June 29–July 3, 2013
Arlington, Texas, USA

Association for Computing Machinery

Advancing Computing as a Science & Profession

DEBS'13

Proceedings of the 7th ACM International Conference on
Distributed Event-Based Systems

Sponsored by:
ACM SIGMOD and ACM SIGSOFT

In cooperation with:
EPTS, European Union-Canada, CSW, RuleML, and ODBMS.org

Supported by:
University of Texas at Arlington, CSE@UTA, and NSF

**Association for
Computing Machinery**

Advancing Computing as a Science & Profession

The Association for Computing Machinery
2 Penn Plaza, Suite 701
New York, New York 10121-0701

ISBN: 978-1-4503-1758-0 (Digital)

ISBN: 978-1-4503-2289-8 (Print)

Additional copies may be ordered prepaid from:

ACM Order Department
PO Box 30777
New York, NY 10087-0777, USA

Phone: 1-800-342-6626 (USA and Canada)
+1-212-626-0500 (Global)
Fax: +1-212-944-1318
E-mail: acmhelp@acm.org
Hours of Operation: 8:30 am – 4:30 pm ET

Printed in the USA

Foreword

It is our great pleasure to welcome you to the *7th ACM International Conference on Distributed Event-Based Systems (DEBS 2013)* here at The University of Texas at Arlington, Arlington, Texas, USA. DEBS is the flagship conference for the dissemination of original research, demonstration of prototypes, the discussion of new practical insights, and the reporting of relevant experience relating to event-based computing. Event-based systems have gained in importance in many application domains, ranging from real-time data processing in web environments, non-traditional applications, such as railroad safety and track monitoring, logistics and networking, to complex event processing in finance and security. The event-based paradigm strengthened by continuous stream data processing has gathered momentum as witnessed by current efforts in areas such as event-driven architectures, big data systems, the internet of things, complex event processing, publish/subscribe systems, business process management, cloud computing, web services, information dissemination, and message-oriented middleware. The DEBS conference brings researchers, students, and practitioners from these various communities together in an international setting to exchange ideas and knowledge about current research work and open challenges. The conference also provides a forum for facilitating the exchange of ideas between academics, vendors, and application developers.

The call for scientific papers attracted 58 submissions from Asia, Canada, Europe, and the United States. The program committee accepted 16 papers that cover a variety of topics, including distributed stream processing, publish/subscribe systems, complex event processing models and languages, and mobility and query optimization. The technical program is complemented by three keynotes talks provided by Roger Barga (Microsoft Research), David Wollman (National Institute of Standards and Technology), and Shailendra Mishra (Paypal). Roger Barga addresses the need for batch-oriented analytics engines that are supported by storage and data processing engines such as Hadoop to also provide real-time analytics capabilities. David Wollman outlines the role of stream and event processing for the Smart Grid and other cyber-physical systems applications. Finally, Shailendra Mishra describes the challenges of complex event processing as a supporting technology for the data cloud and cloud services framework. In addition, Jennifer Maxwell (BNSF Railway) presents an invited experience report on the use of event-based technology for the development of an advanced railroad application.

To place emphasis on the practical use of event-based technologies in distributed environments, the Grand Challenge competition provides a showcase of event-based solutions to problems that are relevant to industry at large using real-life data and queries. This year's challenge involved demonstrating the applicability of event-based systems for real-time analytics over high velocity sensor data collected from a soccer game. In addition to the Grand Challenge competition, demonstration and poster sessions provide an opportunity for groups of students, researchers, and practitioners to showcase their prototypes and research for an international audience. The Doctoral Workshop also acts as a meeting place for students to discuss their research and obtain meaningful feedback as well as interaction with experts in the field.

The DEBS 2013 organizers would like to thank the excellent program committee for their hard work in reviewing the submitted papers. Their constructive evaluation, useful comments, and suggestions were instrumental in achieving the high quality of publications found in these proceedings. We also thank the conference authors for submission of quality papers, responding to the reviewers' comments, and abiding by our proceedings production schedule. We further thank the keynote speakers for contributing interesting and motivating talks. We are also grateful to the Association for Computing Machinery (ACM) and its staff for their support, to our ACM SIGSOFT and ACM SIGMOD sponsors, to the Sheridan Communications staff, and to our in-cooperation partners RuleML, the Event Processing Technical Society, the transatlantic Business Process Management Education Network, the Corporate Semantic Web, and the Object Database Management Systems group for enabling this conference. We sincerely thank The University of Texas at Arlington (UTA) and the UTA Department of Computer Science and Engineering for hosting the conference. We also thank the National Science Foundation for the student travel support for this conference.

Finally, we thank our colleagues who volunteered to help with the organization of the conference: Alex Alves and Brian Connell (industry co-chairs); Qingchun Jiang and Badrish Chandramouli (tutorial co-chairs); Alexander Artikis and Raman Adaikkalavan (poster and demo co-chairs); Gero Muehl and Tore Risch (Ph.D. workshop co-chairs); Zbigniew Jerzak and Holger Ziekow (grand challenge co-chairs); Ugur Cetintemel, Boris Koldehofe, and David Eyers (publicity co-chairs), Nenad Stojanovic and Jonathan Goldstein (industry support co-chairs), Leonidas Fegaras (local organization chair), and Samujjwal Bhandari (web master).

We hope that you find the program stimulating and that the conference will provide you with a valuable opportunity to share ideas with other researchers and practitioners in the distributed event-based community.

Sharma Chakravarthy
Susan D. Urban
DEBS 2013 General Co-Chairs

Peter Pietzuch
Elke Rundensteiner
DEBS 2013 Program Co-Chairs

Suzanne W. Dietrich
DEBS 2013 Proceedings Chair

Table of Contents

Keynote Abstract

Research Session 1: Distributed Stream Processing I

Research Session 2: Content-Based Publish/Subscribe Systems

Industry Session 1: Industrial Views and Usage of Streaming Data

Research Session 3: Distributed Stream Processing II

Research Session 4: CEP Languages and Models

Research Session 5: Mobility and CEP Optimization

Research Session 6/Industry Session 2: Event Processing Issues

Tutorials

DEBS Grand Challenge

Demonstrations

Posters

DEBS 2013 Conference Organization

General Co-Chairs: Sharma Chakravarthy *(The University of Texas at Arlington, USA)*
Susan D. Urban *(Texas Tech University, USA)*

Program Co-Chairs: Peter Pietzuch *(Imperial College, UK)*
Elke Rundensteiner *(Worcester Polytechnic Institute, USA)*

Proceedings Chair: Suzanne W. Dietrich *(Arizona State University, USA)*

Industry Co-Chairs: Alex Alves *(Oracle, USA)*
Brian Connell *(West Global, Ireland)*

Tutorial Co-Chairs: Qingchun (Dustin) Jiang *(Oracle, USA)*
Badrish Chandramouli *(Microsoft Research, USA)*

Poster and Demo Co-Chairs: Alexander Artikis *(NCSR, Greece)*
Raman Adaikkalavan *(Indiana University South Bend, USA)*

Doctoral Workshop Co-Chairs: Gero Muehl *(University of Rostock, Germany)*
Tore Risch *(Uppsala University, Sweden)*

Grand Challenge Co-Chairs: Zbigniew Jerzak *(SAP, Germany)*
Holger Ziekow *(AGT International, Germany)*

Publicity Co-Chairs: Uğur Çetintemel *(Brown University, USA)*
Boris Koldehofe *(University of Stuttgart, Germany)*
David Eyers *(University of Otago, New Zealand)*

Industry Support Co-Chairs: Nenad Stojanovic *(FZI, Germany)*
Jonathan Goldstein *(Microsoft Research, USA)*

Local Organization Chair: Leonidas Fegaras *(The University of Texas at Arlington, USA)*

Web Chair: Samujjwal Bhandari *(Texas Tech University, USA)*

Program Committee: Yanif Ahmad *(Johns Hopkins University, USA)*
Ismail Ari *(Ozyegin University, Turkey)*
Alexander Artikis *(National Center for Scientific Research, Greece)*
Jean Bacon *(University of Cambridge, UK)*
Andreas Behrend *(University of Bonn, Germany)*
Mikael Berndtsson *(University of Skövde, Sweden)*
François Bry *(University of Munich, Germany)*
Alejandro Buchmann *(Technische Universität Darmstadt, Germany)*
Gregory Chockler *(IBM Haifa Research Laboratory, Israel)*
Gianpaolo Cugola *(Politecnico di Milano, Italy)*

Industry Program Committee (continued):

Ludger Fiege *(Siemens, Germany)*
Dieter Gawlick *(Oracle, USA)*
Thomas Heinze *(SAP, Germany)*
Alex Kozlenkov *(Betfair, UK)*
Mike Lefler *(Northrop Grumman, USA)*
Edson Tirelli *(Redhat Drools, Canada)*
Paul Vincent *(TIBCO, USA)*
Phil Windley *(Kynetx, USA)*

Additional reviewers:

Alexander Bauer	Helge Parzyjegla
Adam Betts	Weixiong Rao
Mar Callau	Indrakshi Ray
Dan Chalmers	Gholamreza Safi
Jiang Dawei	Kai Sachs
Nihal Dindar	Thorsten Schöler
Shi Gao	Yanyan Shen
Joshua Garcia	Zhitao Shen
Marco Grawunder	Alexander Shkapsky
Vincenzo Gulisano	Martin Strohbach
Melanie Hartmann	Joseph Sventek
Nikos Katzouris	Muhammad Adnan Tariq
Ivo Krka	David Thomas
Richard Lenz	Samu Varjonen
Feng Li	Matthias Weidlich
Ruben Mayer	Kai Zeng
Christopher Mutschler	

DEBS 2013 Sponsors & Supporters

Sponsors:

In cooperation with:

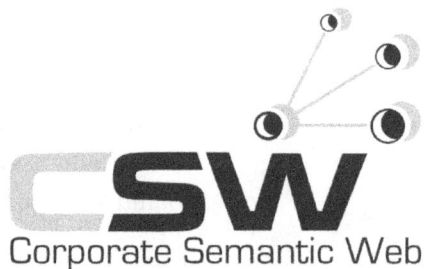 

Supporters:

Frameworks and Data Initiatives for Smart Grid and Other Cyber-Physical Systems

(Invited Keynote)

David A. Wollman

Smart Grid and Cyber-Physical Systems Program Office, Engineering Laboratory,
National Institute of Standards and Technology (NIST)
100 Bureau Drive MS 8200
Gaithersburg MD 20899-8200
+1 301 975-2433
david.wollman@nist.gov

ABSTRACT
I describe the NIST smart grid framework and its applicability as a model for organizational efforts to advance cyber-physical systems, and provide an overview of smart grid data initiatives.

Categories and Subject Descriptors
A.1 [**General Literature**]: Introductory and survey.

General Terms
Management, Measurement, Documentation, Performance, Design, Reliability, Security, Standardization, Verification.

Keywords
Smart grid, interoperability, frameworks, cybersecurity, testing and certification, data analytics, data initiatives, Green Button.

1. INTRODUCTION
The traditional electric grid infrastructure is being modernized to create a new smart grid with advanced sensors, two-way communications and increased intelligence to improve system efficiency, reliability, resiliency and sustainability. Under the Energy Independence and Security Act of 2007, NIST is charged with "primary responsibility to coordinate development of a framework that includes protocols and model standards for information management to achieve interoperability of smart grid devices and systems ..." [1]. Working with traditional electric power industry stakeholders and new entrants from information technology, communications and cybersecurity sectors over several years to address this national priority, NIST has coordinated the development of the NIST Framework and Roadmap for Smart Grid Interoperability [2,3] and established the Smart Grid Interoperability Panel (SGIP), a public-private partnership [4,5] to support NIST to accelerate the standards development process to enable new interoperable smart grid systems and devices. Supported by recent technology deployments, including those funded by the Department of Energy through the American Recovery and Reinvestment Act, new data streams and customer engagement initiatives are now beginning to introduce additional innovation into the electric power industry.

This paper is authored by an employee(s) of the United States Government and is in the public domain.
DEBS'13, June 29–July 3, 2013, Arlington, Texas, USA.
ACM 978-1-4503-1758-0/13/06.

2. SMART GRID
From a systems engineering perspective, the smart grid can be thought of as a complex hierarchical control system-of-systems infrastructure composed of electricity generation, transmission grids and local distribution grids, and end-use applications, as described in numerous publications. An information systems perspective emphasizes the role of distributed intelligence, communications networks, and data management, availability, security and data analytics to support grid and customer operations. Other perspectives are also important; a recent physics perspective [6] emphasizes the need to model the grid's physical behaviors over large spatial (meters to thousands of kilometers) and temporal (milliseconds to hours) scales. Large-scale organizational efforts to improve infrastructures must take into account all of the relevant goals and perspectives, including business, regulatory, and policy. These efforts can also develop industry-based platforms for innovation and organizations with sufficient structure and context to engage and motivate diverse stakeholders and coordinate their efforts and contributions.

2.1 Smart Grid Framework
Frameworks help to organize large stakeholder communities and make clear the vision, principles, underlying structure, and functions of components and systems and necessary improvements to achieve desired systems-of-systems performance within a significant infrastructure. Often frameworks are developed based on common principles and lessons learned from other domains; as an example, ISO/IEC/IEEE 42010:2011 [7] specifies best practices for describing architectures, and its working group has assembled a useful survey of architecture frameworks [8]. Key elements of the NIST smart grid framework [2] address smart grid vision, architectural principles and conceptual model, cybersecurity, testing and certification, identification of applicable standards and gaps, priority action plans to address standards gaps, and the SGIP and its operations.

2.2 Extension to Additional Infrastructures
The NIST smart grid standards process has been recognized as a best practice for effectively engaging stakeholder communities to address key infrastructural goals and objectives, including serving as a model for additional activities such as cloud computing, trusted identities and cybersecurity for critical infrastructures, and as a proposed model for the water industry [9].

3. DATA INITIATIVES

The Federal Government, through the U.S. Chief Technology Officer, has launched Open Data and My Data initiatives in energy and other data across multiple federal agencies and in partnership with the private sector. These initiatives promote public or consumer access to data resources in machine-readable formats and in accordance with policies to rigorously protect privacy, and support entrepreneurs to leverage these data to create innovative applications to benefit consumers.

3.1 Green Button initiative

Following the success of the Blue Button initiative in health information, the White House Green Button initiative was launched in October 2011 to enable consumers to download their own energy usage information from their utilities' websites in a standardized XML-based electronic format, based on standards developed in the North American Energy Standards Board as part of the NIST smart grid framework process. Working directly with the early adopter utilities and their industry partners, an agreement on technical details was reached to enable realization of initial implementations of Green Button in less than four months. A website (www.greenbuttondata.org) and new SGIP priority action plan and technical resources [10] were developed to drive additional standardization and testing and certification to support a vibrant Green Button ecosystem of implementations and applications. Through these efforts, over 16 million U.S. customers now have Green Button data access and can use innovative web applications to help them better understand and manage their energy usage.

3.2 Smart Grid Data Opportunities

The consumer-oriented data initiatives described above represent only a small part of the explosion of smart grid data initiatives and efforts. Additional data streams include phasor measurement unit and smart meter data, which provide increased wide area situational awareness and end-node sensing across the grid. New data analytics capabilities will enable utilities to better manage time-varying renewable energy resources and loads and respond to rapidly changing weather and grid conditions.

4. ACKNOWLEDGMENTS

The summary presented here represents contributions from many NIST staff members and associates working as part of the NIST smart grid team, and of the author and NIST contractor Hypertek, Inc. (Marty Burns), working as part of the U.S. Federal Government interagency Green Button team.

5. REFERENCES

[1] Energy Independence and Security Act of 2007 (December 2007). U.S. Public Law No: 110-140, Sec. 1305. Available at http://www.gpo.gov/fdsys/pkg/BILLS-110hr6enr/pdf/BILLS-110hr6enr.pdf

[2] NIST 2012. *NIST Framework and Roadmap for Smart Grid Interoperability Standards, Release 2.0* (February 2012). NIST Special Publication 1108R2 2012. National Institute of Standards and Technology. Available at http://www.nist.gov/smartgrid/upload/NIST_Framework_Release_2-0_corr.pdf

[3] Wollman, D.A. 2011. Accelerating standards and measurements for the smart grid. In *2011 IEEE International Conference on Acoustics, Speech, and Signal Processing* (Prague, Czech Republic, May 22-27, 2011). ICASSP 2011. IEEE, New York, NY, 5948-5951. DOI=http://dx.doi.org/10.1109/ICASSP.2011.5947716

[4] Smart Grid Interoperability Panel (established November 2009). http://collaborate.nist.gov/twiki-sggrid/bin/view/SmartGrid/WebHome

[5] Smart Grid Interoperability Panel 2.0, Inc. (established 2012 and operational April 2013). http://sgip.org/

[6] Backhaus, S. and Chertkov, M. 2013. Getting a grip on the electrical grid. *Phys. Today* 66, 5 (May 2013), 42-48. DOI= http://dx.doi.org/10.1063/PT.3.1979.

[7] ISO/IEC/IEEE 42010:2011 *Systems and software engineering — Architecture description.* (2011) http://www.iso-architecture.org/ieee-1471/

[8] ISO/IEC/IEEE 42010 2013. Survey of Architectural Frameworks. http://www.iso-architecture.org/42010/afs/frameworks-table.html

[9] Lawson, R.L., Lyman, J.R., and Lyons, B.J. (editors) 2012. *Impact of Municipal, Industrial, and Commercial Water Needs on the Energy Water Nexus: Challenges, Solutions, and Recommendations* (October 2012) Atlantic Council. http://www.acus.org/files/publication_pdfs/403/ee121101waterneeds.pdf

[10] NIST 2013. *User Guide for the NIST Green Button Software Development Kit.* (March 2013) https://collaborate.nist.gov/twiki-sggrid/bin/view/SmartGrid/GreenButtonSDK ; see also http://www.greenbuttondata.org/greentest.aspx for self-testing tools to evaluate Green Button data files.

RIP: Run-based Intra-query Parallelism for Scalable Complex Event Processing

Cagri Balkesen, Nihal Dindar, Matthias Wetter, Nesime Tatbul

ETH Zurich, Switzerland

{cagri.balkesen, dindarn, wetterma, tatbul}@inf.ethz.ch

ABSTRACT

Recognition of patterns in event streams has become important in many application areas of Complex Event Processing (CEP) including financial markets, electronic healthcare systems, and security monitoring systems. In most applications, patterns have to be detected continuously and in real-time over streams that are generated at very high rates, imposing high-performance requirements on the underlying CEP system. For scaling CEP systems to increasing workloads, parallel pattern matching techniques that can exploit multi-core processing opportunities are needed. In this paper, we propose RIP - a Run-based Intra-query Parallelism technique for scalable pattern matching over event streams. RIP distributes input events that belong to individual run instances of a pattern's Finite State Machine (FSM) to different processing units, thereby providing fine-grained partitioned data parallelism. We compare RIP to a state-based alternative which partitions individual FSM states to different processing units instead. Our experiments demonstrate that RIP's partitioned parallelism approach outperforms the pipelined parallelism approach of this state-based alternative, achieving near-linear scalability that is independent from the query pattern definition.

Categories and Subject Descriptors

H.2.4 [**Database Management**]: Systems - Query Processing

Keywords

CEP; Pattern Matching; Stream Processing; Parallelism

1. INTRODUCTION

Complex Event Processing (CEP) has become a critical technology with a wide range of well-known application domains from financial trading to health care. An essential capability for CEP systems is the ability to match patterns over sequences of events. These patterns are typically specified as regular expressions with event variables that are then used to define predicates over individual event occurrences as well as correlations across them. As such, pattern queries can be arbitrarily complex, imposing high computational complexity over the CEP systems that are executing them.

In real-time CEP applications, there is an additional need to detect patterns continuously over streaming event sequences. The time-sensitive nature of events as well as the need to keep up with potentially very high event arrival rates in such settings further exacerbate the performance challenges faced by CEP systems.

For CEP systems to be able to cope with ever-increasing input and query workloads, they must be equipped with techniques that can use modern computing technologies to their advantage. In particular, over the past several years, we have seen an uprising trend in multi-core processing technologies, which presents a ripe opportunity for ensuring high-throughput CEP.

In this paper, the research question we aim to answer is how to exploit inherent parallelism in modern multi-core CPU architectures for scalable processing of CEP queries over event streams. We focus on a common subset of continuous MATCH-RECOGNIZE queries [18] and follow a query execution model based on Finite State Machines (FSMs). Given a query, our goal is to map its FSM execution onto parallel processing units in a multi-core machine. Furthermore, this should be done in a way that scales processing throughput (*i.e.*, the number of input events that can be processed per unit time) with the increasing number of cores, as close to the ideal linear scale-up target as possible.

We propose a novel solution, RIP - a Run-based Intra-query Parallelism technique. RIP distributes input events that belong to individual run instances of a query's FSM to different processing units, thereby providing fine-grained partitioned data parallelism that is independent from the query pattern definition. As we show with a detailed experimental study that is also verified with real-world data workloads, RIP achieves throughput scalability that is very close to the ideal. Furthermore, we compare RIP to a sequential baseline as well as an alternative parallel approach that partitions individual FSM states (as opposed to whole FSM instances in RIP) to different processing units. RIP outperforms this state-based approach under all workload scenarios. In addition to its inferior performance, the state-based approach also has other undesirable limitations such as being query-dependent and bounding scalability by the number of FSM states in the query. In essence, our RIP approach represents partitioned parallelism whereas the state-based approach represents pipelined parallelism. Thus, a significant outcome of this paper is that it clearly shows that partitioned parallelism is a better fit for multi-core CEP than pipelined parallelism.

Partitioned data parallelism for CEP itself is not a new idea [13]. However, previous approaches partition input events directly based on the "PARTITION BY" clause, not at the FSM instance level. Thus, our RIP approach is orthogonal/complementary to these previous approaches in the following ways: (i) Not all CEP queries have "PARTITION BY" clauses, in which case RIP is the only possible approach for data parallelism, (ii) Even in the presence of "PARTITION BY", RIP provides a way to parallelize individual data partitions further, which enables finer-grained partitioning across processing cores. Furthermore, RIP does not suffer from the data skew problem, which is an inherent problem in approaches that are solely based on "PARTITION BY" parallelism.

The rest of this paper is organized as follows: Section 2 describes the data and query models that underlie this work. In Section 3, we describe our basic sequential query processing algorithm and architecture, which sets a baseline for our work. We present out parallel query processing techniques in Section 4. Section 5 provides our experimental results. We summarize the related work in Section 6 and finally conclude the paper in Section 7.

2. DATA AND QUERY MODEL

In this section, we present main assumptions and definitions regarding the data and query model of RIP.

We start with the time domain. We assume that the time domain is a discrete, linearly ordered, countably infinite set of time instants. It is bounded in the past, but not necessarily in the future. Each event has a timestamp and consists of a relational tuple conforming to a schema. Furthermore, we assume that a stream is a totally ordered, countably infinite sequence of events, such that the total order is defined by the timestamps. The CEP annotates each event in the ordered stream by a unique id such that the difference of the ids of two subsequent events is 1. In Example 1 we provide a sample stream specification.

Example 1 *A stream of events that consists of stock market ticks can be specified as follows:*

```
StockTrade(tradeId Long, symbol Char(8), price Float,
          timestamp Long)={
              (1, A, 34.52, <01/19/2006 9:34:01>),
              (2, A, 34.54, <01/19/2006 9:34:01>), ...}
```

Next, we explain how pattern matching queries are specified over a given input stream. Different languages are proposed for pattern matching queries [10, 7, 9, 18]. We use a subset of the MATCH-RECOGNIZE clause [18] to express pattern matching queries. MATCH-RECOGNIZE is originally a proposal for a SQL extension that performs pattern matching on rows. Nevertheless, such queries can also be applied to streams of events which have already supported by some CEP engines [2, 6]. We will briefly discuss a subset of MATCH-RECOGNIZE syntax, our semantics, and then provide an example. By default, contiguous matches are searched in a given stream. However, pattern matching can also be performed in a subset of data, when optional PARTITION BY

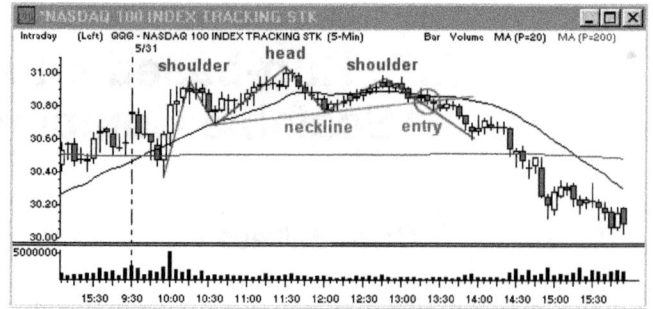

Figure 1: Head and shoulders patterns in a stock trade stream [1]

clause is used, such as looking for patterns for each stock symbol separately. Patterns are specified with regular expressions using pattern variables (PATTERN clause). Each pattern variable is accompanied by a definition in the DEFINE clause. This definition consists of a conjunction of boolean predicates. If an event meets this definition, it can be classified with the corresponding variable. The absence of a definition of a certain variable means that any event can be classified with that variable name. Furthermore, events can be correlated by specifying predicates over pattern variables, such that price of a *StockTrade* event annotated as B must have a price value greater than the event just before itself ($B.price > $ PREV($B.price$)). For example, a pattern specification PATTERN($AB * C$) states that we are looking for an event (classified as A) that is followed by zero ore more events that satisfy the definition of B and by exactly one event that satisfies the definition of C. We call pattern specifications which contain Kleene *,+ variable-length patterns, whereas we call patterns containing neither Kleene * nor Kleene + fixed-length patterns. Please note that search for variable-length patterns might never terminate, such as when predicate of each pattern variable is *true*. In order to avoid that, we assume that the maximum length (MAXLENGTH) of a match is specified in the query. MAXLENGTH clause is an extension to the original proposal. Next, we provide a sample pattern specification from finance domain.

In finance, recognition of chart patterns within stock prices is a common method which is used to predict the future development of stock prices. A well-known pattern is the so-called head and shoulders pattern, which belongs to the family of reversal patterns [4]. If an uptrend of the price is accompanied by the observation of the head and shoulders pattern for a stock, a drop of the price can be forecast for that stock.

Example 2 *Head and shoulders pattern consists of three peaks: (i) the left shoulder that is formed after an uptrend, (ii) the highest peak called the head and (iii) the right shoulder that shows an increase but fails to take out the previous high (head) [3]. The pattern is complete when the price falls below the neckline that is formed by connecting the two low points next to the head [3, 1]. Figure 1 depicts the pattern. A simplified head and shoulders pattern in StockTrade stream can be expressed with MATCH-RECOGNIZE (see Query 1).*

```
SELECT    symbol, left_shoulder_top, head_top,
          right_shoulder_top, point_of_reversal
FROM StockTrade MATCH-RECOGNIZE (
PARTITION BY symbol
MEASURES symbol   AS s_symbol,
         C.price AS left_shoulder_top,
         G.price AS head_top,
         K.price AS right_shoulder_top,
         M.price AS point_of_reversal
PATTERN  (A B* C D* E F* G H* I J* K L* M)
DEFINE
         B AS (B.price ≥ PREV(B.price)),
         C AS (C.price > PREV(C.price)),
         D AS (D.price ≤ PREV(D.price)),
         E AS (E.price < PREV(E.price)
                         AND E.price > A.price),
         F AS (F.price ≥ PREV(F.price)),
         G AS (G.price ≥ PREV(G.price)
                         AND G.price > C.price),
         H AS (H.price ≤ PREV(H.price)),
         I AS (I.price < PREV(I.price)
                         AND I.price > A.price),
         J AS (J.price ≥ PREV(J.price)),
         K AS (K.price > PREV(K.price)
                         AND K.price < G.price),
         L AS (L.price ≤ PREV(L.price)),
         M AS (M.price ≤ PREV(M.price)
                         AND M.price < E.price
                         AND M.price < I.price)
MAXLENGTH 100
)
```

Query 1: Head and shoulders pattern

After specifying a pattern matching query, next we focus on its result tuples. Output of the query is a sequence of matches, where each match contains a sequence of events. Each event in that sequence is classified by a variable such that the sequence of variables conform to the pattern of a given query and the predicates are fulfilled accordingly. Figure 2 depicts a match of Query 1.

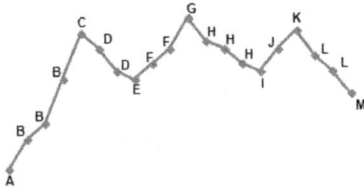

Figure 2: A sample head and shoulders match

Matches can have arbitrary relations depending on the predicates and the input stream, such as a match can include events of another match partially or fully. Some language proposals enable to specify certain match behaviors in the query such as non-overlapping only, or the longest matches [9, 18, 13]. We focus on outputting all matches that can be found, as it is more general and computationally more expensive. Please note that even in the case of non- overlapping match search, all events must be processed as overlapping can only be detected after a match is found, and matches can have arbitrary starts and sizes. Furthermore, we assume that a single event per match is reported which summarizes the events belonging to the match. MEASURES clause is used to specify the fields of a match event in the MATCH-RECOGNIZE proposal such as *head_top* is the high-

est price of the stock in Query 1. Next, we give a sample output event to Query 1.

```
HeadShoulders(Id Float, s_symbol Char(8), left_shoulder_top Float,
         head_top Float, right_shoulder_top Float,
         point_of_reversal Float)={
                    (1, A, 35.0, 37.5, 35.5, 32.1), ...}
```

We use FSM to model pattern matching queries. Since patterns are specified with regular expressions, FSM is a natural choice. Furthermore, It is widely used by other pattern matching engines [16, 10, 11]. Every pattern is transformed into a non-deterministic FSM. Each pattern variable is represented by states in the FSM. An FSM has always a start state (indicated by s_0). The predicates are represented by edges (indicated by p_i). Next, we provide a sample FSM.

Example 3 *FSM of Query 1 is as follows:*

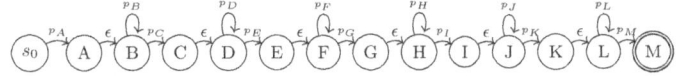

Figure 3: FSM for Query 1

We presented our main assumptions and definitions regarding pattern matching in general. A CEP engine is required to find all possible matches over a given input stream according to a given query regardless of its processing strategy. In the following sections, we discuss how pattern matching queries can be processed sequentially and in parallel.

3. QUERY PROCESSING

This section describes a basic sequential query processing algorithm and architecture for pattern matching.

Figure 4 depicts a simple model of a sequential pattern matching engine. In the figure, the client program feeds the engine with input events and receives the match results. The engine performs three main tasks: receive events, evaluate events, control matches. Next, we discuss each of these tasks.

Input handler is a simple interface that provides event streams to the engine. If PARTITION BY is specified in the query, the input can be partitioned at the input handler. Similarly, match output handler deals with outputting the detected matches, such that it formats the found matches with regard to the output specifications given in the MEASURES clause and sends them to the client. Pattern evaluator performs the main task, which is evaluating events and finding all matches.

Pattern evaluator uses the FSM of the query to evaluate patterns. Each event might contribute to a match and must be evaluated with the FSM. In order to move from one state of the FSM to another state, an event has to be consumed. Furthermore, the movement is only allowed if the event fulfills the predicates of the edge. An exception is the edges that are labeled by an epsilon. These edges do not consume an event and thus it is possible to move to another state without classifying an event. Arriving at a final state means that a match is found. However, finding no edges to move means that the search ended with non-match.

Example 4 *We illustrate execution of part of the head and shoulders query (Query 1), more specifically until the head is*

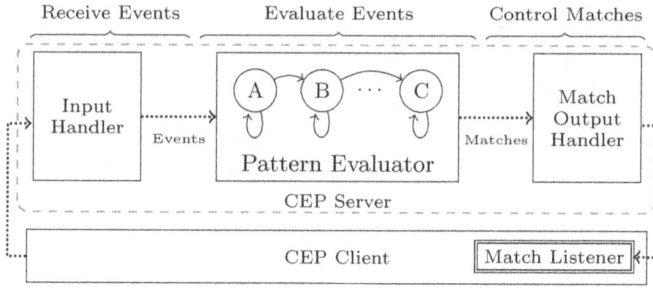

Figure 4: Basic Query Processing Architecture

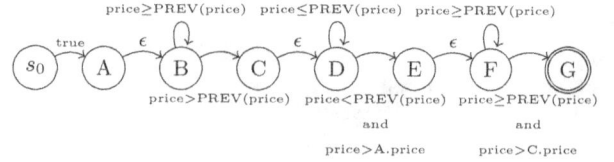

Figure 5: FSM for Example 5

detected. FSM of the query can be found in Figure 5. Please note that Figure 5 depicts the first half of the FSM shown in Figure 3, with explicit predicate definitions.

We call an execution instance of an FSM a "run". Each run holds a pointer to the current state of the FSM (denoted as *curr_state*) and a set of events which conformed to the predicates till the current state (partial match denoted as *PM*). A run might or might not lead to a match. For each incoming event, pattern evaluator creates a new run having the start state of the FSM as its current state and an empty partial match. After that, each run is updated regarding to the incoming event (see Algorithm 1). In Example 5, we illustrate the execution of Algorithm 1.

Algorithm 1: Sequential pattern matching

Input: e : event, R : set of runs, fsm : FSM of the query
Result: R' : updated set of runs

```
1  begin
2  |  R' ← ∅;              // create an empty set of runs
3  |  r_i ← create a new run;
4  |  r_i.current-state ← fsm.start-state;
5  |  r_i.partial-match ← ∅;
6  |  R.add(r_i);                      // add r_i to R
7  |  foreach run r in R do
8  |  |  S ← computeReachableStates(r.current-state, e);
9  |  |  foreach state s in S do
10 |  |  |  if s.evalPredicates(r.partial-match, e) = true
          then
11 |  |  |  |  add e to r.partial-match;
12 |  |  |  |  r.current-state ← s;
13 |  |  |  |  if s is a final-state then
14 |  |  |  |  |  report the r.partial-match;
15 |  |  |  |  |  if s has outgoing edges then
16 |  |  |  |  |  |  r_j ← make a copy of r;
17 |  |  |  |  |  |  R'.add(r_j);
18 |  |  |  |  else
19 |  |  |  |  |  r_j ← make a copy of r;
20 |  |  |  |  |  R'.add(r_j);
21 |  R ← R';
22 |  return R';
```

Example 5 *A StockTrade input stream is given with the following price values for a certain stock symbol:*

```
StockTrade(tradeId Long, price Float)= {(1,33.1),(2,34.0),
                                         (3,33.2),(4,35.0), ...}
```

event (price)	run r_{id}:<curr_state, PM> → <curr_state', PM'>	Prd
$e_1(33.1)$	$r_1 :< s_0, \emptyset > \rightarrow < A, (a_1) >$	p_A
$e_2(34.0)$	$r_2 :< s_0, \emptyset > \rightarrow < A, (a_2) >$	p_A
$e_2(34.0)$	$r_1 :< A, (e_1) > \rightarrow < B, (a_1, b_2) >$	p_B
$e_2(34.0)$	$r'_1 :< A, (e_1) > \rightarrow < C, (a_1, c_2) >$	p_C
$e_3(33.2)$	$r_3 :< s_0, \emptyset > \rightarrow < A, (a_3) >$	p_A
$e_3(33.2)$	$r_2 :< A, (a_2) > \rightarrow -$	p_B
$e_3(33.2)$	$r_2 :< A, (a_2) > \rightarrow -$	p_C
$e_3(33.2)$	$r_1 :< B, (a_1, b_2) > \rightarrow -$	p_B
$e_3(33.2)$	$r_1 :< B, (a_1, b_2) > \rightarrow -$	p_C
$e_3(33.2)$	$r'_1 :< C, (a_1, c_2) > \rightarrow < D, (a_1, c_2, d_3) >$	p_D
$e_3(33.2)$	$r''_1 :< C, (a_1, c_2) > \rightarrow < E, (a_1, c_2, e_3) >$	p_E
$e_4(35.0)$	$r_4 :< s_0, \emptyset > \rightarrow < A, (a_4) >$	p_A
$e_4(35.0)$	$r_3 :< A, (a_3) > \rightarrow < B, (a_3, b_4) >$	p_B
$e_4(35.0)$	$r'_3 :< A, (a_3) > \rightarrow < C, (a_3, c_4) >$	p_C
$e_4(35.0)$	$r'_1 :< D, (a_1, c_2, d_3) > \rightarrow -$	p_D
$e_4(35.0)$	$r'_1 :< D, (a_1, c_2, d_3) > \rightarrow -$	p_E
$e_4(35.0)$	$r''_1 :< E, (a_1, c_2, e_3) > \rightarrow < F, (a_1, c_2, e_3, f_4) >$	p_F
$e_4(35.0)$	$r'''_1 :< E, (a_1, c_2, e_3) > \rightarrow < G, (a_1, c_2, e_3, g_4) >$	p_G
...	...	...

Table 1: Event evaluation sequence for Example 5

Other attributes of StockTrade are avoided for brevity. The query having the FSM shown in Figure 5 is executed over StockTrade stream by a sequential pattern matching engine according to Algorithm 1. The evaluation sequence can be found in Table 1. Table 1 shows new runs created with each incoming event and changes in the states of both the existing and new runs when the corresponding predicate (prd) is executed. p_X denotes the predicate of state X. Dashes($-$) mean that the run is finalized with a non-match. Please note that, reachable states from a given state are the set of states which can be reached by consuming one event. For example, in the FSM shown in Figure 5 reachable states from state A are both state B and C. If multiple edges can be followed, a run is created for each (e.g., r_1 and r'_1 in Table 1). a_1 denotes that the event e_1 was classified by A. In the example, r'''_1 reaches final state G and thus reports a match including events from e_1 to e_4.

We will use the architecture in Figure 4 as a basis for further parallelization approaches. Next, we discuss how the work done by Pattern Evaluator can be parallelized.

4. PARALLEL QUERY PROCESSING

In order to parallelize the basic query processing architecture of Figure 4, the first step is to divide the CEP server thread into three threads, one for each task (*i.e.*, Input Handler, Pattern Evaluator, and Match Output Handler), and to replace method calls between task boundaries with queues accordingly. Of these three threads, Pattern Evaluator has the highest computational cost and therefore is likely to be

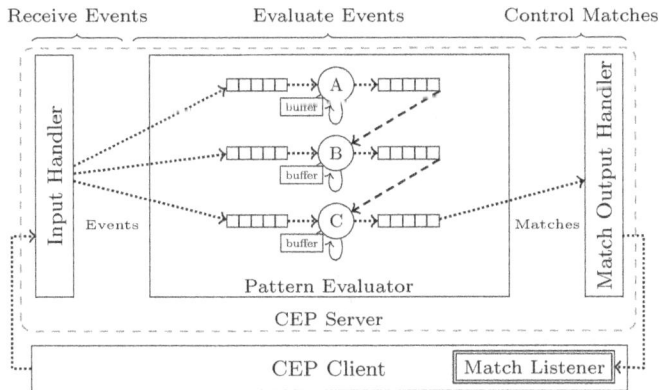

Figure 6: State-based Parallelization

the bottleneck in the face of fast input event arrival and a complex pattern to evaluate. How can the Pattern Evaluator thread be further parallelized?

Given the event evaluation sequence (*e.g.*, Table 1) generated by the sequential pattern matching algorithm (*i.e.*, Algorithm 1), there can be three possibilities:

- *Parallelize by input events:* Each processing unit is assigned a thread that is responsible for a certain partition or a sub-stream of events from the input. For example, approaches that parallelize based on the PARTITION BY attributes of the query implement this possibility [13].

- *Parallelize by state predicates:* Each processing unit is assigned a thread that is responsible for a certain FSM state. This possibility corresponds to the pipelined parallelization approach.

- *Parallelize by runs:* Each processing unit is assigned a thread that is responsible for a certain FSM run instance. This corresponds to the RIP approach that we are proposing in this paper.

Next, we describe two approaches: state- and run-based.

4.1 State-based Parallelization

The idea is to represent each FSM state corresponding to a pattern variable as a processing unit that can run on a dedicated core in parallel. In other words, in the event evaluation sequence, we parallelize the evaluation of each state predicate.

Figure 6 illustrates the basic processing model of our state-based parallelization approach for a pattern that consists of three variables or FSM states (A, B, C). There is exactly one processing unit for each variable in the pattern. Each processing unit has an input queue receiving events of the complete input stream. Except the processing unit of the first pattern variable, all other processing units have a second input queue that contains partial matches from the previous state. The job of a given processing unit (*e.g.*, the one representing variable C) is to evaluate each incoming partial match (*e.g.*, $a_{i-1}b_i$) from the second queue together with the succeeding input event e_{i+1} from the first queue according to all predicates of the corresponding pattern variable (*e.g.*, C). For positive evaluations, the input event is appended to the partial match and the updated partial match is forwarded to the outgoing queue. Note that a processing unit evaluates an event from its first input queue only if it succeeds

events of a partial match that is forwarded from its second input queue. This way, redundant evaluations are avoided. In fact, in total there will exactly be the same number of predicate evaluations as in the sequential case illustrated in Table 1.

For variable-length patterns, a processing unit that represents a pattern variable that is optional (*i.e.*, quantified with * or ?) has to forward each incoming partial match to its output queue in addition to the task described above. Furthermore, a processing unit that represents a pattern variable that allows multiple occurrences of itself (*i.e.*, quantified with * or +) has to keep copies of the partial matches that are put into its output queue in an internal buffer. The partial matches in this buffer have to be evaluated together with the subsequent event. Thus, the processing unit has to work off both its input queues and the internal buffer.

While state-based parallelization is intuitive and can be implemented in practice, we see several potential problems with this approach:

- Communication overhead: Partial matches have to be forwarded among consecutive processing units, causing communication overhead among threads running on different cores. This problem would be even more pronounced in variable-length patterns, which are likely to maintain a higher number of partial matches.

- Replication of input stream: The complete input event stream has to be replicated to each processing unit, since each event has the potential to participate in any of the state predicates depending on the partial matches coming from the preceding processing units. Fortunately, not all of them need to be blindly evaluated at each processing unit, since the processing unit can skip the ones that are earlier than the last event of a partial match.

- Query dependence: The number of processing units, and thus the degree of parallelism is restricted by the number of pattern variables or FSM states in the query. Therefore, this approach would not scale beyond a certain number of cores.

- Load imbalance: It is likely that in a pattern matching query certain states may take longer to evaluate their predicates. This would lead to load imbalance across the processing units, such that processing the state predicates with the most loaded node will create a bottleneck. The load imbalance can be due to several factors, including: selectivity of preceding states, number of predicates for a given state, type of predicates for a given state, and the presence of expensive operators such as Kleene Star.

One solution to query dependence and load imbalance problems of the state-based approach could be state replication. Bottleneck states can be good candidates for replication. Load of a state depends on the number of events it processes and the cost of its predicate. Since the first state of the FSM has to evaluate all the incoming events and likely to filter some of them, we enabled replication of it as an optimization to state-based approach. As a result, we implemented both state-based parallelism approach and its optimized version where the first state of the FSM is replicated.

4.2 Run-based Parallelization

As discussed above, the degree of parallelism in state-based approach is dependent on the number of variables in

7

a query. Loads assigned to each processing unit might be unbalanced; therefore, available resources can not be fully exploited. Moreover, transfer of partial matches between states and thus between processing units seem to have a big overhead. These drawbacks lead to the idea to arrange the evaluations of (event, partial match, state)-triples such that all evaluations of a given run are performed on the same processing unit. We call this approach run-based parallelism. In other words, a partial match remains on a single processing unit until it constitutes a match or it is removed because it cannot end in a match anymore.

In run-based parallelism, each processing unit has an identical task: performing pattern matching on a given sequence of input events. Therefore, the degree of parallelism is independent of the query, unlike state-based approach. In addition to that, since events belonging to the same match stay in a single processing unit, the cost of carrying partial matches around is avoided. However, an important question with this approach is the scheduling of the runs, in other words: "which processing unit will start a run for a given event?". A straight-forward approach could be assigning the processing units in a round-robin manner to the incoming events. For instance, if there are X processing units available, a processing unit i evaluates all runs that start with an event having an id which is congruent to i in modulo X. With the round-robin approach, the input events must be replicated to each processing unit, as pattern matching is sequential by nature such that each processing unit will also need other events. Instead of each incoming event starting a run on another processing unit in a round-robin manner, we took a different approach: we could let n subsequent events start a run on the same processing unit. In other words batches of n events are created and a particular processing unit tries to find all matches that start with events from that batch. Figure 7 depicts the architecture of a pattern matching engine that supports run-based intra-query parallelism (RIP). We can observe that each processing unit has the same task. Besides, each has an input queue for events and an output queue for matches. The event receiver is responsible for forwarding events to the processing units and a match controller collects the matches from the processing units.

With batching, we forward a certain batch only to one processing unit. This way we avoid the replication of events. But how about matches that overlap batches? Beside the batch size n we define another parameter s (size of the shared part of a batch). A processing unit which performs pattern matching on a batch having events with ids $[j; j+n]$ searches for all matches starting between j^{th} and $(j+n-s)^{th}$ events. s events are replicated (i.e., they form the first events of the subsequent batch), so that matches having tail in $(j + n - s; j + n]$ can also be reported. The next question is how to choose a value for the shared part of a batch such that the correctness of the result of a pattern matching query is not violated. For fixed-length patterns with k variables and for variable-length patterns with an upper bound for the match length (MAXLENGTH = k) we simply define: $s = k - 1$. For variable-length patterns where matches can have any length it is more difficult to find an adequate value. The length of the shared part s has to be chosen such that the probability of an occurrence of a match with length $> s + 1$ is almost 0. Furthermore, it is required that $n > s$ and in order to avoid that events belong to more than two batches it should hold

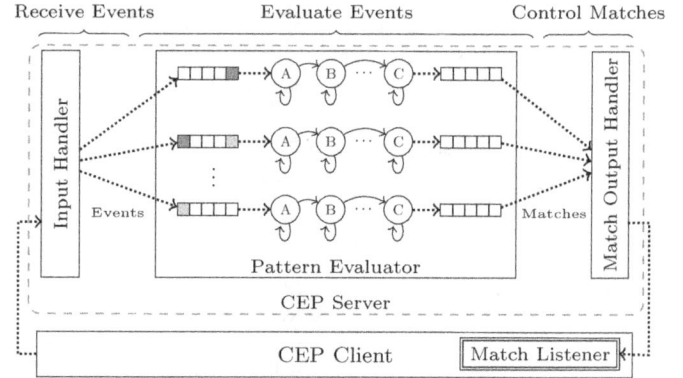

Figure 7: Run-based Parallelization

that $\frac{n}{2} \geq s$. As a result, s events are replicated twice and every event starts exactly one run on exactly one processing unit, but it can contribute to the runs that have started in the previous batch. Shared parts of the batches are shown as shaded boxes in Figure 7.

Due to the reduction of event replication and query independence run-based parallelism approach looks promising. Furthermore, RB+ enables fair scheduling policy. Although different processing units will require different amounts of times, idle processing unit can be assigned to the next batch, and all processing units will be busy at a given time. Thus, different processing times do not create load imbalance across the processing units.

4.3 Discussion

We described two techniques for parallelization of pattern matching: state-based and run-based. In this section, we will analytically compare the performance of these two techniques, focusing on processing time required for event evaluation in each technique.

We start with the processing time of each pattern variable, because in state-based approach each processing unit performs event evaluation for a dedicated pattern variable. The processing time of pattern variable A_i is the number of its incoming events (M_i) multiplied with the time required to evaluate A_i's predicate (p_i) over an event.

$$C_i = M_i * p_i \qquad (1)$$

The number of incoming events for pattern variable A_i depends on the selectivity of the pattern variables before A_i. For our purpose, we assume that the number of incoming events (M_i) for each pattern variable is known. Then, processing time of pattern matching in a sequential pattern matching engine is the sum of processing time of its pattern variables. Assume that there are N pattern variables, total processing time of sequential pattern matching is as follows:

$$C = \sum_{i=1}^{N} C_i \qquad (2)$$

Under these assumptions, the processing time in the case of state-based parallelism is the processing time of the processing unit with the maximum cost. Remember that state-based parallelism performs pattern matching for each state in parallel.

$$C_{SB} = \max_i C_i \qquad (3)$$

Assuming there are X processing units available, in run-based approach the overall processing time of each processing unit is the total cost of sequential processing divided by X. The reason is that in run-based parallelism input is divided into X batches and pattern matching is performed in parallel for each batch.

$$C_{RB} = C/X \qquad (4)$$

If we compare the two approaches with an equal number of processing units (N=X), we can conclude that $C_{RB} \leq C_{SB}$. The state-based approach can only achieve the same performance as run-based approach, if each processing unit has the same load ($C_1 = ... = C_i = ... = C_N$). In all other cases, run-based approach outperforms state-based approach in terms of event evaluation cost.

5. EXPERIMENTS

In this section, we present an experimental study over our parallel pattern matching techniques discussed in this paper. The goal of the experiments is three fold: *(i)* to demonstrate the performance characteristics of each individual parallelization technique in comparison to a sequential execution strategy *(ii)* to study the effects of certain parameters on the performance of corresponding parallelization technique; and finally *(iii)* to quantitatively compare both of the parallelization techniques side-by-side and present the performance superiority of our novel run-based parallelization technique.

5.1 Experimental Setup

We have implemented a prototype pattern matching engine from scratch in Java using Java SE SDK 1.6 and ran all the experiments using the OpenJDK runtime environment. Our prototype contains implementations of the parallel pattern matching techniques, namely state-based and run-based, along with the serial pattern matching implementation as a reference point. Our implementation supports a subset of the `MATCH-RECOGNIZE` query specification as described in Section 2.

In order to replicate a real-world setting, we have conducted all the experiments using a client/server architecture. Basically, the client program is run on a separate machine and sends a continuous stream of events over a Gigabit Ethernet to the server machine which runs our multi-core aware pattern matching engine in isolation. Our implementation uses the Java NIO sockets for efficient communication between the client and the engine where events are sent as byte-streams.

We have used a recent high-end multi-core machine as our experiment platform. The machine comes with 4 processor sockets, each of which is an AMD Opteron 6174 CPU with 12 cores and a clock speed of 2.3 Ghz. The machine uses a Non-Uniform Memory Architecture (NUMA) for memory accesses with a total size of 128 GB main memory. Each core in the socket has private 64 KB L1 and 512 KB L2 caches where the 6 MB L3 cache is shared by all the cores in the socket. We relied on local memory allocations, and due to the first-touch memory allocation policy of Linux, all the allocated memory was local to threads. The machine runs a Debian Linux with kernel version 3.2.16-7.

5.1.1 Datasets

As the workload for our experimental evaluation, we have used two sets of data. The first set of data is generated synthetically to evaluate the performance by changing certain parameters such as selectivity of predicates. The first workload simulates an event stream from a stock market, where each event is a stock trade event as follows:

```
StockTrade(tradeId Long, symbol Char(8), price Float,
          timestamp Long)
```

The size of each event is 24-bytes. Without loss of generality, the queries we have used only use the price attribute for predicate evaluation which is synthetically generated uniformly in the range between 50.0 and 150.0. Using this fixed range serves the purpose of controlling predicate selectivity in queries. In all the experiments, the client generates a fixed number of events (≈ 1.5 Billion) and pushes them to the server with highest possible rate that the pattern matching engine variant running in the server can handle. In the fastest case, the experiment runs for ≈ 30 minutes and gives sufficient data to observe the performance. In addition, to get reliable results, we start the performance measurements after first $\approx 10\%$ of the events are sent and stop it before the final 1% of the events are sent.

As the second workload, we have used real-world stock market data to assess the performance under realistic conditions. As a result, experiments with this workload validate the applicability and performance of our techniques. Data we have used comes from a snapshot of real stock exchange trade and quote (NYSE TAQ [5]) collected from several stock exchanges in the U.S.A. over 3 days between January 3, 2006 and January 5, 2006. In order to use a higher volume event stream, we have explicitly used the quote data which consists of bid/ask prices given by customers as shown below:

```
StockQuote(symbol Char(8), timestamp Int, bid Float,
          bidSize Int, offer Float, offerSize Int)
```

5.1.2 Queries

In our experimental evaluation, we have used a broad number of queries with diverse properties. Here, we briefly summarize the properties of different class of queries that we considered. The first dimension that queries differ is the pattern variables. If a query contains just singleton variables, then it is called a **fixed-length** query (*i.e.*, Q5). Otherwise, it is called a **variable-length** query (*i.e.*, Q1). The second dimension that queries differ is the predicates. If a query contains predicate evaluation against only static values, such as `A.price > 100`, then it is called **static-predicate** query (*i.e.*, Q11). Otherwise, it contains predicates with correlation among values of two different events and/or previous values of those values (*i.e.*, `A.price > B.price` or `A.price > PREV(A.price)`). This type of queries are called **dynamic-predicate** queries. For the interested reader, we provide all the queries used in this paper in Appendix A.

5.1.3 Implementation Variants

We have experimented with the following variants of our pattern matching engine:

- **SEQ:** Sequential (*i.e.* single-threaded) pattern matching engine.
- **SB:** State-based parallel pattern matching engine that uses pipelining.

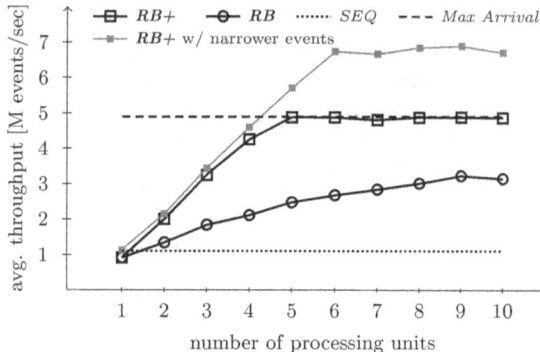

Figure 8: Comparison of run-based techniques

- **SB+:** Optimized version of SB where the first state is duplicated to overcome its certain limitations.
- **RB:** Run-based parallel pattern matching engine where events are distributed in round-robin to all processing units.
- **RB+:** Optimized version of RB. Batches of events of size $n = 5000$ are distributed to processing units. Two subsequent batches, accordingly processing units, have a shared part of size s. A processing unit starts a run for the first $(n - s)$ events in a batch.

In all our experiments, each processing unit is a separate thread.

5.2 Performance of Run-Based Techniques

In this section, we compare the performance of different run-based techniques, **RB** and **RB+** using the synthetic workload and query 8 (**Q8**). The throughput achieved by these techniques with varying number of processing units are shown in Figure 8. To a certain degree, increasing number of processing units (*i.e.* threads) results in a higher throughput. As shown in Figure 8, our optimized version of the run-based, **RB+** scales much faster than **RB** up to a certain point. Surprisingly, the performance of **RB+** stays limited from there on. We have investigated the reason for this result and found out that the execution quickly becomes network-bound in our setup. Using events of size 24-bytes, the Gigabit Ethernet allows only a maximum of ≈ 5 Million events per second connection bandwidth between our client and server. As a result, input path becomes the bottleneck of our evaluation and we are not able to show scalability of our system beyond 10 processing units for this query. In order to prove this situation, we have run the same experiment with narrower events (*i.e.*, 16-byte events by dropping attributes not used in predicates). As can be seen in Figure 8, the performance with narrower events scales better but at some point network becomes the bottleneck again.

On the other hand, although **RB** seems to scale, it does not reach this upper bound even with 10 processing units. The main problem in this technique is the high cost of checking/starting of runs for each event. Based on this experiment, the batching idea clearly shows its benefit over plain **RB**. In the rest of the experiments, we will use **RB+** as it is superior to **RB**.

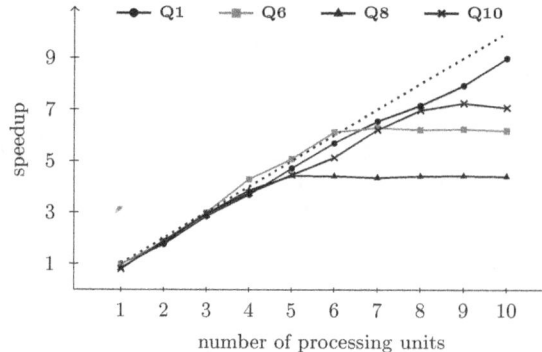

Figure 9: Speedup of RB+ to SEQ for different queries

5.3 Evaluation of Optimized Run-Based Parallelism

In this section, we present the results achieved for our optimized run-based parallelization technique **RB+** with the synthetic workload. Figure 9 shows the speedups attained for four different queries. The four different queries shown in Figure 9 are a representative set of the ones from the entire set of queries we have experimented with, hence only they are shown. We also show the results up to 10 processing units due to the network bandwidth limitation issue as mentioned in Section 5.2. Besides that, our results show a general trend of linear scaling behavior for most of the queries. However, for queries 6 and 8, the maximum speedup is achieved at a low number of processing units and the performance does not further improve. This is mainly due to the reason that per event computation cost of these queries are rather cheaper in comparison to the others. Hence, the input path of the processing, namely the network, becomes a bottleneck earlier in this case. Overall, these experiments show that **RB+** scales well as long as the network is not a limitation. Additionally, it is highly effective independent of the query (*i.e.* run-based parallelism is **query-independent**).

5.4 Effect of Shared Events between Batches

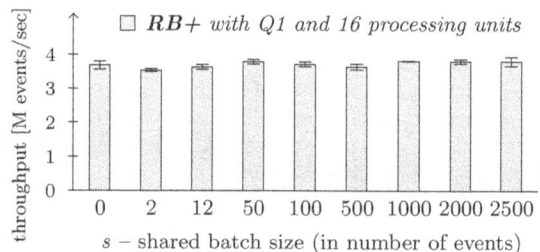

Figure 10: Effect of shared batch size in RB+

The optimized run-based technique **RB+** has a configuration parameter s which is the number of shared events between consecutive batches of different processing units. In this experiment, we investigated whether s has an impact on achievable throughput. Figure 10 shows the results of the experiment where we varied s for evaluation of query 1 (**Q1**) using 16 processing units. Our results mainly show that the size of shared part between batches does not effect

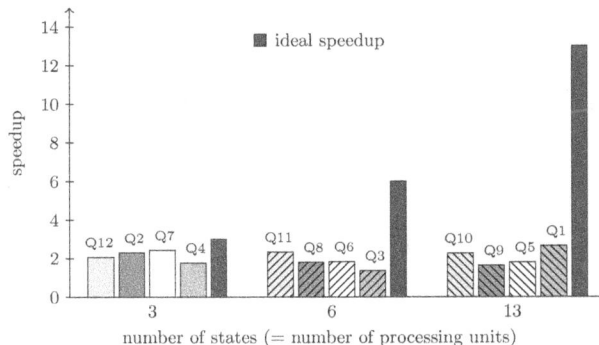

Figure 11: Performance of SB

	Throughput (M Events/sec)	Speedup	# Processing Units
SB	3.34 M	2.32	6
SB+	4.31 M	2.99	7
SEQ	1.44 M	1	1

Table 2: Optimized state-based parallelism (SB+)

the achievable throughput (similar results are observed for different queries).

5.5 Performance of State-Based Parallelism

In this section, we present the results achieved for our state-based parallelization technique **SB** with the synthetic workload. Figure 11 presents the throughput speedups a-chieved for a representative set of queries. The number of finite automata states in each query corresponds to the par-allelism level used for that query (*i.e.*, the number of pro-cessing units). In an ideal case, we would normally expect the speedup achieved for a query to be in line with the num-ber of states. Unfortunately, the results in Figure 11 do not correspond to the expectations. For queries with three state variables, the speedup achieved is close to what we would ex-pect. However, as number of states in a query increase, the speedup achieved does not increase further. The reason for this observation is as follows. State-based parallelism mainly builds up on pipelined parallelism. In the pipelined paral-lelism model, the slowest stage in the pipeline determines the maximum throughput that can be achieved. In a pat-tern matching query, usually different states in a query have different per event costs due to the probability of matches and selectivity of predicates. As a result, unless a query is artificially constructed to have balanced set of states in terms of execution time, it is not possible to achieve a par-allelism speedup proportional to the number of states.

In general, state-based parallelism helps to improve the performance to a certain degree but does not scale with the number of states. As a result, state-based approach is rather **query dependent** where the number of states and the dis-tribution of the workload among the states determine the achievable speedup.

5.6 Evaluation of Optimized State-Based Par-allelism

In state-based technique **SB**, the first state of the au-tomata might constitute the bottleneck when it has a high predicate selectivity with expensive predicates. To reduce its impact on the overall performance, we have implemented an

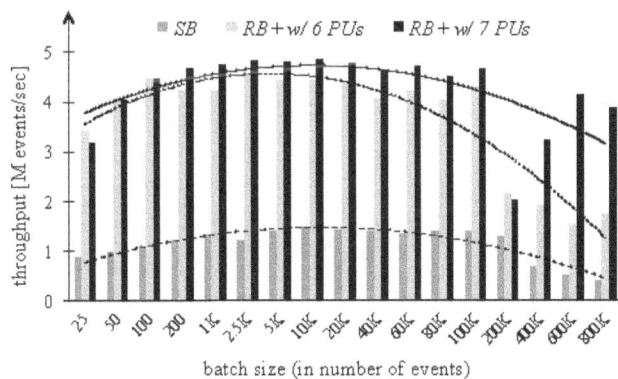

Figure 12: Impact of event distribution batch size

optimized version of the state-based technique called **SB+**. Basically, **SB+** duplicates the first state. For queries where the first state is a bottleneck, this optimization in **SB+** be-comes marginally effective. Table 2 shows the results of an experiment for such a query (**Q11**). However, the general-ity of this optimization is also query dependent and rather limited. Due to this reason, it is not possible to apply this optimization in all the queries of our experiments. Thus, we use **SB** in the rest of the experiments.

5.7 Impact of Batching on Event Distribution

In this section, we investigate the impact of batching on event distribution to processing units. The discussion ap-plies to both of the parallelization techniques and should not be confused with the batching in run-based parallelism.

In all the implementations, the events and partial matches are collected into batches before they are transferred among processing units. The other extreme alternative is event-by-event distribution, which we found out to be a severe performance limitation. The batch-based distribution tech-nique avoids the communication overheads among process-ing units. However, the batch-size of events for distribu-tion becomes a configuration parameter. In the experiment shown in Figure 12, we have varied the event distribution batch size to observe its impact. First of all, we have ob-served a similar behavior for different queries (*i.e.* **query independent**) and we present the results for query 7 (**Q7**). Secondly, in general there is a slight trade-off between a small batch size and a large batch size. Usually, there is a fixed cost for creating a batch and putting it into a queue. With small batch sizes, the frequency of accesses to the queue becomes higher, which means increased synchroniza-tion among processing units. On the other hand, a larger batch size means that an event will reside in the memory for a longer time and in case of Java, would stress the garbage collector more. All in all, regardless of the query, a batch size between 5,000 and 10,000 achieves the best performance in the existence of these trade-offs.

5.8 Comparison of Run-Based and State-Based Techniques

In this section, we quantitatively compare our best run-based parallel pattern matching engine **RB+** and the state-based parallel pattern matching engine **SB**. State-based par-allelism works best when the execution time of different

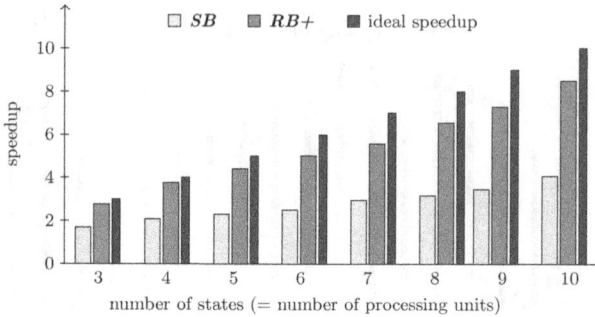

Figure 13: Comparison of parallelization techniques with a balanced query

states are balanced. Although such queries are not common in real-world applications, we also include measurements with such a query in our results. The results of the comparison are shown in Figure 13. Essentially, the results show that even for balanced queries, run-based techniques outperform state-based techniques.

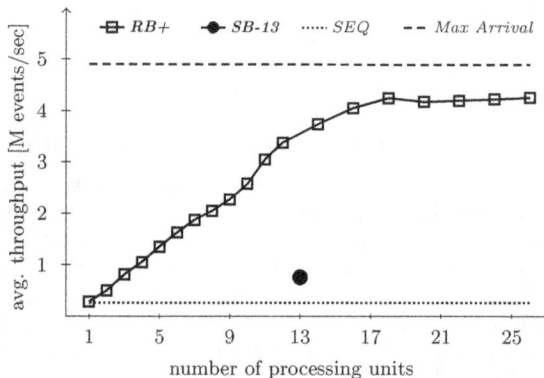

Figure 14: Comparison of parallelization techniques

In order to compare the techniques with a more realistic scenario, we have repeated the comparison experiment using the classic "head and shoulders" pattern. The query (**Q1**) is a rather costly query with 13 pattern variables. Figure 14 shows the achievable throughput for each technique. Note that state-based technique **SB** must use 13 fixed processing units for this query. Despite having sufficient number of states, the state-based parallel pattern matching engine can only achieve a speedup of 2.64. Using the same number of processing units, **RB+** achieves a much better performance. Furthermore, as shown previously, our run-based technique **RB+** has a scaling behavior (*i.e.* ≈15X) up to the point where the network becomes a bottleneck.

5.9 Performance with a Real-World Workload

In this section, we present the performance of our run-based parallelism technique under a real-world workload scenario. The data we used comes from NYSE TAQ [5] as described in Section 5.1.1. We have used the query 1 (**Q1**) which is a classic "head and shoulders" pattern query, and has been discussed throughout the paper. The results of this experiment are shown in Figure 15. The results clearly indicate the performance and the scalability of our run-based

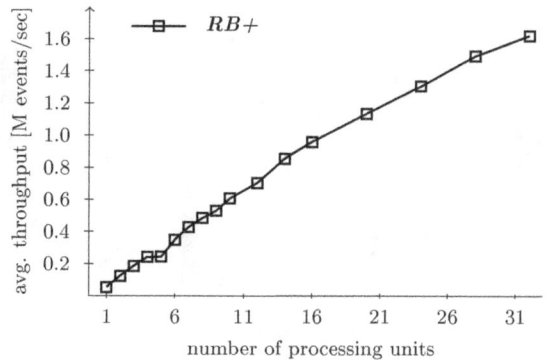

Figure 15: Performance of RB+ with a real-world workload

parallelization technique **RB+**. The performance of our technique is better pronounced under this setting for the following reasons: *(i) cost of query:* even the serial evaluation of this query on the real-world data is expensive, which makes it computation-bound rather than network-bound. As an indication, our serial implementation can handle only up to 68K events per second. *(ii) nature of real-world data:* real-world market data contains a lot of repetitions in values (*i.e.*, in price) due to clustered market activity and once something matches to our pattern, it is likely that many things will match at once (which is not the case with synthetic data). Overall, these reasons make our parallelization technique shine under the real-world dataset and it shows almost a perfect linear scalability.

5.10 Summary of Experiments

In the experiments, we showed the performance characteristics of our parallel pattern matching techniques. The results showed that state-based parallelism is usually **query dependent** and ideal speedups from parallelism could not be achieved easily. On the other hand, we showed that run-based parallelism is more robust to different queries and is **query independent**. Also our quantitative comparison of the techniques concluded that run-based parallelization achieves a superior performance to that of state-based parallelism.

6. RELATED WORK

Recently, there have been many systems proposed for sequential pattern matching on data streams [2, 7, 10, 11, 14, 12]. Each of these systems follows a different approach to optimize high cost of sequential pattern matching. Since our focus is parallelization of pattern matching processing, our work is orthogonal to them. Except ZStream [14], all other systems use some variant of a non-deterministic FSM to detect patterns. ZStream uses tree-based plans to model pattern matching queries. For a given pattern, there exist multiple plans with different costs [14]. ZStream presents a cost-based adaptive optimization where it is possible to adjust the order of evaluations on-the-fly [14]. ZStream can benefit from run-based parallelism, such that multiple query plans can run in parallel. On the other hand, SASE+[7] proposed a shared match buffer to share partial matches across different runs efficiently. Similarly, SASE+ can also use run-based parallelism and use its shared match buffer to maintain partial matches on a single processing unit.

There has been also a few recent works focusing on parallelization of pattern matching processing. Pattern matching can be seen as a stateful operator in a general-purpose streaming system [13]. Hirzel et al. [13] exploit the partitioning constructs provided by the queries (*i.e.*, `PARTITION BY`). Despite being an effective solution, this approach becomes insufficient at times when queries do not contain such constructs. Wu et al. [17] propose a parallelization framework for stateful stream processing operators. Their model splits events in round-robin to different replicas of an operator that are assumed to have an access to a shared state. Their assumption is not feasible for pattern matching, since in this case shared state would consist of set of pointers to an FSM. Additionally, events must be evaluated in a determined order for each active state. Therefore, our approach considers creating parallel tasks from an operator as much independent as possible.

Schneider et al. [15] also consider intra-operator parallelism through data-partitioning. They introduce a compiler and a run time system that automatically extract data parallelism from queries. Additionally, they introduce the concept of safety conditions for automatic parallelization. Given an operator, if one can assign a key to each partition out of the attributes of events, then state of an operator can be partitioned. In this manner, the approach becomes effective without requiring any shared state among replicas.

In a similar effort, Brenna et al. [8] take a different approach and distribute an event processing system across a cluster of machines. They implemented a distributed event pattern matching system based on Cayuga. As a first step, they also apply data parallelism. In contrast to other related work, their focus is also running multiple queries in parallel. In their FSM-based evaluation approach, FSM is decomposed into separate states running on different machines. In this regard, pipelined parallelism of states is achieved. Our state-based parallelization approach also works similarly, where the pipelining is achieved within a machine.

In this paper, our focus is parallelization within a single partition of an event stream. Our approach is complimentary to key-based (*i.e.*, `PARTITION-BY`) parallelization techniques and can be further applied for fine-granular parallelization, especially on multi-core CPUs. We consider two main techniques, run-based and state-based. Lastly, we present an experimental evaluation over both approaches and conclude with the superiority of our run-based parallelization technique.

7. CONCLUSIONS

In this paper, we investigated parallel pattern matching techniques for scaling a CEP query on multi-core architectures. We proposed RIP - a run-based intra-query parallelization approach that achieves linear scale-up, while being query-independent and skew-tolerant. RIP complements previous partitioned parallelism approaches and outperforms its pipelined parallelism alternative. Our focus in this work was throughput, we would like consider other performance criteria such as response time in the future. Further future work directions include analyzing and handling network-bound use cases, extending RIP to be fault-tolerant and to apply in cluster settings, and investigating inter-query parallelism for CEP.

8. REFERENCES

[1] Day trading technical analysis. http://www.daytradingcoach.com/daytrading-technicalanalysis-course.htm. Accessed: 03/11/2012.

[2] Esper. http://www.espertech.com. Accessed: 02/12/2012.

[3] Head and shoulders. http://www.chartpatterns.com/headandshoulders.htm. Accessed: 03/02/2013.

[4] Head and shoulders (chart pattern). http://en.wikipedia.org/wiki/Head_and_shoulders_(chart_pattern). Accessed: 10/11/2012.

[5] NYSE Data Solutions. http://www.nyxdata.com/nysedata/.

[6] Oracle CEP. http://www.oracle.com/technetwork/middleware/complex-event-processing/index.html.

[7] J. Agrawal et al. Efficient Pattern Matching over Event Streams. In *ACM SIGMOD Conference*, Vancouver, Canada, 2008.

[8] L. Brenna et al. Distributed Event Stream Processing with Non-deterministic Finite Automata. In *ACM DEBS Conference*, Nashville, Tennessee, July 2009.

[9] G. Cugola et al. Tesla: a formally defined event specification language. In *Proceedings of the Fourth ACM International Conference on Distributed Event-Based Systems*, DEBS '10, pages 50–61, New York, NY, USA, 2010. ACM.

[10] A. Demers et al. Cayuga: A General Purpose Event Monitoring System. In *CIDR Conference*, Asilomar, CA, 2007.

[11] N. Dindar et al. DejaVu: Declarative Pattern Matching over Live and Archived Streams of Events (Demo). In *ACM SIGMOD Conference*, Providence, RI, 2009.

[12] N. Dindar et al. Efficiently Correlating Complex Events over Live and Archived Data Streams. In *ACM International Conference on Distributed Event-Based Systems (DEBS'11)*, New York, NY, USA, July 2011.

[13] M. Hirzel. Partition and Compose: Parallel Complex Event Processing. In *ACM DEBS Conference*, Berlin, Germany, July 2012.

[14] Y. Mei et al. ZStream: A Cost-based Query Processor for Adaptively Detecting Composite Events. In *ACM SIGMOD Conference*, Providence, RI, June 2009.

[15] S. Schneider et al. Auto-Parallelizing Stateful Distributed Streaming Applications. In *ACM PACT Conference*, Minneapolis, MN, September 2012.

[16] E. Wu et al. High-Performance Complex Event Processing over Streams. In *ACM SIGMOD Conference*, Chicago, IL, June 2006.

[17] S. Wu et al. Parallelizing Stateful Operators in a Distributed Stream Processing System: How, Should you and How much? In *ACM DEBS Conference*, Berlin, Germany, July 2012.

[18] F. Zemke et al. Pattern Matching in Sequences of Rows. Technical Report ANSI Standard Proposal, 2007.

APPENDIX

A. QUERIES

This appendix shows the pattern declarations of all the queries used in our paper.

Query 1 (Q1)

```
1  PATTERN
2    (A B* C D* E F* G H* I J* K L* M
     )
3  DEFINE
4    B AS (B.price ≥ PREV(B.price)),
5    C AS (C.price > PREV(C.price)),
6    D AS (D.price ≤ PREV(D.price)),
7    E AS (E.price < PREV(E.price)
8        AND E.price > A.price),
9    F AS (F.price ≥ PREV(F.price)),
10   G AS (G.price ≥ PREV(G.price))
11       AND G.price > C.price),
12   H AS (H.price ≤ PREV(H.price)),
13   I AS (I.price < PREV(I.price)
14       AND I.price > A.price),
15   J AS (J.price ≥ PREV(J.price)),
16   K AS (K.price > PREV(K.price))
17       AND K.price < G.price),
18   L AS (L.price ≤ PREV(L.price),
19   M AS (M.price ≤ PREV(M.price)
20       AND M.price < E.price
21       AND M.price < I.price)
```

Query 2 (Q2)

```
1  PATTERN
2    (A B+ C)
3  DEFINE
4    A AS (A.price < 70),
5    B AS (B.price > 80
6        AND B.price < 120),
7    C AS (C.price > 130)
```

Query 3 (Q3)

```
1  PATTERN
2    (A B+ C+ D+ E+ F)
3  DEFINE
4    B AS (B.price > PREV(B.price)
5        AND B.price > A.price),
6    C AS (C.price < PREV(C.price)
7        AND C.price > A.price),
8    D AS (D.price > PREV(D.price)
9        AND D.price > A.price),
10   E AS (E.price < PREV(E.price)
11       AND E.price > A.price),
12   F AS (F.price < A.price)
```

Query 4 (Q4)

```
1  PATTERN
2    (A B* C)
3  DEFINE
4    A AS (A.price < 70),
5    B AS (B.price > PREV(B.price)
6        AND B.price > A.price),
7    C AS (C.price > PREV(C.price)
8        AND C.price > 130)
```

Query 5 (Q5)

```
1  PATTERN
2    (A B C D E F G H I J K L M)
3  DEFINE
4    B AS (B.price > PREV(B.price)),
5    C AS (C.price > PREV(C.price)),
6    D AS (D.price < PREV(D.price)),
7    E AS (E.price < PREV(E.price)
8        AND E.price > A.price),
9    F AS (F.price > PREV(F.price)),
10   G AS (G.price > PREV(G.price)
11       AND G.price > C.price),
12   H AS (H.price < PREV(H.price)),
13   I AS (I.price < PREV(I.price)
14       AND I.price > A.price),
15   J AS (J.price > PREV(J.price)),
16   K AS (K.price > PREV(K.price)
17       AND K.price < G.price),
18   L AS (L.price < PREV(L.price)),
19   M AS (M.price < PREV(M.price)
20       AND M.price < E.price
21       AND M.price < I.price)
```

Query 6 (Q6)

```
1  PATTERN
2    (A B C D E F)
3  DEFINE
4    B AS (B.price > PREV(B.price)
5        AND B.price > A.price),
6    C AS (C.price < PREV(C.price)
7        AND (C.price > A.price),
8    D AS (D.price > PREV(D.price)
9        AND D.price > A.price),
10   E AS (E.price < PREV(E.price)
11       AND E.price > A.price),
12   F AS (F.price < A.price)
```

Query 7 (Q7)

```
1  PATTERN
2    (A B C)
3  DEFINE
4    A AS (A.price < 70),
5    B AS (B.price > A.price),
6    C AS (C.price < B.price
7        AND C.price < A.price)
```

Query 8 (Q8)

```
1  PATTERN
2    (A B* C+ D+ E+ F)
3  DEFINE
4    A AS (A.price < 80),
5    B AS (B.price > 80
6        AND B.price < 120),
7    C AS (C.price < 80),
8    D AS (D.price > 80
9        AND D.price < 120),
10   E AS (E.price > 120),
11   F AS (F.price > 130)
```

Query 9 (Q9)

```
1  PATTERN
2    (A B+ C D+ E F+ G H+ I J+ K L+ M)
3  DEFINE
4    A AS (A.price < 70),
5    B AS (B.price > 70
6        AND B.price < 130),
7    C AS (C.price > 130,
8    D AS (B.price > 70
9        AND D.price < 130),
10   E AS (E.price < 70),
11   F AS (F.price > 70
12       AND F.price < 130),
13   G AS (G.price > 130),
14   H AS (H.price > 70
15       AND H.price < 130),
16   I AS (I.price < 70),
17   J AS (J.price > 70
18       AND J.price < 130),
19   K AS (K.price > 130),
20   L AS (L.price > 70
21       AND L.price < 130),
22   M AS (M.price < 70)
```

Query 10 (Q10)

```
1  PATTERN
2    (A B C D E F G H I J K L M)
3  DEFINE
4    D AS (D.price < 100),
5    E AS (E.price > 100),
6    F AS (F.price < 100
7        AND F.price > 60),
8    G AS (G.price > 100
9        AND G.price < 140),
10   H AS (H.price < 100
11       AND H.price > 70),
12   I AS (I.price > 100
13       AND I.price < 130),
14   J AS (J.price < 100
15       AND J.price > 80),
16   K AS (K.price > 100
17       AND K.price < 120),
18   L AS (L.price < 120
19       AND L.price > 80),
20   M AS (M.price > 80
21       AND M.price < 120)
```

Query 11 (Q11)

```
1  PATTERN
2    (A B C D E F)
3  DEFINE
4    A AS (A.price < 80),
5    B AS (B.price < 90
6        AND B.price > 60),
7    C AS (C.price < 100
8        AND C.price > 70),
9    D AS (D.price < 110
10       AND D.price > 80),
11   E AS (E.price < 120
12       AND E.price > 90),
13   F AS (F.price < 130
14       AND F.price > 100)
```

Query 12 (Q12)

```
1  PATTERN
2    (A B C)
3  DEFINE
4    A AS (A.price < 90),
5    B AS (B.price > 110),
6    C AS (C.price < 90)
```

Adaptive Input Admission and Management for Parallel Stream Processing

Cagri Balkesen
Systems Group, ETH Zurich,
Switzerland
cagri.balkesen@inf.ethz.ch

Nesime Tatbul
Systems Group, ETH Zurich,
Switzerland
tatbul@inf.ethz.ch

M. Tamer Özsu
University of Waterloo,
Canada
tamer.ozsu@uwaterloo.ca

ABSTRACT

In this paper, we propose a framework for adaptive admission control and management of a large number of dynamic input streams in parallel stream processing engines. The framework takes as input any available information about input stream behaviors and the requirements of the query processing layer, and adaptively decides how to adjust the entry points of streams to the system. As the optimization decisions propagate early from input management layer to the query processing layer, the size of the cluster is minimized, the load balance is maintained, and latency bounds of queries are met in a more effective and timely manner. Declarative integration of external meta-data about data sources makes the system more robust and resource-efficient. Additionally, exploiting knowledge about queries moves data partitioning to the input management layer, where better load balance for query processing can be achieved. We implemented these techniques as a part of the Borealis stream processing system and conducted experiments showing the performance benefits of our framework.

Categories and Subject Descriptors

H.2.4 [**Database Management**]: Systems

Keywords

Data streams; Adaptive Admission Control; Parallelism

1. INTRODUCTION

Stream processing has matured into an influential technology over the past decade. Numerous applications of stream processing have emerged, ranging from the classical cases such as financial market monitoring to more novel ones such as social feed monitoring [25] or crowd-sourced sensing [27]. A common class of these applications is characterized by a large number of autonomous streaming data sources that are highly dynamic in nature, which leads to input data

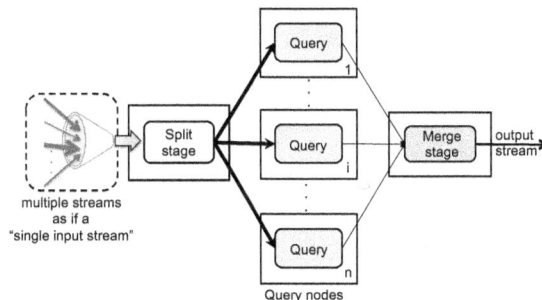

Figure 1: Classic Split-Merge parallelism model.

workloads that dynamically fluctuate over time. This dynamism can be due to several reasons, including: *(i)* intermittent disconnection of data sources due to low connectivity or power, lack of activity, etc.; *(ii)* variability of the rates of each source both among each other and over time; and *(iii)* the skew in the data values that they report. On the other hand, the aggregate input volumes generated by these sources can also get very high and can threaten the quality-of-service (QoS) in a real-time stream processing engine (SPE) by overloading its resources. Therefore, an SPE must be equipped with adaptive admission control and query processing techniques in order to be able to serve these applications in a scalable and resource-efficient manner.

There has been much recent work on scaling stream processing using parallelization techniques [3, 11, 14, 15, 23, 30]. A significant portion of these rely on a classic partitioned parallelism model, where input streams are partitioned and routed to multiple processing units to be processed in parallel [7]. Figure 1 shows the general parallelization framework that these approaches follow.

While there has been much focus on stream partitioning and parallel query evaluation (the middle part of Figure 1), an important problem that has been ignored is the admission control and management of large number of dynamic input data streams. Since partitioned parallelism requires splitting data streams to multiple processing nodes in a load-balanced manner, it is usually assumed that all the input data streams will arrive at a split stage as a single physical data stream as shown in Figure 1. This model is not realistic, and it introduces scalability issues in the split stage, which itself might require parallelization [3, 30].

In this paper, we propose a general framework for explicit management and admission control of input data streams as first-class entities in a parallel SPE (the left half of Figure 1). In a partitioned parallelism setting, this involves three main

15

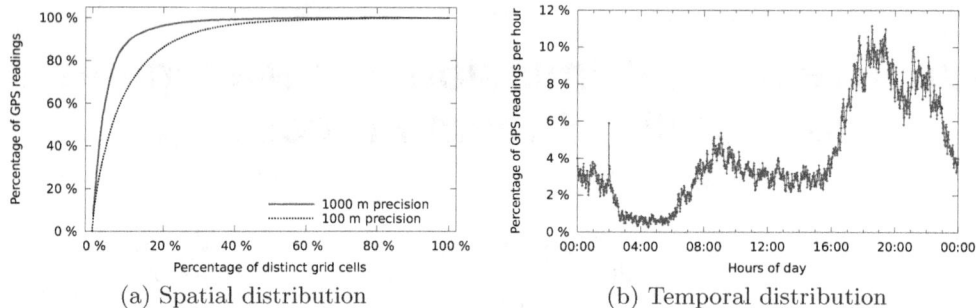

(a) Spatial distribution   (b) Temporal distribution

Figure 2: Skewed and dynamic behavior of data sources in the Uber trace.

tasks: *(i)* accepting and assigning individual input streams to one or more split nodes; *(ii)* continuously monitoring behavior of each input stream; and *(iii)* setting the number of split, query, and merge nodes accordingly. It has been shown that binding all input streams to a single split node would introduce scalability issues [30, 3]. On the other hand, binding each stream to a separate split node would not be resource-efficient. Thus, the first important goal in this problem is to minimize the number of split nodes (and deciding the number of query and merge nodes accordingly). Furthermore, the dynamic nature of the inputs require continuous monitoring of the inputs and performing the admission control tasks adaptively. However, changes in input stream assignment would lead to delay and buffering penalties. Therefore, the second important goal is to minimize the cost of stream redirections.

Adaptive admission control and management of input streams in parallel stream processing systems is important, as it provides the opportunity to observe and react to high and dynamically changing loads as soon as they are received by the system, even before reaching the query processing stage. If done right, it would maximize the scalability and resource-efficiency of the system while maintaining QoS guarantees.

This problem is challenging for several reasons. First, optimal input stream assignment can be reduced to the bin-packing problem, which is known to be NP-hard [6]. Second, minimizing the cost of stream redirections requires having knowledge about future behaviors of inputs, which is usually not available in advance. Therefore, heuristic solutions that predict these behaviors are needed.

Moreover, as our motivating example shall demonstrate, forecasting is not the only way to learn the characteristics of input streams. In many areas, such as financial markets, there are quite well-known periods (*i.e.*, opening-closing hours, crises times, etc.) when high-volume streams will stress SPEs. In fact, many factors such as peak rates, periodicity, rate behavior (rising/falling trend) can be known in advance. By declaratively integrating such knowledge about streams as meta-data into the input stream management, the system can be made more robust and resource-efficient. The following example demonstrates the characteristics and significance of applications that our framework addresses.

1.1 Motivating Application

Large-scale sensor network applications have been prominent use cases of data stream processing. With the emergence of smartphones that are capable of collecting a variety of information such as GPS location, it is now possible to treat everyone carrying a smartphone as a "sensor" in a wide range of useful applications that are called "crowd-sourced sensing applications". For example, in crowd-sourced traffic monitoring, smartphones or in-car GPS systems are used as input data sources that report location information on a continuous basis (*e.g.*, Waze social mobile application [27] or the Mobile Millennium project [12]). Real-time traffic monitoring applications then rely heavily on continuous spatio-temporal aggregation and deep analysis of high-volume streams reporting vehicle location and speed. This can be modeled using the following continuous query:

```
Input(Time, VehicleID, Long, Lat, Speed, ReportType)

SELECT getGridCoordinates(Long, Lat, @precision) AS AreaID,
       COUNT(*), AVG(Speed), MAX(Speed), isQueueEnd(*)
FROM Input [RANGE 60 MINUTE SLIDE 1 MINUTE]
WHERE ReportType = 'traffic'
GROUP BY AreaID;
```

We have analyzed a publicly available real-world trace of 1.2 million GPS position reports from a black car dispatching company called *Uber* that operates in San Francisco [26]. In Figure 2, we plot the distribution of GPS readings from this data trace over space (based on 100m x 100m or 1000m x 1000m tiles over the city map) and time (based on different times of day). While the distribution of GPS reports for different tiles follows a highly skewed, Zipf-like distribution (cf. Figure 2(a)), it also varies significantly throughout the day (cf. Figure 2(b)) due to the changing number of data sources (cars in traffic sending reports) as well as their update rates depending on the peak hours and locations.

As this analysis demonstrates, real-time monitoring applications such as the traffic monitoring case described above, impose a number of unique challenges for stream processing. First of all, it is widely projected that the number of smartphones and GPS devices used by drivers will immensely increase over the next few years [8]. As such, these applications typically involve a very large number of data stream sources. Second, these data sources are highly dynamic and transient (*i.e.*, they can join or leave in an unpredictable way). Third, they may exhibit skewed workloads in terms of their update rates and reported values (*e.g.*, more frequent reports from areas where the traffic is moving faster or where mobile connectivity is stronger). Finally, in order for the results to be useful, live reports must be aggregated and analyzed in a correct and timely manner.

1.2 Scope and Contributions

In this paper, we propose a general framework for adaptive admission control and management of input streams for parallel stream processing. The framework takes as input any available information about input stream behaviors and

Figure 3: Input stream admission and management.

requirements of the query processing layer, and adaptively decides how to assign streams to split nodes. The framework treats input streams as first-class citizens of the system, thereby improving the efficiency and robustness of the query processing layer. We also show how our framework can extend a partitioned parallelism framework and effectively be applied to parallelizing sliding window aggregation queries in SPEs.

2. INPUT STREAM ADMISSION AND MANAGEMENT

In data stream processing, workloads of long running queries fluctuate over time with input rates sometimes increasing by orders of magnitude (cf. Figure 2(b)). When workloads are so unpredictable, it is not possible to provision required resources for query processing in advance.

Our adaptive input stream admission and management framework tries to avoid over-provisioning of resources without sacrificing QoS requirements for highly dynamic streaming workloads. The first major problem for such workloads is the high number of distributed input sources with time-varying input rates. This problem, which is more pronounced in a parallel processing setting, requires dynamically changing the entry points of individual streams to the system. The second problem is that streams are also highly transient, meaning they join/leave over time, which requires an admission control mechanism. Finally, based on the overall volume of streams that enter the system, capacity of the processing layer requires adjustment.

An overview of our framework is shown in Figure 3. In contrast to a classic admission control, our framework eventually accepts all the streams and therefore admission is expected to be always successful. In doing so, the framework utilizes knowledge from both sources and queries in a novel manner. Streams are profiled at runtime and their statistics are used for making forecasts. At the same time, users can also specify meta-data about streams. On the other hand, query knowledge such as windowing and grouping information are inferred from queries. Finally, query load information is also monitored at runtime. We describe the framework and its interaction with the input streams layer in detail in this section. Sections 3 and 4 describe its interaction with the query processing layer.

2.1 The Input Stream Assignment Problem

It is impractical to bind multiple, highly dynamic and transient input streams to a single split node [3, 30]. However, binding only a single stream to each split node may extremely overuse resources. Our solution is to periodically check the behavior of streams along with their meta-data and dynamically re-assign some of the streams to different split nodes. The re-assignment of streams is driven by quality requirements of the query and the behavior of streams.

The problem can be formalized as follows. Assume we are given N input streams with average rates $\{R_1, \ldots, R_N\}$ over a certain period, where the maximum of rates is always less than the node processing capacity C, *i.e.* in the worst case a single stream can be processed by a single split node ($\forall_i R_i \leq C + \epsilon$). We are also given M split nodes each with capacity C, where $M \leq N$. The problem is to partition streams (and rates) into a minimum number k of subsets $M_1, M_2, \cdots, M_k$ such that $\sum_{R_i \in M_j} R_i \leq C + \epsilon, \forall j = 1, \ldots, k$. This problem can be reduced to the bin-packing problem, which is known to be NP-hard, but for which there exist heuristic solutions with guaranteed performance bounds [6]. Some of the well-known heuristic solutions are First Fit Decreasing (FFD) and Best Fit Decreasing (BFD). FFD first sorts items in decreasing order of size and then inserts each item to the first bin that it fits. BFD on the other hand keeps bins sorted in increasing order of free space. Whenever something is inserted to a bin, the bin's order on the list changes with the remaining space.

2.2 Near-Optimal Input Stream Assignment

Time varying stream rates make our problem more challenging than bin-packing where optimization decisions have to be checked periodically. BFD and FFD assume that all bins are initially empty and items can be assigned to any of them. In our context, applying BFD/FFD causes reoptimization from scratch, resulting in a reassignment of all the streams regardless of their previous assignments. This is clearly undesirable, since it has high cost – moving a stream is not a cheap operation as it has delay and buffering penalties on the client side as the experiments demonstrate (Section 6.2). Hence, as a second goal of the optimization, we also need to minimize redirections of streams, *i.e.*, trade off resource optimality against redirection overhead.

Algorithm 1 Input Stream Assignment Strategy Skeleton

1: **for all** split node S **do**
2:    **if** $S.\underline{isOverloaded}()$ **then**
3:       streamsToMove.add($S.\underline{pickStreamsToMove}()$);
4:    **else if** $S.\underline{acceptsNewStream}()$ **then**
5:       bins.add(S);
6:    **end if**
7: **end for**
8: streamsToMove.add(getNewInputStreams());
9: items $\Leftarrow$ sort(streamsToMove, $\underline{PlacementOrder}()$);
10: modifications $\Leftarrow$ runBFDVariant(items, bins);
11: **for all** n in modifications.newNodes **do**
12:    addNewNode(n);
13: **end for**
14: **for all** m in modifications.streams **do**
15:    **if** m.isNewStream() **then**
16:       m.assignStream(m.destNode);
17:    **else**
18:       m.redirectStream(m.srcNode, m.destNode);
19:    **end if**
20: **end for**

Algorithm 1 shows the skeleton of our optimization strategy that is executed periodically. The algorithm iterates through all the split nodes and moves away streams from the overloaded nodes. The streams to be moved along with the new streams are then connected to nodes that have enough capacity. In case of insufficient capacity, new split nodes are added to the system. The stream assignments to nodes are carried out using a variant of the BFD bin-packing algorithm with the goal of using as few nodes as possible. However, the concrete strategy is driven by the heuristics used. Different concrete optimization strategies can be created by customizing the implementation of underlined methods whose general tasks are the following:

isOverloaded: Determines whether a node needs consideration for moving some of its input streams because of insufficient capacity.

pickStreamsToMove: On overload, some of the streams must be moved away from the corresponding node. This method identifies the order in which streams will be moved away from the node until the capacity constraint is satisfied.

acceptsNewStream: Determines whether a given node has enough capacity to accept new input streams (called *accepting node*).

PlacementOrder: Identifies the order in which streams that are waiting to be assigned are considered for placement to accepting nodes.

Our framework's concrete optimization strategy is a specialized implementation of the skeleton (*i.e.*, it customizes the underlined methods). The core of our strategy is based on forecasting rates and utilizing meta-data about streams. In the next two sub-sections, we describe these two components and then finally our concrete optimization strategy.

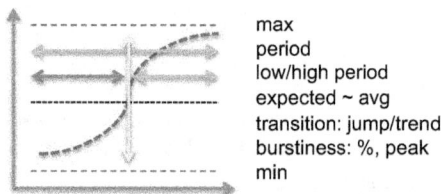

Figure 4: **Modelling behavior of input streams.**

2.3 Forecasting the Input Rate

Part of our solution for input stream assignments is based on predictions about future behavior of input streams rather than their history. History is only employed to make good quality forecasts about future rates of streams. As forecasts become more accurate, the system is better optimized until a point in future instead of a point which lies in the past.

The forecasting model of our system is as follows. Assume that we are given a series of periodic observations of an input stream's rate, denoted by X_i for each period i. The problem is forecasting, at period t, the rate at period $t + k$, denoted by $\hat{X}_{t+k}$. We use Holt-Winters forecasting technique [5], which is a type of exponential smoothing[1]. We especially use Holt's linear trend model (also known as double exponential smoothing) that works particularly well in practice for reasonable term forecasts. As observations arrive, the value for the local mean level (L) and trend (T) for the input rate is updated continuously as follows:

$$L_t = \alpha \cdot X_t + (1 - \alpha)(L_{t-1} + T_{t-1})$$

$$T_t = \gamma \cdot (L_t - L_{t-1}) + (1 - \gamma) \cdot T_{t-1}$$

---

[1]For a survey of time series forecasting, see [4].

Using the updated values of level and trend, the rate forecast at time t, for period $t + k$ is computed as:

$$\hat{X}_{t+k} = L_t + k \cdot T_t$$

The smoothing parameters α and γ can be selected by fitting historical data (we refer the reader to [5] for details). As we shall demonstrate in our experiments, this forecasting technique works quite well for our framework. However, one should note that any sophisticated forecasting technique can be easily plugged into our system, and can be used instead.

2.4 Exploiting External Meta-Data of Streams

In many cases, input data streams often have predictable or known characteristics. Thus, as a first step, our system builds a model for each stream and tries to forecast future rates. This is enabled by continuously monitoring the rate and behavior of each stream. However, beyond that, certain external knowledge can be exploited to improve the modelling and forecasting of streams.

Figure 4 depicts the stream modelling mechanism that we use in our system. Basically, ten essential characteristics of streams are modelled by this mechanism as shown in Figure 4. In the beginning, before a stream is connected to the system, the client can provide information about any of these characteristics as meta-data of the stream. The more information the client provides, the better will be the model in improving the stream assignment optimizations. However, if the client does not give any information about streams, then the model is based on default values of these characteristics that are based on average observations among existing streams. For instance, if the client does not provide any information about the expected or average rate of the stream, then the system assumes a value based on average rates of all existing streams in the system. Among these characteristics, period values give information regarding periodicity of the stream behavior. On the other hand, transition behavior is another important clue about the changes in stream rates. Having information such as "`transition=jump`" means that the stream rate will jump/fall to max/min value. This is very valuable information since it is hard to forecast it by any statistical model. When "`transition=trend`" is given, we can expect that the transition between low and high values will occur with an observable trend, which also greatly improves forecasting accuracy.

2.5 Delta Rate Forecasting with Meta-data

Our concrete optimization strategy for input stream admission and management is called the *Delta Rate Forecasting with Meta-data* **DRF-M**. We employ the rate forecasting-based heuristic (Section 2.3) in our strategy which is enhanced by utilizing stream meta-data. We begin describing it by explaining the concrete implementations of the underlined methods in skeleton strategy shown in Algoritm 1:

isOverloaded: **DRF-M** implementation estimates the latency using an exponentially weighted moving average window of queue size samples, and returns true when this value goes beyond the given threshold, *i.e.*, the QoS metric.

pickStreamsToMove: The main *heuristic* we employ in **DRF-M** is to move the streams with highest expected rate increase, as these are the ones that have the most potential to cause trouble. We call this heuristic *delta-rate-forecast* and it is defined as $\Delta_{RF} = \hat{X}_{t+k} - \hat{X}_{t+1}$. However, if there are meta-data available about the stream, then meta-data

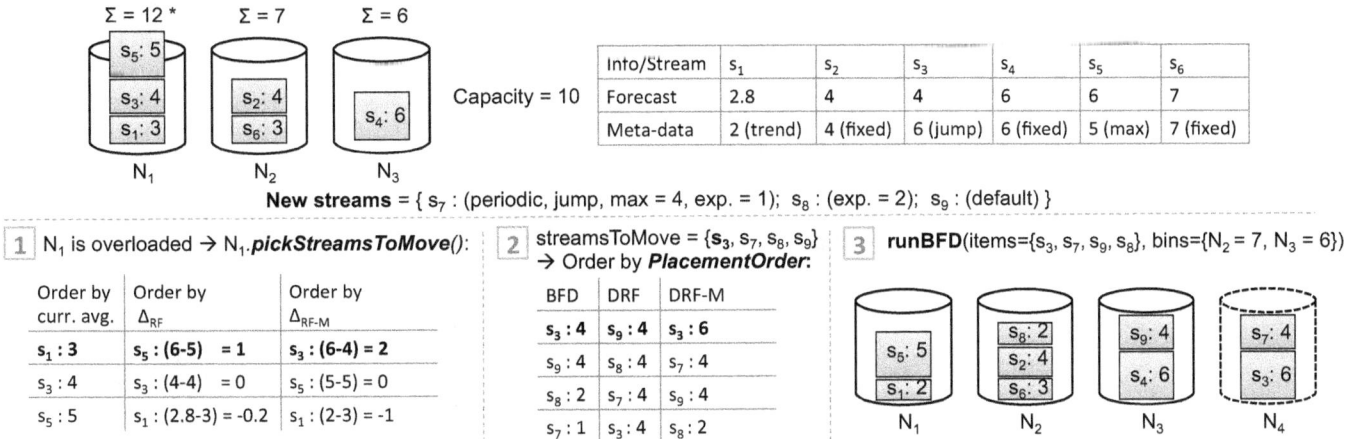

Into/Stream	s_1	s_2	s_3	s_4	s_5	s_6
Forecast	2.8	4	4	6	6	7
Meta-data	2 (trend)	4 (fixed)	6 (jump)	6 (fixed)	5 (max)	7 (fixed)

New streams = { s_7 : (periodic, jump, max = 4, exp. = 1); s_8 : (exp. = 2); s_9 : (default) }

1 N_1 is overloaded → N_1.**pickStreamsToMove()**:

Order by curr. avg.	Order by Δ_{RF}	Order by Δ_{RF-M}
s_1 : 3	s_5 : (6-5) = 1	s_3 : (6-4) = 2
s_3 : 4	s_3 : (4-4) = 0	s_5 : (5-5) = 0
s_5 : 5	s_1 : (2.8-3) = -0.2	s_1 : (2-3) = -1

2 streamsToMove = {s_3, s_7, s_8, s_9} → Order by **PlacementOrder**:

BFD	DRF	DRF-M
s_3 : 4	s_9 : 4	s_3 : 6
s_9 : 4	s_8 : 4	s_7 : 4
s_8 : 2	s_7 : 4	s_9 : 4
s_7 : 1	s_3 : 4	s_8 : 2

3 **runBFD**(items={s_3, s_7, s_9, s_8}, bins={N_2 = 7, N_3 = 6})

Figure 5: Input stream admission and management in action.

based stream rate expectation is used instead of the forecast. For example, if a meta-data about the maximum achievable rate of an input stream is available, then that value can be plugged into the equation instead of a forecast. Hence, in this case $\Delta_{RF-M} = X^m_{t+k} - \hat{X}_{t+1}$, where X^m_{t+k} denotes the meta-data based stream rate expectation at period $t + k$. We then order all the streams of an overloaded node with their $\Delta_{RF}/\Delta_{RF-M}$ and pick streams to move in this order until total rate forecast falls below node processing capacity (i.e., $\Sigma_{RF} \leq C/\Sigma_{RF-M} \leq C$).

acceptsNewStream: To determine whether a node can accept new input streams, our implementation sums up rate forecasts/expectations of a node's input streams (Σ_{RF}) and returns true if Σ_{RF} is below a certain capacity level.

PlacementOrder: In the BFD algorithm, items to be placed in bins are normally considered in decreasing order of size [6]. In our strategy, we consider streams in order of decreasing rate forecasts or meta-data based rate predictions for the next period, $\hat{X}_{t+1}$ or X^m_{t+k} depending on availability.

Figure 5 illustrates the execution of our optimization strategy in action. For this illustration, we assume 3 split nodes ($N_1..N_3$) containing a total of 6 input streams ($s_1..s_6$) deployed on them. The table on the top right shows the forecasts along with meta-data based predictions for stream rates. The capacity of each node is given in terms of tuples that can be processed per unit time (which is 10) and the rates of streams are given as number of tuples that flow per unit time. As the first step of the algorithm, the load of each split node is computed and N_1 is found to be overloaded (12 > 10). The optimization strategy needs to pick streams from N_1 to be assigned to other nodes. Using forecasts and meta-data based predictions from the table, Δ_{RF-M} is computed and s_3 stream is chosen as the victim. Note that if only Δ_{RF} or current average rates were used, the decision would have been different (i.e., 1st and 2nd columns in step 1), and much worse since the chosen streams (as we can see from the meta-data information) are not likely to cause a problem for their nodes, and their redirection is redundant. The second step of the algorithm begins by considering the newly added input streams (cf. line 8 in Algorithm 1) in addition to s_3. This time streams to be moved are ordered according to the *PlacementOrder* heuristic using DRF and meta-data, which is shown on the right-most column in the table. Note the

difference in order when using just DRF in the 2nd column (i.e., no meta-data about new streams, hence all assume a default rate of 4) or decreasing order of average rates (plain BFD) in the 1st column. In the third step, the streams to be moved are considered in the determined order from step 2 and the BFD bin-packing algorithm is executed. As a result, a new split node is added (line 12 in Algorithm 1) and the new stream s_7 and stream s_3 are assigned to that node. Other new streams s_8 and s_9 are assigned to nodes N_2 and N_3, and one optimization period of the algorithm completes.

3. ADAPTIVITY IN PROCESSING LAYER

3.1 QoS Model

Our input stream admission and management framework takes QoS requirements for queries as additional input and uses them in determining the degree of parallelization. More specifically, QoS is specified in terms of maximum result latency (L time units) in the output stream.

We define result latency as the time difference between the arrival timestamp of the last tuple contributing to a query result tuple r and the generation of r's timestamp. All result tuples must have result latency of at most L time units.

3.2 Setting Number of Query and Merge Nodes

The modifications of streams (new assignments or redirections) may result in changing the number of split nodes. As the aggregate input volume changes, this in turn requires adjusting the number of processing nodes (i.e., query and merge nodes) fed by the split nodes. Basically, the optimization decision propagates from the input streams layer to the query processing layer.

The QoS latency metric guides parallelization level (d) adjustment. The optimization goal is to keep the latency during period $i + 1$ below the target. As a first step, the input stream controller determines the number of split nodes in period $i + 1$ (n_s^{i+1}), by considering all streams with their historical, forecasted, and meta-data predicted rates as described in Section 2. Next, the optimizer utilizes total rate expectations from the first step to identify the number of required processing (n_p^{i+1}) and merge (n_m^{i+1}) nodes at period $i + 1$. The total rate forecasts of input streams, Σ_{RF} or Σ_{RF-M} and the per-tuple processing cost of the query op-

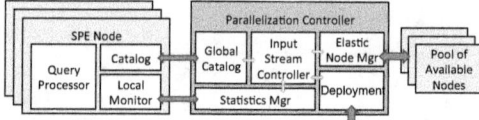

Figure 6: The parallelization controller.

erator (c_{op}) are used to determine the number of processing nodes required for the next period, n_p^{i+1}, using Equation 1a (where H denotes processing headroom of SPE not used for operator execution and C_{op} is the processing capacity of a single node running the query operator).

$$\frac{\Sigma_{RF}}{n_p^{i+1}} \cdot c_{op} = 1.0 - H \qquad (1a)$$

$$\frac{n_p^{i+1} \cdot C_{op}}{n_m^{i+1}} \cdot c_{merge} = 1.0 - H \qquad (1b)$$

Similarly, the number of merge nodes, n_m^{i+1}, is determined using Equation 1b, assuming that all the processing nodes will run close to saturation in the next period. After determining n_p^{i+1} and n_m^{i+1}, the system adjusts parallelization level of a query by instantiating/de-instantiating replicas of the operators. This is supported by dynamic query modifications at runtime [24].

3.3 Architecture and Implementation

In order to implement the techniques proposed in Sections 2 and 3.2, we designed the Parallelization Controller (PC) as a new component that is responsible for dynamic resource management and continuous query optimization in our framework. Figure 6 shows the general architecture of the PC. Queries and streams are admitted to the system via PC's deployment sub-component. The PC has a statistics manager that periodically collects runtime statistics from active SPE (in our implementation, Borealis [1]) nodes. The global catalog keeps track of all deployed queries with their specifications and locations. The input stream controller is responsible for admission and management of all input streams and continuously optimizing their assignments to split nodes. Lastly, the elastic node manager manages a pool of available nodes and is responsible for handling node add/remove requests by the PC. Next, we will briefly discuss the implementation of stream redirection, dynamic query modifications, and state handover.

Stream Redirection: To be able to dynamically redirect streams to different nodes, our system needs to have control over each external input stream. To achieve this, we attach an interface to each stream with several methods. Essentially, the external input client must implement the interface and support its methods. The interface provides methods to suspend/resume the data flow, to establish/drop a connection and to redirect a stream. Whenever a re-assignment of the stream is required, PC calls necessary methods on the relevant client.

Dynamic Query Modifications: Dynamic query modifications involve adding/removing operator replicas to/from a running query and require suspending certain parts of the pipeline. First, to add a new operator, the running split operator is choked for a short period in order to modify it at runtime. Next, a new output stream is added to the choked split operator. After the modification, the split is

resumed without activating the new output stream until the full query modification is complete. In the next step, the new operator is instantiated by retrieving its replica's specification and deployment description from the catalog. The query processor in the new node deploys the operator, its input/output streams and schemas locally. In the third step, the merge operator is choked for a while to add the new input stream. As the last step, merge is resumed and the inactive new output stream of the split operator is activated. Tuples begin flowing on the new stream path from split to merge. Removal of an operator instance follows similar steps.

State Handover: In principle, our parallelization model does not require migrating unprocessed input state during adaptation or load-balancing. Query nodes process all their existing input until the choke point and only ship their partial results to the merge nodes as if they were executing normally, which is then followed by a `stream_end` punctuation to inform the merge operator.

4. INPUT- AND QUERY-AWARE STREAM PARTITIONING

In this section, we describe the integration of stream partitioning techniques and query-awareness into the admission and management of input streams. Stream partitioning and query knowledge is extracted from queries and utilized at the input stream management layer that provides an opportunity to observe and react to dynamic fluctuations in inputs as early as possible. Furthermore, the integration results in robust load-balancing in the processing layer, which is a key requirement for effective parallelization.

There are two main approaches to stream partitioning in the literature: *(i)* content-insensitive, *(ii)* content-sensitive. The former applies to queries with windows and takes only windowing semantics (*i.e.*, size and slide) into account without considering the values that appear in those windows, while the latter applies to queries with key-based processing (*e.g.*, GROUP-BY aggregates) and divides the streams according to the values of those keys.

Given query Q, if it includes key-based processing, then we apply content-sensitive partitioning ("frequency-aware hash-based partitioning"). Otherwise, we apply content-insensitive partitioning (rate-aware pane-based partitioning").

4.1 Frequency-aware Hash-based Partitioning

For queries where evaluation is inherently done on logical partitions identified by keys (*e.g.*, GROUP-BY attributes), typically a hash function is applied over the relevant attributes to identify a processing node for each tuple. This technique can distribute data in a load-balanced manner when the hash function is carefully chosen and the data are uniformly distributed.

In a dynamic setting where there can be a large number of dynamically changing data sources, processing nodes and time-varying fluctuations in the distribution of the data, traditional hashing would result in relocation of keys every time data sources or processing nodes change and would not suffice to achieve load-balancing (cf. Figure 13). What we need, instead, is a hashing technique that not only preserves load-balance in the presence of a data skew, but also minimizes the change in key assignments to processing nodes as data sources or processing nodes join/leave. We, therefore, utilize a consistent-hashing [16] based technique in a novel manner to balance load among processing nodes. It is important to note that using consistent hashing alone does not completely solve the data skew problem. It provides uniform distribution of keys to nodes, where each node will have the number of keys close to the mean number of keys per node. Under data skew, some of the keys appear more frequently than others over a time interval. In this case, nodes that are assigned the more frequent keys end up receiving more load than the others. In order to deal with the data/frequency skew problem, we propose a revised consistent hashing technique where the most frequent keys are divided into sub-keys in a more fine-grained manner and are assigned to multiple processing nodes. We call this stream partitioning approach *frequency-aware hash-based partitioning*.

Our algorithm proceeds in periods of fixed-size time intervals. During each interval, we maintain the frequencies of the K most frequent keys. We partition each such key i into p_i parts, where p_i is proportional to key i's frequency. As tuples arrive for key i, we suffix them with a partition number from 1 to p_i in a round-robin fashion (*i.e.*, key i becomes $i\#j, 1 \le j \le p_i$). This generates p_i distinct keys from each key i, which are treated as if they were separate keys in assigning their corresponding tuples to the processing nodes in the consistent hash table (see Figure 8). It is important to note that this process is carried out on each split node independently so that there is no need for extra communication among the split nodes and hence the mechanism does not need a fully distributed hash table as in peer-to-peer systems. Note that our frequency-aware hash-based partitioning technique is general enough to be applied in other domains that employ consistent hashing (*e.g.*, in distributed key-value stores like Cassandra [18], where temporally skewed accesses are also commonplace).

4.2 Rate-aware Pane-based Partitioning

Our content-insensitive stream partitioning makes novel use of the pane-based technique for parallel processing of sliding window queries. Given a query with window size w and slide s, the main idea is to divide windows into non-overlapping panes of size $gcd(w, s)$ as shown in Figure 7.

Pane-based partitioning is a better approach than window-based partitioning when windows overlap. In this case, independent partitions can be created without replicating the overlapping tuples across partitions [3]. In pane-based partitioning, each tuple belongs to exactly one pane.

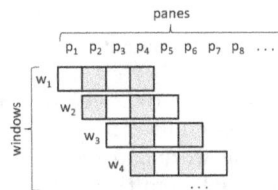

Figure 7: Panes.

In our framework, we assign window-id's and pane-id's to tuples in the split operator (like in [19]), and then distribute panes to the query nodes in a round-robin order. Distributing tuples on a pane-by-pane basis does not work well when input streams are bursty. The reason is that, for time-based windows, bursty or fluctuating input rates may lead to uneven window and pane sizes in terms of number of tuples contained. In this case, we lose control of load-balance over query nodes. This problem is similar to the skew problem in traditional parallel databases, except that, in our case the skew is due to input rates instead of input data distributions. To remedy this problem, we pro-

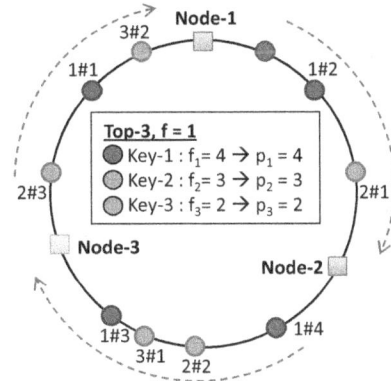

Figure 8: Consistent hashing with further key partitioning.

pose a *rate-aware pane-based partitioning* technique. The *rate-awareness* comes from the fact that the system continuously monitors the expected window and pane sizes and their statistical properties by keeping track of "recently" arrived tuples and their rates. In our approach, a pane is further partitioned into sub-panes if its size is larger than the average size of "recently" arrived panes plus the standard deviation. In this case, the tuples exceeding this average are sent to the next query node in the round-robin sequence. On the other hand, for panes whose size is smaller than this average, our algorithm compensates by routing additional panes/sub-panes to the processing node where such small panes are assigned. This solution smoothly integrates into our framework and automatically preserves load-balance of pane-based partitioning. The overhead we pay in return is continuously maintaining an estimate for average pane size and standard deviation over recent stream history, which is relatively small.

5. QUERY PROCESSING IN ACTION

In this section, we show how our framework can extend a partitioned parallelism model and be effectively applied to parallelizing sliding window aggregation queries in SPEs.

5.1 Query Types

We assume a generic parallelism model as shown in the middle part of the Figure 1. We focus on Select-Map-Aggregate (SMA) queries as our workload to demonstrate the effectiveness of our techniques, as illustrated by the example query of Section 1.1. This query involves a Selection with predicate `ReportType = 'traffic'`, a Map with a user-defined transformation function `getGridCoordinates(Long,-Lat,@precision)`, and a time-based window with size and slide of 60 and 1 minutes, respectively, over which a distributive (`COUNT()`), an algebraic (`AVG()`), a distributive (`MAX()`) and a user defined aggregate function `isQueueEnd()` are applied. The user-defined Map function transforms given GPS coordinates and precision level to a geodetic coordinate system. The user-defined aggregate detects whether a given road segment has a traffic queue-end [9].

5.2 Pane and Window Meta-data

In our framework, split nodes also take part in query processing. Split nodes annotate tuples with meta-data to in-

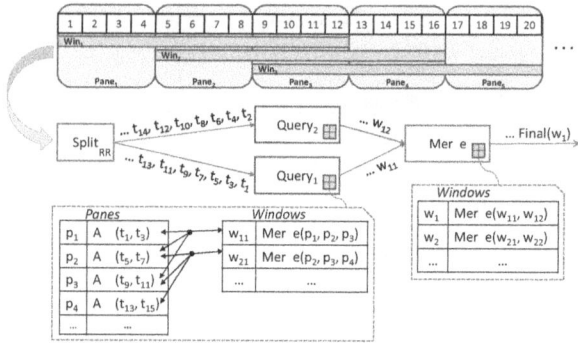

Figure 9: Parallel aggregation pipeline.

form the downstream query, merge, and union nodes about pane- and window-related information that is needed in query evaluation. These include pane-id's and window-id's that are added to the tuples [19], as well as pane-close or window-close punctuations (*i.e.*, additional tuples injected into the streams) signalling the end of a given pane or window.

Consider a query with window size w and window slide s. For count-based windows, a tuple with index i is a window-closer if $((i \geq w) \wedge ((i - w) \bmod s \equiv 0))$. For time-based windows, the same condition can be checked by using i's time field's values. However, when there are multiple tuples with the same time value, the first tuple following a sequence of tuples holding this condition should actually signal a window-close event. A similar discussion applies to pane-close events. Once a tuple is seen that meets the window-close or the pane-close condition, a corresponding punctuation tuple is broadcast to all query nodes. If there are n split nodes, a query node should close a window/pane upon receiving a total of n such punctuations to ensure that all inputs contributing to that window/pane (each might be coming through any one of the n split nodes) are considered.

5.3 Evaluation of Aggregates

Pane-based aggregation decomposes a given query into two sub-queries: *(i)* pane-level sub-query (PLQ) that runs over the panes, and *(ii)* window-level sub-query (WLQ) that runs over the results of the panes. The decomposed evaluation enables parallel processing of a window aggregation as follows. We first partition the input tuples of a window into d partitions. Each of the partitions is processed by a query node that contains a copy of the aggregate operator. Each query node proceeds as if the tuples received for the partition represent the complete window, and generates a partial aggregate for its entire window. This computation benefits from the sharing of pane results and moreover needs reduced internal buffering for distributive and algebraic aggregates. Let us explain this mechanism with an example.

Figure 9 illustrates a parallel aggregation pipeline with 2 query nodes and 1 merge node. The query is a user-defined aggregate with $w = 12$ and $s = 4$ tuples. Therefore, each pane has $w_p = s_p = gcd(12, 4) = 4$ tuples and there are 3 panes per window. For this example, the stream is partitioned with a simple tuple-by-tuple round-robin partitioning. Every query node receives its subset of tuples for corresponding pane partitions (p_i) as a stream from the split operator and is responsible for locally computing the PLQ's for those. PLQ results, (p_i, value) pairs, are stored in a `Panes` table. On the other hand, a `Windows` table keeps

track of window results as (w_{ij}, value) pairs that are evaluated from the PLQ results by applying the merge function, i denoting the window-id and j denoting the index of the node. A Panes table entry has a complete result after all the `pane_close` punctuations arrive. A Windows table entry becomes ready for output when all of its n panes have complete results in the corresponding Panes table. In the example, partial window results w_{11} and w_{12} will be output to the merge node from query nodes 1 and 2, respectively. After all query nodes send a `win_close` punctuation to the merge node, the corresponding Windows table entry becomes ready for final output.

6. EXPERIMENTAL EVALUATION

The goal of this experimental study is to investigate how well our framework achieves its goals. The results demonstrate that: *(i)* the number of processing nodes that our system uses is close to optimal, *(ii)* load is balanced at all times with low overhead, and *(iii)* the adaptivity layer meets QoS bounds.

6.1 Experimental Setup

We implemented our adaptive input stream admission and management techniques as an extension to the Borealis distributed stream processing engine [1]. Additionally, we enriched the query execution framework of Borealis by integrating our techniques for a data partitioned evaluation of SMA queries.

All the experiments were conducted on a shared-nothing cluster of machines, where each machine has an Intel® Xeon® L5520 2.26 Ghz Quadcore CPU and 16GB of main memory. The nodes, each running Debian Linux, are connected by a Gigabit Ethernet.

6.1.1 Workloads

To evaluate our system, we used the query from the motivating example introduced in Section 1.1. The query is a fairly expensive SMA query, which includes a costly mapping function (`getGridCoordinates()`) doing floating point intensive transformation on geographic coordinates and it evaluates four aggregations, one of them being fairly complex (`isQueueEnd()`). Lastly, in order to have a representative number of panes, we fixed the ratio of window size to slide at 100, where actual sizes are varied based on the chosen input rate.

The workload data that we used for our experiments is adapted from the real world traces of Uber [26] that is publicly available [13]. The data is a sample of $1.2M$ position reports collected from black cars in San Francisco. However, it misses some of the attributes such as `Speed`, `ReportType` given in the schema described in Section 1.1 and hence we artificially generated these values (assuming 100% selectivity for the predicate). In order to increase input rates, we replayed the real trace in a faster way. As a result, the data we used in the experiments follow the real trace in terms of skew with the only difference being the input rates.

Additionally, we also synthetically generated different temporal patterns based on the distributions of the real dataset. The constant workload (**constw**) consists of k streams with uniformly distributed rates between a min and a max rate. Tuples arrive with exponentially distributed inter arrival times with the mean equal to the chosen average rate. Pair-

22

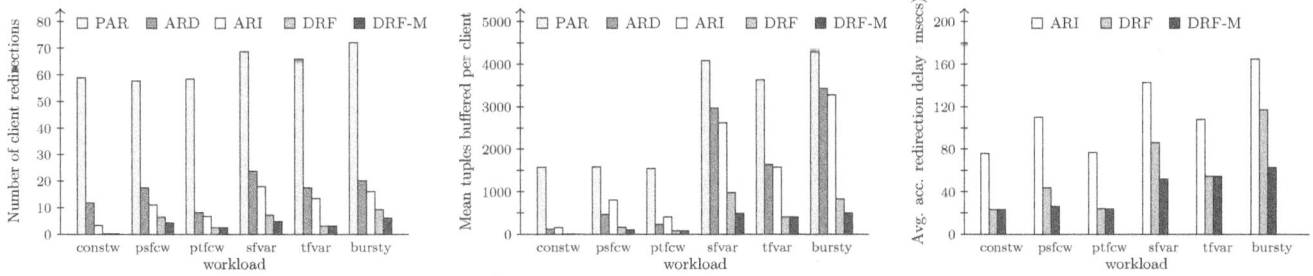

Figure 10: (a) Mean number of client redirections, (b) mean number of buffered tuples, and (c) redirection delay at client side.

step (**psfcw**) and pair-trend (**ptfcw**) fluctuating constant workloads consist of k streams that fluctuate in pairs but opposite of each other while the total load stays constant. We created two workloads where the total load varies. In the step fluctuating version (**sfvar**), rates suddenly change between high and low, whereas in trend fluctuating (**tfvar**) the switch happens with an observable trend. Lastly, for the bursty workload, we used the classical on-off model. During an active period, tuples arrive periodically with a certain rate, whereas in an idle period no data arrives. Duration of active and idle periods follow an exponential distribution. As the total number of streams, we have picked 80. Finally, we define the **load level** as the number of machines that can handle the entire load at hand.

6.1.2 Optimization Strategy Variations

The main optimization strategy of our framework, **DRF-M**, is described in Section 2.5. For comparison, we implemented other strategies by customizing the optimization algorithm shown in Algorithm 1. The baseline algorithm is called *Plain Average Rate BFD* (**PAR**), which simply considers all streams as moveable and all nodes as initially empty. Moreover, it uses only last period average rates instead of forecasts. The other algorithms we consider differ from our strategy in the way they pick streams. *Average Rate Increasing BFD* (**ARI**) picks streams in increasing order of their last period average rates, whereas *Average Rate Decreasing BFD* (**ARD**) picks them in decreasing order. Both rely on last period average rates instead of rate forecasts. Lastly, in order to demonstrate the effectiveness of the meta-data information about streams, we have also implemented **DRF** which relies on just *delta-rate-forecast* heuristic without considering meta-data about the streams.

6.2 Performance of Input Stream Admission and Management

In this experiment, we demonstrate the effectiveness of our input stream admission and management technique **DRF-M**. We discuss the performance in terms of the number of client redirections, the buffering amount at the client, and the delay contribution in the overall query evaluation.

6.2.1 Client Redirections and Buffering

Figure 10(a) shows mean client redirections and Figure 10(b) shows mean client buffering caused by different strategies under different workloads. First, PAR considers reassignment of all streams at each period regardless of the workload. As a result, it shuffles around most of the streams (note that the total number is 80) all the time causing high

amount of client side buffering. Second, the DRF strategy moves streams early by utilizing the forecasts and prevents the problems in advance. This reduces stream movement, as initial movements are provisioned for future rates. As a result, client side buffering is also reduced. The benefit of forecasting is apparent in comparing *sfvar* and *tfvar* workloads where forecasts are more accurate in *tfvar*. Comparing ARI and ARD, we see that ARI performs slightly worse than ARD as it first considers moving low rate streams, which dictates it to move more streams around. Compared to all other techniques, DRF is much better in reducing the number of client redirections and the amount of buffering at the client side. Furthermore, DRF-M, which integrates meta-data knowledge about streams, performs even better. In this experiment, we provided information about peak-rates, trend of rates and burstiness period. In cases where predictions do not perform sufficiently well (*i.e.*, *psfcw*, *sfvar* and *bursty*), DRF-M further improves the performance compared to DRF.

6.2.2 Delay Contribution

Figure 10(c) shows average accumulated delays caused by stream redirections per optimization period. We only include ARI, DRF and DRF-M as others have extremely high delays. The delays are in line with the other experiments, fewer number of redirections and buffering in DRF and DRF-M keep the accumulated delay lower than others. Additionally, DRF-M becomes more robust by integrating meta-data even with a bursty workload.

6.3 Resource Efficiency

In this experiment, we investigate how different strategies perform in terms of resource usage compared to the optimal case that requires solving an instance of the bin-packing problem at each optimization period. To find the optimal number of nodes (*i.e.* bins), we used an approximate method called *wasted-space residual optimality* [17] that provides a tight bound for optimal number of bins required.

Figure 11 shows the result of this experiment. PAR performs very close to the optimal. The reason is that it applies a global optimization in stream assignment by considering all streams at once and does not consider the previous assignments of streams. However, despite being close to optimal in terms of resource efficiency, we have shown in Section 6.2 that global optimization in PAR performs unacceptably poor for admission and management of input streams. Second, rate forecasting can be negative in terms of resource usage as forecasts often tend to overestimate the input rates. DRF can perform similar to the non-forecasting versions

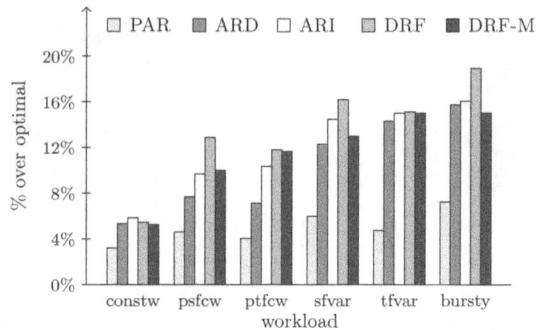

Figure 11: % resource utilization above optimal.

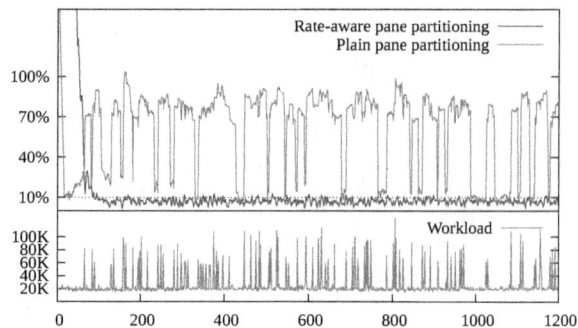

Figure 12: Load-balancing in content-insensitive partitioning.

(ARD, ARI) when forecasting is more accurate, for instance in workloads with an explicitly observable trend (*ptfcw*, *tf-var*). Overall, DRF only needs around 15% more resources than optimal to handle a fluctuating workload with trend. More importantly, our main optimization strategy DRF-M performs even closer to the optimal for *psfcw*, *sfvar* and *bursty* workloads where using meta-data proves better than just forecasts.

To summarize the results of Sections 6.2 and 6.3, the DRF-M strategy is very successful in keeping the delay below a certain threshold by avoiding excessive stream reassignments in a running query, while it requires only $\approx 5\text{-}10\%$ more resources than other strategies and $\approx 15\%$ more than the optimal.

6.4 Impact of Query-awareness in Stream Management for Parallelization

In this section, we evaluate the integration of stream partitioning techniques and query-awareness into the admission and management of input streams. The experiments in this section demonstrate the effectiveness of these techniques in terms of robust load-balancing and low overhead, which are key requirements for effective parallelization.

6.4.1 Content-insensitive Partitioning

Content-insensitive partitioning utilizes window size and slide information from the query and introduces use of panes as discussed in Section 4.2. In this experiment, we evaluate our pane-based partitioning techniques. We use a single splitter node with either plain or rate-aware pane partitioning to compare them. The metric used in the experiment is the **load-balancing ratio** defined as the ratio of mean and standard deviation of CPU loads observed over 16 nodes that split feeds. As the workload, which is specific to this experiment, we use an input stream with a rate uniformly distributed between 18K and 22K for every second. To model the rate-skew, the input rate transiently jumps to 5 times the current rate with a probability of 0.1 at each second. Figure 12 shows the workload at the bottom and the results at the top. First, in both cases the load-balancing ratio is high at the beginning as nodes are idle and most of them do not have enough data to process. However, this period is longer in rate-aware partitioning as it needs a warm-up period to statistically estimate the number of tuples in a pane. After that, rate-aware pane partitioning continuously keeps track of pane-size statistics and dynamically further partitions a pane if there is need. As a result, the load-

balancing ratio is slightly affected by the rate-skew problem and, after the warm-up, the system is able to keep the average load-balancing ratio **below 7%** during the entire run. However, plain pane partitioning is highly sensitive to rate-skew problem as seen in Figure 12. Whenever the rate jumps, the load-balancing ratio also jumps up to 100% causing a high load-imbalance. During the entire run, the average load-balancing ratio is $\approx 60\%$.

6.4.2 Content-sensitive Partitioning

Content-sensitive partitioning utilizes key-based constructs from the query (*i.e.*, GROUP-BY statement in our case) as discussed in Section 4.1. In this experiment, we study the load-balancing performance of our key-based partitioning technique under varying skew. In each experiment, after a warm-up period for collecting key frequency statistics, we measure the mean and the standard deviation of load on the processing nodes. In all experiments, the maximum number of distinct keys is 16K. In the first experiment, we used the real data distributions from the motivating example. In the other ones, we vary the frequency of keys at each experiment by using a Zipf distribution with different parameters. Figure 15 shows the load-balancing property of our key-based partitioning technique on both real data trace and synthetic data with different Zipf and top-K parameters. K on x-axis indicates the number of the most frequent keys that are considered for further partitioning. The percent shown on the y-axis denotes the load-balancing ratio. First of all, as shown previously in Figure 2(a), the real data trace follows a highly skewed Zipfian-like distribution and, not surprisingly, the load-balancing performance of our techniques work equally well on real trace and synthetic data generated with a Zipf distribution. Second, as the skew increases, variation of load between different processing nodes increases significantly if we do not apply further partitioning (*i.e.*, $K=0$). Since there are a few hotspot keys, choosing $K=5$ reduces the ratio below 50% in all the cases. When K increases, *e.g.*, at $K=100$, the variation of load decreases tremendously, almost nearing the keys per node ratio. However, increasing K beyond a certain point does not help as the load-balancing ratio is determined by the keys per node ratio. As a conclusion, by only monitoring and further partitioning the 100-200 most frequent keys we can achieve robust load-balancing even under extreme skew.

6.4.3 Why basic hashing would not suffice?

One might tend to think that basic hash-partitioning may suffice for adaptive parallelization. Assume a hash function

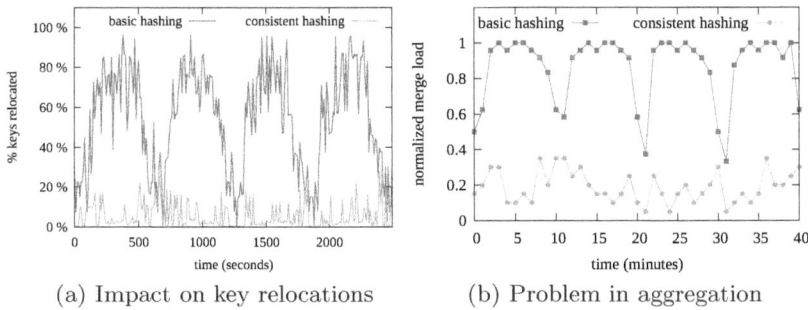

(a) Impact on key relocations   (b) Problem in aggregation

Figure 13: Problem with basic hashing.

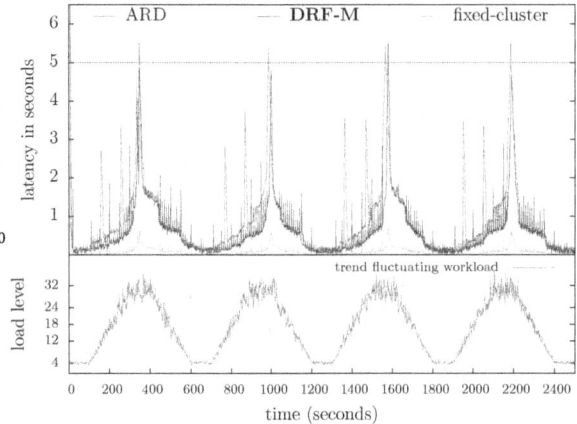

Figure 14: Adaptivity vs. Latency.

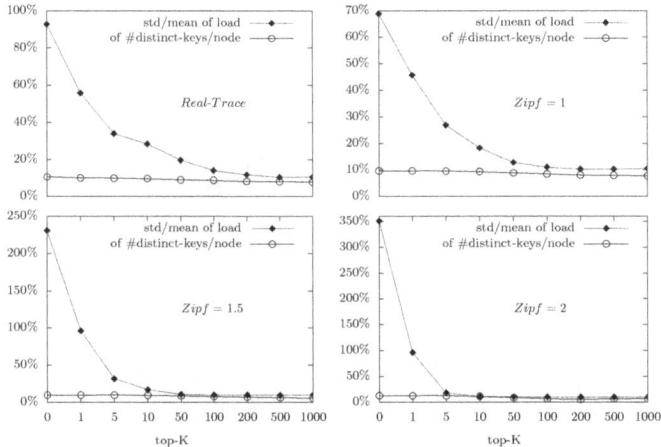

Figure 15: Load-balancing in content-sensitive partitioning under skew.

$h(k) = hash(k)\%N$ where N denotes the number of nodes. We use the same workload as shown in the lower part of Figure 14, where the number of processing nodes changes significantly over time. As N changes at each optimization point, the value of the hash function changes frequently as well. We call each such change a **key relocation**, which causes tuples of a pane to be distributed to excessively many nodes. In an extreme case, no significant aggregation might be done on processing nodes. Even a single pane result must be produced by merging many sub-pane results from several nodes, which in turn increases the merge cost. Figure 13 shows the experiments we conducted to study this effect. Figure 13(a) shows the percentage of all keys that are relocated. In basic hashing, almost all of the keys are relocated as the number of nodes changes. Our technique keeps the number of relocated keys significantly lower. As a result, our technique achieves a lower load level on merge nodes as shown in Figure 13(b).

6.4.4 Load-balancing Overhead

Frequency-aware partitioning needs to keep track of the most frequent K keys for further partitioning. At the implementation level, we use an approximate frequency estimation algorithm on a sample of the stream. In the split node, average per tuple processing cost overhead in comparison to basic hashing is $\approx 17\%$. On the other hand, pane-based partitioning with rate-awareness needs to keep track of pane size statistics. In this case, per tuple processing cost overhead compared to plain round-robin is only $\approx 4\%$. Overall, the load is balanced at all times for a small overhead.

6.5 Adaptivity and QoS Preservation

In this experiment, we study adaptivity, in particular the end-to-end latency behavior when our optimization strategy (DRF-M) is used. For comparison, we use ARD since it is one of the best. The workload used in this experiment is a fluctuating workload with a trend. It begins with a workload saturating 4 machines and goes up to 32. Inspired by the Linear Road Benchmark [2], the QoS metric chosen has a maximum latency of 5 seconds. Results are shown in Figure 14. At the beginning, all the generated streams are assigned randomly, which causes a spike. Latency drops later until load begins to increase. The major difference between the two algorithms is that DRF-M looks at the future (by forecasts), while ARD looks at the past (by average values). Using forecasts, DRF-M optimizes early and keeps the latency low. The early optimizations cause transient peaks but reduce latency later. ARD performs optimizations even earlier than DRF-M, which causes latency to be higher and peaks to be lengthy. When the load-level reaches the max, both algorithms need to shuffle around many streams to achieve optimal assignment. During that time, streams are very fast and this causes a lot of buffering on the clients and nodes resulting in short QoS violations. Finally, we also include the latency measurements with a static cluster of 32 nodes in which nodes are never dynamically added/removed to/from the query. As expected, it has a lower latency but comes with extremely high resource usage. For example, it uses 32 nodes at times when only 3 nodes would suffice for the workload at hand.

6.6 Summary

The experiments show that our system can meet the QoS requirements of fluctuating workloads of highly dynamic and transient input streams while being resource efficient. Integration of input meta-data and query-awareness into the input management enabled our partitioning techniques to achieve robust balancing of load for skewed data and rates with low overhead for maximum utilization of parallelism.

7. RELATED WORK

The advances in parallel processing platforms and the emergence of the pay-as-you-go economic model of the new cloud-based infrastructures motivate the need for elastic scalability in stream processing systems. In order to address this requirement, Recent works introduce capabilities into SPEs to allow flexible scaling up and down of the processing capacity in response to the workload fluctuations [10, 11, 21].

In general, the elastic scalability feature is tightly coupled with the parallelization model. Pipelined parallelism is one of the common models to provide inter-operator/inter-query parallelism (*e.g.*, [29]). In this case, load-balancing/adaptivity requires moving operators and state across different nodes. In order to provide elastic parallelism during runtime, Gulisano et al. [10, 11] use a similar model to pipelining by proposing a technique to split queries into subqueries for allocating them to independent sets of nodes.

The partitioned parallelism model, by contrast, splits input streams into disjoint partitions, each of which is processed by a replica of the query in a parallel fashion. Partitioning usually provides fine-granular intra-operator parallelism and achieves much better load-balancing. In order to provide elastic parallelism in an SPE, Schneider et al. [21] use a partitioned parallelism model that proposes methods for streaming operator elasticity on multi-core CPUs. In one of the earlier works in this area, Flux generalizes the Exchange and RiverDQ approaches of traditional parallel databases to provide online repartitioning of streaming operators such as group-by aggregates [23]. Ivanova et al. [14] instead focus on data partitioning for content-insensitive streaming operators such as windowed aggregates. Very recently, to address the unscalability of partitioning in this work, Zeitler et al. [30] propose a parallelized stream splitting operator (*parasplit*) for massive-volume streams. In addition, once data parallelism is identified, extracting it from queries automatically with a compiler and runtime system constitutes an important step [22].

In terms of admission control, a recent work discusses an auction-based "query admission" to a cloud-resident SPE to increase the system's economic utilization [20]. However, this work mainly focuses on the admission of different user's queries and does not discuss any issues related to the admission control and management of input streams. Another closely related work discusses resource management and admission control for SPEs [28]. By treating the input streams as dummy nodes, the problem of admission control is transformed into a routing and resource-allocation problem with the objective of maximizing the overall system utility. However, the assumptions of this work are rather restrictive, including a fixed-size cluster without elasticity, fixed-rate streams, and no consideration of input stream characteristics. Lastly, Gulisano et al. [11] provide on-demand provisioning for computing resources based on past observations of node loads. However, they also do not consider multiple input streams and their characteristics in their problem.

8. CONCLUSIONS

In this paper, we presented a framework for adaptive admission control and management of input streams for parallel data stream processing. The main goal of this framework is to treat large numbers of dynamic external input streams as first-class citizens of a stream processing engine. By explicitly controlling their admission and managing them, SPEs can better and timely react to dynamically changing workloads. Our main contributions include a near-optimal input stream assignment technique that employs forecasting and meta-data, stream partitioning and adaptivity tech-

niques that employ query knowledge early in the input layer for automatically minimizing the size of the cluster and maintaining load balance. Our results show that these techniques are effective in achieving the goals of our framework.

9. REFERENCES

[1] D. Abadi et al. The Design of the Borealis Stream Processing Engine. In *CIDR*, 2005.
[2] A. Arasu et al. Linear Road: A Stream Data Management Benchmark. In *VLDB*, 2004.
[3] C. Balkesen and N. Tatbul. Scalable Data Partitioning Techniques for Parallel Sliding Window Processing over Data Streams. In *DMSN*, 2011.
[4] P. J. Brockwell and R. A. Davis. *Time Series: Theory and Methods*. Springer-Verlag, 1991.
[5] C. Chatfield and M. Yar. Holt-Winters Forecasting: Some Practical Issues. *Journal of the Royal Statistical Society*, 37(2), 1988.
[6] E. G. Coffman, Jr., M. R. Garey, and D. S. Johnson. *Approximation Algorithms for Bin Packing: A Survey*. 1997.
[7] D. DeWitt and J. Gray. Parallel Database Systems: The Future of High Performance Database Systems. *CACM*, 35(6), 1992.
[8] Gartner. Forecast: Mobile Communications Devices by Open Operating System, Worldwide, 2008-2015.
[9] S. Geisler et al. A Data Stream-based Evaluation Framework for Traffic Information Systems. In *GIS-IWGS*, 2010.
[10] V. Gulisano et al. StreamCloud: A Large Scale Data Streaming System. In *ICDCS*, 2010.
[11] V. Gulisano et al. StreamCloud: An Elastic and Scalable Data Streaming System. *TPDS*, 2012.
[12] J. C. Herrera, , et al. Evaluation of Traffic Data Obtained via GPS-enabled Mobile Phones: The Mobile Century Field Experiment. *Transportation Research Part C: Emerging Technologies*, 18(4), 2010.
[13] Infochimps. http://www.infochimps.com/datasets/uber-anonymized-gps-logs/.
[14] M. Ivanova and T. Risch. Customizable Parallel Execution of Scientific Stream Queries. In *VLDB*, 2005.
[15] T. Johnson et al. Query-aware Partitioning for Monitoring Massive Network Data Streams. In *SIGMOD*, 2008.
[16] D. Karger et al. Consistent Hashing and Random Trees: Distributed Caching Protocols for Relieving Hot Spots on the World Wide Web. In *STOC*, 1997.
[17] R. E. Korf. A New Algorithm for Optimal Bin Packing. In *AAAI*, 2002.
[18] A. Lakshman and P. Malik. Cassandra: A Decentralized Structured Storage System. *OSR*, 44(2), 2010.
[19] J. Li, D. Maier, et al. Semantics and Evaluation Techniques for Window Aggregates in Data streams. In *SIGMOD*, 2005.
[20] L. A. Moakar, P. K. Chrysanthis, C. Chung, S. Guirguis, A. Labrinidis, P. Neophytou, and K. Pruhs. Admission control mechanisms for continuous queries in the cloud. In *ICDE*, 2010.
[21] S. Schneider et al. Elastic Scaling of Data Parallel Operators in Stream Processing. In *IPDPS*, 2009.
[22] S. Schneider et al. Auto-parallelizing stateful distributed streaming applications. In *PACT*, 2012.
[23] M. A. Shah. *Flux: A Mechanism for Building Robust, Scalable Dataflows*. PhD thesis, U.C. Berkeley, 2004.
[24] K. Sheykh-Esmaili et al. Changing Flights in Mid-air: A Model for Safely Modifying Continuous Queries. In *SIGMOD*, 2011.
[25] A. Silberstein et al. Feeding Frenzy: Selectively Materializing Users' Event Feeds. In *SIGMOD*, 2010.
[26] Uber. http://www.uber.com/.
[27] Waze. http://www.waze.com/.
[28] C. H. Xia, D. Towsley, and C. Zhang. Distributed resource management and admission control of stream processing systems with max utility. In *ICDCS*, 2007.
[29] Y. Xing, S. Zdonik, and J.-H. Hwang. Dynamic Load Distribution in the Borealis Stream Processor. In *ICDE*, 2005.
[30] E. Zeitler and T. Risch. Massive Scale-out of Expensive Continuous Queries. In *VLDB*, 2011.

Rollback-Recovery without Checkpoints in Distributed Event Processing Systems

Boris Koldehofe
Institute of Parallel and
Distributed Systems
University of Stuttgart,
Germany
boris.koldehofe@ipvs.uni-
stuttgart.de

Ruben Mayer
Institute of Parallel and
Distributed Systems
University of Stuttgart,
Germany
ruben.mayer@ipvs.uni-
stuttgart.de

Umakishore Ramachandran
College of Computing
Georgia Tech, USA
rama@cc.gatech.edu

Kurt Rothermel
Institute of Parallel and
Distributed Systems
University of Stuttgart,
Germany
kurt.rothermel@ipvs.uni-
stuttgart.de

Marco Völz
Institute of Parallel and
Distributed Systems
University of Stuttgart,
Germany
voelzmo@gmail.com

ABSTRACT

Reliability is of critical importance to many applications involving distributed event processing systems. Especially the use of stateful operators makes it challenging to provide efficient recovery from failures and to ensure consistent event streams. Even during failure-free execution, state-of-the-art methods for achieving reliability incur significant overhead at run-time concerning computational resources, event traffic, and event detection time. This paper proposes a novel method for rollback-recovery that allows for recovery from multiple simultaneous operator failures, but eliminates the need for persistent checkpoints. Thereby, the operator state is preserved in *savepoints* at points in time when its execution solely depends on the state of incoming event streams which are reproducible by predecessor operators. We propose an expressive event processing model to determine savepoints and algorithms for their coordination in a distributed operator network. Evaluations show that very low overhead at failure-free execution in comparison to other approaches is achieved.

Categories and Subject Descriptors

C.2.4 [**Computer-Communication Networks**]: Distributed Systems—*Distributed applications*; C.4 [**Performance of Systems**]: Fault tolerance

Keywords

Reliability, Recovery, Complex Event Processing

1. INTRODUCTION

Event processing systems, also commonly referred to as stream processing or complex event processing (CEP) systems, are nowadays deployed in many business applications including logistic chains, manufacturing, or stock exchange. They allow to integrate and analyze streams of events that stem from many distributed data sources such as sensors. Consumers are provided with event streams that capture correlations of the incoming event streams and this way provide feedback and even trigger interactions with physical processes.

With the increasing scale and inherent distributed deployment of data sources, the paradigm of distributed event processing systems has gained increasing importance. In a distributed event processing system, operators hosted at potentially many different nodes of the network are taking a share in analyzing input streams and producing streams of outgoing events. Since many physical processes, e.g., the control of a manufacturing process, depend on the output of event processing systems, their correctness and performance characteristics are of critical importance. For event processing systems, this imposes strong requirements with respect to availability and consistency of their outgoing streams. In particular, the event streams provided to consumers of event processing systems should be indistinguishable from an execution in which the hosts of some operators fail or event streams are not available during a temporary partitioning of the network.

The efficiency of reliable event processing can be measured with respect to its *runtime overhead* in a failure-free execution as well as its *recovery overhead* in the presence of failures. Currently, dealing with reliability leaves two basic options for event processing systems, known as replication and rollback-recovery. While active replication [18] minimizes the time to deal with host and communication failures, it imposes high processor utilization on the hosts at run-time since the execution of every operator needs to be replicated. Replication also raises significantly the message overhead since event streams targeted to an operator must also be streamed to all of its replicas. Passive replication [5] has slightly different properties, sacrificing recovery-time in order to avoid run-time overhead, but the general problems remain the same. Rollback-recovery [8], on the other hand, requires in its classical form to store checkpoints at regular times to persistent storage. This adds additional run-time overhead regarding bandwidth that is needed to transfer (incremental) state information, which is a burden especially for high bandwidth streams. Furthermore, to ensure the atomic capturing of (incremental) checkpoints, the processing of operators needs to be interrupted inducing event detection latency. Given that an operator state even for simple processing such as aggregation may comprise several Gigabytes [19], minimizing the state for performing a recovery is one of the important research questions in providing large-scale event processing systems. A promising way towards avoiding the need for persistent checkpoints is to recover the state of an operator by replaying logs of incoming event streams [10, 11] (known as "upstream backup"). Yet, the approach is very restrictive regarding operators for which a consistent state can be guaranteed after a recovery.

In this paper, we propose a method for recovery which avoids any interruption of the event processing system and minimizes the amount of state to be transferred in a failure-free execution. The proposed approach relies on the observation that at certain points in time, the execution of an event processing operator solely depends on a distinct selection of events from the incoming streams. So, the operator state only comprises necessary parts of the incoming streams and information about the current event selection on them. Events from incoming streams can be reproduced from predecessor operators, so that only event sources need to provide outgoing streams in a reliable way. However, information about the current event selection is not reproducible and therefore is stored in a *savepoint* and replicated at other operators for failure tolerance.

In this context, our contributions are to propose an expressive, general execution model that enables for any operator to signal on its incoming streams the selection of events that it is currently processing. Such a model can be applied to stream processing as well as complex event processing systems. To illustrate its expressiveness, a comparison to the event specification language *snoop* is drawn. Based on this operator execution model, we propose a *savepoint recovery system* that i) provides the basis in identifying an empty operator processing state, ii) manages the capturing and replication of savepoints and ensures the reproducibility of corresponding events, iii) implements a recovery in which also simultaneous failures of multiple sequential operators can be tolerated.

The paper is structured as follows: Section 2 introduces a general event processing and system model suitable to describe event processing systems. In Section 3, we define the requirements with regard to the reliability of the system. Section 4 sketches our novel approach for rollback-recovery. In Section 5, an expressive operator execution model is introduced that works with *selections* of events. Based on that model, Section 6 shows how operator state is minimized to replicated *savepoints*. The recovery algorithms are described

and their correctness is proved in Section 7. Afterwards, evaluations are provided in Section 8. In Section 9, possible extensions on the proposed recovery method are discussed. Related work is discussed in Section 10. Finally, Section 11 concludes this paper and briefly discusses future work.

2. EVENT PROCESSING & SYSTEM MODEL

2.1 Event Processing Model

The operation of a distributed event processing system can be modeled by an operator graph $G(\Omega \cup S \cup C, L)$ interconnecting sources in S, operators in Ω, and consumers in C in form of event streams in $L \subset (S \cup \Omega) \times (\Omega \cup C)$. In this model, the sources act as producers of basic events like sensor streams, operators perform correlations on their incoming event streams to produce new outgoing events, and consumers define event streams that require reliable delivery. We will later formalize what reliable delivery means.

An *event* e is a tuple of attribute-value pairs, i.e we use $e = (a_1 : v_1, ..., a_m : v_m)$ to refer to the content of an event that comprises m attribute-value pairs. An *event stream* $(p, d) \in L$ of the operator graph is directed from a producer to a destination and ensures that events are delivered to the destination in the order they are produced. Events in a stream are of a distinct *event type*. We call p the predecessor of d and d the successor of p. Accordingly, (p, d) is called an *outgoing stream* of p and an *incoming stream* of d. For an event $e \in (p, d)$ we refer to $SN(e)$ the sequence number of e, which is deterministically assigned and independent of the physical event production time. Events from different incoming streams have a well-defined, global ordering that is independent of the physical time of their arrival at the operator. Any ordering is possible, as long as the local ordering by sequence numbers on single streams is not violated.

Each operator ω performs processing w.r.t. the set of all incoming streams $(in, \omega) \in L$, denoted by I_ω. During its execution, an operator $\omega \in \Omega$ performs a sequence of correlation steps on I_ω. In each correlation step, the operator determines a *selection* σ which is a finite subset of events in each stream of I_ω. A correlation function $f_\omega : \sigma \to (e_1, ..., e_m)$ specifies a mapping from a selection to a finite, possibly empty set of events produced by the operator. The produced events are written in order of occurrence to its outgoing event streams. For each outgoing stream a different set of events may be written.

2.2 System Model

The operators of the operator graph G are hosted by a set of n nodes, each node hosting possibly multiple operators. At any time, each node can fail according to the crash recovery model, where at most $k < n$ nodes are assumed to permanently fail or crash and recover an unbounded number of times. The nodes communicate via communication channels that are established for each event stream in G and guarantee eventual in-order delivery of streamed events. In addition, we will consider event sources and event consumers to be reliable. This means that each event produced by a source will be accessible until all dependent operators have signaled that it can be discarded. Furthermore, event sources must be able to reliably store savepoints from their successors. Similarly, for events streamed to consumers we will use a fault tolerant delivery mechanism so that eventually a consumer receives all events sent to it in the right order.

Note that we do not make any assumptions on timeliness for links connecting sources, operators and consumers, nor do we demand any synchronization of their clocks. The system can be realized as a highly distributed correlation network that involves communication over an Internet-like topology. We will use a monitoring component to suspect faulty processes and trigger reconfigurations on the placement of operators on nodes. The accurateness of this component, however, will only affect the performance, but not the correctness of the proposed method.

3. RELIABLE EVENT PROCESSING

For event processing systems, it is important that detected events capture the status of the monitored real world in a reliable way, i.e., no events of interest are disregarded (*false-negative event detection*) as well as no "wrong" events that did not really occur are delivered to consumers (*false-positive*). Even if the operators of a system are well-defined and sources of an event processing system reliably capture all basic events of the system, the loss of intermediate events in the event processing system can lead to the occurrence of false-negatives or false-positives. For example, consider a business monitoring system for which an operator ω monitors whether customer requests were successfully answered. In this case, ω is required to produce an alarm or confirmation dependent on whether or not a customer request was answered within 10 minutes. The correct detection depends on the successful detection of a customer request, say e_r as well as detecting successful answers, say e_a. In particular, not detecting a successful answer could trigger both a false positive and a false negative, namely an alarm instead of a confirmation.

The major cause for the loss of intermediate events is the failure of nodes. We require a CEP system for a set of given primary event streams and a set of consumers to guarantee the following properties despite of the simultaneous failure of an arbitrary number of nodes:

1. Completeness. Each event that can be detected by the event processing system from a given set of available primary streams will eventually be delivered to every correct consumer interested in the event. Depending on the application, a false-negative event detection can cause that, e.g., decisions are made that base on wrong data in business monitoring systems, or even severe dangers in cyber-physical systems occur.

2. Consistency. The streams the event processing system provides to consumers in an execution with operator failures are indistinguishable from an execution without failures (in particular regarding order and attributes of the comprised events). False-positive events can have similar negative effects as false-negative events, leading to wrong decisions based on faulty information. Also the order of produced events can play a role for event consumers, e.g., if decision-relevant out-of-order events arrive when an irrevocable decision has already been made.

Besides these correctness requirements, we aim with our approach for a low run-time overhead as the main efficiency goal in order to provide high scalability of the system.

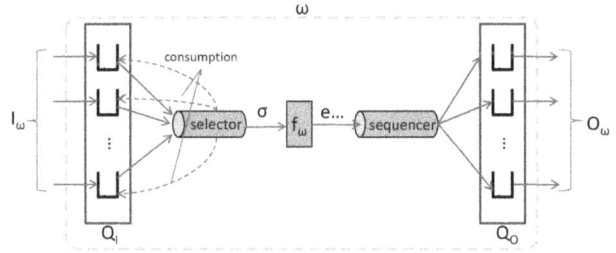

Figure 1: Model of an operator.

4. OVERVIEW OF THE APPROACH

Figure 1 shows a model of the components of an operator. Incoming events from I_ω are cached in queues Q_I from which the *selector* determines selections of events to be mapped to outgoing events by the correlation function f_ω. Further, the selector can exclude events from any further correlations, i.e., events are consumed and removed from Q_I. The produced events are augmented with a sequence number by the sequencer and put into queues Q_O from which they will be transferred to ω's successors. Events are discarded from Q_O only if all successors have acknowledged them.

Note that any approach that allows for the recovery of the state of failed operators requires the replication of state. The difference between distinct recovery methods is how and where state information is replicated, e.g., at standby operators or at a persistent storage for classical rollback-recovery. One important observation from the rollback-recovery approach is that state $\Lambda(T)$ at a point in time T can be seen as state at a previous point in time T_{sp} plus a deviation $\Delta(\Lambda(T_{sp}), \Lambda(T))$ that happened on the state between T_{sp} and T. We are looking for the optimal T_{sp}, when the state of an operator is minimal, so that its replication requires only a minimum of resources.

The state $\Lambda(T)$ of ω comprises the states of Q_I, the selector, f_ω, the sequencer and Q_O. Observe that f_ω implements a mapping in its mathematical sense from selections σ to sets of produced events, or, more precisely, attribute-value-pairs of events from σ are mapped to attribute-value-pairs of produced events, each mapping denoted as a *correlation step*. Although f_ω builds up internal state, in this model there are no dependencies in between two subsequent correlation steps. So, at a point in time between two correlation steps denoted T_{sp}, f_ω is *stateless*. The state of the sequencer just comprises one parameter which is the next SN to be assigned to the next processed event. The state of the selector is harder to determine: In an arbitrary operator implementation, the state may cover manifold relations; e.g., selections could depend on other selections, on intermediate consumptions, even on the results of previous correlation steps. In the general case, taking a snapshot of the processing stack of the selector or implementing a sophisticated state extraction method would be inevitable. However, the selector state can be drastically reduced when a specific operator execution model constrains the scope of possible selections. Finally, the state of Q_I and Q_O comprises all events contained in the queues.

In our *savepoint recovery system*, in order to be able to recover ω once it has failed at a point in time T, the recovery procedure determines an earlier point in time $T_{sp} < T$ with the following properties: (i) f_ω is stateless, (ii) all events

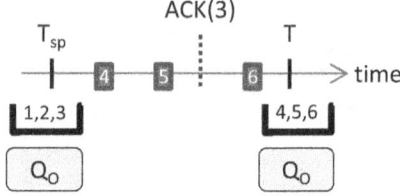

Figure 2: Between T_{sp} and T, all events up to event 3 in Q_O have been acknowledged, so they are not part of $\Lambda(T_{sp})$ w.r.t. the proposed recovery approach.

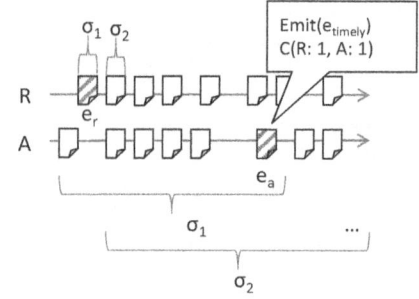

Figure 3: Interface calls to the EE.

that Q_O contained at T_{sp} have been *acknowledged* in the meantime, and (iii) events in Q_I at T_{sp} are eventually available in ω's predecessors. In this process, stateless times of f_ω are indicated to an execution environment by a hook that is installed in the correlation logic. The second property is achieved by a distributed acknowledgment algorithm, which is described in Section 6.2. It synchronizes the points in time T_{sp} for recovery between adjacent operators. Thereby, an *acknowledgment* indicates that an event is not needed anymore in order to achieve consistent event streams at the consumers and therefore can be discarded from Q_O. The algorithm ensures that the latest recovery point T_{sp} at an arbitrary point in time T is always chosen with regard to this property. See Fig. 2 for an example. It shows that despite Q_O is not empty at T_{sp}, it is not necessary to restore it in order to recover $\Lambda(T)$, because all events have been acknowledged in the meantime. Thus, in the following we will not count Q_O as part of $\Lambda(T_{sp})$ with regard to the proposed recovery approach. The third property is also achieved by the acknowledgment algorithm, which only acknowledges events at a predecessor if they are not part of Q_I at T_{sp} anymore.

Now, the relevant, *non-reproducible* state of ω at T_{sp} comprises only the state of the selector and the sequencer, which is captured in a *savepoint* and replicated at ω's predecessors. If ω fails at time T, $\Lambda(T_{sp})$ is restored from the replicated savepoint and replayed events of Q_I from the predecessors. From this point on, the re-execution of ω, i.e., performing a sequence of correlation steps, will allow the operator to fully restore $\Lambda(T)$.

5. EXECUTION MODEL

The following execution model refines the operator model introduced in Section 4 (cf. Fig. 1). It describes the implementation of the selector and the sequencer, and defines the interface of an arbitrary operator's correlation logic to these components. Thereby, we aim to keep the interface simple, so that existing implementations of f_ω can easily be embedded into the proposed system.

Let a window $w(\langle SN_i^{start}, SN_i^{end} \rangle, \cdots)$ on I_ω comprise for each incoming stream $i \in (in, \omega)$ all events between a start event with SN_i^{start} and an end event with SN_i^{end}. Then a selection σ can be defined as the set of all events within w and contains all incoming events on which f_ω executes one correlation step. To implement the mapping f_ω, each the selector and the sequencer, which we together name the *execution environment (EE)*, provide an interface. The interface of the selector is defined as C(*consumption*), with *consumption* being a map of event types and the corresponding number of consumed events. The consumption of x events from a stream $i \in (in, \omega)$ results for the next

selection σ' in: $SN_i^{start'} = SN_i^{start} + x$, i.e., the start event moves further w.r.t. the consumption. Each correlation step has to result in at least one consumption in at least one of the incoming streams to ensure progress. That way, the selector keeps track of the start events of the selections, and just streams events from Q_I in their deterministic order to f_ω until its interface is called and the next selection starts. Events that are marked as consumed by f_ω get deleted from Q_I. The interface of the sequencer EMIT(*event*) takes a produced event from f_ω, assigns it a SN and puts it into Q_O.

Example (Figure 3): Consider the example given in Section 3. In a correlation step, f_ω takes one event of type R (requests), say e_r, and then checks events of type A (answers) e.g. for a matching request ID attribute. The step ends when an event e_a of type A is reached that is either corresponding to e_r or has a timestamp that is more than 10 minutes older than the one of e_r, so that f_ω is sure that the 10 minutes timespan has been violated (given events are ordered by timestamps in streams). In the first case, f_ω would emit an event e_{timely} and would consume e_r and events of type A that have a smaller timestamp than e_r as answers are not expected to appear before the next request. In the second case, an event e_{alarm} is emitted and e.g. delivered to a special agent who will work on the request with a high priority. e_r and events of type A that have a smaller timestamp than e_r are consumed in this case, too.

5.1 Properties

PROPERTY 5.1. (STATE OF AN OPERATOR AT T_{sp}.) *Let T_{sp} be a point in time when an operator ω starts processing a new selection σ_{sp}. Then, $\Lambda(T_{sp})$ of ω comprises:*

- *Events in Q_I.*
- *The state of the selector: For each incoming stream $i \in (in, \omega)$: SN_i^{start} of σ_{sp}.*
- *The state of the sequencer: The SN of the first event to be produced in σ_{sp}.*

Events in Q_I are replayed from predecessors. In order to restore the selector, the SNs of the start events of σ_{sp} have to be restored. Then, the selector can provide to f_ω exactly the same selection that had been provided in the primary execution of the correlation step, which leads to the production of exactly the same events. The subsequent selection σ_{sp+1} depends only on σ_{sp}, and so on, so that all subsequent selections are indistinguishable from a failure-free execution. To restore the sequencer, it is initialized with the SN of the next emitted event.

PROPERTY 5.2. (START EVENTS OF CONSECUTIVE SELECTIONS.) *For a selection σ_s, each start event has a higher or equal sequence number compared to the selection σ_p of a preceding correlation step.*

Selection windows are moved when events are consumed. A consumption always leads to a higher sequence number of the next start event. This property limits the dependencies between event streams. For two consecutive correlation steps (and thereby for the production of events in such steps), the selection start events from a stream in I_ω are never descending.

5.2 Expressiveness

After we have defined how the execution model of our event processing system works, one might ask whether this really reflects the requirements of real-world CEP systems with regard to the detection of event patterns. Does it provide enough expressiveness so that any realistic situation detection can be implemented?

As a reference, we will take the event specification language *snoop* [6] and check whether all event patterns that are formalized in snoop can be implemented in our execution model. This has several reasons: First, snoop has been motivated by real-world event processing scenarios and not just on some academic theoretical models. Such scenarios comprise, amongst others, sensor applications (e.g., hospital monitoring and global position tracking), applications that exhibit causal dependency (e.g., between aborts and rollbacks, bug reports and releases) and trend analysis and forecasting applications (e.g., security trading, stock market analysis). Furthermore, snoop is well-established in the scientific event processing community. But above all, it provides a high expressiveness in comparison to other languages, as Margara and Cugola show in their article [7].

In snoop, complex events can be correlated by *event operators*, which are the following ones: Disjunction, sequence, conjunction, aperiodic and periodic operators. Further, *parameter contexts* in snoop describe which incoming events are considered in the computation of the parameters of a produced event in a correlation step, when there are several possible events to choose from. The following parameter contexts are defined: (i) *Recent*, where only the most recent occurrences are used for correlation. (ii) *Chronicle*, where incoming events are correlated in the chronological order in which they occur. (iii) *Continuous*, where continuously each possible event starts a correlation execution. (iv) *Cumulative*, where all events between a possible start and end event are correlated. For more detailed explanations and examples, please refer to the original snoop paper [6].

PROPOSITION 5.3. (EXPRESSIVENESS OF THE EXECUTION MODEL.) *All event operators and parameter contexts of snoop can be implemented using the execution model that is proposed in this work.*

PROOF. In snoop, *event expressions* define a finite time interval in which one or more atomic happenings, or events, can occur. Thus, they correspond to finite sets of sequential events. So they are equivalent to event selections as they are defined in the execution model. All snoop event operators work solely with event expressions as operands. Thus, the sequence of execution iterations of snoop event operators can be seen as an execution with a sequence of event selections $(\sigma_1, \sigma_2, \sigma_3, ...)$ as operands.

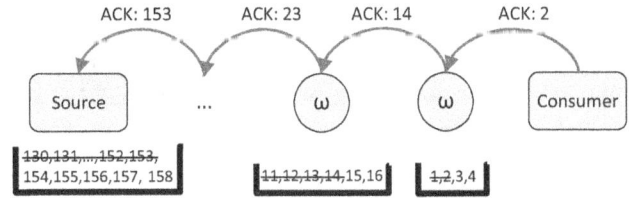

Figure 4: ACK flow and pruning of Q_O.

LEMMA 5.4. *For the operands $(\sigma_1, \sigma_2, \sigma_3, ...)$ of a snoop event operator, the following properties are satisfied:*
(i) $SN_j^{start} \in \sigma_{k+1} \geq SN_j^{start} \in \sigma_k \; \forall j \in (in, \omega)$,
(ii) For all event operators and parameter contexts exists an implementation of f_ω so that when it is executed on σ_1, σ_2, σ_3..., the events produced by f_ω satisfy the semantics of snoop.

PROOF. (i) Proof by contradiction. If $\exists e$ with $e \in \sigma_{k+1} \wedge e \in j : SN(e) < SN_j^{start} \in \sigma_k; j \in (in, \omega)$, then e would be in a later time interval but have a lower SN than the start event of σ_k. This contradicts to the policy that sequence numbers are assigned sequentially.

(ii) is satisfied because given the event selections, f_ω can implement any operations on a selection, especially any functionality of a snoop event operator can be implemented. □

LEMMA 5.5. *None of the parameter contexts demands for the consumption of an intermediate event that is located within the window bounds of the selection of the next event operator execution.*

PROOF. In *Recent*, when an event is detected, all events which cannot become the initiator of an event detection and are ordered between the detection initiator and the event that triggered the detection are consumed. This cannot affect intermediate events, because if an earlier event of a type can potentially start an event detection and is not consumed, then a later event of the same type can potentially start an event detection, too.

In *Chronicle*, events are used for parameter computation in the order they occur and then they are consumed, so no intermediate consumption can occur.

In *Continuous*, no explicit consumptions happen at all.

In *Cumulative*, all events of a selection are consumed. □

As a conclusion of Lemma 1 and Lemma 2, f_ω works on sequential selections that do not demand intermediate consumptions and so it can implement the interface to the EE defined by the execution model. So, our execution model is at least as expressive as the snoop event specification language.

6. CAPTURING AND REPLICATING SAVEPOINTS

6.1 Log and Savepoint Management

6.1.1 Logs of Outgoing Events

Events in Q_I of ω are preserved in the Q_O of its upstream neighbors (a.k.a. predecessors), so that *no additional events* need to be transferred over the network at failure-free run-time. If ω fails, Q_I can be restored when its predecessors re-send their Q_O. Q_O must always contain enough events to restore the successor to its latest acknowledged state $\Lambda(T_{sp})$ which depends on the coordination of savepoints described in Section 6.2. Note, however, that outgoing events are reproduced when an operator recovers, so that events in Q_O are *reproducible* and do not need to be replicated.

6.1.2 Savepoints and Savepoint Trees

Savepoints contain the non-reproducible part of $\Lambda(T_{sp})$, which comprises the state of the selector and the sequencer. They are stored together with Q_O in the volatile memory of the predecessors of ω. If ω's predecessor is an event source, savepoints and events can be stored there in a reliable way, as event sources are implemented fault-tolerant.

So, when ω crashes at a point in time T, its predecessors hold all state information that is necessary to restore $\Lambda(T)$: $\Lambda(T_{sp})$ is restored from the savepoints and events from Q_O at predecessors, and $\Delta(T_{sp}, T)$ is restored by re-running ω from T_{sp} until T. We will determine later the points in time when an operator has to update and distribute its savepoint. To deal with asynchrony, it is necessary that all predecessors store a *complete* savepoint, so that at the recovery of ω a self-consistent savepoint is available, i.e., the information about the start events of σ belong to the same σ, and the next SN fits with that σ. In contrast to that, the re-sent events from incoming streams in I_ω do not have to be consistent w.r.t. the same savepoint, because it is easily possible for an operator that is getting restored to ignore events that stem from older selections and therefore are not part of Q_I.

By now, only one failed operator can be restored at a time, but not several adjacent operators that fail at the same time. To make that possible, the non-reproducible part of $\Lambda(T_{sp})$, namely the savepoint, is replicated at all operators of the transitive closure of the predecessor relation in the operator graph, so that each operator preserves a *tree of savepoints* in its volatile memory.

6.2 Coordination of Savepoints

In order to restore $\Lambda(T)$ of ω, one has to determine the point in time T_{sp} to which it has to be restored in order to allow for the restoring of Q_O at T. This depends on the events that are part of Q_O, more precisely, the earlier the events of Q_O at T had been produced, the earlier is T_{sp}. A trivial implementation would never prune Q_O so that it contains all events an operator has ever produced. In case of a recovery, T_{sp} would be "zero", i.e., the operator would be restored to the point in time when it initially started its work. To avoid that, it is necessary that an operator *prunes* Q_O from time to time, i.e., excludes events from $\Lambda(T)$ and thereby increases T_{sp}. Events can be pruned when they are not necessary for the consistency of the event streams delivered to the consumers anymore. The necessity is defined as follows:

DEFINITION 6.1 (NECESSITY OF EVENTS). *An event e is a necessary event if a consumer is interested in it and has not yet acknowledged its receiving.*

If all consumers interested in e have acknowledged its receiving at a point in time T_{ACK}, a predecessor operator ω can be sure that e is not necessary anymore and delete it (and all earlier events) from its Q_O (see Figure 4). That way, e and

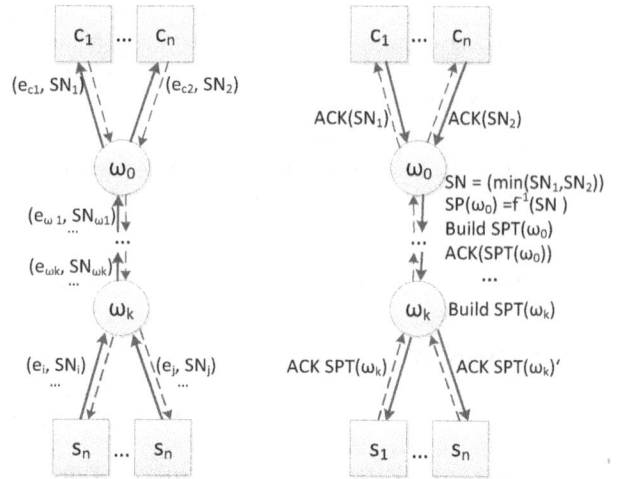

Figure 5: Event and ACK flow in a CEP system.

all earlier events are not part of $\Lambda(T)$ for any $T \geq T_{ACK}$, so that T_{sp} and thereby the savepoint can be adjusted to the correlation step in which the first event following e had initially been produced. This is done by means of the *inverse correlation function* $f^{-1} : e \rightarrow \sigma_e$, which maps $SN(e)$ to the start events of the selection σ_e in which e had been produced. The most efficient implementation of f^{-1} is for each selection to store SN_i^{start} for each stream $i \in (in, \omega)$ together with the produced events in Q_O. For each incoming stream, events that are placed before the corresponding start event of σ_e are discarded from Q_I at T_{sp} and their SNs are acknowledged at ω's predecessors. They proceed in the same way that ω did, prune their Q_O and adapt their T_{sp} to the production of events in Q_O, update their savepoint accordingly in the savepoint tree, and acknowledge SNs from f^{-1} at their predecessors as well as send them the updated savepoint tree for further replication.

To coordinate savepoints, we make use of acknowledgment messages, say ACKs, which contain both the SN of the acknowledged event and the updated savepoint tree. When receiving an ACK, an operator replaces the obsolete part in its savepoint tree, prunes Q_O and checks whether T_{sp} can be updated. If this is the case, the operator sends an ACK to each of its predecessors. That way the ACKs flow *upstream*, i.e., against the flow direction of events, until they will finally reach the event sources signaling that replicated events have become unnecessary and therefore can be discarded. The algorithms for log and savepoint maintenance of an operator are given in Figure 6.

Example: Figure 5 shows the event and ACK flow in the system. On the left graph, events are flowing downstream, starting at the event sources and getting correlated with each other until some events are delivered to consumers. On the right graph, the consumers acknowledge different SNs of received events. The minimal SN acknowledged by all connected consumers at ω_0 signals the latest unnecessary event, Q_O is pruned, the savepoint tree is updated accordingly and sent with an ACK to all predecessors. They store the new savepoint tree, update their own savepoint if applicable, send ACKs to their predecessors, and so on, until finally the ACKs reach the event sources, where the save-

```
1: Map<successor, ACK> latestRecACKs        ▷ Contains latest
   received ACK from each successor
2: Savepoint ownSP            ▷ Contains current own savepoint
3: List<Event> Q_I                   ▷ Queues of incoming events
4: List<Event> Q_O                   ▷ Queues of outgoing events

5: upon ⟨RECEIVEACK⟩(inACK)
6:  latestRecACKs.INSERT(inACK.producer, inACK)
7:  if latestRecACKs.GETOLDESTACKEDSEQ() has changed
    then                           ▷ update own savepoint
8:      sn = inACK.GETACKEDSEQNO()
9:      e_acked = Q_O.GETEVENT(sn)
10:     map < instream, SeqNo > = f^{-1}(e_acked)
11:     Q_I.PRUNE                             ▷ prune Q_I
12:     newSavepoint =
13:     NEW SAVEPOINT(map < instream, SeqNo >, sn)
14:     Q_O.PRUNE(sn)                         ▷ prune Q_O
15:     SavepointTree = NEW SAVEPOINTTREE()
16:     SavepointTree.SETROOT(newSavepoint)
17:     for all ACK in latestRecAcks do
18:         SavepointTree.ADDCHILD(ACK.savepointTree)
19:     end for
20:     newACK = NEW ACK(SavepointTree)
21:     for all predecessors do
22:         SEND(newACK)
23:     end for
24:  end if
25: end
```

Figure 6: Algorithms for log and savepoint maintenance at an operator ω.

```
1: upon ⟨RECEIVEINIT⟩(predecessors, successors)
2:  for all op in predecessors do
3:      SEND(op, RECOVERYREQUEST)
4:  end for
5:  while not received all RECOVERYINFORMATION do
6:      upon ⟨RECEIVERECOVERYNOTIFICATION⟩(predecessor)
7:          SEND(predecessor, RECOVERYREQUEST)
8:      end
9:      upon ⟨RECEIVERECOVERYINFORMATION⟩()
10:         list<RecoveryInformation>.ADD(RecoveryInformation)
11:     end
12:  end while
13:  RESTORESTATE(latestRecoveryInformation)
14: end

15: upon ⟨RECEIVERECOVERYREQUEST⟩(successor)
16:  SavepointTree = latestRecACKs.GET(successor).GET-
     SAVEPOINTTREE()
17:  RecoveryInformation = NEW RECOVERYINFORMA-
     TION(Q_O, latestRecACKs)
18:  SEND(successor, RecoveryInformation)
19: end
```

Figure 7: Algorithms for recovery of an operator ω.

point trees are replicated and all acknowledged events are discarded.

7. ALGORITHMS FOR OPERATOR RECOVERY

7.1 Recovery of the State of Failed Operators

For the description of the recovery algorithm, we will at first assume that operator failures are detected immediately and that failed operators are restarted automatically. Also, we assume that an operator knows his direct predecessors, even after it has crashed and recovered. From this point, we describe how an operator will be able to restore its state w.r.t. the latest available savepoint, so that event streams that were lost through the failure get reproduced. Later, we will describe how the failure detection and operator topology management can be solved in an asynchronous system.

7.1.1 Recovery Procedure

After its restart, a failed operator ω sends to its predecessors a message called RECOVERYREQUEST. When an operator receives such a RECOVERYREQUEST, it answers by sending the *recovery information* necessary for restoring the state of ω, which comprises Q_O (replay of the outgoing stream) and the savepoint tree of ω. ω waits until it has received all recovery information. Then it identifies the answer containing its latest savepoint SP, which is the answer with the highest value for the SN of the next event to be produced. ω restores $\Lambda(T_{sp})$ by initializing the selector with the selection defined in the SP, restores Q_I with the replayed events from the predecessors, and initializes the sequencer with the next SN to be assigned to a produced event.

To cope with multiple simultaneous failures of adjacent operators, ω sends a RECOVERYNOTIFICATION to its suc-

cessors after its recovery. So, if one of those operators is awaiting recovery information from ω, it can detect that the RECOVERYREQUEST might have been lost because of the failing of ω and resend it. This way, a failed predecessor does not lead to an infinite waiting time for receiving all recovery information. From bottom up, failed operators can recover, each sending the necessary recovery information to its successor, until all operators are restored to their latest ACKed state again. The algorithms for the recovery of an operator are listed in Figure 7.

7.2 Control and Adjustment of the Operator Topology

By now, we have assumed an error-free, immediate detection and restart of failed operators. However, in an asynchronous system, a perfect failure detector cannot be implemented to solve that problem. Instead, we have to work with a weaker failure detector abstraction that suspects operators to have failed, but the suspicions might be wrong.

7.2.1 Coordination of Operator Recovery

To cope with that problem, we use a central component called *coordinator*, which has global knowledge about the operator topology and is eventually always up and running, i.e., there might be times when the coordinator is not available, but it will always come back online. The coordinator uses a failure detector with strong completeness (each failed operator will eventually be detected) and eventual weak accuracy (there is a time after which some correct process is never suspected), i.e., an *eventually strong failure detector*. Such a failure detector checks for heartbeat messages that correct operators send in a certain frequency. If a heartbeat message from ω did not arrive at the coordinator within a *time bound* τ, it will be *suspected* to have failed. As we work with an asynchronous system model, the coordinator can never be sure whether the operator has really failed, but it is sure that a failed and not yet fully recovered operator will not send heartbeat messages anymore, so eventually every failure will be detected. The possibility to implement

```
 1: list<operator> operators                      ▷ list of all operators
 2: list<operator> suspected                       ▷ suspected operators
 3: list<operator> progressed                   ▷ operators that have
    participated in the overall computational progress
 4: map<string, list<operator> > replacements              ▷
    replacements of an operator type

 5: procedure MonitoringProcedure()
 6:    while true do                                ▷ infinite loop
 7:       nextCheck ← currentTime() + checkFrequency
 8:       for all operators do
 9:          CheckLiveness(operator)
10:       end for
11:       wait until nextCheck
12:    end while
13: end procedure

14: procedure checkLiveness(operator)
15:    if (currentTime - lastReceivedHeartbeat.time ) >
       τ_operator then
16:       if operator ∉ suspected then
17:          suspected.add(operator)
18:          startReplacement(operator)
19:       end if
20:    else                                         ▷ op is alive
21:       if operator ∈ suspected
22:       and operator ∈ progressed then
23:          recallReplacements(operator)
24:          adaptTau(operator, higher)   ▷ increase τ_operator
25:       end if
26:    end if
27: end procedure
```

Figure 8: Algorithms for monitoring and management of operator topology at the coordinator.

the coordinator in a distributed manner is discussed in Section 9.

If ω is suspected to have failed, a replacement operator ω', i.e., an operator that implements the same correlation function as ω, is installed on a free system resource. When ω' initializes, it starts the recovery procedure described in Section 7.1. Now, it might be the case that the coordinator suspects ω' to have failed, too, so that ω'' is initialized, and so on. That is why suspected operators are not terminated immediately, but rather have the ability to run in parallel with their replacements. When the first of these parallel operators makes some real *progress* in event processing, the coordinator decides on that operator to remain in the topology and terminates all other replacement operators, i.e., they are shut down and their direct successors and predecessors are notified not to send messages to them any longer. The notion of progress is defined as follows:

DEFINITION 7.1. (PROCESSING PROGRESS OF AN OPERATOR.) *An operator ω has made progress after the restoration of its state when it updates its own savepoint for the first time.*

A savepoint update moves forward the point in time to which an operator gets recovered after its failure. That way, liveness of the system is guaranteed and the topology will finally stabilize. Note, that it is no problem for successors and predecessors of ω to cope with multiple replacements running in parallel: As they produce exactly the same events, the duplicates can easily be filtered, and ACKs are sent only to operators from which the ACKed events have been received.

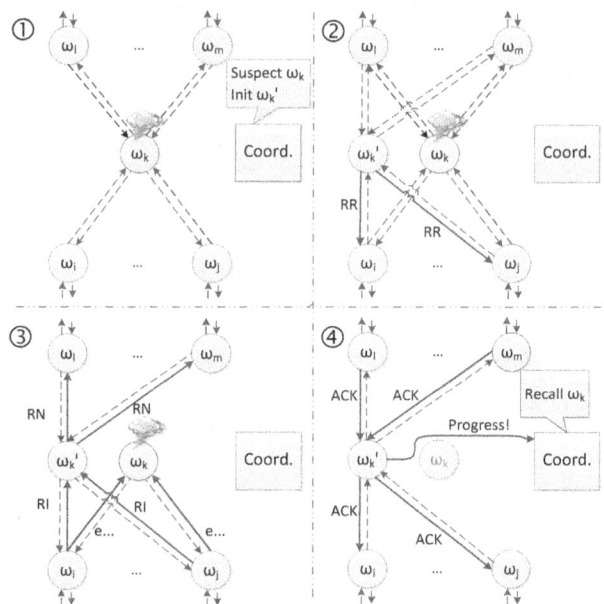

Figure 9: Recovery from an operator failure.

When it turns out that ω had been suspected by mistake, i.e., when the coordinator had suspected ω and received a heartbeat after that, the time bound τ can be adjusted to avoid such false suspicions in the future. We will not go further into detail with the time bound adjustment here as there exist already established algorithms for such problems in the field of eventually strong failure detectors. The algorithms at the coordinator for monitoring and control of the operators are listed in Figure 8.

Example: Figure 9 shows how an operator ω_k fails and is replaced by ω'_k. The coordinator suspects ω_k and starts ω'_k. ω'_k initializes by sending RecoveryRequests to its predecessors, receives recovery information as responses, restores its state and sends RecoveryNotifications to its successors. Now, ω'_k is fully incorporated into event production, and when enough events have been produced so that ACKs are received that make ω'_k update its savepoint, a progress notification is sent to the coordinator. Then, ω_k is deleted from the system, i.e., its successors and predecessors are notified to stop trying to communicate with ω_k.

7.3 Correctness Analysis

For proving correctness and liveness, i.e., completeness and consistency of event streams at consumers (see Section 3), we prove that there are no false-negatives or false-positives and that the overall system makes processing progress despite an arbitrary number of simultaneous operator failures.

PROPOSITION 7.2. (NO EVENT LOSS.) *In spite of the failure and recovery of an arbitrary number of operators at the same time, no necessary event in the sense of Definition 6.1 gets lost in an unrecoverable way.*

PROOF. Let C be a consumer who has not yet received and acknowledged an event e_c. Let ω_{p1} denote a direct predecessor of C, ω_{p2} a direct predecessor of ω_{p1}, and so on. Then the latest savepoint of ω_{p1} is captured with respect to a point in time T_{sp_1} before e_c has been produced. So, e_c is reproducible by a recovered operator ω_{p1}. Further, the latest savepoint of ω_{p2} is captured with respect to a point in time when events that are part of $\Lambda(T_{sp_1})$ of ω_{p1} are reproducible, and so on, so that all necessary events are reproducible. □

PROPOSITION 7.3. (NO FALSE-POSITIVE EVENTS.) *In spite of the failure and recovery of an arbitrary number of operators at the same time, there are not delivered any events to the consumers that would not have been delivered in the failure-free execution of all operators.*

PROOF. Property 5.1 shows that the state of ω at T_{sp} comprises exactly the information that is kept in a savepoint plus events from Q_I. As the savepoint is captured and replicated, it cannot deviate from the original savepoint after the recovery of ω. Further, necessary events from Q_I are either replayed from a preceding Q_O or recursively reproduced, whereas the recursion stops at a point where events from a Q_O are replayed (at the latest from the event sources). Events in Q_O are exactly the same events as sent in outgoing streams. As the recovered ω starts to process the same σ on indistinguishable copies of the events on which it would have been processing in a failure-free operator execution, the produced events are indistinguishable, too. □

PROPOSITION 7.4. (LIVENESS OF THE SYSTEM.) *Events are delivered to the consumers after a finite time interval from their physical occurrence, i.e., the event processing system makes progress in spite of the failure and recovery of an arbitrary number of operators.*

PROOF. As only correct operators send heartbeat messages to the coordinator, failed operators will eventually be suspected and replacements are started. The topology becomes stabilized when an operator signaled processing progress w.r.t. Definition 7.1. So, the liveness of the system is ensured, given that only a finite number of hosts is failing and there are enough correct hosts to run all operators. □

8. EVALUATION

In the evaluation, first of all we want to analyze the overhead of our approach induced at failure-free run-time: We measure the communication overhead and compare it with the overhead that would be induced by an active replication approach. Further, we analyze how the frequency of acknowledgments, the induced communication overhead and the size of Q_O are connected. In doing so, we have implemented the algorithms in an event-based simulation without considering incidental influences like underlying hardware topologies and communication protocols in order to emphasize the *inherent overhead* that would be caused in any implementation on any underlying infrastructure.

As a second aspect, we address the delay that the recovery of operators induces. Thereby, we identify significant parameters and develop a mathematical model of the recovery time of a failed operator.

8.1 Run-time Overhead

Our approach mainly induces run-time overhead with respect to two different aspects: The transmission of ACKs induces communication overhead, and the volatile storage of Q_O and savepoint trees impacts the memory footprint.

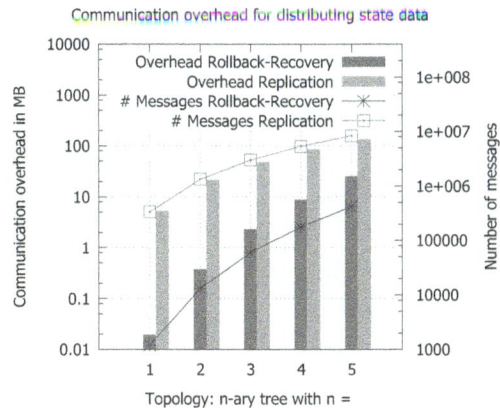

Figure 10: Run-time overhead comparison between rollback-recovery and replication.

8.1.1 Communication Overhead

The only data sent over the communication links at failure-free run-time are ACKs. We compute the size of an ACK as: $S(SimpleACK) + (\#Savepoints \times S(Savepoint))$. $S(SimpleACK)$ is 4 bytes (for the ACKed SN), $S(Savepoint)$ is 4 bytes for the SN of the next produced event, and $n \times 4bytes$ in a n-ary tree for the SNs of the start events in I_ω. An event is considered to be of a size of 16 bytes, 4 bytes for its SN, 4 bytes timestamp and 8 bytes payload. As the simulated operator topology, we chose n-ary trees with a depth of 3 for $n = 1$ to 5, with the root operator connected to 1 consumer and each leave operator connected to 1 source. Event sources produce events with a frequency of 1 event / ms. We compare the overhead with the messaging overhead that would have been caused by duplicate events in the CEP-optimized *active replication* approach [20] developed by Völz et al. We assume a low replication factor of 2 and the best case scenario for the leader election (only one leader at a time), leading to an overhead that approximately equates to the number of events sent through the network regularly, and neglect the overhead that the leader election would cause. Figure 10 shows how much additional data is sent over the network within 5 minutes. As one can see, our rollback-recovery approach induces less communication overhead than the compared active replication approach. Conclusions on this are drawn in Section 8.3.

8.1.2 Memory Consumption

The consumption of main memory at a host that an operator induces can be divided into two different parts: One part is the memory that is used for intermediate results in event processing, containing Q_I and the memory stack of f_ω. This part contains no specific overhead of the rollback-recovery approach, but rather the normal memory footprint of any event processing operator, so that we do not consider this in our evaluations. The other part is the memory used by all data stored solely for the purpose of enabling efficient rollback-recovery. This part is determined by two aspects: The size of the stored savepoint trees of the successors and the size of Q_O. The size of the savepoint trees depends solely on the operator topology and basically consists of one savepoint for each member of the transitive closure of the successor relation and is static (for a static operator topology).

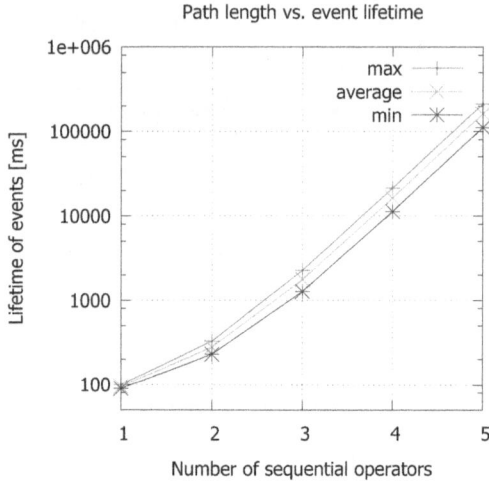

Figure 11: Lifetime of events in the sources against the number of sequential operators between sources and consumers.

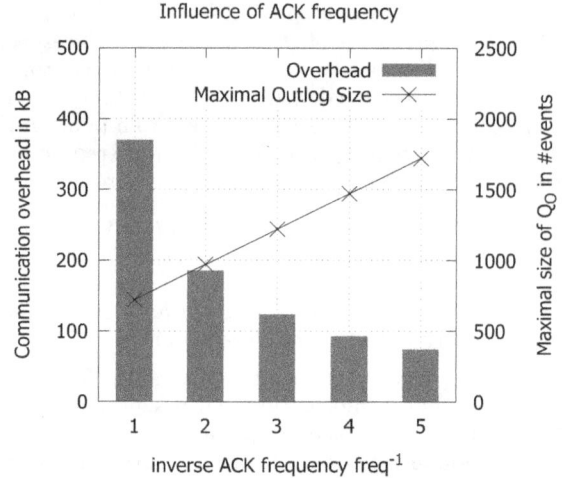

Figure 12: Influence of the ACK frequency at the Consumer on the overall communication overhead and the maximal size of Q_O at the source.

The size of Q_O, however, is dynamic and depends on the amount of produced events of an operator that are (possible through intermediate steps) correlated into an event that is delivered to event consumers and on the point in time between two consecutive ACKs that lead to its pruning.

To determine the maximal memory footprint, we analyze the event sources, as they have to store the maximal save-point trees and events produced by sources have the maximal lifetime, i.e., the time between their production and storage in Q_O and the receiving of their ACK which triggers their deletion from Q_O. We have measured the influence of the complexity of the events delivered to the consumers, i.e., the number of simple source events that are aggregated to a complex event, on the size of Q_O in the event sources. To do so, we built a simple topology containing one event source producing events in a frequency of 1 event / ms, a variable number of sequential operators and one consumer. In each correlation step, an operator takes 10 new events from its incoming stream and produces 1 outgoing event. Figure 11 shows the results: With an increasing complexity of the events delivered to the consumers, the lifetime of events in the outlog of the event sources increases. Conclusions on this are drawn in Section 8.3.

8.1.3   Influence of ACK Frequency

We have further evaluated how the frequency of ACKs influences the maximal size of Q_O at sources and the run-time communication overhead. In doing so, we programmed the Consumer to only acknowledge each *freq*-th event that it receives. The underlaying topology is a binary tree with a depth of 3, the rest of the parameters is as in the preceding scenarios. Figure 12 shows the results: When the ACK frequency decreases, the outlog size increases, but the communication overhead decreases. Conclusions on this are drawn in Section 8.3.

8.2   Recovery Overhead

As the rollback procedures take some time until an operator state is restored, it takes longer for the system to recover from failures in comparison to active replication (where a

replicated operator can take over processing with almost no latency). The recovery time of an operator ω is

$recoverytime(\omega) = T_{fd} + T_{deploy} + T_{rec} + T_{pred}$

with the parameters: (i) $T_{fd} = T_{channel\_delay} + T_{hb\_freq}$: Failure detection latency, depends on the communication delay between operators and the coordinator and on the frequency of heartbeat checks. (ii) T_{deploy}: Allocation of resources and deployment of the replacement operator, mainly depends on the underlying technology such as communication channels and the availability of resources. For example, when using an elastic compute cloud such as Amazon EC2, it can take some minutes until a new node is allocated (this highly depends on the deployed system, users report from about 1 minute up to 15 minutes). The time can be reduced when pre-deployed operators are provided. (iii) $T_{rec} = max(T_{channel\_delay}) + max(size(rec\_inf) \times channel\_rate)$: Recovery of the deployed replacement, depends on the slowest connection to a predecessor and on the size of the recovery information. (iv) T_i: Recovery of predecessor operators in the case of i adjacent failures: $T_{pred} = \sum_{j=1}^{i-1} recoverytime(\omega_j)$. This is the summation of the recovery time of failed predecessors, which need to be recovered successively first in order to recover ω.

8.3   Conclusions on the Evaluation

8.3.1   Run-time Overhead

We see that in comparison to active replication the network load can be reduced drastically by applying the proposed approach. An increasing node degree n causes that more sources participate in the production of simple events that get eventually aggregated to a complex event delivered to consumers. That way, the number of simple events per source aggregated in such a complex event decreases and the frequency of ACKs increases. Therefore, the communication overhead increases faster with rollback-recovery than with active replication. However, this behavior can be controlled by the consumers: If they decrease their frequency of ACKs, the overall network load decreases exponentially, but the size of Q_O at sources increases linearly. Besides the low network load, we do not need to preserve redundant resources as we would in active replication. An additional advantage is that we are able to recover from multiple arbitrary operator failures with rollback-recovery (in fact, all operators can fail at the same time and be restored), a property which would cause *immense* costs in active replication.

8.3.2 Recovery Overhead

Recovery generally takes longer than in active replication. The main parameters highly depend on the communication channels and the provision of nodes to deploy replacement operators. As the size of recovery information is limited to the size of the savepoint tree plus the size of re-streamed Q_O, it can be inferred from the evaluations in Figures 11 and 12 and the calculations given in Section 8.1.1.

9. DISCUSSION

This section briefly discusses possible extensions of the proposed recovery method.

How can intermediate consumptions be handled? Intermediate consumptions, i.e., consumptions of events in an arbitrary order instead of a sequential consumption, build up dependencies between different correlation steps and therefore are involved into the operator state. Such consumptions need to be replayed when restoring an operator state. To make that possible, they can be stored in the operator savepoint, e.g., in a table that connects correlation steps with the intermediate consumptions. Thus, the size of the savepoints and thereby the run-time overhead would increase.

How can the execution model by simplified for stream processing? In stream processing, in contrast to complex event processing, the window sizes of the execution model can be determined without considering the content of the contained events and the correlation function semantics. Therefore, the execution environment can track the selection window movement without needing information from the correlation function f_ω about the number of consumed events. This simplifies the interface between the EE and f_ω: f_ω just has to signal the end of each correlation step.

How can the coordinator be implemented in a distributed manner? When distributing the coordinator functionality over different nodes, it is intuitive to make a predecessor the coordinator of a successor, as they communicate with each other anyway and so heartbeat messages could be piggybacked. In doing so, it is important that each operator has exactly one coordinator responsible for its failure detection and recovery, so that the operator topology stabilizes. To solve this problem for asynchronous systems, concepts of leader election or group membership are necessary, e.g., as used in [9].

10. RELATED WORK

The existing approaches for distributed stream processing systems can be divided in three categories: The first category targets applications characterized as "partial fault-tolerant" [2,14]. In the case of a failure, systems try to produce information which is not perfectly accurate but might still be useful to the receiver. In the second category, information is published tentatively and corrections can be issued at a later point in time that revoke the messages sent before [1,3,4,13]. These solutions are based on two premises: (i) Dependencies of operators on each other's output have to

be within a reasonable limit to keep correction cost acceptable and, more important, (ii) the correction of incorrect messages has to be possible at all. In the scenarios we are examining, decisions might have already been made based on incorrect information that are either very costly or even impossible to correct. Therefore, accurate information is needed at all times.

Solutions that provide accurate information at all times involve the replication of functionality in active or passive replication [18] [5], or rollback-recovery [8] using checkpoints in combination with logs. Among others, these three principles have been applied to distributed stream processing systems; however, none of the current approaches provides all of the necessary properties for large-scale monitoring systems. In the following, we will discuss the proposed solutions individually.

Approaches using active replication [12] incur quadratic overhead in terms of messages during failure-free execution. Checkpointing [15] requires the frequent execution of sophisticated state-extraction algorithms that need either to be specified individually for each operator or require taking a full memory snapshot. Therefore, these approaches either restrict the user to using predefined operators only or require additional expertise to implement the extraction function. On the other hand, a memory snapshot can only be taken if the respective pages are write-locked, which incurs significant additional detection delay during failure-free execution. The approach of "upstream backup" [10, 11] uses a similar construct of a simple ACK to recover from only one single failure at a time without any state replication. However, the approach is very restrictive regarding operators for which a consistent state can really be guaranteed after a recovery. More sophisticated, asynchronous event processing operators need a different execution model that at least allows for independent windows on different incoming streams and therefore inherently possess non-reproducible state that needs to be replicated.

Reliability for distributed complex event processing systems has not been researched as actively as for stream processing systems. Active replication has been applied to CEP as well, providing a leader election algorithm to reduce the message overhead during failure-free runtime [20]. Still, for tolerating n simultaneous failures, $n+1$ replicas are deployed for each operator, creating at least a linear message overhead. An approach for dealing with unreliable communication channels when delivering events to a CEP system has been proposed [16]. However, operator failures are not considered in this approach.

11. CONCLUSION

Although reliability is critical for many applications involving event processing systems, state-of-the-art approaches have clear shortcomings in providing accurate processing and low run-time overhead in a large-scale deployment.

This paper proposed a novel rollback-recovery mechanism for multiple simultaneous operator failures in distributed stream and event processing systems that eliminates the need for checkpoints and does not use persistent memory at operators. It therefore avoids the main drawbacks of previous approaches, which increase processing and network load for creating and maintaining large checkpoints, or burden application developers with defining operator specific mechanisms for checkpointing and recovery.

We defined an event processing model based on the concept of event selections to find points in time when an event processing system has minimal non-reproducible state which is then stored in replicated savepoints. The rest of the operator state can be reproduced from primary event streams, so that only event sources have to maintain events in a reliable way. An algorithm to coordinate savepoint maintenance over multiple levels of operators is provided, allowing to recover from simultaneous operator failures. We proved the algorithm correctness and provided evaluation results demonstrating its behavior in different parameter settings in comparison to active replication. The evaluations have shown that the network load can be reduced drastically, and that the frequency of acknowledgments at event consumers is a design parameter that can be used to balance between memory requirements and network load.

Future work will focus on the further exploration of the proposed recovery scheme. We want to improve the runtime behavior by dynamically adapting the acknowledgment frequency to system properties and by the segmentation of the operator topology by means of reliable persistence layers. Besides, the concept of savepoints can be used for the efficient implementation of operator migration [17]. Furthermore, in order to allow for a better scalability and speedup of the event correlations, we want to explore how the operator execution model can support the parallelization of processing.

Acknowledgment

This work has been supported by contract research "Internationale Spitzenforschung II" of the Baden-Württemberg Stiftung.

12. REFERENCES

[1] M. Balazinska, H. Balakrishnan, S. Madden, and M. Stonebraker. Fault-Tolerance in the Borealis Distributed Stream Processing System. In *Proc. of SIGMOD '05*, pages 13–24.

[2] N. Bansal, R. Bhagwan, N. Jain, Y. Park, D. Turaga, and C. Venkatramani. Towards Optimal Resource Allocation in Partial-Fault Tolerant Applications. In *Proc. of the 27th IEEE Conference on Computer Communications, INFOCOM '08*, pages 1319–1327.

[3] A. Brito, C. Fetzer, and P. Felber. Minimizing Latency in Fault-Tolerant Distributed Stream Processing Systems. In *Proc. of the 29th IEEE Int'l Conference on Distributed Computing Systems, ICDCS '09*, pages 173–182.

[4] A. Brito, C. Fetzer, H. Sturzrehm, and P. Felber. Speculative Out-Of-Order Event Processing with Software Transaction Memory. In *Proc. of the 2nd ACM Int'l Conference on Distributed Event-Based Systems, DEBS '08*, pages 265–275.

[5] N. Budhiraja, K. Marzullo, F. B. Schneider, and S. Toueg. Distributed systems (2nd ed.). chapter "The primary-backup approach", pages 199–216. ACM Press/Addison-Wesley Publishing Co., New York, NY, USA, 1993.

[6] S. Chakravarthy and D. Mishra. Snoop: An expressive event specification language for active databases. *Data Knowl. Eng.*, 14(1):1–26, 1994.

[7] G. Cugola and A. Margara. Processing Flows of Information: From Data Stream to Complex Event Processing. *ACM Comput. Surv.*, 44(3):15:1–15:62, June 2012.

[8] E. N. M. Elnozahy, L. Alvisi, Y.-M. Wang, and D. B. Johnson. A Survey of Rollback-Recovery Protocols in Message-Passing Systems. *ACM Comput. Surv.*, 34:375–408, September 2002.

[9] M. Franceschetti and J. Bruck. A Leader Election Protocol for Fault Recovery in Asynchronous Fully-Connected Networks. Technical report, California Institute of Technology, 1998.

[10] J.-H. Hwang, M. Balazinska, A. Rasin, U. Cetintemel, M. Stonebraker, and S. Zdonik. High-Availability Algorithms for Distributed Stream Processing. In *Proc. of the 21st IEEE Int'l Conference on Data Engineering, ICDE '05*, pages 779–790.

[11] J.-H. Hwang, M. Balazinska, A. Rasin, U. Cetintemel, M. Stonebraker, and S. Zdonik. A Comparison of Stream-Oriented High-Availability Algorithms. Technical Report CS-03-17, Brown University, September 2003.

[12] J.-H. Hwang, U. Cetintemel, and S. Zdonik. Fast and Highly-Available Stream Processing over Wide Area Networks. In *Proc. of the IEEE 24th Int'l Conference on Data Engineering, ICDE '08*, pages 804–813.

[13] J.-H. Hwang, S. Cha, U. Cetintemel, and S. Zdonik. Borealis-R: A Replication-transparent Stream Processing System for Wide-area Monitoring Applications. In *Proc. of SIGMOD '08*, pages 1303–1306, 2008.

[14] G. Jacques-Silva, B. Gedik, H. Andrade, and K.-L. Wu. Language Level Checkpointing Support for Stream Processing Applications. In *Proc. of the 39th IEEE/IFIP Int'l Conference on Dependable Systems and Networks, DSN '09*, pages 145–154.

[15] Y. Kwon, M. Balazinska, and A. Greenberg. Fault-tolerant Stream Processing using a Distributed, Replicated File System. *Proc. of VLDB Endow.*, pages 574–585, 2008.

[16] D. O'Keeffe and J. Bacon. Reliable Complex Event Detection for Pervasive Computing. In *Proc. of the 4th ACM Int'l Conference on Distributed Event-Based Systems, DEBS '10*, pages 73–84.

[17] B. Ottenwälder, B. Koldehofe, U. Ramachandran, and K. Rothermel. MigCEP: Operator Migration for Mobility Driven Distributed Complex Event Processing. In *Proc. of the 7th ACM Int'l Conference on Distributed Event-Based Systems, DEBS '13*.

[18] F. B. Schneider. Implementing Fault-Tolerant Services Using the State Machine Approach: A Tutorial. *ACM Comput. Surv.*, 22(4):299–319, 1990.

[19] Z. Sebepou and K. Magoutis. CEC: Continuous Eventual Checkpointing for Data Stream Processing Operators. In *Proc. of the 41st IEEE/IFIP Int'l Conference on Dependable Systems and Networks, DSN '11*, pages 145–156.

[20] M. Völz, B. Koldehofe, and K. Rothermel. Supporting Strong Reliability for Distributed Complex Event Processing Systems. In *Proc. of the IEEE 13th Int'l Conference on High Performance Computing and Communications, HPPC '11*, pages 477–486.

Ariadne: Managing Fine-Grained Provenance on Data Streams

Boris Glavic
Illinois Institute of
Technology
Chicago, IL
bglavic@iit.edu

Kyumars Sheykh Esmaili
Nanyang Technological
University
Singapore
kyumarss@ntu.edu.sg

Peter M. Fischer
University of Freiburg
Germany
peter.fischer@
cs.uni-freiburg.de

Nesime Tatbul
ETH Zurich
Switzerland
tatbul@inf.ethz.ch

ABSTRACT

Managing fine-grained provenance is a critical requirement for data stream management systems (DSMS), not only to address complex applications that require diagnostic capabilities and assurance, but also for providing advanced functionality such as revision processing or query debugging. This paper introduces a novel approach that uses operator instrumentation, i.e., modifying the behavior of operators, to generate and propagate fine-grained provenance through several operators of a query network. In addition to applying this technique to compute provenance eagerly during query execution, we also study how to decouple provenance computation from query processing to reduce run-time overhead and avoid unnecessary provenance retrieval. This includes computing a concise superset of the provenance to allow lazily replaying a query network and reconstruct its provenance as well as lazy retrieval to avoid unnecessary reconstruction of provenance. We develop stream-specific compression methods to reduce the computational and storage overhead of provenance generation and retrieval. Ariadne, our provenance-aware extension of the Borealis DSMS implements these techniques. Our experiments confirm that Ariadne manages provenance with minor overhead and clearly outperforms query rewrite, the current state-of-the-art.

Categories and Subject Descriptors

H.2.4 [**Database Management**]: Systems—*Query Processing*

Keywords

Data Streams, Provenance, Annotation, Experiments

1. INTRODUCTION

Stream processing has recently been gaining traction in a new class of applications that require diagnostic capabilities, assurance, and human observation [3, 14]. In these applications, there is a common need to provide "fine-grained provenance" information (i.e., at the same level as in database provenance [10]), to trace an output event back to the input events contributing to its existence.

Example. In monitoring and control of manufacturing systems, sensors are attached along a supply chain. Sensor readings are processed by a DSMS in order to detect critical situations such as machine overheating. These detected events are then used for automatic corrections as well as for notifying human supervisors. Human supervisors need to understand why and how such events were triggered to be able to assess their relevance and react appropriately. Figure 1 shows a simplified example of a continuous query that detects overheating. Two sensors feed timestamped temperature readings to the query. Each sensor stream is filtered to remove massive outliers (i.e., temperature t above $350°C$). The stream is aggregated by averaging the temperature over a sliding window of 3 temperature readings to further reduce the impact of sudden spikes. These data cleaning steps are applied to each sensor stream individually. Afterwards, readings from multiple sensors are combined for cross-validation (i.e., a union followed by a sort operator to globally order on time). The final aggregation and selection ensure that a fire alert will only be raised if at least three different sensors show average temperatures above $90°C$ within 2 time units. In this example, the user would want to understand which sensor readings caused an "overheating" alarm event, i.e., determine the tuples that belong to the *fine-grained* provenance of this event.

Challenges and Opportunities: Tracking provenance to explore the reasons that led to a given query result has proven to be an important functionality in many domains such as scientific workflow systems [11] and relational databases [10]. However, providing fine-grained provenance support over data streams introduces a number of unique challenges that are not well addressed by traditional provenance management techniques:

Online and Infinite Data Arrival: Data streams can potentially be infinite; therefore, no global view on all items is possible. As a result, traditional methods that reconstruct provenance from the query and input data on request are not applicable.

Ordered Data Model: In contrast to relational data, data streams are typically modeled as ordered sequences. This ordering can be exploited to provide optimized representations of provenance.

Window-based Processing: In DSMSs, operators like *aggregation* and *join* are typically processed by grouping tuples from a stream into windows. Stream provenance must deal with windowing behavior in order to trace the outputs of such operators back to their sources correctly and efficiently. The prevalence of aggregations leads to enormous amounts of provenance per result.

Low-latency Results: Performance requirements in most streaming applications are strict; in particular low latency should be maintained. Provenance generation has to be efficient enough to not violate the application's latency constraints.

Non-determinism: Mechanisms for coping with high input rates (e.g., load shedding [22, 24]) and certain operator definitions such as windowing on system time result in outputs that are not determined solely by the inputs. Conventional provenance management techniques (e.g., query rewrite [13]) and naive solutions (e.g., tak-

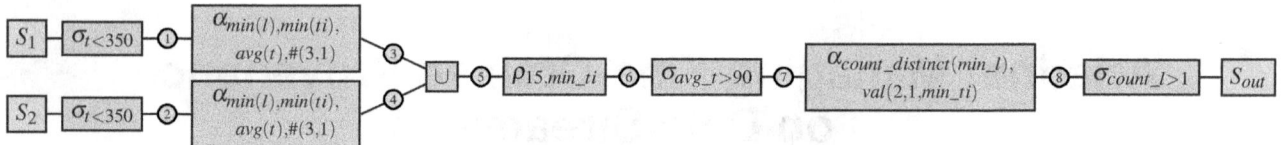

Figure 1: Example Query Network

ing advantage of cheap, fast storage by dumping all inputs and inferring provenance from the complete stream data) are not sufficient to address all of the challenges outlined above.

Contributions and Outline: In this paper, we propose a novel propagation-based approach for provenance generation, called *operator instrumentation*. We use a simple definition of fine-grained provenance that is similar to *Lineage* in relational databases [10]. Our approach annotates regular data tuples with their provenance while they are being processed by a network of streaming operators. Propagation of these provenance annotations is realized by replacing the operators of the query network with operators that create and propagate annotations in addition to producing regular data tuples (we refer to this transformation as *operator instrumentation*). This approach can also be used to compute the provenance of a part of the query network by only instrumenting a subset of the operators. Previous annotation propagation approaches for fine-grained stream provenance [12] are restricted to one-step provenance, i.e., annotating output tuples from an operator with their provenance from the operator's input. Our approach is more general and flexible; provenance can also be propagated through several operators or even a complete query network. By lifting this restriction we are able to overcome many of the shortcomings of these approaches including large storage overhead (tracking provenance through a path in the query network requires storage of all streams on the path) and expensive retrieval (queries over provenance require recursive tracing using the single-step provenance).

We represent provenance as sets of tuple identifiers during provenance generation. Querying provenance is supported by reconstructing complete input tuples from the identifier sets using a new operator called *p-join*. This is achieved by temporarily storing input stream tuples for the reconstruction.[1] A number of optimizations enable us to decouple provenance management from query processing: The *Replay-Lazy* optimization reduces the run-time overhead of provenance computation by propagating a concise superset of the provenance and lazily replaying a query network to reconstruct its provenance. The *Lazy-Retrieval* method avoids reconstructing provenance for retrieval if parts of the provenance will not be needed by the query. Furthermore, we devise a number of compression schemes to reduce the computation cost. We have implemented our approach in Ariadne, a provenance-aware DSMS that is based on the Borealis prototype [1]. More specifically, this paper makes the following contributions:

- We introduce a novel provenance generation technique for DSMS based on annotating and propagating provenance information through operator instrumentation, which allows generating provenance for networks and subnetworks without the need to materialize data at each operator.

- We propose a number of optimization techniques that allow decoupling provenance computation from query processing through the application of lazy generation and retrieval techniques and improve performance by compression.

---

[1]This is in contrast to one-step approaches that also require the storage of intermediate streams.

Method	Applicable to	Runtime Overhead	Retrieval Overhead
Inversion	Invertible	None	High
Query Rewrite	Deterministic	High	-
Operator Instrumentation	All	Low	-

Figure 2: Comparison of Provenance Generation Alternatives

- We present Ariadne, the first DSMS prototype providing support for fine-grained multi-step provenance.

- We provide an experimental evaluation of the proposed techniques using Ariadne. The results demonstrate that providing fine-grained provenance via optimized operator instrumentation has minor overhead and clearly outperforms query rewrite, the current state-of-the-art.

The rest of this paper is organized as follows: Section 2 gives an overview of our approach for adding provenance generation and retrieval to a DSMS. We introduce the stream, provenance, and annotation model underlying our approach in Section 3. Building upon this model, we present its implementation in the Ariadne prototype in Section 4. We cover optimizations of our basic approach in Section 5. We present experimental results in Section 6, discuss related work in Section 7, and conclude in Section 8.

2. OVERVIEW OF OUR APPROACH

We generate and propagate provenance annotations by replacing query operators with special provenance-aware operators. Provenance is modeled as a set of tuples from the input streams that are sufficient to produce a result tuple. Output tuples are annotated with sets of tuple identifiers representing their provenance.

2.1 Why Operator Instrumentation?

There are two well-known provenance generation techniques in the literature that we considered as alternatives to operator instrumentation for generating DSMS provenance: (1) computing inverses and (2) rewriting the query network to propagate provenance annotations using the existing operators of the DSMS. Figure 2 shows a summary of the tradeoffs. *Inversion* (e.g., Woodruff et al. [27]) generates provenance by applying the inverse (in the mathematical sense) of an operator. For example, a join (without projection) is invertible, because the inputs can be constructed from an output tuple. Inversion has very limited applicability to DSMSs, because no real inverse exists for most non-trivial operators. *Query Rewrite*, established in relational systems such as Perm [13], DB-Notes [8], or Orchestra [19], generates provenance by rewriting a query network Q into a network that generates the provenance of Q in addition to the original network outputs. This usually requires changes to the structure of the query network. For example, as explained in [13], a provenance-generating copy of a subnetwork has to be added to and joined with the original subnetwork to support aggregates. This leads to significant additional run-time overhead and incorrect provenance for non-deterministic operators.

In summary, we believe that Operator Instrumentation is the best approach for generating provenance in DSMSs, because it is applicable to a large class of queries while maintaining low overhead in

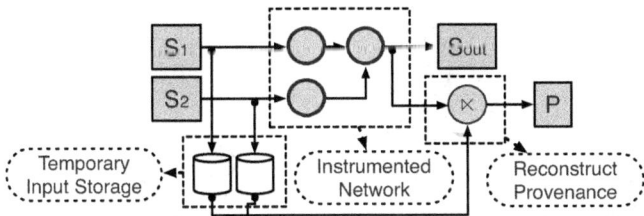

Figure 3: Reduced-Eager Operator Instrumentation

Method	Applicable to	Runtime Overhead	Retrieval Overhead
Reduced-Eager	All	Full Generation (high)	Reconstruct (low)
Replay-Lazy	Deterministic	Minimal Generation (low)	Replay (high)

Figure 4: Trade-offs for Eager vs. Lazy

terms of provenance computation and retrieval. Our experimental results in Section 6 verify our hypothesis.

2.2 The Operator Instrumentation Approach

The key idea behind our operator instrumentation approach is to extend each operator implementation so that the operator is able to annotate its output with provenance information based on provenance annotations of its inputs. Under operator instrumentation, provenance annotations are processed in line with the regular data. That is, the structure of the original query network is kept as is (operators are simply replaced with their instrumented counterparts). Thus, most issues caused by non-determinism are dealt with in a rather natural way, since the execution of the original query network is traced[2]. Provenance can be traced for a single operator (as supported by previous approaches [12]) or for a complete subnetwork. Furthermore, we can trace provenance for a subnetwork by instrumenting only operators in that subnetwork. The only drawback of operator instrumentation is the need to extend all operators. However, as we will demonstrate in Section 4.2, this extension can be implemented with reasonable effort.

With operator instrumentation, provenance can be generated either *eagerly* during query execution (our default approach) or *lazily* upon request. We support both types of generation, because their performance characteristics in terms of storage, runtime, and retrieval overhead are different (see Figure 4). This enables the user to trade runtime-overhead on the original query network for storage cost and runtime-overhead when retrieving provenance

Reduced-Eager: Figure 3 shows an example how we instrument a network for *eager* provenance generation. We temporarily store the input tuples for the instrumented parts of the network (e.g., for input streams S_1 and S_2, since we want provenance for the entire query network). The tuples in the output stream of the instrumented network carry the provenance annotations as described above, i.e., each output is annotated with the set of identifiers of the tuples in its provenance. Provenance is reconstructed for retrieval from the annotations using a new operator called *p-join* ($\bowtie$). For each output tuple t, this operator retrieves all input tuples in the provenance using the set of identifiers from the provenance annotation and outputs all combinations of t with a tuple from its provenance. Each of these combinations is emitted as a single tuple to stream P. We call this approach *Reduced-Eager*, because we are eagerly propagating a reduced form of provenance (the tuple identifier sets) during query execution and lazily reconstructing provenance independent of the execution of the original network. In comparison with using sets of full tuples as annotations, this approach pays a price for storing and reconstructing tuples. However, because compressed representations can be used, this cost is offset by a significant reduction in provenance generation cost (in terms of both runtime

and latency). Since *reconstruction* is separate from generation, we can often avoid reconstructing complete provenance tuples during provenance retrieval, e.g., if the user only requests provenance for some results (query over provenance).

Replay-Lazy: Instead of generating provenance *eagerly* while the query network is running, we would like to be able to generate provenance *lazily* in order to decouple provenance generation from the execution of the query network. Since DSMSs are expected to deal with high rates and low latency requirements, eager provenance computation may incur significant runtime overhead to the critical data processing path. Decoupling most of the provenance computation from query processing enables us to reduce the runtime overhead on the query network and outsource provenance generation to a separate machine and thus improve performance for both normal query processing and provenance computation. For deterministic networks, we can realize lazy generation by replaying relevant inputs through a instrumented copy of the network. We call this approach *Replay-Lazy*. *Replay-Lazy* has to propagate minimal bookkeeping information during query execution to be able to determine which inputs are relevant and, thus, reduce the amount of data that is stored and replayed. We record for each output tuple the parts of the input which are needed for the replay to be executed correctly (by annotating the tuple), which turns out to be a concise superset (constant size) of the actual provenance. *Replay-Lazy* reduces the runtime overhead by just computing this minimal type of provenance, but incurs a higher retrieval cost due to the replay and is only applicable to deterministic networks.

3. PROVENANCE PROPAGATION BY OPERATOR INSTRUMENTATION

Based on the stream data and query model of Borealis [1], we now informally introduce our stream provenance model and discuss how to instrument queries to annotate their outputs with provenance information. A formal treatment can be found in [15].

3.1 Data and Query Model

We model a stream $S = \ll t_1, \dots \gg$ as a possibly infinite sequence of tuples. A tuple $t = (TID; a_1, \dots)$ is an ordered list of attribute values (here a_i denotes a value) plus a tuple-identifier (TID) that uniquely identifies the tuple within stream scope denoted as *stream-id:tuple-id*. A *query network* is a directed acyclic graph (DAG) in which nodes and edges represent streaming operators and input/output streams respectively. Each stream operator in a query network takes one or more streams as input, and produces one or more streams as output. The query algebra we use here covers all the streaming operators from [1].

Selection: A selection operator $\sigma_c(S)$ with predicate c filters out tuples from an input stream S that do not satisfy the predicate c.

Projection: A projection operator $\pi_A(S)$ with a list of projection expressions A (e.g., attributes, function applications) projects each input tuple from stream S on the expressions from A.

Aggregation: An aggregation operator $\alpha_{agg,\omega}(S)$ groups its input S into windows using the window function ω and computes the aggregation functions (agg) over each window generated by ω. For example, the count-based window function $\#(c, s)$ groups a consec-

---

[2]The overhead introduced by provenance generation may affect temporal conditions (e.g., windows based on system time). However, this is not a real drawback, because such conditions are sensitive to other system events in addition to overhead caused by provenance generation.

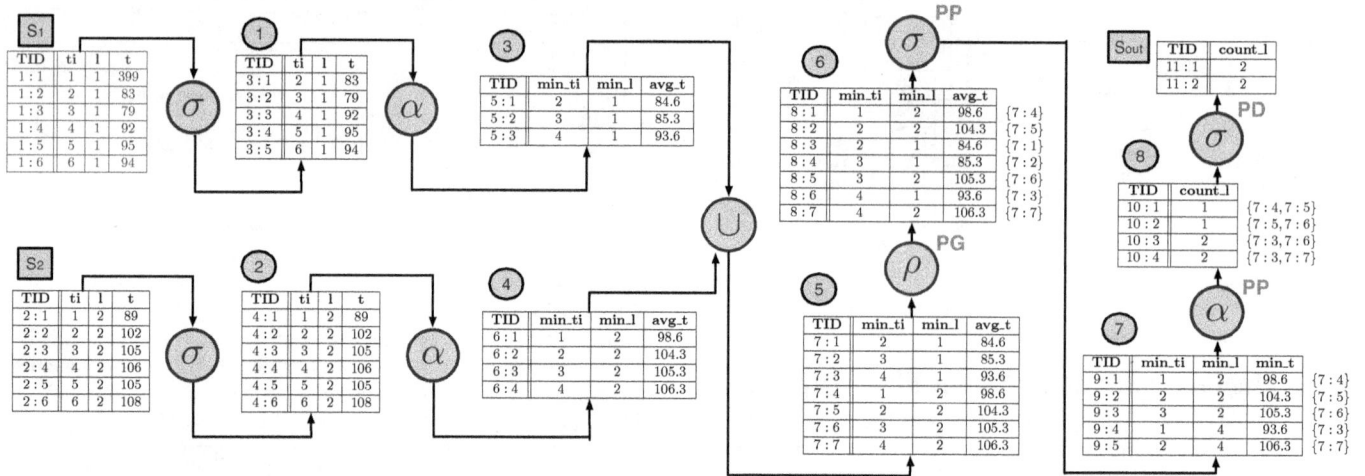

Figure 5: Example Query Network Evaluation with Provenance-aware Operators and Provenance Annotations

S1

TID	ti	l	t
1:1	1	1	399
1:2	2	1	83
1:3	3	1	79
1:4	4	1	92
1:5	5	1	95
1:6	6	1	94

1

TID	ti	l	t
3:1	2	1	83
3:2	3	1	79
3:3	4	1	92
3:4	5	1	95
3:5	6	1	94

3

TID	min_ti	min_l	avg_t
5:1	2	1	84.6
5:2	3	1	85.3
5:3	4	1	93.6

6

TID	min_ti	min_l	avg_t	
8:1	1	2	98.6	{7:4}
8:2	2	2	104.3	{7:5}
8:3	2	1	84.6	{7:1}
8:4	3	1	85.3	{7:2}
8:5	3	2	105.3	{7:6}
8:6	4	1	93.6	{7:3}
8:7	4	2	106.3	{7:7}

Sout

TID	count_l
11:1	2
11:2	2

8

TID	count_l	
10:1	1	{7:4,7:5}
10:2	1	{7:5,7:6}
10:3	2	{7:3,7:6}
10:4	2	{7:3,7:7}

S2

TID	ti	l	t
2:1	1	2	89
2:2	2	2	102
2:3	3	2	105
2:4	4	2	106
2:5	5	2	105
2:6	6	2	108

2

TID	ti	l	t
4:1	1	2	89
4:2	2	2	102
4:3	3	2	105
4:4	4	2	106
4:5	5	2	105
4:6	6	2	108

4

TID	min_ti	min_l	avg_t
6:1	1	2	98.6
6:2	2	2	104.3
6:3	3	2	105.3
6:4	4	2	106.3

5

TID	min_ti	min_l	avg_t
7:1	2	1	84.6
7:2	3	1	85.3
7:3	4	1	93.6
7:4	1	2	98.6
7:5	2	2	104.3
7:6	3	2	105.3
7:7	4	2	106.3

7

TID	min_ti	min_l	min_t	
9:1	1	2	98.6	{7:4}
9:2	2	2	104.3	{7:5}
9:3	3	2	105.3	{7:6}
9:4	1	4	93.6	{7:3}
9:5	2	4	106.3	{7:7}

utive input tuple sequence (length c) into a window and slides by a number of tuples s before opening the next window. The value-based window function $val(c,s,a)$ groups a consecutive sequence of tuples into a window if their values in attribute a differ less than c from the attribute value of the first tuple in the window. The slide s determines how far to slide on a before opening the next window. Note that value-based windows subsume the concept of time-based windows by using a time attribute.

Join: A join operator $\bowtie_{c,j\omega}(S_1,S_2)$ joins two input streams S_1 and S_2 by applying the join window function $j\omega$ to S_1 and S_2. A join window function models the buffering behavior of stream joins. All tuples from both input streams that are in the join's buffer at a point in time are grouped into the same join window. For each join window w, the join operator outputs all pairs of tuples from S_1 and S_2 that belong to w and fulfill the join condition c.

Union: A union operator $\cup(S_1,S_2)$ merges tuples from two input streams S_1 and S_2 into a single stream based on their arrival order.

B-Sort: A b-sort operator $\rho_{s,a}(S)$ with slack s and an order-on attribute a applies bounded-pass sort with buffer size $s+1$ on its input, and produces an output that is approximately sorted on a.

EXAMPLE 1. *Figure 5 shows an execution of the network introduced in Figure 1 for a given input. For now ignore the annotations on operators and tuples in streams 6 to 8. Both input streams (S_1 and S_2) have the same schema with attributes time (ti), location (l), and temperature (t). The left-most filters drop temperature outliers. The results of this step are grouped into windows of three tuples using slide one. For each window we compute the minimum of time (to assign each aggregated tuple a new time value) and location (the location is fixed for one stream, thus, the minimum of the location is the same as the input location), and average temperature. The aggregated streams are merged into one stream ($\cup$) and sorted on time. We then filter out tuples with temperature values below the overheating threshold and compute the number of distinct locations over windows of two time units. Tuples with fewer than two distinct locations are filtered out in the last step. For instance, in the example execution shown in Figure 5, the upper left selection filters out the outlier tuple 1:1 $(1,1,399)$. The following aggregation groups the first three result tuples into a window and outputs the average temperature (84.6), minimum time (2), and location (1).*

3.2 Provenance Model and Annotated Streams

We use a simple provenance model that defines the provenance of a tuple t in a stream O of a query network q as a set of tuples from input (or intermediate) streams of the network. We use $P(q,t,I)$ to denote the *provenance set of a tuple t* from one of the streams of network q with respect to inputs from streams in a set I. For instance, if t is a tuple in stream 3 of the example network shown in Figure 1, then $P(q,t,\{S_1\})$ denotes the set of tuples from input stream S_1 that contributed to t. We omit I if we compute the provenance according to the input streams of the query network.

Note that we require I to be chosen such that the paths between streams in I and O (the stream of t) form a proper query network. For instance, assume that t is a tuple from stream 5 in the network shown in Figure 5. $P(q,t,\{1,2\})$ denotes the set of tuples from streams 1 and 2 that contributed to t. $P(q,t,\{2\})$ would be undefined, because only one of the inputs of the union is included. Formally, our work is based on a declarative definition of provenance, which is used to determine the provenance behavior for each of the operators. Intuitively, the provenance definition for all operators is as follows: For *Selection* and *Projection*, the provenance of t consists of the provenance of the corresponding input tuple. The same is true for *Union* and *BSort*, since only a single tuple is contributing to t. For example, tuple 9:1 in the network shown in Figure 5 was generated by the selection from tuple 8:1. Thus, the provenance set of this tuple is $\{7:4\}$, the same as the provenance set of tuple 8:1. For *Join*, the union of the provenance sets of the join partners generating t constitutes the provenance. Finally, the provenance set for t in the result of an *Aggregation* is the union of the provenance sets for all tuples from the window used to compute t.

We use the concept of provenance sets to define streams of tuples that are annotated with their provenance sets. For a query network q, the *provenance annotated stream (PAS) $P(q,O,I)$* for a stream O according to a set of streams I is a copy of stream O where each tuple t is annotated with its corresponding provenance set $P(q,t,I)$. In the following, we will omit the query parameter q from provenance sets and PAS if it is clear from the context.

EXAMPLE 2. *Consider the PAS $P(6,\{5\})$ for the output of the b-sort operator according to its input shown in Figure 5 (provenance sets are shown to the right of the tuples). Each output t of the b-sort is annotated with a singleton set containing the corresponding tuple from the b-sort's input, e.g., tuple 8:1 is derived from tuple 7:4. Now consider the PAS for the output of the last aggregation in the query according to the input of the b-sort ($P(8,\{5\})$). Each output tuple is computed using information from a window containing two input tuples with one tuple overlap between the individual provenance sets. For example, tuple 10:2 is derived from*

Algorithm 1 InstrumentNetwork Algorithm

1: **procedure** INSTRUMENTNETWORK(q, O, I)
2:     $mixed \leftarrow \emptyset$
3:     **for all** $o \in q$ **do**   ▷ Find operators with mixed usage
4:         **if** $\exists S, S' \in input(o) : S \in I \wedge S' \notin I$ **then**
5:             $mixed \leftarrow mixed \cup input(o)$
6:     **for all** $S \in (mixed \cap I)$ **do**   ▷ Add projection wrappers
7:         $S \leftarrow \Pi_{schema(S)}(S)$
8:     **for all** $o \in q$ **do**   ▷ Replace operators
9:         **if** $\exists S \in I : \text{HASPATH}(S, o) \wedge \text{HASPATH}(o, O)$ **then**
10:             **if** $\exists S' \in input(o) : S' \in I$ **then**
11:                 $o \leftarrow PG(o)$
12:             **else**
13:                 $o \leftarrow PP(o)$
14:     **for all** $o \in q$ **do**   ▷ Drop annotations
15:         **if** $O \in input(o)$ **then**
16:             $o \leftarrow PD(o)$

---

a window of tuples with provenance $\{7{:}5\}$ and $\{7{:}6\}$, and tuple $10{:}3$ is derived from a window with provenance $\{7{:}6, 7{:}3\}$.

3.3 Instrumenting Operators and Networks for Annotation Propagation

We now discuss how to instrument a query network q to generate the PAS for a subset of the streams in q by replacing all or a subset of the operators with annotating counterparts. Three types of *instrumented operators* are used in this approach:

Provenance Generator (PG): The provenance generator version $PG(o)$ of an operator o computes the PAS for all output streams of the operator according to its input streams. The purpose of a PG is to generate a PAS from input streams without annotations. For each output stream S of the operator o, $PG(o)$ creates $P(S, input(o))$ where $input(o)$ are the input streams of operator o.

Provenance Propagator (PP): This version of operator generates the PASs for its outputs from PASs of its inputs. For simplicity, let us explain the concept for an operator o with a single output O and a single input PAS $P(S, I)$. The PP version of o will output $P(O, I)$, i.e., the output will be annotated with provenance sets of O according to I. Intuitively, a PP generates annotated output streams by modifying the annotations from its input streams according to the provenance behavior of the operator.

Provenance Dropper (PD): The provenance dropper version $PD(o)$ of an operator o removes annotations from the input before applying operator o. Provenance droppers are used to remove annotations from streams in networks with partial provenance generation.

The *PG* version of selection generates an annotated output stream where the provenance set of each output tuple t contains the corresponding input tuple, and the *PP* version outputs the input tuples with unmodified provenance sets (for tuples that fulfill the selection condition). Projection, union, and b-sort behave in the same way by creating singleton provenance sets (*PG*) or passing on provenance sets from the input (*PP*). The *PG* operator for aggregation annotates each output tuple t with a provenance set that consists of all identifiers for tuples in the input window that generated t, and the *PP* operator annotates each output tuple t with the union of the provenance sets of all tuples in the window that generated t. The *PG* version of join annotates each output t with a set consisting of the two tuples that were joined to produce tuple t. The *PP* version of this operator unions the provenance sets of the join partners.

Networks with Annotation Propagation: Using the PG and PP versions of operators we have the necessary means to generate

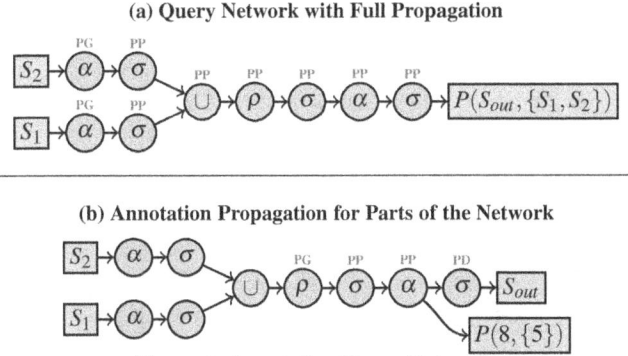

(a) Query Network with Full Propagation

(b) Annotation Propagation for Parts of the Network

Figure 6: Annotating Query Networks

provenance for a complete (or parts of a) query network by replacing all (or some) operators with their annotating counterparts. PD versions of operators are used to remove provenance annotations from streams that are further processed by the network. We use algorithm *InstrumentNetwork* (Algorithm 1) to instrument a network q to compute a PAS $P(O, I)$. First we normalize the network to make sure that the inputs to every operator are either **(1)** only streams from I or **(2)** contain no streams from I. This step is necessary to avoid having operators that read from both streams in and not in I, because the annotation propagation behaviour of these operators is neither correctly modelled by their PG nor PP version. We wrap each stream S in I that is connected to such an operator in a projection on all attributes in the schema of S. This does not change the results of the network, but guarantees that we can use solely PG and PP operators to generate a PAS[3]. The algorithm then iterates through all operators in the query network and replaces each operator that reads solely from streams in I (case 1) with its PG version, and all remaining operators on paths between streams in I and O are replaced with their PP versions. Finally, all non-instrumented operators reading from O are replaced by their PD version. This step is necessary to guarantee that non-instrumented operators are not reading from annotated streams.

A query network instrumented to compute a PAS $P(O, I)$ generates additional PAS as a side effect. Each PP operator in the modified network generates one or more PAS (one for each of its outputs) according to the subset of I its connected to. Thus, additional PAS are generated for free by our approach. We use $P(q)$ (called *provenance generating network* or PGN) to denote a network that generates the PAS for all output streams of network q according to all input streams of q. Such a network is generated using a straightforward extension of Algorithm 1 to sets of output streams.

EXAMPLE 3. *Two provenance generating versions of the example network are shown in Figure 6 (the operator parameters are omitted to simplify the representation). Figure 6(a) shows $P(q)$, i.e., the annotating version of q that generates the PAS $P(S_{out}, \{S_1, S_2\})$ for output stream S_{out} according to all input streams (S_1 and S_2). The left-most filter operators in the network are only attached to input streams and, thus, are replaced by their PG versions. All other operators in the network are replaced by PP operators. The query network shown in Figure 6(b) generates the PAS $P(8, \{5\})$ (An example execution was shown in Figure 5). The output stream of the right-most aggregation is annotated with provenance sets containing tuples of the b-sort operator's input stream. The right-most selection is replaced with its PD version to drop provenance*

---

[3] Adding operator types to the algebra that deal with a mix of annotated and non-annotated streams does not pose a significant challenge. However, for simplicity we refrain from using this approach.

(a) Tuple Layout

Tuple:
TS = P + H bytes

| TID | .... | | Field 1 | | Field n |

T bytes

Tuple Header: H bytes   Payload: P bytes

(b) Provenance Tuple Layout (First)

| #TIDS | TID_1 | TID_2 | .... | TID_{n-1} |

Tuple Header: T bytes   Provenance Payload: (P + H - T)/ T tuple identifiers

---

(c) Provenance Tuple Layout (Intermediate)

| TID_n | TID_{n+1} | TID_{n+2} | .... | TID_{2n-1} |

Provenance Payload: (P + H)/ T tuple identifiers

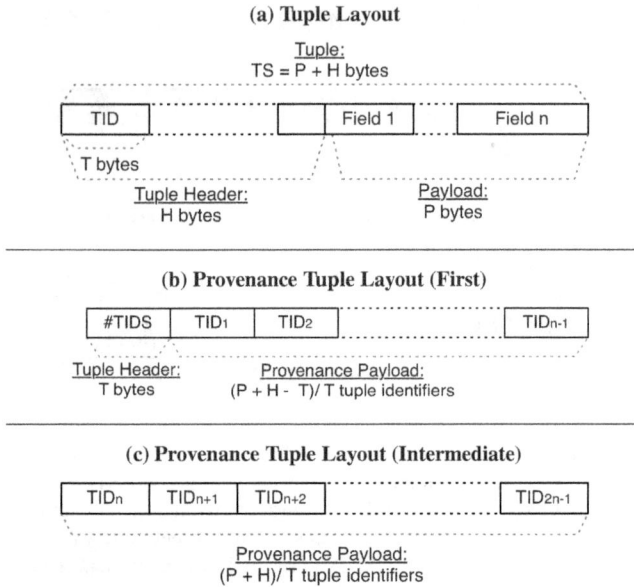

Figure 7: Physical Tuple Layout

annotations before applying the selection. This is necessary to produce the output stream S_{out} without annotations.

4. IMPLEMENTATION

In this section, we present the implementation of the *Ariadne* prototype. Given the overall architecture (outlined in Section 2) and the provenance propagation model (Section 3), three aspects are now of particular interest: (1) Representation of provenance annotations during the computation, (2) implementation of *PG* and *PP* operators, and (3) storing and retrieving the input tuples for *Reduced-Eager*.

4.1 Provenance Representation

The physical representation of provenance annotations and mechanism for passing them between operators is a crucial design decision, because it strongly influences the run-time overhead of provenance generation and how we implement annotating operators. Since these annotations consist of TID sets, they can be of variable size. However, Borealis uses fixed-length tuples that consist of a fixed length header storing information such as TID and arrival time, and a payload which stores the binary data of the tuple's attributes values. The schema of a stream, which is not stored in the stream tuples, is used to interpret the payload of tuples.

We considered three alternatives to pass these variable-size TID-Sets between annotating operators: (1) Modify the queuing mechanism to deal with variable-length tuples, (2) propagate TID-Sets through channels other than Borealis queues, or (3) split large TID-Sets into fixed-length chunks which are then streamed over standard queues. We chose the third approach, as it is least intrusive and retains the performance benefits of fixed-size tuples.

We serialize the provenance (TID-Set) for a tuple t into a list of tuples that are emitted directly after t. Each of these tuples stores multiple TIDs from the set. Figures 7(b) and 7(c) show the physical layout of such tuples. The first tuple (Figure 7(b) in the serialization of a TID-Set has a small header (same size as a TID) that stores the number of TIDs in the set. This header is used by downstream operators to determine how many provenance tuples have to be dequeued. Given that the size of a TID in Borealis is 8 bytes (actually *sizeof (signed long)*), we are saving at least an order of

magnitude of space (and tuples propagated) compared to using full tuples. We adapted the TID assignment policy to generate globally unique TIDs that are assigned as contiguous numbers according to the arrival order at the input streams. If stream-based tuple lookup becomes necessary, we could reserve several bits of a TID for storing the stream ID. This is a trivial extension of our approach and left for future work.

4.2 Provenance Annotating Operator Modes

We extend the existing Borealis operators with new operational modes to implement *PG*, *PP*, and *PD* operators. Operators in both PG- and PP-mode need to perform three steps: (1) retrieving existing provenance-related information from the input tuples, (2) compute the provenance, and (3) serialize provenance annotations along with data tuples. These steps have a lot of commonalities: Serialization (step 3) is the same for all operators. Retrieval (step 1) differs only slightly for *PG* and *PP* modes, but is again the same for all operators. When reading tuples from the input streams in *PG*-mode, the TID of each input tuple is extracted as provenance. In PP-mode we read the provenance sets attached by previous operations. For *PD* we simply discard the retrieved TID set. We factored out these commonalities into a so-called *provenance wrapper*. The provenance wrapper also implements additional common functionality such as buffering and merging of TID-Sets. Hooking into the *dequeue()* and *enqueue()* methods of Borealis, retrieval and serialization can be added trivially. Using the provenance wrapper, the operator-specific part of the provenance computation can thus be expressed with a small amount of code. For Selection, Projection, Union the provenance of a result tuple consists of the provenance of a single input tuple which can be directly determined. B-Sort and Join are slightly more complicated, requiring some lightweight bookkeeping to keep track of the contributing tuples. The most complicated case is aggregation, in particular with overlapping windows: each output tuple may depend on several input tuples, and each input tuple may contribute to several output tuples. This requires fairly elaborate state management, including merging and sharing TID sets. Nonetheless, the amount of code needed for aggregation was about 200 LOC, a fairly small change.

EXAMPLE 4. *Figure 8 shows the provenance computation for the annotating network from Figure 6(b). Recall that this network generates $P(q, 8, \{5\})$. Provenance headers are highlighted in brown and TIDs in a provenance tuple are highlighted in red. We use unrealistically small tuple sizes for presentation purposes. For instance, the aggregation operator uses the provenance wrapper to merge the TID-Sets from all tuples in a window and output them as the TID-Set for the result tuple produced for this window. For instance, the tuple 10:1 is generated from a window containing tuples 9:1 and 9:2. The merged TID-Set for these tuples ($\{7:4, 7:5\}$) is appended to the output tuple queue after tuple 10:1.*

4.3 Input Storage and Retrieval

As mentioned before, we apply a *Reduced-Eager* approach which requires preservation of input tuples at PG operators to be able to reconstruct fully-fledged provenance from TID-Sets for retrieval. We use a Borealis feature called Connection Point for input tuple storage and introduce the p-join operator for transforming TID-Sets into a queryable format.

Input Storage at PG operators: Connection points (CP), introduced by Ryvkina et al. [23] for revision processing in Borealis, provide temporary storage for tuples that pass though a queue. Besides other strategies, CPs support a time-out based strategy for removing old tuples from storage. We set this timeout according to the provenance retrieval pattern of the application, which typically

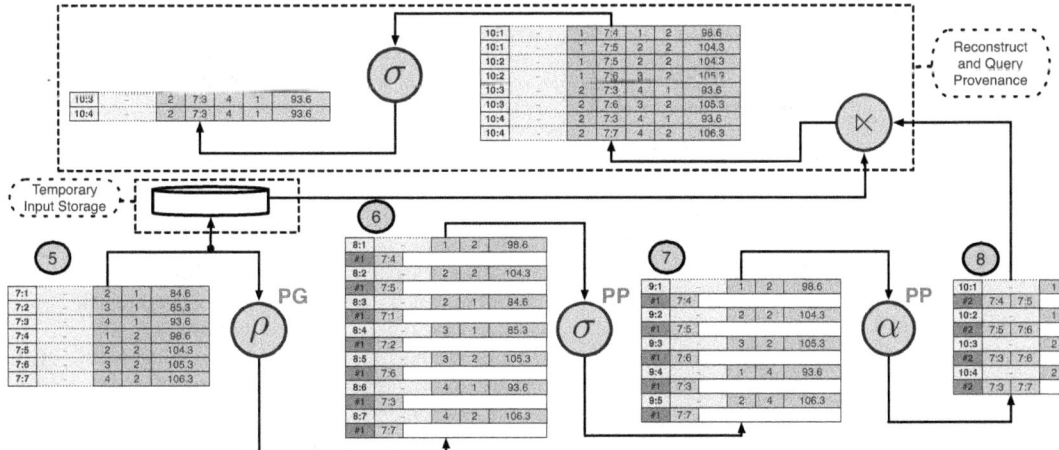

Figure 8: Provenance-enabled Query Network with Retrieval

span several seconds to minutes. Using the provenance itself for more directed expiration as well as utilizing write-optimized, possibly distributed storage technologies are interesting avenues for future work. If a query network q is instrumented to compute a PAS $P(O,I)$, then we add a connection point to each stream in I, i.e., the streams that are inputs of provenance generators.

P-join: Similar to the approach in [13], we have chosen to represent provenance to the consumer using the non-extended Borealis data model. For each result tuple t with a provenance annotation set P, we create as many duplicates of t as there are entries in P. One tuple from the provenance is attached to each of these duplicates. Thus, we effectively list the provenance as a sequence of regular tuples which enables the user to express complex queries over the relationship between data and its provenance using existing Borealis operators. This functionality is implemented as a new operator called p-join. A p-join $\bowtie (S,CP)$ joins an annotated stream S with a connection point CP and, thus, outputs tuples with tuples from their provenance. P-join uses a fast hash-based look-up from a CP (using the TID as the key) to determine the tuples to join with an input tuple instead of using a regular join with an input stream.

EXAMPLE 5. *The relevant part of the running example network with retrieval is shown in Figure 8. Recall that this network was instrumented to generate $P(q,8,\{5\})$. Hence, a CP (the cylinder) is used to preserve tuples from stream 5 for provenance retrieval. The PAS generated by the aggregation operator is used as the input for a p-join with the single CP in the network. The stream produced by the p-join can be shown to a user or be used as input for further processing. Assume the user expected the system to output less alarms and suspects that the threshold for overheating should be raised. To test this assumption she can investigate which alarms (output tuples) have temperature readings (input tuples) in their provenance that are slightly above the threshold (e.g., below 100 degree). This query can be implemented by applying a filter ($avg\_t < 100 \wedge count\_l > 1$) on the output of the p-join as shown in Figure 8.*

5. OPTIMIZATIONS

Reduced-Eager is a solid solution for provenance computation. However, certain challenges in stream processing call for additional optimizations: (1) Typical DSMS workloads rely heavily on windowed aggregation. Such workloads produce large amounts of provenance per result. (2) Stream processing systems treat data as transient and discard data as soon as possible to keep up with high

input data rates. Computing provenance on the fly to deal with the transient nature of streams increases run-time and latency. We address these challenges by developing compressed provenance representations (to reduce the overhead) as well as lazy provenance computation and retrieval techniques (to decouple query execution from provenance generation).

5.1 Provenance Compression

The methods we developed for TID-set compression range between generic data compression to methods which exploit data model and operator characteristics. We mainly target aggregation and focus on techniques that enable provenance computations at operators without having to decompress. Since each presented compression method has its sweet spot, we adaptively combine them.

Interval encoding: exploits the fact that the provenance of a window is the union of the provenance of the tuples in the window. These tuples form contiguous sub-sequences of the input sequence. This method encodes a TID-Set as a list of intervals spanning continuous sequences in the set. For example, consider the interval encoding (Figure 9(b)) for the example network shown in Figure 9(a). The provenance of tuple 3:1 is represented as a single interval [1,4], because the TID-Set forms a single contiguous sequence of TIDs (1 to 4). Interval encoding is most advantageous for queries involving aggregations over long sequences of contiguous TIDs, but introduces overhead if such sequences do not occur - both the start and end TID of an interval need to be stored.

Delta Encoding: Delta encoding utilizes the fact that windows with small slide values overlap to a large extent. Therefore, the TID-Set of a tuple may be encoded more efficiently by representing it as some delta to the TID-Set of one of its predecessors (by encoding which TIDs at the start of the previous set are left out and which TIDs are appended to the end). We repeatedly send a tuple with uncompressed provenance followed by several tuples with their provenance encoded as a delta to the last uncompressed provenance that was sent. While this "restart" approach has a higher space overhead than encoding a TID-Set as a delta to the last delta, we can restore a TID-Set from its delta representation in a single step without the need to apply a long chain of deltas to the last uncompressed provenance.

EXAMPLE 6. *Consider how delta encoding handles the example from Figure 9(b). The provenance header of a delta compressed tuple contains an additional field storing the amount of overlap (number of TIDs) between the delta and the last complete TID-Set that was sent. The TID-Set of the first output tuple of the aggrega-*

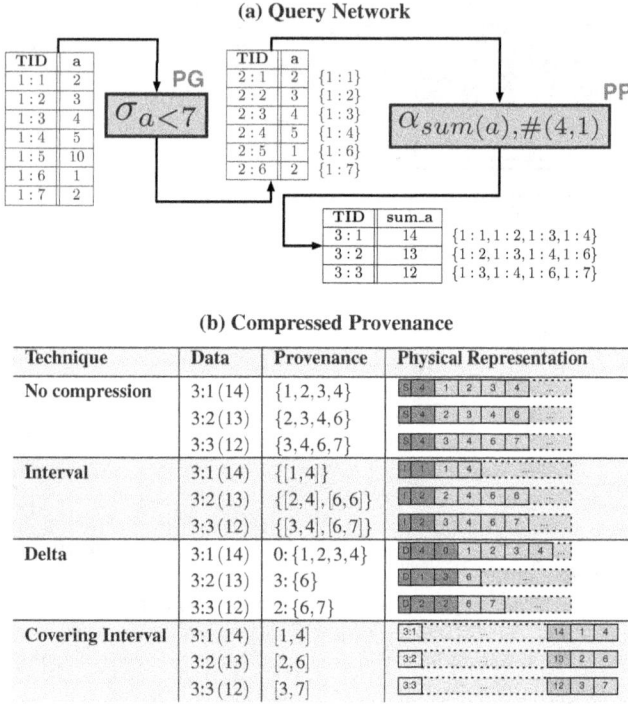

(a) Query Network

(b) Compressed Provenance

Technique	Data	Provenance	Physical Representation
No compression	3:1 (14)	{1,2,3,4}	
	3:2 (13)	{2,3,4,6}	
	3:3 (12)	{3,4,6,7}	
Interval	3:1 (14)	{[1,4]}	
	3:2 (13)	{[2,4],[6,6]}	
	3:3 (12)	{[3,4],[6,7]}	
Delta	3:1 (14)	0:{1,2,3,4}	
	3:2 (13)	3:{6}	
	3:3 (12)	2:{6,7}	
Covering Interval	3:1 (14)	[1,4]	
	3:2 (13)	[2,6]	
	3:3 (12)	[3,7]	

Figure 9: Compression Techniques Example

tion is sent completely. The TID-Set of tuple 3:2 (3:3) shares three (two) TIDs with last full TID-Set (tuple 3:1). The provenance of these tuples is encoded as deltas storing the overlap (3 respective 2) and the additional TIDs ({6} respective {6,7}).

For Delta encoding, we have to cache the last complete TID-Set that was sent and the number of deltas applied to it. Operators in PP-mode may have to reconstruct TID-Sets from the delta representation. For example, an aggregation in PP-mode needs to do so to merge the provenance for a window of tuples. In contrast, Projection can simply pass on delta compressed provenance. The same applies for selection except that selection may filter out a tuple with a complete TID-Set leaving the following deltas orphaned. We handle this situation by reconstructing the full TID-Set for the first orphaned tuple and adapting the following deltas.

Dictionary Compression: If the size of a TID-Set exceeds a threshold we can use dictionary compression techniques (we use LZ77) to compress it. This type of compression can reduce the cost of forwarding significantly for large TID-Sets at the cost of additional processing to compress and decompress TID-Sets.

Adaptive Combination of Compression Techniques: Our prototype combines the presented compression techniques using a set of heuristic rules that determine when to apply which type of compression. Generally speaking, we first choose whether to use intervals or a TID-Set, then apply delta-encoding on-top if the overlap between consecutive TID-Sets is high, and finally apply dictionary compression if the result size still exceeds a threshold.

5.2 Lazy Generation and Retrieval

We now introduce two optimizations that decouple query processing and provenance operations to save computation cost.

Replay-Lazy: The *Replay-Lazy* method introduced in Section 2.2 computes provenance by replaying parts of the input through a provenance generating network. *Replay-Lazy* can be advantageous for several reasons: (1) the cost of provenance generation is only paid if provenance is actually needed, (2) the overhead on regular query processing is minimal, enabling provenance for time-critical applications, and (3) provenance computation is mostly decoupled from query execution. Thus, provenance generation can be performed later or on different resources, e.g. a distributed system.

Replay-Lazy is only applicable to query networks consisting of deterministic and monotone operators. Furthermore there is one critical concept required to make replay feasible: With no additional information, the whole input of the query network (i.e., stream prefix up to this point) has to be replayed through a PGN until the output of interest is produced. This can be avoided if we can compute which parts have to replayed while executing the query. We can prove that for all monotone and deterministic operators, replaying all tuples from the interval spanned by the smallest and largest TID in the provenance of an output tuple (we refer to them as the *covering interval* of a TID-Set) is sufficient. The proof of this property requires induction over the structure of a query network. We sketch the base case here. Consider a consecutive subsequence S of an operator's output stream where the operator reads from the inputs of the network. We have to show that replaying all tuples in the covering interval of S produces S. For example, *Selection* and *projection* generate a single output from a single input tuple solely based on the values of this tuple. Thus, applying them on the covering interval for S will produce S. For *aggregation* we need to guarantee that we open and close windows at the same positions when replaying the covering interval. With regarding to opening, the semantics of Borealis windows yield a opening at the beginning of the stream. Since we take the original window opening as the start of the covering interval, we get exactly the same (first) window opening. For closing, the arguments are analogous. By inductively applying these arguments we can show that replaying the covering interval for a result is sufficient to reproduce this result.

Replay-Lazy in Ariadne is based on these observations. The network is instrumented in the same way as for *Reduced-Eager*, except that we annotate each tuple with its covering interval. Given that these intervals require constant storage space, we can piggyback them on data tuples instead of sending the possibly unbounded TID set in additional tuples. This significantly reduces the amount of data to be propagated, reducing the processing cost on the tuple queues. Furthermore, covering intervals can be generated very efficiently during operator execution. The most complex case is aggregation where we compute the covering interval for a result tuple as the minimum and maximum TID values in the covering intervals for the tuples in the window.

In order to access the tuples belonging to a covering interval, we introduce a new join operator: A c-join $\otimes(S, CP)$ between a stream S and a connection point CP processes each tuple t from S by fetching all tuples included in the covering interval of t from the connection point and emitting these tuples. These tuples are then fed into a copy of the query network that is instrumented for provenance generation. Since this computation does not handle covering intervals one-by-one, but in a streaming fashion, we will encounter some issues with overlapping covering intervals and gaps between covering intervals. The input to a window operator is not necessarily a consecutive subsequence of the input, but a concatenation of subsequences that may have overlap or gaps. Thus, the operator may produce different windows when run over a concatenation of covering intervals. We address this problem by (1) replaying the overlapping parts of covering intervals only once and (2) forcing operators to drop state if there is a gap between consecutive intervals. The c-join operator sends a control tuple after the last tuple from each covering interval. This control tuple instructs downstream operators to drop their internal state (e.g., open windows) and flush their buffers (b-sort).

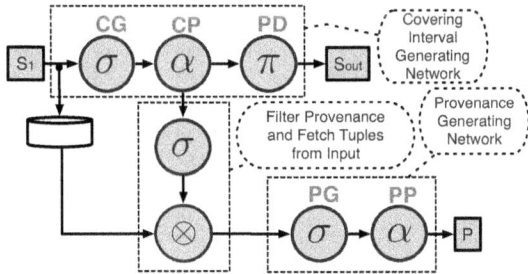

Figure 10: Example for a Replay-Lazy Network

EXAMPLE 7. *Consider the covering intervals shown in Figure 9(b). The TID-Set for tuple 3:1 is covered by the interval* [1,4]. *This covering interval is stored in two additional fields at the end of the data tuple 3:1. For this tuple the covering interval is the same as the interval encoding of the TID-Set. In general, this is obviously not the case. For example, the covering interval for tuple 3:2 contains TID 5 that is not in the provenance of 3:2. Figure 10 shows how to instrument the query network from Figure 9(a) for Replay-Lazy. The operators in the original part of the network are set to produce covering intervals (we refer to the covering interval version of PG and PP-mode as CG and CP-mode). The output of this part of the network is then routed through a selection to filter out parts of the provenance according to the user's preferences. Afterwards, we use a c-join to fetch all tuples with TIDs of the covering interval from the connection point and route these tuples through a provenance generating copy of the query network to produce provenance for tuples of interest.*

Lazy Retrieval: Our provenance generation approaches (both *reduced-eager* and *replay-lazy*) reduce the runtime cost of provenance generation by shifting computational cost to tuple reconstruction when retrieving provenance. If interactive retrieval is used, we only need to reconstruct provenance for tuples when explicitly requested. If the reconstruction result is further processed by a query network (queries over provenance information), we have the opportunity to avoid the cost of reconstruction through a p-join operator if we can determine that parts of the provenance are not needed to answer the retrieval part of the query. To this end we try to push selections that are applied during retrieval of provenance through the reconstruction (p-join) if the selection condition does not access attributes from the provenance, i.e., we use the following algebraic equivalence:[4] $\sigma_c(S \ltimes CP) \equiv \sigma_c(S) \ltimes CP$.

6. EXPERIMENTS

The goal of our experimental evaluation is to investigate the overhead of provenance management with *Ariadne*, compare with competing approaches (*Rewrite*), investigate the impact of varying the provenance generation and retrieval methods (eager vs lazy), and study the effectiveness of the optimizations proposed in Section 5.

Figure 11 shows the query network (called *Basic* network) used in most experiments in its original (a), rewritten (b) and instrumented (c) version. Details of the rewrite can be found in [15]. The Replay-Lazy version closely resembles Figure 10. This query covers the most critical operator for provenance management (aggregation) and is simple enough to study individual cost drivers. In experiments that focus on the cost of provenance generation, we leave out parts of these networks that implement retrieval (the dashed boxes).

---

[4]For conjunctive selection conditions, we can split the condition and push conjuncts that only reference attributes from *schema*(S) through the p-join.

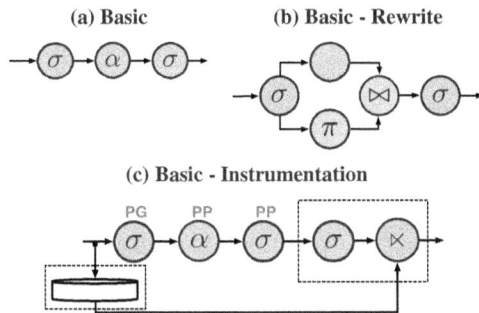

(a) Basic   (b) Basic - Rewrite

(c) Basic - Instrumentation

Figure 11: Experiment Queries

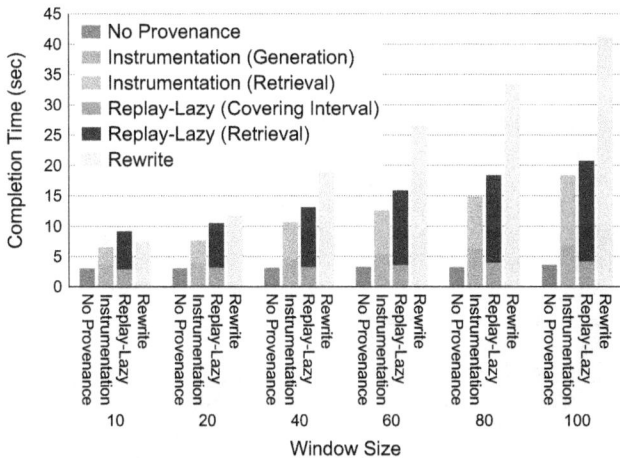

Figure 12: End to End - Varying Amount of Provenance

Setup and Methodology: Since the overhead of unused provenance code turned out to be negligible, we used *Ariadne* also for experiments without provenance generation. All experiments were run on a system with four Intel Xeon L5520 2.26 Ghz quad-core CPUs, 24GB RAM, running Ubuntu Linux 10.04 64 bit. Both the client (load generator) and the server are placed on the same machine. The input data consists of tuples with a small number of numeric columns (in total around 40 bytes), to make the overhead of provenance more visible. The values of these columns are uniformly distributed. All input data is generated beforehand. Each experiment was repeated 10 times to minimize the impact of random effects. We show the standard deviation where possible in the graphs. Our study focuses on the time overhead introduced by adding provenance management to continuous queries, as this is the most discriminative factor between competing approaches. We are interested in two cost measures: (1) **computational cost**, which we determine by sending a large input batch of 100K tuples over the network at maximum load and measuring the *Completion Time*; (2) **Tuple Latency** determined by running the network with sufficient available computational capacity.

6.1 Fundamental Tradeoffs

In the first set of experiments, we study the computational overhead of managing provenance (split into generation and retrieval) using the *Basic* query with *Maximum Load*. We show results for our *reduced-eager* and *replay-lazy* approaches without provenance compression (called *Single* from now on), and compare them with the cost of the network with *No Provenance* as well as *Rewrite*.

End to End Cost: The first experiment (shown in Figure 12) compares the end-to-end cost when *changing the amount of provenance*

47

Method		Number of Aggregations			
		1	**2**	**3**	**4**
No Provenance		3.1	3.9	4.8	5.7
Instr.	Generation	3.9	7.4	14.7	48.6
	Retrieval	3.0	12.9	103.0	2047.0
Replay-Lazy	Cov. Inter.	3.1	4.4	5.2	6.3
	Retrieval	5.2	14.7	91.1	2224.0
Rewrite		7.2	625.0	crash	crash

Figure 13: Varying Aggregations: Completion Time (Sec)

that is being produced per result tuple. This is achieved by changing the *window size* (WS) of the aggregation operator from 10 to 100 tuples (while keeping a constant *slide* SL = 1 and selectivity 25% for the first selection in the network). Provenance is retrieved for all result tuples. The results demonstrate that the general overhead of provenance management is moderate for all methods: an order of magnitude more provenance tuples than data tuples (WS=10) roughly doubles the cost, two orders of magnitude (WS=100) lead to an increase by a factor 5 (*Instrumentation*) to 12 (*Rewrite*). Analyzing the individual methods, we see that the cost of *Instrumentation* is strongly influenced by Retrieval: around 40% at WS=10, and around 65% at WS=100. This cost is roughly linear to the amount of provenance produced. The overhead of provenance generation through Instrumentation is between 20% (WS=10) and 113% (WS=100). Using *Replay-Lazy* the overhead on the original query network (generation of *covering intervals*) is further reduced to 3% (WS=10) and 16% (WS=100), respectively. The price to pay for this reduction is the additional cost of provenance *Replay*, where the cost is similar to the combination of *Instrumentation* Generation and Retrieval, as this method is now applied on all covering intervals to compute the actual provenance. Even for this benign workload, *Rewrite* shows much worse scaling than *Instrumentation* with full *Retrieval*: while roughly on par for WS=10, it requires twice as much time for WS=100.

Nested Aggregations: We now increase the number of aggregations to exponentially increase the amount of provenance per result tuple. We start off with the *Basic* network (WS=10 and SL=1) and gradually add more aggregation operators. The increase of cost for *Instrumentation* is (slightly) sublinear in the provenance size. Most of the overhead can be attributed to *retrieval*, while provenance generation increases moderately due to the TID-Set representation. The overhead of generating *Covering Intervals* for *Replay-Lazy* is around 10% over the baseline (*NoProvenance*), while the effort spent for replaying shows the same behavior as the total cost of *Instrumentation*. Finally, the results (Figure 13) indicate that *Rewrite* does not scale in the number of aggregations as demonstrated by an increase in overhead in comparison to *instrumentation* from 20% (one aggregation) to 3300% (two aggregations). At three aggregations, the execution exhausts the available memory.

6.2 Cost of Provenance Generation

We now focus on window-based aggregation, since it is not used in traditional, non-streaming workloads and produces large amounts of provenance. In addition to the methods shown before, we enable the adaptive compression technique (denoted as *Optimized*). Furthermore, we will no longer consider the *Rewrite* method (its drawbacks are obvious) and *Retrieval* cost (as it is linear with respect to the provenance size). We study the impact of *Window Size* (provenance amount per result), *Window Overlap* (commonality in provenance) and Prefilter *Selectivity* (TID contiguity). These experiments use the *Basic* network.

Window Size: Figure 14(a) shows *Completion Time* for varying WS from 50 to 2000. A front filter selectivity of 25% ensures that there are very few contiguous TID sequences, limiting the potential of *Interval Compression*. As expected, completion time is higher for larger window sizes, but compression mitigates this effect: While the completion time overhead for *Single* increases from 70% to 530%, compression reduces it to 50% and 140%, respectively. Covering Intervals further reduces it to 14% and 70%. The cost savings are even more pronounced for queue sizes and memory consumption, where the overhead is reduced to a small, almost constant factor. For space reasons we omit these graphs.

Window Slide: Reducing the overlap between windows (increasing SL from 1 to 100, WS=100) decreases the overall cost, since far fewer result tuples need to be generated (Figure 14(b)). The logarithmic decline can be explained by the fact that the low load makes the impact of provenance generation negligible for slides bigger than 10. Large slide values result in small overlap between open windows. Hence, they demonstrate the worst-case scenario for the adaptive compression, because maintaining the complex data structures of these techniques does not pay off anymore. Yet, compression performs only slightly worse than the Single approach.

TID Contiguity Besides the specific window parameters such as WS or SL, the performance for window-based aggregates is also influenced by upstream operators affecting the distribution of TID values. We investigate these factors by varying the selectivity of the first selection operator in the *Basic* network between 5% and 100% (Figure 14(c)). Without TID compression, the *Completion Time* is linear to selectivity, because the number of generated output tuples also grows linearly and generation is not affected by TID distribution. Interval compression used by *Optimized* becomes more efficient when increasing selectivity as more and more contiguous TID ranges are created. We therefore see no further increase in cost for selectivities over 75%.

6.3 Influence of Network Load on Latency

In reality, a query network is rarely run at maximum load. Thus, performance metrics such as *Latency* play an important role. We run the *Basic* network (*Generation* and *Retrieval*, WS=100, SL=1, S=25%) and vary the load by changing the size of the batches being sent from the client between 10 and 100 tuples while keeping the frequency of sending batches fixed. Smaller batches are avoided, because they result in very unpredictable performance. For sizes larger than 100 the slowest method (*Single*) would not be able to always process input instantly. As shown in Figure 15, provenance generation does indeed increase the latency, but this increase is very moderate and stays at the same ratio over an increasing load. *Single* results in about 75% additional latency, *Optimized* reduces this overhead to around 60%, while *Covering Intervals* is the cheapest with around 20% overhead.

6.4 Complex Query Networks

We now investigate whether our understanding of the cost of individual operators translates to real-life query networks using the complete running example introduced in Figure 1. We use this network (called **Complex**) to study how our approach translates to a more complex query network with multiple paths and a broad selection of operators. This query does not lend itself easily to straightforward optimizations (limited TID contiguity) and stresses intermediate operators with large amounts of provenance. We vary the amount of provenance created by the network by varying the window size for the aggregations applied before the union operator ("front" windows). As Figure 16 shows, the overhead of *Reduced-Eager* instrumentation without compression (*Single*) is higher than

(a) Window Size (SL = 1, S = 25%)   **(b) Window Slide (WS=100, S = 25%)**   **(c) TID Contiguity (WS=100, SL = 1)**

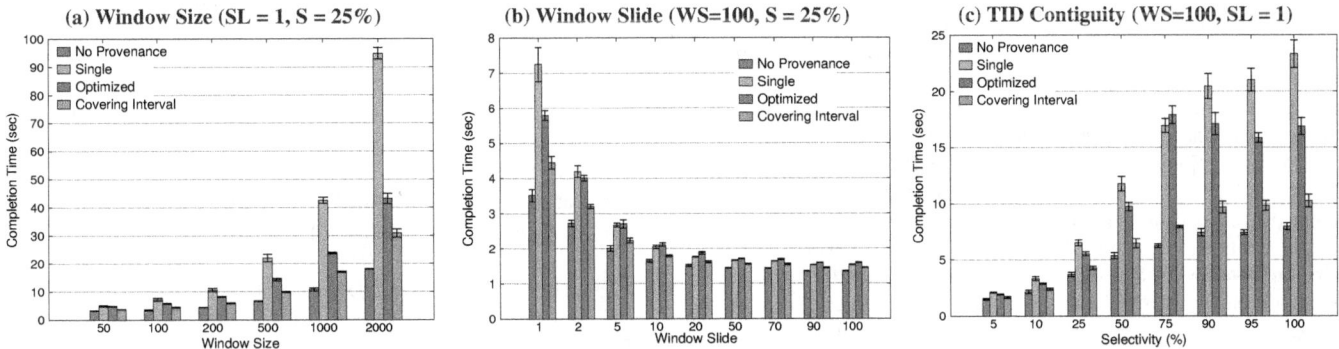

Figure 14: Impact on Completion Time

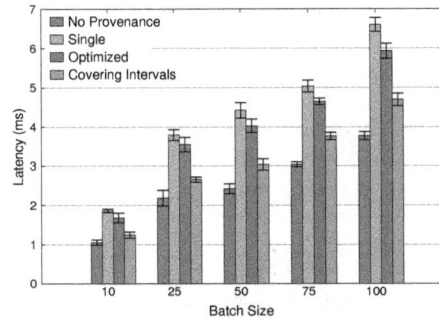

Figure 15: Latency For Varying Load

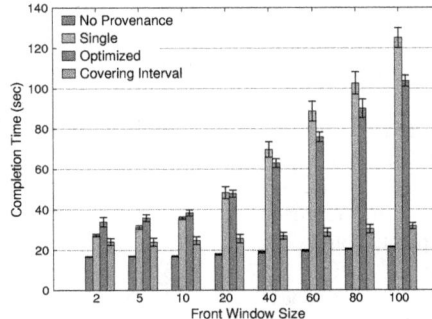

Figure 16: Complex Network

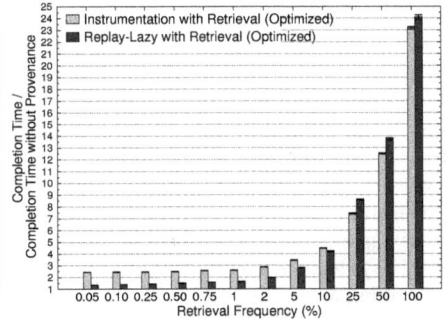

Figure 17: Varying Retrieval Frequency

in previous experiments. The *Optimized* method (adaptive compression) shows its benefits: while more expensive for very small WS values (100% overhead at WS=2), it becomes more effective for larger window sizes. *Covering Intervals* is again very effective with 40% overhead independent of the increase in provenance. Memory measurements support these observations, since the additional provenance does not increase the cost significantly when using compression or covering intervals.

6.5   Varying Retrieval Frequency

Many real-world scenarios do not need provenance for the entire result stream. We therefore study the effect of retrieval frequency (as a simple form of partial provenance retrieval) on the trade-off between *Reduced-Eager* and *Replay-Lazy*. Using the *Nested Aggregation* network with four aggregations (WS=10 and SL=3) and 2 million input tuples we vary the rate of retrieval from 0.05% to 100% (by inserting an additional selection before reconstruction). The results are shown in Figure 17 (overhead w.r.t. completion time of *No Provenance*). For low retrieval frequencies (less than 1%) the cost of retrieval is insignificant. *Reduced-Eager* generates provenance for all outputs and, thus, the overall cost is dominated by provenance generation. Computing covering intervals for *Replay-Lazy* results in a relative overhead of about 13% over the completion time for *No Provenance* (which is constant in the retrieval frequency). *Replay-Lazy* has to compute only few replay requests at low retrieval rates, but in turn pays a higher overhead for higher retrieval rates. *Replay-Lazy* is the better choice for the given workload if the retrieval frequency is 10% or less.

6.6   Summary

Our experiments demonstrate the feasibility of fine-grained end-to-end provenance in data stream systems and the benefits of our approach. *Operator Instrumentation* clearly outperforms *Rewrite*, since provenance generation is more efficient. Furthermore, Re-

duced-Eager allows us to separate generation and retrieval. Replay-Lazy based on covering intervals further reduces the overhead on the "normal" query network and enables us to scale-out. The optimizations for provenance compression are effective in both small-scale, synthetic as well as large-scale, real-life workloads.

7.   RELATED WORK

Our work is related to previous work on provenance management in workflow systems, databases, and stream processing systems.
Workflow Systems. Workflow provenance approaches that handle tasks as black-boxes where all outputs of a task are considered to depend on all of its inputs are not suitable for managing stream provenance [11]. More recently, finer-grained workflow provenance models have been proposed (e.g., allowing explicit declarations of data dependencies [6] or applying database provenance models to Pig Latin workflows [5]). These systems only support non-stream processing models. Furthermore, for stream provenance, data dependencies can be inferred from the well-defined operator semantics, without explicit declarations. Ariadne's compression techniques resemble efficient provenance storage and retrieval techniques in workflow systems (e.g., subsequence compression technique [6] or node factorization [9]). However, due to the transient and incremental nature of streaming settings, we use compression mainly for optimizing provenance generation. Furthermore, it is more critical for our techniques to be efficient in terms of memory usage and encoding/decoding overhead, since compression at an operator may also affect the load on its downstream operators (e.g., it may be necessary to decompress provenance).
Database Systems. There are several different notions of database provenance [10] supported by different systems (e.g., Trio [7], DB-Notes [8], Perm [13]). Like the *lineage provenance semantics* in relational databases [10], Ariadne represents the provenance of an output tuple as a set of input tuples that contributed to its gener-

ation. In principle, our Reduced-Eager operator instrumentation techniques can be extended to support more informative provenance models similar to database provenance models such as provenance polynomials [16] and graph-based models [2]. A major advantage of some of these models is that they are invariant under query equivalence. However, it is unclear what equivalences hold for streaming operators. Given the fundamental differences in the data and query models for streams, investigating whether these existing provenance models or minimization techniques [4, 21] can be adapted to stream provenance is promising future work.

Stream Processing Systems. There is only a handful of related work on managing stream provenance. Vijayakumar et al. have proposed coarse-grained provenance collection techniques for low-overhead scientific stream processing [25, 26]. Wang et al. have proposed a rule-based provenance model for sensor streams, where the rules have to be manually defined for each operation [20]. More recently, Huq et al. have proposed to achieve fine-grained stream provenance by augmenting coarse-grained provenance with time-stamp-based data versioning, focusing specifically on query result reproducibility at reduced provenance metadata storage cost [17] using provenance inference techniques [18]. In this work, provenance generation is based on inversion, as opposed to Ariadne's propagation-based approach. In contrast to *Ariadne*, the approach is only applicable to a small class of streaming operators and does not always guarantee correct provenance.

A common use case for stream provenance data is query debugging. Microsoft CEP server [3] exposes the state of the system through snapshots (containing runtime statistics) and streams of manageability events (e.g., query start, a query failure, stream overflow, etc.). This information can be used to track coarse-grained provenance. The visual debugger proposed in [12] supports fine-grained provenance computation based on identifier annotation and operator instrumentation. Our approach is more general in that we support multi-step provenance, can decouple provenance computation from regular query processing, and compress provenance. We expose provenance as regular stream data and, thus, queries over provenance can be expressed using standard streaming operators.

8. CONCLUSIONS

In this paper, we present *Ariadne*, a prototype system addressing the challenges of computing fine-grained provenance for data stream processing. *Reduced-Eager operator instrumentation* provides a novel method to compute provenance for an infinite stream of data that adds only a moderate amount of latency and computational cost and correctly handles non-deterministic operators. *Replay-Lazy* and *Lazy-Retrieval* provide additional optimizations to decouple provenance computation from stream processing, further reducing the impact on critical paths and saving cost when provenance is not needed. Query networks can also be partially instrumented, catering for use cases like stream debugging that do not always need end-to-end provenance. The effectiveness of our techniques is successfully validated in the experimental evaluation over various performance parameters and workloads.

Interesting avenues for future work include: (i) studying provenance retrieval patterns to exploit additional knowledge for storage decisions and in optimizing computations, (ii) investigating distributed architectures and integration of our system with scalable distributed storage, and (iii) extending our provenance semantics to model the inherent order of streams.

9. REFERENCES

[1] D. Abadi et al. The Design of the Borealis Stream Processing Engine. In *CIDR*, 2005.

[2] U. Acar et al. A Graph Model of Data and Workflow Provenance. In *USENIX TaPP Workshop*, 2010.

[3] M. H. Ali et al. Microsoft CEP Server and Online Behavioral Targeting (Demonstration). In *VLDB*, 2009.

[4] Y. Amsterdamer et al. On Provenance Minimization. In *PODS*, 2011.

[5] Y. Amsterdamer et al. Putting Lipstick on Pig: Enabling Database-style Workflow Provenance. *PVLDB*, 5(4), 2011.

[6] M. K. Anand et al. Efficient Provenance Storage over Nested Data Collections. In *EDBT*, 2009.

[7] O. Benjelloun et al. ULDBs: Databases with Uncertainty and Lineage. In *VLDB*, 2006.

[8] D. Bhagwat et al. An Annotation Management System for Relational Databases. *VLDB Journal*, 14(4), 2005.

[9] A. Chapman et al. Efficient Provenance Storage. In *SIGMOD*, 2008.

[10] J. Cheney et al. Provenance in Databases: Why, How, and Where. *Foundations and Trends in Databases*, 1(4), 2009.

[11] S. B. Davidson et al. Provenance in Scientific Workflow Systems. *IEEE Data Engineering Bulletin*, 32(4), 2007.

[12] W. De Pauw et al. Visual debugging for stream processing applications. In *Proceedings of the International Conference on Runtime Verification*, 2010.

[13] B. Glavic and G. Alonso. Perm: Processing Provenance and Data on the same Data Model through Query Rewriting. In *ICDE*, 2009.

[14] B. Glavic et al. The Case for Fine-Grained Stream Provenance. In *BTW DSEP Workshop*, 2011.

[15] B. Glavic et al. Ariadne: Managing fine-grained provenance on data streams. Technical Report 771, ETH Zurich, 2012. available at: http://cs.iit.edu/~glavic/publications.html.

[16] T. J. Green et al. Provenance Semirings. In *PODS*, 2007.

[17] M. Huq et al. Facilitating Fine-grained Data Provenance using Temporal Data Model. In *VLDB DMSN Workshop*, 2010.

[18] M. Huq et al. Adaptive Inference of Fine-grained Data Provenance to Achieve High Accuracy at Lower Storage Costs. In *e-Science*, 2011.

[19] Z. G. Ives et al. The ORCHESTRA Collaborative Data Sharing System. *ACM SIGMOD Record*, 37(2), 2008.

[20] A. Misra et al. Advances and Challenges for Scalable Provenance in Stream Processing Systems. In *IPAW Workshop*, 2008.

[21] D. Olteanu and J. Závodný. On Factorisation of Provenance Polynomials. In *USENIX TaPP Workshop*, 2011.

[22] F. Reiss and J. Hellerstein. Data Triage: An adaptive Architecture for Load Shedding in TelegraphCQ. In *ICDE*, 2005.

[23] E. Ryvkina et al. Revision Processing in a Stream Processing Engine: A High-Level Design. In *ICDE*, 2006.

[24] N. Tatbul et al. Load Shedding in a Data Stream Manager. In *VLDB*, 2003.

[25] N. Vijayakumar and B. Plale. Towards Low Overhead Provenance Tracking in Near Real-time Stream Filtering. In *IPAW Workshop*, 2006.

[26] N. Vijayakumar and B. Plale. Tracking Stream Provenance in Complex Event Processing Systems for Workflow-Driven Computing. In *VLDB EDA-PS Workshop*, 2007.

[27] A. Woodruff and M. Stonebraker. Supporting Fine-grained Data Lineage in a Database Visualization Environment. In *ICDE*, 1997.

Efficient Content-based Routing with Network Topology Inference

Muhammad Adnan Tariq, Boris Koldehofe, Kurt Rothermel
University of Stuttgart
{first name.last name}@ipvs.uni-stuttgart.de

ABSTRACT

Content-based publish/subscribe has gained high popularity for large-scale dissemination of dynamic content. Yet it is highly challenging to enable communication-efficient dissemination of content in such systems, especially in the absence of a broker infrastructure. This paper presents a novel approach that exploits the knowledge of event traffic, user subscriptions and topology of the underlying physical network to perform efficient routing in a publish/subscribe system. In particular, mechanisms are developed to discover the underlay topology among subscribers and publishers in a distributed manner. The information of the topology and the proximity between the subscribers to receive similar events is then used to construct a routing overlay with low communication cost. Our evaluations show that for internet-like topologies the proposed inference mechanisms are capable of modelling an underlay in an efficient and accurate manner. Furthermore, the approach yields a significant reduction in routing cost in comparison to the state of the art.

Categories and Subject Descriptors

C.2.1 [**Network Architecture and Design**]: Distributed networks; C.2.4 [**Distributed Systems**]: Distributed applications

Keywords

Content-based, Publish/Subscribe, P2P, Underlay, QoS

1. INTRODUCTION

Publish/Subscribe (pub/sub) is an important many-to-many communication paradigm for building large-scale distributed applications such as news distribution, service discovery, stock exchange, electronic auction, network monitoring, environmental monitoring and others. In a pub/sub system, messages are not given explicit destination addresses and are routed according to their content. This enables loose coupling between the producers (*publishers*) and consumers

(*subscribers*) of information. Publishers inject information into the system in the form of events without the knowledge of the relevant set of subscribers. Likewise, subscribers express their interest in certain events by issuing subscriptions without the need to know the set of publishers.

In a content-based pub/sub – which provides the most expressive way to specify events of interest, where subscriptions define restrictions on message content – an important concern is to route events from the publishers to the relevant subscribers with low delay and message overhead [25]. Traditionally, a dedicated network of brokers is used for the intermediate routing of events. However, recent systems use peer-to-peer (in short P2P) model, where subscribers and publishers arrange themselves in a broker-less overlay network and participate in forwarding events. The efficiency of event routing in a broker-less environment is very sensitive to the organization of subscriber and publisher peers in an overlay network. Typically, two approaches are used for organizing the peers in such systems. The first approach uses DHT-based overlays [29] to arrange peers. The content-based filtering is implemented as a separate layer on top of DHTs [13]. The efficiency of this approach is restricted as the overlay network is oblivious to the dynamics in the upper content-based layer [14].

The second approach on the other hand uses the information about the event traffic and user subscriptions to organize peers in semantic (or interest) communities [28, 32, 31], i.e., peers matching similar events are placed in close proximity in an overlay network. Such a semantic organization of peers reduces the pure forwarders, i.e., the peers which participate in forwarding an event without a matching subscription, and as a consequence results in a decrease of overall message overhead as well as an improvement in the average number of overlay hops to deliver events. However, the overlay-level mechanisms alone may not provide desired benefits without the knowledge of the underlying physical network topology (in short underlay). For instance, two apparently independent overlay paths may share common underlying physical links [18] and therefore, the selection of overlay paths solely based on the semantic similarities between the peers may lead to multiple copies of the same messages on the shared underlay links resulting in higher message overhead (bandwidth utilization) and higher end-to-end delays, as illustrated in the following simple example.

EXAMPLE 1. *Figure 1(a) shows a small scenario where five subscribers and a publisher are connected to different routers in an IP (Internet Protocol) network. The subscribers have non-identical but overlapping subscriptions to*

(b) Underlay oblivious tree with max degree 2

(c) Underlay aware tree with max degree 2

(a) Subscribers connected to underlay routers along with their subscriptions and number of received events

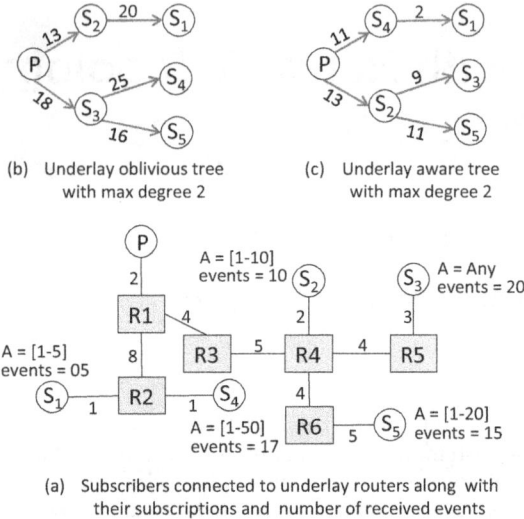

Figure 1: A simple example illustrating the benefits of underlay awareness.

a numeric attribute A and thus receive intersecting (or overlapping) sets of event messages. The overlay in Figure 1(b) organizes the subscribers according to the containment relationship between their subscriptions without the knowledge of the underlying network, similar to the work of Tariq et al. [30]. Clearly, no extra message overhead is incurred (to deliver the events received by each subscriber) at an overlay-level, each subscriber only receives the matching events and forwards a subset of those events to its child subscribers. However, the communication cost in terms of number of packets (or messages) travelled on each underlay link is high (i.e., 327 messages are forwarded in total) because overlay paths induce duplicate messages on common underlay links. Moreover, the delay penalty, i.e., delay in comparison to the unicast delay from the publisher, for individual subscribers is very high, e.g., s_4 experience 3.9 times more delay. In contrast, the overlay in Figure 1(c) takes into account both the underlay topology and the containment relationships between the subscriptions for its organization. Here, the subscriber s_2 has to receive and forward additional events to satisfy the subscriptions of s_3 and s_5 resulting in an overhead of 10 overlay-level messages. However, the delay penalty of subscribers is reduced to at most 1.2 and the communication cost is lowered to 246 underlay messages, which clearly shows that the semantic arrangement alone is not always beneficial in reducing message overhead and delay.

In this paper, we present a novel scheme that exploits the knowledge of event traffic, user subscriptions, and the router-level topology of the underlying network to construct an efficient routing overlay, which minimizes the overall cost of disseminating events in a content-based pub/sub system. Our main contributions can be summarized as follows. First, we develop methods to discover the underlay topology among the peers participating in a pub/sub system. The proposed methods incur low overhead and maintain the topology information in a distributed manner by constructing a *Topology Discovery Overlay* (in short TDO) (cf. Section 4). Second, we propose different strategies to construct a cost efficient pub/sub routing overlay on a TDO, taking into account

the underlay topology as well as the event traffic matched between the subscriber peers (cf. Section 5). Finally, through extensive evaluations, we show that the proposed approach performs well on Internet-like topologies, by leading to substantially low routing cost in terms of message overhead and end-to-end delays (cf. Section 6).

2. SYSTEM MODEL AND PROBLEM FORMULATION

We consider a content-based pub/sub system consisting of a set of N distinct peers. The peers have unique identifiers and are connected to the underlying (IP) network at different points through access links. The underlay is modelled as an undirected graph $G^U = (\mathcal{V}^U, \mathcal{E}^U)$, where $\mathcal{V}^U = (\mathcal{R} \cup \mathcal{P})$ represents the set of routers $\mathcal{R}$ and peers $\mathcal{P}$, and $\mathcal{E}^U \subseteq (\mathcal{P} \times \mathcal{R}) \cup (\mathcal{R} \times \mathcal{R}) \cup (\mathcal{R} \times \mathcal{P})$ represents the set of physical links. Each link $\varepsilon_{i,j}^u = (i,j) \in \mathcal{E}^U$ from $i \in \mathcal{V}^U$ to $j \in \mathcal{V}^U$ is associated with a delay value $d^U(\varepsilon_{i,j}^u)$.

The overlay network is the virtual topology induced by the peers on the underlay. It can be modelled as a graph $G^O = (\mathcal{P}, \mathcal{E}^O)$, where $\mathcal{E}^O \subseteq \mathcal{P} \times \mathcal{P}$ is the set of overlay links. An overlay link is the point-to-point connection between two peers p and q, it is mapped to an *underlay route* consisting of a sequence of physical routers $r_i \in \mathcal{R}$ and physical links determined by IP routing, i.e., $\langle p, q \rangle = \{(p, r_i), (r_i, r_j)....(r_m, q)\}$. The delay of an overlay link $\langle p, q \rangle$ corresponds to the unicast path delay from peer p to q, i.e., $d^O(p,q) = \sum_{\varepsilon^u \in \langle p,q \rangle} d^U(\varepsilon^u)$. Note that the IP network routing is usually asymmetric [18] and therefore, the underlay route from a peer p to another peer q (i.e., $\langle p, q \rangle$) may not be the reverse of the route followed by $\langle q, p \rangle$. The methods developed in this paper, work with asymmetry by treating $\langle p, q \rangle$ and $\langle q, p \rangle$ as two separate overlay links. However, for the ease of presentation, we assume that the underlay routes are symmetric and $d^O(p,q) = d^O(q,p)$. A prefix relation can be defined between peers w.r.t. the overlay links from a common ancestor peer. Let $\langle p, q \rangle = \{(p, r_{q,1}), (r_{q,1}, r_{q,2}), ..., (r_{q,j}, q)\}$ and $\langle p, s \rangle = \{(p, r_{s,1}), (r_{s,1}, r_{s,2}), ..., (r_{s,j+1}, s)\}$ represent overlay links of p with q and s respectively. Then $\langle p, q \rangle$ is said to be a prefix of $\langle p, s \rangle$ w.r.t. p, denoted by $q \leadsto^p s$, iff $r_{q,i} = r_{s,i}, \forall i \in \{1, ..., j\}$ holds. Moreover, the neighbourhood of a peer p in the overlay network is defined as the set of peers to which this peer has direct point-to-point connections (overlay links) and is denoted by $NG(p)$.

Peers act as publishers and/or subscribers, and run a content-based pub/sub protocol to exchange events. The pub/sub overlay is maintained as a spanning tree T of G^O, i.e., $T = (\mathcal{P}, \mathcal{E}_T^O)$, where $\mathcal{E}_T^O \subseteq \mathcal{E}^O$. In the following, we will refer to T as pub/sub overlay or tree. A *path* in T connects a peer p to another peer q over intermediate peers and is defined by a set of overlay (tree) links, i.e., $path(p,q) = \{\langle p, p_i \rangle, \langle p_i, p_j \rangle, ..., \langle p_m, q \rangle\}$. Furthermore, each path is associated with a delay value $D(p,q) = \sum_{\langle i,j \rangle \in path(p,q)} d^O(i,j)$. The dissemination of an event over T induces *routing cost* in terms of delay and message overhead. The routing cost is influenced by three factors, i) rate of false positives, ii) stress on physical links, and iii) relative delay penalty.

False positives measure the excess bandwidth consumption (in terms of extra messages) induced by the pub/sub tree T during the dissemination of events. They are defined as the rate of events that peers receive and forward with-

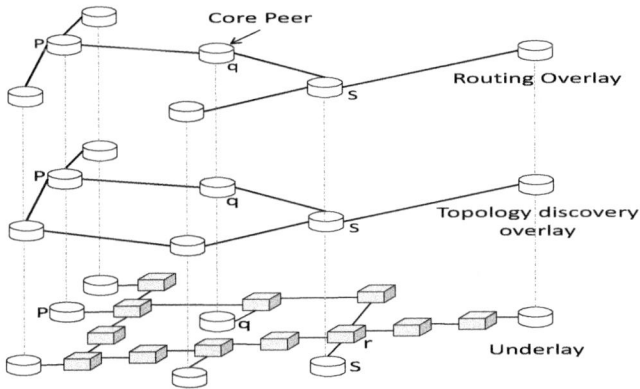

Figure 2: Decomposition into different layers.

out a matching subscription. Let E_ξ be the set of last ψ events published in the system. Each event $e \in E_\xi$ published by a peer p_e is delivered to a set of matching (subscriber) peers S_e by traversing only those links in T that lie on the paths between p_e and S_e. The *routing load* of a link $\langle i, j \rangle \in \mathcal{E}_T^O$, denoted by $\Upsilon(i, j)$, is defined as the number of overlay paths that pass through the link for the dissemination of all the events in E_ξ, i.e., $\Upsilon(i, j) = \sum_{e \in E_\xi} |\{q \in S_e : \langle i, j \rangle \in path(p_e, q)\}|$. Ideally to avoid false positives, the routing load on each link should be induced by the dissemination of only those events that are matched by the subscriptions of both of its adjacent peers.

The *Stress* of a physical link (i, j) is defined as the number of identical copies of a message sent over that link. Similar to false positives, stress measures the excess bandwidth usage and is influenced by the organization (topology) of peers in the pub/sub tree T. Ideally, a message should traverse each physical link at most once.

Relative delay penalty (in short RDP) measures the additional delay introduced by the pub/sub tree T on the delivery of an event from a publisher to all relevant subscribers. It is defined as the ratio of the delay experienced when sending events using the overlay to the delay experienced when sending events using the direct unicast path in the underlay [15]. The RDP value of 1.0 means that the delay at the overlay and the underlay is exactly same.

Given a dynamic set of (subscriber and/or publisher) peers $\mathcal{P}$ and continuously evolving event traffic E_ξ, our objective is to maintain a pub/sub tree T such that

1. the stress induced by the pub/sub tree on the links in the underlay is minimized, and

2. the cost for disseminating events is minimized in terms of false positives and delay, i.e., $\text{cost}(T, \mathcal{P}) = \min \sum_{\langle p, q \rangle \in \mathcal{E}_T^O} \Upsilon(p, q) \, d^O(p, q)$.

3. APPROACH OVERVIEW

Meeting the objectives presented in Section 2 amounts to finding a good trade-off between three contradicting goals: i) to lower the relative delay penalty (RDP), ii) to reduce the rate of false positives, and iii) to minimize stress on underlay links. For instance, lowering RDP may increase stress on some links in the underlay. Consider a mesh overlay where all the peers have point-to-point connections (overlay links) with each other. In this case, RDP between all pairs of peers

is 1.0, however, the stress on the physical links close to the peers is very high [15]. Similarly, organizing subscribers (according to the similarity of their received events) to avoid false positives conflicts with the other two goals (cf. Example 1).

We therefore propose to solve the problem by decomposing it into two layers, the topology discovery layer and the routing layer, as shown in Figure 2. The topology discovery layer focuses on minimizing RDP and link stress without taking into account the subscriptions of peers and the event traffic matched by them. This layer maintains a topology discovery overlay network (TDO), which connects all the participants of a pub/sub system. In general, TDO can use any overlay link from $\mathcal{E}^O = \mathcal{P} \times \mathcal{P}$. However, to lower the delay penalty and limit the duplicate packets on the underlay, only those overlay links are selected, which minimize the overlaps between the mapped underlay routes, i.e., minimize sharing of underlay links or in other words connect peers according to their location in the underlay topology (G^U). Figure 2 shows that the peers are arranged in TDO such that the underlay routes mapped by the corresponding overlay links have minimum overlap. For instance, $q \rightsquigarrow^p s$ and therefore $path(p, s)$ (overlay path from p to s) in TDO passes through q. Connecting subscribers according to the underlay topology may induce higher stress on the last mile links e.g., (s, r) has a stress of 3 in Figure 2. To alleviate this problem, peers actively monitor the bandwidth of their last mile links and impose limits on their degrees (neighbours in TDO).

In general, organizing peers in TDO according to the underlay topology requires tools (or techniques) to infer the underlay route among all pairs of peers in the system. A number of underlay route inference tools and techniques are discussed in Section 4.3. However, these tools are expensive in terms of time and control traffic. Therefore, the topology discovery layer employs methods to limit the underlay route inferences between the peers without much degradation in the quality of TDO in terms of minimizing stress and RDP.

The routing layer runs on top of the TDO and maintains a spanning tree to distribute events (using a subset of overlay links from the TDO), as shown in Figure 2. To reduce the cost of event routing, the selection of links from the TDO is based on end-to-end delays between the peers as well as event traffic consumed or produced by them. In particular, a core-based approach is employed, whereby a small set of peers that experience higher routing load and have low delay paths (in the TDO) act as *cores*. The remaining non-core peers connect to their closest cores by using the lowest cost paths (in terms of dissimilarity of received events and end-to-end delays) in the TDO. The cost of event routing is sensitive to the selection of cores and therefore, various core selection strategies with different performance benefits are developed with complexity ranging from the use of global knowledge to only local neighbourhood-based voting mechanisms.

In the subsequent sections, we first describe the construction of TDO (cf. Section 4) and afterwards present the maintenance of a cost efficient pub/sub routing tree on the TDO (cf. Section 5).

4. TOPOLOGY DISCOVERY OVERLAY

In this section, we tackle the problem of constructing a topology discovery overlay (TDO) with low stress and RDP. In particular, we will describe two approaches to maintain the TDO in a dynamic manner, the landmark approach and the random walk approach. The landmark approach extends the work of Kwon et al. [24] on underlay-aware single source multicast to support multiple sources in a scalable manner, whereas the random walk approach is more sophisticated, it overcomes the limitations of the landmark approach and addresses the trade-off between stress and RDP.

4.1 Landmark Approach

The landmark approach is inspired from the work of Kwon et al. [24], which addresses underlay-aware overlay creation with respect to only a single source. However, in a pub/sub system, every peer can be a publisher and a subscriber at the same time, and hence the TDO should reflect (discover) the underlay topology w.r.t. all the peers participating in the system. For this reason, the direct use of the approach of Kwon et al. [24] is not suitable and would result in an overhead of $O(N^2)$ underlay route inferences, i.e., detection of router-level underlay path between all pairs of peers.

It is a known fact that the router-level network forms a sparse graph [9] and therefore, underlay route inference between all pairs of peers is not necessary to construct a TDO that reflects a highly accurate underlay topology among publishers and subscribers [18]. For this reason, the landmark approach selects a small set of $k_{\mathcal{L}}$ peers as pivots (or landmarks), i.e., $k_{\mathcal{L}} \ll N$, and the underlay topology between the peers is discovered only with respect to the selected landmarks.

The set of landmarks is fixed and globally known to all peers in the system. Moreover, landmarks in the set are selected uniformly and independently from each other. Each peer individually picks a random number ρ in $[0, 1]$ and decides to become landmark if $\rho < \frac{k_{\mathcal{L}}}{N}$. To estimate the total number of peers N in a distributed and scalable manner, a gossip-based aggregation algorithm [16] is used. The same algorithm serves the purpose of distributing the set of landmarks among other peers.

The TDO is maintained as a virtual forest of $k_{\mathcal{L}}$ logical trees, where each tree is associated with a landmark. Each landmark acts as the root of its associated tree while all other peers (including other landmarks) join the tree.

4.1.1 Joining a Landmark Tree

In order to connect to a tree associated with a landmark s_k, a newly arriving peer s_n sends a connection request to the root of the tree (i.e., s_k). On receiving the request, the root s_k discovers the underlay route mapped by the overlay link $\langle s_k, s_n \rangle$ by using one of the underlay route inference techniques described later in Section 4.3. Once the underlay route for $\langle s_k, s_n \rangle$ is discovered, the peer s_n is placed in the tree such that the newly discovered underlay route has minimum overlap with the underlay routes of other members of the tree. This is accomplished by comparing the underlay route of $\langle s_k, s_n \rangle$ with the routes of other neighbours (child peers) at each level of the tree and performing one of the following three mutual exclusive actions [24] until the desired parent is reached.

Let s_t be the current peer in the tree which is processing the connection request from s_n. The algorithm deals with three possible cases as follows:

- *Case 1:* $\exists p \in NG(s_t) : p \leadsto^{s_k} s_n$

  In this case, the connection request is forwarded to the

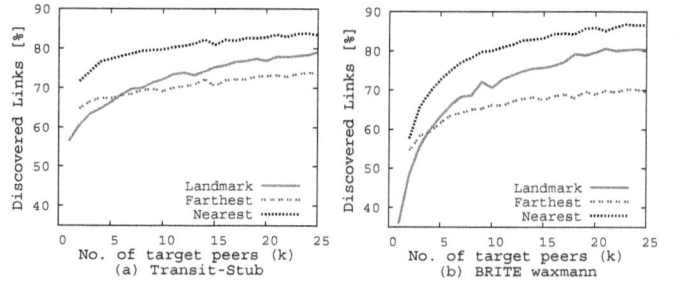

Figure 3: Selection of target peers vs. accuracy of discovered topology.

peer p as it shares a part of the underlay route from s_k to s_n and hence is a more appropriate parent (for s_n) than s_t. For instance, if $\langle s_k, p \rangle = \{(s_k, r_i), (r_i, r_j), (r_j, p)\}$ and $\langle s_k, s_n \rangle = \{(s_k, r_i), (r_i, r_j), (r_j, r_o), (r_o, s_n)\}$, then placing s_n as a child of p in the tree reduces overlapping among the underlay links.

- *Case 2:* $\exists p \in NG(s_t) : s_n \leadsto^{s_k} p$

  In this case, the underlay route of s_n is a prefix of the route mapped by $\langle s_k, p \rangle$ and hence, s_n should become a child of s_t and adopt p as its own child.

- *Case 3:* Neither Case 1 nor Case 2 evaluates to true.

  If no prefix relationship can exist between the underlay routes of s_n and the neighbours of s_t, then s_n joins s_t as a child.

4.2 Random Walk Approach

The TDO maintained by the landmark approach reflects the underlay topology among the participating peers with reasonable accuracy (cf. Figure 3). However, there are some drawbacks associated with the landmark approach. First, the stress induced by the TDO on the underlay links close to the landmark peers is high. Second, the landmark approach is not very resilient against churn and the failure of an existing landmark requires all the peers to join a new landmark tree.

The above drawbacks can be avoided, if the landmarks are not fixed. Each peer is allowed to infer underlay routes to $k_{\mathcal{L}}$ different peers (termed as *target peers*) and use the inferred routes to find a suitable position (to connect) in the TDO. An important consideration in this regard is how each peer selects its target peers? Clearly, the selection of target peers affects the discovery of the underlay topology (among the peers participating in the TDO) and thereby influences the stress and RDP. Figures 3(a) and (b) show the impact of the selection of target peers on the accuracy of discovered underlay topology. The figures depict the percentage of the discovered underlay links on GT-ITM Transit-Stub [34] and BRITE Multi-level [26] topologies, for two target peer selection criteria and the landmark approach. The nearest and the farthest criteria make use of round trip delays for the selection of target peers. The figures show that selecting $k_{\mathcal{L}}$ peers with the lowest delays as targets consistently performs better than the landmark approach. The farthest target selection criterion on the other hand performs worst because the peers with high delays are usually in different

Algorithm 1 Random walk approach

1: **upon event** Receive(RANDWALK, p, $D(p,q)$, $k_{\mathcal{L}}$, TTL) at peer q **do**
2:     TTL = TTL -1
3:     selectionCriteria()
4:     **if** $|NG(q)| > \ell(q)$ **then**
5:         peerToRemove = $\{s_1 : \forall a \in NG(q)\ \ d^O(q,s_1) > d^O(q,a)\}$
6:         **trigger** Send(DISCONNECT, peerToRemove)
7:     **if** $k_{\mathcal{L}} > 0 \wedge \text{TTL} > 0$ **then**
8:         peers[] = randomlySelectNeighbours $(NG(q)$, $\sigma \times |NG(q)|)$
9:         **for all** $t \in$ peers **do**
10:            delay= $D(p,q) + d^O(q,t) - 2\times$ last mile delay of q
11:            **trigger** Send(RANDWALK, t, delay, $\lfloor \frac{k_{\mathcal{L}}}{\lceil peers \rceil} \rfloor$)

12:   **procedure** selectionCriteria **do**
13:     **switch** (heuristic) **do**
14:       **case** DWorst:
15:         delay = $\{d^O(q,s_2) : \forall a \in NG(q)\ \ d^O(q,s_2) > d^O(q,a)\}$
16:       **case** DBest:
17:         delay = $\{d^O(q,s_1) : \forall a \in NG(q)\ \ d^O(q,s_1) < d^O(q,a)\}$
18:       **case** MLink:
19:         delay = $D(p,q)$ // Obtained in the RANDWALK message
20:     **if** $d^O(q,p) <$ delay **then**
21:       $k_{\mathcal{L}} = k_{\mathcal{L}} - 1$
22:       Infer underlay route $\langle q,p \rangle$ using tools from Section 4.3.
23:       **if** $\exists s_1 \in NG(q) : s_1 \rightsquigarrow^q p$ **then** // Case 1
24:         **trigger** Send(CONNECT, s_1, p, $\langle q,p \rangle$)
25:       **else if** $\exists s_1 \in NG(q) : p \rightsquigarrow^q s_1$ **then** // Case 2: Swap s_1 and p
26:         $NG(q) = \{NG(q) \setminus s_1\} \cup p$
27:         **trigger** Send(NEWPARENT, s_1, p)
28:         **trigger** Send(DISCONNECT, s_1)
29:       **else** // Case 3
30:         $NG(q) = NG(q) \cup p$
31:     **if** $p \in NG(q)$ **then**
32:       **trigger** Send(ACK, p)

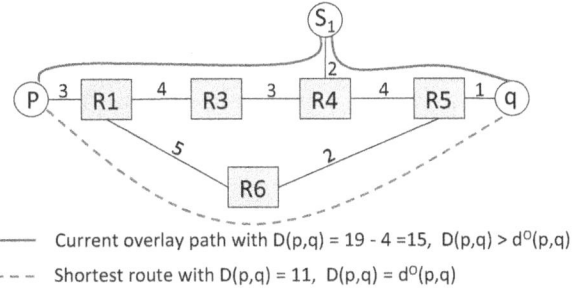

——— Current overlay path with D(p,q) = 19 - 4 =15, D(p,q) > d^O(p,q)
- - - - Shortest route with D(p,q) = 11, D(p,q) = d^O(p,q)

Figure 4: MLink heuristic.

to infer the underlay route to p (cf. Algorithm 1, *lines 13 - 19*):

- *DWorst Heuristic:* This heuristic selects q as a target if the unicast path delay from q to p (i.e., $d^O(q,p)$) is lower than the delay $d^O(q,a)$ to any existing neighbour a of q.

- *DBest Heuristic:* This heuristic is more restrictive than DWorst and selects q as a target only if $d^O(q,p)$ improves on the existing neighbour of q with the lowest delay.

- *MLink Heuristic:* This heuristic selects q as a target, if some underlay links between p and q with lower delays are not discovered yet, i.e., not mapped by the overlay paths in the TDO. The peers are arranged in the TDO according to the prefix relation between their underlay routes and therefore, existence of undiscovered underlay links between p and q can be checked by comparing the delay on the $path(p,q)$ in the TDO (excluding the last mile delays of the intermediate peers) and the unicast delay $d^O(q,p)$, as shown in Figure 4. A smaller unicast delay $d^O(q,p)$ predicts the existence of undiscovered underlay links, which if included in the TDO lead to smaller delay on the $path(q,p)$.

In case peer q is selected as a target, it infers the underlay route of $\langle q,p \rangle$ using tools described in Section 4.3, compares it with the routes to other neighbours, and follows one of the three mutually exclusive cases mentioned in Section 4.1.1 (cf. Algorithm 1, *lines 22 - 30*). Following case 2 or 3 results in the acceptance of peer p as a neighbour of q. However, accepting peer p as a neighbour may violate the degree constraints (i.e., $\ell(q)$) imposed by peer q (to avoid bandwidth bottleneck on the last mile link) and therefore, an existing neighbour with the highest delay may be selected for disconnection (cf. Algorithm 1, *lines 4 - 6*).[2] Finally, the random walk message is forwarded to $\sigma \times |NG(q)|$ randomly selected neighbours along with the number of remaining targets to be selected. (cf. Algorithm 1, *lines 7 - 11*).

4.3 Techniques for Underlay Route Inference

Until now, we assume the availability of some tool to infer the underlay route between the peers. In this section, we give an overview of different techniques and tools which can be used for this purpose.

In general, the techniques to infer the underlay route (or topology) between a pair (or group) of peers mainly fall in

Autonomous systems (AS). Inferring underlay routes between the peers in different AS discover the same backbone links repeatedly and consequently, the TDO may results in higher stress on the underlay links as well as an increase in RDP [19]. The links within a single AS are more diverse and therefore, peers with low delays should be preferred as targets.[1]

The evaluations shown in Figures 3(a) and (b) use global knowledge to select the peers with lowest delays. However, finding $k_{\mathcal{L}}$ nearest peers of a particular peer accurately in a distributed system is very expensive [5]. For this reason, our distributed approach does not focus on finding $k_{\mathcal{L}}$ nearest peers, but rather proposes three simple heuristics to select the target peers using random walk on the TDO.

A newly arriving peer p joins the TDO by sending the connection request to any existing peer. The connection request follows the protocol mentioned in Section 4.1.1 to find an appropriate place (neighbours in the TDO) for the new peer. Once joined, the peer p initiates a random walk (RANDWALK message) on the TDO. The number of peers visited by the random walk is controlled by the Time-to-Live (TTL) value and the neighbourhood selectivity factor (σ). The TTL value determines the number of forwarding hops, while the selectivity factor ($0 < \sigma \leq 1$) specifies the percentage of the neighbours to be included in the random walk at each forwarding hop.

Upon the reception of a random walk (RANDWALK) message from a peer p, the peer q employs one of the following three heuristics to determine its feasibility as a target

---

[1]Similar conclusions are drawn by the work of Jin et al. [19].

[2]To avoid partitions in the TDO, each peer additionally maintains a small set of overlay links to distant peers.

two categories [35]: tomography-based and router-assisted. The tomography-based techniques only discover the logical topology between the peers, induce high computation and communication overhead, and have limited accuracy due to certain assumptions about the statistical properties of the underlying network [35, 18]. We therefore propose to use router-assisted techniques. These techniques take advantage of the router's response to the Internet Control Message Protocol (ICMP) based probe messages to infer the underlay route between the pair of peers. In particular, a peer can find the underlay route to other peers using tools, such as *traceroute, tracepath, tcptraceroute* etc. These tools have been extensively used for underlay topology discovery [24, 6]. Recently, many new tools are proposed to overcome the limitations (e.g., due to load balancing in ISPs [23] or Multi-protocol Label Switching – MPLS) and increase the efficiency (especially the probe redundancy) of the standard tools [7]. A problem with router-assisted techniques is that roughly 1/3 of routers (termed as *anonymous routers*) do not respond to ICMP messages [24, 35, 18]. These anonymous routers appear distinct in different underlay routes and therefore, inflate the discovered underlay topology [18]. Several merging techniques [18, 12] are proposed to detect and collapse the anonymous occurrences of the same router. All these techniques are orthogonal to our work in this paper and can be integrated. Moreover, a reasonable percentage of routers respond to ICMP messages [24, 35, 18] and thereby the inferred underlay routes (with distortions induced by anonymous routers) can still suffice to arrange peers in the TDO minimizing RDP and stress.

Another possibility is to rely on the data available from the internet topology discovery projects [10]. Topology servers such as OSPF [11] can also be used to obtain ISP level (intra-domain) underlay routes by using simple network management protocol (SNMP). Moreover, as pointed out by Kwon et al. [24], the periodic logs of router configuration can be employed. However, underlay route information obtained from these techniques may not be very accurate due to dynamic nature of the internet [35].

5. EVENT ROUTING

Until now, we have described the maintenance of the topology discovery layer. In this section, we address the problem of constructing a cost efficient routing tree T on a TDO, additionally taking into account the end-to-end delay and the event traffic matched between the subscriber peers.

The basic idea of our approach is to reduce the distance (delay) between the peers that consume or produce similar events by placing them nearby in the routing tree T (or in other words, to place peers matching dissimilar events away from each other). Therefore, the first step is to quantify the (dis)similarities between the peers to produce or consume similar events. Intuitively the similarity between two peers increases with the increase in overlapping events and decreases with the non-overlapping event traffic. More precisely, let $\overline{E}_{p_i}$ and $\overline{E}_{p_j}$ denote the events matched (or produced) from the set E_ξ by the peers p_i and p_j respectively. The similarity between peers p_i and p_j is calculated by using the Jaccard function[3] [32], i.e., $\mathrm{sim}(p_i, p_j) = \frac{|\overline{E}_{p_i} \cap \overline{E}_{p_j}|}{|\overline{E}_{p_i} \cup \overline{E}_{p_j}|}$. Accordingly, the dissimilarity between the peers can be derived

---

[3] Jaccard function assigns similarities in metric space [4] i.e.,

as: $\mathrm{dsim}(p_i, p_j) = [1 - \mathrm{sim}(p_i, p_j)] \times \alpha$. The dissimilarity values are normalized in the range $[0, \alpha]$, where 0 means that peers consume/publish exactly same events and α is a penalization constant.

Consequently, each overlay link in the TDO is weighted according to the delay (induced by the underlay) as well as the dissimilarity of its adjacent peers p_i and p_j to receive/publish same events, i.e., $w(p_i, p_j) = d^O(p_i, p_j) + \mathrm{dsim}(p_i, p_j)$. Similarly, the weight of a path in the TDO, i.e., $path(p_i, p_n)$, is defined as: $W(p_i, p_n) = \sum_{\langle i,j \rangle \in path(p_i, p_n)} w(i, j)$. The links with smaller weights $w(p_i, p_j)$ should be preferred in T to reduce the routing cost. However, taking into account the weights of the links alone, for instance, by connecting peers in a minimum (weighted) spanning tree (MST), may results in a very high routing cost (cf. Section 6.2). The reason is that the structure of a tree, i.e., organization of peers, influences the routing load (defined in Section 2) on each (overlay) link and is therefore crucial for achieving lower routing cost. Similarly, source-based trees (i.e., separate shortest weighted path tree for each publisher peer) are not desirable as they impose serious scalability issues in terms of control overhead and size of the routing tables.

We therefore employ a core-based approach to build the pub/sub routing tree T. The approach selects a small set of peers, denoted by C, as cores. In general, any peer in the system can be selected as a core. However, only those k_C peers which have low delay paths in the TDO and participate in the dissemination of many events are selected as cores. The core peers are connected with each other using the minimum weighted paths in the TDO. A separate shortest weighted path tree is maintained by each core peer c, denoted as SPT_c. Each non-core peer p selects one of the core peers as its *relay*, denoted as $rel(p)$, such that $W(p, rel(p)) = min_{c \in C} W(p, c)$, and joins the shortest path tree rooted at $rel(p)$ (i.e., $SPT_{rel(p)}$). A path in T between two peers p and q with different relays is composed of three sub-paths: from p to $rel(p)$, from $rel(p)$ to $rel(q)$ and, finally from $rel(q)$ to q.

Clearly, to realize the core-based approach three main issues should be addressed: i) selection of good candidate peers to act as cores (cf. Section 5.1), ii) discovery and connection to the closest relays by non-core peers (cf. Section 5.2) and, iii) maintenance of the routing tree T in the presence of dynamics that arise due to changes in the event traffic and the subscriptions as well as churn/failures of the core and the non-core peers (cf. Section 5.3).

5.1 Core Selection

The core selection in a distributed environment mandates: i) election of a leader to decide the set of cores (C) and, ii) a structure (e.g., tree) to communicate between the leader and the peers in the system. For this purpose, the peers maintain a spanning tree, denoted as T_C, on the TDO such that the root of the spanning tree acts as a leader. Maintaining a distributed spanning tree in dynamic conditions is a well researched topic [2]. For this reason, we will not discuss the maintenance algorithm in this paper.

In the following, we present various core selection strategies with the variations in selection criteria, required knowledge and performance under different workload scenarios.

---

similarities are non-negative, symmetric and obey triangular inequality.

5.1.1 Strategies Based on Global Knowledge

These strategies assume that the leader has knowledge about the shortest (weighted) paths between all pair of peers in the system (All pairs shortest path – APSP). To acquire APSP knowledge at the leader we used the algorithm of Kanchi et al. [22]. The Kanchi's algorithm works on T_C and has a complexity of $O(N)$ message overhead and $O(N^2)$ message size. Once APSP information is available at the leader, two different core selection strategies can be employed.

Maximum Path Count (MaxPath): This strategy selects the peers with higher routing load as cores. In particular, first k_C highest loaded peers which participate in the dissemination of most events, i.e., a number of shortest paths pass through the peers, are selected as cores.

Shortest Path Cost (SPath): This strategy prefers those peers as cores, whose shortest path trees result in lower routing cost. More precisely, for each peer p, the weights along the shortest paths to all other peers are summed (i.e., $\sum_{\forall q \in \mathcal{P}} W(p,q)$) and the first k_C peers with the lowest values are selected as cores.

5.1.2 Strategies Based on Local Knowledge

Maintenance of APSP information (required by the strategies based on global knowledge) utilizes messages of very large size, i.e., $O(N^2)$, especially on the links near the root of T_C [22]. To overcome the problem, we employ voting-based mechanism where each peer votes for potential candidates to be selected as cores according to its local knowledge. In particular, each peer either votes for itself or its neighbour. The votes are aggregated towards the root (leader) of T_C. To reduce the message size, a small (constant) number of core candidates with higher votes are kept at each aggregation step (each level of T_C). Finally, the root selects the k_C peers with the highest votes as cores. Two different voting strategies are considered.

Closest Neighbour (CNeigh): This strategy promotes peers which are connected by low delay links and receive events similar to their neighbours (in the TDO) as cores. In this strategy, each peer votes for its neighbour with the lowest weight (i.e., neighbour with low delay and receiving similar events).

Selection Potential (SPotent): This strategy is inspired from the centralized heuristic developed by Campos et al. [1] for the construction of a minimum cost multicast tree. In this strategy, each peer votes for itself by measuring its potential to be selected as a core. The selection potential of a peer p is determined by considering three characteristics: i) number of neighbours in the TDO (i.e., $NG(p)$) , ii) sum of weights to all the neighbours (i.e., $\sum_{q \in NG(p)} W(p,q)$) and, iii) worst delay to a neighbour (i.e., $D_W = \{d^O(p,q) : \forall a \in NG(p) \ d^O(p,q) > d^O(p,a)\}$). More precisely, the selection potential of a peer p is calculated as follows:

$$NG(p) + \frac{NG(p)}{\sum_{q \in NG(p)} W(p,q)} + \frac{1}{D_W}$$

5.2 Core Discovery and Connection

Once the core peers are selected and distributed by the leader (root of T_C), the next step is to connect all the non-core peers to their relays (i.e., closest cores) using minimum weighted paths in the TDO. To accomplish this, each core c_i initiates the construction of a shortest path tree (SPT_{c_i}) by

---

Algorithm 2 Core discovery and connection

1: $\forall_{c \in C} \ w(c) = \infty$ // Initialization performed at each peer q

2: **upon event** Receive(CORE_SPT, c_i, $W(c_i, q)$, p) at peer q **do**
3: $\quad w(c_i) = W(c_i, q)$
4: $\quad Rcv(c_i) = Rcv(c_i) \cup p$ // msg for core c_i is received from p
5: $\quad$ **if** $\forall_{t \in C} \ w(c_i) < w(t)$ **then**
6: $\quad\quad$ **trigger** Send(JOIN_CORE, c_i, p)
7: $\quad\quad$ **for all** $v \in NG(q) : v \notin Rcv(c_i)$ **do**
8: $\quad\quad\quad$ weight $= W(c_i, q) + w(q, v)$
9: $\quad\quad\quad$ **trigger** Send(CORE_SPT, c_i, weight, q , v)

---

sending CORE_SPT message to its neighbours in the TDO. Upon the reception of a CORE_SPT message for SPT_{c_i} from a peer p, the peer q checks whether the minimum weight path to c_i improves on the weight of the shortest paths to other cores. If there is no improvement then the message is dropped from further forwarding (to reduce control overhead), otherwise the peer q joins SPT_{c_i} by sending join (JOIN_CORE) message to its parent p on SPT_{c_i}. Moreover, the CORE_SPT message for SPT_{c_i} is propagated to only those neighbours which have not received it yet (cf. Algorithm 2).

To avoid partitions in T, all the cores should also be connected with each other. During the core selection, the leader selects a core with the highest votes (similarly highest load or lowest cost in the case of MaxPath and SPath respectively) as the root core. All other cores connect to the shortest path tree of the root core similar to the non-core peers, as described in Algorithm 2.

5.3 Handling Dynamics

P2P systems are very dynamic in nature and therefore, complete recalculation of routing tree for every minor change in the event traffic or the set of peers ($\mathcal{P}$) is not feasible.

A newly arrived peer requests its neighbours on the TDO to forward the CORE_SPT messages and joins the SPT of the closest core (cf. Algorithm 2, *lines 1 - 6*). Similarly, disconnections (due to leaves/failures) of existing core and non-core peers are handled locally. A peer p on discovering the disconnection of parent q (which may be core itself) on $SPT_{rel(p)}$, joins the SPT of the second closest core. However, if the information about the minimum weight paths to other cores is not available (due to pruning of CORE_SPT message in Algorithm 2), the peer p requests its neighbours on the TDO to forward the CORE_SPT messages and joins similar to the arrival of a new peer. Moreover, the CORE_SPT message of the selected core is forwarded to the child peers (on the SPT of previous $rel(p)$) to detect cycles and update weights to the new core.

The dynamic changes in the subscription and event workload as well as changes in the TDO due to arrivals/disconnections of peers, accumulate over time, so that the current routing tree T becomes suboptimal. In order to adapt to the changes, the leader of T_C periodically starts the core selection process and a new routing tree T is constructed. The time period for the construction of new routing tree T is a system parameter, which is specified by the administrator of the system.

6. PERFORMANCE EVALUATIONS

Experiments are performed using PeerSim [17]. Physical network topologies are generated using BRITE [26] and GT-

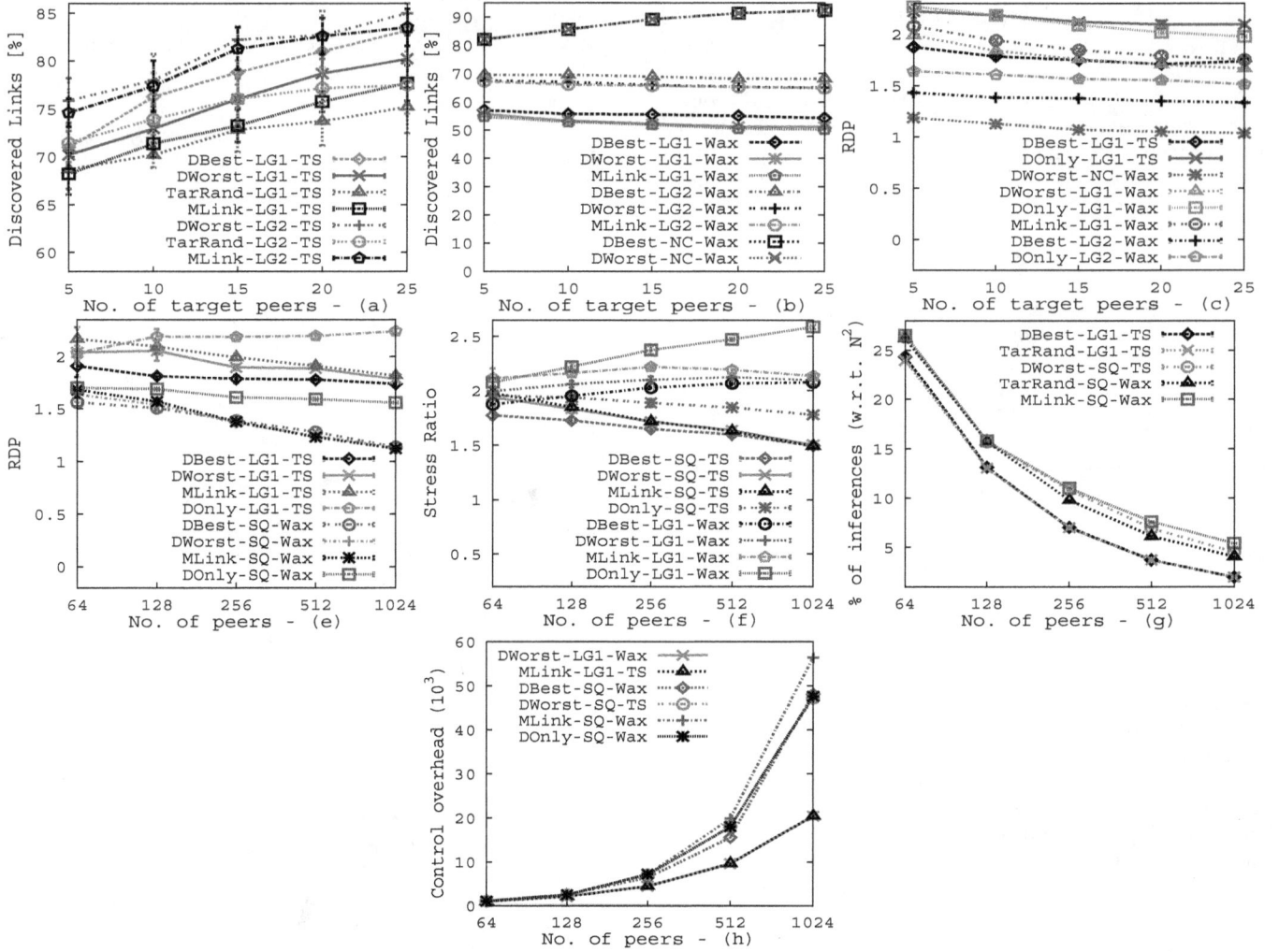

Figure 5: Evaluations for topology discovery overlay (TDO)

ITM [34] tools. BRITE generates a non-hierarchical Wax-man topology (in short Wax) with 1640 routers. GT-ITM generates two layer hierarchy of transit and stub domains (in short TS) comprising 1584 routers. Up to $N = 1024$ peers are used in the experiments, which are connected to random routers (stub domain routers for TS topology). The accuracy of the topology discovery increases with the increase in the number of peers (cf. Section 6.1.2) and therefore, to mimic conservative (strict) settings moderate number of peers are used in the experiments. The last mile delays (between the peers and their access routers) are set to be $5-10\%$ of the average delay between all the routers in the system. To avoid bandwidth bottlenecks on the last mile links, the limits on the degree constraints of the peers are chosen as log_2N (denoted as LG1), $2 \times log_2N$ (denoted as LG2) and $\sqrt{N}$ (denoted as SQ). Moreover, NC represents the scenario where no degree constraints are imposed on the peers. For all the experiments, each peer performs only a single random walk. Unless otherwise stated, the neighbour-hood selectivity factor is set to 0.1 and the number of target peers are chosen as 10.

The content-based schema contains up to 5 integer attributes, where the domain of each attribute is in the range

[0, 10]. Experiments are performed on two different models for the distributions of subscriptions and events. The uniform model (in short UD) generates random subscriptions/events independent of each other. The interest popularity model (in short ZD) chooses five hotspot regions around which subscriptions/events are generated using the widely used zipfian distribution. For the experiments, up to 5000 events are used and each event matches 5% of subscriptions.

6.1 Performance of TDO

We compare our work with two baseline approaches. The first approach maintains TDO by inferring underlay routes to $k_\mathcal{L}$ arbitrary target peers (chosen randomly) and is denoted as *TarRand*. The second approach (denoted as *DOnly*) organizes peers in the TDO solely based on their end-to-end delays to the target peers without using the underlying topology information.

6.1.1 Influence of Target Peers

Figures 5(a) and (b) show the percentage of discovered underlay links versus the number of target peers ($k_\mathcal{L}$), for different (target) selection heuristics and degree constraints.

As expected, the percentage of discovered underlay links increases by relaxing the degree constraints, for both types of topologies and all selection heuristics. Moreover, DBest heuristic performs slightly better by discovering higher percentage of underlay links. It is also worth noting that DBest and DWorst heuristics show similar results in the absence of degree constraints. TarRand on the other hand performs poor, which shows that the proposed heuristics are beneficial for the selection of good target peers. Figures 5(a) and (b) depict that for transit-stub topologies, the percentage of discovered underlay links improves by increasing the number of target peers under all degree constraints. In contrast, the percentage of discovered links decreases very slightly in the presence of degree constraints, for waxmann topologies (Wax). An explanation for such a behaviour lies in the structure of the topologies. However, in the absence of any degree constraints, the percentage of discovered underlay links for Wax improves with the increase in the number of target peers similar to TS, as shown in Figure 5(b). Nevertheless, the slight loss in accuracy for Wax in the presence of degree constraints does not effect the corresponding RDP and Stress. Figure 5(c) plots RDP achieved by the TDO for different numbers of target peers and selection heuristics. RDP is measured as the ratio of delay experienced between all pairs of peers on the TDO to the delay experienced between them using the direct unicast paths in the underlay. It is clear from the figure that for Wax topologies, RDP decreases slightly with the increase in the number of target peers. Moreover, RDP is lowered quiet significantly by relaxing the degree constraints as expected. For instance, in the absence of degree constraints and 10 target peers, the RDP is 1.19 for Wax topologies. Furthermore, DOnly approach which does not utilize topology information results in higher RDP.

6.1.2 Effect of Number of Peers Participating in the System

Figures 5(e) and (f) illustrate the effectiveness of TDO to lower RDP and minimize stress, for different size of peers participating in the system. It is clear from the Figure 5(e) that RDP decreases gradually with the increase in the number of peers. The reason is that the percentage of access routers (i.e., routers directly attached to the peers through the last mile links) increases with the increase in the number of peers and therefore, the organization of peers in the TDO resembles underlay topology more accurately, enabling messages to follow overlay paths which are similar to the underlay routes (except the last mile links to intermediate peers in the TDO), decreasing the delay penalty. For the same reason, only moderate number of peers (up to 1024) are used in the evaluations. Figure 5(f) shows the impact of the number of peers (participating in the system) on stress. Clearly, the total stress introduced by the TDO increases in proportion to the number of participating peers, since more identical messages traverse physical links when more peers join the TDO. In order to compare the effectiveness of the TDO to reduce stress across different peer sizes, Figure 5(f) plots the ratio of total stress introduced (as a result of communication between all pairs of peers) by sending messages on the TDO to the stress introduced when the messages are routed directly on the underlay. The lower value of stress ratio represents higher effectiveness in minimizing stress. Figures 5(e) and (f) show that the performance of all

three selection heuristics becomes almost similar with the increase in the number of peers and the relaxation of degree constraints. The DOnly approach which does not take into account the underlay topology experiences up to 39% higher RDP and 30% rise in stress.

Figure 5(g) shows the influence of the number of peers on the control overhead due to the inference (discovery) of underlay routes between the peers. Underlay route inference techniques are very expensive in terms of computation and communication cost (cf. Section 4.3) and therefore, number of underlay route inferences should be minimized. The figure plots the percentage of underlay route inferences in comparison to the naive approach, whereby underlay routes are discovered between all pairs of peers. The percentage of inferences decreases with the increase in the number of peers mainly because the number of targets are kept constant. Figure 5(h) displays the control overhead due to peer joins during the construction of the TDO. In general, MLink performs slightly more underlay route inferences and produces higher control overhead. This is because in MLink target peers are selected according to the difference between the delays on the paths in the TDO (excluding the last mile delays) and the unicast delays. This may results in TDO connections between arbitrary peers which have high delays or are not located nearby in the underlay topology and hence, resolves in comparatively higher number of disconnections (e.g., when a peer with lower delay sends join message, the neighbour with the highest delay is disconnected), producing slightly more underlay route inferences and join messages.

6.2 Performance of Event Routing

We evaluate three aspects of our event routing approach: i) capability of the proposed core selection strategies to reduce cost of event dissemination (routing cost) in comparison to the baseline approaches, ii) impact of increase in number of cores on the routing cost and the control overhead and, iii) adaptability to dynamic changes in the workload.

We compare our work against three baseline approaches: i) random (*Rand*), ii) similarity-based (*Sim*), and iii) delay-based (*MST*). The first two are core-based approaches. Rand selects k_c random peers as cores, whereas Sim selects cores solely based on the similarity between the peers to produce/consume similar events. The third approach MST maintains a minimum delay spanning tree for the routing of events. Moreover, we implement an optimal routing (*OPT*) algorithm that uses separate shortest path routing trees for the dissemination of each published event [25].

6.2.1 Core Selection Strategies

Figure 6(a) shows the routing efficiency of the proposed core selection strategies and the baseline approaches in comparison to OPT. More precisely, the efficiency of a routing approach (or a strategy) is defined as the ratio of the event routing cost (cf. Section 2) incurred by the approach (or the strategy) to the cost of routing events using OPT. To measure the routing cost around 2000 events are disseminated in the system. Clearly, a lower value for routing efficiency means better approach. The figure depicts that SPath performs better than all other strategies mainly because it uses the global knowledge. However, interestingly SPotent strategy which only exploits the local knowledge to select cores, performs almost similar to the global knowledge based MaxPath strategy. Moreover, all the approaches perform consis-

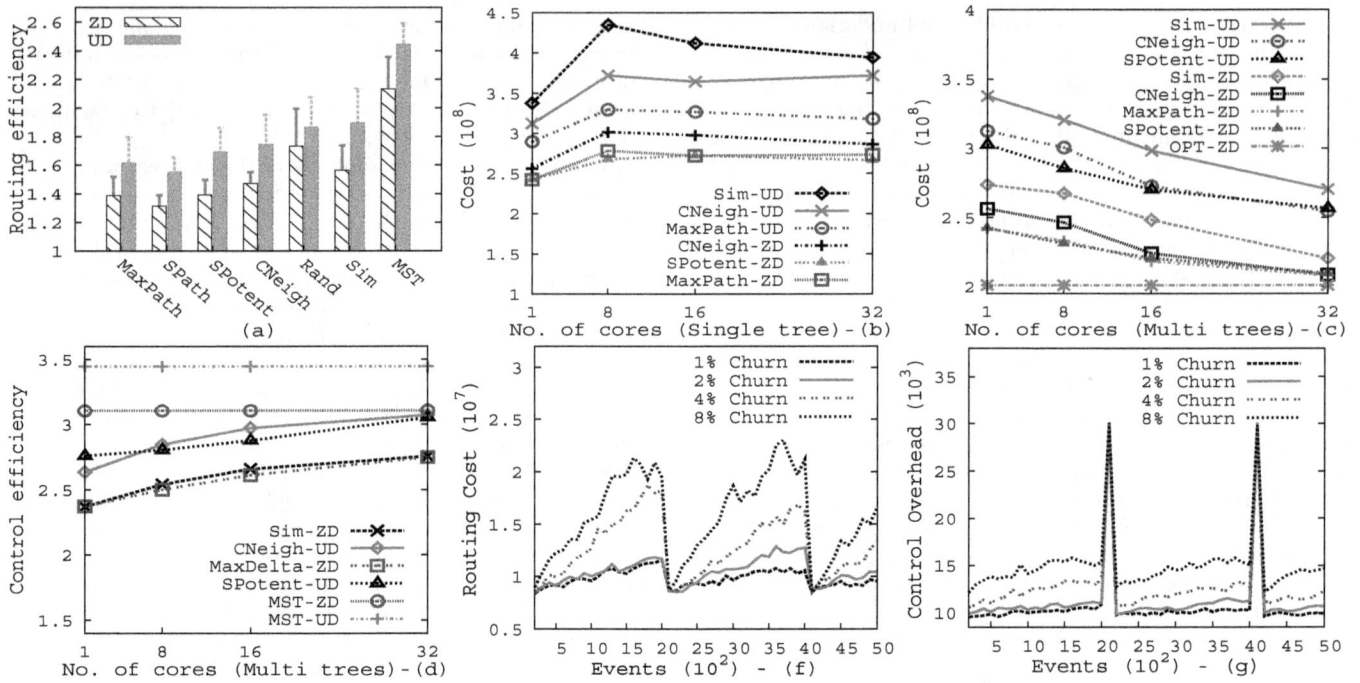

Figure 6: Evaluations for event routing

tently better in case the subscription/event workload follows interest popularity model (i.e., ZD). This is because the subscriptions associated with an interest hotspot consume similar events and placing such subscriptions nearby in the routing tree limits event dissemination to a certain region saving routing cost, whereas for uniformly distributed workload the improvement from nearby placement of the subscriptions consuming similar events is relatively small. For the same reason, Sim achieves better efficiency than Rand for zipfian workload (ZD), whereas both Sim and Rand perform almost same in the case of uniform workload (UD). Another interesting observation is that MST performs even worse than Rand. This is because MST only considers the TDO links with lowest delays, while Rand additionally takes into account the even traffic consumed by the peers (for connecting them to the closest cores) to further reduce the cost of event dissemination.

6.2.2 Impact of Core Size

Figure 6(b) depicts the influence of the number of cores on the communication cost to forward subscriptions as well as route events from the publishers to the interested subscribers. The trend shows that the cost increases with the increase in the number of cores. This is because all the cores in $\mathcal{C}$ are connected with each other through the shortest weighted path tree rooted at the core c_h with the highest votes (cf. Section 5.2). The SPT_{c_h} may not represents shortest (weighted) paths between all pairs of cores in $\mathcal{C}$ and therefore, the communication (such as event dissemination or subscription forwarding) between two peers p and q with different relays (cores) incurs higher cost due to higher weight (delay and dissimilarity in event traffic) on the path between $rel(p)$ and $rel(q)$. Certainly, the communication cost can be decreased, if the cores are connected with each other through shortest weighted paths. Figure 6(c) illus-

trates this point by showing that in the presence of APSP (All pairs shortest weighted paths) between the cores, the communication cost decreases significantly with the increase in the number of cores. Clearly, this reduction in cost comes at the expense of additional control overhead due to the maintenance of k_C shortest weighted path trees. It is worth mentioning that the cores represent only a small fraction of peers in the system (i.e., $k_C \ll N$) and therefore, control overhead is much lower in comparison to the maintenance of APSP w.r.t. all peers in the system. Figure 6(d) depicts the control efficiency of the proposed core selection strategies w.r.t. different core sizes. The control efficiency is defined as the ratio of the complete message traffic generated in the system to the number of matching events received by the peers (i.e., events which are matched by the subscriptions of the peers). The traffic includes all the control overhead induced in the system during leader election, selection of cores, maintenance of SPTs to connect peers and cores in the routing overlay, subscription forwarding and event dissemination. The control efficiency of 1.0 indicates ideal system, whereby events are directly delivered to all the peers with matching subscriptions without incurring any unnecessary message overhead. Figure 6(d) shows that the control efficiency decreases with the increase in core size, mainly due to the maintenance of k_C shortest path trees. However, the control efficiency of the proposed core selection strategies is still better than MST approach. This is because MST does not take into account the event traffic consumed/produced by the peers during the construction of routing overlay and therefore, experiences high control overhead during subscription forwarding and event dissemination.

6.2.3 Adaptability to the Changes in Workload

Figures 6(f) and (g) show the behaviour of the system in the presence of continuously arriving and leaving subscribers. The churn is introduced in the system after the dissemination of every 100 events. The percentage of churn is relative to the total number of peers in the system. During the experiment, SPotent is used as the core selection strategy and subscriptions/events workload is generated using zipfian distribution (ZD). Nevertheless, similar trends are observed for other core selection strategies and uniformly distributed subscriptions/events workload (UD).

Figure 6(f) shows that the cost of event routing increases as more and more events (up to 2000) are disseminated in the system. This is because the joins and leaves of peers (due to churn) are only handled locally to reduce the control overhead (cf. Section 5.3) and as a consequence, the routing overlay degrades overtime resulting in higher routing cost. Figure 6(g) shows the control overhead in terms of the number of overall messages in the system. A slight increase in the control overhead for higher percentages of churn is due to the local handling of peer dynamics, as mentioned above. After every 2000 events, complete recalculation of the routing overlay is initiated by the leader, which significantly lowers the routing cost, as shown in Figure 6(f). Moreover, Figure 6(g) depicts that immediately after the leader initiated recalculation of the routing overlay, the control overhead rises considerably for a small transient period. However, the new routing overlay obtained after the transient period consumes almost identical control traffic.

7. RELATED WORK

Publish/Subscribe Systems: In the recent past, several content-based pub/sub systems have been proposed with the aim to provide communication efficient routing of events from the publishers to the subscribers. Many of these systems [3, 28, 32] focus on minimizing bandwidth usage by clustering subscribers according to their interests, without taking into account the properties of the underlying physical network. As shown in Example 1, these systems could be suboptimal w.r.t. the communication overhead and end-to-end delays.

Few systems [25, 14, 27] consider underlay related QoS metrics such as end-to-end delay, data rate, loss rate etc., to optimize pub/sub overlay for efficient routing of events. Majumder et al. [25] propose an approach that constructs multiple trees to efficiently distributed events in a content-based pub/sub system. The construction of each tree is formulated as a generalized steiner tree problem and an approximation algorithm is developed to build trees with communication cost at most poly-logarithmic factor of the optimum. However, the proposed approach assumes the availability of the content-based workload (subscriptions and matched events) and the properties of the underlying network at a central coordinator, which hinders its scalability. Similarly, XPort [27] targets the construction of an event distribution tree that can be optimized according to the application-defined performance metrics, e.g., minimize average path delay to the root. However, XPort mandates that all the publishers are connected to the root of the event distribution tree.

Nevertheless, some existing pub/sub systems [8] address reliable delivery of events by explicitly taking into account the router-level topology of the underlying network. Generally, these systems rely on the redundancy in the underlay paths between publishers and subscribers to provide resilience against the network failures. In contrast to our work, these systems assume that the topology information is some-

how available. Moreover, the QoS metrics such as delay and bandwidth, which are focused in this paper are not addressed.

Topology-aware Overlay Networks: Previous research in the area of Application Layer Multicast (ALM) has shown that the knowledge of the underlying (router-level) network topology is beneficial to achieve low physical link stress, low RDP and high bandwidth data dissemination [18, 21, 20, 24, 36]. Zhu et al. [36] address the problem of constructing a high bandwidth overlay for ALM. The authors prove that the problem is NP-hard and propose a distributed heuristic, which incrementally improves the bandwidth of the ALM tree by replacing the lower bandwidth overlay links with the higher bandwidth links. Similarly, Jin el al. [21] develop approximation algorithms to construct maximum bandwidth multicast tree (MBMT) and minimum stress multicast tree (MSMT). However, the approximation algorithms are centralized and assume the availability of the complete knowledge about the router-level topology of the underlying network. FAT (FAST Application-layer Tree) [20] uses underlay route inference tools such as traceroute, to discover router-level underlay topology and build a multicast tree on top of the discovered topology to achieve high bandwidth and low RDP. A heuristic, named Max-Delta, is employed to discover the underlay topology in an efficient and scalable manner. The MLink heuristic proposed in this paper is adopted from the Max-Delta heuristic. In particular, we modified the Max-Delta to operate in a completely decentralized environment and without the use of network coordinate system.

Lastly, a huge amount of graph theory literature is available on spanning tree related optimization problems [33] such as Minimum Routing Cost Spanning Tree (MRCT) or Optimum Communication Spanning Tree (OCRT). Nevertheless, all these theoretical approaches cannot be applied for event routing in a content-based pub/sub system, because their focus is to minimize the pairwise distances between the vertices in the input graph without any consideration to the traffic requirements between those vertices. Moreover, these approaches are centralized and are not targeted to handle continuously evolving workload as is the case in P2P-based systems.

8. CONCLUSION

In this paper, we have presented an approach that exploits the knowledge of event traffic, user subscriptions and the router-level topology of the underlying physical network to achieve scalable and communication efficient dissemination of events in a content-based pub/sub system. For this purpose, we have developed methods to discover underlay topology between subscribers and publishers in the system. The proposed methods construct a *Topology Discovery Overlay* (TDO), whereby peers are connected according to the overlapping in the underlay routes. Afterwards, the information of the discovered topology and the proximity between the peer to receive or produce similar events is used to build an event routing overlay. In particular, we have proposed different core selection strategies (exploiting global and local knowledge) to facilitate the construction of a communication efficient event routing overlay on top of TDO. Our evaluations show that for Internet-like topologies, TDO is capable of lowering physical link stress and reducing RDP. Moreover, the proposed core-based approach reduces the cost to disseminate events up to 49% in comparison to the widely used baseline and related approaches.

9. REFERENCES

[1] R. Campos and M. Ricardo. A fast algorithm for computing minimum routing cost spanning trees. *Comput. Netw.*, 2008.

[2] C. Cheng, I. Cimet, and S. Kumar. A protocol to maintain a minimum spanning tree in a dynamic topology. *SIGCOMM Comput. Commun. Rev.*, 1988.

[3] A. K. Y. Cheung and H.-A. Jacobsen. Green resource allocation algorithms for publish/subscribe systems. In *Intl. conf. on distributed computing systems*, 2011.

[4] K. L. Clarkson. Nearest-neighbor searching and metric space dimensions. In *Nearest-neighbor methods for learning and vision: theory and practice.* 2006.

[5] M. Costa, M. Castro, A. Rowstron, and P. Key. PIC: Practical Internet coordinates for distance estimation. In *Intl. conf. on distributed computing systems*, 2004.

[6] B. Donnet and T. Friedman. Internet topology discovery: A survey. *IEEE Comm. Surv. Tuts.*, 2007.

[7] B. Donnet, P. Raoult, T. Friedman, and M. Crovella. Deployment of an algorithm for large-scale topology discovery. *IEEE J.Sel. A. Commun.*, 2006.

[8] C. Esposito, D. Cotroneo, and A. Gokhale. Reliable publish/ subscribe middleware for time-sensitive Internet-scale applications. In *DEBS*, 2009.

[9] M. Faloutsos, P. Faloutsos, and C. Faloutsos. On power-law relationships of the Internet topology. *SIGCOMM Comput. Commun. Rev.*, 1999.

[10] C. T. C. A. for Internet Data Analysis. http://www.caida.org/home/, 2012.

[11] M. Goyal, M. Soperi, E. Baccelli, G. Choudhury, A. Shaikh, H. Hosseini, and K. Trivedi. Improving convergence speed and scalability in OSPF: A survey. *IEEE Commun. Surveys Tuts.*, 2011.

[12] M. H. Gunes and K. Sarac. Resolving anonymous routers in Internet topology measurement studies. In *IEEE INFOCOM*, 2008.

[13] A. Gupta, O. D. Sahin, D. Agrawal, and A. E. Abbadi. Meghdoot: Content-based publish/subscribe over P2P networks. In *Intl. conf. on middleware*, 2004.

[14] M. A. Jaeger, H. Parzyjegla, G. Muehl, and K. Herrmann. Self-organizing broker topologies for publish/subscribe systems. In *ACM sympos. on appl. comput. (SAC)*, 2007.

[15] S. Jain, R. Mahajan, D. Wetherall, and G. Borriello. Scalable self-organizing overlays. Technical Report UW-CSE 02-02-02, University of Washington, 2002.

[16] M. Jelasity, W. Kowalczyk, and M. v. Steen. An approach to massively distributed aggregate computing on peer-to-peer networks. In *Workshop on parallel, distributed and network-based processing (PDP)*, 2004.

[17] M. Jelasity, A. Montresor, G. P. Jesi, and S. Voulgaris. PeerSim: A peer-to-peer simulator. http://peersim.sourceforge.net/.

[18] X. Jin, W. Tu, and S. H. G. Chan. Scalable and efficient end-to-end network topology inference. *IEEE Trans. Parallel Distrib. Syst.*, 2008.

[19] X. Jin, W. Tu, and S.-H. G. Chan. Traceroute-based topology inference without network coordinate estimation. In *IEEE intl. conf. on commun.*, 2008.

[20] X. Jin, Y. Wang, and S.-H. G. Chan. Fast overlay tree based on efficient end-to-end measurements. In *IEEE intl. conf. on commun. (ICC)*, 2005.

[21] X. Jin, W. P. Yiu, S. H. Chan, and Y. Wang. On maximizing tree bandwidth for topology-aware peer-to-peer streaming. *IEEE Transactions on Multimedia*, 9:1580–1592, 2007.

[22] S. Kanchi and D. Vineyard. An optimal distributed algorithm for ALL-pairs shortest-path. *Intl. J. on Information Theories & App.*, 11:141–146, 2004.

[23] S. Kandula, D. Katabi, S. Sinha, and A. Berger. Dynamic load balancing without packet reordering. *ACM SIGCOMM Comput. Commun. Rev.*, 2007.

[24] M. Kwon and S. Fahmy. Path-aware overlay multicast. *Comput. Netw.*, 47:23–45, 2005.

[25] A. Majumder, N. Shrivastava, R. Rastogi, and A. Srinivasan. Scalable content-based routing in pub/sub systems. In *IEEE INFOCOM*, 2009.

[26] A. Medina, A. Lakhina, I. Matta, and J. Byers. BRITE: Universal topology generation from a user"s perspective. Technical report, Boston University, 2001.

[27] O. Papaemmanouil, Y. Ahmad, U. Çetintemel, J. Jannotti, and Y. Yildirim. Extensible optimization in overlay dissemination trees. In *Proc. of ACM SIGMOD intl. conf. on management of data*, 2006.

[28] O. Papaemmanouil and U. Cetintemel. SemCast:: Semantic multicast for content-based data dissemination. In *Intl. conf. on data engineering (ICDE)*, 2005.

[29] I. Stoica, R. Morris, D. Liben-Nowell, D. R. Karger, M. F. Kaashoek, F. Dabek, and H. Balakrishnan. Chord: a scalable peer-to-peer lookup protocol for Internet applications. *IEEE/ACM Transactions on Networking*, 11:17–32, 2003.

[30] M. A. Tariq, G. G. Koch, B. Koldehofe, I. Khan, and K. Rothermel. Dynamic publish/subscribe to meet subscriber-defined delay and bandwidth constraints. In *Proc. of Intl. conf. on parallel computing (Euro-Par)*, 2010.

[31] M. A. Tariq, B. Koldehofe, G. G. Koch, I. Khan, and K. Rothermel. Meeting subscriber-defined QoS constraints in publish/subscribe systems. *Concurrency and Computation: Practice and Experience*, 2011.

[32] M. A. Tariq, B. Koldehofe, G. G. Koch, and K. Rothermel. Distributed spectral cluster management: A method for building dynamic publish/subscribe systems. In *Intl. conf. on dist. event-based systems (DEBS)*, 2012.

[33] B. Y. Wu and K.-M. Chao. *Spanning Trees and Optimization Problems.* Chapman and Hall, 2004.

[34] E. W. Zegura, K. L. Calvert, and S. Bhattacharjee. How to model an internetwork. In *IEEE intl. conf. on comp. commun. (INFOCOM)*, 1996.

[35] X. Zhang and C. Phillips. A survey on selective routing topology inference through active probing. *IEEE Communications Surveys & Tutorials*, 2011.

[36] Y. Zhu, B. Li, and K. Q. Pu. Dynamic multicast in overlay networks with linear capacity constraints. *IEEE Trans. Parallel Distrib. Syst.*, 2009.

StreamHub: A Massively Parallel Architecture for High-Performance Content-Based Publish/Subscribe

Raphaël Barazzutti,[1] Pascal Felber,[1] Christof Fetzer,[2] Emanuel Onica,[1],
Jean-François Pineau,[1] Marcelo Pasin,[1] Etienne Rivière,[1] and Stefan Weigert[2]
1. University of Neuchâtel, Switzerland   2. TU Dresden, Germany
first.last@{unine.ch, tu-dresden.de}

ABSTRACT

By routing messages based on their content, publish/subscribe (pub/sub) systems remove the need to establish and maintain fixed communication channels. Pub/sub is a natural candidate for designing large-scale systems, composed of applications running in different domains and communicating via middleware solutions deployed on a public cloud. Such pub/sub systems must provide high throughput, filtering thousands of publications per second matched against hundreds of thousands of registered subscriptions with low and predictable delays, and must scale horizontally and vertically. As large-scale application composition may require complex publications and subscriptions representations, pub/sub system designs should not rely on the specific characteristics of a particular filtering scheme for implementing scalability.

In this paper, we depart from the use of *broker overlays*, where each server must support the whole range of operations of a pub/sub service, as well as overlay management and routing functionality. We propose instead a novel and pragmatic *tiered approach* to obtain high-throughput and scalable pub/sub for clusters and cloud deployments. We separate the three operations involved in pub/sub and leverage their natural potential for parallelization. Our design, named STREAMHUB, is oblivious to the semantics of subscriptions and publications. It can support any type and number of filtering operations implemented by independent libraries. Experiments on a cluster with up to 384 cores indicate that STREAMHUB is able to register 150 K subscriptions per second and filter next to 2 K publications against 100 K stored subscriptions, resulting in nearly 400 K notifications sent per second. Comparisons against a broker overlay solution shows an improvement of two orders of magnitude in throughput when using the same number of cores.

Categories and Subject Descriptors

C.2.4 [**Computer Systems Organization**]: Computer-Communication Networks—*Distributed Systems*

Keywords

Publish/subscribe; Scalability; Performance

1. INTRODUCTION

Content-based publish/subscribe (pub/sub) [20] is a strong contender for offering an efficient, yet *natural* communication paradigm to developers of large-scale applications. It supports decoupled interactions between the producers (*publishers*) and the consumers (*subscribers*) of information by the means of messages (*publications*). Decoupling occurs both in terms of space and time: publishers and subscribers do not need to know the existence or identity of one another, and no particular synchronization between them is necessary. They only communicate indirectly through a *pub/sub system*. It is the responsibility of this system to *route* publications from the publishers to interested subscribers. Routing is based on *subscriptions* registered by the subscribers to express their interest in specific content. The operation of *matching* the content of the publications against the subscriptions stored in the system is called *content filtering*.

A typical use of pub/sub systems is for composing a collection of independent applications running on different administrative domains or geographical locations. Communication between these applications takes place via a common pub/sub service running on a set of *dedicated servers*, typically set up in a *public cloud* or a *cluster equipped with a public address*, interconnected through a local area network and exposing access points to client applications.

The decoupled and data-centric nature of the pub/sub communication model allows for seamless integration and evolution of large-scale applications. A typical example is *QoS Monitoring as a Service* [36], where an application running on a private cloud is monitored and key performance indicators (KPIs) are generated as publications. These KPIs are propagated to a third-party monitoring service, based on subscriptions generated from a service level agreement (SLA) in order to detect violations of this SLA. Communication takes place via a pub/sub service deployed on a public cloud accessible by both parties. Other applications include e-Health systems [26] that bridge several medical and healthcare institutions sharing information about patients cases, or the canonical example of stock trading [24]. We note that for all these applications, the use of a third-party infrastructure for communication may raise concerns about privacy and data security: publications and subscriptions represent sensitive data that should not be leaked to a third party. As a result, *encrypted content filtering schemes* have gained interest in the recent years [6, 18, 25, 26, 34] as they support filtering of encrypted publications against encrypted subscriptions without needing decryption. Such approaches suffer, however, from a high computational cost and disallow some optimizations, in particular those based on containment relationships between subscriptions (i.e., the fact that a subscription will match a subset of the publications matching another subscription) or on the aggregation of a set of subscriptions into a single one.

Objectives. We argue that the key properties of a pub/sub system running on a public cloud or cluster and supporting large-scale application composition should be as follows.

(1) High throughput and low, predictable delays. The raw performance of the pub/sub service deployed on a public cloud or cluster must be sufficient to support demanding applications, such as high-frequency trading or network monitoring. This requires exploiting parallel processing of incoming subscriptions and publications as much as possible. Since the filtering operation itself is costly, the design must avoid filtering an incoming publication against a given subscription multiple times, which typically happens in overlay brokers systems. Furthermore, delays between the generation of a publication and its dispatching to interested subscribers must remain of the same order as the delay a coupled communication between the producer and consumer of information would take. As a corollary, there should not be significant deviation in the notification time for all subscribers interested in a given publication.

(2) Scalability. The ability to support increasing numbers of publishers/publications, subscribers/subscriptions, and notifications, as well as more computationally intensive filtering schemes, requires several levels of scalability. *Vertical scalability* is required to take advantage of additional resources available on a given node, notably multi- and many-core architectures that can process the pub/sub traffic in parallel. *Horizontal scalability* allows supporting a higher load by adding more nodes to the cluster. Ideally, a linear increase in the number of nodes should result in a linear increase in maximum supported throughput.

(3) Filtering scheme agnosticism. The design and architecture of distributed pub/sub systems should not be dependent on a particular filtering scheme and in particular on the semantics and representations of publications and subscriptions. Most existing distributed pub/sub systems [11, 14, 17, 27, 40] support filtering schemes based on conjunctive predicates ($<, \leq, =, \dots$) over discrete attribute values (integers, strings, ...), and their designs are closely tied to the nature of this particular representation. This applies, for instance, to the construction and maintenance of routing tables between brokers that drive the flow of publications. To minimize inter-broker traffic, these systems typically rely on the ability to determine containment relationships between subscriptions and/or to construct aggregated subscriptions. Yet, such features are not available with all content-based filtering schemes, notably with encrypted approaches [6, 18, 25, 26, 34]. As a matter of fact, there exist no fundamental reasons why content-based routing should be restricted to attribute- and predicate-based filtering: a pub/sub service should be able to integrate virtually any filtering scheme operating on the content of exchanged data using stored filters, as required by the application. Examples include not only encrypted filtering for privacy preservation, but also statistical methods such as Bayesian filtering [37] or even template matching for digital images (for instance, for face recognition) [10]. The architecture of the pub/sub system should be independent of the nature of the filtering

scheme, while still allowing for specific optimizations at the level of a single node.

Contributions. In this paper, we revisit the design of a distributed content-based pub/sub engine for supporting high throughput, low latency, and horizontal and vertical scalability. We propose a novel approach based on a tiered architecture and inspired by dataflow programming techniques, which exploits parallelism in ways similar to MapReduce [19] and stream processing engines inspired from it [2, 5, 9, 33]. A set of independent operators, each spanning an arbitrary number of servers and taking advantage of multiple cores on individual servers, implement the three fundamental operations of content-based pub/sub: *subscription partitioning*, *publication filtering*, and *publication dispatching*. Interactions with the pub/sub system are managed by a set of independent *data converters and connection points* (DCCP) that maintain persistent connections with clients (publishers and subscribers).

We implement our approach in STREAMHUB, a pub/sub engine designed for operating on a public cluster or cloud. STREAMHUB leverages the runtime support of an existing stream processing engine such as S4 [33], Storm [2], or StreamMine [9]. We use the latter engine in our prototype implementation.

Our evaluation on a cluster with up to 384 cores on 48 physical machines indicates that STREAMHUB is able to sustain high-throughput workloads: up to 150 K subscriptions registered per second; and up to almost 2 K publications filtered per second with a population of 100 K stored subscriptions, resulting in an output flow of nearly 400 K notifications per second to interested subscribers.

We note that our contribution is not on the actual filtering scheme itself, which is supported by an independent library that can be chosen arbitrarily as long as it implements a simple and schema-oblivious API. We demonstrate the performance of STREAMHUB using the well-established counting algorithm of SIENA [12], and we leave the integration and comparison of other filtering libraries, and in particular those providing privacy-preserving encrypted matching [6, 18, 25, 26, 34], for future work. Similarly, while STREAMHUB is designed with elastic scalability in mind (i.e., the ability to dynamically adapt the number of servers associated with each operator according to the experienced workload), we leave the implementation of elastic server provisioning for future work and concentrate on the performance and scalability of the architecture with various static configurations.

Outline. The remainder of this paper is organized as follows. We survey previous work on distributed pub/sub systems in Section 2, and we present and motivate our proposed architecture in Section 3. We describe the implementation of STREAMHUB in Section 4, as well as the libraries used in our evaluation for filtering publications and clustering subscriptions. We evaluate our approach and compare it to a broker-based pub/sub system in Section 5, before concluding in Section 6.

2. RELATED WORK

We start by reviewing related work on distributed content-based pub/sub systems. We focus on high-efficiency middleware operating on dedicated machines and do not specifically elaborate on peer-to-peer approaches. Similarly, we do not discuss work targeting the simpler topic-based filtering model.

2.1 Publish/Subscribe Engines

Most earlier work on scalable pub/sub has relied on networks of *brokers*, which are dedicated machines, each performing the whole range of operations that compose the content routing task: (1) management of subscriptions from users and other brokers, (2) filtering of incoming publications against stored subscriptions and dispatching to local interested subscribers, and (3) filtering of incoming publications against routing tables for dispatching to other brokers. Brokers are typically organized in a *broker overlay*, with subscriptions and publications flowing between brokers according to its logical structure, typically a tree or a mesh.

Well-known examples of broker-based pub/sub middleware are SIENA [11], Gryphon [3], and PADRES [27]. In these systems, a client (publisher or subscriber) connects to one of the brokers, which then acts as its single point of contact. Brokers forward subscriptions registered by their clients towards neighboring brokers. These systems are based on a filtering scheme where subscriptions are defined as conjunctions of predicates ($<, \leq, =, \dots$) on a set of discrete attributes values (integers, strings, ...). They rely on the ability to (1) determine containment relationships between subscriptions, and (2) construct aggregated subscriptions representing the interests of sets of subscriptions. Subscriptions are aggregated along the way from consumers to producers of information, taking advantage of containment relationships between subscriptions: a single aggregated subscription may represent the interests of many downstream subscriptions, thus reducing the number of subscriptions managed by the broker and improving filtering performance (see for instance [28]). This approach works well with few publishers and with subscriptions that have certain locality properties (e.g., subscribers with similar interests connect to the same broker). However, it requires complex algorithms for maintaining the consistency of forwarding tables and provides only limited benefits when information flows from many sources or when the subscription representation does not allow for containment or aggregation [6, 10, 18, 25, 26, 34, 37].

In broker overlays, under some workloads, publications may have to traverse a number of brokers that have no local interested subscriber but still have to filter the publication against stored subscriptions. These are called *forwarder-only* brokers. While techniques for rewiring the broker overlay have been proposed to tackle this problem [31], the presence of such forwarder-only brokers is intrinsic to a design where communication flows depend on the filtering scheme and on the current workload of stored subscriptions. Since all brokers play all roles in the pub/sub operation, the allocation of publishers and subscribers to brokers has a strong impact on the balance of load and on the overall filtering efficiency. A bad placement may result in a high number of messages being propagated between brokers. Some optimizations were proposed to address this problem by connecting subscribers with similar subscriptions to the same brokers [15], or by linking publishers and their expected subscribers to the same brokers [16, 32]. Cheung *et al.* [17] proposed to use similar techniques to rewire the PADRES overlay in order to reduce the environmental footprint of the pub/sub system. Again, these mechanisms are dependent on the filtering scheme and require the ability to determine proximity relations between subscribers and publishers. This would not be possible, for instance, with encrypted filtering approaches.

In contrast to systems based on overlay of brokers, the logical connections between the elements in our proposed architecture are independent of the nature of the subscription and publication workloads and of the nature of the filtering scheme. We support scaling each of the pub/sub operations independently by simply adding more processors to the set of nodes that support this operation. We do not require any specific optimization support from the filtering scheme, though we can leverage their existence for improving single-node performance inside filtering libraries. Note that our approach is readily applicable to architectures like Google's GooPS [35], where pub/sub is implemented by regional data centers consisting of clusters of brokers and interconnected by dedicated network links.

2.2 Filtering Mechanisms

Our architecture supports *pluggable* filtering mechanisms. As the design of new such mechanisms is not the focus of this paper, we only briefly discuss below a few well-known algorithms that can be readily used in our STREAMHUB implementation (see Section 4.2.1). Note that this list is far from being exhaustive.

SIENA uses a counting algorithm [12] for efficiently matching publications against subscriptions. Individual predicates are stored in a forwarding table and a subscription is detected as matching when all its predicates have been encountered. We use an implementation of this counting algorithm as the default filter in STREAMHUB for non-encrypted matching. Additional details on its operation are given in Section 4.2.1. Encrypted filtering can be supported for instance by *asymmetric scalar-product preserving encryption* [18], combined with pre-filtering [6] for efficiency. Gryphon [3] inserts the set of subscriptions into a matching tree: leaves contain subscriptions, non-leaf nodes contain tests, and outgoing edges represent the results of the tests. A publication traverses down the tree by following all matching paths and reports a matching subscription for each leaf node reached. PADRES uses a scalable filtering engine [22] that can leverage multiple cores on a shared memory architecture. By splitting the state of subscriptions and using multiple threads synchronized using either locks or transactional memory, the filtering throughput is significantly improved. We also exploit all the cores available on a machine and provide synchronization mechanisms for concurrent accesses to a shared state.

Other examples of filtering mechanisms that can be leveraged in the context of STREAMHUB include, but are not limited to, the following. RAPIDMatch [30] is a tree-based filtering mechanism that takes into account the sparseness of criteria definitions over the whole attribute set in some pub/sub workloads for greater efficiency. TAMA [41] trades accuracy and space complexity for efficiency by clustering range-based subscriptions in predefined sets based on discrete cuts of the definition range of each attribute. The use of discrete cuts leads to the presence of false positives, while the presence of subscriptions in multiple buckets leads to higher memory consumption, in return for faster filtering. Fabret *et al.* [21] use schema-clustering to minimize the number of filtering operations performed, along with techniques to improve cache performance of the algorithm. Filtering mechanisms also exist for boolean expressions [8, 23], XML documents and XPath expressions [4, 13], and compact data representation using Bloom filters [29].

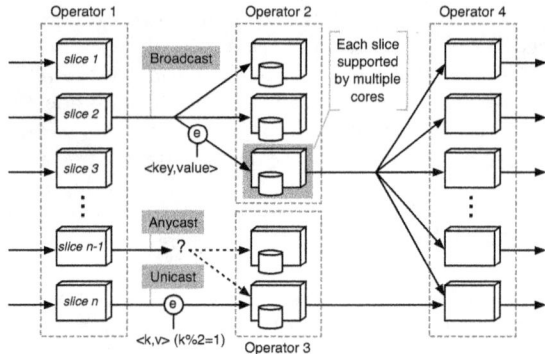

Figure 1: Architectural principles.

2.3 Clustering Subscriptions

Similarly to filtering mechanisms, we support subscription clustering by the means of pluggable libraries. Subscription clustering, as described in Section 4.2.2, splits the whole set of subscriptions maintained by the pub/sub system into clusters according to similarity (if a proximity metric is available on the subscription). This typically increases the level of containment and the potential for aggregation, which in turn improves the performance of the filtering operation. Classical clustering algorithms include K-means [39], Event Space Partitioning (ESP) [38], or R-trees [7].

3. ARCHITECTURE

Our design choices aim at maximizing pipeline, task, and data parallelism in order to support high-throughput and scalable pub/sub. The resulting architecture shares these design principles with big-data processing systems such as MapReduce [19], and in particular with the online models of computation on data *streams* that were inspired from it [2,5,9,33].

Our architecture uses the base construction principles illustrated by Figure 1. It is composed of a set of *operators*, sharing the same code and supporting pipeline parallelism. Operators are organized as a directed acyclic graph (DAG). Communication takes place in the form of *events* flowing through the DAG of operators. Each operator can scale horizontally by using an arbitrary number of operator *slices*, each running on a different server and managing an independent state. Slices scale vertically by partitioning the received event load between all available cores on each server. There is no communication or shared state between the slices of an operator. Event forwarding between operators can use one the three primitives: *anycast* (sending to a random slice of an operator), *broadcast* (sending to all slices of an operator), or *unicast* (sending to a slice of an operator chosen according to a key).

We use a set of three operators. Each implements a different aspect of the pub/sub service: subscription *partitioning*, publication *filtering*, and publication *dispatching*. Thanks to the scalability properties of operators, one can easily adapt the number of physical machines and cores to the load experienced by each of these three operations. This load varies with the nature of the workload, such as the number, complexity, or selectivity of subscriptions. The load also varies with the nature of the filtering schemes. For instance, encrypted filtering requires more processing power than non-encrypted

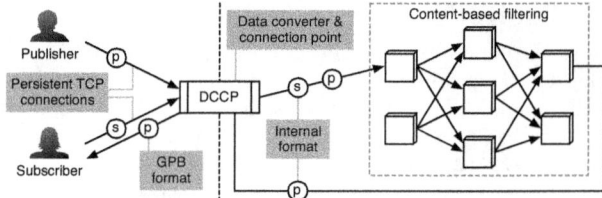

Figure 2: User view of StreamHub.

filtering. To sustain the same publication throughput, one should allocate more slices (servers) to the publication *encrypted filtering* operator.

We present in this section our operators and support mechanisms. We start by describing the endpoints used by external clients to access STREAMHUB. Afterwards, we present the operators that support content-based filtering, as well as the partition of the load onto different slices at each operator. The filtering operation itself is delegated to one or more *filtering libraries*. STREAMHUB also provides optional support for *clustering libraries*, which can partition the state of subscriptions in elaborate ways and speed up the filtering operation. As these libraries are pluggable components whose algorithms do not represent novel contributions of this paper, we describe them in Section 4.

3.1 Connection To and From Clients

The pub/sub operators are typically deployed on a cluster or a cloud, i.e., a set of machines with limited hardware heterogeneity. In our implementation, STREAMHUB, operators are implemented using the same language (C++). As a result, the internal communication and serialization formats between the elements forming the architecture can be selected based on performance criteria. Our implementation uses the efficient binary format provided by Boost libraries[1] for internal propagation of events. In contrast, clients may execute on different platforms and use a variety of languages. The choice of the external format is thus driven by its hardware and language independence. Our implementation uses Google Protocol Buffers (GPB),[2] which provide efficient serialization primitives for subscriptions, unsubscriptions, and publications while hiding language and platform heterogeneity.

Publishers and subscribers need a persistent and public connection point to the cluster or cloud supporting the pub/sub service. Connecting to any of the nodes supporting the pub/sub service is impractical in clouds (due to VM migrations) and often impossible in clusters (as most nodes do not have a public IP address). Our design features components external to the operators implementing the pub/sub service, that act as such persistent connection points. These are also in charge of translating between the external and internal representation format, and henceforth named *Data-Converter & Connection-Points* or DCCPs. Figure 2 presents a user-centric view of the system. Clients connect to a DCCP via a *persistent* TCP connection to enable low end-to-end delay for communication with the pub/sub service and, more importantly, to support asynchronous notifications of matching publications, as clients may not be directly reachable

---

[1]http://www.boost.org/

[2]http://code.google.com/apis/protocolbuffers/

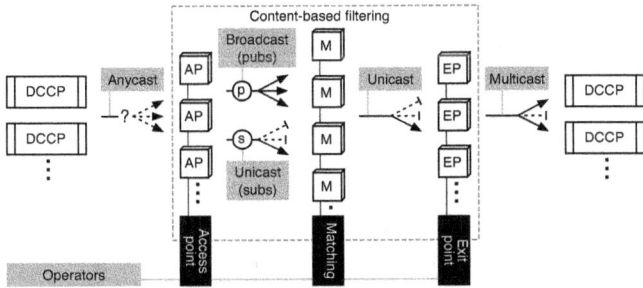

Figure 3: StreamHub processing operators (libraries and states not shown for clarity).

(for instance, they may be located behind a NAT or firewall). We note that this practical impossibility to reach clients directly limits the applicability of rewiring schemes for solutions based on brokers overlays [15–17, 32].

Several DCCPs can be used for the same STREAMHUB deployment, e.g., when the number of opened connections or the necessary bandwidth becomes too high for a single machine, when the cost of conversion creates a bottleneck, or on the same host when several network adapters are available.

3.2 Content-Based Routing Operators

In this section, we present the three operators that form the *core engine* of our scalable pub/sub architecture. These three operators are organized as a pipeline. They are listed in Table 1 and illustrated by Figure 3, together with the communication primitives used for propagating events between them. A detailed example of the path taken by subscriptions and publications within the STREAMHUB engine is shown by Figure 4.

3.2.1 Access Point Operator

The *Access Point* (AP) operator plays the role of the input operator. It receives events from any of the DCCPs. The selection of an AP operator slice by a DCCP is done at random to guarantee good load balancing properties. The role of the AP operator is to *partition* incoming subscriptions among all slices of the *Matching* (M) operator as follows.

Each incoming event has a *key*, which is a data structure that indicates the type of the client request (i.e., a new subscription, an unsubscription, or a publication). Subscriptions are not stored by the AP operator slices but are instead forwarded to the M operator that implements the filtering operation as we describe next. Our architecture can simultaneously support different filtering schemes (such as flat vs. structured data, encrypted publications and/or subscriptions, declarative vs. executable filters). Each filtering scheme is supported by a separate M operator. The choice of the destination operator depends on the *filtering scheme identifier* embedded in subscriptions. The same applies to publications.

Only one of the slices of the M operator holds any given subscription.[3] AP slices hence use unicast communication to select the appropriate M operator slice that will be responsible for an incoming subscription. The default mechanism relies on unicast and routes the subscription based on the

---

[3]Resilience of subscriptions in the presence of nodes faults can be handled at the level of the underlying stream processing engine, for instance using active replication or checkpoint/replay techniques.

hashing of the *subscription identifier* specified in event keys. We note that this selection mechanism is *stateless* and *reproducible*: an unsubscription will be routed from the AP to the M operator using unicast and will arrive at the M operator slice that actually holds the subscription.

Alternatively to this default mechanism, the user can decide to defer selection to a library, denoted by `libcluster` in Figure 4, which supports more complex forms of subscription clustering (see Section 4.2.2). A clustering algorithm can maintain a slice-supported state, which allows for deciding on subscription placement based on the content of that subscription. This incurs additional costs at the AP operator level, in return for a better performance at the M operator level. In case the selection mechanism is not deterministic and reproducible, unsubscriptions need to be broadcast to all slices of the corresponding M operator.

Publications need to be matched against all subscriptions. They are thus broadcast from the AP operator to all slices in the corresponding M operator. Note that our architecture targets deployments in clouds or clusters, which are typically supported by dedicated, high-performance network infrastructures. The broadcast operation of publications in our architecture is designed to take advantage of the availability of IP multicast in such settings for dispatching publications, although our current evaluation does not exploit this feature.

3.2.2 Matching Operator

The *Matching* (M) operator supports publication *filtering*. An M operator is associated with a library, denoted by `libfilter` in Figure 4, operating on the independently-maintained state at each of its slices. This library matches incoming publications against registered subscriptions. Different filtering implementations can be used as `libfilter` for different M operators, but they must comply with a simple API supporting two main operations: (1) storing/removing subscriptions based on their identifiers; and (2) processing a publication and returning a list of matching subscriber identifiers. At this stage, the content of the subscriptions and publications themselves is only accessed by the filtering library, making our architecture oblivious to the nature of the matching operation. The default filtering library provided with STREAMHUB is based on the SIENA counting algorithm [12] and is described in Section 4.2.1. Privacy-preserving filtering can be easily implemented using asymmetric scalar-product preserving encryption [18] or other mechanisms [25, 26, 34]. Recent proposals to reduce the cost of privacy-preserving encrypted filtering through the use of a pre-filtering stage [6] can also trivially be integrated to `libfilter` libraries.

Subscriptions are stored in the state maintained for each slice. This state can be accessed concurrently using read and read-write locks (see Section 4 for implementation details). As filtering only requires reading the subscription set, and since most pub/sub workloads are dominated by publications, this allows for vertical scaling of the filtering operation for each slice of the M operator on multiple cores.

An M operator slice calls its `libfilter` for each incoming publication and generates an output event composed by the publication p and a list of matching subscriber identifiers, $s_1, s_2, \ldots, s_n$. When this list is empty, an output event indicating the lack of matching subscription is generated. The event is then sent to the next operator, the *Exit Point* (EP), using unicast. The routing key for selecting the slice of the EP operator is the identifier of the publication p. As

Operator	Role	Description
AP Access Point	Subscription *partitioning*	– Receives subscription events and dispatches each to a single slice of an M operator. Optionally applies subscription clustering using a `libcluster` library. – Receives publications, forwards them to all slices of an M operator.
M Matching	Publication *filtering*	– Receives subscriptions and forwards them to the `libfilter` library. The `libfilter` library stores the subscription and corresponding subscriber identifier in the operator slice state. – Receives publication events and forwards them to the `libfilter` library, which returns a set of matching subscriber identifiers. The M operator slice forwards each publication and list of matching subscriber identifiers to the EP operator by unicast, using the publication identifier as key.
EP Exit Point	Publication *dispatching*	– Receives a publication and list of matching subscriber identifiers. When all lists are received, prepares the notifications, splits the list of matching identifiers, and dispatches them to corresponding DCCPs.

Table 1: Operators supporting scalable CBR.

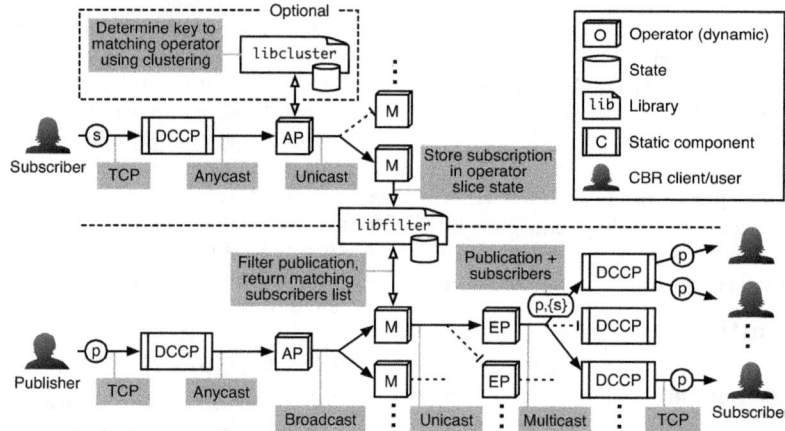

Figure 4: Path taken by subscriptions (top) and publications (bottom) in the StreamHub architecture.

a result, each slice of the M operator processing p will send its list of matching identifiers to the same slice of the EP operator.[4]

3.2.3 Exit Point Operator

The *Exit Point* (EP) operator acts as the output operator of the engine. It shares similarities with the *reduce* phase in the MapReduce terminology [19]. Each incoming publication will be filtered at all slices at the M operator level, but will be processed by a single slice at the EP operator level. An EP operator slice receives the publication and lists of matching subscriber identifiers from all slices of the M operator (or notifications of empty matching lists). Once lists have been received from all M operator slices (or after a timeout to avoid slow M operator slices to delay notifications), the EP operator proceeds with *publication dispatching*: it contacts each DCCP maintaining a connection to at least one interested subscriber and sends it a notification message together with the identifiers of matching subscribers connected to that DCCP. The latter is then in charge of propagating the notification to the actual subscribers.

4. IMPLEMENTATION

We implement our architecture on top of a stream processing engine, STREAMMINE [9]. Other frameworks also present the features and abstractions our implementation requires, such as S4 [33], Storm [2], or Continuous-MapReduce [5].

---

[4]If publications are of significant size, it is possible to have a single slice of the M operator send p and the others sending only their lists.

We present an overview of STREAMMINE in this section, as well as the `libfilter` and `libcluster` libraries supported by our prototype STREAMHUB.

4.1 StreamMine stream processing engine

STREAMMINE is a framework that targets scalable processing of information flows in the form of streams of *events*. Its architecture follows the design principles presented at the beginning of Section 3 and illustrated in Figure 1. STREAMMINE allows defining operators organized in a DAG. Operators are composed of a number of *slices* that typically reside on separate machines in a processing cluster or a cloud, and have unique identifiers (*id*). Slices of the same operator share the same code, in the form of an *event handler*, a function that is called whenever a new event is received and may emit new events for operators downstream in the DAG (for instance, in Figure 1, slices of operator 1 may generate events for operator 2 or 3). The final operator is responsible for propagating the stream of resulting events to the clients of the event-based application.

STREAMMINE provides support for communication among operators and for management of the state that may be maintained by operator slices. Communication between operators is exclusively conducted based on events. Each event is a <key,value> pair. STREAMMINE supports *unicast*, *anycast*, and *broadcast* communication primitives. The operator to which events are sent is chosen upon their creation. STREAMMINE communication primitives are oblivious to the content of events, which may only be used inside event handler functions. All communications take place on pre-established and persistent TCP connections: all slices of one operator are

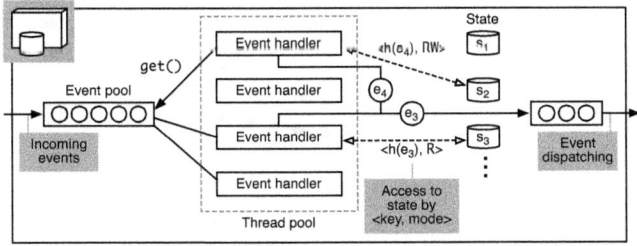

Figure 5: Details of an operator slice from Figure 1 supported by 4 threads.

persistently connected to all slices of the next operator(s) in the DAG.

The *unicast* primitive determines the *id* of the slice in the next operator by using a key and a hash-function (a simple modulo by default). A specific hash-function can be specified by the event handler function, which may implement more sophisticated stream partitioning mechanisms. The *anycast* primitive sends the event to a random slice of the next operator. The *broadcast* primitive sends the event to all slices of the next operator.

STREAMMINE operators slices can be either stateless or stateful, and can be composed of several independent processing threads to support vertical scalability when running on a multi-core processor. All threads of all slices of a given operator support the execution of the same event handling function. Figure 5 presents a detailed view of the state of the greyed slice from Figure 1. Threads from a pool process incoming events from an input queue using a part of the state determined according to the event identifiers. The state of a slice (such as a window of events or summary information from previously processed events) is managed by STREAMMINE, and can be partitioned using the same keys that are used for unicast routing between operators. Each thread accesses the state corresponding to the event to process using the appropriate read-only (R) or read-write (RW) mode. An event with key k_1 can be processed in parallel with another event with key k_2 as long as $k_1 \neq k_2$ or, if $k_1 = k_2$, only when both accesses are read-only.

4.2 Filtering and Clustering Libraries

In the following, we present the filtering and clustering libraries (`libfilter` and `libcluster`) that STREAMHUB currently supports. While these libraries are based on known algorithms and do not represent novel contributions *per se*, they contribute to the overall performance of STREAMHUB as studied in Section 5.

4.2.1 Filtering Libraries

STREAMHUB can support any filtering scheme if implemented through an appropriate `libfilter` library. We listed variants of filtering schemes in Section 2.2. We note that our architecture also supports filtering schemes that need to maintain a state for each of the subscription they store, across the processing of several publications. For instance, a subscriber might wish to receive only the nth publication that matches a given subscription, or be able to send subscriptions on the statistical evolution of publications attributes (e.g., over a window of publications). The corresponding state can be maintained by the `libfilter` in the slice-supported state.

STREAMHUB currently features an attribute-based filtering

scheme library (`libfilter`) that uses a counting algorithm similar to that of SIENA [12]. It organizes predicates for received subscriptions in a forwarding table. An incoming publication will traverse and match in this forwarding table the predicates organized in conjunction sets. Each subscription is associated with a counter that specifies how many of its predicates have been matched so far. When a predicate is satisfied, the counters of all associated subscriptions are increased, and the whole subscription is marked as matched when all predicates of a subscription have been satisfied. Numerical predicates are indexed according to their type $(=, <, >)$ and sorted by values in order to speed up traversals. Therefore, typically only a small part of the graph is traversed by publications. The algorithm generally scales sublinearly in the number of evaluated conjunction sets.

4.2.2 Clustering Libraries

When using multiple slices in the matching operator, each of these slices holds a subset of all subscriptions and filters publications concurrently with other matchers. By default, we partition subscriptions in a simple and deterministic way using a hash. This splits the load among all M operator slices. However, for many filtering schemes, filtering performance can be improved when subscriptions are partitioned in a content-aware manner. These types of subscription clustering are more costly than hash-based partitioning but they result in gains for the publication filtering performance. This is the case of the attribute-based filtering scheme described previously. As similar subscriptions are stored in the same M operator slice, the filtering algorithm may be able to better factorize common predicates and achieve higher filtering performance (this typically depends on the ability of the filtering operator to support containment determination between subscriptions). For pub/sub systems that process more publications than subscriptions, the relative gain can be significant as we show in our evaluation.

STREAMHUB supports various clustering algorithms by the means of `libcluster` libraries, that can optionally maintain state about previous subscriptions. When multiple filtering schemes are supported by multiple M operators, each slice of the AP operator supports a different `libcluster` (or default hash-based unicasting) for each such M operator. Deterministic clustering allows unicasting unsubscriptions while non-deterministic clustering require broadcasting unsubscriptions. STREAMHUB features the two clustering libraries described below.

K-Means [39]: This clustering algorithm performs a partitioning of the subscriptions into K groups and a repetitive re-assignment based on the distance between subscriptions and groups until convergence. The algorithm is stateful and non-deterministic. We implement it in an online manner (*sequential* K-Means) for the dynamic clustering of subscriptions.

Event Space Partitioning (ESP) [38]: The space of subscriptions is represented as a d_s dimensional space, where d_s is the number of attributes. Each M operator slice is responsible for subscriptions that fall within its portion of the space. Subscriptions that intersect multiple domains are managed by the M operator slice that hosts the first attribute in lexicographic order. As the value d_s cannot be known in advance with content-based routing, it will increase when encountering subscriptions with unknown attributes. This clustering mechanism is stateful but deterministic.

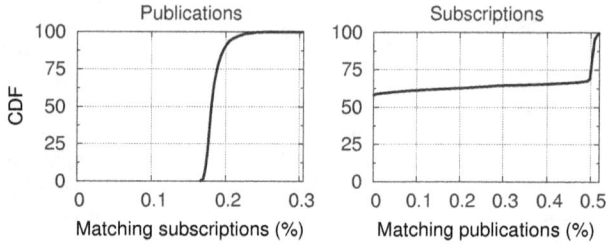

Figure 6: Workload characteristics: cumulative distribution of matching set sizes for publications (left) and matching ratios for subscriptions (right).

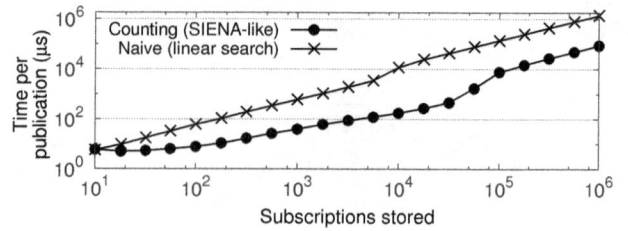

Figure 7: Performance of the counting libfilter for filtering incoming publications with respect to the size of the stored subscriptions set.

5. EVALUATION

In this section, we present the experimental validation of STREAMHUB on a cluster of 48 nodes, each with two quad-core Intel Xeon (E5405) 2 GHz processors and 8 GB of RAM (384 cores total), interconnected with full-duplex 1 Gbps Ethernet. Our implementation uses the C++ language. We configure STREAMMINE to use batching between operators. Up to 16 KB of events can be stored in output buffers for each operator, and sent in batches or after a time limit. Batching allows increasing maximal supported throughput but has an impact on delays, as we demonstrate at the end of this Section.

We first present the characteristics of the pub/sub workload used for the evaluation, followed by the baseline performance of the counting algorithm (libfilter). We then proceed to a operator-by-operator evaluation of the STREAMHUB architecture, highlighting performance and scalability of each of the operators. We describe the impact of subscription clustering (libcluster) and evaluate how the system scales when using an increasing number of nodes. Finally, we present a comparison of our approach with a broker overlay solution running on the same cluster.

5.1 Experimental Workload

We constructed an experimental workload similar to the one used for the evaluation of Meghdoot [24]. It targets an attribute-based filtering scheme. We gathered five years of quotes for 200 randomly selected stocks from Yahoo! Finance [1]. This corresponds to over 250,000 publications. We built synthetic subscriptions based on the same categories as in [24]. These subscriptions contain a variety of ranges and equality predicates on the attributes of stock quotes, namely the symbol, date, exchanged volume, and daily statistics on their price (open, close, high, low). The characteristics of the workload are detailed in Figure 6. They represent a moderately selective type of pub/sub workload: a publication needs to be dispatched to a median of 0.18% of all subscriptions (with 100,000 subscriptions, each publication generates a median of 180 notifications), while a large part of subscriptions do not find publications of interest in the workload but yet need to be processed by the M operator.

5.2 Baseline Filtering Performance

We first evaluate the raw performance of the libfilter filtering library based on the SIENA-like [12] counting algorithm. We compare it to a naive linear-search filtering mechanism acting as a baseline. Figure 7 indicates that the filtering operation cost evolves sublinearly and is at least an order of magnitude better than the naive algorithm above 500 stored subscriptions. Nonetheless, the cost of filtering can grow quite high with large sets of subscriptions, as can be observed on the right side of the graph. This highlights the importance of scaling the processing of incoming publications horizontally and vertically to sustain a high filtering throughput, and to process an incoming publication against subsets of the overall set of subscriptions to reduce dispatching delays.

5.3 Performance of Operators

We now proceed to an operator-by-operator evaluation of STREAMHUB. Our methodology is to add one operator at a time, replacing the operators downstream the DAG by *sink* operators that receive the events but do not process them further. We denote such sink operators as S(AP), S(M), and S(EP). We focus our evaluation on the scalability aspects of each operator. All experiments are based on 180-seconds runs of STREAMHUB, during which the system is fed with subscriptions and/or publications as fast as possible to observe the maximal achievable throughput. When observing the performance of the publication filtering operation, subscriptions are registered before starting the measurement.

In our evaluation, the DCCPs are replaced by *generators* that inject the workload into the AP operator. We first verified that these generators can provide the system with a sufficient throughput of publications and subscriptions and do not represent a bottleneck. Our results (not shown) indicate that the generators are able to nearly saturate the input bandwidth capacity of the nodes that host the AP operator slices. This indicates they will not impair the remainder of the evaluation.

We present the complete operator-by-operator evaluation results in Figure 8. We look primarily at the throughput in terms of bandwidth and events processed.

5.3.1 AP Operator Scalability

The first column of two plots in Figure 8 presents the AP operator scalability. It depicts the maximal input and output throughput of the operator with a publications-only workload. This corresponds to the worst case scenario since publications, unlike subscriptions, need to be broadcast by each AP operator slice to all sink S(M) operator slices. As expected, the input throughput of the AP operator is inversely proportional to the number of sink S(M) operator slices: a copy of each publication needs to be made for every S(M) operator slice and the bottleneck becomes the output bandwidth of AP operators. The planned support for IP multicast between the AP and M operators would boost

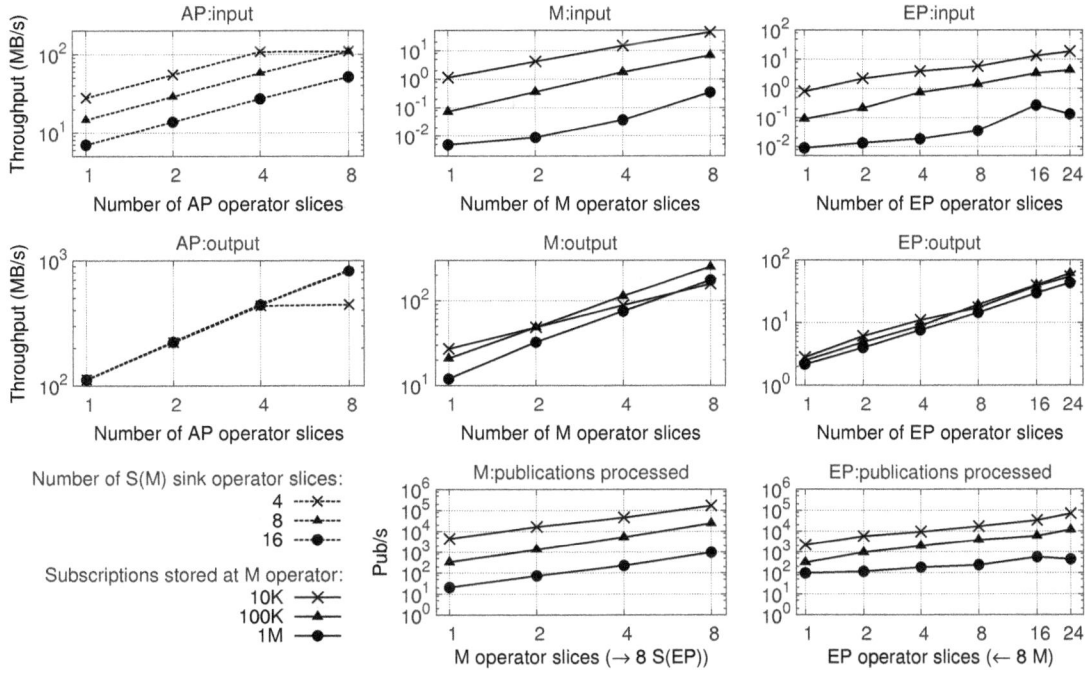

Figure 8: Scaling of StreamHub operators: Input and output throughput for all operators when varying the number of slices and subscriptions. Each operator is evaluated with the downstream operator replaced by a sink. We use one physical machine per slice.

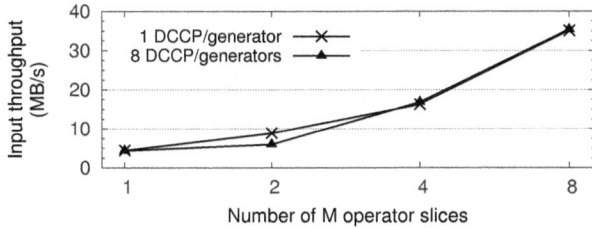

Figure 9: Scaling of the M operator receiving and storing a subscriptions-only workload. The throughput corresponds to the traffic between the DCCP/generators and the AP operator, with 8 AP operator slices.

performance for this operation. We observe nonetheless that this output throughput nearly saturates the cross-bandwidth of the connections between the AP and S(M) operator slices, and is able to saturate the input bandwidth of the S(M) operator slices (serving 104 MB/s of publications to each of them). This indicates that the AP operator will not hinder scalability when the S(M) sink operator slices are replaced by real M operator slices that need to perform the computationally-intensive filtering operation, as confirmed by our next experiment.

5.3.2 M Operator: Subscription Storage Scalability

We start the evaluation of the M operator by assessing the scalability of the subscription storage with a subscriptions-only workload. Figure 9 presents the average bandwidth that the generators are able to push through the AP operator for storage at the M operator level. We use a set of 8 AP operator slices so that the AP operator does not form a bottleneck. We use 1 to 8 M operator slices. We observe that the scalability of the subscription storage is almost linear and STREAMHUB is able to register a flow of 35.4 MB/s with 8 M operator slices, which corresponds to a constant flow of 150,000 subscriptions stored per second. We observe a slight degradation of the throughput when using 8 generators and only 2 M operator slices. The reason was tracked down to overflows in input buffers of the M operator slices, leading to retransmissions of messages from the AP operator and some loss of bandwidth.

5.3.3 M Operator: Publication Matching Scalability

We now investigate the scalability of the filtering operation at the M operator level, i.e., matching each publication against the set of stored subscriptions. We use a set of 8 sink S(EP) operator slices as the downstream operator and 8 AP operator slices for the upstream operator. The second column of three plots in Figure 8 presents the achieved input/output throughput and the number of publications that the M operator filters per second, including transmission to the downstream S(EP) operator. We clearly observe that the architecture scales: the addition of new operator slices to the M operator results in linear increase of its processing capacity. Note that, as expected from the workload characteristics (median matching set of 0.18% of stored subscriptions), the bandwidth requirements are higher for output than for input because the publications are augmented with a potentially large list of matching identifiers.

5.3.4 EP Operator Scalability

We complete the operator-by-operator scalability evaluation by replacing the S(EP) sink operator slices with their real counterparts that perform publication dispatching. We

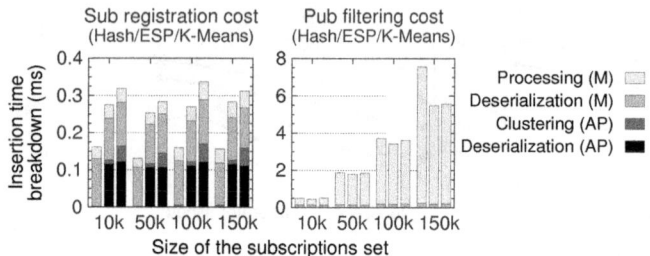

Figure 10: Overhead of clustering for storing subscriptions (left) and impact on filtering efficiency (right). Each group of stacked bars shows the breakdowns of average costs for one subscription or one publication matched against the corresponding subscription set. Each group has three bars for hash-based (no clustering), ESP, and K-Means.

use 8 generators, 8 AP, and 8 M operators slices. We observe in the third column of three plots of Figure 8 the input/output throughput of the EP operator and the number of publications that are effectively dispatched. With a configuration of 8 EP operator slices, STREAMHUB is already able to filter and dispatch from 3.8 K to 17 K publications per second, for respectively 100 K and 10 K stored subscriptions (corresponding to 684 K and 306 K notifications sent out to subscribers per second, respectively).

5.3.5 Discussion

The results of the operator-by-operator evaluation clearly show that the subscription registration and publication filtering operations scale by adding more slices (and thus physical machines) to the operator that supports them. Adequately provisioning the architecture allows handling an arbitrary number of publications and subscriptions. One should point out that the specific workload considered in our evaluation is costlier for the operators that deal with publication dispatching (EP) and matching (M) than for handling and forwarding incoming publications (AP).

5.4 Impact of Clustering

We now investigate the impact of using a `libcluster` library at the AP operator level for clustering subscriptions. Our objective is to evaluate if the additional cost for registering a subscription in the system using content-aware clustering is compensated by the subsequent performance gain when filtering publications against stored subscriptions. We present in Figure 10 the time required to store a subscription at the M operator level (left) and process an incoming publication against the set of stored subscriptions (right). Times are obtained by averaging over 10,000 events. The breakdown distinguishes between the different operations at the AP and M operators: deserializing the event at the AP operator level (for subscriptions when using clustering) and processing it (clustering, storing, or matching) at both the AP and M operators levels.

We observe that the cost of subscription insertion increases due to the additional deserialization and treatment at the AP operator level. On the other hand, the use of clustering yields significant performance gains when matching publications against a large set of subscriptions: for 150 K subscriptions matching is 25 to 27% faster when using K-Means or ESP.

This supports our claim that using a `libcluster` library, when applicable to the filtering scheme being used, may significantly increase the filtering performance or reduce the number of M operator slices required to sustain a given publication filtering throughput requirement. At the same time, the use of a `libcluster` library does not break the separation of concerns and filtering schema agnosticism that underpins the complete architecture.

5.5 Overall Performance

Our last experiment with STREAMHUB relates to the overall provisioning and scaling of the complete architecture. We consider the case where a cluster or a cloud virtual environment needs to be scaled up to increase the throughput of the pub/sub process, with the objective of offering a linearly increasing performance as more physical nodes are added to support the service, and to sustain low and predictable end-to-end delays. As previously demonstrated, the optimal assignment of slices (and thus, physical machines) to operators depends on the nature of the workload. For the purpose of this evaluation, we determined the best configuration for a given budget of machines based on the operator-by-operator experiments. Our architecture is designed to easily support dynamic scaling by migrating slices between physical machines. We leave the integration of such mechanisms and the appropriate decision-making systems to future work. Figure 11 presents the evolution of the publication throughput with clusters of 8 to 32 machines (our other machines are used for 8 generators and 16 sink DCCPs). We observe that the scalability objectives of STREAMHUB are met: there is a linear gain in performance between 8 to 32 machines. The maximal supported throughput between the smaller and the larger configuration when using the ESP partitioning is actually 4.26x higher, which is mostly due to the reduced contention on the AP operator slices. We note that the impact of clustering is consistent with what we observed in Figure 10: throughput is from 10% to 28% better with clustering (see Figure 8). Table 2 presents the average end-to-end delays (between the reception of a publication and the reception of the corresponding notifications by the subscribers) observed by clients, and their variations. In this case, we selected the throughput to be around half of the maximal supported throughput in the 16 and 32 nodes configurations. We consider two settings, with batching and without. Batching increases throughput but also introduces extra delays. Disabling it divides the maximal supported throughput by approximately a factor of 2. In both cases though, the delays are low (around a second with batching, or a fraction of a second without it) and predictable as they show only slight variations between publications.

5.6 Comparison with PADRES

For completeness, we have also performed experiments with the same set of subscriptions and publications using the most recent version of PADRES [27] (v2.0). As detailed in our introduction, PADRES is based on different design choices than STREAMHUB: it establishes and maintains a network of brokers that collectively implement pub/sub functionality and is specific to a particular filtering scheme, while our design dedicates different machines to each operation and is independent from the actual filtering scheme that is used.

Our PADRES setup consists of one publisher, one subscriber, and a varying number of brokers. We verified that

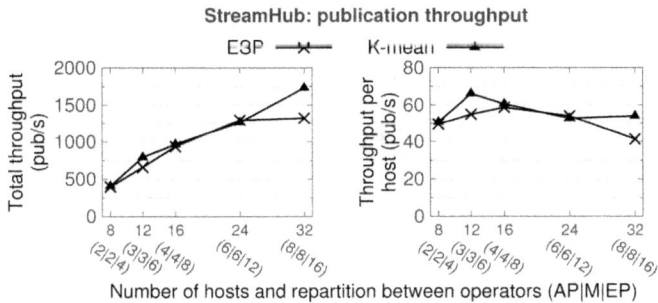

StreamHub: publication throughput

Figure 11: Throughput of StreamHub with 100,000 subscriptions, using `libcluster` and the workload-optimal configurations for each number of available machines. The number of slices at each operator is indicated within parentheses.

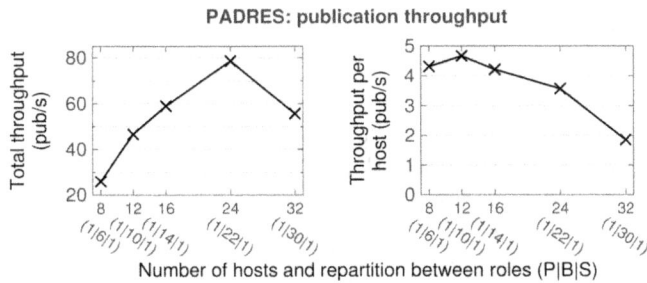

PADRES: publication throughput

Figure 12: Throughput of PADRES with 100,000 subscriptions. The number of hosts is indicated within parentheses: a single publisher (P) and a single subscriber (S) were sufficient to fully load the brokers (B).

neither the publisher nor the subscriber represent a bottleneck in the experiments. The publisher and the subscriber are connected to every broker. Subscriptions and publications are randomly partitioned among brokers. Every machine executes 4 broker instances, which corresponds to half of its available cores. Using all cores on each machines yielded lower performance figures, probably due to contention on resources. Results are averaged over 100 publications, measured after an initial warm-up phase of 2,000 messages to enable JIT optimizations.

Figure 12 shows the throughput achieved with the same 100,000 subscriptions as for Figure 11 and various numbers of brokers. We observe that PADRES scales well for up to 88 brokers (i.e., 22 machines, each running 4 broker processes) but seems to suffer when adding more brokers. Actually, each publication has to be filtered by multiple brokers for propagation to other brokers due to the use of routing tables that are constructed according to the filtering schema that is used. This adds to the overall load and reduces the contribution of each broker to overall throughput (Figure 12, right). We finally observe that the maximal raw throughput achieved in our cluster is two orders of magnitude higher with our architecture than with PADRES. While a part of this difference can be accounted to language and implementation differences, the higher parallelism and independence of operations in our architecture clearly helps improving the filtering throughputs.

Configuration	(AP 4|M 4|EP 8)		(AP 8|M 8|EP 16)	
Batching	16 K	None	16 K	None
Publications/s	500	200	1,000	500
Average delay	1.06 s	0.36 s	0.98 s	0.22 s
Std. dev.	0.28 s	0.17 s	0.3 s	0.15 s

Table 2: End-to-end delays (settings as Figure 11).

6. CONCLUSION

We presented a novel design for high-throughput pub/sub services. We focused on the support of large-scale applications communicating through a managed environment providing the pub/sub service, such as a publicly available cluster or a public cloud deployment. Our architecture is highly parallel and scalable, and can readily support arbitrary complex filtering schemes, including encrypted or state-based filtering. We do so by departing from previous approaches based on broker overlays and by decoupling the architecture and communication flows of the pub/sub system from the filtering scheme(s) and the subscriptions workload. Our implementation, STREAMHUB, splits the pub/sub service into fundamental operations, allocated to horizontally and vertically scalable operators supported by a scalable stream processing engine. The evaluation of STREAMHUB on a cluster with up to 384 cores indicates that it can sustain high throughputs of subscription registrations and publication filtering: we filter thousands of publications against hundreds of thousands of registered subscriptions, resulting in hundreds of thousands notifications sent to clients every second.

This work opens several research perspectives that will be part of our future work on high-throughput pub/sub services for large-scale application compositions. The use of privacy-preserving encrypted filtering is a growing requirement for applications running on multiple private clouds and supported by untrusted public cloud infrastructures providing the pub/sub service. We plan on integrating such encrypted filtering approaches [18, 25, 26, 34]. We recently proposed techniques for lowering their computational cost [6], that we can easily integrate as `libfilter` libraries. Publications and subscriptions will need to be encrypted and decrypted as they enter and leave untrusted public clouds. This can be supported in a parallel and scalable manner at the AP and EP operator levels, and supported by pub/sub-specific key management techniques.

We also plan to support *elastic scaling* of the STREAMHUB architecture. This requires observing the workload experienced by each of the three operators and adapting the number of physical machines for each operator according to the requirements of the corresponding pub/sub operation. To that end, we intend to extend STREAMHUB with a resource provisioner for stream processing.

Acknowledgments. The research leading to these results has received funding from the European Community's Seventh Framework Programme (FP7/2007-2013) under grant agreement number 257843 (SRT-15 project). We are grateful to Abhishek Gupta and Amr El Abbadi for their insights on using Yahoo! finance publication workloads.

7. REFERENCES

[1] http://finance.yahoo.com/.
[2] Storm: Distributed and fault-tolerant realtime computation. http://storm-project.net.

[3] M. K. Aguilera, R. E. Strom, D. C. Sturman, M. Astley, and T. D. Chandra. Matching events in a content-based subscription system. In *PODC*, 1999.

[4] M. Altinel and M. J. Franklin. Efficient filtering of xml documents for selective dissemination of information. In *VLDB*, 2000.

[5] N. Backman, K. Pattabiraman, R. Fonseca, and U. Cetintemel. C-MR: continuously executing MapReduce workflows on multi-core processors. In *MapReduce workshop*, 2012.

[6] R. Barazzutti, P. Felber, H. Mercier, E. Onica, and E. Rivière. Thrifty privacy: Efficient support for privacy-preserving publish/subscribe. In *DEBS*, 2012.

[7] N. Beckmann, H.-P. Kriegel, R. Schneider, and B. Seeger. The R*-tree: an efficient and robust access method for points and rectangles. In *SIGMOD*, 1990.

[8] S. Bittner and A. Hinze. The arbitrary boolean publish/subscribe model: making the case. In *DEBS*, 2007.

[9] A. Brito, A. Martin, T. Knauth, S. Creutz, D. Becker de Brum, S. Weigert, and C. Fetzer. Scalable and low-latency data processing with streammapreduce. In *CloudCom*, 2011.

[10] R. Brunelli. *Template Matching Techniques in Computer Vision: Theory and Practice*. Wiley, 2009.

[11] A. Carzaniga, D. S. Rosenblum, and A. L. Wolf. Design and evaluation of a wide-area event notification service. *ACM TCS*, 2001.

[12] A. Carzaniga and A. L. Wolf. Forwarding in a content-based network. In *SIGCOMM*, 2003.

[13] C.Y. Chan, P. Felber, M.N. Garofalakis, and R. Rastogi. Efficient filtering of XML documents with XPath expressions. In *ICDE*, 2002.

[14] R. Chand and P. Felber. Scalable distribution of XML content with XNet. *IEEE TPDS*, 19, 2008.

[15] A. Cheung and H.-A. Jacobsen. Load balancing content-based publish/subscribe systems. *ACM Trans. Comput. Syst.*, 28(4), 2010.

[16] A. Cheung and H.-A. Jacobsen. Publisher placement algorithms in content-based publish/subscribe. In *ICDCS*, 2010.

[17] A. Cheung and H.-A. Jacobsen. Green resource allocation algorithms for publish/subscribe systems. In *ICDCS*, 2011.

[18] S. Choi, G. Ghinita, and E. Bertino. A privacy-enhancing content-based publish/subscribe system using scalar product preserving transformations. In *DEXA*, Lecture Notes in Computer Science, 2010.

[19] J. Dean and S. Ghemawat. Mapreduce: simplified data processing on large clusters. In *OSDI*, 2004.

[20] P.T. Eugster, P. Felber, R. Guerraoui, and A.-M. Kermarrec. The many faces of publish/subscribe. *ACM Computing Surveys*, 2003.

[21] F. Fabret, H. A. Jacobsen, F. Llirbat, J. Pereira, K. A. Ross, and D. Shasha. Filtering algorithms and implementation for very fast publish/subscribe systems. In *SIGMOD*, 2001.

[22] A. Farroukh, E. Ferzli, N. Tajuddin, and H.-A. Jacobsen. Parallel event processing for content-based publish/subscribe systems. In *DEBS*, 2009.

[23] M. Fontoura, S. Sadanandan, J. Shanmugasundaram, S. Vassilvitski, E. Vee, S. Venkatesan, and J. Zien. Efficiently evaluating complex boolean expressions. In *SIGMOD*, 2010.

[24] A. Gupta, O. D. Sahin, D. Agrawal, and A. El Abbadi. Meghdoot: content-based publish/subscribe over p2p networks. In *Middleware*, 2004.

[25] M. Ion, G. Russello, and B. Crispo. Supporting publication and subscription confidentiality in pub/sub networks. In *SecureComm*, 2010.

[26] Mihalea Ion, Giovanni Russello, and Bruno Crispo. An implementation of event and filter confidentiality in pub/sub systems and its application to e-health. In *CCS*, 2010.

[27] H.-A. Jacobsen, A. Cheung, G. Lia, B. Maniymaran, V. Muthusamy, and R. S. Kazemzadeh. The PADRES publish/subscribe system. In *Handbook of Research on Adv. Dist. Event-Based Sys., Pub./Sub. and Message Filtering Tech.*, 2009.

[28] K. R. Jayaram and P. Eugster. Split and subsume: Subscription normalization for effective content-based messaging. In *ICDCS*, 2011.

[29] Z. Jerzak and C. Fetzer. Bloom filter based routing for content-based publish/subscribe. In *DEBS*, 2008.

[30] S. Kale, E. Hazan, F. Cao, and J. P. Singh. Analysis and algorithms for content-based event matching. In *DEBS*, 2005.

[31] R. S. Kazemzadeh and H.-A. Jacobsen. Opportunistic multipath forwarding in content-based publish/subscribe overlays. In *Middleware*, 2012.

[32] W. Li, S. Hu, J. Li, and H.-A. Jacobsen. Community clustering for distributed publish/subscribe systems. In *CLUSTER*, 2012.

[33] L. Neumeyer, B. Robbins, A. Nair, and A. Kesari. S4: Distributed stream computing platform. In *KDCloud*, Sidney, Australia, 2010.

[34] C. Raiciu and D. S. Rosenblum. Enabling confidentiality in content-based publish/subscribe infrastructures. In *Securecomm*, 2006.

[35] J. Reumann. Pub/Sub at Google. CANOE and EuroSys Summer School, 2009.

[36] L. Romano, D. De Mari, Z. Jerzak, and C. Fetzer. A novel approach to QoS monitoring in the cloud. In *CCP*, 2011.

[37] M. Sahami, S. Dumais, D. Heckerman, and E. Horvitz. A bayesian approach to filtering junk e-mail. In *AAAI Workshop on Learning for Text Categorization*, 1998.

[38] Y.-M. Wang, L. Qiu, D. Achlioptas, G. Das, P. Larson, and H. J. Wang. Subscription partitioning and routing in content-based publish/subscribe networks. In *DISC*, 2002.

[39] T. Wong, R. Katz, and S. McCanne. An evaluation of preference clustering in large-scale multicast applications. In *INFOCOM*, 2000.

[40] Y. Yoon, V. Muthusamy, and H.-A. Jacobsen. Foundations for highly available content-based publish/subscribe overlays. In *ICDCS*, 2011.

[41] Y. Zhao and J. Wu. Towards approximate event processing in a large-scale content-based network. In *ICDCS*, 2011.

DYNATOPS: A Dynamic Topic-based Publish/Subscribe Architecture

Ye Zhao
Dept. of Information and
Computer Science
University of California, Irvine
yez@uci.edu

Kyungbaek Kim
Dept. of Electronics and
Computer Engineering
Chonnam National University,
South Korea
kyungbaekkim@jnu.ac.kr

Nalini
Venkatasubramanian
Dept. of Information and
Computer Science
University of California, Irvine
nalini@ics.uci.edu

ABSTRACT

Emerging societal scale notification applications call for a system that is able to efficiently support simple, yet changing subscriptions for a very large number of users. In this paper we propose DYNATOPS, a dynamic topic-based pub/sub architecture that provides efficient scalable societal scale event notifications for dynamic subscriptions via distributed broker networks. In DYNATOPS, users are moderately repositioned on brokers and brokers are moderately repositioned on the overlay structure for efficient event notifications, to adapt to the publications and subscription dynamics. In contrast to existing self-organized techniques, the broker network reconfiguration in DYNATOPS is executed in a planned manner utilizing a cost-driven reconfiguration process. With extensive experiments, we observe that under highly dynamic subscriptions DYNATOPS can still maintain an efficient dissemination structure that provides 30% less notification delay and overhead in general, and a reconfiguration cost reduction of 80% as compared to other state-of-the-art systems.

Categories and Subject Descriptors

C.2.4 [**Computer-Communication Networks**]: Distributed Systems

Keywords

topic based, publish/subscribe, dynamic subscriptions

1. INTRODUCTION

The recent years have witnessed the growth of societal scale notification systems that have penetrated multiple aspects of our day-to-day life. Key examples include mobile social networks (e.g. Twitter and Foursquare), geomarketing (e.g. shopalerts.att.com), traffic and weather alerts (e.g. www.wunderground.com and weather.gov), emergency response (e.g. www.gdacs.org/alerts and www.mywarn.com),

etc. These systems are large (e.g. Twitter is estimated to reach 500 million users in 2012 and currently handles over 340 million tweets daily), geographically distributed and largely subscription based. The notion of subscriptions in such systems is often simple, and instantiated by an average citizen – deals for local shops, traffic alerts for freeways, weather conditions for zipcodes, and location check-ins from friends. Moreover, we observe an emerging trend that the interests of such users, i.e. subscriptions, are short lived (duration of minutes or hours) and change dynamically based on users' locations or contexts.

For instance, mobile subscribers are often interested in events and information within their immediate vicinity; the dynamically changing location is a key aspect of what constitutes a subscription and consequently a relevant notification in this case. In disasters (e.g. earthquakes), people's information needs (i.e. subscriptions) change with the evolution of the disaster event (e.g. pre-disaster or post-disaster). An individual's region of interest, i.e. subscription, changes as he/she moves into or out of disaster region; people are anxious to check the safety of their beloved ones and the changing locations or statuses of families or friends cause subscription changes as well. Such shifts in notification needs calls for a system that is able to efficiently support simple, yet changing subscriptions for a very large number of users.

Publish/subscribe has for long been a popular communication paradigm to provide customized notifications to users in a distributed environment due to its loose coupling between the information providers (i.e. publishers) and consumers (i.e. subscribers). Pub/Sub systems are either content-based where subscribers receive notifications when the content of the message matches their interest [6, 35, 32, 8, 16] or topic-based [30, 40, 36, 20] when the "topic" of the publication matches their interest.

One of the main incentives for content-based pub/sub is to enable delivery of relevant and meaningful notifications through rich and expressive subscription languages. Here, sophisticated subscription management strategies are usually required to determine matching subscribers and subsequently route only the relevant events; runtime overheads for subscription insertion/removal and event matching are much higher than topic-based implementations [5, 34, 28]. Over the last decade, significant progress has been made in the design of pub/sub systems to address scalability and efficiency of content-based pub/sub [28, 13, 21, 14, 22], largely motivated by the needs of enterprise systems. The design of pub/sub systems taking into account frequently changing subscriptions is beginning to receive interest, especially in the context of content-based pub/sub systems where the emphasis is on designing novel subscription languages and schemas. For example, [28] proposed a parametric subscription language in content-based pub/sub systems to reduce broker runtime complexity in the event of a subscription update. The key idea is to insert variables into subscriptions which may be updated frequently so that only variable update is performed during subscription update. Techniques to manage the overheads due to event matching and dynamic subscription updates are however still a concern.

We conjecture that a topic-based pub/sub system can form the basis of an efficient architecture to deal with the simple, yet changing notification needs of a large number of users; for example by routing events through group multicast to peers that match subscription topics. Subscription insertion/removal and event routing on a broker can be easily done in $O(1)$ time. Indeed, topic-based pub/sub systems have been widely deployed in contexts where events divide naturally into groups (i.e. "topics") and efficient information notification is demanded [23, 9]. More recent topic-based pub sub systems, e.g. Twitter, have scaled to a very large number of users.

In this paper, we propose DYNATOPS, a novel topic-based pub/sub system that provides efficient scalable event notifications for dynamic subscriptions. To enable rapid notifications that can scale to the societal level, in the DYNATOPS system (Section 3), users connect to a distributed broker network that is built on top of a structured overlay for subscription management and publication distribution. DYNATOPS incorporates two unique broker management mechanisms to address subscription dynamicity. First, it uses a **similarity-based user placement** (Section 4) technique to map DYNATOPS users to nearby brokers. Under fast changing subscriptions such as those caused by changing locations of users, conventional user placement policies show a dramatic increase in their subscription management overhead. The proposed technique efficiently groups users sharing similar interests to be managed by the same set of brokers, to effectively alleviate the overhead with regard to subscription updates among brokers. Our experimental results (Section 6) indicate over 40% reduction in brokers' subscription management overhead as compared to other state of the art techniques under highly dynamic subscriptions.

Second, more importantly, to provide efficient event notifications, DYNATOPS incorporates a broker reconfiguration process (Section 5) that is both **subscription and structure-aware**. Unlike existing topic-based pub/sub systems where topology changes are triggered in a self-organizing manner to reflect subscription changes, we propose a cost-driven reconfiguration process that changes topology in a planned manner. The key intuition behind our approach is that reconfiguration of the broker network is achieved by merely moving broker nodes to positions in an overlay structure where routing is already highly optimized - this reduces the effort for reconfiguration in a large scale system. Furthermore, we trigger the reconfigurations only when they are likely to have high utility. The combination of these strategies allows us to reduce notification delay and overhead by 30%, and reduce the cost of reconfiguration by over 80% as compared to other state of the art techniques under highly dynamic subscriptions (Section 6).

2. RELATED WORK

Conventional pub/sub systems assume that clients join the broker environment in one of the following ways: (a) connecting to any broker with no restrictions [27, 35], or (b) connecting to the closest broker [16, 24, 29]. [7] is the first to investigate client placements that optimize delivery delay and system load. However, the work focused on the placement of a few known publishers under fixed subscribers' subscriptions and broker overlay topologies. Such schemes are inefficient in societal scale notification applications where (a) publishers are many (in general the entire user set) and (b) subscriptions change frequently based on user interests. In this paper, we explore a similarity-based user placement that takes into account both the dynamics of user subscriptions and broker load. The proposed technique can effectively reduce subscription management overhead and improve notification efficiency under dynamic subscriptions of users.

Building and reconfiguring overlay networks that take into account nodes' subscriptions for dissemination efficiency has been explored in both content-based and topic-based pub/sub systems. In content-based paradigm, Sub-2-Sub [39] is a content-based protocol that clusters nodes according to their subscriptions to construct a ring for each attribute. [37] proposed a self-organizing algorithm to cluster brokers that supposedly will be target for the same events in the near future. [43] discussed primitives that reconfiguration protocols need to implement to ensure high availability with minimum disruption under topology changes. In topic-based paradigm, many recent topic-based pub/sub systems [38, 42, 20, 36, 31, 19] build and maintain their overlays based on brokers' subscriptions. For rendezvous-based pub/sub systems that maintain topic-routing trees, Magnet [38] clusters nodes with similar subscriptions on a skewed DHT, and explores a customized routing to reduce the number of relay nodes in the multicast trees. When a node's subscription changes, the node needs to rejoin the DHT to be placed onto a new position based on its new subscription. On the other hand, [42, 20, 36, 31, 19] build relay-free overlays without topic rendezvous and explore gossip-based dissemination and/or in-cluster flooding to disseminate event notifications. Tera and StAN [36, 31] creates dedicated topic overlays for each topic. A node joins overlays for the topics that it subscribes to by connecting to a node already in the overlay. SpiderCast and TCO [20, 19] build a single unstructured overlay that strives to maximize clustering of nodes according to their interest in topics. The focus of system is to keep low node degrees while maintaining the topic-connected property as the foundation of the relay-free routing. This is achieved by the neighbor maintenance routine in SpiderCast and the overlay construction algorithm in TCO, both of which can trigger an overlay topology reconfiguration when a node's subscription changes. PolderCast [42] maintains a ring structure for each topic and combines deterministic dissemination over a ring with probabilistic dissemination similar to gossiping. Its overlay management mechanism also triggers topology updates whenever node churns or subscription changes.

While all the above systems trigger topology changes to reflect subscription changes in a self-organizing manner, in this paper we design DYNATOPS with a different philosophy. We argue that in societal scale notification applications where subscriptions are short lived and frequent change is the norm, the topology reconfiguration should be incorporated in a more systematic and planned manner in the sys-

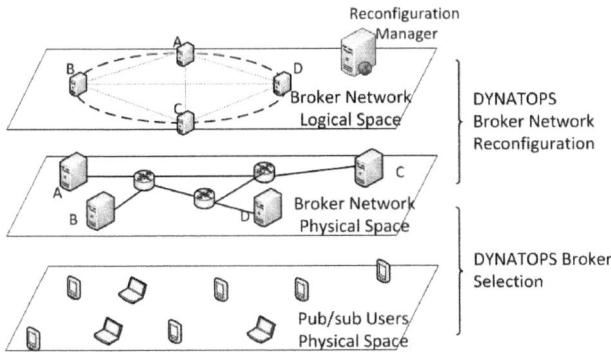

Figure 1: DYNATOPS system overview

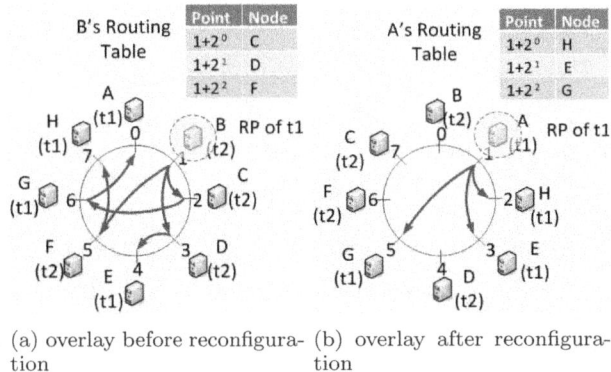

(a) overlay before reconfiguration

(b) overlay after reconfiguration

Figure 2: example of broker network reconfiguration

tem design. This is to reduce the reconfiguration overhead from frequent subscription changes that we already know will happen. This is achieved through built-in mechanisms that detect when sufficient changes have occurred and that deal with those changes through planned overlay reconfigurations. We design a cost-driven reconfiguration process that detects when sufficient changes have occurred and deals with those changes through planned overlay reconfigurations that are likely to have high utility.

3. DYNATOPS OVERVIEW

Figure 1 shows the DYNATOPS system where pub/sub users connect to brokers for topic subscriptions and event publications. To provide scalable and efficient pub/sub services, DYNATOPS maintains a broker network based on structured overlays (e.g. Chord DHT [25]); Brokers are configured onto the overlay as overlay nodes with unique nodeIDs. Similar to [30, 40], DYNATOPS constructs a Rendezvous-based broker network and maintains independent topic routing trees to route event messages of different topics: each topic has a Rendezvous Point (RP), which is an overlay node responsible for the hashed key of the topic name in the DHT, and the RP serves as the root of the corresponding topic routing tree. Every broker determines which trees to join based on the subscriptions of users that connects to it. A broker must join the topic tree when at least one of its users subscribes to the topic, and leaves the tree when all of them unsubscribe to minimize notification overhead. For convenience, we use "broker subscribes to the topic" to refer to the first case and "broker unsubscribes to the topic" to refer to the second case. A topic routing tree

spans all brokers that subscribe to the topic and it is created in a top-down fashion such that the routing path from the root to each of the brokers in the tree is consistent with the default routing path by the underlying key-based routing algorithm. An example of topic routing tree using Chord is shown in Fig. 2a. There are 8 brokers uniformly placed into the structure with their mapped IDs shown on the ring. We considered 2 topics $t1$ and $t2$, and they are hashed to IDs 1 and 4 respectively. Each broker is interested in only one topic. The arrows in the ring indicate the topic routing tree for $t1$ based on the routing table of each broker (we only show one of them in the figure). For event publications, the published messages are first forwarded from publishers to their topic RPs. Then the RP nodes disseminate the messages along the topic routing trees to every single broker that subscribes to the topic.

3.1 Dynamic Mappings

The centerpiece of the DYNATOPS system are two efficient dynamic mapping algorithms in response to users' and brokers' dynamic subscriptions: 1) a simple distributed *similarity-based user placement* algorithm that maps pub/sub users to pub/sub brokers; 2) the *DYNATOPS broker network reconfiguration* algorithm running on a Reconfiguration Manager to manage the broker network structure (i.e. mapping of brokers to overlay nodes in logical space).

The reconfiguration manager is a logically centralized entity that monitors the pub/sub environment, e.g. rates of event publications and subscription changes at brokers, and intelligently adapts the broker network structure for fast and efficient event notifications. It only communicates with brokers periodically with minimal message overhead. To alleviate the concern that the reconfiguration manager may pose a bottleneck or a single point of failure, it can be distributed over multiple servers using a distributed overlay similar to that proposed in our earlier implementations [1].

The aim of the user placement algorithm is to reduce brokers' subscription changes so as to reduce subscription management overhead and alleviate the demand for broker network reconfiguration (described later) when the pub/sub users' subscriptions are dynamic. This is done by dynamically aggregating users with similar subscriptions to be managed together by the same set of brokers.

However, as brokers' subscription change topic routing trees in rendezvous-based pub/sub may involve unrelated relay brokers that are not themselves interested in the topic but that reside on the routing path from the root to subscribed brokers (see example in Figure 2a). The unrelated relay brokers cause excessive delay and overhead in event notifications. Our aim is to eliminate/reduce the unrelated relay brokers. In DYNATOPS we explore the possibility of dynamically altering the broker network structure to match the underlying (possibly changing) subscription needs - i.e a *Structure and Subscription aware Broker Reconfiguration (SSBR)* to map brokers to overlay nodeIDs. The goal of the reconfiguration is to intelligently adapt the broker network based on updated pub/sub environment to construct efficient topic routing trees. Figure 2b shows an example illustrating how DYNATOPS reconfigures the broker network for efficient event notifications based on updated broker subscriptions. We can see that before reconfiguration, event notification in $t1$ takes 3 unrelated relays (Broker C, D and F are not interested in the topic 1), and 3 maximum hops

(Broker A receives the published event after 3 hops). After reconfiguration, the tree changes along with the change of the mapping and of the routing table on each broker. Note, the topic trees are still constructed following the basic routing rules of Chord. For $t1$, the unrelated relays becomes 0 and the maximum hop becomes 1 after reconfiguration.

Figure 3 shows the system architecture for DYNATOPS broker network reconfiguration. DYNATOPS brokers handle the publications and subscriptions from its pub/sub users through the pub/sub manager component. They also periodically report their pub/sub states (e.g. number of publications and subscription summaries) to the reconfiguration manager. Based on the received information, the reconfiguration manager performs a cost-driven reconfiguration computation to seek a balance between potential performance improvement and reconfiguration cost from the network reconfiguration. The reconfiguration manager then coordinates the overlay structure configuration with the structure manager component on each broker through its configuration controller component.

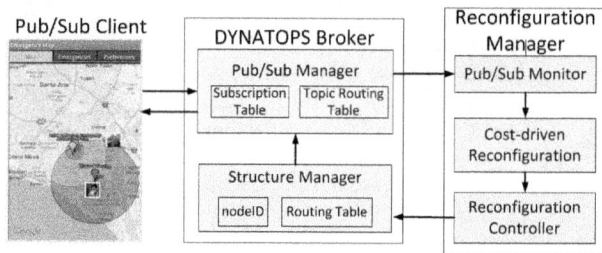

Figure 3: DYNATOPS Broker System Architecture

4. USER PLACEMENT STRATEGY

The core of our user placement strategy is a grouping algorithm that takes as an input the location and subscription of a user, and outputs the broker that is responsible for hosting the user's subscriptions. The goal of the algorithm is to ensure that users with similar subscriptions are grouped and managed by the same set of brokers. The grouping of similar users brings two benefits to the pub/sub system. First, it minimizes the subscription management overhead at brokers. Subscription management overhead incurs in topic-based broker networks when brokers' subscriptions change. The intuition here is that by clustering similar users each broker subscribes to topics that interests all/most of the users it hosts, so that the subscription states of the brokers are more stable and less dependent on a single user's subscription changes. Furthermore, when a user subscribes to a new topic, it is more likely that the topic has also been subscribed by users with similar interests, so that the topic has been subscribed by the broker hosting the user.

Second, it reduces the potential number of brokers that require to subscribe to each single topic. In rendezvous-based pub/sub implementations, the number of brokers subscribing to a topic directly reflects to the size of the topic routing tree and subsequently impacts on the event notification delay and overhead on the specific topic. This is particularly true for DYNATOPS because the broker overlay is configured to eliminate/reduce unrelated relay brokers in topic routing trees so that the tree size is more dependent on the number of brokers subscribed to the topic.

Algorithm 1: User Join Protocol

(1) the user sends the join request to a random broker he knows during bootstrap with its subscriptions. In the case that the user has a connected broker already but changes its subscriptions, the join request is piggybacked to the subscription change message.
(2) the requested broker calculates the *user-broker utility* $Util_{u,b}$ for all its visible brokers (explained later).
(3) the requested broker replies to the user with the broker ID (address) that yields the largest utility value in the last step.
(4) the user joins the system by connecting to the selected broker.

Let P denote the set of topics, we evaluate the similarity of random user u to broker b in their subscriptions $s_u, S_b \subseteq P$ by a *user-broker similarity* metric, $Sim_{b,v}$, which is defined as the normalized size of their intersection, in the range $[0, 1]$. Formally, $Sim_{b,v} = |S_b \cap s_v|/|s_v|$. Our scheme is flexible and can accommodate other similarity metrics (e.g. Jaccard similarity), however, their analysis is out of the scope of the paper. Similarity based user placement will select for each user u a hosting broker that yields the highest user-broker similarity among all brokers. However, user placement based only on similarity metrics may result in severe load imbalance at brokers, especially when users' subscriptions are highly skewed (e.g. when most users only subscribe to a few very popular topics). That is, a few brokers have to host the majority of users due to high similarity of their subscriptions. Hence, to alleviate load imbalance, we also take into account a *load* metric, L_b, to reflect the load level of a broker, with range $[0, 1]$. In this work we assume homogeneity of brokers and define broker load as the normalized amount of local user subscriptions managed by a broker. Formally, $L_b = \sum_{u \in U_b} |s_u|/\sum_{u \in U} |s_u|$. A *user-broker utility* combining the similarity and load metrics is defined as $Util_{u,b} = Sim_{b,u} - w_l \cdot L_b$, where w_l is the relative weight for the load metrics.

The crux of user placement is the user join protocol which is executed every time a user subscribes to a new topic, or unsubscribe an existing topic. We present the join protocol in Algorithm 1.

Ideally the grouping algorithm requires each broker to acquire the global information on the subscriptions and loads of other brokers. This will incur significant overhead when the network size is large. This message overhead is considered as part of the subscription management overhead in DYNATOPS. Hence, we explored two techniques to avoid excessive overhead: 1) instead of maintaining the real-time state of subscriptions and loads of other brokers, each DYNATOPS broker only updates the information every T_{update} period; 2) we explored a clustering technique to divide brokers into clusters and only let brokers in the same cluster exchange the subscription and load information. When a user joins, the broker running the algorithm only evaluates utilities for brokers from the same cluster. We show in our experimental evaluation that a small cluster size (e.g. 10 brokers in a cluster) is good enough for the grouping algorithm to outperform existing techniques.

5. COST-DRIVEN BROKER NETWORK RECONFIGURATION

DYNATOPS aims to reconfigure the broker network to minimize event notification overhead and delays. We provide a formal modeling of the notification performance metrics and use it to drive the broker network reconfiguration process.

Let B denote the set of brokers, and $G(V, E)$ denote the structured overlay topology that DYNATOPS builds its broker network atop. A vertex $v \in V$ is an overlay node with a fixed nodeID. This corresponds to a fixed node position in the overlay geometry too. Its edges to other vertices are links to other overlay nodes. We assume $|V| = |B|$. DYNATOPS configures the broker network by specifying the mapping of the set of brokers B onto the set of overlay nodes V (i.e. nodeIDs) in $G(V, E)$. Therefore, we can define the configuration as a mapping matrix, $X = \{x_{b,v}\}$, between B and V, such that:

$$x_{b,v} = \begin{cases} 1 & \text{if broker } b \text{ is mapped to overlay node } v; \\ 0 & \text{otherwise.} \end{cases}$$

Let S_b be the subscriptions of broker b. In the rendezvous-based pub/sub implementation, given the overlay configuration X and $S = \{S_b : \forall b \in B\}$ as the set of broker subscriptions, the topic routing tree for each topic can be determined easily. The tree is rooted at the topic rendezvous and spans all overlay nodes whose mapped broker subscribes to the topic.

To formalize the performance of the pub/sub system, we formulate the **event overhead**, o_p, for an event in topic p as the total number of forwarded messages required to disseminate it from the RP to all brokers that subscribe to topic p. This overhead can be divided into two parts: (a) **subscriber overhead**, o_p^{sub}, as the number of messages consumed by brokers that subscribe to the topic; and (b) **relay overhead**, o_p^{relay}, as the number of the messages consumed by intermediate unrelated relays who *have not* subscribed to the topic. Meanwhile, we formulate the **broker event delay**, $d_{b,p}$, for an event in topic p to reach a specific subscribed broker b as the delay to forward it from the topic RP to that broker, and it can be easily approximated by the RTTs between brokers during each hop along the path. Given the set of brokers that subscribe to topic p, we formulate the **event delay** as the cumulative broker event delays for all brokers in the set, as: $d_p = \sum_{b:p \in S_b} d_{b,p}$. Note that in the above formulation we opt out the overhead and delay for forwarding the event from its publisher to the RP. This is because we assume any user in the system can be a potential event publisher (regardless of his subscriptions) so that the average path length from publisher to RP is independent of broker network configurations.

To evaluate the performance of event notifications of the pub/sub by taking into account events in all available topics during a time span $(t_0, t_0 + T)$, we define **cumulative relay overhead** and **cumulative delay** under a broker network configuration X as follows:

$$O^{relay}_{(t_0, t_0+T)}(X) = \sum_{p \in P} \sum_{\tau=t_0}^{t_0+T} \delta_p(\tau) \cdot o_p^{relay}(\tau) \quad (1)$$

$$D_{(t_0, t_0+T)}(X) = \sum_{p \in P} \sum_{\tau=t_0}^{t_0+T} \delta_p(\tau) \; d_p(\tau) \quad (2)$$

where $\delta_p(t)$ is the number of events of topic p in time slot t, and $o_p^{relay}(t)$ and $d_p(t)$ are event relay overhead and event delay of the topic routing tree in time slot t. Note that if the brokers' subscriptions are static during the evaluation period, then all the topic routing trees are static, subsequently o_p^{relay} and d_p are static and the above equations can be rewritten as:

$$O^{relay}_{(t_0, t_0+T)}(X) = \sum_{p \in P} N_p^{(t_0, t_0+T)} \cdot o_p^{relay} \quad (3)$$

$$D_{(t_0, t_0+T)}(X) = \sum_{p \in P} N_p^{(t_0, t_0+T)} \cdot d_p \quad (4)$$

where $N_p^{(t_0, t_0+T)} = \sum_{\tau=t_0}^{t_0+T} \delta_p(\tau)$ is the total number of events of topic p during the period.

Now we define our pub/sub performance metric during an evaluation period $(t_0, t_0 + T)$ under configuration X as the **Notification Cost**, $C_{(t_0, t_0+T)}(X)$, as follows:

$$C_{(t_0, t_0+T)}(X) = O^{relay}_{(t_0, t_0+T)}(X) + w_d \cdot D_{(t_0, t_0+T)}(X) \quad (5)$$

where $w_d \geq 0$ is a relative weight of delay performance to overhead performance.

5.1 Reconfiguration Process

A question needs to be answered is *when and how the broker network should be reconfigured*. Since reconfiguration is not cost-free – it may incur both management overhead and potential disruption of event notifications, it is not plausible to reconfigure the broker network whenever subscriptions change on brokers. To avoid frequent reconfigurations, we define *reconfiguration free period*, T_{free}, as the minimum period between two consecutive reconfigurations in DYNATOPS. Intuitively, if the benefit of making a reconfiguration cannot justify the cost of it, the broker network should not be reconfigured. Every T_{free} period, DYNATOPS performs a cost-driven reconfiguration process to evaluate the benefit of reconfiguration against its cost.

Let X be the broker network configuration before reconfiguration, and X' be the new configuration. The benefit of reconfiguration is evaluated as the gain in $C_{(t_0, t_0+T_{free})}$, which reflects the efficiency of event notifications. Formally,

$$Bft(X, X') = C_{(t_0, t_0+T_{free})}(X) - C_{(t_0, t_0+T_{free})}(X') \quad (6)$$

The cost of reconfiguration is the overhead associated with the transition of the broker network from its old configuration X to its new configuration X'. We designed a reconfiguration protocol for efficient broker network transitions in DYNATOPS. We formulate the reconfiguration cost as the upper bound we derived for the message overhead of the protocol to reconfigure the broker network over a Chord DHT (See Section 5.1.2 for the protocol and the discussion on its overhead). Assume $\Gamma(X, X')$ is the number of brokers that have a different mapping in configuration X' compared to X. The reconfiguration cost is:

$$Cst(X, X') = \begin{cases} 0 & \text{if } X' = X; \\ O(|V| + log^2(|V|) \cdot \Gamma(X, X') \\ \quad + |P| log(|V|) \cdot \Gamma(X, X')) & \text{otherwise.} \end{cases} \quad (7)$$

Algorithm 2: reconfiguration process

Step1-online monitoring:
online monitoring the event publications and subscription changes on brokers to estimate $C_{(t_0,t_0+T_{free})}(X)$.

Step2-reconfigurability test:
fast judging the demand of broker reconfiguration from $C_{(t_0,t_0+T_{free})}(X)$. If demand is low, return to step1; Otherwise, continue to step 3.

Step3-reconfiguration computation:
calculating X' to maximize $Bft(X,X') - Cst(X,X')$. If $Bft(X,X') \leq Cst(X,X')$ return to step1; Otherwise, continue to step4.

Step4-reconfiguration protocol:
coordinating the brokers to transit to X'.

Algorithm 2 shows the DYNATOPS reconfiguration process that is periodically executed by the reconfiguration manager.

The reconfiguration manager monitors and estimates the rate of event publications as well as subscriptions to calculate $C_{(t_0,t_0+T_{free})}$. We apply an exponential filter to estimate publication rate in topic p for the next period from the observation in current period:

$$\overline{R}_{pub}^{k+1}(p) = (1 - \alpha_{pub})\overline{R}_{pub}^k(p) + \alpha_{pub}R_{pub}^k(p) \qquad (8)$$

where $\overline{R}_{pub}^{k+1}(p)$ is the estimated publication rate in topic p for the $(k+1)^{th}$ period, and R_{pub}^k is a monitored publication rate for the $(k)^{th}$ period. α_{pub} is the parameter for the filter. In DYNATOPS we set $\alpha_{pub} = 0.3$.

Since it is hard to estimate the dynamics of brokers' subscriptions $S(t)$ for each time slot t in the next evaluation period $(t_0, t_0 + T_{free})$, we simply consider a static S equals $S(t_0)$ as an approximation. Better strategies could be considered by acquiring more context-awareness of the pub/sub users.

The reconfigurability test aims to prune out unnecessary reconfiguration computations when estimated reconfiguration demand is low for the next reconfiguration free period. The intuition here is that when the broker network is already fairly optimized or the event notification cost is low, the marginal benefit of reconfiguration won't be able to justify the cost of it. Hence, we compare the estimated $C_{(t_0,t_0+T_{free})}(X)$ with a cost threshold to decide the necessity for reconfiguration computation. A reconfiguration computation is desired only if it is larger than the threshold. In this paper, we set the threshold to $\beta \cdot maxCst(X,X')$, where $maxCst(X,X')$ is the maximum possible reconfiguration cost in the broker network by equation 7 and $\beta > 0$ is a control parameter (we set it to 0.1 in our implementation).

5.1.1 Reconfiguration Computation

DYNATOPS performs reconfiguration computation to determine optimal topology configuration X' that maximizes $Bft(X,X') - Cst(X,X')$. We prove in [4] that the problem is NP-hard to solve. Instead of solving the problem directly, we first present a sub-problem and propose an efficient algorithm for the problem. We define the basic reconfiguration problem without taking into account the reconfiguration cost: **Structure and Subscription aware Reconfiguration (SSBR)** as follows.

$SSBR(G(V,E), S, N_p^{(t_0,t_0+T)})$: Being aware of the overlay structure $G(V,E)$, brokers subscriptions S and $N_p^{(t_0,t_0+T)}$ as the number of event publications in each topic during a period, solve the following optimization problem:

$$arg \min_X C_{(t_0,t_0+T)}(X) \qquad (9)$$

where $C_{(t_0,t_0+T)}(X)$ is the notification cost defined in equation 5.

The above problem is still NP hard unless we consider the special case where only delay is considered (i.e. $w_d = \infty$) and delay between two brokers is strictly proportional to the number of hops in the overlay (In this case, the problem can be efficiently solved and an optimal solution is available). We present a greedy algorithm with upper bound complexity $O(|P|^2|V|^2 log(|V|))$ (see [4] for proof) for the general case. The algorithm iteratively improves the solution given an initial broker network configuration. We call the algorithm SSBR-Greedy and show it in Algorithm 3. In each iteration, the algorithm explores the neighborhood $Nb(X)$ (we will define later) of the current best configuration X and finds the best neighboring configuration that minimizes the cost function in equation 5. Let $\widetilde{X'}$ be the best among $X' \in Nb(X)$. If $\widetilde{X'}$ is superior to X, then the best configuration moves from X to $\widetilde{X'}$. Otherwise, a local optimal configuration is reached and the algorithm stops. Each iteration the algorithm finds a better configuration with a better $C_{(t_0,t_0+T_{free})}$ than the one of last iteration. They form an improvement path in $C_{(t_0,t_0+T_{free})}$. The algorithm returns all the configurations found on the improvement path.

The neighborhood, $Nb(X)$, of a configuration X is a set of configurations that are directly derivable from X. One immediate available neighborhood of X can be derived by swapping the mapping in X of any two brokers. However, this neighborhood contains $|V|(|V| - 1)/2$ configurations, leading to great computational overhead for the algorithm to examine in each iteration. To improve the algorithm efficiency for online computation, we examine a different yet smaller neighborhood with only $|V| - 1$ configurations.

We introduce the concept of *Broker SSBR Cost*. The broker SSBR cost, c_b evaluates each broker for their contributions to the total SSBR cost in equation 5. It consists of two parts: broker overhead cost, $c_b^O(X)$, and broker delay cost, $c_b^D(X)$. They are defined as follows:

$$c_b^O(X) = \sum_{p \in P} N_p^{(t_0,t_0+T)} \cdot z_{b,p}(X) \qquad (10)$$

where $z_{b,p}(X)$ is a 0-1 variable which equals to 1 if b is an unrelated relay in the routing tree of topic p, and 0 otherwise.

$$c_b^D(X) = \sum_{p \in S_b} N_p^{(t_0,t_0+T)} \cdot d_{b,p}(X) \qquad (11)$$

It is not difficult to derive the following relationship between broker SSBR cost and the total SSBR cost of the system:

$$\begin{aligned} C_{(t_0,t_0+T)}(X) &= \sum_{b \in B} c_b(X) \\ &= \sum_{b \in B}(c_b^O(X) + w_d \cdot c_b^D(X)) \end{aligned} \qquad (12)$$

In each iteration our greedy algorithm finds the broker with the highest broker cost under configuration X and construct a neighborhood $Nb(X)$ consisting of configurations that are derived by swapping the mapping of the broker

Algorithm 3: SSBR-Greedy

Input: $G(V, E), S, N_p^{(t_0, t_0+T)}$
Output: $List of X$ that along the improvement path of
$C_{(t_0, t_0+T)}(X)$

$\widetilde{X}$ = initial configuration; $\widetilde{minC} = C_{(t_0, t_0+T)}(\widetilde{X})$;

$List = []$ **while** $\widetilde{minC} < minC$ **do**

$\quad minC = \widetilde{minC}, X = \widetilde{X}$, List.add(X);
$\quad$ **foreach** $X' \in Nb(X)$ **do**
$\quad\quad tmpC = C_{(t_0, t_0+T)}(X')$;
$\quad\quad$ **if** $tmpC < \widetilde{minC}$ **then**
$\quad\quad\quad \widetilde{minC} = tmpC, \widetilde{X} = X'$;
$\quad\quad$ **end**
$\quad$ **end**
end

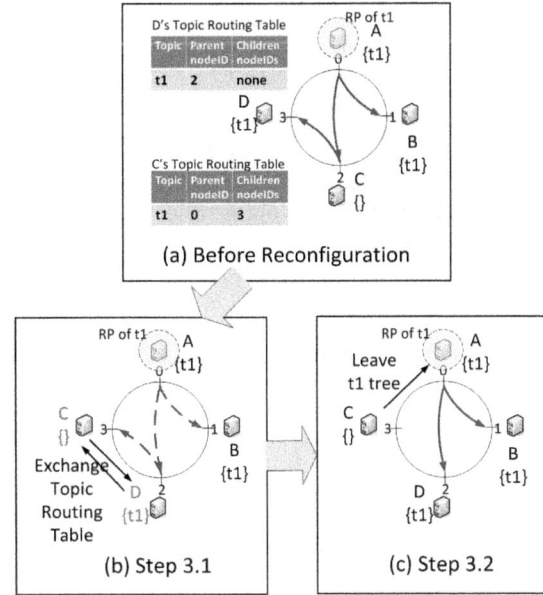

(a) Before Reconfiguration

(b) Step 3.1   (c) Step 3.2

Figure 4: An example of the step 3 of the reconfiguration protocol. Solid lines in (a) shows topic t1's tree before reconfiguration. Broker "C" and "D" are reconfigured. Dashed lines in (b) shows the reconstructed tree after "C" and "D" exchange their data in step3.1. Solid lines in (c) shows the repaired topic routing tree after step 3.2.

with the highest external overhead grade with that of another broker. Apparently the neighborhood contains only $|V| - 1$ configurations. By searching new configurations that have a different mapping for the bottleneck broker who has the worst broker cost, we have a better chance to improve the total cost.

We adapt the SSBR-Greedy algorithm to solve the original reconfiguration computation problem by taking into account reconfiguration cost $Cst(X, X')$, and call the new algorithm DYNATOPS-Greedy algorithm (see Algorithm 4). It consists of two steps: At the first step, the algorithm applies the SSBR-Greedy algorithm to iteratively find new configurations that improves the $C_{(t_0, t_0+T_{free})}$: each iteration the algorithm finds a better configuration with a better $C_{(t_0, t_0+T_{free})}$ than the one of last iteration. They form an improvement path in $C_{(t_0, t_0+T_{free})}$. At the second step, the reconfiguration cost $Cst(X, X')$ of all the configurations X' along the improvement path are taken into account and the best one is selected as the output of the algorithm. The algorithm has the same computational complexity as the SSBR-Greedy algorithm.

Algorithm 4: DYNATOPS-Greedy

Input: $G(V, E), S, N_p^{(t_0, t_0+T_{free})}, X$
Output: X' that maximize $Bft(X, X') - Cst(X, X')$

step one:
$List = SSBR - Greedy()$;
step two:
$C = C_{(t_0, t_0+T_{free})}(X)$;
$bestUtil = 0$;
$X' = X$;
foreach $\widetilde{X}$ in List **do**
$\quad \widetilde{C} = A.get(\widetilde{X})$;
$\quad Util = C - \widetilde{C} - Cst(X, \widetilde{X})$;
$\quad$ **if** $Util > bestUtil$ **then**
$\quad\quad bestUtil = Util$;
$\quad\quad X' = \widetilde{X}$;
$\quad$ **end**
end

5.1.2 Reconfiguration Protocol

The control plane of a DYNATOPS broker consists of two levels: 1) the overlay level, where its overlay nodeID, neighbor table and routing table are maintained; and 2)

the pub/sub level where its topic routing trees (i.e. logical parent nodes and children nodes in trees) are maintained. Each reconfiguration process has a unique version number, a successful reconfiguration will update the control plane of all brokers to the new version where both levels of the control plane must converge. On one hand, DYNATOPS relies on the maintenance protocol of the underlying structure overlay to ensure the convergence of the overlay level of the new control planes of brokers. On the other hand, we designed an efficient reconfiguration protocol to ensure the convergence of the pub/sub level of the new control planes. Taking Chord DHT as an example underlying structure, we show that the entire reconfiguration process incurs $O(|V| + (log^2(|V|) + |P|log(|V|)) \cdot \Gamma(X, X'))$ message overhead where $\Gamma(X, X')$ is the number of nodes to reconfigure. A reconfiguration of the broker network from version number $s1$ to $s2$ consists of following steps:

STEP1: The reconfiguration manager sends a RCFG_INIT message to all brokers. The message contains the new version number $s2$ of the control plane after reconfiguration. Upon receiving the message the brokers replicate their $s1$ control planes to $s2$ and maintains both instances keeping $s1$ as their default control plane to be used by data plane.

STEP2: The reconfiguration manager sends to brokers with new nodeIDs in Chord a RCFG_OVERLAY message. The brokers that receive the message leave and rejoin the Chord ring with their new nodeIDs in $s2$. Once successfully reconfigured, the brokers send a RCFG_OVERLAY_DONE message back to the reconfiguration manager. (According to [25], the step takes $O(log^2(|V|) \cdot \Gamma(X, X'))$ messages to repair the Chord ring)

STEP3: The reconfiguration manager sends to all brokers a RCFG_PUBSUB message to reconfigure the pub/sub level of the control plane. This process is divided into two sub-steps. An example of this process is shown in Figure 4.

- *3.1:* Each reconfigured broker (under a new nodeID in $s2$) forwards its Topic Routing Table data in $s1$ to the broker who takes its $s1$ nodeID in $s2$. This is easily done by key-based routing in the overlay without knowing the real identity of the other broker. The data corresponds to a local view of the topic routing trees it joined (see Figure 4). The brokers replace their $s2$ Topic Routing Table with the received data to restore the topic routing trees in $s2$. We illustrate in the example that the restored topic routing tree is the same as the original tree in structure. However, the tree is not necessarily consistent with the subscriptions at brokers after reconfiguration: broker "C" does not subscribe to t1 but it is a leaf node in the tree. (the step takes $O(log(|V|) \cdot \Gamma(X, X'))$ messages)

- *3.2:* To repair the inconsistency, each reconfigured broker compares its Topic Routing Table with its subscriptions, and initiates tree leave/join requests to fix its incorrect participation/absence in topic trees. The request messages are forwarded to the root of the tree and a top-down fashion update of the tree is incurred. Upon completion of this step, all the topic routing trees in $s2$ correctly reflect both the routing and subscriptions states of the broker network. (the step takes $O(|P|log(|V|) \cdot \Gamma(X, X'))$ messages)

STEP4: The reconfiguration manager sends to all brokers a RCFG_FINISH message. Once the message is received, the brokers make $s2$ as their default control plane and nullify $s1$ when all brokers switched to $s2$. (the step takes $O(|V|)$ messages)

To avoid event losses it is important for each broker to maintain two instances of its control planes ($s1$ and $s2$) during the reconfiguration process. An event published during the reconfiguration is forwarded by the data plane and tagged with the version of the control plane used for table lookup so that its next hop can use the same version to ensure consistency. Moreover, any broker will not activate $s2$ before $s2$ become convergence at all brokers (i.e. STEP4). This way the correctness of event notification is ensured. To cope with uncertain delays in the network, each step of the protocol is enforced by atomic operation [17]. That is, next step will not be triggered unless all brokers have acknowledged accomplishment of the current step.

6. PERFORMANCE EVALUATION

To evaluate the performance of DYNATOPS, we created two models that emulate the real world subscription dynamics, and compared DYNATOPS with several well-known topic-based pub/sub implementations for its subscription management and event publication efficiencies.

6.1 Dynamic Subscriptions Modeling

We considered two models of subscription changes: (1) a location-based subscription model that emulates users' dynamic subscriptions in many geosocial networking applications and location-based services; and (2) a generic Poisson dynamic subscription model that emulates changing interests of users in timely and popular topics.

6.1.1 Location-based Subscription Model

To create a large-scaled dynamic subscription model, we considered a twitter dataset [44] containing 3 million location checkins (in longitude and latitude coordinates) from over 40K Twitter users in the U.S. for 3 months period from Aug. 1st 2010 to Oct. 31st 2010. To convert the dynamic location checkins into dynamic subscriptions, we divided the U.S. geography into grids of one degree of latitude by one degree of longitude, the size of which is about 3500 $mile^2$. This results in 20×60 (i.e. 1200) grids, and we considered each of them as a location topic (i.e. totally 1200 topics). Users' checkins over time at different grids are considered as traces of their movement.

We presented our preliminary findings on users' grid checkins in Fig. 5a and 5b. We observed over 450K grid visits events (we treat users' successive checkins to locations in the same grid as a single event), from which we extracted over 160K unique (user,grid) pairs. 1/3 of them are single-time visit (i.e. a user visits to the grid only once) while the other 2/3 are at least repeated once by the user (Fig. 5a). We also analyzed the linger time of all the events. We treated the lapse of time before a user checked into a new grid as the linger time he/she stayed in the current grid. Our results indicates that about half of the 450K visits have a linger time less than a day. On the other hand, there are 10% of the visits are relatively long-lived, with a linger time over a week (Fig. 5b).

For users' dynamic subscriptions, we assume a user always subscribed to the grids he/she was residing in. Furthermore, during experiments we let each user randomly choose 4 other users as friends, and constantly follow/subscribe to the current grids/locations of his/her friends(Fig. 5c). This mimics a geosocial networking application, e.g. foursquare, where users can share their locations and activities with friends.

To experiment the pub/sub system, we considered 1200 brokers such that each broker is located inside a grid. The RTT delay between a pair of brokers and that between a broker and a user are random variables with their means proportional to their geographical distances.

6.1.2 Generic Poisson Subscription Model

In this model, we emulated a time period of $T = 100hrs$ with time granularity of $\Delta t = 1hr$. We experimented with 50K users, 100 brokers and 1000 topics. Each user subscribes to 5 topics according to the patterns of their subscriptions. The dynamics of subscription changes over time is modeled as a Poisson process. We considered three patterns for users' topic subscriptions:

- Uniform Distribution: users subscribe to topics from the topic space in a uniform random manner.

- Zipf Distribution: topic popularity follows Zipf distribution. The probability for the ith topic in the topic space is proportional to $(i + 1)^{-\sigma}$, $i = 1, 2, \ldots, |P|$.

- Multimodal: users' subscriptions fall into modes. We evenly partitioned the topic space into $m = 100$ modes, and each mode contains $n_{mode} = 10$ topics. A user first randomly select a interested modes and then choose topics uniformly at random from the selected mode.

6.2 Comparison Systems

We evaluated DYNATOPS along multiple dimensions by extensive simulations. The key dimensions that serve as

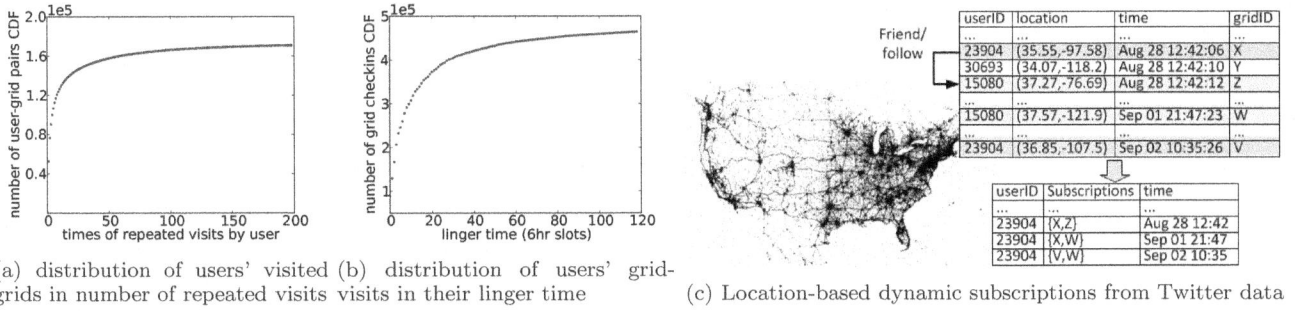

(a) distribution of users' visited grids in number of repeated visits

(b) distribution of users' grid visits in their linger time

(c) Location-based dynamic subscriptions from Twitter data

Figure 5: dynamic subscription model from Twitter dataset

metrics for our study include *subscription management overhead*, as the number of control messages exchanged between brokers to update topic trees when brokers' subscription changes, and to update information in clusters; *notification delay* as the average latency for publications to be delivered from publishers to subscribers; *notification overhead* as the number of messages to deliver event publications; and *reconfiguration overhead* as the number of control messages for the reconfiguration protocol.

We compared DYNATOPS with several existing topic-based pub/sub systems of different categories: 1) *Bayeux*, a well-known pub/sub system atop the Tapestry DHT [10]; Bayeux was picked because it is a rendezvous-based pub/sub system on a structured overlay – providing a common ground for comparing with our system. Unlike DYNATOPS, Bayeux does not optimize its brokers based on subscriptions or perform reconfigurations, giving us an opportunity to test the value of these techniques. 2) *Topic Connected Overlay(TCO)*, a pub/sub overlay [19, 33, 11, 12] that eliminates unrelated relay brokers to provide optimal notification overhead efficiency by connecting brokers that subscribe to the same topic to form a connected subgraph; Since TCO optimizes broker topology at all times for notification efficiency, it again gives us an opportunity to test the performance and efficiency of our cost-driven broker reconfiguration policy. 3) *GeoPS* [26], a pub/sub service specific to location-based subscriptions. It takes advantage of geography-aware overlay hierarchy and geocasting technique for efficient subscription management and publication notifications. Furthermore, to study the value of the proposed schemes, we considered three versions of DYNATOPS system: (a) DYNATOPS(BNR) explores the benefit of the broker network reconfiguration scheme with an equivalent user placement scheme as other systems; (b) DYNATOPS(UP) explores the benefit of the user placement scheme only, and (c) DYNATOPS is the overall mechanism that incorporates both user placement and broker network reconfiguration schemes.

We implemented our simulator and all the above systems in Java. In our simulation, the broker networks of Bayeux and GeoPS were considered to be static. For the Bayeux simulation, brokers join the Tapestry Overlay with random Ids uniformly distributed over the Id space. For the GeoPS simulation, we divided the geography into power-of-2 grids on both edges of a rectangular geography as required by the GeoPS system. Specifically, we divide the U.S. into 32×32 grids (i.e. 1024 in total). TCO requires its broker overlay to be reconfigured whenever topic-connected property is no longer hold due to subscription changes on brokers.

We reconfigure TCO by running the DCB-M algorithm [12] for partitions of nodes having changed subscriptions. Since there is no existing reconfiguration protocol to refer to, we assume the message overhead to conduct each reconfiguration is the number of links that are changed in the network topology. Users are placed on brokers at the start of each simulation, and their subscriptions change over time following the specific subscription model. Since Bayeux and TCO do not have a specific user placement policy, we considered two commonly used policies in the simulation: 1) Static selection, where a user is statically assigned a broker and 2) Location-based selection, where each broker is responsible for users in a specific region and users handover to new brokers when they move to different regions.

6.3 Experimental Results

6.3.1 Basic Results

We experimented DYNATOPS and compared its performance with existing systems under the two subscription models.

location-based subscription model: Figure 6 shows the results for the location-based subscription model. We compared DYNATOPS with Bayeux and GeoPS in their subscription and publication performances. For Bayeux, we considered both static and location-based user placement policies indicated by "Bayeux(static)" and "Bayeux(loc)". Furthermore, we considered proximity neighbor selection(PNS) in its overlay construction, along with location-based user placement, indicated by "Bayeux(loc+PNS)". When experimented with user placement technique, we formed broker clusters (see Section 4) based on their geographical proximity to avoid extensive maintenance overhead, and let each cluster manage users in a continuous geographical area close to it.

We observe that by grouping users with similar subscriptions, DYNATOPS significantly reduces the subscription management overhead against other systems (Fig. 6a). Moreover, we observe that the overhead first decreases with the increase of the cluster size c, which indicates the reduction in topic tree updates in the broker network. Under large cluster sizes (e.g. $c = 50$), however, the overhead for updating brokers' states in a cluster becomes significant, so the total subscription management overhead starts to increase.

Fig. 6b shows the standard deviation in subscription load on brokers. We observe that pure similarity based user placement ($w_l = 0$) worsens the load imbalance on brokers, especially when the cluster size is large. However, the is-

(a) brokers' subscription changes
(b) notification delay
(c) notification overhead
(d) reconfiguration overhead

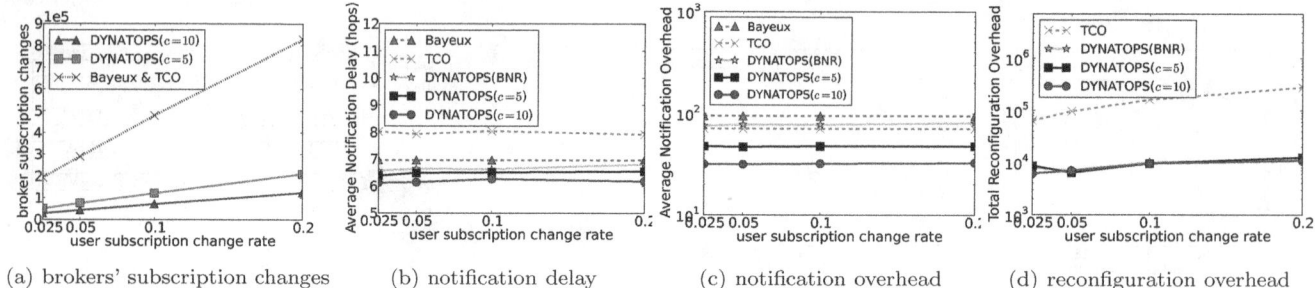

Figure 7: Poisson subscription model results under varying rate of user subscription changes with multimodal pattern

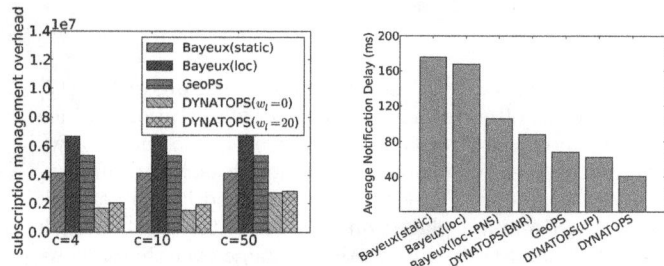

(a) subscription management overhead ($T_{update} = 12hrs$)

(b) standard deviation of brokers' subscription load ($T_{update} = 12hrs$)

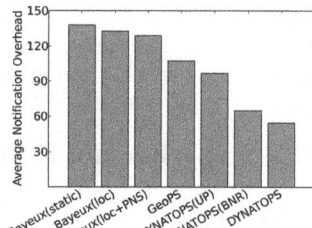

(c) ratio of users' handovers in DYNATOPS to that of GeoPS

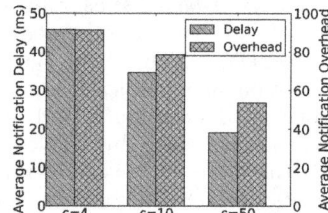

(d) notification delay ($T_{free} = 12hrs$, $c = 10$, $w_d = 1$)

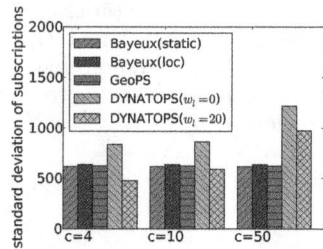

(e) notification overhead ($T_{free} = 12hrs$, $c = 10$, $w_d = 1$)

(f) DYNATOPS notification performance

Figure 6: location-based subscription model results

NATOPS is highly efficient and it provides over 60% improvement against Bayeux and 30% against GeoPS in delay, and over 40% improvement against Bayeux and 20% against GeoPS in overhead (DYNATOPS $w_d = 1$). Furthermore, the notification performance improvement increases as the increase of the cluster size (Fig. 6f). This is because with larger cluster size the user placement makes the brokers' subscriptions more skewed, which favors the broker network reconfiguration to reduce unrelated relays in the topology.

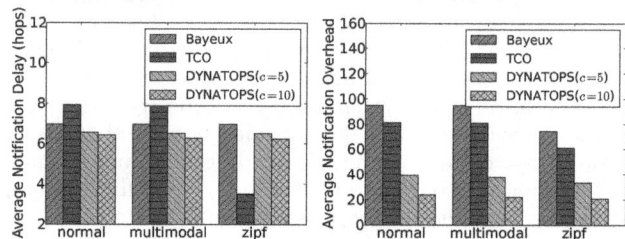

(a) notification delay
(b) notification overhead

Figure 8: Poisson subscription model results in different patterns
(subscription change rate = 0.1, $T_{free} = 10hrs$)

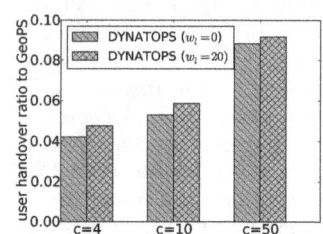

Poisson subscription model: Fig. 7 shows the results of the Poisson subscription model where users subscriptions change with varying Poisson rates. We compared DYNATOPS with Bayeux and TCO for subscription and publication performances. In both Bayeux and TCO, we assume users are statically assigned brokers in a uniformly random manner. For publication performances, we also considered DYNATOPS(BNR) where the user placement is the same as those for Bayeux and TCO, to evaluate DYNATOPS under the broker network reconfiguration technique along. For simplicity, in the experiment we assumed a unit RTT delay between any pair of brokers so that the notification delay is dominated by the number of overlay hops.

Fig. 7a to 7d show the experimental results where users subscriptions follow the multimodal pattern under varying Poisson rate of user subscription changes. We observe that DYNATOPS reduces the number of brokers' subscription changes by 80% against other systems (Fig. 7a), resulting in significantly less subscription management overhead. Fig. 7b and 7c show the publication delay and overhead performances of different pub/sub systems. TCO achieves a better overhead performance than Bayeux and DYNATOPS(BNR) because of the topic-connected property. However, we observe a worse delay performance because its suboverlay construction is not delay aware. On the other hand, DYNATOPS

sue is greatly improved by adjusting the weight for the load factor in the algorithm. We also evaluated the number of user handovers due to mobility in GeoPS and DYNATOPS. We observe that DYNATOPS reduces the user handovers by over 80% against GeoPS as shown in Fig. 6c.

Both user placement and broker network reconfiguration can improve notification delay (Fig. 6d) and overhead (Fig. 6e). This is because by clustering users with the same topic the user placement can reduce the number of brokers that need to subscribe to the topic so as to reduce the size of the topic routing tree. Combining the two algorithms DY-

considering both user placement and broker network reconfiguration outperforms Bayeux and TCO on both delay and overhead. It provides 10% improvement in delay and over 50% improvement in overhead against the compared systems.

We also compared the reconfiguration cost between DYNATOPS and TCO (Fig. 7d). The reconfiguration overhead for TCO increases dramatically with the increase of the rate of users subscription changes. This makes the scheme infeasible to be applied in highly dynamic environment. On the other hand, DYNATOPS's reconfiguration overhead is less sensitive to the rate of users subscription changes. It is over 80% less than that of TCO when users' subscriptions change fast.

The notification performance of each system under different subscription patterns of users are shown in Fig. 8a and Fig. 8b. We observe that TCO has a low delay under zipf pattern where subscription is highly skewed but worse under other subscription patterns. On the other hand, DYNATOPS outperforms other systems under all subscription patterns.

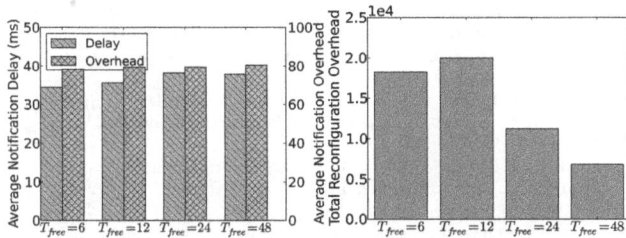

(a) notification performance (location-based model)

(b) reconfiguration overhead (location-based model)

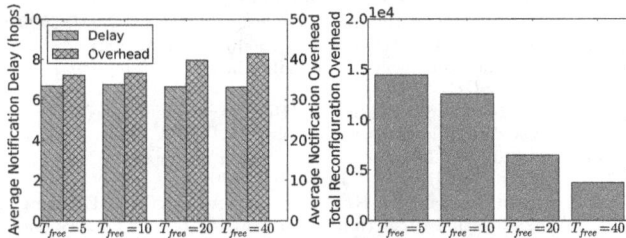

(c) notification performance (Poisson model)

(d) reconfiguration overhead (Poisson model)

Figure 9: results under varying reconfiguration free period. For location-based model, $c = 10$; For Poisson model, subscription change rate $= 0.025$ and $c = 5$.

6.3.2 Reconfiguration free period

To gain better understanding of the performance, we experimented with various reconfiguration free period T_{free} in both location-based and Poisson models. In Fig. 9. We observe that with the increase of the reconfiguration free period, the notification performance degrades slightly and the reconfiguration overhead decreases because less reconfigurations were triggered. It is worth noting that DYNATOPS only experienced a slight degradation in notification efficiency when the reconfiguration free period increases. This is because the user placement technique stabilized brokers subscriptions such that they do not experience dramatic sub-

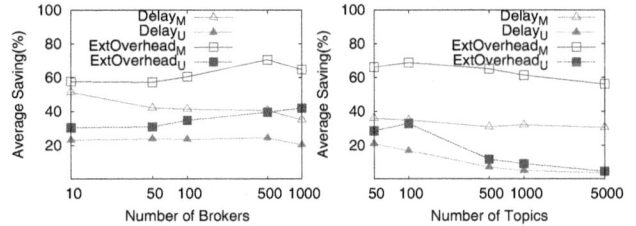

(a) Scaling of Broker Network   (b) Scaling of Topic Space

Figure 10: Performance savings of DYNATOPS configurations against CHash under various size of broker network $|B|$ and of topic space $|P|$. We varied $|B|$ with fixed $|P| = 100$, and varied $|P|$ with fixed $|B| = 100$. "M" denotes multimodal pattern and "U" denotes uniform pattern.

size	varying $|B|$			varying $|P|$		
	10	100	1000	50	500	5000
time	28ms	184ms	96s	98ms	502ms	1.9s

Table 1: The computation time of the DYNATOPS-Greedy algorithm under various size of broker network $|B|$ and of topic space $|P|$. For varying $|B|$, we fixed $|P| = 100$, and for varying $|P|$ we fixed $|B| = 100$.

scription changes over time in spite of dynamic users' subscriptions.

6.3.3 Scalability

We also experimented with various sizes of the broker network and of the topic space to evaluate the time efficiency and performance of the DYNATOPS-Greedy configuration algorithm. We ran the algorithm on a Dell workstation with a QuadCore 2GHz CPU and 2G memory. The performance of the output DYNATOPS configurations are compared against that of a bootstrap configuration from consistent hashing of brokers public keys or IP addresses for their nodeIDs. This is the configuration approach adopted by most existing DHT-based pub/sub systems [30, 40, 41, 15]. The performance was evaluated under two subscription patterns on brokers: uniform distribution subscriptions and multimodal subscriptions. Figure 10 and Table 1 show the performance and computation time of the algorithm. We observe that DYNATOPS configuration always provides improved notification performance against consistent hashing under various size of broker networks and topic spaces. The improvement is larger under skewed subscription patterns than the uniform pattern. Furthermore, the proposed configuration algorithm is efficient to compute DYNATOPS configurations for a large broker network and topic space.

7. DISCUSSION AND CONCLUSION

In this paper, we propose and develop DYNATOPS, a pub sub system for societal scale applications, that can deal with dynamic, yet short lived subscriptions. DYNATOPS users are moderately repositioned on brokers for efficient subscription management and brokers are moderately repositioned on the overlay structure for efficient event notifications, to adapt to the publications and subscription dynamics. Unlike existing systems where the overlay topology changes in a self-organizing manner in response to the changes of subscriptions, DYNATOPS performs planned reconfiguration utilizing a cost-driven reconfiguration process. The proposed approach can significantly reduce the reconfiguration cost while maintaining a high notification performance as compared to state-of-the-art systems.

The centralized reconfiguration requires the participation of all brokers in the structured overlay. To mitigate the scalability concern on the reconfiguration computation and protocol when the network size grows, a hybrid pub/sub network similar to [18] which exploit both unstructured clustering of similar peers and structured rendezvous routing may be adopted. In the hybrid network, only gateway brokers from each cluster of gossip-based unstructured overlays will join the core structured rendezvous network and participate into the structure reconfiguration. The performance of the hybrid structure will be investigated in the future work. We will also extend the centralized configuration manager to a distributed implementation, mitigating any reliability concerns.

We have implemented a prototype of the DNATOPS broker system atop a Chord DHT implementation OpenChord [3]. We will next deploy this broker network on a campus cluster and evaluate the system on an emulated Internet using Modelnet [2]. We are also extending DYNATOPS to implement a large scale mobile alerting system that exploits the geographical and societal correlations inherent in societal scale notification systems.

8. REFERENCES

[1] Farecast. http://www.ics.uci.edu/~dsm/papers/farecast_techreport.pdf.
[2] Modelnet. http://issg.cs.duke.edu/modelnet.html.
[3] Openchord. http://sourceforge.net/projects/open-chord/.
[4] techreport. http://www.ics.uci.edu/~yez/dynatops_tech.pdf.
[5] D. Rosenblum A. Carzaniga and A. Wolf. Achieving scalability and expressiveness in an internet-scale event notification service. In PODC, 2000.
[6] D. S. Rosenblum A. Carzaniga and A. L. Wolf. Design and evaluation of a wide-area event notification service. In TOCS, 2001.
[7] Y. Cheung A. King and H. Jacobsen. Publisher placement algorithms in content-based publish/subscribe. In ICDCS, 2010.
[8] I. Aekaterinidis and P. Triantafillou. Pastrystrings: A comprehensive content-based publish/subscribe dht network. In ICDCS, 2006.
[9] et al. B. F. Cooper. Pnuts: Yahoo!s hosted data serving platform. In VLDB Endow., 2008.
[10] et al B. Y. Zhao. Tapestry: An infrastructure for fault-tolerant wide-area location and routing. In UCBerkeley Tech. Rep., 2001.
[11] H. Jacobsen C. Chen and R. Vitenberg. Divide and conquer algorithms for publish/subscribe overlay design. In ICDCS, 2010.
[12] R. Vitenberg C. Chen and H. Jacobsen. Scaling construction of low fan-out overlays for topic-based publish/subscribe. In ICDCS, 2011.
[13] F. Cao and J. P. Singh. Efficient event routing in content-based publish/subscribe service network. In INFOCOM, 2004.
[14] F. Cao and J. P. Singh. Medym: Match-early with dynamic multicast for content-based publish-subscribe networks. In Middleware, 2005.
[15] A. Post D. Sandler, A. Mislove and P. Druschel. Feedtree: Sharing web micronews with peer-to-peer event notification. In IPTPS, 2005.
[16] G. Li et al. Adaptive content-based routing in general overlay topologies. In Middleware, 2008.
[17] R. Strong F. Cristian, H. Aghili and D. Dolev. Atomic broadcast: From simple message diffusion to byzantine agreement. Information and Computation, 1995.
[18] A. H. Payberah F. Rahimian, S. Girdzijauskas and S. Haridi. Vitis: A gossip-based hybrid overlay for internet-scale publish/subscribe enabling rendezvous routing in unstructured overlay networks. In IPDPS, 2011.
[19] et al G. Chockler. Constructing scalable overlays for pub-sub with many topics: Problems, algorithms and evaluation. In PODC, 2007.
[20] et al G. Chockler. Spidercast: A scalable interest-aware overlay for topic-based pub/sub communication. In DEBS, 2007.
[21] V. Muthusamy G. Li and H.-A. Jacobsen. Adaptive content-based routing in general overlay topologies. In Middleware, 2008.
[22] N. Venkatasubramanian H. Jafarpour, S. Mehrotra and M. Montanari. Mics: An efficient content space representation model for publish/subscribe systems. In DEBS, 2009.
[23] et al H. Liu. Client behavior and feed characteristics of rss, a publish-subscribe system for web micronews. In IMC, 2005.
[24] Y. Huang and H. Garcia-Molina. Publish/subscribe in a mobile environment. Wireless Networks, 2004.
[25] et al I. Stoica. Chord: A scalable peer-to-peer lookup service for internet applications. In SIGCOMM, 2001.
[26] U. Lee J. H. Ahnn and H. J. Moon. Geoserv: A distributed urban sensing platform. In CCGrid, 2011.
[27] R. S. Kazemzadeh and H.-A. Jacobsen. Reliable and highly available distributed publish/subscribe service. In SRDS, 2009.
[28] C. Jayalath K.R. Jayaram and P. Eugster. Parametric subscriptions for content-based publish/subscribe networks. In Middleware, 2010.
[29] O. Kasten L. Fiege, F. C. Gartner and A. Zeidler. Supporting mobility in content-based publish/subscribe middleware. In MIDDLEWARE, 2003.
[30] et al M. Castro. Scribe: A large-scale and decentralized application-level multicast infrastructure. In PJSAC, 2002.
[31] R. Oliveira M. Matos, A. Nunes and J. Pereira. Stan: exploiting shared interests without disclosing them in gossip-based publish/subscribe. In IPTPS, 2010.
[32] G. Muhl. Large-scale content-based publish/subscribe systems. In PhD thesis, Darmstadt Univ. of Technology, 2002.
[33] M. Onus and A. W. Richa. Minimum maximum degree publish-subscribe overlay network design. In INFOCOM, 2009.
[34] R. Guerraoui P. Th. Eugster, P. A. Felber and A. Kermarrec. The many faces of publish/subscribe. In ACM Computing Surveys (CSUR), 2003.
[35] P. R. Pietzuch and J. M. Bacon. Hermes: A distributed event-based middleware architecture. In DCSW, 2002.
[36] et al R. Baldoni. Tera: topic-based event routing for peer-to-peer architectures. In DEBS, 2007.
[37] L. Querzoni R. Baldoni, R. Beraldi and A. Virgillito. Efficient publish/subscribe through a self-organizing broker overlay and its application to siena, 2007.
[38] et al. S. Girdzijauskas, G. Chockler. Magnet: practical subscription clustering for internet-scale publish/subscribe. In DEBS, 2010.
[39] et al S. Voulgaris. Sub-2-sub: Self-organizing content-based publish subscribe for dynamic large scale collaborative networks. In IPTPS, 2006.
[40] et al S.Q. Zhuang. Bayeux: an architecture for scalable and fault-tolerant wide-area data dissemination. In NOSSDAV, 2001.
[41] R. Peterson V. Ramasubramanian and E. G. Sirer. Corona: A high performance publish-subscribe system for the world wide web. In NSDI, 2006.
[42] R. Vitenberg V. Setty, M. Steen and S. Voulgaris. Poldercast: Fast, robust and scalable architecture for p2p topic-based pub/sub. In Middleware, 2012.
[43] V. Muthusamy Y. Yoon and H. Jacobsen. Foundations for highly available content-based publish/subscribe overlays. In ICDCS, 2011.
[44] K. Lee Z. Cheng, J. Caverlee and D. Z. Sui. Exploring millions of footprints in location sharing services. In ICWSM, 2011.

HUGO: Real-Time Analysis of Component Interactions in High-Tech Manufacturing Equipment (Industry Article)

Yuanzhen Ji
SAP AG
Chemnitzer Str. 48
01187 Dresden, Germany
yuanzhen.ji@sap.com

Thomas Heinze
SAP AG
Chemnitzer Str. 48
01187 Dresden, Germany
thomas.heinze@sap.com

Zbigniew Jerzak
SAP AG
Chemnitzer Str. 48
01187 Dresden, Germany
zbigniew.jerzak@sap.com

ABSTRACT

One of the major problems faced by the high-tech manufacturing industry is the need for automated and timely detection of anomalies which can lead to failures of the manufacturing equipment. Failures of the high-tech manufacturing equipment have a direct negative impact on the operating margin and consequently profit of the high-tech manufacturing industry.

Automated and timely detection of anomalies is a difficult problem, the major challenge being the need to understand the interactions between large amount of machine components. Even very experienced system engineers are not aware of all interactions, especially if those need to be derived from high velocity sensor data. This, in turn, makes it impossible to recognize early warning signals and take action before failure happens.

In this paper we present HUGO[1] – a system for real-time analysis of component interactions in high-tech manufacturing equipment. HUGO automatically discovers (based on the available sensor data) correlations between machine components and helps engineers analyze them in real-time so as to be able to detect deterioration of the manufacturing equipment conditions in a timely fashion.

Categories and Subject Descriptors

J.1 [**Administrative Data Processing**]: Manufacturing; I.5.4 [**Pattern Recognition**]: Applications—*signal processing*

Keywords

Equipment Monitoring; Complex Event Processing

1. INTRODUCTION

High-tech manufacturing equipment, such as photolithography systems or vapor depositions systems, contain thousands

---

[1]Hugo Steinhaus was a Polish mathematician and educator, one of the first to propose the method of k-means clustering.

of components which are monitored by hundreds of digital and analogue sensors. The sheer size and complexity of the data which is delivered by the sensors monitoring such systems makes it very challenging for system engineers to detect abnormal behavior leading to failures. The two major challenges faced by the system engineers are: (1) the need to know what to monitor and (2) the ability to extract higher level information from raw sensor data in real-time.

It might be surprising for a laymen to learn that a trained professional does not know which parts of a machine should be monitored. It is, however, important to notice that a systems engineer always seeks to monitor *interactions* of components within a machine. Let us consider a following example: given a sensor monitoring an opening of a valve and a sensor monitoring the operations of a pump, an engineer can observe whether the time between the opening of a valve and the start of the pump operation remains stable or degrades over time. This, in turn, is an indication for an abnormal behavior leading to failures in the future. If we recall that a manufacturing machine contains hundreds of sensors, we can conclude that an engineer is faced with tens to hundreds of thousands of such correlations which he could monitor. The existence of such a big number of correlations makes it impossible, even for experienced engineers, to analyze them manually and detect anomalies timely.

HUGO helps systems engineers to cope with this issue by automatically selecting only meaningful component correlations to monitor. HUGO exposes a set of parameters to drive the selection process. These parameters can be easily adjusted by the system engineers to meet their desired level of insight. HUGO is also able to automatically derive component interaction diagrams with only minimum prior knowledge as to the setup of the machine. Component interaction diagrams represent direct feedback to the engineers tuning the selection process parameters.

Moreover, HUGO allows system engineers to perform real-time analysis of high velocity raw sensor data. Having automatically selected component correlations to monitor, HUGO uses a modified version of the HDDStream [8] algorithm to group sensor readings within each correlation and monitor statistical properties of each group, focusing on the calculation of the long time trend. Combined with rules defined by the system engineers HUGO provides real-time alerting functionality allowing for a timely detection of anomalies.

We have implemented HUGO on top of a commercial Complex Event Processing (CEP) [7] system and evaluated the proposed methods using a real world dataset [6] coming from the manufacturing machine installed at the Infineon Technolo-

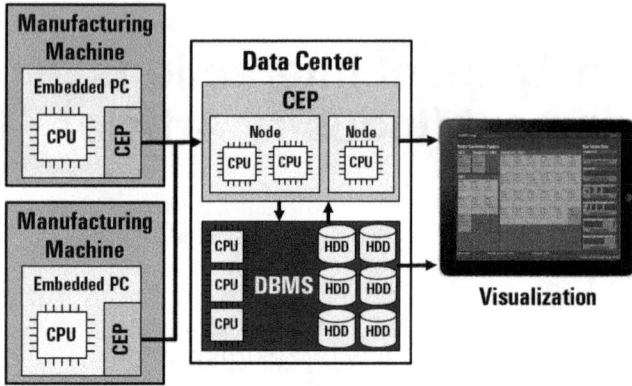

Figure 1: General system architecture

gies AG fabrication plant in Dresden, Germany. Moreover, we have received positive feedback from the Infineon engineers about our evaluation results. Despite this very specific setup we believe that the algorithm and approach of HUGO can be applied to broader set of use cases involving monitoring of high-tech manufacturing equipment.

To summarize, the main contributions we claim in this paper include: (1) a method for automatic detection of most meaningful component correlations for a high-tech manufacturing machine (*what to monitor?*); (2) an extension of the HDDStream clustering algorithm for analysis of temporal dependencies between related machine components (*extracting higher level information from raw sensor data in real-time*); and (3) an evaluation based on real-world data, including feedback from the engineers working with the system.

The remainder of this paper is organized as follows. In Section 2 we describe the overall setup of the HUGO system and its deployment in the target manufacturing environment. Subsequently, in Section 3 we describe how we extended and applied the HDDStream algorithm to perform real-time analysis of temporal dependencies between machine components (Contribution 2). In Section 4 we describe how HUGO uses heuristic rules to automatically select component correlations to be monitored by the system (Contribution 1). Section 5 presents our evaluation over real-world manufacturing sensor data (Contribution 3), followed by an analysis of the related work in Section 6. We conclude with Section 7.

2. SYSTEM DESIGN

The general system architecture is shown in Figure 1. Each manufacturing machine is monitored by a set of embedded sensors, with each sensor monitoring a specific machine component. Producing product items in a manufacturing machine usually involves multiple *processing steps*. A certain *processing step* such as patterning or deposition requires the interaction and collaboration of several machine components, each component being responsible for a certain *processing action*. Same processing steps are repeated for each product item processed on the machine. As a result, the same machine component interactions are also repeated in the iterating processing steps. Sensors embedded in the machine collect information about the processing actions of machine components at a fixed frequency. The high frequency sensor data is collected by a CEP engine which runs on an embedded computer (PLC). The streaming sensor data originating from

each machine is subsequently forwarded to the data center, which consists of a CEP system and a database system. The CEP system is responsible for on-line processing of the raw sensor data by correlating data from different sensors and analyzing the correlations using the extended HDDStream [8] algorithm. In parallel, the raw sensor data and the processing results can be persisted into the database system for further, offline root cause analysis. As a last step, the processing results are visualized through a browser-based user interface and system engineers are notified about the occurrence of critical events. The description of the visualization features as well as the functionality of accessing database from the user interface is out of the scope of this paper.

Monitoring sensors produce either digital or analog signals. Analog sensors monitor aspects such as current flowing through and voltage of different parts of the machine. Binary digital sensors produce a state transition (from 0 to 1 or vice verse) whenever a processing action is taken by the corresponding machine component. Detailed description of the sensors can be found in [6]. To reduce the data processing complexity, we first convert analog signals into digital ones using user-specified rules. Without loss of generality, we consider in the following only digital sensors which produce just two different values: 0 and 1. Nevertheless, the proposed approach can easily be extended and applied to digital sensors producing multiple values.

3. TEMPORAL ANALYSIS

The goal of the sensor data analysis is to monitor whether the interaction between pairs of related components in the machine adheres to certain time regimes. More specifically, we inspect the interaction in terms of the delay between the processing actions taken by the related components. In this section, we describe in detail how sensors are correlated with each other, how the streaming data clustering method is applied to analyze the temporal dependency between machine components, and most importantly, how we tailor a state-of-the-art clustering algorithm HDDStream [8] to solve the specific interaction monitoring problem.

3.1 Correlate Sensor Data for Analyzing

Interdependence between two related machine components is studied by correlating the sensor data from the two components.

Figure 2 shows an example of the signals from a pair of digital sensors over time. It also illustrates how the two sensors are correlated and analyzed. Each transition from the "off" state to the "on" state (the raising edge) of a sensor indicates an occurrence of a processing action. As described in Section 2, processing steps repeat for each production item processed by the machine. Therefore, we can observe a repeating state transition pattern in the signal series. To study the temporal dependency between two processing actions, each raising edge of *Sensor A* is correlated with the following raising edge of *Sensor B* in the same processing step. The delay (Δt) between these two state transitions is measured and subject to clustering. The same correlation procedure is repeated in each iteration of the corresponding processing step, producing a stream of delay measurements. It can be observed in Figure 2 that the first two delay measurements ($t_2 - t_1$ and $t_4 - t_3$) are almost equal, while the third one ($t_6 - t_5$) is significantly longer. As the result of clustering, the first two delay measurements will be assigned to the same

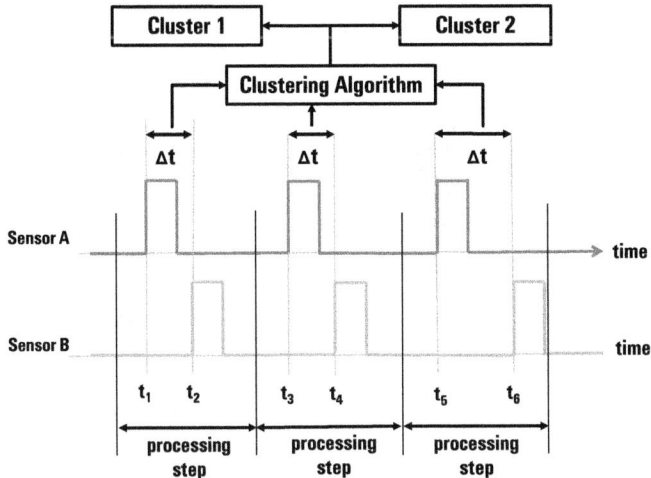

Figure 2: Sensor pair analysis by clustering the delay between temporally adjacent raising edges

cluster (*Cluster 1*) while the third one will be assigned to a second cluster (*Cluster 2*).

Delay measurements are continuously fed into the clustering algorithm. After a certain training period (e.g. 24 hours), data points in clusters which contain only a few members (e.g. less than 10) can be considered as erroneous. This in turn, suggests an abnormal interaction between the corresponding pair of machine components. By means of clustering, system engineers are automatically presented only with the data which is already considered to be a manifestation of an abnormal behavior.

3.2 Tailored Clustering Algorithm

We leverage *HDDStream*, a *density-based* streaming data clustering algorithm proposed in [8] to perform data analyzing. We choose the density-based rather than the *k-means-based* clustering method, because *k-means-based* clustering requires to know the desired number of clusters (k) produced by the algorithm in the final solution, and assumes that the number of clusters remains constant. This assumption does not hold in real-world scenarios of constantly evolving data streams. In contrast, density-based approaches do not demand a priori knowledge of the number of clusters.

Because data streams are unbounded, it is impossible to maintain clusters by keeping all the historical data points. A widely adopted solution is to summarize sets of data points through an appropriate summarizing structure called *micro-cluster* [1]. A micro-cluster only keeps sufficient statistics of a set of data points, for instance, a number N which represents the total number of data points in the cluster, and a vector, of the same dimension of data points, which stores the linear sum or square sum of the N points. Single data points are not maintained by micro-clusters.

HDDStream introduces two types of micro-clusters to cope with the evolving feature of data streams: potential core micro-clusters and outlier micro-clusters. A potential core micro-cluster is a micro-cluster which collects more than N_{min} data points within a limited radius ϵ in a projected subspace, while an outlier micro-cluster is a micro-cluster whose density has not reached the pre-specified density threshold. An outlier micro-cluster may collect more and more data points

over time and evolve into a potential core micro-cluster when its density reaches N_{min}. Vice verse, a potential core micro-cluster may also lose density over time and degrade to an outlier micro-cluster.

The reason for the density loss is that, to give a higher level of importance to the most recent data, each data point in HDDStream is assigned a *weight* via an aging function. The weight of a data point exponentially decreases with time t according to the function $f(t) = 2^{-\lambda \cdot t}$, where $\lambda (> 0)$ is a user-configurable decay factor. For example, given the current time t, the weight for a data point p_i which arrived earlier at t_i is $2^{-\lambda \cdot (t-t_i)}$. Since data points are summarized by micro-clusters, the statistics maintained in the micro-clusters decays over time in the same way. Consequently, HDDStream employs a temporal extension of micro-clusters. Each micro-cluster at time t contains three statistic components for a set C of d-dimensional data points:

- $\overline{CF1(t)}$: a d-dimensional vector of the weighted linear sum of the points in each dimension.

- $\overline{CF2(t)}$: a d-dimensional vector of the weighted square sum of the points in each dimension.

- $W(t)$: sum of the weights of the data points.

3.2.1 Representation of the Radius Threshold

The region covered by a micro-cluster in the dimensional feature space is determined by the current center of the micro-cluster and its radius. The radius threshold ϵ defines the boundary of a micro-cluster. A data point p can be assigned to an existing micro-cluster mc iff the addition of p to mc does not affect the boundary of mc.

For the machine monitoring scenario described in this paper, the target items to be clustered is the temporal delay between pairs of processing actions. Therefore, the data point has only one dimension. As a result, the functions given in [8] for calculating the center and radius of a micro-cluster can be simplified into the following form:

$$center(mc) = CF1(t)/W(t)$$

$$radius(mc) = \sqrt{\frac{CF2(t)}{W(t)} - \left(\frac{CF1(t)}{W(t)}\right)^2}$$

Note that $CF1(t)$ and $CF2(t)$ is now a scalar rather than a vector.

In *HDDStream*, the radius threshold of a micro-cluster is a parameter which can be specialized with an absolute value. In other words, all micro-clusters have the same maximal radius. Whereas, we have the observation that different pairs of related processing actions are usually sensitive to variations in the delay to a different extent. More specifically, if the normal delay between one pair of processing actions is around 10 seconds, then 1 second's variance is already a critical event of which the system engineer needs to be notified. To that end the clustering algorithm must be able to mark a duration measurement with value 9 or 11 as an outlier instead of assigning it to the same micro-cluster as for the delay measurements with value 10. This implies that the radius threshold of a micro-cluster in this scenario must be smaller than 1. However, for another pair of processing actions whose normal delay is around 100 seconds, the deviation of 1 second is normal and tolerable. But if the radius threshold remains smaller than 1, delay measurements with value 100

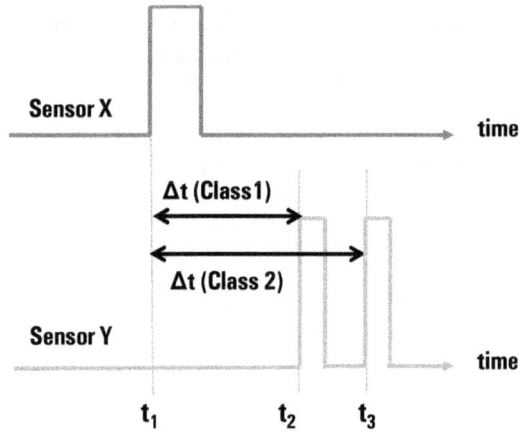

Figure 3: Two-level clustering

```
1   Input: measurement data stream S = p₁, p₂, p₃...
2
3   clusterID = -1;
4   while(S has more data points) {
5     p(value, ts, classID) = next data point from S;
6     if(p belongs to an existing class) {
7       pCoreMC = list of potential core micro-
                  clusters in class p.classID;
8       oMC = list of outlier micro-clusters in
              class p.classID;
9       clusterID = add(p, pCoreMC, oMC);
10      if(clusterID < 0) {
11        Initialize a new outlier micro-cluster
                 omc in class p.classID and add p to it;
12        clusterID = omc.ID;
13      }
14    }
15    else {
16      Initialize a new outlier micro-cluster omc
              in class p.classID and add p to it;
17      clusterID = omc.ID;
18    }
19  }
20  return clusterID;
```

Listing 1: Pseudo code of the clustering algorithm

and 101 will be assigned to two different micro-clusters. Although *HDDStream* includes an on-demand offline procedure in which the online maintained micro-clusters are further grouped to extract the final clusters, and in this procedure the two micro-clusters compressing measurements 100 and 101 respectively will probably be merged together, it is not a desired solution since the offline micro-cluster grouping step introduces additional processing overhead. What is worse, real abnormal situations cannot be distinguished from normal situations until the offline micro-cluster grouping step is performed, which is against the goal of timely anomaly detection.

To cope with this problem, the radius threshold in our solution is expressed as a percentage relative to the center of a micro-cluster. For example, given the radius threshold being 10%, the radius boundary of a micro-cluster with center at 10 is 1 ($= 10 \times 10\%$), while the radius boundary of a micro-cluster with center at 100 is 10 ($= 100 \times 10\%$). The actual radius threshold is derived from the use case itself. For instance, if any deviation bigger than 1% of the regular delay between a pair of processing actions needs to be detected, then the radius threshold will be set to 1%. As a result, the additional offline clustering over the so-far extracted micro-clusters can be skipped and the micro-clusters themselves could be regarded as the final clusters. Nevertheless, the offline procedure can still be applied on demand to improve the quality of the clustering results.

3.2.2 Two-level Clustering

In a single processing step, some processing actions can be conducted multiple times. An example is shown in Figure 3. We can observe that one raising edge of *Sensor X* is followed by two raising edges of *Sensor Y*. To describe the correlation between these two sensors, both delay measurements ($t_2 - t_1$ and $t_3 - t_1$) are required. Although the deviation between these two measurements may be tiny, they represent different interaction semantics and should not be assigned to the same cluster. To guarantee the correct correlation semantics, we assign each delay measurement a *Class ID* (*Class 1* and *Class 2*) before performing clustering. We also tune the clustering algorithm accordingly to ensure that measurements with different class IDs will not be assigned to the same micro-cluster. As a result, all micro-clusters of a certain sensor correlation are maintained in a hierarchical way. A set of

micro-clusters is maintained under each *class ID* and no micro-cluster can belong to two different classes. In the current implementation, the class ID is a simple integer value which is incrementally increased according to the number of so-far encountered different edge correlations in a single iteration of the corresponding processing step. Note that this tuning to the HDDStream algorithm is introduced only to facillitate our sensor data analysis scenario. It does not change the principle of the clustering algorithm.

The example in Figure 3 also shows that there might exist multiple "regular" delay values for a given pair of processing actions. Indeed, the lower bound for the number of regular delay values is exactly the number of classes appeared in the given correlation.

Listing 1 gives the pseudo code of the revised clustering algorithm. The input to the clustering algorithm are delay measurements calculated based on the raw sensor data. Information contained in one data point p includes the value of the delay measurement, a timestamp as well as a class ID. For each newly arrived data point, the algorithm first check whether it belongs to an existing class ($p.classID$). If not, a new outlier micro cluster omc is initialized under the new class ID and the data point is assigned to it. If the class already exists, the algorithm tries to add p to its closest micro-clusters in the class. If p cannot be assigned to any existing micro-cluster in the class, a new outlier micro-cluster will be initialized for p.

The pseudo code of the *add* procedure in Listing 1 is shown in Listing 2.

The distance between a one-dimensional data point p and a micro-cluster mc is defined as follows:

$$dist(p, mc) = p - center(mc)$$

3.3 Analysis Procedure Summary

The overall data analysis procedure is outlined in Figure 4. In the preprocessing step, analog sensor signals are converted into digital signals using user-specified rules. Next, based

```
1   Input: a data point p, pCoreMC and oMC;
2
3   distances: list of distances w.r.t p;
4   for(mc in pCoreMC ∪ oMC) {
5     dist = distance between p and mc;
6     distances.add(dist);
7   }
8   if(!empty(distances)) {
9     mc_closest = getClosestMC(distances);
10    Trial = checkRadiusBoundary(mc_closest, p);
11    if(Trial == true) {
12      Add p to mc_closest;
13      return mc_closest.ID;
14    }
15  }
16  return -1;
```

Listing 2: Pseudo code of the add procedure

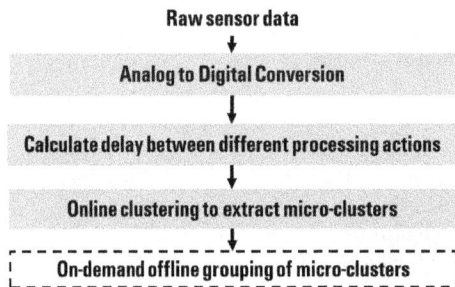

Figure 4: Overall data analysis procedure

on the timestamps included in the sensor data, temporal delay between related processing actions is measured and analyzed with the online clustering algorithm. The outcome of online clustering is a set of micro-clusters. As described in Section 3.2.1, we tune the *HDDStream* algorithm to use a relative percentage instead of an absolute value to define the radius threshold. Because the radius threshold represents the maximum deviation that can be tolerated and it is derived from the use case itself, the online extracted micro-clusters can be regarded as final clusters, making the on-demand offline micro-cluster grouping step only optional.

4. SELECTION OF CORRELATIONS

A high-tech manufacturing machine is composed of a large number of mechanical components. However, not every component pair has a strong correlation in terms of the action delay because they may be involved in different, unrelated processing steps. Due to the high complexity of manufacturing processing steps and the machine itself, system engineers usually have little a priori knowledge about which components are indeed involved in the same processing step and thus worth monitoring. To tackle this issue, we propose a heuristic method for automatically selecting meaningful correlations using a training phase.

The rationale behind the proposed method is, that if a pair of machine components has strong interdependence, then all delay measurements between the corresponding processing actions over time should form only a few densely populated areas in the domain of the delay value. Any measurement whose value does not fall into any of these areas can be regarded as an outlier. When considering the expected clustering result, we would expect the clustering algorithm to produce only a limited number of clusters which summarize the majority of the delay measurements. These clusters are defined as *regular clusters*. Clusters which contain only few members are basicly formed by outliers and are defined as *outlier clusters*. In other words, a component pair is meaningful for monitoring only when one could easily distinguish outlier clusters from regular clusters based on its clustering result.

In the training phase, we first divide all sensors into groups based on, if any, priori knowledge about the manufacturing machine. For instance, a SABRE Electrofill system, which is widely used in the semiconductor industry, contains 3 electro plating cells for copper deposition and 3 postplating cells for wafer-postclean. Machine components in one cell do not interact with components in other cells. Therefore, sensors in the machine can be grouped based on cells and sensors in different groups will never be correlated with each other. If there is no such priori knowledge available for grouping sensors, all sensors will be put into the same group. However, grouping sensors based on priori knowledge is only a manual way to reduce the search space of the correlation selection procedure, thereby saving the computation resources. In the end the results with and without pre-sensor grouping will be identical.

For each sensor group the data analyzing approach outlined in Section 3 is applied to every sensor pair. However, we turn off aging Moreover, due to the lack of knowledge about the actual ordering between the processing actions, both correlation possibilities (*Sensor A to Sensor B* and *Sensor B to Sensor A*) need to be studied. We now consider a single sensor group since the same method can be applied to any sensor group. We only investigate the correlation between different sensors. That is, given N sensors in a group, there are $N \times (N-1)$ possible correlation pairs. At the end of the training phase, the following information can be obtained for each correlation pair:

- number of generated delay measurements: N
- number of produced classes: l
- number of produced clusters: k
- number of delay measurements summarized by each cluster: $N_c = \{N_{c_1}, \ldots, N_{c_k}\}$

To find the most meaningful component correlations, we first sort elements in N_c in the descending order. The resulting list is denoted as $N_c^{\downarrow}$. The lower bound for the number of "regular" delay values between a certain pair of processing actions can be derived from the number of produced classes. Ideally, there should be only one regular cluster in each class ($k = l$), which is also the only cluster in this class, indicating that the corresponding pair of machine components interact without any exception. However, due to the existence of anomalies, usually the number of produced clusters is bigger than the number of classes ($k > l$). Therefore, we introduce an error factor ρ to tolerate outliers existing in the dataset. The rule we used to determine whether a component correlation is meaningful for monitoring or not is as follows:

A component correlation is meaningful for monitoring iff:

1. $k <= \rho \cdot l$, where $\rho \geq 1$, or
2. $\sum(TOP_{\rho \cdot l}(N_c^{\downarrow})) \geq N\theta$, where $\theta \in (0, 1]$

$\rho \cdot l$ defines the upper bound of the expected number of regular clusters. Chosing a bigger ρ means we allow more clusters produced for a given component correlation to be treated as regular clusters. This, in turn, makes it easier for the component correlation under inspection to pass the first condition. Parameter θ, which we name as *coverage* parameter, defines the expected proportion of delay measurements that which covered by the regular clusters. For example, $\theta = 1$ indicates that all delay measurements of the given correlation have to be covered by the allowed number $(\rho \cdot l)$ of regular clusters. By setting a smaller θ, we relax this "coverage" requirement, thereby making the second condition easier to be passed. In general, the above rule is stricter when ρ and θ are set to a value close to 1.

Although this sensor pair selection procedure is mainly applied in the training phase, it can also be applied periodically at runtime to check whether the so-far selected correlations are still valid.

5. EVALUATION

To evaluate our machine health monitoring approach, we used a real-world dataset coming from one manufacturing machine located at the Infineon Technologies AG fabrication plant in Dresden, Germany. The manufacturing machine is monitored by 45 binary digital sensors as described in [6]. However, only 26 of them are active. All active sensors form 3 groups- see Table 1. The monitoring data is generated at the frequency of 100Hz. Each sensor has a unique identifier which is the same as the identifier of machine component being monitored. Each monitoring data is stamped by the time at which the data is produced.

Sensor Group	# Active Binary Sensor	# Possible Correlation Pairs
Group 1	10	90
Group 2	9	72
Group 3	7	42

Table 1: Distribution of active binary sensors in groups

In the experiments, raw sensor data is replayed using a custom data generator, which can preserve the original data producing frequency. Moreover, the generator also allows to configure a *speedup* parameter to further increase the data producing frequency. All the experiments are conducted on a machine with a two-core 2.26GHz CPU and 4GB RAM. We first evaluate the scalability of the proposed solution in terms of the system throughput and the clustering latency with increasing number of correlation pairs under monitoring. System throughput is defined as the number of events that can be processed by the system per second. We then study the influence of the parameter configuration on the result of meaningful correlation selection.

In the scalability test, we only use data from sensor group 1. We set the speedup parameter of the data generator as 100, thereby fixing the input data rate from each sensor at 10,000 events/s. We then vary the number of sensors (n) from 5 to 35 and assume that interdependence exists between every two sensors. Although group 1 has only 10 binary sensors, additional sensor streams can be simulated by inverting the sensor value[2] or shifting the timestamps in an original sensor stream. The same dataset is replayed in each test run and the

[2]Change value 0 to 1 and vice verse.

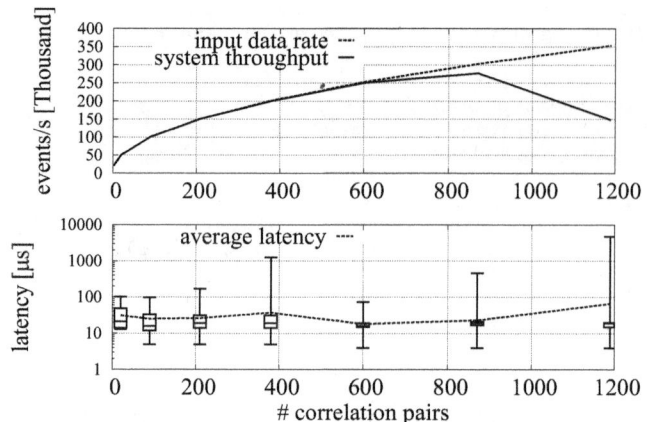

Figure 5: System throughput and clustering latency

actual input rate is calculated by multiplying 10,000 with the number of sensors being monitored ($10,000 * n$). The system throughput is then measured under each simulated workload and compared with the actual input data rate. It can be seen from Figure 5 that the system reaches its throughput capacity when monitoring 870 correlation pairs (30 sensors) simultaneously.

Under each simulated workload, the time needed to cluster the correlation samples (clustering latency) is also measured. We select a certain correlation pair which is a member of all the correlation pairs in each test run, and measure the clustering latency for 100 consecutive correlation samples starting from a fixed data time (12 hours after the time represented by the timestamp of the first raw sensor data in the dataset). Latency measurements are summarized and shown in Figure 5 using boxplot. It can be seen that in general the clustering latency is very small when the system is not overloaded, and starts to increase after the system reaches its capacity.

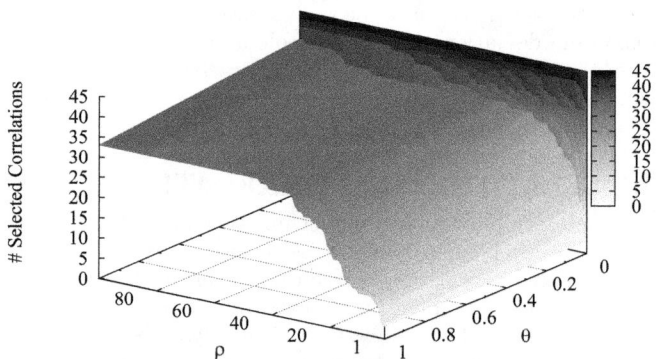

Figure 6: Influence of parameter setting on the correlation selection result

As shown in Figure 5, with a given amount of computation resources and under a certain data rate, there exists an upper bound on the number of correlation pairs that can be monitored by the system.

With naive correlation strategy, a lot of computation resources is indeed wasted since not every component pair is meaningful for correlation. To find out the most meaningful component correlations, we apply the method described in

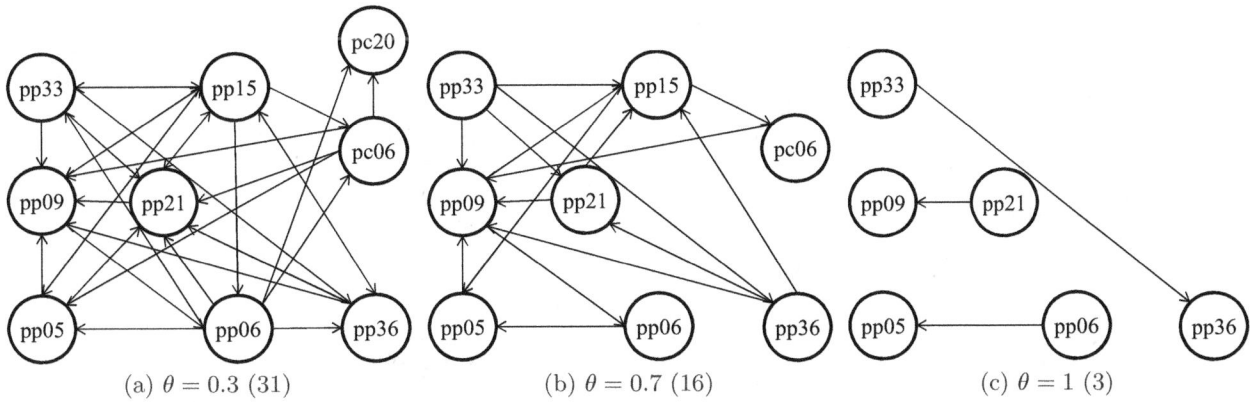

Figure 7: Component interaction diagrams for sensor group 2 with fixed ρ (= 2) and increasing θ

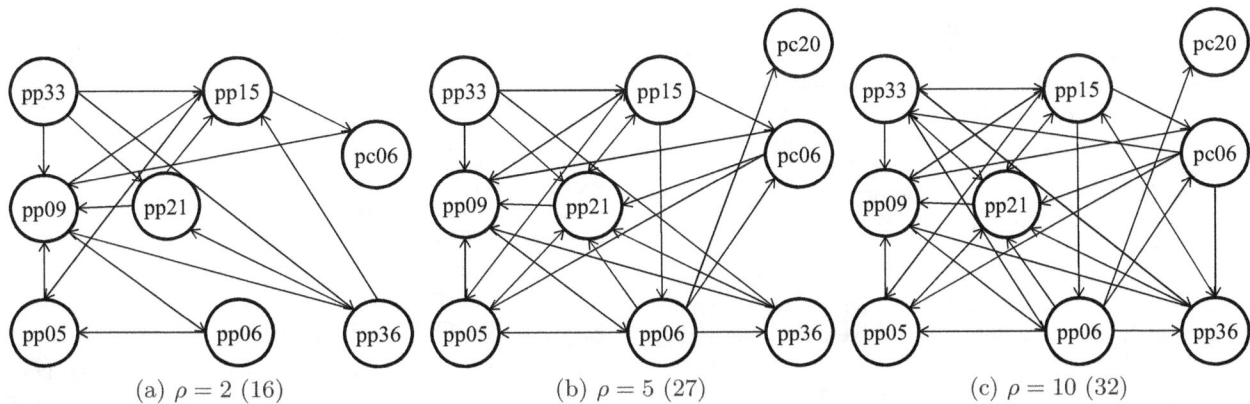

Figure 8: Component interaction diagrams for sensor group 2 with increasing ρ and fixed θ = (0.7)

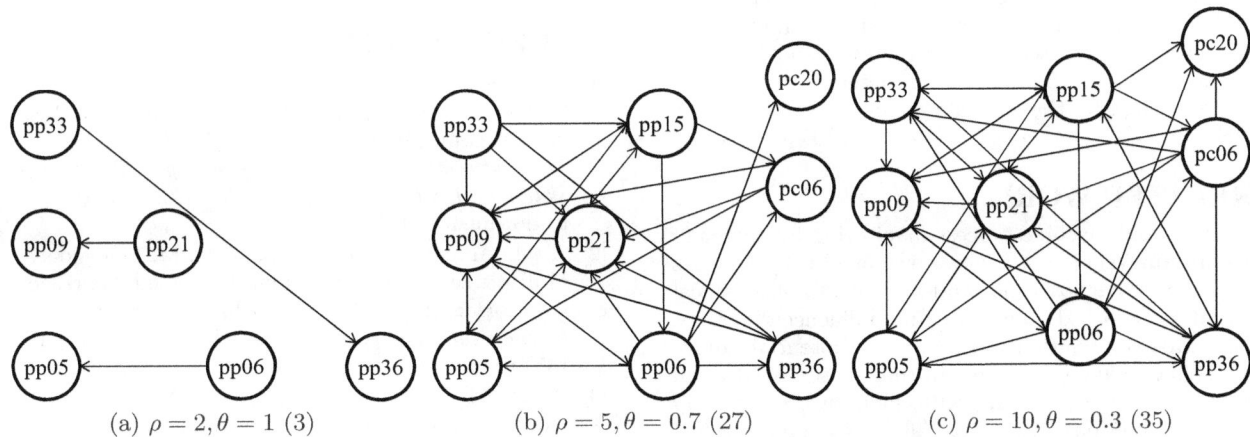

Figure 9: Component interaction diagrams for sensor group 2 with increasing ρ and decreasing θ

Section 4 to 24 hours' sensor data from all 3 sensor groups. Due to the existence of outliers in the given dataset, the number of selected correlation pairs varies with different parameter (ρ and θ) configurations. The stricter the selection condition is, the higher possibility that one of the filtering condition is violated, thereby resulting in a less number of component correlations to be selected by the algorithm. Figure 6 shows the influence of the parameter setting on the selection result for sensor group 1.

One thing that is worth explaining is, even with the most relaxed parameter configuration ($\rho = 100$ and $\theta = 0$) the total number of selected correlations is 45 but not 90 (the number of all possible correlation pairs in sensor group 1). This is because, during the training period, the occurrence of the other 45 correlation pairs was not observed. For example, in each repeating processing step, a signal from sensor pp08 always appears after the signal from sensor pp04, but not the other way round, which is similar to the scenario shown in Figure 2. Therefore, there is only the correlation from pp04 to pp08 but not the correlation in the other direction. Provided with this parameter influence chart shown in Figure 6, system engineers can tune parameters of the algorithm (ρ and θ) to tolerate the existence of outliers in a given dataset.

In addition, for each parameter configuration, we can derive a component interaction diagram for each sensor group based on the selection result. This diagram could help system engineers to understand how machine components interact with each other within the machine. Figure 7a shows the component interaction diagram for sensor group 2 with $\rho = 2$ and $\theta = 0.3$. The number of component correlations appearing in the diagram is given in the brackets below the diagram. Each circle in the diagram represents a machine component. An arrow from component X to component Y indicates that component Y directly depends on component X temporally.

As mentioned above, the number of selected component correlations is influenced by the parameter settings in the filtering rules. We show in Figure 7, 8 and 9, each of which contains a series of 3 component interaction diagrams, how the component interaction diagrams change with the parameter settings. In Figure 7, the error factor ρ is fixed and the coverage parameter θ is changed stepwise from 0.3 to 0.7 and 1. Figure 8 shows the results when θ is fixed and ρ is changed from 2 to 5 and 10. Results for changing ρ and θ at the same time are shown in Figure 9. In all three figures, we see that the component interaction diagrams evolve in a consistent way when we relax or strengthen the selection conditions. Take Figure 8 as an example, when ρ is changed from 2 to 5, more action dependencies between machine components are revealed, but all the existing dependencies shown in Figure 7b can still be found in Figure 8b. Similar behavior can be observed when strengthening the selection conditions: only existing action dependencies are filtered out and no new dependencies can be detected - see Figure 7 and Figure 9. The meaningfulness of these component interaction diagrams have been verified by the Infineon engineers working with the machine.

6. RELATED WORK

Equipment and machine process monitoring by means of sensor data analysis is not a new concept. In [2], authors propose IDES, a diagnosis and control system for mechanical systems. IDES is based on constructing influence diagrams, which describe the relationship between a potential failure and the signal changes of a monitoring sensor. IDES, in contrast to HUGO, is not designed to monitor the temporal component interactions. Authors in [9] present a hierarchical fabrication plant-wide control strategy for semiconductor manufacturing process. Sensors are used to collect metrology data of the wafers that are processed on the high-tech manufacturing equipment. The collected data is then analyzed using the principle component analysis approach. The failure detection is based on evaluation of quality of the product itself, which is different from the component interaction monitoring approach taken by HUGO. In [4] authors present an oil processing plant behavior analysis model SDAEM, whose goal is to analyze time series data such as temperature and pressure monitored by sensors deployed in the plant. Individual sensor data is analyzed by detecting patterns in

historical data using data mining techniques and searching for patterns in real-time data. Similarities between the signal trends of different sensors are detected using the detrended cross correlation method. The approach of HUGO is different from the one of SDAEM in that HUGO detects correlation between machine components which cannot be achieved by comparison of the signal trends. There also exist numerous review papers regarding manufacturing processing monitoring and machinery diagnostics [5, 3]. None of these approaches aims at analyzing the temporal dependencies between related machine components.

7. CONCLUSION

In this paper we have presented HUGO – a system which enables systems engineers to get real-time insight into relevant high-tech manufacturing machine component interactions. HUGO achieves this goal by applying a tailored version of HDDStream [8], a density-based clustering algorithm, on top of the sensor data originating from the manufacturing equipment. The results of clustering are used as the input to the algorithm which automatically filters out meaningless component interactions. HUGO can be easily applied to any type of high-tech machines, providing that they allow for real-time sensor data collection.

We have evaluated HUGO using real world data originating from one of the machines located at the Infineon Technologies AG fabrication plant in Dresden, Germany.

8. ACKNOWLEDGMENT

The authors wish to thank Infineon Technologies Dresden, for providing real-world machine monitoring sensor data. We especially thank Infineon engineers working with the manufacturing machine, for constructive discussions during the work and their feedback to our evaluation results.

9. REFERENCES

[1] C. C. Aggarwal, J. Han, J. Wang, and P. S. Yu. A framework for projected clustering of high dimensional data streams. In *Proceedings of the Thirtieth international conference on Very large data bases - Volume 30*, VLDB '04, pages 852–863. VLDB Endowment, 2004.

[2] A. M. Agogino, S. Srinivas, and K. M. Schneider. Multiple sensor expert system for diagnostic reasoning, monitoring and control of mechanical systems. *Mechanical Systems and Signal Processing*, 2(2):165 – 185, 1988.

[3] R. Du, M. A. Elbestawi, and S. M. Wu. Automated monitoring of manufacturing processes, part 1: Monitoring methods. *Journal of Engineering for Indunstry*, 117:121 – 132, 1995.

[4] A. C. B. Garcia, C. Bentes, R. H. C. de Melo, B. Zadrozny, and T. J. P. Penna. Sensor data analysis for equipment monitoring. *Knowl. Inf. Syst.*, 28(2):333–364, Aug. 2011.

[5] A. K. Jardine, D. Lin, and D. Banjevic. A review on machinery diagnostics and prognostics implementing condition-based maintenance. *Mechanical Systems and Signal Processing*, 20(7):1483 – 1510, 2006.

[6] Z. Jerzak, T. Heinze, M. Fehr, D. Gröber, R. Hartung, and N. Stojanovic. The debs 2012 grand challenge. In

Proceedings of the 6th ACM International Conference on Distributed Event-Based Systems, DEBS '12, pages 393–398, New York, NY, USA, 2012. ACM.

[7] D. C. Luckham. *The Power of Events: An Introduction to Complex Event Processing in Distributed Enterprise Systems*. Addison-Wesley Longman Publishing Co., Inc., Boston, MA, USA, 2001.

[8] I. Ntoutsi, A. Zimek, T. Palpanas, P. Kröger, and H.-P. Kriegel. Density-based projected clustering over high dimensional data streams. In *SDM*, pages 987–998, 2012.

[9] S. J. Qin, G. Cherry, R. Good, J. Wang, and C. A. Harrison. Semiconductor manufacturing process control and monitoring: A fab-wide framework. *Journal of Process Control*, 16(3):179 – 191, 2006.

Proactive Event Processing in Action:
A Case Study on the Proactive Management of Transport Processes (Industry Article)

Zohar Feldman
IBM Research – Haifa
Haifa University Campus
Haifa 31905, Israel
+972 4 8281019
zoharf@il.ibm.com

Fabiana Fournier
IBM Research – Haifa
Haifa University Campus
Haifa 31905, Israel
+972 4 8286489
fabiana@il.ibm.com

Rod Franklin
KLU (Kuehne Logistics University)
Brooktorkai 20, 20457
Hamburg, Germany
+49 40 328 707 231
rod.franklin@the-klu.org

Andreas Metzger
Paluno (The Ruhr Institute for Software Technology)
University of Duisburg-Essen, Germany
Gerlingstrasse 16, 45127 Essen, Germany
+49 201 183 4650
andreas.metzger@paluno.uni-due.de

ABSTRACT

Proactive event processing constitutes the next phase in the evolution of complex event processing. Proactive event processing makes it possible to anticipate potential issues during process execution and thereby enables proactive process management. One industry domain that can expect relevant benefits from applying proactive event processing is transportation. Transportation companies face numerous stochastic issues when managing the shipment of goods. One such issue faced in airfreight is the exact volume, weight, and number of pieces that a shipper wants to have shipped. Because of the high cost of air shipments, discrepancies between what has been booked by a shipper and the actual volume that is delivered impose costs that create problems for all participants in a shipment. One potential approach to addressing this problem is to use real-time monitoring and proactive alerting to assist air freight companies in anticipating actual delivered weights, volumes, and piece counts. In this paper we address the issue of cargo shipments by leveraging real-time monitoring data collected from an industry-standard monitoring system of a large freight forwarding company. Our evidence indicates that by using a novel proactive event-driven software engine, prediction about the weight of shipments can be developed and used in a proactive manner to assist air freight planners in making better estimates and plans for the shipment of goods. We demonstrate that through the use of this proactive approach, predictions concerning over- and under-weight loads can be made days in advance of a shipment, thus enabling the air freight planner to optimize their load plans and thus maximize the revenue that they generate from shipments.

Categories and Subject Descriptors

D.4.8 [**Performance**]: Modeling and prediction, Operational analysis; G.3 [**Probability and Statistics**]: Experimental design; I.2.3 [**Deduction and Theorem Proving**]: Uncertainty, probabilistic reasoning.

General Terms

Design, Experimentation, Management, Performance.

Keywords

Event processing, proactive, predictive, transport and logistics

1. INTRODUCTION/MOTIVATION

Proactive event processing constitutes the next phase in the evolution of complex event processing. Proactive event processing makes it possible to anticipate potential issues during process execution and thereby enables proactive process management [2]. One industry domain that can expect relevant benefits from applying proactive event processing is air freight transportation.

Air freight transportation is an important component of international trade. Manufacturers of goods that are time sensitive, expensive, perishable or used in just-in-time supply networks have come to rely on air freight for the shipment of their products. This reliance has increased as globalization of production has increased [16]. In 2011 over 200 billion revenue ton kilometers were logged by air freight carriers [17]. By 2031 air freight volumes are expected to increase to over 550 billion. Evidence suggests that improved management of transport processes through advanced IT might yield savings of between 10% and 15% [8]. In addition, environmental impacts resulting from the operation of transport and logistics services are significant, so any improvement in efficiency within a logistics network may positively contribute to sustainability objectives. CO_2 emissions from transport activities amounted to approximately 23% of energy related CO_2 emissions in 2005 and are projected to increase by 80% to 130% by 2050 [18].

To efficiently transport freight by air requires that the air cargo companies know precisely the characteristics of the shipment that is booked by the shipper (a.k.a. seller, exporter, customer) so that these companies can properly plan how to handle and transport the shipment. Airline and governmental regulations on what can be shipped by air, as well as limitations in the size of the hold in which the cargo is shipped, require the air cargo company to have a clear picture of what a shipper wants transported. This means that volume, quantity, weight and product data for each package being shipped must be accurately conveyed by the shipper to the air cargo company so the shipment can be efficiently planned and executed.

Unfortunately, many shippers are not able to convey the exact weights, package dimensions or quantities until the moment of shipment. This means that they must estimate these factors when booking carriage with an air cargo company (or via an intermediary freight forwarder). These estimates result in significant problems for the air cargo company since they must often replan their loads at the last minute when the actual shipment arrives. Such replanning activity, while being inefficient and adding cost to the air cargo company, can also result in shipment delays. Given a shipper's need for the timely delivery of their goods, such delays can cause financial penalties to be levied against the shipper by their customers.

The costs associated with variances in what is booked versus what is actually tendered by a shipper provide an incentive to the carrier or freight management company to predict, given a historical performance profile of shipments, whether a planned shipment will be over or under in weight, quantity or volume. Advances in proactive event driven computing hold out hope that such predictions can be made in a reliable manner.

This paper presents the application of a novel software engine instantiating proactive event driven computing principles to the problem of predicting whether a shipment tendered by a shipper through a freight forwarder will vary from its original booking parameters. We examine actual shipments tendered by a large freight forwarder to develop and experimentally validate a prediction capability to determine how well such an approach works in addressing the problem of booked versus actual variances. Over 2 million events from the freight forwarder's tracking and tracing system have been considered, covering five months of business activities.

The paper is organized as follows. Section 2 of the paper describes the concept of proactive event driven computing. Section 3 describes in detail the air freight use case addressed in this work. The predicted model and the event processing network created are given in Section 4. The experiments conducted are described in Section 5. Section 6 concludes the paper and identifies future research directions.

2. PROACTIVE EVENT-DRIVEN COMPUTING

In this section, we overview the concept of proactive event driven computing and describe the proactive event driven engine implemented in this work.

2.1 The Proactive Principle

Event processing is the bridge between the occurrence of events, and the reaction through an adaptation that is required by the situation [1]. A situation may be triggered by the observation of a *raw event*, but is more typically obtained by detecting a (sometimes complex) *pattern* over the flow of events. Many of these patterns are temporal in nature, but they can also be spatial, spatio-temporal, or modal [1]. Event processing deals with these functions: get events from sources, route these events, filter them, normalize or otherwise transform them, aggregate them, detect patterns over multiple events, and transfer them as alerts to a human or as a trigger to an autonomous adaptation system.

In general, event-processing applications to date deal with detection of event patterns and the identification of reactive situations. Examples of event patterns might be a delay in the expected time of arrival of goods to a warehouse or an increasing trend in the temperature measured in a certain container during transportation.

In this paper we relate to the next phase of evolution of event processing applications, namely *proactive event-driven computing*. We refer to proactive event-driven computing as the ability to mitigate or eliminate undesired states, or capitalize on predicted opportunities in advance [3], [2]. This is accomplished through the online forecasting of future events, the analysis of events coming from many sources, and the application of online decision-making processes.

The proactive principle can be illustrated as depicted in Figure 1. For a certain application we define the set of acceptable/desirable states (scoped by the closed curved line in the figure). At time (t − Δ) we forecast that the system is moving outside the set of acceptable/desirable states; i.e., towards the red state that it will reach at time (t). In such a situation, proactive computing allows changing the course of the states (by making a real-time decision), and thus to proactively change the outcomes to remain within the set of acceptable/desirable states; that is, towards the green state in the figure. This means, we have a time window Δ in which to act in order to change the course of states/events. This window of opportunity enables acting ahead of time and taking smarter actions.

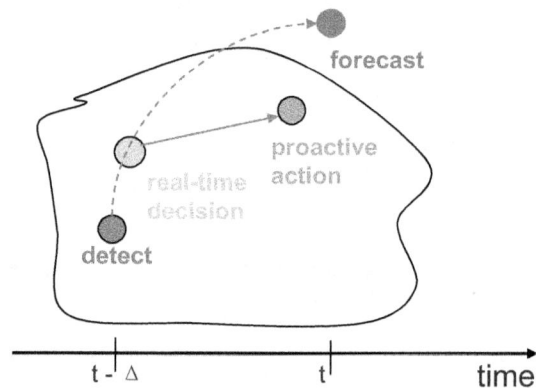

Figure 1: Proactive event driven computing principle

For example, let's assume that we have a passenger flying from A to C via B. At 9:00AM our passenger has to leave airport A. At 8:20AM there are reports regarding severe weather conditions at airport B, which can lead to an airport closure with a 60% probability. At 8:30 AM, our passenger gets a text message regarding potential closure of airport B along with a rescheduled flight itinerary (via alternative airport D), thus ensuring timely arrival at destination C.

Proactive Event-Driven Computing is a new paradigm where a decision is neither made due to explicit users' requests nor as a direct response to past events. Unlike traditional event processing, a decision is made in response to future event(s) that are forecasted from ongoing events and derivations of them. The decisions and actions are often real-time, or near real-time, in the sense that they are done under strict time constraints.

The proactive principle extends the reactive pattern known as sense-and-response or detect-and-act patterns [6] to a novel pattern consisting of four stages [2]:

Detect events and situations using enhanced event processing techniques.

Forecast/predict unexpected future events and states before they occur. Forecasting is done by observing ongoing events, analyzing them, and using predictive analytics techniques.

Decide, within time constraints, how to handle forecasted events and states using real-time optimization techniques. The decision process can be made with or without human intervention.

Act in the best way possible by enacting the decision taken by means of adapting the operational system to either mitigate the problem or reach a desired opportunity.

Proactive capabilities require going beyond the state-of-the-art in several areas. First, in event processing engines, as there is a need to extend event processing to support the concept of future events (*forecast*); secondly, in real-time optimization approaches, as there is a need to make real-time decisions based on events (*decide* and *act*).

2.2 Progress from the State-of-the-Art

The underlying motivation of proactive computing stems from social and economic factors, and is based on the fact that prevention is often more effective than cure [4]. Proactive event-driven applications can be applied to scenarios in a wide range of fields, including medicine, finance, transportation, and security to predict and prepare for future events. In fact, situations in which proactive event-driven computing might be beneficial have already been identified by the authors in the settings of transport and logistics (see [5]). This paper has suggested employing proactive event-driven computing for the run-time management of operational transport and logistics processes. Although this previous work has provided evidence for the challenges involved in managing transport process execution and the opportunities offered by predictive monitoring of those processes, it is only with the paper at hand that an actual implementation and empirical evidence for applying proactive event processing in practice is presented.

As a general observation, proactive systems are still in their infancy. Proactive applications have been developed in an *ad hoc* manner for several years; in particular in the IT infrastructure and management domain. Some examples include proactive security systems [10], proactive routing in mobile ad-hoc wireless networks [11], proactive network management with failure handling [12], as well as quality prediction [15] and proactive SLA negotiation in service oriented systems [13]. However, these are manually tailored applications with *ad hoc* underlying models, limiting their scalability, reusability, and pervasive use. We propose a comprehensive single framework with a seamless underlying model to enable proactive behavior. To this end, at the conceptual level, two modules are required [3]: a *forecasting/predicting* module, capable of predicting future probabilistic system states, and a *(near) real-time decision module*. The forecasting module relies on predictive models that, in combination with real-time pattern detections, produce a future (probabilistic) event. The (near) real-time decision module is triggered by forecasted events provided by the forecasting module, and it is expected to incorporate probabilistic information carried by the event predictions to optimize its actions.

2.3 Prototype Implementation

Building on top of core Future Internet technology components, currently being developed under the European Union's Future Internet Public Private Partnership program (http://www.fi-ppp.eu/), we developed a prototype implementation for a proactive event processing module. This module has been developed as part of the FInest collaboration space, a domain-specific, configurable and extensible set of services for the transport and logistics domain [14].

The FInest proactive event processing module (proactive module for short) provides event-processing facilities to determine relevant situations occurring within and in the context of transport processes. Such events include, for instance, changes in transport orders, critical weather conditions, and violations of transport plans and milestones.

The FInest proactive module has a single programming model and user interface for designing a proactive application that incorporates the four phases of detect-forecast-decide-act introduced in Section 2.1. The proactive platform also includes an integrated run-time platform to develop, deploy, and maintain proactive applications.

The event-driven platform is based on the notion of an *Event Processing Network (EPN)*, a collection of event processing agents, producers, consumers, and global state elements connected by a collection of channels [1]. An *event producer* is an entity at the edge of an event processing system that introduces events into the system. An *event consumer* is an entity at the edge of an event processing system that receives events from the system. An *Event Processing Agent (EPA)* is a software module that processes events [1]. In the context of this work, we apply three types of EPAs as follows (for a comprehensive description and classification of EPAs, please refer to [1]):

Filter or Threshold – This agent takes an incoming event object and applies a test to decide whether to discard it or whether to pass it on for processing by subsequent agents.

Split – This agent takes a single incoming event and emits a collection of event objects. Each of them can be a clone of the original event, or a projection of that event containing a subset of its attributes.

Enrich – This agent takes a single input event, uses it to query data from a global state element, and creates a derived event that includes the attributes from the original event, possibly with modified values, and can include additional attributes.

Each EPA acts on a set of event objects specified by a *context*. An event processing context is defined as a named specification of conditions that group event instances so that they can be processed in a related way. It assigns each event instance to one or more *context partitions*. A context can have one or more context dimensions and can give rise to one or more context partitions.

A *temporal context* consists of one or more time intervals, possibly overlapping. Each time interval, or window, corresponds to a context partition, which contains events that occur during that interval. An example can be an EPA that raises an alert if someone attempts to make more than three withdrawals from an ATM machine within a single day.

A *segmentation context* is used to group event instances into context partitions based on the value of an attribute or collection of attributes in the instances themselves. As a simple example, consider an EPA that takes a single stream of input events in which each event contains a customer identifier attribute. The value of this attribute can be used to group events so there is a separate context partition for each customer. Each context partition contains only events related to that customer so the behavior of each customer can be tracked independently of the other customers.

The proposed proactive engine introduces a new building block named *PRoactive event-processing Agent (PRA)* that extends the functionality of an EPA to process proactive patterns. PRAs, similar to their (reactive) counterparts, analyze incoming events in a particular context, and may derive either an operative decision or a future event, i.e., an event that is predicted to occur in the (near) future. For this purpose, PRAs are equipped with defined predictive and decision models, such as optimization models and rules. In our previous travel example, the relevant proactive agent detects incoming events regarding potential severe weather conditions, forecasts that there is a 60% chance that the original itinerary cannot be completed, decides on a rescheduling, and acts by sending a notification to the passenger along with the new flight itinerary.

Predictive models can be used not only to predict the probability of a future event, but to also predict the value of some numerical or categorical event attributes (e.g., the occurrence time, or the demand for a certain product). By nature, these predictions are made with some level of uncertainty, and thus a proper representation for this uncertainty is imperative. An adaptation of the event processing paradigm to accommodate uncertainty has been discussed in [9], where it is proposed that uncertain attributes are represented by corresponding statistical distributions and probabilities. In addition, [9] points out the need to re-factor some of the core event processing functions and constructs to account for uncertain events that were traditionally regarded as deterministic. For example, a sequence pattern of two events that have uncertain occurrence times can only be detected with some probability; arithmetic expressions, which are used extensively in derivation and assertion, would need to be extended with the notion of probabilistic calculus, having some terms of the expressions represented by statistical distributions. Indeed, these extensions are vital in the proactive event processing architecture as it is possible that the output of PRAs would be routed to standard EPAs and vice versa (e.g., a PRA that emits a future event, processed by a standard aggregation EPA whose output is then run by another PRA to derive a decision).

Event processing applications are directed to operational systems that are required to react and change upon incoming events in real-time, as in the transport and logistics domain. Proactive event driven applications add a new dimension by allowing users to react to events before they actually occur. Proactive event driven applications rely on predictive models which have been determined or trained using historical data. Using those models, future events are predicted and combined with real-time data obtained from the operational environment during execution. This unique combination enables the continuous improvement of forecast accuracy.

3. THE CASE STUDY

This section provides an insight into the industry case study that we use to empirically evaluate the capabilities of proactive event-driven computing. We start with a brief introduction to the transport and logistics domain and then elaborate on Cargo 2000, a standards-based monitoring technology that delivers basic events as input to our proactive event-processing solution. Finally, we provide details of the data set used during the case study.

3.1 The Transport and Logistics Domain

The shipment of goods requires the integration of services from multiple organizations. Freight forwarders, cargo carrying airlines, airport logistics companies, ground handlers, ground transport companies and regulatory agencies all may be involved in the operational business process. Each of these entities, operating independently to achieve internal efficiency and performance objectives, must be coordinated to act in an integrated fashion if customer expectations are to be met.

Due to the complexity of the shipment process, there are numerous kinds of deviations that may occur during transport execution, and that would require dynamic rescheduling of shipments. Examples include booking cancellations and performance violations [5], as well as volume and weight discrepancies. Delays and discrepancies can arise due to internal considerations such as cargo consolidation, where an organization delays a shipment while waiting to obtain a lower cargo price through a more complete container load. In addition, external factors, such as ground handling delays due to congestion or priority shifts can also arise and contribute to less than desired performance. Interestingly, most process-oriented delays arise at the boundaries between the organizations involved in an air cargo shipment.

The case study in this paper focuses on prediction and proactive management of weight discrepancies. Weight discrepancies occur when a difference is observed between the weight that has been booked by the customer and the weight that is actually delivered. As mentioned in the introduction, many shippers are not able to convey the exact weight until the moment of shipment, and even then discrepancies between booking and actual may only be observed at the time the freight is received at the airline. Two specific situations can be differentiated:

- **Hi shows ("over-weight loads"):** In this case more actual freight is delivered than planned, i.e., the ratio of actual vs. planned is greater than 1.

- **Lo Shows ("under-weight loads"):** In this case less actual freight is delivered than planned, i.e., the ratio of actual vs. planned is less than 1.

3.2 Event Monitoring Technology

To support the cross-organizational monitoring of transport processes, IATA (the International Air Transport Association) has established the Cargo 2000 initiative "aiming at implementing a new quality management system for the worldwide air cargo industry. The objective is simple: to implement processes, backed by quality standards, which are measurable to improve the efficiency of air cargo" [7]. This means Cargo 2000 constitutes a tracking and tracing system that allows for end-to-end visibility of the supply chain. Stakeholders involved in the transport process can share agreed Cargo 2000 messages, comprising transport planning, re-planning and service completion events. Cargo 2000 thus enables an unprecedented level of transparency in the supply chain.

Overall, Cargo 2000 is based on the following key principles:

- Every shipment gets a plan (called a *RouteMap*) describing planned transport routes (including flight numbers and airport codes) and booked cargo volumes.

- Every route map has predefined *milestones* with planned times of arrival.

- During process execution, stakeholders receive *events* about successful milestone completion, as well as milestone violations, each including the effective time the milestone has been reached, as well as possible updates of actual cargo volumes.

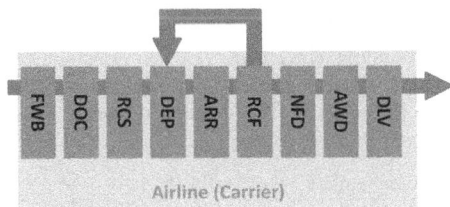

Figure 2: Cargo 2000 Milestones

Figure 2 shows the relevant Cargo 2000 milestones that are addressed in our case study:

- **FWB**: Master Airway Bill Creation (Airway Bill = "A shipping document used by the airlines for air freight. It is a contract for carriage that includes carrier conditions of carriage including such items as limits of liability and claims procedures.", see http://www.finest-ppp.eu/domain-dictionary)

- **DOC**: Truck Arrival at Departure Airline

- **RCS**: Freight Checked in at Departure Airline

- **DEP**: Goods Confirmed on Board

- **ARR**: Flight Arrival at Destination

- **RCF**: Freight Acceptance Arrival Airline

- **NFD**: All Freight and Documents Ready for Pick-up

- **AWD**: Documents Delivery to Import Forwarder

- **DLV**: Freight Delivery to Import Forwarder

A transport leg may involve multiple segments (e.g., transfers to other flights or airlines). In these cases, the RCF service "loops back" to the DEP service (indicated by the "loop-back" arrow in Figure 2).

Air carriers and logistics service providers that have implemented Cargo 2000 are able to track the progress of a shipment by observing the various events occurring along the shipment route. This is a significant advance from the historical "black box" processes that preceded the industry's implementation of the Cargo 2000 standard. However, even though supply chain participants can see the progress of a shipment, this viewing is retrospective, i.e., notifications and event updates occur after the fact. Predictive events are not provided through existing implementations of the Cargo 2000 standard. This paper provides a technical solution to address this gap.

3.3 Industry Data Set

Our case study rests on an industry data set, comprising transport tracking and tracing events from a large freight forwarder's Cargo 2000 system covering five months of business activities. The data set contains over 2 million system messages representing raw events, such as route map updates (replanning), milestone completion, as well as milestone violation. Together, those events represent the execution of approximately 151,000 actual transports.

4. THE PROACTIVE APPROACH

Our goal is to proactively alert about possible substantial discrepancies, either positive or negative, between the freight that has been scheduled by a certain forwarder to be transported on a particular flight, and the actual weight that was delivered by the shippers to go on that particular flight. This means that we aim to address hi- and lo-shows (see Section 3.1) on a per flight basis. A substantial discrepancy, in our case, is interpreted as a deviation of more than 20% of the overall cargo weight, which thus constitutes a buffer. Accordingly, we call a flight *over-loaded* (resp. *under-loaded*) if the overall cargo weight summed over all route maps scheduled by a particular forwarder to include that flight is larger (resp. smaller) than the planned weight (including the buffer of 20%). Our proactive implementation is manifested through the combination of a predictive model that estimates the probability of being either over- or under-loaded, and probabilistic rules that fire alerts based on this prediction. In what follows, we describe in detail these two components as well as the event processing network that encapsulates them.

4.1 The Predictive Model and Probabilistic Rules

We first wish to be able to evaluate the probability of the aforementioned situations, given any other information that we have in hand. Since the weight discrepancies of different route maps are independent of each other, it is sufficient to predict the actual weight per route map, whereas the prediction per flight is obtained by a straightforward aggregation. We use the following notation:

- PW_r – The planned weight of route map r

- AW_r – The actual weight of route map r

- FW_r – The forecasted weight of route map r

- RM_f – The set of all route maps that are scheduled on flight f

- ARM_f – The set of all route maps that are scheduled on flight f and were already delivered to the airline (i.e., completed milestone RCS) in the considered point of time

In order to determine the predictive model, we analyze data about past shipments comprised of informative attributes such as the planned weight, the number of packages, the source and the destination of the shipment, and the shipping airlines. For each shipment, the actual weight was extracted from the milestone completion events. Figure 3 plots the actual versus the planned weights. It appears that in approximately 50% of the shipments, some weight discrepancy is reported; in 38% the actual weight is lower than planned and for the remaining 12%, it is higher. An interesting phenomena that is reflected in the vertical lines passing through the round values of planned weight, is that in many cases the planned weight is merely a rough estimation made by the shipper, probably in the absence of more reliable information. Our first conclusion, which is not surprising, is that given the planned weight, the actual weight is independent of all other attributes. This fact was validated using statistical tests that revealed insignificant differences in the planned-versus-actual deviations between different values of shipment sources and destinations. Moreover, we have discovered that the ratio between the actual weight and the planned weight is independent of all other factors, practically implying the following relation

$$FW_r = Ratio \cdot PW_r,$$

where *Ratio* is a random variable whose distribution function is depicted in Figure 4. The mean for *Ratio* is 0.96 with a standard deviation of 0.58.

Based on the above analysis, at any given time, we forecast the cargo weight of a flight f by the following random variable

$$\sum_{r \in ARM_f} AW_r + \sum_{r \in RM_f \setminus ARM_f} Ratio \cdot PW_r$$

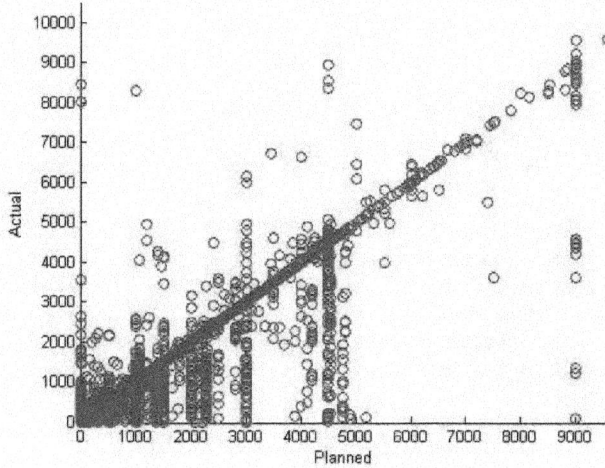

Figure 3: Actual vs planned weights

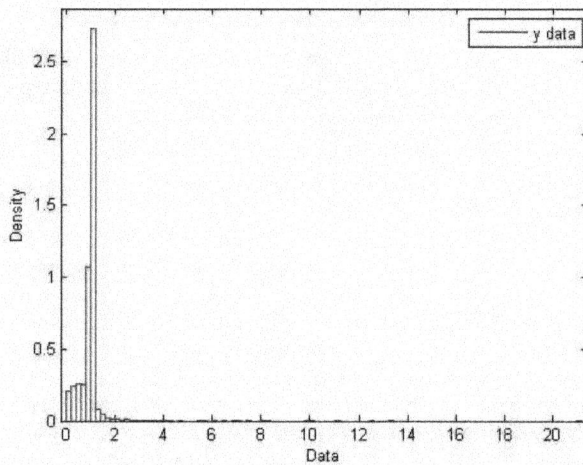

Figure 4: Ratio distribution function

It should be noted that, while the analysis is performed on historical data at a given period in time, the reported numbers and distribution might change over time. It is less likely, however, that the qualitative findings about the independence of the actual/planned ratio would be refuted in future queries. It is therefore expected that updating the predictive model would not require a large amount of repeated analysis of new data, and thus rather an automatic updating process could suffice. In fact, this can be achieved by utilizing an additional EPA that matches planned and actual values of particular items and performs some calculation to update the predictive model.

Equipped with the weight forecasting model from above, we now need a decision mechanism that based on this input fires alerts, considering two objectives: (1) catch as many discrepancies as

possible in advance to allow for an appropriate proactive response to be placed (i.e., achieve high recall), and (2) avoid false alarms as much as possible (i.e., achieve high precision). Obviously, these two objectives are conflicting; improving one might come at the expense of another. As a consequence, we choose the following rules:

1. Alert "over-loaded" if and only if

$$P\left\{ \sum_{r \in RM_f \setminus ARM_f} Ratio \cdot PW_r > \sum_{r \in RM_f} 1.2 \cdot PW_r - \sum_{r \in ARM_f} AW_r \right\} > \delta_o$$

2. Alert "under-loaded" if and only if

$$P\left\{ \sum_{r \in RM_f \setminus ARM_f} Ratio \cdot PW_r < \sum_{r \in RM_f} 0.8 \cdot PW_r - \sum_{r \in ARM_f} AW_r \right\} > \delta_u,$$

where P denotes the probability of the expression enclosed within the curly brackets. The sum on the left hand side of the expressions in the curly brackets represents the predicted weight of all route maps that have not yet been delivered. Informally, expression 1 states that an "over-load" situation is observed if the aggregate of predicted weights per flight (at a given point in time) is greater than what has been planned (plus 20% buffer) reduced by the weight of the actual freight already admitted at the point of prediction. Expression 2, following the same pattern, states that an "under-load" situation is observed if the predicted weights per flight are smaller than what has been planned (minus a 20% buffer) reduced by the weight of the actual freight already admitted at the point of prediction.

The proactive engine accommodates the above rules and expressions both during build-time and execution. The embedded expression builder is extended with a variety of probabilistic functions, such as *prob*, *mean*, etc., allowing for editing "probabilistic expressions", similar to the ones above. Correspondingly, the expression evaluator that is part of the execution engine is extended with logic to compute probabilistic functions (e.g. *mean*, *std.*) and arithmetic operators (e.g. *summation*, *division*) performed on probabilistic attributes. For instance, the sum on the left hand side of the expressions in the curly brackets is determined by the engine as probabilistic (comprised of probabilistic attributes), and thus it is computed by numerical convolution rather than standard arithmetical summation, resulting in a distribution rather than a simple scalar.

Both rules are governed by the threshold parameters δ_o and δ_u.

Increasing the values of these parameters would trigger alerts at higher variance levels, while lower values result in an increased number of alerts due to lower variance tolerances. Tuning these parameters in a way that balances between the two objectives in a satisfactory manner is essential. Such optimization can be conducted empirically as described in Section 5.

4.2 The Event processing Network

To implement a proactive event processing network in our case study, the following event types have been defined based on the raw events found in the data set (cf. Section 3.3):

- *MilestoneUpdate:* an event that indicates the actual values for a specific RouteMap at a certain milestone;
- *MilestoneFlights:* an event that associates the flights to a milestone

- *RouteMapFlight*: an event that associates to each RouteMap its relevant remaining flights.

Table 1 describes the event types along with their main attributes, where those attributes are defined as follows:

- *MilestoneCode:* The Cargo 2000 code of the specific milestone (see Figure 2) the event relates to;
- *RouteMapID:* A unique identifier for each shipment;
- *ActualTimeStamp:* The time stamp of the occurrence of the event given as UTC;
- *Weight:* Cargo weight;
- *FlightID:* A unique identifier for each flight (typically a combination of flight number and calendar date).

Table 2 describes the event processing agents that form the event-processing network of our case study, which is depicted in Figure 5.

The *producer* of the events for the Hi/Lo shows use case is the data set comprising the actual transport events (see Figure 5).

We specified a single *consumer* for the Hi/Lo shows case study in the form of a dashboard (see Figure 6) that shows in real-time the events as they are being processed by the event processing network (the MilestoneUpdate events) and the alerts that are fired by the WeightAlertNotification output event (see Table 2). A screenshot of this dashboard is shown in Figure 6.

Table 1: Event Types defined in Case Study

#	Event name	Attribute name
1.	*MilestoneUpdate*	MilestoneCode
		RouteMapID
		ActualTimeStamp
		Weight
2.	*MilestoneFlights*	MilestoneCode
		RouteMapID
		Array [0..N] of FlightID
3.	*RouteMapFlight*	RouteMapID
		FlightID

Table 2: Processing Agents defined in Case Study

EPA Name	FilterMilestone
EPA type	Threshold/Filter
Context	Temporal: always
Rule (informal definition)	Filters out all event updates which do not belong to the FWB milestone
Rule definition	If MilestoneUpdate.MilestoneCode == 'FWB'
Input type events	MilestoneUpdate
Output type events	MilestoneUpdate

EPA Name	MilestoneFlights
EPA type	Enrich
Context	Temporal: always
Rule (informal definition)	At each milestone event, it is enriched with all its flights
Rule definition	Enrich (MilestoneEvent) with RouteMaps records from RouteMapsFlights
Input type events	MilestoneUpdate
Output type events	MilestoneFlights

EPA Name	RouteMapFlight
EPA type	Split
Context	Temporal: always
Rule (informal definition)	Arranges pairs of a shipment with a flight
Rule definition	Split (MilestoneFlights) by FlightID
Input type events	MilestoneFlights
Output type events	RouteMapFlight

PRA Name	AlertOnFlightDiscrepancy
EPA type	PRA
Context	Segmentation: FlightID
Rule (informal definition)	For each flight it calculates whether there is a probability of being over (under) weight above (under) a certain threshold
Rule definition	See equations 1 and 2 in Section 4
Input type events	MilestoneUpdate
	RouteMapFlight
Output type events	WeightAlertNotification

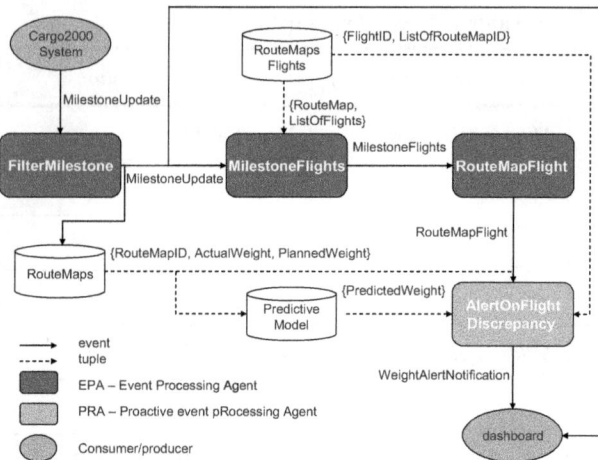

Figure 5: Hi/Lo Shows EPN

5. EXPERIMENTATION AND ANALYSIS

Our experimental study is based on five months of operational data, comprised of approximately 151,000 route maps records (after data cleansing). We divided the data into a training set (80% of the first route maps records) and a test set (20% of remaining route maps). We used the training set to build the predictive model. The test set is used for a simple validation in a simulative mode where all records are converted to appropriate MilestoneUpdate events, and fired into the event processing in the order of their actual occurrence time. Since there are no temporal contexts or temporal patterns of any sort in our event processing network, the actual time of the events is insignificant to the processing, thus the above procedure constitutes a consistent simulation run.

The FInest proactive module allows for the definition of producers and consumers for event data. These are specified during the application build-time and translated into input and output adapters respectively during execution time. The producer applied in our case study is a web-based dashboard that during the execution displays the events as they are being processed by the run-time engine and fires the alerts or notifications whenever an over-load or under-load situation is detected by the proactive event processing agent. The MilestoneUpdate events, as well as the alerts fired by the proactive engine, are displayed on the event dashboard as depicted in Figure 6.

Figure 6 shows the screenshot of the event dashboard that displays a flow of events followed by two alerts, one notifying about a potential overload of flight DL6278T with likelihood of 1.0 and the other about a potential underload of flight AA2101 with likelihood of 0.76. The trigger to each of these two alerts is a milestone event corresponding to these flights that caused firing of the alert (the proactive rule is matched).

Throughout each experiment, we maintain the following sets:

1. **AlertedUnder** – the set of all flights that were alerted by the proactive engine about being possibly under-loaded.

2. **AlertedOver** – the set of all flights that were alerted by the proactive engine about being possibly over-loaded.

3. **ActualUnder** – the set of all flights that were eventually found to be under-loaded.

4. **ActualOver** – the set of all flights that were eventually found to be over-loaded.

All flights that contain only one route map were omitted from the four sets, as these flights cannot be alerted ahead of time. Altogether, there were 586 over-loaded flights and 532 under-loaded flights. As mentioned in the preceding section, we are interested in two performance measures; one is recall, measuring the fraction of the over- and under-loaded flights that the proactive engine catches. The other performance measure is precision, measuring the portion of alerts that were indeed correct out of all alerts that were made. More formally, recall and precision for both under-loaded and over-loaded are calculated by the following equations.

Figure 6: Event dashboard

$$Recall_{over} = \frac{|AlertedOver \cap ActualOver|}{|ActualOver|}$$

$$Precision_{over} = \frac{|AlertedOver \cap ActualOver|}{|AlertedOver|}$$

$$Recall_{under} = \frac{|AlertedUnder \cap ActualUnder|}{|ActualUnder|}$$

$$Precision_{under} = \frac{|AlertedUnder \cap ActualUnder|}{|AlertedUnder|}$$

We conducted several experiments, each experiment corresponds to a different choice of parameters values. The values of the threshold parameters δ_o and δ_u ranged between 0.01 and 0.99 in increments of 0.02.

Figure 7 and Figure 8 show the plots for recall and precision for under-loaded alerts and over-loaded alerts respectively for each selection of parameter values. In both plots, the parameter values are displayed for selected points, i.e., ones that exhibit a somewhat preferable balance between the recall and precision.

Evidently, the over-loaded alerts can be made with very good precision (almost 100%) while catching a good portion of the true over-loaded flights (about 70%). This portion can even get to 75% without compromising the accuracy much. In the under-loaded alerts, the accuracy that can be guaranteed is smaller (75%-80%), though a high recall rate (95%) can be obtained at this level of accuracy.

We also examine the time between when an alert is made for a particular flight, and the time of flight departure. The distribution of the offset times were rather identical in all experiments. A typical distribution of the offsets is displayed in Figure 9. The mean alert time is 58 hours (almost 2.5 days) and the standard deviation is 56. The minimum time is 6 hours, and in some cases the alert was set as long as 14 days before the scheduled flight. These are very encouraging results, as these time ranges allow for a proper reaction to take place.

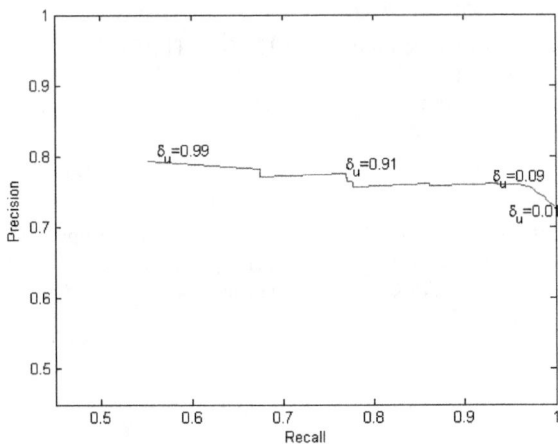

Figure 7: Under-loaded measurements for $0.05 \leq \delta_u \leq 0.95$

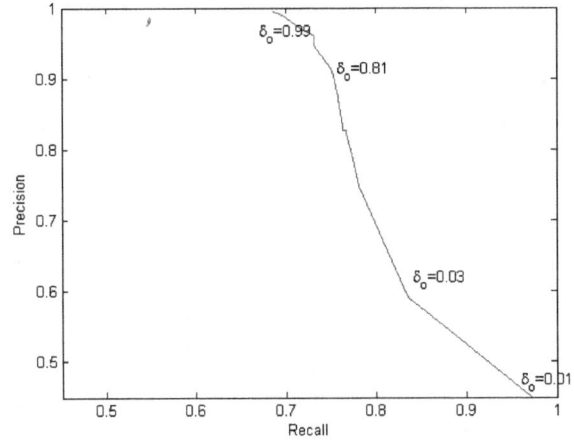

Figure 8: Over-loaded measurements for $0.05 \leq \delta \leq 0.95$

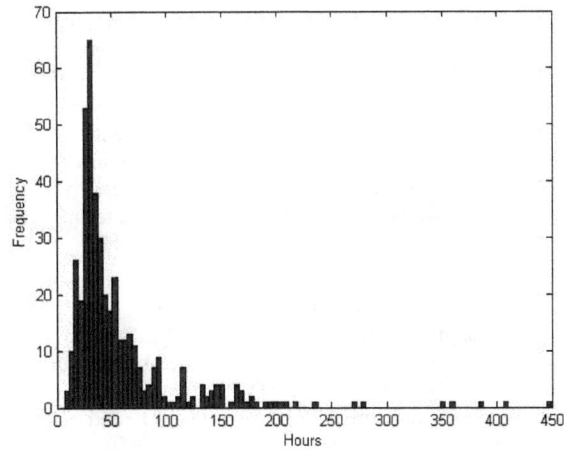

Figure 9: Alert offset time histogram

As mentioned previously, proactive event driven computing comprises a pattern of four stages: detect, forecast/predict, decide, and act. These four stages are expressed in the Hi/Lo shows case study as follows:

Detect events of relevance and apply event processing rules to discover situations of interest by applying event processing rules. ***Forecast/predict*** a potential over-weight (under-weight) flight by analyzing the actual milestone events and applying the predictive model. This step is the core part in our case study.

Decide whether to fire an alarm notifying of a potential over-weight (or under-weight) flight.

Act in terms of either rescheduling the alerted shipments to an alternative route in the case of over-weight; or selling available capacity in the case of under-weight. Note that not acting is also an option that can be followed by the human actor.

6. CONCLUSIONS AND FUTURE WORK

In this work, we explored the benefits of applying a proactive event-driven approach in the domain of transport and logistics, specifically addressing the problem of weight discrepancies in air freight.

Our experimental study shows that our proactive engine can alert about over-loaded and under-loaded situations with a high level of accuracy. Furthermore, the alerts fired by the FInest proactive module notify several days in advance of a potential weight discrepancy, allowing for a timely response by the forwarder and air freight carrier.

The air freight industry, although smaller than maritime or road transport sectors, constitutes an extremely valuable mode of transport for goods characterized by high value to weight, delivery time sensitivity or perishability. Improvements in the ability of air freight companies to plan their loads and improve their operational efficiencies has the potential to increase profits, reduce environmental impact and positively contribute to customer satisfaction. The results of this preliminary application of proactive event monitoring are promising in that they provide industry players with the potential to anticipate issues well in advance of the actual flight and take corrective actions. Since the air cargo industry carries approximately 30% by value of all goods shipped internationally [19] improvements in the ability to plan and ship these goods has a large positive economic value for the global economy.

One possible future direction is to improve the predictive model. Although our findings show that much of the shipment information that was available for us have no predictive value, it is certainly possible that other data elements, such as customer information, may be more valuable. It is also interesting to take the proactive approach a step further from merely alerting to actually recommending and even executing specific actions, such as shipment rescheduling. Ideally, these actions should optimize desirable business objectives such as revenue, image etc., possibly requiring more sophisticated optimization models and techniques.

7. ACKNOWLEDGMENTS
We thank the anonymous referees for their helpful comments. The research leading to these results has received funding from the European Union's Seventh Framework Programme FP7/2007-2013 under grant agreement 285598 (FInest) and 604123 (FIspace).

8. REFERENCES
[1] Etzion O. and Niblet P. 2010. Event processing in action. Manning.

[2] Engel Y, Etzion O., and Feldman Z 2012. A Basic model for proactive event-driven computing. Proceedings of the sixth ACM conference on Distributed Event Based Systems (DEBS'12).

[3] Engel Y. and Etzion O. 2011. Towards proactive event-driven computing. Proceedings of the fifth ACM conference on Distributed Event Based systems (DEBS'11).

[4] Fleming M. 2009. Business Navigation Systems Combine CEP with BPM. IDC report.

[5] Metzger, A. Franklin R., and Engel Y. 2012. Predictive monitoring of heterogeneous service-oriented business

networks: The transport and logistics case. SRII 2012 Global Conference, ser. Conference Publishing Service (CPS), R. Badinelli, F. Bodendorf, S. Towers, S. Singhal, and M. Gupta, Eds. IEEE Computer Society.

[6] Schulte W.R. 2011. How to choose design patterns for event-processing applications. Gartner report #G00214719.

[7] Cesana R. 2004. Cargo 2000 phase 3 specification. IATA/Cargo 2000, Tech. Rep. [Online]. Available: www.cargo2000.com

[8] AEL. 2010. A technology roadmap for logistics: Promoting a comprehensive and integrated European strategy to support and incentivise ICT platforms and green technologies for European transport and logistics operations. Alliance for European Logistics, Tech. Rep.

[9] Artikis A., Etzion O., Feldman Z, and Fournier F. 2012. Event processing under uncertainty. Proceedings of the sixth ACM conference on Distributed Event Based Systems (DEBS'12).

[10] Dolev S., Kopeetsky, and A. Shamir A. 2011. RFID authentication efficient proactive information security within computational security. Theory of Computing Systems, pages 1–18.

[11] Kunz T. and Alhalimi R. 2010. Energy-efficient proactive routing in MANET: Energy metrics accuracy. Ad Hoc Networks, 8(7):755–766.

[12] Fu S. and Xu C.Z. 2007. Exploring event correlation for failure prediction in coalitions of clusters. In ICS.

[13] Mahbub K. and Spanoudakis G. 2010. Proactive SLA negotiation for service based systems. In 6th World Congress on Services.

[14] Franklin R., Engel Y., Hagaseth M., Tjora A., Fournier F., Fleischhauer R., Marquezan C., Metzger A., Stollberg M., and Tschapke S. 2012. Cloud based collaboration platform for transport & logistics business networks. 6th International Scientific Symposium on Logistics, BVL.

[15] Zeng L., Lingenfelder C, Lei H., and H. Chang H. 2008. Event-driven quality of service prediction. Int'l Conference on Service-Oriented Computing–ICSOC 2008, pp. 147–161.

[16] Vision 2050, IATA, p5

[17] World Air Cargo Forecast: 2012 2013, The Boeing Company, p.3, http://www.boeing.com/commercial/cargo/wacf.pdf, accessed 25 January 2013.

[18] Transport, Energy and CO_2: Moving Towards Sustainability, International Energy Agency, 2009, p. 44.

[19] Kasarda J., Appold S., and Mori M. 2006. The Impact of the Air Cargo Industry on the Global Economy, The International Air Cargo Association, Air Cargo Forum, Calgary, CA.

Model-based Validation of Streaming Data

(Industry Article)

Cheng Xu
Department of Information Technology
Uppsala University
Box 337, SE-75105, Sweden
+46 18 471 7345
cheng.xu@it.uu.se

Daniel Wedlund
AB Sandvik Coromant
R&D Application solutions,
Functional Products
SE-811 81 Sandviken, Sweden
daniel.wedlund@sandvik.com

Martin Helgoson
AB Sandvik Coromant
R&D Application solutions,
Functional Products
SE-811 81 Sandviken, Sweden
martin.helgoson@sandvik.com

Tore Risch
Department of Information Technology
Uppsala University
Box 337, SE-75105
+46 18 471 6342
tore.risch@it.uu.se

ABSTRACT

An approach is developed where functions are used in a data stream management system to continuously validate data streaming from industrial equipment based on mathematical models of the expected behavior of the equipment. The models are expressed declaratively using a data stream query language. To validate and detect abnormality in data streams, a model can be defined either as an analytical model in terms of functions over sensor measurements or be based on learning a statistical model of the expected behavior of the streams during training sessions. It is shown how parallel data stream processing enables equipment validation based on expensive models while scaling the number of sensor streams without causing increasing delays. The paper presents two demonstrators based on industrial cases and scenarios where the approach has been implemented.

Categories and Subject Descriptors

H.2.4 [**Database Management**]: Systems – *Parallel databases, Query processing*

Keywords

Equipment Monitoring; data stream management system; data stream validation; parallelization; anomaly detection.

1. INTRODUCTION

Emerging business scenarios such as provision of total care products, product service systems (PSS), industrial product-service-systems (IPS^2), and functional products [3] [4] [5] [14] [15] imply needs to efficiently monitor, verify and validate the functionality of a delivered product in use. This can be done with regard to pre-defined criteria, e.g. productivity, reliability, sustainability, and quality. A functional product in this context mean an integrated provision of hardware, software and services.

In case of machining several factors and dependencies have to be considered, which in turn means that data (e.g. in-process data) from the machining process, information (e.g. about cutting tools), and knowledge (e.g. physical models), from several domains have to be captured, combined and analyzed in a comprehensive knowledge integration framework that includes quality assurance of data, validation of models, learning capabilities, and verification of functionality [10]. A considerable challenge is to scale up data analysis for handling huge amount of equipment.

In this context novel software technologies are needed to efficiently process and analyze the large data streams, in particular related to in-process activities, and to facilitate the steps towards increased automation of the related processes.

In manufacturing industry, equipment such as machine controllers and various sensors are installed. This equipment measure and generate data during the machining process, i.e. in-process. Depending on the case a huge amount of parameters (e.g. power, torque, etc.) at different sample rates (ranging from a couple of HZ to 20 kHZ) need to be processed. Processing data streams from controllers and sensors is critical for monitoring the functional product in use. For instance, the parameters related to the power consumption could help the engineers to analyze the process, compare different application strategies, monitor and maintain the hardware e.g. to get an indication of the degree of tool-wear or when a tool needs to be replaced or machine maintenance is required.

Often a mathematical model of the process can be developed, e.g. to calculate the expected power consumption and detect abnormal behavior. In other cases, when there is no such model pre-defined, a model can be learned based on observing sensor readings during training sessions. This requires a general approach to define the correct behavior of the equipment either analytically or statistically.

Data Stream Management Systems (DSMSs), such as Aurora [1] and STREAM [16], process continuous queries, CQs, over data streams that filter, analyze, and transform the data streams. A simple CQ can be: "give me the sensor id and the power consumption whenever the power is greater than 100W". However, detecting abnormal behavior in equipment often involves advanced computations based on knowledge about the machining process, e.g. theoretical models of the equipment's behavior, rather than just simple numerical comparisons in a query condition. An advanced CQ could be: "given a power consumption model computing the theoretical expected power consumption at any point in time, give me the sensor id whenever the difference between the actual power consumption and the theoretical expected power on the average is greater than 10W during 1 second."

To enable general stream validation based on mathematical models, the system called SVALI (Stream VALIdator) was developed and used in industrial applications. The system provides the following facilities:

1. Users can define and install their own *analytical* models inside the DSMS to validate correct behavior of the data streams. The models are expressed as side-effect free functions (formulae) over streamed data values.

2. For applications where no theoretical model can be easily defined, the system can also dynamically learn a model based on some existing observed correct behavior and then use that *learned* model for subsequent validation.

SVALI is a distributed DSMS extending SCSQ [22] with validation functionality. Many SVALI nodes can be started on different compute nodes. The distributed SVALI architecture enables processing of validations in parallel without causing unacceptable delays by the often expensive computations, as shown in this paper.

The paper is organized as follows. In Section 2 the architecture of a SVALI node is presented. Section 3 presents two general strategies for stream validations in SVALI called *model-and-validate* and *learn-and-validate*, illustrated by real-life industrial examples. Section 4 presents results from simulations on how the parallelization enables scalable processing of expensive validation functions in the applications, and Section 5 discusses related work. Finally, Section 6 summarizes and outlines future work.

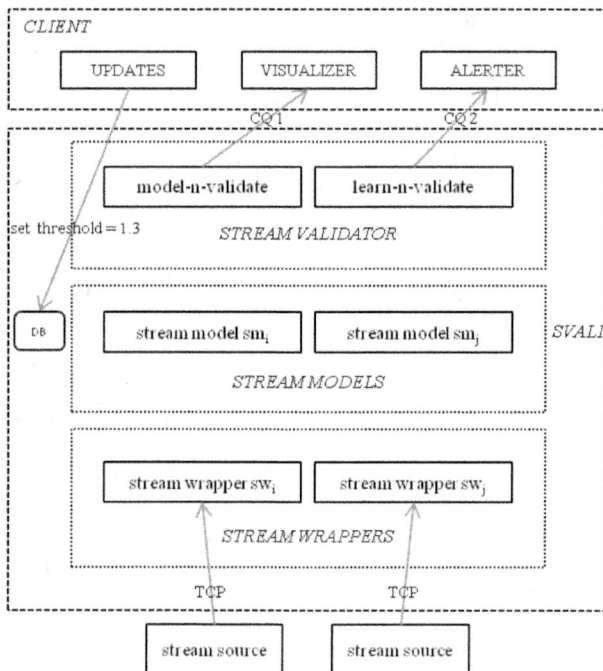

Figure 1. System Architecture

2. SYSTEM ARCHITECTURE

Figure 1 shows the architecture of the SVALI system. Different kinds of data streams are collected from *stream sources* of sensor readings. SVALI is an extensible DSMS where new kinds of stream sources can be plugged in by defining *stream wrappers*. A stream wrapper is an interface that continuously reads a raw data stream and emits the read events to the SVALI kernel. On top of the stream wrappers, equipment specific *stream models* over raw data streams analyze the received stream tuples to validate that different kinds of equipment behave correctly. A stream model is a function over either individual stream tuples or over windows of stream tuples. Stream models are passed as a parameter to the *stream validator* that applies the models to produce *validation streams* where deviations from correct behavior are indicated.

The main-memory *local database* stores meta-data about the streams such as stream models, tolerance thresholds, collected statistics, etc.

For validating streaming data using an analytical stream model the system provides a second order function, called *model_n_validate()*. It validates data streaming from sensors on a set of machines based on a stream model function and emits a *validation stream* of significant deviations for malfunctioning machines.

It is also possible to automatically build at run-time a model of correct behavior based on observed correct streaming data using another second order function called *learn_n_validate()*. During a learning phase it computes statistics of correct behavior of the monitored equipment based on a user provided statistical model. After the learning phase the collected statistics is stored in the local database and used as the reference with which the streaming data will be compared. As for model-and-validate, the system will emit a validation stream when significant deviations from normal behavior are detected.

The validation streams can be used in CQs. For example, in Figure 1 CQ1 is used as input to a visualizer of incorrect power consumption and CQ2 is a stream of alert messages signaling abnormal power consumption.

It is possible to dynamically modify the validation models while a validating CQ is running by sending update commands from the application to the local database. For instance, it is possible to change some threshold parameter used in an analytical model for a particular kind of machine, which will immediately change the behavior of the running validation function.

Usually the process of validation of a single machine's behavior depends on data streaming only from that particular machine combined with data in the local database. The overall detected abnormal behaviors are then collected by merging the individual machines' validation streams. For such CQs, the system automatically parallelizes the execution so that each compute node executes validation functions for a single data stream source independent of streams from other machinery. The system then merges the validation streams before delivering the result to the application. All the nodes contain the same database schema of machine installations and meta-data such as thresholds used in validation models. In the paper it is shown that this parallelization strategy outperforms validation on a single node and enables the delay caused by the monitoring of many machines to be bounded.

3. MODEL BASED VALIDATION

The functionalities of the two kinds of model based validation methods in SVALI are described along with examples of how they are applied on industrial equipment in use.

3.1 Model-and-validate

When the expected value can be estimated based on an analytical stream model, it is defined as a function which is passed as a parameter to the general second order function called *model_n_validate()* that has the following signature:

model_n_validate (Bag of Stream s, Function modelfn,
          Function validatefn)
     -> Stream of (Number ts, Object m, Object x)

The user defined stream model function, *modelfn(Object e)->Object x*, specifies how to compute the expected value *x* based on a stream element *e*. A stream element can be a single stream tuple or a window of tuples.

The user defined validation function, *validatefn(Object r, Object x)->(Number ts, Object m)*, specifies whether a received stream element *r* is invalid compared to the expected value *x* as computed by the model function. In case *r* is invalid the validation function returns the *ts* time stamped invalid measurement *m* in *r*.

The element of the validation stream returned by *model-and-validate()* are tuples *(ts, m, x)*, where *ts* and *m* are computed by the validation function and *x* is computed by the model function.

CQs specification involving model-and-validate calls are sent to a SVALI server as a text string for dynamic execution. It is up to the SVALI server to determine how to execute the CQs in an efficient way. In particular SVALI transparently parallelizes the execution to minimize the delay caused by executing expensive validation functions.

3.1.1 Demonstrator 1

This section demonstrates how model-and-validate is used to validate the power consumption in an industrial case based on a milling scenario. The case, including the framework, meta-data, models, a cutting tool, a machine tool, related equipment to capture the needed in-process data, and a stream server called Corenet was provided by Sandvik Coromant. The streaming process data used in this demonstrator was simulated using real recorded process data from Sandvik Coromant. To be specific, the data was collected from a MoriSeiki 5000 with a Fanuc control system that was equipped with the Kistler sensor system 9255B, and DMG with a Siemens control system. The difference between running Corenet with a recorded file compared to Corenet with connection to a machine is just a matter of configuration. In this paper a consistent behavior was needed to evaluate the performance and therefore it was of benefit to use recorded data from earlier machining attempts.

Figure 2 illustrates how the milling process was performed. The parameters in Table 1 describe the milling process. Tool working engagement is denoted by a_e feed per tooth by f_z, maximum chip thickness by h_{ex}, cutting depth by a_p cutting speed by v_c and the number of cutting edges by z_c.

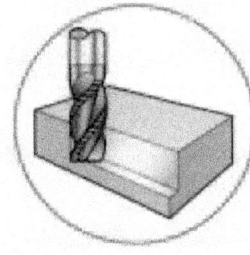

Figure 2. The side milling process

Table 1. Parameters that measured

a_e [mm]	f_z [$mm/tooth$]	h_{ex} [mm]	a_p [mm]	v_c [m/min]	z_c
2	0.0756	0.05	20	200	4
3	0.0641	0.05	20	200	4

This model can be expressed as a formula:

$$P_c = \frac{a_p \cdot a_e \cdot f_z \cdot v_c \cdot z_c \cdot k_c}{\pi \cdot D_{cap} \cdot 60 \cdot 10^3}$$

where

$$k_c = k_{c1} \cdot h_m^{-m_c} \cdot \left(1 - \frac{\gamma_0}{100}\right)$$

$$h_m = \frac{360 \cdot \sin(\kappa_r) \cdot a_e \cdot f_z}{\pi \cdot D_{cap} \cdot \cos^{-1}\left(1 - \frac{2 \cdot a_e}{D_{cap}}\right)}$$

The following parameters are stored in the SVALI local database as meta-data for a specific milling model:

$$k_{c1} = 1950, \, m_c = 0.25$$

The user installs the validation model expressed as functions as shown in Table 2 applied on the JSON objects *r* received in the stream from the equipment called "mill1":

Table 2. Functions installed in SVALI

Model	Corresponding function installed in SVALI
$h_m = \frac{360 \cdot \sin(\kappa_r) a_e \cdot f_z}{\pi \cdot D_{cap} \cdot \cos^{-1}\left(1 - \frac{2 \cdot a_e}{D_{cap}}\right)}$	*Create function hm(Record r)* *->Number* *as 2*pi()*sin(90*pi()/180)*ae(r)*fz(r) /* *(pi()*dcap(r)* acos(1-2*ae(r)/dcap(r)));*
$k_c = k_{c1} \cdot h_m^{-0.25} \cdot \left(1 - \frac{m_c}{100}\right)$	*create function kc(Record r)* *->Number* *as kc1("mill1")*power(hm(r), -0.25)* ** (1-mc("mill1")/100);*
measured power consumption	*create function measuredPower(Record r)* *-> Number* *as r["power"];*
$P_c = \frac{a_p \cdot a_e \cdot f_z \cdot v_c \cdot z_c \cdot k_c}{\pi \cdot D_{cap} \cdot 60 \cdot 10^3}$	*create function expectedPower(Record r)* *-> Number* *as (ap(r)*ae(r)*fz(r)*vc(r)*zt(r)* kc(r))/* *(pi() * dcap(r) * 60000);*

The validation function is defined as:

```
create function validatePower(Record r, Number x)
                        -> (Number ts, Number m)
  as select ts, m
     where m = measuredPower(r)
     and abs(x - m) > th("mill1");
```

The function *th(Chartsring k)* is a table of validation thresholds for each kind of machine *k* stored in the local database. After the model is installed in the SVALI server, a CQ validating a single JSON stream delivered from host "h1" on port 1337 is expressed as[1]:

```
select model_n_validate(bagof(input), #'expectedPower',
                        #'validatePower')
from Stream input
where input = corenetJsonWrapper("h1", 1337);
```

Here, the wrapper function *corenetJsonWrapper()* interfaces a data stream server called "Corenet" delivering JSON objects to SVALI.

3.2 Learn-and-Validate

In cases where a mathematical model of the normal behavior is not easily obtained the system provides an alternative validation mechanism to learn the expected behavior by dynamically building a statistical reference model based on sampled normal behavior measured during the first *n* stream elements in a stream. Once the reference model has been learned it is used to validate the rest of the stream. This is called learn-and-validate and is implemented by a stream function with the following signature:

```
learn_n_validate(Bag of Stream s, Function learnfn,
                Integer n, Function validatefn)
  -> Stream of (Number ts, Object m, Object e)
```

The *learning function, learnfn(Vector of Object f)->Object x,* specifies how to collect statistics *x*, the *reference model*, of expected behavior, based on a sequence *f* of the *n* first streams elements.

As for model-and-validate, the *validation function, validatefn(Object r, Object x)->(Number ts, Object m),* returns a pair *(ts, m)* whenever a measured value *m* in *r* is invalid at time *ts* compared to the reference value *x* returned by the learning function.

The function *learn_n_validate()* returns a validation stream of tuples *(ts, m, x)* with time stamp *ts*, measured value *m*, and the expected value *x* according to the reference model learned from the first *n* normally behaving stream elements.

3.2.1 Demonstrator 2

This part demonstrates how learn-and-validate has been applied in an industrial case, based on a cyclical manufacturing scenario. The case was provided by Sandvik Coromant, including the framework, methods, meta-data, needed systems, equipment, and the generated in-process data [2]. The streaming process data used in this demonstrator was simulated in the same way as in Demonstrator 1.

---

[1] The notation #'fn' specifies the function named 'fn'.

In Figure 3, the blue curve shows the normal behavior of one cycle where the x-axis is time and the y-axis is the measured power consumption. Continuous processing will lead to a certain degree of wear of the equipment. The wear rate is computed by the difference in power consumption between cycles. When the wear rate exceeds an upper limit, indicated by the red curve in the figure, the tool is worn out and should be replaced. Data for this demonstrator was logged using a system from Artis (http://www.artis.de/en/), the visualization in Figure 3 was also generated using that system.

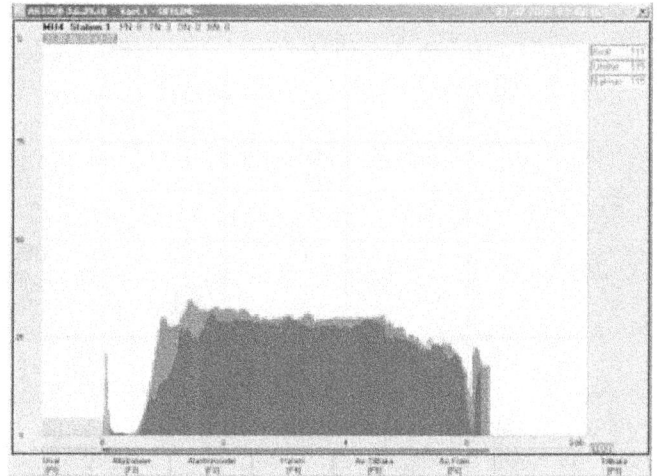

Figure 3. Cyclic behavior curve

The raw cyclic data streams is in this case represented by JSON records *["id":id, "trigger":tr, "time":ts, "value":val]* where *ts* is a time stamp, *id* indicates the identity of a particular machine process, *tr* indicates whether the cycle starts or stops, and *val* is the measured sensor reading to be validated.

Predicate windows: The value *tr* is set by the monitored equipment to 1 when a window starts and 0 when it stops. Such windows with dynamic extents are in SVALI represented as *predicate windows*. Traditional time or count windows cannot be used to identify the cycles when the logic or physical size of the cycle is unknown beforehand and is dependent on a predicate, as in our example. For this SVALI provides a predicate window forming operator *pwindowize(Stream s, Function start, Function stop)->Stream of Window* that creates a stream of windows based on two predicates (Boolean functions) called the *window start condition* and the *window stop condition*.

The window start condition is specified by the *start function, startfn(Object s)->Boolean*. It returns true if a stream element *s* indicates that a new cycle is started, in which case *s* is the *start element* of the cycle. The window stop condition is specified by a stop function, *stopfn(Object s, Object r)->Boolean*, that receives the start element *s* and a received stream element *r* and returns true if the received element indicates that the cycle has ended.

For example:

```
create function cycleStart(Record s) -> Boolean
  as s["trigger"] = 1;
create function cycleStop(Record s, Record r) -> Boolean
  as r["trigger"] = 0 and s["trigger"] = 1;
```

In our example, *pwindowize()* is used to build the reference model from the first two cycles of predicate windows. Analogous to the milling example, the CQ validates a JSON stream delivered from host "h2" on port 1338 based on learn-and-validate. It is expressed as:

```
select learn_n_validate(bagof(sw), #'learnCycle', 2,
                           #'validateCycle')
from Stream s, Stream sw
where s= corenetJsonWrapper( "h2", 1338) and
      sw = pwindowize(s, #'cycleStart', #'cycleStop');
```

Learning function: In our example the learning function computes the average power consumption of the *n* first windows *f* in the stream. It has the definition:

```
create function learnCycle(Vector of Window f)
                           -> Vector of Number
as navg(select extractPowerW(w) from Window w where w in f);
```

The function *navg(Bag of Vector)->Vector* returns the average vector of a set of numerical vectors normalized for possibly different lengths. The function *extractPowerW(Window w)->Vector x* extracts a vector of the power consumptions of each element in window *w*. It has the definition:

```
create function extractPowerW(Window w)  -> Vector of Number
as window2vector(w, #'extractPower');
```

The function *extractPower()* is defined as:

```
create function extractPower(Record r)-> Number as r["val"];
```

The system function *window2vector(Window w, Function fe)->Vector f* creates a new vector *f* by applying the function *fe(Object e)->Object* on each element in window *w*.

Validation function: To validate the current stream window, we first extract the power consumption for the current window as a vector and then compare the extracted vector with the learned vector. This is defined as:

```
create function validateCycle(Window w, Vector e)
                    -> (Number ts, Vector of Number m)
as select timestamp(w), m
    where neuclid(e, m) > th("machine2") and
          m = extractPowerW(w);
```

The function *neuclid(Vector x, Vector y)->Number* returns the Euclidean distance between *x* and *y* normalized for different lengths.

4. PERFORMANCE EXPERIMENTS

To analyze the performance of stream validation in SVALI, the performance of *model_n_validate()* was measured for a set of streams with varying stream rates. Scale-up is simulated by generating many simulated streams with different time offsets based on the raw data provided by Sandvik Coromant. The number of machines is scaled up by increasing the set of streams. The scalability of two queries was investigated:

- Q1: Given the analytical model for the power consumption of a machine process above, produce a validation stream per event of those machines where the power exceeds a threshold 1.2.

- Q2: Given the analytical model for the power consumption of a machine process, produce a validation stream of those machines where the power on average exceeds a threshold 1.2 for 0.1 seconds.

Query Q1 is the example query defined in Sec 3.1.1. Query Q2 uses the following second order functions *measuredPower()*, *expectedPower()* and *validatePower()*:

```
create function measuredPower(Window r)
                -> Vector of Number m
 as window2vector(r, #'measuredPower');
create function expectedPower(Window r)
                -> Vector of Number x
as window2vector(r, #'expectedPower');
create function validatePower(Window r, Vector of Number x)
                -> (Number ts, Vector of Number m)
as select ts(r), m
    where m = measuredPower(r)
    and neuclid(m, x) > th("mill1");
```

Given these three functions, query Q2 validating a bag of streams *bsw* of 0.1 second windows is defined as:

```
model_n_validate(bsw, #'expectedPower', #'validatePower');
```

By simulation, the number of machines is scaled up to 100. Each machine emits a data stream during 30 seconds. To simulate the impact of the performance of streams of different stream rates, the element rate of each stream was randomly chosen between 1 and 10 ms. The validations were done both centrally and in parallel. Central validation first merges streams from all machine processes and then validates them in one process, while parallel validation assigns an independent SVALI process per stream source and then merges the validation streams in a separate process. The parallelization strategy is chosen by the *model_n_validate()* function.

The experiments were made on a Dell NUMA computer PowerEdge R815 featuring 4 CPUs with 16 2.3 GHz cores each. OS: Scientific Linux release 6.2 (Carbon). All simulated stream sources and SVALI nodes run as UNIX processes.

The selectivity of the CQs is defined as the relative stream volume of outgoing tuples from SVALI compared with the incoming ones. Table 3 shows the selectivity of the two queries. The selectivity of the two cases are slightly different because of the randomness in the simulation based on the real data.

Table 3. Query selectivity

	selectivity Q1	selectivity Q2
central validation	14.5%	3.4%
parallel validation	15%	3.5%

Response time of the validation is measured since low latency is critical because decisions are made when the abnormalities are detected.

For the simple query Q1 Figure 4 shows the average delay (response time) per event caused by SVALI as the number of machines is increased, measured by recording the time when each event arrives to SVALI compared with the time when SVALI emits the corresponding processed event. It shows that Q1 has fast response time but still increases with the number of machines. By contrast parallel validation stays around 0.2 ms as the number of monitored machines increases.

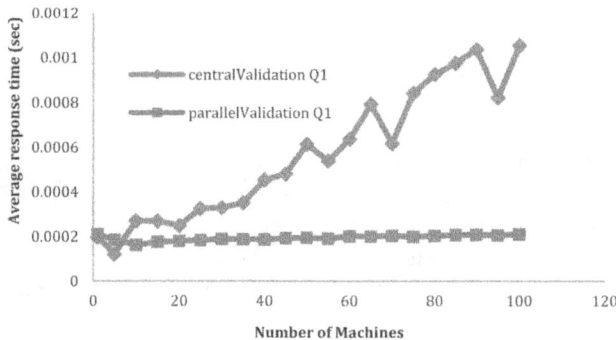

Figure 4. Average response time for Q1

For expensive validations of complex queries like Q2, Figure 5 shows that the central validation does not scale, while the parallel approach remains within bound, i.e. from 1 ms to 2 ms. We also continue increasing the number of simulated machines to explore the capability of our NUMA computer of parallel validation of Q2. In our experiment environment, our system is efficient to handle up to 450 simulated machines.

Both figures show that central validation is slightly faster than the parallel one when the number of machines is small. This is due to the overhead of starting an extra independent validation process for each machine.

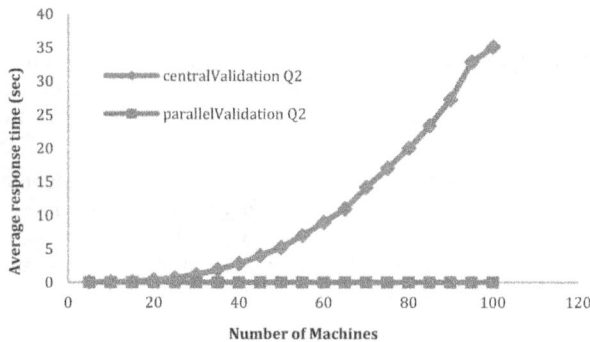

Figure 5. Average response time for Q2

In conclusion, central validation does not scale with the number of machines in particular when validation is expensive, while parallel processing enables scalable validation as long as there are sufficient resources to do the processing.

5. RELATED WORK

This paper complements other work on data stream processing [1] [7] [9] [16] [17] [22] by introducing a general approach to validate normal behavior of streams with non-trivial validation functions.

Several applications of anomaly detection are discussed in [6], such as intrusion detection [8] [11], medical and public health anomaly detection [13] [20] [21], industrial damage detection [12] and so on. Our work belongs to the area of industrial damage detection, i.e. monitoring the behavior of industrial components. Jakubek and Strasser [12] use Neural Networks with ellipsoidal basis functions to monitor a large number of measurements with as few parameters as possible in the automotive field. By contrast, SVALI provides general functionality for monitoring streams from a large number of equipment in parallel, based on plugging in general models.

An adaptive runtime anomaly prediction system called ALERT [19] was developed for large scale hosting infrastructures. The aim was to provide a context aware anomaly prediction model with good prediction accuracy. Rather than anomaly prediction, we mainly focused on supporting online anomaly detection that requires more strict response time. The data streams analyzed in [19] have a fairly low arrival rate, i.e. one sample every 2 seconds and one sample every 10 seconds. By contrast, we show that our system can handle many streams with much higher arrival rates.

Di Wang et al. [20] proposed an active complex event processing system in a hospital environment, where rules are triggered by state changes of the system during CQ processing. In our system, validation models are stored in the SVALI local database and can be modified dynamically by update commands from the application side.

The main focus of [23] is time series data stream aggregate monitoring, while our approach is providing a flexible stream validation framework that can be applied on both individual event monitoring, where only latest event is of interest for processing, and aggregate monitoring, where window aggregation is required for the analysis. This is based on the fact that our stream validation operator treats both raw stream and windowed stream equally.

6. CONCLUSION AND FUTURE WORK

Two general strategies were presented to validate streams from industrial equipment, called *model-and-validate* and *learn-and-validate*, respectively. Model-and-validate is based on explicitly specifying an analytical model of expected behavior, which is compared with actual measured data stream elements. Learn-and-validate dynamically builds a statistical model based on a set of observed correct behavior in streams. We show that the approach is applicable in an industrial setting on real industrial data from real industrial machines.

In our SVALI system, continuous queries validating that equipment behaves correctly are defined declaratively in term of validation functions that are sent to a server, which generates a parallel execution plan to enable scalable computation of validation streams. The experiments show that parallel execution scales better than a central implementation of model-and-validate when increasing the number of streams from monitored machines.

Investigating parallelization of learn-and-validate is future work. Another interesting future work is to regularly refine the learnt model. Furthermore, the impact of complex model functions on the strategy chosen should be investigated, for instance, to validate streaming data based on trends of measured equipment behavior over time. This can be handled by defining complex model functions that compute trends over time rather than the actual expected measurements. This may involve new scalability challenges.

ACKNOWLEDGMENTS

This work was supported by the Swedish Foundation for Strategic Research, grant RIT08-0041 and by the EU FP7 project Smart Vortex [18].

7. REFERENCES

[1] Abadi, D.J., et al.: Aurora: a new model and architechture for data stream management. The VLDB journal, 12(2), 2003.

[2] Alizadeh, Z.: Method for automated tests of wear (Metod för automatisering av förslitningstest). *Project work in Automated Manufacturing,* 2011.

[3] Alonso-Rasgado, T., Thompson, G. and Elfstrom, B.O.: The design of functional (total care) products. *Journal of Engineering Design*, Vol. 15, No. 6, pp.515-540, 2004.

[4] Alonso-Rasgado, T. and Thompson, G.: A rapid design process for Total Care Product creation. *Journal of Engineering Design*, Vol. 17, No.6, pp.509-531, 2006.

[5] Baines, T.S., Lightfoot, H.W., Evans, S., Neely, A., Greenough, R., Peppard, J., Roy, R., Shehab, E., Braganza, A., Tiwari, A., Alcock, J.R., Angus, J.P., Bastl, M., Cousens, A., Irving, P., Johnson, M., Kingston, J., Lockett, H., Martinez, V., Michele, P., Tranfield, D., Walton, I.M., Wilson, H.: State-of-the-art in product-service systems. Proceedings of the Institution of Mechanical Engineers, Part B, *Journal of Engineering Manufacture*, Vol. 221, pp.1543-1552, 2007.

[6] Chandola, V., Banerjee, A., and Kumar, V.: Anomaly detection: a survey. *ACM Computing Surveys*, 41(3), 2009

[7] Cranor, C., Johnson, T., Spataschek, O., Shkapenyuk, V.: Gigascope: A Stream Database for Network Applications. *Proc. SIGMOD Conf.,* 2003.

[8] Gonzalez, F.A. and Dasgupta, D.: *Anomaly detection using real-valued negative selection.* Genetic Programming and Evolvable Machines 4, 4, pp.383-403, 2003.

[9] Girod, L., Mei, Y., Newton, R., Rost, R., Thiagarajan, Balakrishnan, A.H., Madden, S.: XStream: A Signal-Oriented Data Stream Management System. *ICDE Conf.,* 2008.

[10] Helgoson, M., Kalhori, V.: A conceptual model for knowledge integration in process planning, *45th CIRP Conference on Manufacturing Systems*, Procedia CIRP 3 (2012), pp.573-578, Elsevier, 2012.

[11] Hu, W., Liao, Y. and Vemuri, V.R.: Robust anomaly detection using support vector machines. *Proc. of the International Conference on Machine Learning*, pp.282-289, San Francisco, CA, USA, 2003.

[12] Jakubek, S. and Strasser, T.: Fault-diagnosis using neural networks with ellipsoidal basis functions. *American Control Conference.* Vol. 5. pp.3846-3851, 2002.

[13] Lin, J., Keogh, E., Fu, A., and Herle, H.V.: Approximations to magic: Finding unusual medical time series, *Proc. of the 18th IEEE Symposium on Computer-Based Medical Systems.* IEEE, 329-334, Washington, DC, USA, 2005.

[14] Löfstrand, M., Backe, B., Kyösti, P., Lindström, J., Reed, S.: A Model for predicting and monitoring industrial system availability. *Int. J. of Product Development*, Vol. 16, No 2. pp.140-157, 2012.

[15] Meier, H., Roy, R. Seliger, G., Industrial Product-Service Systems-IPS2: *CIRP Annals - Manufacturing Technology*, 59, pp.607-627, 2010.

[16] Motwani, R., Widom, J., Arasu, A., Babcock, B., Babu, S., Datar, M., Manku, G., Olsten, C., Rosenstein, J., and Varma, R.: Query processing, resource management, and approximation in a data stream management system, *1st Biennial Conference on Innovative Database Research (CIDR)*, Asilomar, CA, 2003.

[17] Shasha, D. and Zhu, Z.: Statstream: statistical monitoring of thousands of data streams in real time, *VLDB Conf.*, pages 358-369, 2002.

[18] *Smart Vortex Project* - http://www.smartvortex.eu/

[19] Tan, T., Gu, X., and Wang, H.: Adaptive system anomaly prediction for large-scale hosting infrastructures. *PODC Conf.*, 2010.

[20] Wang, D., Rundensteiner, E., Ellison, R.: Active Complex Event Processing for Realtime Health Care, *VLDB Conf.*, 3(2): pp.1545-1548, 2010.

[21] Wong, W.K., Moore, A., Cooper, G., and Wagner, M.: Bayesian network anomaly pattern detection for disease outbreaks, *20th International Conference on Machine Learning*, AAAI Press, Menlo Park, California, pp.808-815, 2003.

[22] Zeitler, E. and Risch, T.: Massive scale-out of expensive continuous queries, *Proceedings of the VLDB Endowment*, ISSN 2150-8097, Vol. 4, No. 11, pp.1181-1188, 2011.

[23] Zhu, Y. and Shasha, D.: Efficient elastic burst detection in data streams, *9th SIGKDD Conf.*, 2003.

Mobile QoS Management Using Complex Event Processing (Industry Article)

Mauricio Arango
Oracle Corporation
550 W. Cypress Creek Rd.
Fort Lauderdale, FL 33309 USA
mauricio.arango@oracle.com

ABSTRACT

This paper describes a use case and a corresponding prototype of a system that provides end-to-end Quality-of-Service (QoS) management for mobile broadband telecommunications service operations using measurements collected from end-user devices. Traditionally mobile telecommunications systems manage performance by monitoring network elements. With a device-based approach the main source of monitored information are end-user devices, where users run their applications and where they directly experience the effects of variations in performance in the sub-systems that comprise the mobile application delivery chain: data center, network and device.

In this solution, user devices measure and report transaction latencies combined with location data and bandwidth capacity usage. These measurement event streams are collected and analyzed by a CEP application that provides near real-time insight on the state of the network. It identifies problem conditions such as congested base stations and high latency devices, detects opportunities to correct problems and initiates actions when conditions apply, specifically involving offloading of traffic to WiFi networks. Since QoS management in mobile networks is highly dependent on the dynamic location and speed of devices, this CEP application heavily leverages geospatial functions in the selected CEP platform.

Categories and Subject Descriptors

C.2.3 [**Network Operations**]: Network Management, Network Monitoring; C.2.4 [**Distributed Systems**]: Distributed Applications; I.5 [**Pattern Recognition**]: Implementation; I.6 [**Simulation and Modeling**]: Miscellaneous.

Keywords

Complex event processing; real-time analytics; quality of service; location-based services; performance management; network management; mobile communications; multi-agent simulation.

1. INTRODUCTION

Telecommunications service providers have an urgent need to provide services that offer compelling value beyond basic broadband transport services. Mobile users utilize an increasingly large array of applications that require connectivity to data center-based services (cloud-based services).

Additionally, most of the Software-as-a-Service (SaaS) providers are targeting their customers to interact via mobile applications. A key aspect to the success of a mobile application or a mobile SaaS service is to assure a very good user experience. One of the essential factors of user experience is end-to-end quality of service (QoS), which involves performance monitoring and detection and resolution of issues that impact performance. QoS management is an area where mobile service providers can add significant value to their customers. In a cloud-based mobile application, end-to-end QoS management involves multiple complex systems including the network, the data center/cloud platform and service software, and the device platform and application software (see figure 1).

In telecommunications, QoS management is an area of network management where traditional methods involve monitoring of network components, such as base stations and base station controllers, to derive key performance indicators, which are used to determine when it is necessary to take actions to address network conditions that are causing service performance degradation or violations of a service-level agreement (SLA).

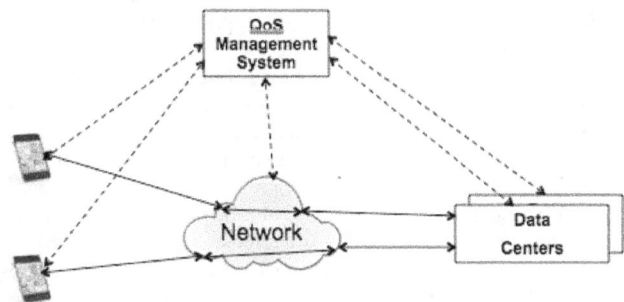

Figure 1. End-to-End QoS Management System

This paper addresses an emerging type of QoS management technique that involves direct monitoring of end-user mobile devices. In our solution, each user device measures and reports transaction latencies combined with location data and bandwidth capacity usage. These measurement streams are collected and analyzed by a complex event processing (CEP) application that tracks performance for each end-user device and also infers network conditions such as congested base stations. Device-based monitoring enables much faster identification of problems experienced by the end user and provides a level of granularity that is generally not available via network-centric monitoring. In the latter case, for example, when detecting a congested base station it is not simple and not always possible to identify all the end-users affected and the level of impact they experience from such network problem. QoS management with device-based monitoring provides a combination of customer experience management and network management. Traditionally these are handled separately but there is need to integrate them in order to rapidly translate from a problem in user experience to the root cause in the network.

QoS management systems can best be thought as event-based applications, whose mission is to monitor continuous changes in devices and network components and to detect relevant situations that need to be reported and that require actions to correct problems or optimize operating conditions. Implementing these applications with a CEP platform product offers high benefits in terms of much shorter development cycles and lower maintenance costs due to the built-in features found in CEP platforms. The CEP platform used to build the described prototype is Oracle Event Processing [10]. Other software components used in the prototype include: Oracle WebLogic Server [14] for JMS message queues for input event collection, Oracle MapViewer [13] for map-based rendering of the CEP application results, and the MASON [9] multi-agent simulation toolkit for building a mobile device and network simulator.

The main contribution of this paper is to show through a concrete example how to build a real-time analytics application for telecommunications using CEP and illustrate the key benefits of CEP technology and platforms in real-time monitoring and management of telecommunications systems. An additional contribution of this work is to show the benefits of using agent-based simulation for developing and testing CEP applications that collect events from a large number of dynamic event sources.

2. QOS MANAGEMENT USE CASE

The scenario in this use case involves a mobile broadband cellular network, a WiFi access network, users with smartphone devices capable of running a multitude of applications and capable accessing both the mobile and the WiFi networks, and data centers hosting server-side application software that users access via their mobile apps. End-to-end transaction latency is measured by a software agent installed in each user device and comprises three main sources of latency: the data center-based server-side of the application, the networks connecting the device-based application and the data center, and the device that initiated the transaction. This case assumes that the most significant sources of latency are the network and the data center and, therefore, does not include device latency in end-to-tend latency calculations.

The sources of monitored data are agents in user devices and data centers. For this use case, direct network monitoring was not included in order to highlight that significant network state insight can be inferred from device-based monitoring. However, whenever possible, having access to both device and network element monitoring can assure higher precision in identifying certain network problems. The network information needed in this system is only the static configurations of mobile and WiFi base station grids. Real-time network status information is inferred from device and data center measurements.

For device measurements, a device agent produces an event every time a transaction is completed. In addition to the transaction latency value, each of these events also includes the corresponding device location in geographical coordinates (latitude, longitude) and a value proportional to the size of the volume of data exchanged in the transaction. The latter is referred to as the traffic load measure and indicates the level of bandwidth usage in a transaction.

The system requires monitoring the quality of service experienced by each user and reporting of all incidents where transaction latency experienced by any application running on a mobile device is above a specified threshold. Also required are notifications of above-threshold average latencies over a specified time window. For each latency violation it is required to determine which are the sources of high latency: the network, the data center, or both. Latency violation notifications are routed to a dashboard system that provides map-based rendering of the state of the network, analogous to real-time air traffic maps used in air traffic control operations. Via inference from device-based measurements, the system is required to detect congested base stations.

The last feature in this solution is a capability to decide when to switch a device from the mobile network to the WiFi network and vice-versa. WiFi offload mechanisms [2][5] are a QoS management tool used to prevent or mitigate congestion impact in a mobile broadband network. In this use case we utilize a centralized decision mechanism that uses device location information to calculate speed and determine when a device becomes a candidate for switching to the WiFi access network. In our example a device is switched to WiFi if it has a high latency incident, is static, and is attached to a mobile base station that is in congested state.

3. IMPLEMENTATION ARCHITECTURE

The implementation architecture is depicted in figure 2. The system comprises four components: the QoS application running on a CEP platform, an event collection message queue system where events from the monitored components are published, a map-based rendering web application that displays the state of the network as perceived by the monitored devices, and an agent-based simulator that simulates the network, devices and data center and generates the device and data center event streams that drive the application.

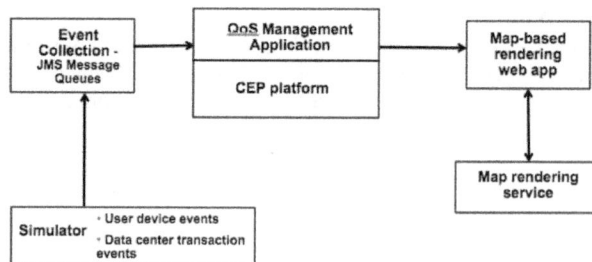

Figure 2. Implementation Architecture

The prototype was designed and implemented as a distributed system where its components are decoupled and operate independently, communicating via asynchronous publish/subscribe mechanisms. The simulator produces event streams that are published to JMS message queues. The QoS management CEP application subscribes to the JMS queues and doesn't communicate directly with the simulator. The CEP application publishes its results to an HTTP pub/sub server, which is part of the OEP platform, and the web-based rendering application subscribes to queues in the HTTP pub/sub server. This design approach leverages the advantages of constructing distributed systems with publish/subscribe mechanisms [7].

3.1 CEP Platform

The mobile QoS management application was implemented on Oracle Event Processing (OEP), which is an enterprise-grade CEP application platform. OEP provides both a development environment and a high-performance Java runtime engine for CEP applications. A CEP application is modeled as an Event Processing Network (EPN) [8][12], which is a directed graph whose nodes are either event sources or sinks or a combination of source and sink at the same time. Source nodes produce events that are consumed by sink nodes. Inputs to a sink node are defined by which source nodes it is connected to. These connections between nodes are unidirectional edges from sources to sinks. A source node may have multiple output edges to different sink nodes. Sink nodes also can have multiple connecting edges to different source nodes.

An EPN has an event-driven [3][6][8] computational model where an EPN node only performs computation when it receives incoming events and the result of computation in a node are new output events sent to its connecting sink nodes.

In the OEP platform, EPN nodes have an additional classification according to more specific functions they perform. The following is a partial list of the OEP node types. Only the ones used in this application are listed:

- *Input adapter* - Receives external raw events from monitored systems such as mobile devices or data centers in our use case, and converts them into the data formats used by events inside an EPN. An input adapter is an event source from the perspective of an EPN.

- *Output adapter* - Produces events from the EPN to be consumed by systems outside an EPN. These systems could be components external to the OEP platform instance or could be other EPNs running on the same or a different OEP platform instance. An output adapter is an event sink from the perspective of an EPN.

- *Processor* - Is a node that operates both as an event sink and as an event source. Processors are the containers of the bulk of the logic implemented in an EPN. This logic is expressed as rules written in CQL (Continuous Query Language) [1][4][11] a declarative language derived from SQL with extensions to handle event streams via the use of time interval and event quantity windows.

- *Channel* - Is a connector buffer between every source and sink and implement the edges in the EPN graph.

3.2 QoS Management Application EPN

This section describes the QoS management application EPN. Since the entire EPN diagram isn't readable in a single diagram in this paper's format, it is split into multiple sections and figures described below.

3.2.1 EPN Input and Device Stream Enrichment

The function of the input and enrichment area of the EPN is to convert external event messages into internal EPN event structures, to map every device event location and base station configuration event to a point in a geospatial grid, to create tables with mobile and WiFi base station configuration information, and to generate an enriched device event stream with additional information including the identifier for the closest mobile base station, the data center latency for the corresponding transaction, the derived network latency, and the device speed.

The EPN has three input event streams, which are generated by a simulator described in a section below. Their role and data contents are:

- *Device status event* – An event of this type is generated by a device every time a transaction is completed by an application in the device. Data on each event includes: device identifier, transaction identifier, location (latitude and longitude), total transaction latency (in milliseconds), and traffic load. The latter field is a metric of the amount of data sent or received during the transaction with range 1-10, where 1 corresponds to very low bandwidth transactions and 10 to very high bandwidth transactions.

- *Data center latency event* – An instance of this event type is generated by a data center every time it services a transaction requested by a device. Data on each event includes: transaction identifier and data center transaction latency.

- *Base station status event* – Events of this type are generated by the network simulator in its initialization phase. These events are used only to load base station configuration information into tables in the EPN. This is not a high frequency stream like the two above. Data on each event includes base station identifier, base station location (latitude and longitude), and base station type (mobile macro base station or WiFi hotspot).

Figure 3 shows first input section (left side) of the EPN. The three outermost source-only nodes in figure 3 are input adapters. Each of these nodes is a Java component that subscribes to a separate corresponding JMS message queue. Each of these queues is assigned to collect events from one of the input event types described above. Event messages are published in the queues by the network simulator. Every time an event message is published, a handler is invoked in the corresponding input JMS adapter object.

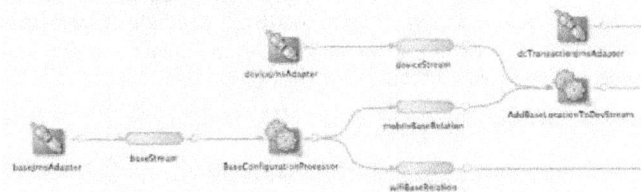

Figure 3. EPN section 1

`deviceJmsAdapter` is the input adapter that subscribes to messages from the device status message queue, which is the queue dedicated to collect mobile device status events from the simulator. Upon arrival of a device status event, the input adapter extracts it from the queue and converts to an EPN `DeviceStatusEvent` Java object. All events inside an OEP

EPN are instantiated as Java objects. In addition to converting an external event into an internal EPN event, this JMS input adapter uses the Oracle Spatial Java Class Library (which is fully integrated as a module in OEP) [11] to map this event's location to a point in a geospatial grid within the EPN. Having all device and base locations mapped to geospatial points permits performing location-based functions like finding the nearest base station to a given device location. `baseJmsAdapter` is another input JMS adapter and it performs similar functions as `deviceJmsAdapter` on the base station status event stream. `dcTransactionJmsAdapter` is the third input JMS adapter and performs similar actions as the two other with the data center latency event stream.

There are two processor nodes in this section, the first one, `BaseConfigurationProcessor` produces two tables, `mobileBaseRelation`, which stores the configuration information (base identifier and location) for all the mobile base stations, and `wifiBaseRelation`, which stores the configuration information for all the WiFi hotspots. These tables are implemented as relation channels. OEP EPN channels can be either stream or relation channels. The other processor in this section is the `AddBaseLocationToDevStream`, which finds the closest mobile base station to the device associated with the last event received and adds the base station identifier into an expanded device status event. The following is the CQL query implemented by this processor:

```
SELECT
  dev.*,
  base.baseId AS baseId,
  distance@spatial(dev.geom, base.geom) AS
    distanceFromBaseStation
FROM deviceStream[NOW] AS dev,
mobileBaseRelation AS base
WHERE NN@spatial(dev.geom, base.geom, 20.0d)
  = true
```

This rule performs a join query of the device event stream and the mobile base station relation in which the condition evaluation in the WHERE clause obtains the location to the nearest mobile base station, using the Nearest Neighbor function (`NN@spatial`) from the Oracle Spatial library. The rule also adds the distance from the device to nearest base station as a new field in the expanded device event.

The next section, shown in figure 4, contains processor `AddDcAndNetLatencyToDeviceStream`, which performs a join query between the device status event stream and the data center latency event stream:

```
SELECT
  devb.*,
  dc.dataCenterTransactionLatency AS
  dcLatency,
  devb.totalTransactionLatency-
  dc.dataCenterTransactionLatency  AS
  networkLatency
FROM
  deviceWithBaseStream [rows 100] AS devb,
  inDcTransChannel [rows 100] AS dc
WHERE (devb.transactionId =
      dc.transactionId)
```

This query results in finding the data center latency event with the same transaction identifier as the current device event and extending the device event with the value for the data center latency for the corresponding transaction. The query also calculates the network latency by subtracting the data center latency from the total transaction latency in the device event. It also expands the device event with the network latency value and feeds the enriched stream to the `devWithBaseAndLatenciesStream` channel.

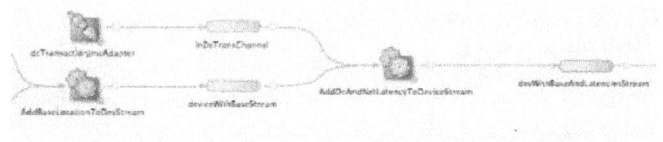

Figure 4. EPN section 2

The last section of the device event enrichment area, shown in figure 5, contains processor `SpeedDetectionProcessor`, which calculates the average speed for every active device as a moving average updated on every device event arrival. Device speed is needed to determine if a mobile device is eligible to be switched to a WiFi network, since one of the requirements for switching a mobile device to a WiFi hotspot is to have low speed or be static. Current techniques perform a speed estimate based on rate of handovers or base station reselections [5], and have lower precision that than location-based methods as the one presented here.

Figure 5. EPN section 3

The following is the CQL code in `SpeedDetectionProcessor`:

```
<view id="DeviceSpeedStream" >
ISTREAM(
  SELECT
  dev.deviceId AS deviceId,
  distance@spatial(dev.geom, PREV(dev.geom))
  / (dev.tstmp - PREV(dev.tstmp)) AS speed
  FROM devWithBaseAndLatenciesStream
  [PARTITION BY deviceId ROWS 50]
  AS dev
  GROUP BY deviceId
)
</view>

<view id="AverageSpeedStream" >
ISTREAM(
  SELECT
  dev.deviceId AS deviceId,
  AVG(dev.speed) AS avgSpeed
  FROM DeviceSpeedStream [PARTITION BY
      deviceId ROWS 50] AS dev
  GROUP BY deviceId
```

```
    )
</view>

<query id="DeviceMovingRule">
  SELECT
   dev.*
   'moving' as motion
  FROM AverageSpeedStream AS avstr,
   devWithBaseAndLatenciesStream AS dev
  WHERE avstr.avgSpeed >= 2

</query>
<query id="DeviceStaticRule">
  SELECT
   dev.*,
   'static' as motion
  FROM AverageSpeedStream AS avstr,
   devWithBaseAndLatenciesStream AS dev
  WHERE avstr.avgSpeed < 2
</query>
```

In the first part of the previous CQL segment, two views are used to construct a stream with the average speed for each device. Views are queries that generate streams or relations used as intermediate stages in a more complex query. The first view partitions the enriched event stream, `devWithBaseAndLatenciesStream`, into multiple streams, one per device and calculates the current speed using the `distance@spatial` function to obtain the distance between the current event for a device and the previous event for the same device. The second view operates on the speed stream and calculates the average speed over a window with 50 events. `ISTREAM` is a CQL function that converts a relation into a stream. The two queries at the bottom are used to determine if the device is static or moving and enrich the device state stream by adding the motion state field in each device state event.

3.2.2 QoS Management Rules

In this section we will describe the remaining portion of the EPN that contains the rules that detect QoS problem situations including devices experiencing high network latency and congested base stations. It also includes rules for responding to solve problem conditions, specifically on detection of a device with low performance (high-latency) and attached to a congested mobile base station, by initiating the action to switch it to a higher capacity and higher cell density WiFi network. Techniques to steer low speed traffic to lower cost and higher density networks such as WiFi are commonly referred in the telecommunications industry as WiFi offload [2][5]. The policy used in this prototype to determine when to perform WiFi offload on a device is to perform a switch when the device is experiencing high network latency and is static, and its current base station is in congested state.

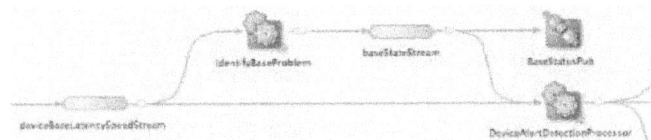

Figure 6. EPN section 4

The first set of rules are contained in the `IdentifyBaseProblem` processor and they are used to detect when a mobile base station becomes congested. The policy conditions defined to signal congestion are to have an average latency of all the transactions it handles within a time window above a predefined threshold and to have an aggregate transaction traffic load over the same time window above a threshold corresponding to the maximum traffic capacity of the base station. Following are the CQL statements in the `IdentifyBaseProblem` processor, where a view is used to generate an intermediate stream with the average latency and the aggregate traffic load, which are used to evaluate the congestion testing conditions in the last two queries. These queries generate a base status stream that is routed to the map-based rendering application by an HTTP publish adapter and is also an input into the next processor that checks the device conditions.

```
<view id="BaseStatusStream" >
ISTREAM(
  SELECT
    devb.baseId as baseId,
    AVG(devb.networkLatency) AS
    averageNetworkLatency,
    SUM(devb.transactionLoad) AS aggregateLoad
  FROM devWithBaseAndLatenciesStream
   [PARTITION BY baseId ROWS 50] AS
   devb
  GROUP by baseId
)
</view>

<query id="SwitchToCongestedBase">
  SELECT
   base.*,
   'CONGESTED_BASE_STATION' AS baseState
  FROM BaseStatusStream as base
  WHERE base.averageNetworkLatency >=
   LATENCY_THRESHOLD AND base.aggregateLoad
   >= LOAD_THRESHOLD
</query>

<query id="SwitchToNormalBase">
  SELECT
   base.*,
   'NORMAL_BASE_STATION' AS baseState
  FROM BaseStatusStream AS base
  WHERE base.averageNetworkLatency <
   LATENCY_THRESHOLD AND base.aggregateLoad <
   LOAD_THRESHOLD
</query>
```

The `DeviceAlertDetectionProcessor` processor contains the rules that detect if a device is experiencing high latency and decide how to respond to this situation. If the device with high latency also is static and its base station is in congested state, a WiFi offload request event is generated. If the device has normal latency, a notification is published to the map-based rendering application via a corresponding HTTP publish adapter. For all other condition combinations the device is signaled as having a high latency alert and WiFi offload is not applied. Except for the WiFi request rule, the other three rules generate device status events that are sent to the map-based rendering application for display. The CQL statements for this processor are:

```
<query id="AlertLatencyMovingRule">
  SELECT*
  FROM devBaseLatenciesSpeedStream AS dev,
  WHERE dev.networkLatency >=
```

```
      LATENCY_THRESHOLD AND dev.motion =
      'moving'
</query>

<query id="NoAlertRule">
  SELECT *
  FROM devBaseLatenciesSpeedStream as dev,
  WHERE dev.networkLatency <
      LATENCY_THRESHOLD
</query>

<query
id="AlertLatencyStaticNormalBaseRule">
  SELECT dev.*
  FROM devBaseLateciesSpeedStream AS dev,
    baseStateStream AS base
  WHERE dev.networkLatency >=
  LATENCY_THRESHOLD AND
    dev.motion = 'static' AND base.baseState
    = 'NORMAL_BASE_STATION'
</query>

<query id="AlertSwitchToWifiRule">
  SELECT dev.*
  FROM devBaseLateciesSpeedStream AS dev,
    baseStateStream AS base
  WHERE dev.networkLatency >=
    LATENCY_THRESHOLD AND
    dev.motion = 'static' AND base.baseState
    = 'CONGESTED_BASE_STATION'
</query>
```

The last section of the application EPN, shown in figure 7, contains processor the `SwitchToWifiProcessor`, whose function is to assign a WiFi hotspot, to every offload request it receives. The hotspot selected is the closest to the given device. The processor publishes the WiFi request with the hotspot identifier to the map-based rendering application via an HTTP publish adapter. In this prototype offload events are consumed by the map-based rendering application, which displays the selected device and base station linked by a connection line (see figure 9). In a production system this event would also be consumed by a response application responsible for executing the action of switching the device.

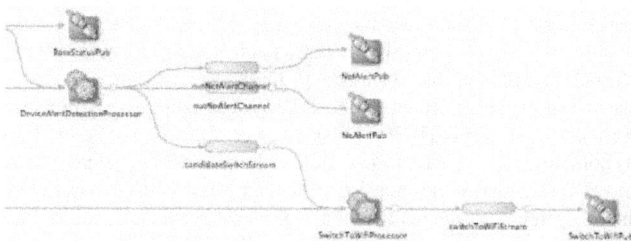

Figure 7. EPN section

3.3 Simulator

The simulator was implemented using the Java-based MASON multi-agent simulation toolkit [9]. This is a tool for building simulators of systems that are composed of many agents with similar but to some extent independent behavior. It fits very well with simulation of mobile telecommunications networks where there are large numbers of users, devices and network components.

The simulation model for this prototype comprises five Java classes: `QoSGrid`, `Network`, `Device`, `BaseStation` and `DataCenter`. There is one instance of `QoSGrid`, `Network` and `DataCenter`, and as many instances as needed, depending on the hardware resources available, of `Device` and `BaseStation`. Each of these instances is an agent and agent's behavior is programmed in Java as part of the corresponding Java class. For example, a device's behavior consists of initiating transactions and moving every certain time interval. After an agent is instantiated it performs a continuous loop consisting of performing actions, scheduling a future time to perform more actions and pausing until the clock advances to the time when it was scheduled to function again.

The MASON toolkit library allows you to schedule agents and handles all the pausing and activation of agents. A device agent simulates a transaction by invoking the network and data center instances, which will return corresponding latencies. The network agent keeps track of the traffic load in the device agents that are assigned to it. In this way it can issue transaction latencies that vary with the aggregate traffic load from its attached devices. As the load in a base station increases, so does the latency of the transactions it handles. Devices are either designed to move along a random walk or to be subject to "forces" that pull them or repel to and from certain points. The simulator supports injection of congestion-causing events, such as a traffic accident, which causes neighboring devices to be static and increase their traffic. The MASON library supports two-dimensional grids. This permits assigning geospatial coordinates to every agent in a simulation model and to perform calculations such as nearest neighbor and distance between two points.

3.4 Map-based Web Application

Results from the CEP application are published to an HTTP publish/subscribe server that implements the Cometd Bayeaux protocol. The HTTP pub/server used in this prototype is OEP's Jetty server. The map-based application is written in JavaScript and runs on any web browser. It subscribes to all the QoS management application channels (equivalent to queues) in the HTTP pub/sub server and reacts to every result event produced by the CEP application. It uses an instance of the mapping service provided by the Oracle Fusion Middleware MapViewer Server product where markers, lines and other objects can be overlayed on maps. A selected map displays the location of every mobile and WiFi base station, which are static objects, and also displays markers corresponding to each device as they move across the geographical region under display.

When high latency is detected in a device or when a base station becomes congested the corresponding markers in the map are modified to signal problem conditions. Figure 8 illustrates a situation where there are multiple devices with a marker labeled '1' in light gray (or yellow). These represent devices with high latency and they surround another marker also labeled '1' in dark gray (or orange), which corresponds to the base station to which all the devices are attached and is in congested state.

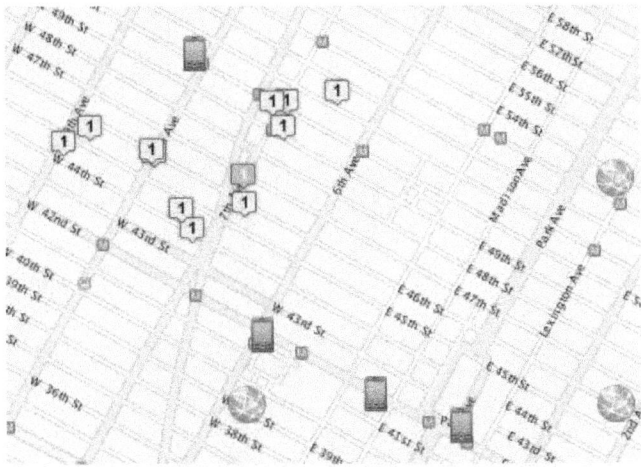

Figure 8. High-latency and congestion rendering

Figure 9 below shows how devices that have been switched to WiFi are tracked, changing the device marker and drawing a line between the device and the selected WiFi access point.

Figure 9. WiFi offload rendering

4. CONCLUSIONS

The applications to manage mobile network operations are inherently event processing applications since they manage systems that are constantly in movement and under continuous variation in their operating conditions due to changes in user location, traffic load, weather conditions and under impact from changes in other massive systems like transportation systems. To efficiently manage such large operations with high quality of service and user experience it is necessary to have a real-time view of the state of the system. This requires continuous monitoring of very large number of components and rapid analysis and response to these high volume and high speed event streams of information. We believe CEP technology and products offer unique advantages towards becoming core foundation components in key next generation systems and applications that are going to be needed to manage mobile telecommunications infrastructures.

In summary, this use case highlights three key benefits of CEP technology and products. First, the EPN model with its distributed, event-driven, asynchronous and graphical programming model features. In our experience, this simple but powerful model of graphs of source and sink nodes makes it easier to think about

event-driven problems and its solutions largely because of its graph-oriented foundation and because it facilitates breaking up the solution into decoupled components communicating asynchronously. Another key benefit is the use of a declarative language like Oracle Event Processing CQL, which largely simplifies the effort of programming the rules within EPN processing nodes. The third highlighted benefit is the integration of a geospatial library in the CEP platform, such as the Oracle Spatial library in OEP. Having access to geospatial functions within CQL and within Java code in adapters and other EPN nodes greatly simplifies the task of developing location-based services, as is the case with the use case presented.

5. REFERENCES

[1] Arasu, A,. Babcock, B., Babu, S., Cieslewicz, J., Datar, M., Ito, K., Motwani, R., Srivastava, U., and Widom, J. 2004. STREAM: The Stanford Data Stream Management System: http://ilpubs.stanford.edu:8090/641/1/2004-20.pdf

[2] Bubley, D. Carrier WiFi Opportunities Enabling offload, onload and roaming. Disruptive Analysis. (August 2011): https://wifimobilize.com/pdf/whitepaper.pdf

[3] Chandy, K.M., Schulte, W.R. 2010. *Event Processing, Designing IT Systems for Agile Companies*. McGraw-Hill.

[4] De Castro Alves, A. 2010. New Event-Processing Design Patterns Using CEP, In *Business Process Management Workshops, BPM 2009 International Workshops*. Springer. Ulm, Germany. (September 2009).

[5] Developing and integrating a high performance HetNet, 4G Americas: http://www.4gamericas.org/documents/4G%20Americas%20 Developing%20Integrating%20High%20Performance%20HE T-NET%20October%202012.pdf

[6] Etzion, O., Niblett, P. 2011. *Event Processing in Action*. Manning Publications Co.

[7] Eugster, P. Th., Felber, P., Guerraoui, R., and Kermarrec, A.M. 2003. The Many Faces of Publish/Subscribe. *ACM Computing Surveys* (June 2003).

[8] Luckham, D. 2007. *The Power of Events*. Addison-Wesley.

[9] MASON Multiagent Simulation Toolkit: http://cs.gmu.edu/~eclab/projects/mason/

[10] Oracle Event Processing: http://www.oracle.com/technetwork/middleware/complex-event-processing/overview/index.html

[11] Oracle Fusion Middleware CQL Language Reference for Oracle Complex Event Processing 11g Release 1 (11.1.1.6.3). (August 2012): http://docs.oracle.com/cd/E23943_01/apirefs.1111/e12048.pdf

[12] Oracle Fusion Middleware Developer's Guide for Oracle Complex Event Processing 11g Release 1 (11.1.1.6.3) for Eclipse. (August 2012): http://docs.oracle.com/cd/E23943_01/dev.1111/e14301.pdf

[13] Oracle MapViewer: http://www.oracle.com/technetwork/middleware/mapviewer/o verview/index.html

[14] Oracle WebLogic Server: http://www.oracle.com/technetwork/middleware/weblogic/ove rview/index.html

Efficient Event Detection by Exploiting Crowds*

Ioannis Boutsis
Department of Informatics
Athens University of
Economics and Business,
Athens, Greece
mpoutsis@aueb.gr

Vana Kalogeraki
Department of Informatics
Athens University of
Economics and Business,
Athens, Greece
vana@aueb.gr

Dimitrios Gunopulos
Department of Informatics &
Telecommunications
University of Athens
Greece
dg@di.uoa.gr

ABSTRACT

Encouraging users to participate in community-based sensing and collection for the purpose of identifying events of interest for the community has found important applications in the recent years in a wide variety of domains including entertainment, transportation and environmental monitoring. One important challenge in these settings is how significant events can be detected by exploiting the data sensed, gathered and shared by the crowd, while respecting the resource costs. In this paper we investigate the use of dynamic clustering and sampling techniques that allow us to significantly reduce utilization costs by clustering low-level streams of events based on their geo-spatial locations and then selectively retrieving the ones that depict the highest interest. Our experimental results illustrate that our approach is practical, efficient and depicts good performance.

Categories and Subject Descriptors

C.2.4 [**Distributed Systems**]

Keywords

Distributed Systems; Mobile Systems; Community-based Participatory Sensing; Sampling; Clustering; Event Detection

1. INTRODUCTION

"Community-based Participatory Sensing" systems where all the members contribute data to the system with the purpose of identifying events of interest for the community, are

---

*This research has been co-financed by the European Union (European Social Fund ESF) and Greek national funds through the Operational Program "Education and Lifelong Learning" of the National Strategic Reference Framework (NSRF) - Research Funding Program:Thalis-DISFER, Aristeia-MMD Investing in knowledge society through the European Social Fund, the FP7 INSIGHT project and the ERC IDEAS NGHCS project. We would also like to thank the anonymous reviewers and our shepherd, Prof. Mohamed Y. Eltabakh.

increasingly gaining popularity in recent years. The data are typically produced in the form of data streams and are generated on ubiquitous and portable devices, such as smartphones and tablets which are outfitted with a wide range of sensing capabilities, like GPS, WiFi, microphones, cameras and accelerometers. By combining data streams from different devices, important information and events of interest can be extracted such as congestion detection or real-time delay estimation as in the VTrack system [35]. Similar examples can be found in a number of domains including location-based services such as personalized weather information and for identifying areas of good WiFi connectivity [12], determining fuel efficient routes [13] and earthquake warning detection systems[27].

One important observation in these systems is that many people may gather in one place when an important event occurs. This happens in various situations such as social events (*i.e.,* conferences, concerts), traffic events (*i.e.,* traffic congestion) or emergency events (*i.e.,* earthquakes, floods). In these situations we are interested in identifying instantly that an event occurs, from the "gathering" of the people in a specific place, and then to analyze the event in more detail to define its nature.

Hence, one fundamental question is how to achieve efficient event detection by exploiting the data observed and provided by the crowd. This is a challenging problem considering the fact that mobile devices often produce more data than the network can deliver or the system can process, while only a subset of the data suffices to provide useful information about the events. In some cases, a small number of observations may yield confident event detection, while in other cases, a large number of observations are required to identify an event precisely.

Supporting efficient event detection in participatory sensing systems is a challenging process, as one needs also to consider the respective costs for the devices when producing and delivering the data, such as the energy consumption and the monetary cost (*i.e.,* 3g cost). It is vital that energy resources are used efficiently, especially when data stream sources are energy-constrained mobile devices and the amount of the users in participatory sensing systems depend on their costs. Thus, a fundamental question is how to define a suitable subset from the available data, to provide results of high quality, with small cost.

Our main idea is that the efficient identification of the important events where many participants are gathered can be achieved through clustering, and the selection of the most important data streams requires an efficient sampling approach. Clustering[1, 4] and sampling[10, 5, 22] in large multidimensional datasets are two major data analysis tasks. However, there is inherent complexity of the clustering techniques, especially when we deal with stream data to detect events that can potentially evolve over time. Sampling on the other hand can reduce the size of the problem by selecting a subset of the data for processing, so that the available resources would be able to process the size of the sample. However, the sample needs to be decided with respect to the input data and the selection criteria. Thus, defining the optimal selection criteria to export a representative sample is a fundamental task when efficient event detection is required. Our goal is to use clustering as well as sampling techniques to select the stream data to be processed, that will enable us to identify core real-world events of interest over time in an accurate and efficient manner.

In this paper we present DENSE, a community-based participatory sensing system that aims to stimulate user participation by encouraging users to be members of the system as part of a dynamic group, so as to identify events of interest as they occur. Users participate in the community by sensing and sharing streams of data. Our technique uses the user's GPS readings to dynamically determine clusters that evolve over time, to identify the locations where important events take place. Then we perform sampling, by selecting a subset of the devices that participate on these clusters to retrieve their data streams. The sampling is based on the amount of data streams that the system can handle, and the selection aims to retrieve the most representative data streams in every cluster. This way we are able to extract important events, with minimal cost. We summarize our contributions below:

- We present **DENSE**, our system that exploits the data gathered and shared by members of the participatory sensing system to achieve efficient detection of events. Our focus is on social events such as concerts, theatrical performances, etc., that involve the gathering of people in dense spatial regions.

- We develop a dynamic clustering technique that allows us to cluster data streams generated from user mobile devices. Our technique extracts and updates the clusters dynamically using the stream data shared by the participants, to identify the locations where events of interest occur.

- We present a sampling scheme that selects k good representative streams with respect to the number, shape of the clusters and the data points distribution.

- We provide a detailed experimental evaluation of our approach on PlanetLab[30] using the T-Drive trajectory dataset[38, 37].

2. SYSTEM ARCHITECTURE AND MODEL

In this section we present the architecture and main components of our system, DENSE (Dynamic EveNt detection in participatory SEnsing Sytems). We then describe the system model and introduce our clustering and sampling model.

2.1 DENSE Architecture

DENSE is a wide-area stream processing middleware that comprises a set of distributed nodes, denoted as n_i, connected via virtual links, denoted as l_j. DENSE is built as

an overlay on top of the Pastry peer-to-peer network and runs on Planetlab [30]. The goal of DENSE is to support the execution of distributed stream processing applications with QoS constraints, while efficiently managing the system resources. A distributed stream processing application is represented as a graph, where nodes represent the functions (that we call *event processing components*) and edges represent the data streaming between the different components based on the application logic. Upon submitting a user request, the system instantiates the appropriate components on the system nodes, in order to perform the processing, required by each application. Examples of application components are streaming components that are responsible to generate the stream data (*e.g.,* accelerometer sensor) or stream processing components (such as aggregation and projection components) that are used to process data streams from multiple mobile devices.

Figure 1 illustrates the DENSE architecture. In our previous work, we have implemented the following modules: i) A *discovery module* used for identifying application components and data streams in the system. ii) A *routing module* that is responsible for routing data streams as well as protocol messages between nodes. iii) A *monitoring module* for building and maintaining resource utilization profiles. iv) A *composition module* that selects and instantiates application components at runtime. v) A *resource management module* named RADAR [7], that attempts to manage the resources dynamically based on the applications' QoS demands and resource availability. We extend the DENSE middleware with: vi) A *clustering module*, which is responsible to determine the clusters dynamically, based on the GPS readings provided by the users. vii) A *k-sampling module*, that determines which of the available data streams will be processed. The sampling and clustering components work in concert, as we describe next.

In the DENSE system, we assume a spatial decomposition of the geographic area into a number of non-overlapping regions, similar to that of [34]. The organization of the area into regions can be done with respect to the size of the geographic area or the number of participants in the region, possibly defining several tiers at different levels of granularity, ranging from small local areas at the lowest tier, to the entire network area at the highest tier; this allows the system to collect streaming data from all users in a scalable manner.

2.2 System Model

In this paper we are interested in identifying events in "dense spatial regions"; these are events that involve the gathering of many people in one place considering the time and location dimensions, such as conferences, theatrical performances, festivals, media events, sporting events, traffic events, natural disasters (*e.g.,* floodings), etc. Our goal is to detect the exact location of such events and then to identify a representative subset of the data streams for further processing. This will allow us to considerably reduce the resource consumption when tracking how these events evolve over time. Note though that, our technique is general and can be used in multiple application scenarios such as determining congested areas or car accidents, earthquake detection, etc.

In our system we exploit streams of data generated by application modules running on the smartphones, for each

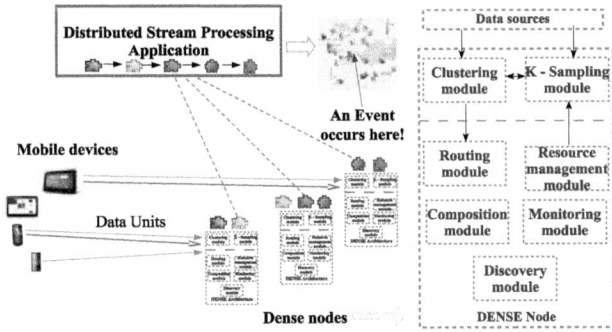

Figure 1: DENSE architecture.

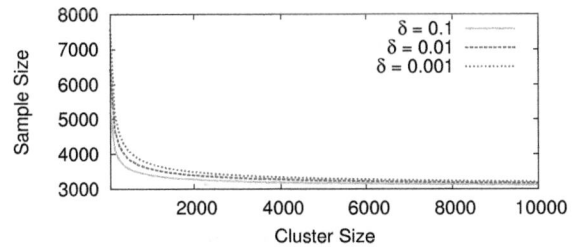

Figure 2: Required sample size to guarantee that a fraction of the cluster will be included in the sample.

$user_i \in U$. A stream of data consists of a sequence of individual chunks of data, called *Application Data Units* (ADUs); these are messages triggered locally at the phone using sensors present on mobile phones such as microphone, camera, GPS, accelerometer, motion sensors, etc., and their exact form is application dependent. An example of such ADUs is: <user_id, accelerometer data, microphone samples, timestamp, latitude, longitude> (for earthquake monitoring). The data units from multiple mobile sensors are streamed into the distributed stream processing system for further processing. The ADUs may vary in size since they may combine several types of data with different characteristics (*e.g.*, they might contain audio samples and accelerometer data for analyzing the congestion levels in a location) and so we must ensure that the amount of ADUs will not exceed the system's processing and communication resources. Thus, only a subset of the users that belong to the clusters, provided by the clustering component, are selected to provide their ADUs. Smartphones are powerful enough to do some local processing instead of sending the raw data streams. For example, in an earthquake monitoring application, the mobiles may process the data sensed from the accelerometer to define if they exceed an "alarm" threshold or to determine if their GPS location is similar to their previous location. The advantage is less communication overhead at the expense of higher processing overhead for the smartphones. However, local processing is application dependant, since it does not provide a benefit for every application (i.e. video processing on smartphones is prohibitive).

We note that the clustering and the sampling components are triggered in our system periodically, and the value of the time period is based on the events that we want to track. Thus, whenever the defined time period expires, both components are utilized to process the received GPS locations, extract the clusters and select the users to sample from.

The **clustering component**, implemented at the nodes of DENSE, will be using the data that include the GPS location of each $user_i$. In order to conserve energy and reduce the cost we state that users should not transmit their data units when their GPS location is identical to their previous one. Thus, our system uses a cache to preserve the users' previous locations, for some time. Nevertheless, after the defined time period has been exceeded and the user has not provided a new location, the system considers that the user has gone offline, so it stops using his last location when defining the clusters.

The **sampling component**, implemented at the source nodes of DENSE is responsible for obtaining the application data streams after deciding which of the mobile nodes will have their data streams processed. This component works in concert with the clustering and the rate allocation component to determine the users that will submit their data.

2.3 How to Select Good Event Representatives

In this section we consider the implications of sampling for our technique. We note, that, random uniform sampling may not be sufficient in our system and we choose to implement and use a method for biased sampling. The problem with random sampling is two-fold: First, if applied in the original dataset with the purpose of speeding up the computation, the use of uniform random sampling may lead to loss of events. To illustrate this, consider the following situation:

Guha *et al.* in [14] present a formulation to link the sample size with the probability that a fraction of the cluster is included in the sample, based on Chernoff bounds. For a dataset D of size n, let u be a cluster of size $|u|$. They consider that a cluster u is included in the sample when more than $\varphi * |u|$ points of the cluster belong to the sample, with $0 \leq \varphi \leq 1$.

Figure 2 illustrates the sensivity of the sample size required by uniform random sampling to guarantee that u is included in the sample, with a probability no less than δ, $0 \leq \delta \leq 1$, for a database of $n = 10,000$ points. As can be observed, in order to guarantee with probability 99%, that 30% of the points of a cluster with 500 points will be included in the sample, we need to sample 35.3% of the database.

However, in [22] they show that using biased sampling we can get a sample that has the same probability to include points from a given cluster with smaller sample size than uniform random sample. Second, since our goal is to retrieve data from devices which are located in small but dense clusters, using uniform sampling we would have to include a large fraction of data items, and this would result in high resource consumption. Furthermore, as we show in our experimental evaluation, even if we consider only the subset of points that belong to the clusters as the dataset D, the use of random uniform sampling provides a worse than biased sampling selection of points, to analyze the events.

3. OUR PROPOSED APPROACH

In this section we illustrate how we employ clustering and sampling to provide efficient event detection.

3.1 Clustering

Clustering is the task of grouping a set of objects in such a way that objects in the same group, denoted as cluster, are more similar to each other, meaning that their attributes are closer in the multidimensional space, than to those in other groups. We take advantage of clustering to define the groups that contain a large number of users in a geo-spatial location. The selection of the clustering approach plays an important role to the identification of the locations where important events take place. Several clustering techniques have been proposed in the literature [1, 32] such as the K-means[16] and K-medoids[29] algorithms. However these algorithms cannot be used in our setting since they typically perform better when the clusters are spherical, and are incapable to detect noise and outliers. Hierarchical clustering[19] has several advantages over K-means and K-medoids algorithms. It can be used to discover clusters of arbitrary shape and is insensitive to the size of the cluster. However, the runtime complexity of hierarchical clustering algorithms is quadratic.

Density-based clustering is a natural and attractive clustering approach for our situation since it can identify arbitrarily shaped clusters, it can handle noise and outliers, and one-pass algorithms that need to examine the raw data only once exist, thus the method's complexity is low. We note also that density corresponds well to human perception of clusters in the Eucledian space. Finally, density based clustering does not demand a prior knowledge of the amount of clusters k as the k-means algorithm does.

There are two well-known clustering algorithms for density-based clustering: (i) DBSCAN [32] and (ii) Optics [4]. DB-SCAN is one of the most common clustering algorithms. In DBSCAN, the definition of a cluster is based on the notion of density reachability. The algorithm's main idea is to instantiate a cluster when at least a predefined number of points are reachable from a point p, meaning that these points are within a specific range from p. All of these points are integrated to the cluster, and the cluster is expanded recursively by examining which of these new points possess the same property, so that their reachable points will be included in the cluster. Optics is similar to DBSCAN, but it addresses one of DBSCAN's major weaknesses, that is the problem of detecting meaningful clusters in data of varying density. This is achieved by ordering (linearly) the points of the database so that that points which are spatially closest become neighbors in the ordering. Additionally, a special distance is stored for each point that represents the density that needs to be accepted for a cluster in order to have both points belong to the same cluster. Afterwards, the algorithm can export the clusters from the ordered list. However, none of these approach deals with mobile data where the clusters need to be managed and updated in real-time.

3.2 Dynamic Clustering

Assuming a data set D, containing a number of points $(x_1, x_2, ..., x_m)$, the goal is to extract a number of non-overlapping subsets $x_1, x_2, ..., x_n$, with $n < m$, identified as *clusters*, whose points are close to each other in the multi-dimensional space, based on the clustering criterion.

Our approach for dynamic clustering shares the same logic with Optics, but is designed to extract efficiently clusters from stream data.

The clustering approach requires two parameters when processing a point: ϵ, that describes the maximum distance to consider, and $MinPts$, describing the minimum amount of points required to form a $cluster_c$. Thus, a point p is considered as a core point if at least $MinPts$ points are found within its $\epsilon - neighborhood$, $Nb_\epsilon(p)$. Similar to Optics we consider a core distance and a reachability distance variable for each point. Each point is assigned a core distance,

core(p), that basically describes the distance to its farthest point among the closest $MinPts$ as:

$$core(p) = \begin{cases} \emptyset & \text{if } |Nb_\epsilon(p)| < MinPts \\ \text{distance to farthest MinPts} & \text{otherwise} \end{cases}$$

The reachability distance of a point p, reach(p), from another point o is defined as the distance between p and o, or the core distance of o:

$$reach(p,o) = \begin{cases} \emptyset & \text{if } |Nb_\epsilon(o)| < MinPts \\ \max(core(o), \text{distance}(o,p)) & \text{otherwise} \end{cases}$$

Intuitively, if o and p are nearest neighbors, this distance is used to examine if $\epsilon' < \epsilon$ to decide if o and p belong to the same cluster.

The clustering process works as shown in Algorithm 1. It traverses through not-processed points, and when a core point p ($core(p)! = \emptyset$) is found, and thus a cluster can be instantiated, it identifies the points within its $Nb_\epsilon(p)$, adds them in a Priority Queue and updates their distances on the defined order. Additionally, it also adds in the Priority Queue and updates the distances, of the points in $Nb_\epsilon(q)$, for every core point q within the $Nb_\epsilon(p)$ recursively. Thus, similar to Optics, the points are ordered based on their spatial distance. The goal of the algorithm is to extract the clusters from the ordered list by traversing through the points and checking the reachability distances among consecutive points. Thus we denote as a $cluster_c$, a group of consecutive points where their reachability distance does not exceed an application dependant predefined value, which plays a crucial role in the amount of extracted clusters [4]. In our experiments we denote that two consecutive points belong to the same cluster when their reachability distance is defined and less than ϵ. Thus, we iterate through points and define as noise the points whose $core(p) == \emptyset$ and $reach(p,o) == \emptyset$, we initiate a $cluster_c$ when p has the attribute $core(p)! = \emptyset$ and $reach(p,o) == \emptyset$ and add all the following points to the same cluster until we find a point with the attribute $reach(p,o) == \emptyset$. We note that, as it is obvious from the algorithm, each point p has a defined reachability variable, either if it has more than $MinPts$ points within its $Nb_\epsilon(p)$ (core point), or if it belongs to the $\epsilon - neighborhood$ of a core point.

Clustering Mobile Data. In our system all the mobile devices define their gps location by providing the following information : <user_id, timestamp, latitude, longitude>, where the $user\_id$ is generated through SHA-1 hashing, the timestamp represents the unix time when the location was retrieved, and the latitude, longitude represent the actual location. In this paper we assume that the noise in the readings of the sensors is negligible.

Periodically all participants examine if their gps locations differ from their previous geographical location and in that case they transmit their new location to the clustering component. Our clustering component receives the GPS readings, and updates the clusters, by using two functions, insert and remove. Thus, for each time period the clustering component: (i) Inserts newly arrived users. (ii) Removes and re-inserts the points for an updated user location. (iii) Removes the points that represent users that have not participated with a new location for a recent time period. Thus, we update the new distances and derive the corresponding

Algorithm 1 Clustering

ClusterData(ϵ, $MinPts$)
Initialize ordered list L
for ($\forall p \in DB$ if p not-processed) **do**
    N = points inside $Nb_\epsilon(p)$
    Set p processed; $L.add(p)$;
    Seeds = new Priority Queue
    if ($core(p)! = \emptyset$) **then**
        update (N, p, Seeds, ϵ, $MinPts$)
        for ($q \in Seeds$) **do**
            N' = points inside $Nb_\epsilon(q)$
            Set q processed; $L.add(q)$;
            if ($core(q)! = \emptyset$) **then**
                update (N', q, Seeds, ϵ, $MinPts$)

update(N, p, Seeds, ϵ, $MinPts$);
coredist = core(p);
for ($\forall o \in N$) **do**
    if ($o! = processed$) **then**
        new-reach = $max(coredist, distance(o, p))$
        if ($reach(o) == \emptyset$) **then**
            o.reach = new-reach; Seeds.add(o, new-reach);
        else
            if (new-reach < reach(o)) **then**
                o.reach = new-reach; Seeds.move_up(o, new-reach);

Insert(p, ϵ, $MinPts$)
N = points inside $Nb_\epsilon(p)$;
for ($\forall l \in N$) **do**
    Set l not-processed;
    if (l belongs to cluster c) **then**
        Set all $n \in c$ as not-processed;

Remove(p, ϵ, $MinPts$)
N = points inside $Nb_\epsilon(p)$;
for ($\forall l \in N$) **do**
    Set l not-processed;
    if (p belongs to cluster c) **then**
        Set all $n \in c$ as not-processed;

Table 1: Insert, Remove

or a new cluster can be formed or it might be a noisy point. In all cases we have to update the distances of the points that belong to the $Nb_\epsilon(p)$. This is done by setting all the points in the $Nb_\epsilon(p)$ as not processed. However, in the case that one of the points in $Nb_\epsilon(p)$ belongs to a cluster c, we need to set as non-processed all the points of the cluster c as well. This happens because a Reachable point receives its reachability distance from the core point, and if this core point does not belong to the $Nb_\epsilon(p)$, to be re-processed, the Reachable point will be assigned with a wrong distance that may affect the extraction of the clusters. However, typically no more than one clusters will be found in the $Nb_\epsilon(p)$.

Remove. When a user has not transmit a new location for some time or has updated his/her current position, the previous position needs to be removed from the dataset. When we remove a point p in case where it is a core or a reachable point then the integrity of the cluster should be investigated, since it can can lead to the removal of some Reachable points from the cluster or to the division of the cluster, if less than $MinPts$ have left to the core points' range after the removal of point p. Thus, we need to set as not processed all the points that belong to the same cluster with p, if p belongs to a cluster and all the points in the $Nb_\epsilon(p)$. In the case that point p is a noisy point it can be easily removed since it does not affect any clusters.

Complexity. Our complexity is similar to Optics, that is, we also achieve a worst case complexity of $O(n \cdot \log n)$ for initializing the clusters. However, at runtime, typically less than n points need to be updated.

3.3 K-Sampling

Once the clusters are identified we select a subset of the mobile devices, to provide the system with the application specific ADUs that may contain data with different characteristics such as audio feeds, accelerometer data, etc. This will allow us to validate and track the event over time.

Suppose there are l data streams originating from mobile nodes in a specific region. The goal of the sampling component is to select a subset of the application data units k, (where $k < l$) to be processed. The sampling component consults the resource management component to determine the maximum amount of data units (k), that the system can efficiently process, depending on resource availability. These k data units should derive from users that belong to the clusters, formed by the clustering component, to analyze the events that takes place in these clusters. Thus, for each time period we select the k most representatives data streams, to analyze the identified clusters. However the selection of the k devices to retrieve their ADUs is not trivial.

First we note that the sample that we will receive from each cluster is proportional to the cluster's size and that at least one point will be selected for each cluster. This happens since when we are limited in resources we would like to extract more data from clusters with a lot of points, since they would represent more important events. Thus we select

clusters (explained below). Finally the formed clusters, extracted for that time period, are provided to the sampling component to define the mobile devices that will provide the application specific ADUs through k-sampling.

Updating the Clusters. The advantage of our approach is that it modifies only the portions of the ordered list that needs to be updated when the data change. Thus, when the points of a cluster remain static, they do not need to be updated. However we can insert and remove points that might affect the existence, the shape or the size of the clusters, and thus we should provide an updated view over time.

The points that are processed can be assigned to three categories: (i) **Core points** which are the points that belong to a cluster, and there are more than $MinPts$ points found within their $Nb_\epsilon(p)$, (ii) **Reachable points** which are the points that belong to a cluster but there are less than $MinPts$ points found within their $Nb_\epsilon(p)$, and they are typically found in the boundaries of the cluster, and (iii) **Noisy points** which are the points that they do not belong to any cluster.

Changing one point can affect multiple neighbor points, meaning that their reachability or core distance should be changed. Since DENSE works with stream data, multiple points can be affected over time, when users update their gps location (points). In order to avoid redundant processing on the same points, when several points change in the same neighborhood we mark the changed and the affected points from the updates as not-processed and remove them from the ordered list L. At the end of the time period we execute our Clustering method that processes only the marked points and then we extract the updated clusters. We state that the ordered list of the algorithm is maintained through executions so that the data will be updated. The insert and remove functions are shown in Table 1.

Insert. When a user transmits a new GPS location, its current position has changed and thus the point p should be inserted in the dataset to compute new clusters, while its previous position (if exists) needs to be removed. Point p might be inserted in the spatial region where a cluster exists

from each $cluster_c$: $max(1, \frac{k}{\sum_{i=1}^{c} am_c} * am_c)$ points, where am_c represents the amount of points in cluster $cluster_c$ and k is the amount of points that the system can process, provided by the resource management component.

Although different techniques can be used to select a subset from each cluster, we aim to retrieve the most representative users. Each user typically represents other users within a range, since they will generate similar data. For instance, all the users driving on the same road will most likely have the same traffic speed, etc., and thus we only need to select one user to represent the others. Hence, our goal is to select the users that will represent the maximum amount of other users in the cluster, based on the distribution of the users and their local density. In order to export these users we define the function `Repr(point p, radius x)` that is able to identify the list of points that can be found within a radius x from point p, along with point p, `Repr(p,x)` $= \{q : \forall q \ s.t. \ distance(p,q) \leq x\}$.

Using Kernels for Density Estimation. Kernel density estimation is based on statistics and more specifically on the kernel theory [11, 36]. Kernel estimation is a generalization form of sampling, where all points have a weight of one but they distribute their weights in the space around them. A kernel function describes the form of this distribution. We choose to implement clustering and then sampling on the clusters based on the kernels, instead of just using the kernels to extract the sample for two reasons. First, the computational function for the kernels depends on the amount of points and thus computing the kernel density estimators for the whole database would increase the complexity compared to computing them only for a small number of points in the clusters. Second, using this technique for the whole database might abandon small clusters where the points are distributed in a sparser manner, although they involve events.

For a data set D, let $(x_1, x_2, ..., x_n)$ be a set of tuples drawn from some distribution with an unknown density f. We are interested in estimating the shape of this function f. Its kernel density estimator is:

$$\hat{f}_h(x) = \frac{1}{n}\sum_{i=1}^{n} K_h(x - x_i) \quad = \frac{1}{nh}\sum_{i=1}^{n} K\left(\frac{x - x_i}{h}\right) \quad (1)$$

where $K(\bullet)$ is the kernel, a symmetric but not necessarily positive function that integrates to one, and $h > 0$ is a smoothing parameter called the bandwidth. A kernel with subscript h is called the scaled kernel and defined as $Kh(x) = 1/h * K(x/h)$. It has been shown that the exact shape of the kernel function does not affect the approximation [11], and a polynomial or a Gaussian function can work well. Thus, for our experiments we choose to use the common Gaussian function as the kernel function:

$$K(u) = \frac{1}{\sqrt{2\pi}}e^{-\frac{1}{2}u^2} \quad (2)$$

However, the standard deviation of the function, that is the bandwidth, plays an important role. In our experiments we choose the bandwidths according to [33], where it has been shown that if Gaussian basis functions are used, and the underlying density being estimated is Gaussian then the optimal choice for h is:

$$h = \left(\frac{4\hat{\sigma}^5}{3n}\right)^{\frac{1}{5}} \approx 1.06\hat{\sigma}n^{-1/5} \quad (3)$$

where $\hat{\sigma}$ is the standard deviation of the samples.

In our setting the values of x_i represent the 2-dimensional points $latitude_i$, $longitude_i$. Thus for the distance $x - x_i$ we use the Euclidean distance among 2-dimensional points:

$$dist(x - x_i) = \sqrt{(lat - lat_i)^2 + (long - long_i)^2}. \quad (4)$$

The kernel density estimator metric for each of the points within a cluster, can be estimated, by combining 1,2,3,4 as:

$$\hat{f}_h(x) = \frac{1}{nh}\sum_{i=1}^{n} \frac{1}{\sqrt{2\pi}}e^{-\frac{1}{2}\left(\frac{dist(x-x_i)}{h}\right)^2} \quad (5)$$

Algorithm 2 Selection of Representative Points (Radius x)

---

for ($\forall p \in cluster_c$) **do**
  Compute $\hat{f}_h(p)$ of point p;
  Add p in the ordered list OL based on $\hat{f}_h(p)$;
repeat
  Select point p with the highest $\hat{f}_h(p)$ in the OL;
  $rep_p = |\texttt{Repr(p,x)}|$;
  Remove all points $q, q \in \texttt{Repr(p,x)}$ from OL;
  Add p to SL;
  Update the $\hat{f}_h(p), \forall p \in OL$ and reorder OL;
until ($|SL| \geq \frac{k}{\sum_{i=1}^{c} am_c} * am_c$)
if ($|SL| < \frac{k}{\sum_{i=1}^{c} am_c} * am_c$) **then**
  Select $\frac{k}{\sum_{i=1}^{c} am_c} * am_c - |SL|$ points $\notin SL$;

Proposed k-Sampling technique. We propose a greedy algorithm to solve the maximization problem, based on the kernel density estimator. The goal of our approach is to greedily select the point that is able to represent the highest number of points, until the resource constraint will be fulfilled. The steps of our algorithm are shown in algorithm 2, and need to be executed for each cluster individually. We select a radius x to identify the range within which a point can be consider as representative for another point. In our experiments we set x dynamically as $\epsilon/\left(2 * \frac{k}{\sum_{i=1}^{c} am_c} * am_c\right)$. First, we estimate the density for every point p as $\hat{f}_h(p)$. That way we are able to identify the points that represent a lot of other points. Then, the points are inserted in an ordered list OL with respect to their kernel density estimator. While less than $\frac{k}{\sum_{i=1}^{c} am_c} * am_c$ points have been selected, we select point p with the highest kernel density estimator value from the ordered list OL and insert it in the list of selected points SL. Then, we remove all the points that belong in the list of `Repr(point p, radius x)` from the ordered list OL, since these points are represented by point p and we note the amount of the representative points rep_p to be used as a weight, as we will discuss later. Moreover, we update the kernel density estimator and the ordered list for the remaining points before continue with the loop, since the kernels might have changed after the removal of the points. For instance a point that was close but outside the radius of p will have a lower density estimator if a lot of neighboring points have been removed. If the algorithm is terminated and the amount of selected points in the list, $|SL|$, are less than $\frac{k}{\sum_{i=1}^{c} am_c} * am_c$ points, then we select $\frac{k}{\sum_{i=1}^{c} am_c} * am_c - |SL|$ points randomly from the points that have not been selected, $p \notin SL$.

After the points have been selected for each cluster we inform the devices that correspond to these points to provide their application-specific ADUs for the sampling. Each of the ADUs will be assigned with a weight, based on the amount of the representative points for point p, denoted as rep_p and thus the processing of each ADU is considered as processing rep_p identical ADUs. Consider for example an application that aims to export the sound pollution within a cluster. Each ADU contains the estimated decibels collected by the mobile device. The average sound pollution in this application will be computed as: $pollution = (sound\_level_p * rep_p)/\sum rep_p$.

4. EXPERIMENTAL EVALUATION

4.1 Experimental Setup

We have implemented our techniques over the DENSE middleware and tested it on the PlanetLab [30] testbed. Our system was implemented in Java6 with approximately 5.7K lines of code.

Event Identification Application: The experimental evaluation scenario used was an application that is able to identify events that happen in a specific spatiotemporal region, such as concerts, sports events or traffic congestion in the city of Beijing in real-time. We used the T-Drive Trajectory Dataset [38, 37], where we extracted a one-week trajectories (from 2-2-2008 until 8-2-2008) that represent 10,357 taxis in the city of Beijing. The total number of points in this dataset is about 15 million and the total distance of the trajectories reaches 9 million kilometers.

The experimental evaluation focuses on the following parameters: (i) **Clustering and Sampling efficiency**, (ii) **Clustering and Sampling Latency**, (iii) **Comparison of our approach with Optics, D-Stream, DBSCAN, Uniform Sampling**, in order to evaluate the benefit of different features of our approach, (iv) **Benefit from the Online Clustering** and (v) **Energy savings**.

4.2 Operation of DENSE

In this section we demonstrate the operation of DENSE in identifying events in a real dataset and also illustrate its superiority over Uniform Sampling.

First, we illustrate the advantage of our approach, when using our dynamic density clustering to identify the events, before sampling is performed. In figure 3 we present the spatial distribution of all the taxis in the dataset, at 6:20 of 7/2/2008. As can be observed most of the points are located near the city center. Note that the latitude distance (39.6 - 40.6) is approximately 110 km and the longitude distance (115.5-117.5) is approximately 170km.

We have executed our online clustering approach for these points and set the parameters as follows: $MinPts = 30$ and $\epsilon = 0.01 \simeq 1km$, which means that we aim to identify clusters with core-points which have at least 30 neighbors inside a radius that is approximately 1km. This is presented in figure 4, where we extracted 24 clusters. Some of these clusters, like the large red cluster in the city center, can be ignored since they reflect events which are repeated every day in specific time periods, like the traffic in the city center. However, our approach is able to identify whether these clusters should be further explored, in case where the size of these clusters differs from the expected size for the specific time period. An advantage of our clustering technique, that can be shown in figure 4, is that it also considers points that are part of a more densely packed cluster individually. This can be easily observed by the small clusters near the large red cluster which should be treated independently, while other

clustering techniques, such as K-Means, would consider all of them as one large cluster.

We state at this point that the selection of the two parameters $MinPts$ and ϵ plays an important role to the identification of the clusters and should be tuned according to the structure of the events that we want to identify. Thus if our goal is to find more dense clusters in an area, we could set a higher number to the $MinPts$ compared to the examined area. For instance we present the same snapshot with figure 5, when $MinPts$ is set to 60 and ϵ is set to 0.01.

In figure 6 we present a snapshot of uniform sampling that contains the same amount of data points as the ones that we extracted through clustering (approximately 35% of the total points). As can be seen the uniform sampling selects users for sampling that cover the whole area, including a lot of outliers. However, since our goal is to identify events in the specific area, if we use uniform sampling we will end up sampling from several users that do not provide any benefit, in terms of event analysis, and thus wasting a lot of resources, which are available for the k-sampling. On the other hand the use of the density clustering enables us to select data only from the users in the clusters, where events occur in order to analyze the events in more detail.

Event Identification: Our technique is based on our belief that when an interesting event occurs there would be a cluster from users that "gathered" at the event. We have validated this belief by identifying several concerts that actually took place in Beijing, retrieved from CHINA DAILY[1]. All the concerts that we examined formed clusters whose center is approximately the location where the event was hosted. For example we investigated a concert that took place in Beijing Concert Hall in Xicheng District on the Feb 7 2008 at 7:30 pm. This is illustrated in figure 4 by the light blue cluster whose center at 6.20 was: 39.90818171987097, 116.37933930159906. The small distance among the cluster's center and the Beijing Concert Hall (approximately 200m) is due to the Beihai Park, where no taxis can enter (and this can be found by the gap in the center of the big red cluster). However, if we analyzed other data as well, such as the direction of the users towards a point we could further increase our confidence about the location of the event. Nevertheless, as the times goes by the cluster's center moves constantly towards the actual location of the event.

The cluster that we study scaled in size over time and its maximum size was observed at 7.20. The observation of the cluster's size over time enables us to approximate the time interval when the event takes place. In most cases, when an event occurs, the size of the users gathering increases over time, until it reaches a peak and then it decreases, which enable us to estimate the actual time of the event as the peak of the cluster's size. Moreover, the retrieved data at that time point will be more accurate for the event. For example the center of the cluster will be much closer to the event's location than it will be an hour later.

4.3 Clustering

In this section we present the advantage of our dynamic clustering compared to the standard Optics algorithm for every iteration, and we present the variation of the clusters with regard to the used variables.

The benefit of our technique relies to the fact that we only need to re-process a subset of the data in order to identify

---

[1]http://www.chinadaily.com.cn

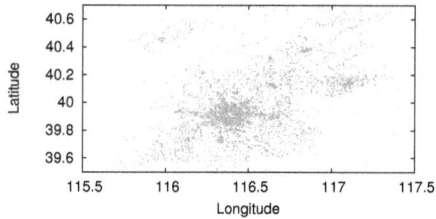

Figure 3: Snapshot of all data points at 6:20 of 7/2/2008

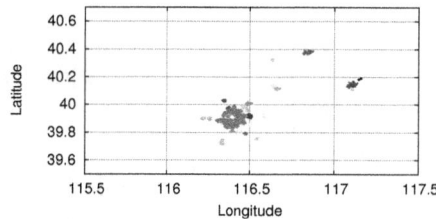

Figure 4: Detection of Clusters using DENSE

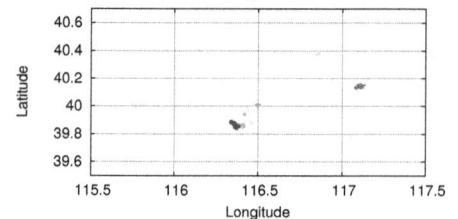

Figure 5: Detection of Clusters using DENSE with $MinPts = 60$

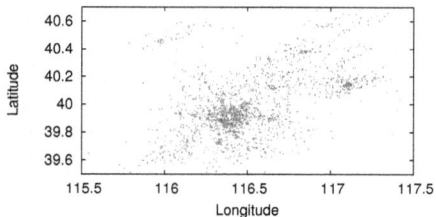

Figure 6: Output with Uniform Sampling

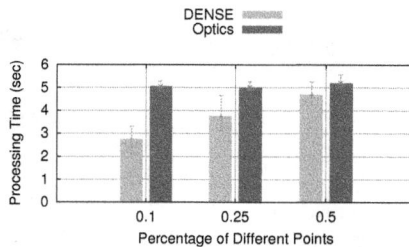

Figure 7: Overhead Comparison

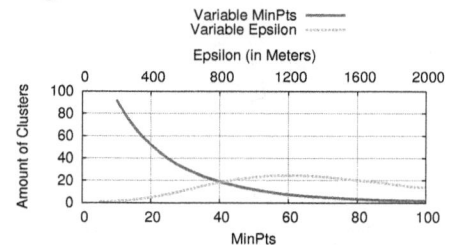

Figure 8: Clusters Variation under different MinPts, Epsilon

the clusters, but the result is identical to the original Optics algorithm. In figure 7 we compare the processing time needed for the clustering for both techniques with confidence intervals, to present the minimum and maximum processing times. The clustering involves the data received in the 7th of February 2008, and the time period to trigger the clustering algorithm is 20 minutes. This experiment was executed in a Intel Core i5 laptop with 4GB of RAM, which is a more controlled environment for the measurements. In our experiments, we use a large time interval as a period (20 minutes), and so the percentage of the taxis that change their geographical location among two sequential time periods is on average, approximately 50%. Note however, that when 50% of the points are updated the percentage of the points, affected due to their relationship is a lot higher, and our technique needs to update all the affected points as well. We compare the processing times using different percentages of points variation. More specifically we compare the techniques when the points that change their location during a time period are 10%, 25% and 50%. As can be seen from the figure DENSE has a great advantage over the standard Optics algorithm when the percentage of changing points is low. This happens since DENSE would not need to re-process most of the points that remain the same (except from those which are affected from the changes). Thus, in a system with numerous points where only a small fraction changes over time (i.e. when a system utilizes static sensors along with the moving ones or when some cars remain static due to congestion or because they have parked) DENSE has a significant performance improvement. However, as the fraction of points that change over time increases the gap is decreased. Note that when all points change, DENSE will reflect an identical processing time with Optics, since all the points will be processed, as in the original implementation.

In figure 8 we present the variation of the amount of clusters under different values for the $MinPts$ and ϵ variables, for the data points at 6:20 of 7/2/2008, and we show why we set the variables as $MinPts=30$points and $\epsilon \simeq 1$km. Note that the x axis is different for each of the variables. We variate the $MinPts$ variable from 10 to 100, while the ϵ variable is set to 1km. It is obvious that when the $MinPts$

value is low a lot of clusters can be identified, however they will not be important events, if the $MinPts$ to form a cluster inside a radium of 1km is small. As the $MinPts$ variable increases the amount of identified clusters is reduced, since we will only identify denser clusters. When the $MinPts$ is set to a high value the clustering will identify only extremely dense clusters, which should be important, but other more sparse but important events will not be identified. Thus, we set $MinPts$ as 30, so that all important events will be identified, without needing to sample from unimportant clusters. Moreover, we variate ϵ from 100m to 2km when the $MinPts$ is set to 30. As can be observed from the figure, the amount of clusters increases when the ϵ value increases, until it reaches 1km. This happens since there are more clusters that can be identified with a specific $MinPts$ value when the radius is increased. However after ϵ has reached 1km it starts decreasing, since the range will be so large that some of the nearby clusters will be merged. However, this might prevent us from identifying events since we will consider two separate events as one. Hence, we have set ϵ as 1km. Nevertheless, the selection should be based on the specific setting and the events that should be identified (i.e. only extremely dense clusters should be considered when we need to identify a major concert).

4.4 Comparison

In this section, we compare DENSE with D-Stream [9], in terms of clustering quality. We choose D-Stream for the comparison since it is a well-known approach that has been proposed in the literature for dynamically clustering streams of data. Like our approach, D-Stream aims to cluster only the subset that changes over time in order to be able to cope with data streams. While our technique manages to achieve that through the ordered list, D-Stream uses grids to divide the spatial area and to avoid re-clustering in grids that have not been changed. The processing time in D-Stream depends on the size of the grids. Dividing the spatial area to smaller grids results on a highest processing time since more grids would typically change over time. However, the values that we set on our experiments for D-Stream produces a slightly faster -less than 5%- processing time than

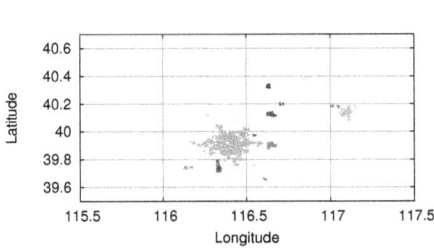

Figure 9: Detection of Clusters using D-Stream

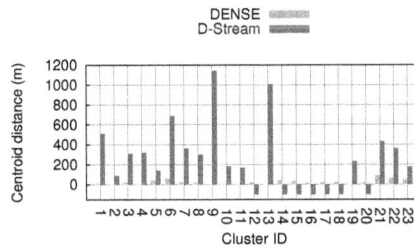

Figure 10: Comparison with DB-SCAN

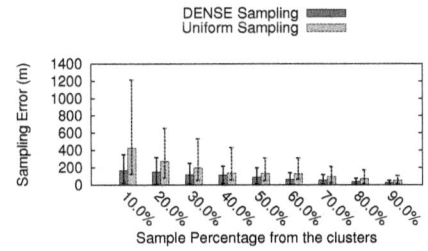

Figure 11: Sampling Error- Distance

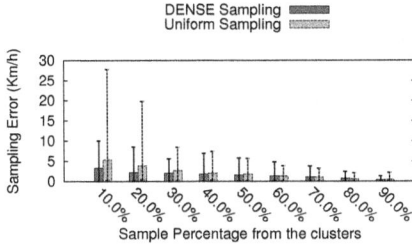

Figure 12: Sampling Error - Speed

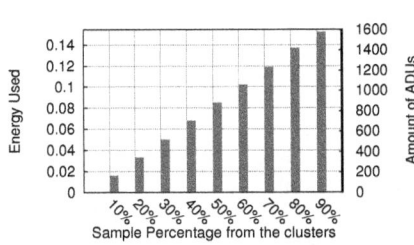

Figure 13: Energy Usage

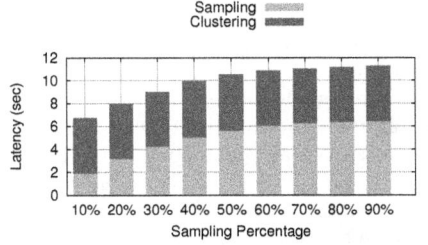

Figure 14: Latency

DENSE. D-Stream identifies dense and transient grids (transient grids have more points than the sparse grids but less than the dense ones), creates a cluster for each dense grid and merges iteratively the clusters of neighboring grids that are either dense or transient. Afterwards, it updates the clusters based on the evolution of the grids. In figure 9 we present the output of D-Stream for the same scenario (data/time) as we illustrated for our dynamic clustering approach. We have set the length of the grids to 0.02, similar to our ϵ radius variable. The disadvantage of D-Stream is that the grid's density represents the whole area of the grid, while in DENSE each point identifies the local density in the defined radius. Hence, a cluster that has its points in the borders of four grids might not be found. This squared structure inevitably lead us to use a smaller $MinPts$ value than in our approach, to be able to instantiate similar clusters. When we set large values for the $MinPts$ (close to 30) to extract the clusters with D-Stream, especially for the transient grids, it produced a lot of small clusters, since there were not enough neighbor grids to be merged with that amount of points. On the other hand, the use of small values led to a few enormously large clusters since several clusters found transient grids and merged together. Thus, we have tuned the minimum points for a transient grid to 12 and for a dense grid to 15 that provides almost the same amount of clusters with DENSE.

As can be observed from figure 9 their approach is able to identify most of the clusters. However, several clusters were merged together, since they were adjacent grids. Consider for example a left grid with a lot of points in its upper-left corner and a neighboring right grid with a lot of points in its lower-right corner. Although these points are far from each other the grids are going to be merged in D-Stream. Hence, this drawback of D-Stream caused the disappearance of the light blue cluster, that we had identified in our use case, and it proves that this technique cannot be used for event detection since a lot of events will be lost. Moreover, we can observe that the use of a smaller $MinPts$ value led to the instantiation of small clusters. However, we could easily prune these clusters when they contain less than 30 points.

In figure 10 we illustrate quality of the clustering for DENSE and D-Stream compared to DBSCAN which is a state of the art density algorithm. DBSCAN was selected for the comparison rather than Optics, so that the comparison would be fair, because DENSE shares the same logic with Optics. Thus, we provide the distance among the centroids of the DBSCAN's clusters compared to respective DENSE and D-Stream clusters. As can be seen from the figure DENSE manages to identify the same clusters with DBSCAN, with a small distance that ranges from 0 to 86m depending on the cluster. That proves that all of the clusters had almost the same points in the result set. On the other hand the D-Stream clustering failed to identify several clusters that DBSCAN found (presented as distance of -100m) and the identified clusters had a distance that ranged from 87 up to 1142 meters, compared to DBSCAN. Thus, we conclude that D-Stream fails to provide similar results to the well-known density clustering techniques.

4.5 Sampling

Finally we examine the effectiveness of our sampling approach. We present the accuracy of DENSE compared to the actual result when all the points from the clusters are used in the processing. Additionally, we compare our approach with performing random uniform sampling on the clusters. We choose uniform sampling for the comparison since it is a common technique for sampling.

We state that the sampling reflects the percentage of points that is used from the clusters. In our database, and for the specific settings we have defined ($MinPts$=30, $\epsilon \simeq$ 1km) the clusters (along with the ones that we filter due to repetition) involve approximately the 30% of the whole database. Thus, when we sample for example 10% of the clusters this is 3% of all the points in the specific time period.

Our goal in the specific experiment is (i) to identify the center of the cluster, when the event actually occurs, as we proved in the use case and (ii) to identify the average speed of the users within the cluster. Although we are not able to extract more interesting events due to the limited data in T-drive, in a real application where we can retrieve multiple types of ADUs from the selected users we could provide more interesting application specific events.

Error Metrics. Since our mechanism is based on sampling, it is expected that the results would have a deviation, compared to the results we would get by processing all the ADUs in the given geographical area. In order to examine the effectiveness of DENSE we rely on two error metrics. First we use the Euclidean distance among the actual center of the cluster and the estimated one through sampling. Hence, we define the sampling error metric Δ_i as the expected absolute difference between the estimate location (lat'_i, lng'_i) and the exact location (lat_i, lng_i) of the cluster's center: $\Delta_i = \sqrt{(lat'_i - lat_i)^2 + (lng'_i - lng_i)^2}$. Moreover, when we compare the average speed among the actual and the one estimated from sampling we use the following error metric: $\Delta_i = \sqrt{(speed' - speed)^2}$.

In figures 11,12 we present the average Sampling Error of all the clusters, produced at 6:20 of 7/2/2008, to identify the center of the cluster and its average speed, along with the minimum and maximum error, for several sampling percentages. We also compare our k-sampling technique by sampling k points, that correspond to the sampling percentage, by performing random uniform sampling on the set of the clusters. Note that, the DENSE system has filtered the large red cluster due to its repetition.

As expected, the output is dependent to the amount of points that we sample, and thus when we use a higher sampling percentage the results are more accurate. However, we can observe that when we use 10% of the sample we get an average error of approximately 165m, and an error of 347m on the worst case. On the contrary the uniform sampling provides an average error of 422m for all the clusters. When the sample size increases to 40%, we can even identify the center of the cluster in less than 111 meters on average and within less than 215 meters in the worst case, presented by the confidence intervals, while the uniform sampling is able to identify the center of the cluster with an error of 133m on average and 431m in the worst case. Moreover, with a sampling percentage of 90% from the clusters, we can identify the events with an error which is less than 22 meters on average. As can be seen our technique outperforms random uniform sampling in all cases and it is able to provide accurate results even with a minimum sampling size.

Figure 12 presents a similar experiment with figure 11, but it illustrates the error of the average speed of the devices within the cluster. As can be observed DENSE can provide accurate results even with a minimum sampling size, since the average error is 3.25km/h when the sample size is 10% and it decreases as the sample size increases. Additionally, we illustrate that our technique outperforms random uniform sampling especially for a small sample, where the selection of the optimal points is very important. The difference among the two sampling techniques compared to the previous experiment is smaller, because the ADUs in the previous experiment depend on the location while in this experiment this is not always the case. For example typically all the taxis in the same geographical location will have a similar speed. However, some of them might have slowed down, stopped or parked.

Figure 13 illustrates the energy savings from the sampling for the same setting with the previous experiment. This derives from the amount of ADUs that were transmitted to the system for processing, since each ADU requires energy from the mobile device to send the ADU and the respective energy consumption for processing the ADU in our system. Thus we present the amount of transmitted ADUs for different sampling percentages and the percentage of the ADUs transmit-

ted out of the total ADUs, since the sampling percentages refer to the amount of ADUs produced from nodes, within the clusters. Thus, for a sample of 10%, where we illustrated that the average error is approximately 165m from the center of the clusters and 3.25km/h from the actual speed in the clusters, we used only 168 points, which is only the 1.6% of all the points in the dataset for the specific timeperiod. Similarly the sample size of 40% is the 6.8% of the whole database with 706 points and the sample size of 90%, whose average error was less than 22 meters and 0.34km/h is approximately 12.7% of all the points. Thus, we conclude that using the clustering to determine the events can filter a lot of outliers and reduce the energy consumption.

Moreover, in figure 14 we present the latency for the clustering and the sampling, for the same experiment. We executed this experiment in a Intel Core i5 laptop with 4GB of RAM, that provides a controlled environment. As can be observed the clustering takes almost the same time, which is approximately 4.8 seconds, for all cases. The sampling time though depends on the sampling size since when it is increased, the algorithm needs to select more points, thus it traverses through the while-clause more times and the selection and the reassignment of the new kernel density estimators increases the processing time. However even for a sample size of 90% our approach takes almost 11.2 seconds, to select the optimal points of 10,357 points, that provides a high accuracy as we presented before. Nevertheless, the latency is low compared to the time interval we consider as period (20 minutes) and as we explained, a smaller time interval would provide lower processing times for the clustering and thus lower latency.

5. RELATED WORK

Participatory Sensing systems have recently become extremely popular for processing high-throughput, low-latency data streams and a number of systems have emerged in the literature [13], [35]. Hull *et al* in CarTel [17] propose a mobile sensor computing system for traffic monitoring. They use a query-oriented programming interface, to handle the data from the sensors, opposed to our stream processing architecture. Additionally, they suggest a "carry-and-forward" delay-tolerant network, which is opposed to our mechanisms that suggest a realtime processing logic.

Distributed stream processing systems have recently become extremely popular for processing high-throughput, low-latency data streams. A number of stream processing systems have emerged in the literature (including our own work on the Synergy middleware [31]). The research in this area is very rich and many papers have been published on detailed aspects of the technology such as data models, operators and query languages, resource management, scheduling, admission control policies, composition and placement algorithms, etc. Although, these research efforts have focused on high performance stream processing engines, our work focuses on the problem of sampling out of the available data streams to identify events of interest when the requested system capacity is incapable to handle all the data streams.

Clustering has been widely studied and many algorithms have been proposed. Several works aim to cluster moving objects that move along paths close to each other for a certain time [23, 6, 20, 18]. However, in our approach the users move towards an event from different places, so they have different directions and speeds. Moreover, we do not need heavy-weight algorithms that constantly track the trajectories of the objects, but we only need to know the location of the active users for each time period. DBSCAN [32] is a well-known algorithm for density clustering, that identifies and clusters dense regions, separated by low density regions. OPTICS [4], that we extend in our approach, is able detect meaningful clusters in data of varying density, while DBSCAN cannot. Several approaches exist that deal with the clustering of data streams [1]. They aim to provide a good clustering using a small amount of memory and time but they do not consider density clustering. D-Stream [9] and DenStream[8], are techniques for density clustering over data streams. As we proved in the experimental section, our technique outperforms D-Stream. DenStream provides an approximation of the actual clusters, based on the DBSCAN, while our approach provides identical results with the OPTICS algorithm. Authors in [25] present SCUBA, that develops moving spatio-temporal clusters and perform intelligent load shedding for the data. As we discussed, moving clusters cannot be used in our approach to cluster the users of an event. Moreover, opposed to DENSE, they consider that every point belongs to a cluster, and they merge moving clusters with similar speed and direction even though their overlap can be only a few points. Finally, they use a grid structure for the clustering and they select the data tuples based on their distance to the centroid while DENSE selects the most representative ones. Authors in [26] propose EDACluster that is also based on grids to perform density clustering.

The research in the area involving the problem of sampling is very rich and several approaches have been proposed. In [24], the authors perform region sampling in sensor networks, to reduce the energy cost rate and use statistics to predict the optimal sampling plan. However DENSE is able to sample only specific regions where events occur. Al-Kateb *et al* in [2] propose an algorithm to extend the reservoir sampling, that selects a uniform random sample of a given size from an input stream of an unknown size, with an adaptive-size reservoir. However, our technique driven by the application logic, outperforms uniform random samples. Halkidi *et al* in [15] study the problem of online clustering, however the focus is on high dimensional sensor data. In [5] they propose a k-sampling technique that aims to select the most recent data, based on the timestamp. Stratified Sampling [10] is another well-known method for efficient sampling from a population, where the members of the population constitute homogeneous subgroups(stratums) and random sampling is performed for each stratum. However, we proved that DENSE outperforms random sampling.

A similar paper to our approach is [22] where the authors propose a technique for biased sampling, where the probability that a given point will be included in the sample depends on the local density of the data set. Our technique differs since we sample only within the clusters. Their approach might abandon clusters of lower density completely, which can lead to unidentified events. Authors in [21] propose Watchdog, an event detection framework that aims to cluster the right sensors to meet user specified detection accuracy during runtime. In order they determine the accuracy detection they generate clusters of each possible size, and examine them using Hidden Markov Models. This approach cannot be used in stream data and when the data size is too large, since the clustering would need a lot of time. Palmer

and Faloutsos in [28] propose an algorithm to sample for clusters, using density information. Their approach works under the assumption that clusters have a zipfian distribution and is designed to identify clusters when they differ a lot in size and density, and there is no noise. Although their approach is an one-pass algorithm it provides an approximation and it is not adaptive, thus, it has to be executed even if no points have changed.

Several event detection approaches have been proposed in the literature to address in-situ event identification, especially for wireless sensor networks that emphasize in the energy savings. Regions of similar sensor data are detected in [34]. Although they use Kernel Density Estimators to identify similar sensor readings this cannot be extended for Participatory Sensing Systems where the mobile devices might produce different readings for the same event (*e.g.*, speed).

Authors in [3] focus on finding events described by a query. This is a complementary approach to ours; we take a more exploratory approach since: (i) they do not focus on the detection of the phenomena (events), but they assume that the description of the phenomena is given, (ii) the selection of the tuples is based on the distance from the phenomenon and thus all the tuples in the specific region will be returned, while we choose good representative users to provide data, (iii) they use different approaches to solve the problem thus they do not provide any clustering or sampling techniques.

6. CONCLUSIONS

In this paper, we have presented DENSE, a system that aims to improve user participation in community-based participatory sensing systems. DENSE makes it easy for users to sense, collect and share data units which are used to identify real life events when they occur. We propose online techniques to cluster the user data and select only a subset of users in these clusters for sampling to identify and track the events over time. The advantage of our technique is that it filters the noisy points through clustering, based on the application logic, and that it considers the data streams that depict the highest interest when selecting the data sample. Detailed experimental results illustrate that our approach is practical, efficient, depicts good performance and is able to provide accurate results with a relatively small sample size.

For our future work we plan to extend our approach to examine the capabilities of the devices in real-time, in terms of availability, battery levels etc., to include the resource capabilities of the devices when we decide which ones should be selected for the sampling.

7. REFERENCES

[1] C. C. Aggarwal, J. Han, J. Wang, and P. S. Yu. A framework for clustering evolving data streams. In *VLDB*, Berlin, Germany, Sep 2003.

[2] M. Al-Kateb, B. S. Lee, and X. S. Wang. Adaptive-size reservoir sampling over data streams. In *SSDBM*, Banff, Canada, July 2007.

[3] M. H. Ali, M. F. Mokbel, and W. G. Aref. Phenomenon-aware stream query processing. In *MDM*, pages 8–15, Mannheim, Germany, May 2007.

[4] M. Ankerst, M. M. Breunig, H.-P. Kriegel, and J. Sander. Optics: ordering points to identify the clustering structure. In *SIGMOD*, Philadelphia, PA, June 1999.

[5] B. Babcock, M. Datar, and R. Motwani. Sampling from a moving window over streaming data. In *SODA*, San Francisco, CA, January 2002.

[6] M. Benkert, J. Gudmundsson, F. Hübner, and T. Wolle. Reporting flock patterns. *Computational Geometry*, 41(3):111–125, 2008.

[7] I. Boutsis and V. Kalogeraki. Radar: Adaptive rate allocation in distributed stream processing systems under bursty workloads. In *SRDS*, Irvine, CA, October 2012.

[8] F. Cao, M. Ester, W. Qian, and A. Zhou. Density-based clustering over an evolving data stream with noise. In *SIAM*, Bethesda, MD, April 2006.

[9] Y. Chen and L. Tu. Density-based clustering for real-time stream data. In *KDD*, San Jose, CA, Aug 2007.

[10] W. G. Cochran. *Sampling Techniques, 3rd Edition*. John Wiley, 1977.

[11] N. Cressie. *Statistics for spatial data*. Wiley & Sons, 1993.

[12] A. Dou, V. Kalogeraki, D. Gunopulos, T. Mielikinen, V. Tuulos, S. Foley, and C. Yu. Data clustering on a network of mobile smartphones. In *SAINT*, Munich, Germany, July 2011.

[13] R. K. Ganti, N. Pham, H. Ahmadi, S. Nangia, and T. F. Abdelzaher. Greengps: a participatory sensing fuel-efficient maps application. In *MobiSys*, San Francisco, California, USA, June 2010.

[14] S. Guha, R. Rastogi, and K. Shim. Cure: an efficient clustering algorithm for large databases. In *SIGMOD*, pages 73–84, Seattle, Washington, USA, June 1998.

[15] M. Halkidi, V. Kalogeraki, D. Gunopulos, D. Papadopoulos, D. Zeinalipour-Yazti, and M. Vlachos. Efficient online state tracking using sensor networks. In *MDM*, Nara, Japan, May 2006.

[16] J. A. Hartigan and M. A. Wong. Algorithm AS 136: A K-Means Clustering Algorithm. *Applied Statistics*, 28(1):100–108, 1979.

[17] B. Hull, V. Bychkovsky, Y. Zhang, K. Chen, M. Goraczko, A. Miu, E. Shih, H. Balakrishnan, and S. Madden. Cartel: a distributed mobile sensor computing system. In *SenSys*, pages 125–138, Boulder, Colorado, USA, Oct-Nov 2006.

[18] C. S. Jensen, D. Lin, and B. C. Ooi. Continuous clustering of moving objects. *IEEE Trans. on Knowl. and Data Eng.*, 19(9):1161–1174, September 2007.

[19] S. Johnson. Hierarchical clustering schemes. *Psychometrika*, 32:241–254, 1967.

[20] P. Kalnis, N. Mamoulis, and S. Bakiras. On discovering moving clusters in spatio-temporal data. In *Advances in spatial and temporal databases*, pages 364–381. Springer, 2005.

[21] M. Keally, G. Zhou, and G. Xing. Watchdog: Confident event detection in heterogeneous sensor networks. In *RTAS*, pages 279–288, Stockholm, Sweden, April 2010.

[22] G. Kollios, D. Gunopulos, N. Koudas, and S. Berchtold. Efficient biased sampling for approximate clustering and outlier detection in large datasets. *IEEE Trans. on Knowl. and Data Eng.*, 2003.

[23] Z. Li, B. Ding, J. Han, and R. Kays. Swarm: mining relaxed temporal moving object clusters. *Proc. VLDB Endow.*, 3(1-2):723–734, September 2010.

[24] S. Lin, B. Arai, D. Gunopulos, and G. Das. Region sampling: Continuous adaptive sampling on sensor networks. In *ICDE*, Cancún, México, April 2008.

[25] R. V. Nehme and E. A. Rundensteiner. Scuba: scalable cluster-based algorithm for evaluating continuous spatio-temporal queries on moving objects. In *EDBT*, Munich, Germany, March 2006.

[26] C. S. d. Oliveira, P. I. Godinho, A. S. G. Meiguins, B. S. Meiguins, and A. A. Freitas. Edacluster: an evolutionary density and grid-based clustering algorithm. In *ISDA*, Rio de Janeiro, Brazil, Oct 2007.

[27] M. Olson, A. H. Liu, M. Faulkner, and K. M. Chandy. Rapid detection of rare geospatial events: earthquake warning applications. In *DEBS*, New York, NY, July 2011.

[28] C. R. Palmer and C. Faloutsos. Density biased sampling: an improved method for data mining and clustering. In *SIGMOD*, Dallas, TX, May 2000.

[29] H.-S. Park and C.-H. Jun. A simple and fast algorithm for k-medoids clustering. *Expert Syst. Appl.*, 36(2):3336–3341, Mar. 2009.

[30] PlanetLab Consortium. http://www.planet-lab.org, 2004.

[31] T. Repantis, X. Gu, and V. Kalogeraki. Synergy: Sharing-aware component composition for distributed stream processing systems. In *Middleware*, Melbourne, Australia, Nov. 2006.

[32] J. Sander, M. Ester, H.-P. Kriegel, and X. Xu. Density-based clustering in spatial databases: The algorithm gdbscan and its applications. *Data Min. Knowl. Discov.*, 2(2):169–194, June 1998.

[33] B. Silverman. *Density Estimation for Statistics and Data Analysis*. Monographs on Statistics and Applied Probability. Chapman & Hall, 1986.

[34] S. Subramaniam, V. Kalogeraki, and T. Palpanas. Distributed real-time detection and tracking of homogeneous regions in sensor networks. In *RTSS*, Rio de Janeiro, Brazil, Dec 2006.

[35] A. Thiagarajan, L. Ravindranath, K. LaCurts, S. Madden, H. Balakrishnan, S. Toledo, and J. Eriksson. Vtrack: accurate, energy-aware road traffic delay estimation using mobile phones. In *SenSys*, Berkeley, CA, Nov 2009.

[36] M. Wand and C. Jones. *Kernel Smoothing*. Monographs on Statistics & Applied Probability. Chapman & Hall, 1995.

[37] J. Yuan, Y. Zheng, X. Xie, and G. Sun. Driving with knowledge from the physical world. In *KDD*, San Diego, California, USA, August 2011.

[38] J. Yuan, Y. Zheng, C. Zhang, W. Xie, X. Xie, G. Sun, and Y. Huang. T-drive: driving directions based on taxi trajectories. In *SIGSPATIAL GIS*, San Jose, CA, November 2010.

Towards Complex Actions for Complex Event Processing

Steffen Hausmann
Institute for Informatics
University of Munich
hausmann@pms.ifi.lmu.de

François Bry
Institute for Informatics
University of Munich
bry@lmu.de

ABSTRACT

Complex actions are a natural extension for complex event processing languages needed by many applications like emergency management. In particular interactions with external actuators that are common in those applications pose challenges that need to be adequately covered. Many approaches towards actions and reactivity in event processing are, however, either too simple or too formal to model complex composite actions in a convenient manner or require a complete knowledge of the actions and of their effects.

This article proposes a pragmatic yet generic approach to complex actions in event processing which adapts to the heterogeneous and incomplete nature of physical actions. The article furthermore introduces a static semantic analysis for rejecting incorrect and undesirable programs which scales with the available information without requiring an a priori, or complete, knowledge of the actions and their consequences. The article finally describes a transformation of complex actions into complex events queries making it rather simple to add complex actions to a wide range of event processing languages.

Categories and Subject Descriptors

D.3.2 [**Programming Languages**]: Language Classifications—*Constraint and logic languages*; F.3.2 [**Logics and Meanings of Programs**]: Semantics of Programming Languages—*Program analysis*

Keywords

Composite Actions, External Actions, Temporal Analysis, Semantic Analysis, Complex Event Processing

1. INTRODUCTION

Many applications are conveniently implemented using complex event processing techniques [19]. However, many implementations focus merely on the deduction of high-level

knowledge in terms of complex events and delegate the execution of reactions, if any at all are modeled within the event processing system, to proprietary often hard coded systems. A large number of applications can substantially benefit from a new generation of event processing systems that integrate the definition of complex events with the capability of modeling the logic of reactions whereas only the execution of basic actions is delegated to external actuators.

One particular field that benefits from such a new kind of systems is emergency management in public infrastructures like subway systems and airports. Nowadays, such infrastructures are operated by humans from a central control room. Composite reactions are executed by isolated and proprietary subsystems with an incomplete knowledge and the information provided by sensor is poorly processed. Moreover, incidents in the past have shown that static procedures and human misinterpretation may result in severe casualties or damages [13, 22].

Emergency management calls for complex event processing with complex actions and fast computable simulations [4] making it possible to derive a more abstract and high level interpretation of the arriving data and to execute composite reactions that are requested by human operators.

Challenges. Although the combination of complex events and reactive rules has already been extensively investigated in the literature, the physical nature of basic actions that are eventually executed by external actuators introduces new aspects that need to be considered to obtain an adequate and effective approach suited, for instance, to emergency management applications as they are described in [25, 18].

Example 1. Smoke is the most dangerous threat to passengers and personnel during a fire in a metro station. Accordingly it is crucial to keep evacuation routes free of smoke as long as possible. This is usually achieved by adapting the ventilation regime so that a flow of fresh air keeps the smoke away from important areas.

To this end, smoke dampers are opened and ventilators are activated to generate the desired air flow that pushes the smoke out of the station. Moreover, warning signals are activated close to the outlet of the ventilation system some time before the leakage of smoke.

From this example we derive the following observations:
Physical Actions Atomic actions are executed by external actuators that interfere with the real world the underlying physical effects of which can hardly be formalised. To estimate, e.g., the effect of an airflow on the distribution

of smoke within an area, complex numeric simulations of physical effects are required [4].

Irreversible Effect Physical actions can often hardly be reversed or compensated as the caused physical effects cannot be easily undone. Once activated, the ventilators can indeed be turned off again, however, the caused airflow has already scattered the smoke what cannot be simply undone by reversing the airflow.

Timing of Actions In contrast to mere sequences of actions that are commonly used in imperative procedures, the exact timing between physical action is often crucial to obtain a desired effect. To be effective, the warning of leaking smoke needs to be issued, e.g., 20 seconds ahead of time and not just in the moment the smoke actually passes out.

Indirect Feedback External actions may fail to achieve their intended goal. However, feedback on their success usually cannot be inferred from the feedback that is provided by the contributing actuators. The adaptation of the ventilation regime is successful when the smoke actually disappeared, not when the dampers and ventilators were activated successfully.

Requirements. Based on these observations we derive the following requirements for complex actions suitable for modern and effective emergency management:

High-Level Language Emergency management has a natural need for expressiveness and ease of use. Complex actions need to be capable of modelling composite workflows in a manner that is convenient and appropriate for humans. Furthermore, complex actions must be tailored to the particularities of physical actions as they are desirable for interactions with external actuators in the infrastructure. At the same time, approaches based on intelligently acting autonomous systems cannot be used. Emergency managers are in charge and need to be in control and consequently they only accept actions that are specified in a deterministic and comprehensible way.

Integration of Events and Actions Instead of dedicating the execution of composite actions to proprietary and specialized systems without an expressive notion of complex events, it seems more appropriate to uniformly integrate the execution of composite actions into the event processing system. Complex event queries are capable of combining the information from various sources to obtain an abstract representation of the infrastructure and its condition that is valuable to control the executed procedures during runtime and to determine, e.g., the result of complex actions.

Expressive Temporal Dependencies Complex actions usually try to achieve a higher level goal that cannot be realised by individual actions but requires the collaboration of multiple actions. To this end, complex actions have a need for temporal dependencies that specify the timing and sequence for several actions in a manner that exceeds the capabilities of ordinary sequences and cases from imperative programming languages. To be valuable, the system must be able to actually execute complex actions according to their temporal dependencies.

Static Semantic Analysis Complex actions require a versatile semantic analysis that identifies errors at compile time which would otherwise only manifest during runtime. As the knowledge on runtime properties of heterogeneous actions is often incomplete, the analysis needs to scale with the available information. Basic properties of complex actions must be verifiable without specific knowledge whereas

more specific properties can be verified if the corresponding knowledge is available.

Contributions. We make the following contributions:

- Identification of orthogonal dimensions that must be supported by expressive complex actions and discussion of limitations that are inherent to external actions.

- Introduction of expressive complex actions tailored to external actions with a clear separation of orthogonal aspects of action execution.

- Discussion of viable temporal dependencies between actions and elaboration of an execution strategy that satisfies those dependencies during runtime.

- Elaboration of a semantics of actions that enables a semantic analysis which ensures crucial properties of complex actions at compile time.

- Suggestion of a transformation scheme that converts complex actions to event queries which can be evaluated on top of a conventional event processing system.

2. FOUNDATIONS OF COMPLEX ACTIONS

2.1 Times Associated with Actions

The underlying time model is a crucial aspects for complex event processing that substantially influences the semantics of complex events. In event processing systems application time is often used in favour of system time to avoid unintuitive effects. In a similar way, the employed time model significantly impacts the semantics of actions and thus similar issues need to be accounted to obtain an appropriate time model for actions.

In general it seems desirable to apply a synchronous time model and that the times associated with an action instance are determined by the corresponding actuator that actually executes it. In this way, the impact of latency and network delays is minimized and in consequence the semantics of actions becomes more meaningful and stable.

We distinguish three different times of actions: one related to the beginning and two related to the ending of an action.

Initiation Time. The initiation time of an action refers to the time the action is deemed to begin.

Success and Failure Times. The end of an action is denoted by the time of its success or failure. Naturally, each action can only either succeed or fail. In the context of emergency management, actions are furthermore considered as failed if they did not succeed within an application dependent amount of time.

Note that these times are subject to a priory unknown runtime effects and cannot be directly influenced. In particular the initiation times of actions can only be affected indirectly: Actions are requested by the event processing system as soon as the premises of the corresponding reactive rule are satisfied. However, this constraints only the earliest possible times at which actions can be conceptually initiated whereas the times of their actual initiation are subject to runtime effects, such as, latency and network delay.

This aspect substantially impacts the way how actions can be executed during runtime and introduces limitations on viable temporal relations that can be actually guaranteed during runtime.

2.2 Indirect Feedback on Physical Actions

Physical actions are requested within the event processing system and executed by external actuators. As a consequence the system has inherently no general knowledge on the progress of requested actions. Instead it depends on the feedback that is provided by the corresponding actuators to determine the current status of running actions. However, due to the heterogeneity of actuators in large infrastructures, the quality of feedback may vary substantially. For instance, not every actuator can provide the feedback that is desired, to determine when and if an action was actually successful, some even cannot provide any feedback at all.

As a consequence, it is often mandatory to rely on indirect feedback from related sensors that allows inferences on the execution status of actions. For instance, to determine whether a ventilator was activated successfully, one can use the information on the current airflow measured by an adjacent anemometer. If even no indirect feedback is available, domain knowledge can be used to specify, for instance, that the activation of the ventilator is successful 20 seconds after the request was emitted by the event processing system.

In summary, it is desirable to obtain the feedback on the execution of actions directly from the actuator, but due to technical limitations the feedback may need to be inferred from other sources including very generic information provided by the event processing system itself. As a consequence, the times associated with external actions need to be adjustable according to the capabilities of the actuators and the requirement of the programmer as there is no suitable default that equally fits all kinds of diverse actions.

2.3 Dimensions of Complex Actions

A language towards complex actions for emergency management must support (at least) the three complementary dimensions of action composition, temporal dependencies, and execution result. A fourth dimension, temporal assertions, seems desirable to increase the quality and robustness of programs but it does not result in a higher expressiveness.

Action composition. Complex actions are composed from several (atomic or complex) sub-actions that are executed in combination to achieve a certain higher level goal that cannot be achieved by single and more basic actions. Naturally, a language for complex actions must support the composition of several actions into one composite complex action.

Note that emergency management requires temporal dependencies that exceed the expressiveness of common sequences and choice as they are available in imperative languages. However, action composition covers only the mere collection of several actions whereas monolytic operators available in other approaches, like sequences, are expressed by means of more generic and expressive temporal dependencies between actions.

Temporal dependencies. Temporal relations are mandatory to specify the timing and execution order of actions which must be satisfied when the action is executed. Commonly used temporal dependencies between actions are for instance *before* and *after* which may additionally specify an optional duration (e.g., *20 seconds after*).

To obtain expressive complex actions, it is crucial that multiple dependencies can be independently specified for the same action. Note that this requirement is often not satisfied by monolytic composition operators which interleave temporal relations and action composition.

To be suitable for external actions with uncertain results, temporal relations must furthermore discriminate between success and failure of actions to allow different reactions based on the result of preceding actions (e.g., *only execute a after b was successful*).

Execution result. Complex actions need a mean to specify whether their intended effect has been accomplished or not, that is, if their execution was successful or failed. Without a notion of success and failure of actions, composite workflows that invoke different alternatives to adapt to the result of preceding actions cannot be easily modeled.

As the desired effect of actions may not only depend on the success of their sub-actions, those means must be expressive enough to specify generic event patterns that verify the success and failure of the desired effects of the complex action.

Temporal assertions. Temporal assertions specify temporal conditions between actions that need to be satisfied during runtime. In contrast to temporal dependencies, these conditions have no effect on the execution of the composite action. It is just verified during compile time that the conditions *will* be satisfied if the action is executed according to its temporal dependencies.

It is desirable that the verification of assertions does not rely on comprehensive domain knowledge on actions, as the available knowledge is in practice often incomplete. However, if specific domain knowledge is actually available for certain actions, it should be considered by the analysis to obtain stronger results.

Temporal assertions do not increase the expressiveness of actions, but they facilitate the development of more robust code as they they specify conditions on the behaviour during runtime that are verified by the system at compile time.

Besides the capabilities of four dimensions, a clear separation of concerns of the orthogonal properties of the dimensions seems desirable. The benefits of a clear separation of concerns that are widely recognised for rule based languages, in particular for rule based event query languages [7]. These benefits can be naturally generalised for complex actions in complex event processing. Without a clear separation of orthogonal concepts, complex actions lose expressiveness and become cumbersome and unintuitive to write. This effect increases the more dimensions are considered for the actions.

2.4 Semantic Analysis for Actions

The clear separation of concerns and a good coverage of the four orthogonal dimensions of actions is arguably desirable for complex actions, in particular for complex actions in emergency management. However, the resulting expressiveness comes at a price, namely the need for a strong semantic analysis capable of rejecting incorrect and faulty programs. The semantic analysis of complex actions should preferably cover at least the three following aspects.

Viability of Temporal Dependencies. Atomic temporal dependencies need to be viable in the sense that they can be actually satisfied by the system during runtime. As the referred time-points of actions can only be affected indirectly, arbitrary temporal dependencies between actions may not necessarily be satisfiable during runtime.

For instance, due to inherent runtime effects, it is impossible for the system to guarantee that two actions are actually initiated at the same time, because the distribution of the action request to the actuator is subject to latency. Note that this still holds if the initiation refers to the time the request is emitted by the system.

Fairness of Actions. Using action identifiers and generic relations to specify temporal dependencies between actions seems desirable. In fact, it is even mandatory to facilitate the integration of multiple independent dimensions without losing expressiveness.

However, the flexibility of temporal dependencies may result in inconsistent specifications, for instance in cyclic dependencies between actions, that prevent sub-actions from being executed. Accordingly, the semantic analysis must verify at compile time whether the temporal dependencies allow that all sub-actions can actually be executed during runtime and that there is no "dead code" that contains actions which will never be executed.

Entailment of Assertions. Specifying temporal assertions is only meaningful if it is verified during compile time that the corresponding assertions of an action will actually be satisfied during runtime.

However, the verification often requires domain knowledge that might not be available for all kinds of physical actions. Accordingly, it is mandatory that the semantic analysis can incorporate such domain knowledge, specified, e.g., in the schema of actions, but does not rely on it to work at all.

3. ACTIONS IN A HIGH-LEVEL LANGUAGE

In the following, we will elaborate complex actions that can be integrated into high-level event query languages. To this end, a short overview of the event query language Dura is given which has been introduced in [16] and which is exemplarily used as a basis for our work. Subsequently, we will extend the event query language with expressive complex actions that aim at a full coverage of the aforementioned dimensions of complex actions.

3.1 Event Processing with Dura in a Nutshell

Dura is a high-level rule based complex event processing language in the spirit of the XML query and transformation language Xcerpt [9] and the rule based event query language XChange^{EQ} [6].

Event queries in Dura are characterized by a pattern based query approach, versatile temporal dependencies between events, versatile negation and grouping capabilities, and a clear separation of query dimensions that is desirable to obtain a high expressiveness of the language [7]. Moreover, Dura comes with stateful objects that represent non-volatile data which can be updated in non-destructive and declarative fashion and support of multiple external time models.

Atomic Event Queries. Events are represented as structured data, similar to structs known from C. Every event has a name, contains a unique identifier and further user defined attributes in its payload, and is associated with a time interval.

Events are queried by means of a pattern based approach, that is, the query pattern resembles the data of the event and variables are specified in the pattern where data should be extracted. In addition, an event identifier is introduced

that precedes the query that is used in composite queries to refer, e.g., to the time of the matched event.

```
event e: smoke{ area{var Area}, amount{var C} }
```

The preceding query matches `smoke` events and binds the value of the `area` and `amount` attributes to variables. Note that either values or composite data can be bound to variables and that the query pattern may be incomplete, omitting irrelevant attributes.

Composite Event Queries. Several event queries are combined by means of the operators `and`, `or`, and `not`. In addition to the mere composition of queries, temporal and other dependencies between events and the data they carry are given in a separate `where` part that is appended to the query.

```
and{
    event e: smoke{ area{var Area}, amount{var C} },
    event f: temp{ area{var Area}, value{var T} }
} where { {e,f} within 2 min, C > 0.1, T > 50 }
```

This query matches `smoke` and `temp` events that occur within 2 minutes in the same area, note the implicit join over the variable `Area`, and which report a temperature above 50°C and a smoke concentration that exceeds 10 percent.

Event queries are purely declarative and do not consume or absorb any events. Accordingly, the same event can be matched by a rule multiple times. For instance, a smoke event may be matched twice if two suited temp events occur within the appropriate amount of time.

Deductive Rules. Deductive rules derive higher level events based on the occurrence of events in the stream. They correspond to materialized views from database systems.

```
DETECT
    fire{ var Area }
ON
    and{
        event e: smoke{ area{var Area}, amount{var C} },
        event f: temp{ area{var Area}, value{var T} }
    } where { {e,f} within 2 min, C > 0.1, T > 50 }
END
```

In their head deductive rules contain a data term with variables which are replaced by the values obtained during the evaluation of the query in the body of the rule. Note that the values for the unique identifier and the time of events are automatically determined by the system.

The given rule derives new `fire` events carrying the originating area of the fire in their payload whenever the query from above matches the stream of events.

3.2 Complex Actions for Dura

Complex actions aim at a high expressiveness with a full coverage of all four dimensions of actions. In the following, complex actions for Dura are introduced in the context of an emergency management related scenario that resembles the one given in the introduction.

Atomic Actions. Atomic actions are specified in a manner similar to the specification of atomic event queries.

```
action a: adapt-ventilation{ var Area }
```

However, instead of extracting values from the pattern, as in case of event queries, the values that are already bound to variables are injected to the corresponding actions as parameters.

Reactive Rules. Reactive rules are the counterpart of deductive rules. They trigger the execution of actions as a reaction to the occurrence of events. Note that there is no automatic conflict resolution for reactive rules matching the same events in Dura. Accordingly, all reactive rules matching the stream of events are always triggered. Conflicts between rules are explicitly resolved by adding further conditions to their event queries.

```
ON
    event e: fire{ var Area }
DO
    action a: adapt-ventilation{ var Area }
END
```

For the sake of simplicity, we assume that an enterprise service bus [10] is available and that external actuators are connected to the bus by means of appropriate adaptors.

Action Composition. Composition of complex actions is expressed in a manner similar to the composition of event queries. Several actions are grouped together by means of the compound operator and identifiers are introduced that refer to the actions they precede.

```
compound{
    action a: open-fire-dampers{ var Area },
    action b: activate-ventilators{ var Area }
}
```

Note that, due to the clear separation of orthogonal dimensions, compound is the only available operator that is required for the composition of actions. It just specifies the actions that are executed in combination with their concrete parameters, but does not describe further dependencies between actions. So in this case, both actions are simply executed concurrently.

Temporal Dependencies. Temporal dependencies between actions are specified in the where part of complex actions. They refer to the actions from the separate compound part by means of the action identifiers and specify the timing of actions. To this end, action identifiers are used in combination with *init*, *succ*, and *fail* to distinguish between the different time-points associated with the actions.

Temporal dependencies are specified by means of conjunctions of inequalities that determine lower bounds for the initiation of actions. For other applications it seems appropriate to furthermore support disjunctions of temporal dependencies that enable non-deterministic actions. However, for emergency management applications the determinism of actions is a crucial requirement and as a consequence, disjunctive dependencies are not further considered here although they can be integrated in our approach. An extension integrating disjunctive dependencies is discussed in Sec. 7.

```
compound{
    action a: open-fire-dampers{ var Area },
    action b: activate-ventilators{ var Area }
} where { succ(a) <= init(b) }
```

The preceding complex action uses temporal dependencies to specify that the ventilators should only be activated after the fire dampers have been successfully opened. Note that this behavior corresponds to a simple sequence of actions that can be also specified by many other approaches that support composite actions. However, due to the clear separation of dimensions more elaborated dependencies can be easily specified whereas approaches that interleave the composition of actions and their temporal dependencies in monolithic operators fail to express the following extension of the preceding example.

```
compound{
    action a: open-fire-dampers{ var Area },
    action b: activate-ventilators{ var Area },
    action c: warn-of-smoke-emission{ var Area }
} where { succ(a) <= init(b),
          init(c) + 20 sec <= init(b) }
```

The complex action is complemented by a third action that warns persons close to the outlet of the ventilation system of the imminent emission of smoke. To be effective, a time delay of 20 seconds between the issue of the warning and the actual emission of smoke is added to the temporal dependencies of the action.

Execution Result. Complex actions usually try to achieve a higher level goal that cannot be realised by individual actions. Naturally, the success of the action depends on the achievement of this goal which often cannot be inferred from the raw success of the comprising actions. As a consequence, Dura employs versatile event queries to specify the success of actions beyond the success of their sub-actions.

The success and failure of complex actions is specified in the dedicated succeeds on part by means of common event queries. The failure of actions is implicitly specified, as in emergency management actions are deemed as failed if they are not successful within a certain amount of time. The where part of the event query specifying the success of the action may as well refer to the time-points of sub-actions by means of their action identifiers.

Similar to the specification of the success of actions, the initiation of external non-composite actions can be specified by means of an initiated on part that is incorporated to the (schema) specification of the atomic action.

```
compound{
    action a: open-fire-dampers{ var Area },
    action b: activate-ventilators{ var Area }
} where { succ(a) <= init(b) }
  succeeds on {
    event e: smoke{ area{var Area}, amount{var C} }
      where { C < 0.2, end(e)-init(a) < 60 sec }
}
```

In this case, the action that is intended to extract smoke from a certain area is deemed successful if the smoke concentration drops below 20% in the respective area within one minute from the beginning of the action and fails otherwise. Note that the where part of the complex action and of the query in the succeeds on part are both referring to the open-fire-damper action by means of the identifier a.

Temporal Assertions. Temporal assertions are specified in the hence part of complex actions. They are denoted in a way that resembles the specification of temporal dependencies but are in general more expressive, as arbitrary combinations of conjunctions and disjunctions of inequalities can be specified. Temporal assertions serve to express additional formulas that must hold during runtime. Assertions that do not necessarily hold during runtime are detected during compile time and result in compilation errors.

Note that domain knowledge, such as, the maximal duration of the corresponding actions and the latency of the system, may be required to verify assertions during compile time. The available domain knowledge is specified in the schema of actions by means of inequalities similar to those of assertions. However, if no additional domain knowledge is available or if it is omitted from the schema, assertions may be falsely rejected due although they are actually always satisfied during runtime.

```
compound{
    action a: open-fire-dampers{ var Area },
    action b: activate-ventilators{ var Area }
} where { succ(a) <= init(b) }
    hence or{ succ(b)-init(a) <= 20 sec,
              fail(b)-init(a) <= 20 sec }
```

Assertions are used in this case to ensure that the sequential execution of open-fire-dampers and activate-ventilators is completed (regardless of its result) within 20 seconds. Recall that assertions do not influence the execution of actions and are just verified during compile time. To actually verify this particular assertion, reliable information on the duration of both actions and the latency needs to be available in the schema of the actions.

Complex Action Rules. Complex action rules assign names to (anonymous) complex actions in a way that resembles procedures that assign names to certain fragments of code.

```
FOR
    adapt-ventilation{ var Area }
DO
    compound{
        action a: open-fire-dampers{ var Area },
        action b: activate-ventilators{ var Area }
    } where { succ(a) <= init(b) }
    succeeds on {
        event e: smoke{ area{var Area}, amount{var C} }
            where { C < 0.2, end(e)-init(a) < 60 sec }
    }
END
```

Accordingly, the specified complex action can be executed by referring to its name adapt-ventilation instead of repeating the entire code of the body of the given rule.

3.3 Satisfying Temporal Dependencies

During runtime complex actions are actually executed by the event processing system according to their temporal dependencies. To this end, the system can defer actions whose initiation is explicitly specified in the temporal dependencies of the complex action.

To obtain clear and reasonable semantics, the system may not implicitly assume dependencies that are not explicitly specified by the user. In general, implicit assumptions are avoided in our approach as they influence the semantics of actions in a way that can easily be overlooked by programmers. Note that this is a major difference to approaches concerned with the planning and scheduling of actions [31].

To satisfy the following temporal dependency, the system simply defers the initiation of b until the success of a has been observed. If several dependencies for the initiation of an action are given, the system simply defers its initiation until all of them are satisfied.

```
where { succ(a) <= init(b) }
```

In contrast, the subsequent temporal dependency is invalid as it does not constrain the initiation of actions and can hence only be observed during runtime but cannot be satisfied in general without considering further dependencies.

```
where { succ(a) <= succ(b) }
```

In summary, temporal dependencies specify lower bounds for the initiation of actions that need to be exceeded before the action is requested by the system. Although the available constraints seem rather limited, we will determine that due to the inherent properties of external actions other dependencies cannot be satisfied in general.

The execution of complex actions can thus be understood as some kind of feedback loop. The event processing system requests the execution of actions which eventually results in the observation of their success or failure. This, in turn, determines the lower bounds for the initiation of further actions which will be eventually exceeded. Eventually these actions will be requested for execution and so forth.

4. SEMANTICS OF COMPLEX ACTIONS

The execution strategy of complex actions combined with the loose structure of temporal dependencies bears some pitfalls. For instance, cyclic dependencies can be specified that prevent some, or even all, actions from being executed during runtime. To overcome those undesirable effects while maintaining the expressiveness of the temporal constraints we elaborate a semantic analysis that is capable of detecting such situations during compile time.

However, to obtain a meaningful analysis, the correctness of an algorithm for the semantic analysis of actions must be verified formally. To this end, a formal semantics of complex actions is required that is generic enough to model physical action but that is at the same time specific enough to formally prove the desired properties.

4.1 Formalization of Complex Actions

For convenience, complex actions are formalized in a more concise manner that omits the verbose syntactic constructs of the language and contains only information that is crucial for the intended analysis.

Definition 1. The set of *variables* is denoted $\mathcal{V} = \mathcal{V}_o \cup \mathcal{V}_a$. For each action identifier f, the variable $f_{\mathrm{init}} \in \mathcal{V}_a$ is called *affected* variable and the variables $f_{\mathrm{succ}}, f_{\mathrm{fail}} \in \mathcal{V}_o$ are called *observed* variables.

Variables correspond to the times associated with actions and accordingly their values are determined by external components. However, the initiation of actions can be deferred by the system and thus the system can determine lower bounds for the value of affected variables whereas the values of observed variables can indeed just be observed.

Note that these notions resemble activated and received time-points from [31].

Definition 2. The set of *atomic temporal dependencies* is a set of triples denoted $\mathcal{C} = \mathcal{V} \times \mathbb{Q} \times \mathcal{V}$.

Informally these triples correspond to temporal dependencies of complex actions. For instance, $(a_{\mathrm{succ}}, 0, b_{\mathrm{init}}) \in \mathcal{C}$ corresponds to the dependency succ(a) <= init(b) from above. For convenience, $(u, d, u'), (v, -d, v'), (w, 0, w') \in \mathcal{C}$ can also be written $u + d \leq u'$, $v - d \leq v'$ and $w \leq w'$. Other relations, like $<$ and $\doteq$, are not considered here, but note that they can be expressed by means of the given ones.

Definition 3. A *complex action* C is formally represented by a conjunction of temporal dependencies $C = \bigwedge_i d_i$ with $d_i \in \mathcal{C}$.

Definition 4. The *assertions* H of complex actions are represented by conjunctions of disjunctions of temporal dependencies $H = \bigwedge_i \bigvee_j d_{ij}$ with $d_{ij} \in \mathcal{C}$.

Definition 5. The *domain knowledge D* on actions is obtained from their schema and represented just like their assertions are by $D = \bigwedge_i \bigvee_j d_{ij}$ with $d_{ij} \in \mathcal{C}$.

For convenience, a conjunction $C = \bigwedge_i d_i$ is represented by a set $C = \bigcup_i d_i$. As the number of dependencies is always finite, both representations are used interchangeably. Moreover, complex actions from Dura are formally identified by their corresponding set of temporal dependencies.

Definition 6. The *variables* of a complex action $C \subseteq \mathcal{C}$ are denoted

$$\text{var}(C) = \left\{ v \mid (v \dot{+} d \dot{\leq} v') \in C \lor (v' \dot{+} d \dot{\leq} v) \in C \right\}$$

Definition 7. The *axiomatic closure* of a complex action $C \subseteq \mathcal{C}$ is a set $C_{\mathcal{A}} \supseteq C$ that contains the following implicit axioms on sub-actions

$$C_{\mathcal{A}} = C \cup \bigcup_{f_{\text{init}} \in \text{var}(C)} \left\{ \perp_{\text{init}} \dot{\leq} f_{\text{init}}, f_{\text{init}} \dot{\leq} f_{\text{succ}}, f_{\text{init}} \dot{\leq} f_{\text{fail}} \right\}$$

whereby the special variable $\perp_{\text{init}} \in \mathcal{V}_o$ refers to the initiation of the complex action.

The additional dependencies that are introduced by the axiomatic closure ensure that no sub-action is initiated before the complex action has been initiated and that the success and failure of sub-actions occur after their initiation.

Example 2. The complex action `adapt-ventilation` from Sec. 3.2 is formally represented by the set $C = \{a_{\text{succ}} \dot{\leq} b_{\text{init}}\}$ with the axiomatic closure

$$C_{\mathcal{A}} = C \cup \{ \perp_{\text{init}} \dot{\leq} a_{\text{init}}, a_{\text{init}} \dot{\leq} a_{\text{succ}}, a_{\text{init}} \dot{\leq} a_{\text{fail}},$$
$$\perp_{\text{init}} \dot{\leq} b_{\text{init}}, b_{\text{init}} \dot{\leq} b_{\text{succ}}, b_{\text{init}} \dot{\leq} b_{\text{fail}} \}$$

The following domain knowledge on `open-fire-damper` actions limits their duration to 5 seconds.

$$D = \left\{ a_{\text{succ}} \dot{-} 5 \dot{\leq} a_{\text{init}} \lor a_{\text{fail}} \dot{-} 5 \dot{\leq} a_{\text{init}} \right\}$$

Note that the system latency can be specified in a similar manner by constraining the time between the initiation of actions and the end of their predecessors.

4.2 Formalizing Viable Temporal Dependencies

By design, complex actions in Dura only support temporal dependencies in their `where` part that specify lower bounds on the initiation of actions. However, this limitation is actually not specific for Dura but applies in general if the initiation of actions can only be indirectly affected.

To satisfy atomic temporal dependencies during runtime, there must be lower bounds for their affected variables so that the temporal dependencies are satisfied for all valid values of their observed variables. In the following we discriminate between *viable* dependencies for which proper lower bounds exist and *observable* dependencies that may not be satisfied in all situations.

There are four different categories of atomic dependencies. Note that atomic dependency with variables that refer to the same action, e.g., $a_{\text{succ}} \dot{-} 5 \dot{\leq} a_{\text{init}}$, are not considered in the following, because they are always observable as the duration of actions cannot be influenced by the system.

$(v_1 \dot{+} d \dot{\leq} v_2) \in \mathcal{V}_o \times \mathbb{Q} \times \mathcal{V}_o$: The variables v_1 and v_2 are both observed variables and hence the system has no

direct influence on their values. Accordingly, those kinds of dependencies are observable dependencies.

$(v_1 \dot{+} d \dot{\leq} v_2) \in \mathcal{V}_o \times \mathbb{Q} \times \mathcal{V}_a$: The value $\ell_2 = v_1 \dot{+} d$ is a lower bound for the affected variable v_2 so that the formula is satisfied for all values of the observed variable v_1. Accordingly those kinds of dependencies are viable dependencies. However, in practice, only $d \in \mathbb{Q}^+$ is reasonable, as the value of v_1 is not determined until it is exceeded.

$(v_1 \dot{+} d \dot{\leq} v_2) \in \mathcal{V}_a \times \mathbb{Q} \times \mathcal{V}_o$: There is no lower bound ℓ_1 for the affected variable v_1 that implies the formula (the assumption there is a bound ℓ_1 leads to a contradiction for $v_2 < \ell_1 + d$). Therefore, those kinds of dependencies are observed dependencies.

$(v_1 \dot{+} d \dot{\leq} v_2) \in \mathcal{V}_a \times \mathbb{Q} \times \mathcal{V}_a$: In general, there are no lower bounds ℓ_1 and ℓ_2 for v_1 and v_2 that imply the formula (the assumption there are such bounds leads to a contradiction for $v_2 < v_1 + d$). Accordingly, those kinds of dependencies are observed dependencies.

In summary, the set $\mathcal{V}_o \times \mathbb{Q}^+ \times \mathcal{V}_a$ exactly corresponds to the set of viable dependencies which can be satisfied during runtime by choosing the right lower bounds for their affected variable. Naturally, viable dependencies are specified in the `where` part of actions whereas observable dependencies are specified in their `hence` part where it is verified by the semantic analysis that they actually hold during runtime.

4.3 Semantics of Complex Actions

In order to prove properties of complex actions, their behaviour must be characterized in a formally precise manner. To this end, we develop a notion of runtime traces that formalizes the behavior of complex actions during runtime.

Definition 8. $\mathbb{P} = \mathbb{Q}^+ \cup \{\infty\}$ and $\mathbb{D} = \mathbb{Q}^+ \cup \{\infty\}$ denote the set of *time-points* and the set of *durations*. Time-points and durations can be added up in a canonical manner

$$+ : \mathbb{P} \times \mathbb{D} \to \mathbb{P}, \ (p, d) \mapsto (p + d).$$

The terms are discriminated to emphasise their different semantics. Durations will be used to describe possible delays during runtime whereas time-points will refer to the absolute times, for instance, at which time an action succeeded.

Definition 9. A *variable assignment* maps variables to values in $\mathbb{D}$ or $\mathbb{P}$. In the following, variable assignments are denoted by sets of variable value pairs as it is known from substitutions used in model theory [2].

Variable assignments can be naturally applied to composite syntactical expressions. For $v_i \in \mathcal{V}$ and $d_i \in \mathbb{Q}^+$

$$\tau(v_1 \dot{+} d_1) = \tau(v_1) + d_1$$
$$\tau\left(\{v_1 \dot{+} d_1, \ldots, v_k \dot{+} d_k\}\right) = \left\{\tau(v_1 \dot{+} d_1), \ldots, \tau(v_k \dot{+} d_k)\right\}$$

Definition 10. Given a complex action $C \subseteq \mathcal{C}$, a variable assignment $\Delta : \text{var}(C) \to \mathbb{P}$ is called a *trace* of C.

Traces are intended to describe the execution of actions. To this end, a trace maps variables corresponding to the initiation, success and failure of sub-actions to actual time-points. Thereby the value $\infty \in \mathbb{P}$ indicates that an action has not been initiated, did not succeed, and did not fail.

Obviously not every arbitrary trace corresponds to how the action is actually executed during runtime. Some sub-actions may, according to the trace, be successful before they begin, the temporal dependencies of the complex action may not be satisfied by the trace, etc. To obtain a more appropriate representation of complex actions, traces need to incorporate the temporal dependencies between actions and the execution strategy for actions.

However, in general, it cannot be known in advance how long it will take to execute an external action and whether the execution will be successful or not. Therefore these runtime effects are abstracted away by means of so-called scenarios.

Definition 11. Given a complex action $C \subseteq \mathcal{C}$, a variable assignment $\Delta : \mathrm{var}(C) \to \mathbb{D}$ is called a *scenario* of C. For convenience $\Delta(v)$ is also denoted Δ_v.

Each scenario describes one particular series of developments for the different outcomes of sub-actions and time delays that can potentially occur during runtime.

Example 3. The scenario $\delta \supseteq \big\{ 7/\bot_{\mathrm{init}}, 1/a_{\mathrm{init}}, 5/a_{\mathrm{succ}},$ $\infty/a_{\mathrm{fail}} \big\}$ describes, e.g., that the action a is initiated 1 ms after it has been requested and succeeds 5 ms after it has been initiated.

Definition 12. For a complex action C the *preconditions* for the determination of a variable $v \in \mathrm{var}(C)$ are denoted

$$\mathrm{pre}_C(v) = \Big\{ v_i \dotplus d_i \ \Big| \ (v_i \dotplus d_i \dot\leq v) \in C \Big\}$$

Informally, the preconditions of a variable f_{init} is the set of lower bounds which must each be exceeded before the action f can be requested by the event processing system. Therefore, the time-point when the action is actually initiated depends on the largest of those bounds and the latency between the request and the initiation which is available from the considered scenario.

Definition 13. Given a complex action $C \subseteq \mathcal{C}$ and a runtime scenario Δ. Then the operator $T_{\Delta,C}$ maps variable assignments to variable assignments with

$$T_{\Delta,C}(\sigma) = \Big\{ \Big(\max \big\{ \sigma\big(\mathrm{pre}_C(v)\big) \big\} + \Delta_v \Big) \Big/ v \ \Big|$$
$$\forall v' \in \mathrm{var}\big(\mathrm{pre}_C(v)\big) : v' \in \mathrm{dom}(\sigma) \Big\}$$

Hereby $\max \emptyset = 0 \in \mathbb{P}$ and thus the operator $T_{\Delta,C}$ is actually a mapping between (incomplete) traces.

T formalizes on step of the feedback loop described in Sec. 3.3. It takes as an argument an incomplete trace that contains the values of variables that have already been observed and adds values for the initiation, success and failure of actions in response to the given (observed) values in compliance with the scenario Δ. To obtain a complete trace, the operator is applied multiple times to incrementally determine values for all variables of the action C.

Note that the operator T makes a transition from merely syntactic formulas on the right to actual time-points that are assigned to v on the left.

Definition 14. The *powers* of T are inductively defined by

$$T^0 = \emptyset, \ T^{n+1} = T(T^n)$$

and the *least fixpoint* of T is denoted $\mathbf{T}$.

As the operator T is monotonic [2], it has a unique least fixpoint. Moreover, the fixpoint is reached after a finite number of iterations. For a formal proof refer to the appendix in the electronic version of this paper [17].

Basically, the fixpoint $\mathbf{T}$ describes, based on one particular scenario, how the action will be executed by the system if the given delays are actually observed during runtime.

Example 4. A complete iteration of T is given in the following example. Note that not only the initiation of actions, but also the time-point of their success and failure are determined by T according to the scenario Δ. For $C = \big\{ a_{\mathrm{succ}} \dotplus 5 \ \dot\leq \ b_{\mathrm{init}} \big\}$ and with $T = T_{\Delta,C_\mathcal{A}}$

$$T^1 = \big\{ \Delta_{\bot_{\mathrm{init}}} / \bot_{\mathrm{init}} \big\}$$
$$T^2 = T^1 \cup \big\{ \Delta_{\bot_{\mathrm{init}}} + \Delta_{a_{\mathrm{init}}} / a_{\mathrm{init}} \big\}$$
$$T^3 = T^2 \cup \big\{ \Delta_{\bot_{\mathrm{init}}} + \Delta_{a_{\mathrm{init}}} + \Delta_{a_{\mathrm{succ}}} / a_{\mathrm{succ}} \big\}$$
$$\cup \big\{ \Delta_{\bot_{\mathrm{init}}} + \Delta_{a_{\mathrm{init}}} + \Delta_{a_{\mathrm{fail}}} / a_{\mathrm{fail}} \big\}$$
$$T^4 = T^3 \cup \big\{ \Delta_{\bot_{\mathrm{init}}} + \Delta_{a_{\mathrm{init}}} + \Delta_{a_{\mathrm{succ}}} + 5 + \Delta_{b_{\mathrm{init}}} / b_{\mathrm{init}} \big\}$$
$$T^5 = T^4 \cup \big\{ \Delta_{\bot_{\mathrm{init}}} + \Delta_{a_{\mathrm{init}}} + \Delta_{a_{\mathrm{succ}}} + 5 + \Delta_{b_{\mathrm{init}}} + \Delta_{b_{\mathrm{succ}}} / b_{\mathrm{succ}} \big\}$$
$$\cup \big\{ \Delta_{\bot_{\mathrm{init}}} + \Delta_{a_{\mathrm{init}}} + \Delta_{a_{\mathrm{succ}}} + 5 + \Delta_{b_{\mathrm{init}}} + \Delta_{b_{\mathrm{fail}}} / b_{\mathrm{fail}} \big\}$$
$$T^6 = T^5 = \mathbf{T}$$

With the concrete scenario δ from Ex. 3 and $T = T_{\delta,C_\mathcal{A}}$

$$\mathbf{T}(\bot_{\mathrm{init}}) = 7, \quad \mathbf{T}(a_{\mathrm{init}}) = 8, \quad \mathbf{T}(a_{\mathrm{succ}}) = 13$$

which means that the complex action is initiated at time 7, a is initiated at time 8 and succeeds at time 13. However, by design, the fixpoint $\mathbf{T}$ may not contain values for all variables of the complex action.

Example 5. For $C = \big\{ a_{\mathrm{succ}} \dotplus 5 \dot\leq b_{\mathrm{init}}, \ b_{\mathrm{succ}} \dotplus 3 \dot\leq a_{\mathrm{init}} \big\}$ the event processing system will neither initiate a nor b during runtime as both actions depend on each other. Accordingly, runtime traces of C must provide ∞ as a time-point of a_{init} and b_{init}. However, the fixpoint of $T = T_{\Delta,C_\mathcal{A}}$ expresses this by containing neither of both variables instead of mapping the variables to ∞.

$$T^0 = \emptyset, \quad T^1 = \big\{ \Delta_{\bot_{\mathrm{init}}} / \bot_{\mathrm{init}} \big\}, \quad T^2 = T^1 = \mathbf{T}$$

This observation leads to the following definition of runtime traces, which informally maps missing values to ∞.

Definition 15. Suppose $C \subseteq \mathcal{C}$ is a complex action. A trace of C is called *runtime trace* if there is a scenario Δ such that for $T = T_{\Delta,C_\mathcal{A}}$ holds

$$\tau|_{\mathrm{dom}(\mathbf{T})} = \mathbf{T}$$
$$\forall v \notin \mathrm{dom}(\mathbf{T}) : \ \tau(v) = \infty$$

and furthermore for all $f_{\mathrm{init}} \in \mathrm{dom}(\mathbf{T})$ holds

$$\mathbf{T}(f_{\mathrm{init}}) \neq \infty \implies \big(\mathbf{T}(f_{\mathrm{succ}}) \neq \infty \iff \mathbf{T}(f_{\mathrm{fail}}) = \infty \big) \ \ (\star)$$

Runtime traces formally describe how complex actions are executed during runtime based on a scenario that describes the time delays that occur and determines the results of actions. They are used in the following to formally analyse the runtime properties of complex actions.

The condition $(\star)$ ensures that actions eventually either succeed or fail if they are initiated. This fundamental assumption seems very natural for actions in general and in particular for emergency management purposes. It is thus directly incorporated into the definition of runtime traces. Note that less generic properties of specific actions can be specified in the domain knowledge associated with their schema when necessary.

5. SEMANTIC ANALYSIS OF ACTIONS

5.1 Preliminaries

Definition 16. A *disjunctive temporal problem* (DTP) [29] is a conjunction of disjunctive constraints $\bigwedge_i \bigvee_j c_{ij}$, where the c_{ij} have the form $l \leq v - v' \leq u$, v and v' represent variables that designate time-points, and $l, u \in \mathbb{Q}$.

Checking the consistency of a DTP is known to be NP-hard and there are extensions with the domain $\mathbb{Q} \cup \{\infty\}$ and with support of strict inequalities [29, 5].

In the following, the execution of complex actions that is formalized by runtime traces is expressed by means of solutions to disjunctive temporal problems. In this way, the entailment of assertions can be reduced to the inconsistency of a DTP which can be verified by established approaches.

Definition 17. A *dependency graph* is a directed weighted graph given by a triple $G = (V, E, w)$ of the set of vertices $V \subseteq \mathcal{V}$, the set of edges $E \subseteq V \times V$ and the weight function $w : E \to \mathbb{Q}$. Furthermore, the notation $v \overset{p}{\leadsto} v'$ indicates that there is a *path* p from v to v' in the graph.

A complex action C is represented by means of a dependency graph G_C by adding an edge $v \longrightarrow v'$ labeled $-d$ to the graph for each $(v' \dot{+} d \leq v) \in C$. Note that a similar representation is used to solve simple temporal problems, a variation of DTPs, in polynomial time [12].

The graph representation of a complex action is used in the following to conveniently verify fairness properties of the action by checking properties of the graph.

Definition 18. The *canonical domain knowledge* of a complex action C is a DTP that corresponds to $(\star)$ from Def. 15. With $v \doteq \infty$ abbreviating $\perp_{\text{init}} \dot{+} \infty \leq v$ it is denoted

$$C_{\mathcal{D}} = \bigwedge_{f_{\text{init}} \in \text{var}(C)} \left(\left(f_{\text{succ}} \doteq \infty \land f_{\text{fail}} \dot{<} f_{\text{succ}} \right) \lor \left(f_{\text{fail}} \doteq \infty \land f_{\text{succ}} \dot{<} f_{\text{fail}} \right) \lor f_{\text{init}} \doteq \infty \right)$$

5.2 Formal Properties of Complex Actions

For space limitations we just give the intuition behind the proofs here and refer the interested reader to the appendix in the extended electronic version of this paper [17].

Definition 19. A complex action $C \subseteq \mathcal{C}$ is *fair* iff for all $f_{\text{init}} \in \text{var}(C)$ there is a runtime trace τ with $\tau(f_{\text{init}}) \neq \infty$.

The preceding definition formalizes the notion of fairness from Sec. 2.4. Accordingly an action is fair, if for each of its sub-actions there is at least one scenario in which the sub-action is actually executed. That is, the complex action contains no "dead code" which is never executed during runtime.

THEOREM 1. *A complex action C is fair iff $G_{C_{\mathcal{A}}}$ is acyclic and there is no node v and no action f_{init} such that $v \leadsto f_{\text{succ}}$ and $v \leadsto f_{\text{fail}}$ are paths in $G_{C_{\mathcal{A}}}$.*

Algorithm 1: Viability, Fairness, and Entailment Test

input : a complex action C with assertions H and domain knowledge D

if $C \setminus (\mathcal{V}_a \times \mathbb{Q}^+ \times \mathcal{V}) \neq \emptyset$ **then** /* ensure viability */
    | **fail** C cannot be reliably executed;

$(V, E, w) \leftarrow (\emptyset, \emptyset, \emptyset)$; /* initialize graph structure */

foreach $(v + d \leq v') \in C_{\mathcal{A}}$ **do** /* populate graph */
    | $V \leftarrow V \cup \{v, v'\}$;
    | $E \leftarrow E \cup \{(v', v)\}$;
    | $w \leftarrow w \cup \{(v', v) \mapsto -d\}$;

if (V, E, w) *is cyclic* **then** /* ensure fairness */
    | **fail** C is not fair;

if $v \leadsto f_{\text{succ}}$ *and* $v \leadsto f_{\text{fail}}$ *are paths in* (V, E, w) **then**
    | **fail** C is not fair; /* ensure entailment */

if $C_{\mathcal{A}} \land C_{\mathcal{D}} \land D \land \neg H$ *is inconsistent* **then**
    | **fail** the assertions H are not necessarily satisfied;

PROOF (SKETCHED). Paths in the graph correspond to temporal dependencies and because of $(\star)$ actions either succeed or fail. Accordingly, if there are cyclic dependencies in the graph or the execution of an action depends on the success and failure of one of its predecessors, the preconditions of the actions cannot be met and thus it is never executed and the complex action is not fair. □

The following theorem establishes a relationship between runtime traces which formalize the execution of actions and solutions of disjunctive temporal problems which are derived from the temporal dependencies of the complex action.

THEOREM 2. *A trace τ of a complex action C is a runtime trace iff the variable free formula $\tau(C_{\mathcal{A}} \land C_{\mathcal{D}})$ holds.*

PROOF (SKETCHED). By definition of T, the values in $\mathbf{T}$ satisfy the constraints from $C_{\mathcal{A}}$. Moreover, the definition of runtime traces excludes solutions of $C_{\mathcal{A}}$ that do not satisfy $(\star)$ which is formalized by $C_{\mathcal{D}}$. Accordingly, runtime traces satisfy $C_{\mathcal{A}} \land C_{\mathcal{D}}$ and conversely from every solution of $C_{\mathcal{A}} \land C_{\mathcal{D}}$ an appropriate scenario can be constructed that specifies a runtime trace. □

Definition 20. The assertions H of a complex action C with domain knowledge D are *entailed* iff for all runtime traces τ of C that conform to D the variable free formula $\tau(H)$ holds.

Accordingly, assertions are entailed, if they hold for every runtime trace of the corresponding actions, that is, if they hold for every way an action can be executed during runtime.

THEOREM 3. *The assertions H of a fair complex action C with the domain knowledge D are entailed iff the disjunctive temporal problem $C_{\mathcal{A}} \land C_{\mathcal{D}} \land D \land \neg H$ is inconsistent.*

PROOF (SKETCHED). Runtime traces correspond to the solutions of $C_{\mathcal{A}} \land C_{\mathcal{D}}$. However, not all runtime traces obey the restrictions specified by the domain knowledge. Accordingly, runtime traces that conform to the domain knowledge must satisfy D and thus they are solutions of $C_{\mathcal{A}} \land C_{\mathcal{D}} \land D$.

To verify that all those traces imply the assertions H, it suffices to show that $(C_{\mathcal{A}} \land C_{\mathcal{D}} \land D) \Rightarrow H$ is valid and thus that $C_{\mathcal{A}} \land C_{\mathcal{D}} \land D \land \neg H$ is inconsistent. □

These established connections are exploited by Algorithm 1 to check the fairness of actions and entailment of assertions by means of basic graph properties and the inconsistency of disjunctive temporal problems which can be verified in finite time by approaches like [5]. The comlexity of Algorithm 1 is dominated by the complexity of checking the consistency of DTPs which is known to be NP-hard [29].

6. COMPLEX ACTIONS IN CEP SYSTEMS

To obtain a generic approach that is applicable to a wide range of event processing systems, we represent the execution of actions by means of events and translate complex actions and reactive rules to regular complex event queries. In this way, we obtain the functionality of complex actions by actually evaluating a set of conventional event queries.

For the sake of simplicity, we assume that complex actions have a proper name and anonymous complex actions have been eliminated in a preprocessing step by introducing complex action rules for them.

6.1 Modelling Actions by Means of Events

Each action that is conceptually available in the language is mapped to four special types of events representing the request, initiation, success, and failure of the action. For instance, the open-fire-dampers action is represented by the following four types of events.

```
open-fire-dampers$request    open-fire-dampers$initiated
open-fire-dampers$succeeded   open-fire-dampers$failed
```

The payload of these events contains the parameters of the action and additional internal information, such as, a unique identifier to discriminate different instances of the same action and, if applicable, a reference to the identifier of the composite action that caused its execution. Moreover, the time-points associated with actions correspond to the occurrence times of the respective events.

6.2 Translation of Reactive Rules

Conceptually, reactive rules trigger the execution of actions. They are thus translated to deductive rules that derive request events which are distributed to the according actuators where they trigger the actual execution of the action. The reactive rule from Sec. 3.2 is thus converted to

```
DETECT
    adapt-ventilation$request{ payload{var Area} }
ON
    event e: fire{ var Area }
END
```

Recall that the identifier and the time of events are determined by the system. Accordingly, the identifier of the request event designates the identifier of the respective action.

6.3 Translation of Complex Actions

In the following, the basic ideas of translating complex actions will be introduced based on the complex actions adapt-ventilation from Sec. 3.2.

Temporal Dependencies. Temporal dependencies referring to certain time-points of actions occur for instance in the where part of actions and of event queries contained in the succeeds on part. Therefore, the contained references to actions need to be converted to references to events.

To this end, queries of events related to the corresponding actions are introduced and the references to time-points

of actions are subsequently converted into references to the time of the introduced events. For instance, the query

```
event e: smoke{ area{var Area}, amount{var C} }
    where { C < 0.2, end(e)-init(a) < 30 sec }
```

taken from the succeeds on part of the adapt-ventilation action contains init(a) which refers to the initiation of the open-fire-dampers action. The query is thus converted to

```
and{
    event bot$init: adapt-ventilation$initiated{ id{var I} }
    event a$init: open-fire-dampers$initiated{ ref{var I} }
    event e: smoke{ area{var Area}, amount{var C} }
} where { C < 0.2, end(e)-end(a$init) < 30 sec }
```

Note that the join between the identifier of the complex action adapt-ventilation and the identifier referred by the initiation event of the open-fire-dampers action is mandatory to distinguish open-fire-dampers actions related to this instance of the complex action from those that just happen to be initiated at the same time and relate to other action instances or other complex actions.

In a similar manner, the preconditions $\{\perp_{\mathrm{init}}\dot{+}0,\ a_{\mathrm{succ}}\dot{+}0\}$ of the activate-ventilators actions from the same complex action are translated to the following query.

```
and{
    event bot$init: adapt-ventilation$initiated{ id{var I} },
    event a$succ: open-fire-dampers$succeeded{ ref{var I} }
} where { end(bot$init) + 0ms <= now(),
          end(a$succ) + 0ms <= now() }
```

It matches whenever the activate-ventilators can be initiated without violating any temporal dependencies of the complex action, that is, when all lower bounds that constrain the initiation of activate-ventilators are exceeded.

Action Composition. The semantics of composite actions specify that each sub-action is executed as soon as the lower bounds for their initiation are exceeded. To obtain the same behaviour by means of deductive rules, all sub-actions of a composite action are separated into independent rules, each of them responsible for the execution of one particular action in accordance with the temporal dependencies of the complex action.

To this end, the event query that monitors the preliminaries of each sub-action is determined as discussed above. These queries are subsequently included in the body of declarative rules that derive the appropriate request events. Note that the event query corresponding to the preliminaries of a sub-action always contains a query for the initiation of the complex action and thus the parameters required for the execution of sub-actions can be obtained from the payload of the queried initiated event.

```
DETECT
activate-ventilators$request{ ref{var I}, payload{var A} }
ON
and{
    event bot$init:
      adapt-ventilation$initiated{ id{var I}, payload{var A} }
    event a$succ: open-fire-dampers$succeeded{ ref{var I} }
} where { end(bot$init) + 0ms <= now(),
          end(a$succ) + 0ms <= now() }
END
```

Accordingly, the execution of the activate-ventilators action is handled by the given deductive rule. Note that the query for adapt-ventilation$initiated events has been extended to extract the area that is passed to the action activate-ventilators as a parameter.

Execution Results. Translating the execution result specified in the succeeds on part of a complex action is straight forward. References to sub-actions in the where part of the query are rewritten as it has been described above and a deductive rule with the obtained query is created that derives the corresponding adapt-ventilation$succeeded event.

To obtain the query for the failed event, the same procedure is applied to the negation of the succeeds on query. To this end, the query in the succeeds on part needs to be timely bounded with respect to at least one time-point of an action. Due to space limitations, the simple but rather longish rules are only contained in the appendix of [17].

7. EXTENSIONS

Conditional Actions. Temporal dependencies of complex actions specify the execution order of actions relative to their initiation and success. However, in some situations it may be more suitable to specify the execution of actions in relation to the current state of the infrastructure, static data, or the occurrence of certain events instead of referring to the initiation and success of preceding actions.

This functionality can be added to Dura by means of conditional actions that block the execution of actions until a given event query matches. Recall, that in Dura event queries integrate queries for static and dynamic data.

```
compound{
    action a: request-operator-confirmation{ ... }
    IF event e: request-confirmed{ ref{id(action a)} }
        where { end(e)-succ(a) <= 20 sec }
    THEN action b: ...
}
```

The former action requests a confirmation from the operator and only executes the action b if the request is confirmed within 20 seconds. The translation of conditional actions corresponds to the translation of the execution result of actions. But instead of deriving succeeded and failed events, the corresponding request events are derived.

Disjunctive Temporal Dependencies. To obtain a deterministic specification of actions, the where part of complex actions must not contain disjunctive dependencies, such as

$$\text{or}\{ \ succ(a) <= init(b), \ succ(a) <= init(c) \ \}$$

However, if all temporal dependencies in a disjunction refer to the initiation of the same action, they correspond to a join of different execution branches and the execution of the complex action remains deterministic.

$$\text{or}\{ \ succ(a) <= init(c), \ fail(b) <= init(c) \ \}$$

The translation of temporal dependencies to event queries also applies for this kind of disjunctive constraints, it just needs to be slightly extended to ensure that the action is only initiated once, e.g., if in this example a is successful and b fails. The proposed semantic analysis can be reused by applying it to every disjunct of the disjunctive normal form of the corresponding dependencies. Accordingly, the analysis rejects the complete action if it rejects a single disjunct, as the dependencies must be met in any case.

8. RELATED WORK

Many approaches combining event detection and reaction rules have been proposed and studied by the research community. In fact, many of them are capable of specifying reactions to events in one way or another.

Complex Event Processing Most event processing systems support some kind of reactivity [19]. However, reactions are often dedicated to proprietary systems by means of remote procedure calls or some imperative host languages without a notion of complex actions. Notable exceptions are works from Paschke et. al. [23] and Behrends et. al. [3]. Although the proposed languages are capable of specifying composite workflows they still lack a language level support of complex actions that is tailored to physical actions and conveniently integrates complex events. Furthermore they do not provide a semantic analysis that verifies, e.g., fairness properties of actions.

Active Databases Active databases [1, 15, 14] realise automatic reactions in response to events by means of event-condition-action (ECA) rules. ECA rules are well established and have been intensively studied [24], but due to their origin in databases, events and actions are often related to (composite) updates of the internal knowledge base or trigger basic remote procedure calls. The authors of [8] argue that it is possible to realize workflows by means of ECA rules, but identify substantial shortcomings of hand coded rules that mimic imperative constructs like sequences.

Logic Based Formalisms The event calculus [27, 21] and the situation calculus [20] provide logic based frameworks which are commonly used for abductive planning and reasoning about the implications of actions based on a formal description of actions and their effects. Many extensions have been proposed that support composite actions and the specification of workflows [26, 11]. However, the focus of these formal and thus rather minimalistic formalisms is on reasoning about actions given a formal specification of their effects in contrast to high-level actions intended for emergency managers that are executed as events occur.

Temporal Constraint Satisfaction Temporal constraint satisfaction problems [12, 28] are commonly applied in problems related to planing and scheduling. In particular approaches that analyse the presence of dynamic plans that adhere to given constraints and cover events with contingent durations [31, 29] and disjunctions of events [30] are related to the semantic analysis of complex actions. However, our analysis focuses on the validation of fairness properties of actions that can fail during runtime, whereas those approaches try to determine dynamic plans for the execution of actions.

9. CONCLUSIONS

This work introduces complex actions with a clear separation of orthogonal dimensions and expressive temporal dependencies that naturally integrate complex events and actions in a high-level language. Thereby the specific particularities of physical actions as they are desirable, for instance, for emergency management have been considered. Moreover, we demonstrated how to realize complex actions by means of common complex event queries.

To compensate for inconsistent specifications of actions that are possible due to the desirable flexibility of our approach we have elaborated a semantic analysis that is tailored to physical actions and that scales with the in practice often varying degree of available knowledge on actions.

The proposed approach has been applied to implement the use cases of an emergency management related project [18]. And although this has been our main motivation for this work, our findings generalize to other applications that rely on external or physical actions.

10. ACKNOWLEDGMENTS

We would like to thank N. Eisinger and S. Brodt for valuable suggestions and discussions on our work. This work has been partly founded by the European Commission within the project "EMILI— Emergency Management in Large Infrastructures" under grant agreement number 242438.

11. REFERENCES

[1] R. Adaikkalavan and S. Chakravarthy. SnoopIB: interval-based event specification and detection for active databases. *Data and Knowledge Engineering*, 59(1):139–165, 2006.

[2] K. R. Apt, H. A. Blair, and A. Walker. Towards a Theory of Declarative Knowledge. In *Foundations of deductive databases and logic programming*, pages 89–148. Morgan Kaufmann, 1988.

[3] E. Behrends, O. Fritzen, W. May, and F. Schenk. Combining ECA Rules with Process Algebras for the Semantic Web. In *Proc. Int. Conf. Rules and Rule Markup Languages for the Semantic Web*, pages 29–38. IEEE, 2006.

[4] M. Bettelini, S. Rigert, and N. Seifert. Optimum Emergency Management Through Physical Simulation— Findings from the EMILI Research Project. In *Proc. World Tunnel Congress*, 2013.

[5] S. Brodt and F. Bry. Temporal Stream Algebra. Technical report, University of Munich, 2012. http://www.pms.ifi.lmu.de/publications/.

[6] F. Bry and M. Eckert. Rule-based composite event queries: the language XChangeEQ and its semantics. In *Proc. Int. Conf. Web Reasoning and Rule Systems*, pages 16–30. Springer, 2007.

[7] F. Bry and M. Eckert. Rules for Making Sense of Events: Design Issues for High-Level Event Query and Reasoning Languages. In *AI Meets Business Rules and Process Management, Proc. AAAI Spring Symposium*. AAAI, 2008.

[8] F. Bry, M. Eckert, P.-L. Pătrânjan, and I. Romanenko. Realizing Business Processes with ECA Rules: Benefits, Challenges, Limits. In *Proc. Int. Workshop on Principles and Practice of Semantic Web*, pages 48–62. Springer, 2006.

[9] F. Bry and S. Schaffert. Towards a declarative query and transformation language for XML and semistructured data: Simulation unification. *Proc. Int. Conf. Logic Programming*, 2401:255–270, 2002.

[10] D. Chappell. *Enterprise Service Bus*. O'Reilly, 2004.

[11] N. K. Cicekli and Y. Yildirim. Formalizing Workflows Using the Event Calculus. In *Proc. Int. Conf. Database and Expert Systems Applications*, pages 222–231. Springer, 2000.

[12] R. Dechter, I. Meiri, and J. Pearl. Temporal constraint networks. *Artificial Intelligence*, 49(1-3):61–95, 1991.

[13] K. Fridolf. Fire evacuation in underground transportation systems: a review of accidents and empirical research. Technical report, Lund University, 2010.

[14] S. Gatziu and K. R. Dittrich. Detecting composite events in active database systems using Petri nets. In *Proc. Int. Workshop on Research Issues in Data Engineering*, pages 2–9. IEEE, 1994.

[15] N. H. Gehani, H. V. Jagadish, and O. Shmueli. Composite Event Specification in Active Databases: Model and Implementation. In *Proc. Int. Conf. Very Large Data Bases*, pages 327–338. Morgan Kaufmann, 1992.

[16] S. Hausmann, S. Brodt, and F. Bry. Dura: Concepts and Examples. Technical report, University of Munich, 2011. http://www.emili-project.eu/index.php?id=481.

[17] S. Hausmann and F. Bry. Towards Complex Actions for Complex Event Processing (Extended Version with Appendix). Technical report, University of Munich, 2013. http://www.pms.ifi.lmu.de/publications/.

[18] R. Llopis, X. Fust, J. a. González, J. L. Marín, N. Seifert, M. Bettelini, S. Rigert, V. Janev, P. Kroner, and D. Siller. Evaluation of our Simulation and Training Environment SITE and of our Use Case Implementations. Technical report, 2012. http://www.emili-project.eu/index.php?id=544.

[19] D. Luckham. *The Power of Events: An Introduction to Complex Event Processing in Distributed Enterprise Systems*. Addison Wesley, 2001.

[20] J. McCarthy and P. J. Hayes. Some philosophical problems from the standpoint of artificial intelligence. *Machine Intelligence*, 4:463–502, 1969.

[21] R. Miller and M. Shanahan. Some Alternative Formulations of the Event Calculus. In *Computational Logic: Logic Programming and Beyond*, pages 452–490. Springer, 2002.

[22] Fire Investigation Summary Düsseldorf. Technical report, National Fire Protection Association, 1998.

[23] A. Paschke, A. Kozlenkov, and H. Boley. A Homogeneous Reaction Rule Language for Complex Event Processing. *Proc. Int. Workshop Event Driven Architecture and Event Processing Systems*, 2007.

[24] N. W. Paton and O. Díaz. Active database systems. *ACM Computing Surveys*, 31(1):63–103, 1999.

[25] N. Seifert, M. Bettelini, and S. Rigert. Concrete Use Case Models (Main Report). Technical report, 2011. http://www.emili-project.eu/index.php?id=481.

[26] M. Shanahan. Event Calculus Planning Revisited. In *Proc. European Conf. Planning*, pages 390–402. Springer, 1997.

[27] M. Shanahan. The Event Calculus Explained. In *Artificial Intelligence Today*, volume 1600 of *LNCS*, pages 409–430. Springer, 1999.

[28] K. Stergiou and M. Koubarakis. Backtracking algorithms for disjunctions of temporal constraints. *Artificial Intelligence*, 120(1):81–117, 2000.

[29] I. Tsamardinos, T. Vidal, and M. E. Pollack. CTP: A New Constraint-Based Formalism for Conditional, Temporal Planning. *Constraints*, 8(4):365–388, 2003.

[30] K. B. Venable and N. Yorke-Smith. Disjunctive temporal planning with uncertainty. In *Proc. Int. Joint Conf. Artificial Intelligence*, pages 1721–1722. Morgan Kaufmann, 2005.

[31] T. Vidal and H. Fragier. Handling contingency in temporal constraint networks: from consistency to controllabilities. *Journal of Experimental and Theoretical Artificial Intelligence*, 11(1):23–45, 1999.

Reliable Speculative Processing of Out-of-Order Event Streams in Generic Publish/Subscribe Middlewares

Christopher Mutschler[1,2]
christopher.mutschler@fau.de

[1] University of Erlangen-Nuremberg
Department of Computer Science
Programming Systems Group
Erlangen, Germany

Michael Philippsen[1]
michael.philippsen@fau.de

[2] Fraunhofer Institute for Integrated Circuits IIS
Locating and Communication Department
Sensor Fusion and Event Processing Group
Erlangen, Germany

ABSTRACT

In surveillance, sports, finances, etc., distributed event-based systems are used to detect meaningful events with low latency in high data rate event streams. Both known approaches to deal with the predominant out-of-order event arrival at the distributed detectors have their shortcomings: buffering approaches introduce latencies for event ordering and stream revision approaches may result in system overloads due to unbounded retraction cascades.

This paper presents a speculative processing technique for out-of-order event streams that enhances typical buffering approaches. In contrast to other stream revision approaches our novel technique encapsulates the event detector, uses the buffering technique to delay events but also speculatively processes a portion of it, and adapts the degree of speculation at runtime to fit the available system resources so that detection latency becomes minimal.

Our technique outperforms known approaches on both synthetical data and real sensor data from a Realtime Locating System (RTLS) with several thousands of out-of-order sensor events per second. Speculative buffering exploits system resources and reduces latency by 40% on average.

Categories and Subject Descriptors

C.2.4 [**Computer-Comm. Networks**]: Distrib. Syst.—*Distrib. Applications*; D.1.3 [**Programming Techniques**]: Concurrent Programming—*Distributed Programming*

Keywords

Distributed Event Processing; Out-of-Order Event Processing; Publish/Subscribe; Message-oriented Middleware.

1. INTRODUCTION

Event-based systems (EBS) are the method of choice for a near-realtime, reactive analysis of data streams in many fields of application such as surveillance, sports, stock tradings, RFID-systems, and fraud detection in various areas [1].

EBS turn the high data load into events, and filter, aggregate, and transform them to higher level events until they reach a level of granularity that is appropriate for an end user application or to trigger some action. Often the performance requirements are high so that event processing needs to be distributed over several nodes. Many applications also demand event detection with minimal delays. For instance, our distributed EBS detects events to steer an autonomous camera control systems to points of interest, see Fig. 1. This obviously requires low detection latencies.

To process high rate event streams, an EBS usually splits the computation over several event detectors, linked by publish/subscribe to build an event detection hierarchy. These event detectors are distributed over the available machines. Events arrive at the distributed detectors out-of-order because of various types of delay. Ignoring the wrong order causes misdetection. Event detectors themselves cannot reorder the events with low latency because in general event delays are unknown before runtime. Moreover, as there are also dynamically changing application-specific delay types (like for instance a detection delay) there is no a-priori optimal assignment of event detectors to available nodes. Hence, in a distributed EBS the middleware deals with out-of-order events, typically without any a-priori knowledge on the event detectors, their distribution, and their subscribed events.

Buffering middleware approaches withhold the events for some time, sort them, and emit them to the detector in order. The main issue is the size of the ordering buffer. If it is too small, detection fails. If it is too large, it wastes time and causes high detection latency. Note that waiting times add up along the detection hierarchy. The best buffer sizes are unknown and may depend on some dynamic, unpredictable behavior. In addition, there is no need to buffer

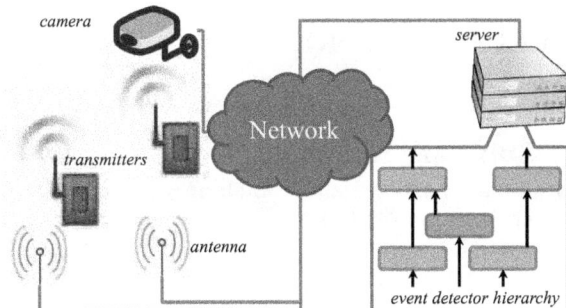

Figure 1: Automatically controlled camera system.

events that cannot be out-of-order or that can be processed out-of-order without any problems. Buffering middlewares are the basis of reliable event detection, but they are also too costly for many types of events and do not benefit from faster CPUs (as they are bound by the waiting times).

Speculative middlewares, the other approach to cope with out-of-order event arrivals, speculatively work on the raw event stream. As there is no buffering, this is faster. Whenever an out-of-order event is received, falsely emitted events are retracted and the event stream is replayed. The effort for event retraction and stream replay grows with the number of out-of-order events and with the depth of the detection hierarchy. This is a non-trivial challenge for the memory management, may exhaust the CPU, and may cause high detection latencies or even system failures. In contrast to buffer-based approaches, a stronger CPU helps, but the risk of high detection latencies remains.

To combine the advantages of both, this paper proposes to add a novel speculative processing to a buffering EBS. The most important requirements are: (1) The middleware can neither exploit the events' semantics nor their use by the event detectors because both of them are highly application-specific. Hence, methods for strong synchronization of event detectors are no viable option. (2) In spite of the speculation, the buffering middleware must keep event detection reliable, i.e., false-positive or false-negative detection must be avoided to prevent system failures. Hence, it is no option to use imprecise approximative methods or to discard events that would cause a system overload.

Our key idea is to use buffering to sort most of the events but to let a snapshot event detector speculatively and prematurely process those events that will be emitted soon. Event detectors are restored when a replay occurs. The degree of speculation is adapted to suit the CPU availability, ranging from full speculation on an idle CPU to plain buffering on a busy CPU. Our technique works without knowledge on internal event semantics, can be used for any publish/subscribe-based buffering middleware, and does not use query languages or event approximation.

The rest of the paper is organized as follows. Sec. 2 reviews related work. Sec. 3 provides basic definitions of the time-model and introduces the K-slack buffering that we use in the rest of the paper to present the novel speculation. The main contributions of this paper are covered in Sec. 4: a speculative event processing and snapshot recovery, two methods to efficiently retract events across the detection hierarchy, and a greedy method to adapt the amount of speculation at runtime to optimize detection latency by efficiently exploiting unused system resources. Sec. 5 evaluates our methods before Sec. 6 concludes.

2. RELATED WORK

As we know of no attempt to fully combine buffering and speculation in an EBS, we discuss both fields in turn.

2.1 Buffering Techniques

As we have explained above, buffering is needed for reliable event detection but also introduces latency. Below we sketch some known buffering EBS and show that for each of them an added speculative component might improve latency.

To deal with communication errors and timing uncertainties caused by the lack of a global clock in distributed sys-

tems O'Keeffe et al. [2] use time intervals instead of event time stamps. Buffered events are only emitted when time intervals safely overlap. Therefore, as latencies are high, an added speculative component that lowers the upper interval margin can reduce detection latency.

Punctuations [3, 4] are special annotations embedded into data streams to indicate (1) the end of a subset of data, and (2) that no event will be generated with a lower time stamp. For negative patterns like A!BC, where no B shall occur in between A and C, a buffering unit must use timed punctuations that introduce latency because firing a punctuation on each event will exhaust the system. An added speculation unit can help because punctuations can also be fired speculatively, so that events can be consumed earlier.

Srivastava et al. [5] model stream time differences and clock-skews between data sources. Their heartbeat stream synchronization among buffers introduces latency. Speculation can help by processing events before the heartbeats actually occur or by emitting the heartbeats prematurely.

SASE [6, 7, 8] and Cayuga [9, 10, 11, 12] both are event processing engines for RFID-readings that work with Non-deterministic Finite Automata generated from event queries. They assume that events are delayed for at most K time units, K to be set a-priori. Although both systems use query languages they can be applied for arbitrary middlewares. But their conservative and a-priori configuration causes high detection latencies in their delay buffers. Speculation can help by processing events before they have been buffered sufficiently long, i.e., for K time units.

2.2 Speculative Techniques

Known EBS speculation techniques are either based on query languages and window operators, are imprecise and approximate events, are unreliable, or use a-priori knowledge for their configurations. Hence, as they do not fulfill all the above-mentioned requirements for general purpose publish/subscribe middleware, known speculation techniques cannot be used as add-ons to a buffering system.

Approximative techniques [13, 14, 15, 16] use partial or imprecise events to generate the most likely query results first and refine the results incrementally on corrected and more precise events. To limit latency and resource consumption, some of the authors only retract events that have a strong impact on the generated output or use partial events to restore the correct state for the replay. However, as all those systems use query languages and are imprecise, they are unsuitable as a generic speculation component.

Another way to limit the degree of speculation (and hence latency and resource consumption) is to automatically discard older and unprocessed events from their queues and to process more recently received events instead [17]. However, this is only applicable to state-less event detectors. In general, event detector states depend on the discarded events so that detection fails if they are dropped.

A commit action resolves the speculation (the essence of transaction systems) into a reliable event detection step [18, 19]. But every out-of-order event increases the number of transactions, i.e., the degree of speculation, and results in potential CPU overload and hence system failure. That is why buffering EBS stay away from transaction speculation.

Window query approaches [20] pipe events through operator graphs that are constructed from queries. The degree of speculation is set by limiting historical operator states.

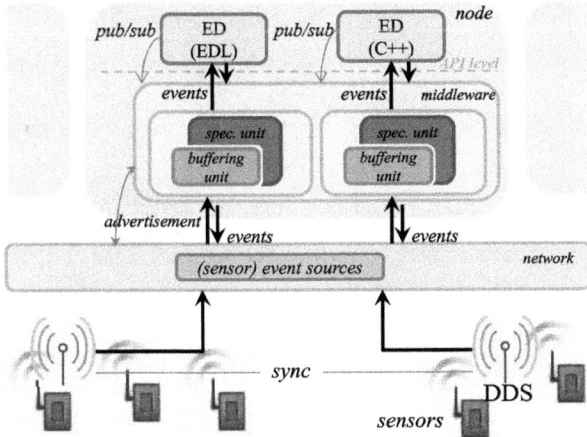

Figure 2: Distributed publish/subscribe EBS.

Unfortunately, window operators (such as multi-joins) need event detector definitions in a particular query language and are hence not general purpose.

Complex Event Detection and Response (CEDR) [21] speculatively generates events out of event streams that also may contain revision tuples enhanced with time stamp corrections. Upon a revision event arrival, CEDR only adjusts the time stamps of the generated event instead of retracting the event. But this brakes stateful event detectors that may already have consumed the generated event with the old time stamp, and may have generated a (false-positive) event because of the old time stamp.

Chandramouli et al. [22] limit speculation either by sequence numbers or by *cleanse*. The receiver can use the former to deduce disorder information in the rare cases when particular events are generated at stable rates. The latter only works for a punctuation-based environment, which must incorporate the event definition to limit query windows by setting the punctuation to the latest event time stamps of the event detector. Since the middleware technique cannot access this information, it cannot be used as a generic buffering extension.

3. BUFFERING EBS ENVIRONMENT

In this section, we illustrate the buffering in the hosting EBS that we extend with our novel speculative technique. Although Sec. 4 will build on top of this buffering, the novel speculation can easily be adopted by other buffering EBS because our speculation is general purpose and quite generic.

As can be seen in Fig. 2, our EBS consists of several data distribution services (DDS) that collect sensor data (for example an antenna that collects RFID readings), and several nodes in a network that run the same event processing middleware. The middleware creates a reordering buffer per event detector (ED). This is wrapped with the new speculation unit. The middleware deals with all types of delays such as processing and networking delays or detection delays[1] and does not need to know the complex event pattern that the detector implements (either in a native programming language [23] or in some EDL [6]). The detector does not need

[1]If events are generated with earlier time stamps than the time stamps of the events that cause them, they have a detection delay and can only be inserted into the event stream long after they have actually happened.

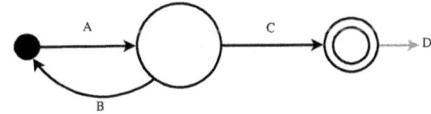

(a) Example for A!BC.

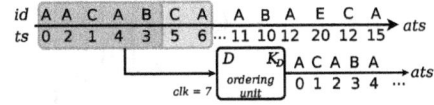

(b) Sorting window over event stream.

Figure 3: Out-of-order examples.

to know on which machine other event detectors are running nor their runtime configurations. The application code of the event detector assumes that the events are received in correct order with respect to their occurrence time stamps. At startup the middleware has no knowledge about event delays but just notifies other middleware instances about event publications and subscriptions (advertisement) [24]. The middleware is therefore generic and encapsulated.

Since our speculative buffer asks the event detector to provide and to restore snapshots, event detectors have to provide additional functionality. However, in many cases this can easily be achieved as snapshots are handled transparently to the (application) code in the event detector that is used to process the event stream.[2]

3.1 Time Model Semantics

We use the following terminology throughout the paper:
Event type, instance and time stamps. An event type defines an interesting occurrence and is identified by a unique ID. An event instance is an instantaneous occurrence of an event type at a point in time. It can be a primitive (sensor) or a composite event. An event has three time stamps: an occurrence, a detection, and an arrival. All time stamps are in the same discrete time domain according to our time model. An event appears at its occurrence time stamp ts, or just time stamp for short. It is detected at its detection time stamp dts. At arrival time stamp ats the event is received by a particular EBS node. The occurrence and the detection time stamp are fixed for an event at any receiving node whereas the arrival time stamp may vary at different nodes in the network.
Out-of-order event. Consider an event stream $e_1, \cdots e_n$. Events of type ID are used to set the local clock. Then e_j is out-of-order if there do not exist e_i, e_k, with $e_i.id = e_k.id = $ID and $e_i.ats \leq e_j.ats$ so that $e_i.ts \leq e_j.ts \leq e_k.ts$, i.e., $e_j.ats$ does not fit between two consecutive clock updates, see Sec. 3.2.
Event Stream. The input of an event detector is a potentially infinite event stream that usually is a subset of all events, holds at least the event types of interest for that detector, and may include some irrelevant events as well.

3.2 K-slack in a detector hierarchy

Consider the following example. To detect that a player kicked a ball, we wait for the events that a ball is near the player and then, that the ball is kicked, a peak in acceler-

[2]The application code does not need to care about data synchronization or side-effects as the middleware assures that no events are being processed by the detector while taking or restoring a snapshot.

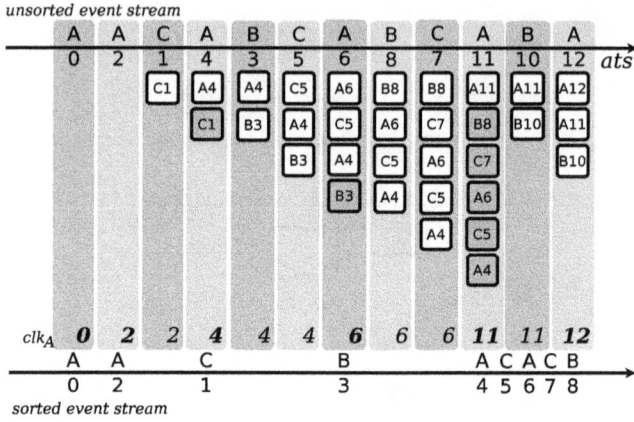

Figure 4: Ordering unit for event detector A!BC

ation. Between the two events there may not be the event that the ball leaves the player, because in that case the ball would just have dropped to the ground. More formally: if we receive event A (near) and subsequently C (acceleration peak) and not B (not near) in between, we generate event D.[3] Figure 3(a) gives a finite state automaton for event D. To simplify, we leave out the differentiation of transmitter IDs for player identification.

An exemplified event stream is depicted in Figure 3(b). The events in the stream are out-of-order and a naive processing of events will not lead the event detector to generate event D out of A4/C5 and will detect D out of A2/C1.[4]

To achieve a correct detection, the buffering middleware of our hosting EBS mounts a dynamically generated ordering unit based on K-slack between the event input stream and the event detector. K-slack [7, 25, 26] assumes that an event e_i can be delayed for at most K time units.

K-slack is a standard approach that works as follows (with dynamic buffer-resizing). A local clock clk is extracted out of the event stream by setting it to the occurrence time stamps of particular event types [26]. Hence, whenever clk is updated we can deduce the maximal delay of all events e_i that have been received since the last clk update by $\delta(e_i)=clk-e_i.ts$. Hence, for a particular event detector the ordering unit (that takes a stream with potential out-of-order events and produces a sorted event stream) must set K to the maximal delay of all its subscribed events, i.e., $K=\max_i [\delta(e_i)]$. This gives the initial size of the dynamically-sized buffer for event ordering. Hence, whenever we receive a new event we just insertion-sort it into the buffer. Whenever clk is updated and $e_i.ts+K\leq clk$ holds for some tail events e_i in the buffer, we emit those e_i to the output stream and purge them from the buffer as we can be sure that there will not be any event to be received in the future that has a time stamp lower than $e_i.ts$.

Fig. 4 shows the internals of the event ordering unit for the input stream of Figure 3(b). clk is set whenever an event of type A is received, see the bold values in the clk_A line. At the beginning when A0 and A2 are received, there are no measurements and K is still 0, which means that both

---

[3]This is similar to the book shelf reading example that is often used in applications combining RFID systems and EBS.
[4]Certainly this problem only arises when events are merged. However, this is necessary because we split computing across several event detectors and must iteratively summarize preliminary results (events).

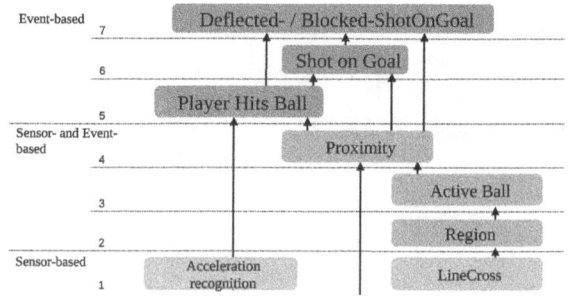

Figure 5: Event processing hierarchy.

events are immediately passed to the output stream, without being delayed at all (they fulfill $e_i.ts+K\leq clk_A$). When C1 is received, it is pushed to the buffer and waits until A4 updates clk_A. As the delay for C1 is 3=4-1, we set $K=3$ and emit C1 ($e_i.ts+K=1+3\leq clk_A$ =4). A4 is buffered at least until clk_A equals 7=4+K. With A6 the maximal delay of B3 is 3=6-3, K holds, and B3 is passed to the output stream. Hence, we extract both a local clock clk_A and K from the event stream to delay both late and early events as long as necessary to avoid out-of-order event processing at the event detector (after an initial calibration of the ordering unit).

Fig. 5 shows an event processing hierarchy for a *blocked shot on goal*. Each event detector in this hierarchy has its own dynamically parameterized ordering unit, and is configured to detect events with low latency. For instance, the *player hits ball* (level 5) event detector implements a pattern similar to that of Fig. 3(b). Its ordering unit introduces a latency of more than one second to guarantee an ordered event input to the detector. This delays the detection of a *shot on goal* (level 6) for at least one second (and the *blocked shot on goal* may be delayed even longer).

3.3 Motivation

Even if we use minimal K-values for all the detectors across the hierarchy, the resulting combined latencies may be unnecessarily high and a speculative processing may be the better option.

Assume the example in Fig. 3(b) needs a minimal $K_D=3$. This delays the detection of any event in upper processing hierarchies by at least 3 time units since event D can only be detected with 3 time units delay. However, assume that events of type B are rare. Then it may be advantageous not to delay the detection of D until we preclude the occurrence of B, but to retract a false-detection of D in the rare cases when B actually occurs. For the event stream in Fig. 3(b) we can hence detect D out of A4/C5 before clk is set to 8 (A4 is emitted at $clk=7$ whereas C5 must wait at least until $clk\geq 8$). If there is a B to cancel the detection of D later we retract D. Hence, the event detector that is used to detect D generates preliminary events that can be used to trigger event detectors on higher levels with low latency.

Hence, the key idea is to combine both techniques and to let the speculation unit wrap a K-slack buffer to process a portion of events prematurely.

4. SPECULATIVE PROCESSING

Added speculation results in improved detection latency if there are no out-of-order events at all, because nothing that an ordering unit emits and a detector generates has ever to

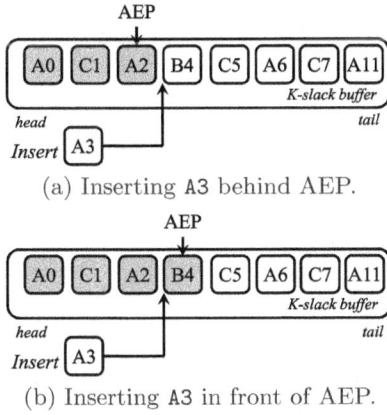

(a) Inserting A3 behind AEP.

(b) Inserting A3 in front of AEP.

Figure 6: K-slack's event insertion and AEP.

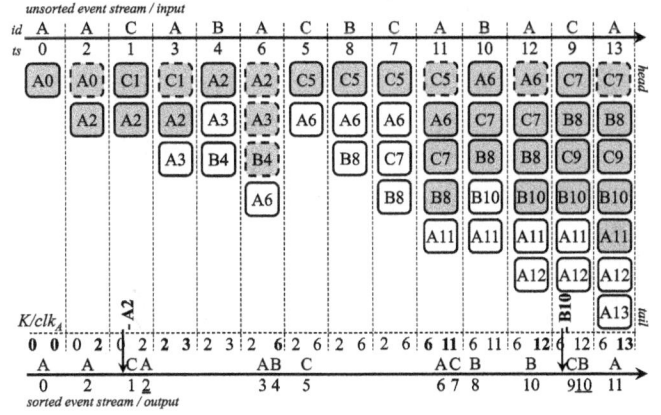

Figure 7: Speculative ordering unit with $\alpha = \frac{1}{3}$.

be retracted from further up the detector hierarchy. But the more out-of-order events there are and the deeper the detection hierarchy is, the more complex becomes the retraction work as more memory is needed to store the detector states and as more CPU time is needed to perform the retraction. Hence, in naive speculation approaches, the cost of purging the effects of false speculation can easily outweigh its beneficial effects and can easily increase the latency beyond what pure non-speculative buffering would have caused.

Therefore, the amount of speculation must be limited so that the CPU and memory are used at full capacity on the one side, but without getting exhausted on the other side. System parameters must be deduced at runtime and the speculative ordering units must be continuously adapted to the current system and event load. From now, we use the following terminology:

Event emission and replay. The ordering unit emits events to the event detector to process them. An event is emitted *prematurely* if it is emitted before K-slack would emit it. When an event detector produces an event and sends it to the middleware we say an event is *generated*. Whenever the ordering unit detects a miss-speculation the event stream is replayed. In those cases particular (premature) events are emitted repeatedly to the event detector, see Sec. 4.1.

Event retraction. Whenever the ordering unit detects a miss-speculation, events may have been mistakenly processed and need to be retracted. We have to consider two different issues. First, events have been emitted to the event detector in a wrong order and the event stream is immediately replayed. This is solved by *snapshot recovery*, see Sec. 4.2. Second, the event detector may have generated events based on the incorrectly ordered event input. These events may already have been inserted into the ordering units' buffers of upper level event detectors or may even have been emitted prematurely. Hence, events must be retracted throughout the entire detector hierarchy, see Sec. 4.3.

4.1 Event Emission and Replay

Our speculative event processing technique extends K-slack buffering approches. It puts most of the input events in order but it does not buffer them as required for a perfectly correct order. Instead of buffering an event e_i for K time units, we only buffer e_i as long as

$$e_i.\text{ts} + \alpha \cdot K \leq clk, \qquad \alpha \in [0;1], \qquad (1)$$

with a new attenuation factor α. The attenuation factor

is used to adjust the speculation component. The larger α is, the fewer events are emitted prematurely, i.e., $\alpha=1$ is essentially a K-slack without speculation. Smaller values for α switch on speculation. For $\alpha=0$, there is no buffering/ordering at all because the inequation always holds (except for events with negative delays[5]). For instance, a classic event ordering unit with $K=5$ and $\alpha=1$ will emit an event with $ts=20$ that is received at $clk=22$ not before clk is at least 25. Only then $e_i.\text{ts}+K=20+5\leq25=clk$. Pure buffering middlewares will not just emit the events but they will also purge them from the buffer. In the example with $K=5$ but with $\alpha=0.6$ the speculative buffer prematurely emits the event already at $clk=23$ ($20+0.6\cdot5=23$). With $\alpha\leq0.4$ emission is even instantly at $clk=22$.

With speculation, events are emitted but no longer instantly purged from the buffer. They may be needed for the event replay later. Hence, the K-slack buffer is enhanced with an *already emitted pointer* (AEP) that is a reference to the last element in the buffer that has already been emitted speculatively.

A newly arriving event is inserted into the sorting buffer according to its time stamp. For instance, in Fig. 6(a) and 6(b) A3 is inserted between A2 and B4. The events from the buffer's head to AEP (shown in grey) have already been emitted. Depending on α, clk, K, and AEP there are two possible cases:

$\mathbf{e_i.ts > e_{AEP}.ts}$: If the time stamp of the recent event e_i is larger than that of the AEP, no false-speculation has occurred, and hence no events need to be retracted or replayed. In Fig. 6(a) A0 to A2 have been prematurely emitted, and A3 is not missing in the stream that is already on the go.

$\mathbf{e_i.ts \leq e_{AEP}.ts}$: If the time stamp of the new event is smaller that that of the AEP the falsely emitted events must be retracted by means of the methods that we describe in Sec. 4.3. The AEP is set to e_i and the events from the buffer's head to the new AEP are replayed. In Fig. 6(b) the event B4 must be retracted, and A3 can be emitted prematurely before replaying B4.

Whenever clk is updated the speculative buffer emits all the events that fulfill inequation (1). Events are purged only if the regular non-speculative K-slack buffer would purge them.

Fig. 7 shows how the speculative buffer for the event detector from Fig. 3(a) works with $\alpha=1/3$ and an initial $K=0$.

---

[5]This may be the case if different events are used to set clk.

Figure diagram (speculative ordering buffer, vertical orientation with event rows A0, C1, A2, A3, B4, A6, C5, B8, C7, A11, A12, B10, C9, A13, and snapshot events s_0–s_{11}).

K/clk$_A$

0	0	0	2	2	2	3	2	3	2	6	2	6	2	6	2	6	6	11	6	116	6	12	6	12	6	13

A A C A AB C ACB B CB A

0 2 1 2 34 5 67 8 10 9 10 11

sorted event stream / output

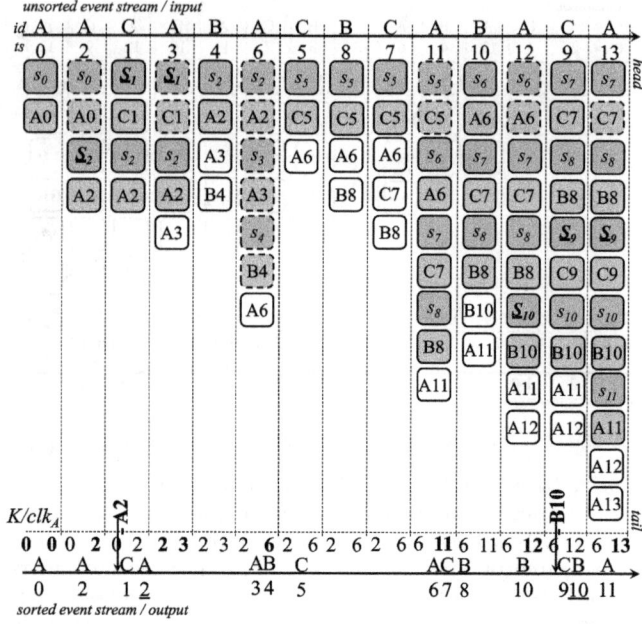

Figure 8: Speculative ordering unit with snapshot recovery and $\alpha = \frac{1}{3}$.

The orientation of the buffer is now vertical, the head is on top. Events of type A are used to set the internal clock clk_A, and K is adjusted by means of dynamic K-slack, see the bold values. Dashed events will be purged from the buffer. Prematurely emitted events are in grey. The AEP, although not explicitly visualized, points to the lowest grey event. Retraction is shown with negative events that point to the output stream. Replayed events are underlined.

At the beginning, we have no measurements of event delays, so we emit A0 and A2 (speculatively). When C1 is received, we detect that we incorrectly emitted A2 before, and replay the correctly ordered sub-stream, i.e., we emit C1, and again A2. K is set to 2 as soon as A3 arrives. A3 is not yet emitted, because $e_i.ts+\alpha \cdot K=3+\frac{1}{3} \cdot 2=3.67>3=clk$. C1 can now be purged as $K=2$ tells us that there cannot be out-of-order events with $ts<3-K=1$. We insert B4 into the buffer. With A6, we evaluate the currently buffered events, emit A3 ($3.67 \leq 6=clk_A$) and B4 ($4.67 \leq 6=clk_A$), and purge the buffer by erasing each event that satisfies $e_i.ts+K \leq clk$, i.e., A2, A3, and B4 that are now safe (by means of the rules of pure K-slack). Although clk is not updated on reception of C5, we can prematurely emit C5 because it fulfills $e_i.ts+\alpha \cdot K=5+\frac{1}{3} \cdot 2=5.67 \leq 6=clk$, and since A6 has not been processed before, we do not need to replay. B8 and C7 are both queued until reception of A11. We then process A6, C7, and B8, and purge C5. With A12 we prematurely emit B10 because $e_i.ts+\alpha \cdot K=10+\frac{1}{3} \cdot 6=12 \leq 12=clk$. We insert C9 in front of the AEP and thus detect another false speculation. Hence, we relocate the AEP and replay C9 and B10.

Whenever the event detector generates an event out of a prematurely emitted event, the middleware attaches the original K-value difference, i.e., K^+, so that the ordering units of higher level event detectors can calculate the event delay, and hence their new K-value, appropriately.

4.2 State Recovery

If speculation was too hasty the speculative ordering unit relocates the AEP and replays the event stream. However,

---

Algorithm 1: Adding a newly received event e.

Data: Event e, OrderingBuffer *buffer*, Mutex m, WorkerThread *workerThread*

begin

  UpdateK($clk-e.ts+e_i.K^+$); // update K if needed

  while $!m.acquireLock()$ **do**   // lock buffer

      $workerThread$.interrupt();

  BufferIterator $it \leftarrow buffer$.tail;

  repeat

    $it \leftarrow it$.previous;

    if $it.GetTime() \leq e.GetTime()$ **then**

      $buffer$.insertAfter(it, e);

      break;

  until $it = buffer$.head;

  if $e.GetTime() < buffer.head.GetTime()$ **then**

    $buffer$.push_front($buffer$.head, e);

  if $AEP.ts > e.ts$ **then**   // it.next is snapshot

    Event $s \leftarrow it.next$.pop();

    s.SetTime(e.GetTime());   // adjust ts

    $buffer$.insert_before(it, s); // move snapshot

    $buffer$.emit(s);   // re-init detector

    $buffer$.SetAEP(it);   // relocate AEP

  m.releaseLock();

  $workerThread$.wakeUp();

---

although the ordering unit may revise incorrect events by means of the retraction methods that we describe in Sec. 4.3, the event detector that processes the emitted events may still be in a wrong state due to these events. Hence, for a replay the internal variables of the event detector must be reverted to the state they had before the event detector processed the first incorrect premature event to avoid inconsistencies.

Such a state recovery is difficult because of three reasons. First, since the ordering middleware transparently handles out-of-order event streams the event detector does not even know that an ordering unit exists. Second, even if the event detector knows that there is a speculative ordering unit, and it processes retraction events to revert its state, it nevertheless has no clue about α and K, and hence how many states it needs to keep. Third, in many cases retraction cascades, which are the core reason why speculation must be limited, can be interrupted earlier and resolved faster. But this is only possible from within the ordering middleware, see Sec. 4.3.2.

Our solution is to let the middleware trigger both state backup and recovery. This avoids side-effects by out-of-order events in the detector and the application programmer does not need to care about retraction events or recovery. On demand, the event detector has to be able to provide all the data that is necessary to later on be restored to this snapshot. The key idea is to ask the event detector for a snapshot whenever a premature event e_i is going to be emitted and to insert this snapshot as an exceptional event e_s with $e_s.ts=e_i.ts$ into the ordering buffer, directly in front of the prematurely emitted event e_i. The snapshot then represents the event detector state that has been in place before e_i was prematurely emitted.

Whenever events are replayed to an event detector, the detector switches back to an earlier state as soon as it receives such an exceptional event e_s encapsulating that earlier state. Only the first/earliest buffered snapshot event is emitted in

Algorithm 2: Event emission, replay, and buffer purge.

Data: OrderingBuffer *buffer*, Mutex *m*, Clock *clk*
begin
  while *true* **do**
    if *m.acquireLock()* **then**
      while $AEP \neq buffer.tail()$ **do**
        CheckAndBreakOnInterrupt();
        if $AEP.GetTime() \leq clk - \alpha \cdot K$ **then**
          SnapshotEvent $s \leftarrow$ MakeSnapshot();
          $buffer.insert\_before(AEP, s)$;
          $buffer.emit(AEP)$;
          $AEP \leftarrow AEP.next()$;
          if *AEP.isSnapshotEvent()* **then**
            $AEP \leftarrow AEP.next$;
        else
          break;
      // buffer purge by K-slack constraints
      while $buffer.head().GetTime + K < clk$ **do**
        if $buffer.head = null$ **then**
          break;
        if $buffer.head() \neq AEP$ **then**
          $buffer.pop\_front()$;
        else
          break;
      $m.releaseLock()$;
    else
      $m.sleep()$;

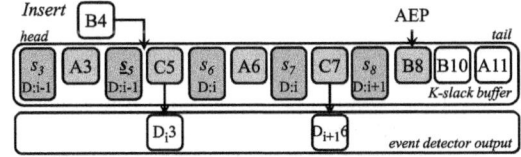

(a) D3 and D6 generated prematurely.

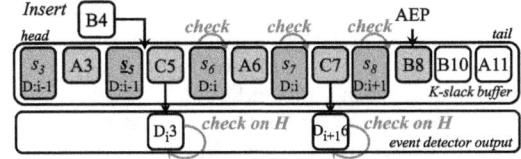

(b) On-Demand Retraction.

Figure 9: Event retraction on reception of B4.

event detector processing, inserts the (out-of-order) event at its correct position, reinitializes the event detector, and relocates the AEP, if needed. With its termination it triggers the worker thread to proceed. The worker threads are also triggered by *clk* updates, and are also used to purge the obsolete events from the buffer.

4.3 Event Retraction

If some event is missing in the speculatively emitted stream, we restore the snapshot of the subscribing event detector and replay the event stream. What remains open is that this event detector may itself already have generated events based on the incomplete event stream. These events must be retracted/eliminated from event streams subscribed by detectors on higher hierarchy levels. Since this may lead to a heavy retraction cascade we must limit the degree of speculation.

Consider the example event detector of Fig. 3(a) and the speculative buffer in Fig. 9(a). For this example we assume that the event detector numbers the generated D events. The event detector has already speculatively processed the grey events A3 to B8 and has already generated D_i3 out of A3/C5 and $D_{i+1}6$ out of A6/C7 when an event B with time stamp 4 arrives. Since the subscribing event detector itself has incorrectly generated D_i3, we must restore the event detector's state, replay C5 to B8, and retract D_i3 from the streams of higher level event detectors.

Moreover, $D_{i+1}6$ may be wrong as well because of two reasons. First, the event detector may not have reached the D-state in presence of B4, because of some internal state variables that are not shown. Second, even if it would reach the D-state then instead of $D_{i+1}6$ it should have produced D_i6. Hence, in addition to be able to replay event streams the middleware must also be ready to invalidate events that have been generated based on prematurely emitted events.

The key idea to restore a correct state at a higher level event detector H is to send a retraction event that identifies the events that have incorrectly generated so that H's ordering unit can fix that and replay the event stream.

Below we present two techniques to handle event retractions across the detection hierarchy: *Full Retraction* and *On-Demand Retraction*.

4.3.1 Full Retraction

The key idea of *Full Retraction* is to instantly retract all events that may have been generated incorrectly as soon as the AEP is relocated. For this purpose, an event detector's

---

a replay, the remaining snapshots are skipped. During a replay, event detectors are also asked for snapshots, and existing snapshots in the ordering buffer are replaced by new ones. Snapshot events are purged from the buffer like any other events.

Fig. 8 shows the ordering unit of Fig. 7 with snapshot processing. On top of each emitted grey event there is a special snapshot event in the buffer (denoted by s_{ts}) holding the state of the detector before the premature event was processed. Consider the replay situation at C1 in column 3. The snapshot s_2 that has been taken when A2 has been emitted speculatively (column 2) is still in the buffer. For the replay, this snapshot is emitted first, followed by C1 and A2. The procedure is similar when C9 arrives.

If two subsequent snapshots do not differ, we just store a reference to the prior snapshot. Nevertheless speculation needs extra storage. The space needed grows with the degree of speculation and depends on the complexity of the event detector's state space.

Algs. 1 and 2 show how the speculation works. We use worker threads that iterate over the ordering units and that are used by the event detectors for event processing (Alg. 2). While such worker threads may be busy with processing events, a new event may be received, and Alg. 1 is called upon reception. For any event we receive, we first calculate its delay and update K by means of classic K-slack, if necessary. Note that as events may have been generated prematurely we have to add K^+, i.e., the premature emission time that we attached to the event, on top of the event's delay. Next, since this event may be out-of-order, Alg. 1 acquires the lock on the ordering unit's buffer, i.e., stops the

ordering buffer must not only store the prematurely emitted events and the snapshots but must conceptually also hold a list of events that the detector has generated from the prematurely emitted events, i.e., D_i3 and $D_{i+1}6$ in the example. When an out-of-order event is inserted into the buffer, we first collect all events that may have been incorrectly generated, and send a (conceptual) retraction event for each of them to the ordering unit of each subscribing higher level event detector H. When this ordering unit receives such a retraction event it purges this event from its buffer, and performs its own retraction and replay. Hence, a retraction event reuses the replay and snapshot recovery used for out-of-order events. For instance, in Fig. 9(a) we insert B4 between A3 and C5, instantly send retraction events for -D_i3 and -$D_{i+1}6$, tell the event detector to restore the appropriate snapshot, and start the replay.

Although retraction of every single incorrectly generated D event would work, there is a more efficient way to achieve the same effect. The idea is to exploit an event counter i that the ordering unit attaches to the detector's state as it has been done by the event detector before.[6] Instead of sending several retraction events (-D_i3 and -$D_{i+1}6$ in the example), it is sufficient just to send the event *counter* D:i-1 to the upper level detector. This detector can then purge all D events from its buffer that have a larger counter.

But the event counter not only helps to reduce the number of retraction events that need to be sent to higher level detectors. With the counters stored in the states, there is no longer a need to keep lists to the generated events. In the example, there is no need to store the lists C5->D_i3 and C7->$D_{i+1}6$. Instead the counter values are piggybacked to the states s. This reduces the necessary footprints.

The advantage of full retraction is that the ordering units of higher level event detectors purge retracted events from their buffers and replay their event streams immediately. If the event detector's state changes and/or the prematurely generated events differ, full retraction works as efficient as possible. Full retraction is essentially the state-of-the-art in the related work.

4.3.2   On-Demand Retraction

With full retraction and its purging of generated events, the detectors have to perform their detection work again. This consumes CPU cycles. But consider state-less detectors that will generate exactly the purged events again. It is obvious that for those detectors most of the retraction work is wasted. The efficiency of full retraction and the achievable degree of speculation strongly depend on the internal structure of the event detector and its generated events.

The key idea of *on-demand retraction* is not to send the retraction events immediately upon AEP relocation. Instead we replay the event stream and only retract events if snapshots change and/or if events are not generated again during replay. In more detail, whenever we emit events during replay we check if the following two properties hold:

(1) Snapshots are equal. If we replay the event stream, and the snapshots do not differ we can abort the replay process. Because the upcoming premature events in the replay cause the same snapshots and hence generate the same events both the snapshots and the previously generated premature events remain valid. We assume that event detectors solely process events emitted by the middleware. Other input, e.g., system calls or file handles, are not allowed.

(2) Generated events are equal. The events and their counters that are generated again during replay are marked as updates, and the ordering unit of the higher level event detector H checks if the previously generated premature event equals the recently generated update event. If it does, the ordering unit of H does not reinsert the new event, does not relocate the AEP, and hence does not trigger an unnecessary retraction cascade.

Fig. 9(b) shows on-demand retraction for the example. When B4 is inserted into the buffer, the event detector is reset to use the snapshot $\underline{s}_4=\underline{s}_5$, and works on the replayed events. The event detector will reach some state s_5' after processing B4 speculatively (not shown in Fig. 9(b)). If $s_5'=\underline{s}_5(=\underline{s}_4)$, i.e., if the state of the event detector is not affected by B4, we can abort replay and retraction because all the subsequent snapshots and the prematurely generated events will remain unchanged.

However, if the state of the event detector is affected, we replay the event streams, and whenever an event is generated, we set the *update* flag before we send it to the ordering unit of H. The ordering unit of H then checks the updated event w.r.t. equality and discards it if there is no change.

If the event detector is state-less or events that cause a replay do not change much of the output, on-demand retraction considerably reduces retraction work that would be introduced by full retraction across the detector hierarchy. See also the evaluation in Sec. 5.

4.4   Runtime α-adaptation

Speculation uses additional system resources to reduce event detection latency. The remaining question is how to set the attenuation factor α that controls the degree of speculation. The ideal value of α results in best latencies but also avoids exhausting the available system resources and hence system failure.

We now present a runtime α-adaptation algorithm that achieves this goal. It is safe because when either no runtime measurements are available or when a critical situation occurs, e.g., a CPU load that is higher than some threshold, α is (re-)set to its initial value $\alpha_0=1$ in order to prevent a system failure. Moreover, α-adaptation only has a local effect because α only effects replay and retraction of a single ordering unit. The CPU load on machines that run other detectors are not affected much because the speculative buffer of an upper level event detector only inserts and/or retracts events but does not start a replay (which in general depends on its own α).

The key idea of our runtime α-adaptation is to use a control loop similar to the congestion control mechanism known from the transmission control protocol (TCP) [27]. Congestion control tries to maximize throughput by doubling the data rate, i.e., the congestion window size that holds the number of to-be-acknowledged packets, at each time unit. When the data rate becomes too high for the link, data packets are timed out because packets are lost in the network, and the window size is reduced to 1. The maximal window size is saved and a new iteration begins. The window size is doubled again until it reaches half the window size of the previous iteration. Then its size is incremented until again packets are lost and the next iteration starts over.

---

[6]The time stamps cannot be used as event counter because the ordering middleware has no influence on their generation and they are not said to be increasing.

Algorithm 3: α-adaptation.

Data: α, α_s, *lastMinimum*, **bool** *slowmode*, b_l, b_u, b_c

begin

  if $b_u < b_c$ **then**   // reduce speculation

      $lastMinimum \leftarrow \alpha$;

      $\alpha \leftarrow 1$;

      $slowmode \leftarrow$ false;

  if $b_c < b_l$ **then**   // increase speculation

      $\alpha_{target} \leftarrow 0$;

      if *slowmode* **then**

          $\alpha_{target} \leftarrow \alpha - \alpha_s$;

      else

          $\alpha_{target} \leftarrow \alpha/2$;

          if *(1- lastMinimum) / 2* $> \alpha_{target}$ **then**

             slowmode $\leftarrow$ true;   // goto slow mode

             $\alpha_{target} \leftarrow \alpha - \alpha_s$;

      $\alpha \leftarrow \alpha_{target}$;

To adapt that idea, we use α as the congestion window size, and the CPU workload as a load indicator. Whenever we evaluate the CPU load we adjust the value of α. To measure the CPU load accurately, the middleware repeatedly (after each time interval t_{span}) sums up the times that event detectors need for event processing, i.e., t_{busy}, and relates it to the sum of the times the worker threads have available, t_{span}. The resulting busy factor b_c is

$$b_c = 1 - \frac{t_{busy}}{t_{span}}.$$

For instance, with a time interval t_{span}=0.5s and an accumulated t_{busy}=0.41s the busy factor b_c is 0.41s/0.5s=0.82. This means that 82% of the available resources are used and that about 18% of the system resources are still available (assuming that no other processes interfere with the EBS). The busy factor grows with decreasing values of α.

To adjust α we specify a target zone $[b_l; b_u]$, i.e., an interval of the *lower* and the *upper* target values for b_c. If the busy factor is below b_l, CPU time is available and α is decreased by halving its value. This is similar to the doubling the congestion control window size. α is the inverse of the window size and halving α increases speculation. If the busy factor grows above b_u, CPU time becomes critical, and the current α is kept (called α_{best}) before α is set to its initial value α_0=1. From there α is again halved until its value is about to be set below the bisection line $(1-\alpha_{best})/2$. From then on α is lowered in small steps of α_s, to slowly approach the target zone. Alg. 3 gives the pseudo code for the α-adaptation.

Our evaluation shows that the busy target interval [0.8; 0.9] in combination with α_s=0.05 works reasonably well. Of course, b_c is not only affected by the choice of α. In burst situations or when a detector reaches a rare or slow area of its state space, t_{busy} may peak. In such cases, the runtime α-adaption reacts appropriately by resetting α and hence by giving more resources to the detector.

5. EVALUATION

For the evaluation we have analyzed position data streams from a Realtime Locating System (RTLS) installed in the main soccer stadium in Nuremberg, Germany. This RTLS tracks 144 transmitters at the same time at 2,000 sampling points per second for the ball and 200 sampling points per second for players and referees. Each player has four transmitters, one at each of his limbs. The sensor data consists of absolute positions in millimeters, velocity, acceleration, and Quality of Location (QoL) for any direction [28].

Soccer needs these sampling rates. With 2,000 sampling points per second for the ball and a velocity of up to 150 km/h, two succeeding positions may be more than 2cm apart. Soccer events such as pass, double pass, or shot on goal happen within a fraction of a second. A low latency is required so that a hierarchy of detectors can help the human observer, for example a reporter, or a camera systems that should smoothly follow events of interest, to instantly work with the live output of the system.

We present results from applying our event processing system and our algorithms on position data streams from the stadium. Our platform consists of several 64-bit Linux machines, each equipped with two Intel Xeon E5560 Quad Core CPUs at 2.80 GHz and 64 GB of main memory that communicate over a 1 Gbit fully switched network. For our tests we organized a test game between two amateur league soccer clubs and processed the incoming position streams from the transmitters.[7]

For all benchmarks we replay position stream data in our lab's computing cluster. To focus on the experimental results more clearly, we perform all the work on just one machine. Our event processing middleware, i.e., the methods for speculative processing, pub/sub-management, etc., take around 9,000 lines of C++ code. On top of that we implemented over 70 event detectors with more than 16,000 lines of C++ code that are used to detect more than 750 different event types. The event detection hierarchy has 15 levels, and we replay a snippet of the event stream from the soccer match. The duration of the test event stream is 65 seconds and consists of 2.2 million position events plus 25,000 higher-level events that are generated by the event detectors (not including prematurely emitted events or retraction events). The data stream also incorporates some burst situations. The average data rate of the processed data streams is 2.67 MBytes/sec.

We let the event detectors work on the data streams, and discuss the generated results. For all our experiments we use only one worker thread to make the results more clear and to avoid side-effects. Sec. 5.1 shows that speculative processing can considerably reduce both latencies and detection delays. Sec. 5.2 evaluates the α-adaptive speculation in detail. Sec. 5.3 and 5.4 provide measurements on the resource consumption during the event stream replay versus full speculative and pure buffering approaches.

5.1 Latency reduction

Fig. 10 shows that added speculation can significantly reduce latency of buffering middlewares. For the benchmark we measured the latency of the *pass* event detector. This detector subscribes to 6 different event types and detects a (unsuccessful) *pass* event.

When we replay the event data stream to a pure dynamic K-slack buffering (α=1, straight line) it updates K upon ordering mistakes and finally ends up with a detection latency of 1458ms at the end of the stream replay. The average latency for the 65 seconds is 1276ms. In contrast, our

---

[7]FIFA rules do not allow a continuous operation in premier league matches.

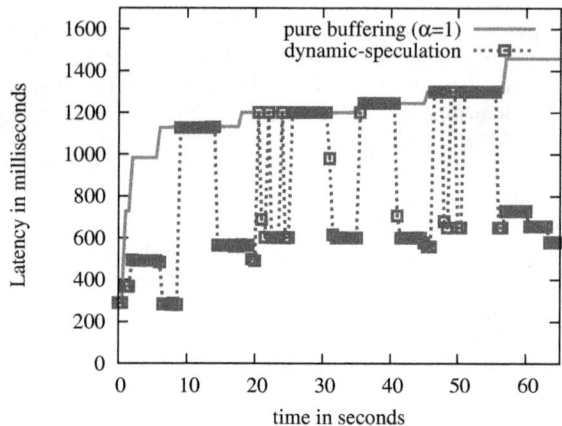

Figure 10: Latencies of (speculative) buffering.

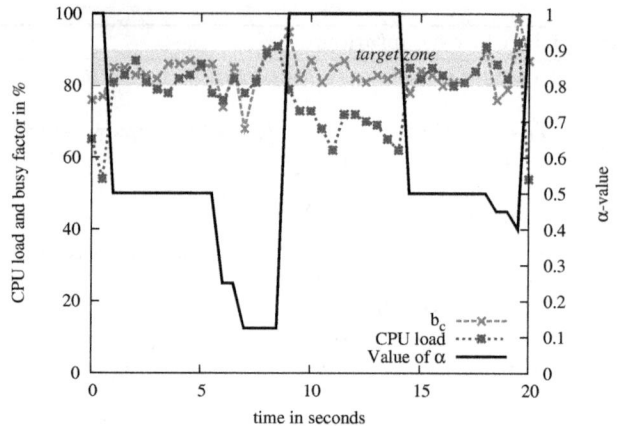

Figure 11: Adaptation of α.

dynamic α-adaptation reaches a much smaller detection latency (dotted line). At the beginning, α starts at $\alpha_0=1$ and around 290ms of latency. As the CPU is not fully loaded α-adaptation switches on speculation. This brings detection latency down to 280ms, where pure buffering already has 1128 ms latency. Note that the latency of pure buffering increases much more than that of dynamic speculation as α-adaptation outweighs the growth of the K-slack buffer. At several points the event streams, and hence the busy factor burst. That causes α to back off, leading to a higher detection latency again. Afterwards, α-halving resumes and the latency approaches its minimum again. The average latency of the dynamic speculation is below 800ms, i.e., about 40% better than what pure buffering can achieve.

These results show that our speculative buffering technique strongly reduces the detection latency of events at runtime. Throughout the entire 65 seconds the CPU load was tolerable, and at the critical burst situations α-adaptation can avoid system failures, see Sec. 5.2. Hence, camera movements can be triggered about 40% faster than with pure buffering techniques. The latencies of other event detectors behave similarly.

We did not show the latency of full speculation ($\alpha=0$) because it consumes too much CPU power and causes event processing to fail. See Sec. 5.3 for more details. Other variants with static α-values would just result in latencies that represent the original latency divided by the static α-value.

5.2 Runtime α-adaptation

In the above measurements there are several bursts where α has to back off due to high system loads. To discuss the performance of our α-adaptation in more detail, let us zoom into the first 20 seconds of the event stream, see Fig. 11.

With a busy factor target zone [0.8; 0.9], we start from $\alpha=1$ (straight line). We evaluate and (possibly) halve α every $t_{span}=0.5$ seconds, and as a result the busy factor b_c (dashed line) grows. After 7 seconds α is 0.125, we cease halving, and b_c stays in its target zone between 0.8 and 0.9. For a while, both the busy factor b_c and the CPU load fluctuate within the target zone before a growing frequency of incoming events requires more and more detection work. After 8.5 seconds into the benchmark b_c reaches 0.95 (the CPU load at that time was at 91%), α is immediately reset to 1, and as a result both b_c and the CPU load drop instantly. Then α is evaluated and after 16 seconds α-halving starts over. But this time halving stops at the bisection line (1.0-

0.125)/2=0.43. From there α takes small steps of 0.05 per t_{span} to bring b_c and CPU load back into the target zone.

The α-adaptation algorithm not only decreases α to efficiently use the available CPU power but also rapidly stops speculation if the system is almost overloaded in burst situations, to avoid system failure and to absorb the bursts. Moreover, b_c is a sufficiently good indicator of the CPU load. Only if the CPU load is low, b_c slightly overestimates because of task switches and thread sleeping.

5.3 Resource Consumption

To measure the resource consumption we replay the event stream snippet three times. Fig. 12 shows the resulting CPU loads. We recorded the CPU loads for pure K-slack buffering ($\alpha=1$, straight line), dynamic α-adaptation (dotted line), and fully speculative processing ($\alpha=0$, dashed line).

Pure buffering exhibits a comparatively lazy CPU load of 50-70% for the entire 65 seconds. That is because events are buffered for a sufficiently long time and the event detectors neither receive retraction events nor are they asked for snapshots or get restored. In contrast, full speculation causes a high CPU consumption above 90% for the entire 65 seconds. In the benchmark the CPU consumption reaches 100% a few times. This is prohibitive because event detection then takes longer than it should. The resulting higher delays cause a ripple effect since the K-values of the detectors further up the detection hierarchy are not prepared to deal with the extra delay and purge events or process them out-of-order. Hence, detectors may get stuck in invalid states and event processing fails. Even worse, there is another reason for system failure: when event processing is slowed down, the queue of incoming events that await being processed often outgrows the available buffer space.

Fig. 12 also shows that to achieve the good detection latencies discussed in Sec. 5.1 the dynamic speculation makes reasonable and efficient use of the available resources. The CPU load stays within a non-critical target zone that gives the dynamic α-adaptation enough room to react to bursts and to avoid system failures. Hence, if detection latencies in an application are too high, one simply needs to use a stronger CPU. Then there is more room for speculation and hence latency reduction.

Speculation also needs more main memory. On our benchmark, pure buffering took only 1,120 KBytes of buffer space, averaged over the 65 seconds. There are two reasons for the demand being that small. First, only the events but not the

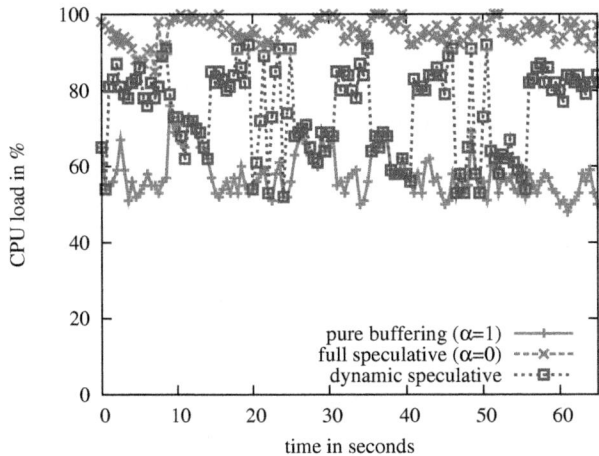

Figure 12: CPU loads with varying α.

detectors' snapshots need to be stored. And second, since an event is usually input to more than one detector we store it only once and insert a reference to it into the ordering units. In contrast, as an event detector's state has an average size of around 800 Bytes, full speculation required 21,100 KBytes for an event detector's buffer on average. Dynamic speculation is better and only took 14,850 KBytes on average, i.e., with only 14 MBytes of additional main memory per detector one can buy a latency reduction of 40%.

States of event detectors from the lower levels are considerably smaller (below 50 bytes) than the states from higher level detectors (one unique detector has a state size of 800 KBytes). Beyond that, event detectors of lower levels are snapshot more frequently than higher level event detectors since the event load is considerably higher.

5.4 Evaluation of Retraction Techniques

To evaluate the two retraction techniques we replay the real event stream from the first half of the soccer match (45 minutes). For each of the two retraction techniques we record the number of events that are prematurely generated and retracted from a *player-hits-ball* event detector.

On-demand retraction is much more light-weighted and in general also helps reduce latency. Over the 45 minutes, full retraction affected 5,623 ball hit events, whereas on-demand retraction only had to work on 735 events. With full retraction, the resulting retraction cascade affected 117,600 events across the detector hierarchy, compared to 12,300 events for on-demand retraction. To explain the advantages of on-demand retraction, more than just the event counts need to be considered. Compared to full retraction it is more costly for the on-demand retraction to process snapshots and to check for state changes. More work takes more CPU power away so that α-adaptation selects a lower degree of speculation, which results in a higher latency. On the other hand, the many retraction events of full retraction are quicker to deal with – but there are so many of them.

On-demand retraction works best for event detectors with small states or with states that do not change much (or not for every single event). For example, event detectors that directly process sensor data or low-level events. For such detectors, on-demand retraction can (1) abort the retraction cascade from the bottom of the event hierarchy, and (2) check detector state changes quickly because snapshots are small or not even necessary.

But there are rare event detectors that work better with full-retraction. The *pass* detector is an example. First, it changes its state on almost every event received. Thus, all its checking of snapshots and of generated events is useless work. Second, full retraction only affects 819 events. On-demand retraction can only reduce that number by 27 which is not enough to amortize its cost.

In total, choosing on-demand retraction *for all detectors* is better than full retraction. In the benchmark averaged over all detectors the α-value of full retraction was 0.81 whereas on-demand retraction only achieved an average α-value of 0.69. Nevertheless, on-demand retraction achieved a 15% better detection latency than full retraction. It is future research and an optimization problem of its own to automatically deduce and assign the best retraction technique *for each individual detector* at runtime. That might improve performance even more.

5.5 Discussion

We first showed that our speculative buffer with dynamic α-adaptation reduces latency considerably. We zoomed into the details and proved that our method exploits available system resources progressively until we reach a predefined level. Comparing the resource consumption of our approach to full-speculative as well as buffering approaches shows that we achieve a perfect trade-off between latency reduction and resource consumption.

We deliberately did not present results on the efficiency of taking and restoring snapshots. While memory consumption has shown to be moderate but tolerable, the time for taking snapshots was too small in our benchmarks to matter at all. Hence, there is also no need for more sophisticated mechanisms like transactional memories etc. However, depending on both the event detectors' states and the events, this may be an option for improvement for other applications.

6. CONCLUSION

Our speculative buffer extension achieves reliable and low-latency event processing under the predominance of out-of-order events. Any buffering middleware can use our speculation to process buffered events earlier and hence to reduce detection latency by exploiting available CPU and memory resources whereas conservative buffering approaches can natively not use them. Our speculation needs no a-priori knowledge of event delays nor the internal description of the event detectors and the system adaptively adjusts the degree of speculation at runtime.

An evaluation of the presented methods on position data stream from a Realtime Locating Systems (RTLS) in a soccer application shows that our dynamic speculation outperforms other speculative and buffering techniques. On average, we achieved a 40% reduction of latency.

Future work will refine the α-adaptation to incorporate event loads and latencies per event detector more specifically. Moreover, we will investigate approaches that automatically deduce and select the best retraction technique for each individual event detector at runtime.

Acknowledgements

This work is supported by the Fraunhofer Institute for Integrated Circuits IIS whose RTLS called RedFIR we have used. We are grateful to the researchers at the Fraunhofer IIS for sharing their work and system with us.

7. REFERENCES

[1] M. Stonebraker, U. Çetintemel, and S. Zdonik, "The 8 requirements of real-time stream processing," *SIGMOD Rec.*, vol. 34, no. 4, pp. 42–47, 2005.

[2] D. O'Keeffe and J. Bacon, "Reliable complex event detection for pervasive computing," in *Proc. 4th Intl. Conf. Distributed Event-Based Systems*, (Cambridge, UK), pp. 73–84, 2010.

[3] P. A. Tucker, D. Maier, T. Sheard, and L. Fegaras, "Exploiting punctuation semantics in continuous data streams," *IEEE Trans. Knowledge and Data Engineering*, vol. 15, no. 3, pp. 555–568, 2003.

[4] J. Li, K. Tufte, V. Shkapenyuk, V. Papadimos, T. Johnson, and D. Maier, "Out-of-order processing: a new architecture for high-performance stream systems," in *Proc. VLDB Endow.*, vol. 1, (Auckland, NZ), pp. 274–288, 2008.

[5] U. Srivastava and J. Widom, "Flexible time management in data stream systems," in *Proc. 23rd ACM Symp. Principles Database Systems*, (Paris, France), pp. 263–274, 2004.

[6] E. Wu, Y. Diao, and S. Rizvi, "High-performance complex event processing over streams," in *Proc. ACM Intl. Conf. Management of Data*, (Chicago, IL), pp. 407–418, 2006.

[7] M. Li, M. Liu, L. Ding, E. Rundensteiner, and M. Mani, "Event stream processing with out-of-order data arrival," in *Proc. 27th Intl. Conf. Distrib. Comp. Systems Workshops*, (Toronto, CAN), pp. 67–74, 2007.

[8] J. Agrawal, Y. Diao, D. Gyllstrom, and N. Immerman, "Efficient pattern matching over event streams," in *Proc. ACM Intl. Conf. Management of Data*, (Vancouver, CAN), pp. 147–160, 2008.

[9] A. Demers, J. Gehrke, M. Hong, M. Riedewald, and W. White, "Towards expressive publish/subscribe systems," in *Proc. 10th Intl. Conf. Extending Database Technology*, (Munich, Germany), pp. 627–644, 2006.

[10] A. Demers, J. Gehrke, B. Panda, M. Riedewald, V. Sharma, and W. White, "Cayuga: a general purpose event monitoring system," in *Proc. 3rd Biennial Conf. Innovative Data Systems Research*, (Pacific Grove, CA), pp. 412–422, 2007.

[11] L. Brenna, A. Demers, J. Gehrke, M. Hong, J. Ossher, B. Panda, M. Riedewald, M. Thatte, and W. White, "Cayuga: a high-performance event processing engine," in *Proc. ACM Intl. Conf. Management of Data*, (Beijing, China), pp. 1100–1102, 2007.

[12] L. Brenna, J. Gehrke, M. Hong, and D. Johansen, "Distributed event stream processing with non-deterministic finite automata," in *Proc. 3rd Intl. Conf. Distributed Event-Based Systems*, (Nashville, TN), pp. 3:1–3:12, 2009.

[13] M. Balazinska, Y. Kwon, N. Kuchta, and D. Lee, "Moirae: history-enhanced monitoring," in *Proc. 3rd Biennial Conf. Innovative Data Systems Research*, (Pacific Grove, CA), pp. 375–386, 2007.

[14] A. S. Maskey and M. Cherniack, "Replay-based approaches to revision processing in stream query engines," in *Proc. 2nd Intl. Workshop Scalable Stream Processing Systems*, (Nantes, France), pp. 3–12, 2008.

[15] D. Anicic, S. Rudolph, P. Fodor, and N. Stojanovic, "Retractable complex event processing and stream reasoning," in *Proc. 5th Intl. Conf. Rule-based Reasoning, Programming, and Applications*, (Fort Lauderdale, FL), pp. 122–137, 2011.

[16] C.-W. Li, Y. Gu, G. Yu, and B. Hong, "Aggressive complex event processing with confidence over out-of-order streams," *Comp. Science and Technol.*, vol. 26, no. 4, pp. 685–696, 2011.

[17] E. Ryvkina, A. S. Maskey, M. Cherniack, and S. Zdonik, "Revision processing in a stream processing engine: a high-level design," in *Proc. 22nd Intl. Conf. Data Engineering*, (Atlanta, GA), pp. 141–143, 2006.

[18] A. Brito, C. Fetzer, H. Sturzrehm, and P. Felber, "Speculative out-of-order event processing with software transaction memory," in *Proc. 2nd Intl. Conf. Distributed Event-Based Systems*, (Rome, Italy), pp. 265–275, 2008.

[19] B. Wester, J. Cowling, E. B. Nightingale, P. M. Chen, J. Flinn, and B. Liskov, "Tolerating latency in replicated state machines through client speculation," in *Proc. 6th USENIX Symp. Networked Systems Design and Implementation*, (Boston, MA), pp. 245–260, 2009.

[20] M. Liu, M. Li, D. Golovnya, E. Rundensteiner, and K. Claypool, "Sequence pattern query processing over out-of-order event streams," in *Proc. 25th Intl. Conf. Data Eng.*, (Shanghai, China), pp. 784–795, 2009.

[21] R. S. Barga, J. Goldstein, M. Ali, and M. Hong, "Consistent streaming through time: a vision for event stream processing," in *Proc. 3rd Biennial Conf. Innovative Data Systems Research*, (Pacific Grove, CA), pp. 363–374, 2007.

[22] B. Chandramouli, J. Goldstein, and D. Maier, "High-performance dynamic pattern matching over disordered streams," in *Proc. VLDB Endow.*, vol. 3, (Singapore), pp. 220–231, 2010.

[23] Z. Jerzak and C. Fetzer, "BFSiena: a communication substrate for StreamMine," in *Proc. 2nd Intl. Conf. Distributed Event-Based Systems*, (Rome, Italy), pp. 321–324, 2008.

[24] G. Mühl, L. Fiege, and P. Pietzuch, *Distributed event-based systems*. Springer, Berlin, 2006.

[25] S. Babu, U. Srivastava, and J. Widom, "Exploiting k-constraints to reduce memory overhead in continuous queries over data streams," *ACM Trans. Database Systems*, vol. 29, no. 3, pp. 545–580, 2004.

[26] C. Mutschler and M. Philippsen, "Distributed low-latency out-of-order event processing for high data rate sensor streams," in *Proc. 27th Intl. Conf. Parallel and Distributed Processing Symposium*, (Boston, MA), pp. 1133–1144, 2013.

[27] M. Allman, C. Hayes, and S. Ostermann, "An evaluation of TCP with larger initial windows," *SIGCOMM Comput. Commun. Rev.*, vol. 28, no. 3, pp. 41–52, 1998.

[28] T. v. d. Grün, N. Franke, D. Wolf, N. Witt, and A. Eidloth, "A real-time tracking system for football match and training analysis," in *Microelectronic Systems*, pp. 199–212, Springer Berlin, 2011.

Dynamic Expressivity with Static Optimization for Streaming Languages

Robert Soulé
Cornell University
soule@cs.cornell.edu

Michael I. Gordon
Massachusetts Institute of
Technology
mgordon@mit.edu

Saman Amarasinghe
Massachusetts Institute of
Technology
saman@mit.edu

Robert Grimm
New York University
rgrimm@cs.nyu.edu

Martin Hirzel
IBM Research
hirzel@us.ibm.com

ABSTRACT

Developers increasingly use streaming languages to write applications that process large volumes of data with high throughput. Unfortunately, when picking which streaming language to use, they face a difficult choice. On the one hand, dynamically scheduled languages allow developers to write a wider range of applications, but cannot take advantage of many crucial optimizations. On the other hand, statically scheduled languages are extremely performant, but have difficulty expressing many important streaming applications.

This paper presents the design of a hybrid scheduler for stream processing languages. The compiler partitions the streaming application into coarse-grained subgraphs separated by dynamic rate boundaries. It then applies static optimizations to those subgraphs. We have implemented this scheduler as an extension to the StreamIt compiler. To evaluate its performance, we compare it to three scheduling techniques used by dynamic systems (OS thread, demand, and no-op) on a combination of micro-benchmarks and real-world inspired synthetic benchmarks. Our scheduler not only allows the previously static version of StreamIt to run dynamic rate applications, but it outperforms the three dynamic alternatives. This demonstrates that our scheduler strikes the right balance between expressivity and performance for stream processing languages.

Categories and Subject Descriptors: D.3.4 Programming Languages]: Processors

Keywords: Stream Processing; StreamIt

1. INTRODUCTION

The greater availability of data from audio/video streams, sensors, and financial exchanges has led to an increased demand for applications that process large volumes of data with high throughput. More and more, developers are using *stream processing* languages to write these programs. Indeed, streaming applications have become ubiquitous in government, finance, and entertainment.

A streaming application is, in essence, a data-flow graph of streams and operators. A *stream* is an infinite sequence of data items, and an *operator* transforms the data. The *data transfer rate* of an operator is the number of data items that it consumes and produces each time it fires. In *statically scheduled* stream processing languages, every operator must have a fixed data transfer rate at compile time. In contrast, *dynamically scheduled languages* place no restriction on the data transfer rate, which is determined at runtime.

Without the restriction of a fixed data transfer rate, dynamic streaming systems, such as STREAM [2], Aurora [1], and SEDA [17], can be used to write a broader range of applications. Unfortunately, many optimizations cannot be applied dynamically without incurring large runtime costs [11]. As a result, while dynamic languages are more expressive, they are fundamentally less performant. Using fixed data transfer rates, compilers for static languages such as Lime [3], StreamIt [15], Esterel [4], and Brook [5] can create a fully static schedule for the streaming application that minimizes data copies, memory allocations, and scheduling overhead. They can take advantage of data locality to reduce communication costs between operators [7], and they can automatically replicate operators to process data in parallel with minimal synchronization [6]. This paper addresses the problem of how to balance the tradeoffs between *expressivity* and *performance* with a hybrid approach.

In an ideal world, all applications could be expressed statically, and thus benefit from static optimization. In the real world, that is not the case, as there are many important applications that need dynamism. We identify four major classes of such applications:

- *Compression/Decompression.* MPEG, JPEG, H264, gzip, and similar programs have data-dependent transfer rates.

- *Event monitoring.* Applications for automated financial trading, surveillance, and anomaly detection for natural disasters critically rely on the ability to filter (e.g. drop data based on a predicate) and aggregate (e.g. average over time-based or attribute-delta based window).

- *Networking.* Software routers and network monitors such as Snort [13] require data-dependent routing.

- *Parsing/Extraction.* Examples include tokenization (e.g. input string, output words), twitter analysis (e.g. input tweet, output hashtags), and regular expression pattern matching (e.g. input string, output all matches).

While these applications fundamentally need dynamism, only a few streams in the data-flow graph are fully dynamic. For instance, an MPEG decoder uses dynamism to route i-frames and p-frames along different paths, but the operators on those paths that process the frames all have static rates. Financial computations require identifying events in data-dependent windows, but static rate operators process those events. A network monitor recognizes network protocols dynamically, but then identifies security violations by applying a static rate pattern matcher.

Based on this observation, we developed our hybrid scheduling scheme. The compiler partitions the streaming application into coarse-grained subgraphs separated by dynamic rate boundaries. It then applies static optimizations to those subgraphs, which reduce the communication overhead, exploit automatic parallelization, and apply inter-operator improvements such as scalarization and cache optimization.

We have implemented this hybrid scheduling scheme for the StreamIt language. To evaluate its performance, we compared it to three scheduling techniques used by dynamic systems (OS thread, demand, and no-op) on a combination of micro-benchmarks and real-world inspired synthetic benchmarks. In all three cases, our hybrid scheduler outperformed the alternative, demonstrating up to 10x, 1.2x, and 5.1x speedups, respectively. In summary, this paper makes the following contributions:

- An exploration of the tradeoffs between static and dynamic scheduling.

- The design of a hybrid static-dynamic scheduler for streaming languages that balances expressivity and performance.

- An implementation of our hybrid scheduler for the StreamIt language that outperforms three fully dynamic schedulers.

Overall, our approach yields significant speedup over fully dynamic scheduling, while allowing stream developers to write a larger set of applications than with only static scheduling.

2. STREAMIT BACKGROUND

Before presenting the design of our hybrid scheduler, we briefly describe the StreamIt language. The left-hand side of Figure 1 shows a snippet of StreamIt code used for video processing. The right-hand side shows a graphical representation of the same code, which we will use throughout this paper. The program receives a video stream as input, and decodes it by applying a sequence of operations: Huffman decoding, inverse quantization, and an inverse discrete cosine transformation.

The central abstraction provided by StreamIt is an operator (called a *filter* in the StreamIt literature). Programmers can combine operators into fixed topologies using three composite operators: *pipeline*, *split-join* and *feedback-loop*. Composite operators can be nested in other composites. The example code shows four operators composed in a pipeline. The operators are VideoInput, Huffman, IQuant, and IDCT.

Each operator has a *work* function that processes streaming data. To simplify the code presentation, we have elided the bodies of the work functions. When writing a work function, a programmer must specify the *pop* and *push* rates for that function. The pop rate declares how many data items from the input stream are consumed each time an operator

```
1  float->float pipeline Decoder {
2      add float->float filter VideoInput() {
3          work pop 1 push 1 {
4              float input, result;
5              input = pop();
6              /* details elided */
7              push(result);
8          }
9      }
10     add float->float filter Huffman () {
11         work pop * push 1
12         { /* details elided */ }
13     }
14     add float->float filter IQuant () {
15         work pop 64 push 64
16         { /* details elided */ }
17     }
18     add float->float filter IDCT () {
19         work pop 8 push 8
20         { /* details elided */; }
21     }
22 }
```

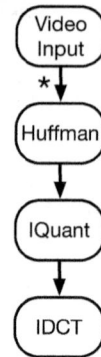

Figure 1: StreamIt code for video processing.

executes. The push rate declares how many data items are produced.

When all pop and push rates are known at compilation time, a StreamIt program can be statically scheduled. In the example, all of the operators except Huffman have static pop and push rates. If a pop or push rate can only be determined at run time, then the character * is used instead of a number literal to indicate that a rate is dynamic. An * appears on both line 11 of the Huffman operator, and in the graphical representation.

To access the data items that are popped and pushed, StreamIt provides built-in *pop()* and *push()* functions, such as appear in lines 5 and 7. These functions implicitly read from an input stream or write to an output stream.

There are several execution paths for the StreamIt compiler, which use different scheduling strategies. The next section reviews these different strategies.

3. RELATED WORK

Table 1 presents an overview of various approaches for scheduling stream processing languages, which we contrast with our hybrid scheduling technique. Our scheduler appears in the last row, shaded in grey.

The simplest approach is **sequential scheduling**. All operators are placed into a single thread, with no support for parallel execution. The StreamIt Library [15] uses this approach, and implements dynamism by having downstream operators directly call upstream operators when they need more data.

In **OS thread scheduling**, each operator is placed in its own thread, and the scheduling is left to the underlying operating system. This approach is used by some database implementations, and is similar to the approach used by the SEDA [17] framework for providing event-driven Internet services. To improve performance, SEDA increases the number of times each operator on the thread executes. This optimization, called *batching* [9], increases the throughput of the application at the expense of latency. This form of dynamic scheduling is easy to use, since all scheduling is left to the operating system. However, without application knowledge, the operating system cannot schedule the threads in

Scheduling Scheme	Approach	Benefits and Drawbacks
Sequential	Operators are placed in a single thread and execute sequentially.	No parallelism, but low latency.
OS Thread	Each operator gets its own thread. The operating system handles the scheduling.	Easy to implement. Suffers from lock contention, cache misses, and frequent thread switching.
Demand	Fused operators are scheduled to run when data is available.	Uses fusion to reduce the number of threads and batching to improve throughput. It is not spatially-aware, does not optimize across operators, and has no data parallelization.
No-op	Implements dynamism by varying the size of the data. Always sends a data item, but the data item can be a nonce.	Does not implement data-parallelization. Increased costs associated with sending no-op data values.
Hardware Pipelining	Stream graph is partitioned into contiguous, load-balanced regions, and each region is assigned to a different core.	Low latency, but load-balancing is very difficult, leading to low utilizations.
Static Data-Parallelism	Data-parallelism applied to coarse-grained stateless operators. Double buffering alleviates stateful operator bottlenecks.	No dynamic applications. Increases throughput at the expense of latency.
Hybrid Static/Dynamic	Partition into coarse-grained components with dynamic boundaries. Apply static optimizations to the components.	Allows for dynamic data transfer rates, is spatially-aware, implements fusion, batching, cross-operator, and data-parallel optimizations.

Table 1: Overview of scheduling approaches. Our scheduler appears in the last row, shaded in grey.

an optimal order, so there are frequent cache misses, unnecessary thread switches, and increased lock contention.

In **demand scheduling**, the scheduler determines which operators are eligible to execute by monitoring the size of their input queues. When an operator is scheduled, it is assigned to a thread from a thread pool. One example of a system using this technique is Aurora [1]. Aurora does not map threads and operators to cores with consideration to their data requirements, i.e., it is not spatially aware. However, it does provide two optimizations that improve on basic demand scheduling. First, like SEDA, it implements batching. Second, it implements a form of operator *fusion* [9], by placing multiple operators on the same thread to execute. Fusion reduces communication overhead and the frequency of thread switching. Like Aurora, our hybrid scheduler implements both the fusion and batching optimizations. Unlike Aurora, our scheduler data-parallelizes operators. With *data-parallelization* replicas of the same operator on different cores process different portions of the data concurrently. Additionally, our scheduler can optimize across fused operators, such as by performing scalarization to further reduce inter-operator communication costs.

One common approach that static languages use to implement dynamic scheduling is **no-op scheduling**. With this approach, special messages are reserved to indicate that an operator should perform a *no-operation*. An operator always produces a fixed number of outputs, but some of those outputs are not used for computation. CQL [2] implements a variation of this approach. In CQL, each operator always produces a bag (i.e. a set with duplicates) of tuples. The size of the bag, however, can vary. Therefore, an operator can send an empty bag to indicate that no computation should be performed by downstream operators. As a result, it suffers from increased costs associated with sending no-op values. In contrast to our scheduler, CQL does not data-parallelize operators.

With **hardware pipelining**, neighboring operators are fused until there are fewer or equal operators as cores. Each

fused operator is then assigned to a single core for the life of the program. This allows upstream and downstream operators to execute in parallel. The StreamIt infrastructure includes a compilation path that mainly exploits this approach [7] for several different target platforms, including clusters of workstations [14], the MIT Raw microprocessor [16], and Tilera's line of microprocessors [18]. The hardware pipelining path supports dynamic rates, but it cannot fuse operators if they have dynamic data transfer rates. The challenge for hardware pipelining is to ensure that each fused set of operators performs approximately the same amount of work, so that the application is properly load balanced. For real-world applications, this is difficult [6]. Dynamic data transfer rates make the problem even harder, because there is no way to statically estimate how much work an operator with a dynamic data transfer rate will perform. Consequently, hardware pipelining was largely abandoned as a compilation strategy by StreamIt, except when targeting FPGAs.

With **static data-parallelism**, the compiler tries to aggressively fuse all operators, and then data-parallelize the fused operators so that they occupy all cores. One complication for this strategy is that operators with stateful computations cannot be parallelized, and therefore introduce bottlenecks. There are compilation paths of the StreamIt compiler [6] that target commodity SMP multicores and Tilera multicore processors using the static data-parallelism approach. The StreamIt compiler offsets the effects of stateful operator bottlenecks by introducing *double buffering* between operators. With double buffering, non-parallelized operators can execute concurrently, because the buffer that a producer writes to is different from the buffer from which the consumer reads.

Our **hybrid scheduler** extends the static data-parallelism path of the StreamIt compiler. The static data-parallelism strategy is scalable and performant across varying multicore architectures (both shared memory and distributed memory) for real world static streaming applications [6], but

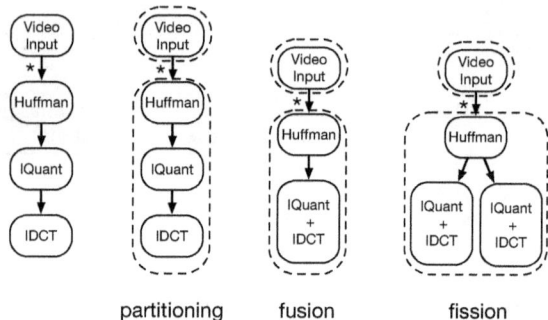

partitioning   fusion   fission

Figure 2: The data-flow graph is first partitioned into static subgraphs. Solid edges are streams from producers to consumers. The asterisk indicates a dynamic communication channel, and the dashed line indicates the static subgraphs. Each static subgraph is optimized by fusing and then parallelizing.

does not include the expressiveness of dynamic data transfer rates. In this work we achieve scalable parallelism with minimal communication for a wider set of streaming applications. Our strategy partitions the application into static subgraphs separated by dynamic rates, and applies the static data-parallelism optimizations to the subgraphs.

4. COMPILER TECHNIQUES

In practice, many streaming applications contain only a small number of operators with dynamic data transfer rates, while the rest of the application is static. This observation motivates our design. The high-level intuition is that the compiler can partition the operators into subgraphs separated by dynamic rate boundaries. It can then treat each subgraph as if it were a separate static application, using a *static data-parallelism* scheduler. In other words, within a subgraph, operators communicate through static buffers, and the compiler can statically optimize each subgraph independently of the rest of the application.

The compiler for our hybrid scheduler therefore extends a static data-parallelism compiler in two ways. First, it must partition the application into subgraphs. Second, it must assign subgraphs onto threads and cores. This section discusses the techniques used by the compiler to support our hybrid scheduler. Section 5 presents the runtime techniques for scheduling each of the partitions.

4.1 Partitioning

To partition the application, the compiler runs a breadth-first search on the data-flow graph to find weakly connected components obtained by deleting edges with *dynamic communication channels*. A *dynamic communication channel* is an edge between two operators where either the producer, the consumer, or both have dynamic rate communication.

If there exists an edge with a dynamic communication channel where the endpoints belong to the same weakly connected component, the compiler reports an error stating that the application in invalid. In future work, we are exploring extensions to this algorithm which would allow the compiler to also partition along static edges instead of reporting an error.

The result of the partitioning algorithm is a set of sub-

graphs that can each be treated as a separate static application. This allows us to leverage the static compiler and optimizer almost *as-is* by running them on each subgraph independently.

We have implemented partitioning as an extension to the StreamIt compiler. As discussed in Section 3, our extension modifies the static data-parallel compilation path of the compiler. Other compilation paths in the compiler support dynamic data rates. However, in contrast to our extension, they do not target SMP multicores, and do not allow either fission or fusion optimizations.

Using StreamIt as a source language has two implications for the partitioning algorithm. First, because the data-flow graphs in StreamIt are hierarchical, the compiler must first turn composite operators into their constituent operators to flatten the data-flow graph. Second, partitioning must respect the topological constraints enforced by the StreamIt language. In StreamIt, the operator-graph must be a *pipeline*, *split-join*, or *feedback-loop* topology. Our current implementation only partitions the graph into pipeline topologies. Although the partitioning algorithm works for other topologies, the StreamIt language would need to add split and join operators that can process tuples out-of-order. A static *round-robin* join operator, for example, would interleave the outputs of dynamic rate operators on its input branches, resulting in errors.

Although dynamic split-join topologies would be useful to implement applications such as an MPEG decoder, which routes i-frames and p-frames along different paths for separate processing, we have found that many applications only use dynamic rates within pipeline topologies at the ingress or egress points of the data-flow graph. This is consistent with the use of dynamic rates for filtering or parsing data before or after some heavy-weight computation. Examples of such applications include automated financial trading, anomaly detection, and graphics pipelines.

4.2 Optimization

Once the graph is partitioned, the compiler can optimize each subgraph independently. Ideally, our modified compiler could treat the static optimizer as a black-box, and simply re-use the existing static data-parallel compilation path to first fuse operators to remove the communication overhead between them, and then data-parallelize (or performs *fission* on, in StreamIt terminology) the fused operators.

However, we had to slightly modify the standard fusion and fission optimizations to support dynamic rates. Our compiler does not data-parallelize operators with dynamic communication channels. In general, they could be parallelized, as long as there were some way to preserve the order of their outputs. We plan to address this in future work. This restriction impacts the fusion optimizations. Operators with dynamic input rates but static output rates are not fused with downstream operators. Although such a transformation would be *safe*, it would not be *profitable* because the fusion would inhibit parallelization. Figure 2 illustrates the changes to the operator data-flow graph during the partitioning and optimization stages of our compiler.

4.3 Placement and Thread Assignment

The static data-parallel compilation path of the StreamIt compiler assigns operators to cores using a greedy bin-packing algorithm that optimizes for spatial locality. That is, the

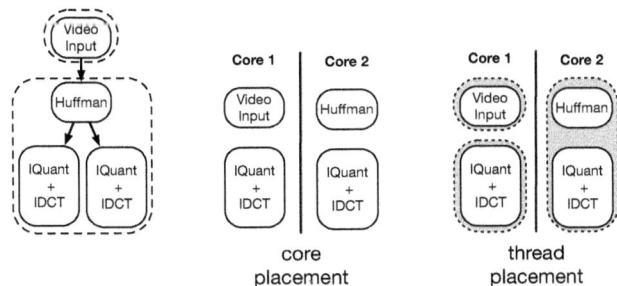

Figure 3: Operators are first assigned to cores and then to threads. Operators on the same thread appear in the same shaded oval.

mapping algorithm tries to place producers and consumers on the same core, while at the same time balancing the workload across available cores. The work estimates come from a static analysis of the operator code [7].

To support dynamic rate partitions, we extend the compiler to not only assign operators to cores, but additionally assign operators to threads. In Figure 3, the partitioned operators are first mapped to cores and then assigned to threads. As will be explained in Section 5.1, each static subgraph is placed on its own thread. Data-parallelized static rate operators on the same core as their producer are placed in the same thread as their producer. Data-parallelized static rate operators not on the same core as their producer are assigned to different threads. In Figure 3, the `VideoInput` and `Huffman` operators are each assigned to separate threads, because they are in separate static subgraphs. The data-parallelized `IQuant+IDCT` operator on core 1 is in its own thread. The data-parallelized `IQuant+IDCT` operator on core 2 is placed on the same thread as its producer.

5. RUNTIME TECHNIQUES

Section 4 discusses the compiler techniques used to support our hybrid scheduler. This section presents the runtime techniques. At runtime, operators in different subgraphs communicate through dynamically-sized queues, adding the flexibility for dynamic rate communication. Within a subgraph, communication is unchanged from the completely static version. Operators communicate through static buffers, even across cores. Each subgraph runs in its own thread, which allows operators to suspend execution midway through a computation if there is no data available on its input queues. Threads run according to the *data-flow order* of the operators they contain, meaning that upstream subgraphs run before downstream subgraphs. This ordering makes it more likely that downstream subgraphs have data available on their input queues when they execute. If data is not available for an operator, the thread blocks, and the next thread runs. Finally, batching is used to reduce the overhead of thread switching.

5.1 Suspending and Resuming Subgraphs

To support dynamic rate communication between operators, we need to consider two questions: (1) what happens if a producer needs to write more data than will fit into an output buffer, and (2) what happens if a consumer needs to read more data than is available from an input buffer?

If a producer needs to write more data than will fit into an output buffer, we need to grow the buffer. In other words, the writer must not block. If a writer could block, then it might never produce enough data for a downstream operator to consume, leading to deadlock. Therefore, we use dynamically-sized queues for communication between the subgraphs. If a producer needs to write more data than will fit into the queue, the queue size is doubled. There is a small performance hit each time a queue needs to be resized. The total number of resizings is logarithmic in the maximum queue size experienced by the application. For most applications, resizing only happens during program startup, as the queues quickly grow to a suitable size. Our current implementation does not decrease queue sizes. In ongoing work, we are investigating adaptive schemes which would adjust the queue size as the workload changes.

Supporting dynamic consumers is more difficult. A stateful operator may run out of data to read partway through a computation. For example, an operator that performs a run-length encoding needs to count the number of consecutive characters in an input sequence. If the data is unavailable for the encoder to read, it needs to store its current character count until it can resume execution. The challenge for dynamic consumers is how to suspend execution, and save any partial state, until more input data becomes available.

To support this behavior, we needed an implementation that is tantamount to coroutines. We chose to use Posix threads that are suspended and resumed with condition variables, although user-level threads would be a viable alternative. Threads are, after all, the standard abstraction for saving the stack and registers. However, using threads had three implications for our design. First, prior versions of StreamIt use one thread per core. We needed to modify the runtime to support running multiple threads per core, one at a time. Second, we needed to add infrastructure for scheduling multiple threads. Finally, switching between threads had a significant negative impact on performance. We needed to explore techniques to offset that impact.

We considered several alternatives to using threads that we thought might incur less of a performance hit. However, we were not able to find a better solution. Closures, such as provided by Objective-C blocks or C++0x lambdas are not sufficient, as they cannot preserve state through a partial execution. We considered adding explicit code to the operators to save the stack and registers, but that code would be brittle (since it is low-level, and breaks abstractions usually hidden by the compiler and runtime system), and not portable across different architectures. A dynamic consumer could invoke an upstream operator directly to produce more data, but the scheduling logic would get complicated as each upstream operator would have to call its predecessor in a chain. On Stack Replacement [10], which stores stack frames on the heap, would work, but there was no readily available implementation to use.

5.2 Scheduling

The code generated by the static data-parallel path of the StreamIt compiler uses only one thread per core. Each operator in the thread executes sequentially in a loop. At the end of each loop iteration, the thread reaches a barrier. The barrier guarantees that all operators are in synch at the beginning of each global iteration of the schedule.

To support dynamic rate communication, we extend the

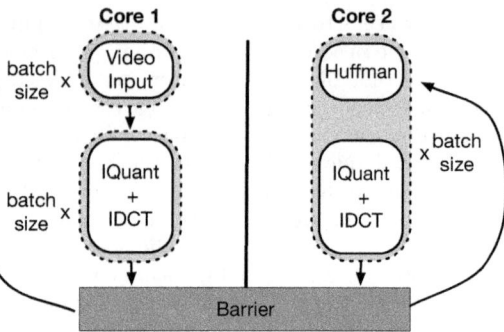

Figure 4: Each thread executes in data-flow order on its assigned core. Each thread is responsible for scheduling the next thread on its core. The solid arrow indicate control transfer.

StreamIt compiler to multiplex multiple threads on the same core. This complicates the scheduler, as it has to coordinate between the various threads.

To prevent multiple threads on a core from being eligible to run at the same time, each thread is guarded by a condition variable. A thread will not run until it is signalled. Our original design had a *master* thread for each core that signalled each thread when they were scheduled to run. However, we found that the biggest performance overhead for our dynamic applications comes from switching threads. To reduce the number of thread switches, we altered our design so that each thread is responsible for signaling the subsequent thread directly. The solid arrows in Figure 4 indicate the transfer of control between threads. Switching from the master thread approach to our direct call approach resulted in an 27% increase in throughput for an application with 32 threads.

The first operator assigned to a thread is the *leader* of that thread. In Figure 4, `Huffman` is the leader of the first thread on core 2. Threads run according to the data-flow order of the leaders. Running in data-flow order makes it more likely that downstream subgraphs have data available on their input queues when they execute.

At program startup, all dynamic queues are empty. As execution proceeds, though, the queues fill up as data travels downstream. This allows for *pipelining*, meaning that downstream operators can execute at the same time as upstream operators. In Figure 4, `Huffman` executes on the data that `VideoInput` processed in the previous iteration. Sometimes, an upstream operator might not produce data. This might occur, for example, with a selection operator that filters data. When this occurs, there is a slight hiccup in the pipelining that resolves when more data travels downstream.

To guard against concurrent accesses to a dynamic queue by producers and consumers, the *push* and *pop* operations are guarded by locks. A lock-free queue implementation would be an attractive alternative to use here, as it could allow for greater concurrent execution [12].

5.3 Batching

As mentioned in Section 5.2, the abandoned master thread approach taught us that the biggest performance overhead for our dynamic applications comes from switching threads. This insight led us to implement the *batching* optimization.

With batching, each thread runs for *batch size* iterations before transferring control to the next thread. When the batch size is increased, more data items are stored on each dynamic queue. Batching increases the throughput of the application and reduces thread switching at the expense of increased memory usage and latency. As we will show in Section 6.1.3, running an application with the batch size set to 100 can triple the performance.

6. EVALUATION

Overall, our design strikes a balance between static and dynamic scheduling. It allows for dynamic communication between static components, and for aggressive optimization within the static components.

Because all of the scheduling strategies discussed in this paper are sensitive to variations in both the application structure and the input data set, we first evaluate our system using a set of micro-benchmarks. All of the micro-benchmarks are parameterizable in terms of computation, parallelism, and communication, allowing us to better explore tradeoffs that different scheduling strategies make. The micro-benchmarks are designed to highlight the effects of altering one of these parameters.

Each section starts with the intuition or question that motivates the experiment, followed by a discussion of the setup and results. Section 6.1 evaluates the overhead we can expect for our hybrid scheduler as compared to fully static scheduling. Section 6.2 evaluates what performance improvement we can expect compared to completely dynamic schedulers.

The benchmarks in Section 6.3 model the structure of three applications, and use parameterized workloads for the application logic. These applications make use of a predicate-based filter; an operator for computing volume-weighted average price; and a Huffman encoder and decoder. These experiments help to understand how our scheduler behaves for real-world applications.

To make the material more accessible, we have grouped the results together in Figures 5, 6, 7, and 8. Each experiment has two figures associated with it. On the left is a topology diagram that illustrates the application that was run in the experiment. On the right is a chart that shows the result. In all topology diagrams, a number to the left of an operator is its static input data rate. A number to the right indicates its static output data rate. An asterisk indicates that the rate is dynamic.

In many of the experiments, we vary the amount of work performed by an operator. One work unit, or one computation, is defined as one iteration of the following loop:

```
1  x = pop();
2  for (i = 0; i < WORK; i++) {
3      x += i * 3.0 - 1.0;
4  }
5  push(x);
```

Each subsection below discusses an experiment in detail. All experiments were run on machines with four 64 bit Intel Xeon (X7550) processors, each with 8 cores (for a total of 32), running at 2.00GHz, and an L3 cache size of 18MB. All machines ran Debian 2.6.32-21 with kernel 2.6.32.19. Overall, the results are encouraging. Our hybrid scheduler outperforms three alternative dynamic schedulers: OS thread, demand, and no-op.

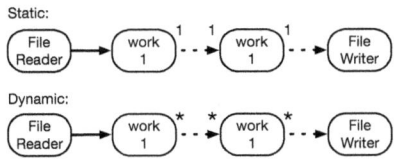

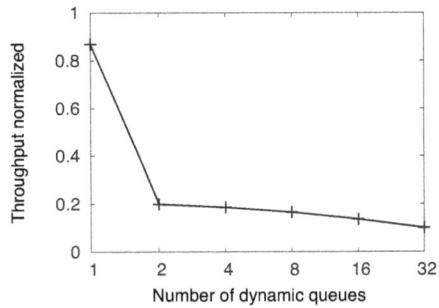

(a) *Dynamic scheduling shows a 5x slowdown with two dynamic queues compared to static scheduling.*

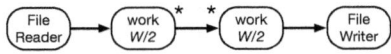

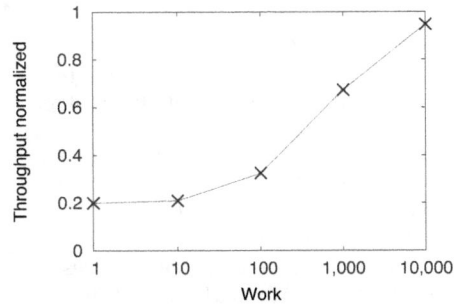

(b) *Larger operator workload amortizes dynamic scheduling overhead.*

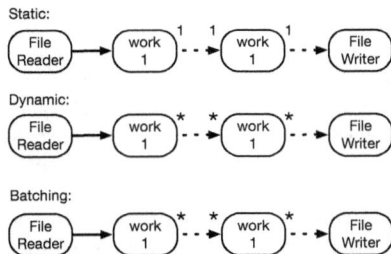

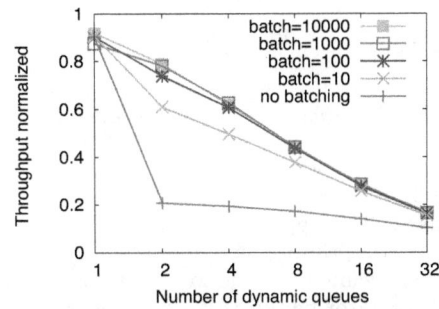

(c) *Batching can further ameliorate the effects of thread switching.*

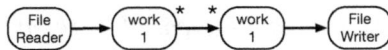

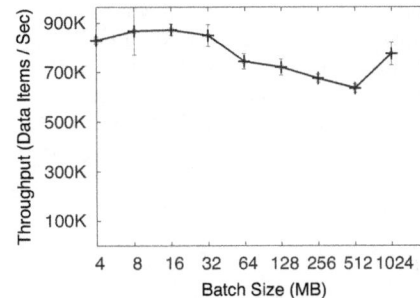

(d) *Batching beyond the cache size hurt performance.*

Figure 5: Experiments with fused operators.

6.1 Comparison to Static Schemes

We expect that the runtime mechanisms used to support dynamic communication will have higher overhead than the fully static equivalents. This is the tradeoff that the hybrid compiler makes in order to get better expressivity. The following set of experiments quantify the overhead of supporting dynamic communication.

6.1.1 Worst-Case Overhead without Batching

How does the communication overhead from dynamism compare to that of the static scheduling?

The worst-case scenario for our scheduler is if the operators do not perform any computation, so the communication overheads cannot be amortized. Figure 5 (a) shows the worst-case overhead for dynamic scheduling as compared to static scheduling. The application is a pipeline of $n + 1$ operators communicating through n dynamic queues. Each operator forwards any data it receives without performing any computation. The results are normalized to a static application, also of $n + 1$ operators, where all operators are fused. The experiment is run on a single core.

The y-axis is the normalized throughput and the x-axis has increasing values of n. As expected, there is significant overhead for adding dynamism. For the simple case of a single dynamic queue, there is a 5x decrease in throughput. The throughput decreases linearly as we add more queues. When there are 31 queues, there is a 10x performance hit.

The biggest detriment to performance comes from switching threads. In the experiment in Section 6.1.3, we show that the overhead from thread switching can be ameliorated by increasing the batch size.

6.1.2 Operator Workload

How does operator workload affect the performance?

Operators for most applications perform more work than in Section 6.1.1. Figure 5 (b) shows the effect of operator workload on our scheduler. The application is a pipeline of two operators communicating through a dynamic queue, running on a single core. We define W as the total workload for the application. Each operator performs $W/2$ computations, and we run the application with increasing workloads.

The results are shown normalized to a static application with two fused operators. The y-axis shows the throughput and the x-axis shows workload. As the operator workload increases, communication overheads are amortized. The 5x overhead with the identity filter improves to 1.48x overhead when the two operators perform 1,000 computations combined. Performance can be further improved with the batching optimization.

6.1.3 Batching

How does batching affect the performance?

In contrast to operator workload, the batch size is fully under control of the system. That is fortunate, because it means we can ameliorate the worst-case behavior from Section 6.1.1. The experiment in Figure 5 (c) demonstrates that batching improves the performance of a dynamic application. It repeats the experiment from Section 6.1.1, with increasing batch sizes. In the chart, each line is the dynamic application run with a different amount of batching.

The graph shows that increasing the batch size can significantly improve the throughput. The 5x overhead with the identity filter improves to 1.64x overhead when the batch size is set to 100. As the batch size increases, so does the throughput. However, as the next experiment shows, there is a limit.

6.1.4 Batching vs. Cache Size

Does batching too much negatively affect the performance?

Batching causes more data to be stored on the dynamic queues. The experiment in Figure 5 (d) tests if increasing the batch size beyond the cache size hurts performance. The application consists of two identity operators in a pipeline.

We ran the experiment with increasing batch sizes, shown in the x-axis. Although there is a lot of variance in the data points, we see that the performance does start to degrade as the batch size outgrows the cache size at 18MB. The performance degradation is not excessive, though, because streaming workloads mostly access memory sequentially, and can therefore benefit from hardware pre-fetching.

6.1.5 Dynamism with Parallelism

How does dynamism affect parallelism?

Adding dynamism to applications introduces bottlenecks into the operator graph, since operators with dynamic communication rates are not parallelized. The experiment in Figure 6 (a) explores how this bottleneck affects performance.

We compare two version of an application: one static and one dynamic. Both version consist of three operators in a pipeline. In the dynamic version, the first and second operators communicate through a dynamic queue. For each data item, the first operator does 100 computations, and the third operator does 900 computations. The second operator simply forwards data.

We increased the degree of parallelism for both applications. In the static case, all operators are fused and parallelized. In the dynamic case, only the third operator is parallelized.

The effects of the bottleneck introduced by the dynamic rate are apparent, as the static case outperforms the dynamic case. However, neither case sees dramatic improvements when parallelized, and indeed the static case sees a drop in performance after 16 cores. There was not sufficient parallelized work to offset the extra communication costs. In the next experiment, we increase the operator workload.

6.1.6 Parallelism and Increased Workload

How does operator workload affect the fission optimization?

Figure 6 (b) repeats the experiment in Figure 6 (a), but with an increased operator workload. For each data item, the first operator does 1,000 computations, and the third operator does 9,000 computations. The static version of the application effectively parallelizes the work, getting a 17x speedup over the non-parallelized version. The dynamic version also sees a performance improvement, despite the bottleneck, achieving 6.8x increase in throughput.

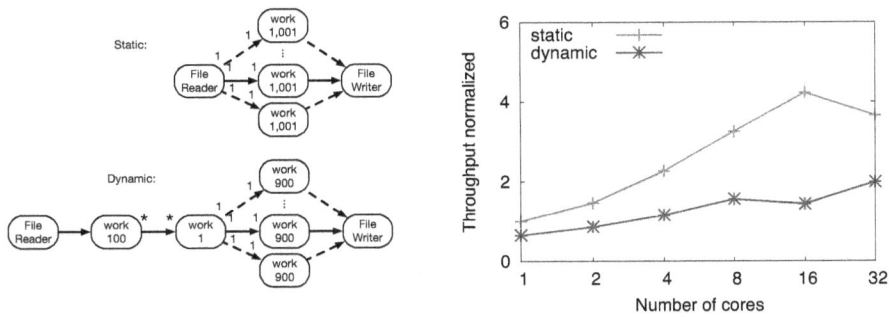

(a) *Dynamic rates introduce a bottleneck for data parallelization.*

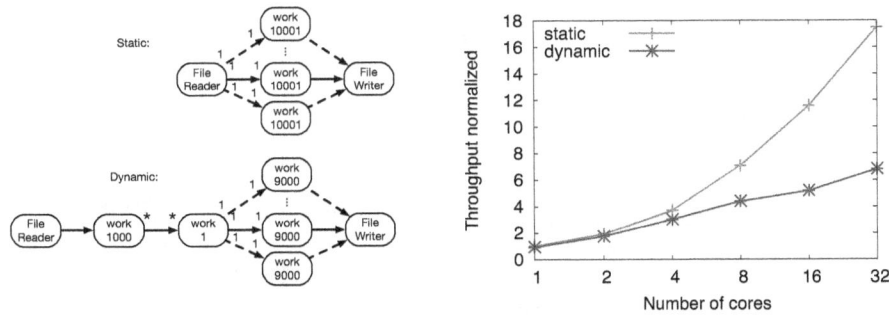

(b) *Larger operator workloads offset the impact of the bottleneck.*

Figure 6: Experiments with parallelized operators.

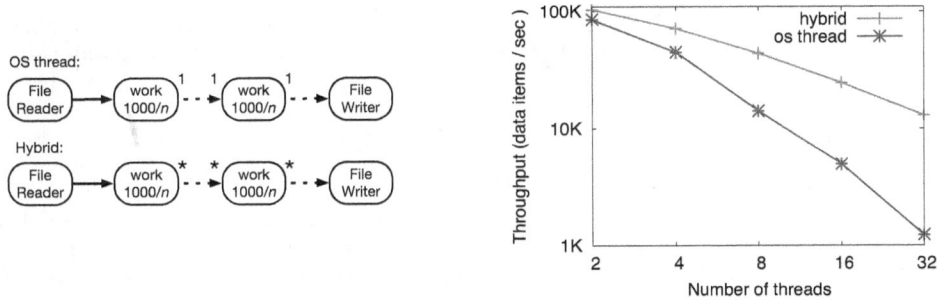

(a) *The hybrid scheduler outperforms the OS thread scheduler by as much as 10x.*

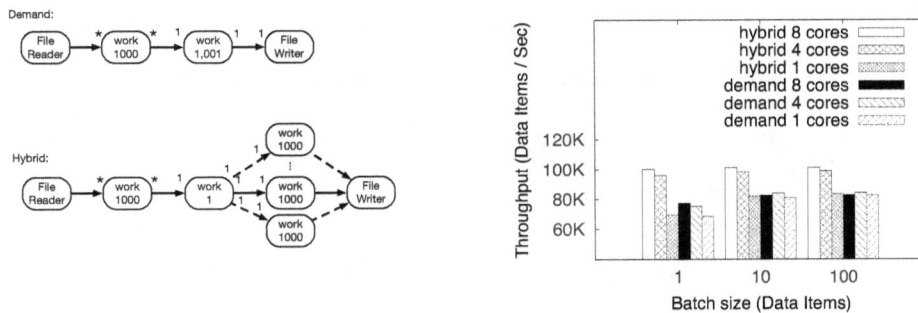

(b) The hybrid scheduler outperforms the demand scheduler by 1.2x with a modest workload.

Figure 7: Comparing the hybrid scheduler to OS thread and demand scheduling.

6.2 Comparison to Dynamic Schemes

Our hybrid scheduler makes a tradeoff between performance and expressivity, trying to balance both demands. The last section demonstrates that, as expected, adding support for dynamic rate communication hurts performance. The real test of our scheduler, though, is to see if adding the static optimizations yields better performance when compared to other dynamic schedulers. In the following experiments, we compare our hybrid scheduler to OS thread, demand, and no-op schedulers. In all three cases, our hybrid scheduler outperforms the alternative.

6.2.1 OS Thread Scheduling

How does out scheduler compare to OS thread scheduling?

The experiment in Figure 7 (a) compares our hybrid scheduler to an OS thread scheduler. The application consists of n operators arranged in a pipeline. We ran the application with both schedulers on one core with an increasing number of operators. Recall that we ran all experiments on Debian 2.6.32-21 with kernel 2.6.32.19.

All communication between operators is through dynamic queues, and in both the hybrid and OS thread version, each operator executes in its own thread. In the hybrid version, our scheduler controls the scheduling of the threads, so that each thread executes in upstream to downstream order of the operators. In the OS thread scheduler version, the operating system schedules the threads. The results show that the hybrid version significantly outperforms the OS thread approach. In an application with 8 operators, it is 3.1x faster. When there are 32 operators, it is 10.5x faster.

6.2.2 Demand Scheduling

How does our scheduler compare to demand scheduling?

As discussed in Section 3, the demand scheduler in Aurora uses fusion and batching to increase performance, but does not support data-parallelization. It is not an inherent limitation of demand schedulers that they could not support data parallelization. However, it is more difficult to implement data-parallelization for demand schedulers than it is for static schedulers, because it requires machinery to ensure the correct ordering of data. Quantifying the overhead for that machinery is out of scope for this paper. Our comparison is faithful to the Aurora implementation.

The experiment in Figure 7 (b) compares our hybrid scheduler to a demand scheduler. The application consists of three operators in a pipeline. The first does 1,000 computations of work, the second is the identity filter, and the third does 1,000 computations. Since both the hybrid and demand schedulers perform fusion, it does not matter how many operators are downstream from the second operator, as they would be fused into a single operator during optimization. The same application was run in both experiments, but for the demand scheduler, data-parallelization was disabled. Since both the demand scheduler and the hybrid scheduler implement batching, we increased the batch size for different runs of the experiment. We ran both versions of the program on 1, 4, and 8 cores. The hybrid version on 4 and 8 cores outperforms the demand scheduler by 1.2x on 4 cores, and 1.3x on 8 cores. Although these improvements are modest, Section 6.1.6 showed that increasing the workload in the parallelized operators would increase the performance gains of the hybrid scheduler.

6.2.3 No-op Scheduling

How does our scheduler compare to no-op scheduling?

In no-op scheduling, special messages are reserved to indicate that an operator should perform a no-operation. Using this approach, a statically scheduled streaming language can simulate the behavior of a dynamically scheduled language. Because the no-op scheduler is static, it can be optimized with the static optimizer to take advantage of fusion and data-parallelization. However, because replicas receive no-op messages instead of actual work, the workload among replicas is often imbalanced.

To compare our hybrid scheduler with a no-op, we implemented two applications, bargain trade finder and predicate-based filtering, with both systems. The results for this experiment are discussed in detail in Sections 6.3.2 and 6.3.3. In both cases, the hybrid scheduler was about 5x faster than the no-op scheduler.

6.3 Real-World Inspired Benchmarks

The applications in this section are designed to model the structure and workload of three real world applications. The first application, Huffman encoder and decoder, is compared to the demand scheduler described in the previous section. The next two applications, bargain trade finder and predicate based filtering, are compared to a no-op scheduler. In all three experiments, the hybrid approach exhibited improved performance over the alternative approach.

6.3.1 Huffman Encoder and Decoder

Many audio and video processing applications make use of a Huffman encoder for data compression. It serves as a good example of an operator that, by its very nature, cannot be expressed statically. Implementing a Huffman encoder operator with the no-op scheme, for example, would not make sense, since the operator would always output a maximum length byte string, with some of the bytes filled in as no-op padding, loosing the benefits of the encoding.

Our synthetic application has a Huffman encoder at the application ingress, and a decoder at the egress. Three operators are in-between the encoder and decoder, emulating additional processing (i.e., busy looping rather than doing the actual computation) that would be performed for data transmission over a lossy channel.

For the experiment, we increased the number of available cores, which allowed our hybrid scheduler to take advantage of the data parallelization. The demand scheduler does not perform data parallelization, which is consistent with the Aurora implementation. Figure 8 (a) shows the results. The hybrid scheme outperforms the demand scheduler by 20% when run on 8 cores. However, when we ran the experiment on 16 cores, we exceeded the benefits of parallelization.

6.3.2 Bargain Trade Finder

A *volume weighted average price*, or VWAP, is a computation often used in financial applications. It keeps a sum of both the price of trades and the volume of trades that occur during a given time window. By time we refer to application time, as embodied by a time attribute of each data item. And by window, we refer to a sequence of data items

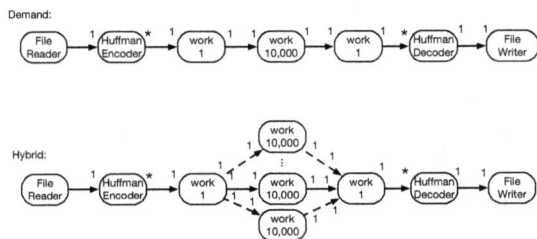

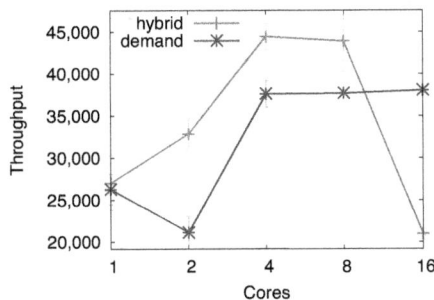

(a) *The hybrid scheduler outperforms the demand scheduler by 1.2x for a Huffman encoder and decoder..*

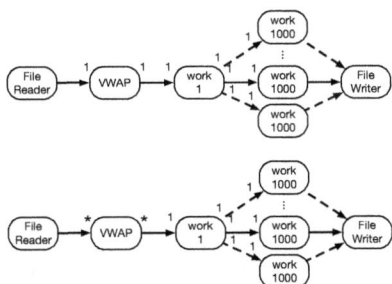

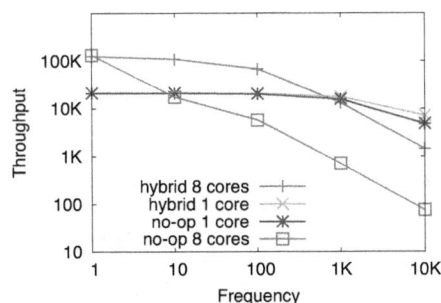

(b) *The hybrid scheduler can perform 5.1x faster than the no-op scheduler for applications that use VWAP.*

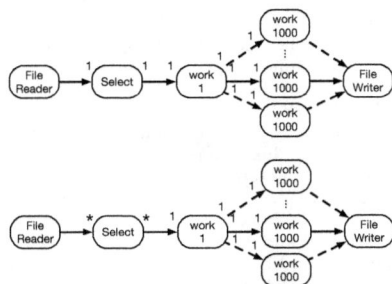

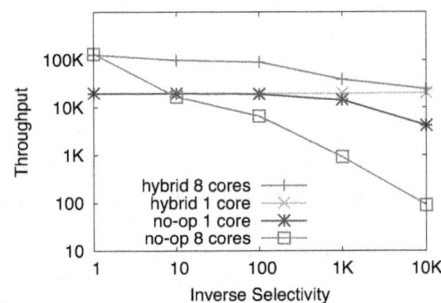

(c) *The hybrid scheduler can perform 4.9x faster than the no-op scheduler for predicate-based filtering.*

Figure 8: Experiments with real-world inspired synthetic benchmarks.

for which the time attribute differs at most by a prescribed amount. At the end of that window, it sends the average.

A hedge fund might use a VWAP operator in an application for finding bargains transactions [8]. A bargain occurs when a stock price dips below its average price over a past time window. To emulate the bargain finder application, we placed three operators in a pipeline. The first operator is the VWAP, for computing the rolling average. The remaining two operators represent the static work needed to perform a transaction once a bargain has been identified.

We implemented the bargain finder application using both our hybrid scheduler, and a no-op scheduler. Both schedulers parallelize the third operator. For both configurations, we varied the frequency of the input data. In the graphs in Figure 8 (b), a frequency of 10 means that on average every

10th input data item would produce the next window. That is, a total of 10 trades appear in the time window.

Figure 8 (b) shows the results. The hybrid scheme on 8 cores shows a 5.1x performance improvement over the best no-op version when the frequency is 10. When the frequency is greater than 1,000, the hybrid scheme on 1 core exhibits better throughput than the other configurations.

6.3.3 Predicate-Based Filtering

Many applications are only interested in processing *significant events*, where the definition of significant is application-dependent. For these applications, it is necessary to filter data based on some predicate. For example, ocean-based sensors constantly monitor tidal heights. If the tidal height exceeds some threshold, it can then be correlated with other

169

measurements, such as wind speed and barometric pressure, to predict the onset of a storm.

To emulate this application, we implemented an operator that that scans incoming data for items that match a predicate (e.g., data items above a threshold). The application consists of three operators. The first is the filter, and the remaining two operators process the significant events.

For the experiment, we varied the selectivity of the data. In Figure 8 (c), an inverse selectivity of 10 means that on average, for every 10 inputs, the selection filters 9. Put another way, 1 in 10 inputs would result in meaningful downstream computation. The hybrid scheduler shows significant performance improvements over the no-op version. When the inverse selectivity is 10, the hybrid scheduler shows a 4.9x higher performance compared to the best no-op version.

7. OUTLOOK AND CONCLUSION

This paper presents the design of a hybrid static/dynamic scheduler for streaming languages. Stream processing has become an essential programming paradigm for applications that process large volumes of data with high throughput.

In ongoing work, we are investigating mapping these hybrid scheduling techniques to a distributed architecture. Our current prototype uses shared memory segments for dynamic queues, but other implementations are possible. For example, prior work on distributed versions of StreamIt used remote memory spaces to run on the TILERA [18] architecture, or sockets in a Java-library implementation [15].

The first contribution of this paper is to explore the trade-offs between dynamic and static scheduling. While statically scheduled languages allow for more aggressive optimization, dynamically scheduled languages are more expressive, and can be used to write a wider range of applications, including applications for compression/decompression, event monitoring, networking, and parsing.

The second contribution of this paper is the design of a hybrid static-dynamic scheduler for stream processing languages. The scheduler partitions the streaming application into static subgraphs separated by dynamic rate boundaries, and then applies static optimizations to those subgraphs. Each static subgraph is assigned its own thread, and the scheduler executes the threads such that upstream operators execute before downstream operators.

The third contribution of this paper is an implementation and evaluation of our hybrid scheduler in the context of the StreamIt language. When compared against three alternative dynamic scheduling techniques, OS thread, demand, and no-op, our scheduler exhibited better performance.

In summary, our approach shows significant speedup over fully dynamic scheduling, while allowing developers to write a larger set of applications. We believe that our scheduler strikes the right balance between expressivity and performance for stream processing languages.

Acknowledgements

We thank the anonymous reviewers for their helpful comments. We thank Bill Thies for his feedback on this work, and Robert Kleinberg for his suggestions on Section 4.1. This work is partially supported by NSF CCF-1162444.

8. REFERENCES

[1] D. J. Abadi, D. Carney, U. Çetintemel, M. Cherniack, C. Convey, S. Lee, M. Stonebraker, N. Tatbul, and S. Zdonik. Aurora: A new model and architecture for data stream management. *The VLDB Journal*, 12(2):120–139, Aug. 2003.

[2] A. Arasu, S. Babu, and J. Widom. The CQL continuous query language: Semantic foundations and query execution. *The VLDB Journal*, 15(2):121–142, June 2006.

[3] J. Auerbach, D. F. Bacon, P. Cheng, and R. Rabbah. Lime: A Java-compatible and synthesizable language for heterogeneous architectures. In *Proc. ACM Conference on Object-Oriented Programming Systems, Languages, and Applications*, pages 89–108, Oct. 2010.

[4] G. Berry and G. Gonthier. The ESTEREL synchronous programming language: Design, semantics, implementation. *Science of Computer Programming*, 19(2):87–152, Nov. 1992.

[5] I. Buck, T. Foley, D. Horn, J. Sugerman, K. Fatahalian, M. Houston, and P. Hanrahan. Brook for GPUs: Stream computing on graphics hardware. In *Proc. ACM International Conference on Computer Graphics and Interactive Techniques*, pages 777–786, Aug. 2004.

[6] M. I. Gordon, W. Thies, and S. Amarasinghe. Exploiting coarse-grained task, data, and pipeline parallelism in stream programs. In *Proc. 12th ACM International Conference on Architectural Support for Programming Languages and Operating Systems*, pages 151–162, Oct. 2006.

[7] M. I. Gordon, W. Thies, M. Karczmarek, J. Lin, A. S. Meli, A. A. Lamb, C. Leger, J. Wong, H. Hoffmann, D. Maze, and S. Amarasinghe. A stream compiler for communication-exposed architectures. In *Proc. 10th ACM International Conference on Architectural Support for Programming Languages and Operating Systems*, pages 291–303, Dec. 2002.

[8] M. Hirzel, H. Andrade, B. Gedik, V. Kumar, G. Losa, M. Mendell, H. Nasgaard, R. Soulé, and K.-L. Wu. Streams processing language specification. Research Report RC24897, IBM, Nov. 2009.

[9] M. Hirzel, R. Soulé, S. Schneider, B. Gedik, and R. Grimm. A catalog of stream processing optimizations. Technical Report RC25215, IBM, Sept. 2011.

[10] U. Hölzle, C. Chambers, and D. Ungar. Debugging optimized code with dynamic deoptimization. In *Proc. ACM Conference on Programming Language Design and Implementation*, pages 32–43, 1992.

[11] A. H. Hormati, Y. Choi, M. Kudlur, R. Rabbah, T. Mudge, and S. Mahlke. Flextream: Adaptive compilation of streaming applications for heterogeneous architectures. In *Proc. 18th International Conference on Parallel Architectures and Compilation Techniques*, pages 214–223, Sept. 2009.

[12] M. M. Michael and M. L. Scott. Simple, fast, and practical non-blocking and blocking concurrent queue algorithms. In *Proc. 15th ACM Symposium on Principles of Distributed Computing*, pages 267–275, 1996.

[13] M. Roesch. Snort- lightweight intrusion detection system for networks. In *Proc. 13th USENIX Large Installation System Administration Conference*, pages 229–238, 1999.

[14] J. Sermulins, W. Thies, R. Rabbah, and S. Amarasinghe. Cache aware optimization of stream programs. In *Proc. ACM SIGPLAN/SIGBED Conference on Languages, Compilers, and Tools for Embedded Systems*, pages 115–126, June 2005.

[15] W. Thies, M. Karczmarek, and S. Amarasinghe. StreamIt: A language for streaming applications. In *Proc. 11th International Conference on Compiler Construction*, volume 2304 of *LNCS*, pages 179–196, Apr. 2002.

[16] E. Waingold, M. Taylor, D. Srikrishna, V. Sarkar, W. Lee, et al. Baring It All to Software: Raw Machines. *IEEE Computer*, 30(9):86–93, 1997.

[17] M. Welsh, D. Culler, and E. Brewer. SEDA: An architecture for well-conditioned, scalable Internet services. In *Proc. 18th ACM Symposium on Operating Systems Principles*, pages 230–243, Oct. 2001.

[18] D. Wentzlaff, P. Griffin, H. Hoffmann, L. Bao, B. Edwards, C. Ramey, M. Mattina, C.-C. Miao, J. F. Brown III, and A. Agarwal. On-chip interconnection architecture of the tile processor. *IEEE Micro*, 27(5):15–31, Sept. 2007.

Towards Unified and Native Enrichment in Event Processing Systems

Souleiman Hasan

Digital Enterprise Research
Institute, National University of
Ireland, Galway

souleiman.hasan@deri.org

Sean O'Riain

Digital Enterprise Research
Institute, National University of
Ireland, Galway

sean.oriain@deri.org

Edward Curry

Digital Enterprise Research
Institute, National University of
Ireland, Galway

ed.curry@deri.org

ABSTRACT

Events are encapsulated pieces of information that flow from one event agent to another. In order to process an event, additional information that is external to the event is often needed. This is achieved using a process called event enrichment. Current approaches to event enrichment are external to event processing engines and are handled by specialized agents. Within large-scale environments with high heterogeneity among events, the enrichment process may become difficult to maintain. This paper examines event enrichment in terms of information completeness and presents a unified model for event enrichment that takes place natively within the event processing engine. The paper describes the requirements of event enrichment and highlights its challenges such as finding enrichment sources, retrieval of information items, finding complementary information and its fusion with events. It then details an instantiation of the model using Semantic Web and Linked Data technologies. Enrichment is realised by dynamically guiding a spreading activation algorithm in a Linked Data graph. Multiple spreading activation strategies have been evaluated on a set of Wikipedia events and experimentation shows the viability of the approach.

Categories and Subject Descriptors

H.3.3. [**Information Storage and Retrieval**]: Information Search and Retrieval---*information filtering.*

General Terms

Algorithms, Experimentation, Languages, Theory.

Keywords

Information Completeness; Event Enrichment; Event Processing; Linked Data; Spreading Activation.

1. INTRODUCTION

Event-based technology is becoming more widely needed with the rise of new applications ranging from Smart Homes to Smart Cities and the Internet-of-Things [1]. Event-based systems enable a decoupled mode of interaction between participants which makes it suitable for large-scale and distributed environments

such as sensor networks and mobile environment [11]. There are estimates that by the end of 2020 fifty billion devices will be connected to mobile networks [20] which would push event-based technology to its limits.

While the basic information item in an event-based system is an event, it is not uncommon that normal users require the system to handle information that is not encoded in the event. Such information typically comes from legacy databases or web data sources. This causes an information completeness problem for events to be sufficient for tasks such as subscription matching. One current solution to the information completeness issue is to develop external, static and dedicated event processing agents that retrieve information from legacy data sources and enrich the event before it is propagated for further processing. For example, an energy consumption event is generated by a smart electric heater containing the heater's serial number. An enricher retrieves information about the room and floor of the heater from a building management system database and adds it to the event which can then be considered when matching users' interests in high energy consumption events from that specific room or floor.

Future applications of event-based systems are large-scale applications such as the Internet-of-Things where the number of tasks that require information not included in events increases. In these environments the enrichment agents can quickly become difficult to develop and maintain. We argue that the problem lies in the approach taken in current event-based middleware where an event is considered as a closed world. For example, if a subscription tests a specific property that is not included in the event, then that is considered a negative match by default. No attempt is made to try and complement information in the event before judging on positive or negative matching.

The need to complement incomplete events has been recognized by the event processing community. Hinze et al. [15] states that "event enrichment calls for an understanding not only of the events but also for the external sources of information". Hohpe and Woolf [16] dedicates a set of patterns such as message translator, content enricher, and aggregator to address several problems that can be classified under event incompleteness. Teymourian et al. [25] investigates the improvement of expressiveness and flexibility of complex event processing systems via the usage of background knowledge about events and their relations to other concepts in the application domain.

Patterns by Hohpe and Woolf [16] reflect the current state-of-the-art and practice in the design of event processing networks where dedicated agents are assigned with well-defined tasks to overcome some incompleteness issues. For example, they propose the use of dedicated event enrichment agents to access a database and retrieve necessary information that is added to events before they propagate to consumers. However, such agents are ad-hoc and tailored to the particular situations they are designed for. That contradicts with the event processing vision detailed by Etzion and Niblett [10] which calls for a unified and declarative way to process events. Enrichment agents are non-native to the paradigm, and as event processing systems scale out to large and highly heterogeneous environments, the maintenance of such enrichment agents becomes difficult.

Other related work focuses on the fusion of background knowledge with events using a query answering paradigm that spans events and background knowledge. However, such approaches make some assumptions that may not hold in many situations. For example, the work of Teymourian et al. [25] assumes that the background knowledge and events have the same data format and semantics, and that the knowledge base is accessible via a query service making the federation of the query feasible.

We think that in order to make advancement with respect to the event incompleteness problem, it is crucial to deal with the abstract characteristics of the problem and to integrate it into the event processing paradigm so it becomes a native component of event processing engines. Event enrichment can be done closer to the producer's side or closer to the consumer's side. In this paper we explore enrichment which is unified with consumption logic (matching) as consumers can better judge the content completeness of events with respect to their information needs. The contribution of this paper is threefold:

- A unified and native model of event enrichment is proposed along with its formalism.

- An instantiation of the model based on dereferenceable Linked Data and spreading activation is presented.

- An evaluation framework for event enrichment based on assessment of event completeness and enrichment precision is discussed.

The rest of this paper is organized as follows: Section 2 motivates the problem of information incompleteness in event processing systems while Section 3 outlines the dimensions of information incompleteness and the challenges for event enrichment. Section 4 explains the main concepts of the proposed model, its formalism and some potential implications. Section 5 details an instantiation of the proposed model based on Linked Data and spreading activation. Experiment and evaluation are explained in Section 6 and Section 7 summarizes related work. The paper concludes and discusses some potential future directions in Section 8.

2. MOTIVATIONAL SCENARIO

A sustainability officer is an employee who is responsible for assuring the company commitment to its social responsibility programs. For example, the sustainability officer would be interested in situations where energy consumption, and hence CO_2 emissions, of a particular department or building is excessive with regard to company or international standards [7,13].

In order for the sustainability officer to do the job, an event-based middleware is set up. Various energy-related sensors and real-time sources are instrumented so events flow into the middleware. Events in such a scenario are encapsulated with minimal information recording for instance a device name and the amount of energy used. An example attribute-value event describing the energy consumption of a heater is shown in Example 1.

Example 1: An Energy Consumption Event

> *{(type, "energy consumption"),*
>
> *(device, "heater1"),*
>
> *(consumption, "high")}*

Non-technical users such as the sustainability officer tend to include higher level and business concepts and checks in their subscriptions to events. Examples of these are the *"room"* or the *"floor"* where the event was originated, or the *"business unit"* or *"project"* with which the device is associated. One example subscription is shown in Example 2.

Example 2: A Subscription for High Energy Consumption

> *{(type= "energy consumption")*
>
> *and (floor= "second floor")*
>
> *and (consumption="high")}*

The events do not have information about the *"floor"* to answer the subscription in Example 2. Thus, in order to meet information requirement for this subscription, additional information sources in the enterprise such as data about the building would need to be exploited. Dedicated software agents need to be developed to enrich events with sufficient information. A large number of subscriptions may require dedicated enrichment agents. As a result, enrichment routines can become a burden to develop and maintain.

3. EVENT ENRICHMENT

The event-based interaction paradigm is based on the principle of decoupling the various parties which are involved in the interaction, namely event producers and consumers. The main advantage of decoupling the production and consumption of events is an increased scalability by "removing explicit dependencies between the interacting participants" [11]. The three common dimensions of decoupling between event producers and consumers are space, time and synchronization [11]. Thus, the only feasible way of interaction between participants becomes confined to exchanging events which carry payloads of information, making such a system event centric.

While the inherent feature of decoupling has its own virtues, it introduces other challenges in the event-based paradigm. An important one is the fact that event producers should have minimal assumptions on the information needs of event consumers. As a result, the content of an event payload becomes independent of consumers' needs. This can lead to information incompleteness on the consumers' side because there is not enough information in the event to process it.

If an event consumer ignores the concerns of information incompleteness and tries to conduct matching between its subscription and events, this may result in a high false positives or false negatives rate due to lack of relevant information in the events needed for the correct matching result. Thus, the consideration of the various dimensions of incompleteness becomes crucial to decrease the number of false positives/negatives in the matching process.

3.1 Dimensions of Incompleteness

Event incompleteness is a relative concept; it does not only depend on the event but also on the event consumption logic that is implemented by an event consumer. Event consumers may vary from simple User Interface agents to complex event processing engines. In order to simplify the discussion on event consumers, we limit discussion to content-based matchers of single events using a subscription language to match events. These are common in the publish/subscribe paradigm and are usually implemented using a message-oriented middleware [9]. However, generalization to other types of event consumers is possible in light of the formalism we present in Section 4.1.

Given a particular event consumption logic, event incompleteness has a broad set of orthogonal dimensions. We have defined the dimensions based on an analysis of the enterprise integration patterns of Hohpe and Woolf [16]. This analysis produces general dimensions of incompleteness as follows:

1. **Event Format:** The event lacks the syntactical structure that can be processed by an event consumer. For example, let an event be as follows:

   "energy consumption of the heater in the second floor is high"

   This event is in plain text language syntax and thus cannot be processed by an event consumer which uses the subscription from Example 2. This is because the subscription expects attribute-value syntax not available in the event.

2. **Event Semantics:** The event lacks references to an interpretation scheme that can be used by an event consumer to understand what the event payload really means. For example, let an event be as follows:

   {"energy consumption", "second floor", "high"}

   This event is in tuple structure. It lacks the reference scheme according to which an event consumer which uses the subscription from Example 2 can interpret the actual indication of the term *"high"*.

3. **Complementary Background Knowledge:** The event lacks the amount of information required by an event consumer, and the complementary information resides in an enrichment source. For example, let an event be as follows:

   {(type, "energy consumption"), (device, "heater1"), (consumption, "high")}

   This event cannot be processed by an event consumer which uses the subscription from Example 2 because the event lacks any information about the *"floor"* in which the event occurred. This complementary information is likely to exist in a building management system database which has a fact such as *{("heater1", exists_in, "second floor")}*.

4. **Complementary Transformation:** The event lacks the amount of information required by the event consumer, and the complementary information can be obtained via a reasoning process over the event. For example, let an event be as follows:

   {(type, "energy consumption"), (device, "heater1"), (watt_hour, "1500")}

   Let the event consumer use the following subscription:

   {(type="energy consumption") and (device="heater1") and (kilowatt_hour= "1.5")}

   The event lacks the property *"kilowatt_hour"* and thus is incomplete with respect to the consumer. However, this information can be obtained by a calculation on the actual event itself using a reasoning rule such as: *kilowatt_hour= watt_hour/1000*.

5. **Temporal Segmentation:** A single event does not have the amount of information required by an event consumer, and the complementary information resides in other events which occurred previously or are going to occur in the future. For example, it is common to have three-phase electricity power feeds to buildings. Clamp-on power monitoring sensors are usually installed on every 1-phase cable entering the building. This results in three events arriving at a specified rate one after the other:

   {(type, "power consumption"), (consumer, "building"), (watt_phase1, "3000")}

   {(type, "power consumption"), (consumer, "building"), (watt_phase2, "2800")}

   {(type, "power consumption"), (consumer, "building"), (watt_phase3, "3200")}

   Let an event consumer use a subscription such as the following:

   {(type= "power consumption") and (consumer ="building") and (watt_all_phases="9000")}

   The consumer finds that all the events lack the knowledge about the three-phases power consumption. However, such information can be obtained by temporally aggregating three events from all the phases in order to get the overall power consumption that can be processed by the consumer.

3.2 Challenges for Event Enrichment

The term *event enrichment* is used in this paper to refer to any process that is done on events in order to overcome fully or partially an event incompleteness problem that spans one or more of the event incompleteness dimensions explained in Section 3.1.

For the sake of simplicity throughout the rest of this paper, we leave the temporal segmentation dimension to future work. Reasoning for complementary transformation over events is assumed to be done beforehand with the result stored in a knowledge base. That turns the complementary transformation dimension into the complementary background knowledge dimension. Given the final set of incompleteness dimensions, four fundamental challenges are recognized:

1. Determination of the Enrichment Source (ES)

The first challenge to face event enrichment is the decision on which enrichment source(s) to use. The challenge comes from the fact that event producers and consumers are decoupled and potentially have various perspectives of where complementary information for an event may exist. Determining the enrichment source may be statically stated by the event producer or consumer making this challenge easy to overcome. However, if sources are not known beforehand then a source discovery process is needed. Some possible enrichment sources include:

- **Wikis**: The Wikipedia online corpus for instance *"http://en.wikipedia.org/wiki/"* can be considered as a textual domain-agnostic enrichment source.

- **Relational Databases**: An example is a Building Management System (BMS) relational database described by the connection string *"Server=www.example.com\rdbms; Database=BMS-DB;"*

- **Linked Data** [2]: The DBpedia corpus for example can be addressed by its domain *"http://dbpedia.org/resource/"*.

2. Retrieval of Information Items from the enrichment Source

The access and retrieval mechanism poses a challenge to the enrichment process as it affects its ability to retrieve atomic information items from the enrichment source. Retrieval of information items can be quite challenging if network transfer has reliability issues or if the retrieval speed forms a bottleneck in the system. The exact retrieval mechanism will depend on the selected enrichment source. Some example retrieval mechanisms include:

- **Wikis**: A retrieval mechanism for Wikipedia is a search operation against its search API followed by an HTTP GET request to get a Wikipedia article as the information item.

- **Relational Databases**: A retrieval mechanism for a relational database is a SQL query against a query interface, with the retrieved rows as the information items.

- **Linked Data**: A retrieval mechanism for the DBpedia corpus for instance is looking up (dereferencing) URIs [3] of the resources, with the RDF [17] graphs of these URIs being the information items retrieved.

3. Finding Complementary Information for an Event in the Enrichment Source

The ability of the enrichment process to retrieve atomic information items from an enrichment source is faced with the challenge to determine which of the information items can complement an event and should be retrieved. Several ways to find complementary information are:

- **Wikis**: To find complementary information in the Wikipedia corpus, articles related to a term in the event can be searched and then links from these articles are followed one step deep and ultimately all the resulting articles are retrieved.

- **Relational Databases**: To find complementary information in a relational database, one can formulate a SQL query with some specific primary keys coming from the event.

- **Linked Data**: To find complementary information in the DBpedia corpus, a spreading activation [5] of URIs can be conducted starting from seed URIs and following the links in the data cloud with some termination conditions.

4. Fusion of Complementary Information with the Event

The final challenge is integrating and fusing the complementary information items with the event. This challenge stems from the several formats and semantics of data models that are used by the enrichment source and by the event. Multiple instances of fusion are presented in Example 3.

Example 3: Fusion Methods

Let an event be the attribute-value map

> *{(type, "energy consumption"),*
> *(device, "heater1"),*
> *(consumption, "high")}.*

Let the enrichment source be a relational database with the relations *<heater, room>* and *<room, floor>* containing respectively the rows:

> *<heater1, room123>*
>
> *<room123, second floor>*

One possible fusion method is to add two attribute-value pairs to the event so it becomes:

> *{(type, "energy consumption"),*
> *(device, "heater1"),*
> *(consumption, "high"),*
> *(room, "room123"),*
> *(floor, "second floor")}*

Another fusion method is to add one attribute value pair which contains the location to the event so it becomes:

> *{(type, "energy consumption"),*
> *(device, "heater1"),*
> *(consumption, "high"),*
> *(location, "room123, second floor")}.*

4. UNIFIED AND NATIVE ENRICHMENT MODEL

The key pillar of the proposed model is the recognition of enrichment as a core task of event processing engines. In addition, the enrichment behaviour of an event processing engine can be dictated to the engine using a uniform and declarative mechanism. The cornerstone of the model is the concept of an *enrichment element* that is a declarative specification for the engine to enrich events with complementary information items.

The model proposes that the enrichment element is described using a set of declarative language constructs similar to the ones used currently for matching purposes. In order to systematically characterize the language constructs needed for the enrichment element, we propose four language clauses that are mapped to the four enrichment challenges as follows:

1. **ENRICH FROM** clause which allows the engine to determine the enrichment source(s) explicitly.

2. **RETRIEVE BY** clause which allows the engine to determine the retrieval mechanism for atomic information items.

3. **FIND BY** clause which specifies the approach which would dictate the retrieval of a subset of information items from the enrichment source(s) that can complement the event.

4. **FUSE BY** clause which defines the fusion approach to integrate retrieved complementary information with the incomplete event.

The next issue is to determine who is responsible for defining the enrichment elements. Reviewing the clauses of an enrichment element shows that some of these can be specified by the event producer and/or the event consumer. Specifically, the enrichment source and retrieval mechanism can be defined by the producer who may know them at the time of producing the event.

The model proposes that all the enrichment clauses are described by the event consumer. That is because the consumer has a better understanding of the information need at the consumption side. This is also aligned with scenarios where the event producer has little assumptions on information needs of the consumers and where decoupling is the norm. This adds to our previous work on loose semantic coupling and approximate matching in event processing systems [14].

Consequently, the model suggests that the enrichment element co-exists with the matching element which forms subscriptions in current systems. The resulting subscription which contains enrichment and matching elements is called a *unified subscription*.

By having unified subscriptions, enrichment can be brought to the core of the event processing engine. It operates based on the enrichment element and uses the matching element to conduct an enrichment process over the incoming incomplete events and enrichment source(s) to produce enriched events that can then be matched against the matching element. It is called a *native enricher* in this model. While implementation details of the enricher are left to particular instantiations, the proposed model suggests that the enricher not only uses the enrichment clauses to operate, but also the matching element to guide the enrichment process. Figure 1 depicts the proposed enrichment model.

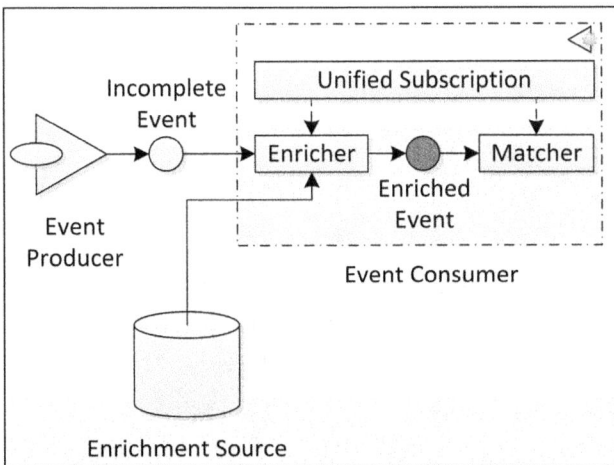

Figure 1. Unified and native enrichment model

Example 4 presents a simple instantiation of the enrichment clauses and the native enricher.

Example 4: Instantiation for Plain Text Events

Events are represented as bags of words. Let an event be as follows:

{"energy", "consumption", "heater1", "high"}

Let the matching element of subscriptions be represented as a bag of words as follows:

{"energy", "second", "floor", "high"}

The semantics of the event matching is that all words in the matching element need to be found in the event for a positive match, otherwise it is a negative match.

We assume that the enrichment source for the system is an enterprise wiki of text articles called *enterprise-wiki*. The wiki contains an article titled *"second floor"* which contains the term *"heater1"*. The wiki can be searched via a term search API which returns a list of articles containing the term. The API is accessible via a RESTful web service. When the API is searched with the term *"heater1"* the article titled *"second floor"* is returned.

The enrichment clauses are defined as the following:

- ENRICH FROM specifies the name of the wiki.

- RETRIEVE BY specifies the access protocol.

- FIND BY specifies the search mechanism.

- FUSE BY defines the fusion method to extract words from the retrieved article's title or from the article content, and if to add the new words to the event or to replace its words by the new found words.

A full example unified subscription becomes:

```
ENRICH FROM 'enterprise-wiki'.
RETRIEVE BY 'HTTP GET'.
FIND BY 'term search'.
FUSE BY 'title terms' 'add'.
{"energy",     "second",     "floor",
"high"}.
```

When the event *{"energy", "consumption", "heater1", "high"}* arrives to the system, the native enricher uses the words in the event to search the *enterprise-wiki* using each word at a time. Assuming that the enricher firstly retrieves the article titled *"second floor"*, it extracts the single words from the article's title and adds them to the event. The enriched event becomes as follows:

{"energy", "consumption", "heater1", "high", "second", "floor"}

Other articles are retrieved and fused similarly. The matching element is then evaluated against the enriched event. As a result, the matcher finds a positive match.

4.1 Formalism

The model is represented using the quadruple $(\mathcal{L}, E, ES, U)$, where:

- $\mathcal{L}$ is the unified subscription language.

- E is the set of events.

- ES is a set of information items that form the source of enrichment.

- U is the universe which contains all the possible information items.

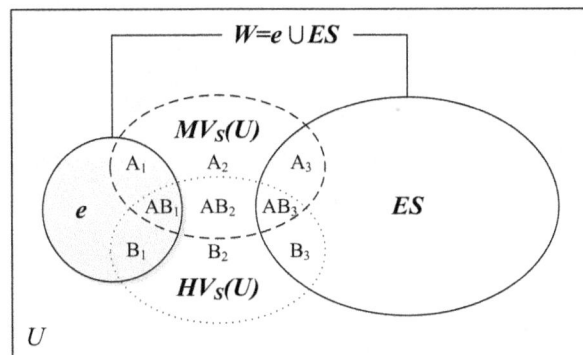

Figure 2. The universe U, the event e, the enrichment source ES, the world W, the enrichment view HV_S, and a matching view MV_S

The model has two underlying assumptions concerning valid information items and common information items. Valid information items are those which are considered to be true facts. Given an event $e \in E$, we assume that the only valid information items are those which exist in the event e or in the enrichment source ES. In other words, this assumption is equivalent to a Closed World Assumption (CWA) where the world $W = e \cup ES$. In fact, it is worth mentioning that traditional event processing systems usually make a closed world assumption at the matching stage, where the world $W = e$. The principal assumption that the world is limited to the event causes the incorrect decisions of the matcher in judging many positive and negative matches.

The other assumption concerns common information items between events and the enrichment source. We assume that there is no intersection between the content of e and ES, i.e. $e \cap ES = \Phi$. The purpose of this assumption is to simplify the description of the model. However, in reality the event may have been published with some information items that also exist in the enrichment source. Nevertheless, the model is easily extended to the case where $e \cap ES \neq \Phi$. When conducting enrichment in practice, the information items in ES which are already in e can simply be discarded to turn the assumption into a valid assumption. Figure 2 illustrates the various concepts of the model.

Let S be a subscription in L, S is a pair (H_S, M_S), where:

- H_S is the enrichment clauses element of S.
- M_S is the matching predicates element of S.

The model is described through the following definitions.

Definition 1: Boolean Matching Element

Let S be a unified subscription and I a set of information items:

$$M_S \text{ is a Boolean matching element} \qquad (1)$$

$$\Leftrightarrow M_S(I) \in \{True, False\}$$

Definition 2: Approximate Matching Element

Let S be a unified subscription and I a set of information items:

$$M_S \text{ is an approximate matching element} \qquad (2)$$

$$\Leftrightarrow M_S(I) \in \Re$$

Definition 3: Unknown Matching Result

Let S be a unified subscription and I a set of information items:

$$M_S(I) = Unknown \qquad (3)$$

$$\Leftrightarrow (M_S \text{ is a Boolean matching element}$$

$$\wedge M_S(I) \notin \{True, False\})$$

$$\vee (M_S \text{ is an approximate matching element}$$

$$\wedge M_S(I) \notin \Re)$$

Definition 4: Matching View

Let S be a unified subscription and I a set of information items:

$$MV_S \text{ is a matching view of } S \text{ on } I \qquad (4)$$

$$\Leftrightarrow M_S(MV_S(I)) \neq Unknown$$

Definition 5: Enrichment View

Let S be a unified subscription and I a set of information items:

$$HV_S \text{ is an enrichment view of } S \text{ on } I \qquad (5)$$

$$\Leftrightarrow HV_S(I) = \{ii : ii \in I, ii \text{ is retrieved during enrichment}\}$$

Definition 6: Complete Event

Let S be a unified subscription and e an event from E:

$$e \text{ is complete with respect to } M_S \Leftrightarrow \qquad (6)$$

$$\exists MV_S \text{ where } M_S(MV_S(e)) = M_S(MV_S(W))$$

Definition 7: Enriched Event

Let S be a unified subscription, e an event from E, ES the enrichment source, HV_S the enrichment view of the H_S element of S, $\oplus$ the FUSE BY operator of H_S:

$$ee \text{ is the enriched event of event } e \text{ according to } H_S \qquad (7)$$

$$\Leftrightarrow ee = e \oplus HV_S(U)$$

Definition 8: Valid Enrichment

Let S be a unified subscription, e an event from E, ES the enrichment source, HV_S the enrichment view of the H_S element of the unified subscription S:

$$HV_S(U) \text{ is valid} \Leftrightarrow HV_S(U) \setminus HV_S(W) = \Phi \qquad (8)$$

Definition 9: Successful Enrichment

Let S be a unified subscription, e an event from E, ES the enrichment source, HV_S the enrichment view of the H_S element of S, $\oplus$ the FUSE BY operator of H_S:

$$HV_S(U) \text{ is successful} \Leftrightarrow HV_S(U) \text{ is valid} \wedge \qquad (9)$$

$$e \oplus HV_S(U) \text{ is complete with respect to } M_S$$

Definition 10: Minimal Successfully Enriched Event

Let e be and event from E and ES be the enrichment source. Let $S_1, S_2 \ldots S_n$ be a set of unified subscriptions in L where the matching element of all of them is the same M_S, while they vary in the enrichment elements being $H_{S1}, H_{S2} \ldots H_{Sn}$ respectively. Let $HV_{S1}, HV_{S2} \ldots HV_{Sn}$ be the set of enrichment views corresponding to the subscriptions. Let $ee_1, ee_2 \ldots ee_n$ be the enriched events of e according to the enrichment views respectively:

$$ee_k \text{ is a minimal successfully enriched event} \Leftrightarrow \qquad (10)$$

$$ee_k \setminus \{ii : ii \in ee_k\} \text{ is not complete with respect to } M_S$$

An ideal event enrichment process would always turn events into minimal successfully enriched events. Ideally the areas in Figure 2 of $MV_S(W)$ and $HV_S(W)$ would be identical for at least one MV_S. Besides, the enrichment view would be valid, i.e. $HV_S(W) = HV_S(U)$. Thus, the areas A_1, B_1, A_2, B_2, AB_2, A_3, and B_3 become all empty. The definition above can be interpreted as a hard constraint, meaning that an enrichment process is considered successful for an event only if it produces a minimal successfully enriched event. This interpretation is suitable in many cases such as when the matching element M_S is a Boolean matching element.

However, there are cases where the event processing system may accept approximation. One example is when the matching element M_S is an approximate matching element. In such cases, it is suitable to adapt definition 10 to a softer interpretation, leading to Definitions 11 and 12.

Definition 11: Cost of Transformation into a Minimal Successfully Enriched Event

Let e be an event from E and ES the enrichment source ES, let $S_1, S_2 \ldots S_n$ be a set of all possible subscriptions in L where the matching element of all of them is the same M_S, while they vary in the enrichment elements being $H_{S1}, H_{S2} \ldots H_{Sn}$ respectively. Let $ee_{m1}, ee_{m2} \ldots ee_{mk}$ be the set of minimal successfully enriched events of e according to the various enrichment clauses elements H_{S1}, H_{S2}... H_{Sn}. Let S be a subscription with the enrichment element H_S. Let ee be the enriched event of e according to H_S. We define the cost function $MSECost$ as follows:

$$MSECost : W \times W \to \Re^+ \cup \{0\} \qquad (11)$$

$$MSECost\ (ee, ee_{mi})\ is\ the\ min\ cost\ to\ turn\ ee\ into\ ee_{mi} \qquad (12)$$

$$MSECost\ (ee_{mi}, ee_{mi}) = 0 \qquad (13)$$

Definition 12: Approximately Minimal Successfully Enriched Event

Let ee be a successfully enriched event and ee_{mi} any minimal successfully enriched event:

$$ee\ is\ an\ approximately\ minimal\ successfully\ enriched \qquad (14)$$
$$event \Leftrightarrow Min_{ee_{mi}} (MSECost\ (ee, ee_{mi})) > 0$$

4.2 Implications

This section discusses three of the potential implications of the proposed model:

- **Sharing and Re-usability of Enrichment Elements**: This stems from the core concept of recognizing enrichment routines as separate and modular declarative language elements. In deployments where a large number of producers and consumers exist, it is possible that only a small set of consumers would have the knowledge and expertise to provide well defined enrichment elements along with matching elements through unified subscriptions. Other consumers will keep writing classical matching subscriptions without specifying enrichment logic. This forms an opportunity for the event processing engine to enrich events according to the provided enrichment routines by expert users and forward the enriched events to normal users who would get more complete events.

- **Distribution of Enrichment**: When the event processing system is distributed into a set of brokers, there is an opportunity to distribute enrichment elements on the nodes to achieve an optimal overall completeness. With a suitable algebra for enrichment elements, coverage and ordering relationships can be defined for enrichment elements to avoid redundant enrichment and to account for optimized distributed enrichment plans.

- **Approximation in Event Processing Engines**: Building on the case when enrichment is done automatically by native enrichers may introduce some approximately complete events rather than fully complete events. Matching over partially complete events would need to account for the still missing information. This provides a good motivation for approximate matching in event processing systems which was investigated previously by the authors [14] based on the need for loose semantic coupling in heterogeneous systems.

These implications and others are subject to further investigation in the future.

5. A LINKED DATA INSTANTATION OF THE EVENT ENRICHMENT MODEL

This section details the implementation of the proposed model (refer to Figure 2): the event model, the enrichment source model, the matching element of subscriptions and the enrichment element along with a native enricher. The instantiation is designed for Linked Data events. Linked Data along with its core RDF graph model can be seen as a generic model for events, making the concepts applied in this instantiation also applicable in other implementations. A large amount of openly accessible Linked Data has been published on the web in the recent years making it easier to experiment with Linked Data events to study the enrichment model. Linked Data has also been used as a mechanism to link contextual data within different domains including finance, life sciences, public sector and energy [8].

5.1 Event Model

Events are instantiated as Linked Data events. Thus, an overview of Linked Data is given before proceeding.

Linked Data

Emerging from research into the Semantic Web, Linked Data proposes an approach for information interoperability based on the creation of a global information space. Linked Data leverages the existing open protocols and standards of the World Wide Web (WWW) architecture for sharing structured data on the web. The overall objective of Linked Data is to provide flexible data publishing and consumption. Berners-Lee [3] summarizes Linked Data in four principles:

1. Using URIs as names for things.

2. Using HTTP URIs so that people can look up those names.

3. When someone looks up a URI, providing useful information using standards such as RDF [17].

4. Including links to other URIs so that people can discover more things.

Event Model

An event is instantiated as a labelled directed graph. The resource description framework (RDF) is used to represent information about events using statements or triples. A statement consist of a *(subject, property, object)* triple. Subjects are references to information resources and are represented as URIs. Objects may be URIs or literal values. Properties come from various vocabularies (the RDF name of ontologies) and are represented as URIs of terms in these vocabularies. One subject may have multiple statements with the same property and different objects.

The resulting event can be represented as follows: Let E be the set of events conforming to the event model, P the set of properties, $URIs$ the set of all URIs and Lit the set of all Literals such as strings and numbers, then an event can be seen as a finite set of triples as follows:

$$e \in E \Leftrightarrow e = \{(s, p, v) : (s, p, v) \in URIs \times P \times (URIs \cup Lit)\} \quad (15)$$

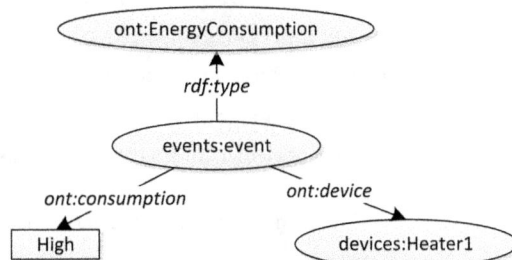

Figure. 3. An example event

A URI can be written using prefixes for clarity. For example the URI *http://www.example.com#event* can be written as *example:event* with the prefix *example* representing the part *http://www.example.com*. Figure 3 illustrates an example event where *ont* represents a prefix for the vocabulary of terms in the energy domain, *devices* a prefix for instances of devices in the environment, and *events* a prefix for all event instances.

5.2 Enrichment Source Model

The enrichment source is instantiated as a labelled directed graph. RDF is used to represent enrichment information. The enrichment source is a set of triples *(subject, property, object)* following the Linked Data principles. Let *ES* be the enrichment source, *P* the set of properties, *URIs* the set of all URIs and *Lit* the set of all Literals such as strings and numbers then:

$$ES = \{(s, p, v) : (s, p, v) \in URIs \times P \times (URIs \cup Lit)\} \quad (16)$$

Figure 4 illustrates an example enrichment source where *building* is a prefix for instances such as rooms and floors.

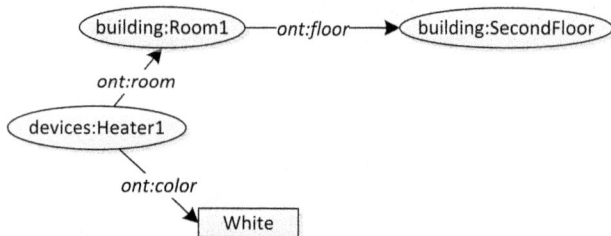

Figure. 4. An example enrichment source

The enrichment source is assumed to be accessible by dereferencing URIs associated with it. Dereferencing a URI means sending an HTTP request to its host, specifying the content type to be returned such as RDF, and finally receiving the HTTP response. The validity of a triple as required by Definition 8 is judged by its existence in the event or in the enrichment source.

5.3 Matching Element Model

The instantiation of the matching element of a subscription is a simplified version of the SPARQL patterns [23] which can contain basic graph patterns with variables. The matching element uses property paths in the place of properties to describe a regular expression of properties, or a path. The matching element is a Boolean matching element as defined in Definition 1. A matching view as defined in Definition 4 is the set of all triples that forms a solution to the graph pattern. Example 5 presents an example matching element.

Example 5: A Matching Element

The following matching element matches any event of type energy consumption whose URI has a path to the second floor URI within three nodes:

```
?event rdf:type ont:EnergyConsumption.
?event (?p){3} building:SecondFloor.
```

5.4 Enrichment Element Model

The instantiation of the enrichment element of a subscription is as follows:

- ENRICH FROM specifies the domain URI of the enrichment source.

- RETRIEVE BY specifies dereferencibility as the method for retrieval, notated as DEREF.

- FIND BY specifies how to explore the enrichment source to find complementary information. We propose a spreading activation strategy to be used by the enricher as explained in Section 5.5. The enrichment view defined in Definition 5 is the set of all triples whose subjects are activated during the spreading activation.

- FUSE BY realizes the $\oplus$ operator of the model presented in Definition 7. The RDF UNION is a suitable instantiation.

Example 6 presents a unified subscription that enriches from an enterprise Linked Data cloud, retrieves by dereferencibility, finds via a spreading activation strategy called *UniformWeightsAllAdjacent* and fuses via union. It aims at matching any event of type energy consumption whose URI has a three-links path to the *"second floor."*

Example 6: A Unified Subscription

```
ENRICH FROM <www.myenterprise.org>
RETRIEVE BY 'DEREF'
FIND BY 'Spreading Activation'
        'UniformWeightsAllAdjacent'
FUSE BY 'UNION'
{?event rdf:type ont:EnergyConsumption.
?event (?p){3} building:SecondFloor.}
```

The minimality of enriched events as defined in Definition 8 is realized by removal of triples from an enriched event. Finally, the approximation between an enriched event and a minimal successfully enriched event defined by the function *MSECost* in relations (11), (12) and (13) is realized by the cardinality of the relative complement operation '\' on sets of triples. Thus, the cost to turn an enriched event *ee* into a minimal successfully enriched event *ee_m* is composed of two costs:

- The cost to include all the successful enrichment triples in *ee_m* into *ee*. That is equivalent to $|ee_m \setminus ee|$.

- The cost to remove all unnecessary enrichment triples from *ee*. That is equivalent to $|ee \setminus ee_m|$.

The first point measures the completeness while the second measures the precision. These two measures and their combination form the basis for evaluation as shown in Section 6.

5.5 Native Enricher

The enrichment model is realized through a spreading activation algorithm [5]. Spreading activation (SA) originated in cognitive psychology as a network processing model for a supposed model of human memory. Applications of SA can be found in Artificial Intelligence, Cognitive Science, Databases, Information Retrieval, etc. The pure spreading activation model incorporates a processing technique for a generic graph data structure such as the RDF graphs. It is based on the idea of marking some nodes as active and then spreading the activation into other nodes iteratively. The way that spreading takes place and the semantics of the active nodes depends on the application. The processing is defined by a sequence of iterations that continue until a termination condition is activated. Each iteration consists of one or more pulses and a termination check [6].

Each pulse of the spreading activation consists of three stages: pre-adjustment, spreading and post-adjustment [6]. The spreading phase consists of a number of activation waves where each node calculates activation inputs transferred to it from its neighbors, which can be done using the formula:

$$I_j = \sum_i O_i w_{ij} \qquad (17)$$

Where I_j is the total input to node j, O_i is output of neighbor i and w_{ij} is a weight associated with the edge from node i to node j. When a node computes its total input I_j it calculates its output O_j as a function of I_j:

$$O_j = f(I_j) \qquad (18)$$

The function can be simply a threshold function which decides if the node j is activated or not. The output of the node is in turn sent to neighboring nodes in the next pulse and so on. Activation spreads from the initially activated nodes to further nodes in the network. Pure SA may fall in a deadlock and run forever unless controlled. Constraints can be enforced in the pre-adjustment stage. Four sorts of constraints can be recognized [6]:

- **Distance Constraint**: The SA should decay as it reaches nodes far from the initially activated nodes.

- **Fan-out Constraint**: The SA should cease at nodes with very high connectivity.

- **Path Constraint**: The SA should be selective in the path it spreads in making use for example of the semantics of labels on the edges.

- **Activation Constraint**: Using various thresholds can affect the behavior of the SA.

Spreading activation within the enricher along with the Linked Data instantiation of the event and the enrichment source models can realize the enrichment model. Spreading Activation can be used to explore the enrichment source and retrieve a set of triples to be fused in the event. In order to guide SA in the enrichment source, we propose a path constraint to favor some links over the others. The path constraint that we propose is based on ranking the links connected to a spread node based on their semantic relatedness with terms in the matching element and then just follow the top two or three links. The semantic relatedness used in the experiment is a WordNet-based measure called the Path measure. More on WordNet and semantic measures can be found in [4].

6. EXPERIMENT

In order to demonstrate how to evaluate a particular instantiation of the proposed enrichment model, an experiment has been conducted in association with the Linked Data instantiation of the enrichment model described in Section 5. The experiment has been done on real-world data, namely events extracted from Wikipedia, and uses the DBpedia dataset as an enrichment source.

A set of event subscriptions is generated where each subscription conforms to the unified language instantiation in Section 5. Matching elements use the property path variables to express a path of predicates between an event and a value. The minimal successfully enriched events for each subscription are calculated in order to form a baseline to measure the effectiveness of enrichment.

The purpose of the experiment is to compare three strategies of event enrichment which vary the mechanism used by the enricher to find complementary information items in the enrichment source. The variation is expressed by different parameters to the

spreading activation algorithm in the FIND BY clause of the subscription enrichment element. The three strategies are:

- **UniformWeightsAllAdjacent**: A spreading activation strategy where activation from one node spreads equally to all adjacent nodes.

- **UniformWeightsRandomAdjacent**: A spreading activation strategy where activation from one node spreads equally to a random set of adjacent nodes.

- **DifferentWeightsSemRel**: A spreading activation strategy where activation from one node spreads unequally to a set of adjacent nodes based on the semantic relatedness of the adjacency edges and the terms in the matching element of the subscription.

The key difference between the evaluated strategies is that the former two guide enrichment independently from the matching element of the subscription while that last strategy actually benefits from the fact that enrichment logic and matching logic exist together in the unified subscription. The last strategy guides the enrichment algorithm according to semantic relatedness between the terms in the matching element and terms on the links in the enrichment source. Thus, the last strategy, if confirmed to perform better than the other two, proves that a unified subscription with enrichment and matching together unified and native to the event processing engine is a beneficial approach to event enrichment.

It is worth mentioning that the objective is not to investigate the best approach for enrichment in the particular Linked Data instantiation but rather to demonstrate how evaluation can be conducted. Investigating the best performing enrichment strategies for Linked Data events is indeed an important future direction.

6.1 Event Set and Enrichment Source

The event set used in this experiment is a structured representation of events in Wikipedia[1]. DBpedia [2] is a community project to extract structured information from Wikipedia. DBpedia is one of the efforts under the Linked Open Data initiative which targets the publication of structured data on the web according to the Linked Data principles [3]. The data model used to represent DBPedia data is RDF. The event set used for this experiment is a subset of the current version the English DBpedia[2]. It contains all resources of type `dbpedia-owl:Event`. Each event is a triple of the form `<eventURI, rdf:type, dbpedia-owl:Event>`.

The size of the event set is around 24,000 events. Examples of various event types found in the event set are: *"Football Match"*, *"Race"*, *"Music Festival"*, *"Space Mission"*, *"Election"*, *"10th-century BC Conflicts"*, *"Academic Conferences"*, *"Aviation Accidents And Incidents In 2001"*, etc.

The enrichment source is the set of all triples that are stored on the online DBpedia and can be retrieved by looking up DBpedia resource URIs. Events are played sequentially and pushed to the native enricher which searches the enrichment source for complementary information, fuses it with the events and forwards them to the event matcher.

---

[1] http://www.wikipedia.org/

[2] http://downloads.dbpedia.org/3.8/en/. Last modified on the 1st of August 2012. Accessed on 25th of February 2013.

6.2 Unified Subscription Set

The subscription set consists of four subscriptions. The matching element of subscriptions was automatically generated using the following method:

1. We start by the seed URI of the 1966 FIFA World Cup Final *http://dbpedia.org/resource/1966_FIFA_World_Cup_Final* and retrieve resources linked to it to build a path-shaped graph of 4-triples long. Figure 5 shows the resulting full path-shaped graph.

2. For the first subscription, we pick the first triple and consider it as the matching element.

3. For the second subscription, we pick the first two triples and construct a matching element as defined in Section 5 using the two terminal URIs of the two-triples long path as subject and object and a property path variable in between.

4. We repeat the last step for subscriptions 3 and 4.

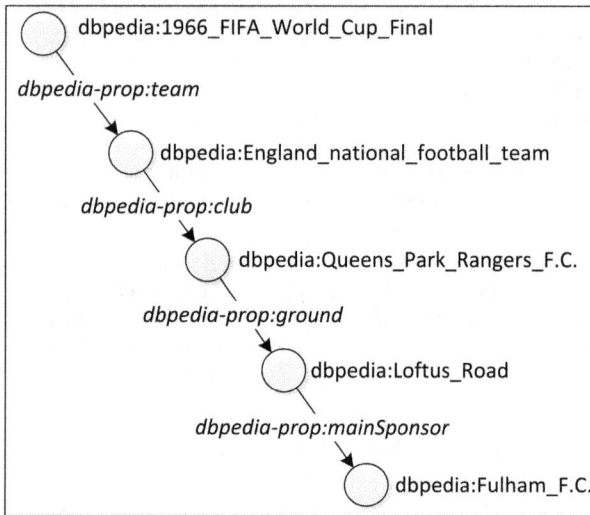

Figure 5. The base path-shaped graph used to generate the matching elements of the subscriptions

The resulting matching elements are shown in Table 1. Subscriptions range in complexity with respect to the length of the property path in their matching elements with the most complex subscription being the one with the longest property path. To form the final unified subscriptions, each matching element is concatenated with an enrichment element which consists of the four clauses ENRICH FROM, RETREIVE BY, FIND BY and FUSE BY. The evaluated three strategies are passed as parameters to the FIND BY operator.

Table 1. Matching elements of the unified subscription set

ID	Matching Element

1	`?event rdf:type dbpedia-owl:Event.`
	`?event (?p){1}`
	`  dbpedia:England_national_football_team.`

2	`?event rdf:type dbpedia-owl:Event.`
	`?event        (?p){2}`
	`  dbpedia:Queens_Park_Rangers_F.C..`

3	`?event rdf:type dbpedia-owl:Event.`
	`?event (?p){3}`
	`  dbpedia: Loftus_Road.`

4	`?event rdf:type dbpedia-owl:Event.`
	`?event (?p){4}`
	`  dbpedia: Fulham_F.C..`

6.3 Minimal Successfully Enriched Events Construction

In order to generate the event data that can be considered a minimal successfully enriched event with respect to each subscription, the following methodology has been used:

For each matching element of a subscription, a SPARQL [23] query is formed and executed against the DBpedia online SPARQL API. The query uses optional joins and filters to match all the events in DBpedia with all possible cases of their associated values or predicates. Example 7 shows the generated query for subscription 3.

Example 7: A Generated SPARQL Query

```
SELECT DISTINCT ?event ?team ?club
WHERE
  {?event a dbpedia-owl:Event .
    OPTIONAL
      {?event  dbpedia-prop:team  ?team .
        FILTER (!isLiteral(?team))
        OPTIONAL
          {?team dbpedia-prop:team  ?club .
            FILTER (!isLiteral(?club) )}}}
```

When the SPARQL queries are executed, the result contains all the events with possible values for the specified path. These events with their associated data are minimally complete as a matching decision can be made upon them for the specified subscription.

6.4 Evaluation Criteria

Given a subscription S and an event e. Let ee be the enriched event of e according to S. Let e_m be the closest minimal successfully enriched event to ee according to relations (11), (12) and (13) and their instantiation in Section 5.4. We define the following metrics for evaluating the effectiveness of the enrichment approach:

$$Completeness = \frac{|ee \cap e_m|}{|e_m|} \tag{19}$$

$$Precision = \frac{|ee \cap e_m|}{|ee|} \tag{20}$$

$$F_5 Score = \frac{(1+5^2)*Precision*Completeness}{5^2*Precision+Completeness} \tag{21}$$

The intersection is realized via an intersection between the set of triples that form each graph ee and e_m. The cardinality of events here is realized through the number of triples in the set that corresponds to each graph. The *F-Score* is a composite measure which is useful to summarize the effectiveness of an enrichment approach in one number for a subscription rather than two numbers. We argue that completeness and precision are not equally important. To evaluate an enrichment approach based on information completeness, the completeness measure should be given more weight. That is why the F_5Score is chosen in this evaluation. Depending on the application domain and constraints, other weighting may be considered.

6.5 Results

Figure 6 illustrates the combined F_5Score achieved by each enrichment approach for each subscription and averaged on events. The chart shows the superiority of the semantic relatedness-based approach and confirms the hypothesis that an enrichment approach which makes benefit from the enrichment logic unified with the matching logic is more effective than enrichment that is only based on enrichment logic.

There is also a trend showing that the enrichment effectiveness decreases for more complex subscriptions. The decreasing effectiveness is due to the fact that a longer property path requires more spreading to reach relevant triples while spreading may fade before that. From an empirical perspective, this raises the issue that the evaluation of an enrichment approach shall factor in the effect of the several types and complexities of subscriptions in the results. It is noticeable that the trend is sometimes broken on subscriptions 2 and 4 for some approaches. This is due to the small sample of subscriptions that represent each complexity level used in the experiment. A larger number of subscriptions is supposed to make the trend more apparent.

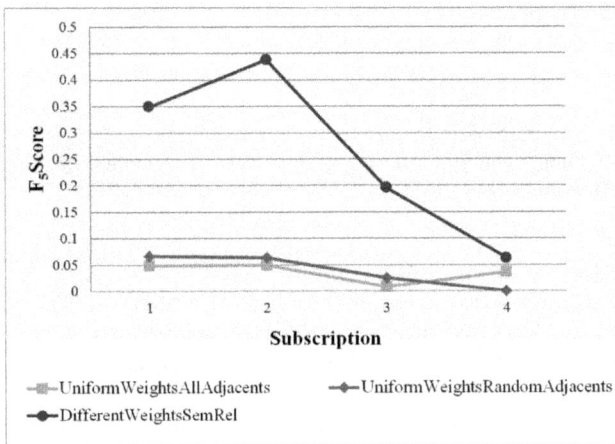

Figure 6. The combined F_5Score achieved by the enrichment approaches for each subscription

7. RELATED WORK

Related work to the event enrichment problem can be found in the event processing and middleware community as well as work in the database community on incompleteness. Hinze et al. [15] recognizes event enrichment among the features most required by event-enabled applications. Nevertheless, event enrichment is still widely addressed by ad-hoc dedicated agents which are tailored specifically to some situations. This is reflected in the set of enterprise integration patterns presented in [16]. Such approaches are non-native to the event processing paradigm where enrichment behaviour is pushed to the end user and less integrated with the rest of the features of event processing engines.

There are several research efforts to address the challenges of integrating background knowledge bases with event streams. Teymourian et al. [25] describes an approach based on a SPARQL-based query language where queries refer to event streams as well as the knowledge base. The authors recognize a set of categories of queries according to which they propose a set of execution plans. Similarly, Le-Phuoc et al. [18] proposes an approach to unify streams and background knowledge using Linked Data. They investigate methods to optimize the

continuous queries over the resulting dynamic Linked Data based on cost-based optimization within time windows. Both approaches form good examples of efforts to address the need for using background knowledge bases with event-based systems. However, some assumptions are already made in these approaches such as the access mechanism to the knowledge base, the data models and the feasibility of using join operators. These assumptions may not hold in some situations and thus the event enrichment problem is not addressed natively within the event-processing paradigm.

While enrichment is generally understood as a process to fuse data from an external source with the events, there has been some work which tackled other aspects of enrichment. Petrovic et al. [22] proposes an approach to semantically match events with subscriptions. At one stage of the proposed system, events get enriched with synonyms of the terms that are used within the events. Such enrichment is interesting as it shows the semantic dimension of the problem. However, the approach does not tackle the enrichment problem in the general terms.

Some work from the database community identifies the problem of incomplete databases and incomplete queries. While the proposed approaches are more attached to databases in general and the relational model in particular, it still gives good insight on the problem. Some focus on missing tuples and missing values such as [12]. Some are more aligned to the query answering perspective such as [19] and [24]. While other works focus on improving the quality of incomplete databases [21].

8. CONCLUSIONS

This paper discussed the information incompleteness problem in event processing systems due to the decoupling principle. The dimensions of event incompleteness have been discussed along with challenges to overcome the incompleteness issue. A model for event enrichment has been proposed. The model is based on unifying enrichment within the event consumer logic and a native enricher that tackles incompleteness before matching. To validate the model, an instantiation using Linked Data events and a Linked Data cloud as an enrichment source has been discussed. The instantiation proposes spreading activation as a potential enrichment approach. Various strategies of spreading activation have been evaluated using a set of Wikipedia events and DBpedia as the enrichment source. Evaluation has been done using a composite completeness and precision measure and it showed a superiority of the spreading activation strategy that is based on semantic relatedness over the other two approaches. This indicates the benefit of the unified subscription model.

The proposed model has implications on various aspects of event processing. Namely, sharing and re-usability of enrichment elements which may help improve the overall information completeness of events, distribution of enrichment which can improve the overall enrichment time, and approximation in event processing systems.

Future work includes further investigation of the aforementioned implications, investigating proper optimization approaches for the native enricher such as caching and indexing is of potential importance in real-time situations. The same also applies to optimizing the precision aspect of enrichment where higher precision means less unnecessary retrieval operations and thus a better performance. Additionally, improvement of enrichment approaches and algorithms for specific instantiations is important to improve the completeness, precision and time performance.

9. ACKNOWLEDGMENTS

This work has been funded by Science Foundation Ireland under Grant No. SFI/08/CE/I1380 (Lion-2).

10. REFERENCES

1. Atzori, L., Iera, A., and Morabito, G. The internet of things: A survey. *Computer Networks 54*, 15 (2010), 2787–2805.

2. Auer, S., Bizer, C., Kobilarov, G., Lehmann, J., Cyganiak, R., and Ives, Z. DBpedia: A Nucleus for a Web of Open Data. *The Semantic Web 4825*, (2007), 722–735.

3. Berners-Lee, T. Linked Data- Design Issues. 2006. http://www.w3.org/DesignIssues/LinkedData.html.

4. Budanitsky, A. and Hirst, G. Evaluating wordnet-based measures of lexical semantic relatedness. *Computational Linguistics 32*, 1 (2006), 13–47.

5. Collins, A.M. and Loftus, E.F. A spreading-activation theory of semantic processing. *Psychological review 82*, 6 (1975), 407.

6. Crestani, F. Application of spreading activation techniques in information retrieval. *Artificial Intelligence Review 11*, 6 (1997), 453–482.

7. Curry, E., Hasan, S., and O'Riain, S. Enterprise Energy Management using a Linked Dataspace for Energy Intelligence. *Second IFIP Conference on Sustainable Internet and ICT for Sustainability*, IEEE (2012).

8. Curry, E., O'Donnell, J., Corry, E., Hasan, S., Keane, M., and O'Riain, S. Linking building data in the cloud: Integrating cross-domain building data using linked data. *Advanced Engineering Informatics 27*, 2 (2012), 206–219.

9. Curry, E. Message-Oriented Middleware. In Q.H. Mahmoud, ed., *Middleware for Communications*. John Wiley and Sons, Chichester, England, 2004, 1–28.

10. Etzion, O. and Niblett, P. *Event Processing in Action*. Manning Publications Co., 2010.

11. Eugster, P.T., Felber, P.A., Guerraoui, R., and Kermarrec, A.M. The many faces of publish/subscribe. *ACM Computing Surveys (CSUR) 35*, 2 (2003), 114–131.

12. Fan, W. and Geerts, F. Capturing missing tuples and missing values. *Proceedings of the twenty-ninth ACM SIGMOD-SIGACT-SIGART symposium on Principles of database systems*, (2010), 169–178.

13. Hasan, S., Curry, E., Banduk, M., and O'Riain, S. Toward Situation Awareness for the Semantic Sensor Web: Complex Event Processing with Dynamic Linked Data Enrichment. *The 4th International Workshop on Semantic Sensor Networks 2011 (SSN11)*, (2011), 60–72.

14. Hasan, S., O'Riain, S., and Curry, E. Approximate Semantic Matching of Heterogeneous Events. *6th ACM International Conference on Distributed Event-Based Systems (DEBS 2012)*, ACM (2012), 252–263.

15. Hinze, A., Sachs, K., and Buchmann, A. Event-based applications and enabling technologies. *Proceedings of the Third ACM International Conference on Distributed Event-Based Systems - DEBS '09*, (2009), 1.

16. Hohpe, G. and Woolf, B. *Enterprise integration patterns: Designing, building, and deploying messaging solutions*. Addison-Wesley Professional, 2004.

17. Klyne, G. and Carroll, J.J. Resource Description Framework (RDF): Concepts and Abstract Syntax. 2004. http://www.w3.org/TR/2004/REC-rdf-concepts-20040210/.

18. Le-Phuoc, D., Dao-Tran, M., Xavier Parreira, J., and Hauswirth, M. A native and adaptive approach for unified processing of linked streams and linked data. *The Semantic Web--ISWC 2011*, Springer (2011), 370–388.

19. Levy, A. Obtaining complete answers from incomplete databases. *Proceedings of the International Conference on Very Large Data Bases*, (1996), 402–412.

20. OECD. Machine-to-Machine Communications: Connecting Billions of Devices. *OECD Digital Economy Papers No. 192*, 2012.

21. Parssian, A., Sarkar, S., and Jacob, V.S. Assessing information quality for the composite relational operation join. *Proc. Seventh Int'l Conf. Information Quality*, (2002), 225–237.

22. Petrovic, M., Burcea, I., and Jacobsen, H.-A. S-ToPSS: semantic Toronto publish/subscribe system. *Proceedings of the 29th international conference on Very large data bases - Volume 29*, VLDB Endowment (2003), 1101–1104.

23. Prud'Hommeaux, E. and Seaborne, A. SPARQL query language for RDF. *W3C working draft 4*, January (2008).

24. Razniewski, S. and Nutt, W. Checking query completeness over incomplete data. *Proceedings of the 4th International Workshop on Logic in Databases*, (2011), 32.

25. Teymourian, K., Rohde, M., and Paschke, A. Fusion of background knowledge and streams of events. *Proceedings of the 6th ACM International Conference on Distributed Event-Based Systems*, ACM (2012), 302–313.

MigCEP: Operator Migration for Mobility Driven Distributed Complex Event Processing

Beate Ottenwälder, Boris Koldehofe,
Kurt Rothermel
Institute of Parallel and Distributed Systems
University of Stuttgart, Stuttgart, Germany
{beate.ottenwaelder,boris.koldehofe,
kurt.rothermel}@ipvs.uni-stuttgart.de

Umakishore Ramachandran
College of Computing
Georgia Institute of Technology,
Atlanta, GA, USA
rama@cc.gatech.edu

ABSTRACT

A recent trend in communication networks — sometimes referred to as fog computing — offers to execute computational tasks close to the access points of the networks. This enables real-time applications, like mobile Complex Event Processing (CEP), to significantly reduce end-to-end latencies and bandwidth usage. Most work studying the placement of operators in such an environment completely disregards the migration costs. However, the mobility of users requires frequent migration of operators, together with possibly large state information, to meet latency restrictions and save bandwidth in the infrastructure.

This paper presents a placement and migration method for providers of infrastructures that incorporate cloud and fog resources. It ensures application-defined end-to-end latency restrictions and reduces the network utilization by planning the migration ahead of time. Furthermore, we present how the application knowledge of the CEP system can be used to improve current live migration techniques for Virtual Machines (VMs) to reduce the required bandwidth during the migration. Our evaluations show that we safe up to 49% of the network utilization with perfect knowledge about a users mobility pattern and up to 27% of the network utilization when considering the uncertainty of those patterns.

Categories and Subject Descriptors

C.2.1 [**Network Architecture and Design**]: Distributed networks; C.2.4 [**Distributed Systems**]: Distributed applications; E.1 [**Data Structures**]: Graphs and networks

Keywords

mobility; complex event processing; migration

1. INTRODUCTION

Over the last decade, the deployment of powerful mobile sensors and large scale sensor networks, monitoring mobile objects or locations, increased tremendously. Examples are off-the-shelf smartphones [5] and CCTV camera networks [25]. They enable novel real-time applications, such as continuous video monitoring of suspects [13], or traffic information systems [18], which provide information of interest to consumers.

Complex Event Processing (CEP) is a key paradigm to realize such applications. Changes in sensor measurements are modeled as events, while the application is modeled as set of event-driven operators. Such operators take streams of events as input, process them and produce new event streams.

Virtualized computing environments, i.e., clouds or fogs [3], provide elastic resources, which is highly appealing to support large-scale CEP systems. Cloud data-centers offer virtually endless resources to execute a vast amount of operators, however, impose a high communication latency since it requires transfering events from a user through the core network to the data center. Fog-computing, a resource paradigm proposed by Cisco [3], allows for processing on resource-constrained devices near users, like routers, for low end-to-end latencies. A federation of both clouds and fogs can support highly heterogeneous systems, where network-intensive operators are placed on distributed fog nodes and computational-intensive operators in the cloud.

In *Distributed CEP (DCEP)* [21], research [20, 22] has shown that the placement of operators has a significant impact on important performance metrics, such as network utilization and end-to-end latency. Furthermore, in *Mobile CEP (MCEP)* systems, where consumers and sensors are mobile, bandwidth and latency of streams are expected to change frequently with continuous location updates. For example, the number of available camera streams or the latency between the access point of a mobile sensor and the fog node where an operator is placed varies. To ensure the system's performance it has to constantly adapt the placement through migrations to new fog nodes.

However, each migration comes with a cost because operators are associated with local state, e.g., a cached portion of the event stream or a street map. This state can accumulate up to several GB of data [24] that have to be transferred during a migration. Frequently performing migrations to find better placements thus can significantly decrease system performance. For example, migrating GBs of state with each cell change of a consumer in a GSM network, while only several MBs of data are streamed to and from operators increases the network utilization.

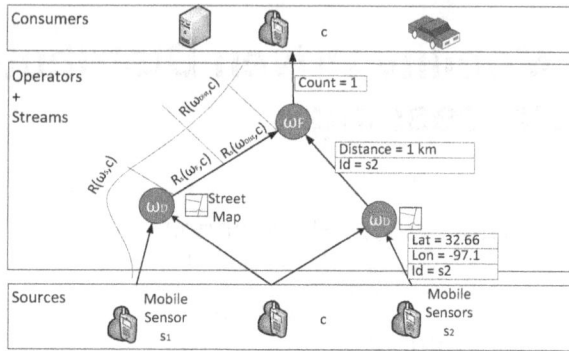

(a) Operator Graph

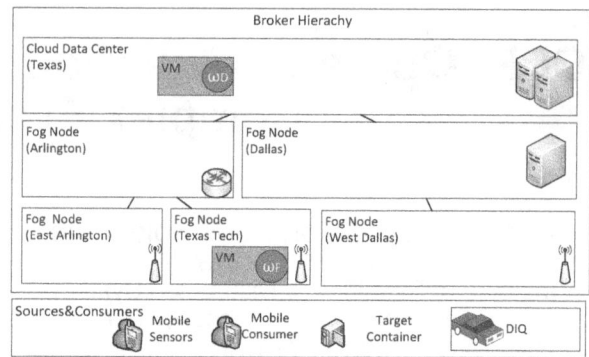

(b) Broker Hierarchy

Figure 1: System Model and CEP Operator Graph

In this paper, we propose methods for providers of virtualized environments to support operator migrations in MCEP systems. These methods exploit application knowledge of the MCEP system and predicted mobility patterns to plan the migration ahead of time. First, it allows us to amortize the migration costs by selecting migration targets that ensure a low expected network utilization for a sufficiently long time. Second, it allows us to serialize the operator for the migration and migrating parts of the operator a priori in away where unnecessary events are not migrated and bandwidth is reduced. In more detail, our contributions are:

1. The definition of a probabilistic data structure, called *Migration Plan (plan)*, which defines future targets and times for the migration, and a distributed algorithm to create such plans.

2. A migration algorithm, which uses a plan to minimize the network utilization while keeping the end-to-end latency below a threshold.

3. An analysis and evaluation study of the cost imposed by the creation and execution of a plan and its benefits.

The remainder of the paper is structured as follows: Section 2 introduces the underlying system model and Section 3 clarifies the problem. We present in Section 4 our plan-based migration approach. In Section 5 we present findings from our analysis. The approach's evaluation is presented in Section 6. Section 7 discusses related work before we conclude the paper and give an outlook on future work in Section 8.

2. SYSTEM MODEL

2.1 MCEP model

The operation of a MCEP system is commonly modeled by a directed, acyclic *operator graph* $G = (\Omega \cup S \cup U, L)$ where Ω denotes the set of operators, S the set of sources (e.g., range queries [18] or a mobile sensor in a smartphone), U the set of consumers, $L \subseteq (\Omega \cup S \times \Omega \cup U)$ the event streams between operators, sources, and consumers. For example, Figure 1(a) depicts an operator graph that can detect the number of friends that were closer than 1 km to a user c over the last hour. Primary events are location updates of users, associated with a source-specific id, which are streamed to ω_D. Operator ω_D utilizes a street map to compute the distance

between a friend and c. Operator ω_F then counts the number of distances smaller than $1km$ with disjoint source-ids and publishes the result on a social platform or the mobile device of the consumer. More sophisticated operator graphs can report about dangerous traffic situations [18] or allow monitoring of suspects [13].

Each $\omega \in \Omega$ encapsulates an arbitrary function that allows detecting patterns on deterministically ordered event streams. Events of those streams are managed in a set of dedicated queues Q. The number of buffered events in Q depends on the operators' semantics, which determine the selection and consumption of events from the queues [6,21].

We refer to these dynamically changing queues as *mutable state*, while the *immutable state* of an operator is the part of the operator that is read-only and fixed in size. For example, the map of ω_D, a database for face recognition, or the executable code of the operator. Intermediate results, i.e., states of variables in an operator's implementation, are denoted as *computational state*.

2.2 Broker Hierarchy

The operator graph is deployed on a federation of k distributed brokers $\{b_1 \ldots b_k\}$. Similar to typical mobile infrastructures, e.g., GSM networks or location services [9], brokers are organized in a spatially-partitioned hierarchy. The communication delay to mobile consumers decreases in a root to leaf direction.

The broker hierarchy is implemented through a combination of cloud data-centers and fog nodes (see Figure 1(b)). The latter can be routers or nearby workstations, that provide virtualized resources*. Such a hierarchy roughly approximates the network topology, since core network devices on the path from the consumer to the data center can be utilized for the processing. Within this mobile infrastructure each $\omega \in \Omega$ is hosted by its own dedicated VM that provides the execution environment for the operator.

Mobile consumer and sources share event streams over a wireless interface with the broker hierarchy. In order to improve their expected link quality, they greedily connect to the topologically closest broker, denoted as leaf broker. Since processing tasks are deemed to consume a lot of energy, those mobile devices are only thin clients, leaving all the processing to the infrastructure.

---

*Such in-network virtualization, i.e., fog computing [3], is currently promoted by companies like Cisco.

3. PROBLEM DESCRIPTION

A placement $P_{ts,te}$ is the assignment of operators $\omega \in \Omega$, of a given operator-graph G, to brokers in between time t_s to time t_e. When a mobile source or consumer connects via new access-points to new leaf brokers the end-to-end latencies and the network utilization can increase since now more brokers are potentially involved in transferring event streams. For example, when the source in Figure 2 changes its connection from the leaf broker b_1 to b_2, it also means that from now on all streams for ω_D, placed on b_1, have to be transferred from b_2 to b_1, possibly over multiple hops in the broker hierarchy. In order to improve the system performance, the system has to adapt the placement $P_i = P_{ts,te}$ at time t_e to a new placement P_{i+1} via migrations $M_j, .., M_k$ of one or multiple operators. To reduce the network utilization imposed by keeping ω_D at b_1 the system migrates ω_D to b_2, which can also affect the placement of ω_F.

Note, that also migrations themselves may impose a significant cost in terms of network utilization, given that a migration requires transferring the whole state of an operator to a new migration target which can be as large as several GB. Therefore, it is important to account for those costs when performing a migration. Instead of always deploying the best possible placement, a placement should only be deployed if its migration costs can be amortized by the gain of the next placement. This gain depends on many dynamic parameters such as the mobility of sensors and consumers as well as the actual workload of the event processing system.

The decision to initiate a migration may also be unavoidable in some cases for ensuring the responsiveness of the CEP system, e.g., to allow users to respond to traffic situations in real-time. In this case, the global end-to-end latency has to stay, at least on average, below a consumer-defined restriction R_c. In particular, it has to stay below the restriction on all paths in G from any source $s_i \in S$ to a consumer $c \in U$. On these paths, the detection is delayed due to communication delays between neighboring operators and the computational delay, the time that an operator requires to process a new input event. To ensure that the global end-to-end latency stays below R_c, the sum of the computational delay $d_c(\omega)$ and in- and outgoing streaming delay $d_{in/out}(\omega)$ of all those coordinated ω has to stay below a local $R_{(\omega,c)}$. For instance, in Figure 1(a) ω_D and ω_F reserve a part of their restriction for the global optimization.

When preserving latency constraints it is also important to consider the downtime of operators during migrations, as a consequence of having to halt an operator and start it again at the migration target. When all state is already available on the migration target at the migration time we achieve a minimal downtime, since the operator can start processing immediately. Consider, for example, in Figure 2, the map and event streams can already be transferred to b_2 before the source connects to b_2 and the operator ω_D has to be migrated to b_2. However, uncertain future locations of the source may lead to a situation where the network utilization is increased because the state is copied to b_2 but the source never connects to b_2 and a migration is unnecessary. This requires to migrate the operator and its state to future placements where the expected network utilization is low.

The *mobile migration problem* addressed in this paper is to find a sequence of placements $P_1, P_2, ..., P_p$ and Migrations $M_1, M_2, ..., M_m$ for an operator graph G in a broker

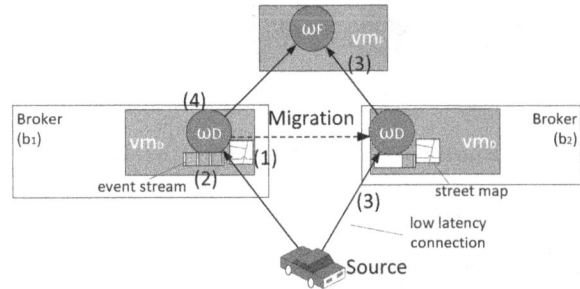

Figure 2: Migration

hierarchy, where the overall network utilization is low and the consumer defined latency restriction is met.

More formally, we consider the average bandwidth-delay product during a time interval as the metric to express network utilization. Let $bdp(P_i)$ be the sum over the average bandwidth-delay product of links in the broker network in a placement P_i. Then, the cost for a placement in between time t_s and t_e is $C_{pla}(P_i) = bdp(P_i) * (t_e - t_s)$. We can define the costs $C_{Mig}(M_j)$ for each migration M_j, accordingly. Furthermore, let $d(s_i, c)$ be the end-to-end latency from any source $s_i \in S$ to any consumer $c \in U$ over a path $(\omega_1, \omega_2, ..., \omega_n)$ in the operator-graph.

An optimal sequence of migrations is found if:

1) $C_{tot} = \sum_{i=0}^{p} C_{pla}(P_i) + \sum_{i=0}^{m} C_{Mig}(M_i)$ is minimal

subject to

2) $\forall c \in U : \sum_{i=0}^{|S|} d(s_i, c) \leq R_c$ at all time

4. PLAN-BASED MIGRATION APPROACH

The MCEP live migration system assigns a dynamically updated live *Migration Plan (plan)* to each operator. The plan defines for an operator a set of future migration targets, a deadline by when an operator needs to be ready to execute at its migration target, and a time when the migration will be initiated such that the migration deadline can be met.

At the time when according to the plan a migration needs to be initiated for an operator, the live migration system will begin to copy first the execution environment (VM) and immutable state (step (1) in Figure 2), then relevant mutable state that is required for future selections when the operator starts executing at the migration target (e.g., only one of three possible events in step (2)). Since the latter state allows to recompute computational state at the target, we don't need to transfer computational state. In the meantime the operator will continue to execute at its original placement until the transfer of state has been completed. Finally, at the times indicated in the plan, events are streamed to the new placement (step (3)) and the resources taken up by an operator at its original location are released (step (4)).

The performance characteristics of the live migration depend on how plans are created, as well as how they are adapted to the dynamics of the MCEP systems, i.e., where sources and consumers are connected to the broker hierarchy, how the usage of resources changes as well as how the load of the event system varies.

In this section, we first propose a simple model for a plan that triggers migrations at discrete time steps (see Subsection 4.1) and later show how to coordinate an operator's plan with the plans of its neighbors. Furthermore, we will show

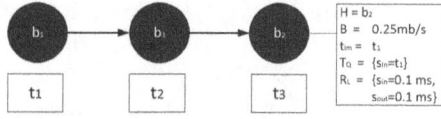

Figure 3: Basic Migration Plan

how to refine the basic mechanisms to deal with the inherent uncertainties which follow from the mobility of sources and consumers, variations in the workload, and resource usage in the broker hierarchy (see Subsection 4.2).

4.1 Creating a Migration Plan

The live migration system continuously anticipates the movement of its connected sources and consumers, as well as the load of event streams and latencies between the operators connected in the MCEP system in order to determine a plan. For mobile sources and consumers, this is achieved by dead reckoning mechanisms [28] or relying on information from navigation systems. The event load on links is estimated on average over the most recent traffic measurements, while latencies can be estimated via regular ping messages between neighbors or using Vivaldi Coordinates [8].

The quality of a created plan depends on the accuracy of this information; in fact unforeseen behavior may degrade the performance properties of our system and in the worst case even violate constraints. For now, however, to understand the basic principle of the proposed migration scheme we will treat this information as if it was accurate.

In this context we will answer

- How far and at which granularity do we have to plan migrations ahead?

- What are possible migration targets that can be incorporated in the migration plan of a single operator?

- How should the migrations of multiple operators be best coordinated?

We address this by first proposing the basic Migration Plan model, which allows studying migrations at varying granularities. In order to select possible migration targets, we propose the *time-graph model*, that allows finding migration targets, depending on the plans of other operators. The proposed coordination algorithm negotiates the plans with dependent operators and migration targets, in order to find minimum cost plans for each operator and reserve resources to ensure the execution of an operator at all times.

Migration Plan Model

A plan describes the upcoming migration behavior of an operator ω, determining when it is going to be hosted at which broker, as well as its expected resource requirements. In other words, it is the trajectory of an operator in the broker hierarchy. As depicted in Figure 3 for ω_D of the example, the plan provides an expected placement of an operator for a sequence of discrete time steps $t_i \in TS = \{t_0, ..., t_{max}\}$. An expected placement is a 5-tuple $ep = (H, B, t_{im}, T_Q, R_L)$, where H is the expected host of the operator, B the average expected bandwidth of the operator's outgoing stream, t_{im} is the time, at which the transfer of immutable state has to be initiated, T_Q a deterministic starting point for each queue $q \in Q$ from which events on the mutable state has to

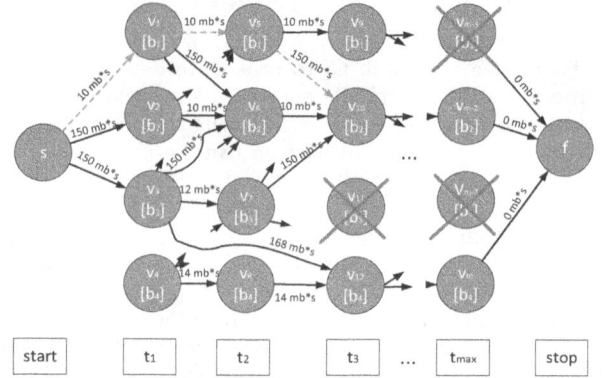

Figure 4: Timegraph Example

be transferred, and R_L indicates which part of the latency restriction is reserved for the incoming and outgoing streams L of ω.

Since consumers and sources are constantly connected to leaf brokers, we can use the same abstraction to model and share their movements. For example, the plan indicates for a mobile sensor to which leaf broker it will be connected to and the expected size of its sensor stream.

Time Graph

The *time-graph* $= \{V_{tg}, E_{tg}\}$ (see Figure 4) is a data-structure that allows for each individual operator ω to identify costs and durations of future migrations and placements. The time-graph for a single $\omega \in \Omega$ comprises migration targets which are suitable to fulfill the constraints of a placement. Note, that even not performing a migration imposes a cost by streaming events over the in- and outgoing streams.

Each vertex $v_{tg} \in V_{tg}$ represents the possible placement of ω at a broker b, starting at time step $t_i \in TS$ and ending at the next time step $t_{i+1} \in TS$. For example vertex v_1 in Figure 4 is labeled with b_1 at t_1, which represents the placement at broker b_1 starting at t_1. Two special vertices which do not indicate future placements, labeled as s and f in Figure 4, represent the start and end of all possible sequences of migrations and placements.

Each directed edge $e_{tg} = (v_j, v_k) \in E_{tg}$ represents the migration between brokers or no migration if e_{tg} connects the same broker. Furthermore, an edge indicates that a migration starting at time step t_j of v_j is expected to be completed at time step t_k of v_k. For example, when the migration from b_3 to b_4 is started at time t_1, then all state is expected to be transferred by t_3 and ω can start processing.

The edge weight $w_{j,k}$ of $(v_j, v_k) \in E_{tg}$ represents the costs that are expected to occur in the time interval $[t_j, t_k)$ – the average bandwidth-delay products weighted with that interval (see Section 3). This comprises the expected migration costs $C_{Mig}(v_j, v_k)$ and expected placement costs $C_{pla}(v_{tg})$ at the broker of v_j during $[t_j, t_k)$. Note that the placement costs are not only considered in the case that an edge represents no migration but also if it represents a migration. This is because ω still processes events at the previous broker, while the migration happens in the background. The edge weight of $10mb*s$ between two subsequent vertices of b_1 are the placement costs during that time step, while the edge weight of $168mb*s$ between v_3 and v_{12} comprises the placement costs of $2 * 12mb * s$ at b_3 and migration costs of $144mb * s$.

```
 1: stablePlan, tmpPlan, neighborPlans, TG ← ∅
 2: upon trigger generatePlan( )
 3:   if notInAwaitState() then
 4:     await notWaitForFeedback() ∧ noTargetCoordination()
 5:     TG ← createTimeGraph(TG)
 6:     path ← determineShortestPath(TG)
 7:     P ← createInitialPlan(path)
 8:     if P deviates from tmpPlan then
 9:       tmpPlan ← P
10:       trigger send planUpdatedMsg(P) to all neighbors
11:     else
12:       tryInitTargetCoordination()
13:     end if
14:   end if
15: end

16: upon receive planUpdatedMsg(plan) from neighbor n
17:   neighborPlans[n] ← plan
18:   trigger generatePlan()
19: end

20: upon receive planAcceptedMsg()
21:   tryInitTargetCoordination()
22: end

23: function tryInitTargetCoordination()
24:   if allFeedbackReceived() ∧ noPlanGeneration() then
25:     checkNeedSendPlanAcceptedMsg()
26:     checkNeedSendReservationRequest(tmpPlan)
27:   end if
28: end

29: upon receive reservationReplyFromTargets(tmpPlan)
30:   if tmpPlan is executable on all targets then
31:     stablePlan ← tmpPlan
32:   else
33:     trigger generatePlan()
34:   end if
35: end

36: upon timeout(timer in regular intervals)
37:   if checkMonitoring() ∨ checkLatencyRrestriction() then
38:     trigger generatePlan()
39:   end if
40: end
```

Figure 5: Generating a Migration Plan

Migration Plan Creation

We now detail a distributed algorithm for the creation of the basic plan for an individual operator ω (see Algorithm 5), executed at the operator's current host. The algorithm finds a shortest weighted path in a time-graph (TG) that is local to ω and generates an executable plan ($stablePlan$) from this path. The time-graph is maintained using the set of plans from all neighbors in the operator graph ($neighborPlans$) and the anticipated event loads and restrictions given by the expected placements in these plans.

The first plan is created after the deployment of an operator. Afterwards, the plan creation is triggered concurrently when the latency restrictions are no longer preserved on the current broker, predictions on the outgoing bandwidth and collected latencies deviate beyond a threshold (Line 36-40) from previous predictions, or the plan of the neighboring operators changes (Line 16-19).

In the first step of the plan generation the *time-graph* is created, which models the expected placement and migration costs for this operator for the next TS time steps (Line 5). In a subsequent step an initial plan is determined by traversing the shortest path in the time-graph. This path contains a sequence of migration targets and times to migrate between them, where the expected overall network utilization is low and the latency restrictions are expected to be preserved (Line 6-7). We replace a previous stable plan with the newly found plan only if this new plan deviates in the expected placements at any time step (Line 8). However, before implementing the new plan it is consolidated by coordinating it with the neighboring operators (Line 10) and the brokers that are selected as migration targets. Migration targets might not have enough resources to execute the plan or neighbors adapt their own plan due to the plan that is to be consolidated. In both cases another iteration of the plan generation is triggered (Line 18/33).

Maintaining the time-graph in a stable manner. Algorithm 6 outlines the creation of the time-graph TG. At first a set of brokers that have in general enough resources to execute the operator are selected as possible future migration targets (Line 2). Then it populates an empty graph with the start and a stop vertex (Line 3).

In the following steps vertices for each combination of discrete time steps TS, starting at the current time now, and possible migration targets ($Targets$) are created (Line 4-5). However, vertices are omitted when the associated broker comes not into consideration to host an operator at $ts+now$ (e.g., v_{11} in Figure 4). This is the case when latency restrictions are not expected to be preserved or a local information on the migration targets, resource reservations indicates that not enough resources to execute the operator at the potential migration target are available.

When the vertex v is created, the algorithm anticipates which migrations are possible and which previously created vertices are therefore connected to v over a directed edge (Line 7-14). This requires to estimate the size of the mutable state, according to the average size of the queues and the time t_{mig} that it takes to migrate all state between any possible host b_p and the host b of v. Since t_{mig} may span over more than one time step, the vertex that represents b_p at time step $now+ts-t_{mig}$ is selected as source of the edge e. However, the operator has to continue its execution at b_p during the the migration, which means that all vertices labeled with b_p between $ts+now-t_{mig}$ and $ts+now$ have to exist (Line 10).

The weight of this new edge is the sum of the placement costs $C_{pla}(v)$ of all vertices representing b_p — the sum over the average bandwidth-delay product between the b_p and the expected placement from the neighbors plan weighted with the time intervals during the given time steps — and migration cost $C_{Mig}(v_j, v_k)$ between b_p and b.

Initial Migration Plan. In order to extract an initial plan (see Lines 6-7 of Algorithm 5) we find the shortest path in the time-graph (the dashed line in Figure 4). At each time step of the shortest-path a broker is determined that represents the expected host ($ep.H$) for an expected placement ep of the plan. Expected values for the bandwidths ($ep.B$) are taken from the bandwidth estimation for the operators outgoing stream. Furthermore, the starting time for the migration of immutable state ($ep.t_{im}$) is computed for each time t_i by subtracting the migration time t_{mig}. The first event of each queue $q \in Q$ ($ep.T_Q$) is then captured according to a window-model, e.g., [18]. Those windows determine the set of events in q that are required for the correlation at a discrete time, therefore if we model the windows position

```
 1: function createTimeGraph( Time-Graph G )
 2:     Targets ← getPossibleTargets()
 3:     s, f ← createStartAndStopNode(G)
 4:     for ∀ts ∈ TS do
 5:         for ∀b ∈ Targets do
 6:             if shouldCreateVertex(b, G, ts + now) then
 7:                 v ← createVertex(G, ts + now, b)
 8:                 for ∀b_p ∈ Targets do
 9:                     t_mig ← estimateStateMigrationTime(b_p, b)
10:                     if checkEdgeCondition(b_p, b) then
11:                         e ← edge(ts + now − t_mig, b_p, ts, b, G)
12:                         w_e ← calculateEdgeWeight(e, t_mig)
13:                     end if
14:                 end for
15:             end if
16:         end for
17:     end for
18: end
```

Figure 6: Time Graph Maintenance

at t_i we can approximate the first required event from the windows bounds.

Coordination. An operator starts the coordination of plans by sending the plan to each neighbor (Line 10 of Algorithm 5). Then the operator waits until it received at least one feedback message from each neighbor until it starts the coordination with the selected targets (Line 24/26). A feedback can either be a changed plan of a neighbor or an acceptance of the plan. Note, that we even consider a plan that was sent concurrently by a neighbor and still in transmission when the plan coordination was started as feedback.

When a neighbor receives a plan, it re-evaluates its own plan before it decides on a feedback (Line 18). If the newly determined plan deviates from the current plan, the operator starts to coordinate its own plan, by sending a changed plan of its own as feedback (Line 10). Otherwise, the operator will send the feedback to all neighbors that recently updated their plans that it accepts their plans (Line 12/25). To reduce the number of coordination steps when neighbors concurrently generate plans, we ensure that a plan is only generated if all feedback is available and the plan is not coordinated with migration targets (Line 3-4). In the analysis we show that this coordination eventually terminates.

The coordination with migration targets happens in two steps. First, a request is sent to all migration targets, asking if i) they have enough resources available to host the operator ii) they can ensure the local latency restrictions. If this is not the case, the plan is rejected and re-evaluated at the initiator of the coordination, with a time-graph that does not create vertices for brokers that rejected the plan.

Although, these conditions are already checked when the time-graph is created, other plans of other operators compete for the resources. Therefore, plans have to reserve the resources at the migration target in a second step. This enables a broker to approximate its future resource utilization. If all future migration targets can execute the plan the resources are reserved and previous reservations of the previous plan are revoked.

Stability

Updated plans of neighbors bear the potential to make the plan of an operator unstable if the mobility is inaccurately captured or communication characteristics keep changing (e.g., diverging bandwidths). For example, if the operator generates a new plan with each location update of a source that instantly triggers a migration of an operator to a new host, we arbitrarily increase the network utilization.

To alleviate the mobility problem in the basic plan, we allow to restrict the number of time steps for the creation of the plan. The longer a consumer or source does not deviate from its predicted location, the more time steps can be considered for the time-graph. The intuition behind that can be seen in Figure 4. Edge weights that include migration costs are typically higher than for edges between the same broker. Therefore it is unlikely that an edge from any broker b_i to another broker b_j is considered for the shortest path if only few time steps are included, even if a potential migration target promises lower placement costs. At the same time we make sure that an operator eventually can migrate, even with a small number of time steps, by gradually decreasing the initial migration cost from the current host to neighbors the longer an operator stayed at a broker.

To ensure that a plan does not continuously change, only because of a small deviation in the measured bandwidth or latency, edge weights are only replaced in a time-graph if these measurements change beyond a threshold.

Properties

The number of brokers that are selected in Line 2 of Algorithm 6 has a severe impact on the performance of the live-migration system. Modelling all brokers, in a large-scale scenario with thousands of broker, is computationally costly, because the number of vertices and edges grows cubically. The number of vertices, per time step in the time-graph, grows linearly within each time step with the number of brokers n_b, thus the complexity is $O(n_b * |TS|)$. More severe is the number of edges, which grows quadratically per time step, because we connect each broker with all other brokers of the next time step. Thus the complexity is $O(n_b^2 * |TS|)$, which is cubic if the number of brokers n_b equals $|TS|$. Furthermore, each broker has to acquire information about the latency, bandwidth and available resources of these brokers, to determine the placement costs, which can only be determined by regularly sending messages between the broker.

Although selecting all brokers as migration targets gives a near-optimal solution to the mobile migration problem, we decrease the network and computation costs by only selecting the most relevant broker. To increase the scalability, we utilize the spatial-temporal locality property. Mobile objects move only within local bounds, e.g., do not connect to the system from London and seconds later from New York. Hence, good future migration targets are found close to the current broker that hosts the operator. Hence, each broker keeps coarse grained information on brokers responsible for far away locations, and fine-grained information on nearby broker.

4.2 Uncertainty-aware Migration Plans

So far, we presented plans as sequences of definite placements. However, since these sequences represent the predicted future, it comprises various uncertainties. Sources and consumers can change their movement pattern, e.g., vehicles changing their routes, or they hand-off between adjacent leaf broker at unexpected times. Data-rates of event streams can also vary, e.g., when an operator detects less events than expected.

Depending on how the system captures the movement of mobile devices, the actual future connection to a leaf broker is predicted more or less accurately. Simple dead reckoning mechanisms predict future locations based on the direction and speed of the last few reported locations, which is typically only accurate for nearby locations. The next sequence of leaf brokers and when a source or consumer connects to them is therefore highly uncertain. This can be improved by using more definite locations of navigation systems. Learning connection patterns between neighboring leaf broker gives a more accurate view than dead reckoning, but less accurate than the path of a navigation system. For example, while driving on a highway vehicles will connect with high probability to the same sequence of leaf broker that cover subsequent sections of that road and with a low probability take the next exit that may require to connect to another leaf broker.

Since data-rates of event streams can vary, it is possible that placing an operator ω at its planned migration target imposes higher costs compared to an optimal placement. In case the placement costs dominate over the migration costs, it is beneficial to stall the decision for a concrete migration target until it is certain that the placement can be improved. However, dependent operators, e.g., with large state, now require the information about all possible migration targets of ω to plan their migrations.

In this context we have to answer:

- What is a meaningful representation of an uncertain connection and migration decision?

- Given the uncertain representation of neighbors what are the best migration targets incorporated in a plan?

We address the question of the uncertainty-aware representation by expanding the plan to a *Markov chain*. The second one is addressed by a set of heuristics that aim to minimize the expected overall migration and placement costs of a single operator.

Uncertainty-aware Migration Plan Model

An uncertainty-aware plan is represented as *Markov chain*, as depicted in Figure 7. It allows for more than one expected placement at the same time step, connecting adjacent time steps with probabilistic state-transitions. We distinguish two kinds of uncertainty-aware plans. First, *temporally skewed migrations*, describe that instead of migrating at a fixed time step a mobile consumer/source or operator will initiate the migration within a temporal interval of discrete time steps. For example, a vehicle's connection change from b_1 to b_2 according to the plan in Figure 7 is performed with probability 0.5 at time t_1 and with probability 0.5 at t_2. Second, *spatially skewed migrations*, allow to describe multiple migration possibilities at the same time step, e.g., if a transition from b_1 to b_3 at t_2 in Figure 7 were included.

Creating the Uncertainty-aware Migration Plan

This section describes how the system creates uncertainty-aware plans for a consumer or source to indicate the possible future leaf broker and its data-rates. Furthermore, upon receiving uncertainty-aware plans, an operator has to adapt its own plan. To this end it can select from a pool of policies that aim to minimize the expected bandwidth-delay product but vary in their complexity.

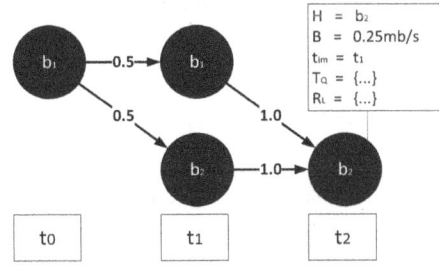

Figure 7: Uncertainty-aware Migration Plan

Planning for consumers and sources. Dead reckoning methods and navigation systems provide a sequence of time-stamped uncertain future locations[†] for mobile sources and consumers. This allows us to determine the expected placements ep of the plan for a set of future time steps $t_i \in TS$. Expected hosts ($ep.H$) are all future leaf brokers responsible for the future location at t_i. The average over the monitored recent traffic determines the expected bandwidth ($ep.B$). Probabilities for state transitions from previous time steps t_{i-1} are estimated based on the proportion of the overlap of the uncertain location with the leaf brokers area weighted by the extent of the uncertain location.

This method changes for learned connection patterns of consumers and sources. These learned patterns describe how probable it is for a source or consumer to change its connection to another leaf broker after it stayed connected for a certain amount of time to its current leaf broker. Such learned probabilities are maintained in a graph where each vertex represents a broker and has an edge to all neighboring brokers the source or consumer can connect to next. Each edge in the graph is annotated with the probability to change the connection and the average time a source or consumer is connected to a broker before it connects to the neighbor.

Such a graph can then be exploited to find a sequence of expected hosts $ep.H$ for an uncertainty-aware plan. A simple algorithm follows paths in the graph sequentially from broker to broker, starting from the current leaf broker of a mobile source or consumer. The algorithm keeps track of the annotated times of edges while traversing the graph and reports a broker as $ep.H$ at a $t_i \in TS$ if the next edge traversal increases the sum of annotated times on that path beyond t_i. State-transition probabilities of the uncertainty-aware plan are equivalent to the probability that a connection changes. Thresholds on the probability that a path represents the actual connection pattern can reduce the number of states.

Policies of operators. In the following section we present policies to process and create uncertainty-aware plans.

Naive Policy: Since each sequence of state transitions in a neighbors probabilistic plan resembles the sequence of brokers of the basic plan creation, the naive approach is to create a plan using multiple time-graphs; in particular, one time-graph for each possible combination of these individual sequences. For example, if the operator ω_D of our running example receives the plan of Figure 7 from the source and a basic plan from ω_F it creates one time-graph with the sequence $seq_1 = \{b_1, b_2, b_2\}$ and one with the sequence $seq_2 = \{b_1, b_1, b_2\}$ of ω_Ds plan. All shortest paths in these

---

[†]Note, this can be a typical GPS normal distribution

time-graphs are then combined to a plan, where each shortest path represents one sequence of state transitions in the resulting plan. Consider the case when the resulting shortest path of the time-graph for seq_1 leads to the sequence $seq_3 = \{b_3, b_4, b_4\}$ and for seq_2 to $seq_4 = \{b_3, b_3, b_4\}$. Since the probability for ω_F to follow the basic plan is 1 and the probability of the source to connect according to the sequence seq_1, respectively seq_2, is 0.5, each of those resulting sequences has the probability of $1 * 0.5$ to represent the actual migration sequence of ω_D. When both are combined to a single plan it looks structurally similar to Figure 7. This policy allows an operator to accurately follow the uncertain movement of a neighbor by creating an uncertain plan for the operator. However, it yields a high computational cost, because it requires to maintain many time-graphs.

Weighted Sum: This policy modifies the cost function to determine the placement costs C_{pla} in a time-graph, in order to create a plan that minimizes the overall expected placement and migration costs. It uses the weighted sum over the bandwidth-delay products to all expected hosts at a time $t_i \in TS$ in a neighbor's plan to determine placement costs $C_{pla}(v_j)$ for a vertex v_j at that time. The weight is the individual probability that an expected placement is chosen, i.e., the summed product of all state transitions on sequences to that expected placement, e.g., 0.5 for both expected placements at t_2 and 1 for the expect placement at t_3 in Figure 7. The computational costs are far lower than for the naive approach.

Temporal Adjustment: Since temporally skewed migrations of neighbors only indicate that the migration between any pair of brokers b_j, b_k can vary in time, the shortest path is determined in a time-graph that only considers one sequences of transitions between those in the neighbors plans. For example only for sequence $seq_1 = \{b_1, b_2, b_2\}$ of the example in Figure 7. An operator can then calculate a temporally skewed plan of its own or use this plan to find the single sequence of brokers with the lowest expected bandwidth-delay product. This is done by determining the probability that the operator is allowed to migrate at another time step in a predefined temporal interval $[t_i - t_s, t_i + t_e]$, instead of the time t_i at which the *ith* migration occurs according to the shortest path. Let $seq_3 = \{b_3, b_4, b_4\}$ be the initial resulting sequence, then for a t_s of 1 $seq_3' = \{b_3, b_3, b_4\}$ and $seq_3'' = \{b_4, b_4, b_4\}$ are also considered. The operator can then choose between selecting the sequence with the lowest expected overall bandwidth-delay product, according to the weighted sums at each time step, as plan or to use all of them as a temporally skewed plan. Like the naive approach this approach also allows an operator to follow the uncertain movement of a neighbor, however, with a smaller accuracy and computational cost.

Changes in data-rates: The last policy is the only one that creates an uncertainty-aware plan without previously receiving such plans from neighbors. Since a time-graph comprises estimated costs on future placements and migrations, the actual costs at the time of an estimated migration might differ. Recall that an operator with small state can defer its migration to such a time. In order to reflect these scenarios in the plan, we select the k shortest paths from a single time-graph, since they are the most likely paths to actually have the lowest costs. For example, due to a deviation in the bandwidth it can be good to also consider the edge from b_1 to b_2 at t_1 in Figure 4.

```
1:  upon timeout migrationTimer(time t)
2:     nextMigration ← findNextTarget(t)
3:     if nextMigration.t_im = t ∧ ¬stateMigrated then
4:         trigger send immutalbeState to nextMigration.H
5:     end if
6:     for ∀tq ∈ nextMigration.T_Q do
7:         if shouldMigrate(tq) then
8:             initiateMutableStateTransfer(tq)
9:             initiateStreaming(tq)
10:        end if
11:    end for
12:    if allStateAtTarget(nextMig.t_i) then
13:        stopOperator()
14:        trigger send start() to nextMigration.H
15:    end if
16: end
```

Figure 8: Execution of a Migration Plan

Each of these k paths represents a sequence of transitions in the plan. The probabilities that these paths represent the actual shortest path are determined by estimating the probability that the estimated cost for one of these paths is lower than for all the other paths and therefore describes the actual migration behavior. We therefore understand the sum of all weights W_{tg} on these paths as random variable X_{tg}. The confidence interval $(min(X_{tg}), max(X_{tg}))$ is given by the interval that determines how far bandwidths and latencies can deviate before the time-graph is created anew. However, without the knowledge of the real distribution within that interval, we can either assume that values are distributed according to a rather typical distribution, such as poison or uniform, learn those distributions, or use hints from the application on the actual distribution of bandwidths from in and outgoing streams. The continuous solution for the probability, that the j-th path has the lowest cost is then:

$$P_{min}(X_j) = \int_{y=min(X_j)}^{max(X_j)} \prod_{x \neq j} P(X_x > y)$$

For example, the weights for all depicted paths in Figure 4 including only brokers of b_1 and b_2 accumulate to the same costs. Therefore the probability for both paths in the interval $[t_1, t_2]$ is 0.5.

4.3 Executing a Migration Plan

Algorithm 8 allows the operator to implement the migration according to the probabilistic state transitions in a plan. It decides on one of the possible placements from the plan and informs the live-migration system about when to transfer and initialize an operator at the migration target. The algorithm serializes the migration of immutable and mutable state, while it continues processing at the previous broker until the migration target starts processing.

At each time step $t \in TS$ (see Line 1) of the plans, the algorithm checks if any possible migration needs to be initiated. It starts at the state that models the current placement, e.g., b_1 at t_1 in Figure 7. For the next possible migration according to this plan, e.g., from b_1 to b_2 at t_2, the operator checks if it has to start transferring the immutable state before the next time step. For uncertainty-aware plans this is checked for the sequence that currently has the lowest expected bandwidth-delay product (see Line 2-3). The migration itself starts out by sending the VM and immutable state to the selected migration target (see Line 4). This is skipped if the immutable state already started to be transferred in a previous time step.

In the next step (see Line 6-11), we determine if parts of the mutable state have to be transferred before the next step. This is done by estimating for each queue Q the size of the mutable state that is currently available in all queues starting from T_Q on and how long it takes to migrate these states. In this step, we also inform the neighbors in the operator-graph that they have to start streaming to the migration target and eventually stop streaming to the current host. They in return inform the migrating operator about the first event they transferred to the migration target, which indicates when to stop the streaming of mutable state from the current host to the migration target.

In a final step (see Line 12-15), the previous broker stops the processing at the time when mutable and immutable state is available at the migration target. Finally, it initializes the operator, in a rollback-recovery like fashion [17] at the target.

5. ANALYSIS

5.1 Locality of Plan Generation

The overhead in terms of messages to generate a plan depends on where the plan is generated. Which is either locally at each operator ω or at a central coordinator, e.g., at a dedicated node in the cloud. Note that a time-graph with vertices for all combinations of placements of operators increases the total number of vertices to the power-set. This is why it is more scaleable, even for a central coordinator, with a global view on all operators, to maintain a single time-graph for each operator.

A locally generated plan imposes the overhead to exchange plans (and feedback) with neighbors, which happens in average at a frequency $f_p(\omega)$ with an average size m_p for each message. In the central case all changes in measured and estimated bandwidths have to be sent to the coordinator, which happens in average at a frequency of $f_m(\omega)$ and with an average size of m_m for each message. Stable plans are sent to individual operators with a frequency $f_s(\omega)$. Other messages, i.e., to reserve resources at targets and collect information of latencies on links between neighbors, are nearly the same for both possibilities. A locally generated plan pays off, iff:

$$\sum_{i=0}^{|\Omega|} f_p(\omega_i) * m_p > \sum_{i=0}^{|\Omega|} f_m(\omega_i) * m_m + f_s(\omega_i) * m_p$$

5.2 Threshold for migration generation

In this section we derive a threshold, that determines when a potential second path in the time-graph is shorter than the selected shortest path. This gives a bound on when it is safe to not generate a new plan. Let $(v_1, ..., v_v)$ be the currently selected minimal path and $(v'_1, ..., v'_v)$ any other path. Let D be difference in their overall costs of the edge weights w.

$$D = \sum_{i=0}^{|E|-1} w((v_{i+1}, v_i)) - \sum_{i=0}^{|E|-1} w((v'_{i+1}, v'_i))$$

Only if D is positive, a second path can be shorter. Thus if the change in all weights stays in the bounds of the following threshold at the ith edge, D is guaranteed to be negative and

the selected path is shorter.

$$\frac{|w((v_{i+1}, v_i)) - w((v'_{i+1}, v'_i))|}{2}$$

5.3 Termination

An important property of the coordinated plan generation algorithm is that it eventually terminates, i.e., no new shorter path is selected, iff the estimated latencies on links and bandwidths incorporated in a time-graph do not change while the plan is generated. We claim that, with each newly selected shortest path for the plan generation of an operator the overall costs C_{tot}, the sum over all placement and migration costs, strictly monotonically decreases. We show the termination property by a proof of contradiction.

PROOF. Assume that the total costs C_{tot} increase to C'_{tot} after a new shortest path is selected for an operator ω. The only links that can now increase the placement costs are those directly involved in sharing event streams with neighboring operators of ω. The only migration costs that can be increased are those imposed by ω. Since these costs are used to calculate the edge weights of the time-graph, at least the previous shortest path would have been shorter. $\square$

6. EVALUATION

We implemented the migration approach with the Omnetpp simulator [26]. The traffic simulation package SUMO [1] enabled us to model realistic traffic patterns of vehicles on an OpenStreetMap graph [11]. The approach was tested with a generic operator graph resembling Figure 1(a), that allowed us to extract meaningful thresholds[‡].

Brokers were organized in a hierarchical tree data-structure, where each tier contained a dynamic number of $nb_x * nb_y$ simulated cloud or fog-nodes. With each level in the hierarchy the computational power increased quadratically, while the latency between neighbors in the hierarchy were similar. Vehicles were always connected to a leaf-node of the tree that managed the area where the car was located in. Over the course of 1000 simulated seconds approx. 1000 vehicles drove in an area of the size $7.7x3.5km$. Each connected vehicle published approx. one event per second. Each measurement was taken approx. 5 times.

We initially distributed all virtual brokers in the broker hierarchy randomly and tested three possible migration approaches: i) the *static* approach that didn't perform any migration, ii) the *greedy* approach that greedily selected every few seconds the broker with the best placement cost, and iii) our *MigCEP* approach.

6.1 Impact of state and streaming size

Since the *MCEP* approach is designed to consider the state and streaming size for an optimal sequence of migrations, we studied their influence on the main performance criteria, the network utilization. Furthermore, an increase in the number of brokers on the same area increases the number of hand-overs in the system, the main source of dynamics. Therefore, we also evaluated the impact of the number of brokers in the hierarchy on the network utilization.

In the experiment, we gradually increased the *event size* of one of the sources in the operator graph from 50 to 250 bytes

---

[‡]For simplicity we omitted source c. We parametrized the operator graph regarding the state size, event size, and detection rate.

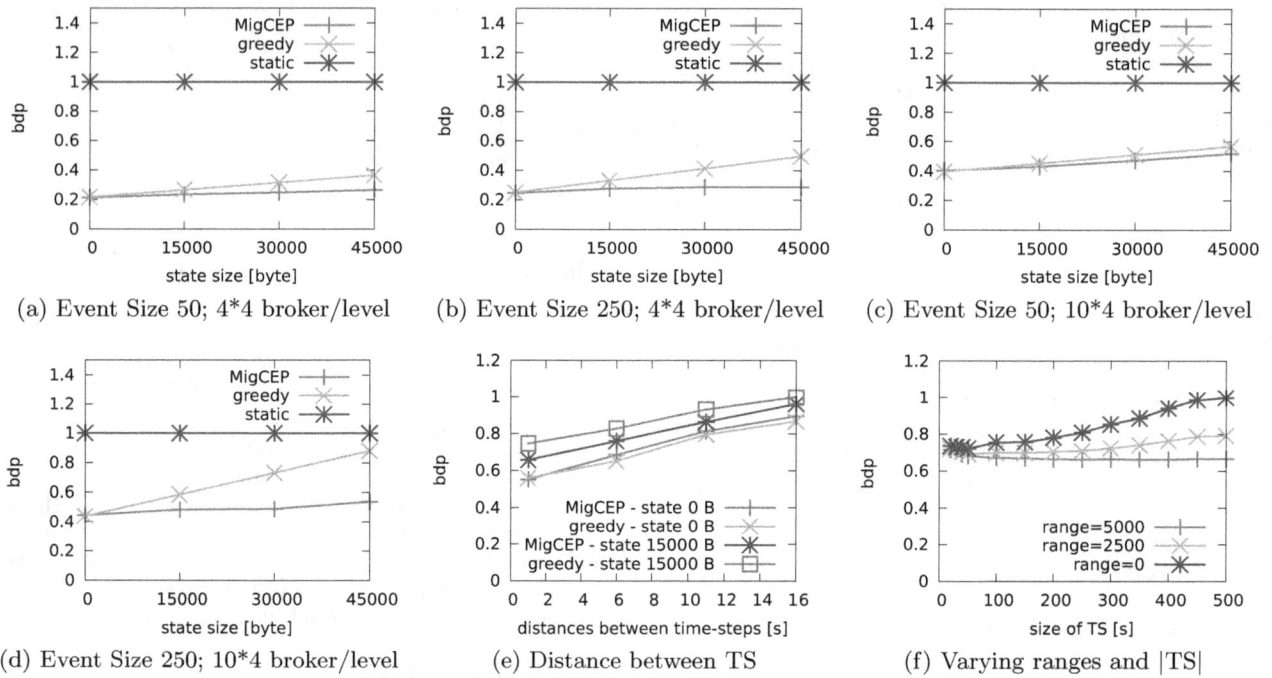

(a) Event Size 50; 4*4 broker/level   (b) Event Size 250; 4*4 broker/level   (c) Event Size 50; 10*4 broker/level

(d) Event Size 250; 10*4 broker/level   (e) Distance between TS   (f) Varying ranges and |TS|

Figure 9: Evaluation of basic time-graph based approach

and the immutable *state size* of the operator that received those events from 0 bytes to 60000 bytes. The number of brokers varied from 21 fog-nodes in a quad-tree with a single cloud data-center root to a tree with one simulated cloud data-center as root and a flat topology of 40 fog-nodes. The information from the simulated navigation system of the vehicle was used to generate plans for vehicles. On the y-axis in Figure 9 (a-d) the results of the average bandwidth-delay product (bdp) is depicted, relative to the *static* approach. The x-axis depicts the immutable state size in bytes.

The results demonstrate the strength of our approach in both broker hierarchies. Our approach outperforms by far the static approach, since it adjusts the placements. While the resulting migration and placement costs are comparable to the greedy approach when the size of immutable state is low, the benefit increases the larger the immutable state is, since our approach amortizes the migration costs. The system had to adapt the placement of the operator more often in the case of larger event sizes (Figure 9(b) and 9(d)) which is why the benefit is more distinguished in those cases. The overhead averaged on low 27 additional coordination messages (resource reservations, plan updates, and feedback) per coordination — independent of event and state size.

6.2 Impact of vertices in the time-graph

The performance of the plan generation depends on the number of vertices in the time-graph. This number changes with the granularity of migration times in a sequence of time-steps TS and the number of selected brokers.

The distance between time-steps dictates the system on when it can perform a migration. The longer the distance, the less vertices in the time-graph; however, the less chances to find the optimal time for a migration. Figure 9(e) depicts the results, relative to the maximal measured bdp, for varying distances between 1 and 16 seconds, effectively reducing the number of vertices by $\frac{1}{4}$ with each larger step.

It demonstrates that the increase in the bdp is linear, while the number of vertices multiplicativly decrease.

Moreover, the number of time-steps of TS dictates how far into the future a prediction is made. In the experiment we increased this size from 10 to 500. We also restricted the number of brokers that are considered for the time-graphas possible target, by only selecting nearby brokers that manage ranges that are no more than 0, 2500, or 5000 meters away. This includes brokers in higher or lower levels of the hierarchy responsible for the same range. Figure 9(f) shows that a larger range gives a better prediction since more brokers were involved. However, the performance only gracefully degrades with fewer brokers. Few time-steps limited the opportunity for planning migrations and too many time-steps reduce the chance to place the operator on the right broker in the future.

6.3 Impact of uncertainties

The future placements typically encounter a lot of uncertainties, depending on how the mobility pattern and communication characteristics are captured. The general setup to test the policies dealing with these uncertainties (Section 4.2) was to deploy both ω_{FS} as state-less operators and ω_D as state-full operator. For the *naive* and *weighted sum* policy (ws), we tested the three methods to capture mobility patterns, uncertain locations from the *dead reckoning* approach (linear), certain locations that could stem from a *navigation* system (navi), and *learned* transitions between leaf broker (learned). For the *temporal* policies we restricted the simulation to the *learned* temporal transition on the path of the navigation system, since the policy is only expressive for this capture method. To test the k-shortest path approach we also randomly increased and decreased the event-sizes. Hence, the placement of one of the ω_{FS} had to be constantly adapted for an optimal placement.

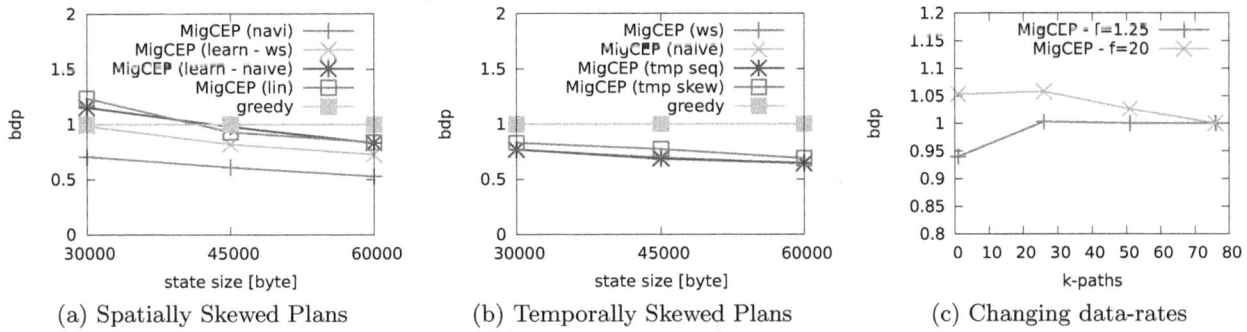

| (a) Spatially Skewed Plans | (b) Temporally Skewed Plans | (c) Changing data-rates |

Figure 10: Impact of uncertainty

The x-axis of Figure 10(a) and Figure 10(b) depicts the varying state size. The average bandwidth-delay product depicted on the y-axis shows the effect of different methods to capture the mobility using different policies on the network utilization; using the greedy approach as baseline. Each policy increased the network utilization less severe than the greedy approach after the state size crossed a specific threshold. That threshold is the point where the reduction in the migration rate makes up for less optimal anticipated placements. Depicted in Figure 10(c) are the results for different numbers of sequences selected form the k-shortest path approach, where the frequency f in the change in the event-size ranged from every 20 seconds to every 1.25 second. The results are depicted relative to the *bdp* value of the largest k for each frequency. For the high-change rate, more paths increased the possibility for wrong placement decisions, however, for slow change rates the system had a better chance to adapt itself.

7. RELATED WORK

The placement of operators has already been studied in context of DCEP [7, 20, 22, 23]. However the main focus of these work are systems where sensors and consumers aren't mobile and the communication characteristics rarely change. Therefore none of the systems considered the impact of migration costs on the placement, nor do they have to consider the mobility of a consumer, which influences the time when it is required to trigger a migration.

Previous work in DCEP focused on uncertainty in detecting events, e.g., on noisy events captured by sensors [16] or predicted future events [10]. However, none of them studied the impact on the system resources when planing future placements with uncertain location information.

Mobility-aware publish-subscribe systems [14,15] dynamically adapt filter operators to new access points of publishers or subscribers. However, filter operators are stateless and therefore none of these systems considers the migration cost itself in the optimization.

Live migration [12,19] in cloud computing environments is used to increase data-access locality, energy saving, or load balancing. A typical goal is to reduce the downtime, the time during which the execution is stopped. On the one hand, pre-copying techniques [4] copy disk-images, i.e., the complete state of the operator, and memory-pages in advance before the processor state. This can arbitrarily increase the bandwidth, because events that are potentially deleted from the queues Q as soon as the VM starts at the target are also migrated. On the other hand, post-copying [12] techniques

transfer first the processor state and then the pages. This can increase the latency if the next required page is not migrated yet, even to such an extent, that latency restrictions are not preserved.

Content-delivery networks improve end-user performance, data availability, and reduce server load by migrating data. They have been considered for mobile environments [2] and cloud environments [27]. However, they do not have to consider dependencies between different operators.

8. CONCLUSION

In this paper we presented methods to improve the overall network utilization for real-time applications with defined end-to-end latency restrictions in future mobile infrastructures. Using a MCEP system as example, we demonstrated that it pays off to plan migrations ahead of time according to the mobility of users or dependent migrations. Costly migrations of state, in terms of network utilization, can be amortized by selecting suitable targets in a time-graph data structure that models the expected costs. Furthermore, we presented how application knowledge improves live-migration systems. Execution environments that are typically used in DCEP provide the possibility to find a better serialization of operators, because they allow a live-migration system to infer which state has to be transferred.

Our ongoing work will focus on further optimization possibilities. We tested the system with only simple prediction mechanisms for data-rates, however, more sophisticated ones could greatly improve the performance. So far, we did not consider the fact that different operators might require the same mutable state—an overlapping set of ingoing event-streams. Finding such overlaps would allow the system to coordinate the migration of multiple operators while migrating the immutable state only once, thus further improving the network utilization.

Acknowledgment

This work is supported by contract research "CEP in the Large" of the Baden-Württemberg Stiftung. The authors would like to thank the reviewers and D. Lillethun for their helpful comments.

9. REFERENCES

[1] M. Behrisch, L. Bieker, J. Erdmann, and D. Krajzewicz. SUMO - Simulation of Urban MObility: An Overview. In *Proc. of 3rd Int. Conference on Advances in System Simulation (SIMUL)*, pages 63–68, Barcelona, Spain, Oct. 2011.

[2] M. M. Bin Tariq, R. Jain, and T. Kawahara. Mobility Aware Server Selection for Mobile Streaming Multimedia Content Distribution Networks. In F. Douglis and B. D. Davison, editors, *Web Content Caching and Distribution*, pages 1–18. Kluwer Academic Publishers, Norwell, MA, USA, 2004.

[3] F. Bonomi, R. Milito, J. Zhu, and S. Addepalli. Fog Computing and Its Role in the Internet of Things. In *Proc. of 1st MCC workshop on Mobile Cloud Computing*, pages 13–16. ACM, 2012.

[4] R. Bradford, E. Kotsovinos, A. Feldmann, and H. Schiöberg. Live Wide-Area Migration of Virtual Machines Including Local Persistent State. In *Proc. of 3rd Int. Conference on Virtual Execution Environments (VEE)*, pages 169–179. ACM, 2007.

[5] A. T. Campbell, S. B. Eisenman, N. D. Lane, E. Miluzzo, R. A. Peterson, H. Lu, X. Zheng, M. Musolesi, K. Fodor, and G.-S. Ahn. The Rise of People-Centric Sensing. *IEEE Internet Computing*, 12(4):12–21, 2008.

[6] S. Chakravarthy and D. Mishra. Snoop: An Expressive Event Specification Language For Active Databases. *Data & Knowledge Engineering*, 14(1):1–26, 1994.

[7] G. Cugola and A. Margara. Deployment Strategies for Distributed Complex Event Processing. *Springer Computing*, 95(2):129–156, 2013.

[8] F. Dabek, R. Cox, F. Kaashoek, and R. Morris. Vivaldi: A Decentralized Network Coordinate System. In *Proc. of 2004 Conference on Applications, Technologies, Architectures, and Protocols for Computer Communications (SIGCOMM)*, pages 15–26. ACM, 2004.

[9] C. du Mouza, W. Litwin, and P. Rigaux. SD-Rtree: A Scalable Distributed Rtree. In *Proc. of the 23rd Int. Conf. on Data Engineering (ICDE)*, pages 296–305. IEEE, Apr. 2007.

[10] Y. Engel, O. Etzion, and Z. Feldman. A Basic Model for Proactive Event-driven Computing. In *Proc. of 6th ACM Int. Conference on Distributed Event-Based Systems (DEBS)*, pages 107–118. ACM, 2012.

[11] M. Haklay and P. Weber. OpenStreetMap: User-Generated Street Maps. *IEEE Pervasive Computing*, 7(4):12–18, Dec. 2008.

[12] M. R. Hines, U. Deshpande, and K. Gopalan. Post-Copy Live Migration of Virtual Machines. *SIGOPS Oper. Syst. Rev.*, 43(3):14–26, July 2009.

[13] K. Hong, S. Smaldoney, J. Shin, D. Lillethun, L. Iftodey, and U. Ramachandran. Target Container: A Target-Centric Parallel Programming Abstraction for Video-based Surveillance. In *Proc. of 5th ACM/IEEE Int. Conf. on Distributed Smart Cameras (ICDSC)*, pages 1–8, Aug. 2011.

[14] S. Hu, V. Muthusamy, G. Li, and H.-A. Jacobsen. Transactional Mobility in Distributed Content-Based Publish/Subscribe Systems. In *Proc. of 29th IEEE Int. Conf. on Distributed Computing Systems (ICDCS)*, pages 101–110, June 2009.

[15] K. Jayaram, C. Jayalath, and P. Eugster. Parametric Subscriptions for Content-Based Publish/Subscribe Networks. In *Proc. IFIP/ACM/USENIX Conf. on Middleware*, pages 128–147, 2010.

[16] G. G. Koch, B. Koldehofe, and K. Rothermel. Higher Confidence in Event Correlation Using Uncertainty Restrictions. In *Proc. of 28th Int. Conf. on Distributed Computing Systems (ICDCS) Workshops*, pages 417 –422, June 2008.

[17] B. Koldehofe, R. Mayer, U. Ramachandran, K. Rothermel, and M. Völz. Rollback-Recovery without Checkpoints in Distributed Event Processing Systems. In *Proc. of 7th ACM Int. Conf. on Distributed Event-Based Systems (DEBS)*. ACM, 2013.

[18] B. Koldehofe, B. Ottenwälder, K. Rothermel, and U. Ramachandran. Moving Range Queries in Distributed Complex Event Processing. In *Proc. of 6th ACM Int. Conf. on Distributed Event-Based Systems (DEBS)*, pages 201–212. ACM, 2012.

[19] R. K. K. Ma and C.-L. Wang. Lightweight Application-Level Task Migration for Mobile Cloud Computing. In *Proc. of 26th IEEE International Conference on Advanced Information Networking and Applications (AINA)*, AINA '12, pages 550–557. IEEE Computer Society, 2012.

[20] P. Pietzuch, J. Ledlie, J. Shneidman, M. Roussopoulos, M. Welsh, and M. Seltzer. Network-Aware Operator Placement for Stream-Processing Systems. In *Proc. of 22nd Int. Conf. on Data Engineering (ICDE)*, pages 49–60. IEEE Computer Society, 2006.

[21] P. Pietzuch, B. Shand, and J. Bacon. Composite Event Detection as a Generic Middleware Extension. *IEEE Network*, 18(1):44–55, Feb. 2004.

[22] S. Rizou, F. Dürr, and K. Rothermel. Solving the Multi-operator Placement Problem in Large-Scale Operator Networks. In *Proc. of 19th Int. Conf. on Computer Communication Networks (ICCCN)*, pages 1–6. IEEE Communications Society, Aug. 2010.

[23] B. Schilling, B. Koldehofe, and K. Rothermel. Efficient and Distributed Rule Placement in Heavy Constraint-Driven Event Systems. In *Proc. of 13th IEEE Int. Conf. on High Performance Computing and Communications (HPCC)*, pages 355 –364, Sept. 2011.

[24] Z. Sebepou and K. Magoutis. CEC: Continuous Eventual Checkpointing for Data Stream Processing Operators. In *41st Int. Conf. on Dependable Systems Networks (DSN)*, pages 145–156, June 2011.

[25] J. Shin, R. Kumar, D. Mohapatra, U. Ramachandran, and M. Ammar. ASAP: A Camera Sensor Network for Situation Awareness. In *Proc. of 11th Int. Conf. on Principles of Distributed Systems (OPODIS)*, pages 31–47. Springer-Verlag, 2007.

[26] A. Varga. The OMNeT++ Discrete Event Simulation System. In *Proc. of the European Simulation Multiconference (ESM)*, June 2001.

[27] P. Wendell, J. W. Jiang, M. J. Freedman, and J. Rexford. DONAR: Decentralized Server Selection for Cloud Services. In *Proc. of ACM SIGCOMM*, SIGCOMM '10, pages 231–242, New York, NY, USA, 2010. ACM.

[28] O. Wolfson, A. P. Sistla, S. Chamberlain, and Y. Yesha. Updating and Querying Databases that Track Mobile Units. *Distributed and Parallel Databases*, 7:257–387, July 1999.

Opportunistic Spatio-temporal Event Processing for Mobile Situation Awareness

Kirak Hong, David Lillethun,
Umakishore Ramachandran
College of Computing
Georgia Institute of Technology
Atlanta, Georgia, USA
{khong9, davel, rama }@cc.gatech.edu

Beate Ottenwälder, Boris Koldehofe
Institute of Parallel and Distributed Systems
University of Stuttgart
Stuttgart, Germany
{beate.ottenwaelder,
boris.koldehofe}@ipvs.uni-stuttgart.de

ABSTRACT

With the proliferation of mobile devices and sensors, mobile situation awareness is becoming an important class of applications. The key requirement of this class of applications is low-latency processing of events stemming from sensor data in order to provide timely situational information to mobile users. To satisfy the latency requirement, we propose an opportunistic spatio-temporal event processing system that uses prediction-based continuous query handling. Our system predicts future query regions for moving consumers and starts processing events early so that the live situational information is available when the consumer reaches the future location. In contrast to existing systems, our system provides timely information about a consumer's current position by hiding computation latency for processing recent events. To evaluate our system, we measure the quality of results and timeliness of live situational information with various query parameters. Our evaluation shows that we can achieve highly meaningful query results with near-zero latency in most cases.

Categories and Subject Descriptors

C.2.1 [**Network Architecture and Design**]: Distributed networks; C.2.4 [**Distributed Systems**]: Distributed applications

Keywords

mobility; complex event processing; situation awareness

1. INTRODUCTION

The explosive growth of sensors in the environment is enabling many future applications. Vehicles and mobile communication devices (i.e., smartphones and tablets) have a variety of sensors that they lacked only a few years ago [5]. Large scale camera deployments around transportation infrastructure, such as airports, seaports, and highways are becoming common as well. For example, there are hundreds of cameras monitoring the highways in the Atlanta metro area [1]. These sensors could enable applications such as one that notifies drivers of live road conditions near them, warning of traffic, accidents, or obstructions on the road. Such information could also be used in live, adaptive traffic routing applications. Furthermore, urban sensor deployments can enhance community safety, for example, by notifying police officers of suspicious individuals based on their behaviors.

These applications, often classified as mobile situation awareness, provide situational information to mobile users based on the events from various sensors that are widely deployed in the environment. Mobile situation awareness is naturally event-based, processing primitive events from sensors using application-specific algorithms to generate high-level events including situational information, and finally either reporting the situational information to a human or using it for automated decision making. In this context, events are spatio-temporal in nature – they occur at a particular place and time – and mobile users typically make continuous queries about their surroundings, i.e., situational information based on recent, nearby events.

As a specific example, consider a user who is driving from New York to Los Angeles. The user may have a vehicular application to automatically detect driving conditions along the route (e.g., traffic, accidents, road obstructions, or construction) and reroute the user around those problems. However, it is not practical to process the events along this whole cross-country route for the entire trip. Furthermore, an accident along the route near LA may not be relevant if it happens while the user is only just leaving NY. Therefore, the application should only process events in the vicinity of the user, according to some reasonable, application-defined range. Timely delivery of events is critical for this application, however, since there is no point in notifying the user's vehicle of an accident or bad traffic after the user passes the last exit on the highway before the problem – it is too late for the user to do anything useful with that information. This is an example of an application where an approximate result is better than a late result.

Complex Event Processing (CEP) is a well-known paradigm to generate such situational information. To generate situational information, CEP applications use operator graphs consisting of multiple operators that perform online processing of events. Online processing of events allows asynchronous, low-latency generation of situational information since events are processed as they come. In a traditional, infrastructure-based CEP application, a single operator graph would take input from all the sensors in the infrastructure and perform continuous computation to generate live events.

However, for a mobile situation awareness application, it is not scalable to continuously perform live computation on all of the sensors everywhere. Furthermore, mobile users are typically only interested in events occurring within a certain area around them. Computing events outside that area results in wasted computation. The reduction in needed computation when only processing events in a range around the mobile user, vs. processing all events, is substantial [19]. A naive solution would be to start the operator graph anew in different locations as the mobile user moves to those locations. However, processing of some historical events is typically necessary before live event processing can begin. Often the user is interested in recent events, not only ones happening right now. It also may be the case that some historical context is needed to correctly process new events. Events must be processed in temporal order, so there is a processing delay to deal with the historical events before live event processing begins. Therefore, if the operator graph is started in a location only when a user moves to that location, the user will then be in a different location by the time the operator graph has finished processing the historical events. This could potentially lead to a situation where the operator graph is constantly trying to "catch up" to the user, resulting in processing events in inappropriate locations and never actually getting to process any "live" events.

We propose to address this problem by processing the historical events for a location before the mobile user arrives at that location, so that live event processing begins at the moment the user arrives, if not before. Two existing technologies enable this just-in-time computation: future location predictions for the mobile user placing the query, and processing time estimations for the CEP algorithms. Several location prediction algorithms already exist [32], and profiling techniques can be used to estimate processing time. Our system treats both of these as black boxes, allowing different location prediction and processing time estimation algorithms to be plugged in. However, two important challenges still remain. First, if the speed of the mobile user is too fast compared to the processing time, the historical event processing may take longer than the user takes to get to the new location. To mitigate this, we propose using parallel resources to enable pipeline processing of future locations in several time- steps look-ahead. Second, the location predictor may not give a single, accurate location prediction. To mitigate the imperfection of location prediction algorithms, we propose taking several predictions for each time-step look-ahead and opportunistically compute the events for all of those locations, as our parallel resources allow. When the user arrives at that time, the prediction among those that is closest to truth (the user's actual position) will be selected and its events returned.

Our research contributions include 1) a system architecture that enables spatio-temporal event processing for mobile situation awareness applications; 2) methods for (a) starting event processing at predicted future locations in advance of a mobile user's arrival, (b) pipelining multiple future prediction points to allow completion of event processing by the time the mobile user arrives, and (c) selecting multiple location points from a predictor to opportunis-

tically compute events at future locations; 3) metrics for assessing the quality of results and timeliness of mobile situation awareness applications; and 4) an experimental evaluation of our system and methods.

The remainder of this paper is structured as follows: Section 2 discusses related work. Section 3 presents the system architecture. Section 4 discusses our opportunistic event processing method. Section 5 evaluates our system and Section 6 discusses future work and concludes.

2. RELATED WORK

Many complex event processing systems [25, 20, 2, 7, 18] provide methods to efficiently detect interesting patterns on various sensor data for situation awareness applications. To reduce latency for processing events, some CEP systems exploit parallelism [8, 13] while others support adaptive placement of operators [28, 24]. However, these systems are designed to support CEP on a fixed infrastructure of sources. In contrast, our system supports CEP for mobile devices, such as smart vehicles, which requires migrating an operator graph to a new region when a user moves. Koldehofe et al. [19] propose a system that supports CEP on moving ranges. However, they do not address the latency of processing historical events when an operator graph moves to another region. We use this work as a baseline for our approach to prove the efficacy of opportunistic event processing in terms of timeliness and quality of results.

Research in spatio-temporal databases has developed various representations of spatio-temporal objects and methods for querying and storing spatio-temporal objects [9, 23, 10]. These spatio-temporal databases are complementary to our system since they can serve as a spatio-temporal event storage module in our system. Predictive query handling on spatio-temporal databases [16, 12] allows answering queries about the future locations of mobile objects, e.g., the ten nearest neighbors after five minutes, based on location prediction of mobile objects. In contrast, our system delivers just-in-time situational information about the recent state of the current location. Hendawi et al. [12] precompute query results to improve scalability and reduce the latency of query handling. However, their work combines on-demand query results with precomputed query results to provide complete results with various best-effort latencies. Our system provides query results with near-zero latency, although query results may not be complete due to inaccurate location predictions.

Mobile publish-subscribe systems adapt streaming based on consumer location changes [15, 22]. Cilia et al. [6] support pre-subscriptions to new locations before the consumer arrives to improve the bootstrapping process of mobile event-based applications. Low-latency event delivery is achieved through exploiting parallelism [31] and adaptation of routing paths [30]. However, the above work does not deal with the computational latency for delivering situational information since they focus on delivering individual events rather than complex events that are generated by processing the individual events.

Large-scale situation awareness [27] is receiving increased attention due to the proliferation of sensors and advances in analytics, such as computer vision. Target Container [14] is a distributed system providing a high-level, handler-based programming abstraction that helps domain experts write large-scale surveillance applications on camera networks. SLIP-

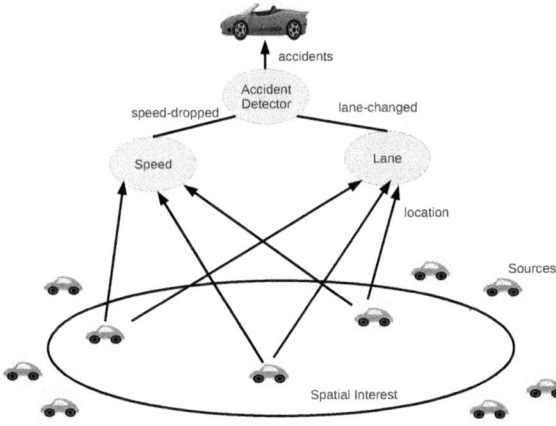

Figure 1: Example operator graph for mobile situation awareness

stream [26] offers a stream-oriented programming model that ensures automatic scalability of interactive perception applications. However, these systems focus on processing live streams from cameras, which potentially requires a huge amount of system resources in the large scale. In contrast, our system performs analysis of sensor data based on user queries and caches the query results for later use, resulting in efficient use of system resources.

Meissen et al. [21] present an approach to predict the future context of a user and efficiently deliver information based on the knowledge discrepancy between the situation-awareness system and the user. However, they focus on identifying knowledge discrepancy based on various operations, including set and relational algebra. In contrast, we focus on reducing computational latency with opportunistic event processing.

3. SYSTEM ARCHITECTURE

In this section, we discuss the details of our system architecture including the spatio-temporal event and query model, the logical modules for event processing, and the fog-based distributed architecture of our system.

3.1 Spatio-temporal Query Model

To support mobile situation awareness, our system collects various types of sensor data called events from widely deployed heterogeneous sensors such as smartphones, connected vehicles, and traffic monitoring cameras. Every event must have a set of required properties including a type, a location, and a timestamp. A location and timestamp property can be either a point or a range, regarding the type of event. The required properties are set by a producing sensor, specifying where and when a certain type of event is generated. Besides the required properties, each event may have optional application-specific properties for sensor data, which can be either structured (e.g., integer, string) or unstructured (e.g., audio or video).

Using events collected from various sensors, our system provides situational information to mobile users. Situational information is generated by executing an application-specific operator graph on the collected events. An operator graph consists of multiple operators, where each represents a piece of computation. Each operator takes one or more input types of events and produces an output type of event. Connecting edges between operators define the logical flow of events. Take Figure 1 as an example of using an operator graph for mobile situation awareness. In the example, each car continuously reports location events, including its identifier and geographical position, to the operator graph. By consuming speed and location events, two leaf operators in the operator graph detect speed-patterns and lane switches of each car. The root operator is an accident detector, which incorporates the speed and lane information to detect an accident if many cars reduced their speed and avoided a specific lane at the same time. The final outcome of this operator graph, accidents, are the situational information that our system delivers to mobile users. Note that a real application may also include heavy-weight operators, such as computer vision algorithms, and sensor streams may be unstructured, such as video.

To receive situational information, a mobile user registers a continuous query with a number of parameters listed in Table 1. An *operator graph* as the application-specific situation awareness logic that generates situational information from sensor events. The *spatial interest* and *temporal interest* defines a space and time range based on a user's current location and current wallclock time that define the selection of interesting events as an input to the operator graph. For example, a navigation system may want to display all recent accidents at nearby locations. Detecting such recent events requires processing both live and historical events, which require a mobile user to specify her temporal interest based on the duration from the current wallclock time. The user also specifies her spatial interest based on her current location to receive most relevant information.

A mobile user also sets a *location sensitivity* that indicates a distance threshold for updating the spatial scope of the situation awareness based on the user's current location. For example, a car navigation system has to show up-to-date information while a car is moving. It can set the location sensitivity at 100 meters so it can receive updated situational information for a new region whenever the user moves more than one 100 meters.

Temporal Ordering

Note that it's crucial that our system injects events to operator graphs in a temporal order. If events are not temporally ordered, the application logic of each operator has to go through past events that are already processed, and perform its algorithm again to find certain patterns using updated sequence of events. Take for example an operator that detects a linear drop in speed values over the last 30 seconds. If delivered in the right temporal order, e.g., $\{speed, t_1, l_1, 30\frac{km}{h}\}$, $\{speed, t_2, l_2, 20\frac{km}{h}\}$, $\{speed, t_3, l_3, 10\frac{km}{h}\}$, it's a sequential process to just compare the last two events with every new event arrival. Delivered in the wrong temporal order $\{speed, t_3, l_3, 10\frac{km}{h}\}$, $\{speed, t_2, l_2, 20\frac{km}{h}\}$, $\{speed, t_1, l_1, 30\frac{km}{h}\}$, means that the operator either detects an increase in the speed or has to sort the events and look at each event again to check if it is now a linear drop. Our ordering model assumes that live-events from the same sensor arrive in temporal order over a FIFO channel, so that a local time-stamp in the arrival order according to a local clock allows for a total ordering of events for the processing of the operator. Historical events that are injected

Query Parameter	Description	Example
spatial interest	a mobile user's interested region, in terms of distance from the user's current location	500 meters from here
temporal interest	a mobile user's interested time duration, in terms of duration from current wallclock time	recent 5 minutes
operator graph	operator graph implementing situation awareness logic	Figure 1
location sensitivity	distance threshold to update the scope of situation awareness (i.e., Our system switches to a new operator-graph if the user moves more than this threshold from the previous location.)	100 meters

Table 1: Query Parameters for Mobile Situation Awareness

to create historical situations are buffered before being collected by the operator and deterministically time-stamped at that buffer.

Operator Graph Switch

When a user moves to another region, our system needs to provide updated situational information for the region. Following the results of [19], it is beneficial to create and initialize an operator graph on demand based on user mobility, instead of deploying a vast amount of operator graphs for all possible regions. Consider again the example that a consumer is interested in accidents that happened in the last hour in a 5 km perimeter. The current operator graph already processes up-to-date events from a previous region. Integrating historical events from the new region that were not previously detected means that the current operator graph cannot process these events in the previously established temporal order. For example location l_1 was not part of the previous region, suddenly this wrong temporal ordering $\{speed, t_2, l_2, 20\frac{km}{h}\}$, $\{speed, t_3, l_3, 10\frac{km}{h}\}$, $\{speed, t_1, l_1, 30\frac{km}{h}\}$ is possible. To continuously provide situational information while a user is moving, our system creates a new operator graph for the user's updated spatial interest and terminates the previous operator graph. The new operator graph starts processing historical and live events for a new region and asynchronously delivers situational information to the user. After processing all historical events, the operator can provide live situational information by processing live events from a specific region. In order to distinguish results, they are stamped with the *spatial interest* and the interval of the maximal and minimal time-stamp from events that are used to generate the situational information.

3.2 Logical Modules for Event Processing

Figure 2 shows the logical structure of our spatio-temporal event processing architecture. Each client has a *query subscriber* through which a mobile user registers a continuous query with a server. The registered query is handled by the server's *query processor* that creates an operator graph and executes it by injecting relevant spatio-temporal events matching the continuous query. While running, the operator graph generates high-level events for situational information such as car accidents on highways, which are then asynchronously delivered to the current user through the query subscriber.

Our system includes a *spatio-temporal event storage* that stores primitive events from sensors as well as high-level events that are generated from operator graphs to serve future queries without redundant computation. All events in the spatio-temporal event storage are indexed by loca-

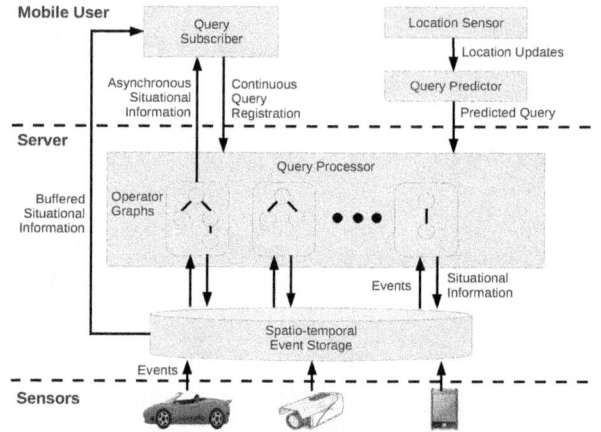

Figure 2: Conceptual view of our system architecture: Each component represents a logical module that is distributed over multiple physical nodes.

tion, time, and type properties. An administrator given TTL value specifies a lifecycle of the events stored in the event storage. After an event is expired based on its TTL value and timestamp, our system removes the event from the spatio-temporal event storage. By removing old events, our system efficiently uses its storage space by keeping events that are more effective for situation awareness.

A *query predictor* is a key contribution in our system that allows opportunistic event-processing based on location predictions. The query predictor runs on the client-side and sends requests for creating and running operator graphs on a user's future locations. Detailed mechanisms of this component are discussed in Section 4.

3.3 Fog-based Distributed Event Processing

To serve a large number of continuous queries while each query potentially involves processing a large number of event streams, we need to run operator graphs on distributed computing resources. One design choice can be using the cloud, since it provides virtualized system resources on demand. Using the cloud, our system can elastically scale up and down regarding the number of users and sensor streams for event processing. However, there are two critical drawbacks for the cloud-based approach. The first problem is the network latency to deliver situational information from the cloud to mobile devices. If our system is running in the cloud, it collects events and delivers situational information through the Internet. Satyanarayanan, et al. [29], show that WAN latencies can be high and that these latencies interfere with interactive applications. We argue that sensor applications are vulnerable to the same issue due to the sense-process-actuate loop, as would be any other applications with feedback loops. In short, WAN latencies prevent our system from providing timely information to mobile users. Another problem of using the cloud is the core network traffic. Although network traffic is invisible to mobile users, using geographically centralized cloud can potentially burden the underlying network infrastructure.

In order to alleviate these problems, we propose deploying our system on computational resources located near the edge of the network. *Fog computing* is a new resource paradigm proposed by Cisco [4] that supports large–scale, latency–sensitive applications. The key idea is to maintain highly available computing and storage resources in the middle of the network infrastructure, providing resources from the core to the edge. In contrast to the cloud, these hierarchical and geographically distributed resources allow applications to perform low–latency processing near the edge. Although no commercial fog products are deployed in a production environment yet, we envision our system running in the edge network to which mobile users can communicate with low latency. This may be accomplished using smart routers, middleboxes, or simply a local cluster, and we shall henceforth refer to any computational resources at the edge of the network as "fog nodes". On each of the distributed nodes, we run an instance of the spatio-temporal event storage and query processor to store events and execute operator graphs based on the events.

To allow fog-based distributed event processing, sensors send events to nearby fog nodes after receiving a connection endpoint (e.g., IP address) from a well-known name server. The name server maintains a directory including each fog node and their responsible spatial regions. Similarly to the sensors, a mobile user can find a nearby fog node through the name server to register a continuous query. Once an operator graph is created at the fog node, the mobile user receives situational information from the fog node that is running the operator graph. If the operator graph's region overlaps the region of multiple fog nodes, events are asynchronously aggregated from the multiple fog nodes to the node running the operator graph. When a user moves away from the current operator graph, our system finds a new fog node to create a new operator graph for a new region.

To select the best fog node to run an operator graph, our system uses a simple heuristic based on the current and expected workload of candidate fog nodes. At runtime, our system monitors the workload at each fog node in terms of processor utilization, per-event processing time for each individual operator graph, and event rate for different event types. The latter is done by monitoring the average event rates on fine-grained regions in individual grids for different event types that span the region of a fog node.

Upon a request for creating a new operator graph, our system finds candidate fog nodes whose responsible regions overlap with the new operator graph's region. Among the candidate nodes, our system first selects a node with highest event rate for the operator graph by summing up event rates for fine-grained regions within the overlap between the fog node's region and the operator graph's region. Once a fog node is selected, our system estimates how the processor utilization would change at the selected fog node if it starts

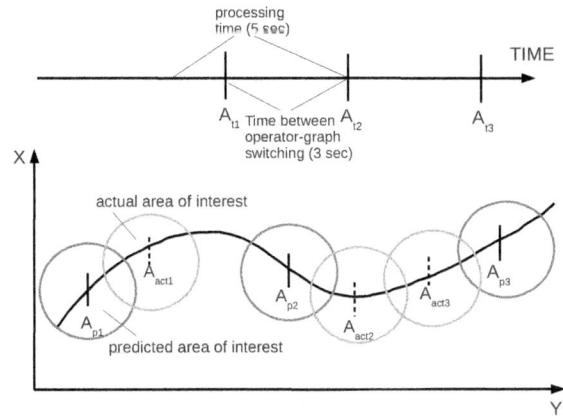

Figure 3: Examples for predictive query execution: operator graphs do not match with predicted locations and may require more time to execute than it takes to switch from one operator graph to the next

running the new operator graph. The estimated workload is calculated based on the average per-event processing time of the operator graph and expected event rate for the entire region of the new operator graph. If the estimated processor utilization stays below a certain threshold, our system selects the fog node to run the new operator graph. Otherwise, our system selects the fog node with the next highest event rate for the operator graph and estimates workload again. The intuition behind this approach is to find a fog node that minimizes the network utilization for aggregating events, while ensuring that the node has enough computational capacity to run the operator graph.

4. OPPORTUNISTIC EVENT PROCESSING

This section details the problem of processing latency for historical events when switching to a new operator graph and our solution to minimize the latency using opportunistic event processing mechanism.

4.1 Problem Description

If a mobile user moves to a new location that is farther than its distance threshold (location sensitivity), our system creates a new operator graph with an updated region and starts processing historical events matching to the mobile user's temporal interest (e.g., recent 5 minutes). Although situational information is asynchronously generated and delivered to the user while processing the historical events, the mobile user can only receive live situational information after processing all historical events in temporal order. Because of the processing latency of historical events, switching to a new operator graph causes a delay before receiving live situational information. Since low-latency is a key requirement in mobile situation awareness, such a delay can be a significant problem. Another problem caused by the latency of processing historical events is the meaningfulness of situational information. By the time when recent situational information is delivered, a mobile user may already moved away from the previous location, which makes some situational information meaningless as they are outside of the mobile user's current spatial interest.

4.2 Solution Overview

To give timely situational information, an operator graph must have processed all historical events when a user switches to this operator graph. In the ideal case, there may be no historical events for the operator graph's region and therefore is the processing latency for historical events zero. However, if the region contains historical events matching to the user's temporal interest, we should start the operator graph earlier before the user switches to the operator graph, giving enough time to process all historical events. To start operator graphs earlier, our system performs opportunistic computing based on the prediction of a mobile user's future locations. A location predictor based on a well-known prediction techniques, e.g., a linear dead-reckoning or locations from the navigation system, provides a generic location model for the predicted future locations. This is a set of predicted locations associated with a probability that this location represents the actual location of a consumer. Using the predicted locations, our system creates operator graphs for each future location and starts running the operator graphs before a mobile user reaches one of the future locations.

The quality and timeliness of the resulting situations detected by the predicted operator graph highly depends on where and when an operator graph is initialized. The location prediction only gives uncertain future locations, which makes it highly probable that the spatial interest does not match with the predicted operator graph' region. Consider, for example, in Figure 3 the predicted spatial region A_{p1} deviates from the actual spatial interest A_{act1} and the circles that indicate those interests only partially overlap with each other. Since processing of historical events takes time, it is also possible that the consumer moves faster to new locations than the operator graph requires to process all historical events. Consider again Figure 3, the temporal axis shows that a consumer moves within 3 seconds from A_{act1} to A_{act2} while the processing takes 5 seconds.

In this context we discuss a quality metric that allows a user to decide if the results of a predicted operator graph are meaningful, in spite of the partial overlap with the actual spatial interest. Furthermore, we discuss how the processing time of an operator graph can be anticipated. Both metrics are based on the number of events that are contained in this overlapped region (see Subsection 4.3). To maximize the probability that the consumer receives timely results, we describe the basic query prediction mechanism. To avoid the problem of late processing in face of fast movements we extend that algorithm by pipelining future operator graphs for not only the next predicted location, but for more subsequent locations (see Subsection 4.4). We also provide a method to maximize the probability that a user gets results with a desired quality from the system, based on over-provisioning of operator graphs (see Subsection 4.5).

4.3 Metrics

Quality of Results

We break the quality of results down to two metrics, the *completeness* and the *effectiveness*. The completeness indicates how many events covered by the spatial interest of a consumer are not included in the processing of results, and therefore describes the event-loss. The effectiveness indicates how many events are included in the processing but

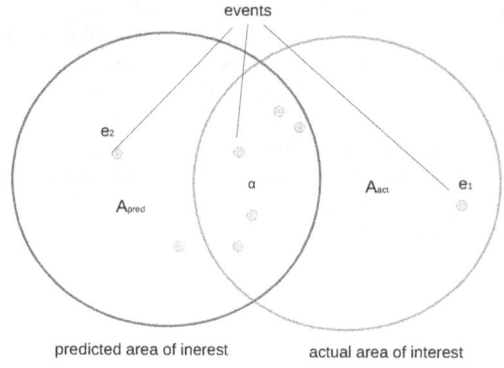

events

e_2

A_{pred} α A_{act} e_1

predicted area of inerest   actual area of interest

Figure 4: Quality of Results

not covered by the spatial interest of a consumer, and therefore describes the noisiness.

Since imprecise location predictions lead to overlaps in the actual spatial interest and the predicted operator graph's region, not all events that lie in the spatial interest are included in the resulting situation. For example event e_1 in Figure 4 is not included in the area of the predicted operator graph. An interesting observation, however, is that most of the relevant events in this example lie within the overlap. Our metric captures such an inhomogeneous event distribution by giving a value close to one if most of the relevant events are in the overlap, and close to zero if most of the events are not in the overlap. More formally, let V_{ov} be the number of events in the overlap and V_i be the number of events in the spatial interest of the consumer:

$$completeness = \frac{V_{ov}}{V_i} \qquad (1)$$

The effectiveness considers that events can be included in the processing of resulting situations of an operator graph that are not relevant to the consumer. For example, event e_2 in Figure 4. The effectiveness is therefore represented by a value of the domain $[0, 1]$, where 1 is the ideal case where all events that are processed lie within the overlap. More formally, let V_{ov} be the number of events in the overlap and V_p be the number of events in the predicted operator graph's region:

$$effectiveness = \frac{V_{ov}}{V_p} \qquad (2)$$

The involved actual spatial interest of the consumer and the operator graph's region can have a low overlap, but the resulting situations may still be meaningful to the consumer when the effectiveness and completeness are close to 1.

We can estimate the effectiveness and completeness for two circular regions A_{q_1}, A_{q_2} under the assumption of spatially evenly distributed events. Let α be the overlap of those areas, and er be the average event rate. Observe that the estimation is independent of the event rate:

$$E(completeness) = \frac{er * \alpha}{er * A_{q_1}} = \frac{\alpha}{A_{q_1}} \qquad (3)$$

and

$$E(effectiveness) = \frac{er * \alpha}{er * A_{q_2}} = \frac{\alpha}{A_{q_2}} \qquad (4)$$

```
1:  P ← ∅ // set of predicted locations
2:  q_curr ← initial_query // current operator graph
3:  Q ← ∅ // set of predicted operator graphs

4:  upon locationUpdate(Location currentLoc )
5:    if currentLoc - previousLoc > location_sensitivity then
6:      stopOperatorGraphs(q_curr)
7:      switchToNewOperatorGraph(currentLoc,Q)
8:      P ← getNextPredictedLocations(currentLoc)
9:      Q ← generateQueries(P)
10:     startOperatorGraphs(Q)
11:     previousLoc ← currentLoc
12:   end if
13: end

14: function switchToNewOperatorGraph(Location currentLoc,
     Set-of-operator-graphs Q_L)
15:   q_curr ← selectNext(Q_L)
16:   discardOperatorGraps(Q_L − q_curr)
17:   deliverHistoricEvents(q_curr)
18:   initiateLiveNotification(q_curr)
19: end
```

Figure 5: Basic Query Prediction

Timeliness

The time an operator graph takes to process historical events depends on the complexity of the algorithm that is realized with the operator graph, the available resources of the executing platform and the number of input events. In order to approximate the processing time for a given platform and number of events the operator graph can be profiled on different platforms. The time in between those sampling points can then be interpolated. Let $C_i()$ be the function to determine this interpolated time, T be the temporal interest, R be the spatial region of the operator graph and $ev(R)$ be an average value of events per second in the spatial range estimated from the historical events already available in that area, then the anticipated processing time computes T_c to:

$$T_c = C_i(ev(R) * T) \qquad (5)$$

Note that if another operator graph for the same spatial region is already deployed for another consumer, this result can be reused. Reusing effectively reduces the processing time on historical events, for the consumer specific operator graph that reuses results, to zero.

4.4 Query Prediction

We now outline an algorithm for the predictive query system. To explain the basic principles of the algorithm, we first describe how the system predicts future locations and initializes the next operator graph each time the mobile user moves farther than the *location sensitivity* user-defined parameter (Algorithm 5). Thereafter, we extend the algorithm to initialize operator graphs for destinations that are farther away, to deal with fast moving consumers (Algorithm 6).

Predicting the next operator graph

An initial operator graph is deployed when the consumer initiates its query at its initial location (*initial_query*). Henceforth, the system keeps track of the operator graph that currently processes events on behalf of the consumer Q_{curr} and set of future operator graphs Q that already process events for the next expected location of the consumer.

With every location update from the consumer, the query processor compares the current location (*currentLoc*) of the consumer with the location that was reported the last time the consumer switched to a new operator graph (*previousLoc*). If these locations deviate more than the *location_sensitivity*, the system stops the processing for the current operator graph and releases its resources (Line 5-6).

In the next step (Line 7) the system selects one operator graph from the set of future operator graphs. Policies to select the next operator graph q_{curr} — specified by the domain expert that designed the operator graph — are to switch to the operator graph which has process on an area of interest that has the highest overlap with the current spatial interest of the consumer, the highest completeness, or effectiveness. Operator graphs that are not selected are stopped and their resources are freed (Line 15-16). The system delivers then all historical situations from the spatio-temporal event storage that have been detected so far and afterward delivers live-situations detected by this operator graph (Line 17-18).

At last the system selects and initializes future operator graphs (Line 8-9). The system retrieves a set of future locations from the location predictor, representing possible locations for the center of the future region of the operator graph the consumer will switch to, and initialize the operator graph at each of that locations (Line 15-17). The number of retrieved locations is a system parameter that is set by a system administrator prior to the deployment of an operator graph. In Section 4.5 we address a more sophisticated solution for the operator graph selection (Line 18).

Pipelining

When the consumer moves with a high frequency from one location to another it can happen that the processing of historical events takes longer than moving further than the threshold *location_sensitivity*. In such a case it is useful to pipeline more than one set of operator graphs. This means that operator graphs are not only processing for the next possible switch of operator graphs due to an movement beyond the threshold *location_sensitivity*, but also for a sequence of movements to new operator graphs that are further away.

Algorithm 6 presents the extended algorithm to consider this issue. The basic idea is to maintain an *eagerness* parameter that dictates how many predicted locations we look ahead. This can be set by a system administrator or dynamically adjusted according to the expected processing time T_c (see Equation 5).

The basic difference to Algorithm 5 is that iteratively more operator graphs are added (Line 11-19). With every new step of this iterative process, the location predictor is called, however, with the predicted locations of the previous prediction as input. The intuition is that those locations represent the next actual locations (Line 11). Note, that this exponentially increases the number and uncertainty of predicted locations for a high *eagerness*, which is traded-off for a timely delivery of results.

For each step until the eagerness is reached the operator checks, if an operator graph is already deployed due to a previous location update. In such a case (Line 13), the system selects and initializes a new set of operator graphs at each of the predicted location (Line 16-17). Moreover, if an operator graph is already deployed through a previous location update, the system checks if the predicted locations deviate beyond a threshold (e.g., $100m$) from the previous

```
1: P ← ∅ // set of predicted future locations
2: q_curr ← initial_query // current operator graph
3: Q[] ← ∅ // set of predicted operator graphs
4: currStep ← 0

5: upon locationUpdate(Location currentLoc )
6:   if currentLoc - previousLoc > location_sensitivity then
7:       stopOperatorGraphs(q_curr)
8:       switchToNewOperatorGraph(currentLoc,Q[currStep])
9:       P ← currentLoc
10:      for step ∈ [currStep + 1, currStep + eagerness] do
11:          P ← getNextPredictedLocations(P)
12:          if notExists(Q[step])
13:              ∨ locationDeviates(Q[step], P) then
14:              stopOperatorGraphs(Q[step])
15:              Q[step] ← generateQueries(P)
16:              startOperatoGraphs(Q[step])
17:          end if
18:      end for
19:      inc(currStep)
20:  end if
21: end
```

Figure 6: Opportunistic Query Prediction

```
1: function generateQueries( Locations P_L )
2:   Q_L ← ∅
3:   s_tot ← 0
4:   S ← calcInitialCosts(P_L, S)
5:   while P_L ≠ ∅ do
6:       p ← selectAndRemoveNext(P_L)
7:       if ∄q ∈ Q_L : canExecute(OperatorGraph(p)) then
8:           if s_tot + S[p] ≤ s_max then //stop if resource cap
9:               Q_L ← Q_L ⋃{OperatorGraph(p)}
10:              s_tot = s_tot + S[p]
11:          end if
12:      end if
13:  end while
14:  return Q_L
15: end
```

Figure 7: Query Generation

predictions. In this case the operator graphs that already process for that step will be stopped and their resources will be freed (Line 14), before a new set of operator graphs is initialized.

Reuse of Results

Situational information of operator graphs can be reused, since it is buffered in the spatio-temporal event store. Which applies if multiple consumer deploy the same operator graph for the same spatial-interest. The main idea is to use a reference-counting mechanism for operator graphs that match in the spatial interest and overlap in the temporal interest. When initializing operator graphs (Line 8 of Algorithm 6) the system has then to check if other operator graph for the same spatial interest already exist. If this is the case a reference associated with the trees is increased. Moreover, instead of instantly releasing resources of operator graphs, the system decides according to the reference count if other consumers still require the operator graph.

4.5 Opportunistic Prediction

We now focus on the opportunistic algorithm to select a set of operator graphs for each predicted location. Its task is to select future operator graphs, s.t. the probability is maximized that the next time the *location_sensitivity* is exceeded an operator graph can be found that ensures a consumer-defined completeness and effectiveness. The method of choice to achieve the desired qualities is an over-provisioning of operator graphs. This means, that instead of only one operator graph, multiple-operator graphs process at the same time on historical data for slightly different areas of spatial interests. Which raises the problem that, depending on the number of over-provisioned operator graphs, the required resources and the overall time to process all operator graphs increases. Therefore it's crucial to stay below a specific maximal resource cap s_{max}, which express the maximum tolerable number of events that can be processed in parallel.

Selecting all predicted locations as centers for the areas of interest of operator graphs is one opportunity. However,

dependent on the number of retrieved queries, the overhead in terms of processing all events can be large.

To find a good approximation that selects a set of operator graphs from that set of predicted locations and stays below a resource limit s_{max}, we'll first discretize the problem and then reduce it to a set coverage problem. For the discretization we assume that only the predicted locations are valid future locations of the consumer, which is true if the number of predicted locations is infinite. The universe U for the set coverage problem is the set of events that is covered by all interest areas of the operator graph selected by the simple approach. The interest areas of those operator graphs represent the subsets $G \subset U$. The problem is then to select a minimum number of subsets $G' \subset G$, s.t., all elements of U are covered. However, we have to consider two additional constraints to the classical set coverage problem: i) all areas of not selected subsets $N \subset G$ must overlap with areas of selected subsets $G' \subset G$, s.t., completeness and effectiveness for all sets in N are expected to be ensured, and ii) the overall expected resource usage s_{tot} stays below s_{max}. The first constraint strives to ensure the quality, while the second one strives to ensure the resource limits.

Constraint Set Cover Algorithm

We adapted the greedy Johnson's Algorithm [17] to solve the set coverage problem (see Algorithm 7) to consider our constraints. It computes a set of operator graphs Q that have a high probability to ensure the results quality. It does this on the basis of a set of selected probabilistic locations P and a map S where the resource requirement of individual operator graphs, with the area of interest centered at each $p \in P$ is maintained. The algorithm starts out by receiving a set of predicted locations P_L and estimating the resource requirement of the operator graphs as if at each of those locations we center the area of interest of an operator graph and only this operator graph would process historical events (Line 2-3).

Henceforth, the algorithm tries to add sequentially for each predicted location $p \in P_L$ a new operator graph (Line 4-14). Which p is selected next depends on a policy that an domain-expert specified while developing the situation aware application with the operator graph. Choosing the next predicted location of P_L with the highest probability, will favor operator graphs that have a high probability for an overlap with the actual location, possibly only selecting few operator graphs. Choosing the operator graph with the lowest expected cost $S[p]$, will deploy many operator graphs, possibly at unlikely locations. Choosing the lowest cost factor $(1 - p) * S[p]$, will trade-off the benefits of the previously described policies (Line 5).

An operator graph is said to be executable at the next selected location p if no other operator graph $q \in Q$ is already selected that satisfies the consumers requirements on completeness and effectiveness, which can be checked according to Equation 1 and Equation 2 (Line 6-7). The algorithm stops if the overall expected costs s_{tot} exceed the limit s_{max} or all point $p \in P$ are covered.

5. EVALUATION

In this section, we evaluate our system by measuring the timeliness and quality of results, based on realistic spatio-temporal events and user mobility. Timeliness is a delay between switching to a new operator graph and receiving live situational information after processing historical events. Our system predicts future locations and starts running operator graphs on the locations before user arrival, therefore provides near-zero latency for receiving live situation updates when switching to the new operator graphs. Quality of results are measured in terms of completeness and effectiveness as defined in Section 4. In our approach, the quality of results can degrade if location predictions are inaccurate. To compensate such prediction errors, we opportunistically deploy multiple operator graphs for future locations, increasing chances to find a better operator graph with higher quality of results. As provided in the subsequent subsections, our system outperforms on-demand query processing that starts operator graph after user arrival both in terms of timeliness and quality of results.

5.1 Experimental Setup

To evaluate our system, we conducted simulations using SUMO [3], a well-known traffic simulator that generates realistic mobility patterns of vehicles on a real road network. Our simulations monitored the traffic in the downtown area (3.791 km x 2.872 km) of Atlanta for 20 minutes based on the road network obtained from Open Street Map [11]. We originally simulated 1000 vehicles for each simulation but the random trip generator of SUMO automatically pruned out some invalid routes after generating trips, which resulted in 884 vehicles per simulation on average. For each simulation, we observed 282,951 events on an average, meaning each vehicle reported about 320 events on an average.

During the simulation, we recorded each vehicle's geographical location at every second, which is used in two different ways in subsequent experiments. In one case, we treated the location reports as anonymous spatio-temporal events that are used by operator graphs to generate situational information. In the other case, we use the trajectory of individual vehicles to simulate mobile users receiving situational information through continuous queries.

When measuring the quality of results and timeliness, we use four different event processing mechanisms, namely *zero*, *eager-oracle*, *eager*, and *lazy*. *Zero* represents an ideal case for both opportunistic event processing and on-demand event processing, which assumes zero computing cost for event processing. In this case, *location sensitivity*, a user-given parameter for the operator graph switch, is ignored and an operator graph is created upon every fine-grained location update. At each location, the created operator

graphs provide up-to-date situational information immediately since the cost to process historical events is zero, resulting in perfect quality of results at any given time and location.

Eager-oracle is an ideal case for our opportunistic event processing that assumes an oracle predictor that knows the exact future locations of all mobile users. Since our system knows the exact future locations, it can run operator graphs on the exact locations before user arrival. However, unlike the *zero* case, operator graphs are created at coarse-grained locations defined by *location sensitivity* since the computing cost is not zero. While a mobile user is keep moving, the user's spatial interest may be slightly different from the current operator graph region at each moment, resulting in degrades in quality of results. In the following experiments, *zero* provides perfect completeness and effectiveness while *eager-oracle* provides an upper bound quality of results for our opportunistic event processing mechanism.

Eager represents opportunistic event processing with a realistic location predictor, called *dead-reckoning*. Dead-reckoning is a process of predicting future locations based on the current location, estimated speed, and estimated direction. We used simple linear dead-reckoning, using the last ten location histories to estimate future direction and speed, and predict future locations based on this estimate. To compensate for decreased completeness due to the erroneous nature of location prediction, we create four opportunistic operator graphs for each prediction.

The last case, *lazy*, represents on-demand event processing that creates an operator graph and starts processing historical events upon user arrival. Because of processing latency for historical events, a user cannot immediately receive up-to-date situational information, which results in degradation of both timeliness and quality of results.

5.2 Quality of Results Comparison

This section compares different event processing mechanisms by measuring the quality of results. We measured two metrics, completeness and effectiveness, at each fine-grained location of individual vehicles based on the overlapping events between the mobile user's actual spatial interest and the current operator graph's region. Although both metrics are measured, we only present completeness in this paper since they show the same trend. We also vary user-given parameters as well as processing latency for historical events in order to investigate each parameter's impact on the quality of result. For each experiment, the following default parameters are used, except one parameter that is selected as a control variable.

Location Sensitivity	=	100 meters
Spatial Range	=	500 meters
Temporal Range	=	60 seconds
Processing Latency	=	4 seconds

Figure 8 shows completeness for different event processing mechanisms while varying location sensitivity. In this experiment, smaller location sensitivity means more fine-grained, and more frequent operator graph switches while a user is moving. As shown in the figure, both *eager* and *eager-oracle* provide better quality of results as location sensitivity decreases because the distance between two successive operator graphs depends on the location sensitivity, and the quality of service degrades as operator graphs are spread

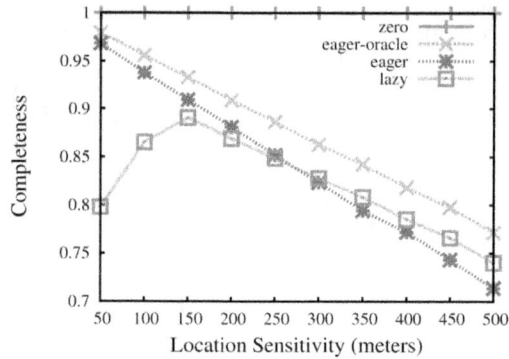

Figure 8: Completeness of query result with different location sensitivity

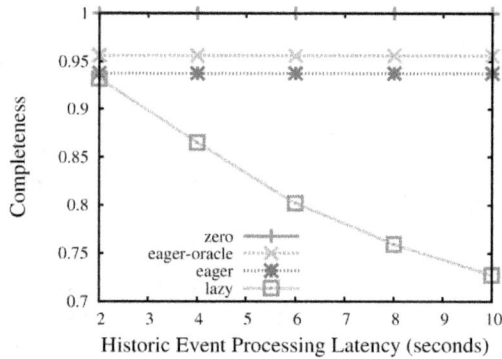

Figure 10: Completeness of query result with different spatial interest

eager and *eager-oracle* are not affected by historical event processing latency because they process events in advance through our opportunistic event processing mechanism. The difference in quality of results between the two is due to the imperfect location predictions in *eager*. However, *lazy* shows decreasing completeness when historical event processing latency increases. The decreased completeness is caused by user mobility, since a requesting mobile user can be far away from the requested location by the time a new operator graph is ready to begin "live" processing.

Figure 10 shows changes in the completeness when the range of a mobile user's spatial interest changes. In this experiment, all event processing mechanisms show the same trend that wider spatial interest yields a better quality of results. Although quality of service decreases between two subsequent operator graphs because of missing events and unnecessary events, the number of events that are missed or unnecessarily included can be negligible at large spatial interest.

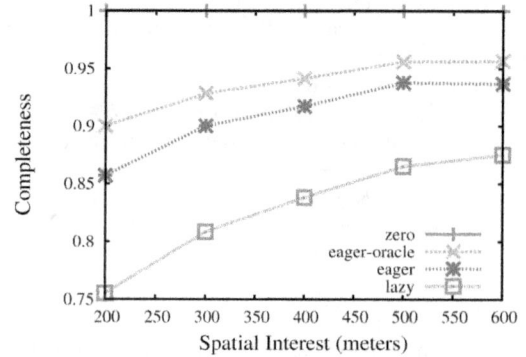

Figure 9: Completeness of query result with different processing latency

farther apart. *Eager* shows a steeper decrease in quality of results since the prediction error also increases when predicting far-away future locations. In contrast to opportunistic event processing mechanisms, on-demand event processing, or *lazy*, shows that it achieves peak completeness at 150 meters of location sensitivity. At small location sensitivities, we observed that an operator graph cannot catch up to the fast-moving vehicles since the vehicles moves away from the operator graph's region before the operator graph finishes processing historical events. On-demand event processing cannot handle such fast-moving vehicles with a small location sensitivity, thus showing the necessity of opportunistic event processing. At large location sensitivities, *lazy* shows a similar trend to *eager-oracle* because the quality of results decreases between two subsequent operator graphs while there is no uncertainty of future location involved.

Figure 9 presents completeness while varying historical event processing latency. When a user switches to a new operator graph, the operator graph should process recent historical events to provide up-to-date situational information. In realistic scenarios, processing latency for historical events depends on the number of events and complexity of operators. However, we used processing latency as a control variable in this experiment to show the impact of processing latency on the quality of results. As shown in Figure 9,

5.3 Timeliness Comparison

This section compares the timeliness of situational information between opportunistic event processing and on-demand event processing. We compare timeliness by measuring the delay between a mobile user's arrival at a new location and receiving live situational information about that location. In on-demand event processing, the delay is exactly the same as the historical event processing latency since live situational information is only available after processing all the historical events. In the opportunistic event processing mechanism, however, the new operator graph might already be created and have processed all the historical events. In this case, the delay for live situational information is zero since the mobile user can immediately receive the information.

In this experiment, we used a dummy operator graph that takes a uniform random latency from one to three seconds to process historical events, while both the server and client modules are running on the same local machine. In a realistic scenario, timeliness will be also affected by network latency between a mobile user and a server that is running an operator graph. For opportunistic event processing, we use the *dead-reckoning* predictor to predict future locations

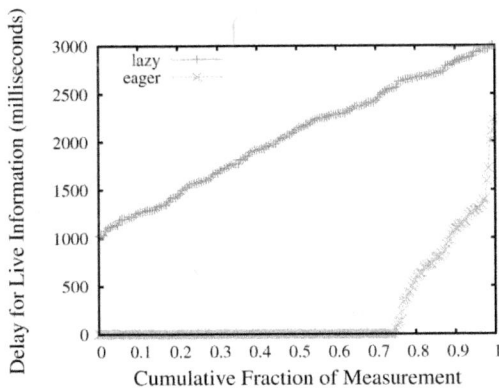

Figure 11: Timeliness of Opportunistic and On-demand Event Processing

while four operator graphs are opportunistically created at each prediction.

Figure 11 shows the cumulative distribution function (CDF) for the timeliness of both on-demand and opportunistic event processing mechanisms. On-demand event processing, labeled as *lazy*, creates an operator graph after user arrival and therefore it suffers from poor timeliness caused by the historical event processing latency. The delay for receiving live situational information is uniformly distributed between one to three seconds, following the distribution of event processing latency. However, our approach of opportunistic event processing (labeled as *eager*) provides zero latency in more than 70% of time because the operator graphs have already been created and the historical events processed when the user arrives at the future location. In few cases, our system has to create operator graphs on demand, which causes the same amount of delay with the on-demand event processing. Another cause of delay in opportunistic event processing is that a vehicle moved too fast and therefore the operator graph did not process all historical events yet.

6. CONCLUSION

The abundance of sensors in the environment enables many exciting new applications. Mobile situation awareness applications are one such class of applications that are furthermore spatio-temporal event-based as well as latency-sensitive. Event-based applications are typically programmed using a complex event processing (CEP) model, however there are challenges when the system includes mobile consumers with an interest in nearby, recent situational information that must be addressed.

It is necessary to update the spatio-temporal range of operator graphs as mobile users move through time and space in order to keep the results relevant, as well as to allow the application to scale and avoid wasted computation. However, mobile situation awareness applications often require recent historical events as well as current, live events. The processing of these recent historical events each time the location of the query changes causes a delay to delivering query results and processing live events.

In this paper, we have proposed a system and method to address the problems caused by this delay. The metrics of interest that we improved are the timeliness and quality of

results for mobile spatio-temporal queries. Our contributions include: 1) the system architecture, 2) the method for eager computation of historical events, including a pipelining method to look several steps into the future and an opportunistic computing method to compensate for partially inaccurate location prediction results, and 3) a simulation evaluation that shows that our system and method achieve the near-zero latency goal, as measured by the timeliness metric, while improving the quality of results over an on-demand computation method.

There are two significant areas of future work. The first is to develop an actual mobile situation awareness application and use its operator graph to simulate our method using real algorithms and workloads. The second, as fog computing technology develops and testbeds become available, is to create a real implementation of our system using a fog computing platform.

Acknowledgment

This work is supported by contract research "CEP in the Large" of the Baden-Württemberg Stiftung. The authors would like to thank the reviewers and K. Rothermel for their helpful comments.

7. REFERENCES

[1] Georgia Navigator. http://www.511ga.org, 2013.

[2] ADI, A., AND ETZION, O. Amit - the situation manager. *The VLDB Journal 13*, 2 (May 2004), 177–203.

[3] BEHRISCH, M., BIEKER, L., ERDMANN, J., AND KRAJZEWICZ, D. Sumo-simulation of urban mobility-an overview. In *SIMUL 2011, The Third International Conference on Advances in System Simulation* (2011), pp. 55–60.

[4] BONOMI, F., MILITO, R., ZHU, J., AND ADDEPALLI. S. Fog Computing and Its Role in the Internet of Things. In *Proceedings of the 1st MCC workshop on Mobile Cloud Computingputing* (New York, NY, USA, 2012), MCC '12, ACM, pp. 13–16.

[5] CAMPBELL, A. T., EISENMAN, S. B., LANE, N. D., MILUZZO, E., PETERSON, R. A., LU, H., ZHENG, X., MUSOLESI, M., FODOR, K., AND AHN, G.-S. The rise of people-centric sensing. *IEEE Internet Computing 12*, 4 (2008), 12–21.

[6] CILIA, M., FIEGE, L., HAUL, C., ZEIDLER, A., AND BUCHMANN, A. P. Looking into the past: enhancing mobile publish/subscribe middleware. In *Proceedings of the 2nd international workshop on Distributed event-based systems* (New York, NY, USA, 2003), DEBS '03, ACM, pp. 1–8.

[7] CUGOLA, G., AND MARGARA, A. Tesla: a formally defined event specification language. In *Proceedings of the Fourth ACM International Conference on Distributed Event-Based Systems* (New York, NY, USA, 2010), DEBS '10, ACM, pp. 50–61.

[8] CUGOLA, G., AND MARGARA, A. Low latency complex event processing on parallel hardware. *J. Parallel Distrib. Comput. 72*, 2 (Feb. 2012), 205–218.

[9] DU MOUZA, C., LITWIN, W., AND RIGAUX, P. SD-Rtree: A Scalable Distributed Rtree. In *Proc. of IEEE 23rd International Conference on Data Engineering* (Apr. 2007), ICDE 2007, pp. 296–305.

[10] GÜTING, R. H., BÖHLEN, M. H., ERWIG, M., JENSEN, C. S., LORENTZOS, N. A., SCHNEIDER, M., AND VAZIRGIANNIS, M. A Foundation for Representing and Querying Moving Objects. *ACM Trans. Database Syst. 25*, 1 (Mar. 2000), 1–42.

[11] HAKLAY, M., AND WEBER, P. Openstreetmap: User-generated street maps. *Pervasive Computing, IEEE 7*, 4 (oct.-dec. 2008), 12 –18.

[12] HENDAWI, A. M., AND MOKBEL, M. F. Panda: A Predictive Spatio-Temporal Query Processor. In *Proceedings of the 20th International Conference on Advances in Geographic Information Systems* (New York, NY, USA, 2012), SIGSPATIAL '12, ACM, pp. 13–22.

[13] HIRZEL, M. Partition and compose: parallel complex event processing. In *Proceedings of the 6th ACM International Conference on Distributed Event-Based Systems* (New York, NY, USA, 2012), DEBS '12, ACM, pp. 191–200.

[14] HONG, K., SMALDONE, S., SHIN, J., LILLETHUN, D. J., IFTODE, L., AND RAMACHANDRAN, U. Target container: A target-centric parallel programming abstraction for video-based surveillance. In *ICDSC* (2011), pp. 1–8.

[15] JAYARAM, K., JAYALATH, C., AND EUGSTER, P. Parametric subscriptions for content-based publish/subscribe networks. In *Middleware 2010* (2010), I. Gupta and C. Mascolo, Eds., vol. 6452 of *Lecture Notes in Computer Science*, Springer Berlin / Heidelberg, pp. 128–147.

[16] JEUNG, H., YIU, M. L., ZHOU, X., AND JENSEN, C. S. Path prediction and predictive range querying in road network databases. *The VLDB Journal 19*, 4 (Aug. 2010), 585–602.

[17] JOHNSON, D. S. Approximation algorithms for combinatorial problems. In *Proceedings of the fifth annual ACM symposium on Theory of computing* (New York, NY, USA, 1973), STOC '73, ACM, pp. 38–49.

[18] KOCH, G. G., KOLDEHOFE, B., AND ROTHERMEL, K. Cordies: Expressive event correlation in distributed systems. In *Proceedings of the 4th ACM International Conference on Distributed Event-Based Systems* (New York, NY, USA, 2010), DEBS '10, ACM, pp. 26–37.

[19] KOLDEHOFE, B., OTTENWÄLDER, B., ROTHERMEL, K., AND RAMACHANDRAN, U. Moving Range Queries in Distributed Complex Event Processing. In *Proceedings of the 6th ACM International Conference on Distributed Event-Based Systems* (New York, NY, USA, 2012), DEBS '12, ACM, pp. 201–212.

[20] LI, G., AND JACOBSEN, H.-A. Composite subscriptions in content-based publish/subscribe systems. In *Middleware '05: Proceedings of the ACM/IFIP/USENIX 2005 International Conference on Middleware* (New York, NY, USA, 2005), Springer-Verlag New York, Inc., pp. 249–269.

[21] MEISSEN, U., PFENNIGSCHMIDT, S., VOISARD, A., AND WAHNFRIED, T. Resolving Knowledge Discrepancies in Situation-aware Systems. *Int. J. Pervasive Computing and Communications 1*, 4 (2005), 327–336.

[22] MUTHUSAMY, V., PETROVIC, M., GAO, D., AND JACOBSEN, H.-A. Publisher mobility in distributed publish/subscribe systems. In *Proceedings of the Fourth International Workshop on Distributed Event-Based Systems (DEBS) (ICDCSW'05) - Volume 04* (Washington, DC, USA, 2005), IEEE Computer Society, pp. 421–427.

[23] PFOSER, D., JENSEN, C. S., AND THEODORIDIS, Y. Novel Approaches in Query Processing for Moving Object Trajectories. In *Proceedings of the 26th International Conference on Very Large Data Bases* (San Francisco, CA, USA, 2000), VLDB '00, Morgan Kaufmann Publishers Inc., pp. 395–406.

[24] PIETZUCH, P., LEDLIE, J., SHNEIDMAN, J., ROUSSOPOULOS, M., WELSH, M., AND SELTZER, M. Network-aware operator placement for stream-processing systems. In *Proceedings of the 22nd International Conference on Data Engineering* (Washington, DC, USA, 2006), ICDE '06, IEEE Computer Society, pp. 49–.

[25] PIETZUCH, P. R., SHAND, B., AND BACON, J. Composite Event Detection as a Generic Middleware Extension. *Network, IEEE 18*, 1 (jan/feb 2004), 44 – 55.

[26] PILLAI, P. S., MUMMERT, L. B., SCHLOSSER, S. W., SUKTHANKAR, R., AND HELFRICH, C. J. Slipstream: scalable low-latency interactive perception on streaming data. In *Proceedings of the 18th international workshop on Network and operating systems support for digital audio and video* (New York, NY, USA, 2009), NOSSDAV '09, ACM, pp. 43–48.

[27] RAMACHANDRAN, U., HONG, K., IFTODE, L., JAIN, R., KUMAR, R., ROTHERMEL, K., SHIN, J., AND SIVAKUMAR, R. Large-Scale Situation Awareness With Camera Networks and Multimodal Sensing. *Proceedings of the IEEE 100*, 4 (april 2012), 878 –892.

[28] RIZOU, S., DÜRR, F., AND ROTHERMEL, K. Fulfilling end-to-end latency constraints in large-scale streaming environments. *IEEE International Performance Computing and Communications Conference 0* (2011), 1–8.

[29] SATYANARAYANAN, M., BAHL, P., CACERES, R., AND DAVIES, N. The case for VM-based cloudlets in mobile computing. *IEEE Pervasive Computing 8*, 4 (October - December 2009).

[30] TARIQ, M. A., KOCH, G. G., KOLDEHOFE, B., KHAN, I., AND ROTHERMEL, K. Dynamic publish/subscribe to meet subscriber-defined delay and bandwidth constraints. In *Proceedings of the 16th international Euro-Par conference on Parallel processing: Part I* (Berlin, Heidelberg, 2010), EuroPar'10, Springer-Verlag, pp. 458–470.

[31] WANG, Z., ZHANG, Y., CHANG, X., MI, X., WANG, Y., WANG, K., AND YANG, H. Pub/sub on stream: a multi-core based message broker with qos support. In *Proceedings of the 6th ACM International Conference on Distributed Event-Based Systems* (New York, NY, USA, 2012), DEBS '12, ACM, pp. 127–138.

[32] WOLFSON, O., SISTLA, A. P., CHAMBERLAIN, S., AND YESHA, Y. Updating and querying databases that track mobile units. *Distrib. Parallel Databases 7* (July 1999), 257–387.

Adaptive Online Scheduling in Storm

Leonardo Aniello
aniello@dis.uniroma1.it

Roberto Baldoni
baldoni@dis.uniroma1.it

Leonardo Querzoni
querzoni@dis.uniroma1.it

Research Center on Cyber Intelligence and Information Security and
Department of Computer, Control, and Management Engineering Antonio Ruberti
Sapienza University of Rome

ABSTRACT

Today we are witnessing a dramatic shift toward a data-driven economy, where the ability to efficiently and timely analyze huge amounts of data marks the difference between industrial success stories and catastrophic failures. In this scenario Storm, an open source distributed realtime computation system, represents a disruptive technology that is quickly gaining the favor of big players like Twitter and Groupon. A Storm application is modeled as a topology, i.e. a graph where nodes are operators and edges represent data flows among such operators. A key aspect in tuning Storm performance lies in the strategy used to deploy a topology, i.e. how Storm schedules the execution of each topology component on the available computing infrastructure. In this paper we propose two advanced generic schedulers for Storm that provide improved performance for a wide range of application topologies. The first scheduler works offline by analyzing the topology structure and adapting the deployment to it; the second scheduler enhance the previous approach by continuously monitoring system performance and rescheduling the deployment at run-time to improve overall performance. Experimental results show that these algorithms can produce schedules that achieve significantly better performances compared to those produced by Storm's default scheduler.

Categories and Subject Descriptors

D.4.7 [**Organization and Design**]: Distributed systems

Keywords

distributed event processing, CEP, scheduling, Storm

1. INTRODUCTION

In the last few years we are witnessing a huge growth in information production. IBM claims that "every day, we create 2.5 quintillion bytes of data - so much that 90% of the data in the world today has been created in the last two

years alone" [15]. Domo, a business intelligence company, has recently reported some figures [4] that give a perspective on the sheer amount of data that is injected on the internet every minute, and its heterogeneity as well: 3125 photos are added on Flickr, 34722 likes are expressed on Facebook, more than 100000 tweets are done on Twitter, etc. This apparently unrelenting growth is a consequence of several factors including the pervasiveness of social networks, the smartphone market success, the shift toward an "Internet of things" and the consequent widespread deployment of sensor networks. This phenomenon, know with the popular name of *Big Data*, is expected to bring a strong growth in economy with a direct impact on available job positions; Gartner says that the business behind Big Data will globally create 4.4 million IT jobs by 2015 [1].

Big Data applications are typically characterized by the three *V*s: large *volumes* (up to petabytes) at a high *velocity* (intense data streams that must be analyzed in quasi real-time) with extreme *variety* (mix of structured and unstructured data). Classic data mining and analysis solutions quickly showed their limits when faced with such loads. Big Data applications, therefore, imposed a paradigm shift in the area of data management that brought us several novel approaches to the problem represented mostly by NoSQL databases, batch data analysis tools based on Map-Reduce, and complex event processing engines. This latter approach focussed on representing data as a real-time flow of events proved to be particularly advantageous for all those applications where data is continuously produced and must be analyzed on the fly. Complex event processing engines are used to apply complex detection and aggregation rules on intense data streams and output, as a result, new events. A crucial performance index in this case is represented by the average time needed for an event to be fully analyzed, as this represents a good figure of how much the application is quick to react to incoming events.

Storm [2] is a complex event processing engine that, thanks to its distributed architecture, is able to perform analytics on high throughput data streams. Thanks to these characteristics, Storm is rapidly conquering reputation among large companies like Twitter, Groupon or The Weather Channel. A Storm cluster can run *topologies* (Storm's jargon for an application) made up of several processing components. Components of a topology can be either *spouts*, that act as event producers, or *bolts* that implement the processing logic. Events emitted by a spout constitute a *stream* that can be transformed by passing through one or multiple bolts where its events are processed. Therefore, a topology represents a graph of stream transformations. When a topology is submitted to Storm it schedules its execution in the cluster, i.e., it assigns the execution of each spout and each bolt to one of the nodes forming the cluster. Similarly to batch data analysis tools like Hadoop, Storm performance are not generally limited by computing power or available memory as new nodes can be always added to a cluster.

In order to leverage the available resources Storm is equipped with a *default scheduler* that evenly distributes the execution of topology components on the available nodes using a round-robin strategy. This simple approach is effective in avoiding the appearance of computing bottlenecks due to resource overusage caused by skews in the load distribution. However, it does not take into account the cost of moving events through network links to let them traverse the correct sequence of bolts defined in the topology. This latter aspect heavily impacts the average event processing latency, i.e., how much time is needed for an event injected by a spout to traverse the topology and be thus fully processed, a fundamental metric used to evaluate the responsiveness of event processing applications to incoming stimuli.

In this paper we target the design and implementation of two general purpose Storm schedulers that, like the default one, could be leveraged by applications to improve their performance. Differently from the default Storm scheduler, the ones introduced in this paper aim at reducing the average event processing latency by adapting the schedule to specific application characteristics[1].

The rationale behind both schedulers is the following: (i) identify potential *hot edges* of the topology, i.e., edges traversed by a large number of events, and (ii) map an hot edge to a fast inter-process channel and not to a slow network link, for example by scheduling the execution of the bolts connected by the hot edge on a same cluster node. This rationale must take into account that processing resources have limited capabilities that must not be exceeded to avoid an undesired explosion of the processing time experienced at each topology component. Such pragmatic strategy has the advantage of being practically workable and to provide better performances.

The two general purpose schedulers introduced in this paper differ on the way they identify hot edges in the topology. The first scheduler, named *offline*, simply analyzes the topology graph and identifies possible sets of bolts to be scheduled on a same node by looking at how they are connected. This approach is simple and has no overhead on the application with respect to the default Storm scheduler (but for negligible increased processing times when the schedule is calculated), but it is oblivious with respect to the application workload: it could decide to schedule two bolts on a same node even if the number of events that will traverse the edge connecting them will be very small. The second scheduler, named *online*, takes this approach one step further by monitoring the effectiveness of the schedule at runtime and re-adapting it for a performance improvement when it sees fit. Monitoring is performed at runtime on the scheduled topology by measuring the amount of traffic among its components. Whenever there is the possibility for a new schedule to reduce the inter-node network traffic, the scheduled is calculated and transparently applied on the cluster

---

[1]The source code of the two schedulers can be found at `http://www.dis.uniroma1.it/~midlab/software/storm-adaptive-schedulers.zip`

preserving the application correctness (i.e. no events are discarded during this operation). The online scheduler thus provides adaptation to the workload at the cost of a more complex architecture. We have tested the performance of our general purpose schedulers by implementing them on Storm and by comparing the schedules they produce with those produced by the default Storm scheduler. The tests have been conducted both on a synthetic workload and on a real workload publicly released for the DEBS 2013 Grand Challenge. The results show how the proposed schedulers consistently delivers better performance with respect to the default one promoting them as a viable alternative to more expensive ad-hoc schedulers. In particular tests performed on the real workload show a 20% to 30% performance improvement on event processing latency for the online scheduler with respect to the default one proving the effectiveness of the proposed topology scheduling approach.

The rest of this paper is organized as follows: Section 2 introduces the reader to Storm and its default scheduler; Section 3 describes the *offline* and *online* schedulers; Section 4 reports the experiments done on the two schedulers. Finally, Section 5 discusses the related work and Section 6 concludes the paper.

2. STORM

Storm is an open source distributed realtime computation system [2]. It provides an abstraction for implementing event-based elaborations over a cluster of physical nodes. The elaborations consist in queries that are continuously evaluated on the events that are supplied as input. A computation in Storm is represented by a *topology*, that is a graph where nodes are operators that encapsulate processing logic and edges model data flows among operators. In the Storm's jargon, such a node is called a *component*. The unit of information that is exchanged among components is referred to as a *tuple*, that is a named list of values. There are two types of components: (i) *spouts*, that model event sources and usually wrap the actual generators of input events so as to provide a common mechanism to feed data into a topology, and (ii) *bolts*, that encapsulate the specific processing logic such as filtering, transforming and correlating tuples.

The communication patterns among components are represented by *streams*, unbounded sequences of tuples that are emitted by spouts or bolts and consumed by bolts. Each bolt can subscribe to many distinct streams in order to receive and consume their tuples. Both bolts and spouts can emit tuples on different streams as needed. Spouts cannot subscribe to any stream, since they are meant to produce tuples only. Users can implement the queries to be computed by leveraging the topology abstraction. They put into the spouts the logic to wrap external event sources, then compile the computation in a network of interconnected bolts taking care of properly handling the output of the computation. Such a computation is then submitted to Storm which is in charge of deploying and running it on a cluster of machines.

An important feature of Storm consists in its capability to scale out a topology to meet the requirements on the load to sustain and on fault tolerance. There can be several instances of a component, called *tasks*. The number of tasks for a certain component is fixed by the user when it configures the topology. If two components communicate through one or more streams, also their tasks do. The way such a communication takes place is driven by the *grouping* chosen by the user. Let A be a bolt that emits tuples on a stream that is consumed by another bolt B. When a task of A emits a new tuple, the destination task of B is determined on the basis of a specific grouping strategy. Storm provides several kinds of groupings

- *shuffle grouping*: the target task is chosen randomly, ensuring that each task of the destination bolt receives an equal number of tuples

- *fields grouping*: the target task is decided on the basis of the content of the tuple to emit; for example, if the target bolt is a stateful operator that analyzes events regarding customers, the grouping can be based on a customer-id field of the emitted tuple so that all the events about a specific customer are always sent to the same task, which is consequently enabled to properly handle the state of such customer

- *all grouping*: each tuple is sent to all the tasks of the target bolt; this grouping can be useful for implementing fault tolerance mechanisms

- *global grouping*: all the tuples are sent to a designated task of the target bolt

- *direct grouping*: the source task is in charge of deciding the target task; this grouping is different from fields grouping because in the latter such decision is transparently made by Storm on the basis of a specific set of fields of the tuple, while in the former such decision is completely up to the developer

2.1 Worker Nodes and Workers

From an architectural point of view, a Storm cluster consists of a set of physical machines called *worker nodes* whose structure is depicted in Figure 1. Once deployed, a topology consists of a set of threads running inside a set of Java processes that are distributed over the worker nodes.

A Java process running the threads of a topology is called a *worker* (not to be confused with a worker node: a worker is a Java process, a worker node is a machine of the Storm cluster). Each worker running on a worker node is launched and monitored by a *supervisor* executing on such worker node. Monitoring is needed to handle a worker failure.

Each worker node is configured with a limited number of *slots*, that is the maximum number of workers in execution on that worker node. A thread of a topology is called *executor*. All the executors executed by a worker belong to the same topology. All the executors of a topology are run by a specific number of workers, fixed by the developer of the topology itself. An executor carries out the logic of a set of tasks of the same component, tasks of distinct components live inside distinct executors. Also the number of executors for each component is decided when the topology is developed, with the constraint that the number of executors has to be lower than or equal to the number of tasks, otherwise there would be executors without tasks to execute. Figure 1 details what a worker node hosts.

Requiring two distinct levels, one for tasks and one for executors, is dictated by a requirement on dynamic rebalancing that consists in giving the possibility at runtime to scale out a topology on a larger number of processes (workers) and threads (executors). Changing at runtime the number

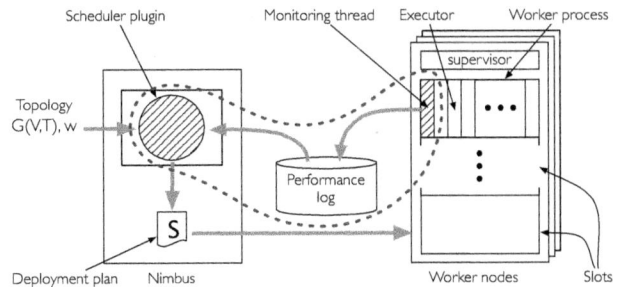

Figure 1: A Storm cluster with the Nimbus process controlling several Worker nodes. Each worker node hosts a *supervisor* and a number of *workers* (one per slot), each running a set of *executors*. The dashed red line shows components of the proposed solution: the offline scheduler only adds the plugin to the Nimbus process, while the online scheduler also adds the performance log and monitoring processes.

of tasks for a given component would complicate the reconfiguration of the communication patterns among tasks, in particular in the case of fields grouping where each task should repartition its input stream, and possibly its state, accordingly to the new configuration. Introducing the level of executors allows to keep the number of tasks fixed. The limitation of this design choice consists in the topology developer to overestimate the number of tasks in order to account for possible future rebalances. In this paper we don't focus on this kind of rebalances, and to keep things simple we always consider topologies where the number of tasks for any component is equal to the number of executors, that is each executor includes exactly one task.

2.2 Nimbus

Nimbus is a single Java process that is in charge of accepting a new topology, deploying it over worker nodes and monitoring its execution over time in order to properly handle any failure. Thus, Nimbus plays the role of master with respect to supervisors of workers by receiving from them the notifications of workers failures. Nimbus can run on any of the worker nodes, or on a distinct machine.

The coordination between nimbus and the supervisors is carried out through a ZooKeeper cluster [17]. The states of nimbus and supervisors are stored into ZooKeeper, thus, in case of failure, they can be restarted without any data loss.

The software component of nimbus in charge of deciding how to deploy a topology is called *scheduler*. On the basis of the topology configuration, the scheduler has to perform the deployment in two consecutive phases: (1) assign executors to workers, (2) assign workers to slots.

2.3 Default and Custom Scheduler

The Storm default scheduler is called *EvenScheduler*. It enforces a simple round-robin strategy with the aim of producing an even allocation. In the first phase it iterates through the topology executors, grouped by component, and allocates them to the configured number of workers in a round-robin fashion. In the second phase the workers are evenly assigned to worker nodes, according to the slot availability of each worker node. This scheduling policy produces workers that are almost assigned an equal number of executors, and distributes such workers over the worker nodes at disposal so that each one node almost runs an equal number of workers.

Storm allows implementations of custom schedulers in order to accommodate for users' specific needs. In the general case, as shown in Figure 1, the custom scheduler takes as input the structure of the topology (provided by nimbus), represented as a weighted graph $G(V,T), w$, and set of user-defined additional parameters (α, β, ...). The custom scheduler computes a *deployment plan* which defines both the assignment of executors to workers and the allocation of workers to slots. Storm API provides the *IScheduler* interface to plug-in a custom scheduler, which has a single method *schedule* that requires two parameters. The first is an object containing the definitions of all the topologies currently running, including topology-specific parameters provided by who submitted the topology, which enables to provide the previously mentioned user-defined parameters. The second parameter is an object representing the physical cluster, with all the required information about worker nodes, slots and current allocations.

A Storm installation can have a single scheduler, which is executed periodically or when a new topology is submitted. Currently, Storm doesn't provide any mean to manage the movement of stateful components, it's up to the developer to implement application-specific mechanism to save any state to storage and properly reload them once a rescheduling is completed. Next section introduces the Storm custom scheduler we designed and implemented.

3. ADAPTIVE SCHEDULING

The key idea of the scheduling algorithms we propose is to take into account the communication patterns among executors trying to place in the same slot executors that communicate each other with high frequency. In topologies where the computation latency is dominated by tuples transfer time, limiting the number of tuples that have to be sent and received through the network can contribute to improve the performances. Indeed, while sending a tuple to an executor located in the same slot simply consists in passing a pointer, delivering a tuple to an executor running inside another slot or deployed in a different worker node involves much larger overheads.

We developed two distinct algorithms based on such idea. One looks at how components are interconnected within the topology to determine what are the executors that should be assigned to the same slot. The other relies on the monitoring at runtime of the traffic of exchanged tuples among executors. The former is less demanding in terms of required infrastructure and in general produces lower quality schedules, while the latter needs to monitor at runtime the cluster in order to provide more precise and effective solutions, so it entails more overhead at runtime for gathering performance data and carrying out re-schedulings.

In this work we consider a topology structured as a directed acyclic graph [8] where an upper bound can be set on the length of the path that any input tuple follows from the emitting spout to the bolt that concludes its processing. This means that we don't take into account topologies containing cycles, for example back propagation streams in online machine learning algorithms [10].

A Storm cluster includes a set $\mathcal{N} = \{n_i\}$ of worker nodes ($i = 1...N$), each one configured with S_i available slots ($i = 1...N$). In a Storm cluster, a set $\mathcal{T} = \{t_i\}$ of topologies are deployed ($i = 1...T$), each one configured to run on at most W_i workers ($i = 1...T$). A topology t_i consists of a set C_i of interconnected components ($i = 1...T$). Each component c_j ($j = 1...C_i$) is configured with a certain level of parallelism by specifying two parameters: (i) the number of executors, and (ii) the number of tasks. A component is replicated on many tasks that are executed by a certain number of executors. A topology t_i consists of E_i executors $e_{i,j}$ ($i = 1...T$, $j = 1...E_i$).

The actual number of workers required for a topology t_i is $\min(W_i, E_i)$. The total number of workers required to run all the topologies is $\sum_{i=1}^{T} \min(W_i, E_i)$. A schedule is possible if enough slots are available, that is $\sum_{i=1}^{N} S_i \geq \sum_{i=1}^{T} \min(W_i, E_i)$.

Both the algorithms can be tuned using a parameter α that controls the balancing of the number of executors assigned per slot. In particular, α affects the maximum number M of executors that can be placed in a single slot. The minimum value of M for a topology t_i is $\lceil E_i/W_i \rceil$, which means that each slot roughly contains the same number of executors. The maximum number of M corresponds to the assignment where all the slots contain one executor, except for one slot that contains all the other executors, so its value is $E_i - W_i + 1$. Allowed values for α are in $[0, 1]$ range and set the value of M within its minimum and maximum: $M(\alpha) = \lceil E_i/W_i \rceil + \alpha(E_i - W_i + 1 - \lceil E_i/W_i \rceil)$.

3.1 Topology-based Scheduling

The *offline scheduler* examines the structure of the topology in order to determine the most convenient slots where to place executors. Such a scheduling is executed before the topology is started, so neither the load nor the traffic are taken into account, and consequently no constraint about memory or CPU is considered. Not even the stream groupings configured for inter-component communications are inspected because the way they impact on inter-node and inter-slot traffic can be only observed at runtime. Not taking into account all these points obviously limits the effectiveness of the offline scheduler, but on the other hand this enables a very simple implementation that still provides good performance, as will be shown in Section 4. A partial order among the components of a topology can be derived on the basis of streams configuration. If a component c_i emits tuples on a stream that is consumed by another component c_j, then we have $c_i < c_j$. If $c_i < c_j$ and $c_j < c_k$ hold, then $c_i < c_k$ holds by transitivity. Such order is partial because there can be pairs of components c_i and c_j such that neither $c_i > c_j$ or $c_i < c_j$ hold. Since we deal with acyclic topologies, we can always determine a linearization ϕ of the components according to such partial order. If $c_i < c_j$ holds, then c_i appears in ϕ before c_j. If neither $c_i < c_j$ nor $c_i > c_j$ hold, then they can appear in ϕ in any order. The first element of ϕ is a spout of the topology. The heuristic employed by the offline scheduler entails iterating ϕ and, for each component c_i, placing its executors in the slots that already contain executors of the components that directly emit tuples towards c_i. Finally, the slots are assigned to worker nodes in a round-robin fashion.

A possible problem of this approach concerns the possibility that not all the required workers get used because, at each step of the algorithm, the slots that are empty get ignored since they don't contain any executor. The solution employed by the offline scheduler consists in forcing to use empty slots at a certain point during the iteration of the components in ϕ. When starting to consider empty slots is controlled by a tuning parameter β, whose value lies in $[0,1]$ range: during the assignment of executors for the i-th component, the scheduler is forced to use empty slots if $i > \lfloor \beta \cdot C_i \rfloor$. For example, if traffic is likely to be more intense among upstream components, then β should be set large enough such that empty slots get used when upstream components are already assigned.

3.2 Traffic-based Scheduling

The *online scheduler* produces assignments that reduce inter-node and inter-slot traffic on the basis of the communication patterns among executors observed at runtime. The goal of the online scheduler is to allocate executors to nodes so as to satisfy the constraints on (i) the number of workers each topology has to run on $(\min(W_i, E_i))$, (ii) the number of slots available on each worker node (S_i) and (iii) the computational power available on each node (see Section 3.2.1), and to minimize the inter-node traffic (see Section 3.2.1). Such scheduling has to be performed at runtime so as *to adapt the allocation to the evolution of the load in the cluster*. Figure 1 shows the integration of our online scheduler within the Storm architecture. Notice that the performance log depicted in the picture is just a stable buffer space where data produced by monitoring components running at each slot can be placed before it gets consumed by the custom scheduler on Nimbus. The custom scheduler can be periodically run to retrieve this data emptying the log and checking if a new more efficient schedule can be deployed.

3.2.1 *Measurements*

When scheduling the executors, taking into account the computational power of the nodes is needed to avoid any overload and in turn requires some measurements. We use the CPU utilization to measure both the load a node is subjected to (due to worker processes) and the load generated by an executor. Using the same metric allows us to make predictions on the load generated by a set of executors on a particular node. We also want to deal with clusters comprising heterogeneous nodes (different computational power), so we need to take into account the speed of the CPU of a node in order to make proper predictions. For example, if an executor is taking 10% CPU utilization on a 1GHz CPU, then migrating such executor on a node with 2GHz CPU would generate about 5% CPU utilization. For this reason, we measure the load in Hz. In the previous example, the executor generates a load of 100MHz (10% of 1GHz).

We use L_i to denote the load the node n_i is subjected to due to the executors. We use $L_{i,j}$ to denote the load generated by executor $e_{i,j}$. We use CPU_i to denote the speed of the CPU of node n_i (number of cores multiplied by single core speed).

CPU measurements have been implemented by leveraging standard Java API for retrieving at runtime the CPU time for a specific thread (*getThreadCpuTime(threadID)* method of *ThreadMXBean* class). With these measures we can monitor the status of the cluster and detect any imbalance due to node CPU overloads. We can state that if a node n_i exhibits a CPU utilization trend such that $L_i \geq B_i$ for more than X_i seconds, then we trigger a rescheduling. We refer

to B_i as the capacity (measured in Hz) and to X_i as the time window (measured in seconds) of node n_i. One of the goals of a scheduling is the satisfaction of some constraints on nodes load.

We don't consider the load due to IO bound operations such as reads/writes to disk or network communications with external systems like DBMSs. Event-based systems usually work with data in memory in order to avoid any possible bottleneck so as to allow events to flow along the operators network as fast as possible. This doesn't mean that IO operations are forbidden, but they get better dealt with by employing techniques like executing them on a batch of events instead of on a single event and caching data in main memory to speed them up.

In order to minimize the inter-node traffic, the volumes of tuples exchanged among executors have to be measured. We use $R_{i,j,k}$ to denote the rate of the tuples sent by executor $e_{i,j}$ to executor $e_{i,k}$, expressed in tuples per second $(i = 1...T; j, k = 1...E_i; j \neq k)$. Summing up the traffic of events exchanged among executors deployed on distinct nodes, we can measure the total inter-node traffic. Once every P seconds, we can compute a new scheduling, compare the inter-node traffic such scheduling would generate with the current one and, in case a reduction of more than $R\%$ in found, trigger a rescheduling.

3.2.2 *Formulation*

Given the set of nodes $\mathcal{N} = \{n_i\}$ $(i = 1...N)$, the set of workers $\mathcal{W} = \{w_{i,j}\}$ $(i = 1...T, j = 1...\min(E_i, W_i))$ and the set of executors $\mathcal{E} = \{e_{i,j}\}$ $(i = 1...N, j = 1...E_i)$, the goal of load balancing is to assign each executor to a slot of a node. The scheduling is aimed at computing (i) an allocation $A_1 : \mathcal{E} \rightarrow \mathcal{W}$, which maps executors to workers, and (ii) an allocation $A_2 : \mathcal{W} \rightarrow \mathcal{N}$, which maps workers to nodes.

The allocation has to satisfy the constraints on nodes capacity

$$\forall k = 1...N \sum_{\substack{A_2(A_1(e_{i,j}))=n_k \\ i=1...T; j=1...E_i}} L_{i,j} \leq B_k \qquad (1)$$

as well as the constraints on the maximum number of workers each topology can run on

$$\forall i = 1...T$$
$$|\{w \in \mathcal{W} : A_1(e_{i,j}) = w, j = 1...E_i\}| = \min(E_i, W_i) \quad (2)$$

The objective of the allocation is to minimize the inter-node traffic

$$\min \sum_{\substack{j,k:A_2(A_1(e_{i,j}))\neq A_2(A_1(e_{i,k})) \\ i=1...T; j,k=1...E_i}} R_{i,j,k} \qquad (3)$$

3.2.3 *Algorithm*

The problem formulated in Section 3.2.2 is known to be NP-complete [9, 18]. The requirement of carrying the rebalance out at runtime implies the usage of a quick mechanism to find a new allocation, which in turn means that some heuristic has to be employed. The following algorithm is based on a simple greedy heuristic that place executors to node so as to minimize inter-node traffic and avoid load imbalances among all the nodes. It consists of two consecutive phases.

In the first phase, the executors of each topology are partitioned among the number of workers the topology has been

Data:
$\mathcal{T} = \{t_i\}$ $(i = 1...T)$: set of topologies
$\mathcal{E} = \{e_{i,j}\}$ $(i = 1...T; j = 1...E_i)$: set of executors
$\mathcal{N} = \{n_i\}$ $(i = 1...N)$: set of nodes
$\mathcal{W} = \{w_{i,j}\}$ $(i = 1...T; j = 1... \min(E_i, W_i))$: set of workers
$L_{i,j}$ $(i = 1...T; j = 1...E_i)$: load generated by executor $e_{i,j}$
$R_{i,j,k}$ $(i = 1...T; j, k = 1...E_i)$: tuple rate between executors $e_{i,j}$ and $e_{i,k}$

begin
    // First Phase
    foreach topology $t_i \in \mathcal{T}$ **do**
        // Inter-Executor Traffic for topology t_i
        $IET_i \leftarrow \{\langle e_{i,j}; e_{i,k}; R_{i,j,k}\rangle\}$ sorted descending by $R_{i,j,k}$
        foreach $\langle e_{i,j}; e_{i,k}; R_{i,j,k}\rangle \in IET_i$ **do**
            // get least loaded worker
            $w* \leftarrow \mathrm{argmin}_{w_{i,x} \in \mathcal{W}} \sum_{A_1(e_{i,y}) = w_{i,x}} L_{i,y}$
            if $!assigned(e_{i,j})$ **and** $!assigned(e_{i,k})$ **then**
                // assign both executors to w^*
                $A_1(e_{i,j}) \leftarrow w^*$
                $A_1(e_{i,k}) \leftarrow w^*$
            else
                // check the best assignment of $e_{i,j}$ and $e_{i,k}$ to the workers that already
                // include either executor and to w^* (at most 9 distinct assignments to consider)
                $\Pi \leftarrow \{w \in \mathcal{W} : A_1(e_{i,j}) = w \vee A_1(e_{i,k}) = w\} \cup \{w^*\}$
                $best\_w\_j \leftarrow null$
                $best\_w\_k \leftarrow null$
                $best\_ist \leftarrow MAX\_INT$
                foreach $\langle w\_j, w\_k \rangle \in \Pi^2$ **do**
                    $A_1(e_{i,j}) \leftarrow w\_j$
                    $A_1(e_{i,k}) \leftarrow w\_k$
                    $ist \leftarrow \sum_{x,y: A_1(e_{i,x}) \neq A_1(e_{i,y})} R_{i,x,y}$
                    if $ist < best\_ist$ **then**
                        $best\_ist \leftarrow ist$
                        $best\_w\_j \leftarrow w\_j$
                        $best\_w\_k \leftarrow w\_k$
                    end
                end
                $A_1(e_{i,j}) \leftarrow best\_w\_j$
                $A_1(e_{i,k}) \leftarrow best\_w\_k$
            end
        end
    end

    // Second Phase
    $IST \leftarrow \{\langle w_{i,x}; w_{i,y}; \gamma_{i,x,j}\rangle : w_{i,x}, w_{i,y} \in \mathcal{W}, \gamma_{i,x,j} = \sum_{A_1(e_{i,j}) = w_{i,x} \wedge A_1(e_{i,k}) = w_{i,y}} R_{i,j,k}\}$ sorted descending by $\gamma_{i,x,j}$
    foreach $\langle w_{i,x}; w_{i,y}; \gamma_{i,x,j}\rangle$ **do**
        $n* \leftarrow \mathrm{argmin}_{n \in \mathcal{N}} \sum_{A_2(A_1(e_{i,y})) = n} L_{i,y}$
        if $!assigned(w_{i,x})$ **and** $!assigned(w_{i,y})$ **then**
            $A_2(w_{i,x}) \leftarrow n^*$
            $A_2(w_{i,y}) \leftarrow n^*$
        else
            // check the best assignment of $w_{i,x}$ and $w_{i,y}$ to the nodes that already
            // include either worker and to n^* (at most 9 distinct assignments to consider)
            $\Xi \leftarrow \{n \in \mathcal{N} : A_2(w_{i,x}) = n \vee A_2(w_{i,y}) = n\} \cup \{n^*\}$
            $best\_n\_x \leftarrow null$
            $best\_n\_y \leftarrow null$
            $best\_int \leftarrow MAX\_INT$
            foreach $\langle n\_x, n\_y \rangle \in \Xi^2$ **do**
                $A_2(w_{i,x}) \leftarrow n\_x$
                $A_2(w_{i,y}) \leftarrow n\_y$
                $int \leftarrow \sum_{j,k: A_2(A_1(e_{i,j})) \neq A_2(A_1(e_{i,k}))} R_{i,j,k}$
                if $int < best\_int$ **then**
                    $best\_int \leftarrow int$
                    $best\_n\_x \leftarrow n\_x$
                    $best\_n\_y \leftarrow n\_y$
                end
            end
            $A_2(w_{i,x}) \leftarrow best\_n\_x$
            $A_2(w_{i,y}) \leftarrow best\_n\_y$
        end
    end
end

Algorithm 1: Online Scheduler

configured to run on. The placement is aimed to both minimize the traffic among executors of distinct workers and balance the total CPU demand of each worker.

In the second phase, the workers produced in the first phase have to be allocated to available slots in the cluster. Such allocation still has to take into account both inter-node traffic, in order to minimize it, and node load, so as to satisfy load capacity constraints.

Algorithm 1 presents the pseudo-code for the online scheduler. This is an high level algorithm that doesn't include the implementation of many corner cases but shows instead the core of the heuristic.

In the first phase, for each topology, the pairs of communicating executors are iterated in descending order by rate of exchanged tuples. For each of these pairs, if both the executors have not been assigned yet, then they get assigned to the worker that is the least loaded at that moment. Otherwise, the set Π is built by putting the least loaded worker together with the workers where either executor of the pair is assigned. Π can contain three elements at most: the least loaded and the two where the executors in the pair are currently assigned. All the possible assignments of these executors to these workers are checked to find the best one, that is the assignment that produces the lowest inter-worker traffic. At most, there can be 9 distinct possible assignments to check.

Similarly, in the second phase the pairs of communicating workers are iterated in descending order by rate of exchanged tuples. For each pair, if both have not been allocated to any node yet, then the least loaded node is chosen to host them. If any or both have already been assigned to some other nodes, the set Ξ is built using these nodes and the least loaded one. All the possible allocations of the two workers to the nodes in Ξ are examined to find the one that generates the minimum inter-node traffic. Again, there are at most 9 distinct allocations to consider.

4. EVALUATION

Our experimental evaluation aims at giving evidence that the scheduling algorithms we propose are successful at improving performances on a wide range of topologies. We first test their performance on a general topology that captures the characteristics of a broad class of topologies and show how the algorithms' tuning parameters impact on the efficiency of the computation, comparing the results with those obtained by using the default scheduler. Then, in order to evaluate our solution in a more realistic setting, we apply our scheduling algorithms to the DEBS 2013 Grand Challenge dataset by implementing a subset of its queries. Performance were evaluated on two fundamental metrics: the average latency experienced by events to traverse the entire topology and the average inter-node traffic incurred by the topology at runtime.

All the evaluations were performed on a Storm cluster with 8 worker nodes, each with 5 slots, and one further node hosting the Nimbus and Zookeeper services. Each node runs Ubuntu 12.04 and is equipped with 2x2.8 GHz CPUs, 3 GB of RAM and 15 GB of disk storage. The networking infrastructure is based on a 10 Gbit LAN. These nodes are kept synchronized with a precision of microseconds, which is sufficiently accurate for measuring latencies in the order of milliseconds. Such synchronization has been obtained by leveraging the standard NTP protocol to sync all the nodes with a specific node in the cluster.

4.1 Reference Topology

In this section we analyze how the tuning parameters actually affect the behavior of scheduling algorithms and consequently the performances of a topology. In order to avoid focusing on a specific topology, we developed a reference topology aimed at capturing the salient characteristics of many common topologies.

Workload characteristics.

According to the kind of topologies we deal with in this work (see Section 3), we consider acyclic topologies where an upper bound can be set on the number of hops a tuple has go through since it is emitted by a spout up to the point where its elaboration ends on some bolt. This property allows us to assign each component c_i in the topology a number $stage(c_i)$ that represents the length of the longest path a tuple must travel from any spout to c_i. By grouping components in a same *stage*, we obtain a horizontal stratification of the topology in stages, such that components within the same stage don't communicate each other, and components at stage i receive tuples from upstream components at stages lower than i and send tuples to downstream components at stages greater than i. This kind of stratification has been investigated in [19]. Recent works on streaming MapReduce [21, 20, 11] also focus on the possibility to model any computation as a sequence of alternated map and reduce stages, supporting the idea that a large class of computations can be structured as a sequence of consecutive stages where events always flow from previous to subsequent stages.

These considerations led us to propose the working hypothesis that a chain topology can be employed as a meaningful sample of a wide class of possible topologies. Chain topologies are characterized by two parameters: (i) the number of stages, that is the horizontal dimension and (ii) the replication factor for each stage, that is the vertical dimension corresponding to the number of executors for each topology component. We developed a *reference topology* according to such working hypothesis. Taking inspiration from the MapReduce model [14], in the chain we alternate bolts that receive tuples using shuffle grouping (similar to mappers) to bolts that are fed through fields grouping (similar to reducers). In this way we can also take into account how the grouping strategy impacts on the generated traffic patterns.

Figure 2 shows the general structure of the reference topology. It contains a single spout followed by an alternation of *simple* bolts, that receive tuples by shuffle grouping, and *stateful* bolts, that instead take tuples by fields grouping. Stateful bolts have been named so because their input stream is partitioned among the executors by the value embedded in the tuples, and this would enable each executor to keep some sort of state. In the last stage there is an *ack* bolt in charge of completing the execution of tuples.

Each spout executor emits tuples containing an incremental numeric value at a fixed rate. Using incremental numeric values allows to evenly spread tuples among target executors for bolts that receive input through fields grouping. Each spout executor chooses its fixed rate using two parameters: the average input rate R in tuples per second and its variance V, expressed as the largest difference in percentage of the actual tuple rate from R.

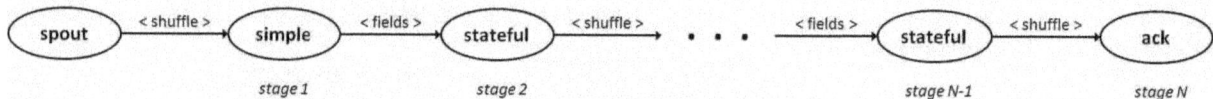

Figure 2: Reference topology.

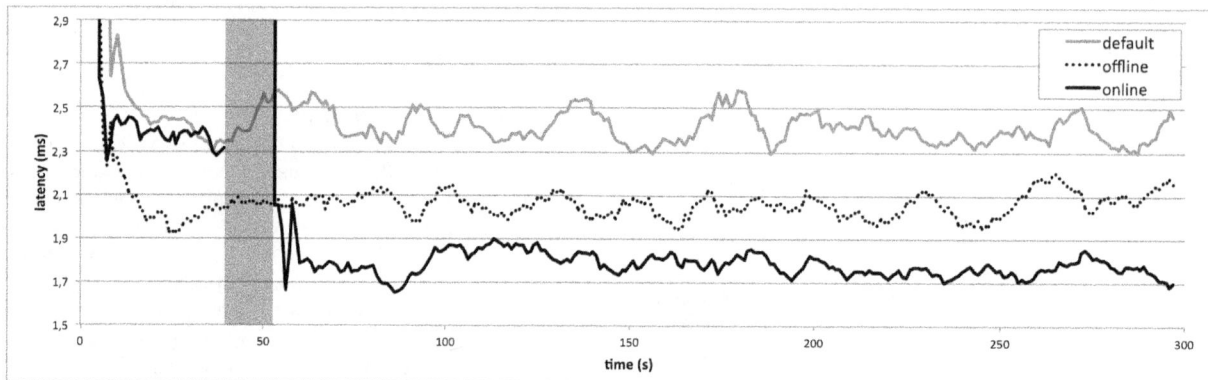

Figure 3: Tuple processing latency over time, for default, offline and online schedulers.

The i-th spout executor sets its tuple rate as $R_i = R(1 - V(1 - 2\frac{i}{C_0-1}))$ where C_0 is the number of executors for the first component, that is the spout itself, and $i = 0, ..., C_0 - 1$. Therefore, each spout executor emits tuples at a distinct fixed rate and the average of these rates is exactly R. In this way, the total input rate for the topology can be controlled (its value is $C_0 \cdot R$) and a certain degree of irregularity can be introduced on traffic intensity (tuned by V parameter) in order to simulate realistic scenarios where event sources are likely to produce new data at distinct rates.

In order to include other factors for breaking the regularity of generated traffic patterns, bolts in the reference topology have been implemented so as to forward the received value with probability 1/2 and to emit a different constant value (fixed for each executor) the rest of the times. The traffic between executors whose communication is setup using fields grouping is affected by this mechanism since it makes the tuple rates much higher for some executor pairs. This choice models realistic situations where certain pairs of executors in consecutive stages communicate more intensively than others.

Evaluation.

The first experiments were focussed at evaluating the runtime behavior of the proposed schedulers with respect to the default one. Figure 3 reports how event latency evolves over time for an experiment. Each points reported in the figure represents the average of latencies for a 10 events window. The reference topology settings used in this test include 7 stages, and variable replication factors: 4 for the spout, 3 for the bolts receiving tuples through shuffle grouping and 2 for the bolts receiving tuples through fields grouping.

At the beginning all schedules experiences a short transient state where the system seems overloaded and this heavily impacts measured latencies. This transient period lasts approximately 15-20 seconds and is characterized by large latencies. In the subsequent 20 seconds time frame (up to

second 40) it is possible to observe some characteristic behavior. The performance for all three schedules are reasonably stable, with both the default and online schedulers sharing similar figures, and the offline scheduler showing better results. This result proves how the topology-based optimizations performed by the offline scheduler quickly pay-off with respect to the default scheduler approach. The online scheduler performance in this timeframe are instead coherent with the fact that this scheduler initializes the application using a schedule obtained applying exactly the same approach used by the default scheduler (hence the similar performance). However, during this period the active scheduler collects performance measures that are used later (at second 40) to trigger a re-schedule. The shaded interval in the figure shows a "silence" period used by the active scheduler to instantiate a new schedule. The new schedule starts working at second 50 and quickly converges to performance that are consistently better with respect to both the default and the offline scheduler. This proves that the online scheduler is able to correctly identify cases where a different schedule can improve performance, and that this new schedule, built on the basis of performance indices collected at runtime, can, in fact, provide performance that surpass a workload-oblivious schedule (like the one provided by the offline scheduler).

We then evaluated how the proposed schedulers behave as the number of stages increases for different replication factors. As the number of stages increases, the latency obviously becomes larger as each tuple has to go through more processing stages. With a small replication factor traffic patterns among executors are quite simple. In general, with a replication factor F, there are F^2 distinct streams among the executors of communicating bolts because each executor of a stage possibly communicate to all the executors at the next stage. The offline scheduler does its best to place each of the F executors of a bolt c_i where at least one of F executors of the component c_{i-1} has been already placed, which means that, in general, the latency of up to F streams out

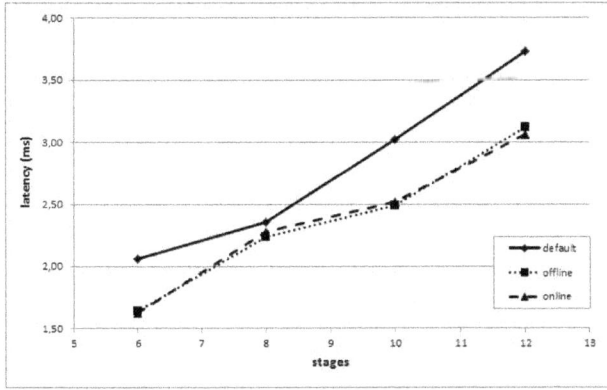

Figure 4: Average latency as the number of stages varies, with a replication factor of 2 for each stage.

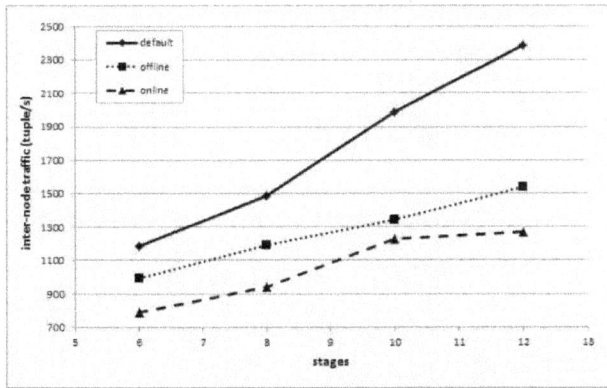

Figure 6: Average latency as the number of stages varies, with a replication factor of 4 for each stage, for default, offline and online schedulers.

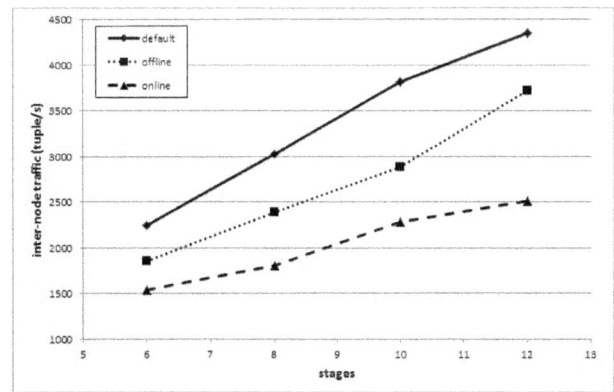

Figure 5: Average inter-node traffic as the number of stages varies, with a replication factor of 2 for each stage.

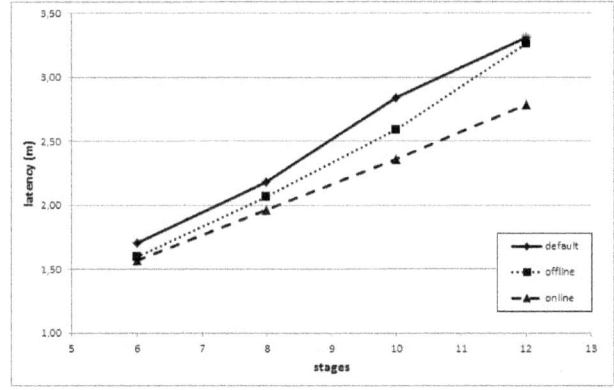

Figure 7: Average inter-node traffic as the number of stages varies, with a replication factor of 4 for each stage, for default, offline and online schedulers.

of F^2 is improved. Therefore, about $1/F$ of the tuples flowing among consecutive components get sent within the same node with a consequent latency improvement. As the replication factor increases, the portion of tuples that can be sent locally gets lower and the effectiveness of the offline scheduler becomes less evident. The precise trend also depends on whether the streams that are optimized are intense or not; however, the offline scheduler is is oblivious with respect to this aspect as it calculate the schedule before the topology is executed. On the other hand, the online scheduler adapts to the actual evolution of the traffic and is able to identify the heaviest streams and consequently place executors so as to make such streams local.

These evaluations have been carried out setting the parameters $\alpha = 0$ and $\beta = 0.5$, considering an average data rate $R = 100$ tuple/s with variance $V = 20\%$.

Figures 4 and 5 report average latency and inter-node traffic for a replication factor 2, i.e. each component is configured to run on 2 executors. Latencies for offline and online schedulers are close and always smaller with respect to the default scheduler. The low complexity of communication patterns allows for only a little number of improvement actions, which are leveraged by both the schedulers with the consequent effect that performances prove to be very similar. The results about the inter-node traffic reflect this trend and

also highlight that the online scheduler produces schedules with smaller inter-node traffic. Note that smaller inter-node traffic cannot always be directly related to a lower latency because it also depends on whether and to what extent the most intense paths in the topology are affected.

Figures 6 and 7 the same results for a replication factor set to 4. While the online scheduler keeps providing sensibly lower latencies with respect to the default one, the effectiveness of offline scheduler begins to lessen due to the fact that it can improve only 4 out of 16 streams for each stage. Such a divergence between the performances of offline and online schedulers is also highlighted by the results on the inter-node traffic; indeed the online scheduler provides assignments that generate lower inter-node traffic.

We finally evaluated the impact of the α parameter on the schedules produced by our two algorithms. Figures 8 and 9 report results for a setting based on a 5 stages topology with replication factor 5, $R = 1000$ tuple/s and $V = 20\%$.

In such setting a topology consists of 30 executors, and we varied α from 0 to 0.2, which corresponds to varying the maximum number of executors per slots from 4 to 8. The results show that the offline scheduler slightly keeps improving its performances as α grows, for what concerns both the latency and the inter-node traffic. The online scheduler pro-

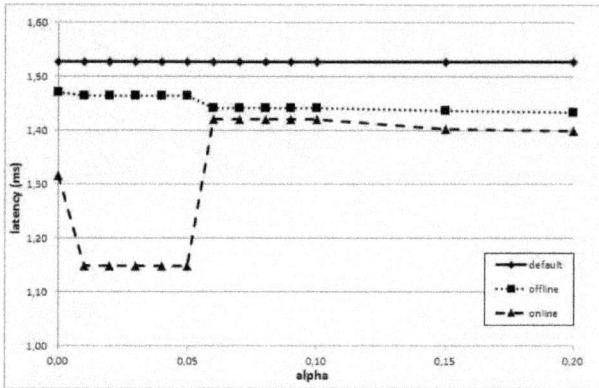

Figure 8: Average latency as α varies for default, offline and online schedulers.

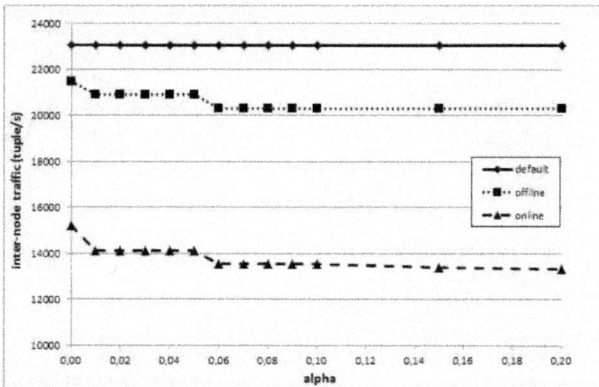

Figure 9: Average inter-node traffic as α varies for default, offline and online schedulers.

vides its best performances when α is 0.05, that is when the upper bound on the number of executors is 5. Larger values for α provide larger latencies despite the inter-node traffic keeps decreasing. This happens because there is a dedicated thread for each worker in charge of dequeuing tuples and sending them to the others workers, and placing too many executors in a single slot makes this thread a bottleneck for the whole worker.

4.2 Grand Challenge Topology

We carried out some evaluations on the scenario described in the Grand Challenge of DEBS 2013, considering in particular a reduced version of the first query. In such scenario, sensors embedded in soccer players' shoes emit position and speed data at 200Hz frequency. The goal of the first query is to perform a running analysis by continuously updating statistics about each player. The instantaneous speed is computed for each player every time a new event is produced by the sensors, a speed category is determined on the basis of computed value, then the global player statistics are updated accordingly. Such statistics include average speed, walked distance, average time for each speed category.

The topology includes three components: (i) a spout for the sensors (*sensor* component in the figure, replication factor 8, with a total of 32 sensors to be simulated), (ii) a bolt that computes the instantaneous speed and receives tuples by shuffle grouping (*speed* component in the figure, replica-

tion factor 4), (iii) a bolt that maintains players' statistics and updates them as new tuples are received by fields grouping from the speed bolt (*analysis* component in the figure, replication factor 2).

Figure 10 shows how latency (top) and inter-node traffic (bottom) evolve over time. It can be noticed that most of the time the offline scheduler allows for lower latencies and lighter traffic than the default one, while the online scheduler in turn provides better performances than the offline one as soon as an initial transient period needed to collect performance indices is elapsed. The performance improvement provided by the online scheduler with respect to the default one can be quantified in this setting as oscillating between 20% and 30%. These results confirms that the optimizations performed by the online scheduler are effective also in real workloads where they provide noticeable performance improvements.

5. RELATED WORK

There exist alternative distributed event and stream processing engines besides Storm. Similarly to Storm, these engines allow to model the computation as continuous queries that run uninterruptedly over input event streams. The queries in turn are represented as graphs of interconnected operators that encapsulate the logic of the queries.

System S [6] is a stream processing framework developed by IBM. A query in System S is modeled as an Event Processing Network (EPN) consisting of a set of Event Processing Agents (EPAs) that communicate each other to carry out the required computation. The similarity to Storm is very strong, indeed EPNs can be seen as the equivalent of Storm topologies and EPAs as the analogous of bolts. S4 [23] is a different stream processing engine, developed by Yahoo, where queries are designed as graphs of Processing Elements (PEs) which exchange events according to queries' specification. Again, the affinity with Storm is evident as the PEs definitely correspond to the bolts.

Another primary paradigm of elaboration in the scope of Big Data is the batch oriented MapReduce [14] devised by Google, together with its main open source implementation Hadoop [27] developed by Apache. The employment of a batch approach hardly adapts to the responsiveness requirements of today's applications that have to deal with continuous streams of input events, but there are scenarios [7] where it still results convenient adopting such an approach where the limitations of the batch paradigm are largely offset by the strong characteristics of scalability and fault tolerance of a MapReduce based framework.

An attempt to address the restrictions of a batch approach is MapReduce online [13], that is introduced as an evolution of the original Hadoop towards a design that fits better to the requirements of stream based applications.

Other works [21, 20, 11] try to bridge the gap between continuous queries and MapReduce paradigm by proposing a stream based version of the MapReduce approach [3] where events uninterruptedly flow among the map and reduce stages of a certain computation without incurring in the delays typical of batch oriented solutions.

The problem of efficiently schedule operators in CEP engines has been tackled in several works. Cammert et al. [12] investigated how to partition a graph of operators into subgraphs and how to assign each subgraph to a proper number of threads in order to overcome common complications

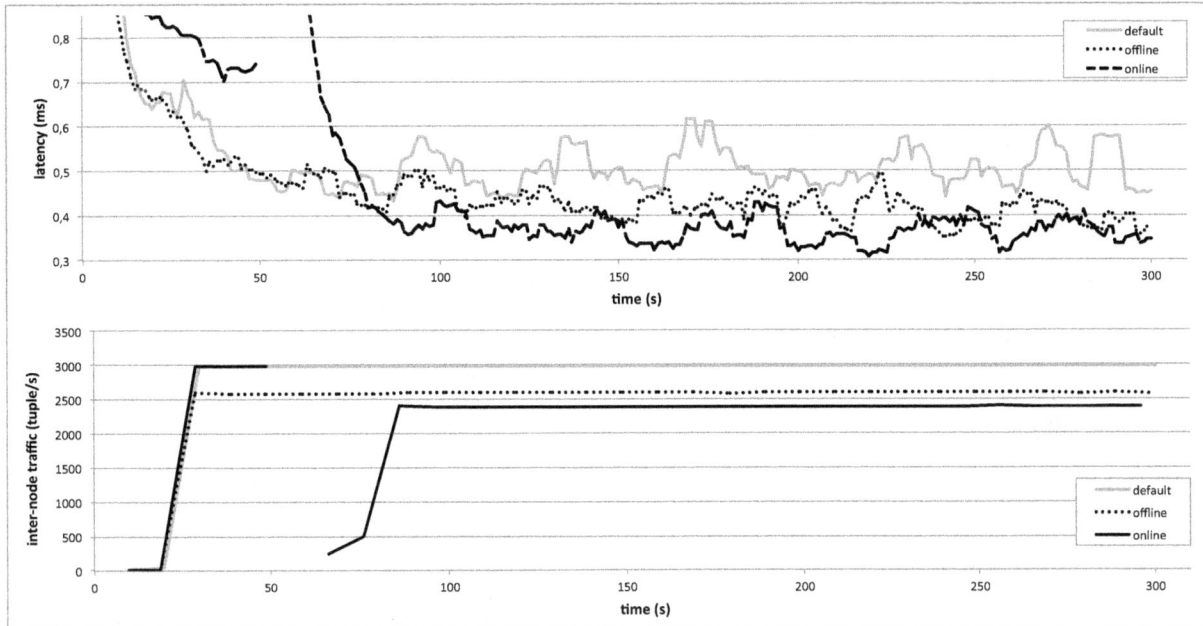

Figure 10: Latency (top) and traffic (bottom) over time for default, offline and online schedulers for the first query of DEBS 2013 Grand Challenge.

concerning threads overhead and operators stall. Moakar et al. [22] explored the question of scheduling for continuous queries that exhibit different classes of characteristics and requirements, and proposed a strategy to take into account such heterogeneity while optimizing response latency. Sharaf et al. [25] focus on the importance of scheduling in environments where the streams to consume are quite heterogeneous and present high skews; they worked on a rate-based scheduling strategy which accounts for the specific features of the streams to produce effective operators schedules.

Hormati et al. [16] and Suleman et al [26] propose works conceived for multi core systems rather than clusters of machines. Differently from our solutions, the former aims at maximizing the throughput by combining a preliminary static compilation with adaptive dynamic changes of the configuration that get triggered by variations in resource availability. The latter focuses on chain topologies with the goal of minimizing execution time and number of used cores by tuning the parallelism of bottleneck stages in the pipeline. On the other hand, Pietzuch et al. [24] are concerned with operator placement within pools of wide-area overlay nodes. They proposed a stream-based overlay network in charge of reducing the latency and leveraging possible reuse of operators. The solution proposed in this paper, differently from [24], does not consider the efficient use of the network as a first class goal, nor does consider operator reuse possible. SODA [28] is an optimized scheduler specific for System S [6] which takes into account several distinct metrics in order to produce allocations that optimize an application-specific measure ("importance") and maximize nodes and links usage. One of the assumptions that drives their scheduling strategy is that the offered load would far exceed system capacity much of the time, an assumption that cannot be made for Storm applications. Xing et al. [30] presented a methodology to produce balanced operator mapping plans for Borealis [5]. They only consider node load and actually ignore the impact of network traffic. In a later work, Xing et at. [29] described an operator placement plan that is resilient to changes in load, but makes the relevant assumption that operators cannot be moved at runtime.

6. CONCLUSIONS

Storm is an emerging technology in the field of Big Data and its employment in real scenarios keeps increasing as well as the open source community that supports and develops it. The wide range of use cases Storm is expected to support and their relevant complexity make the evolution of Storm quite challenging and push for general purpose new features able to fit to most use cases. The work presented in this paper goes along this line. We designed and implemented two generic schedulers for Storm that adapt their behavior according to the topology and the runt-time communication pattern of the application. For Storm users that do not want to create from scratch ad-hoc schedulers for their applications, such adaptive schedulers represent good alternatives to the usage of the default scheduler provided by Storm. Experiments show the effectiveness of the approach as the latency of processing an event is below 20-30% with respect to the default Storm scheduler in both tested topologies.

Acknowledgments

We would like to thank the anonymous reviewers and our paper shepherd, Peter Fischer, for all the useful comments and suggestions that greatly helped us in improving this paper. This work has been partially supported by the TENACE project (MIUR-PRIN 20103P34XC).

7. REFERENCES

[1] Gartner says big data creates big jobs: 4.4 million it jobs globally to support big data by 2015. http://www.gartner.com/newsroom/id/2207915.

[2] Storm. http://storm-project.net/.

[3] Streammine3g. https://streammine3g.inf.tu-dresden.de/trac.

[4] Data never sleeps infographic. http://www.domo.com/learn/7/236#videos-and-infographics, 2012.

[5] D. J. Abadi, Y. Ahmad, M. Balazinska, M. Cherniack, J. hyon Hwang, W. Lindner, A. S. Maskey, E. Rasin, E. Ryvkina, N. Tatbul, Y. Xing, and S. Zdonik. The design of the borealis stream processing engine. In *Proceedings of the 2nd Biennial Conference on Innovative Data Systems Research*, 2005.

[6] L. Amini, H. Andrade, R. Bhagwan, F. Eskesen, R. King, P. Selo, Y. Park, and C. Venkatramani. Spc: a distributed, scalable platform for data mining. In *Proceedings of the 4th international workshop on Data mining standards, services and platforms*, 2006.

[7] L. Aniello, L. Querzoni, and R. Baldoni. Input data organization for batch processing in time window based computations. In *Proceedings of the 28th Symposium On Applied Computing*, 2013.

[8] R. Baldoni, G. A. Di Luna, D. Firmani, and G. Lodi. A model for continuous query latencies in data streams. In *Proceedings of the 1st International Workshop on Algorithms and Models for Distributed Event Processing*, 2011.

[9] S. Bansal, P. Kumar, and K. Singh. An improved duplication strategy for scheduling precedence constrained graphs in multiprocessor systems. *IEEE Transactions on Parallel and Distributed Systems*, 2003.

[10] Y. Baram, R. El-Yaniv, and K. Luz. Online choice of active learning algorithms. *The Journal of Machine Learning Research*, 2004.

[11] A. Brito, A. Martin, T. Knauth, S. Creutz, D. Becker, S. Weigert, and C. Fetzer. Scalable and low-latency data processing with stream mapreduce. In *Proceedings of the 2011 IEEE Third International Conference on Cloud Computing Technology and Science*, 2011.

[12] M. Cammert, C. Heinz, J. Kramer, B. Seeger, S. Vaupel, and U. Wolske. Flexible multi-threaded scheduling for continuous queries over data streams. In *Proceedings of the 2007 IEEE 23rd International Conference on Data Engineering Workshop*, 2007.

[13] T. Condie, N. Conway, P. Alvaro, J. M. Hellerstein, K. Elmeleegy, and R. Sears. Mapreduce online. In *Proceedings of the 7th USENIX conference on Networked systems design and implementation*, 2010.

[14] J. Dean and S. Ghemawat. Mapreduce: simplified data processing on large clusters. *Communications of the ACM*, 2008.

[15] C. Eaton, D. Deroos, T. Deutsch, G. Lapis, and P. Zikopoulos. *Understanding Big Data*. Mc Graw Hill, 2012.

[16] A. H. Hormati, Y. Choi, M. Kudlur, R. Rabbah, T. Mudge, and S. Mahlke. Flextream: Adaptive compilation of streaming applications for heterogeneous architectures. In *Proceedings of the 2009 18th International Conference on Parallel Architectures and Compilation Techniques*, 2009.

[17] F. P. Junqueira and B. C. Reed. The life and times of a zookeeper. In *Proceedings of the 21st annual symposium on Parallelism in algorithms and architectures*, 2009.

[18] Y.-K. Kwok and I. Ahmad. Dynamic critical-path scheduling: An effective technique for allocating task graphs to multiprocessors. *IEEE Transactions on Parallel and Distributed Systems*, 1996.

[19] G. T. Lakshmanan, Y. G. Rabinovich, and O. Etzion. A stratified approach for supporting high throughput event processing applications. In *Proceedings of the 3rd ACM International Conference on Distributed Event-Based Systems*, 2009.

[20] A. Martin, C. Fetzer, and A. Brito. Active replication at (almost) no cost. In *Proceedings of the 2011 IEEE 30th International Symposium on Reliable Distributed Systems*, 2011.

[21] A. Martin, T. Knauth, S. Creutz, D. Becker, S. Weigert, C. Fetzer, and A. Brito. Low-overhead fault tolerance for high-throughput data processing systems. In *Proceedings of the 2011 31st International Conference on Distributed Computing Systems*, 2011.

[22] L. A. Moakar, A. Labrinidis, and P. K. Chrysanthis. Adaptive class-based scheduling of continuous queries. In *Proceedings of the 2012 IEEE 28th International Conference on Data Engineering Workshops*, 2012.

[23] L. Neumeyer, B. Robbins, A. Nair, and A. Kesari. S4: Distributed stream computing platform. In *Proceedings of the 2010 IEEE International Conference on Data Mining Workshops*, 2010.

[24] P. Pietzuch, J. Ledlie, J. Shneidman, M. Roussopoulos, M. Welsh, and M. Seltzer. Network-aware operator placement for stream-processing systems. In *Proceedings of the 22nd International Conference on Data Engineering*, 2006.

[25] M. A. Sharaf, P. K. Chrysanthis, and A. Labrinidis. Preemptive rate-based operator scheduling in a data stream management system. In *Proceedings of the ACS/IEEE 2005 International Conference on Computer Systems and Applications*, 2005.

[26] M. A. Suleman, M. K. Qureshi, Khubaib, and Y. N. Patt. Feedback-directed pipeline parallelism. In *Proceedings of the 19th international conference on Parallel architectures and compilation techniques*, 2010.

[27] T. White. *Hadoop: The Definitive Guide*. O'Reilly Media, Inc., 2012.

[28] J. Wolf, N. Bansal, K. Hildrum, S. Parekh, D. Rajan, R. Wagle, K.-L. Wu, and L. Fleischer. Soda: an optimizing scheduler for large-scale stream-based distributed computer systems. In *Proceedings of the 9th ACM/IFIP/USENIX International Conference on Middleware*, 2008.

[29] Y. Xing, J.-H. Hwang, U. Çetintemel, and S. Zdonik. Providing resiliency to load variations in distributed stream processing. In *Proceedings of the 32nd international conference on Very large data bases*, 2006.

[30] Y. Xing, S. Zdonik, and J.-H. Hwang. Dynamic load distribution in the borealis stream processor. In *Proceedings of the 21st International Conference on Data Engineering*, 2005.

Real-time Probabilistic Data Association over Streams[*]

Mert Akdere[†]
Google, Inc.
Mountain View, CA, USA
makdere@gmail.com

Jeong-Hyon Hwang
University at Albany, SUNY
Albany, NY, USA
jhh@cs.albany.edu

Uğur Çetintemel
Brown University
Providence, RI, USA
ugur@cs.brown.edu

ABSTRACT

The Probabilistic Data Association (PDA) problem involves identifying correspondences between items over data sequences on the basis of similarity functions. PDA has long been a topic of interest in many application areas such as real-time tracking and surveillance. Despite its significance, however, it has largely been ignored by the event-processing community. Our work rectifies this situation by studying PDA in the context of continuous event processing.

Specifically, we formulate PDA as a continuous probabilistic ranking problem with constraints and efficiently solve it using fast constraint resolution. Our solutions are built on a top-k approximation to the problem guided by resource-aware optimization techniques that adaptively utilize the available resources to produce real-time results. User-defined data association constraints are used to restrict the solution space and quickly eliminate inconsistent solution candidates. We also derive the runtime complexity of our solutions and experimentally evaluate these solutions using a prime PDA application: real-time tracking of moving objects within a camera network. Our evaluation results demonstrate the superiority of our solutions over traditional constraint programming formulations.

Categories and Subject Descriptors

H.2 [**Database Management**]: Systems

Keywords

data association; data streams; probabilistic databases; ranking; constraint resolution

---

[*]This work has been supported by the National Science Foundation under CNS-0721703 and CAREER award IIS-1149372.
[†]Work done while at Brown University.

1. INTRODUCTION

The data association problem refers to identifying correspondences between items over data sequences [19, 20]. A classical application area for data association is *tracking* [20], where the task is to map a given set of measurements to a set of tracks (or objects). Probabilistic data association (PDA) is a type of data association technique that uses similarity functions to create data association hypotheses together with association scores [2, 3]. In tracking applications, each hypothesis would represent a mapping of measurements to tracks.

PDA is an important task with many applications in diverse domains. As mentioned, a major target of PDA is the area of tracking and surveillance applications such as visual tracking where the task is to track people (or objects) in video streams [2], ocean surveillance (tracking of ships and submarines), and air defense and traffic control systems [3]. Document classification and topic intensity tracking is also an application of PDA where each document (e.g., e-mail) is classified into topics and the evolution of topic trends are of interest [1]. Yet another interesting application is found in the domain of law enforcement where the task is to associate crime incidents committed by the same individuals or group of individuals based on suspect traits and crime similarities [27].

PDA is often cited as one of the biggest challenges in tracking applications [19] and has long been a topic of interest. However, despite its importance and wide applicability in a variety of applications, it has largely been ignored by the event-processing community. In this paper, we explore the PDA problem from the perspective of probabilistic query processing [16]. Specifically, we consider the PDA problem as a constrained probabilistic ranking problem with possible worlds semantics [6, 7].

In the possible worlds semantics, relations are defined to be uncertain: an uncertain relation represents a set of possible relation instances. In most cases, this is achieved by adding an *existence probability / confidence* field to each relation. This added field represents the membership probability of a tuple in a relation. Based on this definition of uncertain relations, a probabilistic database is defined as a set of uncertain relations and can be viewed as a probability distribution over database instances. There is a close relationship between the data association problem and the possible worlds semantics: the PDA problem can be defined over an uncertain relation consisting of tuples describing data associations together with association scores. In this formulation, each possible world instance represented by the uncertain relation would be a separate data association hypothesis.

We apply the above formulation to represent the PDA problem. Assuming a continuous influx of tuples that represent data associations and the probabilities of these associations, we consider the *PDA query* whose goal is to find the maximum probability possible world among those that can be defined according to the input tuples. We also present two efficient query execution methods that both emphasize efficient partial-exploration of the underlying possible worlds in the presence of association constraints. The first one is based on *Constraint Programming* (CP) [23] and leverages existing powerful constraint solvers [22] for efficiency and generality. The second approach is a form of *Ranked Search* that efficiently explores only the high-probability possible worlds, selectively pruning them with constraint elimination methods. The latter has the benefit of solving the PDA problem with low computational overhead.

Since exploring all possible worlds is intractable, our solutions use a *top-k approximation* approach which maintains only the k possible worlds with the highest probabilities. This approach has the benefit of limiting the constraint space and avoiding the decline of data association speed. In contrast to previous solutions that relied on pre-defined, fixed k values [2, 3], our solutions adjust the value of k to effectively balance processing overhead and association accuracy. These solutions tackle the challenges of detecting possible worlds that make limited contributions to association accuracy, as well as improving association accuracy while negligibly increasing computational overhead.

We illustrate these solutions using a running example, *visual tracking*, throughout the paper. While we heavily use visual tracking to explain our techniques with concrete examples and to demonstrate their potential impact in a real-world application, our goal is not to specifically solve this tracking problem per se. In what we describe below, the only application-specific component is the "cooking" functionality that processes the raw data (i.e., images in our example application) to extract the data on which our techniques operate. As such, our techniques are quite general and readily applicable to other PDA applications.

We note that our solutions go beyond the existing results on probabilistic query processing research in two aspects. First, probabilistic databases have limited support for the specification and efficient execution of domain constraints, which play a central role in PDA. Second, continuous PDA is fundamentally a stream processing problem as it involves temporal sequences. Prior work studied mostly static data and one-time queries (e.g., [7, 14]). To effectively support real-time tracking of moving objects, our solution has a time threshold that bounds the time to be spent on processing incoming data and strives to produce most accurate results within this time limit.

The paper makes the following contributions:

(i) Our high-level contribution is the first use of continuous, probabilistic query processing techniques on an important class of applications that involve PDA and that have so far remained outside the scope of the event-processing community.

(ii) We integrate efficient constraint resolution methods into probabilistic query evaluation. We first describe how we can use a constraint solver for this purpose.

This is important in that a class of constraints that are already efficiently supported by existing solvers can be immediately used. Next, we propose a general search-based method for the resolution of generic constraints and then present methods to integrate efficient constraint resolution techniques into the solution. We also discuss the computational complexity of these methods.

(iii) We describe an adaptive parameter tuning technique that can be used to trade off processing overhead with association accuracy. With additional optimizations, we show that processing times can be significantly reduced with only modest accuracy losses.

(iv) We use a real-world PDA application, a visual tracking application that we deployed locally, for experimentally evaluating our techniques. The results reveal that our approach outperforms a widely cited generic solution for PDA [3]. (Our claim concerns the solution of the generic PDA problem and not the heavily optimized, specialized PDA solutions that exist for the tracking application.)

In the rest of the paper, we first describe the PDA problem in Section 2. Then, we present our solutions to the PDA problem in Section 3. Constraints for PDA and resolving these constraints are described in Section 4. Section 5 presents our technique for balancing accuracy and execution time. An experimental evaluation of our techniques is given in Section 6. Related work is in Section 7 and we conclude the paper in Section 8.

2. THE PDA PROBLEM

In this section, we first discuss and formulate the PDA problem, using a generic PDA application context. Next, we discuss the complexity of the PDA problem and its relationship with the PDA constraints. Finally, we present the visual tracking application which is used as the running example throughout the paper.

2.1 Generic PDA Application Model

We consider a generic PDA application in terms of the following main components: (i) data items, (ii) high-level objects and (iii) similarity functions. *Data items* are the basic units between which we would like to establish associations (i.e., links). In general, each *object* represents a set of associated data items and is uniquely identified by an *object id*. However, the complete semantics of objects, their representation and management (i.e., object creation/deletion) are application dependent. In a tracking application, each object could represent a person, with its data items identifying the appearances of the person. Similarly, in a document classification system objects and items could represent a list of topics and documents, respectively. In addition, applications could either choose to perform their own object management (e.g., by defining a priori a set of objects, such as a fixed set of document topics) or allow the system to self-manage the objects. In system-based object management, new objects are automatically created for the received data items and object deletion is performed when no item is assigned to an object for a user-specified time interval. For now we assume that there exists a fixed set of objects. Finally, a *similarity function* computes a similarity value between a given object and a data item. Then, within this general setup, the primary goal of a PDA application is to find the maximum score associations, represented via objects, between data items based on the results obtained from the similarity functions.

2.2 Problem Definition

First, we consider the PDA problem on a non-streaming (i.e., traditional) probabilistic database. Later, we generalize it to the streaming scenario. In the non-streaming case, the input to the system is an uncertain relation U (see Figure 1) consisting of tuples of the form $<$ *item id*, *object id*, *probability* $>$. Each tuple of the relation U represents the association of a data item and an object together with a probability. Tuple probabilities are derived from the computed similarity values by normalization.

	item id	object id	probability	TupleID
Mutual Exclusion Group I	1	1	.3	t1
	1	2	.7	t2
Mutual Exclusion Group II	2	1	.4	t3
	2	2	.6	t4

PW	Probability
{t1,t3}	.12
{t1,t4}	.18
{t2.t3}	.28
{t2,t4}	.42

Figure 1: An example uncertain relation, U, representing the associations between two data items and two objects given for the non-streaming PDA problem

Each tuple is also part of a mutual exclusion group (MEG) [10, 15]. A MEG is a set of tuples from which only one can exist in a database instance. A separate MEG is formed for each data item to represent the basic constraint that each item is to be associated exactly with a single object. Then, the PDA problem is equivalent to finding the maximum probability possible world, W, represented by the relation U. Observe that W consists of a single assignment for each data item and represents the set of assignments for which the overall probability is maximized. Data items are associated with each other if they are assigned to the same object. In Figure 1, all of the possible worlds and their probabilities are listed for the given uncertain relation. In this case, the possible world $\{t2, t4\}$, which assigns both items to object 2 is the maximum probability possible world.

Current probabilistic databases allow a tuple to be part of only a single mutual exclusion group [10, 15] and as far as we know not much research has been done on the interplay of constraints and probabilistic databases. In this scenario (i.e., when each tuple is part of a single MEG and there are no additional constraints), the problem is solvable in linear time (in the number of tuples) by selecting the tuple with the maximum probability for each MEG. However, in many PDA applications, there is a number of additional constraints restricting the space of valid data associations and the complexity of the PDA problem depends on the given set of constraints. We discuss the problem complexity in Section 2.3 and present example constraints in the context of the visual tracking application in Section 2.4. With additional constraints, the PDA problem becomes a constraint optimization problem which can be formalized as follows:

PDA Problem (non-streaming): Given an uncertain relation U representing the associations between n data items and m objects,

$$maximize \prod C[i][X_i]$$
$$s.t.\ X_i \in D_i, \text{ constraint_list}$$

where X_i is a variable that represents the ith data item from U and has the domain $D_i = \{1, 2, \ldots, m\}$, and $C[i][j]$ is the probability of the assignment of the ith data item to the jth object.

The solution to the constraint problem is a list of assignments of the form $X_i = x_i$ for $1 \leq i \leq n$. The assignment $X_i = x_i$ assigns the ith data item to the x_i^{th} object. Hence, the solution also encodes the maximum score possible world that satisfies the given list of constraints.

In our system, we support generic boolean constraints on the set of assignments and user-defined function-based constraints as part of the *constraint_list*. For instance, a simple example constraint is $X_1 \neq X_2$ which disallows assigning items 1 and 2 to the same object. We discuss the set of supported constraints, constraint resolution techniques and example constraints for the visual tracking application in Section 4.

PDA Problem (streaming): Now, we consider the same problem in the context of probabilistic data streams. The streaming PDA problem is mainly a continuous / iterative version of the non-streaming PDA problem. We assume that a high-level PDA application continuously receives new data items. Moreover, upon the receipt of each set of new items, the high-level application computes the similarity values between all pairs of new items and existing objects.

In the streaming probabilistic data scenario, the tuples of the uncertain relation U are modified to be of the form $<$ *time point*, *item id*, *object id*, *probability* $>$. The new attribute *time point* is used to represent the iteration number (i.e., the points at which new tuples are appended to the database). For instance, in a visual tracking application, the video frame number could be used as the time point attribute. In this way, all of the data items extracted from the same frame would be identified with the same time point value. Finally, we can now define the streaming PDA problem as the problem of computing the set of maximum score assignments at each point in time for all of the received data items across all points in time.

2.3 Complexity of the PDA Problem

In Section 2.2, we showed that the PDA problem can be expressed as a constraint optimization problem. In this section, we discuss the complexity of the PDA problem based on the constraint optimization formulation. Constraint optimization problems (hence, also the PDA problems) are equivalent to constraint satisfaction problems (CSP) [28] to which an additional set of "soft" constraints (i.e., preferential constraints which need not be satisfied) are added to represent the score functions. A CSP is defined as a triple (X, D, C), where X is a set of variables, D is a set of domains and C is a set of constraints and the goal is to find an assignment for all of the variables that satisfy the given set of constraints.

CSPs are in general NP-complete and tractable only for a few very restricted cases such as the well-known 2SAT case, where the variables are all binary-valued and all of the constraints are binary (i.e., defined over 2 variables) [28]. Generally, constraint solvers apply search-based methods, such as the branch-and-bound algorithms, backtracking algorithms and heuristic methods [29] to solve the CSPs. In our constraint-programming based solution to the PDA problem (Section 3.2.1), we employ a constraint solver to demonstrate this approach. The exact complexity of a PDA problem mostly depends on the given set of constraints. Therefore, it is essential to use efficient constraint resolution techniques whenever applicable. For this purpose, in our second solution to the PDA problem, the Ranked Search method (Section 3.2.2), we allow the integrated use of specific constraint resolution techniques. This is discussed in more detail in Section 4.

2.4 Running Example: Visual Tracking Application

In this section, we describe the visual tracking application which is used as the running example in the rest of the paper. In the visual tracking application, we consider the tracking of people and image features (e.g., corner features [21]) extracted from video streams. In the case of tracking people, using similarity functions based on image processing techniques, we compute the similarity score of a blob and a person. A blob is defined as a connected region of foreground pixels in an image and a person is represented as a series of blobs and related information. Therefore, the task of tracking people (i.e., high-level objects) reduces to the act of associating blobs (i.e., data items) across images. This process is illustrated in Figure 2 where blobs are denoted with rectangles and blob associations are shown with arrows. Tracking features is a similar task but performed on image features instead of blobs. Further information on the detection of blobs and features, and the camera network setup used in collection of video streams for experimentation are provided in Section 6.

Figure 2: Illustration of tracking and data association using a video captured with our local camera network. Solid lines indicate the correct data associations.

We can represent the tracking application as shown in Figure 3. We identify each frame and person using a frame number (*Frame#*) and person id (*PersonID*). The blobs extracted from the same frame are assigned unique ids (*BlobID*). Each tuple describes the score (*MatchScore*) of associating a blob and a person. The association score is computed using similarity functions (discussed in Section 6). Also, we assigned each tuple with a unique *TupleID* for illustration purposes. Observe that, the *Frame#*, *BlobID*, *PersonID* and *MatchScore* fields correspond to the *time point*, *item id*, *object id* and *probability* fields discussed in Section 2.2, respectively. Within this setup, for each possible world derived from the given data stream, the probability of that possible world can be computed. For instance, in the possible world {t2, t3}, the first blob in frame 1 is person 2 and the second blob is person 1. The scores of tuples in the same mutual exclusion groups can generally be used to derive probabilities. In this example, we do not perform this step since it is not necessary for the PDA query. As mentioned before, the score of a possible world is defined to be the product of the scores of its assignments.

The data stream in Figure 3 is ordered according to the key (Frame#, BlobID, PersonID). This ordering occurs in-

Frame#	BlobID	PersonID	MatchScore	TupleID		PW[1]	Score
1	1	1	.9	t1		{t1,t3}	.81
1	1	2	.8	t2		{t1,t4}	.63
1	2	1	.9	t3		{t2,t3}	.72
1	2	2	.7	t4		{t2,t4}	.56
2	1	1	.6	t5			
...	...	...	...	...		Mutual Exclusion Groups:	
						(t1,t2), (t3,t4)	

Figure 3: Representation of a single-camera tracking application as a probabilistic data stream

herently as frames are received in-order from a camera and the processing follows the same order. A possible world for a given snapshot of the input stream at a frame number f, represents a complete data association for all of the received frames (from 1 to f). When a new frame, $f+1$, is received, a new possible world, including associations for frame $f+1$, is to be formed. Figure 3 represents a single-camera scenario. In the multiple-camera case, the input stream is augmented with a *CameraID* field, and the processing is done in terms of synchronized sets of frames.

In the above example, the mutual exclusion groups defined on Frame# and BlobID, are used to specify the underlying assumption that each blob is to be assigned to only a single person (e.g., $t1 \vee t2$). However, a number of other additional constraints could be specified as part of a tracking application. For instance, we could require a person (i) to be assigned at most one blob in a frame and (ii) not to be assigned blobs in cameras with non-overlapping views. Supporting such constraints efficiently is discussed in Section 4.

3. PDA QUERY EXECUTION

The PDA query is the database specification of the streaming PDA problem defined in Section 2.2. Hence, the goal of the PDA query is to continuously compute and output the most likely possible world (i.e., the data association hypothesis with the highest score) at each point in time. Each output possible world must represent a complete data association hypothesis covering all of the query points in time.

In the tracking application, the task is to track all of the people (or features) observable by the cameras. As discussed in Section 2.4, this task corresponds to a continuous data association problem on a probabilistic data stream (see Figure 3). In the context of the tracking application, we use the PDA query to perform the association between the people/features detected in the camera network. As mentioned before, we assume that all of the tuples with the same Frame# / time point, called a *frame set*, are appended to the input data stream. In the rest of the paper, we use the PDA query mainly within the tracking application framework to easily express our execution methods and related optimizations.

Finally, the PDA query supports a range of constraints which are commonly used in PDA applications. These include pairwise inequality constraints on association items, unique assignment constraints and other user-defined constraints; all supported through a single interface. Constraints and their enforcement are discussed in Section 4.

3.1 Top-k Approximation

A naive method to execute the PDA query would be to repeatedly enumerate all of the possible worlds from the input stream and output the possible world with the maximum probability that satisfies the given set of constraints as the answer upon the arrival of each new frame set (or in a generic PDA application, upon the arrival of the tuples of a new point in time). However, the number of possible worlds is exponential in the number of association items, and thereby prohibits the naive enumeration approach. In addition, each possible world represents a complete data association hypothesis for all of the received frames. Therefore, the hypothesis space keeps growing exponentially as more frames (and consequently more data items) are received.

A more practical, but inexact (i.e., approximate) approach to executing the PDA query would be to incrementally produce the output hypothesis (i.e., possible world) at each frame set by extending the output hypothesis for the previous frame set. More specifically, at each frame set we would expand the previous output hypothesis with associations for the newly received data items. While this approach would be efficient, it would not be optimal to only build upon the single best hypothesis at each frame, because a lower ranking hypothesis may end up ranking higher as new "evidence" (i.e., frames) is observed. As the best hypothesis for a frame set may be significantly different from the previous best hypothesis, computing multiple hypotheses makes it more likely to find the best hypotheses in the next frame sets. In other words, keeping multiple hypotheses enables some degree of error recovery in the data associations of the earlier frames. Finally, another reason for computing multiple hypotheses is that the ranking results are based on uncertain information and therefore the distinction between the top ranked possible worlds is not absolute.

As such, the Multi-Hypothesis Tracking (MHT) model [2, 3, 4] has been the most widely adopted approach to real-time PDA. While multiple realizations of this model are possible, the common idea is to keep track of k-best hypotheses, where k is decided (often in an ad-hoc manner) subject to real-time processing constraints. We also adopt this popular and practical *top-k approximation* model as the basis of our solution; however, as we describe below, we extend and significantly improve upon the existing solutions. At each point in time, we incrementally compute the k-best hypotheses based on the most recent k-best hypotheses. Each hypothesis is formed from a combination of a previous hypothesis with a set of assignments for the most recent point in time.

3.2 Execution Methods

In this section, we discuss different top-k based execution methods for the PDA query. In each case, we assume that we are given a set of data associations corresponding to the most recent point in time, together with the previous k-best possible worlds to start with. Given this input, the expected output of the query is the new top-k possible worlds and their scores.

3.2.1 Constraint Programming

Our first solution is based on a constraint programming (CP) [23] formulation of the PDA problem. The main advantage of a CP-based approach is that it enables the use of existing powerful constraint solvers [22] to solve the PDA problem. In addition, a variety of constraint types, already efficiently supported by the constraint solvers, are immediately available for use. Given m objects (all of the objects

belonging to a possible world) and n association items (blobs or features) received at this point in time, we define a CP for the PDA problem as follows:

CP for PDA problem:

$$maximize \prod C[i][X_i]$$
$$s.t.\ X_i \in D_i,\ constraint\_list$$

where $X_1, X_2, \ldots X_n$ are variables with domains $D_i = \{1, 2, \ldots m\} \cup \{m + i\}$ $(1 \le i \le n)$ and $C[i][j]$ is the score of assigning the ith item to the jth object.

This formulation is very similar to the constraint program given in Section 2.2 except for the variable domain definitions. In this case, the first m objects are previously existing objects, whereas the $(m + i)^{th}$ object represents the creation of a new object for the ith data item. For the tracking application, new objects represent the possibility that a new person enters the camera view. The solution to the CP, an assignment for each X_i, specifies a complete assignment for the items at this point in time.

Given the previous k-best possible worlds (i.e., parent possible worlds), our CP-based method initially creates k separate CPs, one for each parent possible world. All of these CPs are then solved to obtain k new possible worlds, where each possible world is the best solution based on its parent possible world. More specifically, each CP is formed by combining the corresponding parent possible world and the new data associations obtained after the parent possible worlds are constructed. Then, these CPs and their solutions are inserted into a priority queue. Using the queue, we obtain a new set of k-best possible worlds. Our CP-based method bears some similarity to Murty's algorithm [5]. The key difference of our method is that it can effectively prune the search space, as explained below, using constraint resolution.

Algorithm 1 CP-based algorithm for PDA problem

1. state $\leftarrow \{(cp_1, soln_1), \ldots, (cp_k, soln_k)\}$
2. topk $\leftarrow \emptyset$
3. **while** $|topk| \le k$ **do**
4. $\quad (cp, s) \leftarrow$ state.pop()
5. $\quad$ topk.insert(s)
6. $\quad cp_{new} \leftarrow cp$.update(s)
7. $\quad s_{new} \leftarrow cp_{new}$.solve()
8. $\quad$ state.insert(cp_{new}, s_{new})

Algorithm 1 shows the overall operation of our CP-based method. The priority queue mentioned above is denoted as *state* (see line 1). At each iteration of the while-loop (lines 3-8), the current best solution is taken from the priority queue (*state*) and added to the results list (*topk*). Furthermore, the CP of the best solution is modified to obtain the next best solution, which is then added to the priority queue. If the solution is a set of assignments $X_i = j_i$ for $1 \le i \le n$ and $j_i \in 1, \ldots, m + n$, then the modification to the CP consists of adding a new constraint, $\lor X_i \ne j_i$, to remove the current solution from the solution space.

As mentioned before, a constraint solver performs an efficient search on the space specified by the domains of the problem variables [22]. Hence, our CP method can be viewed as a search-based MHT implementation with embedded constraint resolution techniques. For comparison, we also implemented a search-based MHT algorithm as outlined in [4]

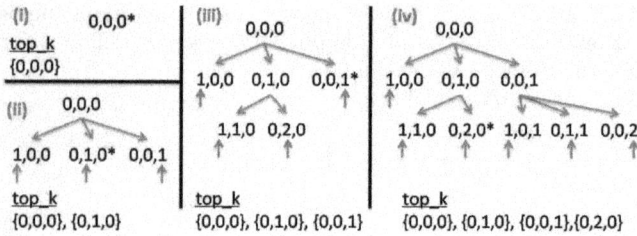

Figure 4: Example execution of *Ranked Search*

which performs a breadth-first search on the set of assignments using score-based bounds for pruning. However, in our experiments it was outperformed by our CP solution. Therefore, we do not provide the results for the previous search-based method in this paper.

3.2.2 Ranked Search

Consider the case where each tuple belongs to a single mutual exclusion group (MEG) and there are no additional constraints. Then, the possible world with the highest score consists of the maximum score assignment of a data item to an object for each MEG. If we sort the tuples for each MEG by score, the 0th-index tuple (i.e., the highest scoring tuple) in each group will constitute the maximum score possible world. In this case, the solution is found immediately after sorting. Therefore, the run-time complexity of finding that solution is $O(nm \log m)$, where n is the number of items at the current point in time and m is the number of objects. $\{0, 0, 0\}$ in Figure 4 (i) represents the maximum score possible world which consists of the 0th tuple for each of three 3 MEGs.

Given the above possible world, the next best possible world must consist of the 1st tuple for one of the three MEGs and the 0th tuple for the other MEGs. As Figure 4 (ii) shows, such a possible world has a single 1 together with 0s in its set of indices. Figures 4 (iii) and (iv) illustrate the process of finding the 3rd and 4th best possible worlds by incrementing one of the values in the index set.

In Figure 4, the possible world with the next highest score (denoted with a * sign) is added to the top-k list. The newly added world is also expanded using index increments to obtain a set of next possible worlds. In the figure, each index-set has a pointer to its leftmost modified index (see the up arrows). During each expansion, only the indices before the index pointer can be modified. This restriction guarantees the distinctness of the possible worlds that are examined. In other words, each branch of the search tree explores a distinct sub-space.

The expansion process mentioned above has the following properties:

(i) Let the sum of the values of an index-set be s. Then, the index-set is at level s of the tree and is reachable in s steps.

(ii) All possible values of the index-set are reachable from the root of the search and no value is produced more than once (based on the property that only the modifications before the index-pointer are allowed).

(iii) All ancestors of an index-set have less or equal values at each index position and therefore have higher score values.

The run-time complexity of our *Ranked Search* algorithm is $O(nm \log m + n(k - 1))$. The second term represents the worst case scenario for the number of nodes expanded during the search process. The search tree in Figure 4 is used for illustration purposes only. In practice, a priority queue, enabling immediate access to the possible world with the best score, is used. The described *Ranked Search* algorithm only works for the case in which there is a single parent possible world at the previous point in time (i.e., $k = 1$). To handle the more general case with multiple possible worlds, we only need to modify the algorithm (i) to generate a separate root index-set for each parent possible world and (ii) to make index increments aware of the parent possible world by skipping the indices of the tuples not belonging to the parent possible world. The rest of the algorithm is unchanged and each index-set, regardless of its parent possible world, is inserted into the same priority queue.

Finally, constraints and their evaluation constitute an important part of the *Ranked Search* method. To support the use of constraints, we modify the algorithm so that it adds a possible world to the top-k list if and only if that possible world satisfies the constraints. As discussed before, in this case the complexity of the problem depends on the given set of constraints. We discuss how to efficiently resolve constraints using constraint-based pruning strategies in Section 4.

4. PDA CONSTRAINTS

We consider a variety of commonly used constraints in PDA applications. We support generic boolean constraints on data associations, and user-defined function-based constraints. In Section 4.1, we present generic constraint resolution techniques for boolean and function-based constraints. Then in Section 4.2, we discuss how to utilize existing specific constraint resolution techniques using as example a *bipartite matching* [25] algorithm for efficiently supporting a commonly used *unique assignment* constraint.

4.1 Generic Constraint Resolution

In the CP-based method, boolean constraints on assignments are embedded in the CPs. For instance, based on the physical locations of the cameras, we might know that two items, X_1 and X_2, cannot be the same object: $X_1 \neq X_2$. This is called a *pairwise inequality* constraint. On the other hand, the user-defined function-based constraints cannot be handled in this way. Such constraints are evaluated separately: each possible world, obtained as the solution to a CP, is checked for satisfying the function-based constraints. If the constraints are not satisfied, the CP is modified as described in Section 3.2.1 to obtain the next best solution.

In the Ranked Search method, both boolean and function-based constraints are evaluated together on possible worlds before being added to the top-k list. In the case where a possible world fails a boolean constraint, we only need to consider modifying the variables that are part of the constraint to obtain a solution. Therefore, during the expansion process in Section 3.2.2, the index incrementing operation is only performed on the variables of the failed constraint(s). For instance, in the case of the pairwise inequality constraint $X_1 \neq X_2$, the index incrementing operation will only change the variables X_1 and X_2. The other child possible worlds are pruned, without being formed, since it is certain that they cannot satisfy the constraints. To handle the user-defined function-based constraints, we provide an interface that allows functions to return the set of assignments to change for satisfying the constraints. Given this information, function-based constraints can be handled similarly.

4.2 Specific Constraint Resolution

We observe that not all constraints can be handled efficiently using the generic constraint resolution methods described in Section 4.1. Specifically, in the cases where the violation of a constraint is caused by a large subset (or all) of the assignment items, the generic methods may take a long time for resolving the constraints. For this kind of constraints, it can be more efficient to use specific constraint resolution techniques. In this section, we discuss how we can utilize existing efficient solutions for such constraints in our framework.

Constraint solvers are already equipped with optimized algorithms for resolving specific constraints including *AllDifferent, Range, Sequence* constraints and others [22]. These constraint resolution techniques can be utilized by embedding the query constraints in the CPs. In this section, we consider the unique assignment constraint, which specifies that a given set of items are to be assigned to distinct objects. The unique assignment constraint can be solved efficiently using the *AllDifferent* constraint, which forces its argument variables to assume different values from one another. Observe that the unique assignment constraint can also be expressed as multiple pairwise inequality constraints in which case the solution will be much less efficient.

The Ranked Search method is ill-suited to efficiently solve the unique assignment constraint since its solution would be based on pairwise inequality constraints. The worst-case scenario would be the case of bipartite matching in which all of the variables are to be assigned different values. This is a common constraint in the case of feature tracking in which all of the features are to be matched against each other. However, there is an efficient algorithm, the Hungarian Method [25], that solves the bipartite matching problem in polynomial time. We can incorporate this algorithm within the Ranked Search method by replacing the index incrementing operation with the Hungarian method for the cases where the unique assignment constraint is violated. Observe that we can use this method to handle constraints on subsets of variables by solving a subproblem in which only the constrained variables are free and the rest of the variables are fixed. This hybrid constraint resolution technique enables the Ranked Search method to efficiently solve complex constraints using specialized algorithms. The Ranked Search algorithm will correctly compute the set of top-k possible worlds as long as the integrated constraint resolution methods are optimal.

5. OPTIMIZATIONS

5.1 Reducing the Computation Time

Until now, we assumed that the parameter k for a query has a user specified and fixed value (similar to top-k queries). In practice, however, it is not clear how to set this value. In addition, it is likely that different k values are better fitting for data association at different time points, thereby requiring an adaptive mechanism to adjust the value of k during runtime. The reason is that, depending on the score distribution, the top possible world scores could be very similar

or really far apart. In the latter case, lower ranked possible worlds, though still within top-k, are unlikely to lead to top-k possible worlds at the next point in time and therefore will not contribute to the query result.

Based on this observation, we propose an adaptive mechanism that dynamically adjusts the k-value based on a statistical test, instead of using a fixed value, and reduces the computation time without significantly changing the query results. At a high level, we keep track of the change between the scores of the top possible world and the top i^{th} possible world. When this change has a low probability, according to the gathered statistics, we stop generating possible worlds (i.e., k is set to i) and return the result.

More specifically, we define a variable CR_i, the change rate of the top i^{th} possible world:

$$CR_i = \frac{p_i - p_{i+1}}{p_1}$$

where p_j is the score of the top j^{th} possible world. We assume that change rates are i.i.d. variables with mean μ and variance σ^2. Then based on the Chebyshev's Inequality [18] we have:

$$P(|CR_i - \mu| \geq c\sigma) \leq \frac{1}{c^2}$$

where $c > 0$ is a constant. We use a cumulative version of this inequality:

$$P(|\sum_1^n CR_i - n\mu| \geq c\sqrt{n}\sigma) \leq \frac{1}{c^2}$$

Here, $\sum_i^n CR_i$ is the cumulative change rate of the top n^{th} possible world and $\sum_i^n CR_i = \frac{p_1 - p_{n+1}}{p_1}$. Finally, we remove the absolute sign from the inequality to only consider the cases where the argument has a positive value. Otherwise the cumulative change rate is less than its expected value, which means that the possible world scores are close to each other. Therefore, given a probability threshold, $\frac{1}{c^2}$, our stopping condition is simply the given inequality test. This method is used together with a timeout mechanism or a maximum k value for the cases when the test always passes.

5.2 Improving the Association Accuracy

In this section, we first discuss how to measure the accuracy of the PDA query results and then present methods to increase accuracy without increasing the query processing times.

5.2.1 Accuracy Metrics

Given the ground truth (GT) data association for a PDA problem, there are various forms of accuracy metrics for data association [26]. An intuitive metric, variations of which are widely used by tracking applications, is the sequential accuracy, in which pairs of items associated with the same object in sequential time points / frames are identified and compared with the GT. If the GT also has the given items assigned to a single object, the item is said to be correctly associated, or a true positive (TP). If the association only exists in the query result but not in the GT, it is called a false positive (FP). Finally, if the association exists in the GT but not in the result, it is a false negative (FN). Then, the well-accepted precision and recall metrics of Information Retrieval can be applied: precision = $\frac{TP}{TP+FP}$ and recall = $\frac{TP}{TP+FN}$. Observe that, this metric focuses on individual item associations instead of continuous object tracking.

Hence, it is possible that each object is tracked correctly for a small number of frames but a high accuracy score is obtained. For instance, consider a single object video stream of 10 frames, for which 5 different 2-frame long objects are output as the tracking results (i.e., every two frames tracking fails and a new object is detected). In this case, the sequential accuracy would have 100% precision and 50% recall. For this reason, we can also use an object-based metric that compares the objects in the query result with the GT. In this case, we compare the first detected item for the object that an item is assigned to in the query result, with the first detected item of the corresponding object in the GT. TPs, FPs and FNs are defined similarly to the sequential accuracy metric.

Our top-k approximation method is based on the assumption that given relevant score assignments for data items (i.e., not conflicting with the GT), there is a strong correlation between high possible world scores and accuracy. This relationship is demonstrated experimentally in Section 6.

5.2.2 Hypothesis Sampling

In general, we expect the accuracy of the query results and the top possible world scores to increase with increasing values of k (until the maximum score possible worlds are obtained). Therefore, the first method of increasing accuracy is to increase the k-value. However, the value of k is limited due to computational reasons. Depending on the specified constraints and for large values of k, both the CP-based method and the Ranked Search method may take a long time to find the top-k possible worlds. In the worst case, an exponential number of possible worlds may need to be enumerated. In addition, a lower-ranked possible world in a frame set could lead to a high score possible world in later frame sets as the change in scores across frame sets is unlikely to be the same for all possible worlds. Given a fixed k value, such possible worlds could be prematurely eliminated. Finally, high score possible worlds tend to be very similar in terms of their assignments, which reduces the ability to recover from erroneous assignments.

We now add an additional *sampling step* to the Ranked Search method to address the mentioned issues. After the top-k possible worlds are found, we sample from the rest of the already computed possible worlds. The sampled possible worlds that satisfy the constraints are added to the top-k list. The sampling itself can be done uniformly at random or weighted by score. As future work, we plan to explore various sampling techniques and measure their effectiveness. Observe that the newly added possible worlds (i) are not necessarily high-score possible worlds and (ii) increase assignment *diversity* (as they originate from different parent possible worlds). Finally, notice that the sampling does not notably increase the computation time as it is performed over the already computed possible worlds; i.e., no additional iterations are performed to form new possible worlds.

6. EXPERIMENTS

6.1 Experimental Setup

In this section, we present an experimental evaluation of our algorithms using the visual tracking application described in Section 2.4.

6.1.1 Testbed

We have set up a 24 camera network (indoors) over a 100 Mbps wired LAN in our department as our testbed. In our setup, each camera [8] captures 5 frames (of size 640x480 pixels) per second (fps) and continuously forwards frames to a desktop computer in the same LAN for processing/storage. Although we had to limit the frame rate to avoid overloading the network, in our experiments we report processing times (per frame) that demonstrate that our system can easily cope with much higher data rates.

Video streams are processed by our computer vision (CV) library which extracts blobs and other image features and stores them in a central database. Our framework supports both real-time tracking on live videos and tracking on recorded videos using the central database (for debugging and retrospective analysis). For repeatability purposes, in the experiments reported here we use previously recorded videos. Our CV library, tracking application and all other tools are implemented in C++. We use the VXL library [9] for image processing and the ILOG [22] constraint solver to solve constraint programs.

6.1.2 Cooking Images: From Raw Data to Relations

We now describe how we "cook" the images within our visual tracking system. Notice that cooking is in general application-specific; we simply apply common practice and techniques and describe them for completeness and to facilitate repeatability.

Color-histogram and location-based matching [19] are the two similarity functions used to compute data association scores in this study. A color-histogram represents the color distribution of the pixels in a given image region. Our color-histogram implementation is a 3-dimensional histogram with 8 bins in each dimension based on the RGB color space [19]. The color-histogram matching function computes a score based on the similarity of the color-histogram of a data item with the color-histograms of an object. We use an intersection-distance based function for computing the similarity of two color-histograms. The intersection-distance function first normalizes each color-histogram and then sums the minimum of the values in the two histograms for each bin. On the other hand, for the location-based matching function, we model the motion of objects using a Kalman-filter [17] and use its prediction results in location estimation. In our experiments, matching score is computed as a weighted combination of the color-histogram and location-based similarity functions.

The objects considered for tracking in the experiments are people and foreground image features. There are a variety of image features available for tracking. In this study, we use a corner feature [21] provided by the VXL computer vision library. In addition, in a tracking application each object must be represented with a model based on the information required by the similarity functions. The representation model for objects is application dependent. In our implementation, the object representation models consist of a motion model and a bag of color-histograms.

In our experiments, we normalized each similarity function to return a unit value. In addition, to avoid numerical underflows, we use the logarithm of each assignment score and maximize the sum of the log-scores instead of the product of the scores. The scores reported in the experiments are log-scores unless otherwise stated.

We note that it is common practice to derive probability values from the scores assigned by user-defined similarity functions in many real-world applications (such as handwriting recognition, document classification, and keyword-based Web search) in a manner similar to the way we describe it here for visual tracking. The discussion of better probabilistic models is outside the scope of this paper. Our approaches do not make any assumptions about how the probability values are derived and thus can work with alternate interpretations.

In Section 6.2, we present experiments on the relation between accuracy and possible world scores using synthetic datasets. Then in Section 6.3 we present experimental results using real datasets.

6.2 Tracking Accuracy

In this experiment, we use a single-camera synthetic video stream of 10 frames formed by rotating a single image 2 degrees clockwise (with respect to its upper left corner) per frame. 42 features, extracted from the foreground pixels in the original image, are rotated with the image. Hence, each feature performs a circular motion with the same angular speed. As a result, we know the exact feature locations (i.e., the ground truth) in all frames using which we can precisely compute tracking accuracy. This is a common "trick" used when evaluating tracking solutions.

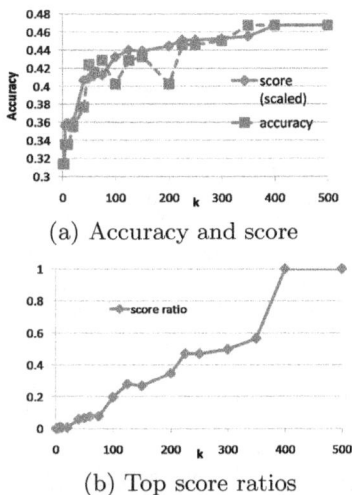

(a) Accuracy and score

(b) Top score ratios

Figure 5: Score and Accuracy Relationship

We tracked the features using Ranked Search with different k values (from 1 to 500). The accuracy vs. score comparison for the top possible world obtained with each value of k is provided in Figure 5(a). The used accuracy metric is the object-based metric described in Section 5.2. The shown curve is the precision curve and in this case it is the same with the recall curve as we used bipartite matching and each false negative also caused a false positive (and vice versa). The score values are normalized to fit in the accuracy interval. The general trends (i) increasing score with increasing k value and (ii) increasing accuracy with increasing score are displayed. Based on this result, in the rest of the experiments, we use increasing score values as indicators for increasing accuracy.

We should point out that the association accuracy reported in our experiments is fundamentally a function of the quality and resolution of the underlying raw data and the similarity functions used. As such, the nominal accuracy values achieved are not an indication of how well our proposed algorithms work. These values should be interpreted in a relative manner; e.g., our algorithms should not unnecessarily degrade the best possible accuracy achievable in our setting in order to improve processing efficiency.

The maximum achieved object-based accuracy ($\approx 48\%$) is low. However, with the sequential accuracy metric, we obtained values between 90% for $k = 1$ and 93% for $k = 500$ on the same results. The high sequential accuracy shows that while frame-by-frame tracking is accurate, feature-to-object mappings are less accurate. The reason is the lack of prior information on the feature motion models. In addition, the color-histogram function was not used in this experiment since the features across frames are identical (the color-histogram would therefore provide certain information).

The scores shown in Figure 5(a) and the rest of the section are log-based. However, in Figure 5(b), we show how the actual score value (i.e., not log-based) changes with k-value for the same results in Figure 5(a). The values are normalized using the best score.

6.3 Tracking Methods and Performance

6.3.1 CP-based method vs Ranked Search

In this experiment, we compare PDA query execution methods using a video stream of 268 frames from 3 video cameras (804 total frames). In this case, we are tracking 2 people walking towards each other, crossing paths and leaving the camera views in separate directions. The query execution times for each method is shown in Figure 6(a). A uniqueness constraint (i.e., blobs in the same camera are assigned to different objects) is enforced. As mentioned in Section 3.2.1, our CP-based solution can be viewed as a search-based MHT implementation with embedded constraint resolution techniques. In contrast to previous MHT implementations [2, 3, 4, 5], our CP-based solution effectively prunes its search space using constraint resolution.

The CP-based method, despite using the *AllDifferent* construct (Section 4.2), is unable to handle large values of k and requires seconds for processing k values greater than 50. The Ranked Search method (without the constraint resolution techniques) performs much better. The best performance is obtained with the Ranked Search method using the constraint resolution (Ranked Search + CR) techniques. Observe that, while the Ranked Search method in general requires longer execution times for the larger k values, in some cases it can take longer times for smaller values of k as well. The reason is the lack of CR techniques which makes the execution time mainly dependent on the constraint instances. While there are only 2 people in this video, there are also noise blobs being observed due to imperfect detection of foreground pixels which makes the problem harder. The query results obtained with all the execution methods are the same and we show the best score obtained with each value of k in Figure 6(b).

6.3.2 Constraint Resolution

I. Generic Constraint Resolution: In this experiment, we analyze how the query execution times change with (i) the number of tracked objects and (ii) different levels and types

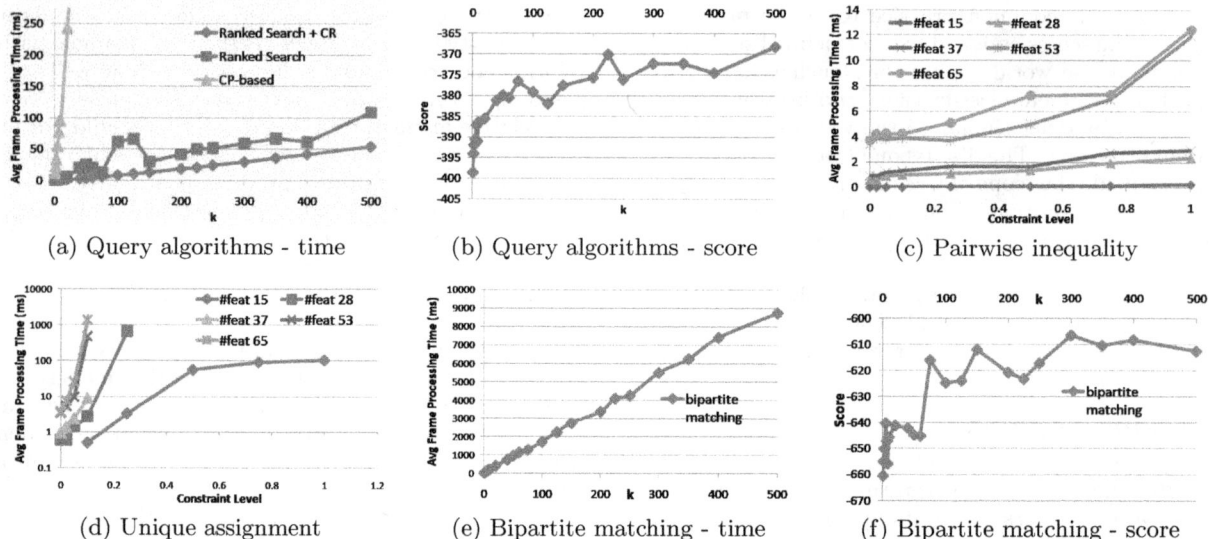

(a) Query algorithms - time

(b) Query algorithms - score

(c) Pairwise inequality

(d) Unique assignment

(e) Bipartite matching - time

(f) Bipartite matching - score

Figure 6: Comparison of PDA query execution methods and constraint resolution techniques

of constraints using a fixed value of $k = 10$ and generic constraint resolution techniques (Section 4.1). The test video contains 20 frames from a single camera.

Local Constraints: Local constraints are constraints that affect only a small subset of the variables [23]. As a local constraint example, we consider the pairwise inequality constraint (Section 4.1) (affects only 2 variables). In Figure 6(c), we show the average query execution times (per frame) for tracking different number of features (15, 28, 37, 53 and 65) under different constraint levels. The constraint level specifies the ratio of the features on which pairwise inequality constraints are placed. The results show that the increase in the number of features for low constraint levels does not notably affect the execution time. However, the execution time becomes more sensitive to the number of features as the constraint level increases.

Global Constraints: Now we consider the unique assignment constraint (Section 4.2) which is a *global constraint* (affects all variables). In Figure 6(d), we show the execution times for tracking different number of features with varying levels of the unique assignment constraint. In this case, the constraint level specifies the ratio of the features on which a unique assignment constraint is placed. When the constraint level is 1, the problem is equivalent to the bipartite matching problem. The results show that it is much harder to solve the unique assignment constraint with the generic constraint resolution methods. We can only obtain the full range of results for the case with 15 features. With a larger number of features, we ran out of memory before we could find the top-10 possible worlds.

II. Specific Constraint Resolution - Bipartite Matching: In this experiment, we focus on the specific constraint resolution techniques within the context of bipartite matching (i.e., one-to-one matching of features to objects Section 4.2). The test video contains 23 frames with an average number of 38 features per frame. We execute feature tracking for different k values (from 1 to 500). The average query execution times are given in Figure 6(e). The execution time increases linearly with the value of k. We were unable to compute the top-10 possible worlds using generic CR techniques for more

than 15 features and level-1 unique assignment constraint. With specific CR techniques, however, we could obtain these results for $k = 500$. In addition, we show the score curve for the best score obtained with each value of k in Figure 6(f).

6.3.3 Adaptive-k Processing

In this experiment, we analyze the effects of the adaptive-k mechanism using different threshold values and frame processing time limits, described in Section 5.1, on the score and execution time performance of the Ranked Search algorithm. We track the people in a video of 23 frames using the Ranked Search algorithm with the adaptive-k setting. The time limit specifies the maximum time allowed for processing a single frame, which is used to time out processing when the adaptive-k test is unable to stop processing. Average per frame query execution times are shown in Figure 7(a) for different values of the threshold and the time limit.

With a 250ms time limit, the adaptive-k mechanism is unable to notably reduce the computation time even with the larger values of the threshold. As discussed in Section 5.1, the threshold indirectly specifies the maximum cumulative drop in possible world scores before processing is stopped. The fact that the adaptive-k mechanism is unable to stop processing means that the possible worlds generated in 250ms are all within the score limits specified by the threshold.

For larger values of the time limit, the adaptive-k mechanism is able to reduce the average frame processing time. However, this is possible due to a trade-off between score and processing time. The score values obtained in the experiment are shown in Figure 7(b). For a 750ms time limit, we can use a threshold value of 0.05, to reduce the average computation time by 142ms ($\approx 19\%$) and still obtain a similar top possible world score. Similarly with 500ms time limit, we can use a threshold of 0.075 and reduce the average computation time by 57ms ($\approx 11\%$) without a significant loss in the best-score. The vertical lines in Figure 7(a) indicate this reduction in computation for these accuracy-cut based threshold values. For larger threshold values, the achieved best-score is smaller. The reason is that the possible worlds

228

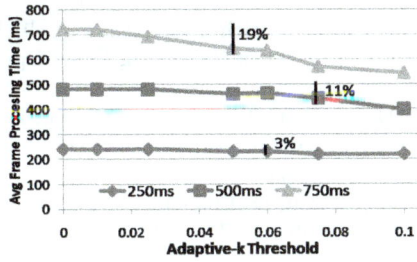

(a) Adaptive-k vs. time

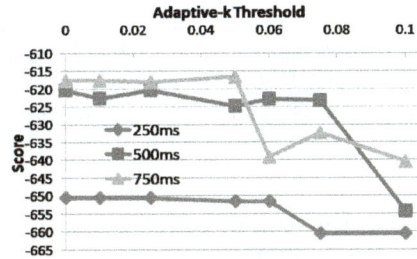

(b) Adaptive-k vs. score

Figure 7: Ranked Search with Adaptive-k

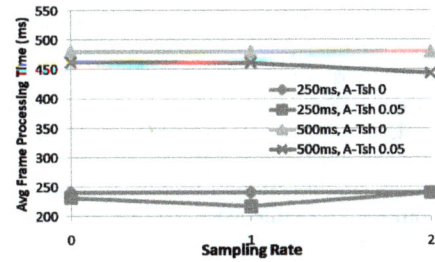

(a) Sampling - time

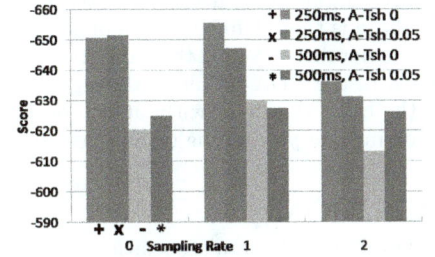

(b) Sampling - score

Figure 8: Hypothesis sampling

that generate these best-scores are prematurely eliminated during processing.

6.3.4 Hypothesis Sampling

In this experiment, we focused on the effects of sampling on per frame average execution time and score performance of the Ranked Search algorithm. For comparability purposes, we used the same 23-frame video with the Adaptive-k experiment (Section 6.3.3). There are three different dimensions for the algorithm settings used in this experiment: (i) frame processing time limit (250ms and 500ms) (ii) adaptive-k mechanism (used with a threshold of 0.05 or not used) and (iii) uniform sampling with different rates. The sampling is done as an additional step as discussed in Section 5.2.2. The experiment results for all combinations are shown in Figures 8(a) and 8(b).

The sampling rates, 0, 1 and 2, specify the ratio of sampled possible worlds to the already computed top-k possible worlds. For instance, with a sampling rate of 1, if top-10 possible worlds are computed using the Ranked Search algorithm, then 10 additional possible worlds are sampled from the rest of the computed possible worlds. In Figure 8(a), as predicted in Section 5.2.2, we show that sampling does not increase the execution time of the tracking algorithm. In Figure 8(b) we compare the best-score obtained for each setting of the tracking algorithm. The results show that in all cases a higher score is obtained with a larger time limit. However, it is still possible to improve the achieved score using sampling. For the sampling rate 2, the score is improved significantly for the 250ms time limit, approaching the score obtained with the 500ms time limit, both with the adaptive-k mechanism and without it. The relative score improvement for the 500ms case is less. Yet with a sampling rate of 2, a score of -610 is achieved, which is the best observed score in this case, and beats all non-sampling based scores and the scores achieved with 750ms time limit shown in the adaptive-k experiment.

7. RELATED WORK

Multi-Hypothesis Tracking (MHT) [2, 3, 4] is a widely used data association model with many applications, that forms multiple hypotheses for object tracking. Similar to our work, in MHT implementations [2, 5] a top-k approximation is used for finding high score data association hypotheses. In [5], an MHT implementation based on the bipartite matching algorithm is provided applying to one-to-one matching problems only. As in our CP-based method, the problem is repeatedly divided into separate problems which are solved optimally till top-k solutions are found. However, our techniques for improving the efficiency and accuracy, as well as our integrated constraint resolution framework, are novel and, as we demonstrated experimentally, provide significant benefits enabling real-time PDA with high accuracy.

Other data association methods include the Global Nearest Neighbors (GNN) [19] method, in which each data item is assigned to the object it most likely belongs to. However, in GNN items are assigned independently and without any constraints. In addition, GNN is unable to recover from erroneous assignments. Another data association method is the Joint Probabilistic Data Association Filter (JPDAF) [20], which unlike MHT and GNN is an object-based approach. In JPDAF, multiple items could be assigned to an object and each object model is updated based on a weighted combination of the data items assigned to it. Observe that, in JPDAF there is no specific data association, instead an object-based view, describing the model of each object, is provided to the user.

A top-k query on uncertain data computes the best k results according to a given rank function. In prior research on probabilistic databases, top-k queries were extensively studied [6, 10, 11, 13] and there has been different formulations of top-k queries targeting different applications. For instance, in [6], definition for two types of top-k queries are given: *U-Topk* and *U-k Ranks*. The U-Topk query returns k tuples which has the highest probability of being the top-k tuples in all possible worlds. In the U-k Ranks query, the result is a list of k tuples where the ith tuple has the highest probability for being the ith ranked tuple in all possible worlds. The PDA query introduced in this paper involves a top-k approximation and can be viewed as a continuous top-k query. However, our main goal is to find high score possible worlds at each frame instead of finding the best-k hypotheses for a single frame. In addition, the PDA query results are complete possible worlds, not partial assignments obtained from possible worlds.

In [12], authors consider the duplicate detection problem for data integration and cleaning. The proposed solution is to view the dirty database as a probabilistic database and the clean database is then defined as one of the instances of the probabilistic database. While this definition is similar to our formulation of the PDA problem, their goal (to answer queries over the clean database without computing it) and methods (involving query rewriting techniques) are different.

8. CONCLUSIONS

Continuous probabilistic data association is a data-driven stream processing challenge that arises in a variety of real-world applications. We described how continuous query processing techniques can support PDA, showing experimental evidence that they can improve upon the existing solutions in terms of generality and performance.

Our primary contributions include algorithms for probabilistic constrained ranking over data streams and a resource-aware tuning approach that produces real-time results with modest losses in accuracy. We use a visual tracking application over a smart camera network to evaluate our solutions.

There are several open directions for future work on PDA. In addition to live PDA, many applications would like to extract data associations over stored, historical data. Such a functionality can greatly benefit from standard tools such as indexing, as well as novel execution strategies that look for associations at different spatio-temporal granularities. Another promising direction is the integration of the cooking process with PDA processing over the relational representation, which was the topic of this paper. In our model, cooking is handled independently and separately by application-specific logic, after which our PDA algorithms kick in. Here, there are opportunities for new cross-layer optimizations by, for example, using on-demand computation of the similarity scores, i.e., by extracting only those image features required by the PDA algorithm.

9. REFERENCES

[1] Krause, A., et al. Data Association for Topic Intensity Tracking. ICML, 497-504, 2006.

[2] Cox, I. J. and Hingorani, S. L. An Efficient Implementation of Reid's Multiple Hypothesis Tracking Algorithm and Its Evaluation for the Purpose of Visual Tracking. Pattern Anal. Mach. Intell. 18(2), 1996.

[3] Reid D.B. An Algorithm for Tracking Multiple Targets. IEEE Trans. on Automatic Control 24(6), 843-854, 1979.

[4] Blackman, S. Multiple Hypothesis Tracking for Multiple Target Tracking. IEEE A & E Systems Magazine 19, 2004.

[5] Murty, K. G. An Algorithm for Ranking All the Assignments in Order of Increasing Cost. Operations Research 16, 1968.

[6] Soliman, M. A., Ilyas, Ihab F., and Chang, K. C. Top-k Query Processing in Uncertain Databases. ICDE, 896-905, 2007.

[7] Dalvi, N. and Suciu, D. Efficient Query Evaluation on Probabilistic Databases. The VLDB Journal 16, 2007.

[8] DCS-900 Camera. http://www.dlink.com/products/?pid=270.

[9] Vision-X Libraries. http://vxl.sourceforge.net.

[10] Hua, M., Pei, J., Zhang, W., and Lin, X. Ranking Queries on Uncertain Data: A Probabilistic Threshold Approach. SIGMOD, 673-686, 2008.

[11] Re, C., Dalvi, N. N., and Suciu, D. Efficient Top-k Query Evaluation on Probabilistic Data. ICDE, 886-895, 2007.

[12] Andritsos, P., Fuxman, A., and Miller, R. J. Clean Answers over Dirty Databases: A Probabilistic Approach. ICDE, 2006.

[13] Ge, T., Zdonik, S., and Madden, S. Top-k Queries on Uncertain Data: On Score Distribution and Typical Answers. SIGMOD, 375-388, 2009.

[14] J. Widom. Trio: A System for Integrated Management of Data, Accuracy, and Lineage. CIDR, 262-276, 2005.

[15] Benjelloun, O., et al. Databases with Uncertainty and Lineage. VLDB Journal 17(2), 243-264, 2008.

[16] Suciu, D., et al. Probabilistic Databases. Morgan & Claypool Publishers, 2011.

[17] Kalman, R. E. A New Approach to Linear Filtering and Prediction Problems. Transactions of the ASME 82(D), 35-45, 1960.

[18] Ross, S. A First Course in Probability. Prentice Hall, 2008.

[19] Forsyth, D. A. and Ponce, J. Computer Vision: A Modern Approach. Prentice Hall, 2002.

[20] Bar-Shalom, Y. Tracking and Data Association. Academic Press Professional, 1987.

[21] Smith, P., Sinclair., D. et al. Effective Corner Matching. BMVC, 1-12, 1998.

[22] IBM ILOG CP Optimizer. www.ilog.com

[23] Marriott, K., and Stuckey, P. J. Programming with Constraints: An Introduction. MIT Press, 1998.

[24] Kanagal, B. and Deshpande, A. Online Filtering, Smoothing and Probabilistic Modeling of Streaming Data. ICDE, 1160-1169, 2008.

[25] Papadimitriou, C. H., et al. Combinatorial Optimization: Algorithms and Complexity. Prentice-Hall, 1998.

[26] Manohar, V. et al. Performance Evaluation of Object Detection and Tracking in Video. ACCV, 151-161, 2006.

[27] Brown, D. E. and Hagen, S. Data Association Methods with Applications to Law Enforcement. Decision Support Systems 34(4), 369-378, 2003.

[28] Apt, K. Principles of Constraint Programming. Cambridge University Press, 2003.

[29] Kumar, V. Algorithms for Constraint-Satisfaction Problems: A Survey. AI Magazine, 1992.

The Hidden Pub/Sub of Spotify (Industry Article)

Vinay Setty
University of Oslo, Norway
vinay@ifi.uio.no

Gunnar Kreitz
Spotify and KTH – Royal
Institute of Technology,
Stockholm, Sweden
gkreitz@kth.se

Roman Vitenberg
University of Oslo, Norway
romanvi@ifi.uio.no

Maarten van Steen
VU University and The
Network Institute
Amsterdam, The Netherlands
steen@cs.vu.nl

Guido Urdaneta
Spotify, Stockholm, Sweden
guidou@spotify.com

Staffan Gimåker
Spotify, Stockholm, Sweden
staffan@spotify.com

ABSTRACT

Spotify is a peer-assisted music streaming service that has gained worldwide popularity. Apart from providing instant access to over 20 million music tracks, *Spotify* also enhances its users' music experience by providing various features for social interaction. These are realized by a system using the widely-adopted pub/sub paradigm. In this paper we provide an interesting case study of a hybrid pub/sub system designed for real-time as well as offline notifications for *Spotify* users. We firstly describe a multitude of use cases where pub/sub is applied. Secondly, we study the design of its pub/sub system used for matching, disseminating and persisting billions of publications every day. Finally, we study pub/sub traffic collected from the production system, derive characterizations of the pub/sub workload, and show some interesting findings and trends.

Categories and Subject Descriptors

C.2.4 [**Computer-Communication Networks**]: Distributed Systems—*Distributed applications*

Keywords

Pub/Sub Systems,Event Notifications,Workload Analysis

1. INTRODUCTION

Spotify is a successful peer-assisted music-streaming service that provides access to over 20 million tracks to its users residing in 20 countries. The technical architecture providing the streaming service and user behavior of *Spotify* have been described in two recent studies [1, 2]. However, little has been said about the technical details of one of *Spotify*'s most engaging features: its ability to facilitate sharing and following of various music activities among its users in real time.

In this paper, we explain how the architecture allows the users to follow playlists, artists, and the music activities of their friends. The distinctive feature of the architecture is that this entire range of social interaction is supported by pub/sub, a popular communication paradigm that provides a loosely coupled form of interaction among a large number of publishing data sources and subscribing data sinks [3]. Thus, this paper adds a new unique application to a currently known list of large-scale systems that report benefits from using pub/sub, which includes application integration [4], financial data dissemination [5], RSS feed distribution and filtering [6], and business process management [7].

The end-to-end architecture of the pub/sub engine at Spotify is the main focus of our study. The subscriptions are topic-based. The engine is hybrid: It allows relaying events to online users in real time as well as storing and forwarding selected events to offline users who come online at a later point. The architecture includes a DHT-based overlay that currently spans three sites in Sweden, UK, and USA. The architecture is designed to scale: It stores approximately 600 million subscriptions at any given time and matches billions of publication events every day under its current deployment.

We study the performance of the system based on recently recorded traces. The objective of the study is twofold: First, we characterize the workload of the pub/sub system in terms of event publication rates, topic popularity, subscription sizes, subscription cardinality, and temporal subscription/unsubscription patterns. Unfortunately, there exist precious few characterizations of subscriptions and synthetic workload generators for pub/sub systems [8]. In view of this shortage, the value of our characterization is that it can be used towards corroborating the validity of synthetic workloads as well as their generation. One particularly surprising finding that we explain in the paper is that the event publication rate for a topic is not correlated with the topic popularity.

The second goal of the study is to analyze the message traffic produced by the pub/sub system and derive trends and patterns. In particular, we show that the traffic due to the activity of following friends dominates the total traffic of social interactions.

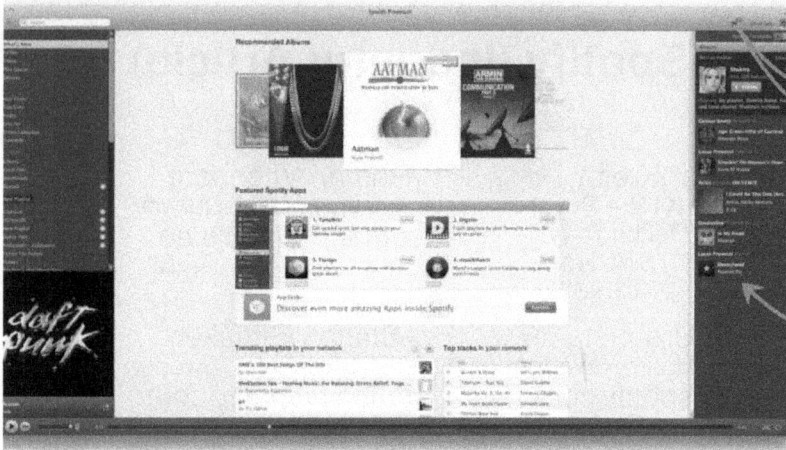

Figure 1: Spotify Desktop Client Snapshot

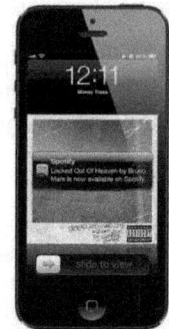

Figure 2: Push Notification

2. SPOTIFY PUB/SUB MODEL AND FEATURES

Spotify pub/sub follows the well-known topic-based pub/sub model. Users can subscribe (or follow) topics, which can be any of the following types:

Friends: *Spotify* allows its users to integrate with their Facebook account, and, once this integration is done, by default all Facebook friends who are also *Spotify* users become topics that can be followed. A *Spotify* user can also follow another *Spotify* user even if they have not integrated their Facebook account by finding each other by sharing music or Playlists.

Playlists: Playlists (collections of music tracks) in the Spotify system have URIs, allowing users to subscribe to playlists created by others. Additionally, a user can search for publicly available user-created Playlists within the *Spotify* client. Subscribing to a Playlist allows users to receive future updates to the Playlist. By default, a Playlist can only be modified by its creator, but a Playlist can also be marked as "collaborative", making it world writable.

Artist pages: *Spotify* has dedicated pages for each artist and allows users to follow them. This allows users to get notifications about new album releases or news related to the artist.

Any user can become a subscriber of the topics of the types mentioned above. A subscription is generally a pair of strings, the username of the subscriber and the topic name. The following are the publication events related to the above mentioned topic types:

Friend feed: When a user plays a music track, creates or modifies a Playlist, or marks an artist or a track or an album as favorite, an event notification is sent to all the friends following the user. Optionally, these events can also be published on the associated Facebook wall of the user. The friend feed can be seen at the bottom-right pane of the desktop client as shown in Figure 1.

Playlist updates: Whenever a Playlist is modified by adding or removing a track or renaming the Playlist, the subscribers of the Playlist are notified about the update via friend feed. The pub/sub system is also responsible for instantly synchronizing the Playlist information across all the devices of all the subscribers of the Playlist.

Artist pages: Whenever a new album related to an artist is added in *Spotify* and whenever a playlist is created by an artist a notification is sent to all the followers of that artist.

It is worth mentioning that all of the publication events mentioned above are delivered to subscribers in real-time (best-effort as well as guaranteed delivery) when the user is online, some of them can also be delivered as offline notification via Email, and they can be retrieved by the user in the future. For example, when a new album is added for a famous artist with millions or followers, (a) an instant notification event is sent to the *Spotify* client software used by all the followers of the artist who are currently online, (b) an email notification is sent to the offline followers, and (c) the event is also persisted so that current and future followers can retrieve the historical events related to the artist in the future. The persistence of the update is also essential to support multiple devices of the same user i.e. a user logged into one device may want to retrieve the notification on a different device at a later point in time.

3. ARCHITECTURE FOR SUPPORTING SOCIAL INTERACTION

In this section we describe the technical architecture of the system that facilitates the social interaction between users based on the popular pub/sub communication paradigm. The pub/sub system at one end consists of publishers generating publication events and at the other end consists of subscribers, which are essentially *Spotify* clients. The pub/sub system is hosted across several data-centers (referred to as sites within *Spotify*). There are currently three sites: Stockholm - Sweden, London - UK and Ashburn - USA. These sites are not limited to hosting the pub/sub system, their

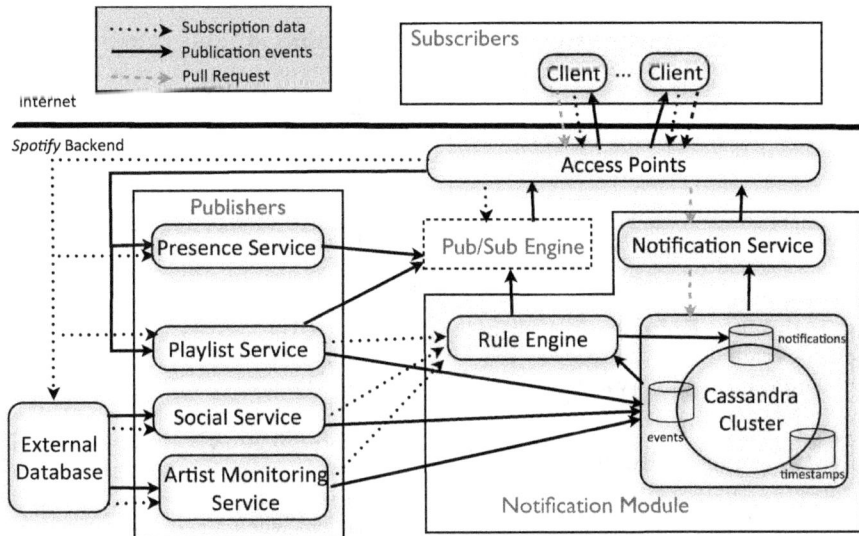

Figure 3: Architecture Supporting Social Interaction

main purpose is to host the music streaming service and all the back-end services necessary for *Spotify* to function.

3.1 Architecture Overview

A high-level architecture consisting of subscribers, publishers, and two core components, the *Pub/Sub Engine* and the *Notification Module*, that are essential for enabling the social interaction between users is shown in Figure 3. The two core components are crucial for supporting high-performance real-time event delivery and reliable offline notifications in a resource-efficient manner.

Whenever designing a system for delivering publication events, the architects have to address a fundamental trade-off between latency and reliability. In order to address this trade-off the system supports three essential event flow paths.

Real time to online clients: The real-time delivery of events is done by Pub/Sub Engine. However, Pub/Sub Engine is light-weight i.e. it does not make the incoming events persistent, also there are no acknowledgments in place to detect failures, which results in a best-effort delivery of publication events without any guarantees but with low latency. Notice that in Figure 3 the Pub/Sub Engine directly receives input from three different sources: the Presence service, the Playlist service, and the Notification Module. Output is delivered to the subscribers via Access Points.

Persisted to online clients: The motivation for having this event-flow path for the delivery of publication events is purely based on the application requirement. The requirement is that some publication events like an album release or a Facebook friend joining *Spotify* are classified as critical for the users, and these critical publications must be delivered reliably, and at least once across all devices. This event flow path is realized by Notification Module by storing the incoming publication events in the Cassandra cluster [9] for reliable and offline delivery. This will be explained in detail later in Section 3.3.

Persisted to offline clients: Whenever a client comes online, it can retrieve the publication events from the Notification Module by sending a pull request with the time-stamp of the last seen event. This path is shown in Figure 3. The client may receive the same notification twice: once when it was online last time and another time when it came back online. However, the client software can distinguish already seen publications using the time-stamp of the publications.

3.2 Subscribers and Publishers

The *Access Points* (APs) act as an interface to all the external clients. From a pub/sub perspective, APs are responsible for relaying client join/leave messages to various services, relaying subscription/unsubscription requests from clients to the pub/sub service, and relaying publication messages from the pub/sub service to clients. The APs are responsible for maintaining the mapping between the TCP connection to the client software and the topics and vice versa. This mapping is crucial for relaying subscriptions, unsubscriptions and publications.

All *Subscribers* in the pub/sub system are client software instances running on user devices. The client is a proprietary software application available for several desktop and mobile devices. A snapshot of the desktop client is shown in Figure 1. There are two ways of subscribing to a topic: Firstly, when a user explicitly follows a particular user, artist or playlist from the client interface and secondly, the social relations established from Facebook connections. In the former case subscription to the topic is done explicitly, while in the latter case subscriptions are done implicitly.

Whenever the client subscribes to a topic, the subscription information is sent to the Access Points. This information includes the user name of the subscriber and the corresponding URI for the service, as listed in Table 1. However, since the subscription information is needed by both the Pub/Sub Engine and the Notification Module there are two distinct subscription flow paths:

Table 1: List of topic types and corresponding services

Topic Type	URI	Service	Notification Type
User	hm://presence/user/<user-name>/	Presence	Friend-feed
Playlist	hm://playlist/user/<user-name>/playlist/<playlist-id>/	Playlist	Friend-feed, In-Client, Push and Email
Artist	hm://notifications/feed/artist-id%notification-type/	Artist Monitoring	In-Client, Push and Email
Social	hm://notifications/feed/username%notification-type/	Social	In-Client, Push and Email

Subscriptions to the Pub/Sub Engine: The client sends a list of topics and the URI of the relevant service to an AP, which are eventually forwarded to the Pub/Sub Engine.

Subscriptions to the Notification Module: If the subscription request is for the Social service, the Artist monitoring service or the Playlist service, the request is forwarded from an AP to the respective services. These services are then responsible for providing the subscription information to the Notification Module.

The *Publishers* of the pub/sub system are services running in the *Spotify* sites. All publications for the topics mentioned in the previous section are generated from four services, listed below and shown in Figure 3. The specific topics for these services are used in the form of URIs for communication and matching purposes and they are listed in Table 1. These URIs use a protocol internal to Spotify, denoted hm (Hermes).

The Presence Service is responsible for receiving friend feed events generated by users from client software. Whenever a user takes an action to trigger friend feed (as described in Section 1) the client generates a message to the user topic type via APs. The Presence service then stores the event in main memory and forwards the received event to the Pub/Sub Engine (shown in Figure 3 and explained in detail in Section 3.4) to be matched and delivered to the client software of the subscribers. All the events from the Presence service that are intended for the subscribers of a user are delivered to clients in real time in a best-effort manner (i.e., no fault-tolerance techniques are used and hence no delivery guarantees). Also, Presence events are not persisted in secondary memory. Instead, only the last seen event is stored in main memory, due to the significantly higher volume of traffic compared to other services. All Presence events can be seen at a friend feed pane at the bottom-right corner of the Spotify desktop client software as shown in Figure 1.

The Playlist Service is mainly responsible for tracking playlist modifications made by users. As explained in Section 1, a playlist can be subscribed in two ways: a user can explicitly subscribe to playlists, and, in addition to that, by default all users are also subscribed to the playlists of their friends. The Playlist service treats the publications for these two types of subscriptions differently. playlist updates from friends are shown in friend feed and are delivered via Pub/Sub Engine, and the rest are delivered via the Notification Module. The playlist service also provides subscription lists (i.e., given a playlist, all the subscribers of the playlist; and, given a user, all the subscribed playlists of the user).

The Social Service is responsible for managing the social relations of *Spotify* users as well as integration with Facebook. The Social service generates a publication event when a Facebook friend of an existing user who is not already using *Spotify* joins *Spotify*. It also provides an interface to obtain all the friends of a user who are subscribers to the friend feed from the given user. Finally, it is also responsible for posting user activities on the Facebook wall for those users who opted for this feature.

Artist Monitoring Service is responsible for generating publication events whenever there is a new album or track for an artist and new playlists created by an artist. Note that the artist monitoring-service is essentially a batch job running at regular intervals (typically once a day) that queries an external database to detect any new album releases for the artist.

A summary of all topics types that can be subscribed by the clients and the corresponding services producing publications are listed in Table 1.

3.3 Notification Module

The publication events for all the topics are delivered to clients in several ways. The Notification Module receives the publication events from all services, except the Presence service, and then classifies them and delivers them to the subscribers in the form of the following **Notification Types**:

In-client notification: Some events like artist updates and new Facebook friends joining *Spotify* are shown in a notification icon at the top-right corner of the *Spotify* desktop client, as shown in Figure 1. Note that unlike friend feed, in-client notifications are persisted for guaranteed delivery.

Push notifications: Push notifications are for mobile devices. The Notification service forwards the events to the corresponding push notification services provided by the vendors of the user devices. An example of the push notification is shown in Figure 2.

Email notifications: When a user is not online, events like artist, playlist and friend updates are sent via email excluding the users who have opted out of this service.

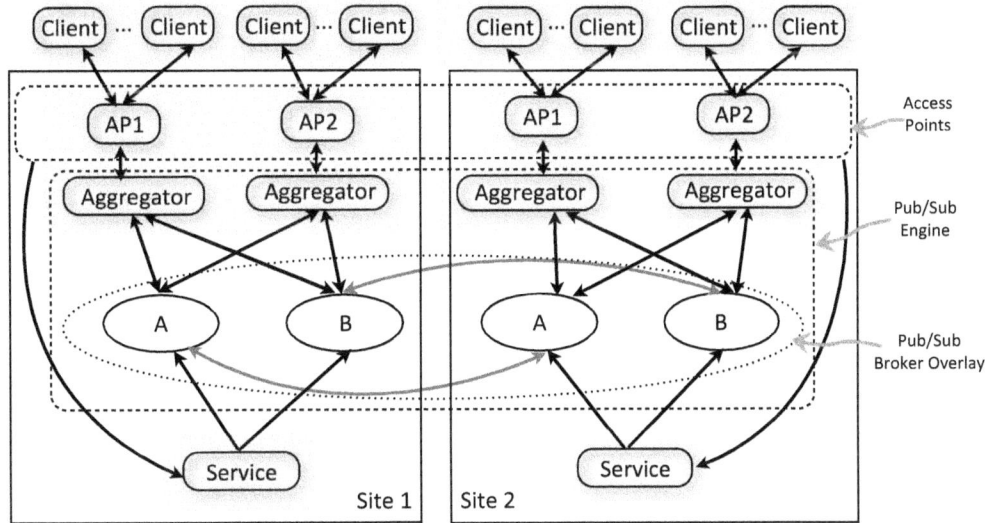

Figure 4: Real-Time Pub/Sub

A summary of the topics and the notification types with which they can be delivered to the subscribers is listed in Table 1.

An important component of the Notification Module is the Rule Engine. It has the logic for classifying every publication event into one of the above mentioned notification types. The rules are embedded in the Rule Engine, but the subscription information is obtained from the respective publication services. The rules are based on the following parameters:

- Online status of the user.

- Client device type (desktop or mobile).

- User subscription preferences on email notifications.

Depending on the notification type, the Rule Engine will forward the publication event to Pub/Sub Engine and Cassandra for persistence.

3.3.1 Publication Event Persistence

The motivation for persistence of publication events is driven by the following goals: reliable delivery of publications, offline delivery and future retrieval of publications, and a smooth way to deliver publication events to the same user but using clients from different devices. All publication events generated from the playlist, Social and Artist services are persisted in a Cassandra cluster in a column family called *events*, as shown in Figure 3. It is worth noting here that each publication event is stored as (topic, subscriber) pairs in the Cassandra cluster. This is a significant blowup of data for the topics with millions of subscribers. Since the persistence of these events requires significant storage and computing resources the following measures are taken:

- Presence events, which are of significantly higher volume (as shown with workload analysis in Section 4), are not persisted.

- Each publication event in the *events* column family has an expiry date of 90 days by default (i.e., no events are retained over 90 days).

Once the events are written to the *events* column family, each event is processed by the Rule Engine, which constantly polls *events* and detects the new events. Based on the generated rules, the Rule Engine decides if the events are to be sent to the Pub/Sub Engine for real-time delivery or written back to the Cassandra cluster but to a different column family called *Notifications* along with the notification type to be used. The *Notification service*, which polls the *Notifications* column family, delivers the publication events using the Notification Type suggested by the Rule Engine.

Finally, to support pull requests from clients, the column family *Timestamps* is used for keeping track of the timestamp of the last seen event for each client. Whenever a client connects to an AP, a request is sent to the Notification service with the time-stamp of the last seen event, and the Notification service responds with all publications that were generated after than the given time-stamp. Note that time synchronization is not a problem here since the clients adhere to the clock of an AP. The time-stamp check also helps avoid duplicate delivery of publication events and, once a notification is read on one device it will be shown as read in all the other devices of the same user.

3.4 Pub/Sub Engine

The Pub/Sub Engine consists of *Aggregators*, responsible for aggregating subscriptions and distributing publications. The core component of the Pub/Sub Engine is a DHT overlay of broker servers managing subscriptions, publication matching, and delivery. A diagram with the different components of the Pub/Sub Engine is shown in Figure 4.

The *Aggregators* sit between the APs and the pub/sub broker overlay. When a client connects to *Spotify* via an AP, it also sends a set of subscriptions by sending all the friends, playlists and artists the user is interested in. Each subscriber-topic pair is considered a separate subscription. All subscriptions are managed for matching purposes in main memory. In order to scale w.r.t. the number of subscriptions and publication events, the Aggregators are crucial. The Aggregator locally aggregates all the subscriptions for a given topic and sends a single subscription on their behalf to the pub/sub broker overlay. The Aggregator distributes the publication to the APs in the reverse direction. The Aggregator is also responsible for hashing the subscription to a respective broker in the pub/sub broker overlay.

The *pub/sub brokers* are organized as a DHT (Distributed Hash Table) overlay with the subscription as the key. The overlay of pub/sub brokers have the following responsibilities:

Managing subscriptions: pub/sub brokers are responsible for receiving subscription requests from Aggregators and storing the subscriptions in memory. The brokers are responsible for maintaining the mapping between the topics and the corresponding Aggregator where the subscription came from. This mapping is absolutely crucial for routing the publications to the right Aggregator. Pub/sub brokers also receive unsubscription requests for a topic from the Aggregators when there are no more online subscribers for that topic.

Matching publications: pub/sub brokers match the incoming publications from the publisher services against in-memory subscriptions.

Forwarding matched publications: Once the matching entries are found the publication is forwarded to all the corresponding Aggregators.

Cross-site forwarding: The broker overlay is also responsible for forwarding publications to a different site if there are any subscribers. Note that the pub/sub broker overlay spans all the sites.

Each broker in a site has a one-to-one corresponding broker in other sites which exchange their subscriptions and publications from the corresponding sites. For example, as shown in Figure 4, broker A in Site 1 has a corresponding broker A in Site 2 (i.e., all the subscriptions obtained within Site 1 and managed at broker A, are also forwarded and replicated at corresponding broker A of Site 2 and vice-versa). Whenever there is a publication for a subscription at the broker A of Site 1, if there is a matching subscription registered from the broker A of Site 2, the publication is forwarded via a cross-site link to the broker A of Site 2. Then the broker A of Site 2 forwards the publication to the corresponding subscriber in Site 2 via an AP. This cross-site DHT overlay of pub/sub brokers facilitates interaction among *Spotify* users that follow each other but are connected to different sites.[10]

Load Balancing: Since all subscriptions are in memory, it is crucial to have a scalable solution to manage them. The DHT organization of the pub/sub brokers is the key to scale in-memory storage of over 600 million subscriptions. The pub/sub broker overlay is also designed to distribute the load publication matching and forwarding load among the brokers.

4. ANALYSIS OF SPOTIFY PUB/SUB WORKLOAD

In this section we study the different characteristics and patterns emerging from the pub/sub traffic at *Spotify*. The main goal of the study is to characterize the workload used by a deployed pub/sub system, thereby serving as a reference for workload-modeling purposes in the pub/sub community in both industry and academia. Another goal of this study is to analyze the message traffic produced by the *Spotify* pub/sub system and derive trends and patterns. All the results presented in this paper are based on traces collected from production data. The traces were collected during 10 days from Thursday, 10 Jan 2013 to Saturday, 19 Jan 2013.

4.1 Analysis of Traces From The Presence Service

In this section, unless explicitly mentioned, we study the subscriptions and publications given as input to the Presence service. We restrict our analysis to the Presence service due to its dominance of the pub/sub workload in *Spotify*, which is illustrated later in this section. In order to simplify our analysis, at any time we consider only users with desktop clients, who have been online at the Stockholm site and have produced at least one publication in the studied time period, and their corresponding subscribers.

We study the following characteristics of the workload:

- The distribution of **Topic Popularity**: The Complimentary Cumulative Distribution Function (CCDF) of the percentage of the total number of subscribers subscribing to a topic, shown in Figure 5.

- The distribution of **Subscription Size**: The CCDF of the percentage of total number of topics subscribed by a single subscriber, shown in Figure 6.

- The distribution of **Publication Event Rate (per-topic)**: The CCDF of the percentage of total publication events generated for the chosen time period, shown in Figure 7.

It is easy to see that log-log plots CCDFs of topic popularity and subscription size Figure 6 follow a distribution close to a power law. The CCDF of Publication Event Rate, on the other hand, does not follow power-law. There is a sharp deviation around 0.0005% of the total number of publication events.

Notice that the CCDF of topic popularity and subscription size are similar to the typical degree distribution in social networks [11]. This behavior is due to the fact that subscriptions and topics in *Spotify* pub/sub are predominantly defined by the social relations between *Spotify* users. Also, as mentioned in Section 1, it is known that when a Facebook friend of a *Spotify* user joins *Spotify*, by default they become subscribers of each other. This observation motivates the use of social graphs as workload for academic works on topic-based pub/sub systems as done in [10, 12].

Next we study the distribution of the number of publications attracted by subscriptions. We call it *Subscription Cardinality* per subscriber, which we define as the percentage of total publications events matching the topics subscribed by a subscriber. It is mathematically expressed as below:

$$C(S) = \frac{\sum_{t_S \in S} ev(t_S)}{\sum_{t \in \mathcal{T}} ev(t)} * 100$$

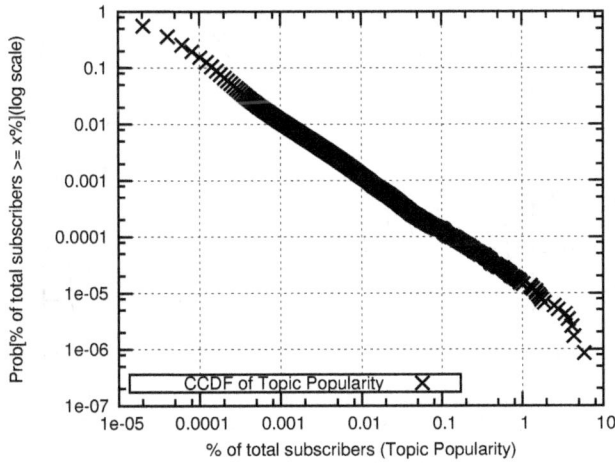

Figure 5: CCDF of Topic Popularity

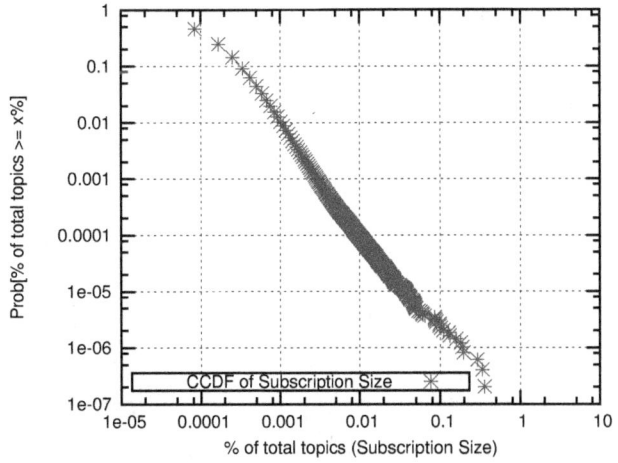

Figure 6: CCDF of Subscription Size per user

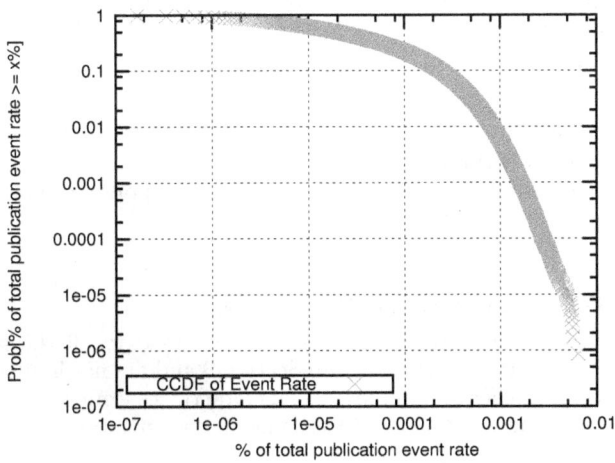

Figure 7: CCDF of Publication Event Rate per topic

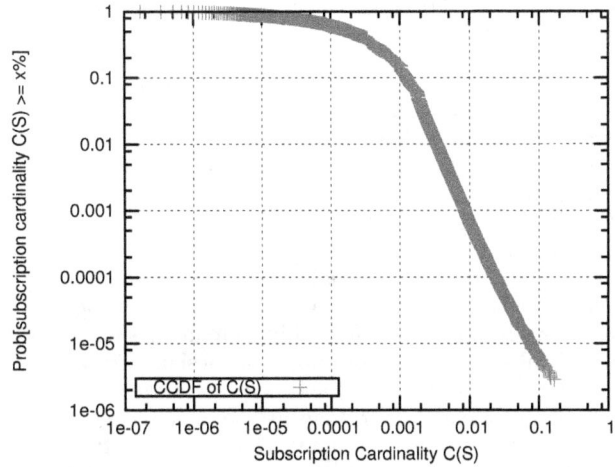

Figure 8: CCDF of Subscription Cardinality per user

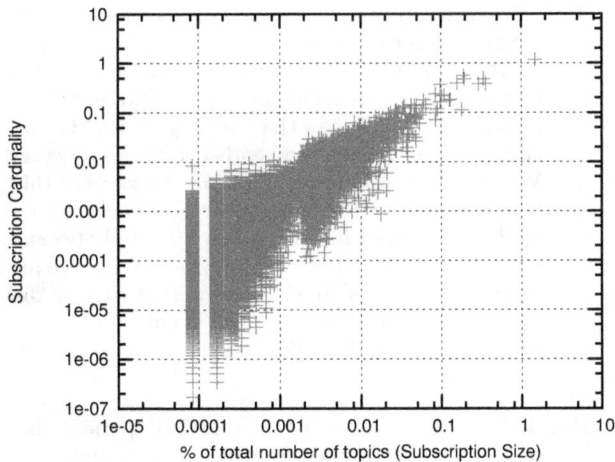

Figure 9: Relationship between subscription cardinality and subscription size (%of total number of topics)

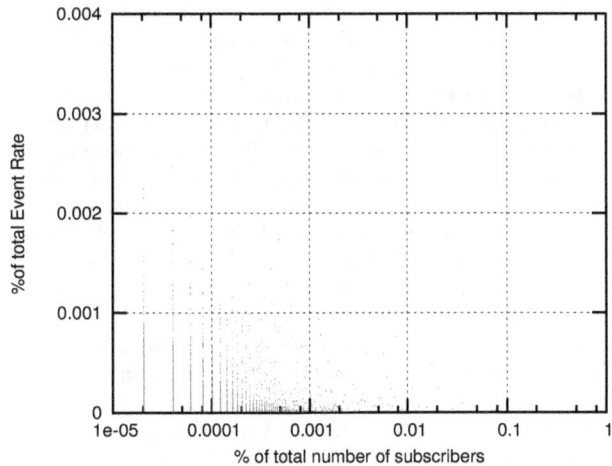

Figure 10: Relationship between topic Popularity (% of total number of subscribers) and Publication Event Rate

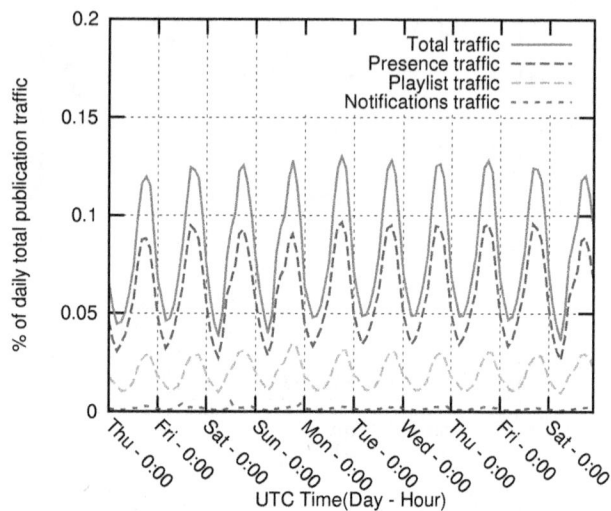

Figure 11: Pattern of publications generated per service-basis

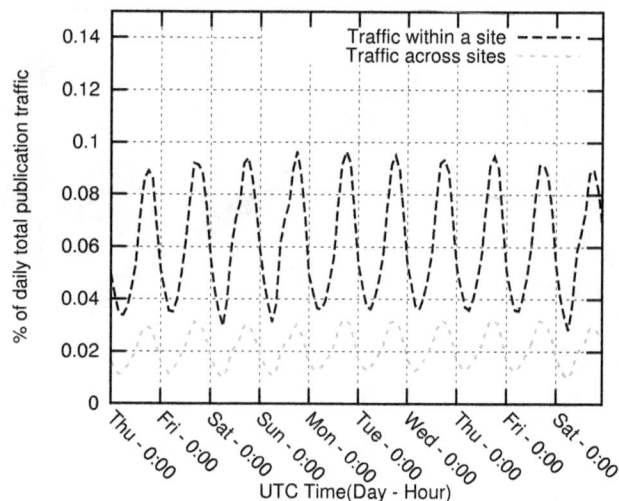

Figure 12: Publication traffic within the sites vs across the sites

Where, $\mathcal{T}$ is a global set of all topics, $S \subseteq \mathcal{T}$ is a set of topics subscribed by a subscriber, $ev(t)$ is the publication event rate of topic t. Thus, a subscriber with a subscription cardinality of, for example, 0.1%, receives 0.1% of all publications in the system.

In Figure 8 the x-axis is the cardinality of a subscription $C(S)$ and y-axis is the probability that a subscription has cardinality greater than or equal to that of corresponding value in x-axis (in other words CCDF). This distribution is an interesting result for the pub/sub community since cardinality of subscriptions is an important design parameter for many pub/sub systems [13] and they are generally estimated probabilistically. Our analysis shows a diverse subscription cardinality ranging from 0.2% to as low as 10^{-7}%. Also more than 90% of the subscribers have $C(S) < 0.001$% which shows a very low cardinality.

Each subscriber is allowed to subscribe to an arbitrary number of topics and that results in arbitrary subscription sizes for the subscribers. A study about the relationship between subscription sizes and the corresponding matching events is crucial to understand the resources needed to handle the publication traffic at the brokers. We do this study by considering each subscriber's subscription cardinality and the corresponding subscription size. We show in Figure 9 that, as the number of topics followed by a subscriber (i.e., subscription size) increases, the number of publications received by the subscriber (i.e, the cardinality) also increases linearly. In Figure 9 we show a 1% random sample of all the points due to significantly high number of data points slows down the pdf rendering.

As suggested earlier, the subscription workload for the *Spotify* pub/sub system is characterized by a social graph. However, when we study the topic popularity (number of subscribers of each topic) and the corresponding publication event rate for that topic, we see no correlation at all. i.e. a topic with very few subscribers can lead to significantly more publications than topics with many subscribers. This behavior is shown in Figure 10. We conjecture that the reason for this is that, unlike social networks, the activity in *Spotify* pub/sub is determined by the music listening behavior of users. This implies that a frequent listener of

music in *Spotify* does not necessarily have a high number of subscribers, similarly a user with many subscribers is not necessarily a frequent listener of music. We leave the confirmation of this conjecture for future research. Again we show a 1% random subset of the original data points to improve pdf rendering speed.

4.2 Pub/Sub Traffic Analysis

The following measurements correspond to all the publisher services mentioned in Section 3 and are not limited to the Presence service. We also include traces from all sites for these measurements for the same 10 days mentioned earlier.

4.2.1 Publication Traffic

First we study the distribution of publication traffic by separately decomposing it per service.

The Presence Traffic: From Figure 11 it is easy to observe that, for the Presence service, there is a periodic pattern of publication traffic on a daily basis with peak traffic towards the evening around 6 PM and the lowest traffic around 2 AM in the morning. Also, the traffic is slightly lower during weekends compared to weekdays. Without further analysis it is easy to see that this pattern is similar to the pattern for playbacks as observed in [2]. The reason for this pattern is simply because the publications generated by the Presence service are due to the playback of music tracks. It is easy to observe from Figure 11 that Presence events are the majority among the publication traffic, followed by Playlist events.

Playlist Traffic: There is a similar daily periodic pattern in the Playlist publication traffic, with highest traffic around 6 PM and lowest traffic around 2 AM. However, in contrast to the Presence service, the Playlist service traffic has slightly higher traffic on Sunday compared to the weekdays.

Notifications Traffic: For Notifications traffic, which includes updates to artist pages and updates from the

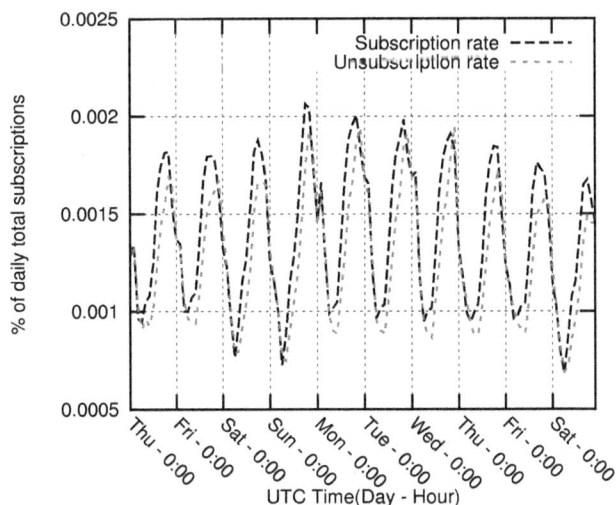

Figure 13: Subscription and unsubscription rate

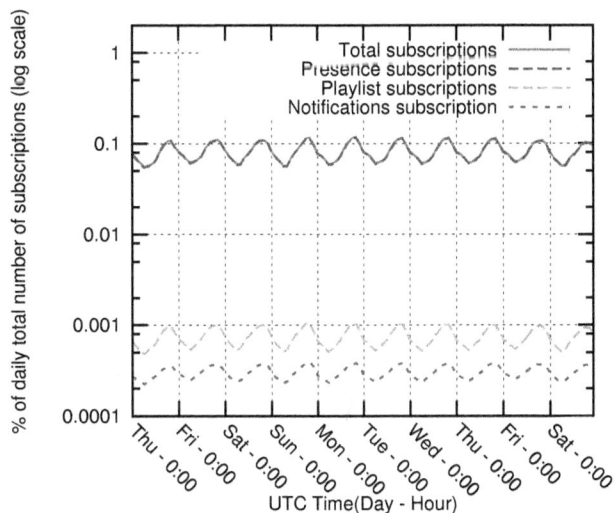

Figure 14: Pattern of percentage of total number of subscriptions

Social service, one can observe small spikes with notifications every day stemming from batch jobs launched for artist updates. Notice the significantly low traffic due to notification module compared to the Presence service and the Playlist service. This is in consistent with the hybrid design principle for real-time notification for the Presence service and offline notification for artist pages and social updates.

Next we compare the total publication traffic (from all services) generated from within the same site (local site) against the publication traffic generated from the rest of the sites (called remote sites). Remote traffic is due to the music activity of users in a remote site for which there is at least 1 subscriber in the local site. As we can observe from Figure 12, remote traffic is nearly an order of magnitude lower than local traffic. This result is in accordance with the design of *Spotify* pub/sub with each site having a pub/sub system designed to handle high local traffic, and low remote traffic with cross-site links at the pub/sub broker overlay (as described in Section 3.4).

4.2.2 Subscription Traffic

Figure 13 shows the pattern of subscriptions and unsubscriptions. There is a periodic pattern in subscriptions and unsubscription rates as well, and this is due to users joining and leaving *Spotify* at regular intervals. This periodic churn behavior can help model the churn of subscribers in a pub/sub system. Many research works [10, 14, 13] in the area of pub/sub use synthetic churn workloads or adapt churn traces from other peer-to-peer systems like file-sharing services or Skype. In this paper we characterize churn using traces from an actually deployed pub/sub system. Again, similar to publication traffic, subscription requests exhibit a daily pattern of evening peaks and early morning troughs as well. However, the weekly pattern of subscription patterns is significantly different from weekly pattern of publication traffic due to the simple fact that subscription traffic is due to the users logging in and out of the system while publication traffic is due to the playback of music. An interesting observation to make in Figure 13 is that the curve for unsubscription rate is ahead of the curve for subscriptions

approximately 2 hours on average. Also the rate of subscriptions and unsubscriptions match approximately, hence the number of subscriptions for a small period remain constant. This hypothesis is confirmed by Figure 14, which shows that there is little variation in the number of subscriptions for the chosen time period. In Figure 14 we can also see that the number of subscriptions is dominated by the Presence service. This is because *Spotify* users by default have more subscriptions to follow their friends than subscriptions to follow Playlists, artists and album pages. This also confirms our previous claim that the Presence traffic dominates *Spotify* pub/sub traffic.

4.3 Summary

Here is the summary of important observations from the analysis of the *Spotify* pub/sub workload:

- Topic popularity and subscription sizes follow a distribution close to a power law, similar to degree distributions in social graphs.

- The Publication Event Rate does not follow power law distribution.

- Subscription cardinality is significantly low (max 1%) and varies from 1% to as low as 10^{-7}%, indicating subscriptions with diverse subscription cardinality.

- Subscription cardinality of a subscriber is linearly proportional number of topics subscribed by that subscriber.

- The Publication Event Rate of a topic bears no relation to its popularity.

- Publication traffic shows a daily pattern. It is lowest at 2 AM and highest around 6 PM. It also shows a weekly pattern with slightly lower traffic during weekends.

- Publication traffic from local sites is much higher compared to publication traffic from remote sites.

- Subscription and unsubscription rates significant churn in subscriptions. However, the total number of subscriptions does not change much in a 10-day period.

- Both subscription and publication traffic is dominated by traffic related to the Presence service.

5. RELATED WORK

Pub/sub systems have been a subject of research for several decades, and a large number of topic-based pub/sub systems have been proposed in that period. Many academic research systems like Scribe [14], Bayeux [15], Tera [16], SpiderCast[17], Vitis [12], PolderCast[10] have focused on topic-based pub/sub. Several topic-based pub/sub systems have been proposed in the industry as well [4, 5].

However, supporting social interaction between *Spotify* users poses a specific set of requirements. There is a need to handle publications with different levels of criticality. As a result, there is a need for resource-efficient real-time delivery of events as well as reliable and offline delivery. *Spotify* also demands at-least-once delivery of events across all devices of the same user. In addition to that, there are multiple services generating publication events which need to be efficiently channeled via different paths to the subscribers. These requirements result in the need for a hybrid pub/sub system with different event flow paths.

Given the lack of real data, researchers in academia rely on synthetic workload generation techniques [14, 16, 18, 17]. Even though there have been some characterizations of pub/sub workloads from real systems in the past [6, 19, 8], they all mainly focus on characterizing the distribution of topic popularity in the workload. To the best of our knowledge, this work is the first to characterize the distributions of topic popularity, subscription sizes, distribution of per-topic publication event rate and its relationship with topic popularity, as well as the distribution of subscription cardinality and its relationship with subscription sizes. All of the analyses have been performed based on an actual deployed system.

6. CONCLUSIONS

In this paper, we presented the architecture of a system that allows *Spotify* users to follow playlists, artists, and the music activities of their friends. The architecture is realized by pub/sub, a popular communication paradigm. We described how a hybrid system with a scalable Pub/Sub Engine driven by a DHT overlay of brokers that facilitates real-time delivery of events and also a Notification Module to persist important events for offline notification as well as future retrieval of events. We did an extensive study of the system by analyzing real traces collected from an actual deployed system. We characterize the system workload, which helps model pub/sub workloads for research. We also analyze the pub/sub traffic at *Spotify* to derive trends and patterns.

Acknowledgments

We would like to thank the following engineers of *Spotify* specifically, for their invaluable inputs and support for this paper: Tommie Gannert, Mikael Goldmann and Javier Ubillos.

7. REFERENCES

[1] G. Kreitz and F. Niemela, "Spotify – large scale, low latency, P2P music-on-demand streaming," in *P2P*, 2010.

[2] B. Zhang, G. Kreitz, M. Isaksson, J. Ubillos, and G. Urdaneta, "Understanding user behavior in spotify," in *IEEE INFOCOM*, 2013.

[3] P. Eugster, P. Felber, R. Guerraoui, and A. Kermarrec, "The many faces of publish/subscribe," *ACM Computing Surveys*, 2003.

[4] J. Reumann, "GooPS: Pub/Sub at Google." Lecture & Personal Communications at EuroSys & CANOE Summer School, 2009.

[5] "Tibco rendezvous." http://www.tibco.com.

[6] H. Liu, V. Ramasubramanian, and E. G. Sirer, "Client behavior and feed characteristics of RSS, a publish-subscribe system for web micronews," in *IMC*, 2005.

[7] G. Li, V. Muthusamy, and H. Jacobsen, "A distributed service-oriented architecture for business process execution," *ACM Transactions on the web*, 2010.

[8] A. Yu, P. Agarwal, and J. Yang, "Generating wide-area content-based publish/subscribe workloads," in *Network Meets Database (NetDB)*, 2009.

[9] A. Lakshman and P. Malik, "Cassandra: a decentralized structured storage system," *SIGOPS*, 2010.

[10] V. Setty, M. van Steen, R. Vitenberg, and S. Voulgaris, "Poldercast: Fast, robust, and scalable architecture for P2P topic-based pub/sub," in *Middleware*, Springer-Verlag New York, Inc., 2012.

[11] A. Mislove, M. Marcon, K. P. Gummadi, P. Druschel, and B. Bhattacharjee, "Measurement and analysis of online social networks," in *SIGCOMM*, IMC, 2007.

[12] F. Rahimian, S. Girdzijauskas, A. Payberah, and S. Haridi, "Vitis: A gossip-based hybrid overlay for internet-scale publish/subscribe enabling rendezvous routing in unstructured overlay networks," in *IPDPS*, 2011.

[13] G. Li, *Optimal and Robust Routing of Subscriptions for Unifying Access to the Past and the Future in Publish/Subscribe*. PhD thesis, Graduate Department of Computer Science, University of Toronto, 2010.

[14] M. Castro, P. Druschel, A.-M. Kermarrec, and A. Rowstron, "Scribe: a large-scale and decentralized application-level multicast infrastructure," *IEEE Journal on Selected Areas in Communications*, 2002.

[15] S. Zhuang, B. Zhao, A. Joseph, R. Katz, and J. Kubiatowicz, "Bayeux: an architecture for scalable and fault-tolerant wide-area data dissemination," in *NOSSDAV*, 2001.

[16] R. Baldoni, R. Beraldi, V. Quema, L. Querzoni, and S. Tucci-Piergiovanni, "Tera: topic-based event routing for peer-to-peer architectures," in *DEBS*, 2007.

[17] G. Chockler, R. Melamed, Y. Tock, and R. Vitenberg, "Spidercast: a scalable interest-aware overlay for topic-based pub/sub communication," in *DEBS*, 2007.

[18] G. Chockler, R. Melamed, Y. Tock, and R. Vitenberg, "Constructing scalable overlays for pub-sub with many topics," in *PODC*, 2007.

[19] Y. Tock, N. Naaman, A. Harpaz, and G. Gershinsky, "Hierarchical Clustering of Message Flows in a Multicast Data Dissemination System," *Parallel and Distributed Computing and Systems (PDCS 05)*, 2005.

Event Stream Database Based Architecture to Detect Network Intrusion (Industry Article)

Vikram Kumaran
Cisco System, Inc.
vkumaran@cisco.com

ABSTRACT

This paper presents a novel network intrusion detection architecture built on a real-time streaming database platform. The architecture addresses both misuse and anomaly detection and is built to handle the high data volume, velocity and variety of traffic seen in enterprise networks through the use of in-memory stream processing. Traditional intrusion pattern detection systems look at the internal attributes of individual events to determine malicious intent; our architecture supports and extends that paradigm by adding the ability to detect both malicious and anomalous intrusion patterns in multi-step event sequences. The approach uses context based stream partitioning to minimize noise in input streams. The solution employs event labeling to reduce dimensionality and manage complexity of raw input streams. The architecture allows for aggregating alerts from an ensemble of detectors to provide a more reliable result by minimizing false positives. Furthermore, it allows domain experts to define high-level rules to filter trivial alerts. In this publication we will present the internals our architecture, its merits, along with a detailed description of our reference implementation.

Categories and Subject Descriptors

C.2 [**Communication/Networking and Information Technology**]: Security and Protection, Network Operations

Keywords

Stream Database; Intrusion Detection; Real-time Pattern Detection.

1. INTRODUCTION

Ours is a world of connected devices. The number of machines on the Internet grows by leaps and bounds every passing day. In a world of networked devices it has always been necessary to separate private information from public information; on the other side, there always has and will be malicious attempts at breaking that barrier. Intrusion detection is a critical step in protecting networks and it has moved beyond the capabilities of individual network operators looking at traps and alerts and deciphering intention. Intrusion detection requires a complete architecture that supports automated classification of behavior as normal, *misuse* (detecting known malicious attacks) or *anomalous* (detecting hitherto unknown attacks), along with the ability to bring in domain expertise to build rules to tease out important

alerts among all the alarms going off. In this paper we present an architecture that addresses these challenges.

Intrusion detection and prevention in real-time is a hard problem and there are many open challenges to be addressed. Most real-world commercial systems have accepted the approach of misuse-detection by matching network traffic with known intrusion signatures. However a library of signatures is never a complete set as new methods of intrusion are devised and variations are attempted. To deal with zero-day detection the community has devised algorithms that detect anomalous traffic. Anomaly detection is different than the traditional signature based approach, as one has to deal with a combinatorial explosion of valid but rare traffic patterns. When you add to the complexity of misuse and anomaly detection the volume of traffic in networks, the diversity of network traffic, and the inability of these systems to present alerts in a manner that domain expert can understand and act on, the problem becomes very challenging [17]. The shear volume of false positives that they tend to generate has muted the adoption of these systems. Work in this area has shown network traffic, not as a single stream but combination of many sub-streams with different characteristics (namely: application, protocol, hosts, port numbers etc.). By aggregating the results of different anomaly detection techniques that work differently for different sub-stream, the number of false positives can be managed to a large extent [18].

This paper describes a new architecture that handles both misuse and anomaly detection using a real time streaming database platform. Real-time streaming databases have been effectively used to identify critical situations in large distributed sensor networks [7]. In the next section we discuss literature related to our approach, followed by an architecture discussion and a detailed description of our reference implementation. We discuss automated detection mechanisms and how alerts can be combined with user defined rules to build complex detection schemes. Finally, we conclude comparing our architecture with the current state of art, by demonstrating how our system is a complete solution for the problem.

2. RELATED WORK

Successful intrusion detection systems with high success rates balance both signature based and anomaly detection [14]. Detecting predefined signatures exhibits low false positive rates but can be fooled easily when the attacks employ variations [12]. While the low false positives have encouraged many commercial systems like MacAfee and Sourcefire [22] to embrace a signature based approach, it is a manually intensive process to build comprehensive and accurate libraries. This approach is also limited by its inability to catch intrusions on day zero. Orthogonal to the signature based techniques are the anomaly detection algorithms. Early attempts relied on statistical measures to catch traffic outliers [13]. As interest in this area increased, techniques from machine learning like, support vector machines [10], neural networks [23] genetic algorithms [3], artificial immune systems [19] and many more, have been used with some success. Unlike signature-based approaches these techniques are primarily built for and are able to identify zero-day attacks. However these models are trained on attack-free datasets to catch outliers. This by its very nature leads to lots of false positives in the real world, as the closed world assumption typically does not hold [17]. Everything that is anomalous is not malicious; the possible combinations of acceptable but novel behavior are plenty. One approach that has successfully addressed the false positive count is the use of hybrid systems that employ multiple algorithms on the same data stream in parallel. Using a well-chosen methodology to combine alerts from multiple algorithms and determine intervention [18, 9]. In the following sections of this paper, we build on solutions provided above to define a complete IDPS platform that includes both misuse and anomaly detection and provides the flexibility for network operators to manage false positive alerts.

One of the interesting questions that come as we start to build systems that detect patterns of intrusion is the question of salient attributes in the data that are critical indicators of malicious access. Typically most systems discussed above have looked at payload and individual audit events to determine intrusion. There has been recent interest to not just focus on intrusive inspection of individual packets of network traffic but look at the traffic flow as a whole and build models that are based on flow patterns across the network [1]. Packet inspection starts becoming prohibitive at today's network speeds; add to that, the challenge created by encrypted protocols, and large distributed networks, we start to see the value of flow based detection, as a complementary approach in the arsenal [8]. In our architecture we allow for both, payload based detection and flow based detection to provide a comprehensive view of the network state.

At a high level one can think of intrusion detection as detecting patterns in network events similar to other solutions implemented in event processing systems process today [2]. Real-time database event management systems are used today in many places to process voluminous streams of data coming from various sensors to identify higher-level semantically salient events. They are used to analyze real-time events in many areas including control systems, network monitoring and sensor networks [7]. In our architecture we use a real-time event data stream-processing engine as the platform to build our intrusion detection system. We believe that event stream processing platforms provide the ability to efficiently handle large volume of data and provide powerful event processing languages that can be used to build sophisticated pattern detection mechanisms.

In the next section we will define a comprehensive architecture that can build context aware derived data streams, identify both known and zero-day attacks, with the capability to control false positives by using ensemble of parallel detection algorithms and domain expert defined rules. In the subsequent section we will elaborate on this architecture how it can be used as a platform to build a complete network intrusion detection system.

3. ARCHITECTURE

A high level view of our architecture is shown in Fig 1. The architecture breaks the IDPS system into four distinct modules that build on each other to achieve intrusion detection. The four modules abstract layers of information and structure over the raw stream and finally deliver actionable alerts for the network operator or an automated policy engine.

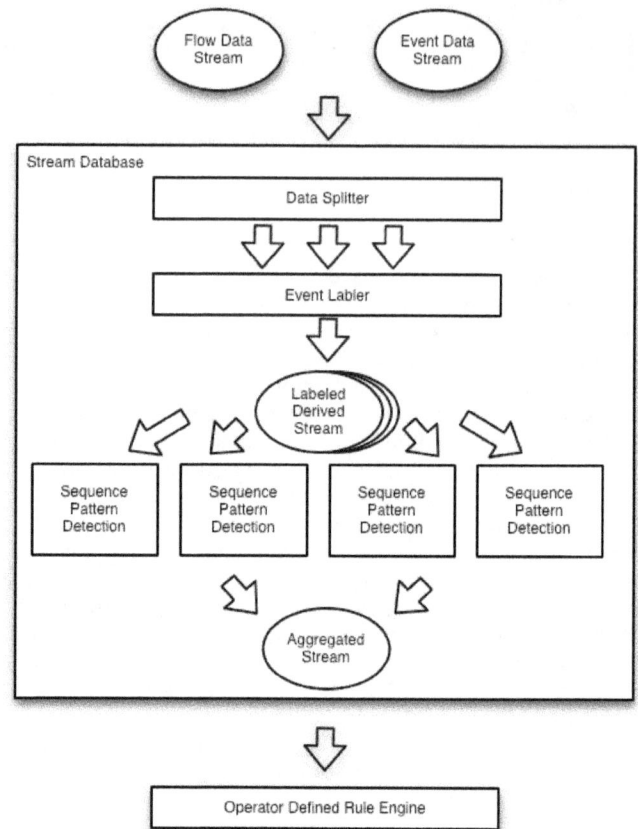

Figure 1. High Level Architecture Diagram

The *Data Splitter* module splits incoming event streams into distinct streams based on one or more specific characteristic that fall under the following four categories.

- *Physical* attributes like physical location, device type, MAC address etc.

- *Communication* attributes like communication protocols.

- *Network and Flow* characteristics like the bandwidth, throughput, number of connections etc.

- *Packet* content, in cases where we do deep packet inspection content of a network packet can be used to separate events into different streams

The *Event Labeler* looks at different streams and tags events. All tags used are predefined along with conditions that would trigger an event to be tagged. The precondition for a tag could be one or more of the following triggers

- *Threshold* based triggers set valid range or enumerations for attributes. If and when a value is found that is not within range or in the filter list the event is tagged with an appropriate label. For example, we could have a valid set of IP addresses a host can connect-to and if we notice that there has been a violation the event would be labeled as such.

- *Stochastic* triggers are based on statistical anomalies, like identifying an event with bandwidth being more than 2 standard deviations above historic mean.

- *Pattern* triggers look for specific value in an attribute or combination of attributes within that single event. An example would be finding a text snippet that identifies a worm in the network packet content, or noticing prohibited connection between two hosts using a disallowed communication protocol in a flow event.

The *Detection Module* runs both misuse and anomaly detection algorithms against the labeled derived streams and issues alerts on a match. Unlike the *Event Labeler* where the focus is on summarizing information in multiple attributes within an event into a set of labels with no concern for distinguishing malicious or normal traffic, the detection module looks for patterns that are malicious both within single events and in sequence of events. The different detection mechanisms are run in parallel on multiple streams. These parallel alerts are aggregated and when there is agreement between different algorithms a single alert event is sent. This prevents both event flooding and minimizes false alerts; a typical problem in intrusion detection systems.

The *Rules Module* contains human defined if-then rules that use the alerts generated by the previous steps as asserted facts and runs a standard Rete algorithm to determine subsequent action. This module helps network operators bring contextual information from outside systems not intrinsic to the event streams.

The architecture described above provides a complete solution and builds on the successful ideas of earlier research as described in previous sections to provide an effective intrusion detection platform. In the subsequent section we will describe in a little more detail the mechanisms and algorithms implemented within the modules described above.

4. REFERENCE IMPLEMENTATION

The key challenges faced by an IDS system are volume and velocity of data. Given the large volume and speed, the acceptable latency in analyzing the data is very small, new data is constantly streaming through the network and the traditional 'store-first-and-query-later' approach will not be able to meet the needs [6]. However, the workload characteristics are a perfect fit for a stream query processing system. We use in our architecture Cisco Prime Analytics (previously known as Truviso) platform's implementation of continuous query language called TruSQL; a superset of SQL [6].

While the details of TruSQL can be found in the publication by Franklin et. al. [6], here we will try to provide sufficient details to understand its application in our architecture. TruSQL defines a notion called a *stream* that is an ordered unbounded relation. The *stream* is ordered usually on a time attribute. TruSQL then lets you define queries on these streams. Unlike tables, *streams* are unbounded. TruSQL uses the idea of a time *window* to provide a bounded sequence of relations over which the SQL query is applied. Here is an example of a TruSQL query with a window clause.

```
SELECT url, count(*) url_count
FROM url_stream <VISIBLE '5 minutes'
ADVANCE '1 minute'>
WHERE url LIKE '%Order.do%'
GROUP BY url
ORDER BY url_count desc
LIMIT 10
```
Query 1: Example TruSQL Continues query

The above query should be very familiar to anybody who has seen SQL, the primary difference is the VISIBLE and ADVANCE keywords. The VISIBLE keyword specifies the time bound of 5 minutes over the stream and the ADVANCE keyword shifts the visible window by one minute every minute to move the window along as new data enters the stream. This is a typical continues

query in TruSQL. The language provides other windowing mechanisms like tumbling windows and landmark widows that facilitate different types of aggregations and filters on the stream.

One other feature that the platform provides is the ability to write multiple queries on streams, with all the richness and expressivity of SQL. These queries are called derived streams, as they themselves are unbounded streams of tuples emitted by the query after crunching through the raw stream. These derived queries can execute in parallel on raw streams and can also be chained to produce higher-level analytics.

The key take away is that, stream processing by doing bulk of the processing in memory as the data tuple enters the system, provides a very efficient, low latency solution for real-time analytics [6] and is a perfect fit for IDS as we will show in this paper.

4.1 Data Splitter

Data Splitter is the first module in our architecture that processes events published by our event collectors from sources like NetFlow, syslog, system traps etc.

The splitting of the raw stream into sub streams based on physical, communication, flow and packet characteristic is a simple matter of defining the right WHERE clauses in the continuous query to produce a derived stream. By providing different filter criteria on the query applied on a raw stream we can create context aware parallel streams from the same source and by simple inner/outer joins on the raw streams we can combine multiple streams into one, as well.

Shown below is an example of two continues queries that split a single Cisco NetFlow raw stream into two types of derived streams based on different characteristics: the first stream looks at flow events that is connected with traffic from and to a specific host on the network and the second creates a derived stream that only has flow events for SSH traffic.

```
CREATE STREAM 10_1_1_70_traffic_stream
    ( event_time cqtime,
      source_ip4,
      dest_ip4,
      counter_bytes
    ) AS
SELECT event_time, source_ip4,
    dest_ip4, src_port,
    dest_port, counter_bytes
FROM netflow_stream
WHERE source_ip4 = 10.1.1.70
  OR dest_ip4 = 10.1.1.70;
```

Query 2: Derived stream filtered on a specific host

```
CREATE STREAM ssh_traffic_stream
    (source_ip4, dest_ip4,
     traffic_bytes,
     event_time cqtime,
    ) AS
SELECT source_ip4, dest_ip4,
    src_port, dest_port,
    sum(counter_bytes) traffic_bytes,
    cq_close(*) as window_close_time
FROM netflow_stream <slices '1 minute'>
WHERE
    Nbar_app = 'ssh'
GROUP BY
    source_ip4, dest_ip4, dest_port, src_port;
```

Query 3: Derived stream filtered on communication protocol

These two queries create two independent parallel derived streams over which other processing can be done as will be shown below.

4.2 Event Labeler

The *Event Labeler* labels events based on attribute values in a stream. The three typical mechanisms for tagging events are threshold based, stochastic or pattern based labels. As we are building these streams using SQL it is possible to add more sophisticated logic as long as it can be expressed using SQL. The Cisco Prime Analytics system is built on top of Postgres and hence supports standard Postgres user defined functions (UDF), which can accommodate more detailed algorithms for labeling events. The queries below are simple illustration of how event labels can be applied to events.

```
SELECT source_ip4,
       dest_ip4,
       traffic_bytes,
       event_time,
      (CASE WHEN
                traffic_bytes > 1000,000
                THEN 'HIGH'
        ELSE 'LOW'
        END) as traffic_label
FROM
       ssh_traffic_stream;
```

Query 4: Event labeled based on a threshold value

```
SELECT sts.source_ip4,
       sts.dest_ip4,
       Sts.avg_bytes,
       sts.event_time,
      (CASE
        WHEN
              (hst.avg_traffic-sts_avg_bytes)>
              hst.std_dev*2
              THEN 'ABNORMAL'
       ELSE 'NORMAL'
       END) as traffic_label

FROM
     (SELECT source_ip4, dest_ip4,
        AVG(traffic_bytes) as avg_bytes,
        cq_close(*) as event_time,
        FROM
        ssh_traffic_stream
              <slices'10 minutes'>) as sts,
              historic_ssh_traffic as hst
     GROUP BY source_ip4, dest_ip4
```

Query 5: Event label based on stochastic attributes

```
SELECT source_ip, msg,
      (CASE WHEN
 msg ~ E'Authorization failed .?\(.*f\df\d'
        THEN 'ACCESS_ALERT_386'
        ELSE 'NORMAL'
        END) as alert_label
FROM syslog_stream;
```

Query 6: Event label based on pattern in attribute

The queries above are given as examples of how event labeling is done in principal. In the real implementations the setup requires user-defined functions to manage the mapping of patterns to labels instead of simple case statements. The mapping is managed through event-mapping tables that define how patterns,

thresholds and stochastic rules correspond to labels. This meta-table is the knowledge based that is used by a event-label UDF to dynamically assign labels to events on the stream in real-time. For stochastic labeling to work we need to have static tables defined with pre-calculated baseline statistics on historic data for comparison. In the case of pattern based queries Postgres supports regular expressions that can be used to match text patterns in attributes. In the examples above we only have constraints on single attribute and define only one label, but in a realistic implementation multiple attributes can be considered to produce a label and one attribute can generate multiple labels. Event labeler in our reference implementation works more like the derived stream definition below, where event attributes are sent to a user defined function that returns a list of labels for that event.

```
CREATE STREAM ssh_labeled_traffic_stream
       (source_ip4 as text,
        dest_ip4 as text,
        traffic_bytes as integer,
        event_time as timestamp cqtime ,
        event_labels as text[]

       ) AS
SELECT source_ip4, dest_ip4,
     traffic_bytes, event_time,
     Event_labler_udf(source_ip4, dest_ip4,
   traffic_bytes) as event_labels
FROM ssh_traffic_stream;
```

Query 7: Event labeling using a user defined function.

4.3 Detection Module

The output from the *Event Labeler Module* is a stream of labeled events. The next module in our architecture is the *Detection Module*. This module contains multiple sub-modules: each sub-module would implement different detection algorithms some are targeted towards misuse detection based entirely on attributes within the event, some towards misuse detection based on a sequence of events, some detect anomalous events based on individual event attributes and some identify anomalous sequence of events. The idea of multiple detection algorithms is based on the principal that by attacking the problem through different means we can gather more evidence to corroborate and identify true malicious events, minimizing false positives [11]

As described in earlier sections, there have been numerous techniques implemented over many years of research on network intrusion detection. The architecture described above and stream databases provide a perfect platform to implement many of these algorithms. In our reference implementation we model multiple techniques for both misuse and anomaly detection to demonstrate the platform's capability. Our implementation serves as a reference and shows the power and extensibility of the architecture. We can add more detection modules as necessary depending on the use case.

4.3.1 Intra-Event Intrusion Detection

For Intra-event misuse detection, the two algorithms we implement are signature based intrusion detection and event label classification. We describe the approaches below. These detection modules can work on the same stream or different parallel streams as necessary

Signature Based Intrusion Detection: Events have textual information that represents the context of the event. It could be error messages printed as part of a syslog event or it could be text extracted from TCP packets. Events could contain contextual information about host IP, communication protocol, destination port etc. We use an approach similar to the one suggested by Sommer et al. [16]. The query (8) below shows an example of how we can combine contextual information and regular expression signatures to catch salient events

```
SELECT "WEB_ATTACK" as alert_type
   FROM network_traffic_stream
   WHERE dest_ip << inet '192.168.1/24'
     AND protocol = 'TCP'
     AND dest_port = 80
     AND payload ~ E'*conf\/httpd\.conf'
```

Query 8: Combining contextual information with regex

The query's WHERE clause does a context aware regex match to determine a web attack. Obviously it is not possible to custom code queries for each alert type. In a real life system the rules are managed through a rules table with rows that define the stream to apply the rule along with context filters for the where clause and the regular expression for the payload. The rules are picked up from these meta-tables and used in matching signatures on events within a context. This is very similar in design to the *Event Labeler* meta-table design.

Classification Based Intrusion Detection: As we described in the *Event Labeler* module, every event is labeled with a set of event labels based on the attributes of the event. The classification needs to be segmented based on context, like communication protocol, etc. to get better accuracy in model predictions. The *Data Splitter module* splits raw streams into parallel streams based on context and the *Event Labeler* labels events based on event attributes, followed by the classifier. We train a Naïve Bayes classifier on the event labels to classify events as malicious or normal. The NB classifier is trained on historic, labeled, data. The reason we choose Naïve Bayes is because they are very simple to implement, are very fast at classification (an important feature for stream processing). NB is also competitive when compared to other methods used in intrusion detection [15]. The NB classifier is implemented as user defined function in the database and event labels are passed to it for classification.

Anomaly detection from just a single event's attributes can be done in many ways and in our reference implementation we choose a statistics based anomaly detection algorithm, as it does not require supervision or explicit labeling of normal and anomalous behavior and can catch zero day events without training.

Statistical Anomaly Detection: We look at the statistics of attributes like the number of connections to and from a host, the number of bytes coming in and going out of each host, applications on a host that generates traffic etc. and compare the averages from baseline historic 'normal' behavior to current behavior by calculating the Mahalanobis distance. Using a threshold to mark a flow event as anomalous or normal we catch malicious behavior. This is a simple mechanism for detecting outliers and has been used by other researchers for many years to successfully catch anomalies in their network [21]. What you consider "normal" differs considerably depending on the type of traffic. The Data Splitter modules splits streams based on different contextual attributes and the statistical parameters would be specific to the type of traffic in the stream. The context aware split of streams is important for reduced false alerts. The previous modules in the architecture, by segregating and contextualizing the stream, make it possible for this module to have better success rate.

4.3.2 Discrete Event Sequence Intrusion Detection

The detection modules described above focus on individual events, but in a real network malicious intrusion, individual events by themselves can be considered normal, as the intrusion attempt evolves over time, spanning multiple 'normal' events. Detecting known patterns or anomalous patterns in discrete sequence of events is an important challenge for intrusion detection.

As described earlier stream database provide windowing mechanism and event labeler labels individual events with one or more event tags. If we consider the possible event tags as an alphabet the sequence of events in a time window represents a string in that alphabet. Here is a simple query (9) to highlight the concept of converting a stream of events into a string.

```
SELECT t.host_id,
       regexp_matches(t.event_str,
E'((?:B|D){3,} P)(?=.*?[^H])')
   FROM
     (SELECT source_ip as host_id,
         array_to_string(array_agg(
       CASE WHEN (counter_Kbytes > 10000)
             THEN 'B' ELSE '' END ||
       CASE WHEN (dest_ip << inet '192.168.1/24')
             THEN 'D' ELSE '' END ||
       CASE WHEN (protocol = 'TCP')
             THEN 'P' ELSE '' END ||
       CASE WHEN (port = 80)
             THEN 'H' ELSE 'O' END), '')
             as event_str
       FROM netflow_stream
       GROUP BY source_ip) as t;
```

Query 9: Converting event label alphabet into strings

We can then use well studied methods in identifying know patterns and anomalous patterns in strings to catch misuse or anomaly detection as described below

Regular Expression Based Matching: As shown in the query (9) above, sequence of events can be represented as a string in a well defined alphabet and based on experience with known patterns of behavior during an intrusion we can detect these sequences in the event stream by defining regex patterns. For example if an external machine tries to connect to multiple ports on a specific destination devices within a very short period of time it might represent a misuse behavior and we can write a very regex pattern to catch that. This assumes prior knowledge of behaviors and is not ideal for zero day scenarios, but is an important arsenal in network intrusion detection. Based on experience we build libraries that can be matched against input event sequences to catch misuse. As described in earlier detection modules, these patterns are kept in a meta-table and matched against the event sequence string for the current time window to catch intrusion.

Clustering Based Anomaly Detection: We apply standard similarity based clustering techniques like k-medoid algorithm to get the set of medoids (event strings) that represent normal traffic by training on baseline data set of event 'strings' recorded during network operations with just normal traffic. The clustering algorithm is typically run offline, on historic data. As events arrive, we compare the strings in the current time window with the medoids of the training set, using a longest common subsequence (LCS) similarity measure. We mark the current event sequence as anomalous if the LCS is above the threshold for the closest medoid. This is similar to the kernel-based techniques described by Chandola et al. [20]. The training of the model should be re-done on a periodic basis to adjust for change in baseline behavior.

As always, there are new and better algorithms that are being developed and we would want to take advantage of them in our architecture. Our platform is flexible enough to accommodate most algorithms but there are some specific criteria we need to validate, as we are dealing with data rates that are very high.

Firstly, while the model building through training can be done in a batch mode through a time consuming process, the model checking to see if an event or an event sequence is normal or malicious needs to happen at network speeds. Secondly the modeling algorithm needs to scale to large datasets, as the training data sets are typically very large.

All the algorithms in the reference implementation have their advantages and disadvantages. They are very successful in detecting some types of intrusion while generating false positives in other contexts. To mitigate that problem, the architecture uses an ensemble of detectors to catch misuse and anomalies. Aggregating from an ensemble minimizes alert floods and helps manage false alerts. Aggregation of alerts is done through simple rules. In the case of anomaly detection, we forward alert along only if there is corroboration of multiple alerts raised for the same host within the current time window by multiple detectors. The number of detectors that need to corroborate is customizable.

4.4 Rules Module

Individual events or event sequences that have been labeled as malicious are then streamed to the final module in our architecture, which is the *Rules Module*. As described earlier the rules module provides an interface for a human expert to define rules on the alerts coming from the earlier modules. The module unlike the other modules described before lives outside the stream database platform, and in our reference implementation we implement it using the Drools rules engine [5]. Rule (1) below shows a simple if-then rule.

```
RULE "Ignore Backup"
    WHEN
        a:Anomaly (type == "HIGH_TRAFFIC",
                   host=="10.1.1.70")
        Time (hour < 23)

    THEN
        Server.email("Unusual traffic on host " +
                     a.getHost())
END
```
Rule 1: Sample Domain Expert Defined If-Then Rule

The *Rules Module* is critical to add another layer of filtering by experts to customize and fine-tune alerts specific to the network in which the system is operating. The rules also give domain experts the ability to bring in contextual data from outside the streams, like customer information or infrastructure information. In the example shown above (Rule 1) we ignore high traffic alert at between 11-12 in the night because the expert knows that, data backups are running during that time.

The reference implementation described above highlights the power of the platform and is flexible enough to be extended and to accommodate the needs of real life use cases.

5. CONCLUSION

Network intrusion detection is a complex problem that needs a large bag of tricks to work together for a good solution in the field. There is no one silver bullet or machine-learning algorithm that will solve the problem. Over many years researchers have found different approaches that work well within certain contexts. In this paper we have presented an architecture that is based on common wisdom about network intrusion solution. Our goal with this architecture has been to build a platform that will scale to the volume of data that stream within IT networks today, a platform that can compute and respond with sufficient speed to facilitate real-time action. A stream database is an ideal platform that can

handle both the volume of data and can provide actionable insight in real time for network applications [4].

Network traffic audit logs come from many sources: NetFlow, syslog, SNMP, traps etc. While the data sources are rich in terms of information, raw data streams need to be collected and collated based on context for detection mechanisms to work accurately. A noisy data stream is not suitable for building accurate models, which leads to missed detection. Our architecture provides a clean way to split raw data streams based on event attributes into context aware derived streams that are ideal for further analysis and pattern recognition.

When dealing with varied data streams the number of dimensions that is considered in intrusion detection quickly becomes unmanageable. In our architecture we provide an event labeling methodology to transform raw attribute data and combination of attributes into a smaller salient set of event labels and attributes that provide a more streamlined and manageable set of dimensions over which patterns and machine learning algorithms can be applied.

Intrusion can be classified as either known malicious behavior or unknown zero day attacks that are observed through anomalies in the network traffic. Misuse is detected by matching pre-built patterns while anomaly is detected through statistical or other machine learning methods targeting outliers. Our architecture recognizes the need for both types of detection and supports both type of detection techniques running in parallel on event streams. The architecture supports multiple detectors in parallel that can be expanded as the research continues and newer and better algorithms are discovered. One more feature that is important to highlight in our architecture is the ability aggregate alerts from multiple detectors to only report when there is strong evidence of intrusion. This is very important to prevent alert storms and false positives.

We also acknowledge in our architecture that alert management has an aspect of context that is usually obtained through years of experience managing the network. Domain experts need to be able to automate their knowledge to filter known spurious alerts and correlate different alerts based on their preference and intuition. The ability to add custom rules in the architecture allows domain experts to manage the alert streams the way they would prefer to manage the network.

All the features and capabilities described above provide a complete and customizable platform to detect intrusion in real time in the enterprise. Stream databases and network intrusion detection is a perfect match and our architecture leverages the power of stream based real-time analytics to solve the problem of intrusion detection.

6. ACKNOWLEDGMENTS
My thanks to Cisco Prime Analytics team for help and advice on using the TruCQ stream database.

This paper does not necessarily reflect the views of all Cisco Systems. Not all advice or views in this paper may be appropriate for your particular business or circumstances.

7. REFERENCES
[1] A. Sperotto, G. Schaffrath, R. Sadre, C. Morariu, A. Pras, and B. Stiller. 2010. An Overview of IP Flow-Based Intrusion Detection. Commun. Surveys Tuts. 12, 3 (July

2010), 343-356. DOI=10.1109/SURV.2010.032210.00054
http://dx.doi.org/10.1109/SURV.2010.032210.00054

[2] Amer Farroukh, Mohammad Sadoghi, and Hans-Arno Jacobsen. 2011. Towards vulnerability-based intrusion detection with event processing. In Proceedings of the 5th ACM international conference on Distributed event-based system (DEBS '11). ACM, New York, NY, USA, 171-182. DOI=10.1145/2002259.2002284 http://doi.acm.org/10.1145/2002259.2002284

[3] Chris Sinclair, Lyn Pierce, and Sara Matzner. 1999. An Application of Machine Learning to Network Intrusion Detection. In Proceedings of the 15th Annual Computer Security Applications Conference (ACSAC '99). IEEE Computer Society, Washington, DC, USA, 371-.

[4] Chuck Cranor, Theodore Johnson, Oliver Spataschek, and Vladislav Shkapenyuk. 2003. Gigascope: a stream database for network applications. In Proceedings of the 2003 ACM SIGMOD international conference on Management of data (SIGMOD '03). ACM, New York, NY, USA, 647-651.

[5] Drools, http://www.jboss.org/drools/

[6] Franklin, M. J., Krishnamurthy, S., Conway, N., Li, A., Russakovsky, A., & Thombre, N. 2009. Continuous analytics: Rethinking query processing in a network-effect world. In CIDR Conference.

[7] Gianpaolo Cugola and Alessandro Margara. 2012. Processing flows of information: From data stream to complex event processing. ACM Comput. Surv. 44, 3, Article 15 (June 2012), 62 pages.

[8] Gregor Schaffrath and Burkhard Stiller. 2008. Conceptual Integration of Flow-Based and Packet-Based Network Intrusion Detection. In Proceedings of the 2nd international conference on Autonomous Infrastructure, Management and Security: Resilient Networks and Services (AIMS '08). Springer-Verlag, Berlin, Heidelberg, 190-194.

[9] Hervé Debar and Andreas Wespi. 2001. Aggregation and Correlation of Intrusion-Detection Alerts. In Proceedings of the 4th International Symposium on Recent Advances in Intrusion Detection (RAID '00), Wenke Lee, Ludovic Mé, and Andreas Wespi (Eds.). Springer-Verlag, London, UK, UK, 85-103.

[10] Hu, W., Liao, Y., & Vemuri, V. R. 2003. Robust anomaly detection using support vector machines. In Proceedings of the international conference on machine learning, 282-289.

[11] Kai Hwang, Min Cai, Ying Chen, and Min Qin. 2007. Hybrid Intrusion Detection with Weighted Signature Generation over Anomalous Internet Episodes. IEEE Trans. Dependable Secur. Comput. 4, 1 (January 2007), 41-55.

[12] Karen A. Scarfone and Peter M. Mell. 2007. SP 800-94. Guide to Intrusion Detection and Prevention Systems (Idps). Technical Report. NIST, Gaithersburg, MD, United States.

[13] Lunt, T. F., Jagannathan, R., Lee, R., Whitehurst, A., & Listgarten, S. 1989. Knowledge-based intrusion detection. In AI Systems in Government Conference, 1989., Proceedings of the Annual, 102-107. IEEE.

[14] M. Ali Aydin, A. Halim Zaim, and K. Gokhan Ceylan. 2009. A hybrid intrusion detection system design for computer network security. Comput. Electr. Eng. 35, 3 (May 2009),

[15] Nahla Ben Amor, Salem Benferhat, and Zied Elouedi. 2004. Naive Bayes vs decision trees in intrusion detection systems. In Proceedings of the 2004 ACM symposium on Applied computing (SAC '04). ACM, New York, NY, USA, 420-424.

[16] Robin Sommer and Vern Paxson. 2003. Enhancing byte-level network intrusion detection signatures with context. In Proceedings of the 10th ACM conference on Computer and communications security (CCS '03). ACM, New York, NY,

[17] Robin Sommer and Vern Paxson. 2010. Outside the Closed World: On Using Machine Learning for Network Intrusion Detection. In Proceedings of the 2010 IEEE Symposium on Security and Privacy (SP '10). IEEE Computer Society, Washington, DC, USA, 305-316.

[18] Shashank Shanbhag and Tilman Wolf. 2009. Accurate anomaly detection through parallelism. Netwrk. Mag. of Global Internetwkg. 23, 1 (January 2009), 22-28.

[19] Steven Andrew Hofmeyr. 1999. An Immunological Model of Distributed Detection and its Application to Computer Security. Ph.D. Dissertation. The University of New Mexico. Advisor(s) Stephanie Forrest. AAI9926862.

[20] Varun Chandola, Arindam Banerjee, and Vipin Kumar. 2012. Anomaly Detection for Discrete Sequences: A Survey. IEEE Trans. on Knowl. and Data Eng. 24, 5 (May 2012), 823-839.

[21] Wang, K., & Stolfo, S. 2004. Anomalous payload-based network intrusion detection. In Recent Advances in Intrusion Detection, 203-222. Springer Berlin/Heidelberg.

[22] Young, G., & Pescatore, J. 2009. Magic quadrant for network intrusion prevention system appliances. Gartner Core RAS Research Note G, 167303, 1-12.

[23] Zhang, Z., Li, J., Manikopoulos, C. N., Jorgenson, J., & Ucles, J. 2001. HIDE: a hierarchical network intrusion detection system using statistical preprocessing and neural network classification. In Proc. IEEE Workshop on Information Assurance and Security, 85-90.

Tutorial: Stream Processing Optimizations

Scott Schneider
IBM Watson Research Center,
Yorktown Heights, NY, USA
scott.a.s@us.ibm.com

Martin Hirzel
IBM Watson Research Center,
Yorktown Heights, NY, USA
hirzel@us.ibm.com

Buğra Gedik
Computer Engineering Dept.,
Bilkent University, Turkey
bgedik@cs.bilkent.edu.tr

ABSTRACT

This tutorial starts with a survey of optimizations for streaming applications. The survey is organized as a catalog that introduces uniform terminology and a common categorization of optimizations across disciplines, such as data management, programming languages, and operating systems. After this survey, the tutorial continues with a deep-dive into the fission optimization, which automatically transforms streaming applications for data-parallelism. Fission helps an application improve its throughput by taking advantage of multiple cores in a machine, or, in the case of a distributed streaming engine, multiple machines in a cluster. While the survey of optimizations covers a wide range of work from the literature, the in-depth discussion of fission relies more heavily on the presenters' own research and experience in the area. The tutorial concludes with a discussion of open research challenges in the field of stream processing optimizations.

Categories and Subject Descriptors

D.3.4 [**Programming Languages**]: Processors—*optimization*; H.2.4 [**Database Management**]: Systems—*query processing*; D.4.8 [**Operating Systems**]: Performance—*operational analysis*

Keywords

Stream processing, optimizaition, data parallelism, fission

1 Introduction

We are living in an increasingly connected and instrumented world, where a large number and variety of data sources are available from various software and hardware sensors. These data sources often take the form of continuous data streams. Examples can be found in several domains, such as live stock ticker data in financial markets, call detail records in telecommunications, video streams in surveillance, production line status feeds in manufacturing, and vital body signals in health-care. In all of these domains there is a need to gather, process, and analyze data streams, detect emerging patterns and outliers, extract valuable insights, and generate actionable results. Most importantly, this analysis often needs to happen in near real-time.

Stream processing is a computational paradigm that enables carrying out these tasks in an efficient and scalable manner. Streaming applications are programs that process continuous data streams on-the-fly, as the data flows through the system. Various research communities have independently developed programming models and systems for streaming. While there are differences both at the language level and at the system level, each of these communities ultimately represents streaming applications as a *graph* of streams and operators. Since operators run concurrently, stream graphs inherently expose parallelism. At the same time, many streaming applications require high performance, and as a result each community has developed optimizations that go beyond this inherent parallelism.

Unfortunately, while there is plenty of literature on streaming optimizations, the literature uses inconsistent terminology. Furthermore, different communities have different assumptions that are often taken for granted. To address the terminology issue, this tutorial includes a survey of streaming optimizations using a uniform terminology. To address the diverse assumptions, the survey clarifies conditions that specify when the optimizations can be applied without changing the semantics of the applications, as well as when they are expected to improve the performance. This part of the tutorial is based on a survey paper by the authors [18].

Handling large volumes of live data in short periods of time is a major characteristic of streaming applications. Thus, supporting high throughput processing is a critical requirement for streaming systems. It necessitates taking advantage of multiple cores and/or host machines to achieve scale. This requires language and system level techniques that can effectively locate and efficiently exploit data parallelism in streaming applications. This latter aspect, called *fission*, is the focus of the second part of the tutorial.

Many streaming optimizations are limited in terms of the speedup they can bring, due to their strong dependence on application characteristics such as pipeline depth or filter selectivity. In contrast, the main limiting factor for data parallelism is the number of available cores, which can be easily scaled by providing additional hardware. As such, fission is a fundamental optimization that can provide good scalability as long as resources are available and the application is free of non-parallelizable bottlenecks.

This tutorial formalizes the problem of fission and provides details on how to apply it safely (no impact on appli-

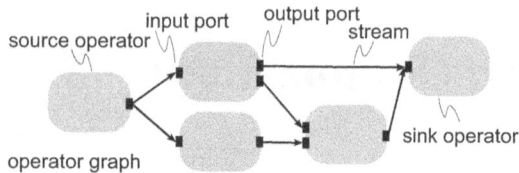

Figure 1: Basic concepts related to streaming applications.

cation semantics), transparently (no or minimal intervention from the application developers), and elastically (adaptive to run-time dynamics). Additional details on these topics can be found in our recent work [30].

This tutorial concludes by discussing open research challenges. The discussion includes both broad challenges valid for multiple optimizations, and in-depth challenges specific to fission. For example, the programming model design plays a big role in making many optimizations easier or harder to apply. Specifically, for fission, the programming model can help by providing well-defined interfaces for state.

The optimization techniques covered in this tutorial will help application developers to better understand performance trade-offs, compiler and run-time designers to implement safe and profitable optimizations, and researchers to explore new areas in streaming optimizations that are in need of technical innovations.

2   Background

This section provides a brief overview of fundamental concepts related to stream processing applications.

Operator Graphs

A stream processing application is organized as a *graph*, formed by a set of *operators* connected to each other by *streams*. A stream is a series of *data items*, where each data item consists of a set of *attributes*. Operators are generic data manipulators. They can have input and output ports. An operator fires when a data item is delivered to one of its input ports. During its firing, an operator can perform processing and produce data items on its output ports. Streams connect output ports of operators to input ports of other operators using FIFO semantics. A *source* operator does not have any input ports. It performs edge adaptation to receive data from an external source and converts it into a stream. Similarly, a *sink* operator does not have any output ports. It performs edge adaptation to deliver data from a stream to an external sink. Figure 1 illustrates these concepts.

State in Operators

A streaming operator that does not maintain state across firings is called *stateless*. For instance, a projection operator that drops some of the attributes of each data item is a stateless operator. Operators that maintain state across firings are called *stateful* operators. For instance, an operator that computes the maximum value of an attribute over the last 10 data items is stateful.

A special case of stateful operators is *partitioned stateful* operators. Such operators maintain independent state for non-overlapping sub-streams defined by a *partitioning attribute*. A typical example is the computation of volume weighted average price for each stock symbol in a financial trading stream, independently over the last 10 transactions involving each stock symbol. In this case, the partitioning attribute is the stock symbol and the data items with

a specific stock symbol value constitute a sub-stream. Independent state, which takes the form a window containing the last 10 data items, is maintained for each sub-stream.

Selectivity of Operators

Streaming operators with a single input and a single output port have a notion of *selectivity* associated with them. Selectivity is the number of data items produced per data item consumed. For example, a selectivity value of 0.1 means 1 data items is produced for every 10 consumed. Selectivity is an important property, as it is used in establishing safety and profitability in many optimizations. Many streaming operators have *dynamic selectivity*, where the selectivity value is not known at development time, and can change at runtime (such as data-dependent filtering, compression, or time-based windows).

Operators can be categorized based on their selectivities. Operators that always produce one data item for each data item consumed are said to have a selectivity of *exactly-one*. Operators that produce zero or one data items for each data item consumed have a selectivity of *at-most-one*. Finally, all other operators have *unknown* selectivity. An example of unknown selectivity is *prolific* operators, which produce more than one data items for each data item consumed.

We assume a programming model that does not restrict the selectivity of operators, even though we categorize the operators based on their selectivity and use this information for safety and profitability analysis. In contrast, *synchronous data flow* (SDF) languages [24] assume that the selectivity of each operator is fixed and known at compile time. While this provides an opportunity for the compiler to create static execution schedules, the resulting inflexibility reduces the set of applications that can be expressed in this model mostly to the signal processing domain.

Flavors of Parallelism

There are three main forms of parallelism that can be found in streaming applications. The first is *pipeline* parallelism, where an operator processes a data item at the same time its upstream operator processes the next data item. Since different operators in an operator graph can be executed on different cores, processors, or machines, this kind of parallelism is inherently present in streaming applications.

The second is *task* parallelism, where different operators process a data item in parallel. Task parallelism takes place when the data items produced by an operator are consumed by more than one downstream operator. For instance, in a video processing application, a frame generated by an operator can be used to perform face detection and background detection in parallel. Again, this kind of parallelism is inherent in the operator graph.

The third is *data* parallelism, where different data items are processed by the same operator in parallel. This is typically achieved by replicating the operator in question and routing data items to different replicas. There are two aspects of data parallelism that stand out. First, it needs to be extracted from the streaming application, as the operator graph needs to be modified to include new operator instances, a splitter needs to be included to route data items to replicas, and a merger is needed at the end to bring the results back. Second, it requires additional mechanisms to preserve the application semantics. For instance, the merger should reorder the data items so that the original order before the split is reestablished.

Safety and Profitability

An optimization is *safe* if the programs generated by applying it are guaranteed to maintain the semantics of the original program. Data parallelism is safe if the operators that are replicated are stateless or partitioned stateful. In the latter case, the routing needs to be done according to the partitioning key, so that each sub-stream is routed to a single replica. Equally importantly, safe data parallelism requires a reordering at the merger, details of which depend on the selectivity of the replicated operators.

Safety alone is not enough to make an optimization useful in practice. For that, we also need to make sure that the optimization applied increases the throughput. In the case of data parallelism, the optimization has a configuration option: the number of replicas. Determining the best setting that maximizes the throughput is the *profitability* problem.

The fission optimization aims at performing safe data parallelism that is profitable. It also aims at performing this *transparently*, such that the application developers do not need to explicitly deal with parallelizing their application.

Adaptive Optimization

The profitability of many optimizations depends not only on application characteristics (such as where the bottleneck is), but also on system dynamics (such as the workload and resource availability). As a result, ideally, the profitability decisions should be *adaptive*. For instance, when there is an increase in the workload availability, the number of replicas in fission would need to be increased.

An important challenge in making optimization profitability decisions adaptive is to satisfy the *SASO* properties of control systems: stability (do not oscillate wildly), accuracy (eventually find the most profitable operating point), settling (quickly settle on an operating point), and overshoot (steer away from disastrous settings).

3 Optimization Catalog

With the definitions from the previous section in place, this section surveys 11 common optimizations for streaming applications. The survey is presented in the form of a catalog, where each optimization has a subsection of its own, and all subsections follow a similar structure. This presentation format is inspired by catalogs for other concepts in computer science, such as design patterns or refactorings. For a more detailed version of this catalog, see our prior work [18]. Each subsection is structured as follows:

Name: For optimizations known under multiple names, we picked what we believe should be the definitive term.

Tag line: Brief summary of what the optimization does.

Figure: Before-and-after picture for the optimization.

Profitability: When and how the optimization is expected to improve performance.

Safety: Conditions to be checked to establish that the optimization preserves semantic equivalence.

Literature: Pointers to the most influential or unique work in the area (for a more thorough literature review see [18]).

Operator Reordering

Change the order in which operators appear in the graph.

Profitability: The core idea of operator reordering is to hoist selective operators upstream so they can eliminate some data items early. That way, expensive operators downstream can spend less time by not processing those data items. If operators A and B are equally selective, it is more profitable to put the less expensive one first. If operators A and B are equally expensive, it is more profitable to put the more selective one first.

Safety: Operator reordering is a common optimization in the relational domain. In that domain, safety is established via algebraic equivalence: $A(B(S)) \equiv B(A(S))$. However, in practice, many streaming operators are not simply relational operators. In that case, one way to establish safety from first principle is as follows. Reordering is safe if both operators are stateless, operator A reads only portions of data items that B forwards unmodified, and vice versa.

Literature: Graefe identified a special case where reordering is particularly profitable: when the merger at the end of a data-parallel region is immediately followed by the splitter at the beginning of the next data-parallel region, swapping them avoids a choke-point [16]. Eddies are a dynamic technique for finding the most profitable ordering of operators with independent selectivities [6]. Rather than literally rewriting the graph, Eddies instead change the data-item routing. Hueske et al. present a static analysis for Java that establishes reordering safety from first principle [20].

Redundancy Elimination

Eliminate operators that are redundant in the graph.

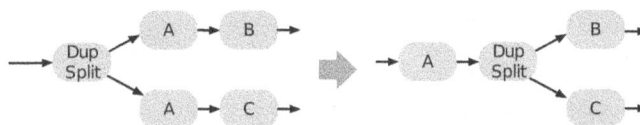

Profitability: Eliminating redundant operators is profitable if resources are limited. For example, if a redundant task takes time away on a core that could be put to better use, eliminating that task improves overall performance. A common cause for redundancy is compilation based on instantiating simple templates. In some cases, redundancy is not immediately obvious, and instead needs to be exposed by other optimizations. Another common cause for redundancy is multi-tenancy, where many users independently launch similar applications that can share subgraphs.

Safety: By definition, finding redundancy requires identifying equivalent computations. While this is undecidable in general, it can often be trivially established based on identical code, or more generally based on algebraic equivalences. One thing to look out for in redundancy elimination is that the state of the operators needs to be combinable as well.

Literature: The Rete algorithm is a seminal example for detecting and eliminating redundancies in a massively multi-tenant system, where applications are frequently launched and retracted [11]. NiagaraCQ applied similar ideas in the context of streaming XML processing [9]. Pietzuch et al. also eliminate redundancy at application launch time, while performing distributed placement [29].

Operator Separation

Separate an operator into multiple constituent operators.

Profitability: Operator separation can be profitable in and of itself via pipeline parallelism. If A_1 and A_2 each have roughly half of the cost of A, and their cost exceeds the communication overhead, then they can exploit an additional core to improve overall throughput. But often, operator separation is profitable by enabling other optimizations, such as fission or operator reordering. For example, MapReduce applications often separate the Reduce operator to extract a Combine operator, which they then reorder and piggy-back on the Map operator [10]. This optimization is valid in streaming systems as well.

Safety: Operator separation is among the more difficult optimizations to establish safety for. To do this from first principles, one must analyze the low-level code and establish all data dependencies. But there are several special cases where operator separation is easier. For example, an idempotent operator such as a Select or an associative Aggregate can be simply repeated. A Select operator can also be separated to filter one conjunct at a time. A Project operator can be separated to map one attribute at a time.

Literature: Algebraic equivalences for separating Select, Project, and other operators can be found in standard database text books [12]. Yu et al. present a compiler analysis that separates Aggregate operators with the help of user annotations [37]. Decoupled software pipelining separates general code by analyzing data dependencies from first principle [28].

Fusion

Fuse multiple separate operators into a single operator.

Profitability: Fusion is the dual of operator separation. Its main performance advantage comes from reduced communication overhead, and from enabling traditional (non-streaming) compiler optimizations on the fused operator. However, fusion requires sharing the same machine and potentially the same thread, thus using fewer available resources. In other words, with fusion, there is less opportunity for task or pipeline parallelism.

Safety: Fusion is among the easiest optimizations to establish safety for. It is usually safe, except when there are conflicts with placement constraints. For example, the user may request colocation, isolation, or exlocation of operators based on scarce resources such as FPGAs or network cards.

Literature: Fusion is a central optimization for the StreamIt programming language, because applications in that language tend to consist of a large number of fine-grained operators [15]. In Aurora, fusion is called superbox scheduling [8]. The COLA fusion optimizer for System S takes other placement safety constraints into account while striving for the most profitable solution [22].

Fission

Replicate an operator for data-parallel execution.

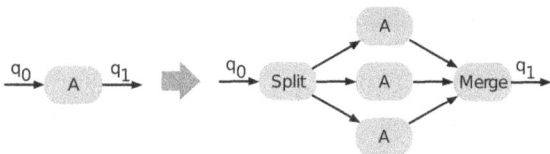

Profitability: Fission is most profitable when applied to an operator with a high processing cost per data item, and when the overhead of parallelization is low. In the ideal case, fission has the potential of improving throughput by a factor of N on N cores. In practice, speedups of $8\times$ or even $16\times$ are not uncommon, but the speedup is rarely ideal and usually tops out eventually. Besides parallelization overhead, load imbalance can also often get in the way, and is the subject of a separate optimization later in this section.

Safety: To be safe, fission must address state and ordering, and avoid deadlocks. In terms of state, fission is easiest if there is either no mutable state or if the state can be partitioned such that each data-parallel operator replica owns a disjoint subset. Otherwise, stateful fission requires synchronization. In terms of ordering, fission is trivially safe when no ordering is required; otherwise, ordering must be enforced by the runtime system, for example, via sequence numbers. Fission can cause deadlocks if there is a circular wait condition, where the splitter waits for buffers to be drained before sending data, but the merger waits for a data item with a particular sequence number before draining buffers.

Literature: The StreamIt compiler derives large benefits from fission of stateless operators with static selectivity [14]. Schneider et al. explored how to make fission safe in the more general case of partitioned-stateful and selective operators [30]; that work is the topic of the deep-dive in Section 4. Finally, Brito et al. propose using transactional memory to make fission safe in the case of arbitrary operator state [7].

Placement

Place the logical graph onto physical machines and cores.

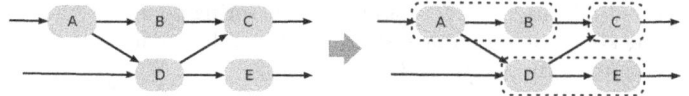

Profitability: Placement is profitable if it maximizes resource utilization while minimizing communication. Assume a distributed streaming system. On the one hand, colocating operators on the same machine can cause resource contention, for instance, on cores or the disk. On the other hand, spreading operators around too much can cause unnecessary cross-machine communication. A good placement finds profitable middle ground between these extremes.

Safety: The safety of placement is easy to establish, unless there are special resource constraints. For instance, a particular operator may only work on a GPU, which may be available only on certain machines. Another safety challenge consists in dynamically changing the placement of a stateful operator, because the state must be migrated transparently.

Literature: An early version of the StreamIt compiler explored placement on a multi-core with non-uniform memory access [15]. Pietzuch et al. explored placement in a stream-based overlay network [29]. And SODA combines placement with job admission in a distributed streaming engine that runs on a cluster [36].

Load Balancing

Avoid bottleneck operators by spreading the work evenly.

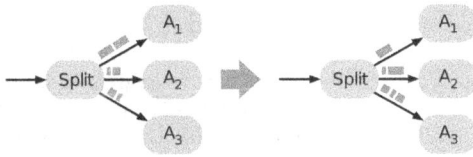

Profitability: The throughput of a stream graph is usually bounded by its slowest operator. Load balancing strives to spread the work around evenly so that all nodes in the system can operate near capacity. Thus, the profitability of load balancing depends on how imbalanced the load was to begin with, and how well it can be balanced. In the case of data parallelism (fission), load balancing can be accomplished at the splitter by routing data items to each operator replica that add up to roughly the same amount of work.

Safety: Balancing load by routing data items to data-parallel replicas assumes that all replicas are qualified to handle all data items they receive. This is easy if they are stateless, but more challenging when they have state. Besides data-item routing, another approach to load balancing is operator placement, which of course is subject to its own safety constraints explained in the previous subsection.

Literature: A good resource for load balancing via routing data items is the River work [5]. On the other hand, examples for load balancing via operator placement include the StreamIt compiler [15] as well as Amini et al.'s work [2].

State Sharing

Share identical data stored in multiple places in the graph.

Profitability: On general-purpose hardware, applications are unlikely to just flat run out of memory. Rather, they would experience throughput and latency degradation due to exceeding the L1 cache, L2 cache, or even main memory. Therefore, state sharing is profitable if it helps keep data closer to the processor, thus avoiding the slower layers of the memory hierarchy. Another performance advantage of state sharing is that it can help avoid data copies, allocation, and serialization, all of which cost time.

Safety: State sharing is typically combined with fusion, because it is easier to share state when running in the same process. If each operator still has its own thread, safe state sharing must avoid race conditions by properly handling mutability, synchronization, and scheduling. Another concern with state sharing is avoiding memory leaks by releasing the shared state when none of the co-owners need it anymore.

Literature: Brito et al. tackle general state sharing between data-parallel operator replicas using transactional memory [7]. A more restrictive case is sharing window state only, which both StreamIt [14] and CQL [3] support. Finally, an even more restrictive, but common and profitable, case shares the state of a queue between two pipelined operators [31].

Batching

Communicate or compute over multiple data items as a unit.

Profitability: Batching improves throughput by amortizing some fixed overheads over multiple data items, such as

communication, indirect calls through layers of the stack, and bringing code and auxiliary data into the cache or into registers. Batching trades throughput against latency: individual data items have longer latency because they wait for a batch to fill. Therefore, in systems where latency matters, batching must ensure data items are still processed within their deadlines. Batching creates inner loops that traditional (non-streaming) compilers are good at optimizing.

Safety: In latency-critical systems, users may view the adherence to deadlines as a safety issue rather than a profitability issue. Aside from that, batching poses few safety challenges. One thing to look out for is potential deadlocks in cyclical graphs, if an operator waits for a batch to form at its input, but that batch does not fill up because of missing output from the same operator.

Literature: The SEDA architecture relies on a dynamic batching controller for picking a profitable batch size [35]. Aurora refers to batching as train scheduling [8]. StreamIt performs batching statically, calling it execution scaling [31].

Algorithm Selection

Replace an operator by a different operator.

Profitability: The idea of operator selection is, of course, to pick a less expensive operator. In some cases, there is a choice between multiple operators with equivalent functionality, and it depends on the data characteristics which one is less expensive. In other cases, the default operator is more general, and the other operator is less general but faster.

Safety: Algorithm selection poses a safety question when the operators differ not just in performance, but also in functionality. In other words, if the faster operator is less general, we must establish that it is applicable based on the configuration. There are even cases where strict semantic equivalence can be sacrificed for performance. An example for that is using an approximation algorithm. This usage of algorithm selection is a variant of load shedding, discussed below.

Literature: The SEDA architecture enables an operator to pick a different algorithm to provide degraded service [35]. Borealis enables an operator to switch to a different algorithm based on a control input [1]. And the SODA optimizer offers algorithm selection at the granularity of entire jobs, to run a variant of a job that is cheaper but lower-quality [36].

Load Shedding

Degrade gracefully during overload situations.

Profitability: The core idea of load shedding is to sacrifice some accuracy so requests do not pile up when the offered load exceeds the processing capacity. This is often a latency issue: by dropping some data items, the remaining ones that are not dropped get processed fast enough to satisfy their deadlines. Sometimes, there are also priorities involved: by dropping less important data items, the more critical ones need not get dropped.

Safety: Given that Section 2 defines safety as semantics preservation, load shedding is by definition unsafe. However, the alternative (not shedding load) is also unsafe if it

```
composite Main {
  type
    Entry = tuple<uint32 uid, rstring server, rstring msg>;
    Summary = tuple<uint32 uid, int32 total>;
  graph
    stream<Entry> Messages = ParSrc() {
      param  servers:     "logs.*.com";
             partitionBy:  server;
    }
    stream<Summary> Summaries = Aggregate(Messages) {
      window  Messages:   tumbling, time(5), partitioned;
      param   partitionBy:  uid;
      output  Summaries:  uid = Any(uid), total = Count();
    }
    stream<Summary> Suspects = Filter(Summaries) {
      param  filter:      total > 100;
    }
    () as Sink = FileSink(Suspects) {
      param  file:        "suspects.csv";
             format:      csv;
    }
}
```

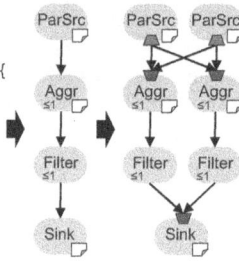

Figure 2: Example SPL program (left), its stream graph (middle), and the parallel transformation of that graph (right). The paper icons in the lower right of an operator indicate state, and the numbers in the lower left indicate selectivity.

means that the system crashes or otherwise fails to live up to its specification, such as quality of service. Therefore, the goal cannot be safety, but rather maximizing accuracy within the constraints of load and resources.

Literature: The Scout operating system uses a data-flow model for its network layer, among other things to enable informed load-shedding decisions [26]. The Aurora streaming engine implements priority-based load shedding [33]. And Compact Shedding Filters ship the task of load shedding from the server to data-generating sensors to avoid unnecessary network communication [13].

4   Fission

This section presents a deep-dive into the fission optimizations, which was briefly mentioned in the optimization catalog (Section 3). The catalog is platform and language agnostic. However, in order to study an optimization in practice, we must look at a specific platform and language. We will first introduce the System S platform and the SPL language [17], and then discuss applying fission there.

System S and SPL

The programming model behind SPL is asynchronous, as it allows operators to have dynamic selectivity. The System S platform allows for distributed execution.

Figure 2 presents a sample SPL program [17] on the left. The program is a simplified version of a common streaming application: network monitoring. The application continually reads server logs, aggregates the logs based on user IDs, looks for unusual behavior, and writes the results to a file.

The types Entry and Summary describe the structure of the *tuples* in this application. A tuple is a data item consisting of attributes, where each attribute has a type (such as uint32) and a name (such as uid). The stream graph consists of operator invocations, where operators transform streams of a particular tuple type.

The first operator invocation, ParSrc, is a source that produces an output stream called Messages, and all tuples on that stream are of type Entry. The ParSrc operator takes two parameters. The partitionBy parameter indicates that the data is *partitioned* on the server attribute from the tuple type Entry. Thus, {server} is this operator's partitioning *key*.

The Aggregate operator invocation consumes the Messages stream, indicated by being "passed in" to the Aggregate operator. The window clause specifies the tuples to operate on, and the output clause describes how to aggregate input tuples (of type Entry) into output tuples (of type Summary). This operator is also partitioned, but this time the key is the uid attribute of the Entry tuples. Because the Aggregate operator is stateful, we consider this operator invocation to have *partitioned state*. The Aggregate operator maintains separate aggregations for each instance of the partitioning key ({uid} in this case).

The Filter operator invocation drops all tuples from the aggregation that have no more than 100 entries. Finally, the FileSink operator invocation writes all of the tuples that represent anomalous behavior to a file.

The middle of Figure 2 shows the stream graph that programmers reason about. In general, SPL programs can specify arbitrary graphs, but the example consists of just a simple pipeline of operators. We consider the stream graph from the SPL source code the *sequential semantics*, and the fission optimization seeks to preserve such semantics.

The right of Figure 2 shows the stream graph that the runtime will actually execute. First, the compiler determines that the first three operators can have data parallelism, and it allows the runtime to replicate those operators. The operator instances ParSrc and Aggregate are partitioned on different keys. Because the keys are incompatible, the compiler instructs the runtime to perform a *shuffle* between them, so the correct tuples are routed to the correct operator replica. A shuffle is a bipartite graph between the end of one parallel region and the beginning of the next. The Filter operator instances are stateless and can accept any tuple. Hence, tuples can flow directly from the Aggregate replicas to the Filter replicas, without another shuffle. Finally, the FileSink operator instance is not parallelizable, which implies that there must be a merge before it to ensure it sees tuples in the same order as in the sequential semantics.

Safety

In the context of fission, *safety* means preserving an application's sequential semantics. Doing so requires support in both the compiler and the runtime.

Compiler

The compiler's task is to decide which operator instances belong to which parallel regions. Furthermore, the compiler picks implementation strategies for each parallel region, but not the degree of parallelism. One can think of the compiler as being in charge of safety while avoiding platform-dependent profitability decisions.

As usual in compiler optimization, the approach is conservative: the conditions may not always be necessary, but they imply safety. The conditions for parallelizing an individual operator instance are:

- **No state or partitioned state:** The operator instance must be either stateless, or its state must be a map where the *key* is a set of attributes from the input tuple. Each time the operator instance fires, it only accesses its state for the given key. Safe fission gives each operator replica a disjoint partition of the key domain.

- **At most one predecessor and successor:** The operator instance must have fan-in and fan-out ≤ 1. This means parallel regions have a single entry and exit where the runtime can implement ordering.

254

The conditions for forming larger parallel regions with multiple operator instances are:

- **Compatible keys:** If there are multiple stateful operator instances in the region, their keys must be compatible. A key is a set of attributes, and keys are compatible if their intersection is non-empty. Using the intersection as the region key ensures that the splitter is at most as fine-grained as any individual operator's key.

- **Forwarded keys:** Care must be taken that the region key as seen by a stateful operator instance o indeed has the same value as at the start of the parallel region. This is because the split at the start of the region uses the key to route tuples, whereas o uses the key to access its partitioned state map. All operator instances along the way from the split to o must forward the key unchanged.

- **No shuffle after prolific regions:** A prolific region is a region with prolific operators. Prolificacy causes tuples with identical sequence numbers. Within a single stream, such tuples are still naturally ordered. But after a shuffle, this ordering could be lost. Therefore, the compiler does not allow a shuffle at the end of a prolific region.

The compiler must establish the previously described safety conditions. We must first distinguish an operator definition from an operator invocation. The *operator definition* is a template, such as an Aggregate operator. It provides different configuration options, such as what window to aggregate over or which function (Count, Avg, etc.) to use. Since SPL users have domain-specific code written in C++ or Java, we support user-defined operators that encapsulate such code. Each operator definition comes with an *operator model* describing its configuration options to the compiler. The *operator invocation* is written in SPL and configures a specific instance of the operator, as shown in Figure 2. The operator instance is a vertex in the stream graph.

We take a two-pronged approach to establishing safety: *properties* in the operator model for operator definitions and *program analysis* for operator invocations in SPL. This is pragmatic and requires some trust: if the author of the operator deceives the compiler by using the wrong properties in the operator model, the optimization may be unsafe. Operator models must specify whether or not they have *state*, how *selective* they are, and whether or not they *forward* all attributes on input tuples.

In most cases, analyzing an SPL operator invocation is straightforward given its operator model. However, operator invocations can also contain imperative code, which may affect safety conditions. State can be affected by mutating expressions. Selectivity can be affected if the operator invocation calls submit to send tuples to output streams. Our compiler uses data-flow analysis to count submit-calls. If submit-calls appear inside of if-statements, the analysis computes the minimum and maximum selectivity along each path. If submit-calls appear in loops, the analysis assumes that selectivity is Unknown.

Runtime

The System S runtime has a concept of *Processing Elements* (PEs), which are a group of operators that the fusion optimization has been applied to. They execute inside of a single operating system process. The runtime support for fission is mostly concerned with PEs, as parallel regions are composed of PEs.

The runtime has two primary tasks: routing tuples to parallel channels, and enforcing tuple ordering. Parallel regions should be semantically equivalent to their sequential counterparts. In a streaming context, that equivalence is maintained by ensuring that the same tuples leave parallel regions in the same order regardless of the number of parallel channels.

Routing and ordering are achieved through the same mechanisms: *splitters* and *mergers* in the PEs at the edges of parallel regions. Splitters exist on the output ports of the last PE before the parallel region. Their job is to route tuples to the appropriate parallel channel, and add any information needed to maintain proper tuple ordering. Mergers exist on the input ports of the first PE after the parallel region. Their job is to take the streams from each parallel channel and merge their tuples into one, well-ordered output stream. The splitter and merger must perform their jobs invisibly to the operators both inside and outside the parallel region.

When parallel regions only have stateless operators, the splitter routes tuples in round-robin fashion, regardless of the ordering strategy. When parallel regions have partitioned state, the splitter uses the attributes that define the partition key to compute a hash value. It then uses that hash to route the tuple, ensuring that the same attribute values are always routed to the same operators.

There are two classes of ordering strategies: implicit and sequence number based. Implicit ordering strategies can be applied to parallel regions that contain only stateless, non-selective operators. In such cases, the splitter and merger can conspire on the order in which tuples are split to, and merged out of, a parallel region. In these cases, no extra information is needed on the tuples themselves to maintain the correct order.

Sequence number based ordering strategies are required when operators in a parallel region are stateful, selective, or prolific. While there are various kinds of specializations, the general idea is that the splitter attaches sequence numbers to all tuples, and the merger uses those sequence numbers to put the tuples back in order.

Profitability

The previous section is concerned with how to discover opportunities to safely extract data parallelism, and how to safely execute it in a runtime system. However, discovering where fission can be safely applied does not answer the basic question: is it profitable? In the context of fission in a streaming system, solving profitability means finding how many parallel channels to use in a parallel region.

In synchronous streaming systems, it may be possible to answer the profitability question statically, at compile time. But in asynchronous streaming systems with user-defined operators, it is impractical to determine profitability statically, which means the decision must happen at runtime.

The following sections describe what problems a solution to dynamic profitability for fission must solve.

Control Algorithm

Dynamically determining the number of parallel channels in a parallel region means that there must be a runtime control algorithm. The input to the control algorithm must be a runtime metric that system implementers wish to use to determine profitability. Fission in particular, and data parallelism in general, tend to pay attention to throughput. However, one could devise an objective function which also uses latency, so as to cap the potential harm to latency while improving throughput. The control algorithm's job is to determine the number of parallel channels that maximizes this objective function.

However, observing *only* throughput and latency may not be enough for a control algorithm to obey all of the SASO properties described in Section 2. Instead, the control algorithm needs a metric to tell it whether operators in a parallel channel have reached their capacity limit. Detecting capacity limitations drives the algorithm, and observing the effect on the objective function checks the accuracy of that capacity detection.

The general approach for the control algorithm is to detect when all of the active parallel channels can not handle any more capacity. In such a case, there is evidence that adding parallel channels will increase throughput. The control algorithm then increase the number of channels, and after the next period, determines if throughput increased. If throughput increased, then it will stay at at least this number of channels, and then evaluate capacity again. If throughput decreased, then it will backtrack by decreasing the number of channels.

State Management

Operators in a parallel region may have partitioned state. As the control algorithm changes the degree of parallelism, operators that were maintaining state for a partition may become dormant, and the tuples they would have handled will be routed elsewhere. To maintain sequential consistency, the operators that remain active in the parallel region must adopt the partitions from the dormant operators. The same issue arises when parallel channels are added: in order to maintain an even spread, the new channels must adopt some partitions that existing channels are responsible for. Adopting partitions means that state must be migrated across operators.

State migration across operators in a streaming system involves several challenges. First, in normal operation, the tuples are always flowing. If an operator migrates a partition's state, then receives a tuple in that partition, sequential consistency will be violated. Hence, in order to maintain sequential consistency, tuples must not flow in the parallel region while partition state is in flux. In order to ensure that tuples do not flow during state migration, the splitter and all of the operators in the parallel region must obey a protocol that stops their flow while state is moving, and starts it again once state has settled.

A second challenge is avoiding too many state transfers while maintaining an even partition distribution among the operators. As the number of parallel channels expands and contracts, operators donate and adopt partitions. However, any given donation or adoption phase should transfer only the minimal amount of state. Balancing minimal state transfers with maintaining an even distribution requires collusion between the operators and the splitter. All of the operators must be able to deterministically decide which partitions they must donate or adopt, and the splitter must agree with these decisions. The splitter's goal is to use a hashing algorithm that is likely to produce a balanced distribution of partitions while minimizing state movement. In practice, consistent hashing schemes can solve these problems [21].

5   Open Research Problems

So far this paper was mostly about existing work. The preceding sections aimed to help users either hand-optimize their code, or understand automatic optimizations applied to their code. They also aimed to help implementers build more efficient streaming systems. In contrast, this section is about what is missing in existing work. By exploring which challenges are still open, and have not been fully solved yet, it aims to help researchers come up with new ideas. These open challenges are grouped into subsections. Each subsection first describes a broad spectrum of high-level research opportunities that apply across the range of optimizations from Section 3. Following that, each subsection makes the discussion more concrete for the fission optimization from Section 4. That way, each subsection highlights both high-level longer-term and specific shorter-term opportunities.

Programming Model Challenges

A *programming model* for stream processing is either a stream programming language (such as StreamIt [34], CQL [3], or SPL [17]), or a library that exposes the functionality of a streaming system as a framework (such as SVM [23], S4 [27], or Storm [32]). Programming model design is an exercise in juggling several, sometimes conflicting, goals. The programming model needs to be expressive enough so the domain of applications it works for is not too narrow. At the same time, it needs to be amenable to static analysis and have clear semantics to facilitate optimizations. A new programming model needs a foreign-code interface for incorporating legacy code written in other languages. And the more familiar a new programming model looks and feels, the easier it is to adopt by a broad community.

Our own work with fission taught us several programming model lessons. One is that even when the programming model is a new language, optimizations must also take libraries in existing languages into account. For fission, that meant providing operator models that assert properties about state, selectivity, etc.; and providing an API for state to be called from C++ but handled by the streaming runtime system. Another lesson was that since partitioning plays such a central role in fission, it should be a first-class concept in the language as well.

Optimization Combination

If a streaming system supports two or more of the optimizations described in Section 3, one question is how to combine them. One approach is to just apply them one by one. The order of optimizations matters. For instance, performing operator separation early opens up opportunities for other optimizations such as operator reordering. Conversely, fusion should happen late, as it makes other optimizations more difficult. But rather than performing optimizations separately one by one, another option is to truly combine them, making a unified profitability or safety assessment. Since different optimizations have their own cost models, combining them leads to new research challenges.

Being a particularly profitable optimization, fission is a prime candidate for combining with other optimizations, such as fusion, load balancing, placement, and batching. Of course, fission can be extended not just with other optimizations, but also with transformations for different purposes than optimization. For instance, both fission and fault tolerance can be accomplished by replicating operators.

Interaction with Traditional Compilers

We use the word *traditional* compiler to refer to a compiler for a non-streaming language such as Fortran, C, or Java. Traditional compilers play a role at both ends of compiling a streaming language. First, besides new features for supporting stream processing, a streaming language usually also has features in common with traditional languages, such as expressions with function calls, arithmetic, variable accesses, and so on. Compiler analysis on such expressions is used to establish safety properties for optimizations. Second, many compilers for streaming languages generate source code for non-streaming languages, which must then still be compiled by a traditional compiler. The traditional compiler comes with its own traditional optimizations, such as function inlining or loop unrolling. Overall performance is best if the code generated by the streaming compiler is easy to optimize by the non-streaming compiler.

Fission is a prime example for an optimization that can benefit from traditional compiler analysis. The analysis can discover information about state, ordering, selectivity, and attribute forwarding that drives the safety decisions for fission. One challenge with this is to analyze general or even legacy code. At the other end, examples of streaming optimizations that interact with downstream traditional compiler optimizations include batching and fusion more than fission. Batching gives rise to loops that a traditional compiler can unroll and optimize. And fusion gives rise to function calls that a traditional compiler can inline. The challenge is to ensure that generated code does not obscure these opportunities. For example, calls are easier to inline if they are monomorphic and part of the same compilation unit.

Dynamic Optimization

A *dynamic* optimization is performed at runtime, as opposed to static optimizations that are performed before the application starts. Some optimizations, such as load balancing or load shedding, are dynamic by nature. But many optimizations, in particular those that modify the operator graph such as operator reordering and fusion, are more typically static. Dynamic optimizations have the advantage that they can use profiling information with statistics about the currently ongoing run, and can even adapt to changes in load or resources. The challenge for dynamic optimizations is to satisfy the SASO properties of control systems outlined earlier in Section 2. Eddies are an example for operator reordering at runtime without actually changing the graph [6], whereas Flextream is an example of pausing the application to rewrite the graph at runtime [19]

In the case of fission, an important dynamic optimization is *elasticity*, which means dynamically changing the degree of parallelism. The main challenge here is profitability: picking the degree of parallelism that yields the best performance. This is complicated when there are multiple parallel regions, each of them with its own degree of parallelism, or when parallel regions nest. Another challenge with dynamic fission is state migration for stateful operators. While the authors have done some work along those lines, there are opportunities for further improvement by minimizing the disruption while the degree of parallelism is being changed.

Benchmarks

Demonstrating that an optimization indeed improves performance requires benchmarks. Everyone can make up a micro-benchmark, but the question is how representative that is of real applications. Realistic benchmarks are required to evaluate both generality (does the optimization work for real cases?) and profitability (is the effect large enough to matter in practice?). The LinearRoad benchmark is an advanced streaming application in the transportation domain [4]. The BiCEP micro-benchmarks demonstrate whether or not relational streaming engines implement certain optimizations [25]. And the StreamIt benchmarks encompass 65 audio, video, and digital signal processing workloads [34]. Together, they offer different viewpoints from different communities on the rapidly evolving field of stream computing.

Fission nicely illustrates the challenges in curating a benchmark suite. On the one hand, the StreamIt benchmark suite is the most comprehensive set of streaming applications available, totaling 33,000 lines of code, including 30 realistic applications and 35 micro-benchmarks. On the other hand, all of these applications are in the media-processing domain. Only 25% of StreamIt benchmarks have any stateful operators, which would simplify both the profitability and safety problems for fission. However, stateful operators appear to be more prevalent in commercial applications for transportation, communication, finance, science, and health-care.

Generality of Optimizations

The approach to establishing safety is almost always conservative: optimizers err on the side of caution by finding sufficient conditions, not necessary conditions. The idea is to support the common case, and not optimize uncommon cases when their safety conditions are too difficult to prove. Unfortunately, as discussed above under benchmarks, it is often not known what the common cases are in practice. Hence, generalizing an optimizer to make its safety conditions more liberal is fertile ground for intricate research challenges. Such work needs to be motivated with workload characterization to demonstrate practical relevance.

To make the discussion concrete, consider the safety conditions for fission. Fission can be more or less conservative when it comes to state, ordering, topology, and user code. In each case, there is a spectrum from more restrictive and easier to handle cases to more liberal but harder to handle cases. For state, the spectrum ranges from stateless to partitioned stateful to arbitrary stateful operators. Ordering is easier to handle for static selectivity than for dynamic selectivity. The internal topology of a data-parallel region can range from a single operator to a simple pipeline of operators to a general subgraph. And in terms of user code, the spectrum ranges from built-in operators only to code that is user-defined in the streaming language to user-defined legacy code in a foreign language to code-generation.

6   Conclusion

This tutorial aims at helping users understand streaming optimizations and performance trade-offs, helping implementers optimize their streaming systems and languages, and helping researchers select relevant and original problems. The tutorial starts with a survey of stream processing optimizations, in the form of a catalog for easy cross-referencing. Following the broad survey comes a deep-dive into fission, a particularly effective optimization that introduces data parallelism. The tutorial concludes with a discussion of open research questions, both for streaming optimizations in general and for fission in particular.

Acknowledgments

We thank our co-authors from prior work: Kun-Lung Wu worked on the fission optimization with us [30], and Robert Soulé and Robert Grimm worked on the optimization catalog with us [18]. The optimization catalog is currently under submission for a journal article.

7 References

[1] Daniel J. Abadi, Yanif Ahmad, Magdalena Balazinska, Uğur Cetintemel, Mitch Cherniack, Jeong-Hyon Hwang, Wolfgang Lindner, Anurag S. Maskey, Alexander Rasin, Esther Ryvkina, Nesime Tatbul, Ying Xing, and Stan Zdonik. The design of the Borealis stream processing engine. In *Conference on Innovative Data Systems Research (CIDR)*, pages 277–289, 2005.

[2] Lisa Amini, Henrique Andrade, Ranjita Bhagwan, Frank Eskesen, Richard King, Philippe Selo, Yoonho Park, and Chitra Venkatramani. SPC: A distributed, scalable platform for data mining. In *Workshop on Data Mining Standards, Services and Platforms (DM-SSP)*, pages 27–37, 2006.

[3] Arvind Arasu, Shivnath Babu, and Jennifer Widom. The CQL continuous query language: semantic foundations and query execution. *Journal on Very Large Data Bases (VLDB J.)*, 15(2):121–142, 2006.

[4] Arvind Arasu, Mitch Cherniack, Eduardo Galvez, David Maier, Anurag S. Maskey, Esther Ryvkina, Michael Stonebraker, and Richard Tibbetts. Linear road: A stream data management benchmark. In *Very Large Data Bases (VLDB)*, pages 480–491, 2004.

[5] Remzi H. Arpaci-Dusseau, Eric Anderson, Noah Treuhaft, David E. Culler, Joseph M. Hellerstein, David Patterson, and Kathy Yelick. Cluster I/O with River: Making the fast case common. In *Workshop on I/O in Parallel and Distributed Systems (IOPADS)*, pages 10–22, 1999.

[6] Ron Avnur and Joseph M. Hellerstein. Eddies: Continuously adaptive query processing. In *International Conference on Management of Data (SIGMOD)*, pages 261–272, 2000.

[7] Andrey Brito, Christof Fetzer, Heiko Sturzrehm, and Pascal Felber. Speculative out-of-order event processing with software transaction memory. In *Conference on Distributed Event-Based Systems (DEBS)*, pages 265–275, 2008.

[8] Don Carney, Uğur Cetintemel, Alex Rasin, Stan Zdonik, Mitch Cherniack, and Mike Stonebraker. Operator scheduling in a data stream manager. In *Very Large Data Bases (VLDB)*, pages 838–849, 2003.

[9] Jianjun Chen, David J. DeWitt, Feng Tian, and Yuan Wang. NiagaraCQ: A scalable continuous query system for internet databases. In *International Conference on Management of Data (SIGMOD)*, pages 379–390, 2000.

[10] Jeffrey Dean and Sanjay Ghemawat. MapReduce: Simplified data processing on large clusters. In *Operating Systems Design and Implementation (OSDI)*, pages 137–150, 2004.

[11] Charles L. Forgy. Rete: A fast algorithm for the many pattern/many object pattern match problem. *Artificial Intelligence*, 19:17–37, 1982.

[12] Hector Garcia-Molina, Jeffrey D. Ullman, and Jennifer Widom. *Database Systems: The Complete Book*. Pearson / Prentice Hall, second edition, 2008.

[13] Bugra Gedik, Kun-Lung Wu, and Philip S. Yu. Efficient construction of compact shedding filters for data stream processing. In *International Conference on Data Engineering (ICDE)*, pages 396–405, 2008.

[14] Michael I. Gordon, William Thies, and Saman Amarasinghe. Exploiting coarse-grained task, data, and pipeline parallelism in stream programs. In *Architectural Support for Programming Languages and Operating Systems (ASPLOS)*, pages 151–162, 2006.

[15] Michael I. Gordon, William Thies, Michal Karczmarek, Jasper Lin, Ali S. Meli, Andrew A. Lamb, Chris Leger, Jeremy Wong, Henry Hoffmann, David Maze, and Saman Amarasinghe. A stream compiler for communication-exposed architectures. In *Architectural Support for Programming Languages and Operating Systems (ASPLOS)*, pages 291–303, 2002.

[16] Goetz Graefe. Encapsulation of parallelism in the Volcano query processing system. In *International Conference on Management of Data (SIGMOD)*, pages 102–111, 1990.

[17] Martin Hirzel, Henrique Andrade, Buğra Gedik, Vibhore Kumar, Giuliano Losa, Mark Mendell, Howard Nasgaard, Robert Soulé, and Kun-Lung Wu. Streams processing language specification. Research Report RC24897, IBM, 2009.

[18] Martin Hirzel, Robert Soulé, Scott Schneider, Buğra Gedik, and Robert Grimm. A catalog of stream processing optimizations. Research Report RC25215, IBM, 2011.

[19] Amir Hormati, Yoonseo Choi, Manjunath Kudlur, Rodric M. Rabbah, Trevor N. Mudge, and Scott A. Mahlke. Flextream: Adaptive compilation of streaming applications for heterogeneous architectures. In *Parallel Architectures and Compilation Techniques (PACT)*, pages 214–223, 2009.

[20] Fabian Hueske, Mathias Peters, Matthias J. Sax, Astrid Rheinländer, Rico Bergmann, Aljoscha Krettek, and Kostas Tzoumas. Opening the black boxes in data flow optimization. In *Very Large Data Bases (VLDB)*, pages 1256–1267, 2012.

[21] D. Karger, E. Lehman, T. Leighton, R. Panigrahy, M. Levine, and D. Lewin. Consistent hashing and random trees: Distributed caching protocols for relieving hot spots on the world wide web. 1997.

[22] Rohit Khandekar, Kirsten Hildrum, Sujay Parekh, Deepak Rajan, Joel Wolf, Lung Kun-Wu, Henrique Andrade, and Bugra Gedik. COLA: Optimizing stream processing applications via graph partitioning. In *International Conference on Middleware*, pages 308–327, 2009.

[23] Francois Labonte, Peter Mattson, William Thies, Ian Buck, Christos Kozyrakis, and Mark Horowitz. The Stream virtual machine. In *Parallel Architectures and Compilation Techniques (PACT)*, pages 267–277, 2004.

[24] E. A. Lee and Messerschmitt D. G. Synchronous data flow. *Proceedings of the IEEE*, 75(9), 1987.

[25] Marcelo R. N. Mendes, Pedro Bizarro, and Paulo Marques. A performance study of event processing systems. In *TPC Technology Conference on Performance Evaluation & Benchmarking (TPC TC)*, pages 221–236, 2009.

[26] David Mosberger and Larry L. Peterson. Making paths explicit in the Scout operating system. In *Operating Systems Design and Implementation (OSDI)*, pages 153–167, 1996.

[27] Leonardo Neumeyer, Bruce Robbins, Anish Nair, and Anand Kesari. S4: Distributed stream processing platform. In *Workshop on Knowledge Discovery Using Cloud and Distributed Computing Platforms (KDCloud)*, 2010.

[28] Guilherme Ottoni, Ram Rangan, Adam Stoler, and David I. August. Automatic thread extraction with decoupled software pipelining. In *International Symposium on Microarchitecture (MICRO)*, pages 105–118, 2005.

[29] Peter Pietzuch, Jonathan Ledlie, Jeffrey Shneidman, Mema Roussopoulos, Matt Welsh, and Margo Seltzer. Network-aware operator placement for stream-processing systems. In *International Conference on Data Engineering (ICDE)*, pages 49–61, 2006.

[30] Scott Schneider, Martin Hirzel, Buğra Gedik, and Kun-Lung Wu. Auto-parallelizing stateful distributed streaming applications. In *International Conference on Parallel Architectures and Compilation Techniques (PACT)*, pages 53–64, 2012.

[31] Janis Sermulins, William Thies, Rodric Rabbah, and Saman Amarasinghe. Cache aware optimization of stream programs. In *Languages, Compiler, and Tool Support for Embedded Systems (LCTES)*, pages 115–126, 2005.

[32] Storm. http://storm-project.net/. Retrieved April, 2013.

[33] Nesime Tatbul, Uğur Cetintemel, Stan Zdonik, Mitch Cherniack, and Michael Stonebraker. Load shedding in a data stream manager. In *Very Large Data Bases (VLDB)*, pages 309–320, 2003.

[34] William Thies and Saman Amarasinghe. An empirical characterization of stream programs and its implications for language and compiler design. In *Parallel Architectures and Compilation Techniques (PACT)*, pages 365–376, 2010.

[35] Matt Welsh, David Culler, and Eric Brewer. SEDA: An architecture for well-conditioned, scalable internet services. In *Symposium on Operating Systems Principles (SOSP)*, pages 230–243, 2001.

[36] Joel Wolf, Nikhil Bansal, Kirsten Hildrum, Sujay Parekh, Deepak Rajan, Rohit Wagle, Kun-Lung Wu, and Lisa Fleischer. SODA: an optimizing scheduler for large-scale stream-based distributed computer systems. In *International Conference on Middleware*, pages 306–325, 2008.

[37] Yuan Yu, Pradeep Kumar Gunda, and Michael Isard. Distributed aggregation for data-parallel computing: Interfaces and implementations. In *Symposium on Operating Systems Principles (SOSP)*, pages 247–260, 2009.

Tutorial: Open Source Application Integration

Introducing the Event Processing Capabilities of Apache Camel

Christoph Emmersberger
Universität Regensburg
Universitätsstraße 31
93053 Regensburg
christoph@emmersberger.org

Florian Springer
Senacor Technologies AG
Wieseneckstr. 26
90571 Schwaig b. Nürnberg
florian.springer@senacor.com

ABSTRACT

"Interesting applications rarely live in isolation." ([1], xxix) With this sentence G. Hohpe and B. Woolf start the introduction to their book *Enterprise Integration Pattern: Designing, Building, and Deploying Messaging Solutions*. While the statement is valid now for more than ten years, Gartner estimates today the cost increase targeting integration aspects for midsize to large companies at about 33% within the next three years (cf. [2]). The expected increase will be mainly driven by the integration of cloud services and mobile devices. Since event processing addresses clearly problems arising with the growth of computational distribution, particularly with the increasing number of mobile devices or cloud services, integration is a topic that needs to be addressed by event processing functionalities.

One of the frameworks within the integration domain is *Apache Camel*. Since it's initial release in 2007, the framework has gained quite some attention - not only within the open-source arena. *Apache Camel* has a strong focus on enterprise application integration since it implements well known *Enterprise Integration Patterns (EIP's)* (cf. [1]).

This work reveals the event processing capabilities of *Apache Camel* alongside a logistics parcel delivery process. The delivery process facilitates the scenario descriptions to exemplify the event processing functionalities within a real-world context. All coding examples, supporting the functionality demonstration, are setup around the shipment of parcels.

General Terms

Software Engineering

Keywords

Integration Framework, Event Processing

1. INTRODUCTION

"Enterprise Application Integration is the creation of business solutions by combining applications using common mid-

dleware." ([3], 2) Middleware specifies a technology stack which is capable to mediate between applications with the overall goal of improving the supply-chain relationships in a distributed application environment. One of the frameworks supporting the mediation between applications coming from the open-source domain is the integration framework *Apache Camel*. The first version of *Camel* has been released in version 1.0 the 2nd July 2007 - just three and a half month after the development had started (cf. [4]).

Regardless of the short development period, the first release covered already two domain specific languages (DSL's) based on Java and XML, the core routing functionality, an initial set of components, examples and a proper project setup [5]). Since than, *Camel* has become an Apache top level project in January 2009. Beside those organizational changes, the project has faced continuous growth which can be exemplified by

- the growing number of committers (starting at seven being a group of more than 30 today),

- an increasing code base which is today more than ten times the size of the first release and

- the growing number of components from an initial set of 18 to todays 140 components (including external components) listed at the *Camel* website (cf. [6]).

In August 2009, *Camel* has experienced a major release (cf. [7]). Since that time, it is available in version two which is still actively maintained. Having said that *Camel* is a middleware technology and "(...) middleware can be regarded as containing the roots of a hierarchical approach to events and event processing (...)" ([8], 37), we can also identify a clear relationship between enterprise application integration and event processing.

Within this tutorial paper we introduce *Apache Camel's* event processing capabilities. The first section gives a brief introduction into the context of a parcel delivery process. The process description does not claim to be generally valid; it's aim is furthermore to serve as consistent basis for all use case descriptions when characterizing the individual event processing functions and their corresponding *Camel* implementation.

After having a rough overview about the supply-chain interactions, the second section brings event processing and it's functionalities into the focus of this work. In this connection we'll cover the the topic's: *"Event type and event object"*, *"event producer, consumer and channel"*, the *"event processing network"* and *"event processing agents, context and state"*.

The subsections *event processing network, event producer, consumer and channel* and *event type* provide an introduction into the concepts of *Apache Camel* while creating cross references to event processing *building blocks* ([9], 59). The section on *event processing agents, context and state* will be covered in a software pattern like structure (cf. [1], xli and [10], 7). Since it is unquestionable a topic of it's own, setting a well defined structure for a pattern, we do not intend to impose any standardization along that line. Instead the pattern like descriptions collates the commonalities of both structures to describe event processing agent functionalities in a consistent manner.

Name identifies the event processing function. The intention of the name is also to provide a brief summary of the described functionality.

Context provides background information on requirements the event processing function aims to resolve. The context information is grouped around the parcel delivery process (cf. chapter 2)

Problem summarizes the problem that is being addressed by the event processing function in general without any contextual description.

Solution describes how *Camel* addresses the problem conceptually. The solution is based upon a graphical representation and a textual description that explaining the solution design.

Example demonstrates the implementation of the solution design with the *Apache Camel* framework. The description contains listings and descriptive elements that explain the implementation approach.

Finally this paper concludes in chapter 4 with a summary of *Camel's* event processing capabilities and discusses possible extensions supporting today's event processing needs.

2. BACKGROUND: PARCEL DELIVERY

A common parcel logistics delivery process (cf. [11], 171), starting with a customer order and ending with reconciliation and invoicing activities, serves as industrial context on which we will discover different event processing functionalities and their corresponding implementation within *Camel*. The generalized process consists of *Order Management, Delivery Disposition, Delivery Execution* and *Order Reconciliation* (see figure 1).

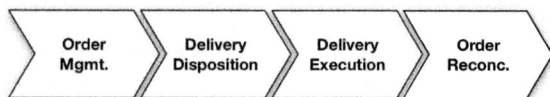

Figure 1: Parcel Delivery Process

Order Management enables the placement of transportation orders across multiple distribution channels. The distribution channel is e.g. an internet portal, an application installed at the customer location, a call center or even a mobile application. An electronic order triggers the physical pickup of an item before the delivery execution can start.

Delivery Disposition is the scheduling component within the parcel delivery process. Amongst others, it defines the size of the delivery area and schedules transportation routes. For distributing the scheduling information, the disposition step needs to integrate with the delivery execution, i.e. sorting sites, navigation systems and scan facilities.

Delivery Execution realizes the actual transport process encompassing *Pickup, Sortation, Transportation* and *Delivery*. At all stages, multiple devices with different hard and software configurations provide status information about an individual order, e.g. mobile scan devices during *Pickup* and *Delivery*, fixed installed scan systems during the *Sortation* process and positioning information while the *Transportation* is being conducted.

Order Reconciliation covers the invoicing and customer care activities. In case of any failures within the delivery process, customers may receive a refund and an insurance claim needs to be opened. Otherwise a monthly bill is created and the incoming payments will be monitored against payment transactions.

3. EVENT PROCESSING

Middleware is, beside other technologies, one of the established technology stacks which has clearly adopted the event processing paradigm ([8], 27-29 and 36-38). This section discovers *Camel's* implementation of the main event processing concepts ([9], 40-47) starting with *event types and objects*, highlighting the *event producer, consumer and channel* concept, integrating the components into an *event processing network* and finally discussing the interaction of *event processing agents, context and state*.

Event types and event objects Events are a representation for something which has happened. As a computational element for the technical representation, an event object is a concrete instance of an event type. All event objects, which belong to an event type, carry the same semantics within their object structure. Event types, objects and their implementation within *Camel* are covered in section 3.1.

Event producer, consumer and channel Producer and consumer are both event processing elements that communicate with each other. While an event producer obtains the role for generating events, the event consumer receives the results. An event channel fulfills the mediation role between producer and consumer. It's main task is to route events from the producer to the appropriate consumer. All three elements and their technical interaction are described in section 3.2.

Event processing networks An event processing network combines all processing elements, notably *event producer* and *consumer, event channel, event processing agent* including *context* and *state* elements into an executable application unit. This does not necessarily imply that all elements need to be executed within a single execution node. In section 3.3 you'll find an in depth explanation on how the combination can be achieved within *Camel*.

Event processing agents, context and state An agent is a software component with the purpose of processing events. The main functionalities of an agent can be summarized as *filtering*, *matching* and *derivation* with support of *context* and *state* information. While *filtering*, *matching* and *derivation* are core functions within event processing, the processing of *context* and *state* is required for event reasoning which means the detection of any conditions that lead to the event generation (cf. section 3.4)

3.1 Event Types and Event Objects

An event is a representation for something which has happened in reality (cf. [12], 151 and [8], 255-256 and [9], 4). Considering the parcel delivery process of figure 1, the central event which triggers all subsequent activities is a customer order for the transportation service, also known as *Shipment*. While the actual instance of an event is called *event object*, the structural definition is captured within an *event type*.

Listing 1 and 2 disclose the relationship between *event type* and *event object*. The *event type* in listing 1 defines, that a shipment order consists of *ShipmentDetails*, *Sender* and *Receiver*. *ShipmentDetails* describes the nature of the *Shipment*, particularly the size and weight of the item; *Sender* and *Receiver* specify the geographical nodes and the distance that needs to be covered by the *Shipment*.

Listing 1: Event Type - Shipment Order

```
1 <?xml version="1.0"?>
2 <xsd:schema version="1.0" ... >
3   <xsd:element name="Shipment"
4     type="tns:ShipmentType"/>
5   <xsd:complexType name="ShipmentType">
6     <xsd:sequence>
7       <xsd:element name="ShipmentDetails"
8         type="tns:ShipmentDetailsType"/>
9       <xsd:element name="Sender"
10        type="tns:SenderType"/>
11      <xsd:element name="Receiver"
12        type="tns:ReceiverType"/>
13    </xsd:sequence>
14  </xsd:complexType>
15  ...
16 </xsd:schema>
```

In contrast to the *event type*, which describes the semantical structure of an event, the *event object* captures what is actual happening or has happened - in our example the concrete request of an order. The *event object* is therefore an instance of an *event type* which contains actual values within the structure of the event type. Listing 2 shows an instance of the *Shipment* with concrete values. While *Weight*, *Length*, *Width* and *Height* define the physical consistency of the Shipment, the *ParcelType* provides a classification information, in our case "Small Parcel". This classification information is not necessarily required, since it could be derived by some *context* information, e.g. when conducting a lookup against a context store. For the purpose of simplicity we decided to retain the attribute and discuss the topic of *context* in section 3.4.

Adding one more comment to the given XML listing: It is of course not an imperative need to specify an *event body* as XML structure. *Camel* supports any Java object type in its message body since the body is of type *"java.lang.object"*

(cf. [13], 14). It is therefore possible to process any event that can be serialized into a Java object.

Listing 2: Event Object - Shipment Order

```
1 <?xml version="1.0" encoding="UTF-8"?>
2 <tns:Shipment ... >
3   <tns:ShipmentDetails>
4     <tns:ParcelType>
5       Small Parcel
6     </tns:ParcelType>
7     <tns:Weight>1.87</tns:Weight>
8     <tns:Length>55</tns:Length>
9     <tns:Width>25</tns:Width>
10    <tns:Height>12.5</tns:Height>
11  </tns:ShipmentDetails>
12  <tns:Sender ... />
13  <tns:Receiver ... />
14 </tns:Shipment>
```

Having introduced the abstract relationship between *event type* and *event object*, we need to investigate the logical structure of an event and it's attributes. Since the XML-based example above represents only the payload, which is usually wrapped in the *event body* within the context of event processing, we need to discover what other attributes are required to create an event. In addition we need to find out, if these elements find an implementation representation within the *Camel* framework.

According to ([9], 62-64), the abstract, logical structure of an event is split into three sections: An *event header*, a *payload* and an *open content* section. The following enumeration describes each element and it's role within event processing.

Header: Covers system defined event attributes e.g. a *type identifier*, a property that flags if it is an *event composition*, the *temporal granularity* and additional *event indicators* such as the *occurrence* and *detection time*, *event source*, *identity* and *certainty*. Header attributes support an efficient processing of the events since they reduce the need to lookup frequently used information.

Payload: Contains data attributes that are specified by the event type. The payload data is the actual, computational representation of what has happened (cf. listing 1 and 2).

Open content: Defines additional data that may be included in the even instance. This encompasses any binary attachment such as any document, audio or video file. However, it is also possible to attach structure or un structured text.

The logical event structure has its representation within *Camel* as *message* object, consisting of *headers*, a *body* and an *attachment* (cf. [13], 13). When taking a look at the *headers* object, we can identify a unique *messageId*. In spite of the *messageId* there exist no other predefined message headers and it is necessary to extend the research also to the surroundings of the *message object* to find additional information like the ones defined by the *event indicators*, e.g the *event source*.

In figure 2 we find an abstract illustration that explains how the message object is embedded within the broader context of an *exchange object*. An *exchange* may contain two message objects, an in and an out object. The reason for that implementation can be found within the concept of *message exchange pattern (MEP)*. *Camel* knows basically two styles of exchanging messages: *InOnly* and *InOut* ([13], 14-15) . While some interaction scenarios manage the processing of a "fire and forget" style (i.e. *InOnly* pattern), others require still the information about the original request message (i.e. *InOut* pattern). To implement this behavior, the exchange contains the information about the pattern style and the option to store two messages.

In addition of the processing behavior, the exchange has also an attribute indicating the *endpoint* where the message camel from respectively the *event source* (cf. section 3.2). Beyond that, the concept involves also the knowledge about it's creation time (i.e. *properties.CamelCreatedTimestamp*), the execution context (i.e. *fromRouteId*) as well as the information if any processing failure. The advantage of carrying exception information outside of the actual message is, that the the exception handling needs only to look at this information rather than parsing the entire message body.

If it is required to add any additional event indicators, this can be handled by setting custom properties within the *message header* or the *exchange properties*.

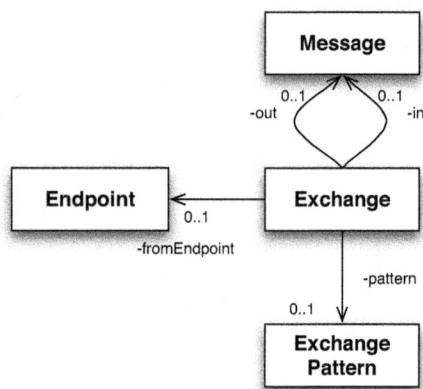

Figure 2: Camel Exchange and Message Model

Reviewing the overall *Camel* implementation it is fair say, that the message and exchange concept provides everything which required by an *event type and object* perspective to fulfill the needs required for event processing.

The next section introduces now the concepts of *event producer*, *consumer*, *event channel* and tries to discover their implementation within the *Camel* framework.

3.2 Event Producer, Consumer and Channel

Event producer and *consumer* are entities that interact with each other in an *event processing network* (cf. section 3.3) by sending and receiving events (cf. [9], 42). Taking an example from the parcel delivery process (cf. figure 1), a customer may submit a shipment order in a customer portal. The order is being sent to the order system which keeps track about the fulfillment degree of all customer orders (cf. figure 3). Before the order system is in capable to confirm that the order can be processed, it requires additional information about the feasibility from the scheduling system since the order system does not know anything about capacities and their utilization. The scheduling system responds

upon the scheduling request and enables the order system to send out an order confirmation to the customer's inbox in the portal application.

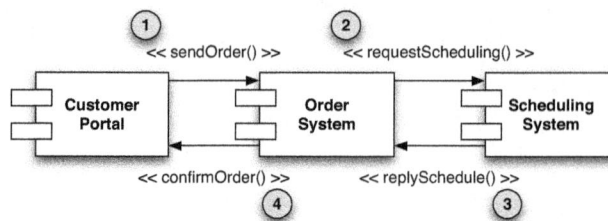

Figure 3: Order Submission

Under the condition of each *participant* acting either as *producer* or *consumer*, the example (cf. figure 3) demonstrates that each participant can obtain multiple roles depending upon the communication direction. At first, when sending the order request, the customer portal holds the event producer role before it turns into an event consumer when finally receiving the order confirmation. Since the role change does not affect any internal semantics or structure of data within the customer portal, it is possible to combine both roles into a single element, called *participant* (cf. [9], 33 and [14], 298). The *Camel* implementation of a participant element is realized via the so called *Component* object (cf. [13], 188-236).

"Components are the primary extension point in Camel" ([13], 189) and implement basically an endpoint factory. Since any *endpoint* is capable to send and receive events, a *component* exposing an endpoint is suitable to realize an *event producer* as well as a *consumer*. What might become a surprise is, that the generic *Component* concept is also capable to realize the concept of an *event channel*. First of all, an event channel is capable to receive events, similar to the behavior of an *event consumer*. Secondly, it acts like an *event producer* when sending events to one or more destinations. Finally, an *event channel* may also modify an input event or make routing decisions (cf. [9], 189).

Since a *Camel Component* provides basically a configurable endpoint to which someone can send events or may retrieve events, it is possible to cover the first and second statement. In addition the endpoint configuration may also contain information on how to modify (e.g. change header information) or apply routing decisions. Figure 4 provides an overview about the object dependencies in *Camel* between, *producer*, *consumer*, *component* and *endpoint*.

Component is a factory for *endpoint* objects. Components can be added to an *EPN* via configuration and inclusion to the *Camel Context* (cf. section 3.3).

Endpoint realizes an addressable element that can send and receive event objects. The endpoint address is specified as *Unified Resource Identifier (URI)* (cf. [15]).

Producer provides a channel on which clients can send event objects in an *endpoint*. The endpoint needs to be individually configured.

Consumer consumes events from an *endpoint*. Consuming events requires an individual configuration, including the appropriate endpoint addressing.

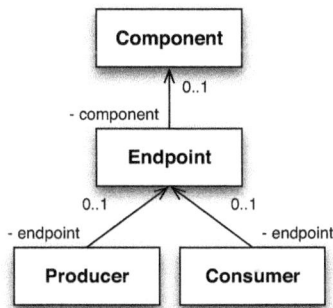

Figure 4: Abstract Component Model

Having gained a first insight into the *component* concept and its adoption to realize *event producer*, *consumer* and *channel* we'd like to give you an example that should provide some clarification. As example, we have selected two implementations within *Camel* that act like *event channels*, since a channel realizes both communication directions.

The first component is called *SEDA-component* and realizes the concept of a *staged event-driven architecture* endpoint (cf. [16]). This endpoint implements in our example (cf. listing 3) an endpoint that can receive events. Nevertheless, a SEDA endpoint may be also used to send events; it can therefore act in both *consumer* and *producer* role. In addition, the component has also the capability to configure basic routing rules such as the enablement of multiple consumers, similar to a topic based communication, as well as some blocking and sizing parameters.

The second component we have decided to use as an event channel is the *JMS-component*, since the Java Message System (JMS) ([17]). is a well known implementation of the *event channel* concept.

Listing 3 shows the mediation between two systems. The first system, in our case the order system, is capable to call a SEDA queue directly while the second system, responsible for scheduling and routing, can only understand JMS messages (cf. figure 3). The communication direction, respectively the indication of which component acts as *event producer* or *consumer*, is described by the *Camel DSL*, a processing language with simple routing expressions. In our example it is a simple *"from().to()"* clause based upon the fluent builder concept (cf. [13], 30, 132).

Listing 3: Endpoint URI Examples

```
1 from("seda://shipmentOrder" +
2     "?multipleConsumers=false")
3 .to("jms:topic:schedule?transacted=true");
```

As already stated, a component can be addressed via an *URI* scheme. In contrast to the *URI* specification (cf. [15], 16-25), *Camel* implements a simplified *URI* structure (cf. [13], 19, 25) to configure and address an *endpoint* individually (cf. listing 3). A *Camel* endpoint URI is based upon a *scheme*, a *context path* and *options*.

Scheme: The scheme references the component that needs to be instantiated. The component identifier needs to be uniquely.

Context path: Identifies the resources within the process-

ing context unique. This is required to address the individual component instance when calling an endpoint.

Options: Options configure the endpoint behavior. The set of options is different for each component since the behavior depends upon the underlying component provider (e.g. the scheduling system)

Having seen now, how *Camel* realizes *event types* and *event objects* (3.1), and knowing how *event producer*, *consumer* and *channel* (3.2) are implemented and interact within the framework, it is time to discover the complete interaction of all elements within the *event processing network*.

3.3 Event Processing Networks

"An event processing network (EPN) is a collection of event processing agents, producers, consumers, and global state elements (...)" (cf. [9], 43). As we have seen in 3.2, most of the elements can be express via components. To combine these components, *Camel* provides two essential elements called *context* and *route*.

Context: The *Camel Context* is a container at runtime level, providing *Camel's* core services, particularly the elements *Registry*, *Type converter*, *Components*, *Endpoints*, *Routes*, *Data formats* and *Languages* (cf. [13], 16).

Route: A *Camel Route* realizes a concrete implementation of a message flow that can be executed on *Camel's* routing engine. It is possible to define multiple routes within a *context*, where each contains a unique identifier (cf. [13], 17).

To get an impression on how a *Camel Context* and *Camel Routes* are structured, we have created a simple listing 4 that provides some clarification. The listing is based upon the Spring DSL (cf. [13], 18) and is embedded in a Spring application context (cf. [18], 27). A *context* element, named *"camelContext"* contains a single *route* with a unique identifier *"camelRoute"*; in addition to that single route it would be possible to add more routes within that context where all can access the same set of core services provided by the *context*. Two core services that must to be registered in our example are the SEDA and JMS component, since they are directly referenced from the route and will be instantiated. Another one is of course the registry that administers all *context paths* for all endpoints to enable a proper endpint resolution when processing the messages.

Listing 4: Context and Route - Application Context

```
1 <?xml version="1.0" encoding="UTF-8"?>
2 <beans xmlns:camel=
3     "http://camel.apache.org/schema/spring"
4     xsi:schemaLocation=
5     "http://camel.apache.org/schema/spring
6     http://camel.apache.org/schema/spring/
            camel-spring.xsd" ... >
7   <camel:camelContext id="camelContext">
8     <camel:route id="camelRoute">
9       <camel:from uri="seda://shipmentOrder"/>
10      <camel:to uri=
11        "jms:topic:schedule?transacted=true"/>
12    </camel:route>
13    ...
```

```
14    </camel:camelContext>
15 </beans>
```

As we have seen in the example of listing 4, *Camel Context* and *Camel Routes* enable the collection of components (e.g. *event producer, consumer* and *channel*). We might want to anticipate the result of section 3.4 to conclude that it is also possible to collect *agents, context* and *state* elements within the concept.

The following section explains the concept of *agents, context* and *state* in detail and points out concrete implementation strategies for each agent functionality.

3.4 Agents, Context and State

An *event processing agent* is a piece of software that implements the processing logic between an *event producer* and a *consumer* (cf. [9], 42, 51). Each agent provides a specific set of event processing functionality that can be assembled within an *event processing network*. The main tasks of an agent are therefore the mediation between *producer* and *consumer*, particularly the grouping of events according to their processing context. This can be achieved e.g. by *filter, split, translate, aggregate* and *enrich* functionalities.
In addition to these functions, *agents* are also responsible to process *context* and *state* information which enables also the correct routing from the event producing to the event consuming component (cf. [9], 51, 145). The context of an event may have multiple dimensions, e.g. *temporal-, spatial-*, or *state-oriented*, where each context dimension can occur in combination with each other one. Identifying the right context for an event can only be conducted, if there is a *global state* element available acting as reference data.

Agent functionality can be reused in different application scenarios. To support the reuse, we have proposed a simplified pattern schema (cf. section 1) containing *name, context, problem, solution* and *example* descriptions.
Even if our intention is not to set a standard, the proposed structure may contribute to the ongoing discussion about standardization within the event processing community (cf. [19]). One of the positive effects a pattern based approach might have is that "[c]learly-defined and commonly-accepted levels of abstraction enable the development of standardized tasks and interfaces." ([20], 48).

The subsequent paragraphs focus on the agent functionality description for *filtering, splitting, translation, aggregation* and *enrichment* based on the logistics parcel delivery process (cf. figure 1). Even if the industrial background is taken from logistics, we have kept the examples general to enable the adoption towards other industry domains.

3.4.1 Filter Agent Pattern

"A [f]ilter agent (...) performs filtering only and has no matching or derivation steps (...)" ([9], 317). To eliminate uninteresting events it utilizes a *filter expression*. The agent processes events in a stateless manner (cf. [9], 51)
Name: *Filter Agent*
Context: The logistics of parcel delivery is characterized by automated sorting processes. Sorting machines pickup the labeling information required for routing parcels physically to their corresponding gates . While the parcels are being processed on conveyor belts, the capturing of the label information is being conducted based on barcode scans or image recognition. It extracts a huge amount of address

data that needs to be distributed to the subsequent delivery nodes.
Problem: Since subsequent processing nodes are only interested in events for their delivery area, it is required to select the particular parcel information and distribute it to the corresponding node. However each node needs the flexibility to change the size of the delivery area, since it must be capable to take over the operation of a nearby delivery area, in case of e.g. low volumes or operational issues in a processing node.
Solution: Providing the flexibility to dynamically change the area, all address events will be published on a single topic. Each node within the delivery network is responsible to create a *filter expression* matching the predefined delivery area. This way it can be assured that each node receives only events for it's field of activity.

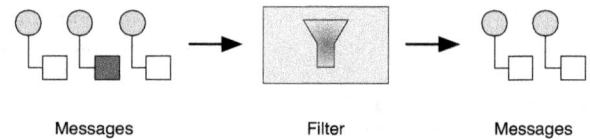

Figure 5: Filter Agent

Example: In the example we are sending address events captured by the sorting machine that contain *name, street, city* and *zipCode* information. For the purpose of simplicity, we assume that a *zipCode* identifies a section of a delivery area and can not be split into the responsibility of two processing nodes. An active delivery node can serve one to many *zipCode* areas at once while an inactive node maintains zero. As an additional restriction we have defined that a processing node can only serve a coherent, ascending sequence of *zipCodes*. All these restrictions have certainly not a direct, representation in the real parcel delivery process. However they help us to realize a simple *filter expression* as you can see in the in listing 5 by a *predicate*.
The *predicate* evaluates all incoming events for a *minZip-Code* and a *maxZipCode* and routes all events within that range to the responsible processing node. *Camel* executes the filtering request within the route by calling the *filter()* expression with a predicate parameter.

Listing 5: Filter Agent
```
1 public class FilterRoute extends
2     SpringRouteBuilder {
3   @Override
4   public void configure() throws Exception {
5     Predicate deliveryArea =
6       or(
7         body().isGreaterThan(minZipCode),
8         body().isLessThan(maxZipCode));
9     from("direct://start-body-filter")
10      .filter(deliveryArea)
11      .to("log://after-body-filter?level=INFO")
12      .end();
13  }
14 }
```

3.4.2 Split Agent Pattern

A split agent "(...) takes a single incoming event and emits a stream of multiple event objects ()" ([9], 52). It can be used

264

to partition an incoming event and distribute the individual parts to different consumers (cf. [9], 126).

Name: *Split Agent*

Context: Several customers are having distributed production facilities while maintaining a single administration office that sends out the collected order requests for the entire customer organization. The centralized, batch oriented order processing provides the customer the opportunity to centralize the purchase and accounting department at a single location rather than having multiple employees sitting in each production facility.

Problem: Distributing the bulk of orders is difficult, since the pickup of parcels at the customer's production facilities needs to be executed by different logistics processing nodes. Assigning the individual responsibility for the processing nodes is not possible based on the entire set of order events.

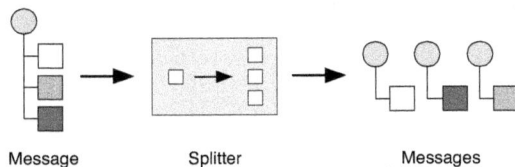

Message   Splitter   Messages

Figure 6: Split Agent

Solution: To enable the responsibility assignment across the logistics network it is required to partition the order collection into single orders where each order contains only the address information of the parcel's sender and recipient. This can be achieved by conducting a split operation on the incoming collection.

Example: The solution can be achieved by splitting the incoming order collection into it's individual parts. *Camel* provides the *split()* expression for conducting those operations. One of the requirements to implement the split expression successfully is to have either a *Collection*, an *Array* or a *NodeList* (cf. [21], 23-24).

Listing 6: Split Agent
```
1 public class SplitRoute
2   extends SpringRouteBuilder {
3   @Override
4   public void configure() {
5     from("direct://start-split")
6       .split(body())
7       .to("log://split-route?level=INFO");
8   }
9 }
```

3.4.3 Translate Agent Pattern

A translate agent is stateless and "(...) takes a single event as its input, and generates a single derived event which is a function of the input event, using a derivation formula" ([9], 125). Its usage ranges from simple type conversions to complex event transformations modifying event attributes.

Name: *Translate Agent*

Context: The marketing and sales department has figured a way, to extract product data as XML documents from their master spreadsheet where they maintain all product information. They have also found a documentation section from the customer portal provider stateing that there is a Java interface where product data can be updated.

Problem: Unfortunately the Java interface can not serialize XML documents directly and it provides only a remote method invocation interface. The interface is therefore only capable to directly process Java objects. What makes the situation even more complicated is, that some of the extracted attributes do not match to the data structure specified within the interface documentation.

Solution: The only way to support the marketing and sales department in their goal to update the companies portal automatically based on the extracted XML data is to translate the XML product data into the format required by the portal software. It is therefore required to translate, the XML *InputStream* into an object of *Product.class*.

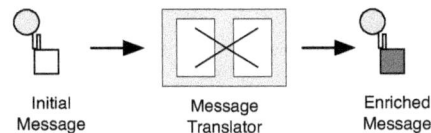

Initial   Message   Enriched
Message   Translator   Message

Figure 7: Translate Agent

Example: The XML document that can be extracted from the spreadsheet has a *product* container with the attributes *name*, *size*, *weight* and a *price* (cf. listing 7). Since the specified *Product.class* object has only a description element and no *size* and *weight* attributes, it is required to translate these attributes into a single element.

Listing 7: Extracted XML-based Product
```
1 <?xml version="1.0" encoding="UTF-8"?>
2 <Product>
3   <Name>Parcel</Name>
4   <Size>max. 60x30x15 cm</Size>
5   <Weight>up to 2 kg</Weight>
6   <Price>4.90</Price>
7 </Product>
```

The proposed implementation for that translation is a *TypeConverter* (cf. [13], 88-91). Since the default set of *TypeConverter* does not cover the specific translation between the XML-based product document and the Java-based *Product.class*, it is necessary to extend the existing set by a custom converter (cf. listing 8).

Listing 8: Translate Agent - Type Converter
```
1 @Converter
2 public class TranslateConverter {
3   @Converter
4   public Product convertInputStreamToProduct(
5       InputStream inputStream) {
6     final XPath xPath = XPathFactory.
7       newInstance().newXPath();
8     final Document document =
9       createXMLDocument(inputStream);
10    return createProduct(document);
11  }
12  private Product
13    createProduct(Document document) { /*...*/
14    return product;
15  }
16  private Document createXMLDocument(
17    InputStream inputStream) { /*...*/
```

```
18      return null;
19  }
20 }
```

To trigger the translation, it is necessary to add a *convertBodyTo(Product.class)* expression to your route. At execution time, the route identifies the object type that reaches at the conversion point and searches for a matching type converter in the *Camel Context* registry.

When the type conversion succeeds, the translate agent sends out the *Product.class* object by executing a remote method invocation (cf. listing 9)

Listing 9: Translate Agent - Route

```
1 public class TranslateRoute
2      extends SpringRouteBuilder {
3  @Override
4  public void configure() {
5    from("direct://start-translate")
6      .convertBodyTo(Product.class)
7      .to("rmi://portal:1099/products");
8  }
9 }
```

3.4.4 Aggregate Agent Pattern

An aggregate agent "(...) takes as input a collection of events and creates a single derived event (...)" ([9], 126). Even if this definition describes the input as *collection* of events it is not within the meaning of a Java *collection* type where a *collection* represents a container object that embraces multiple objects. We want to emphasize that the *aggregate agent* operates on multiple input events and generates a single output event.

When aggregating events, it is sometimes required to execute an aggregation function such as calculating e.g. a sum, an average or the maximum and minimum of a certain event attribute.

Name: *Aggregate Agent*

Context: Since the competition within the parcel delivery market has increased and the prices became more volatile, the marketing and sales department wants to gain an insight into the average price for products and services offered by their competitors.

Problem: Calculating the average market price requires the aggregation of all competitors prices. As soon as one of the competitors changes the price, it is necessary to recalculate the average value.

Solution: To enable the reaction upon any price change, the proposed solution is to aggregate a new average price as soon as one of the competitors updates it's price table. The aggregation will be implemented via an aggregation strategy hiding the complexity of calculating the average value.

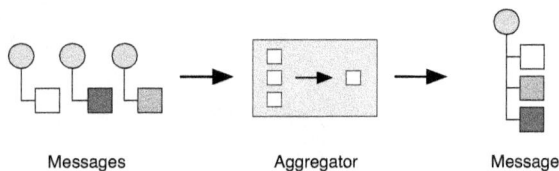

Messages   Aggregator   Message

Figure 8: Aggregate Agent

Example: Listing 10 shows the implementation of a *Camel*

aggregation strategy. The strategy has as a public *aggregate()* function which takes an old and a new exchange object as parameter values. While the old exchange contains all events that have been collected until the completion criteria is met, the new exchange involves the latest event object. Based on these event objects, it is possible to calculate an average product price and return the calculated value as *exchange* object.

Listing 10: Aggregate Agent - Aggregation Strategy

```
1 public class Aggregator
2      implements AggregationStrategy {
3  private final static List<Product> PRODUCTS =
4    new ArrayList<Product>();
5  public Exchange aggregate(
6      Exchange oldExchange,
7      Exchange newExchange) {
8    final Product oldProduct =
9      getProductFromExchange(oldExchange);
10   final Product newProduct =
11     getProductFromExchange(newExchange);
12   if (null != newAggregateProduct) {
13     if (!PRODUCTS.contains(
14       newAggregateProduct)) {
15       PRODUCTS.add(newAggregateProduct);
16     }
17   }
18   newExchange.getIn().setBody(
19     calcAvgProductPrice());
20   return newExchange;
21 }
22 private Product getProductFromExchange(
23     Exchange exchange) { /* ... */
24   return product;
25 }
26 private double calcAvgProductPrice() {
27   /* ... */
28   return ProductPrice;
29 }
30 }
```

Beside the actual calculation logic and the call of the aggregation strategy (*aggregate()*), the definition of the completion criteria is the most important element that needs to be defined. The criteria defines either the size (*completionSize()*) or the time frame (*completionInterval()* and *completionTimeout()*) that triggers the execution of the aggregation strategy. To assure that the average price is being calculated for every new product event, we have decided set the *completionSize* to one (cf. listing 11).

Listing 11: Aggregate - Agent Route

```
1 public class AggregateRoute
2      extends SpringRouteBuilder {
3  @Override
4  public void configure() {
5    final Aggregator aggregator =
6      new Aggregator();
7    from("direct://start-aggregate")
8      .aggregate(body(), aggregator)
9        .completionSize(1)
10     .to("log://aggregate-route?level=INFO");
11 }
12 }
```

3.4.5 Enrich Agent Pattern

An enrich agent "(...) takes a single input event, uses it to query data from a global state element, and creates a derived event which includes the attributes from the original event, possibly with modified values, and can include additional attributes." ([9], 126).

Name: *Enrich Agent*

Context: A customer places an order by providing with the physical characteristics and the distance information derived by the points of transfer (e.g. sender and receiver). In contrast to the described order event of section 3.1, he does not offer any product classification that can be consulted for payoff.

Problem: To create an accurate bill, it is required to classify the order into the appropriate product category, e.g *small parcel*, *parcel* or *oversized parcel*, each having an individual price tag.

Solution: To conduct the mapping of the provided information, it is required to lookup the event context in the global state element. This can be achieved by implementing the *enrichment* pattern that implies in the concrete instance the querying of the product database based on the assigned order event to return the corresponding product category.

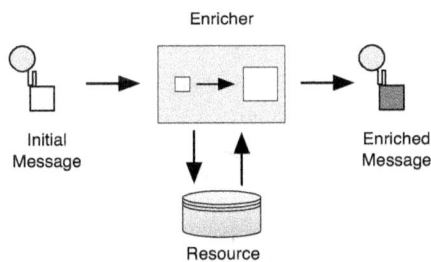

Figure 9: Enrich Agent

Example: The implementation is realized by adopting the aggregation strategy since an aggregation strategy is capable calculating a new output event based on two input exchanges (cf. listing 12).

Listing 12: Enrich Agent - Aggregation Strategy

```
1 public class Enricher implements
2     AggregationStrategy {
3   public Exchange aggregate(
4       Exchange oldExchange,
5       Exchange newExchange) {
6     final Context originalContext =
7       oldExchange.getIn().getBody(
8         Context.class);
9     final List<Context> context =
10      newExchange.getIn().getBody(List.class);
11    /* ... */
12    oldExchange.getIn().
13      setBody(originalContext);
14    return oldExchange;
15  }
16 }
```

What makes the difference compared to a regular aggregation agent is, that one of the exchanges processed within the aggregation strategy is being retrieved by a sub-route that queries the global state. The query is conducted based on a copy of the original incoming event. Listing 13 demonstrates this behavior where the main route calls the sub route when executing the *enrich()* expression.

Listing 13: Enrich Agent - Route

```
1 public class EnrichRoute
2     extends SpringRouteBuilder {
3   @Override
4   public void configure() {
5     configureMainRoute();
6     configureEnrichRoute();
7   }
8   private void configureMainRoute() {
9     from("direct://start-enrich")
10      .enrich("direct://start-enrichment",
11        new Enricher())
12      .to("log://enrich-route?level=INFO");
13  }
14  private void configureEnrichRoute() {
15    from("direct://start-enrichment")
16    .process(
17      new Processor() {
18        public void process(
19          Exchange exchange) { /* ... */
20          exchange.getIn().setBody(context);
21        }
22      }
23    )
24    .to("log://enrichment-route?level=INFO");
25  }
26 }
```

4. CONCLUSION

Within this work we have demonstrated, that *Camel* as an integration framework clearly realizes event processing concepts. It provides all the basic requirements needed for *event types and objects* while maintaining an extension mechanism to add additional, upcoming features targeting their structural semantics (cf. section 3.1).

What might be a surprise is, that *Camel's* generic component concept can serve as an abstraction for *event producer, consumer and channel* (cf. section 3.2). Nevertheless, it has been proven that the concept is sound since its adoption can be exemplified with the number of 140 realizing components, all acting either as *event producer, consumer* or implementing a *channel*. The introduction to the interaction of event processing networks by realizing *Camel context* and *Camel route* completes the frameworks support for the event processing building blocks.

Finally the paper contributes towards the ongoing standardization effort by introducing the agent functionalities for filtering, splitting, translation, aggregation and enrichment (cf. section 3.4).

Since we have seen, that *Camel* provides such a variety of functions and knowing that it is a lightweight framework, it might be a good candidate to be used for assembling services within a data cloud. An indication supporting this observation is, that *Camel* provides already many components that support the integration of modern technologies and services.

5. REFERENCES

[1] G. Hohpe and B. Woolf. *Enterprise Integration Patterns: Designing, Building, and Deploying Messaging Solutions*. Addison-Wesley Longman Publishing Co., Inc., Boston, MA, USA, 2003.

[2] D. Chandrasekhar. Gartner predictions 2013 for application integration: My take. Technical report, Reality Check, 2013.

[3] W. A. Ruh, F. X. Maginnis, and W. J. Brown. *Enterprise Application Integration: A Wiley Tech Brief*. John Wiley & Sons, 2002.

[4] J. Strachan. Initial checkin of camel routing library, 03 2007.

[5] C. Ibsen. Apache camel was awesome from v1.0 onward. Technical report, DZone, 2013.

[6] The Apache Software Foundation. Apache camel. Technical report, Apache Software Foundation, 2013.

[7] The Apache Software Foundation. Happy 5 years birthday apache camel. Technical report, Apache Software Foundation, 2013.

[8] D. C. Luckham. *Event Processing for Business: Organizing the Real-Time Enterprise*. John Wiley & Sons, 2011.

[9] O. Etzion and P. Niblett. *Event Processing in Action*. Manning Publications Co., 2011.

[10] R. v. Ammon, C. Silberbauer, and C. Wolff. Domain specific reference models for event patterns - for faster developing of business activity monitoring applications. In *VIPSI 2007*, October 2007.

[11] C. Emmersberger, F. Springer, and C. Wolff. Location based logistics services and event driven business process management. In D. Tavangarian, T. Kirste, D. Timmermann, U. Lucke, and D. Versick, editors, *Intelligent Interactive Assistance and Mobile Multimedia Computing*, number 53 in Communications in Computer and Information Science, pages 167–177. Springer, 2009.

[12] D. C. Luckham. *The Power of Events: An Introduction to Complex Event Processing in Distributed Enterprise Systems*. Addison-Wesley, November 2001.

[13] C. Ibsen and J. Anstey. *Camel in Action*. Manning Publications Co., 2011.

[14] N. M. Josuttis. *SOA in Practice - The Art of Distributed System Design*. O'Reilly Media, Inc., first edition edition, 2007.

[15] T. Berners-Lee, R. Fielding, and L. Masinter. Uniform resource identifier (uri): Generic syntax. Request for Comments 3986, The Internet Engineering Task Force (IETF), Network Working Group, http://tools.ietf.org/pdf/rfc3986.pdf, January 2005.

[16] M. Welsh. Seda: An architecture for highly concurrent server applications. Project report, Harvard University, http://www.eecs.harvard.edu/ mdw/proj/seda/, May 2006.

[17] M Hapner, R. Burridge, R. Sharma, J. Fialli, and Stout K. Java message service - the jms api is an api for accessing enterprise messaging systems for java programms. Specification Version 1.1, Sun microsystems, April 2002.

[18] Spring. Spring java application framework. Reference Documentation 3.0, Spring Source, http://static.springsource.org/spring/docs/3.0.x/spring-framework-reference/pdf/spring-framework-reference.pdf, 2011.

[19] R. v. Ammon, C. Emmersberger, T. Ertlmaier, O. Etzion, T. Paulus, and F. Springer. Existing and future standards for event-driven business process management. In *Proceedings of the Third ACM International Conference on Distributed Event-Based Systems, DEBS 2009*. ACM, July 2009.

[20] F. Buschmann. *Pattern oriented software architecture: a system of patters*. John Wiley & Sons, 1st edition, July 1996.

[21] P. Kolb. Realization of eai patterns with apache camel. Studienarbeit 2127, Institut für Architektur von Anwendungssystemen, Universität Stuttgart, 04 2008.

Tutorial: Why is Event-driven Thinking Different from Traditional Thinking about Computing?

Opher Etzion
IBM Haifa Research Lab
Israel
opher@il.ibm.com

Jeffrey M. Adkins
IBM Global Business Services
USA
jmadkins@us.ibm.com

ABSTRACT

We observed that many of the applications that are event-based by nature are designed and developed using the conventional thinking about programming, and do not employ event based thinking. The developers are doing a kind of event processing without acknowledging it. One of the main reasons is the fundamental thought differences between event-driven thinking and the design of traditional request-driven applications.

This tutorial concentrates on the thought process and the modeling aspects. It starts with the ontology and semantics of the term events, continues with the inter-relationships among events and other entities (processes, decisions, objects, actors), and discusses the pragmatics of modeling of event-driven logic within a computational independent model.

Categories and Subject Descriptors

D.2.1 [**Software Engineering**]: Requirement/Specification methodologies; D.2.2 [**Software Engineering**]: Design tools and techniques;

General Terms

Event processing, Event-based systems, Business user modeling.

Keywords

Event-based systems – ontology, Event-based systems - modeling

1. INTRODUCTION – BRIEF HISTORY OF EVENT PROCESSING

This section of the tutorial provides common denominator for the discussion, and survey event processing functionalities, and event processing development tools. It provides motivation for the rest of the tutorial by providing thoughts about the state of the practice of event processing in 2013,

2. THE MAJOR DIFFERENTIATION FACTORS OF EVENT-BASED THINKING

This section of the tutorial explains the differences between the traditional thinking, based on the "request/response" paradigm, and reactive event-based thinking. It explains the roots of the differences - temporal orientation, hidden state, and flow of control. It focuses on the role of the human vs. the role of the computer in both cases, and explains what happens behind the scenes of event processing systems.

3. THE ONTOLOGY OF EVENTS AND EVENT INFLUENCE

This section of the tutorial explains the basic concepts and relationships among them in event-driven thinking. It starts with the various interpretations of the term "event" and provides the linguistics perspective and its relations to actors, processes, observers, aspect and reaction. It also discusses the uncertainty aspect in event ontology.

4. ANATOMY OF REACTIVE SYSTEMS

In this section of the tutorial we discuss the 4Ds paradigm that describes reactive systems: Detect, Derive, Decide, and Do. Each of these four components is described in detail:

- The Detect part describes becoming aware of changes that happen outside a system's awareness boundary.

- The Derive part describes the combination of information and event to derive events that are not directly detectable, and discusses various relationships among events: correlation and causality.

- The Decide part describes how an organization decides how to react when an event occurs, and discusses various types of decisions.

- The Do part discusses various type of actions that are done as a reaction.

This section concludes by discussing time-to-value in event-based systems and various roles of human and computers, from notification systems to autonomic computing

5. PRAGMATICS – A COMPUTATIONAL INDEPENDENT MODEL FOR EVENT-BASED SYSTEMS

This section describes the vision for the next generation of event-based system modeling, based on computational independent model that uses pure business concepts, yet can be translated to execution. The basic part of the model will be discussed.

6. SUMMARY AND OPEN ISSUES

The tutorial is summarized with a discussion about open issues, research challenges and pragmatic challenges

Tutorial:
Event-based Systems Meet Software-defined Networking

Boris Koldehofe, Frank Dürr, Muhammad Adnan Tariq
Institute of Parallel and Distributed Systems
University of Stuttgart
$\langle firstname.lastname \rangle$@ipvs.uni-stuttgart.de

ABSTRACT

Software-defined networking (SDN) is a recent development in the area of communication networks with tremendous support by key players building the next generation of computer hardware and software. This development will have significant impact on how communication middleware—in particular, future distributed event-based systems—can be designed. While currently the communication middleware has no possibility to directly influence the properties of its underlying communication channels on the network layer, SDN enables communication middleware to control and flexibly adapt the forwarding of communication flows in the underlying network. In addition to the immediate implication to local area networks such as data center networks, campus networks, or company networks, novel trends like network virtualization may even support Internet-wide distributed applications to benefit from SDN in the future. This paper gives an introduction on how to utilize SDN-concepts for improving the performance of event-based middleware and to test their behavior.

Categories and Subject Descriptors

C.2.1 [**Network Architecture and Design**]: Distributed networks; C.2.4 [**Distributed Systems**]: Distributed applications; D.2.11 [**Software Architectures**]: Data abstraction

Keywords

Software-defined Networking, Event-based Systems, Content-based Routing, Publish/Subscribe, Network Virtualization

1. INTRODUCTION

The success of the Internet and its underlying network protocol (IP) and transport protocols (TCP, UDP) allows for the implementation of large-scale distributed applications by connecting hosts and services all over the world. Although these protocols have proven to be highly versatile,

there is still a gap between the communication functionality required by distributed applications and the simple functionality offered by the Internet protocols. For instance, distributed systems often require asynchronous communication between multiple at design time unknown senders and receivers together with expressive addressing concepts like message channels, or content-based addressing, whereas TCP/IP and UDP/IP are restricted to simple addressing concepts (IP addresses and port numbers) and basic connection-oriented and connection-less services (byte streams and datagrams). This gap is typically filled by communication middleware systems implementing powerful communication paradigms on top of the basic Internet protocols.

Currently, we can observe a clear separation between communication middleware and network protocols. Basically, the communication middleware is interfacing with the network through sockets that give the application little possibilities to influence the behavior of the underlying protocols. In particular, the communication middleware has no influence on how packets are routed in the physical network. Therefore, higher-level routing functionality is often implemented on the application layer in overlay networks on top of the IP network. This strict separation has made it very hard for the communication middleware to support application requirements like guarantees on end-to-end latency since the application overlay is unaware about the real topology of the underlying network. Although this problem can be alleviated by using topology inference mechanisms, these mechanisms are not perfect and induce an overhead. And even if the communication middleware was aware of the physical network topology and all alternative routes on the network layer, it could not influence the routing algorithms of the distributing routing protocols to utilize these routes. Moreover, the implementation of forwarding functionality "in software" on the application layer does not utilize the potential of fast forwarding hardware typically available in switches and routers. Therefore, goals like line-rate data forwarding or low-latency forwarding have been very challenging to achieve so far.

At this point, *software-defined networking* (SDN) is an important development with high potential to overcome many of these limitations. SDN is currently a big trend in networking with strong support from both academia and industry giving applications and middleware systems more control over the communication network, e.g., allowing application designers to build their own network topologies by programming flows in the underlay network rather than in the overlay network.

The basic concept of SDN is the separation of network management (control plane) and forwarding functionality (forwarding plane). The control plane is implemented by a logically centralized controller, which configures the forwarding tables (also called flow tables) of switches to define routes of communication flows in the network. By installing its application-specific control logic in the SDN controller, the communication middleware can control the forwarding of their flows directly on the network layer. In order to facilitate the calculation and optimization of routes, the controller exposes topology information and traffic statistics to the control logic as a global view onto the network.

Packet forwarding is implemented by the switches. Typically, multi-layer switches are used which can make forwarding decisions for communication flows based on layer 2-4 header fields such as source and destination MAC addresses, IP addresses, port numbers, or VLAN ids. This configuration can either be performed proactively before packets of a flow are to be forwarded, or reactively whenever a switch receives packets without matching flow table entry.

There are several advantages offered by SDN:

- *Great flexibility:* Rather than relying on "hard-coded" protocols and control logic implemented by the switches, the control logic can be easily changed through the controller. This concept also enables applications or middleware systems to "program" the network according to their specific needs like quality of service or security requirements.

- *Ease of implementation and testing:* Network control is greatly simplified by the concept of logical centralization and the global view onto the network. Control logic can be implemented using modern programming languages such as C++, Java, or Python, and utilizing powerful integrated developing environments like Eclipse. Instead of falling back to network simulation, the real control logic implementation can be tested and debugged more easily using network emulation. Moreover, centralized control simplifies the verification of control logic compared to distributed protocols, and enables stricter notions of consistency during network updates (strict vs. eventual consistency).

- *High performance:* Although control functionality is implemented in software, packet forwarding can utilize the hardware support of switches enabling low-latency forwarding and line-rate throughput. Moreover, network resources can be optimized based on a global view onto network resources, and the time to react to link and switch failures can be reduced.

With OpenFlow [21], a standard protocol for SDN is available that is already implemented by hardware switches from major vendors and software switches like Open vSwitch [23] which is highly popular to connect virtual machines in data centers. Moreover, several open source controller implementations are available, e.g., NOX (C/Python) [18], or the Java-based controllers Floodlight [7], Beacon [6], and Open-Daylight [22].

In this paper, we approach SDN from the perspective of event-based systems by

1. giving an introduction to the general principle of SDN (Section 2),

2. illustrating a general approach for writing event-based applications in SDN and showing its concrete application to content-based publish/subscribe (Section 3),

3. proposing an evaluation methodology (Section 4),

4. and highlighting research challenges (Section 5).

2. PRINCIPLES AND DESIGN DECISIONS

In this section, we first introduce the underlying principles of SDN, and then propose basic design decisions for implementing SDN-supported communication middleware systems. We conclude with a discussion in generalizing SDN by utilizing the concept of virtual networks to also leverage high performance of distributed applications at Internet-scale.

2.1 Basic Principles of SDN

SDN clearly separates two concerns: Network control implemented by the logically centralized network controller and packet forwarding performed by the switches. Although the controller is logically centralized, it can be physically distributed by running several instances of controllers to increase the availability—e.g., using redundant controllers—or scalability—e.g., by scaling out control logic to several physical machines. The notion of logical centralization implies that for the control logic performing flow programming, this distribution should be transparent.

SDN enables the controller to modify the flow tables of switches. A flow table entry defines actions that the switch should perform on packets of a certain flow, where the flow is defined by the matching criteria of the entry using layer 2 to 4 header fields. Examples of flows are a TCP connection (defined by source/destination IP addresses and source/destination port numbers), packets from a specific MAC address, or packets labeled with a certain VLAN tag. Actions include the forwarding of the flow's packets on certain ports or packet header manipulations like IP or MAC address rewriting.

The definition of flow table entries can either be done proactively a priori to receiving packets of a certain flow, or reactively when the switch receives a packet of an unknown flow without a matching flow table entry for the first time. Using the reactive strategy, a switch forwards packets without matching flow table entry to the controller, which decides on suitable actions and can set suitable flow table entries for future packets of this flow (e.g., to define a route for the flow through the network). After the flow table entry has been configured, forwarding is performed by the switches without contacting the controller again. Typically, hardware switches can perform forwarding at line-rate using dedicated hardware like ternary content-addressable memory (TCAM) for matching flow table entries and incoming packets.

Moreover, the controller can also query the switches for traffic statistics like the number of forwarded packets or bytes over a certain port (link). By implementing standard protocols like the Link Layer Discovery Protocol (LLDP) or Address Resolution Protocol (ARP), the controller can discover the network topology (links between switches and between hosts and switches). Based on this information, the control logic implemented by the switch can dynamically calculate routes for flows.

OpenFlow defines a standard protocol between controller and switch for flow programming and additional basic functions like the mentioned gathering of traffic statistics.

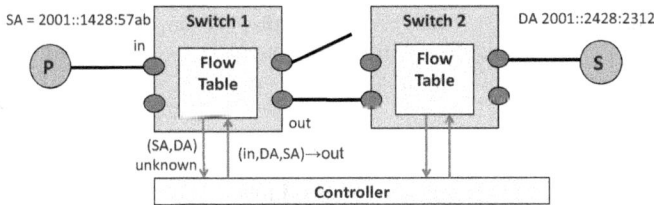

Figure 1: Programming a flow between a publisher and a subscriber

Using the example of a publish/subscribe systems, Figure 1 illustrates the basic principle in establishing a flow between a publisher p and a subscriber s. In this example, flow tables do not contain any flow entries initially. When p forwards the first packet of the flow, Switch 1 receiving the first packet will not be able to make a forwarding decision as its table does not contain an entry matching the source address and destination address fields of the IP-header. Instead the packet will be forwarded to the controller. The controller—once receiving the packets of s—may identify Switch 2 as a suitable target to forward these packets and establish a new flow from port in to port out for all packets comprising the source IP address (2001::1428:57ab) and destination IP address of s (2001::2428:2312). In addition, the controller may install a flow entry also at Switch 2 to establish the path from p to s. Once the flows are programmed, the packets will be forwarded along the path without involving the controller anymore.

2.2 Designing SDN-supported Communication Middleware

For a communication middleware to benefit from SDN and the high forwarding performance of (hardware) switches, the goal is to push the forwarding functionality of the communication middleware onto the switches and let the communication middleware implement the control logic of the physical network to program suitable flow table entries at the switches. Since the the communication middleware usually supports more expressive addressing and message filtering concepts like content-based filters, it is not straight forward to find a mapping to the basic addressing and matching concepts supported by the network such as MAC or IP addresses, and exact or longest prefix matching on bit strings.

In fact, a lot of research in publish/subscribe (e.g., [25, 4, 16, 9, 3, 30, 31]) has addressed the problem of efficiently matching events and filters, and identified this process to be one of the potential performance bottlenecks. Therefore, leveraging the line-rate and low-latency forwarding performance of switches by finding suitable mappings from content-filters to flow table entries is a promising but challenging effort.

A key decision in finding the mapping is the use of suitable header information of packets. As we have already introduced, OpenFlow supports different layer 2 to 4 header fields. The choice of those fields has a number of implications for the design of a middleware such as the number of flow entries that can be used (since the physical network is usually shared between the communication middleware and other applications, we can only reserve a certain amount of address space for the middleware). A limited number of flow entries, for example, may limit the maximum number

of groups that can be established for a group communication middleware. Note, that these limitations are likely to persist also in the future as the size of the TCAM memory dictates the cost of a switch and is therefore considered as a precious resource. Nevertheless, the availability of distinct flows also depends on the concrete standard supported. For instance, the OpenFlow standards 1.0 and 1.1 only support IPv4 (32 bit IP addresses) while later versions support IPv6 addresses (128 bit). Moreover, a group forwarding feature which facilitates the forwarding to multiple ports was only introduced in OpenFlow 1.1.

A critical issue is to ensure the interoperability with other applications sharing the same network. For example, adding a flow by overwriting the MAC or IP destination address fields may restrict the hosts which are reachable in the network. Applications may not even be aware of these restrictions, and, therefore, this might result in faulty and unexpected behavior. A solution is to utilize only specific address ranges that avoid the collision with other applications. For instance, a content routing application may utilize a dedicated range of the address space for IP multicast as it can be seen as an advanced group communication service.

Moreover, certain matching operations like longest prefix matches might only be available for certain addresses (in particular, IP addresses). As we will see later, such a feature is beneficial for mapping content-based filters to the matching operations supported by switches.

Another important restriction to keep in mind is the fact that some switches might not support fast matching on arbitrary combinations of header fields. Therefore, one has to carefully select those fields that are supported in hardware by the switch.

Note, that in many cases it will be inevitable to utilize special header fields in order to capture the dynamics like a new process is joining or leaving the middleware. Those packets will always be forwarded to one of the controllers of the communication middleware to determine changes to the group communication topology. The controllers in order to adapt the network topology may rely on additional information by encoding the topic or the content as part of the address field.

2.3 Internet-scale SDN-based Middleware

While it seems unlikely that an Internet service provider (ISP) will provide applications or the middleware direct access to its switches and routers, the advent of virtual networks will allow applications to configure and access a network of virtual switches that can even spread across multiple ISPs. SDN will also here be the paradigm to flexibly configure the behavior of virtual switches, which then can be mapped to their physical counterparts without loss of performance.

Figure 2 illustrates the reference architecture we envision for the configuration of group communication middleware in such a Future Internet. In this architecture, *network virtualization* serves as a basic abstraction to allocate a network of virtual switches and links. While state of the art approaches already allow for the allocation of virtual networks of a single ISP [29], we will assume in line with current research initiatives such as [1, 27] that an application can allocate a virtual network over multiple ISPs. For instance, in Figure 2 the virtual network consists of four switches from three different ISPs. This way it will be possible to provide access

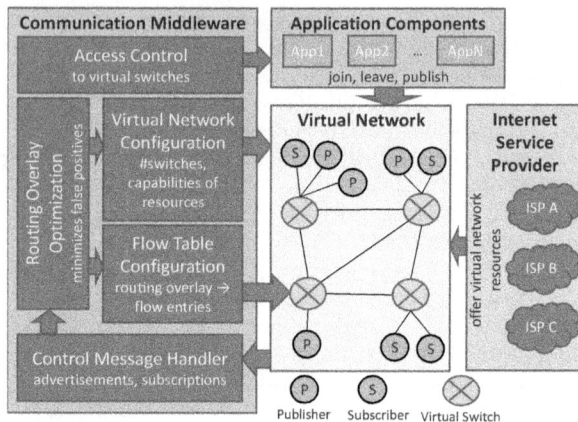

Figure 2: Architecture for configuration of virtual networks.

points very close to publishers and subscribers and to establish routes within the network that provide predictable end-to-end connectivity. The ISPs will provide the middleware with the characteristics of the virtual links connecting virtual switches such as latency or bandwidth as well as a specification of the capabilities of the virtual switches like flow table sizes, supported actions (e.g., address re-writing, IPv6 support), fast matching capabilities on certain tuples of header fields, etc.

Once the middleware has selected an appropriate network of switches and connected individual application components to the switches (cf. *virtual network configuration* and *access control* in Figure 2), we still need an abstraction to configure the virtual switches (in particular, their forwarding tables) to minimize the bandwidth consumption inside the virtual network, and to map the configuration to the ISP's physical infrastructure (cf. *flow table configuration* in Figure 2). It will be crucial that the mapping of virtualized resources to the physical resources can happen without sacrificing the performance of the switches. In our reference architecture, we rely on SDN and the OpenFlow standard as the abstraction to configure the virtual switches as well as the physical switches.

The virtual switches are configured by the control logic of the communication middleware executed by the controller. All control messages are received by the *control message handler*, and changes to the content-based routing overlay are computed accordingly by the *overlay optimization* component. The *flow table configuration* component then implements those changes by reconfiguring appropriate switches of the virtual network. The component decides whether and on which switches a new flow table entry needs to be established or where changes to the current flow tables are required.

In a second mapping stage, the flow tables of virtual switches are mapped to physical switches of the ISP to implement the (virtual) switches and (virtual) links of the virtual network. To this end, the ISP again can rely on the OpenFlow abstraction to program the flow tables of physical switches. This implementation of the virtual network topol-

ogy through the configuration of physical switches ensures that flows along virtual links can benefit from the forwarding performance of the physical hardware switches.

3. SDN-BASED PUBLISH/SUBSCRIBE

Based on our finding in [13], we illustrate next how event-based systems can be realized in SDN to yield line-rate performance. In particular, we focus on implementing content-based publish/subscribe, a key paradigm for interactions between loosely coupled application components (content publishers and subscribers).

3.1 Background

The basic idea of content-based routing is to utilize the diversity of information exchanged between application components to increase the efficiency of forwarding. Using content-based forwarding rules (also called content filters) installed on content-based routers (also termed brokers), bandwidth-efficiency is increased by only forwarding content to the subset of subscriber with an actual interest in the published content.

Many middleware implementations for content-based publish/subscribe have been developed over the last decade (e.g., [25, 4, 16, 9, 3, 30, 31]). These approaches have proven to efficiently support content-based routing between a large number of distributed application components. However, implemented on the application layer, their performance regarding throughput, end-to-end latency, and bandwidth efficiency is still far behind the performance of communication protocols implemented on the network layer. As pointed out earlier, a standard multilayer switch or hardware router can forward packets at line-rate achieving data rates of 10 Gbps and more using dedicated hardware such as TCAM memory. Moreover, they allow for switching delays of only few microseconds. Finally, routing on the network layer is more bandwidth efficient since it avoids sending the same information over the same physical link multiple times, in contrast to an overlay network where multiple logical links might share the same physical link.

Therefore, it it is highly attractive to implement content-based routing directly on the network layer. However, since changes to existing standard network protocols and hardware seemed to be unrealistic (as the slow support of the highly anticipated IPv6 standard shows), current research refrains from network layer implementations, and instead tries to improve application layer approaches along several dimensions: (1) inferring the underlay topology from the overlay topology [33, 10, 14, 5], (2) specific hardware allowing for efficient matching of advertisement and subscriptions on network brokers [28], and (3) reducing the expressiveness of content-routing to topic-based publish/subscribe [11].

Inferring the underlay topology using, for instance, latency spaces as proposed by Vivaldi [5], comes at a significant cost. Despite this effort, it is still hard to accurately infer advanced link state information such as the current link utilization based on observations on end systems.

Relying on dedicated hardware for matching dramatically reduces the scope to which such a middleware can be deployed.

Therefore, it seems reasonable to sacrifice the expressiveness of content-based publish/subscribe if line rate forwarding becomes the major requirement. For instance, LIPSIN [11] proposes topic-based publish/subscribe utilizing IP multicast for line-rate forwarding.

3.2 Publish/Subscribe Operations

As a first step we detail how subscriptions and advertisements are performed utilizing the middleware design decisions made in the earlier section. An application component specifies its interest in receiving certain information by sending a subscription sub_1 to the OpenFlow switch to which the component is connected. The header of the subscription message contains IP_{fix} as a destination address. This destination address is used to identify a new subscription that has to be forwarded to the control handler to build the mentioned global view on subscriptions. We simply achieve the forwarding to the control handler by *not* installing a flow table entry for the address IP_{fix}. Since the default action of OpenFlow is to forward every packet without matching flow table entry to the controller, the controller receives the subscription automatically without the need for an extra flow table entry.

When a new subscription sub_1 is received by the control handler, the routing overlay optimization algorithm is executed to determine the flows for the new subscription. In general, the subscriber will be connected to all flows that cover the subscription sub_1 (i.e., all flows that forward events matching sub_1). This possibly requires the creation of new outgoing ports to existing flow table entries by adding or updating actions (entries) in the flow tables of one or multiple OpenFlow switches. This is performed by the flow table configuration component by sending Flow-mod messages to the corresponding switches. Moreover, the routing overlay optimization algorithm may instruct the flow table configuration to create new flows (or remove existing flows) to optimize event routing from publishers to subscribers.

Similarly, an application component expresses its intent to publish a particular kind of information by issuing an advertisement to the OpenFlow switch. The advertisement is also forwarded to the controller using the address IP_{fix}. By following the same chain of steps, new flows will be created or existing flows are updated ensuring that each subscriber will be covered by the resulting set of flows.

In the following, we will describe in more detail two possible realization of a content-based publish/subscribe system using our OpenFlow architecture, namely, channelization and in-network filtering.

3.3 Channelization

An important concern in a content-based publish/subscribe system is to avoid forwarding of events to the paths in the network where only non-matching subscriptions are connected. From this point of view, channelization is one promising way to reduce the forwarding of unnecessary events by mapping advertisements and subscriptions to a limited set of channels such that the event dissemination within each channel is very efficient with respect to the reduction of unnecessary events. In the setting of our flow-based approach, channels are attractive because they can be easily mapped to flows as shown below.

Typically, two approaches can be used to create channels. The first approach uses absolute (structural) similarity between the subscriptions and the advertisements (such as the area occupied by the intersection of two subscriptions) to calculate their closeness to be placed in the same channel.

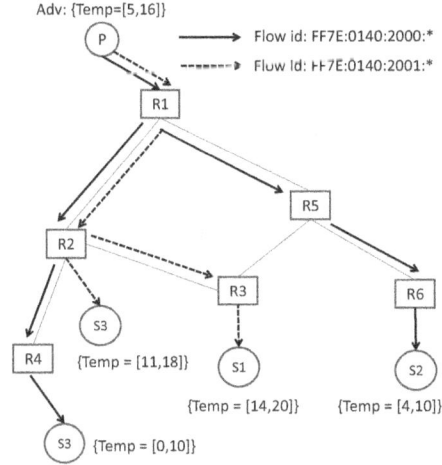

Figure 3: Channelization example.

This approach restricts the content-based model to predefined attributes with ordered data types and known domain (i.e., numeric attributes).

An alternative approach, which often yields more efficient channelization and places no more restrictions on the content-based model, is to rely on the event traffic published/matched by the advertisements/subscriptions in the recent past. However, in addition to control messages dealing with advertisements and subscriptions, the routing overlay optimization requires information on recently published events that in this case needs to be collected in the control network. In this case, each subscriber/publisher periodically forwards the list of recently received events to IP_{fix} which then will be used by the routing overlay optimization algorithm to recalculate and install new channels. Alternatively, this information can also be collected asynchronously from the per-flow statistics (flow packet counter) maintained at each OpenFlow switch by the flow table configuration component.

The routing overlay optimization algorithm will in both cases rely on channelization methods like spectral clustering [32] to create clusters of subscribers and publishers. Each channel is treated as a separate flow and is assigned a unique address from the range of IPv6 multicast addresses reserved by the application (cf. Figure 3). The maximum number of channels is limited by the range of reserved addresses. However, at runtime the number of channels utilized by the system depends on the channelization algorithm and can be dynamically adjusted according to the subscriptions and the advertisements (as well as the event traffic in case of second approach) in the system. Our initial results show for uniform as well as Zipfian distributions—modeling the diversity of interest of subscribers—up to 100 channels are sufficient to perform efficient content-based filtering in publish/subscribe systems.

Once the channels are calculated, the routing overlay optimization calculates for each channel a minimum spanning tree which overall results in minimum bandwidth consumption. The flow table configuration component installs a separate flow for each channel by adding/updating actions in flow table entries of the OpenFlow switches in the network. In addition, it is necessary to send the flow id (i.e., IPv6

275

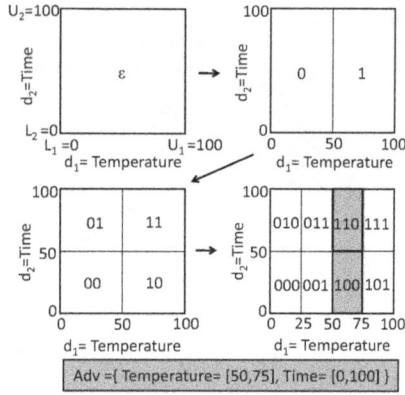

Figure 4: Decomposition of 2-dimensional space.

address) of all channels to which it is supposed to forward its publications to each publisher along with the aggregated subscription of those channels. This step is necessary because a publisher may publish an event that matches subscriptions belonging to multiple different channels. If the channel information is not available at the publishers, then each event should initially be sent to the controller to determine the matching flows (channels), which significantly increases the bandwidth utilization of the link to the controller as well as effects the line-rate forwarding of events.

3.4 In-network Filtering

The channelization approach does not allow for the possibility to prune unnecessary messages within each channel. An event forwarded on a channel is always delivered to the subscribers (issuers) of all the participant subscriptions. In this section, we present an approach to facilitate the filtering (pruning) of events within the switch network. First, we detail the method to decompose subscriptions, advertisements, and events into a spatial representation. Later, we describe how the spatial representation can be used to perform in-network filtering of events in the network of switches.

3.4.1 Spatial Indexing

The content-based schema consisting of d attributes can be modeled geometrically as a d-dimensional space (denoted as Ω) such that each dimension represents an attribute. We employ spatial indexing to divide the d-dimensional space into regular sub-spaces that serve as enclosing approximations for subscriptions, advertisements, and events [31]. As illustrated in Figure 4, any subspace can be identified by a binary string called a *dz-expression*. In particular, dz-expressions fulfill following properties:

1. The shorter the dz-expression the larger is the corresponding sub-space in Ω.

2. A sub-space represented by dz-expression dz_1 is *covered by* the sub-space represented by dz_2, iff dz_2 is a prefix of dz_1.

The subscription/advertisement can be composed of several dz-expressions. For instance, in Figure 4, the spatial representation of advertisement $Adv = \{Temperature = [50, 75] \wedge Time = [0, 100]\}$ requires two dz-expressions $\{100, 110\}$. Nevertheless, an event is represented by the

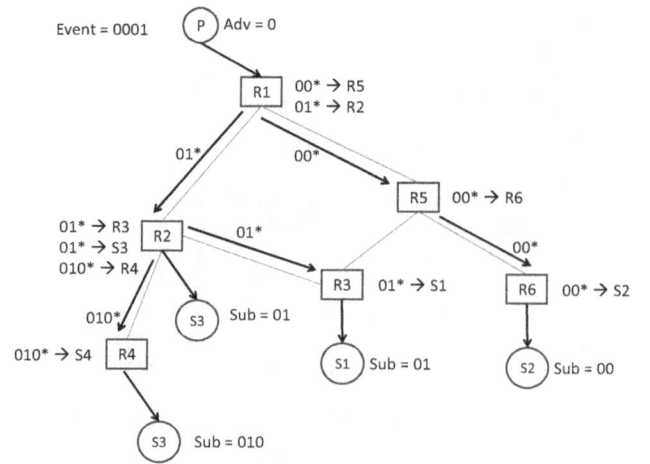

Figure 5: In-network filtering example.

smallest (finest resolution) sub-space that encloses the value represented by it.

3.4.2 Event Filtering

The content routing optimization uses the covering (or containment) relation between the spatial representations of newly arrived and the existing advertisements/subscriptions to set up flows between publishers and subscribers. In particular, each flow is associated with a sub-space and is identified by the corresponding dz. On the arrival of new advertisement Adv_1, the routing optimization algorithm checks for the containment relation between the dz of Adv_1 and the dz associated with the existing flows[1], and performs one of the three actions: (1) If the dz of Adv_1 is covered, then the newly arrived advertisement is mapped to the existing flows. For instance, a newly arrived advertisement 0 is mapped to the existing flows 00 and 01. (2) If dz of an existing flow is covered, then the existing flow is divided into sub flows. For instance, existing flow 0 is divided into sub flows 00 and 01 on the arrival of an advertisement 00. (3) If no containment relation exists, then a separate flow is created for the newly arrived advertisement.

Similarly, the arrival of a new subscription may divide an existing flow into sub flows. For instance, in Figure 5, the arrival of $sub = \{00\}$ divides flow 0 into two sub-flows $\{00*, 01*\}$ (note that only few least significant bits from the bits representing the range of reserved IPv6 addresses are shown to reduce complexity). The symbol $*$ is used to represent standard wildcard/masking operations, which are supported by hardware switches for matching IP addresses using Class-less Interdomain Routing (CIDR). Such wildcards are naturally supported by TCAM memory typically used in switches to store "don't care" values ($*$) besides 0 and 1. Therefore, an event (e.g., 0100) can be matched against the dz of the flow (e.g., 01$*$) in hardware by the switch during forwarding. The creation of two sub flows reduces unnecessary events by limiting the forwarding of events matching 01$*$ to the OpenFlow switches $R5$ and $R6$ as well as subscriber $S2$ in the example. Likewise, the advent of subscrip-

---

[1]In case an advertisement is represented by multiple dz-expressions, the covering relation is checked for each dz separately.

tion $sub = \{010\}$ creates a new flow $010*$ to avoid forwarding of events matching $011*$ to the network path connecting subscriber $S3$.

3.4.3 Discussion

It is worth noting that the total sub-spaces (created as a result of spatial indexing) depend on the number of decompositions of the d-dimensional space. Each decomposition step generates sub-spaces with finer granularity, capable of representing subscriptions/advertisements with higher accuracy. For instance, using the decomposition of Figure 4, a subscription $sub_1 = \{Temperature = [0, 100] \land Time = [0, 25]\}$ can be represented by the sub-spaces $\{000, 001, 100, 101\}$. These sub-spaces do not provide an accurate representation, and hence may match events that do not belong to the original subscription (sub_1) resulting in the dissemination of unnecessary events in the switch network. However, if another decomposition step is performed on dimension d_2, then sub_1 can be accurately mapped by the newly generated sub-spaces, i.e., $\{0000, 0010, 1000, 1010\}$.

Clearly, fine-grained sub-spaces are desirable as they avoid forwarding of unnecessary events. However, the decomposition steps needed to generate sub-spaces with finer granularity also increase the length of the dz-expressions (representing those sub-spaces). In practice, the length of dz-expression and hence the number of sub-spaces are limited by the range of IPv6 multicast addresses reserved by the application.

An important research challenge in this direction is to develop methods to lower the number of bits needed to perform efficient in-network filtering of events. For instance, one promising solution is to perform spatial indexing only on those dimensions that correspond to more selective attributes (i.e., filtering on the attributes results in less number of unnecessary messages). The attributes for the spatial indexing can be dynamically selected by the controller as a result of periodic collection of traffic statistics from the OpenFlow switches. We envision the study of different methods to perform efficient in-network filtering of events utilizing a smaller number of bits as an ongoing future work.

4. EVALUATION AND TESTING

In this section, we describe different alternatives to evaluate the performance of SDN-based communication middleware.

In general, the evaluation of communication middleware has to consider different network-centric performance metrics. First, from the provider's point of view, the *bandwidth-efficiency* is of great importance for the scalability of the middleware regarding the overall number of messages that can be delivered without overloading the underlying physical network. On the one hand, false positives should be kept to a minimum to avoid unnecessary messages wasting bandwidth. On the other hand, the existing physical network resources have to be utilized efficiently using optimized routes that avoid bottlenecks and balance load across alternative paths.

Secondly, the maximum *throughput* of messages is an important performance metric from an application's point of view. The throughput is determined by bottlenecks such as bandwidth limitations of links or processing limits of switches. Therefore, it does not only require optimized routing to avoid network bottlenecks, but also efficient forwarding mechanisms in switches for fast forwarding decisions.

Ideally, messages should be forwarded at *line-rate* to fully utilize the physical network resources.

Thirdly, delay-sensitive applications require low end-to-end delay from the publisher of a message to the subscribers. Besides calculating short paths, the latencies of switches again play an important role. Typically, very low forwarding latencies in the order of microseconds require hardware support.

SDN-supported communication middleware promises to achieve high scalability, throughput, and low latencies by taking advantage of hardware switches, which directly perform message forwarding on the network layer. In order to evaluate all of these properties, the tools for evaluating the system performance have to be chosen carefully. Next, we will discuss different alternatives for the evaluation of such SDN-based communication middleware systems.

4.1 Simulation

As first alternative, network simulators can be used for the evaluation. Since the essential feature of SDN is to execute forwarding directly on the network layer, the network simulator has to support layer 3 forwarding based on IP addresses (preferably IPv6 since mapping content-based publish/subscribe attributes to IP addresses requires a larger address space as shown). This makes simulators targeted at overlay networks like PeerSim [24] unsuitable. Instead, simulators including network layer support such as ns3 [19] are required, which today also provide SDN implementations to simulate OpenFlow switches.

Although simulators are well-suited to evaluate the bandwidth-efficiency also in larger scenarios and with different network topologies, they suffer from two drawbacks: First, the control logic has to be re-implemented for the simulated controller rather than using the code of the actual controller. Secondly, and more importantly, performance metrics depending on the processing power cannot be evaluated realistically. In particular, this includes the latencies of switches and the controller (if messages are also forwarded via the controller).

4.2 Emulation

A second alternative is to use network emulation rather than simulation. A prominent tool for emulating software-defined networks is Mininet [15]. Mininet uses virtualization technologies to emulate several OpenFlow switches on a single host. A real controller can be connected to these switches. Therefore, the real control logic can be used for the experiments, in contrast to simulated controllers. As a consequence, also the performance of the real controller can be taken into account. Moreover, the emulated network has the same flexibility as simulated networks since different topologies can be configured easily.

However, since switches are emulated, they do not reflect the performance (in particular, latency) of physical switches. Moreover, the performance of the machine hosting the emulated network limits the size of the network that can be evaluated.

4.3 Testbeds

Testbeds consisting of physical switches and controllers are the last alternative for performing evaluations. Obviously, a testbed of OpenFlow hardware switches provides realistic results with respect to forwarding performance (throughput

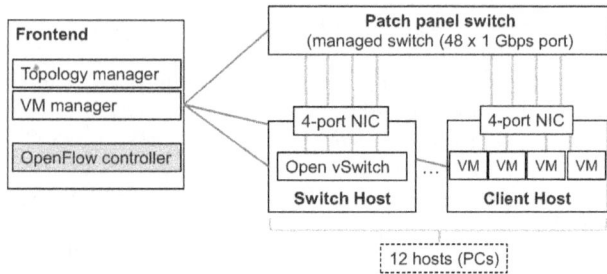

Figure 6: SDN testbed using commodity hardware.

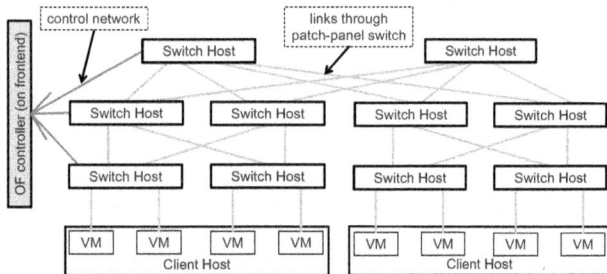

Figure 7: Exemplary network topology (depicted links are point-to-point connections through the patch-panel switch).

and delay). However, considering the price of an OpenFlow switch (several thousand US dollars), experiments are usually restricted to smaller scenarios. Public testbeds such as the European OFELIA testbed [20], which is open to research projects, can provide an alternative.

We have implemented another alternative testbed at the University of Stuttgart consisting of commodity PC hardware and virtualization technologies as used in datacenters (cf. Figure 6). This testbed consists of a cluster of hosts (commodity rack PCs), each equipped with a 4-port Gigabit Ethernet network interface controller (NIC). Some of these hosts act as OpenFlow switches (*switch hosts*) with four physical ports by executing a production-grade software switch (Open vSwitch [23]) attached to the 4-port NIC. The other hosts act as end systems (*client hosts*) with publishers and subscribers by executing four virtual machines on each host. Each virtual machine is connected to one port of the 4-port NIC. A *frontend machine* executes the SDN controller (connected to the hosts through a separate on-board NIC), and manages the virtual machines and network topology (see below).

The network topology can be any topology where switches have at most four links. For instance, Figure 6 shows a hierarchical Fat Tree topology found in data centers [2]. However, also other topologies can be configured like a flat mesh topology. In order to be able to quickly switch between topologies without physical rewiring, we added a *patch-panel switch* (standard managed switch; non-OpenFlow) between the hosts to configure point-to-point connections from ports to switches. Changing the topology just requires changing the mapping between ports of the patch-panel switch through the topology manager executed on the frontend.

This setup can be considered to be a compromise between network emulation and a testbed of hardware switches. It is able to achieve line-rate forwarding performance. Since

the software switch performs forwarding in kernel space, it is faster than user space forwarding solutions. However, it does not reach the low forwarding latency of hardware switches. To also achieve very low forwarding latency, the 4-port NICs can be replaced by 4-port NetFPGA boards [17] which perform forwarding in hardware at the cost of a higher price than a commodity 4-port NIC (in this case, also the patch-panel switch should be replaced by direct cables to remove the artificial extra forwarding latency).

Finally, we would like to mention another cost-efficient solution for smaller testbeds like the one shown in Figure 7. In this scenario, a single 48-port hardware OpenFlow switch is sufficient to replace the ten hosts equipped with 4-port NICs implementing software switches. A prerequisite is that this 48-port hardware switch can be partitioned into ten 4-port logical switches (plus 8 unused ports) as proposed, for instance, in OpenFlow's companion standard OF-CONFIG [21]. The hardware switch achieves line-rate throughput and low forwarding latency. However, the physical memory for flow table entries is shared between the logical switches.

5. RESEARCH PROBLEMS

We conclude this paper by discussing open research problems in building event-based systems with SDN.

Minimizing flow table size. Typically, a switch only has up to 150,000 flow table entries which are shared between all applications. In this paper, we have outlined two approaches that can adjust the trade-off between the number of flow table entries and bandwidth efficiency (number of false positives). However, further research is required to find an optimal solution given a restricted number of flow table entries.

Scalable controller. The controller has to perform computational complex tasks such as optimal route calculation (distribution trees) or subscriber clustering. In particular, these tasks become challenging in large-scale and highly dynamic systems with larger topologies, many publishers and subscribers, high churn rates, dynamic link state, etc. Although a single controller might look like a potential bottleneck at first sight, it could still be implemented scalably by utilizing, for instance, the large resources of data centers ("the cloud"). This requires suitable algorithms that scale up to many cores and scale out to multiple machines. Another possibility to improve scalability is a distributed controller as described next.

Decentralized control and coordination. Although we assumed a single logical controller in this paper, the control plane could be distributed to several controllers to improve scalability and robustness. However, this raises several questions: How many controllers do we need and where to place them [8]? And how to coordinate controllers in order to achieve a consistent and optimal behavior, while letting each controller base its decisions on a local and/or aggregated view? For instance, controllers could be organized hierarchically, or in a (flat) peer-to-peer topology, both requiring different coordination concepts.

Correct operation and verification. Distributed protocols make it hard to achieve correct operation such as loop-free forwarding or constant reachability, in particular, during transitional phases like the re-configuration of distribution trees. However, central control and a globe view on the system—as used in this paper—facilitate the design of correct algorithms and ease the verification of the running system as first approaches demonstrate [12, 26].

Quality of Service (QoS). Many applications such as network control systems rely on QoS properties like a maximum end-to-end delay. This requires the implementation of resource reservation mechanisms or scheduling algorithms for forwarding. Since forwarding is done on the network layer, we can benefit from existing layer 3 protocols and the access to switches/routers—assuming suitable interfaces for virtualized switches/routers—, which are likely to outperform application layer approaches.

Virtual network abstractions. Providing a virtual network spanning resources from multiple providers is a problem that we did not focus on in this paper. However, for achieving optimal performance one question is how many and which physical switches and routers should be exposed in the virtual network? In a multi-provider (ISP) scenario, one might also be able to choose from switches of alternative providers based on advanced optimization metrics like monetary costs.

6. CONCLUSION AND FUTURE WORK

In this paper, we have shown that software-defined networking provides a powerful abstraction to configure communication middleware—in particular, middleware for event-based systems—with the potential to yield significant performance gains.

As we pointed out many research problems exist to understand and utilize the full potential of SDN. Our research focus will be on extending the apparoaches along this direction as well as understanding how even more complex event-based systems can benefit from SDN.

7. REFERENCES

[1] B. Ahlgren, P. A. Aranda, P. Chemouil, S. Oueslati, L. M. Correia, H. Karl, M. Söllner, and A. Welin. Content, connectivity, and cloud: ingredients for the network of the future. *IEEE Communications Magazine*, 49(7):62–70, 2011.

[2] M. Al-Fares, A. Loukissas, and A. Vahdat. A scalable, commodity data center network architecture. In *Proceedings of ACM SIGCOMM 2008*, pages 63–74, Seattle, WA, Aug. 2008.

[3] J. A. Briones, B. Koldehofe, and K. Rothermel. SPINE : Adaptive Publish/Subscribe for Wireless Mesh Networks. *Studia Informatika Universalis*, 7(3):320–353, 2009.

[4] A. Carzaniga, D. S. Rosenblum, and A. L. Wolf. Design and evaluation of a wide-area event notification service. *ACM Transactions on Computer Systems*, 19(3):332–383, 2001.

[5] F. Dabek, R. Cox, F. Kaashoek, and R. Morris. Vivaldi: a decentralized network coordinate system. *ACM SIGCOMM Computer Communication Review*, 34:15–26, 2004.

[6] D. Erickson. Beacon. https://openflow.stanford.edu/display/Beacon/Home.

[7] Project Floodlight: open source software for building software defined networks. http://www.projectfloodlight.org/.

[8] B. Heller, R. Sherwood, and N. McKeown. The controller placement problem. In *Proceedings of the First Workshop on Hot Topics in Software-defined Networks (HotSDN)*, pages 7–12, 2012.

[9] H.-A. Jacobsen, A. K. Y. Cheung, G. Li, B. Maniymaran, V. Muthusamy, and R. S. Kazemzadeh. The PADRES publish/subscribe system. In *Principles and Applications of Distributed Event-Based Systems*, pages 164–205. 2010.

[10] X. Jin, W. Tu, and S. H. G. Chan. Scalable and efficient end-to-end network topology inference. *IEEE Transactions on Parallel and Distributed Systems*, 19(6):837–850, 2008.

[11] P. Jokela, A. Zahemszky, C. Esteve Rothenberg, S. Arianfar, and P. Nikander. LIPSIN: line speed publish/subscribe inter-networking. In *Proceedings of the ACM SIGCOMM conference on Data communication*, pages 195–206, 2009.

[12] A. Khurshid, W. Zhou, M. Caesar, and P. B. Godfrey. VeriFlow: Verifying network-wide invariants in real time. In *Proceedings of the First Workshop on Hot Topics in Software-defined Networks (HotSDN)*, pages 49–54, 2012.

[13] B. Koldehofe, F. Dürr, M. A. Tariq, and K. Rothermel. The power of software-defined networking: Line-rate content-based routing using openflow. In *Proceedings of the 7th MW4NG Workshop of the 13th International Middleware Conference 2012*, pages 3:1–3:6, 2012.

[14] M. Kwon and S. Fahmy. Path-aware overlay multicast. *Computer Networks*, 47(1):23–45, 2005.

[15] B. Lantz, B. Heller, and N. McKeown. A network on a laptop: Rapid prototyping for software-defined networks. In *Proceedings of the Ninth ACM Workshop on Hot Topics in Networks (HotNets 2010)*, Monterey, CA, Oct. 2010.

[16] G. Mühl. *Large-Scale Content-Based Publish-Subscribe Systems*. PhD thesis, TU Darmstadt, November 2002.

[17] Netfpga. http://netfpga.org/.

[18] noxrepo: open source control platforms Nox and Pox for software defined networks. http://www.noxrepo.org/.

[19] ns3. http://www.nsnam.org/.

[20] Ofelia. http://www.fp7-ofelia.eu/.

[21] Open Networking Foundation. OpenFlow management and configuration protocol (OF-CONFIG v1.1.1). Technical report, Mar. 2013.

[22] OpenDaylight. http://www.opendaylight.org/.

[23] Open vSwitch. http://openvswitch.org/.

[24] Peersim p2p simulator. http://peersim.sourceforge.net/.

[25] P. Pietzuch. *Hermes: A Scalable Event-Based Middleware*. PhD thesis, University of Cambridge, Feb 2004.

[26] M. Reitblatt, N. Foster, J. Rexford, C. Schlesinger, and D. Walker. Abstractions for network update. In *Proceedings of the ACM SIGCOMM Conference on Applications, Technologies, Architectures, and Protocols for Computer Communication*, pages 323–334, 2012.

[27] B. Rochwerger, D. Breitgand, E. Levy, A. Galis, K. Nagin, I. M. Llorente, R. Montero, Y. Wolfsthal, E. Elmroth, J. Cáceres, M. Ben-Yehuda,

W. Emmerich, and F. Galán. The reservoir model and architecture for open federated cloud computing. *IBM Journal of Research and Development*, 53(4):1–11, 2009.

[28] M. Sadoghi, H. Singh, and H.-A. Jacobsen. fpga-ToPSS: line-speed event processing on fpgas. In *Proceedings of the 5th ACM international conference on Distributed event-based system (DEBS)*, pages 373–374, 2011.

[29] G. Schaffrath, C. Werle, P. Papadimitriou, A. Feldmann, R. Bless, A. Greenhalgh, A. Wundsam, M. Kind, O. Maennel, and L. Mathy. Network virtualization architecture: proposal and initial prototype. In *Proceedings of the 1st ACM workshop on Virtualized infrastructure systems and architectures (VISA '09)*, 2009.

[30] A. Tariq, B. Koldehofe, G. Koch, and K. Rothermel. Providing probabilistic latency bounds for dynamic publish/subscribe systems. In *Proceedings of the 16th*

ITG/GI Conference on Kommunikation in Verteilten Systemen (KiVS), pages 155–166, 2009.

[31] M. A. Tariq, B. Koldehofe, G. G. Koch, I. Khan, and K. Rothermel. Meeting subscriber-defined QoS constraints in publish/subscribe systems. *Concurrency and Computation: Practice and Experience*, 23(11):2140–2153, 2011.

[32] M. A. Tariq, B. Koldehofe, G. G. Koch, and K. Rothermel. Distributed spectral cluster management: A method for building dynamic publish/subscribe systems. In *Proceedings of the 6th ACM International Conference on Distributed Event-Based Systems (DEBS)*, pages 213–224, 2012.

[33] M. A. Tariq, B. Koldehofe, and K. Rothermel. Efficient content-based routing with network topology inference. In *Proceedings of the 7th ACM International Conference on Distributed Event-Based Systems (DEBS)*, 2013.

Tutorial: Personal Big Data Management in the Cyber-physical Systems – The Role of Event Processing

Nenad Stojanovic
FZI, Research Center for
Information Technology
Haid-und-Neu-Str. 10-14,
76131 Karlsruhe, Germany
nstojano@fzi.de

Ljiljana Stojanovic
FZI, Research Center for
Information Technology
Haid-und-Neu-Str. 10-14,
76131 Karlsruhe, Germany
stojanov@fzi.de

Roland Stuehmer
FZI, Research Center for
Information Technology
Haid-und-Neu-Str. 10-14,
76131 Karlsruhe, Germany
stuehmer@fzi.de

ABSTRACT

In this paper we present an overview of the role that Event Processing can have for the management of personal information in cyberphysical systems. In particular, we present the challenges for this process, mainly related to the Internet of Things and Big Data processing, 2) elaborate on current efforts in developing an event-driven platform that supports the above mentioned requirements and c) present examples from one real-life scenario (remote patient monitoring).

In the central part we present the platform for realizing such an approach. The platform consists of three main components: a distributed publish/subscribe enabled service bus responsible for collecting events from heterogeneous, distributed sources, Event Cloud, a peer-to-peer semantic-based repository responsible for the storage of events and distributed Complex Event Processing responsible for the complex combination of events in real-time. Two main advantages of the platforms are its scalability (cloud-based nature) and the expressivity of the requests that can be defined (combination of real-time and historical queries) based on Web technologies such as RDF and SPARQL.

Categories and Subject Descriptors

H.3.4 [Information Systems]: SYSTEMS AND SOFTWARE Information networks

Keywords

Cyberphysical Systems, Mobile Event Processing, Health Monitoring

1. INTRODUCTION

With the growing success of the new generation mobile technologies the mobile computing devices become more and more popular, the most people has his/her own mobile computing device (e.g. smart phone or tablet computer). On another hand the electronic sensors special the physiological sensors are used more and more in our daily life rather than only in lab environment [1]. Nowadays almost every mobile device has been integrated several sensors such as accelerometer, gyroscope and GPS and the additional sensors including physiological sensors like heartbeat rate sensor or skin conductance sensor can also be connected easily through bluetooth network. Therefore much personal information of users and the environment information of the users can be detected in real time through their mobile device.

How to cope with this enormous quantity of the real time (personal and environmental) information, i.e. which of them are useful and which of them should be monitored, is one of the main challenges of the modern life, which can be treated as real time Big Data challenge [2] [3]. In order to get the benefits of the information surrounding people, new technologies are needed for mobile event-driven processing in the sensor-rich environments (like IoT, Internet of Things), its integration with the server-based processing, incl. real-time and analytical processing (mining of historical information), as well as new knowledge (pattern) management methods to enable the description of complex situations that should be managed and ensure their evolution over time, as the context changes.

In this paper we introduce an approach for using complex event processing technologies (CEP) in a mobile, sensor-enabled environment to process the personal and environmental information of the user in real-time, monitor the important and critical situation and provide the suitable recommendations to the users. Such an architecture will enable the exchange of contextual information (events) between heterogeneous services, providing the possibilities of optimizing and personalizing the execution of the services themselves, resulting in context-driven adaptivity. This infrastructure leads to the concept of the Event Marketplace (similar to a service marketplace) where events coming from different event producers (as illustrated above) can be arbitrary combined by different event consumers.

We argue that the proposed solution can scale regarding the distribution of services (sources) and the throughput of interesting information that can be exchanged and can be easily extended with new services (openness). In addition, the platform uses its cloud-computing nature to be "elastic" as such, could also be turned to operate in the "pay as you go" mode. It has governance that can enforce different non-functional quality criteria (e.g. that a critical event cannot be lost in this huge distributed processing environment) and we have introduced the notion of Event Level Agreement (ELA) that formalize these principles. Moreover, the platform is an active mediator, it can recommend dynamically interesting information which one (service) should (ad-hoc) subscribe to in order to be able to better adapt its execution to the current opportunities.

In order to demonstrate the validity of the approach we present a business case study from the eHealth domain, which is oriented toward real-time remote monitoring of patients with the goal to enable early detection of the potentially dangerous situations and ensure the proper reaction. The demonstration system is based on the commercially available wearable cardio sensors (measuring the performances of the heart's work, like heart rate, heart rate variability or ECG) and the usage of the Android-based smartphones. The system has been tested on the group of patients suffering from the hypertension [1] (high blood pressure). Preliminary results have shown that the presented approach is very promising, especially from the point of view of modeling complex monitoring/diagnostic situations.

We argue that there is a huge application potential of these systems in the general domain of Personal Big Data Management in the Cyber-physical Systems since the technologies for sensing psychophysiology[2] of people are getting ever more non-intrusive and inexpensive and managing people's psychophysiological status has become a key factor for healthier life (e.g. less stress) or more efficient work (e.g. better attention).

It is important to note that (unexpected) opportunities finding is one of the main advantages of the Marketplace: the platform can inform not only that something that was expected happened (done by subscribing to existing complex event patterns in advance), but also can recommend, based on the currently available events, to track some new information that might help in optimizing service execution (realized by recommending to subscribe to some complex event patterns in real time). More concrete examples will be provided in later sections. This feature is based on the event-driven contextualization of the actors (service) that leads to so called situational awareness, i.e. based on the current "flow" of events related to an actor, the platform is aware of the current situation it is involved in.

The paper is structured in the following way: In the second section we describe the motivation of the approach and introduce the requirements for the remote personal monitoring. Our solution is explained in section 3, containing the main technique used. Section 4 introduces the use case and example of the approach. The validation details are provided in the section 5. Afterwards we describe the related works and the conclusion.

2. MOTIVATION AND REQUIREMENTS

Cyber-physical systems (CPS) represent engineered systems where functionalities and salient characteristics emerge from the networked interaction of computational and physical components. Example CPSs include automobiles, aircraft, air traffic control, power grids, oil refineries, medical devices, patient monitoring, and smart structures. One of the main challenges for these systems is the real-time processing of various signals coming from different sensor-based subsystems.

A very important development in CPS in recent years is ever increasing role of different human sensing techniques in the control of a CPS system. The example are wearable sensors which measure in real-time some healthy-related parameters like heart rate, respiratory level, physical activity level, with the main goal to include the psychophysiological[3] status of a user (e.g. stress level, attention level) in the interaction with the environment and the socio/technological systems. Well known applications are modern remote patient monitoring systems, or advance augmented reality systems.

This development implies the need for an advance in processing real-time signals produced in the CPS systems since a) the psychophysiological sensing has become very non-intrusive, producing a large amount of useful data that should be processed locally in a more intensive way (not only on the server because of the privacy reasons), b) the need for an extensive contextualization of these signals and complex processing ahead

of time (different ways of predictions, especially nowcasting) is emerging and c) there is a strong requirement for providing some guarantees for the performances of the processing, by real-time monitoring/managing the performances of the system.

In order to make the explanation of the approach more understandable, we introduce here a motivating example that is going beyond patient monitoring (i.e. fitness monitoring) will be used in further sections. The sketch is presented in **Error! Reference source not found.** that we briefly describe:

- The Marketplace is collecting real-time data from different sources, like smartphones, social media, environmental sensors
- Smartphones are sensing the GPS location and the signals from wearable sensors, like heart-beat rate, speed, distance
- The Marketplace offers a recommendation service for the running competition, that provides a suitable person as a competitor (theoretically the Marketplace can provide the service Your competitor, that would simulate a perfect competitor for the user)
- A user defines preferences for the competitor. In the case illustrated in Figure 1 it is: "*Someone who wrote a tweet about competition in last two weeks*"
- During the running the user is activated the request for finding a companion for running: "*Notify me if my current running performances vary and there is someone in my proximity who satisfies my **preferences** for running in a company*". Note that this request can be automatically triggered.
- The Marketplace is executing this complex query (preferences and request) on the real-time streams and historical data stored in the marketplace (see the query syntax in later sections)
- A recommendation event "*There is a lady with a dog*" is generated and delivered to the first runner's phone as soon as a person satisfying the request will appear.
- If the user accepts this recommendation, another service from the Marketplace will start a discussion process with another runner.

Therefore, modern sensor technologies enable that wearable sensors detect much information about the personal status such as heartbeat rate, skin conductance, blood pressure (that belongs to the psychophysiological parameters) and the environment information like air humidity and atmospheric pressure. With the development of the modern computer technologies the mobile computing devices (e.g. smart phone or tablet computer) become more and more powerful and the sensors can be integrated or connected to the mobile computing devices in an easier way. Therefore the personal data and the environment information can be collected easily through the sensors that the user is wearing on and the carried mobile devices. Furthermore powerful hardware of the mobile device enables processing of sensor data in real time on the mobile device using CEP (complex event processing).

Figure 2 shows the overview of the proposed system. Although the mobile device has been becoming more powerful, the performance of the mobile device is still limited comparing to the traditional desktop system. In additional the limited battery capacity restricts the durative stable performance of the mobile device. Regarding such issues we use an additional server infrastructure to support the mobile device as shown in Figure 2.

---

[1] http://en.wikipedia.org/wiki/Hypertension

[2] http://en.wikipedia.org/wiki/Psychophysiology

[3] http://en.wikipedia.org/wiki/Psychophysiology

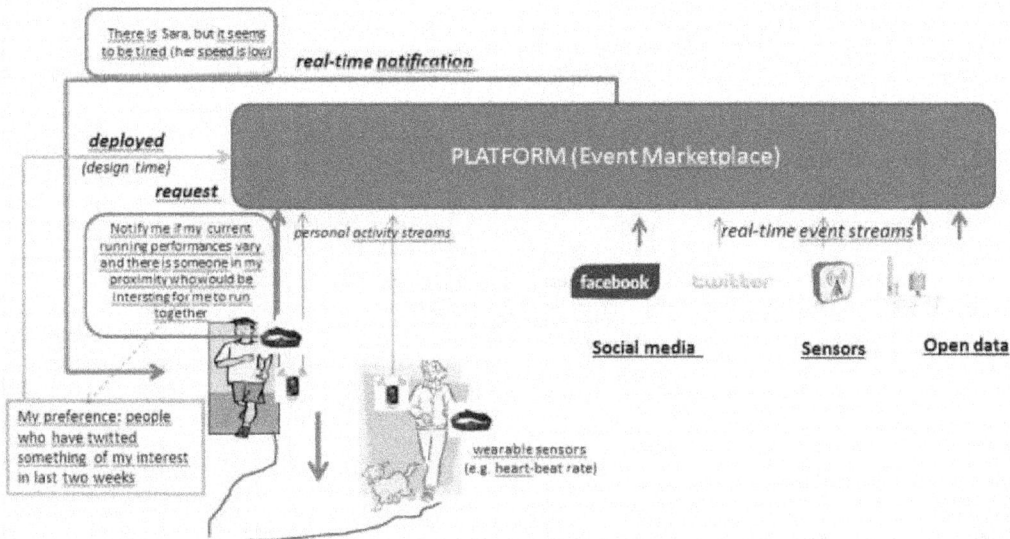

Figure 1: Data-driven querying in action

Figure 2: Overview of the processing flow

The mobile device collects the personal data (physiological data) and environment information sensed by the integrated or connected sensors, while the server infrastructure collects the information from external event sources, such as social media (e.g. Facebook and twitter) or environmental open data (e.g. weather information from the weather stations) and also connects to the domain knowledge bases taking advantage of the large storage space of the server infrastructure. As shown in the figure two CEP engines are used in MCEP system; one is a light weight engine running on the mobile device that is used for preprocessing of the mobile sensing (but including complex event patterns) and another is the full-functioning CEP engine that runs on the server infrastructure and detects more complex event patterns involving different types of events (e.g. from environmental sensors, social web). Both engines work collaboratively. As the result of monitoring and complex processing the recommendations are directly shown to the user on the mobile device.

Since the most sensor data are collected by mobile device, processing the sensor data directly on the mobile device can improve the performance of system regarding the possible slow network transmission rate and high costs. Additionally the privacy of the data must be considered, as the personal data including physiological data of the user has been collected and used in the

monitoring. Some users want to use such data only on the mobile device on the local and don't permit to transfer the data to the server, therefore the system is required to have the ability to process the data on the mobile device.

Regarding the limited performance and the possible abrupt tasks (e.g. the incoming phone call or activities of other Apps) of the mobile device, the mobile device may not able to afford the execution of deployed patterns. In the case of such situations dynamic pattern execution is required, which enable to flexible deploy the patterns on the mobile device or on the server including changing the pattern deployment in the run time.

Figure 3 illustrates the components required for realizing this type of processing, which will be detailed in the next section.

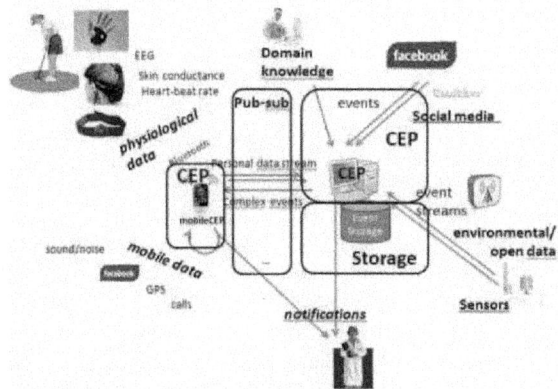

Figure 3: Processing blocks

3. OUR APPROACH

Based on the requirements defined in the previous section, in this section we introduce our approach and the main technologies that are used to realize it.

3.1. Platform

The conceptual architecture for our platform is depicted in Figure 4. We introduce the components briefly before explaining how each of them is needed in the overall functionality.

283

The Distributed Service Bus (DSB) provides the SOA and EDA (Event Driven Architecture) infrastructure for components and end user services. It acts as the basis for service deployments, and processes (BPEL, BPMN), routing synchronous and asynchronous messages from services consumers to service providers. Based on the principles of the system integration paradigm of Enterprise Service Bus the DSB is distributed by nature.

The Governance component allows users to get information about services and events, as well as specifying QoS requirements as SLA contracts using the WS-Agreement standard. The Governance component extends a standard Service-based governance tool (OW2 Petals Master) by adding governance mechanisms for event-based systems. Its role is to provide ways to govern services and events. It provides standards-based APIs and a graphical user interface.

The Event Cloud provides storage and forwarding of events. The role of the Event Cloud is a unified API for manipulating events, real-time or historic. To that end, it contains a peer-to-peer (P2P) network to store histories of events durably in a distributed fashion. In the same way the list of subscribers is distributed across the peers to notify subscribers if a given new event is stored at any node and a corresponding matching subscription exists in the system. Subscriptions may use a simple set of operators such as conjunctive queries to filter out an interesting event according to the numerous information it holds. More complex queries are executed in the DCEP component.

The DCEP component (Distributed Complex Event Processing) has the role of detecting complex events and reasoning over events by means of event patterns defined in logic rules. To detect complex events, DCEP subscribes to the Event Cloud for any simple event defined in the event patterns at a given point in time. DCEP supports traditional event operators such as sequence, concurrent conjunction, disjunction, negation, etc., all operators from Allen's interval algebra, window operators, filtering, enrichment, projection, translation, and multiplication. Out-of-order event processing is supported (e.g. events that are delayed due to different circumstances such as network anomalies).

The Platform Services component incorporates several functional additions to the platform as a whole. The Query Dispatcher has the role of decomposing and deploying user subscriptions in pieces supported by the Event Cloud and DCEP respectively, taking into account the expressivity supported by the two target components. The Event Metadata component stores information about events, such as source descriptions, event type schemas, etc, to enable the discovery of relevant events for an event consumer and to provide data to the subscription recommender. The ESR and SAR component forms the Event Subscription Recommender (ESR) and Service Adaptation Recommender (SAR). However, both ESR and SAR components are not in the focus of this paper.

The next basic scenario is concerned with how to subscribe to complex event patterns, including checking of privacy: The request for detecting a new complex event is again started from a service or end user connected to the DSB (cf. Figure 1). The request is sent to the Governance component which has the role of checking the permissions of the requestor for all of the simple event streams contained in the event pattern. After that the request is forwarded to the Query Dispatcher. Its role is the decomposition of the query into the parts which can be handled locally in the nodes of the Event Cloud and the parts which must be handled by DCEP. The resulting parts are then deployed respectively. Non-functional properties are propagated along with the queries. Thus the Event Cloud and DCEP can monitor and

enforce them. Finally a new stream and metadata is created for the complex events, just like in the previous case of registering a simple event stream. Now, however, the stream contains complex events of a given type: yet, requirements such as non-functional properties, the possibility of discovery and offering subscriptions through WS-Notification apply here in the same way.

Simple events are created on the DSB. They are published by event sources using WS-Notification. The streams of events are handed over to the Event Cloud and transformed to the internal event format of the platform (RDF format). An XML schema will be provided so that services can produce events without knowing the RDF event format of the platform. For this schema a generic mapping will be available. After the events are received by the Event Cloud it will route them to their final storage nodes. At these nodes there will be information about all subscribers which must be notified. For the sake of argument, the DCEP component

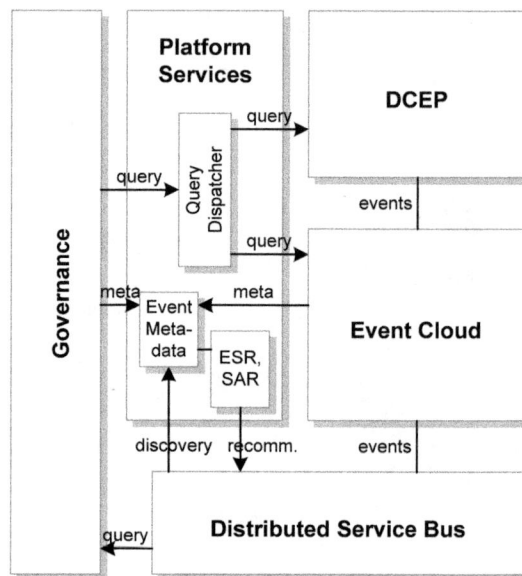

Figure 4: Conceptual Architecture

will be among this set of subscribers because the given event in our scenario is part of a complex event pattern which was registered with DCEP earlier. So, next the DCEP is notified about the event. After notifications for all events of an event pattern arrive, DCEP detects a complex event and in turn notifies the Event Cloud to store and disseminate the complex event using the stream ID of the complex event stream and respectively the right topic on the DSB. The circle is closed from event sources on the DSB to event sinks on the DSB.

Big Data Processing Language

We propose a language to combine real-time data and contextual (historic) data. The language supports use cases as depicted in our introduction and it is suited to be evaluated in a distributed setting. The language is Big Data Processing Language, BDPL. We modelled BDPL as close to SPARQL 1.1 as possible. Exceptions are being made for necessary event operators and the denotations of events compared to non-event historic data. Event derivation (the process of materializing the resulting event) is handled through a CONSTRUCT clause as proposed by SPARQL 1.1. The pattern to be matched is modelled in the WHERE clause. A pattern can contain several events combined with event operators (e.g. SEQ, WINDOW) nested in a sliding time window. The referenced paper describes the event operators' matching semantics in terms of the event's time stamps along with an execution model of our language. Each event is filtered further by its content using graph patterns as defined in SPARQL 1.1. The clause, however, is denoted with EVENT here to distinguish the real-time parts of the query from the optional historic parts. Bound variables are allowed to join events on values in the individual event instances. We extended our underlying engine ETALIS [4] to execute XPATH functions such as fn:contains() to be more expressive with regard to handling XML data types.

The query syntax can be described in plain English as such: We use a subset of the SPARQL 1.1 language: CONSTRUCT queries without operators UNION and OPTIONAL, subqueries, or LIMIT clauses. We distinguish graph patterns (using syntax EVENT and GRAPH) into real-time data and historic data respectively. The real-time parts may be combined with temporal operators such as time windows from [4] to enable temporal processing.

Intuitively, a query is fulfilled if there is a mapping [5] for all variables from the real-time parts and a compatible mapping for the historic data at the time of the real-time answer. Operationally this means that the real-time part is applied to the streams. When there is a result the variable mapping will be checked for compatibility with all historic parts in the query. An inner join is performed on the mappings to derive if they are compatible.

Events

The Linked Data principles [6] are a methodology of publishing structured data and to interlink the data to make them more useful. The principles apply to event modelling. Linked Data is used to reference data from different sections of our distributed storage. Also Linked Data can be employed by end users to reference public contextual data which is not contained in the events.

There is an event ontology from which the event types are inherited. This ontology can be extended by any user by referencing the RDF type: Event as a super class. The ontology makes use of related work by reusing the class "Event" from Dolce Ultralight based on DOLCE [7]. The event format supports interval-based events as well as point-based events by using either just :endTime for a point or both, :startTime and :endTime for an interval. Using the mentioned lists, the event can link to two other events in different streams which were used as input to create the event. These linked events can have further linked events themselves. This allows modelling of composite events [8].

We are developing this event model to satisfy requirements of an open platform addressing *variety* in big data. As such, data from the Web must be reused and be extensible for broader participation. The event schema itself and future updates to the schema can be tracked on-line at [10].

4. USE CASE

Arrhythmia is a common medical condition which includes a broad range of heart-related pathologies. Although not all of them are permanent or require medical attention, they may provide hints to the development of serious heart diseases. The ECG has been a cornerstone for the detection and diagnosis of such conditions for a long time. However, its interpretation is mostly based on medical experts or specialized hardware only available in clinical environments. There is a definite need for automatic, lowcost physiological monitoring solutions that are easy to use, accurate, and can be used in home or ambulatory settings. However, the main problem is not caused by the interpretation of the ECG data since there are many algorithms that can classify arrhythmia from a clear signal. The problem is caused by the interference of the ECG signal and motion (so called motion

artifact), that makes the signal less clear and less usable for the diagnosis. Moreover, other contextual parameters like the air temperature or humidity are also influencing the precision of the detection process. Therefore, the processing infrastructure should be able to define and process a more complex context, including the historical information.

In this paper we present a solution that uses presented infrastructure for collecting and processing ECG data. ECG data is sent through a gateway to the Platform, creating a huge traffic (pro patient 256 events per second). The contextual information accounts the physical activity of the patients, like the type (walking, stairs claiming) and the intensity. In this use case we use the Bioharness 3 sensors (http://www.zephyranywhere.com/products/bioharness-3/), which measures many relevant parameters: heart rate, ECG, posture, body tempereature, R-R interval

The following listing shows an event generated from a simple heartbeat sensor. The event schema combines a sensor schema in namespace nissa: with the Facebook namespace user. The Facebook URI is an example use of Linked Data where more RDF data about the user are obtained by following the URI.

```
@prefix :        <http://events.event-processing.org/types/> .
@prefix nissa:   <http://www.nissatech.rs/ns/types/> .
@prefix geo:     <http://www.w3.org/2003/01/geo/wgs84_pos#> .
@prefix xsd:     <http://www.w3.org/2001/XMLSchema#> .
@prefix rdf:     <http://www.w3.org/1999/02/22-rdf-syntax-ns#> .
@prefix user:    <http://graph.facebook.com/schema/user#> .

<http://events.../nissa1340688541673999872#event>
    a                     nissa:HeartbeatAlert ;
    :endTime              "2012-12-22T13:31:13Z"^^xsd:dateTime ;
    :location [ a         geo:Point ;
    geo:lat   "8.40118890000001"^^xsd:double ;
    geo:long  "49.008156"^^xsd:double .
] ;
    :message              "This is a heartbeat alert (currently at 91) sent
from Android." ;
    :screenName           "firstname.lastname" ;
    :stream               <http://streams.../PersonalMonitoring#stream> ;
    uctelco:phoneNumber   "12345" ;
    user:id               "12345" ;
    user:link             <http://graph.facebook.com/12345#> ;
    nissa:acc             "50.0"^^xsd:double ;
    nissa:battery         "96"^^xsd:int ;
    nissa:calories        "0.08778622072179713"^^xsd:double ;
    nissa:distance        "12.5"^^xsd:double ;
    nissa:duration        "26"^^xsd:int ;
    nissa:heartRate       "91"^^xsd:int ;
    nissa:sessionId       "6"^^xsd:int ;
    nissa:speed           "1.2"^^xsd:double ;
    nissa:steps           "10"^^xsd:int ;
```

The following listing shows a BDPL query for patient monitoring. The purpose of the query is to specifically alert patients who are near a location were reports of increased heartbeat rates were recorded e.g., climbing a steep hill. The construct clause defines the warning created. The where clause requires one location event in real-time and 10 previous reports from history. Privacy is supported by our backend on a per-stream level, so for this query we assume access permission for the stream PersonalMonitoring#stream.

```
PREFIX :    http://events.event-processing.org/types/
...
CONSTRUCT {
        :e rdf:type :UCTelcoEsrRecom .
        :e :stream <http://streams.../Recommendation#stream> .
        :e uctelco:phoneNumber ?phone .
        :e :message "More than 10 alerts were caused here in the past week." .
        :e :location [ geo:lat ?latitude1 ;
                       geo:long ?longitude1 ].
        :e nissa:heartRate ?heartRate2 .
}
WHERE {
        EVENT ?id1 {
            ?e1 rdf:type :UCTelcoGeoLocation .
            ?e1 :stream <http://streams.../GeoLocation#stream> .
            ?e1 :location [ geo:lat ?latitude1; geo:long ?longitude1 ] .
            ?e1 uctelco:phoneNumber ?phone;
        }
        GRAPH ?id2 {
            ?e2 rdf:type nissa:HeartbeatAlert .
            ?e2 :stream <http://streams.../PersonalMonitoring#stream> .
            ?e2 :location [ geo:lat ?latitude2; geo:long ?longitude2 ] .
            ?e2 nissa:heartRate ?heartRate2 .
            ?e2 :screenName ?screenName .
            FILTER (abs(?latitude1 - ?latitude2) < 0.1 &&
abs(?longitude1 - ?longitude2) < 0.5)
        }
} HAVING(COUNT(?e2) >= "10"^^xsd:int)
```

Some experimental results

The presented use case has been tested in two medical institutions and the validation of medical results is in progress. Initial validation has shown that the detection of specific types of arrhythmia outperforms current methods, since the better contextualization enables better understanding of the particular situations the user is involved in. This is an interesting advantage that is based on the possibility of our approach to integrated a huge amount of data in real-time and make decision correspondingly (note that the task is to detect arrhythmia as early as possible).

However, in this paper we present a part of the evaluation of the underlying processing architecture and query language (BDPL) that enables above mentioned contextualization.

Apart from the qualitative comparison we conducted experiments to gain empirical performance data of our engine. To that end we set up a distributed test with one event *simulator node*, one or more nodes for event processing and one *collector node* to receive and examine resulting complex events. Time measurements were taken comparing timestamps in the events (referred to as *source time* or *application time*). To make timestamps comparable across machines we synchronized clocks every minute with the same atomic clock (NTP) service. The environment for our tests was as follows: Java 1.6.0_26-b03 64bit, Java heap size: 1GB, SWI Prolog 5.10.2 64bit, Debian Linux 6.0.2.

For benchmarking we used a query adapted from Q3 of SRBench [10]. The query was altered to derive precisely one complex event per each simple event in the stream. Using such a 1:1 ratio we could measure end-to-end throughput and latency using all nodes.

```
PREFIX om-owl:   <http://knoesis.wright.edu/ssw/ont/sensor-observation.owl#>
PREFIX weather:  <http://knoesis.wright.edu/ssw/ont/weather.owl#>
PREFIX rdf:      <http://www.w3.org/1999/02/22-rdf-syntax-ns#>
PREFIX geo:      <http://www.w3.org/2003/01/geo/wgs84_pos#>
PREFIX xsd:      <http://www.w3.org/2001/XMLSchema#>
PREFIX :         <http://events.event-processing.org/types/>

CONSTRUCT {
        :e rdf:type :SRBench-q3.
        :e :stream <http://streams.event-processing.org/ids/srbench#stream>.
        :e :sedTime ?time
}
WHERE {
        EVENT ?id1 {
                ?e1 :stream <http://streams..../srbench#stream>.
                ?e2 om-owl:procedure ?sensor ;
                    a weather:windSpeedObservation;
                    om-owl:observedProperty weather:_windSpeed;
                    om-owl:result [ om-owl:floatvalue ?value ].
                ?e1 :endTime ?time
                }
}
```

Figure 5 shows throughput and latency for one processing node. Latency includes network access between our nodes for sending events (simulator node) and for evaluating events (collector node). The red curve shows our test of increasing the event rate gradually every 1000 events. The event rate peaks at about 200 events per second. That is the throughput of our implementation of BDPL. At higher event rates the load is increasingly buffered and latency (blue curve) starts to grow. During the experiments the latency including networking averaged at about 5ms per event. Exceptions can be seen on the blue curve on the left of Figure 5 during cold start and on the right of Figure 5 at saturation of throughput.

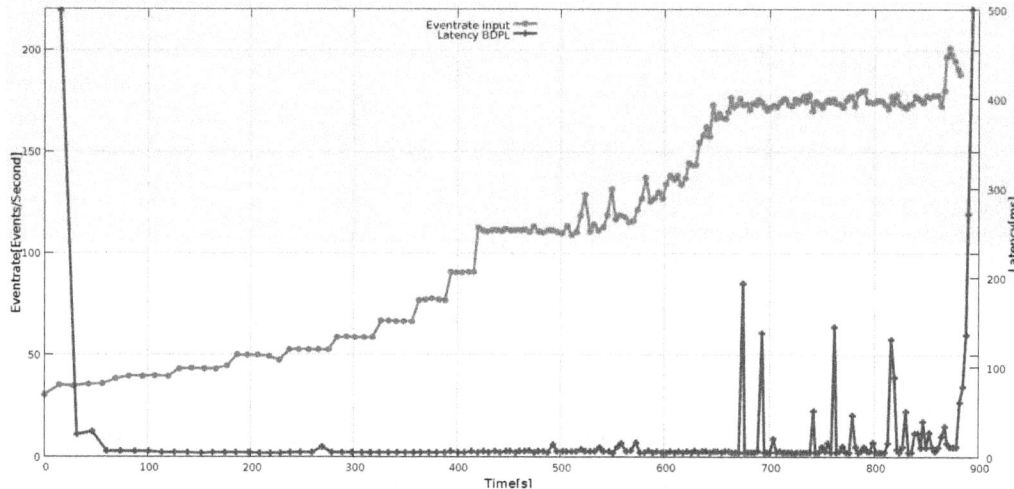

Figure 5: Throughput and latency for one processing engine

Figure 6 shows another experiment in the same setup but with two processing nodes. The two nodes share the load by processing their partitions of the simulated stream in parallel. The achieved throughput is about 350 events per second. The speedup of using two nodes is 1.75.

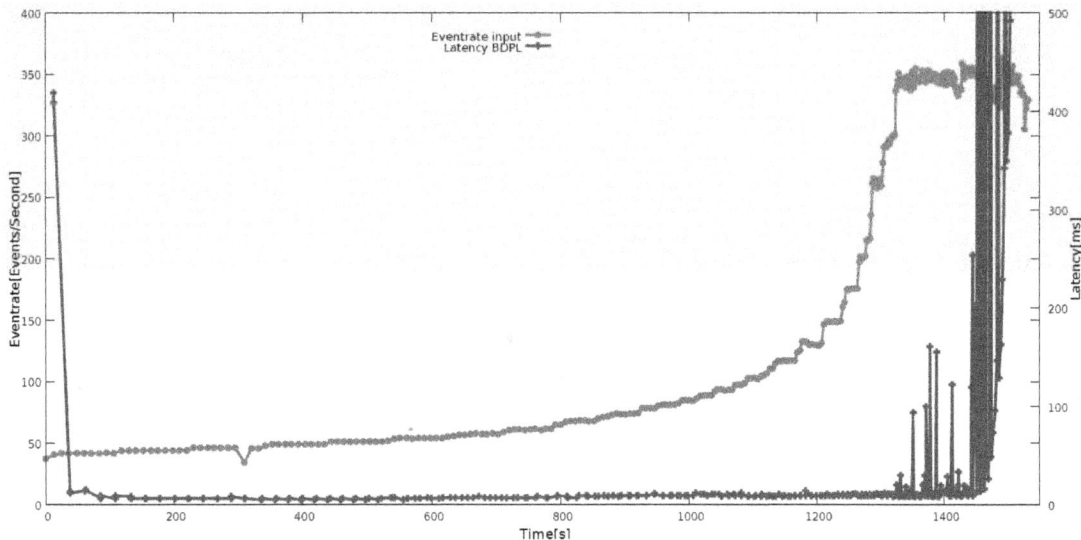

Figure 6: Throughput and latency for two distributed processing engine

5. RELATED WORK

In this section we will present some of the related work from different fields of research that are relevant to our approach.

Mobile and distributed CEP

The most relevant work is [11], which describes a in mobile device embedded CEP system. It combines a DDS (data distribution service) to provide the MPH (mobile patient healthcare) service or traffic update service to the user. Comparing to our system it doesn't use personal data and has no collaboration between the CEP engines.

Another similar work is [14], the authors presented a CEP system on the mobile device, which aims provide Medical monitoring. It uses only simple CEP engine, provides the service in a special field has no dynamic pattern management.

Other related works are the distributed CEP systems. The DHEP [12] project develops an industry system of distributed CEP, which can support interoperability between heterogeneous event processing systems. In [13] the authors develop a platform called DiCEPE (Distributed Complex Event Processing) that focuses on the integration of CEP engines in distributed systems, and which is capable of using various communication protocols. These both systems are not used on the mobile device and have not dynamic pattern management in the systems.

eFitness/eHealth

There is much work in the domain of remote personal monitoring that can be related to different types of the psychophysiological monitoring (e.g. heart rate, hear rate variability, skin conductance) in order to determine some parameters of the user's healthy status (e.g. fitness level, stress level, cardio arrhythmias, ...). In this subsection we present only the most important systems related to using smartphones and wearable (nonintrusive) sensors.

Recently, much research effort is put into more sophisticated approaches of using smartphone sensor data for personal health or physical activity monitoring. Furthermore, a large number of mobile applications is available in popular app stores.

From a scientific perspective, a smartphone application to monitor wellbeing is presented by [15]. The authors propose an application which consumes real-time data from different smartphone sensors in order to compute an overall score of wellbeing in several dimensions such as social activity and sleep. Compared to our work, the main difference is that this approach does not make use of external sensors and does not allow the manual definition of interesting situations by taking into account temporal and spatial operators provided by complex event processing. Another approach, the BALANCE system proposed by [16], aims at encouraging healthier lifestyles to its users. This approach is especially interesting as it combines data entered manually (about food eaten) and sensor data in order to compute the caloric expenditure of a user. However, the authors only investigate one aspect of personal health monitoring, while today's smartphones offer the opportunity to monitor a much wider range of habits and we argue that especially the combination and aggregation of heterogeneous data is promising.

From a practical perspective, applications like the Nike+ ecosystem are becoming more popular. Nike+ combines several available hardware sensors with a smartphone application and a community, allowing users to track sports activities in real-time and to compare themselves with our people through an online community. Even if this is a very interesting application, the potential of such combined applications is much bigger, as Nike+ currently relies on simple metrics (such as NikeFuel, an overall fitness score or burned calories during running).

Other very interesting apps are:

SuperBetter [4] helps to achieve predefined health goals — or recover from an illness or injury — by increasing the personal resilience of the user. It is a gamification-based app that is helping people to be more motivated to do physical exercises.

ShapeUp [5] is an app that helps co-workers to compete, support, and challenge each other with a shared goal of better health. It supports three steps: 1) tracking progress: it enables setting the goals, tracking progress, comparing results with peers, and sharing own successes; 2) finding supporters: it searches the network and browse profiles to find colleagues to support the user

---

[4] https://www.superbetter.com/
[5] https://mywellvolution.shapeup.com/

287

and 3) joining fun challenges: it finds the challenges the user will like, invite the colleagues, and spread good health.

Daily challenge6is another gamification-based app that helps in improving physical activity.

As an example of the traditional systems we mention CardioNet[7], the leading provider of ambulatory, continuous, real-time outpatient management solutions for monitoring relevant and timely clinical information regarding an individual's health. CardioNet's initial efforts are focused on the diagnosis and monitoring of cardiac arrhythmias, or heart rhythm disorders, with a solution that it markets as Mobile Cardiac Outpatient Telemetry™ (MCOT™). Through its Cardiocore division, CardioNet is offers core lab services to pharmaceutical and devise sponsors as they mover new products through the development process. However, although wearable and better than 24h medical holters[8], these sensors are quite intrusive comparing to sensors that have been recently promoted on the market.

From the sensing point of view, the most advance model is Zypher BioHarness™ 3 sensor[9] that enables the capture and transmission of comprehensive physiological data on the wearer via mobile and fixed data networks – enabling remote monitoring of human performance and condition in the real world. BioHarness™ 3 has applications in any field requiring high-level wireless and remote physiological monitoring, including research, training and tele-health situations. The most important feature is very complex measurement, including Heart Rate, R-R Interval, Breathing Rate, ECG, Posture, Activity Level and Peak Acceleration.

6. CONCLUSION

In this paper we present a novel approach of using CEP on the mobile device combining the server infrastructure taking advantage of the in mobile device integrated sensors in order to achieve a flexible monitoring of the user. The proposed system combines the personal data of the user, environment information and the external data source to determine the actual situation of the user and deploys the suitable patterns to perform the special monitoring in the detected situation and provide the useful recommendations to the visitor.

The approach has been validates in a business use case involving patients suffering from hypertension. Preliminary results have shown that the presented approach is very promising, especially from the point of view of modeling complex monitoring/diagnostic situations.

Acknowlegements. This work was in part supported by the European Commission (Project PLAY, Grant 258659). We would also like to thank the remaining PLAY project consortium who are completing the entire platform.

REFERENCES

[1] WILHELM, F. H. AND P. GROSSMAN. "Emotions beyond the laboratory: Theoretical fundaments, study design, and analytic strategies for advanced ambulatory assessment." Biological Psychology. 2010

[2] http://www.gigaspaces.com/Big-Data/Challenges

[3] McKinsey Global Institute. Big Data: The next frontier for innovation, competition and productivity, 2011

[4] Anicic, D., Fodor, P., Rudolph, S., & Stojanovic, N. (2011, March). Ep-sparql: a unified language for event processing and stream reasoning. In Proceedings of the 20th international conference on World Wide Web (pp. 635-644). ACM

[5] Pérez, J.; Arenas, M. & Gutierrez, C. (2009), 'Semantics and complexity of SPARQL', ACM Trans. Database Syst. 34(3), 16:1--16:45

[6] Berners-Lee, T. (2006), 'Linked Data', http://www.w3.org/DesignIssues/LinkedData.html accessed 2010-08-12.

[7] Gangemi, A.; Guarino, N.; Masolo, C.; Oltramari, A. & Schneider, L. (2002), Sweetening Ontologies with DOLCE, in 'Proceedings of the 13th International Conference on Knowledge Engineering and Knowledge Management. Ontologies and the Semantic Web', Springer-Verlag, London, UK, pp. 166--181.

[8] Carzaniga, A.; Rosenblum, D. S. & Wolf, A. L. (2001), 'Design and evaluation of a wide-area event notification service', ACM Trans. Comput. Syst. 19(3), 332--383.

[9] Harth, A. & Stühmer, R. (2011), 'Publishing Event Streams as Linked Data', Technical report, Karlsruhe Institute of Technology, http://km.aifb.kit.edu/sites/lodstream/.

[10] Zhang, Y.; Duc, P.; Corcho, O. & Calbimonte, J.-P. (2012), SRBench: A Streaming RDF/SPARQL Benchmark, in 'ISWC 2012', Springer Berlin Heidelberg, , pp. 641-657.

[11] Lee, J. H., Cheol, R., Jo, J. C., & You, Y. D. (2009, May). Embedded CEP engine used in DDS-based mobile devices for differentiated services for customers. InConsumer Electronics, 2009. ISCE'09. IEEE 13th International Symposium on(pp. 645-646). IEEE.

[12] Björn Schilling, Boris Koldehofe, Udo Pletat and Kurt Rothermel, Distributed Heterogeneous Event Processing, DEBS 2012

[13] Fawaz Paraiso, Gabriel Hermosillo, Romain Rouvoy, Philippe Merle, Lionel Seinturier, A Middleware Platform to Federate Complex Event Processing, Sixteenth IEEE International EDOC Conference (2012)

[14] Mohomed, I., Ebling, M. R., Jerome, W., & Misra, A. (2006, September). HARMONI: Motivation for a health-oriented adaptive remote monitoring middleware. In fourth international workshop on ubiquitous computing for pervasive healthcare applications (UbiHealth 2006), Irvine, California, USA, September.

[15] Lane, D.; Mohammod, BeWell: A Smartphone Application to Monitor, Model and Promote Wellbeing. In: IEEE Pervasive Health. 2012.

[16] Denning, Tamara, Andrew, Adrienne, Chaudhri, Rohit, Hartung, Carl, Lester, Jonathan, Boriello, Gaetano, and Duncan, Glen: Balance: Towards a usable pervasive Wellness Application with Accurate Activity Inference

---

[6] http://meyouhealth.com/daily-challenge/

[7] http://www.cardionet.com

[8] http://en.wikipedia.org/wiki/Holter_monitor

[9] http://www.zephyr-technology.com/products/bioharness-3/

The DEBS 2013 Grand Challenge

Christopher Mutschler
University of
Erlangen-Nuremberg
and
Fraunhofer Institute for
Integrated Circuits IIS
91058 Erlangen, Germany
Christopher.Mutschler@fau.de

Holger Ziekow
AGT International
Hilpertstr. 35
64295 Darmstadt, Germany
HZiekow@agtinternational.com

Zbigniew Jerzak
SAP AG
Chemnitzer Straße 48
01187 Dresden, Germany
Zbigniew.Jerzak@sap.com

ABSTRACT

The ACM DEBS 2013 Grand Challenge is the third in a series of challenges which seek to provide a common ground and evaluation criteria for a competition aimed at both research and industrial event-based systems. The goal of the Grand Challenge competition is to implement a solution to a real-world problem provided by the Grand Challenge organizers. The 2013 edition of the Grand Challenge focuses on real-time, event-based sports analytics. The 2013 Grand Challenge data set was collected during a football match carried out at a Nuremberg Stadium in Germany and is complemented with a set of continuous analytical queries which provide detailed insight into the match statistics for both team managers and spectators.

Categories and Subject Descriptors

C.2.4 [**Distributed Systems**]: Distributed applications

Keywords

event processing, streaming, cep

1. INTRODUCTION

Event-based systems are increasing their footprint in different sectors of our economy. Typical use cases include algorithmic trading [5], information integration [2], and monitoring of key performance indicators in manufacturing domain [4]. With this edition of the DEBS 2013 Grand Challenge we want to explore a slightly different industry branch – sports and entertainment.

The goal of this year's Grand Challenge is to demonstrate the applicability of event based systems for providing real-time, continuous analytics for both managers of sport teams as well as spectators of sports events. The explicit focus of the 2013 Grand Challenge is on analytics for football games. To that end we provide a data set collected during a real football game and couple it with analytical queries. The

goal of the analytical queries is twofold. On one hand side they provide the competitive edge to team managers allowing them to take better more insightful decisions in real time. Examples of such decisions include, e.g., substitution of underperforming players or monitoring of the weaknesses of the opponent team. On the other hand side the ability to operate on real time data allows for new and enriched experience for spectators both in stadiums as well as in front of TV screens. Typical examples of such improved experience include live, interactive in game statistics and analysis.

We hope that both data and queries presented in the DEBS 2013 Grand Challenge will drive stronger adoption of real-time event-based systems. We also hope that both data and queries will become helpful tool for evaluation of event based systems which goes beyond the scope of the DEBS 2013 Grand Challenge.

The remainder of this paper is structured as follows: in Section 2 we present the technical details of the real-time location system RedFIR which was used for collecting the raw data. In Section 3 we provide a detailed description of the recorded raw data. In Section 4 we provide a description of continuous queries to be executed on top of the recorded data. We conclude with Section 5.

2. REDFIR SYSTEM

The RedFIR tracking system is a Real-Time Locating System (RTLS) based on time-of-flight measurements, where small transmitter Integrated Circuits emit burst signals [3]. A centralized unit processes this microwave signals and extracts time of arrival (ToA) values. ToA values are the basis for time difference of arrival (TDoA) values, from which x, y, and z coordinates are derived. In the following, we describe the technical aspects of the RedFIR system installed in the main soccer stadium in Nuremberg, Germany, where the data for this challenge has been recorded.

The RedFIR system operates in the globally license-free ISM (industrial, scientific, and medical) band of 2.4 GHz and allows a usage of around 80 MHz. Miniaturized transmitters ($61x38x9$ mm) use this available bandwidth to generate short broadband signal bursts together with identification sequences. The locating system is able to receive an overall of $50,000$ of those signal bursts per second.

Figure 1 illustrates the signal processing chain of the RedFIR system. The system distinguishes fixed reference transmitters for configuration purposes, i.e., six transmitters located at the corners and the lateral ends of the midline, from M moving transmitters, i.e, the balls or the mobile transmit-

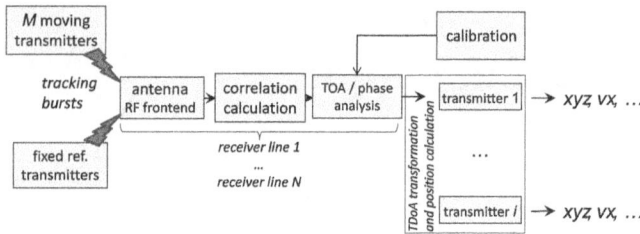

Figure 1: The signal processing chain of the RedFIR system

ters carried by the players. All transmitters emit tracking burst signals, which are received by N receiving antennas that are located on top of the flood light poles and the roofs of the stands. The installation in the soccer stadium in Nuremberg provides 12 antennas that receive signals from up to 144 different transmitters. Balls emit around 2000 tracking bursts per second whereas the remaining transmitters emit around 200 tracking bursts per second.

For each of the 12 receiver lines dedicated FPGAs correlate the individual burst sequences, and a CPU analyzes the resulting ToA and signal phase measurements. The receivers are synchronized so that the RedFIR system can determine time difference of arrival (TDoA) values out of the ToA values for each particular tracking burst between pairs of receivers. This allows the RedFIR system to avoid taking the time of transmission into account and thus alleviates the need to synchronize the transmitters. The RedFIR system can calculate the positions using only the timing information from the receivers. With the given number of receiving units $N=12$, the system derives N-1=11 TDoA-value streams.

Burst signals can be reflected by metallic surfaces as well as the playing field. This means that the receiving antennas might receive a given signal on multiple paths, which might negatively impact the quality of measurements. To avoid using the wrong propagation path an unscented Kalman filter (UKF) monitors several propagation paths at the same time and chooses a reliable line-of-sight (LOS) path for the tracking signal. Hence, at any time the most likely propagation path is used for positioning and ToA calculation [6].

In a final step the TDoA streams and the carrier phase signals serve as inputs to an extended Kalman filter (EKF), one per transmitter, to calculate the x, y, and z coordinates as well as other statistical information – see Section 3. The EKF uses hyperbolic positioning in order to calculate intersection points between measurements. The position information is further improved by using measurements of the carrier phase signal together with the ToA measurements - this allows to increase the accuracy for measurements of relative movements.

The miniature transmitters themselves are splash-proof (in case of the player transmitters) or integrated into the football. Hence, they are charged by an inductive principle. Figure 2 shows the charging cradle for a ball (charging units for the small transmitters are only a few centimeters long) and the suspension of the transmitter within the ball. Both ball and player transmitters can be fully charged within a few hours. The batteries run for over 3 hours, i.e., more than enough for a game with interruptions, stoppage time, and extra time. Moreover, the transmitter are application-specific integrated circuits (ASIC) and can be used as arbitrary wave-

Figure 2: A glass model of the ball's transmitter and inductive charger

form generators (AWG) operating at 2.4 GHz, i.e., they are re-programmable.

3. DATA

The DEBS 2013 Grand Challenge data set was recorded during a training game between two teams of 8 players. The game, during which the data has been collected, was played on a half-size field. The game duration was two halves of thirty minutes each. Figure 3 shows a schematic view of the playing field. Each corner of the field is marked with its coordinates used throughout the DENS 2013 Grand Challenge. The goal areas of both teams are marked with dashed lines. Since the playing field is not a perfect rectangle it is possible to approximate the field as a rectangle using following coordinates: $(0, 33965)$, $(0, -33960)$, $(52483, 33965)$, and $(52483, -33960)$.

Each player and a referee had two sensors embedded in their shin guards. Goalkeepers were additionally equipped with two sensors located in their gloves. Each ball used during the game had one sensor located approximately in the middle of the ball. Listing 1 gives an overview of the sensor to player assignment. Each sensor is identified by a unique

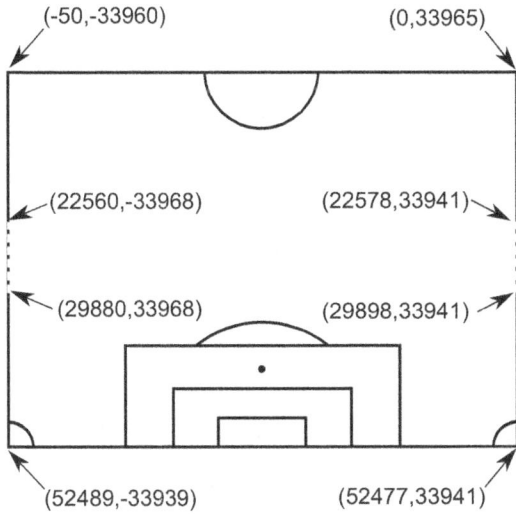

Figure 3: Playing field dimensions and goal areas (dashed lines)

number – its id. The sensor embedded in the left shin guard of a referee has an id of 105.

```
   Referee
      Left Leg: 105, Right Leg: 106

   Balls
5     1st Half: 4, 8, 10
6     2nd Half: 4, 8, 10, 12

8  Team A
9     Goalkeeper A ( Left Leg: 13, Right Leg: 14,
                     Left Arm: 97, Right Arm: 98)
      Player A1 (Left Leg: 47, Right Leg:16)
      Player A2 (Left Leg: 49, Right Leg: 88)
      Player A3 (Left Leg: 19, Right Leg: 52)
      Player A4 (Left Leg: 53, Right Leg: 54)
5     Player A5 (Left Leg: 23, Right Leg: 24)
6     Player A6 (Left Leg: 57, Right Leg: 58)
7     Player A7 (Left Leg: 59, Right Leg: 28)

9  Team B
      Goalkeeper B ( Left Leg: 61, Right Leg: 62,
                     Left Arm: 99, Right Arm: 100)
      Player B1 (Left Leg: 63, Right Leg: 64)
      Player B2 (Left Leg: 65, Right Leg: 66)
      Player B3 (Left Leg: 67, Right Leg: 68)
5     Player B4 (Left Leg: 69, Right Leg: 38)
6     Player B5 (Left Leg: 71, Right Leg: 40)
7     Player B6 (Left Leg: 73, Right Leg: 74)
8     Player B7 (Left Leg: 75, Right Leg: 44)
```

Listing 1: Assignment of sensors (ids) to players and balls

Sensors in the shin guards and gloves produce data with 200Hz frequency. The sensor in the ball produces data with 2000Hz frequency. The total data rate during the game reaches roughly 15,000 position events per second. Listing 2 shows the schema of the raw data set provided as input for the DEBS 2013 Grand Challenge.

```
  sid,       //sensor id
  ts,        //time stamp
  x, y, z,   //sensor coordinates
  |v|,       //velocity
5 |a|,       //acceleration
6 vx, vy, vz, //direction vector
7 ax, ay, az //acceleration vector
```

Listing 2: The input data schema

sid is a unique identifier of the sensor which produced a signal used for the calculation of the position event by the RedFIR signal processing chain – see also Listing 1. *ts* is a time stamp of the given measurement in picoseconds. Time stamp with value 10,753,295,594,424,116 designates the start of the match. Time stamp 14,879,639,146,403,495 marks the end of the match. The first half of the game ends at 12,557,295,594,424,116. The second half begins at 13,086,639,146,403,495. *x*, *y*, and *z* describe the position of the sensor in mm – coordinates (0,0,0) are located at the center of a full size football field. $|v|$ describes is the velocity of the sensor in m/s. *vx*, *vy*, and *vz* represent directed velocity vectors with a normalized size of 10,000. The speed of the sensor in the *x*-direction v_x in SI-units (m/s) can be calculated as:

$$v_x = |v| \cdot vx \cdot 10^{-4} \cdot 10^{-6} \qquad (1)$$

$|a|$ represents the acceleration of the sensor in m/s^2. *ax*, *ay*, and *az* represent directed acceleration vectors with a normalized size of 10,000. The acceleration of the sensor in the *x*-direction in m/s^2 is calculated analogously to that of the velocity:

$$a_x = |a| \cdot ax \cdot 10^{-4} \cdot 10^{-6} \qquad (2)$$

The value of acceleration $|a|$ is zero when the ball is not moving. Due to the geometry of the football field, and hence the antenna placements over the available areas, the absolute and relative precision in the *x* and *y* horizontal plane is highly accurate, i.e., positions only deviate a few centimeters. Relative movements in the vertical plane (*z*) are also resolved with high accuracy. However, due to the limited capabilities of antenna placement in the vertical axis the resolution of the vertical plane cannot compete with that of the horizontal plane. Specifically, it is possible that values for the *z* coordinate become negative.

Raw sensor data for the whole game can be downloaded from the following link: http://lafayette.tosm.ttu.edu/debs2013/grandchallenge/full-game.gz. The total file size is 2.6 GB and it contains a total of 49,576,080 position events. The provided data file is sorted according to the time stamp of the events. The meta data file containing all game interruptions can be downloaded from the following link: http://lafayette.tosm.ttu.edu/debs2013/grandchallenge/referee-events.tar.gz.

For reference purposes we also provide a video recording of the whole game. The video has been recorded using a static camera showing a vertical view of the game. We provide two separate files, one for each half of the game. Both files are 1.7GB in size and are encoded using a standard H.264/MPEG-4 AVC standard. The file containing the footage of the first half of the game can be downloaded here: http://lafayette.tosm.ttu.edu/debs2013/grandchallenge/RedFIR_2012_1.mov, the file containing the footage of the second half is available here: http://lafayette.tosm.ttu.edu/debs2013/grandchallenge/RedFIR_2012_2.mov.

Please note that the video is not fully aligned with the game as recorded by the RedFIR system. The sensor recordings start approximately 5 seconds earlier.

4. QUERIES

In this section we provide a description of four analytical queries which should be implemented as a part of the DEBS 2013 Grand Challenge. The goal of the queries is to provide continuous analysis on top of streaming data [1]. Therefore, in the remainder of the paper we assume that all queries are standing queries consuming the raw input data as defined in Section 3.

Each query, unless explicitly stated otherwise, should provide its results as a continuous stream of events. Result events, unless specified differently in the query, should be produced immediately upon the update from the input event. Results can be provided by simply writing to stdout or to a set of files, one for each result stream. It is also possible to use single output file, prefixing each result stream with a unique id.

4.1 Running Analysis

The goal of the running analysis query is to quantify and track how well each of the players moves on the playing field. The major indicators are the speed and distance covered by each player as a function of time. Each run undertaken by a player can be assigned to one of predefined intensity categories, according to its speed. We define the following intensities: standing (till $1km/h$), trot (till $11km/h$), low speed run (till $14km/h$), medium speed run (till $17km/h$), high speed run (till $24km/h$), and sprint (faster than $24km/h$). The goal of the query is to quantify, on a per player basis, the distribution of run intensities and corresponding distances.

To that end the running analysis query should return two classes of results: (1) current running statistics and (2) aggregate running statistics. The current running statistics report the current running intensity of the player as well as the distance covered with that intensity. The result schema for the current running statistics is given in Listing 3.

```
  ts_start ,
  ts_last ,
  player_id ,
  intensity ,
5 distance ,
6 speed
```

Listing 3: Current running statistics output stream schema

Where ts_start represents the start of the run with the given intensity, ts_stop represents the time stamp of the last event which updated the given result. $player\_id$ is the identifier of a player for which the measurement is made, and $intensity$ describes the intensity of the run. Running intensities can be returned as integers with 0 corresponding to standing and 5 corresponding to sprint. $distance$ is the length of the run with the given intensity. Distance should be calculated in meters in the horizontal plane only. $speed$ is the average speed of the given intensity run. The current running statistics result stream should be returned with a frequency of at most $50Hz$. Intermediate values can be aggregated using an average function.

Aggregate running statistics provides a cumulative view on the running performance of a given player. It contains information on all intensities a player has been running with in the past, as well as distances covered for each intensity. The aggregate running statics should be calculated for different window lengths, thus allowing to compare the current as well

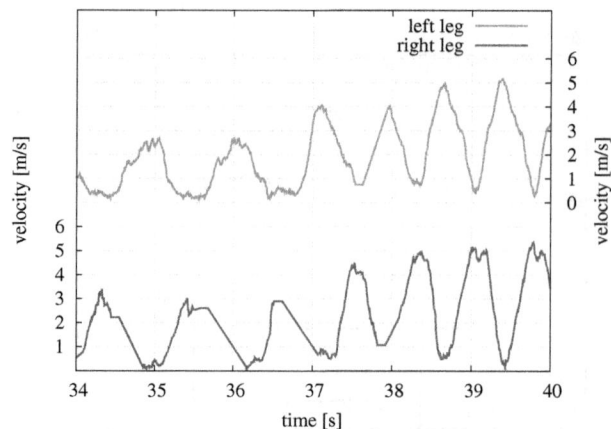

Figure 4: Velocity of the left and right leg of a player

as past performance of the given player. The result schema for the aggregate running statistics is given in Listing 4.

```
  ts ,
  player_id ,
  standing_time , standing_distance ,
  trot_time , trot_distance ,
5 low_time , low_distance ,
6 medium_time , medium_distance ,
7 high_time , high_distance ,
8 sprint_time , sprint_distance
```

Listing 4: Current running statistics output stream schema

where ts represent the latest time stamp which updated the statistics, the $player\_id$ is the player identifier, $intensity\_time$ is the time a given player spent in the given intensity (in milliseconds), $intensity\_distance$ is the distance covered with the given intensity (in meters). The aggregate running statistics must be calculated using following time windows: 1 minute, 5 minutes, 10 minutes, 20 minutes and the whole game duration. Each window will provide its results in a separate stream – the aggregate running statistic query will produce 5 result streams in total. Each result stream should be updated with a frequency of at most $50Hz$.

Every running intensity, which has been active for less than a second must be counted on top of the next intensity with a duration longer than 1 second. For example, if a player is in a trot state for a 2 seconds, then in a low speed run state for 0.8 seconds, and then in a medium speed run state for 2 seconds, the time of the low speed run must be counted on top of the medium speed run. Please note that the requirement to count only intensities active for at least one second requires to delay the output until a reliable measurement has been made. Specifically, this might imply longer delays in output if a player changes frequently between run intensities – e.g. oscillating between trot and low intensity run.

In order to accommodate for the noise in the raw velocity measurements as well as to accommodate for the location of the sensors, the actual speed of the run should be computed using both sensors. Figure 4 shows that the speed of individual sensors does not reflect the actual speed of the player. Moreover, it has to be noted that due to interference it is possible that the system has not received certain position

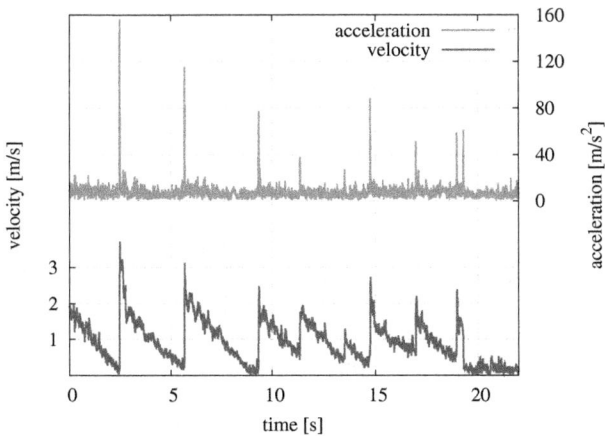

Figure 5: Velocity and acceleration of the ball

events – see for example the right leg velocity between 35.5 and 36.2 seconds. A good approximation of the player speed is the average speed of both left and right sensor over the last second.

4.2 Ball Possession

The goal of the ball possession query is to calculate the ball possession for each of the players as well as for each team. A player (and thereby his respective team) can obtain the ball whenever the ball is in his proximity and he hits it. A ball is in proximity of the player when it is less than one meter away from him. The distance of one meter applies to the distance between the sensor within the ball and any of the two sensors in the player's shin guards. A ball is hit whenever its acceleration or velocity peaks.

A ball will stay in the possession of a given player until another player hits it, the ball leaves the field, or the game is stopped. Specifically, a ball may leave the player's proximity and will still remain in his possession. The ball possession is calculated as time between the first ball contact (hit) and the last ball contact (hit).

Reliable detection of a ball hit is difficult. For the purpose of the Grand Challenge two approaches can be used. The first approach relies on detection of the acceleration threshold of 55 m/s^2. This value depends heavily on the fitness of the players as well as hit type. In professional games values of up to 100 m/s^2 are common. The second approach relies on monitoring of the changes in the ball velocity whenever the observed velocity changes by more than 100% within 15 milliseconds a ball hit may be assumed. Figure 5 illustrates both the acceleration as well as velocity values for a ball in play over the period of 22 seconds.

The ball position query should return two classes of results: (1) per player ball possession stream and (2) per team ball possession. The per player ball possession stream should contain following information – see Listing 5.

```
ts, player_id, time, hits
```

Listing 5: Per player ball possession output stream schema

where *ts* is the latest time stamp of the event which lead to the update of the ball possession, *player_id* is the identifier of the player owing the ball, *time* is the total time of the ball

possession for a given player, and *hits* is the total number of ball contacts for a given player. Per player ball possession result stream should be updated with the frequency of at most 50Hz.

The per team ball possession result stream must contain following statistics – see Listing 6.

```
ts, team_id, time, time_percent
```

Listing 6: Team ball possession output stream schema

where *ts* is the latest time stamp of the event which lead to the update of the team's ball possession, *team_id* is the team identifier. A team should be identified either as "A" or "B". *time* is the total time of the ball possession for a given team, *time_percent* is a percentage of the ball possession time for a given team w.r.t. the total ball possession time of both teams. The per team ball possession should be calculated using five different time windows: 1 minute, 5 minutes, 10 minutes, 20 minutes and the whole game duration. In total five team ball possession result streams should be returned. Each of the team ball possession result streams should be updated with the frequency of at most 50Hz.

4.3 Heat Map

The goal of the heat map query is to calculate statistics about the presence of each player in a given region of the playing field. For this purpose we define a fixed size grid with X columns along the x-axis and Y rows along the y-axis. Each row and column is of equal size. The parameters X and Y should be implemented with following values 8 and 13 (a grid of 104 cells), 16 and 25 (a grid of 400 cells), 32 and 50 (a grid of 1600 cells), 64 and 100 (a grid of 6,400 cells), respectively. The goal of the heat map query is to calculate how long each player spent in the given cell. The system should return results for all grid sizes in parallel using a separate result stream for each grid configuration.

The system must calculate for each cell and each player the percentage of time that the given player spent in the respective cell. The statistics should be calculated using five different time windows: 1 minute, 5 minutes, 10 minutes, 20 minutes and the whole game duration. In total 20 result streams must be returned by the system. Each result stream must be updated once per second and contain the following information – see Listing 7

```
ts, player_id,
cell_x1, cell_y1, cell_x2, cell_y2,
p_time
```

Listing 7: Heat map output stream schema

ts represent the time stamp of the latest event updating the heat map statistics. *player_id* is the player identifier for which the heat map is returned. *cell_x*1, *cell_y*1, *cell_x*2, *cell_y*2 are the coordinates of the lower left and upper right corner of the cell, respectively. *p_time* is the percentage of time that given player spent in the cell during the period specific to the result stream.

Given the large total number of cells in the result streams following optimizations are possible. Instead of returning one event per cell, it is possible to return one event per whole heat map. The event schema should be the following – see Listing 8.

```
  ts, player_id,
  cell1_x1, cell1_y1, cell1_x2, cell1_y2, p_time1,
  cell2_x1, cell2_y1, cell2_x2, cell2_y2, p_time2,
  cell3_x1, cell3_y1, cell3_x2, cell3_y2, p_time3,
5 ...
```

Listing 8: Combined heat map output stream schema

All fields are equivalent to the ones specified in Listing 7. The major difference is the fact that this event schema contains all cells for a given heat map resolution. A further optimization is possible where only fields with changed values (since the last update event) are included.

4.4 Shot on Goal

The aim of the shoat on goal query is to detect when a player hits the ball in an attempt to score a goal. A shot on the goal is defined as any shot that would hit (or closely miss) the goal of the opposing team. Shots on goal include unsuccessful attempts that are, e.g., blocked by a defending player or saved by the goal keeper.

A shot is detected if a player with hits the ball with a minimal acceleration of 55 m/s^2, and the projected movement of the ball would cross the goal area within 1.5 seconds after the hit. The goal areas are defined as rectangles with the following coordinates:

- Goal area 1: $x > 22578.5$ and $x < 29898.5$ with $y = 33941.0$ and $z < 2440.0$

- Goal area 2: $x > 22560.0$ and $x < 29880.0$ with $y = -33968.0$ and $z < 2440.0$

A hit distorts the speed values of the ball. Therefore, data is preprocessed by a Kalman-filter and stabilizes over time – see Figure 5. To allow for corrective measures we do not require shot detection until the ball has moved 1 meter away from the hit location.

It is open to the challenge participants to decide to which degree the ball movement projection should considers the physics of a flying ball. A base-line solution extrapolating the motion vector is acceptable. Extended solutions taking into account, e.g., the curvature of the ball trajectory (bent balls) are also possible.

For the duration of the shot the result stream should be updated with motion values of the ball and the ID of the shooting player according to the following schema – see Listing 9.

```
  ts, player_id,
  x, y, z,
  |v|, vx, vy, vz,
  |a|, ax, ay, az
```

Listing 9: Shot on goal output stream schema

ts represent the time stamp of the latest event updating the shot on goal statistics. *player_id* is the identifier of the player trying to score a goal. x, y, and z are the current coordinates of the ball. $|v|$, vx, vy, and vz represent the current velocity and velocity vectors of the ball. $|a|$, ax, ay, and az represent the current acceleration and acceleration vectors of the ball.

The result stream should be updated with the frequency of the sensor data until an exit condition occurs. Exit conditions are: (1) the ball leaves the field, or (2) the direction of the ball movement changes so that (the proximity of) the goal area would no longer be hit.

5. SUMMARY

In this paper we present the ACM DEBS 2013 Grand Challenge. We provide a detailed description of the Grand Challenge data set along with a description of four analytical queries. The goal of this paper is to provide a long living reference for all willing to use the data and queries for benchmarking and evaluation of event based systems beyond the scope of the ACM DEBS 2013 Grand Challenge. To that end the authors of this paper explicitly encourage comments or questions regarding both the data as well as queries specified in this paper.

6. ACKNOWLEDGMENTS

This work is supported by the Fraunhofer Institute for Integrated Circuits IIS. We would like to thank the researchers at the Fraunhofer IIS for sharing their work and RedFIR system with us. This work is also is partially sponsored by European Commission's Seventh Framework Program under grant agreement No. 257843 — project SRT-15 (http://srt-15.eu). Finally, we would like to thank all ACM DEBS 2013 Grand Challenge participants who provided us with continuous feedback and improvements regarding the description of the DEBS Grand Challenge. Thank You!

7. REFERENCES

[1] A. Arasu, S. Babu, and J. Widom. The cql continuous query language: semantic foundations and query execution. *VLDB*, 15(2):121–142, 2006.

[2] S. Chaudhuri, U. Dayal, and V. Narasayya. An overview of business intelligence technology. *Communications of the ACM*, 54:88–98, 2011.

[3] T. v. d. Grün, N. Franke, D. Wolf, N. Witt, and A. Eidloth. A real-time tracking system for football match and training analysis. In *Microelectronic Systems*, pages 199–212. Springer Berlin, 2011.

[4] Z. Jerzak, T. Heinze, M. Fehr, D. Gröber, R. Hartung, and N. Stojanovic. The DEBS 2012 Grand Challenge. In *DEBS 2012: 6th ACM International Conference on Distributed Event-Based Systems*, Berlin, Germany, July 2012. ACM.

[5] N. Leavitt. Complex-event processing poised for growth. *Computer*, 42(4):17–20, 2009.

[6] T. Nowak and A. Eidloth. Dynamic multipath mitigation applying unscented kalman filters in local positioning systems. *International Journal of Microwave and Wireless Technologies*, 3:365–372, 2011.

Grand Challenge: The BlueBay Soccer Monitoring Engine

Hans-Arno Jacobsen[1], Kianoosh Mokhtarian[1], Tilmann Rabl[1], Mohammad Sadoghi[2],
Reza Sherafat Kazemzadeh[1], Young Yoon[1], Kaiwen Zhang[1]

[1]Middleware Systems Research Group (MSRG), University of Toronto
[2]IBM T.J. Watson Research Center

ABSTRACT

This paper presents the design and implementation of a custom-built event processing engine called BlueBay developed for live monitoring of soccer games. We experimentally evaluated our system using a real workload and report on its performance. Our results indicate that BlueBay achieves a throughput of up to 790k events per second, therefore processing the game's input sensor stream about 60 times faster than real-time. In addition to our custom implementation, we also investigated the applicability of off-the-shelf general-purpose event processing engines to address the soccer monitoring problem. This effort resulted in two additional and fully functional implementations based on Esper and Storm.

Categories and Subject Descriptors

H.4.0 [**Information Systems Applications**]: General

Keywords

BlueBay; DEBS Grand Challenge; event processing

1. INTRODUCTION

Complex Event Processing (CEP) systems in today's connected world define an exciting new area of research with rich potential applications and challenges. For the past two years, the ACM International Conference on Distributed Event-based Systems (DEBS) has organized annual Grand Challenge competitions aimed at promoting a common ground and common evaluation criteria for CEP applications. The DEBS 2013 Grand Challenge [8], which is the focus of this paper, considers the problem of event monitoring in a soccer game. This is an application scenario that is reminiscent of a wide variety of use cases that are made feasible as availability and accuracy of small wireless sensors increase and the ability of CEP systems for live processing of sensor data improves. Furthermore, while our events of interest in a soccer game are domain-specific and related to detection of various game conditions, they are at the same time representative of the challenges in the wider spectrum of application scenarios that involve continuous stream processing.

In this context, this paper presents multiple approaches to address the DEBS 2013 Grand Challenge. Our first solution is an event processing system called *BlueBay* that we designed and built from scratch for monitoring of soccer games. We discuss BlueBay's modular design that enables easy plugging of new types of soccer analysis queries and report on its performance in terms of throughput and delay, as well as the flexibility in tuning the trade-off between the two. Our results indicate that BlueBay achieves a throughput of 350k events/sec with a 90-percentile per-event delay of 0.005 ms. Alternatively, BlueBay can achieve a higher throughput of 790k events/sec with a 99-percentile delay of 15 ms.

In addition to BlueBay, we also investigated the use of existing open-source off-the-shelf CEP engines to solve the Grand Challenge problem. Our efforts in this regard resulted in two additional fully functional soccer monitoring implementations based upon Esper [2] and Storm [6]. We discuss our experience in the process of developing these solutions in qualitative terms and compare the relative performance of our implementations in quantitative terms.

Section 2 presents our multi-stage event processing pipeline that is intended to provide a unified framework under which our CEP solutions execute. Section 3 elaborates on different approaches that we considered in order to address the Grand Challenge monitoring problem. This includes Esper and Storm which resulted in working implementations, as well as STREAM and StreamIT that we were unable to use for the Grand Challenge problem. Section 4 presents the main contribution of this paper, namely the BlueBay engine and Section 5 reports on our experimental evaluation results.

2. MULTI-STAGE MONITORING PIPELINE

Figure 1 illustrates our soccer game monitoring pipeline consisting of three stages, namely, *(i)* the *sensor data collection and dispatching* stage, *(ii)* the *processing* stage, and *(iii)* the *visualization and distribution* stage. We briefly discuss each stage.

2.1 Stage 1: Data Collection and Dispatching

The first stage in our monitoring pipeline involves sensor data collection and dispatching. The input sensor stream originates from transmitters attached to the ball, the referee's and players' feet, as well as the goal keepers' feet and arms. A sensor reading contains the sensor's unique identifier sid, its x, y and z space coordinate, its vx, vy and vz velocity vector components, its ax, ay and az acceleration vector components, velocity vector magnitude $|V|$, and acceleration vector magnitude $|A|$. Each sensor's stream has a frequency of 200 events per second for the feet and arm transmitters, and 2000 events per second for the ball transmitter.

As shown in Figure 1, sensor readings collected from the soccer field are fed into our monitoring pipeline either directly or indirectly. A direct feed is suitable for online monitoring of a live game.

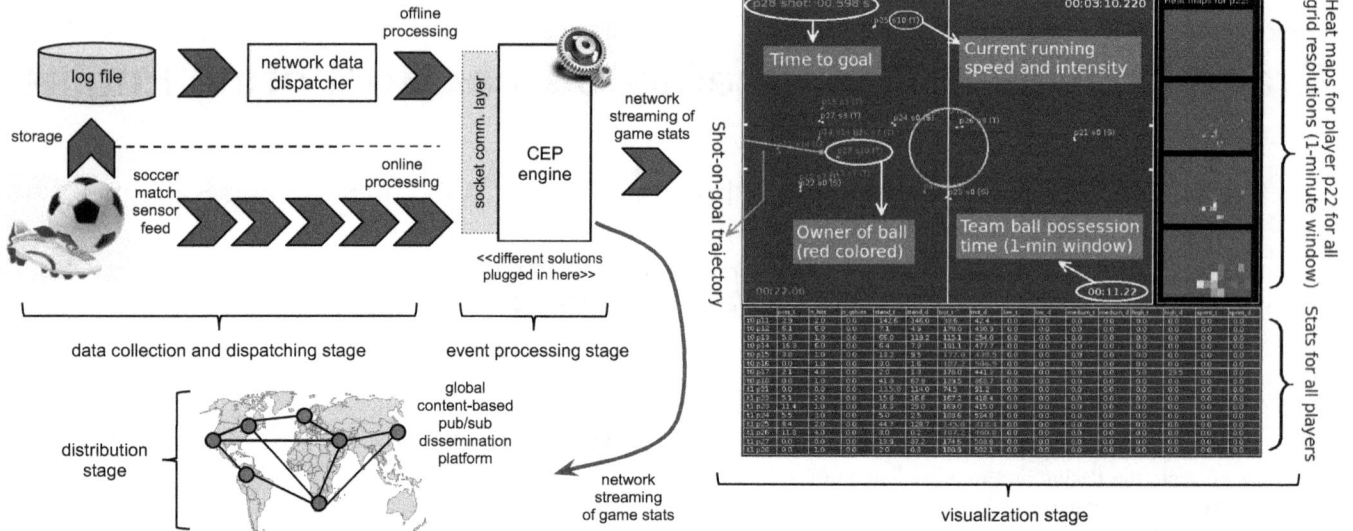

Figure 1: Unified soccer match monitoring pipeline.

Alternatively, sensor data streams can be timestamped and logged into a file (currently in CSV format), and fed into the pipeline at a later point. To support the offline processing mode, we developed a *network data dispatcher* that reads a game's sensor data log file and dispatches sensor readings over a socket connection.

2.2 Stage 2: Continuous Query Processing

The DEBS 2013 Grand Challenge outlines four continuous monitoring queries to detect different game conditions (*e.g.*, shots on goal) and gather various game statistics (*e.g.*, ball possession). The queries are executed in the second stage of our pipeline using different CEP engines that we developed for this purpose. In what follows, we give a brief overview of these monitoring queries (a more elaborate description can be found here [8]). We defer the discussion of different CEP engines to execute these queries to Section 3.

Query 1 (Q1) – Players' running performance: Q1 concerns monitoring of the players' running activity during the game based on 6 intensity classes (*i.e.*, *stop*, *trot*, *low*, *medium*, *high* and *sprint*). Players transition between these classes according to the momentary value of their speed. Q1 produces two types of outputs: *(i)* The intensity statistics output is produced at a maximum frequency of 50 Hz, and *(ii)* the aggregate intensity statistics output is produced based on four different time windows.

Query 2 (Q2) – Ball possession statistics: Q2 computes the time that the ball is in possession of a player or team. The criteria that must be satisfied for a player to possess the ball is to hit it such that his foot is within 1 meter of the ball and as a result of the hit the ball's acceleration reaches at least 55 m/s^2. Q2 produces outputs in two forms: *(i)* The per-player ball possession output reports the number of ball hits and the length of time each player possessed the ball, and *(ii)* the per-team ball possession output reports the percentage of time that the ball was in possession of each team.

Query 3 (Q3) – Heat map: Q3 produces statistics of the aggregate time that each player spends in different regions of the soccer field (*a.k.a.*, the *heat map*). For this purpose, four grid structures with different cell sizes are defined dividing the field from just about a hundred cells (in the least granular grid) to several thousand cells (in the most granular one). Q3 outputs the percentage of time that each player spends in each cell over different time windows.

Query 4 (Q4) – Shots on goal: Q4 detects players' shots on goal and produces an output stream that identifies the shooter and tracks the ball's motion towards the targeted goal. The necessary

conditions that constitute a shot on goal require that the ball is hit by a player (similar to Q2), that it remains within the field, and that the extrapolation of the ball's trajectory indicates that it would be located within the goal posts' coordinates no later than 1.5 seconds after it was hit by the player, provided that the ball is not diverted.

2.3 Stage 3: Visualization and Distribution

The final stage in the pipeline is to provide the results of the query processing stage to the end-users. We envision two usage scenarios for these results. The first scenario involves the use of a graphical user interface to visualize the movement of the ball and players in real-time and to display various statistics in sync with the game play. We developed such a graphical monitoring panel that can be used by team coaches or TV reporters to analyze a live game (see Section 2.3.1 for more detail). Alternatively, the CEP engine's output can be multicast over the Internet for soccer enthusiasts. We believe that a content-based pub/sub network [4, 5] is a suitable choice for this purpose. Next, we discuss these alternatives in turn.

2.3.1 The Graphical Monitoring Panel

We have developed a GUI-based monitoring panel to visualize the soccer game and the related analysis information. In addition to a user friendly illustration of the information, this is a necessary tool for verifying the correctness of the different types of analysis (i.e., false positives and negatives). In our experience, given the huge volume of generated events, this verification would not have been feasible without our visualization tool (Figure 1 illustrates a screen shot and a sample video is available at [7]). We have designed this tool such that it displays the result of important event processing steps, a few examples of which include:

- The detected running speed and intensity is shown next to each player. Besides verifying the speed values, this helped us find significant fluctuations in the detected intensities in small (20 ms) intervals, if proper smoothing was not applied on the raw data.

- Every time a ball hit by a player is detected, the ball turns red and gradually goes back to its original color (white). This helped reveal false positive and false negative detection of ball hits.

- The tool highlights the player identified as the ball possessor. A timer tracks the reported ball possession time for each team (for the 1-minute window). This feature has contributed a lot to the high accuracy of our ball possession analyzer.

- Heat maps at different grid resolutions are displayed for a selected player (for the 1-minute window). Highlighted areas of the map track the player in the field, while his older positions gradually fade away as they fall outside the 1-minute window.

- Every time a shot-on-goal is detected, the ball's predicted trajectory and time to reach the goal is displayed and continuously updated until we leave the shot-on-goal state. Moreover, for every ball hit that is identified as a shot-on-goal, we visualize the ball's estimated next-1-second trajectory. This feature has helped us to tune and verify the accuracy of our shot-on-goal detector.

- A table of statistics displays for each player the time and distance spent in each running intensity level, ball possession time, and the number of ball hits. The table is continuously updated with recently changed values highlighted for easy tracking.

2.3.2 Pub/Sub-Based Dissemination Network

For the dissemination of query results, we envision the use of a distributed content-based pub/sub system [4, 5]. Soccer fans use the content-based filtering capabilities of these systems to tune into the statistics related to specific players or track various game conditions. For example, `subscription=[player: 'Ronaldo', condition: 'ball-hits']` encodes a user's interest to track Ronaldo's ball hits. As illustrated in Figure 1, the output of the query execution stage is fed into the pub/sub network during the game. This stream is matched against subscriptions at a broker and flows towards the users based on their subscription interests.

3. USE OF EXISTING CEP ENGINES

We now discuss the results of our investigation in the application of different off-the-shelf CEP engines to solve the Grand Challenge monitoring problems (see Section 2.2). We found that while some engines were sufficiently capable to address our query processing needs, others were not suitable for our purposes.

3.1 Esper

We used Esper open-source edition [2] (version 4.9.0) and successfully implemented all four challenge queries. The Esper distribution comes with a CEP engine and an event processing language (EPL) which provides a powerful interface into the vast capabilities of the CEP engine. The approach we took in our implementation is based on a logical decomposition of each of the challenge queries. At a high-level, this involves three phases: We first *pre-process* the raw sensor stream in order to augment it with game metadata information such as sensor type (*i.e.*, ball, referee, foot or hand sensor), player id, and team association (metadata is supplied as part of the challenge [8]). Next, in the *processing* phase, we formulate the challenge queries as smaller sub-queries that are continuously evaluated on the augmented stream and incrementally compute the final outcome (Figure 2 illustrates formulation of Q2 in EPL). Finally, the *reporting* phase uses time-triggered sub-queries to produce a sampled output of query results at designated frequencies.

We observed that Esper EPL features elaborate constructs (*e.g.*, windows, contextual partitioning, aggregation, expressions) that are directly applicable towards our stream processing needs. The Esper framework also supports seamless integration with the Java language at two key levels. First, it facilitates interfacing with the CEP engine for the input and output of events to and from the engine. Second, it allows incorporation of Java code snippets and functions as part of the evaluation of an EPL query. We used the former capability to inject raw sensor readings from our network data dispatcher and collect the computed output results using a Java

```
insert into preprocessed_stream
select *,
  msrg.GameSetting.getId(s_id) as id,
  msrg.GameSetting.getType(s_id) as t_id,
  msrg.GameSetting.getSubtype(s_id) as subt_id
from msrg.EsperSensorEvent

insert into b_position_stream
select * from preprocessed_stream where t_id = 2

insert into b_relative_pos
select
  b.s_id as b_s_id, b.ts as b_ts, b.id as b_id,
  b.t_id as b_t_id, b.subt_id as b_subt_id,
  b.x as b_x, b.y as b_y, b.ax as b_ax, b.ay as b_ay,
  b.v as b_v, b.a as b_a, p.ts as p_ts, p.s_id as s_id,
  p.id as p_id, p.t_id as p_t_id, p.subt_id as p_subt_id,
  p.x as p_x, p.y as p_y, p.z as p_z,
  java.lang.Math.sqrt((p.x-b.x)*(p.x-b.x)+
    (p.y-b.y, 2)*(p.y-b.y, 2)) as dist
from preprocessed_stream as p unidirectional,
  b_position_stream.std:unique(s_id) as b
where (p.t_id = 3 or p.t_id = 4) and (b.t_id = 2)

create expression minDist
{(select min(dist) from b_relative_pos.std:unique(p_id))}

insert into b_possession
select *,
  msrg.GameSetting.getBallOwner(p_t_id,b_v,b_x,b_y) as owner
from b_relative_pos
where msrg.GameSetting.ballIn(b_x, b_y) = 1 and b_a > 0.5
  and minDist() = dist and dist <= 1000

insert into b_possession_percent
select *,
  sum(b_ts - prev(b_ts, 1)) as time_total,
  sum((b_ts - prev(b_ts, 1))
    * msrg.GameSetting.equalStr(owner,prev(owner,1),'teamA'))
    as time_teamA,
  sum((b_ts - prev(b_ts, 1))
    * msrg.GameSetting.equalStr(owner,prev(owner,1),'teamB'))
    as time_teamB
from b_possession.win:time(10 seconds)

select *,
  b_ts, owner, time_total,
  time_teamA/time_total as teamA_ownership_percent,
  time_teamB/time_total as teamB_ownership_percent
from pattern [every timer:interval(1 second)] unidirectional,
  b_possession_percent.std:unique(owner)
```

Figure 2: Query 2 implementation in Esper.

callback method. We used the latter capability to encode the game-specific domain knowledge as stateless static Java functions, *e.g.*, to compute the ball trajectory (Figure 3 lists other Java functions).

Finally, we would like to reflect on our experience in working with Esper. We found that Esper's high-level language gives great flexibility and is suitable for fast development and ease of change. In fact, after a steep learning curve to become familiar with its capabilities, we were able to formulate all queries in a matter of a few days time. We therefore believe that in a use case with changing requirements an Esper-based solution is of great value. Also, as an added advantage of Esper's support of the Java language our solution can be incorporated easily into other programs.

3.2 Storm

Storm is a distributed stream processing system built for real-time Web scale stream processing [6]. A Storm *topology* is a directed acyclic graph that consist of data sources (*spout*) as roots and data processing nodes (*bolts*) as inner nodes and leaves. Spouts emit tuples that are consumed and processed by bolts. Spouts and

`getId(s_id)`	Returns unique id for players, referee & ball wearing sensor `s_id`.
`getType(s_id)`	Returns type of entity (*i.e.*, team of players, referee & ball) wearing sensor `s_id`.
`getSubtype(s_id)`	Returns id for showing where sensor `s_id` is worn (*i.e.*, left/right leg/arm).
`equalStr(a, b, c)`	Returns 1 if a=b=c and 0 otherwise.
`ballIn(x, y)`	Returns 1 if x, y is a coordinate within field boundaries.
`getBallOwner(t_id, v, x, y)`	Returns 'ballout' if (x, y) is within field or 'stopped' if v!=0. Otherwise, returns 'teamA' or 'teamB' based on `t_id`.

Figure 3: Java functions from `msrg.GameSetting` **used in Figure 2.**

Figure 4: Storm topology excerpt for Query 3

bolts can have multiple instances that run in parallel. The way data is streamed to these instances is specified by *stream groupings*.

The most basic stream grouping is a *shuffle grouping* that randomly distributes data to bolt instances. A more advanced grouping is the *field grouping* that sends tuples with equal values in a given field to the same bolt. A Storm topology can be specified in various programming languages.

Although spouts and bolts must be individually implemented, Storm takes care of the distribution of tasks (spout or bolt instances) and the reliable transmission of tuples between the two. A Storm system consists of a master node that distributes tasks, code and worker nodes that execute subsets of a topology. A Storm cluster is backed by a Zookeeper cluster [3], which keeps all state information and makes the cluster reliable and failure resilient.

We implemented all four queries in Storm using Java. Figure 4 shows part of the topology that computes Q3 (heat maps). Since all data comes from the sensor stream, there is only a single spout. As a first step, the sensor readings have to be matched with the players. This can be done with an arbitrary degree of parallelism using a shuffle grouping. Next, the sensor readings from the two feet of each player have to be joined to a single position. This is done with a field grouping and a maximum degree of parallelism in terms of the number of players. From the stream of each player's position, the individual heat maps are computed and sent to the output bolt which sends the results to the GUI or to standard output.

3.3 StreamIT

StreamIT [9] provides a high-level language with stream manipulation primitives. We unsuccessfully attempted to implement the challenge queries using StreamIT. We now list the limitations of StreamIT which prevented us from completing the queries:

Limited I/O support: StreamIT has restricted I/O capabilities.

Lack of powerful stateful operators: Communication between blocks in a StreamIT pipeline is regulated through different queues. Therefore, each block is essentially stateless and accesses additional data by peeking at various queues. This queue-based approach is not suitable to formulate the finite-state machine model required for our monitoring queries (such as Q2 and Q4).

Lack of library support: We believe that it would have been more beneficial if StreamIT was provided as a library, where the code produced by StreamIT could be modified in its lower level form.

3.4 STREAM

STREAM is a data stream management system to evaluate continuous queries developed by Stanford [1]. The main features of STREAM are to support a declarative continuous query language (CQL) that unifies access to an incoming (structured) data stream and traditional stored data (in form of tables).

CQL is formulated over either streams (an unbounded bag of events) or relations (a finite time-varying bag of events). CQL is also extended with a sliding time- and count-based window semantics, essentially, the sliding window is a snapshot of an observed finite portion of the event stream. There are three classes of operators in CQL. These classes of operators are distinguished based on their input/output semantics: (1) Relation-to-relation, which takes relations as input and produces a relation as output; (2) stream-to-relation, which takes streams as input and produces a relation as output; and (3) relation-to-stream, which takes relations as input and produces a stream as output. Another notable feature of

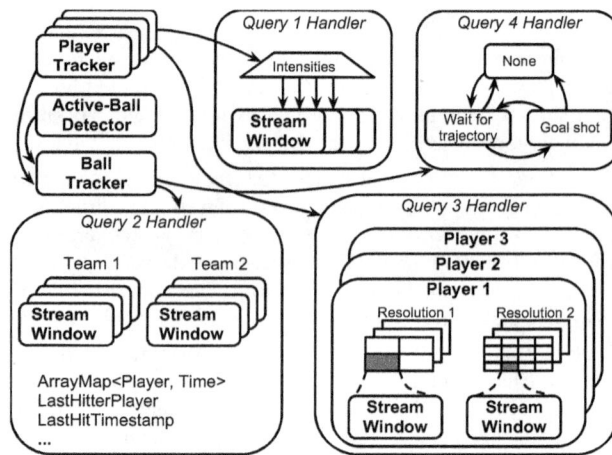

Figure 5: High level diagram of the BlueBay engine.

CQL is the partitioning operator that partitions a stream into a set of sub-streams based on the values of selected attributes in the event stream. Despite the novel features of STREAM, the lack of direct support for user-defined functions (needed to implement complex finite-state machine behavior required by the DEBS Challenge queries) prevent us from including STREAM in our evaluation.

4. THE BLUEBAY ENGINE

BlueBay is the event processing engine that we have developed for analyzing a soccer game's sensor data. This engine is designed in a modular fashion to serve as a general framework for adding any type of soccer analysis query fairly easily (some discussed below), while it is also optimized for speed: With an efficient C++ implementation, it achieves a throughput of up to 790k events per second, handling the sensor events of a whole minute in only one second, *i.e.*, 60 times faster than real time.

BlueBay Components. The internal components of the Blue-Bay engine are illustrated in Figure 5 and briefly described in the following. The *Active-Ball Tracker* tracks which of the ball sensors is the one that we should be monitoring; only one of the balls is the one being played with. There are periods of a few seconds where there are temporarily more than one ball in the field, during which the Active-Ball Tracker should not be misguided until the extra ball is removed. Once the relevant ball sensor is identified, a *Ball Tracker* tracks the state of the ball—position, speed and acceleration, denoised with proper filters (exponential-weighted moving average). The Ball Tracker also monitors the acceleration of the ball and detects potential ball hits. We found that the acceleration is greatly impacted when the ball hits the ground, thus we take only the XY component of the acceleration into account (based on a threshold of $75\ m/s^2$). BlueBay also includes a *Player Tracker* for individual players which tracks the position and speed of the foot sensors. The speed is denoised with a sliding window moving average filter to cut out considerable fluctuations in the speed value as the players' feet takes every step. A value of {running speed, duration} is output every time the speed value is steady enough, with an output frequency of no more than 50 Hz and no less than 5 Hz. Upon every potential ball hit, the hitting player is identified based on the position of the foot sensors. Then, the *Trajectory Estimator* predicts the trajectory of the ball in the next few seconds. The Trajectory Estimator takes into account the current (denoised) position and speed of the ball as well as gravity and air resistance.

Stream Window. A common data structure used in the different components of BlueBay is a sliding window which keeps timestamped data values—entries of the form {timestamp, value, duration}—such as a 1-minute window on how much time a player has spent in a grid cell or the time a player has run at an intensity level. The key feature of this window, to which we refer as *Stream Window*, is its efficiency. It performs all insertion and retrieval operations in constant time and, more importantly, consumes only constant memory. This is achieved by bucketizing the timestamps at some granularity, and maintaining a list (in practice a circular buffer) of fixed length, irrespective of the input rate. For example, to track the distance run by a player at the "sprint" intensity level in the past 5 minutes, we need to keep track of the (timestamped) distance values computed on each Player Tracker report (at 5 to 50 Hz). Instead of maintaining a sliding list of all values having a timestamp of no older than 5 minutes, we aggregate all values having a timestamp between T ms and T+999 ms in one bucket, and only maintain their sum and count, *i.e.*, 300 buckets. Compared to maintaining a full list of individual values, we do not lose any noticeable precision by such bucketization; in the worst case when we are pushing some outdated events out of the window, they may be leaving up to 1 second late. More formally, by maintaining the events of a sliding window of length T seconds in a Stream Window with N buckets, we may return the desired value (sum, max, count for the window) for the past T to $T(1 + 1/N)$ seconds, rather than exactly T. We use small buckets throughout BlueBay (*e.g.*, $N > 100$), except for the substantial number of heat map Stream Windows where we use $N = 20$; we report the heat map of the past 60 to 63 seconds for the 1 minute window.

Query analyzers. Given the above components, we conduct different types of analysis fairly easily. As illustrated in Figure 5, Q1 of the challenge can be readily handled by pushing the output of the aforementioned Player Tracker into Stream Windows—a Stream Window for each defined running intensity level. Similarly for Q2, we receive every ball hit along with the hitting player id from the Ball Tracker, and we can track the per-player and per-team possession time with a simple counter and a Stream Window (for each given window length), respectively. The heat map analyzer (Q3) is nothing but a collection of Stream Windows tracking data received from the Player Trackers. These windows, of different lengths and for the different grid resolutions, a total of 34,000 windows, easily fit into a few hundred MB of memory and perform all operations in constant time. Finally, the shot-on-goal analyzer (Q4) only needs to wait for ball hits from the Ball Tracker, and compare the trajectory given by the Ball Tracker with the position of the goals. This analyzer consists of a finite-state machine. Every time the ball is hit, we enter a waiting state for up to a maximum distance (50 cm) or a maximum time (1 second) since the hit. At that point, we have a reasonable estimate of the ball's trajectory and the time to hit the goal. Accordingly, we either enter the shot-on-goal state or go back to the no-shot state. In the former case, the trajectory is monitored upon every ball sensor event until the ball changes direction, becomes too slow, or leaves the field.

Other types of analysis. The components introduced above enable various new types of soccer analysis, such as the following.

- Ball passes and their success rate for each player and each team can be counted. We are signaled when a new player receives the ball (upon his first hit), and we know who has hit the ball last. We have already implemented this additional analysis in BlueBay.

- A player's running statistics with and without the ball, and at the time of attack and defense can be analyzed using a counter/Stream Window on the Player Tracker's output.

- Offsides can be detected by waiting for ball hits from the Ball Tracker, and forming a black list of players who are not allowed to receive that pass based on their positions at the time of hit.

- The success of a player for man-marking his assigned opponent player can be analyzed through a Stream Window to which we periodically push the distance of the two players.

- The defense-to-attack time for a team can be tracked by monitoring the Ball and Player Trackers, and maintaining a single time counter representing when, which team last acquired the ball.

Efficiency. Since almost all operations in this challenge can be done in $O(1)$ time, it is a matter of efficient implementation techniques that enables a throughput boost in query processing. A few of these techniques employed by BlueBay are as follows. First, for different components we avoid using hash maps to track per-sensor data (even though lookups are $O(1)$). Instead, we assign an *index* $\in [0, Num\ Entities - 1]$ to each entity, such as a sensor or a player. The index for each sensor/player is looked up only once per event in an id-to-index hash map. Then, all the remaining entity lookups, such as updating the position of a player, is done using array-based maps. Moreover, we note that the main body of the analysis consists of a substantial amount of mathematical operations. We avoid the unnecessary use of floating point operations where int64 precision would suffice, while carefully handling cases where there is a risk of overflow (*e.g.*, multiplying two values of picoseconds since epoch). We use efficient, array-based circular buffers instead of linked lists or elastic vectors wherever the data size is fixed, which is often the case—Stream Windows. Finally, the data dispatcher (see Section 2.1) that executes as a separate process and loads the entire data in advance eliminates the impact of disk I/O in the critical path of event processing.

Parallelization. BlueBay can run in single and multi-threaded modes. For the latter, we note that the events emitted to different output streams, per query and sometimes per sub-query, should not contain *reordered timestamps*. Thus, we do not run an arbitrary-size thread pool to handle the events. Rather, we run one thread per query, with the ball possession and shot-on-goal analyzer combined in one since they include common steps. Our code profiling analysis has shown that the most time consuming event processing step in BlueBay is the *emission of heat map statistics*—over half a million Stream Windows that should emit data. Even just iterating over all the windows for all players takes up to a few dozen milliseconds. We therefore designate a number of sub-threads in the thread handling the heat map query, which are responsible for the different grid resolutions. Reordering of output events across different grid resolutions is fine since they belong to different output streams. Once the emission timer fires, the heat map thread launches these sub-threads and blocks until they are all done, before handling any new heat map input event. We also note that in all query analyzers, we disable emission to stdout or file by default, since it involves significant I/O that will not let us analyze the actual performance of the event processing engine. Note that, however, we do perform all the string formatting and preparation of the final output; we just do not print it (*i.e.*, sprintf to memory buffers rather than printf to stdout).

5. EVALUATION

We experimentally evaluated the performance of the BlueBay system in terms of throughput and per-event delay—the time it takes from when an event is received from the data dispatcher to when processing is finished and a possible output event is emitted. Our evaluations are conducted on a PC workstation with Intel Xeon 3.20 GHz 4-core CPU with 6 GB of memory. We measure the throughput as the number of events processed per seconds (e/s), and as a *speedup*. A speedup of s indicates that s seconds worth of sensor data are processed in 1 second worth of actual processing time (*i.e.*, events processed s times faster than real-time).

Implementation	Q1	Q2	Q3	Q4
BlueBay	141x	165x	30x	187x
Esper	7.5x	2.4x	6.3x	2.3x
Storm	9.7x	8.6x	9.8x	8.6x

Table 1: Event processing speedup using different approaches.

BlueBay running all four challenge queries in non-threaded mode achieves an average throughput of 364k e/s, and an average speedup of 27.6x. Table 1 compares the per-query speedup of different implementations and Figure 6 plots the instantaneous throughput for BlueBay. By enabling the multi-threaded mode in BlueBay, the performance is on one hand increased and on the other hand impacted by some noticeable overheads (discussed below). The overall throughput can be increased to 790k e/s (2+ times higher).

As described earlier, in the threaded mode, we allow a query of type X to be processed while a query of type Y is taking some time. We can enforce the different query threads to run at more or less the same pace by limiting the input queue size of the threads. A queue size of 1 enforces that no thread can start working on a new event (it is not given one) until another thread finishes the previous event. A queue size of ∞ makes the threads completely independent. The queue size also governs a trade-off between throughput and per-event delay: A limited queue size ensures that when a thread is falling behind (typically the event triggering heat map emissions), the other threads are paused after some point, giving the full CPU to the busy thread (sub-threads handling heat map emissions; see Section 4). Figure 6 illustrates BlueBay's performance in multi-threaded mode with different queue sizes (q).

Note that unlike I/O-involved jobs where threading immediately boosts the performance by avoiding wasting CPU cycles, here, all threads carry out CPU-heavy jobs, so for small queue sizes the overhead of threading is more significant than the obtained throughput increase in Figure 6. A major part of this overhead is that of the safe enqueuing/dequeuing of events for the threads which takes a non-negligible time compared to the only-a-few-microsecond processing time for most events. Another, less significant factor is the slight performance drop by turning on additional monitoring features such as collecting delay information and tracking the 99-percentile delay; turning on these features in the non-threaded mode drops the aforementioned throughput of 364k to 346k e/s. Finally, unlike I/O-involved jobs, here, the overhead of the many context switches between the CPU-intensive threads is non-negligible.

The trade-off between throughput and delay is illustrated in Figure 7. We can observe in this figure that the throughput can be increased only up to some point, after which some threads (the heat map thread) have a hard time catching up; hence, the jump in the delay value. In particular, the average/99-percentile processing delay for the last three queue sizes, 4k, 16k and 64k is 2.9/15 ms,

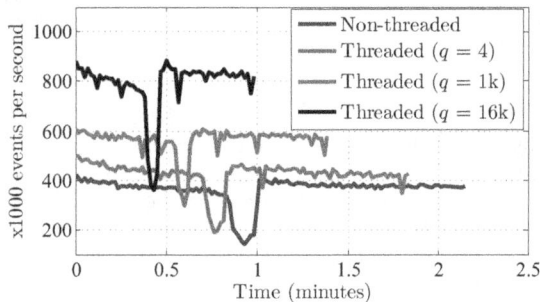

Figure 6: BlueBay's throughput (best viewed in color): x-axis is processing time and higher throughput executions end earlier (drops in graphs correspond to moments of missing ball data).

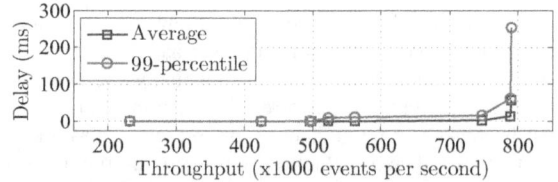

Figure 7: Trade-off between throughput and per-event delay. Points from left to right represent experiments with thread queue sizes of 1, 4, 16, 256, 1k, 4k, 16k and 64k, respectively.

13/61 ms and 56/253 ms, respectively. The average throughput for these cases is 747k, 789k and 790k e/s. This pattern which can be seen in Figure 7 shows the maximum throughput. For non-threaded executions (not shown in the figure), the average/90-percentile delay and throughput are 0.004/0.005 ms and 346k e/s, respectively.

It is noteworthy that the rather complex relationship between throughput, delay and queue size is mainly due to: (i) the substantial unevenness between the work taken for the different events—in particular the *emission* of heat maps (even only preparing the output without the final push to stdout/file), and to a lesser extent, the running statistics—and (ii) the enforcement of one thread per query (and one per sub-query for heat maps) to avoid reordering of timestamps in the output streams, described in Section 4.

Summary. Among the scenarios described, we recommend to use BlueBay in non-threaded mode for monitoring of live soccer games. In this mode, BlueBay processes sensor events 27+ times faster than real-time with less than a few microseconds of delay for 99% of events (maximum delay is 75 ms for heat map emission). For offline monitoring of pre-recorded games, however, a slightly higher delay is not an issue and the multi-threaded mode with a queue size of 4k (or 16k) is recommended. This provides a throughput of 747k e/s (/789k e/s), a speedup of 57x (/60x) and a 99-percentile delay of 15 ms (/61 ms).

6. CONCLUSION

We presented the design of the BlueBay event processing engine that serves as a framework for conducting various types of analysis over the sensor data stream of a soccer game. BlueBay provides the flexibility to trade off between processing throughput in favor of per-event processing latency (and vice versa). Our measurements carried out using a commodity PC demonstrate that it can achieve a throughput of up to 790k events/sec. Moreover, we investigated the applicability of several existing CEP engines to address the Grand Challenge problem. This effort resulted in two additional implementations based upon Esper [2] and Storm [6]. Finally, we reported on our experience in the development process.

7. REFERENCES

[1] A. Arasu et al. Stream: the stanford stream data manager (demonstration description). In *SIGMOD'03*.
[2] Esper Tech Inc. The Esper complex event processing platform.
[3] P. Hunt, M. Konar, F. P. Junqueira, and B. Reed. ZooKeeper: Wait-free coordination for internet-scale systems. In *USENIX ATC'10*.
[4] H.-A. Jacobsen, A. K. Y. Cheung, G. Li, B. Maniymaran, V. Muthusamy, and R. S. Kazemzadeh. The PADRES publish/subscribe system. In *Principles and Applications of Distributed Event-Based Systems*. IGI Global'10.
[5] R. S. Kazemzadeh and H.-A. Jacobsen. Opportunistic multipath forwarding in content-based publish/subscribe overlays. In *Middleware*, 2012.
[6] N. Marz. Storm - distributed and fault-tolerant realtime computation. http://www.storm-project.net/.
[7] Middleware Systems Research Group. Soccer game monitoring – sample video, 2013. http://msrg.org/datasets/blue-bay.
[8] C. Mutschler, H. Ziekow, and Z. Jerzak. The DEBS 2013 Grand Challenge. In *DEBS 2013: Proceedings of the 7th ACM International Conference on Distributed Event-Based Systems*, Arlington, TX, USA, July 2013. ACM.
[9] W. Thies, M. Karczmarek, and S. Amarasinghe. Streamit: A language for streaming applications. In *Compiler Construction*.

Grand Challenge: SPRINT Stream Processing Engine as a Solution[*]

Yingjun Wu[†1], David Maier[†‡2], Kian-Lee Tan[†3]
[†]School of Computing, National University of Singapore, Singapore 117417
[‡]Computer Science Department, Portland State University, Portland, OR 92701, USA
{yingjun[1], tankl[3]}@comp.nus.edu.sg, maier@cs.pdx.edu[2]

ABSTRACT

A stream processing engine, named *SPRINT*, is designed and implemented to efficiently process queries over high-speed sensor data streams from soccer games. SPRINT adopts several novel strategies, including a lock-free ring buffer, frame-based sliding windows, and dynamic parallel computation, to pursue three objectives: high speed, high precision, and low space consumption. Experiments show that SPRINT can achieve these three goals simultaneously.

Categories and Subject Descriptors

H.4 [**Information Systems Applications**]: Miscellaneous

General Terms

Performance, Experimentation

Keywords

Stream Processing Engine, Complex Events, DEBS Grand Challenge

1. INTRODUCTION

The DEBS 2013 Grand Challenge provides an opportunity to develop a stream processing engine for high-speed sensor data analysis in real time. The challenge aims at processing multiple queries over high-speed sensor data streams from a soccer game. Solutions are evaluated from different perspectives including correctness, throughput, and innovation. To tackle this challenge, we designed and implemented *SPRINT*, a stream processing engine, to evaluate multiple continuous queries in parallel. Experiments show

[*]This work is funded by the NExT Search Centre (grant R-252-300-001-490), which is supported by the Singapore National Research Foundation under its International Research Centre @ Singapore Funding Initiative and administered by the IDM Programme Office.

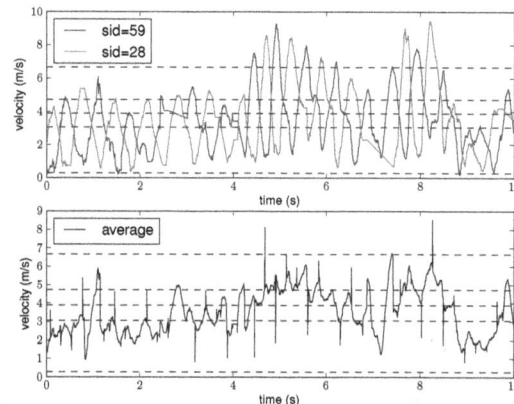

Figure 1: Sensor-generated velocity streams.

that SPRINT can elegantly handle complex queries while meeting the strict requirements of the challenge.

The paper is organized as follows. Section 2 generally reviews the problems and requirements proposed in the challenge and discusses the solution ideas. Section 3 describes the design and implementation of SPRINT in detail. Section 4 analyzes the performance of SPRINT from different perspectives. We discuss related work and conclude the paper in Section 5 and 6, respectively.

2. PROCESSING CHALLENGE QUERIES

The grand challenge requires us to evaluate four complex queries online. In this section, we generally describe the key ideas for solving these queries.

2.1 Query 1: Running Analysis

This query aims calculating instantaneous and aggregated running statistics for each player. The reported results need to satisfy two requirements: (1) all required statistics must be returned as streams at the frequency of at most 50 Hz; (2) a running-status interval with duration less than one second should be counted on top of the next intensity.

Sensor-generated instant velocity cannot directly reflect players' real running speeds. As stated in the problem description, each sensor generates streaming data of one leg's movement. Although the player's speed can be calculated as the average of two sensors, the obtained data are in fact dependent on the player's stride frequency, making it an un-

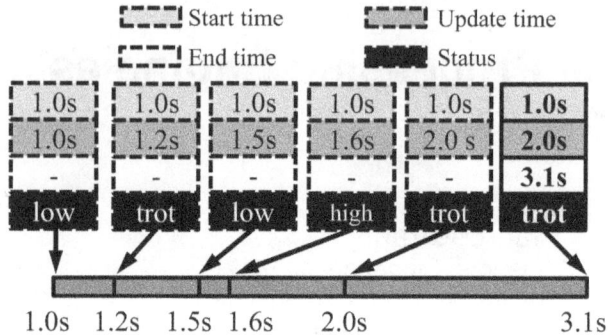

Figure 2: An example of the frame data structure.

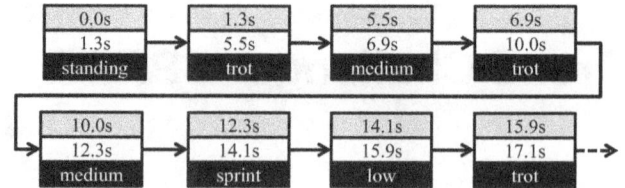

Figure 3: An example of compressed linked list for each player.

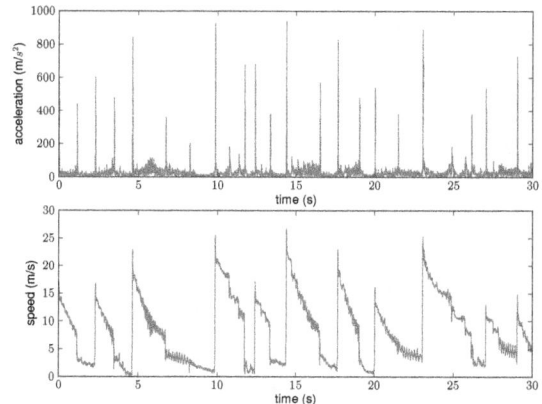

Figure 4: Ball acceleration and velocity. The upper figure shows the acceleration of the ball, and the lower figure shows the velocity of the ball at the same points in time.

reliable indicator of running speed. Figure 1 illustrates this problem with two velocity streams generated from sensors with $sid = 59$ and $sid = 28$, both associated with the same player. The upper-half is the original data, and the lower-half is the corresponding average velocity stream of the two sensors. The series of dashed lines from bottom up represent the thresholds for each running status, i.e., *standing, trot, low, medium, high* and *sprint*. Obviously, the average velocity stream is not stable enough for reliable measurement. SPRINT uses two methods to address this problem. First, every running status with duration less than 0.1 second will be removed as noise. Second, additional cross-status sections are inserted between every two sibling status pair, i.e., *standing-to-trot, trot-to-low, low-to-medium, medium-to-high, high-to-sprint*, in which range the velocities can be regarded as either status. Consequently, data dithering can be controlled in a tolerable range, making the velocity stream stable.

To generate a reliable measurement, we introduce a special data structure, called a *frame* [5], with four fields attached: *start_time, update_time, end_time*, and *status*. Figure 2 illustrates the usage of frames. At first, as a new tuple comes in, we create a frame with *start_time* and *update_time* containing its timestamp, and *status* containing its running intensity. The frame remains unchanged until a tuple with new running intensity is detected. At this time point, if the difference between the current timestamp and *update_time* is less than 1 second, then the *update_time* and *status* fields are modified to the current timestamp and running intensity. Otherwise, the *end_time* is filled in with the current timestamp, marking the frame as a reliable measurement, and the frame is further reported and inserted into a compressed linked list with the *update_time* field omitted. As an example, the frame in Figure 2 will finally report a 2.1-second-long trot running status. Obviously, the frame data structure ensures any reported status is reliable.

In this query, every player has a corresponding linked list for the purpose of recording the running performance trends. Figure 3 gives an example of such a compressed linked list. To aggregate window-range statistics, a pointer is used to trace through the linked list and accumulate the results. This kind of linked list is also referred as a frame-based sliding window, which will be further elaborated in Section 3.

2.2 Query 2: Ball Possession

This query aims at calculating ball-possession percentages for each player as well as for the whole team. The key point

is to efficiently detect the ball-hit event, which occurs when the ball acceleration peaks. Figure 4 shows the change of ball acceleration and velocity in a certain time interval. As suggested in the figure, the ball velocity oscillates with a regular pattern (possibly due to sensor rotation). Once the ball acceleration peaks, the velocity value changes drastically. As the changing pattern of ball velocity is more apparent and robust compared to the ball acceleration, SPRINT implements a velocity-based detection method to monitor the ball-hit events.

The velocity-based detection of ball-hit events continuously keeps track of the ball velocity. Once a sudden change in ball velocity is detected, SPRINT reports a ball-hit event, and then searches for the player who kicked the ball. Here, we define the "sudden change" as a change of +5 or -2 speed units (m/s) in 0.015 second. The player search uses an approximate nearest-neighbor search method. If no player is found in a one-meter-radius range, then the ball-hit event is simply treated as an outlier and discarded. Moreover, we use the "blind eye" method to improve processing efficiency. When the ball is kicked, the acceleration and velocity will stay at a high value for a certain time interval before dropping to normal. Therefore, once the ball-hit event is confirmed, SPRINT pauses velocity monitoring for 0.5 seconds and resumes it afterwards. All tuples in this half-second interval are ignored, since they are irrelevant to the event processing.

Similar to Query 1, the window-range statistics are also held in a frame-based sliding window. However, instead of

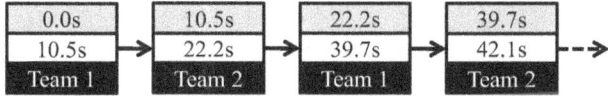

Figure 5: An example of compressed linked list for each team.

maintaining linked lists for both teams, SPRINT only holds a single list to keep track of the possession-exchange event. The reason is that the possession lists for two teams can be serialized, as only one team can hold the possession at any time. An example of a frame-based sliding window in this query is illustrated in Figure 5. Obviously, the two teams control the ball alternately during the game.

2.3 Query 3: Heat Map

This query requires calculating statistics for a heatmap monitoring players' position distributions over a group of equally-sized cells partitioned from the entire field. Output streams should be generated with different window lengths for different combinations of parameters: 8×13 (a grid of 104 cells), 16×25 (800 cells), 32×50 (1,600 cells), and 64×100 (6,400 cells). A simple solution to this query is to partition the field into a grid of 6,400 (64×100) cells and store the corresponding data for each player to record how much time they spend in each cell, since the 6,400 cells are of the minimum granularity and can easily constitute the larger granularity cells. In other words, for each player, an array of 6,400 slots is maintained to record time spent within certain time intervals at each cell. Obviously, the output streams for the paramater combinations of 64×100, 32×50, and 16×25, can be accumulated by summing up the values from their corresponding smaller-granularity cells.

Obtaining heatmap values for the 8×13 combination is much more difficult, as its corresponding 104 cells cannot be exactly aligned with the 6,400 lower-granularity cells. To solve this problem, we store additional cells for the unaligned part and monitor the time span each player spends in each of these unaligned cells. When generating the results, data in corresponding cells are accumulated.

One problem in this query is that keeping track of all 6,400 cells for each player for a long time interval (10 minutes for example) consumes too much memory resource. Interestingly, this problem can also be solved with frame-based sliding windows, as described already for the previous two queries. A linked list is still maintained for each of the players. Within each frame, three fields are maintained: the cell ID, the start time the player enters the cell, and the end time the player leaves the cell. As most players only move in a certain small range and are unlikely to run across the whole field, the linked list for a particular player can be extremely short, greatly reducing memory consumption.

2.4 Query 4: Shot on Goal

The aim of this query is to detect when a player shoots the ball in an attempt to score a goal. Apparently, the set of goal-attempt events is a subset of the set of ball-hit events. We therefore first detect the ball-hit event with a separate detector, using the similar method presented in Query 2. As a result, the detection for a goal attempt will be delayed until a ball hit is determined. Once a ball hit is confirmed, we subsequently estimate whether the ball could reach the

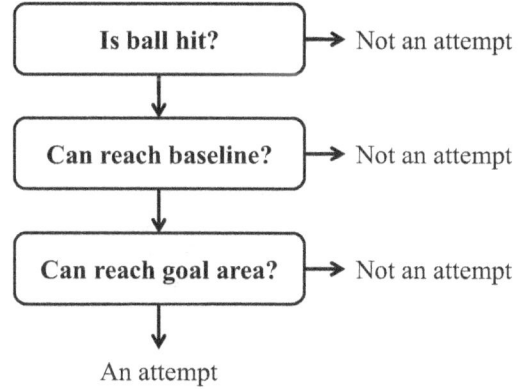

Figure 6: The procedure of detecting goal attempts.

baseline within 1.5 seconds from its current position. If possible, then further computation estimates the ball's position at the exact time that it reaches the baseline, according to its current velocity and position. If the estimated position falls into the goal area, the corresponding tuple will be output until another ball hit is detected or the ball leaves the field. The procedure of detecting goal attempts is shown in Figure 6.

3. ARCHITECTURE

This section describes the architecture of SPRINT, which is implemented in C++. To meet the strict requirements from the grand challenge, SPRINT largely takes advantage of multi-core techniques for the purpose of processing multiple queries in parallel. To optimize system performance, SPRINT adopts several innovative ideas, including a lock-free ring buffer, frame-based sliding windows, and dynamic computation method.

As shown in Figure 7, the overall architecture of SPRINT comprises three main components: preprocessor, shared ring buffer, and a group of parallel query processors. The preprocessor continuously reads tuples from the input data stream and feeds the parsed tuples into the shared ring buffer. The shared ring buffer is used to bridge and synchronize the incoming data and the query processing. Four independent parallel query processors run simultaneously for individual query tasks.

3.1 Lock-free Ring Buffer

SPRINT adopts the one-producer-multiple-consumer model to handle the incoming stream data. Traditionally, the producer-consumer model calls for expensive locking strategies to prevent data race. Instead, SPRINT follows the lock-free ring buffer model proposed in LMAX Disruptor [1]. The LMAX-style ring buffer brings two benefits to our SPRINT system. First, the circular buffer reuses allocated memory efficiently and thus helps to avoid memory allocation operations, which could lead to severe overhead in high-speed stream processing. Second, the lock-free ring buffer adopts CAS locks, introduced in C++ 11, to eliminate the expense incurred by traditional locks.

To maximize the memory bandwidth, we also set the message size to 4 KB, which is the default page size in most operating systems. The preprocessor (query processors) writes (reads) a 4 KB message block containing multiple tuples at

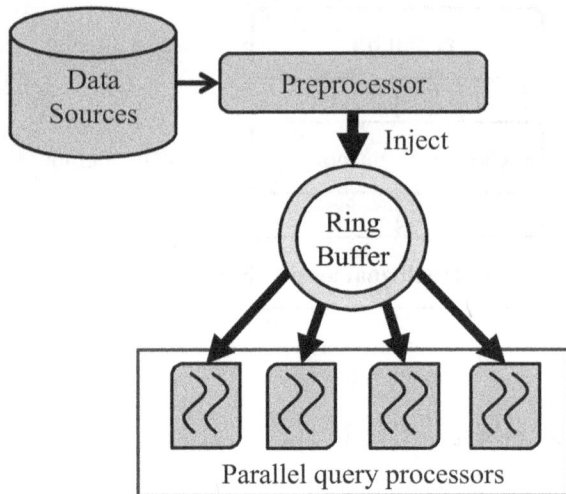

Figure 7: The architecture of SPRINT system.

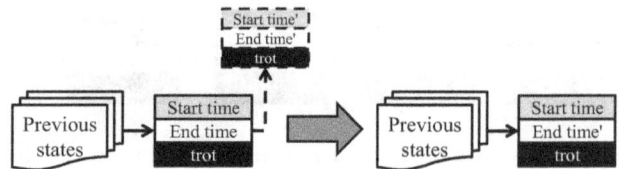

Figure 8: The merging procedure.

one time, instead of writing (reading) tuples one by one. In this way, the time for memory fetching is minimized, further improving the system throughput.

3.2 Frame-based Sliding Windows

Generally, stream processing engines need to perform analysis in a sliding-window manner. One common method to implement sliding windows is to split the window into equal-sized subwindows, or named panes [4] [7], and gradually move the window foward. However, this approach can still be memory intensive. Consider Query 3. For each of the 16 players, 6,400 cells are maintained for every pane, with sliding interval equivalent to 1 second. Thus, to generate the aggregated statistics with window size of 10 minutes (600 seconds), $6400 \times 600 \times 16$ cells should be stored in memory, which may be unacceptable due to the memory constraints.

To tackle this problem, we employ a new data structure, called a *frame*, to greatly reduce memory requirements. Our key idea is to use a linked list of frames to compress the content of sliding windows by only tracking state transitions. Adjacent panes with equal states are merged to eliminate redundant information. In each frame, we only maintain three fields for *start_time*, *status*, and *end_time* to record the start time and end time of the current state.

To better demonstrate the usage of frame-based sliding windows, we recall how we use such sliding windows in Query 1. To record the players' running status, a linked list is stored for each player. At the beginning, the linked list is empty. Once a reliable measurement is made, we encapsulate the measurement in a frame, containing the start time, end time, and running status, and insert it into the linked list. The length of the linked list keeps growing until the earliest frames can be removed. For example, if the largest window size required is 10 minutes, and the current timestamp is 20m 10s, then all frames with end time less than 10m 10s can be dropped.

To strictly meet the required reporting frequency, we can also set a constraint on the time span of a certain frame, computed as $end\_time - start\_time$. For example, if we want to report the instant running intensity with a frequency of 50 Hz, then we can constantly check the equation $end\_time -$

$start\_time \le 0.02$ for every update of the temporal frame. Once the constraint is violated, the frame is reported and an attempt made to insert it into linked list. If the *status* field is exactly the same as the end frame of the linked list, then the two frames will be merged. Figure 8 illustrates such a merging procedure.

To report the aggregated statistics for a certain window interval, we only need to search for the corresponding starting frame and calculate the statistics through the list. Note that for each query, we only maintain one frame-based sliding window with the size equivalent to the longest required window range. If three different window-range aggregations are needed, we then hold three pointers in the sliding window, indicating the appropriate starting frame for each.

Frame-based sliding windows also work with the other queries for the purpose of calculating window-range statistics. Note that other fields, such as the *update_time* field in Query 1, can be included in the frames if necessary.

3.3 Parallel Computation

Our system effectively employs multi-core techniques. We implement multi-core computation at two different levels: inter-query and intra-query. At the inter-query level, multi-core computation helps perform four independent queries concurrently. It mainly benefits from the lock-free ring buffer described above, as well as the dynamic computation discussed later. The intra-query level multi-core computation speeds up individual query processing by performing inner jobs in a parallel mode.

In SPRINT, Query 1 and Query 3 are easily parallelized. Figure 9 illustrates the parallel strategy adopted by SPRINT. As is shown in the figure, SPRINT follows a partition-and-merge paradigm to handle intra-query parallel computation. For Query 1 and Query 3, the input streams can be decomposed according to player ID, since the computation for each player is totally independent. To load-balance the parallel query threads, each processing thread is associated with an equal number of players. As the data comes in, each tuple is mapped to the corresponding processing thread by the job mapper. The processing thread then computes on-demand intermediate results. After that, the intermediate results are sent to a collector, where multiple results are combined and output streams are generated. Note that Query 3 can also be decomposed by cells. However, cell-based decomposition could lead to load-imbalance problems, so we do not incorporate it.

3.4 Dynamic Computation

SPRINT processes four queries in parallel using a global shared ring buffer. Each query uses its private pointer to fetch data from the shared ring buffer and then process it. A data slot is only feed after all four queries have read it. Consequently, as the processing of these four queries are of

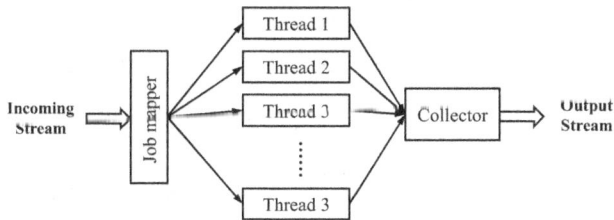

Figure 9: Intra-query level multi-core computation.

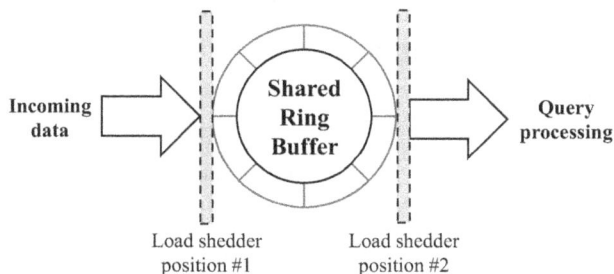

Figure 10: Load shedding strategies.

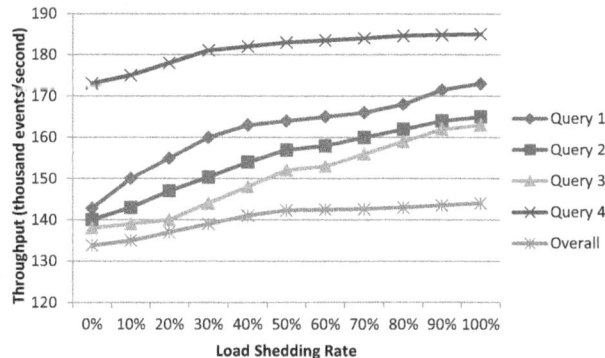

Figure 11: Throughput performance by counting input events.

different speeds, the slowest one determines the consumption progress of the ring buffer. Given the high data rate, it is difficult to make the total throughput of four queries match the incoming data rate with accurate processing of every input data. Instead, a load shedding strategy is needed to adaptively match the consumption rate of the shared ring buffer with the incoming data rate, i.e., query processing should never block the incoming data due to filling of the ring buffer. Moreover, load shedding must take the workload balancing of the four queries into account, since different queries have different tolerance to load shedding.

The shared ring buffer is the central component for load shedding. In the architecture of SPRINT, the load shedder could be placed in two positions: either at the endpoint of the incoming data or the start point of the queries, as shown in Figure 10. Based on these possibilities, our load shedding strategy evolved as follows.

Global shedding. The load shedder is placed in position #1 in Figure 10 and controls load shedding by configuring a global shed factor. As long as the ring buffer is full, indicating congestion, SPRINT increases the global shed factor to drop a great percentage of the incoming data. The advantage of global shedding is its easy implementation. However, it is too crude, as it treats all four queries collectively as a single black box.

Speeding up the straggler. Instead of treating the queries as a black box, we open it up and check which query performs slowest, i.e., is the straggler [6]. The load shedder is placed in position #2 in Figure 10. Instead of reading data consecutively, each query skips its read pointer in the ring buffer to drop some data in order to bridge the relative processing speed gap with other queries. Each query owns a shed factor to control the skipping of its read pointer. When congestion is detected, we check which query is the straggler, and increase the corresponding shed factor. This operation continues iteratively until the congestion is eliminated. Compared with global shedding, this strategy is more precise, but still treats individual queries as black boxes.

Shedding based on tolerance. Different queries have different tolerances for load shedding. Thus we further open up the black boxes to control the load shedding more intelligently. Each query is configured with a *shed tolerance*, which is the maximum shed factor that the query can accept. We define the *tolerance distance* to be the difference between the shed tolerance and the current shed factor. When ring buffer congestion occurs, we increase the shed factor of a query with the largest tolerance distance at the time to alleviate the congestion. This operation is also done iteratively until the congestion is eliminated. Consequently, we are able to minimize the negative side-effects of load shedding. One remaining issue is that finding a suitable set of shed tolerances is nontrivial. In our implementation of SPRINT, we employ empirically determined values.

4. EVALUATION

In this section, we evaluate the SPRINT system from three perspectives: throughput, precision, and recall. All the experiments are conducted on a machine with four 2.00 GHz Intel processors and 2 GB memory. The underlying operating system is CentOS 5.8. We directly take the raw sensor dataset as the data stream source.

Throughput. In our experiments, *throughput* refers to the number of input events consumed per second. To measure the throughput of SPRINT, we first run each query separately to judge single-query performance. Then all the queries are run simultaneously to test overall system performance. The load-shedding rate is set manually and does not take advantage of the tuning strategy introduced in the previous section. To minimize the influence of ring-buffer size, we generate the results only after the throughput value stabilizes, i.e., when the ring buffer can be assumed full. Note that we have muted all the output information during the experiments, since the I/O performance can be quite slow and is usually system dependent.

Figure 11 shows the system throughput as the load-shedding rate varies. As is illustrated in the figure, the throughput of Query 4 is much higher than the other three queries, and remains relatively stable with the variation in load-shedding rate. The relation is Query 4 does not involve window-range aggregation operations, and its query logic tends to be quite simple. The overall throughput turns out to be close to the single-query throughput, as the performance of multiple queries benefits from the parallel computation strategy.

305

However, when the load shedding rate goes up, the overall throughput does not change too much, as parallel computation also brings synchronization overhead.

Precision and recall. As the ball possession and shot on goal statistics have already been provided, we can verify the correctness of Query 2 and Query 4 by comparing our results with the provided referee events. For Query 2, instead of evaluating the correctness of ball possession, we measure the ball-hit events. Table 1 presents the experimental results on precision and recall for Query 2 and Query 4. The load-shedding rate is variously set to 0%, 25%, 50%, 75%, and 100%. Obviously, no output is genereated when the load-shedding rate is set to 100%. As the load-shedding rate increases, the precision of the results remains high, and the recall also does not drop much even when the load-shedding rate reaches 75%. The major reason is that the input data rate is quite high (2000 Hz for the ball) and load-shedding does not prevent generating correct results.

Table 1: Experimental results on Queries 2 & 4.

	Load-shedding	Precision	Recall	F-Score
	0%	93.3%	90.8%	92.0%
	25%	93.3%	90.8%	92.0%
Query 2	50%	90.1%	87.9%	88.9%
	75%	91.5%	75.1%	82.5%
	100%	0.0%	0.0%	0.0%
	0%	84.2%	79.6%	82.0%
	25%	84.2%	79.6%	82.0%
Query 4	50%	83.3%	72.1%	77.3%
	75%	81.8%	62.8%	71.1%
	100%	N/A	0.0%	0.0%

As a reference, we also list the first 15 ball-hit events detected in Table 2. Note that, as our experiment shows, the referee events have around 3-5 seconds lag with the events in the dataset.

Table 2: First 15 ball-hit events.

Estimated Time	Reference Time	Player
0.01s	4.08s	Leo Langhans
2.31s	5.23s	Christopher Lee
4.64s	7.46s	Vale Reitstetter
9.86s	10.75s	Luca Ziegler
12.40s	15.74s	Vale Reitstetter
14.40s	17.47s	Christopher Lee
17.67s	20.48s	Kevin Baer
20.04s	23.07s	Christopher Lee
23.05s	25.53s	Luca Ziegler
29.04s	33.07s	Roman Hartleb
30.01s	34.16s	Erik Engelhardt
30.96s	35.00s	Roman Hartleb
47.47s	47.08s	Christopher Lee
50.21s	52.85s	Vale Reitstetter
53.22s	55.61s	Christopher Lee

To conclude, we have demonstrated the efficiency and effectiveness of SPRINT system in performing multiple complex queries in real time.

5. RELATED WORK

High-performace stream-processing systems are attractive in both academic and industrial communities. Representative works include Storm [2], a distributed real-time computation system, and StreamInsight [3], a commercial platform for complex event processing. These systems are general purpose but hard to optimize for the queries in DEBS 2013 Grand Challenge, since their underlying components are highly interdependent. Aiming at high performace, SPRINT is built from scratch and maximizes the efficiency of queries via several novel designs as mentioned in Section 3.

6. CONCLUSION

In this paper, we introduced a stream processing engine, named SPRINT, to tackle the DEBS 2013 Grand Challenge. SPRINT adopts several novel data structures, including a lock-free ring buffer and frame-based sliding windows, to evaluate the multiple online queries concurrently. The system can also dynamically tune the load shedding rate to adapt to the runtime environment. Experiments showed that SPRINT can simutaneously achieve the three requirements of high speed, high precision, and low space consumption. As future work, we want to further investigate missing-data problems, which occur quite frequently in sensor-generated data streams. We are also looking for a novel stream cleaning method to better filter out noise. Finally, we plan to upgrade our SPRINT system to a general distributed stream processing engine, which could enjoy better generality and scalability.

7. REFERENCES

[1] Lmax disruptor. https://github.com/lmax-exchange.
[2] Storm. https://github.com/nathanmarz.
[3] M. H. Ali, C. Gerea, B. S. Raman, B. Sezgin, T. Tarnavski, T. Verona, P. Wang, P. Zabback, A. Ananthanarayan, A. Kirilov, M. Lu, A. Raizman, R. Krishnan, R. Schindlauer, T. Grabs, S. Bjeletich, B. Chandramouli, J. Goldstein, S. Bhat, Y. Li, V. Di Nicola, X. Wang, D. Maier, S. Grell, O. Nano, and I. Santos. Microsoft cep server and online behavioral targeting. *Proc. VLDB Endow.*, 2(2):1558–1561, Aug. 2009.
[4] J. Li, D. Maier, K. Tufte, V. Papadimos, and P. A. Tucker. No pane, no gain: efficient evaluation of sliding-window aggregates over data streams. *ACM SIGMOD Record*, 34(1):39–44, 2005.
[5] D. Maier, M. Grossniklaus, S. Moorthy, and K. Tufte. Capturing episodes: may the frame be with you. In *Proceedings of the 6th ACM International Conference on Distributed Event-Based Systems*, pages 1–11. ACM, 2012.
[6] M. Zaharia, A. Konwinski, A. D. Joseph, R. Katz, and I. Stoica. Improving mapreduce performance in heterogeneous environments. In *Proceedings of the 8th USENIX Conference on Operating Systems Design and Implementation*, pages 29–42, 2008.
[7] Y. Zhu and D. Shasha. Statstream: Statistical monitoring of thousands of data streams in real time. In *Proceedings of the 28th International Conference on Very Large Data Bases*, pages 358–369. VLDB Endowment, 2002.

Grand Challenge: Real-time Soccer Analytics Leveraging Low-Latency Complex Event Processing

Martin Jergler, Christoph Doblander, Mohammedreza Najafi, Hans-Arno Jacobsen
Middleware Systems Reseach Group (MSRG)
Technical University Munich, Germany
{jergler, doblande, najafim, jacobsen}@in.tum.de

ABSTRACT

In this paper, we present a real-time capable event-based system, which is tailored towards analytical query processing in the context of soccer games. The main challenge is to meet the application's strict real-time and low-latency requirements in face of streams of high-velocity sensor data. We describe a workflow-like architecture for query processing based on a publish/subscribe model. Queries are structured into computational tasks that are arranged sequentially and/or in parallel. Tasks are connected by preallocated ring buffers providing total event ordering and fast as well as decoupled event access. Our evaluation results show the effectiveness of the proposed system in terms of low-latency processing under real-time conditions. Speeding up the system by a factor of 50 compared to real-time introduces almost no latency overhead.

Categories and Subject Descriptors

H.3.3 [**Information Search and Retrieval**]: [Information filtering]

General Terms

Experimentation, Performance, Measurement

Keywords

Event Processing, Complex Event Processing, Publish/Subscribe, DEBS Grand Challenge

1. INTRODUCTION

Today, complex event processing (CEP) systems obtain growing attention from both industry and academia. In order to further encourage research and provide a common basis for evaluation and comparison of CEP systems, the ACM International Conference on Distributed Event-based Systems (DEBS) initiated a grand challenge for the event processing community. Being the third in a row, the ACM DEBS 2013 Grand Challenge focuses on real-time processing of high-velocity sensor data to address a set of analytical queries, which are provided by the challenge committee. In particular, these queries are centered around a use case that targets at the

continuous computation of statistics in soccer games. These analytics reflect the most recent considerable statistics of a match like ball possession, detection of shots on the goal, and running analysis as well as spatial distribution of players during the game [9].

1.1 DEBS 2013 Grand Challenge

In the given scenario, wireless sensors are attached to players and the ball in order to collect position information at discrete points in time [9]. A single sensor is located within the ball and two sensors are located near players' feet (1 sensor per leg). Based on this information, the actual challenge is to design and implement a (centralized) event processing system that consumes the raw sensor streams, computes the analytical queries and returns a set of result streams representing the most recent match statistics. In addition to system correctness, performance is the most critical factor. To ensure the real-time characteristics, the system has to meet strict latency requirements and provide high throughput.

All data provided with the challenge has been gathered in a real game setting recorded at the stadium of Nuremberg. The match took place at a half-sized field and was comprised of two half-times taking 30 minutes each. The corresponding data set primarily consists of the raw sensor measurements, which were generated at a rate of 200 Hz for players' sensors and 2000 Hz for the ball. The format of this input stream is represented by a 13-tuple:

$$(\mathtt{sid}, \mathtt{ts}, \mathtt{x}, \mathtt{y}, \mathtt{z}, |\mathtt{v}|, |\mathtt{a}|, \mathtt{vx}, \mathtt{vy}, \mathtt{vz}, \mathtt{ax}, \mathtt{ay}, \mathtt{az})$$

where $\mathtt{sid}$ is a unique event-identifier, $\mathtt{ts}$ is the point in time the event was produced in picoseconds, and $\mathtt{x}$, $\mathtt{y}$, $\mathtt{z}$ represent the position of the sensor in a three-dimensional space; furthermore, $|\mathtt{v}|$ (in $\mu m/s$), $\mathtt{vx}$, $\mathtt{vy}$, $\mathtt{vz}$ represent a vector for the speed and $|\mathtt{a}|$ (in $\mu m/s^2$), $\mathtt{ax}$, $\mathtt{ay}$, $\mathtt{az}$ describe the absolute acceleration. In addition to raw sensor events, which comprise 2.6 GB of flat data in total, various meta-data is provided. This includes referee events like game interruptions, player substitutions and a mapping of $\mathtt{sid}$s to players.

1.2 Analytical Queries

There are four analytical queries for the given scenario defined by a corresponding result schema [9]. Results have to be produced with the same rate as the raw sensor events are issued to the system.

Query 1 - Running Analysis calculates performance statistics for each player. For that account, six different categories of running intensities are defined (i.e., stop, trot, low, medium, high, and sprint). The query has to compute the duration each player spends within these intensity intervals. Moreover, the distance a particular player covered in the respective interval within a given time frame has to be reported. The query returns two classes of results; the (1) current and the (2) aggregated running statistics. The result stream for (1) is defined as (ts_start,

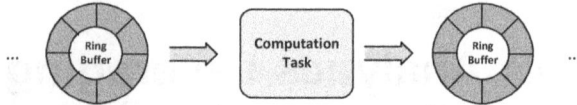

Figure 1: Publish/Subscribe principle with ring buffers

ts_stop, player_id, intensity, distance, speed); for (2) the result is defined as (ts, player_id, standing_time, standing_distance, low_time, low_distance, medium_time, medium_distance, high_time, high_distance, sprint_time, sprint_distance) whereby the aggregation is calculated over four different time windows (i.e., 1, 5, 20 minutes, and the whole game).

Query 2 - Ball Possession computes ball possession statistics of (1) individual players as well as (2) the whole team. The ball is considered to be possessed by a player if it is in his proximity (i.e., less than one meter) and he hits the ball (i.e., acceleration greater $55m/s^2$). A ball is associated with a particular player until another player acquires possession according to the aforementioned criteria. The result schema is defined as (ts, player_id, time, hits) for players and (ts, team_id, time, percentage) for teams. The latter one is again computed over four different time windows (i.e., 1, 5, 20 minutes, and the whole game).

Query 3 - Heatmap calculates statistics for the percentage distribution of individual players over distinct regions of the field. These regions are defined by a grid with X rows along the x-axis and Y columns along the y-axis, which is layered above the field. X and Y are parameterized with four different configurations; i.e., 8 and 13 (i.e., 104 cells), 16 and 25 (i.e., 400 cells), 32 and 50 (i.e., 1600 cells), and 64 and 100 (i.e., 6400 cells). The query calculates the percentage each player resides in a particular cell according to each of these grid configurations. Moreover, statistics are calculated over four different time windows (1, 5, 10 minutes, and the whole game). Altogether, this results in 16 result streams being updated every second and having the following format: (ts, player_id, cell_x1, cell_y1, cell_x2, cell_y2, percentage), whereby a cell is identified by its lower left (x1, y1) and its upper right corner (x2, y2).

Query 4 - Shot On Goal is supposed to identify situations within the game, in which a player hits the ball in order to score a goal. This is defined as any shot that would hit (or closely miss) the other team's goal. More formally, the ball is shot by a player (i.e., acceleration greater $55m/s^2$) and the projected movement of the ball crosses a plane that represents the opponent's goal within 1.5 seconds. For the whole duration this situation is detected, the query returns a result stream with the following schema (ts, player_id, x, y, z, |v|, vx, vy, vz, |a|, ax, ay, az). Result events are produced with the same rate as sensor events.

1.3 Core Concepts Of Our Approach

In this paper, we propose an event-based system that enables query processing for the given scenario [9]. Our approach is highly optimized in terms of achieving low-latency processing while ensuring real-time operation. In general, the system architecture revolves around a publish/subscribe principle based on ring buffers. A ring buffer is a preallocated data structure that enables fast access to the data in FIFO order. Query processing is structured into computation and aggregation tasks that are connected by ring buffers. Each task consumes data from its input ring buffer and writes results to its output ring buffer(s). Output data serves as input for the subsequent tasks. Figure 1 depicts this principle exemplary for a single task. Essentially, each query is represented by a workflow that arranges task elements either sequentially or in parallel.

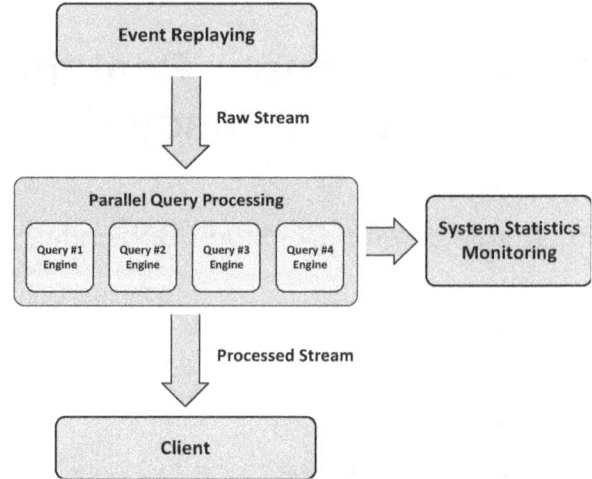

Figure 2: High-level system architecture

The parallel execution pattern facilitates the real-time throughput of our system. Furthermore, in combination with a non-blocking implementation of the ring buffer structure over the Disruptor pattern (cf. Section 2), we achieve low-latency processing. Although, we provide a centralized Java implementation of our system, we argue that the general design is also applicable for distributed executions. In a distributed publish/subscribe-based infrastructure, for instance, the workflow can be implemented as a set of subscriptions [7, 8]. A particular subscription could express its interest in results (i.e., publications) of previous tasks to realize the ring buffer mechanism, then perform its own computation, and emit the result as a new publication. Although, a distributed publish/subscribe-based system would probably provide a higher throughput, it may increase the latency at the same time.

As our centralized approach aims primarily for low latency, we traded memory and CPU efficiency for lowering latency. Our system foregos a higher level language for query expression in order to reach the bottom line of latency achievable on a JVM (Java Virtual Machine [2]) over modern multi-core machines.

The remainder of this paper is structured as follows. We present background information about the Disruptor pattern and the ring buffer implementation in Section 2. The system architecture and the conceptual query processing is described in Section 3. Moreover, we present our evaluation results with focus on latency measurements in Section 4, provide a short discussion about hardware acceleration for CEP in Section 5, and summarize further ideas for optimizing our approach in Section 6.

2. DISRUPTOR & RING BUFFERS

Disruptor is a library that was first presented at QCon San Francisco 2010 and open-sourced by LMAX Trading under the Apache 2.0 license [3]. The main goal of this library is to create an abstraction for low-latency message-passing between threads. Similar approaches are Akka [4], a message passing framework for Scala, and the Actor model of concurrency implemented in Erlang [6]. Another similar approach is Kilim [11], which provides lightweight threads and facilities for fast messaging between threads. In our approach, we leverage the Disruptor pattern to organize the communication between the ring buffer threads.

The JVM executes byte code and includes a garbage collector to release memory for objects that are no longer referenced. To achieve continuous and predictable low-latency, the Java garbage collection cycles have to be reduced to a minimum. With the Disruptor pattern and the usage of pre-allocated ring buffers, memory

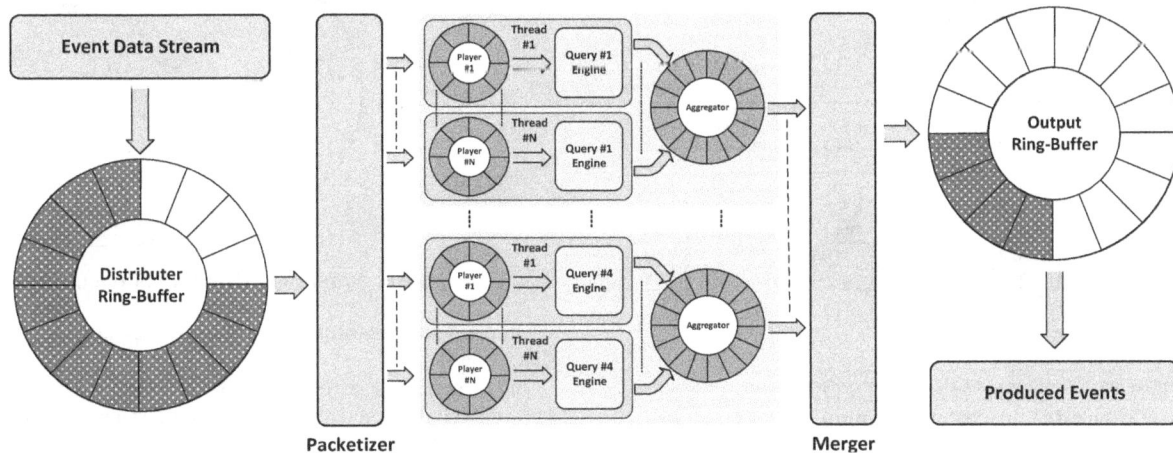

Figure 3: Conceptual overview of query processing

allocations during runtime are largely avoided. Elements in the ring buffers are reused constantly and only temporary variables for storing intermediate results are instantiated. This method provides almost constant memory consumption throughout the whole runtime: Garbage collection load is reduced and multi-threading is alleviated. Synchronization between multiple threads is achieved by different strategies. In general, a combination between spin and block waiting strategies is used. Spin waiting (cf. Listing 1) takes a lot more CPU cycles than block waiting strategies but provides lower latency. Because our system requires more threads (i.e., greater 70) than CPU cores are usually available, we opted for a combination of both. The *Packetizer*, cf. Figure 3, is set to a aggressive spin waiting strategy, all others use a block waiting strategy. Usage of the block waiting strategy causes more latency but uses the CPU more efficiently.

```
public long waitFor(final long sequence, Sequence cursor,
      final Sequence dependentSequence, final
   SequenceBarrier barrier)
      throws AlertException, InterruptedException
{
      long availableSequence;
      while ((availableSequence = dependentSequence.get
         ()) < sequence)
      {
            barrier.checkAlert();
      }
      return availableSequence;
}
```

Listing 1: Spin waiting strategy [3]

3. ARCHITECTURE

A high-level overview of our system architecture is depicted in Figure 2. The *Event Replaying* module issues the raw sensor data to the processing system. The *Parallel Query Processing* module distributes input events among the queries, processes them and forwards the results to the *Client* module. System performance is measured by the *System Statistics Monitoring* module.

3.1 Event Replaying

The *Event Replaying* module reads the raw sensor measurements from disk and forwards the information to the processing module. To simulate the provided game-scenario in real-time, event forwarding is controlled by the system. A waiting strategy based on thread yielding ensures exact event replay according to the timing

information incorporated in the raw data. Once timing is guaranteed, events are inserted in the first ring buffer (cf. Figure 3).

3.2 Parallel Query Processing

In this section we describe the processing concept for each query over our publish/subscribe workflow model, leveraging the ring buffer structure.

3.2.1 Query 1 – Running Analysis

Since running analysis only refers to individual players, the calculation can be parallelized. The statistics are merged afterwards to generate the result stream. Initially, the incoming events are split and all events for a given player are forwarded to a dedicated ring buffer for this player. Consequently, the calculation of the statistics is executed in parallel. Every event is processed as it arrives and the output is throttled according to the defined frequency of 50Hz. Basically, this query is comprised of two parts, the current running statistic and the aggregated statistics. Both queries rely on the distance the player covered since the last event.

The processing module for this query calculates the distance by averaging the position of both feet-sensors first. Then, the distance since the last measurement is computed. Every time a state-change occurs (i.e., the player entered a different intensity interval), a new time frame is initialized. The average speed for a given time frame is calculated by summing up the speed of the individual events and averaging them. This strategy is based on the assumption that the timespans between the single events for a given player are equal. The system can therefore rely on the speed given by the input events. The resulting data is reported to the next ring buffer. All players report to the same output ring buffer which further processes the events and streams them to a Web front end (Figure 6).

The second part of the query is the aggregation per player over the different time windows. First of all, the current statistics are aggregated over time slots with a length of 0.8 seconds. These intermediary aggregates are stored in a queue structure (depicted in Figure 4). The queuing mechanism enables an efficient final aggregation over all time intervals (i.e., 1, 5, 20 minutes and the whole game). Every time the pre-aggregation for a new 0.8 second timeslot is completed (`current_ts`), the queue is updated and the accumulated value is recalculated for all intervals (n): `value = value - t[current_ts - n] + t[current_ts]`.

Our queue implementation provides $\mathcal{O}(1)$ complexity for insertion (i.e., `offer()`) and extraction (i.e., `poll()`) based on point-

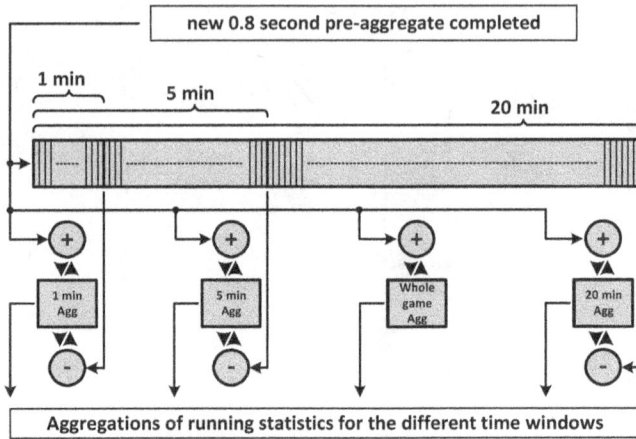

Figure 4: Low-cost aggregation strategy

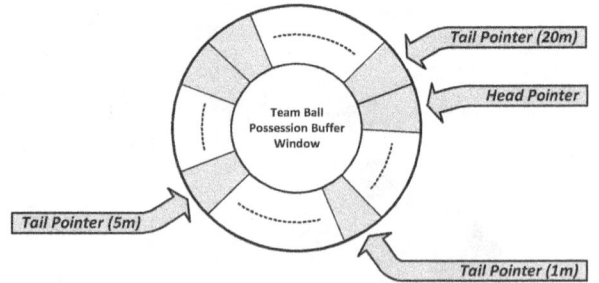

Figure 5: Rotational structure of queue buffer

ers. In general, the queue is implemented based on an array that is initialized with the capacity to store all relevant data (i.e., the 0.8 second aggregations) for the 20 minute time window. To enable the fast queue operations, a *head pointer* identifies the current start index of the array and three different *tail pointers*, with fixed distances from the *head*, point to the end index in the array according to the corresponding time windows (cf. Figure 5).

For aggregation, each new element representing a time interval of 0.8 seconds is inserted at the *head* and added to the aggregate for all time windows. At the same time, the aggregates stored at the *tail pointers* indexes are subtracted from this aggregate (e.g., the aggregate specified by *tail pointer* for the 1 minute window is subtracted from the 1 minute aggregate). Finally, all pointers are incremented.

3.2.2 Query 2 – Ball Possession

Compared with the running analysis, the calculation of ball possession statistics imposes a more sophisticated challenge to our workflow-based architecture: Player events have to be correlated with ball events and therefore parallelism in query processing is much harder to achieve. In particular, parallelism would require thread synchronization and affect performance negatively (i.e., especially latency). For that reason, we opted for a sequential computation and divided the query in two processing tasks that are connected by a ring buffer structure to store intermediary results.

Due to the high rate of raw sensor measurements, the first task acts as an event filter that applies only cheap computations to reduce the amount of events being relevant for the final and accurate computation of the ball possession. The crucial point within this query is the determination of the distance between players and the ball. Moreover, this calculation has to be performed at the rate of incoming events resulting in a vast amount of computations. Usually, the distance between two points is calculated based on the Euclidean norm (i.e., the L2-norm[1] in a 2-dimensional space). We argue that this computation is too expensive for applying it to all events. Instead, we use the L1-norm[2] to identify pairs of player and ball events that are very likely to represent positions with a distance of less than one meter. The threshold for the distance filter according to the L1-norm is set to 1.42 (i.e., slightly higher than $\sqrt{2}$) which captures all combinations of player and ball events that are guaranteed to be less than one meter apart from each other. All

event pairs passing through the filter are forwarded to the intermediary ring buffer.

In the second task for this query, the event pairs are inspected in more detail. First of all, the absolute distance of player and ball is calculated based on the L2-norm. Then the acceleration value of the ball sensor in analyzed to detect situation that fulfill both criteria (i.e., distance less than one meter and acceleration of ball greater than $55m/s^2$).

Based on this information both result streams (i.e., statistics for individual players and for the teams) can be calculated by aggregation. For the player statistics, a new aggregate is instantiated every time the ball possession changes. The hit counter is set to one, the timestamp representing the obtainment of the ball is recorded and a timer is started. If there is no change in ball possession, statistics are just updated (i.e., the hits and timer are incremented). Aggregation for the team statistics is calculated in a similar manner. The difference is that ball possession changes only if a player from the other team acquires ball possession. Times are recorded as for players and the percentage distribution is based on these timings.

3.2.3 Query 3 – Heatmap

The third query addresses the percentage distribution of individual players over distinct regions of the soccer field. Therefore, the field is split into cells by applying four different grid structures (cf. Section 1.2). Furthermore, statistics are aggregated over four different time windows ending up in 16 result streams and comprising 34016 events per second. To reduce the huge number of individual results, we decided to alter the schema and only emit one large event that contains the distribution for a player over all cells in a given grid and in a given time window. Although this query resembles some similarity with Query 1 (i.e., the statistics are calculated per player), the large amount of statistical data that has to be managed and reported by the system poses a special challenge in terms of low-latency and real-time processing. Similar to the calculation of the running statistics, our approach tackles this problem by leveraging parallelism and efficient aggregation. However, instead of parallelizing only single players, we also parallelize the computations for the individual grid structures for each player.

Consequently, the query processing for a player in a given grid is structured into three computational tasks that are arranged sequentially and connected by ring buffers: (1) The calculation of the absolute player position, (2) the computation of the coordinates within the grid structure, and (3) the aggregation of the information for the different time windows. The calculation of the absolute position is done by averaging the latest sensor measurements from both leg sensors. In the next step, this position is mapped onto the respective grid structure in order to determine the cell coordinates this position corresponds to. For the aggregation of the heatmap statistics over the different time windows, we use the same strategy as for aggregation in Query 1. First of all, the statistics are pre-aggregated for time slots of 1 second (i.e., the result stream

---

[1]L2-norm: $\|x\|_2 = \sqrt{\sum_i |x_i^2|}$
[2]L1-norm: $\|x\|_1 = \sum_i |x_i|$

rate). Therefore, a two-dimensional array represents the soccer field for a given grid structure. Every time a new grid position for the player is determined, the counter in the respective array cell is incremented. After one second, these intermediary statistics are pushed to a queue like the one depicted in Figure 4, which has the capacity to store such pre-aggregates for 10 minutes. Furthermore, when a new aggregate is computed, it is added to an array that represents the current statistics over a particular time window. At the same time the last element (i.e., pre-aggregated statistics array) is extracted from the queue and subtracted from this aggregation. Since the current statistics array only contains the number of occurrences of players in particular cells, the values are divided by the total number of occurrences to get the percentage distribution.

3.2.4 Query 4 – Shot On Goal

Similar to the second query, the workflow for Query 4 contains two tasks that are arranged sequentially. The first tasks acts as an event filter to efficiently detect shots. After a shot has been detected a vector representing the projected movement of the ball is calculated and intersected with the plane that represents the goal area. In case of intersection, all following ball events are analyzed until the ball leaves its trajectory.

3.3 Monitoring

Since latency is not a bell shaped curve, reporting mean and standard deviation would skew the system performance. Therefore, we measured latency at the percentile. More specifically, the latency was measured in nanoseconds and describes the time between replaying an event from the file and the output of the result that has been influenced by this event. In a real scenario, this would correspond to the latency between an incoming sensor event over a wireless network and the time the result is sent to a consumer over the network. For people watching an information screen, the value at the 87.50 percentile or even lower would be enough, since the network delays are in the millisecond range. A live betting exchange which would have a low latency connection to this kind of analysis or share the same datacenter would require a very predictable result stream. Since the situation on the soccer field can change rapidly, the betting rates can change rapidly as well. For this kind of scenario, we also included measurements at the 99.805 percentile. Each latency measurement was recorded with a histogram component [1] and the results were printed to the console.

3.4 Client

To allow a scenario where many people can follow real-time data of a football match without technical hurdles, the client is implemented in HTML5. Data is streamed to the *Client* over the websocket protocol, an extension of the HTTP protocol widely implemented in browsers. The charts refresh automatically. To not overload the client, the traffic has to be further throttled to 1 message per 500 milliseconds. A more comprehensive implementation could consider client specific throttling, e.g., 2 seconds for mobile phones and 300 milliseconds for clients with broadband internet connections.

4. EXPERIMENTAL EVALUATION

The latency benchmarks were conducted on an Intel i7-3520M 2.90GHz Dual Core, an i7-3720QM 2.6GHz Quad Core and a machine with two Intel Xeon E5-2665 CPU 2.4GHz Octo Cores. The same benchmark was executed on all machines with the same command-line flags. The program was invoked with the following arguments: `java -d64 -Xmx4g -jar target/ Debs2013 .jar -file=full-game > q1log.txt`. Latency measure-

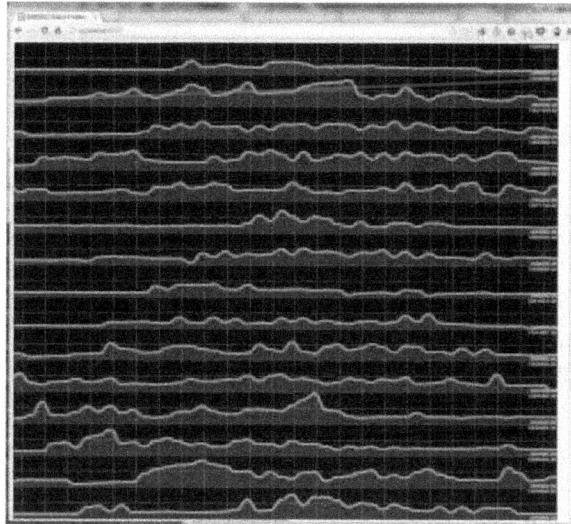

Figure 6: Running speed: HTML5 user interface

PERCENTILE	50.000	87.500	96.875	99.219	99.805
1x2 i7	9.2	18.4	38.9	1,471.4	9,206.7
1x4 i7	49.7	59.2	61.2	69.5	76.9
2x8	30.1	52.2	80.7	108.9	145.1
2x8 aff.	12.7	39.9	48.9	71.7	83.1
4x6 spin.	3.9	4.5	5.3	12.0	1,883.0

Table 1: Query 1 - Latency at percentile in μs

ments have been rounded to 1 digit microseconds and the results are depicted in Table 4 for Query 1 and Table 4 for Query 3.

It is interesting to note that the 87.5 percentile measurements with a Dual Core CPU are faster than the results of a Quad Core processor (cf. Table 4). This can be explained by better cache affinity and the higher clock rate. However, the Quad Core processor is still predictable at the 99.805 percentile, since the machine never overloaded. The Dual Octo Core Xeon processor is predictable over the whole time. The code could have been more optimized towards a 16 core machine. Initial runs on the dual processor machine without manually setting the CPU affinity resulted in worse results, see Table 4. Therefore, the CPU affinity was set to the second processor (i.e., cores 7-15). This was done with the following command: `taskset -p 0x0000FF80 <pid>`. This setting avoids switching between the processors which lowers latency significantly. The latency of Query 3 behaves similar. The performance improvements caused by thread affinity on the dual processor machine were not as high as in the first query. The latency on the Xeon 4x6 was really low compared to the other processors on Query 1. This can be explained because more cores than threads are available and with the given clock rate it can keep up with the incoming events. Therefor, we were able to leverage the SpinWaiting strategy on all event processors. This caused huge improvements in the lower percentiles, while the 99.805 percentile shows that the latency is not always predictable. We think that optimizing the JVM garbage collector settings could have im-

PERCENTILE	50.000	87.500	96.875	99.219	99.805
1x2 i7	6.7	10.6	27.6	365.2	9.298.0
1x4 i7	36.3	39.9	51.7	83.7	118.0
2x8	15.1	17.0	28.3	64.5	90.2
2x8 aff.	14.9	16.9	22.5	67.4	93.9
4x6 spin.	346.8	686.5	1,261.3	28,097.0	28,859.0

Table 2: Query 3 - Latency at percentile in μs

X	RATE	50.000	87.500	96.875	99.219	99.805
1	13315	27.3	60.2	411.2	3,598.4	9,150.7
2	25399	29.0	67.6	647.9	8,321.2	16,471.8
4	52130	26.9	58.0	907.4	8,023.6	10,284.9
8	105271	27.9	70.4	1,205.7	9,553.1	15,107.1
16	208869	24.1	150.7	4,792.5	11,652.0	14,103.9
32	372625	26.5	84.5	713.5	8,353.0	10,781.4
48	510290	21.9	215.9	11,932.4	13,974.3	14,288.9

Table 3: Query 1 - Speedup by factor X on dual core machine. Latencies at percentile in μs

proved the results at that percentile. Query 3 on the Xeon 4x6 with a `SpinWaiting` strategy performed a lot worse because it uses more threads than cores available. The `BlockWaiting` or `YieldWaiting` strategies were much worse. Experiments with running only a few players show that Query 3 can run faster but with all players there is too much parallelism.

To measure throughput we sped up the input-rate beginning with 1 (i.e., real-time) up to 48 (i.e., 48 times faster than real-time.) The benchmark was conducted on a laptop equipped with an Intel i7-3530M Dual Core processor running at 2.90 GHz and a Samsung SSD. Despite the speedup, the latency at the percentile did not deteriorate. In case of excessive queuing, the latency would have increased a lot. The limiting throughput factor was disk speed because the file could not be replayed faster than a 48 times speedup of real-time.

5. HARDWARE ACCELERATED EVENT PROCESSING

In this section, we speculate on possible future directions for accelerating event processing through FPGAs and GPUs.

5.1 FPGA-based Approaches

Field-Programmable Gate Arrays (FPGAs) constitute affordable and reconfigurable hardware platforms. An appropriate query design based on FPGAs could result in significant performance and latency improvements. However, FPGA-based systems are difficult to design and require a careful analysis of the application scenario (i.e., the query characteristics). In general, queries can be divided into two categories: (1) Memory intensive and (2) non-memory-intensive queries. For (2), as long as all queries fit into the FPGA on-board memory, a performance gain is almost guaranteed. As opposed to (1), where FPGAs may not be suitable due to their limited storage capabilities. Here, the FPGA must be bound to an external memory unit (e.g., the Xilinx AC701 board with DDR3 SDRAM memory). The logic segment of the query resides on the FPGA and the part that requires buffering resides on the external memory, limiting efficient system exploitation. Initial results for leveraging FPGAs for event processing can be found in [10].

5.2 GPU-based Approaches

General purpose computing on graphic processing units (GPU) is a further option for improving event processing performance. However, the latency penalty resulting from the use of GPUs makes it difficult to profitably apply GPUs for problems like the DEBS 2013 Grand Challenge aiming at achieving low-latency processing.

Current GPU technology does not support direct access of GPU memory to the filesystem. Therefore, the data has to pass through the system's main memory to reach the GPU. This imposes an excessive transmission latency. Main memory access latency for the current generation of Nvidia GPUs is, for instance, between 200-400 cycles [5]. Worse yet, total system latency is increased by addition of main memory reads, the actual GPU execution, and the write operations for results back to main memory. GPUs can be more beneficial when the latency offered by the execution on the processor goes beyond this lower bound. Basically, GPUs generate a massive increase in computational throughput, but the cost is a significant rise in latency. Therefore, GPUs are well-suited for applications that require excessive data-parallel computations in a way that the memory access latency can be hidden by computations.

There is a new trend of processors, namely accelerated processing units (APUs). These processors include both CPU and GPU units on the same die. This can significantly reduce data sharing and reduce the GPU-CPU access latency, which could offer an edge in high-performance computing while preventing costly transmission penalties. AMD's Trinity (with Radeon HD 7000) and Intel Ivy Bridge (with Intel HD Graphics 4000) are examples of these hybrid processors. Full utilization of both CPU and GPU is a promising way forward to further improve the results of this work.

6. CONCLUSIONS

Our Java-based approach still leaves room for improvements and optimizations. For instance, it is possible to further reduce garbage collection cycles by tuning respective JVM parameters and reusing variables more extensively. In addition, the current implementation uses too many threads, which causes many context switches. For that reason our system uses a blocking strategy for some event processors, which worsens our latency results. For Query 1, this may be avoided by using one thread per team and leveraging a more aggressive strategy (e.g., `SpinWaiting` or `YieldWaiting`) instead of having one thread per player. The current libraries for multi-core processing largely focus on task parallelism or message passing. Nevertheless, threads are necessary to abstract from the underlying number of cores. An idea for achieving this would be the incorporation of an optimizer, which considers the result of a sample benchmark as cost function and various system specifications as constraints. Based on these enhancements, scheduling strategies for throughput or latency could be optimized. Another idea would be to change the thread priority if a particular event processor falls behind and introduces higher latency. However, this has to been done very carefully as it could also effect other processes and consequently lead to an unpredictable system.

7. REFERENCES
[1] Gil Tene, HdrHistogram Library, 2013.
[2] Java Virtual Machine, 2013.
[3] LMAX Trading, Disruptor Library, 2013.
[4] Scala Akka Library, 2013.
[5] *NVIDIA CUDA 5.0 Programming Guide. NVIDIA Corporation*, Oct. 2012.
[6] J. Armstrong. *Programming Erlang: Software for a Concurrent World*. Pragmatic Bookshelf, 2007.
[7] H.-A. Jacobsen et al. The PADRES Publish/Subscribe System. In *Principles and Applications of Distributed Event-Based Systems*. IGI Global, 2010.
[8] G. Li et al. A distributed service-oriented architecture for business process execution. *TWEB'10*.
[9] C. Mutschler, H. Ziekow, and Z. Jerzak. The DEBS 2013 Grand Challenge. In *DEBS 2013: Proceedings of the 7th ACM International Conference on Distributed Event-Based Systems*, Arlington, TX, USA, July 2013. ACM.
[10] M. Sadoghi et al. Multi-query stream processing on FPGAs. ICDE '12, pages 1229–1232, 2012.
[11] S. Srinivasan and A. Mycroft. Kilim: Isolation-typed actors for java. ECOOP '08, pages 104–128, 2008.

Grand Challenge: MapReduce-Style Processing of Fast Sensor Data

Kasper Grud Skat Madsen   Li Su   Yongluan Zhou
{kaspergsm, lsu, zhou}@imada.sdu.dk
University of Southern Denmark

ABSTRACT

MapReduce is a popular scalable processing framework for large-scale data. In this paper, we first briefly present our efforts on rectifying the traditional batch-oriented MapReduce framework for low-latency data stream processing. We investigated how to utilize such a MapReduce-style platform for fast sensor data processing by taking the DEBS Grand Challenge 2013 as an example. Both the analysis and experiments verify that our approach can obtain highly scalable solutions.

Categories and Subject Descriptors

H.2.4 [**Systems**]: Query Processing

Keywords

Sensor Data; MapReduce; Scalability; Sharing Computation

1. INTRODUCTION

There is a recent interest in building large-scale platforms for processing fast data streams, such as MapReduce online [2], Muppet [4] and STORM [1]. Such platforms support massive out-scaling to achieve high data throughput, and at the same time they employ techniques to reduce the data processing latency. Under the same trend, we have studied how to further improve the MapReduce-style frameworks for fast data stream applications with native support for window computation as well as autonomic load management to achieve high cluster utilization and low operational cost when running over a public cloud.

More specifically, we have developed a research system, called Enorm, that adopts an extended MapReduce computation framework that enables eager data processing rather than lazy and batch-based processing as in the traditional MapReduce framework. Furthermore, Enorm natively maintains window-based computation states at the platform level rather than the application level as done in previous stream

platforms and hence allows us to automatically share common computation among overlapping windows.

The DEBS Grand Challenge 2013 [5] is to provide real-time complex analysis over high velocity sensor data, for a soccer match. In this paper, we presented a highly scalable solution, which is implemented in Enorm. The main contributions of this paper include:

1. We researched how to parallelize the processing of real-time high velocity sensor data in a MapReduce-style framework to achieve high data throughput. We designed a parallel solution for the problem in DEBS Grand Challenge 2013. To prove the validity of our design, we conducted experiments on Amazon EC2 which show that throughput will increase as more computing resources are deployed.

2. We presented the feature of automatically sharing common computations among overlapped windows. We built a cost model which could be used to evaluate the effectiveness of sharing. We also provided experimental results to show that conducting sharing properly increases the throughput.

In the following sections, we will briefly introduce the computation framework of Enorm and present a parallel solution to the DEBS Grand Challenge by using Enorm. Finally we will report and discuss the experimental results followed by a conclusion of the paper.

2. COMPUTATION FRAMEWORK

In Enorm, the input data are modeled as a number of continuous streams of tuples in the form of $\langle id, value, ts1, ts2 \rangle$. id is the unique identifier of a tuple, $value$ is the value of the tuple. It is in an arbitrary form and opaque to the system. $ts1$ and $ts2$ are two timestamps associated with a tuple. We use two timestamps to identify the window that a tuple belongs to. Typically, if the event is a computation result over a sliding window, then $ts1$ and $ts2$ indicate the start and end points of the window. $ts1$ and $ts2$ can also be identical which indicates that the tuple has only one timestamp.

Window. In the traditional MapReduce framework, the *reduce* function takes a key and a list of values associated with that key as the input. To perform window operations over streaming data, one can invoke the *reduce* function over each window of the input stream after receiving the whole content of the window.

However, such a lazy evaluation approach will incur excessive latency. There are some existing efforts to address this issue. For example, MapReduce Online [2] solves the latency problem, by modifying the original MapReduce architecture to allow pipelining data between tasks, while maintaining the original MapReduce interface.

As another example, Muppet [4] reformulates the *reduce* function to an *update* function such that only one input key-value pair is taken at each invocation rather than the whole list of values associated with the key. Users can manually program the *update* function to decide when all the data of a window will arrive and output the results for the window.

Although platforms, like Muppet or MapReduce Online, can solve the latency problem, they rely on the application to handle window maintenance, such as window creation, tuple insertion, tuple expiration, etc. Moreover, there exists a wealth of research results on how to efficiently maintain windows and share overlapped window computations [3]. Most of these techniques are application independent.

Pushing the window maintenance and sharing to the application level is quite undesirable. To address these problems, we present Enorm which natively supports window maintenance and sharing. Enorm supports a time-based sliding window, which is defined on a time domain that is consistent with the timestamps of the input data. A sliding window is specified by two parameters: *interval* and *slide*, where *interval* is the length of the window and *slide* is the sliding frequency of the window. Tuple-based windows can be simulated by a time-based window in Enorm by assigning a unique sequence number to each tuple and using it as the timestamp. Given the user-defined windows, Enorm will generate some *segments*. Tuples will be automatically sent to the segments they belong to. Computation results of the segments can be reused to compute multiple final window outputs. We refer readers to the literature, such as [3], for how to generate an optimal set of partial windows.

The computation framework contains the following functions:

Map. The *map* function, $map(key, tuple) \rightarrow list(key, tuple)$, takes a tuple as input and produce zero or more output tuples. This is logically similar to the *map* function in the traditional MapReduce framework.

Compute. The *compute* function, $compute(key, tuple) \rightarrow list(key, tuple)$, also takes a key-tuple pair and returns a list of tuples. In addition, *compute* is associated with a local storage to keep track of the current state of the computation.

When the *compute* function processes a new tuple, Enorm will check if it is the end of a *segment*. If so, *compute* should return the results for that window. Furthermore, the two timestamps $ts1$ and $ts2$ of each output *tuple* would be set as the start and end time of the window.

Results returned from a *compute* function are prepared in a way that they can be merged to generate the final results. To realize the sharing of window computation, we perform the computation for segments and merge their results to generate final results for the complete windows.

Consolidate. The consolidate function, $consolidate(key, list(tuple)) \rightarrow list(key, tuple)$, takes a key and a list of tuples as its input and produces a list of key-tuple pairs. It is usually used to merge the results produced by the *compute* instances to generate the results over the complete windows.

There are two types of *consolidate* functions: *windowed* or *non-windowed*. A non-windowed consolidator will be handled analogously to the *reduce* function in the MapReduce framework. Enorm collects the outputs from the previous function, groups them according to their keys and then invokes the function over a list of tuples with the same key. For windowed ones, Enorm will arrange input according to the window specifications. For each key, it will generate a

Event	Fired
clock<ts,playerid>	50Hz clock per player
gameInterrupted<ts>	On game interruption
gameContinued<ts>	On game continuation
ballHit<ts, playerid>	When a player hits the ball
ballOut<ts>	When ball left playing field
goalShot<ts, playerid>	When shot on goal is detected

Table 1: Events

list of tuples for each window, and invoke the function for each list of tuples.

When the user needs to perform window computation, window specifications should be applied to either a pair of *compute* and *consolidate* functions (with *compute* followed by *consolidate*) or a single *consolidate* function. In the former case, the *compute* function can be used to perform eager processing to achieve lower latency. The following *consolidate* can perform sharing of computations among multiple windows. The latter case is a lazy evaluation where Enorm will collect all the data that belong to the target window and invoke the *consolidate* function after all the data within the target window have arrived. Enorm also supports a single *compute* function. In this case the *compute* function is updating the state of all the complete windows. Hence the final results of windows could be directly returned by the *compute* function.

Partition. For each function, we need to define how to partition its input tuples for parallel processing. There are currently two types of partitioner: *random* and *keyed*, which would partition the tuples randomly and based on their keys respectively.

Processing Engine. The processing engine of Enorm is implemented in Java. It can be deployed on a large cluster and a master node is used to handle the submitted jobs and distribute the tasks across the cluster. Each job is partitioned into components and each *component* will be automatically and dynamically parallelized onto a number of processors.

3. SCALABLE PROCESSING OF SENSOR DATA STREAMS

DEBS Grand Challenge 2013 specifies four queries to be handled concurrently. We propose one MapReduce-style job (Figure 2), which is scalable and handles all four queries concurrently.

3.1 Sharing Computation Between Windows

It is quite common that multiple windows of different length are specified in a query (e.g. query 1 in DEBS 2013 Grand Challenge). For these multiple-window queries, there will be overlaps between the instances of different windows, which means there is duplicated computation for the overlapped data. To eliminate this duplication, Enorm supports sharing the computation of overlapped data between windows. The sharing strategy is: the start and end timestamps of window instances (from different window specifications) divide the time-ordered input data stream into multiple disjoint segments. One complete window instance may cover multiple sequential segments. Each segment will only be processed once. The results of complete window instances are merged from the results of the segments they are cov-

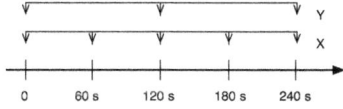

Figure 1: Segments Split in Enorm

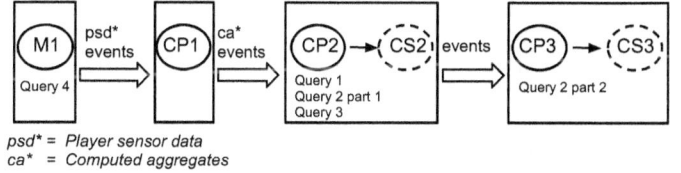

psd* = Player sensor data
ca* = Computed aggregates

Figure 2: Logical job specification

ering. We present an example of segment split in Figure 1, where X is a window whose interval and slide are both 60 seconds and Y is a window whose interval and slide are both 120 seconds. We get several segments of 60 seconds in Figure 1. By using this sharing strategy, every input tuple will only be updated in the segment it belongs to. Hence the update workload keeps the same no matter how many windows there are in a query. The cost of sharing computation between windows consists of two parts: (1) the cost of updating the computation results of the segments and (2) the cost of consolidating results from all the segments to obtain the results of the complete window instances.

In our analysis, we assume that within one query, the cost of consolidating two segments is a constant independent on the lengths of the segments. In the following section, we present a cost model to evaluate the effectiveness of computation sharing.

3.1.1 Cost Model of Sharing Computation

In a query Q, there are multiple windows $W_1, W_2, ..., W_n$. The input rate of Q is represented as v and the output frequency is denoted as f. C_u is the average cost of updating the computation results of a segment for an input tuple and C_f is the average cost of consolidating two segments. The total computation cost with and without sharing are separately denoted as E_s and E_w. At time t, we have:

$$E_w = n \cdot v \cdot t \cdot C_u$$

The cost without sharing will increase linearly with the number of windows in Q.

E_s consists of the cost of updating and consolidating segments. In E_s, the segment update cost at time t equals to: $v \cdot t \cdot C_u$, which has no relation with the number of windows in Q. The consolidation cost equals to $t \cdot f \cdot \sum_{i=1}^{n} M_i \cdot C_f$, where M_i is the average amount of segments that are involved in consolidating window W_i. At time t, M_i is a fixed number which is decided after the intervals and slides of all the windows in Q are specified. We omit describing the computation of M_i due to the space limit. By summing these two parts, we have:

$$E_s = v \cdot t \cdot C_u + t \cdot f \cdot \sum_{i=1}^{n} M_i \cdot C_f$$

From the above equations we can see for queries that have very high input rate v and consist of multiple windows, sharing computation between windows could save $(n-1)/n$ update cost, where n is the amount of windows. Because M_i and C_f are fixed constants for a given query, the consolidation cost is mainly decided by the output frequency f. High output frequency will introduce high consolidation cost. The feature of sharing computation in Enorm is suitable for queries that have multiple windows, high input rates and relatively low output frequency. Decision about whether sharing should be conducted can be made by calculating $E_s - E_w$. This cost model should be calculated offline when

the query is submitted and the query-dependent parameters, C_f and C_u, can be provided by the users.

3.1.2 Cost Analysis for DEBS 2013 Grand Challenge

Based on the DEBS Grand Challenge 2013, results of query 1 and query 2 should be calculated in windows of 1 minute, 5 minutes, 20 minutes and the whole game duration separately. The output frequency of query 1 and query 2 are both 50Hz. Results of query 3 should be calculated in windows of 1 minute, 5 minutes, 10 minutes and the whole game duration separately. The output frequency of query 3 is 1Hz.

In the three queries, the start and end timestamp of the complete window instances will split the input data into consecutive 1-minute segments. We calculated the cost of processing with and without sharing computation based on the cost model. Assume T is the total amount of input player sensor readings. The input rate is 200 tuples per second for each player, the consolidation function will therefore be called every 4 player sensor readings. For query 1 and query 2, we have :

$$E_s - E_w = [T \cdot C_u + \frac{45 \cdot T}{4} \cdot C_f] - [4 \cdot T \cdot C_u]$$

In query 1 and query 2, the update cost C_u and the consolidation cost C_f are almost the same, which means $E_s - E_w$ is negative for both query 1 and query 2.

For query 3, based on the cost model:

$$E_s - E_w = [T \cdot C_u + \frac{T}{5} \cdot C_f] - [4 \cdot T \cdot C_u]$$

In query 3, the actual time players spent in the cells will be calculated after update and consolidation. The percentage of time that players spent in each cell, will be calculated based on the actual time to produce the final results, which costs the same processing time with or without sharing computation. The update cost of query 3, C_u, lies in computing the current player location and updating corresponding cells in the four grids. Four cells will be changed per input tuple. The consolidation cost of query 3, C_f, lies in summing up the values of the cells that have the same location in the heat maps of multiple segments. There are totally 11304 cells in the heat maps of a segment. Hence the consolidation cost of query 3 is much more expensive than the update cost. Therefore, $E_s - E_w$ is negative for query 3.

Based on the above evaluation, conducting sharing computation between windows will not enhance the performance for the queries specified in the DEBS 2013 Grand Challenge, which is mainly caused by the high output frequency of the queries and the expensive consolidation cost of query 3.

3.2 Overview of Query Plan Design

Our objective is to design an Enorm job that can handle the DEBS Grand Challenge problem with low output latency and high throughput. There are two principles that we should follow when designing the query plan:

1. Make components that have heavy workload parallel. Overloaded instances will delay the processing of input data and hence will increase the latency and limit the throughput. Parallelization is needed to avoid overloaded instances.

2. Reduce the volume of data transferred between components. As components could be executed over different nodes in the cluster, high volume data transferring would affect the throughput and introduce latency.

In the following paragraphs, M1 is a *map* function, CP1, CP2 and CP2 are *compute* functions. Both CS2 and CS3 are *consolidate* functions.

Four queries are specified in the DEBS 2013 Grand Challenge. Query 2 and query 4 both take the ball sensor data as input, while query 1 and query 3 both take the player sensor data as input. Based on principle 2, we allocate the ball sensor data processing of query 2 and query 4 together (M1 in figure 2) and the player sensor data processing of query 1 and query 3 together (CP1 in figure 2). This allocation ensures both ball sensor data and player sensor data are processed only once.

After processing the ball sensor data and the player sensor data, the events in table 1 will be detected and some aggregated results, such as aggregated player position statistics, will be produced for the following processing. The volume of the aggregated data is much lower than the raw sensor data. Therefore, the raw sensor data should be processed in the early phases to decrease the volume of transferred data. M1 and CP1 are put at the beginning of the plan for this reason. Because the data rate of the ball sensor is lower than the total data rate of player sensors, we put M1 ahead of CP1 to reduce the latency of query 4. The final plan is presented in figure 2.

The workload of M1 and CP1 in figure 2 are quite high because of their high input rates. To achieve high throughput in M1 and CP1, they are designed to be parallel. Details about how the parallelism of M1 and CP1 works will be presented in the following subsections. M1 is responsible for hit detection, goal shot detection, calculation of shot projection and producing outputs for ball positions during goal shot. CP1 receives events and player sensor data from M1. CP1 calculates the partial aggregated player running statistics and aggregated player location statistics. CP2 receives these partial aggregated results from CP1, it produces the final player running statistics and player heat map. CP2 can be maximally scaled to a number of instances equal to the number of players. Because CP2 only receives the compressed data and events, we deem such a degree of parallelism sufficient. CP3 only receives ball hit events and some other events from CP2 and it will produce the team ball possession statistics. CP2 can maximally be scaled to the number of teams. Because the input volume of CP3 is quite small (only events), the processing will be very fast in CP3 instances. Because of its capability of parallelism and efficient data transferring, the design presented in figure 2 can achieve quite high throughput with low overall latency. Based on our experiments, this design works quite well for the problem in DEBS 2013 Grand Challenge and the principles and the analysis presented in this paper could be applied to similar applications with even higher input rates as the solution is scalable. Details of the various functions in the design are presented in the following subsections.

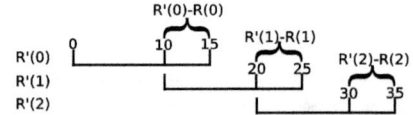

Figure 3: Partitioning M1 example (t=0, s=10 and o=5)

3.3 Input & Data cleaning

Enorm reads the input files concurrently and interleaves the sensor data and game interruption/continuation events, such that all tuples sent to M1 are ordered by timestamps.

The output frequency of sensors are not exactly 200Hz, which brings some trouble in calculating player location. It is important the sensor readings are fairly synchronized, as the player location is based on the average location of two leg sensors. Due to the unstable sensor frequency, paring sensor readings sequentially from both legs of a player will introduce uncontrollable difference between timestamps of the two paired sensor readings. To solve this problem we do data cleaning to pair the leg sensor readings of players correctly. The strategy is: in case the difference between the timestamps of the leg sensors of a given player is more than 1/200 second, the oldest leg sensor reading will be discarded. This check discards 13.6% of the leg sensor data. The sensor position reading is also not always precise. The distance between every pair of leg sensors is measured such that if the measured distance is more than 2.5 meters, it is considered to be erroneous and this pair of leg sensor data will be discarded. This accounts for 0.05% of data.

3.4 M1 function

M1 is a *map* function, which is primarily used to detect events (Table 1). Each M1 instance must have all the newest player sensor data and enough new ball sensor data to do precise goal shot detection. M1 sends player sensor data and events along to the next function. The ball sensor data are not sent along, as they are no longer needed.

3.4.1 Input Partitioning

The input data of M1 are partitioned into multiple ranges with same length. Assume the component where M1 locates has $|N|$ instances which are indexed as: $m_1.m_2....,m_N$. All the ball and player sensor data sent to M1 are partitioned such that sensor data with timestamp in range $R(Y) = [t + Y \cdot s, t + (Y + 1) \cdot s]$, where s is the length of range and t is the offset, will be sent to the M1 instance with index Y modulo $|N|$. $R(Y)$ should not span any window edge. To guarantee the processing speed can catch up with input rate, the parallel degree N should satisfy $N \geq V_{in}/V_p$, where V_{in} is the input rate and V_p is the processing rate of each node. Satisfying the requirement for parallelism, the time interval between a tuple is received and until M1 starts processing the tuple, is maximally $V_{in} \cdot s/V_p - s$. Hence s should be set as small as possible to decrease this delay.

Ball hit event detection requires the newest ball location and the newest player sensor locations, which can be achieved using the above partitioning because all the ball and player data within the same range $R(Y)$ will be sent to the same M1 instance. Goal shot event detection requires collecting ball sensor data from the moment of a ball hit until the ball moves one meter away from the hit location. The calculation of a goal shot projection requires 1.5 seconds of ball sensor data are collected after the goal shot is detected. The above input partitioning cannot satisfy these requirements because ball hit could happen at the end of a range. To correctly detect goal shot in each M1 instance, we change the above input partitioning to guarantee that, at timestamp ts when a hit h is detected, ball sensor data in the range $[ts, ts+1.5]$ is available at the M1 instance that has detected hit h. Considering a ball hit could be detected at the end of a range $R(Y)$, we duplicated data within the first 1.5 seconds of range $R(Y+1)$ to range $R(Y)$. More formally, we introduce an overlap o which defines the amount of duplicated data. The range function is redefined to be

$$R'(Y) = [t + (Y+1) \cdot s, t + (Y+1) \cdot s + o]$$

In the above equation, $R'(Y)$ is equal to $R(Y)$ plus the overlap o, which is set to be 1.5 seconds for the input partitioning of M1. Figure 3 shows an example with offset of 0, slide of 10 and an overlap of 5. To guarantee each instance can finish processing the data of the last range before it starts receiving new data, the values of s and N should satisfy: $(s+o) \cdot V_{in}/V_p \leq N \cdot s$, where $N > V_{in}/V_p$. While satisfying the above condition, s should be set as small as possible to decrease the tuple processing delay. A small s means more data will be duplicated because of the overlap, which in turn requires N to be large to satisfy the above condition.

Ball hit detection is only done for the data within range $R(Y)$. The data in range $R'(Y) - R(Y)$ are only used to handle goal shot detection for ball hits detected in $R(Y)$ and will not be sent to the next component.

3.4.2 Event detection

Ball hit is detected when the acceleration of the ball reaches more than 45 m/s^2. To eliminate duplicated hit detection, a new ball hit event will not be emitted until the ball acceleration decreases to less than 4 m/s^2 and more than 200 milliseconds has passed since the last ball hit. The player who hit the ball, is determined by locating the closest leg sensor to the ball, and determining which player it belongs to.

Ball out is simply detected when the ball leaves the playing field.

Goal shot is detected after a ball hit event happened. Ball sensor readings are collected from the moment of a ball hit and until the ball has moved one meter away from the hit position. If a goal shot is detected, CP1 will continue producing output of the ball positions until the goal shot ends.

3.5 CP1 function

CP1 is a *compute* function that receives player sensor data and events as input from M1. Similar to M1, the player sensor data output from M1 is partitioned into multiple ranges. Data within the same range will be sent to the same CP1 instance. CP1 calculates the aggregated player position statistics and the aggregated player running statistics separately for data within different ranges.

3.5.1 Input Partitioning

Assume the component where CP1 locates has $|N|$ instances which are indexed from 1 to $|N|$ separately. Similar to the M1 function, all the player sensor data input to CP1 are partitioned such that player sensor data with timestamp in range $R(Y) = [t + Y \cdot s, t + (Y+1) \cdot s]$ will be sent to the

CP1 instance with index Y modulo $|N|$. Again, the ranges should not span any window edge. The calculation of N and s has been described in Section 3.4.1.

Receive player sensor data: For each of the partitioned ranges that is specified to a CP1 instance, CP1 will produce aggregated tuples containing: time start, time end, player, intensity, average speed and location statistics for the player data within this range. The results will be sent along with 50Hz frequency.

In query 3, four grids are defined with different columns and rows. Every grid divides the playing field into a fixed amount of cells. The percentage of time every player spent in every cell will be calculated and output with 1Hz frequency. Because there is no limitation of the parallelism of CP1, we calculate the aggregated player position statistics in CP1 to decrease the workload of CP2. For each partitioned range $R(Y)$, the aggregated location statistics consists of the new values of the different cells which are calculated from all the player sensor data within $R(Y)$.

Receive event: Events are duplicated to all the instances of CP2. If a game interruption event is received, all the aggregated values (described above) will be sent to the CP2 instances and the calculation of player sensor data will be paused until a game continuation event is received.

3.6 CP2 & CS2 function

CP2 and CS2 are *compute* and *consolidate* functions respectively. According to the analysis of the cost of sharing computation between overlapping windows in Section 3.1, we decided not to use sharing in our implementation. But we still make sharing optional in our design to show how it can work under situations where it is beneficial. Sharing of computation is performed by the help of CS2 and CS3. We draw them with dashed lines in Figure 2 to indicate that they are optional and only needed when we employ sharing of computation.

The CP2 function will receive aggregated player running statistics, aggregated player location statistics and events. These data are partitioned by player id, which means the component where CP2 and CS2 are located maximally can be parallelized to the number of players.

Non-Shared. If sharing is not conducted, CS2 will not exist in the component where CP2 locates. Each CP2 instance has the global information of the players that are assigned to it. After receiving the aggregated player running statistics, the aggregated player location statistics or ball hit events, the CP2 instance will update the player running state and the player heat map state for all the current complete window instances. Besides the aggregated running statistics, CP2 will also update player running state after receiving a ball out event or game interruption event. Query 1, 2 and 3 in DEBS 2013 Grand Challenge all have 4 concurrent window instances of different length at any time. The outputs of query 1 (player running intensity), part 1 of query 2 (player ball possession) and query 3 (player heat map) will be produced with the required frequency. The time is counted by received clock events.

Shared. If computation between windows are shared, CP2 and CS2 are co-located on the same component. As has been described in section 3.2, CP2 only updates the current segment. Based on the output frequency of each query, CS2 merges the results of the segments to produce

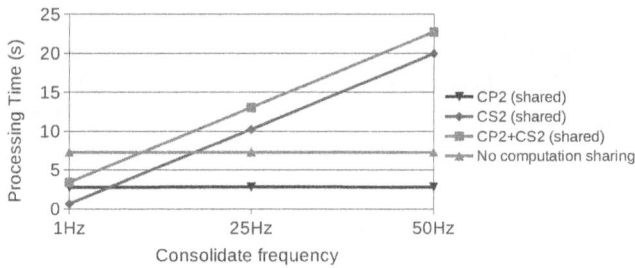

Figure 5: Sharing computation

windows. When finishing calculating the results of complete windows, CS2 will produce query outputs.

3.7 CP3 & CS3 function

CP3 and CS3 are separately *compute* and *consolidate* functions. If sharing is conducted, CP3 and CS3 must be co-located in the same component. CP3 calculates the team ball possession statistics (part 2 of query 2) based on the received events, which include ball hit, ball out, game interruption, game continue and clock events. Because we need the global team information to calculate the team ball possession, the input data that belongs to one team should be partitioned to the same CP3 instance. The component where CP3 (CS3) locates is designed to be maximally parallelized to the number of teams. The input rate of this component is relatively low, which makes its processing very light.

Non-Shared. If sharing is not conducted, each CP3 instance updates the team ball possession statistics based on the input events for all the current complete window instances. The outputs are produced with the required frequency, where time is counted by received clock events.

Shared. In this case, CP3 will only update the team ball possession statistics of the current segment. The consolidation function CS3, will be called with the output frequency to calculate the results of all the current complete windows and produce outputs. The time is counted by the received clock events.

4. EXPERIMENT

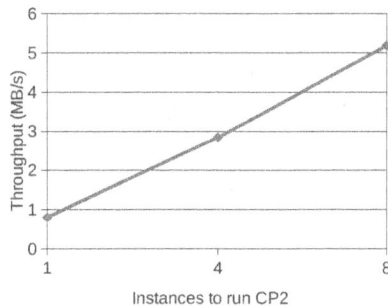

Figure 4: Throughput

The experiments were conducted on Amazon Elastic Compute Cloud, using first-generation medium instances. The scalability and sharing of computation experiments was done using a dedicated instance for the Enorm master daemon.

Scalability. As CP2 handles the heaviest workload, we study its scalability in this set of experiments. Three experiments were conducted by using 1, 4 and 8 dedicated instances, respectively, to process the CP2 function. We simplify the implementation by combining the M1 and CP1 function into one and use only one instance to execute it. Figure 4 shows how the throughput increases as the number of instances used to process the CP2 function are increased. As can be seen from the figure, a nearly linear increase of throughput is achieved by adding more instances of CP2.

Sharing Computation Between Windows. The following experiment was done to examine the benefits of sharing computation between overlapped windows. The experiment was conducted on a single machine. The job was modified to only process query 1 and query 2 without writing output to disk. The cost of writing the output to disk, is independent on the frequency of consolidation.

Figure 5 shows the consolidation cost is low for consolidation frequencies below 1Hz. After 1Hz the cost increases rapidly. The compute cost remains fairly constant, which is expected (Section 3.1.1). As suggested by this result, in general, sharing computation outperforms non-sharing when the consolidation frequency is low. However, non-sharing is more preferable when an application requires a high output frequency which incurs very frequent consolidation.

Latency. We define the latency as the time between a tuple is received (in input) and its processing is finished. The experiment was conducted by randomly selecting 0.1% of the input tuples, and calculating the average latency. The average latency when processing all four queries together, without writing any output to disk, is calculated as 1524 milliseconds. We choose to calculate the average latency of processing all queries, as our implementation handles all queries in one job.

5. CONCLUSION

In this paper, we presented how to use Enorm to parallelize the processing of high-velocity sensor data. We also built a cost model that can be used to evaluate the effects of sharing computations of overlapped windows. For the problem described in DEBS Grand Challenge 2013, we designed a parallel Enorm job. Our experimental results show that the throughput can be increased by parallelizing the job.

6. REFERENCES

[1] http://www.storm-project.net.
[2] T. Condie, N. Conway, P. Alvaro, J. M. Hellerstein, K. Elmeleegy, and R. Sears. Mapreduce online. In *NSDI'10*, pages 21–21, San Jose, California, 2010.
[3] S. Krishnamurthy, C. Wu, and M. Franklin. On-the-fly sharing for streamed aggregation. In *SIGMOD '06*, pages 623–634, Chicago, IL, USA, 2006.
[4] W. Lam, L. Liu, S. Prasad, A. Rajaraman, Z. Vacheri, and A. Doan. Muppet: Mapreduce-style processing of fast data. *PVLDB*, 5(12):1814–1825, Istanbul, Turkey, 2012.
[5] C. Mutschler, H. Ziekow, and Z. Jerzak. The DEBS 2013 Grand Challenge. In *DEBS 2013: Proceedings of the 7th ACM International Conference on Distributed Event-Based Systems*, Arlington, TX, USA, July 2013. ACM.

Grand Challenge: The TechniBall System

Avigdor Gal, Sarah Keren, Mor Sondak,
Matthias Weidlich
Technion - Israel Institute of Technology
avigal@ie.technion.ac.il
{sarahn,mor,weidlich}@tx.technion.ac.il

Hendrik Blom, Christian Bockermann
TU Dortmund
hendrik.blom@tu-dortmund.de,
christian.bockermann@udo.edu

ABSTRACT

In this work we present the solution to the DEBS'2013 Grand Challenge, as crafted by the joint effort of teams from the Technion and TU Dortmund. The paper describes the architecture, details the queries, shows throughput and latency evaluation, and offers our observations regarding the appropriate way to trade-off high-level processing with time constraints.

Categories and Subject Descriptors

H.3.4 [**System and Software**]: Distributed Systems

Keywords

event processing, real-time event processing

1. INTRODUCTION

The ACM DEBS Grand Challenge series seeks to provide a common ground and evaluation criteria for event-based solutions, by offering problems that require event-based systems and that can be evaluated using real-life data and queries. The 2013 challenge [16] involves real-time complex analytics over high velocity sensor data using the example of analyzing a soccer game. The input data comes from sensors in player shoes and a ball used during a soccer match. The real-time analytics involves continuous computation of four main statistics types, namely ball possession, shots on goal, heat maps, and running analysis of team members.

This paper presents the *TechniBall* solution that was developed at the Technion – Israel Institute of Technology together with the Technical University in Dortmund. The proposed solution strikes a balance between the use of high-level complex event processing language (Esper [9]) and a fast low-level processing of events that arrive at the pico-second level (*streams* [5]).

The paper is structured as follows: In Section 2 we detail the overall architecture and discuss implementation aspects.

Section 3 presents the queries that support the required analytics. We share our experiences in building and running the system in Section 4 and conclude with related work discussion (Section 5) and future work (Section 6).

2. ARCHITECTURE

The TechniBall solution is based on a shell for defining data flows and manages parallelization. From within the shell, events undergo initial processing and are then routed to a CEP engine for pattern recognition (see Figure 1).

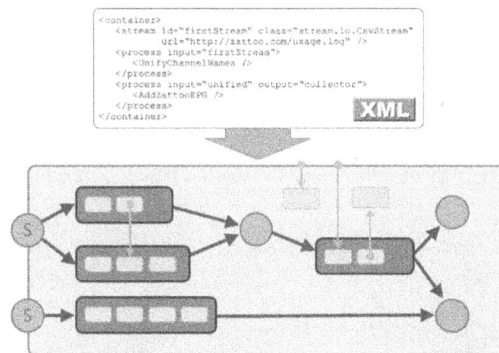

Figure 1: Generic architecture description

For the shell, we used the open-source *streams* framework [6], which provides a description language consisting of sources, sinks and processors. The data flow is defined in high-level XML and is compiled into a computation graph for a stream processing engine (e.g., the *streams runtime* or a topology for the *Storm* engine [15]). *Streams* provides a clean and easy-to-use Java-based middleware to design and implement data stream processes on different stream processing engines. It promotes simple software design patterns such as JavaBean conventions and dependency injection to allow for a quick setup of streaming processes. *Streams* also supports rapid prototyping and allows for direct integration of custom processor classes into the configuration. TechniBall uses the latest *streams* version 0.9.10-SNAPSHOT.

As the CEP engine, we were looking for a platform that easily integrates into a java project and supports the needed expressive power. We chose Esper [9] following the recommendations in [7]. Esper enables rapid development of applications that process large volumes of incoming events in real-time. Esper filters and analyzes events using a declarative high-level, SQL-like language, responding to conditions of interest with minimal latency. We used Esper 4.6.0 for Java, open-source software available under the GNU General Public License (GPL). We implemented a single custom Esper processor using the *streams* API, directly including Esper queries into the XML description of the data flow graphs using a simple `esper.Query` tag. Figure 2 shows the definition of a computation graph with a single input stream and a process that includes the Esper process.

```
<container id="sample-config">
  <properties>
    <!-- define attribute types of attributes
         used in ESPER queries below -->
    <esper.types>...</esper.types>
  </properties>

  <!-- define a stream implemented by the custom soccer stream
       class that has been optimized for the DEBS data  -->
  <stream id="soccer" url="file:/path/to/game-data"
       class="stream.io.FastSoccerStream" />

  <!-- define a process node connected to the soccer stream
       that applies the esper engine and send results to the
       queue "R"                        -->
  <process input="soccer">
    <stream.esper.Query output="R" types="${esper.types}">
        Esper QUERY
    </stream.esper.Query>
  </process>

  <!-- define a process connected to "R" that simply prints
       out all items to stdout   -->
  <process input="R">
    <PrintData />
  </process>
</container>
```

Figure 2: Esper query embedded in *streams*

The TechniBall implementation comes as a single executable Java archive that includes the *streams* runtime and the Esper engine. It receives as input a data flow graph definition in an XML file. For the DEBS challenge we crafted distributed processing of multiple threads. To comply with the challenge specification, we created a virtual machine image running Ubuntu Server Edition 12.10 (64bit, kernel 3.5.0). We tested this image with a virtual machine that features the predefined 4 cores (@2.8 GHz) and 4 GB RAM. Figure 3 (next page) provides an overall architecture of the TechniBall system. The *streams* framework provides stream and queue implementations (circles) and the notion of processes (dark shade boxes), which read from these and execute a list of processors (light shade boxes) for each item read. The top left stream, S, represents the data input. Items are read from the stream as simple hash-maps, which can contain arbitrary serializable values, allowing for dynamically adding new fields to the data that can be consumed by subsequent processors.
A single reader process reads in the data and applies a set of operations (processors) to each element of the stream. These elements provide pre-processing such as joining meta-information to each sensor measurement (player ID, sensor type). The final processor of the reader process dispatches copies of the sensor measurements to several queues, each of which is processed by its own process. The modularity of the solution allows processing several queries in a single thread. The shaded optional processor `GameView` can be added to display a live view of the game (see Figure 12).

3. CHALLENGE QUERIES

We now turn our attention to the four queries posed by the challenge. For most of the query implementations, the input data events need to be preprocessed by applying a chain of processors that have been implemented using the *streams* API. The data pre-processing enriches the data using a metadata file, which contains the player names, associates the transmitter IDs with a player ID (`pid`) and adds fields for the type of sensor (leg, arm, left, right). The player ID provided by the metadata is artificially set up and numbers the players from 0 to 17, where ID 0 is assigned to the referee sensors and all ball sensors are assigned a negative ID. In addition, all players of team A are assigned odd IDs and the players of team B are equipped with even IDs. This allows (a) for using arrays as data structures with the `pid` as the index to player data and (b) for using the *modulo* operator to determine to which team the player belongs. Other operators add flags for signaling whether the game is currently active or compute the player from the leg sensors. The enriched events are marked as $E1$ in Figure 3.
After pre-processing, the enriched events are distributed into three queues, Q_1, Q_2, and Q_3 that are processed by separate threads, each of which handles a different query. The shot detection is part of query 2 and is required in query 4, so queue Q_4 is fed with the detected shots. Query results are assigned a reference and sent to result queue R, from which a process reads and emits the items to standard output.

3.1 Query 1 – Running Analysis

Query 1 keeps track of each players current running distance and reports on the intensity of the runs (e.g. trotting). The process for the running analysis is shown in Figure 4.

```
<process input="Q:1">
    <!-- Track current intensity for each player -->
    <stream.soccer.AddIntensity />

    <!-- Aggregate the intensity levels for each player
         and emit results to the queue "R"       -->
    <stream.soccer.AggregateCurrentIntensity output="R" />
</process>
```

Figure 4: The process definition for the running analysis.

We implemented a processor that keeps track of the intensity level for each player. According to the challenge requirements, intensities need to stay stable over a full second before they are regarded as a new intensity state. Our `AddIntensity` processor implements this tracking of player intensities, aggregates the information of all sensors for each player, and emits the stable intensity levels. For computing the aggregated intensities, we implemented two alternative approaches: First, we created an Esper query to aggregate the events directly. The query in Figure 5 performs aggregation for the trot level for a 1min time window:

```
<esper.Query condition="%{data.pid} @gt 0"  output="R">
  SELECT pid AS player,
    sum(case when intensity=1 then distance else 0 end)
        as trot_distance,
    sum(case when intensity=1 then (ts_stop - ts_start)
        /1000000000 else 0 end) as trot_time
    FROM Data.win:time(60000 sec) GROUP BY pid
</esper.Query>
```

Figure 5: Esper implementation of Query 1

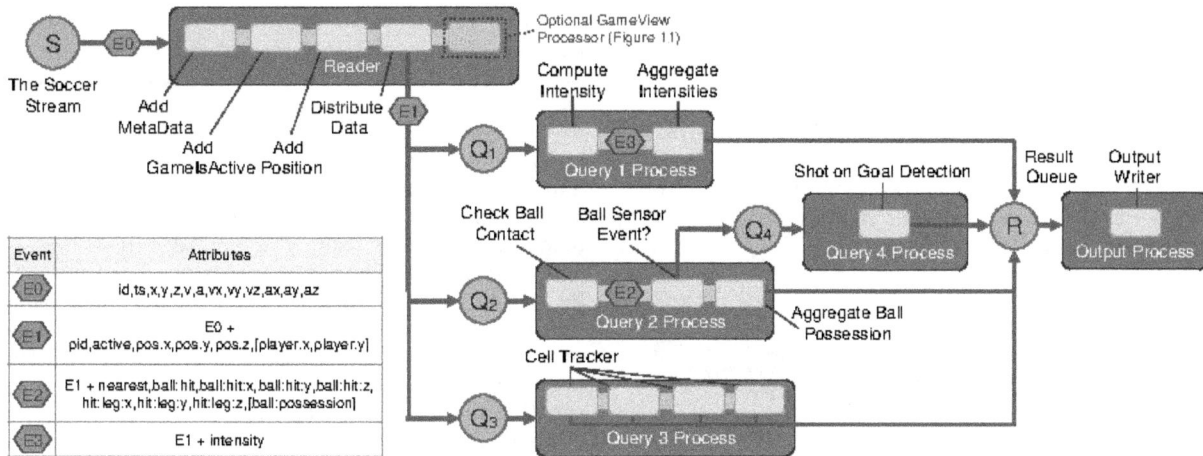

Figure 3: TechniBall overall architecture

An alternative solution directly implemented the aggregation as a separate processor `AggregateCurrentIntensity` using the *streams* API, exploiting some of the features added in the pre-processing step such as direct array lookup of data structures using the `pid` value.

3.2 Query 2 – Ball Possession

The ball possession query requires information from several event types: The player current positions need to be handled and maintained; the ball position needs to be assessed; and the condition for a ball hit needs to be constantly checked. Finally, the ball possession status needs to be maintained and the times of possession need to be aggregated according to the windows sizes. Figure 6 shows the XML definition of the process that handles the ball possession query.

```
<process input="Q:2">
   <!-- Add details on hits of the ball -->
   <stream.soccer.CheckBallContact />

   <!-- Handle possession changes and aggregate the
        possession times for the required windows    -->
   <stream.soccer.AggregateBallPossession output="R" />

   <!-- Send ball events for shot on goal detection -->
   <Enqueue condition="%{data.pid} @lt 0" queue="Q:4" />
</process>
```

Figure 6: Ball possession query

The `CheckBallContact` processor keeps track of the current player positions and checks whether the *ball hit* condition is fulfilled for any incoming ball event. Keeping track of players is done in constant time using the `pid` value from the pre-processing step as index to an array holding player positions. The *ball hit* condition is only checked for ball sensors which are within the field boundaries, thus, this processor automatically chooses the active ball for its computations. If a ball hit is detected, the `ball:hit` field of the event is set to the `pid` of the player that hit the ball. In addition, this processor maintains the current possessor of the ball. Once the possessor changes, the possession time of the last player is emitted. If the ball leaves the field or the game

is interrupted, possession is transferred to player with `pid` 0 (referee). The processor `AggregateBallPossession` maintains sliding windows for each of the requested windows and aggregates the possession times provided by the previous processor. Upon changes of the possession, the current aggregations are emitted to the result queue. An alternative version for this aggregation can be performed by the Esper query shown in Figure 7 (showing only the aggregation by player as an example).

```
<process input="Q:2">
   <stream.soccer.CheckBallContact />

   <!-- Use Esper to aggregate the ball hits grouped
        by player over a sliding window      -->
   <stream.esper.Query condition="%{data.ball:hit} > 0" output="R">
     SELECT max(ts) AS ts, pid AS player,
        sum('ball:possession') AS time,
        sum('ball:hit') AS hits
     FROM Data GROUP BY pid OUTPUT LAST EVERY 1 EVENTS;
   </stream.esper.Query>
   <Enqueue condition="%{data.pid} @lt 0" queue="Q:4" />
</process>
```

Figure 7: Esper aggregation of ball possession

3.3 Query 3 - Heat Map

The heat map tracking is directly implemented in a Java processor within *streams*. `CellTracker` allows for specifying the granularity of the grid and pre-initializes the memory required to track all cells for each player. Each of the cell objects allocates memory for keeping the aggregation windows at initialization time as well. This is a direct memory-to-speed tradeoff – by pre-allocating the memory and using a customized data structure, we ensure updates of our heat-maps in $\mathcal{O}(1)$: With the player ID (pid), added in the pre-processing phase, the cell updates for the grid for each event is then possible in constant time. From the x and y coordinates of the sensor we directly compute the index of the cell and the player ID is then used as the index of the counts that need to be updated. The output format of `Cell-Tracker` is slightly different from the format proposed in the challenge description: instead of emitting an item for each

321

cell (one line per cell), we emit a compressed form of the cell array as

$$cell\_times : [\ldots, i : v_i, (i+1) : v_{i+1}, \ldots] \; \forall \, i : v_i > 0.$$

Thus, we emit the index of the cell and its value for all entries larger than 0. The rest of the provided fields of the emitted result items for the heat map queries match the format requested in the challenge description. Figure 8 provides one instance of `CellTracker` for each grid resolution.

```
<process input="Q:3">
    <soccer.CellTracker gridx="8" gridy="13" output="R" />
    <soccer.CellTracker gridx="16" gridy="25" output="R" />
    <soccer.CellTracker gridx="32" gridy="50" output="R" />
    <soccer.CellTracker gridx="64" gridy="100" output="R" />
</process>
```

Figure 8: Heat map with the four cell tracker instances

3.4 Query 4 – Shot on Goal

The shot on goal query requires a shot/hit of the ball as a trigger and then checks if the ball is directed towards the opponents goal. Processing this query is done together with the ball possession query, as this query already emits information about detected hits.

The `ShotOnGoal` processor computes the future position of a ball based on such a *ball hit* event and checks whether this position passes the goal areas as specified in the challenge description within the pre-defined amount of time. The future position is projected from the current position based on the direction and speed of the ball (including gravity). Essentially, the respective processor can be in three states, *initial*, *hit detected*, and *shot-on-goal detected*. We transition from *initial* to *hit detected* if the `ball:hit` flag is set for a ball event, recording the position of the leg that hit the ball. As soon as the ball is more than 1m away from this position, we check whether it would reach the goal accordingly and, if so, transition from *hit detected* to *shot-on-goal detected*. Whenever being in this state, we emit the relevant event and check whether the conditions for terminating the shot-on-goal are satisfied. If so, we transition to state *initial*.

3.5 Query Result Formats

To meet the challenge requirements regarding the result output formats, we provide a single output process, which prints out the result items emitted by the different query implementations to standard output. This leads to writing mixture of result items from different queries to a single standard output. Two additions allow simple inspection and parsing. First, we add a field `query` to each emitted line, which references the query for which this item has been emitted. Secondly, we encode each item as a JSON object and separate items by a line break. The JSON encoding allows adding fields. For example, for the heat maps, we emit items with the additional fields `query`, `grid` and `win`, which identify the query, the grid resolution and the window, to which the output line belongs.

4. EVALUATION

In this section we outline our evaluations of the *TechniBall* system. All experiments were performed using the Open-JDK Java virtual machine version 1.7.0_21 on an Intel Core

i7-3770 CPU machine with 3.4 GHz with 16 GB of main memory. The game data is read from a ramdisk to eliminate disk latency. Java was started with 4 GB of heap space.

4.1 Reading and Parsing

To optimize the reader implementation to the data at hand, we compared different implementations for reading and parsing events from the file into objects. Java's line reader is capable of reading about 3.3 million lines per second – parsing this into numbers is the hard part. As can be seen in Figure 9(left), the default `split` and parse number functions results in rather poor performance. Using the StringTokenizer and custom parsing improves this. `FastSoccerStream` reads lines and directly parses numbers without splitting the lines into substrings. This leads to a data rate of about 922.000 events per second.

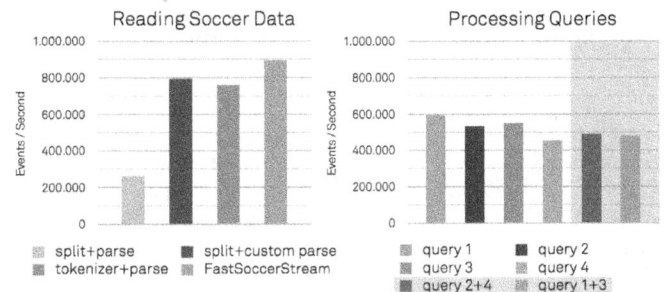

Figure 9: Reading and processing throughput

4.2 Processing Queries

With a basic knowledge of the upper bound of simply reading the data, we investigated the throughput of processing the challenge queries. Here, the combined use of *streams* and Esper was used with an attempt to gain the best of both worlds. We have built upon the abilities of *streams* to perform fast processing of enrichment, filtering, and computation. Esper, on the other hand, kicked in as soon as complex reasoning was needed, making use of its high level query language.

We have implemented queries using both Esper queries and *streams* code, trying out the trade-offs of declarative application specifications, rapid programming, maintainability, execution timing requirements, etc. The heavy emphasis on throughput in the challenge led the implementation away from Esper queries, in the direction of *streams* coding. In the remainder, we report on the performance obtained purely with the custom implementations in *streams*. Figure 9 shows the throughput for each of the queries: For each of those measurements, we set up a single process that reads from the `FastSoccerStream`, joins the meta-data (player ID,...) and applies some basic computations. After that we added the query processor and ran the setup. This was done for each query processor separately. The throughput (events per second) of running each query are shown in Figure 9 (right). Some of the queries work on the same events (e.g., running analysis and heat map do not require ball events) we also tested the throughput of combining queries 1 and 3 (running analysis and heat map) and queries 2 and 4 (ball possession and shot-on-goal). The combined throughput is shown in the shaded part of Figure 9 (right).

In addition we were interested on the latency induced by the query processing. As latency measurement, we computed the time it takes for an event to traverse the data flow graph until it is integrated into the statistics. The time was measured using the Java wall-clock time, which has a granularity of nanoseconds. Figure 10 shows the average latency induced by each of the queries. The average for latency for query processing is at 2356,512 nanoseconds per event.

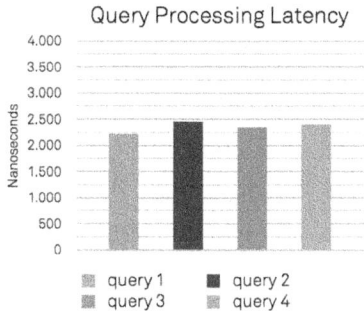

Figure 10: Latency induced by queries (in nanoseconds).

4.3 Going Parallel

Next we tested the throughput of parallel processing of all queries according to the setup of Figure 3 (*standard setup*). In addition we were interested in scaling up the throughput with different combinations of queries within the data flow setup. The *standard setup* features a single queue for each query. The other extreme is a single process that manages all queries (*single-threaded*). This setup is faster due to the required queue-synchronization in the *standard setup*, but does not provide the best overall throughput. By combining queries (e.g., q1+q3) within one process, we add parallelization with fewer synchronization overhead. In our experiments, the setup *q1+q2 || q2+q4* showed the best overall performance, with an average of about 281.000 events per second.

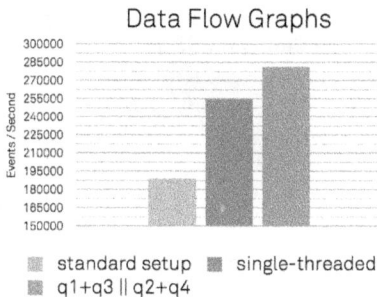

Figure 11: Parallelization impact on throughput

4.4 Data Visualization

Albeit the focus on pure throughput measurements, we have also been interested in a feedback of the raw data by means of a visual representation of the sensor measurements. For this, we implemented a simple `GameView` processor that displays the data with a soccer field visualization (see Figure 12). This feature highlights the player that possesses the ball and shot-detections, allowing the assessment of output statistics like ball possession while "watching the game."

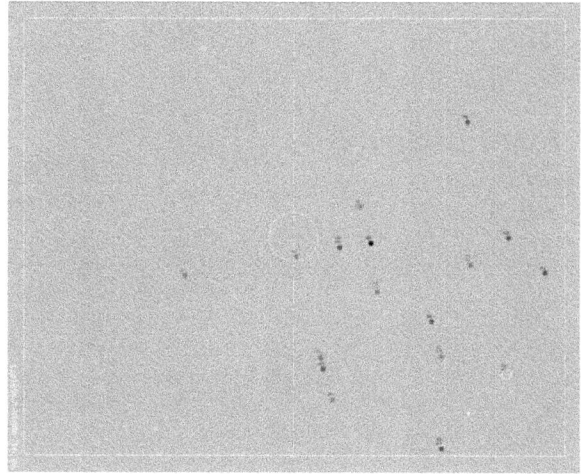

Figure 12: Visualization by the `GameView` processor

5. RELATED WORK

Our work combines a stream processing run-time with a CEP engine, thereby following the conceptual model of an event processing network as put forward by Etzion and Niblett [10]. Here, event processing agents are realized either as *streams* processors or Esper queries. Event channels are implemented by the structure of the *streams* data flow graph. As such, our work follows a stream-oriented model for event processing, rooted in Kahn process networks [12] for non-blocking data flow, so that event streams are modeled by event tuples.

Recently, various data stream engines have been proposed in the literature, such as Storm [15], S4.io [17], MOA [4] and Apache Kafka [14]. The *streams* framework [5, 6] has been designed as a middle-layer API that allows for an implementation of components for stream processing while being able to use these components as building blocks for designing data flow graphs that can be executed with the *streams-runtime* or compiled into Storm topologies. For example, the processors we implemented for the DEBS challenge, can directly be wrapped into Storm bolts (wrapping into bolts is provided by *streams*). As the DEBS challenge is focused on a single stream of data and a single processing node, we decided for the use of the *streams-runtime* as there is no need for the distribution features provided by Storm. *streams* can integrate MOA classifiers as building blocks that can be added to the stream graph. Likewise, we implemented processors for specifying Esper queries within the XML.

Turning to the definition of event processing agents, the Esper Query Language (EQL) is inspired by early query languages such as CQL [2] that declaratively describe the input streams, relevant event contexts, and event production. Our choice for Esper was motivated by a recent survey [7]. However, queries may also be defined based on active rules or logic programming. Active rules (aka Event-Condition-Action rules) are explicitly triggered by event occurrences.

Triggers are defined in event algebra featuring operators such as 'sequence' and 'and' as done, e.g., in Snoop [8]. Query languages based on logic programming employ temporal and action logics. The Event Calculus [13] and derived dialects [3] define axioms that relate to point-based events and the initialization and termination of fluents, properties that change with the occurrence of events. The Etalis system [1] is an example for an implementation of this model.

6. CONCLUSIONS

The paper presents a solution to the DEBS 2013 grand challenge. The solution is based on query parallelization and data stream flow control, using *streams* and Esper.

The proposed solution is based on the framework developed for the INSIGHT European project.[1] The goal of the INSIGHT project is to radically advance our ability of coping with emergency situations in smart cities by developing innovative technologies, methodologies, and systems that will put new capabilities in the hands of disaster planners and city personnel to improve emergency planning and response. The INSIGHT architecture requires a CEP engine that operates on top of a stream processing engine.

The grand challenge, as designed, tests correctness and throughput. We believe, however, that this dataset can serve as a benchmark testing for other aspects of event processing as well. For example, uncertainty management of sensor data and patterns (see a book chapter on the topic [11]) is an intriguing topic that can be tested using this dataset. A task that involves probabilities of analysis such as the *shot-on-goal* query can use this dataset as a benchmark.

An interesting aspect with the high-level description of the data flow graph is the partitioning of data and queries into several threads of execution. For the *TechniBall* setup we chose to divide this into three main parallel computation processes. However, with more CPUs or even additional nodes for computing, this could be massively distributed on a larger set of processors. Finding the most efficient distribution and reasoning about strategies to generally find adequate partitionings of such data flow graphs will be a focus of our future work.

Acknowledgement

We thank Ella Rabinovich for useful discussion. This research has received funding from the European Union's Seventh Framework Programme (FP7/2007-2013) under grant agreement number 318225.

References

[1] D. Anicic, S. Rudolph, P. Fodor, and N. Stojanovic. Stream reasoning and complex event processing in etalis. *Semantic Web*, 3(4):397–407, 2012.

[2] Arasu et al. Stream: The stanford stream data manager. *IEEE Data Eng. Bull.*, 26(1):19–26, 2003.

[3] A. Artikis, G. Paliouras, F. Portet, and A. Skarlatidis. Logic-based representation, reasoning and machine learning for event recognition. In *DEBS*, pages 282–293. ACM, 2010.

[4] A. Bifet, G. Holmes, R. Kirkby, and B. Pfahringer. Moa: Massive online analysis. *The Journal of Machine Learning Research*, 99:1601–1604, 2010.

[5] C. Bockermann. The *streams* framework, 2012. URL http://www.jwall.org/streams/.

[6] C. Bockermann and H. Blom. The streams framework. Technical Report 5, TU Dortmund University, 12 2012.

[7] H.-L. Bui. *Survey and Comparison of Event Query Languages Using Practical Examples*. PhD thesis, LMU München, 2009.

[8] S. Chakravarthy and D. Mishra. Snoop: An expressive event specification language for active databases. *Data Knowl. Eng.*, 14(1):1–26, 1994.

[9] EsperTech. Esper complex event processing engine, 2013. URL http://esper.codehaus.org/.

[10] O. Etzion and P. Niblett. *Event Processing in Action*. Manning, 2010.

[11] A. Gal, S. Wasserkrug, and O. Etzion. Event processing over uncertain data. In *Reasoning in Event-Based Distributed Systems*, pages 279–304. Springer, 2011.

[12] G. Kahn. The semantics of simple language for parallel programming. In *IFIP Congress*, pages 471–475, 1974.

[13] R. A. Kowalski and M. J. Sergot. A logic-based calculus of events. *New Generation Comput.*, 4(1):67–95, 1986.

[14] J. Kreps, N. Narkhede, and J. Rao. Kafka: A distributed messaging system for log processing. In *NetDB*, 2011.

[15] N. Marz. Storm - distributed and fault-tolerant realtime computation, 2013. http://www.storm-project.net.

[16] C. Mutschler, H. Ziekow, and Z. Jerzak. The DEBS 2013 Grand Challenge. In *DEBS*. ACM, 2013.

[17] L. Neumeyer, B. Robbins, A. Nair, and A. Kesari. S4: Distributed stream computing platform. In *ICDMW*, pages 170–177. IEEE, 2010.

---

[1] www.insight-ict.eu

Grand Challenge: Implementation by Frequently Emitting Parallel Windows and User-Defined Aggregate Functions

Sobhan Badiozamany
Uppsala University
Sweden

Lars Melander
Uppsala University
Sweden

Thanh Truong
Uppsala University
Sweden

Cheng Xu
Uppsala University
Sweden

Tore Risch
Uppsala University
Sweden

Emails: Firstname.Lastname@it.uu.se

ABSTRACT

Our implementation of the DEBS 2013 Challenge is based on a scalable, parallel, and extensible DSMS, which is capable of processing general continuous queries over high volume data streams with low delays. A mechanism to provide user defined incremental aggregate functions over sliding windows of data streams provide real-time processing by emitting results continuously with low delays. To further eliminate delays caused by time critical operations, the system is extensible so that functions can be easily written in some external programming language. The query language provides user defined parallelization primitives where the user can express queries specifying how high volume data streams are split and reduced into lower volume parallel data streams. This enables expensive queries over data streams to be executed in parallel based on application knowledge. Our OS-independent implementation was tested on several computers and achieves the real-time requirement of the challenge on a regular PC.

Categories and Subject Descriptors

H.2.4 [**Database Management**]: Systems – *Parallel databases, Query processing*

Keywords

Parallel data stream processing; continuous queries; spatio-temporal window operators.

1. INTRODUCTION

Monitoring a soccer game requires a system than can process, in real-time, large volumes of data to dynamically determine physical properties as they appear. This requires a system having the following properties:

- To keep up with the very high data flow the system must deliver high throughput while processing expensive computations over high volume data.

- Response in real-time requires continuous delivery of query results with low latency.

- Continuous identification of physical phenomena, such as moving balls and players, requires complex spatio-temporal algebraic computations over windows.

Our EPIC (Extensible, Parallel, Incremental, and Continuous) DSMS provides very high throughput and low latency through parallelization, extensibility, and user defined incremental aggregation of windowed data streams. The high level query language provides numerical data representations and data stream windows as first class objects, which simplifies complex numerical computations over streaming data and enables automatic query optimization. To provide very high performance of low level numerical and byte processing functions the system is easily extensible with user defined functions over streams and numerical data, which allows accessing external systems and plugging in time-critical user algorithms.

EPIC extends the SCSQ system [9] with several kinds of data stream windows and incremental evaluation of user-defined aggregate functions over the windows. In particular the window operator *FEW* (Frequently Emitting Windowizer) decouples the frequency of emitted tuples from a window's slide.

To process expensive queries with high-throughput and low latency the system provides application specific stream parallelization functions where general *distribution queries* specify how to parallelize and reduce outgoing data streams.

2. THE EPIC APPROACH

First FEW and its incremental user-define aggregation are presented in sections 2.1 and 2.2, and then the solution is outlined in section 2.3.

Figure 1 shows the overall data stream flow of the implementation. The thickness of the arrows in all data flow diagrams in this paper correspond to the relative volume of the data streams. Each node in the dataflow diagram is a separate OS process, called a *query processing node,* in which a partial continuous execution plan is running. The topology of the dataflow diagram is completely expressed in the query language where it is possible to specify continuous sub-queries running in parallel [9]. The system automatically creates OS processes running the execution plans of the sub-queries and the communication channels between them (local TCP). In the Grand Challenge implementation, the query processing nodes all run on the same computer and the OS is responsible for assigning CPUs to the processes. The system can also distribute query processing nodes over several computers but those features are not used here.

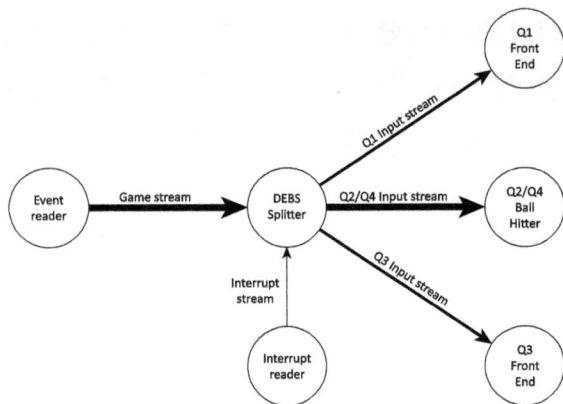

Figure 1. High level data stream flow

2.1 Frequently Emitting Windowizer, FEW

EPIC provides window forming operators that support several kinds of windows, including time, count, and predicate windows [5][2][7]. The windows are formed by *window functions* mapping streams to streams of objects of type *Window*. For example, the window function

tWindowize(Stream s, Number length, Number stride) -> Stream of Window ws

forms a stream *ws* of timed windows over a stream *s* where windows of *length* time units (seconds) slide every *stride* time units. To avoid copying, the windows are represented by pointers to their first and last elements. When a window slides the pointers are updated.

A naive implementation of *tWindowize()* would emit tuples only when the formed windows slide. This causes substantial delays, in particular for large windows. For example, when forming a 10 minutes window, it is not practical to wait 10 minutes for the aggregation to be emitted. To be able to emit aggregation results before a complete window is formed, we have introduced a window function having a parameter *ef*, the *emit frequency*:

fewtWindowize(Stream s, Number length, Number stride, Number ef) -> Stream of Window pw

The window forming function *fewtWindowize()* forms partial time windows, *pw*, every *ef* time units. The emitted partial windows are landmark sub-windows of the elements of the window being formed. When the formed window is complete it is emitted as well before it slides, and then the landmark is reset to the start time of the newly slided window.

The FEW windows are required when:

- The results must be emitted before the window is formed.
- The results must be emitted more often than the slide (not used in this application).

2.2 User-defined incremental window aggregate functions

The windowing mechanism in EPIC supports incrementally evaluated user defined aggregate functions [1][8]. These are defined by associating *init()*, *add()*, and *remove()* functions with a user defined aggregate function:

- *init() -> Object o_new* creates a new *aggregation object*, *o_new*, which is used for accumulating changes in a window.
- *add(Object o_cur, Object e) -> Object o_nxt* takes the current aggregation object *o_cur* and the current stream element *e* and returns the updated aggregation object *o_nxt*.
- *remove(Object o_cur, Object e_exp) -> Object o_nxt* removes from the current aggregation object *o_cur* the contribution of an element *e_exp* that has expired from a window. It returns the updated *o_nxt*.

A user defined aggregate function is registered with the system function:

aggregate_function(Charstring agg_name, Charstring initfn, Charstring addfn, Charstring removefn) -> Object

For example, the following shows how to define the aggregate function *mysum()* over windows of numbers:

```
create function initsum() -> Number s as 0;

create function addsum(Number s_cur, Number
e) -> Number s_nxt as res + e;

create function removesum(Number s_cur,
Number e_exp) -> Number s_nxt as s_cur -
e_exp;
```

These functions are registered to the system as the aggregate function *mysum()* by the function call:

```
aggregate_function('mysum','initsum','addsum
','removesum');
```

After the registration *mysum()* can be used in CQs as:

```
select mysum(w) from Window w where w in
fewtWindowize(s, 10, 2, 1);
```

In this simple example the aggregation object is a single number. It can also be arbitrary objects, including dictionaries (temporary tables) holding sets of rows, which is used in the Challenge implementation to incrementally maintain complex spatio-temporal aggregations.

2.3 Solution outline

In Figure 1 the *Event Reader* node reads the full-game CSV file and produces the *Game* stream consisting of events for both balls and players. The *Event Reader* then scales the time stamps by subtracting the start time. It also transforms the position, velocity, and acceleration values to metric scales. To avoid the *Event Reader* becoming a bottleneck it is implemented as a foreign function in C. To speed up the communication we use binary representation of all events communicated between query processing nodes, while the input and output log files use the CSV format.

The *Interrupt Reader* node produces the *Interrupt* stream, which contains referee interruptions, by reading and transforming the provided game interruptions files.

The *DEBS Splitter* node merges the two input streams based on the time stamps in the streams and produces parallel input streams for the different queries. It also filters out those event stream tuples of the *Game* stream that are in-between game interruptions. The nodes *Q1 Front End*, *Q2/Q4 Ball Hitter*, and *Q3 Front End* receive parallel data streams required for the four Grand Challenge queries Q1-Q4. Q2 and Q4 share some downstream computations executed by *Q2/Q4 Ball Hitter node*.

In EPIC the *splitstream()* system function provides customizable distribution and transformation of stream tuples. The user can provide customizable splitting logic as a *distribution query* over an incoming tuple that specifies how a tuple is to be distributed, filtered and transformed.

The distribution query for the *DEBS Splitter* in Listing 1 is passed as an argument to *splitstream()*.

```
1 select i, ev from Integer i
2 where (i = 0 and isPlayer(ev)) or
3        (i = 1) or
4        (i = 2 and isPlayer(ev));
```

Listing 1. DEBS Splitter distribution query

The result of the query are pairs *(i, ev)* specifying that an incoming event *ev* is to be sent to output stream number *i*. In the DEBS splitter distribution query three output streams enumerated by *i* are specified. They produce the corresponding streams *Q1 Input*, *Q2/Q4 Input*, and *Q3 Input*. The Boolean function *isPlayer(v)* returns true if *v* is a player sensor reading.

To speed up the processing, shared computations are made in separate nodes. In Figure 1 the *Q1 Front End* and the *Q3 Front End* nodes perform stream preprocessing and reduction for queries 1 and 3, respectively, while the *Q2/Q4 Ball Hitter* node detects hits to the ball needed by queries 2 and 4.

2.3.1 Query Q1: Running Analysis

Figure 2 shows the topology of Q1. The aggregated running statistics for different time windows are computed in parallel based on the common current running statistics produced by the *Q1 Front End* node. The stream containing player sensor readings is sent to the *Q1 Front End* node (see Listing 1), which produces the running statistics. The running statistics is then broadcasted to four other nodes to compute the aggregated running statistics of different time window lengths.

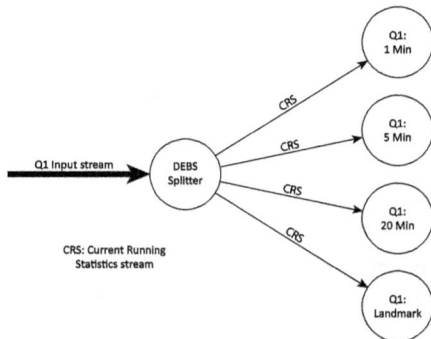

Figure 2. Query 1 data stream flow

2.3.1.1 Incremental maintenance of running statistics

In order to make the result more reliable for the current running statistics, we first create a *1 s* tumbling window and then calculate the statistics for each player over that window. The window length *1 s* was chosen experimentally to produce stable results. Both running and aggregate statistics utilize user defined aggregate functions to maintain arrays of the two types of statistics for each player.

2.3.1.2 Current running statistics

For each incoming player sensor reading in the current *1 s* window, the following statistics tuple for each player is incrementally maintained in an array:

(ts_start, ts_stop, pid, left_x_start, left_y_start, left_x_stop, left_y_stop, right_x_start, right_y_start, right_y_stop, right_y_stop, sum_speed, count)

The time stamp *ts_start* stores the first time when a sensor reading of player *pid* arrives to the current window, while *ts_stop* stores the last sensor reading. The elements *left_x_start*, *left_y_start*, *right_x_start*, and *right_y_start* are the position readings of the left and right foot of the player at time *ts_start*, while *left_x_stop*, *left_y_stop*, *right_x_stop*, and *right_y_stop* are the corresponding foot position readings at time *ts_stop*. To incrementally calculate the average velocity the elements *sum_speed* and *count* are also included. *ts_start*, *left_x_start*, *left_y_start*, *right_x_start*, and *right_y_start* are updated only when the first sensor reading of the player *pid* arrives to the window, while all the other elements are updated every time a sensor reading of *pid* arrives. Here, no remove function is needed for the aggregation, since we are maintaining a stream of tumbling windows where the statistic will be re-initialized every time the window tumbles.

With the statistics above, the current running statistics for a given player is calculated as the Euclidian distance between the average position of the first and last update during the time window.

2.3.1.3 Aggregate running statistics

We have chosen to log the result tuple of Q1 in CSV format every *1 s* since the current running statistics are not emitted more often than once per second. Four FEW time windows were defined for aggregating running statistics with lengths 1 minute, 5 minutes, 20 minutes, and the entire game. All windows slide and emit results every *1 s*. FEW is critical for early emission while the first windows are being formed.

Aggregate running statistics over the window are incrementally maintained in an array similar to current running statistics.

The stream from the *Q1 Front End* node contains the elements *ts_start*, *ts_stop*, *player_id*, *intensity*, *distance*, and *speed*. The difference *ts_stop – ts_start* is used to incrementally maintain the duration of a player being in the corresponding running *intensity* class. Analogously, the moving distance is maintained for the corresponding intensity classes by incrementally associating the incoming distance with the right intensity.

2.3.2 Query Q2: Ball Possession

Figure 3 shows the data flow of queries Q2 and Q4 combined. The *Q2/Q4 input* stream consists of player, ball, and interrupt sensor readings. The *Q2/Q4 Ball Hitter* computes the *Ball Hitter* and the *Ball* streams. The *Ball Hitter* stream contains ball hitter events, which occur when a player *pid* at timestamp *ts* hits the ball. The *Ball* stream contains *Ball Hitter* events interleaved with ball sensor readings. The *Q2/Q4 Ball Hitter* node emits the *Ball* stream to the *Shot on Goals* query processing node, which executes the final stages of query Q4. The *Ball Hitter* stream contains only ball hitter events and is sent to the *Player Possession* node, which calculates and broadcasts the same *Player Ball Possession* stream to four *Team Possession* query processing nodes. The *Team Possession* nodes log every *10 s* statistics of team ball possessions for the two teams with the different window lengths: 1 minute, 5 minutes, 20 minutes, and a landmark window of the entire game. As an alternative, we also measured reporting team possessions every *1 s* resulting in the same latency and throughput.

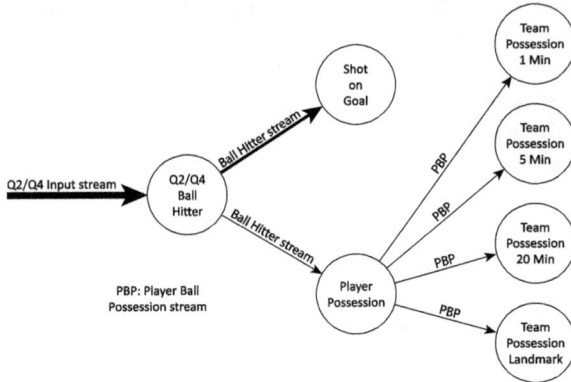

Figure 3. Query 2 and Query 4 data stream flow

2.3.2.1 The Q2/Q4 Ball Hitter query processing node

In order to compute a stream of ball hitters, we maintain acceleration of the ball *ballacc*, its position *bx, by, bz*, the shortest distance from a player to the ball *sdist*, and the player *pid*.

For every input ball sensor reading, the *Q2/Q4 Ball Hitter* node incrementally updates the ball acceleration and the ball position accordingly. When a player sensor reading arrives, it incrementally maintains *sdist*.

A ball hitter event is emitted when both the following criteria hold:

➤ C1: The ball acceleration reaches a predefined threshold: *ballacc > 55 m / s²*.

➤ C2: The shortest distance *sdist* is within the player's proximity: *sdist < 1 m*.

There are 36*200 player sensor readings per second. In addition, after being hit, the ball acceleration remains high for a while, in particular before the ball leaves the player's proximity. Therefore, the two conditions C1 and C2 will hold for a short period of time within which several ball hitter events could be reported for the same actual ball hit by the player. To avoid generating false *ball hitter* events, we employ a *dropping policy* to drop player sensor readings occurring significantly later than the last report time. The dropping policy is expressed by the following query condition over a player sensor reading *v*:

```
ts(v)-lrts > epsilon;
```

Here, *lrts* is the latest timestamp when a ball hitter event was reported, and *epsilon* is the minimum time period between two reports. Because Q4 is more sensitive to the *ball hitter* events, we have empirically tuned this parameter to *0.2 s* to get the best possible accuracy of Q4.

2.3.2.2 The Player Possession query processing node

The *Player Possession* node emits the *Player Ball Possession (PBP)* stream consisting of the variables *fts, pid*, and *hits*, which state that the player *pid* possessed the ball *hits* times, starting from first time the player hits the ball, *fts*.

The *Player Possession* node increases the variable *hits* if a ball hitter event *bhe* is from the same player *pid*. Otherwise, it will emit ball possession events for player *pid* and then reset the variables. The total possession time is the interval between the timestamps *bhe* and *fts*.

2.3.2.3 The Team Possession query processing nodes

There are four *Team Possession* nodes, each with different window length: 1 minute, 5 minutes, 20 minutes, and a landmark of the whole game. For the received *Player Ball Possession* stream they compute team possession statistics as follows:

- Incrementally calculate the sum of the ball possessions of all players in each team when a corresponding player ball possession arrives.
- When a report is logged, the following two percentages are calculated:

$$P_A = \frac{sumTeamA}{sumTeam\,A + sum\,TeamB}$$

$$P_B = \frac{sumTeamB}{sumTeam\,A + sum\,TeamB}$$

Here FEW windows are used to frequently report while the first windows are being formed. For example, the results must be regularly delivered every *10 s* while the *team possession landmark* window is being formed.

2.3.3 Query 4: Shot on Goal

The *Shot on Goal* node receives three different kinds of events in the *Ball* stream:

- A ball hitter event marks a shot and contains a time stamp and the *pid* of the shooting player.

- A ball event contains the current ball sensor reading.

- An interrupt event indicates a game interruption. It is good practice to reset the shot detection when an interruption occurs.

Q4 shares detection of a ball hit with Q2. However, the logic for detecting a shot is slightly different for the two queries: Q2 is specified stricter than needed for Q4. To share computations this stricter logic is also used for Q4.

The operation of Q4 is straightforward; it is an iteration over the *Ball* stream to keep track of the state of a shot:

1. Wait for the next ball hitter event.

2. Check ball events until the ball has travelled one meter.

3. Return ball events as long as the ball is approaching the opposite team's goal.

The calculation of the ball direction uses basic linear algebra over the ball sensor readings.

Gravity is accounted for to an extent. The expected time for the ball to travel to the goal line is multiplied twice with the acceleration constant *g*, and added to the height of the goal bar. The actual ball trajectory is not considered, but the current calculation should be an adequate approximation.

Using the Q2 requirements for detecting a ball hit has the drawback that some events are not detected, such as the header at 12:19 in the second half our example *Game* stream, since the ball is more than one meter away from any sensor. Whether that is technically a "shot" is questionable.

Curve balls need special attention. For example, at 26:07 in the first half there is a curve ball goal. In this case the direction of the ball is pointing outside the goal posts, while the ball later curves inwards and comes to rest inside the goal.

To handle curve balls we have introduced a state *pending*, indicating that a shot is not yet dismissed, but could later be become a shot on goal. The model adds two meters of margin on both sides of the goal posts and the shot is considered pending if it points in the direction of the margin area.

Bounces are considered as long as the direction of the bounce is within the negative distance of the goal bar plus gravity. While the instructions do not account for bounces at all, this limit should add some correctness to the algebra.

Shots that are bounces, which we detect, are not included in the provided list of shots on goal. In the second half of the game there are four shots on goal that are bounces. They are at 4:11, 19:39, 24:36 and 29:29. Setting the bounce threshold to zero, i.e. not considering bounces creates a result in accordance to the specification. Viewing the video makes it apparent that the specification is not correct in this regard.

2.3.4 Query 3: Heat Map
In Query 3 a grid on the field is formed where the cells are numbered in row order, for example from 0 to 6399 in a 64 X 100 grid. Given the position of a player *(x,y)*, the function *cell_id(x,y,grid_size)* returns the corresponding cell number for a given grid size. Query results for lower resolution grids are computed by aggregating the results for the higher resolution grids. Thus we incrementally maintain the results only for the highest resolution.

Note that the results of longer windows cannot be built on top of the results from a shorter window. This is due to the *1 s* stride parameter in all the queries. For example, the 5 minute window can't be built on top of the results produced by the 1 minute window, since the 5 minute window needs to remove the contributions made to the statistics by the expired elements, i.e. the elements with the time stamp $ts - 300 s$, where ts is the current time stamp. Those elements are too old to be in the 1 minute window. Nevertheless, the definition of longer windows in terms of shorter ones could have been utilized if the stride was one minute instead of the one second stride in the Challenge specification.

2.3.4.1 Q3 Front End
Figure 4 shows the dataflow diagram for query Q3. As specified in Listing 1 the *Q3 Input Stream* contains all player sensor readings. The *Q3 Front End* node produces the *One Second HeatMap (OSHM)* stream by forming *1 s* tumbling windows over the incoming tuples. Thereby incremental user defined aggregate functions are used to maintain statistics per second in a table *heamap1s(pid, cell_id, ts, cnt)* local per window. Here ts is the latest time stamp player *pid* has been present in the cell identified by *cell_id* cell identifier in the highest resolution grid (64 X 100). *cnt* is the total number of sensor readings for player *pid* in the cell in the current window.

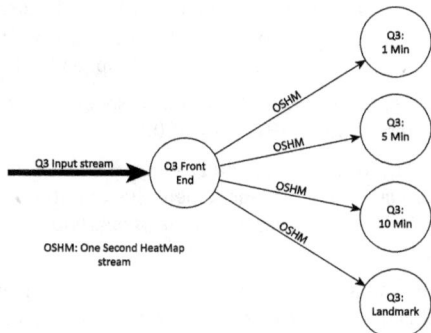

Figure 4. Query 3 data stream flow

The *OSHM* stream is produced by emitting all the rows accumulated in the table during the past second.

The *Q3 Front End* significantly reduces the stream volume by summarizing it. It receives 200 tuples per second from 36 sensors, in total 7200 tuples/second. It emits at maximum the total number of cells all the players have been present in the highest grid resolution during one second, which is about 70 tuples per second, i.e. a factor 10 reduction in stream flow.

2.3.4.2 Q3 query nodes
The *OSHM* stream is broadcasted to four Q3 query nodes *Q3 1 Min*, *Q3 5 Min*, *Q3 10 Min*, and *Q3 Landmark*. These nodes run parallel CQs over time windows with lengths 1, 5, 10 minutes, and whole game, respectively. The windows are formed by the FEW window specification *fewtWindowize(oshm, length, 1, 1)*, where *length* is 60s, 300s, 600s and the whole game duration, respectively. The stride and the emit frequency are both *1 s*. The emit frequency is needed so that sub-windows are emitted while the window is being formed the first time.

Similar to *Q3 Front End*, the Q3 query nodes incrementally maintain user defined aggregates by updating the following local tables inside each window as the input stream elements arrive:

heatmap(pid, cell_id, ts, cnt)

sensor_count(pid, total_cnt)

In table *heatmap*, the attribute *cell_id* is the cell player *pid* has been present in, *ts* is the latest time player *pid* was in the cell, *cnt* is the number of times the player has been present in the cell. To enable translation of *cnt* into percentages per cell, the Q3 query nodes also maintain *total_cnt* per player, which stores the total number of position reports in all cells for a given player during the window in question.

Since Q3 query nodes only maintain the statistics for the highest resolution in a given window length, at reporting time they compute lower resolutions by aggregating grid cells per player to fill the bigger cells in the higher resolutions.

The Q3 query nodes log the output CSV streams to files. Since each Q3 query nodes cover all grid settings in a given window size, the produced log files contains output stream elements for more than one grid setting. We use the following grid identifiers to tag streams per grid: *6400* for 64 X 100, *1600* for 32 X 50, *400* for 16*25, and *104* for 8 X 13 grid setting.

The size of these log files is huge (ca 400,000 rows/s) since they cover all movements between grid cells over several very long windows. Here it becomes important to use SSD as storage medium, which is fast at writing big blocks in parallel, while disk arm movements for writing different log files has been observed to slow down the entire system throughput with a factor of around two.

3. PERFORMANCE
We measured the performance of our implementation based on both throughput and delay. The throughput was measured as the total execution time per query and for all queries in parallel over the entire game. The latency was measured by propagating the system wall clock of the entry time of the latest event contributing to each result tuple. The delay was calculated by subtracting the propagated entry time from the wall time when a result tuple is delivered. The throughput is measured per query while the latency is measured per output stream.

We ran our experiments on a VMware virtual machine with Windows Server 2008 R2 x64, running on a laptop with the following specifications: Dell Latitude E6530, CPU: Intel Core i7-3720QM @2.60 GHz, RAM: 8 GB, Hard Disk Device: ST500LX003-1AC15G, OS: Windows 7 64-bit.

Figure 5 illustrates the throughput of the individual queries as well as all queries running together. Queries Q1, Q2, and Q4 take around 5 minutes to finish separately, while Q3 takes considerably longer time, which is mainly due to intensive report computations in the Q3 query nodes. To investigate the log writing time, *Q3* and the *all queries* columns have a watermark indicating how much time it takes to execute them without logging to disk, showing that this takes around 35 % of the Q3 alone time and 25 % of all queries together. We also investigated whether it would be favorable to parallelize the logging of the result stream for Q3 query nodes, but that turned out to be slower in our current environment.

Since all queries run in parallel according to the dataflow diagrams, running all of them together takes approximately the same time as running the slowest one, Q3.

Figure 6 shows the average delay per output stream while running all queries together. Notice that Q2 and Q4 are time critical queries since they immediately report real-time phenomena. By contrast Q1 and Q3 report delayed statistics aggregated over time.

The VMware virtual machine containing our implementation of the Grand Challenge can be downloaded from http://udbl2.it.uu.se/DEBS/. There is also a zip archive that can be run on any Windows machine.

4. RELATED WORK

In the stream processing community, there has been a lot of work for developing query languages over data streams [5]. [7] introduced a formal specification of different kinds of windows over data streams and provided a taxonomy of window variants. The notation of report (emit) frequency was proposed in SECRET [2] without any actual implementation. SECRET is a descriptive model to help users understand the result of window-based queries from different stream processing engines. Esper [4] also allows a report frequency but does not have user defined window aggregate functions. Furthermore Esper's sliding window model is different from FEW because the slides are triggered by window content changes rather than explicitly specified time periods.

To efficiently calculate the aggregate result over long windows with small strides, [6] and [1] use delta computations to reduce the latency and the memory usage. The focus of [8] is to extend a DSMS with online data mining facilities by user defined aggregate functions over windows. The implementation described in this paper shows that EPIC is general enough to define very complicated user defined aggregations as functions while in [1] and [8] the aggregates are defined as updates.

5. CONCLUSIONS

We have addressed the Grand Challenge by expressing continuous queries in a high level language that supports incremental evaluation of aggregate functions over windows and frequently emitting windowing. We meet the real-time requirements of the real-time queries on a virtual machine running on a laptop. The extensibility of the query engine was used for supporting high throughput and low latency of time critical operations.

ACKNOWLEDGMENTS

This work was supported by the Swedish Foundation for Strategic Research, grant RIT08-0041 and by the EU FP7 project Smart Vortex.

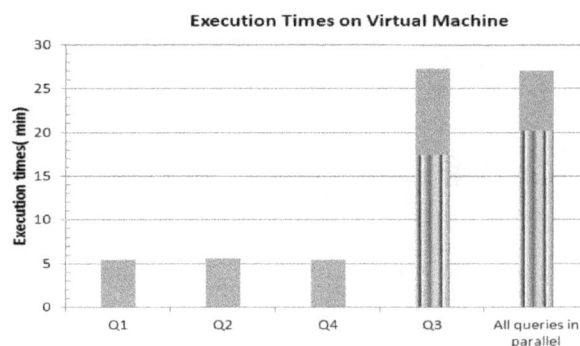

Figure 5. Performance

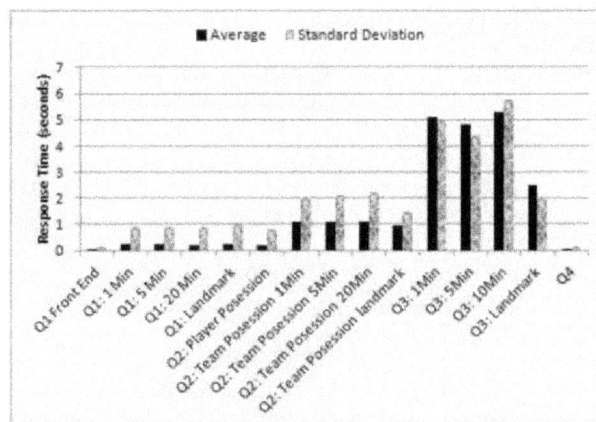

Figure 6. Delays

REFERENCES

[1] Bai, Y., Thakkar, H., Wang, H., Luo, C., and Zaniolo, C.: A Data Stream Language and System Designed for Power and Extensibility. *Proc. CIKM Conf.*, 2006.

[2] Botan, I., Derakhshan, R., Dindar, N., Haas, L., Miller, R. J. and Tatbul, N. SECRET: A Model for Analysis of the Execution Semantics of Stream Processing Systems. *Proc. VLDB Conf.*, 2010.

[3] Botan, I., Fischer, P. M., Florescu, D., Kossmann, D., Kraska, T., and Tamosevicius, R. Extending XQuery with Window Functions. *Proc. VLDB Conf.*, 2007.

[4] http://esper.codehaus.org/

[5] Law, Y-N, Wang, H., and Zaniolo, C.: Relational Languages and Data Models for Continuous Queries on Sequences and Data Streams. ACM TODS 36, 2, (May 2011).

[6] Li, J., Maier, D., Tufte, K., Papadimos,V., and Tucker, P. A. Semantics and evaluation techniques for window aggregates in data streams. *Proc. SIGMOD Conf.*, pp. 311 - 322, 2005.

[7] Patroumpas, K. and Sellis, T. Window specification over data streams. *Proc. EDBT Conf.*, 2006.

[8] Thakkar, H., Mozafari, B. and Zaniolo, C.: Designing an Inductive Data Stream Management System: the Stream Mill Experience. *Proc. 2nd International Workshop on Scalable Stream Processing Systems*, 2008.

[9] Zeitler, E. and Risch, T.: Massive scale-out of expensive continuous queries, *Proc. of the VLDB Endowment*, ISSN 2150-8097, Vol. 4, No. 11, pp.1181-1188, 2011

Demo: Do Event-Based Systems have a Passion for Sports?

Christopher Mutschler
Univ. Erlangen-Nuremberg
and
Fraunhofer Institute for
Integrated Circuits IIS
91058 Erlangen, Germany
christopher.mutschler@fau.de

Nicolas Witt
Fraunhofer Institute for
Integrated Circuits IIS
91058 Erlangen, Germany
nicolas.witt@iis.fraunhofer.de

Michael Philippsen
University of
Erlangen-Nuremberg
91058 Erlangen, Germany
michael.philippsen@fau.de

ABSTRACT

The ubiquity of sensor data calls for automatic processing to extract valuable information. Realtime Locating Systems (RTLS) provide many parallel position data streams for interacting objects, and event-based systems are the method of choice to analyze them.

We demonstrate a distributed event processing system for position stream data from a Realtime Locating System used for a soccer application. Our system can deal with the insufficient knowledge on object and system behavior, and thus the event data loads at runtime. To do so, it dynamically adapts to the variations in the observed environment: events are ordered with respect to their delays, event detectors are reconfigured and migrated between nodes at runtime, and the system is scalable as the number of trackable objects and sensors changes. We demonstrate the efficiency of our system architecture and provide tools to visualize data and to configure detection units at runtime.

Categories and Subject Descriptors

C.2.4 [**Computer-Comm. Networks**]: Distrib. Syst.—*Distrib. Applications*; D.1.3 [**Programming Techniques**]: Concurrent Programming—*Distributed Programming*

Keywords

Self-Management, Sensor Streams, Distributed Event Processing, Publish/Subscribe, Message-oriented Middleware.

1. INTRODUCTION

With wireless localization techniques we can track moving objects in almost arbitrary environments. Realtime Locating Systems (RTLS) can track many objects simultaneously and provide accurate positions at high data rates [1].

By automatically processing this position information, we ease analyses in many fields of applications. Consider the quantitative analysis of sports games like soccer [2]. To detect meaningful data about players, teams and games, and to display information like percentual ball possession on television, we currently require several human observers that count certain events. Further scenarios arise in training.

Cones are placed at specific points on the field, time keeping is assured by light barriers, and velocities are either calculated as a result of previous measurements or are directly determined with lasers. However, such setups are both time-consuming and error-prone. Thus, qualitative results are not objectively correct and are highly doubtful.

A low latency analysis of position data streams provided by an RTLS aids in the implementation of all such scenarios. The aim is to automatically derive events such as passes, ball possessions, or shots from the position data streams. In training, the system implements virtual time gates and sends their results to, for instance, a tablet PC on the field where the trainer can immediately use this information to improve the training or to compare the performance to previous exercises or to other players.

Event-based processing of position data streams is the way to go. Since many interesting incidents, i.e. events, depend on common lower-level events, it is obvious to calculate these basic events only once, and to form an event hierarchy from them. Fig. 1 shows such an event hierarchy to detect a blocked shot on goal. By splitting a pattern into various sub-events, we can reuse those sub-events for the detection of other high-level events. Lower software complexity, no coupling between event implementations, no memory synchronization, implicit parallelism, and better maintenance are further benefits that facilitate the development of event-based systems.

2. SYSTEM ARCHITECTURE

Fig. 2 shows our distributed event-based system (EBS) consisting of several data distribution services (DDS), i.e.,

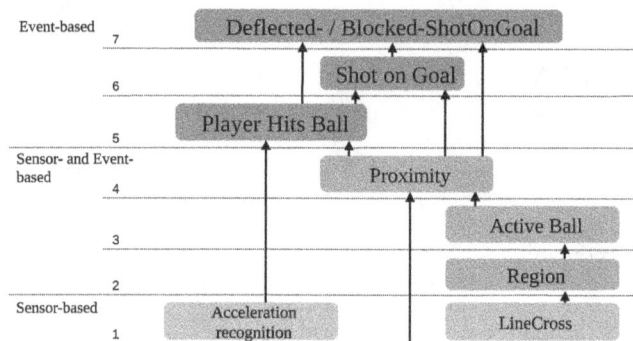

Figure 1: Hierarchy for blocked shot on goal [3].

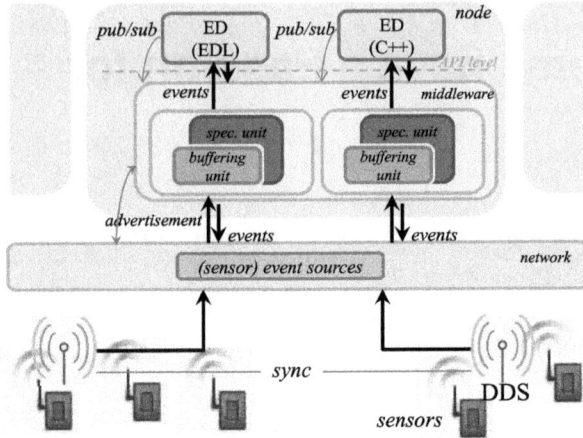

Figure 2: Distributed event processing system.

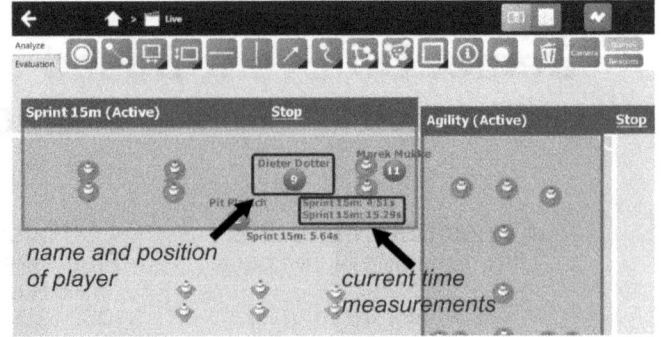

Figure 3: Screenshot of the trainer's GUI: s/he can interactively create virtual training scenarios and *drag & drop* them onto the field/screen. Times and analysis are presented without noticeable delay.

the units that take microwave signals received by antennas to calculate the transmitters' positions, and several nodes in a network that run the same event processing middleware. The middleware creates a reordering buffer per event detector (ED), wrapped with a speculation unit to reduce latency. The middleware deals with all types of delays such as processing and networking delays or detection delays[1] and does not need to know the complex event pattern that is implemented in the ED. EDs can hence be implemented in a native programming language or in some description language. The detector does not need to know on which machine other detectors are running nor their runtime configurations. At startup the middleware has no knowledge about event delays but just notifies other middleware instances about event publications and subscriptions by advertisements [4]. The middleware is therefore generic and encapsulated.

On top of the middlewares there are EDs spread over the available computing nodes. These EDs then work on an event-based interaction level and implement a message-dependence as, for instance, the one depicted in Fig. 1. In total, our system is used to detect over 500 different event types out of around 80 different EDs, depending on the scenario of use. The complexity of EDs variates from low-level detection to highly sophisticated algorithms.

Since the system and object behavior and thus the event loads are unknown a-priori, a static allocation and configuration of the EBS is rarely an optimal solution. Hence, our EBS implements dynamic low-latency reordering of events per event detector [3], migrates event detectors for latency optimization or system overload avoidance [5], and implements speculation to exploit unused system resources for further latency reduction [6].

3. DEMONSTRATION

We present details of our distributed event-based system and our tools that are used to process and visualize sensor data and events. On a distributed system of laptops we run both a virtual replica of the positioning and database system that is used to collect and store sensor data in the main soccer stadium in Nuremberg, Germany, and the distributed event-based system used to analyze the streams and to de-

tect the events. On a tablet PC we demonstrate the tools and GUIs that are used by the trainers and professionals for qualitative analysis, see Fig. 3.

Visitors can design their own exercises and statistic graphs of the previously collected position and event data. Moreover, since the position streams from the stadium can be replayed to the EBS, visitors can also design and configure training scenarios for a realtime analysis as if the data would be gathered in the stadium. We also show our implementation to tackle the DEBS 2013 Grand Challenge [2].

4. CONCLUSION

We sketched the architecture of a distributed event processing system that works with high-volume position sensor streams and that can deal with the challenges and requirements of the sports applications. Its unique features are the basic building blocks that are geared towards low-latency, self-configuration, and reconfiguration at runtime.

5. REFERENCES

[1] T. v. d. Grün, N. Franke, D. Wolf, N. Witt, and A. Eidloth, "A real-time tracking system for football match and training analysis," in *Microelectronic Systems*, pp. 199–212, Springer Berlin, 2011.

[2] C. Mutschler, Z. Jerzak, and H. Ziekow, "The DEBS 2013 Grand Challenge," in *Proc. 7th Intl. Conf. Dist. Event-Based Systems*, (Arlington, TX), 2013.

[3] C. Mutschler and M. Philippsen, "Distributed Low-Latency Out-of-Order Event Processing for High Data Rate Sensor Streams," in *Proc. 27th Intl. Conf. Parallel and Distrib. Processing Symp.*, (Boston, MA), pp. 1133–1144, 2013.

[4] G. Mühl, L. Fiege, and P. Pietzuch, *Distributed event-based systems*. Springer, Berlin, 2006.

[5] C. Mutschler and M. Philippsen, "Runtime Migration of Stateful Event Detectors with Low-Latency Ordering Constraints," in *Proc. 2013 Intl. Conf. Pervasive Computing and Communications Workshops*, (San Diego, CA), pp. 609–614, 2013.

[6] C. Mutschler and M. Philippsen, "Reliable Speculative Processing of Out-of-Order Event Streams in Generic Publish/Subscribe Middlewares," in *Proc. 7th Intl. Conf. Dist. Event-Based Systems*, (Arlington, TX), 2013.

---

[1]Events that are generated with earlier time stamps than those of the events that cause them can only be inserted into the event stream long after they have actually happened.

Demo: Measuring and Estimating Monetary Cost for Cloud-based Data Stream Processing

Thomas Heinze[1]   Patrick Meyer[1]   Zbigniew Jerzak[1]   Christof Fetzer[2]

[1]SAP AG
Dresden, Germany
firstname.lastname@sap.com

[2]System Engineering Group
Technische Universität Dresden, Germany
christof.fetzer@tu-dresden.de

ABSTRACT

In recent time due to the availability of cloud-based data streaming systems like Yahoo! S4 or Twitter Storm and virtually unlimited resources using a public cloud infrastructure it is possible to run stream processing tasks with a new dimension of computational complexity. However, the required resources in terms of CPU, memory, and network bandwidth differ depending on the use case and applied data streaming system. For the user of such a system this is directly visible in the monetary cost he has to spent for the used resources. Therefore, he would like to maximize the ratio between gained performance and his monetary cost.

In our demonstration we present an approach to measure and estimate the monetary cost for data streaming systems. We present a general scheme to model monetary cost for any combination of a cloud-based data streaming system and a major public cloud provider. Our model can be used as a starting point for optimizing the ratio between monetary cost and performance of streaming systems in general.

Categories and Subject Descriptors

C.2.4 [**Distributed Systems**]: Distributed applications

Keywords

Monetary Cost, Cloud-based data stream processing

1. INTRODUCTION

In the past, the major metrics for evaluating a data streaming system have been throughput, latency, and computational accuracy. By the raise of cloud computing, offering an illusion of unlimited resources, and data streaming systems like Twitter Storm [1] and Yahoo! S4 [6], which allow to scale across a large number of hosts, such performance goals become more easily achievable. However, the required resources to process such tasks depend on many different factors like the streaming system and the use case [2]. In

context of cloud computing a "pay per use" model is used. This causes that the different required resources are directly visible to the user by the bill he has to pay for his cloud setup. Therefore, a user is interested in improving the ratio between spent cost and provided quality of service. However, currently no tool to analyze the monetary cost for data streaming systems is available.

In this demonstration we present a model to measure and estimate the required cost for applications on top of cloud-based data streaming systems. Our model can be used with an arbitrary combination of a cloud provider and a data stream processing engine. It measures the monetary cost on a fine-granular level, allowing to find the most costly parts of a query. The demonstration comprises a graphical user interface showing detailed information on the spent monetary cost.

The problem of monetary cost as a new metric for data management systems has been outlined by Florescu et al. [3]. Kossmann [5] shows, that the monetary cost of executing a transactional database workload differs based on the used architecture as well as the cloud provider cost model. We are only aware of one work [4], which tried to optimize a data streaming system deployment towards minimizing the trade-off between cost and latency, however, it is specific to the used system and cloud environment.

2. MONETARY COST

The monetary cost to pay for a given setup depends on the cost model of the cloud provider, which differs between the various providers. For defining a generic cost model we studied the pricing schemes of the major public cloud vendors. All of them calculate the cost by the used RAM, CPU, and/or network capacity. We model the prices for storage as fixed cost for our system, because data streaming systems are using mostly in memory computing. Each provider uses individual intervals for charging the cost, varying between price per month to price per hour, and provides different hardware images. We scale the prices to the same time scale (1 hour) and resource size (1 core, 1 GB RAM, 1 GB network traffic). In summary, the following parameters need to be specified for a given cloud cost model: the price p_{CPU} for using one CPU core for one hour, price p_{RAM} for using a gigabyte of main memory for one hour and the prices $p_{NET_{\leftarrow}}, p_{NET_{\rightarrow}}$ per gigabyte for incoming or outgoing network traffic.[1]

---

[1]Due to space constraints we omit the details on how to model special offerings, different types of hosts (on demand, reserved instances) and fixed cost.

We assume that the data streaming system can be used by one or more users in parallel. The users deploy queries on top of the set of available hosts, where an individual host can be shared by several users. A query describes a certain computation task, which can be split into several atomic operations like filter, aggregation, or join modeled as operators.

Our model is able to calculate the cost to pay on three different levels: the total cost, the cost per query, and the cost per operator inside a query. The total cost p for the current setup can be given as $p = used_{CPU} \cdot p_{CPU} + used_{RAM} \cdot p_{RAM} + used_{NET_{\leftarrow}} \cdot p_{NET_{\leftarrow}} + used_{NET_{\rightarrow}} \cdot p_{NET_{\rightarrow}}$, where $used_{CPU}$, $used_{RAM}$, $used_{NET_{\leftarrow}}$ and $used_{NET_{\rightarrow}}$ represent the number of used CPU's, RAM, and network bandwidth respectively. To calculate the cost per operator, the cost for one host is split proportionally to the used RAM and CPU for all operators running on the host like shown in Figure 1. For the network consumption the used bandwidth is measured. The cost for a single query can be calculated by summing up the costs of all its operators. The different usage metrics are constantly measured and the cost values are updated accordingly. The calculated cost value expresses always the expected cost for the current cost interval (the current hour), the concrete cost is derived at the end of an interval and added to the total cost to pay.

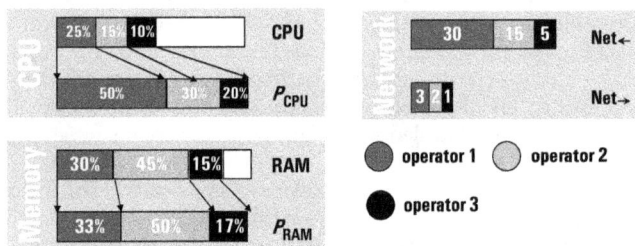

Figure 1: Calculating the cost per operator

Using our model we are also able to estimate the cost for executing a query before deploying it on top of the system. Therefore, we use current system information about the performance of already running queries e.g. the required processing time for filtering or aggregating events. In addition, we use an approach similar to Viglas et al. [7] to estimate the event rates per operator. By combining these two measures the required resources are estimated from which the spent cost can be derived. The cost estimation allows a user to judge the cost of queries before actually deploying them and to rewrite a query if needed. In addition, a user can specify quality of service (QoS) constraints like maximal latency, minimal throughput or required availability.

3. OUR DEMONSTRATION

To illustrate our model, we built a demonstration system presented in Figure 2, where a user can visualize the monetary cost for a cloud-based data streaming system. A user-defined query can be added to a system with certain QoS constraints, and is executed on top of a commercial cloud-based streaming system. We run the system in a private cloud environment with up to 10 VM's and we are able to switch between different cost models within the demonstration. Based on constantly measured memory, network, and CPU consumption the cost values are updated to reflect e.g.

a changing input rate of the query and can be compared with the estimated cost. In addition, a detail view similar to an explain functionality of a database is provided, which presents a break down of the cost of a query into cost per operator to allow to identify the most expensive parts of a query.

(a) List queries view

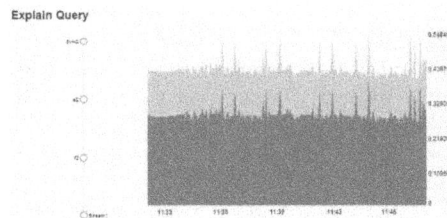

(b) Detailed cost view

Figure 2: Screenshots of our demonstration

4. CONCLUSION

In this demonstration we presented a generic cost model, which allows to measure and estimate the monetary cost for a cloud-based data streaming engine. It can be used as a starting point for improving the ratio between monetary cost and achieved performance.

5. REFERENCES

[1] Twitter Storm: http://storm-project.net/.

[2] M. Dayarathna, S. Takeno, and T. Suzumura. A performance study on operator-based stream processing systems. In *Workload Characterization (IISWC), 2011 IEEE International Symposium on*, pages 79–79, 2011.

[3] D. Florescu and D. Kossmann. Rethinking cost and performance of database systems. *ACM SIGMOD Record*, 38(1):43–48, 2009.

[4] A. Ishii and T. Suzumura. Elastic stream computing with clouds. In *Cloud Computing (CLOUD), 2011 IEEE International Conference on*, pages 195–202, 2011.

[5] D. Kossmann, T. Kraska, and S. Loesing. An evaluation of alternative architectures for transaction processing in the cloud. In *Proceedings of the 2010 SIGMOD International Conference on Management of Data*, pages 579–590, 2010.

[6] L. Neumeyer, B. Robbins, A. Nair, and A. Kesari. S4: Distributed stream computing platform. In *Data Mining Workshops (ICDMW), 2010 IEEE International Conference on*, pages 170–177, 2010.

[7] S. D. Viglas and J. F. Naughton. Rate-based query optimization for streaming information sources. In *Proceedings of the 2002 ACM SIGMOD International Conference on Management of data*, pages 37–48, 2002.

Demo: Elastic MapReduce-style Processing of Fast Data

Kasper Grud Skat Madsen   Yongluan Zhou
{kaspergsm, zhou}@imada.sdu.dk
University of Southern Denmark

ABSTRACT

MapReduce is a popular scalable processing framework for large-scale data. In this paper we demonstrate Enorm, which represents our efforts on rectifying the traditional batch-oriented MapReduce framework for low-latency data stream processing. Most existing work have focused on how to extend the MapReduce framework for low-latency data stream processing, but overlooked the problem of obtaining runtime elasticity.

The demonstration focuses on two important features in Enorm. (1) sharing aggregate computations among overlapping windows and (2) runtime elasticity.

Categories and Subject Descriptors

H.2.4 [**Systems**]: Query Processing

Keywords

MapReduce; Elasticity; Sharing Computation

1. INTRODUCTION

There is a recent interest in building large-scale platforms for processing fast data streams, such as MapReduce online [2], Muppet [4] and STORM [1]. Such platforms supports general computations and massive out-scaling to achieve high data throughput, and at the same time they employ techniques to reduce the data processing latency.

We have developed a research system, called Enorm, that adopts an extended MapReduce computation model which supports eager data processing rather than lazy and batch-based processing. Enorm natively maintains window-based computation states at the platform level rather than the application level as done in previous MapReduce-style systems and hence allows us to automatically share common computations among overlapping windows.

Conventional batch-based systems only allows defining the set of computing units at job submission. In most cases that is acceptable as the job describes a finite computation and the resources required to process the job can be estimated beforehand. State-of-the-art stream-based systems are designed to execute long-standing jobs, whose input properties are usually hard to predict at job submission. This poses great challenges to the users of the system: the input rate might be fluctuating heavily over the runtime and the user

has to predict the needed resources for the job, which are then fixed.

Elasticity is the ability to change the number of "computing units" for a given computation. In this paper we explain the computation framework of Enorm and briefly how elasticity is supported. For the demonstration, we present

1. Two jobs solving the same problem (one with sharing of computation, one without). Attendees of the demonstration, can adjust parameters of the jobs and interactively see how the jobs perform in comparison.

2. A job undergoing periodical elastic adaptations. Only a single feature will be demonstrated, but it will show the benefits this provides.

2. COMPUTATION FRAMEWORK

The input data into Enorm, is modeled as a set of continuous streams of tuples with schema $\langle key, value, ts_1, ts_2 \rangle$. ts_1 and ts_2 are two timestamps associated with a tuple. Typically, if the tuple represents a computation result over a sliding window, then ts_1 and ts_2 indicate the start and end points of the window. ts_1 and ts_2 can also be identical which indicates that the tuple has only one timestamp.

In the traditional MapReduce framework, the *reduce* function takes a key and a list of values associated with that key. To perform window operations over streaming data, the *reduce* function can be invoked over each window of the input stream, after having received all the content of the window. A lazy evaluation approach like this, incurs excessive latency.

There are several existing efforts addressing the latency issue. For example, MapReduce Online [2] which solves the latency problem, by modifying the original MapReduce architecture to allow pipelining data between tasks, while maintaining the original MapReduce interface. As another example, the MapUpdate framework [4] reformulates the *reduce* function to an *update* function such that only one input key-value pair is used for each function invocation. The end-user can program the *update* function to decide when all the data of a window will arrive and output the results for the window. Approaches like this clearly solves the latency problem, but still relies on the application to handle window maintenance, such as window creation, tuple insertion, tuple expiration, etc.

Pushing window maintenance and sharing to the application level is undesirable, because there exists a wealth of research results on how to efficiently maintain windows and do sharing [3], most of which are application independent. We thus present Enorm which natively supports window maintenance and sharing of computation.

Enorm supports a time-based sliding window, which is defined on a time domain that is consistent with the timestamps of input data. Users can apply more than one window specification to the same computation. Given the user-defined windows, Enorm will generate some segments so that the computation results of the segments can be reused to compute multiple final window outputs. We refer readers to the literature, such as [3], for how to generate an optimal set of segments. The computation framework contains the following functions:

Map. $map(key, tuple) \rightarrow list(key, tuple)$ takes a tuple as an input and produce zero or more output tuples. This is logically similar to the *map* function in the traditional MapReduce framework.

Compute. $compute(key, tuple) \rightarrow list(key, tuple)$ takes a key-tuple pair and return a list of tuples. In addition, *compute* is associated with a local storage to keep track of the current state of the computation.

Consolidate. $consolidate(key, list(tuple)) \rightarrow list(key, tuple)$ takes a key and a list of tuples as its input and produce a list of key-tuple pairs. It is usually used to merge the results produced by the *compute* instances to generate the results over the complete window.

There are two types of *consolidate* functions: *windowed* or *non-windowed*. A non-windowed consolidator will be handled analogously to a *reduce* function in the MapReduce framework. For a windowed consolidator, Enorm will arrange input according to the window specifications. For each key, it will generate a list of tuples for each window, and invoke the function for each list of tuples.

Window specifications should be applied to either a pair of *compute* and *consolidate* functions (with *compute* followed by *consolidate*) or a single *consolidate* function. In the former case, the *compute* function can be used to perform eager processing to achieve lower latency. The following *consolidate* can perform sharing of computation among multiple windows. The latter case is a lazy evaluation where Enorm will collect all the data that belongs to the target window and then invoke the *consolidate* function.

Partition. For each function, it must be specified how to partition the input tuples. There are currently two types of partitioners in Enorm: *random* and *keyed*, which will partition the tuples randomly and based on their keys respectively.

Processing Engine. Enorm can be deployed on a large cluster. It uses a master node to handle the submitted jobs and distribute the "computing units" across the cluster. A logical job can be divided into several components, each containing a chain of functions which Enorm will treat as integral units when parallelizing the computation. Note that a component can be parallelized only when the functions in the component have "compatible partitioners", e.g. they have partitioners based on the same key or they can both use random parallelization. One can also put a function with random partitioner and another function with a keyed partitioner together into one component. Then the component can be partitioned using the keyed partitioner of the latter function.

Scaling. The computation framework supports efficient runtime adaptation of parallelization degrees of the components. For convenience, denote the component to be scaled as C_x and its immediate upstream component as C_{x-1}. We choose to present two scaling strategies:

1. Migrate. The affected instances of C_x will be paused at the start of the adaptation. Meanwhile, new parallel instances of C_x will be created at the new location as necessary. Then C_{x-1} will redirect part of the input to the new instances. If C_x has a keyed partitioner and contains stateful functions, then a migration of states must be performed. Finally all the paused instances as well as the new instances of C_x will resume the processing.

2. Split. In our computation framework, the functions that maintain states are the compute functions and by default the compute functions does not assume the inputs are partitioned based on the input key. Furthermore, although the consolidate functions have keyed partitioners, they are stateless operations and hence they can be scaled efficiently too. Based on these observations, a scaling strategy is to split C_x into a few components such that each of them contains either functions with random partitioners or functions with keyed partitioners.

3. STORY LINE

The demonstration consists of two parts: a poster and a system demonstration.

Poster. The poster graphically shows how (1) sharing of aggregate values can be done automatically and (2) how to dynamically scale a component C, which uses a random partitioner and has a single function which requires no migration of state.

System demonstration. Two implementations of one job processing high velocity input and calculating the average values over sliding windows are provided. Implementation 1 uses sharing of computation and implementation 2 does not. The inputrate, number of windows and frequency of consolidation can interactively be adjusted. The two jobs will then be executed and when done, a comparison of their performance will be graphically displayed on the screen.

To show the simple scaling capabilities and benefits, a job will be continuously running and subjected to dynamic scaling. Enorm continuously shows how many tasks are used to process any given component together with the processing speed (tuples/second) of the system.

4. "TAKE-AWAY" MESSAGE

In this paper, we briefly presented Enorm. We showed how Enorm supports sharing of computations, and provided a demonstration setup with tuneable parameters. Furthermore we briefly presented the elasticity of Enorm and provided a demonstration which shows important aspects of the system while undergoing a scaling operation.

5. REFERENCES

[1] http://www.storm-project.net.
[2] T. Condie, N. Conway, P. Alvaro, J. M. Hellerstein, K. Elmeleegy, and R. Sears. Mapreduce online. In *NSDI'10*, pages 21–21, San Jose, California, 2010.
[3] S. Krishnamurthy, C. Wu, and M. Franklin. On-the-fly sharing for streamed aggregation. In *SIGMOD '06*, pages 623–634, Chicago, IL, USA, 2006.
[4] W. Lam, L. Liu, S. Prasad, A. Rajaraman, Z. Vacheri, and A. Doan. Muppet: Mapreduce-style processing of fast data. *PVLDB*, 5(12):1814–1825, 2012.

Demo: Approximate Semantic Matching in the COLLIDER Event Processing Engine

Souleiman Hasan

Digital Enterprise Research Institute
National University of Ireland, Galway
souleiman.hasan@deri.org

Kalpa Gunaratna

Kno.e.sis Center
Wright State University
Dayton OH
USA
kalpa@knoesis.org

Yongrui Qin

School of Computer Science
University of Adelaide, SA
Australia
yongrui.qin@adelaide.edu.au

Edward Curry

Digital Enterprise Research Institute
National University of Ireland, Galway
ed.curry@deri.org

ABSTRACT

This demo presents a use case from the energy management domain. It builds upon previous work on approximate semantic matching of heterogeneous events and compares two semantic matching scenarios: exact and approximate. It illustrates how a large number of exact matching event subscriptions are needed to match heterogeneous power consumption events. It then demonstrates how a small number of approximate semantic matching subscriptions are needed but possibly with a lower true positives/negatives performance. The demo is delivered via the COLLIDER approximate event processing engine currently under development in DERI.

Categories and Subject Descriptors

D.2.12 [**Software Engineering**]: Interoperability---*data mapping, interface definition languages*; H.3.3 [**Information Storage and Retrieval**]: Information Search and Retrieval---*information filtering*.

Keywords

Approximate Event Matching; Loose Semantic Coupling; Semantic Matching.

1. INTRODUCTION

Event-based systems are decoupled in space, time, and synchronization which supports scalability [2]. However, scaling out to include participants from diverse domains poses a significant challenge in terms of the semantic interpretation of events. Current systems assume the existence of a mutual agreement between event producers and consumers on event semantics, which adds explicit dependencies between participants. In large-scale scenarios, such as the Internet-of-Things, high levels of semantic heterogeneity exist among events where different terms may be used to describe same concepts or event types.

If event consumers, or subscribers, are coupled to the underlying schema of events, they need to write many exact matching subscriptions to address the semantic heterogeneity in the events. We have previously proposed [3] an approximate semantic

matching paradigm for event processing systems to work in such scenarios. This approach is implemented in the COLLIDER event processing engine which focuses on semantic approximation and its implications on event processing systems, especially on event enrichment and complex event processing.

Using approximate semantic event processing, a relatively small number of subscriptions are needed to match heterogeneous events. This facilitates the scalability of the system and the adoption by non-technical users. However, approximate matching may result in some false positives/negatives due to approximation. This demo focuses on these aspects of approximate semantic event matching within an energy management scenario.

2. DEMONSTRATION

The demo targets energy management within an office scenario where a user is interested in matching power consumption events in order to take energy saving actions [1]. Heterogeneity exists due to different sensors' manufacturers each using their own event description. The demo shows how a single subscription is used to match several event types using approximate matching semantics, whereas exact matching requires several subscriptions, typically one for each event type to achieve the same result.

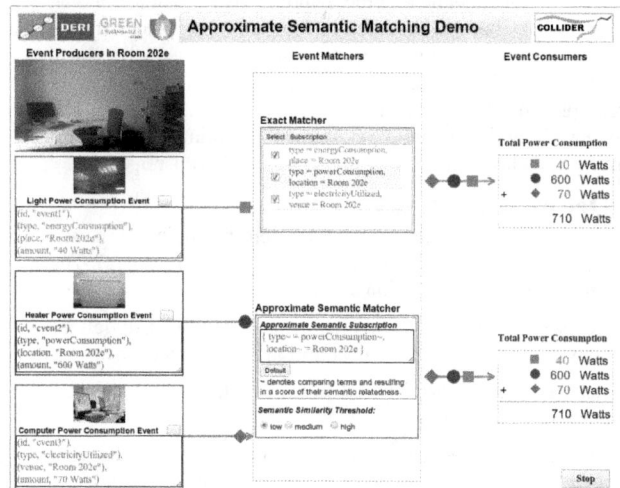

Figure 1. A screenshot from the demo application

2.1 Demo Setup

The main components of the demo are the set of events, the subscriptions and the matchers.

2.1.1 Events

There are three types of power consumption events, namely from sensors monitoring a light, a heater and a laptop. Each event has slightly different properties and descriptions. For example, the event types of *event 1, event 2, and event 3* are described using the terms *"energyConsumption"*, *"powerConsumption"*, and *"electricityUtilized"* respectively. However, these event types are semantically similar to each other in the energy domain. An example is an energy consumption event of a light that exists in *"Room 202e"* and consumes *40 watts* as illustrated in Figure 1. It is represented as a set of attribute-value pairs as the following:

{(id, "event 1"), (type, "energyConsumption"), (place, "Room 202e"), (amount, "40 Watts")}.

2.1.2 Subscriptions

There are two types of subscriptions in the demo: exact matching subscriptions and approximate matching subscriptions. There are three exact subscriptions, one for each event, and one approximate subscription for all the events. The exact matching subscriptions that target *event 1, event 2*, and *event 3* are respectively:

{type=energyConsumption, place=Room 202e}.

{type=powerConsumption, location=Room 202e}.

{type= electricityUtilized, venue=Room 202e}.

The approximate subscription is expressed in a COLLIDER language variant for attribute-value pairs as shown in Figure 1. It contains the *tilde* operator ~ after attributes and values to dictate that the approximate matcher shall match similar terms to the specified terms in the subscription. The approximate matching subscription targets all events and uses *powerConsumption~* to semantically match *"energyConsumption"*, *"powerConsumption"*, and *"electricityUtilized."* It also uses *location~* to semantically match the terms *place, location*, and *venue*. It is expressed as follows:

{type~ =powerConsumption~, location~ =Room 202e}.

2.1.3 Matcher Settings

There are two matchers behind the demo: an exact matcher and an approximate matcher as illustrated in Figure 1. The exact matcher can be set to match events against registered exact subscriptions. In order to match all three events, all three exact matching subscriptions must be registered in the exact matcher. The approximate matcher can be set with a matching threshold to determine how the events match the approximate subscription.

2.2 Demo Workflow

The objective of the use case is to identify the total power consumption of the events that match the user subscription(s). The basic steps in this demonstration application are as follows.

1. The user selects the exact matching subscriptions and defines an approximate matching subscription for the matchers.

2. The user selects and forward plays events to the exact and approximate matchers.

3. The exact matcher uses a subscription to match each event making the total power consumption matched 710 watts.

4. The approximate matcher obtains the correct total amount of power consumption of 710 watts when the threshold is low. If the threshold is medium or high the matched events become less and the total power consumption of matched events becomes less than 710 watts.

3. COLLIDER ARCHITECTURE

The approximation functionality of the demo is delivered via the COLLIDER event processing engine. COLLIDER is currently developed in DERI to study the various aspects of approximation in event processing and the potential impacts of uncertain matching on event enrichment and complex event processing.

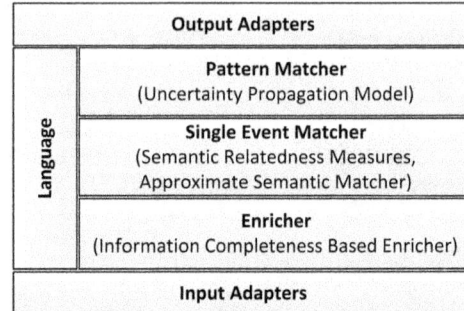

Figure 2. The COLLIDER engine architecture

Figure 2 shows a high level architecture of COLLIDER. Its components are briefly discussed in the following:

1. **Input and Output Adapters:** They allow the engine to interact with event producers and consumers respectively.

2. **The Language Module:** It is responsible for parsing the users' event subscriptions and complex event patterns.

3. **Enricher**: It enriches events which arrive at the engine to improve their information completeness with respect to potential event subscriptions.

4. **Single Event Matcher:** Approximate matching is enabled via a set of semantic relatedness measures as described in [3]. These measures are used to score the similarity between an event and a subscription based on the scores of each pair of terms. Approximate matching results in uncertain values that propagate to the pattern matcher.

5. **Pattern Matcher:** It propagates uncertainties from single event matching to obtain the uncertainty values for derived complex events.

This demo leverages the capability of the approximate single event matcher in COLLIDER while the other modules are out of the scope of this paper.

4. ACKNOWLEDGMENTS

This work has been funded by Science Foundation Ireland under Grant No. SFI/08/CE/I1380 (Lion-2).

5. REFERENCES

1. Curry, E., Hasan, S., and O'Riain, S. Enterprise Energy Management using a Linked Dataspace for Energy Intelligence. *Second IFIP Conference on Sustainable Internet and ICT for Sustainability*, IEEE (2012).

2. Eugster, P.T., Felber, P.A., Guerraoui, R., and Kermarrec, A.M. The many faces of publish/subscribe. *ACM Computing Surveys (CSUR) 35*, 2 (2003), 114–131.

3. Hasan, S., O'Riain, S., and Curry, E. Approximate Semantic Matching of Heterogeneous Events. *6th ACM International Conference on Distributed Event-Based Systems (DEBS 2012)*, ACM (2012), 252–263.

Demo: ALERT – Real-Time Coordination in Open Source Software Development

Dominik Riemer
FZI Forschungszentrum Informatik
Haid-und-Neu-Str. 10-14
76131 Karlsruhe
+49 721 9654724
riemer@fzi.de

Ljiljana Stojanovic
FZI Forschungszentrum Informatik
Haid-und-Neu-Str. 10-14
76131 Karlsruhe
+49 721 9654804
stojanovic@fzi.de

Nenad Stojanovic
FZI Forschungszentrum Informatik
Haid-und-Neu-Str. 10-14
76131 Karlsruhe
+49 721 9654852
nstojano@fzi.de

ABSTRACT

In this demo, we present the final version of the ALERT system. ALERT aims to improve collaboration and coordination of developers in open source software development. In this sense, ALERT provides active support for developers in form of real-time notifications. The system is based on an event-driven architecture which integrates data from several information sources used by developers, e.g., forums, source code management systems and issue trackers. This data is acquired by push sensors, preprocessed by several middle-tier components and send to a complex event detector in order to provide real-time decision support for multiple daily development tasks.

Categories and Subject Descriptors

H.3.4 [**Information Systems**]: Systems and Software

Keywords

Intelligent Complex Event Processing, Semantic Technologies, Open Source Software Development.

1. INTRODUCTION

FLOSS (Free/Libre open source software) communities, and in particular those formed around large projects, have demonstrated that they are capable of producing complex software systems with high quality standards, enough for the many companies that use them in very demanding production, mission-critical environments. However, as those communities grow, individual developers devote a large fraction of their effort to tasks related to communication with their peers, and to gain knowledge of specific aspects of the project [Yamauchi00] [Mockus02] [Crowston05]. Although this communication is obviously needed, developers cannot be expected to read all the information produced by their project, neither that would be an efficient approach.

Existing tools and policies have been designed to focus on discussions and to link knowledge to artifacts, such as issue tracking systems, which are organized around tickets (which can correspond with actions to address bug reports, for example); or mailing lists and forums, which are organized around topics. However, very little has been done to filter all this information, so that the developers get notified of what is of their interest, which means that they still have to devote significant amounts of time just to be informed about what could be of their interest.

In addition, finding relevant information for their tasks, despite the use of those tools and policies, is still a complex, error-prone task, which also consumes a lot of the time of developers.

Taking all the problems mentioned above into account, the ALERT project has identified several problem areas, which it addresses:

- Classification of development tasks, so that similar tasks can be grouped, or tasks that were already defined or even addressed in the past can be compared to current tasks.
- Identification of developers best suited to specific tasks. Again, when tasks are organized in tickets, this would mean suggesting the ticket to the most appropriate developers, so that it is fixed in the most efficient manner possible.
- Localization of relevant context information. When performing any kind of development activity, a developer usually has to look for many related information, and in general, the easier it is to find this information, the easier and better the activity is accomplished. Therefore, providing information related to any artifact (such as lines of code, tickets, email messages, etc.) would contribute to improve development efficiency.
- Selective notification. In many cases, developers do not search for specific information, but are notified of events happening in the project of their interest. Therefore, automated support systems that can learn what information developers need, and which are capable of routing that information to them, will significantly help to shorten the time developers devote just to be informed.

2. COMPLEX EVENT PROCESSING

Establishing real-time situational awareness was one of the most important objectives within the ALERT project. Especially in the field of open source software (OSS), where developers are usually working independent and geographically distributed, there is a high demand for improving collaboration and coordination between developers. CEP in ALERT aims at finding relevant situations by aggregating heterogeneous information sources. One example is the ad-hoc generation of a list of recommended developers after a bug has been classified as important based on a high amount of discussions in a message board. The architecture of the component around complex event processing is shown in Figure 1.

In addition, one of the most important assets in complex event processing is the management of event patterns. As event patterns can be deployed and remove on-the-fly at runtime, users can easily add new situations of interests and receive notifications based on these patterns. In ALERT, we introduced a new methodology based on *goal-driven* notifications. During several user workshops, we identified the need for a methodology which supports the identification of required patterns from a developer's perspective.

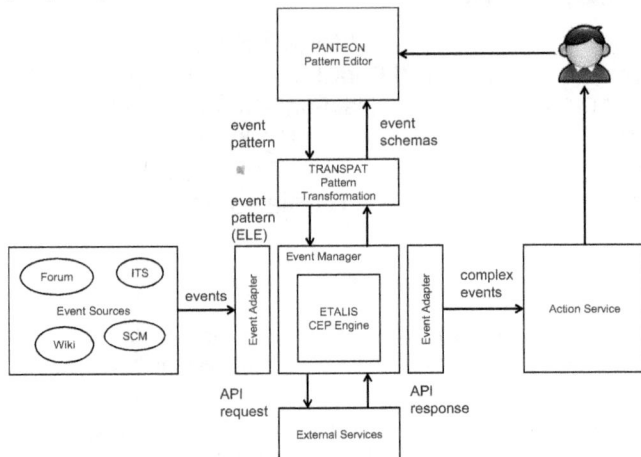

Figure 1: CEP Architecture

At first, we built an initial hierarchy of goals developers aim to achieve with real-time notifications. Goals in this sense are related to the fulfilment of a non-technical objective related to a software development process. For instance, we a high-level goal could be "decrease bug resolution time" or "improve the assignment of developers to new issues". We chose the abstraction of specific technical-oriented event patterns to non-technical goals in order to improve the reusability of event patterns among a community and to improve the alignment between business goals and their technical representation. After several goals had been identified in several user workshops, we constructed a hierarchical goal model. Based on this model, users can add new situations of interest which are related to a specific goal. Additionally, we developed a pattern classification model based on the complexity of an event pattern in order to provide a better abstraction and to ease the communication with developers and end users. This classification is driven by the developer's point of view meaning the kind of patterns a developers needs to define in order to be notified.

Based on the classification of a pattern, this step is followed by the selection of appropriate events. In this phase, the PANTEON tool is used to select the appropriate events from a list of sources. Users are also allowed to select filter operations on single events. Note that we integrated the selection of named entities extracted by the KEUI component described above. This enables users to not only select text-based raw properties of events, but also extracted concepts from unstructured content. If a pattern is consisted of multiple events, users can select between operators (e.g., AND and SEQ). Finally, the output of events (meaning the part of the events which is used by the action manager for a specific notification) can be selected in the PANTEON editor. One important new functionality is the recommendation of related patterns by using different similarity measures. As a result, the user receives recommendations on similar situations of interests within a specific goal.

3. DEMO IMPLEMENTATION

The ALERT system is comprised of several components connected through a publish/subscribe broker. Currently, data from the KDE community is imported (which contains around 250.000 issues, and 70.000 forum posts). In addition, the system is connected to information sources from mailing lists and KDE's source code management systems and receives live events from these systems. All components have been integrated in a single user interface which supports all functionalities described above. The Alert user interface is illustrated in figures 2 and 3.

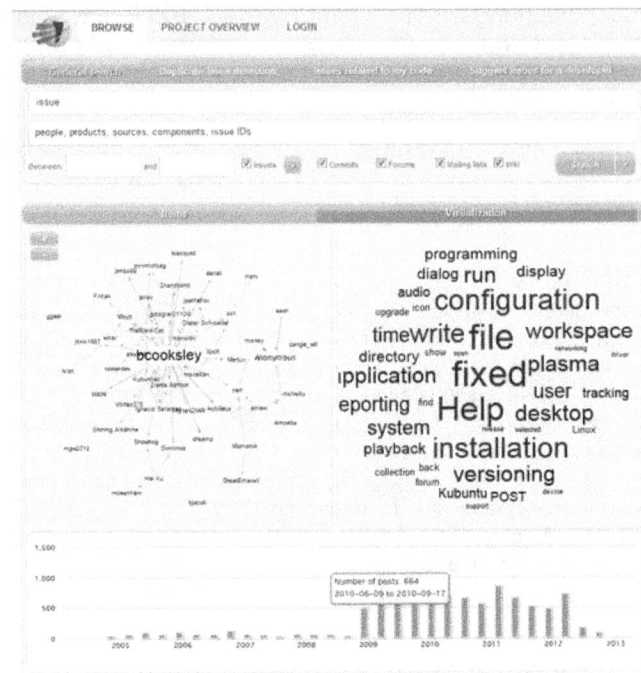

Figure 2: Advanced Search

We will demonstrate the search functionalities, supported by live events created in the underlying systems, the integration of several event types by using semantic event schemas and the creation and deployment of complex notification rules. In addition, we demonstrate more complex scenarios such as real-time recommendation of developers most suitable for a specific bug resolution based on their identified competencies.

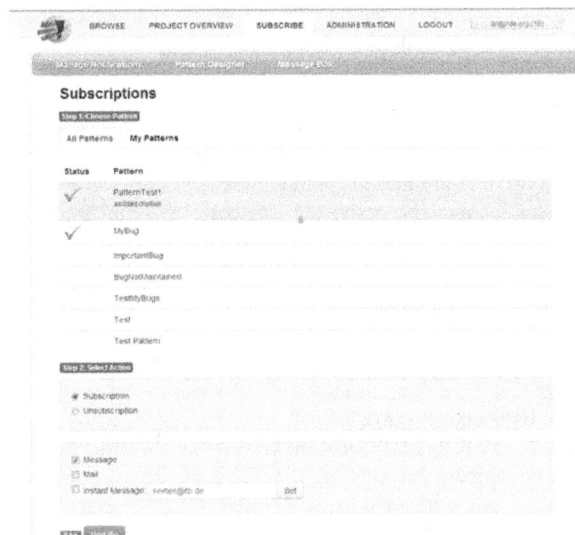

Figure 3: Pattern Subscription Editor

Demo: A System for Dynamic Real-Time Personal Fitness Monitoring

Nenad Stojanovic
FZI, Research Center for
Information Technology

Haid-und-Neu-Str. 10-14,
76131 Karlsruhe, Germany
nstojano@fzi.de

Dominik Riemer
FZI Forschungszentrum Informatik
Haid-und-Neu-Str. 10-14
76131 Karlsruhe
+49 721 9654724
riemer@fzi.de

Yongchun Xu
FZI Forschungszentrum Informatik
Haid-und-Neu-Str. 10-14
76131 Karlsruhe
+49 721 9654
Xu@fzi.de

ABSTRACT

In this demonstration, we present a system for real-time monitoring of personal fitness performance indicators. The system uses smartphone and wearable sensors for gathering information (measurements) from the user in order to enable improving the fitness activity. The main advantages are 1) dynamic fitness monitoring, which enables adapting on-the-fly the situations to be detected to the current performances and the context of the user and 2) extended contextualization, based on the combination of the mobile and server side CEP, that ensures that the most relevant context will be taken into account.

Categories and Subject Descriptors

H.3.4 [Information Systems]: SYSTEMS AND SOFTWARE Information networks

Keywords

Wearable Sensors, Mobile Event Processing, Personal Monitoring

1. INTRODUCTION

Modern smartphones available today offer real-time access to a high variety of sensors, including GPS sensors for tracking a user's current location, accelerometers for identifying their activity and microphones for measuring the noise level, to name but a few. Furthermore, an increasing number of additional external (wearable) sensors (e.g., heart beat rate measuring devices) is available and can be integrated with smartphone via standard interfaces, extending the amount of information that is related to the user and can be obtained through a smartphone. Therefore, smartphones have become very powerful devices for capturing users' behavior and there are plenty of apps that are leveraging this capability. Moreover, the interest of data acquisition on aspects of the daily live is currently being forced by the quantified self (QS) movement, which aims at improving general wellbeing through self-tracking. Self-tracking opens up new opportunities for personal knowledge management, as smartphones are usually a permanent companion in most people's life and therefore enable the opportunity to monitor activities, habits, identify situations of interest and actively support in improving individual lifestyles.

The combination of sensor data, external data and mobile applications, together with the establishment of user communities enable users to not only track their daily activities, but also to compare themselves to others doing similar activities.

However, while looking at smartphone applications available today, it is obvious that most use cases are focused on a single (monitoring) aspect (or a single sensor respectively) of physical activities, e.g., tracking the pulse during sports activities. Although interesting, these apps are just the tip of the iceberg. More sophisticated approaches should focus on the combination of heterogeneous data sources and their relationships, the integration of background knowledge on the user's habits and preferences. We argue that smartphone apps should be aware of not only what the user is doing but also what she/he should do (in order to achieve some goals). Indeed, instead of just monitoring the user's physical activity (e.g. by storing the monitored data), the apps should suggest how to improve/increase the physical activities of the user (e.g. by detecting problems and suggesting improvements). Key factor for achieving this is the real-time awareness of the situation(s) the user is involved in (real-time situational awareness), whereas Complex Event Processing (CEP) is the right technology to achieve it.

In this demo we present a CEP-driven approach for increasing situational awareness based on the personal data collected from the smartphone and wearable sensors which are usually used in the fitness activities (e.g. heart-rate monitors). The approach enables notifying the user about the situations when her/his performances can be improved or damaged (awareness creation), whereas the relevance of the situations will be dynamically determined based on the current user's context. The context will include the information gathered from the server-side, providing additional knowledge for improving current fitness activity.

The approach is based on the combination of (mobile) client- and server- side event processing in order to enable the most efficient detection of the situations of interest (for improving fitness activity). There are two main advantages of this approach:

- dynamic fitness monitoring, which enables adapting on-the-fly the situations to be detected to the current performances and the context of the user

- extended contextualization, based on the combination of the mobile and server side CEP, that ensures that the most relevant context will be taken into account.

We argue that this approach will enable the development of more real-time aware mobile applications that will interact with the environment (sensors) and social web.

2. MOTIVATION

Through processing the personal data and the environment information, which is sensed by sensors of the mobile device, in real time we can monitor the user's situation and provide the meaningful recommendations, which can be useful to the user. Such a system (MCEP – mobile complex event processing) is based on CEP technologies on the mobile device. In following we provide a motivating example that will be used in the demo as well

Assume that Massimo is a middle-age 45 years old employee in an IT company. Since his work is very exciting and challenging and includes the necessity of frequent business travels, he has poor nutrition habits and sedentary lifestyles due to the need of optimizing the available time at the meeting places. After a medical examination he is told that he has high blood pressure and too high levels for the HDL cholesterol, which is one of the risks for developing further cardiovascular diseases. Despite Massimo is fully convinced that he should improve his lifestyle behavior, he has little support to adopt healthier lifestyles. Occasionally Massimo hears that the Health Monitoring system, which provides dynamic remote monitoring based on mobile complex event processing in real-time, can support him to improve his lifestyle behavior, he decides to use it. Massimo downloads the app and installs it on his smartphone. He also buys a non-intrusive wearable cardio activity sensor that continually captures some parameters of the heart's work and determines the real time activity level of the user and sends this information to the central system by using his smartphone. Following the situated and personalized initial delivery of lifestyle guidance, Massimo now carries out physical activities at least twice per week. Once Massimo starts physical activity such as jogging, the Complex Processing component of the system recognizes after some minutes the current activity as Jogging. As a consequence the Jogging monitor patterns are instantly delivered to the Massimo's smartphone. Meanwhile the environmental humidity sensor close to Massimo's real physical position detects the humidity event "too high". In the same way the system will learn what are the optimal physical conditions (including environmental parameters) that will enable Massimo the best relation between the level of the physical activity and the stable healthy status. Such contextual information support the Jogging monitor pattern to combine speed, heart rate and humidity events and matching with the current Massimo preferences and medical history (available through Massimo's personal health record) build an adaptive suitable recommendation and deliver in real time through the smartphone: Under the current humidity condition you should slow down the jogging speed! With the help of our system Massimo improves his lifestyle behaviour as well as his health status.

3. SYSTEM ARCHITECTURE

Our system consists of several components which have been developed during EU projects such as PLAY (www.play-project.eu) and is divided into a mobile part (as seen in the left part of Figure 1) and a server part (as seen in the right part). The mobile device consumes events from several external sensors, measuring biometrical data such as pulse, heart rate and a user's breathing rate (Zypher Bioharness - http://www.zephyr-technology.com/products/ bioharness-3/). Furthermore, internal sensors from mobile sensors are used. For instance, we developed a system for activity recognition based on accelerometer data. In addition, we take weather data from environmental sensors and other external sources into account.

These events are consumed by a mobile CEP engine in order to detect relevant situations, e.g., an increasing heart rate after 5 km of jogging in bad weather conditions.

External events, such as social media sources and environmental sensors are processed server-side. Server-side events are combined with complex events sent from the mobile device to the server in order to detect more complex situations, taking the situation of other users into account. In addition, the server deploys event patterns in the mobile device depending on the current context of the user. One advantage of our system is that patterns are not only deployed dynamically based on specified context conditions, but patterns are also adjusted in form of individual preferences and habits. For instance, a pattern is connected to a certain goal which might be different in several contexts (e.g., a jogging performance of 5 km per hour might be too fast during bad weather conditions or a goal to run 10 km per week should be downgraded due to heart problems). This feature enables highly dynamic management of event patterns but, as this computation is done server-side, still ensures lightweight event processing on the corresponding mobile devices which ususaly have limited computing power and other restrictions such as battery state.

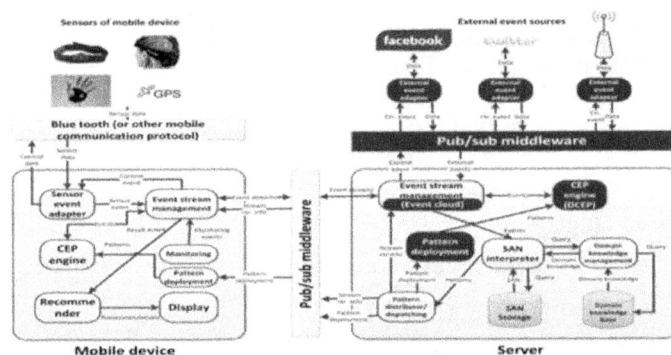

Figure 1: System Architecture

4. SETUP OF THE DEMO

In our demo, we present a prototype of the described system. In order to show the usefulness, we simulate real data which has been recorded in advance. This data captures accelerometer data, GPS data and biometrical data and is processed in real-time during the demonstration.

We modeled multiple patterns which monitor a user's overall wellbeing and detect specific situations (opportunities and threats) during a certain activity (e.g., running and walking). Based on the current context, which is detected based on parameters like current activity, time and location, these patterns are dynamically deployed while pattern-specific parameters are adopted at design-time prior to the pattern deployment. Furthermore, we demonstrate the computation of recommendations based on detected situations.

The demo consists of the Android-based application and a web application which visualizes the current position of an example user, health- and fitness related key performance indicators at a certain timestamp as well as patterns currently deployed. Finally, computed recommendations are sent to the mobile device.

Poster: MADES - A Multi-Layered, Adaptive, Distributed Event Store

Tilmann Rabl[1], Mohammad Sadoghi[2], Kaiwen Zhang[1], and Hans-Arno Jacobsen[1]
[1]Middleware Systems Research Group, University of Toronto
[2]IBM T.J. Watson Research Center

ABSTRACT

Application performance monitoring (APM) is shifting towards capturing and analyzing every event that arises in an enterprise infrastructure. Current APM systems, for example, make it possible to monitor enterprise applications at the granularity of tracing each method invocation (i.e., an event). Naturally, there is great interest in monitoring these events in real-time to react to system and application failures and in storing the captured information for an extended period of time to enable detailed system analysis, data analytics, and future auditing of trends in the historic data. However, the high insertion-rates (up to millions of events per second) and the purposely limited resource, a small fraction of all enterprise resources (i.e., 1-2% of the overall system resources), dedicated to APM are the key challenges for applying current data management solutions in this context. Emerging distributed key-value stores, often positioned to operate at this scale, induce additional storage overhead when dealing with relatively small data points (e.g., method invocation events) inserted at a rate of millions per second. Thus, they are not a promising solution for such an important class of workloads given APM's highly constrained resource budget. In this paper, to address these shortcomings, we present **M**ulti-layered, **A**daptive, **D**istributed **E**vent **S**tore (MADES): a massively distributed store for collecting, querying, and storing event data at a rate of millions of events per second.

Categories and Subject Descriptors

H.2.4 [**Database Management**]: Systems—*Distributed databases*

Keywords

APM; MADES; event processing; event storage

1. INTRODUCTION

In this paper, we present the **M**ulti-layered, **A**daptive, **D**istributed **E**vent **S**tore (MADES): a massively distributed store for collecting, querying, and storing event data. MADES is specialized in storing monitoring data as produced by APM systems. Our target workload consists of small periodically reported data points. In order to support the necessary data rates, we propose a hierarchical architecture of short-term in-memory stores (*on-line stores*) that cluster and aggregate the incoming data and use compression and bulk insertion to significantly reduce the load on the long-term storage (*historic store*). MADES employs push-based communication (*publish/subscribe paradigm*) (PS), in which the on-line stores' data is pushed periodically to the historic store as well as to other on-line stores. Data movement among the on-line stores achieves not

only implicit in-memory replication of data, but also improves efficiency for evaluating continuous queries in which data from multiple sources must be aggregated and joined together over a given sliding window. Moreover, our multi-layered on-line store organization scheme enables each on-line store to adapt to its load by pushing down the excess load to other on-line stores in the lower-layer and ultimately to the historic store. Finally, our proposed architecture naturally provides the elasticity aspect demanded in cloud infrastructures because as new (virtual) machines are added (or removed) from the enterprise infrastructure, a new lightweight instance of the on-line store is also loaded on the newly added machine to collect execution data from the local monitoring agents.

In other words, MADES multi-layered architecture comprises (1) a lightweight on-line store that is capable of answering the desired continuous queries to monitor the system health and publish the measurement results and (2) a durable historic store for enabling extensive data analytics over historic data. Essentially, the on-line store acts as a distributed (adaptive, replicated) cache, with specialized query and compression capabilities, for the historic store and in this way, MADES's novel on-line store design paves the way to provide real-time health and reduce the load on the historic store through bulk insertions of reordered and compressed data. The on-line store is in-memory only and is deployed close to the data monitoring agent (optimally on the same host), while the historic store is durable and deployed on dedicated machines. Moreover, MADES on-line store must be able to deal with (sudden) node addition and removal which not only happens in case of system failures, but also in scaling out the application, e.g., when additional nodes are employed in times of high loads or during system failover and reboots.

2. MADES QUERY LANGUAGE

In the APM use case two classes of (continuous) queries are prevalent: (1) time series queries that retrieve continuous measurements of a specified metric and (2) aggregation queries that computes an aggregation function over multiple time series queries.

Our time series query language can be formalized similar to traditional database SPJG (continuous) queries: selection (σ_c), projection (π), join ($\times$, $\bowtie_c$), and group by (Γ) operators. In fact, we adapt PADRES SQL (PSQL) [2], an expressive SQL-based declarative language for registering continuous queries on event streams over either a time-based or a count-based sliding window model. Essentially the sliding window is a snapshot of an observed finite portion of the event stream.

3. MADES ARCHITECTURE

MADES comprises two main components: the lightweight on-line store and the durable historical store. An architectural overview of MADES is demonstrated in Figure 1. The on-line store nodes are deployed preferably on the production machines directly, where the data is been generated by the monitoring agents. This way the data insertion by the agents is a local function call instead of a remote procedure call or communication over the network. In contrast, the

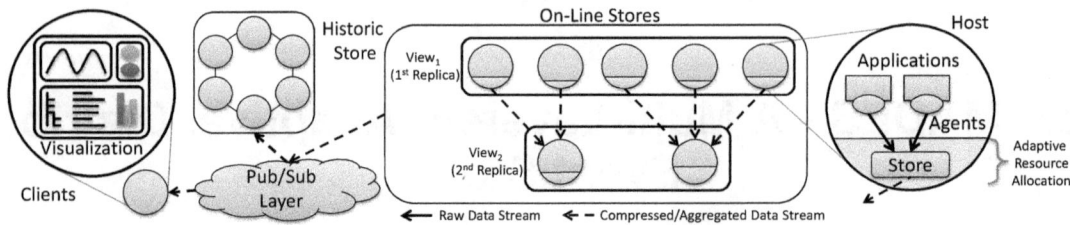

Figure 1: High-Level Overview of MADES Architecture

historical store is deployed on dedicated machines and can leverage any modern key-value store. MADES utilizes Cassandra [3], because of its high performance in the APM scenario [5].

An overview of the on-line store can be seen in Figure 2(a). The on-line store is purely based on main-memory in order to keep the overall overhead on the production hosts low. The size of the store is dependent on the capacity of the host and may be changed based on the requirements of the production system. This makes the store highly adaptive within a single machine and elastic across all machines. Either upon reaching the allocated memory limit or periodically, the data is published and subsequently pushed into the historic store. The data that is produced by an agent or pushed from another on-line store (on a higher layer) is re-ordered and stored in a columnar fashion. The columnar storage is specially attractive in the APM context because the data has a highly regular pattern of metric name followed by (aggregated) measurement values. This column-based storage model enables an effective compression scheme, such as run-length encoding, which is essential in order to keep a low memory footprint while maintaining a low processing overhead.

In particular, most metrics tend to have long consecutive sequences of the same value (low entropy) especially during normal operation of the enterprise system, in which resource failures and usage fluctuations account for a small fraction of the entire enterprise infrastructure. Therefore, when operating on data with low entropy, then any simple and fast compression scheme is far more effective. This is evident for measurements that are generated with a higher frequency than the monitored events and for error reporting metrics that often have long sequences of null (or 0) values. Furthermore, both the on-line store as well as the historic store can operate directly on the compressed data. The overall approach has several advantages, not only the memory footprint is highly decreased by the compression, but also due the columnar alignment, huge space savings is made possible because metric names (which account for a large fraction of each tuple's size) do not have to be stored multiple times. The processing of the compressed data results in a faster operation including scanning and filtering while reducing network traffic as well. Furthermore, bulk insertion through compression and data aggregation (i.e., summarization) substantially reduces the insertion rate of the historic store in MADES.

Not all queries are concerned only with the data that is produced on a single machine. Consider the average CPU utilization over a subset of all monitored machines; in order to compute efficiently these *derived metrics*, we direct all relevant data (followed by aggregation of the data) to a single on-line store in the middle-layer of our MADES multi-layered architecture (as shown in Figure 2(b).) These middle-layer on-line stores are selected based on the excess of resources. If no such node is available, then the final aggregation must be processed on the client at the cost of increased processing (and network traffic) on the client-side.

The on-line stores also act as clients to the historic store. All on-line stores periodically push data to the historic store and the clients. Therefore, all communications, e.g., among on-line stores, between on-line and historic stores, and between on-line stores and clients (e.g., system administrator), are abstracted in form of the decoupled and highly distributed PS paradigm. As a result, both clients and historic stores are modeled as subscribers of monitoring data, while the on-line stores are producers of monitored data. Due

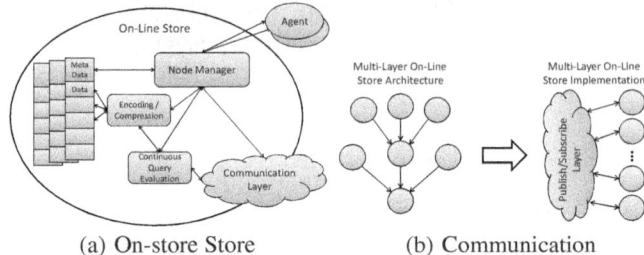

(a) On-store Store   (b) Communication

Figure 2: Overview of MADES Architecture

to MADES multi-layered on-line store design, each layer of the on-line stores also subscribes to a subset of the on-line stores in the preceding layer (depicted in Figure 2(b).) MADES PS communication layer is built over PADRES [2], an open-source PS system.

Apart from adopting the push-based communication of the PS abstraction, for the purpose of data insertion and data propagation, the on-line stores also comprise notifications and query capabilities. In order to retrieve the most recent history of each metric, the client can directly query the on-line nodes for the latest measurements. Furthermore, clients can subscribe to certain metric or aggregation of metrics. This is beneficial for keeping a client user interface up-to-date as well as enable (partial) data replication for higher availability. The data replication naturally arises because the data is replicated (with a different degree of aggregation) in each layer of MADES. Essentially, each layer in our event store provides a different view of the same raw data. Most important, the problem of view maintenance is much simpler in our context because APM's generated data follows a read- and append-only characteristics. Moreover, since all on-line stores are regularly sending their data to the historical store, the historic store has also a relatively up-to-date view of the of the on-line stores (providing yet another redundant form of data replication but durable.)

4. RELATED WORK

MADES builds upon the well-established query language and semantics in streaming database [2], yet MADES distinguishes itself in fundamental respects from state-of-the-art systems, including Ganglia [4] and Nagios [1]: (1) MADES is optimized (with a highly constrained budget) for the write-dominated, append-only APM workloads with millions of insertions per seconds (2) MADES introduces novel multi-layered, distributed on-line stores which are lightweight in-memory stores to process not only continuous queries, but also to enable many layers of aggregation and compression by orchestration within its multi-layered architecture.

5. REFERENCES

[1] C. Gaspar. Deploying nagios in a large enterprise environment. In *LISA'07*.
[2] H.-A. Jacobsen, V. Muthusamy, and G. Li. The PADRES event processing network: Uniform querying of past and future events. *it - Information Technology'09*.
[3] A. Lakshman and P. Malik. Cassandra: a decentralized structured storage system. *SIGOPS Review'10*.
[4] M. L. Massie, B. N. Chun, and D. E. Culler. The Ganglia Distributed Monitoring System: Design, Implementation, and Experience. *Parallel Computing'04*.
[5] T. Rabl, M. Sadoghi, H.-A. Jacobsen, S. Gómez-Villamor, V. Muntés-Mulero, and S. Mankowskii. Solving Big Data Challenges for Enterprise Application Performance Management. *PVLDB*, 5(12):1724–1735, 2012.

Poster: Converging Runtime and Historic Detection of Areas of Congestion Within an Urban Bus Network

David Evans
School of Computing and Mathematics
University of Derby
Derby DE22 1GB, UK
d.f.evans@derby.ac.uk

David Eyers
Department of Computer Science
University of Otago
Dunedin 9052, New Zealand
dme@cs.otago.ac.nz

ABSTRACT

The event calculus (EC) has been used previously to model the behaviour of individual buses in a public transport system. Using this for usefully answering questions about traffic conditions means getting high performance from the backward chaining behaviour of a typical event calculus inference mechanism written in a logic programming language. In seeking to find periods of congestion in the historical data as well as to detect congested traffic as it happens, we have tightly coupled an event calculus implementation with a geospatial database system. We thus go beyond the forms of caching or windowing typically used for managing such spatial data within an EC system.

Our approach can answer historical and real time queries using the same query engine and EC predicates, allowing us to combine complex event processing and longer-term database operations without needing to degrade the precision of results through the introduction of time windows. We are exploring its use on a dataset containing temporal-spatial locations of buses operating over an urban setting that spans several years.

Categories and Subject Descriptors

C.2.4 [**Computer-Communication Networks**]: Distributed Systems—*Distributed applications*; H.2.8 [**Database Management**]: Database Applications—*Spatial databases and GIS*

Keywords

Event calculus, geospatial database

1. INTRODUCTION

Distributed event-based systems have been used as the model for sensor systems that analyse vehicle movement [2]. Subsequent work has examined use of the event calculus (EC) [4] to model this movement and evaluate queries about it, including detecting congestion [1]. However, that work focused on importing data into the runtime environment of an event calculus implementation. This means that a system using, for example, a logic programming language must provide a set of features to handle spatial data.

Spatial database systems provide such facilities, efficiently, as a matter of course. The focus of this paper is to demon-

strate that the elegant model provided by the event calculus can work well when directly coupled with a spatial database. In doing so, we provide the best of both worlds. The EC gives natural logical expression of rich event semantics while the database assists with high speed execution over large spatial datasets. Furthermore, this leads to consistent expression of historical and real-time queries. EC predicates can express either using the same interface, and the spatial database provides effective caching and indexing of historical data. We avoid applying time windows within the EC predicates, allowing for the use of the full extent of indexed records in the database. If the database becomes overloaded, query limiting can be applied over the existing stored data, allowing administrators to determine and apply the specific precision tradeoffs that are necessary.

We explore these ideas in the context of congestion on the roads as experienced by buses.

2. AN EVENT CALCULUS MODEL THAT UTILISES A GEOSPATIAL DATABASE

A typical EC implementation uses predicates of the form `happens(Event,Time)` to model events—each an instantaneous occurrence in time that is identified by a given Prolog term. Prolog allows a variable such as `Event` to be bound to a compound term like `bus(Id)`. The unification process means that `Id` in this example can be used to parameterise the event; this form of parametrising a compound term is a Prolog idiom and is very natural for the programmer. Alongside this `happens/2` predicate, `holds_at(U,T)` is true if fluent `U` holds at time `T`. Fluents are named states of the world that hold over half-open time intervals. `holds_at/2` forms the core of an implementation of the EC in Prolog and is the mechanism for querying historical data.

The primary event that we care about uses compound terms of the form `bus(Id,Easting,Northing)` to represent a sighting of a bus with vehicle ID `Id`. `Easting` and `Northing` together representing the location of the bus as coordinates in a local, Cartesian coordinate system. Alongside this event we define the

```
congested_region(Easting,Northing,R)
```

fluent which holds if the geographical region centred on the point `Easting` and `Northing` and having size `R` is congested. This fluent is deliberately abstract in the sense of not specifying the precise shape of the region nor how `R` is measured.

The computation of large (in geographical terms) congested regions is achieved by a recursive subdivision of the region into smaller areas, i.e.,

```
holds_at(congested_region(Easting,Northing,R),T) :-
    geo_decomposition(Easting,Northing,R,NewEasting,
        NewNorthing,NewR),
    holds_at(congested_region(NewEasting,NewNorthing,
        NewR),T).
```

This evaluation bounds the maximum potential search complexity using a geographical windowing function; predicate

```
geo_decomposition(Easting,Northing,R,
    NewEasting,NewNorthing,NewR)
```

holds when `NewEasting`, `NewNorthing`, and `NewR` are part of a geographical subset of the region `Easting`, `Northing`, `R`.

To define regions we spatially subdivide the plane into a rectangular grid, which has numerous advantageous properties: the grid squares tessellate a region easily, so we can guarantee that the regions provide complete coverage; there is a regular, recursive subdivision of squares into half-width, half-height sub-squares; and the centre points of horizontal and vertical neighbours of a given region are all equidistant.

2.1 Recording and querying the bus sighting events

Data are created over time by software subscribing to a stream of bus sighting events. When a bus sighting event is received it is added into the bus sighting table. This effectively validates the predicate

```
happens(bus(Id,Easting,Northing),Time)
```

based on that bus sighting. Also, each sighting is checked against a set of stored geographical regions, which represent `congested_region/3` fluents that are unterminated. These fluents are the way that EC expresses queries over incoming data, as opposed to fluents describing historical information. Any bus sighting might cancel the congestion condition in a particular region. If any such fluents are terminated, fluents regarding congestion regions geographically containing this region may terminate also and so on, recursively.

We are now in a position to explain the linkage between the geospatial database and the event calculus inference system. The goal is efficient checking of the

```
holds_at(congested_region(Easting,Northing,R),T)
```

fluent (which is described above). In the process we must determine the truth of the

```
happens(bus(Id,Easting,Northing),Time)
```

predicate, so we make a single database query that is simultaneously parameterised with `Id`, `Easting`, `Northing` and `Time`. The database uses traditional indices for `Id` and `Time` and a spatial index for the point that (`Easting`, `Northing`) defines (in the case of PostgreSQL and PostGIS [6] this will be a GiST index). Furthermore, our scheme for geographical decomposition means that the CONGESTEDREGION table stores rows that represent memoised

```
holds_at(congested_region(Easting,Northing,R),T)
```

predicates. We use these when new bus sightings arrive to increase the speed of evaluation and store new predicate evaluations back in the CONGESTEDREGION table for improved performance in the future. Note that to take advantage of the database indices, we store variables from different parts of the predicate in a single table, including `Easting`, `Northing`, and `R`.

When a query is made of a geographical region and a time, we first consult `congested_region` fluents recorded in the CONGESTEDREGION table in the database. If the table contains a row that covers the fluent parameters then the fluent holds. If not then either the fluent does not hold or a conclusion about the region in question requires consulting subregions according to `geo_decomposition/5`. As subregions are checked to determine whether congestion has occurred, fluents describing these regions' congestion are memoised and corresponding rows inserted into the CONGESTEDREGION table. This speeds up any subsequent queries that depend on these fluents.

3. CONCLUSION

We have described a means of reasoning about spatial events by combining the elegance of the event calculus with the efficiency of a spatial database. The approach is not limited to the Simple Event Calculus as used in this paper but is appropriate for EC extensions, such as those described by Mueller [5].

Our next step is to complete an implementation, already begun, that operates on data from the TIME project [2]. These data can be thought of as a stream of bus sightings covering the city of Cambridge, UK. As described by Bejan et al., in 2009 there were 115 buses contributing sightings on a typical weekday [3] and a sighting of each bus is taken around every 20 seconds. Data have been collected for most days since 2007 and a real-time feed of sightings is still available. This represents a large and continuing dataset that is perfect for evaluating the efficiency of our unification of run-time and historic congestion detection, as well as allowing us to fine-tune the interactions between Prolog and the spatial database engine.

4. REFERENCES

[1] A. Artikis, M. Sergot, and G. Paliouras. Run-time composite event recognition. In *Proceedings of the 6th ACM International Conference on Distributed Event-Based Systems*, DEBS '12, pages 69–80, New York, NY, USA, 2012. ACM.

[2] J. Bacon, A. R. Beresford, D. Evans, D. Ingram, N. Trigoni, A. Guitton, and A. Skordylis. TIME: An open platform for capturing, processing and delivering transport-related data. In *Proceedings of the IEEE consumer communications and networking conference*, pages 687–691, 2008.

[3] A. Bejan, R. Gibbens, D. Evans, A. Beresford, J. Bacon, and A. Friday. Statistical modelling and analysis of sparse bus probe data in urban areas. In *Proceedings of the 13th International IEEE Conference on Intelligent Transportation Systems*, pages 1256–1263, Madeira Island, Portugal, September 2010. IEEE Intelligent Transportation Systems Society.

[4] R. Kowalski and M. Sergot. A logic-based calculus of events. *New Generation Computing*, 4:67–95, 1986.

[5] E. Mueller. *Commonsense Reasoning*. Elsevier Science, 2010.

[6] PostGIS Project Steering Committee. PostGIS—spatial and geography objects for PostgreSQL. http://postgis.net, accessed 26 February 2013, 2013.

Author Index

www.ingramcontent.com/pod-product-compliance
Lightning Source LLC
Chambersburg PA
CBHW080906220326
41598CB00034B/5494